W9-CTX-641

VIRGINIA WILLS AND
ADMINISTRATIONS, 1632-1800

Virginia Wills and Administrations 1632-1800

AN INDEX

OF

WILLS RECORDED IN LOCAL COURTS OF VIRGINIA, 1632-1800, AND OF ADMINISTRATIONS ON ESTATES SHOWN BY INVENTORIES OF THE ESTATES OF IN-TESTATES RECORDED IN WILL (AND OTHER) BOOKS OF LOCAL COURTS, 1632-1800.

Compiled by
CLAYTON TORRENCE

REFERENCE

Baltimore
GENEALOGICAL PUBLISHING CO., INC.
1981

Originally published by The National Society
of the Colonial Dames of America
Richmond, Virginia, 1930
Reprinted: Genealogical Publishing Co., Inc.
Baltimore: 1965, 1972, 1977, 1978, 1981
Library of Congress Catalogue Card Number 65-29031
International Standard Book Number 0-8063-0328-X
Made in the United States of America

CONTENTS

1. FOREWORD . . . . page vii

2. EXPLANATION OF THE NATURE OF THIS WORK " viii

3. INDEX . . . . " 1-476

4. APPENDIX: Norfolk City and Fredericksburg Hustings Courts; Kanawha County; Nottoway County; Pendleton County; Prince George County (1787-92); District of West Augusta; Chesterfield County (some items); Petersburg Hustings Court, 1784 - 1799 (Inclusive) . . . . pages 477-483

FOREWORD

The completion and publication of this Index brings to a conclusion a labor of love. The idea of compiling such a work had its genesis in my mind during my boyhood. At an early age I became interested in family history. There was a Virginia tradition in my family and this inspired questioning which led to investigation. I was hundreds of miles from official records and home places of my Virginia forefathers; and consequently the data of which I was in search were difficult to locate. By slow degrees I built up something of a family record. Several years later it was my good fortune to find my home in Virginia. The records of Virginia are inexpressibly precious to me. I have studied them from almost every point of view. I have long had the desire that anyone of Virginia descent should have an opportunity of locating the source from which his or her family came. This Index of Wills and Administrations 1632-1800 grouped under (1) Family names; (2) counties; (3) baptismal names of persons, will, I hope, be a help in such an undertaking.

The first "notes" for this Index were made twenty years ago. Work towards its completion has been done as time could be found in which to do it; but at last it is finished. Gathering material for this work was done by Mary Lightfoot Garland, Elizabeth Green Neblett Torrence and myself. Mary Lightfoot Garland, Elizabeth G. N. Torrence and Mary Turner Rust assumed the burden of "aphabetizing" the items.

Several years ago Mrs. Granville G. Valentine, of Richmond, President of the Virginia Society of the Colonial Dames of America, became interested in the completion and publication of this Index. Her interest was responsible for placing the matter before the National Society of the Colonial Dames of America and obtaining therefrom the funds necessary to completing and publishing the work. Without this encouraging help the Index would never have been completed and sent to the press. I can simply say that whoever may find this work helpful owes a debt of gratitude, far beyond repayal, to Mrs. Valentine and "The Dames." I wish to acknowledge here my gratitude to them for bringing about for me what is so rare in human life—the realization of a dream of youth.

To Mary Lightfoot Garland, those whom this Index helps owe unbounded thanks. The joyous spirit of her labor is concealed in every line. Her interest in this work has never for one instant flagged. Her confidence in the final outcome thereof has kept it going. Her unyielding loyalty to "the cause" has carried her on journeys far and varied in its behalf. Miss Garland visited at least half of the counties of Virginia yet possessing records of wills and administrations prior to the year 1800 and listed the documents for this work. To Elizabeth Green Neblett Torrence is due thanks for generous contribution of time and labor towards the completion of this work; and to Neblett, daughter beloved, who "cut the cards," and Mary Turner Rust (friend incomparable to our household), who "dealt" them—thanks.

I am not Virginian born; but, Virginian by choice. However, I lay claim to "the blood" through two great-grandparents. The exigencies of life carried them to the far south. It has been my happy privilege to return to their native land. Twenty-seven years ago I came to Virginia to live. No day since that early spring when I came in young manhood's dawn upon her soil to live has she failed to yield me inspiration and joy. So to whom but to Virginia could I inscribe this book—and to those nearest and dearest—Virginians—Elizabeth, Clayton, Neblett and Norman: my wife, and our "trinity of love" for whom I am indebted to—Virginia.

CLAYTON TORRENCE.

In Virginia.
16 November, 1930.

◉————————————◉

AN EXPLANATION OF THE NATURE OF THIS WORK

The arrangement of the "Index" is according to *surnames;* following the *surname* will be found the names of *counties* (in alphabetical arrangement where more than one county name is represented) in which wills or administrations of persons of the respective surname are recorded. The *county* name is followed by the *baptismal* names of individuals whose wills or inventories are recorded in the respective counties. The *baptismal name* is followed by the *year* in which the will or inventory was recorded (in some instances the date of record not being given in the record book the *year* in which the document was made is given instead); and the *year* is followed by a *letter* indicating the nature of the document recorded: w=will; i=inventory; a=administrator's bond or estate account (given in absence of inventory); n.w.=nuncupative will.

Copies of documents listed in this "Index" may be obtained (by payment of the regular fee) from the Clerk of Circuit Court of the county in which the document is stated to be on record.

The spelling of surnames given in this "Index" is in accordance with the spelling of that specific surname as given in the document of record. Those using this "Index" would do well where variations in spelling of surname are known or suspected, to go carefully through all surnames beginning with the same initial letter in order to catch up all items given under variations in the spelling of the surname.

This "Index" has as its objective the classification by surname and county of residence of the testators of wills and the inventories of estates of parties dying intestate whose inventories were recorded in the county courts of Virginia (colony and state) between 1632 and 1800. Every item in this "Index" is of record in the archives of the county under whose name it is entered. All counties in Virginia, of formation prior to the year 1800, and which still possess any books in which wills and inventories for the period 1632-1800 are recorded have been visited and these documents listed. The year 1632 is named as a "beginning" period owing to the fact that the records of the original Accomack County extend back to that year[1]. The year 1800

---

[1]First volume of Accomack County records which is in the office of the Clerk of Circuit Court for Northampton County, Eastville, Virginia. A copy of this volume is in the Department of Archives, Virginia State Library, Richmond.

was chosen arbitrarily as the period for terminating this "Index." A limit in point of time had to be placed upon this work, so the ending of the eighteenth century was chosen. Before the organization of county courts wills and administrations were proved before the "general court'" of the colony; but, these earlier records have long since disappeared. Even after the organization of county courts there is evidence of the record of some wills in the "general court." The records too have disappeared. So far as the records remaining show, the earliest wills and administrations of record in Virginia are in the old "county court" books. In the year 1634 the colony was divided into eight "shires," or counties, each with its court of record these eight being Accomack, Charles City, Charles River (York), Elizabeth City, Henrico, James City, Warrosquyoake (Isle of Wight) and Warwick River (Warwick). After the year 1634 the counties formed were by subdivisions of the original territory of these original eight counties[1].

During the long course of years since 1634 many of the record books of these old county courts have disappeared; some have been lost through destruction by fire; some were wantonly destroyed by invading armies, and some have gone in the natural order of decay of such material where it is not properly cared for.

In compiling this "Index" no attempt has been made to go beyond the series of books in which wills and inventories were actually recorded.

The following list indicates the condition of will and inventory records as at present preserved in the several counties of Virginia which were organized prior to the year 1800 which records have been used in the compilation of this "Index." The date following the county name indicates the year in which the county was organized and the word "complete" is used to describe a sequence in the will and inventory records of a county; the counties marked with an asterisk * are now in the State of West Virginia[2].

Accomack (1632-1642; original county; records complete)[3]; Accomack (1663; complete); Albemarle (1744; complete from 1749); Amelia (1735; complete); Amherst (1761; complete); Augusta (1745; complete); Bath (1791; complete); Bedford (1754; complete); Berkeley* (1772; complete); Botetourt (1770; complete); Brooke* (1797; complete); Brunswick (1720 formed; organized 1732 when records begin; complete);Buckingham (1761; destroyed); Campbell (1782; complete); Caroline (1728; destroyed); Charles City (1634; original; one volume of general records 1655-1665; wills and inventories prior 1769 missing; from 1769 complete); Charlotte (1765; complete); Chesterfield (1749; complete); Culpeper (1749; complete); Cumberland (1749; complete); Dinwiddie (1752; destroyed); Elizabeth City (1632; destroyed); Essex (1692; complete); Fairfax (1742; complete); Fauquier (1759; complete); Fincastle (1772; extinct 1777; will records in Montgomery County); Fluvanna (1777; complete); Franklin (1786; complete); Frederick (1743; complete); Gloucester (1651; destroyed); Goochland (1728; complete); Grayson (1793; complete); Greenbrier* (1778; complete); Greensville (1781; complete); Halifax (1752; complete); Hampshire* (1754; wills as listed under specific surnames in this "Index"); Hanover (1721; only remaining volume 1733-5); Hardy* (1786; complete); Harrison* (1784; complete); Henrico (1634; original; fragmentary: those remaining: 1677-1718, 1725-37, 1744-57, 1767-69, 1774-82 [re-recorded], 1781-1800); Henry (1777; complete); Isle of Wight (1637; was under name of Warrosquyoake 1634-1637; some few wills during 1650s;

---

[1]For a presentation of the subject of the formation and organization of the Virginia counties see Morgan P. Robinson's *Virginia Counties: Those Resulting From Virginia Legislation* (Bulletin of the Virginia State Library, Vol. 9, Jan.-July, 1916, Nos. 1, 2 and 3). This work, scholarly in every detail and masterly in its grasp of the subject, is one for which Virginia and Virginians owe a lasting debt of gratitude to Mr. Robinson.

[2]This "Index" does not include the will records of the county of Kentucky formed in the year 1777 and its subsequent divisions which in 1792 became the State of Kentucky.

[3]The records of the original Accomack County (1632-1642) are in custody of the authorities of Northampton County, and wills and inventories entered in this "Index" from these records are marked "Northampton"; to save confusion.

from 1661 complete except that some of books are damaged); James City (1634; destroyed); Kanawha* (1789; complete); King and Queen (1691; destroyed); King George (1721; records in existence, wills 1752-1800 [some pages missing from the books]; inventories 1721-1765; bonds 1739-1790 [executors, administrators, etc.], fiduciary accounts 1794-1807); King William (1702; some fragments)[1]; Lancaster (1651; complete); Lee 1793; destroyed); Loudoun (1757; complete); Louisa (1742; complete with the exception of first pages from the first will book); Lunenburg (1746; complete); Madison (1793; complete); Mathews (1791; destroyed); Mecklenburg (1765; complete); Middlesex (1673; some wills, etc. in order books 1673-94; will books preserved 1698-1734 and 1740-1795, though a number of pages are missing from the volume 1713-34 and first ten pages from volume 1748-60); Monongalia* (1776; destroyed); Montgomery (1777; complete); Nansamond (organized 1637 under name of "Upper Norfolk," and changed to Nansamond in 1642. The Nansamond records totally destroyed); New Kent (1654; destroyed); Norfolk (organized 1636 under name of "New Norfolk" and in 1637 became "Lower Norfolk," and in 1691 Norfolk County; records continuous from 1637, though some volumes very badly damaged, pages illegible, etc.; gaps here and there in the record books); Northampton (1642; complete; these records include the records of the original Accomack County, 1632-1642); Northumberland (1648; wills and inventories remain for periods: 1652-1672, 1706-20, 1710-13, 1718-29, 1738-1800); Nottoway (1789; complete); Ohio* (1776; complete); Orange (1734; complete); Patrick (1791; complete); Pendleton (1788; complete); Pittsylvania (1767; complete); Powhatan (1777; complete); Prince Edward (1754; complete); Prince George (1702; remaining volumes 1713-28 and 1787-92); Prince William (1731; remaining volumes cover periods 1734-1744 and 1778-1803); Princess Anne (1691; complete); Randolph* (1787; complete); Old Rappahannock (1656; became extinct 1692; complete; records kept in Essex Court); Richmond (1692; complete 1699-1800; first will book 1692-99 missing); Rockbridge (1778; complete); Rockingham (1778; destroyed); Russell (1786; destroyed); Shenandoah (organized under name of "Dunmore" in 1772 and name changed in 1778 to Shenandoah; records continuous from 1772, and complete); Southampton (1749; complete); Spotsylvania (1722; complete); Stafford (1664; will and inventory records remaining for 1699-1709, 1729-1748, 1748-1763, 1780-89); Surry (1652; sequence in volumes to 1800, though some pages are almost illegible and one volume badly damaged); Sussex (1754; complete); Warwick (1634; destroyed); Washington (1777; complete); Westmoreland (1653; wills and inventories 1653-1677 and 1691-1800 appear to be complete; there is a gap in the wills, etc. between 1677 and 1690); Wood* (1798; but no will records prior to 1800); Wythe (1790; complete); Yohogania (1776; major portion of territory fell within Pennsylvania on adjustment of boundary line 1780; and other portion added to Ohio County in 1786); York (1634; organized as Charles River and name changed to York in 1642; records continuous from 1633, and complete).

---

[1]The King William County records were burned in 1885. Fragments of record books picked up after the fire are bound in 17 volumes; but these fragments include comparatively few items prior to 1790, and these items are very largely composed of deeds. The will and inventory books evidently suffered almost total destruction.

VIRGINIA WILLS AND
ADMINISTRATIONS, 1632-1800

VIRGINIA WILLS AND
ADMINISTRATIONS—1632-1800

AARON
Amherst
Danl. 1765 a.
ABELL
Shenandoah
Joseph 1772 w.
ABBAY
Northumberland
Eliz. 1796 w.
Jno. 1791 i.
ABBETT
Culpeper
Roger 1762 w.
William 1762 w.
ABBEY
Lancaster
Will 1713 i.
Wm. 1740 i.
ABBINGTON
Westmoreland
Brookes 1716 i.
ABBIT
Stafford
Wm. 1742 i.
ABBITT
Culpeper
Edward 1750 i.
Spotsylvania
John Jos. 1722 a.
ABBOT
Accomack
Jno., Sr., 1694 w.
Jno. 1709 i.
Jno. 1746 i.
Middlesex
Jno. 1776 i.
ABBOTT
Accomack
Jno. 1732 n. w.
Richd. 1748 i.
Mason 1750 i.
Geo. 1751 i.
Roger 1753 w.
Mary 1756 i.
Robt. 1764 w.
Robt. 1766 i.
Richd. 1770 i.
Jno. 1780 i.
Geo. 1789 i.
Robt. 1791 i.
Eliz. 1795 w.
Robt. 1795 i.
Culpeper
Ann 1779 w.

Halifax
Joseph 1788.
Middlesex
Saml. 1779 i.
Northampton
Wm. 1678 w.
Jno. 1655 i.
ABDAIL
Northampton
Hancock 1774 i.
ABDEEL
Northampton
Thos. 1750 i.
Jacob 1754 i.
Eliz. 1755 i.
Hancock 1755 w.
Thos. 1786 w.
Abel 1787 w.
Jacob 1791 w.
ABDEL
Northampton
Luke 1786 i.
ABDELL
Northampton
Jno. 1724 w.
Wm. 1728 i.
Thos. 1739 w.
Nottingham 1745 w.
Henry 1799 i
ABDILL
Accomack
Elisha 1796 i.
ABDUL
Northampton
Eliz. 1755 w.
ABEL
Frederick
John 1764 w.
ABERNATHY
Brunswick
Jesse 1777 w.
Chas. 1796 w.
James 1799 w.
Frederick
William 1780 w.
ABINGTON
Westmoreland
Lawrence 1670 w
ABNEY
Albemarle
Abner 1752 w.
Augusta
Jno. 1788 w.
Halifax
Geo. 1766 w.

Spotsylvania
Dannett 1732 w.
ABNUTT
Frederick
James 1798 w.
ABRAHAM
Northampton
Jno. 1677 w.
Princess Anne
Richd. 1702 w.
Westmoreland
Thos. 1754 i.
ABREL
Berkeley
James 1795 i.
ABRELL
Berkeley
John 1772 w.
ABRIL
Berkeley
James 1790 w.
ABSHEIR
Augusta
Peter 1761 i.
ABSOLOM
Princess Anne
Edwd. 1753 i.
Jno. 1776 w.
ABSTON
Halifax
Francis 1762 w.
ABYOON
Norfolk
George 1790 i.
George 1781 w.
ACKERS
Richmond
Wm. 1714 i.
ACKIS
Princess Anne
Jno. 1728 w.
Adam 1731 w.
Katherine 1734 w.
Wm. 1734 w.
Francis 1743 w.
ACKISS
Princess Anne
Adam 1753 i.
Geo. 1763 i.
John 1790 i.
Wm. 1790 w.
ACKWORTH
Accomack
Patience 1797 w.

ACRA
Middlesex
Jno. 1791 i.
ACRES
Augusta
Simon 1750 i.
Lancaster
Wm. 1688 w.
ADAIR
Augusta
Wm. 1763 w.
ADAM
Fairfax
James 1792 i.
Robert 1789 w.
ADAMS
Accomack
Thos. 1751 i.
Amelia
Wm. 1767 w.
David 1799 w.
Augusta
Saml. 1748 a.
Margt. 1770 w.
Thos. 1788 w.
Pittsylvania
Robt. 1784 i.
Bedford
John 1797 w.
Brunswick
Edwd. 1752 i.
Wm. 1758 w.
Wm. 1763 i.
Eliz. 1769 i.
Peter 1773 w.
Thos. 1778 w.
Henry 1780 w.
Mary 1780 w.
Isaac 1781 w.
Campbell
Robt. 1785 i.
Robt. 1790 w.
Charlotte
Wm. 1769 w.
Chas. 1783 i.
Jno. 1797 i.
Culpeper
Robert 1771 w.
Cumberland
Wm. 1778 w.
Fairfax
John 1752 i.
Elenor 1750 w.
Gabriel 1750 w.
James 1787 i.
Fauquier
John 1781 w.
Fluvana
Jas. 1789 w.
Jas., Sr., 1791 i.
Goochland
Robt. 1740 w.

Henrico
Thos. Bowler 1795 w.
Henry
Joseph 1783 i.
Isle of Wight
Thomas 1663 i.
David 1748 i.
Loudoun
Elizabeth 1758 i.
Gabriel 1761 w.
Norfolk
Jno. 1683 w.
Lot 1788 i.
Northumberland
John 1768 i.
Orange
Benj. 1786 w.
Powhatan
Peter 1796 i.
Pittsylvania
Robt. 1784 i.
Prince Edward
Wm. Robt. 1792 w.
Prince George
James 1722 i.
Thos., Sr., 1722 w.
Southampton
Henry 1770 w.
Robt. 1779 i.
Thos. 1782 w.
Benj. 1795 w.
Surry
Jas. 1720 i.
Peter 1735 w.
Thos. 1735 w.
Patrick 1769 w.
Thos. 1771 w.
Mary 1779 w.
Martha 1784 i.
Sussex
Benj. 1756 w.
Thos. 1788 w.
York
Jos. 1747 w.
ADCOCK
Essex
Burrough 1717 w.
Jno. 1720 i.
Henry 1738 w.
ADDAMAN
Brunswick
Thos. 1735 i.
ADDAMS
Halifax
Jno. 1769 w.
Lancaster
Jno. 1698-9 i.
Louisa
Thos. 1792 i.
York
Thos. 1659-w.

ADDISON
Accomack
Nathan 1738 i.
Hezekiah 1764 i.
Elijah 1774 w.
Nathan 1788 w.
Jno. 1789 i.
Jonathan 1790 w.
Jonathan 1797 i.
Nathan 1798 i.
Northampton
Jno. 1716-17 w.
Jno. 1736 w.
Arnold 1737 i.
Arnold 1739 i.
Thos. 1750 w.
Jno. 1765 w.
Jno., Sr., 1782 w.
Littleton 1791 w.
Prince William
William 1736 i.
ADDLERMAN
Loudoun
Daniel 1792 i.
ADEUSTONE
York
Jno. 1678 w.
ADKEY
Westmoreland
Jno. 1720 nw.
ADKINS
Accomack
Robt. 1717 w.
Charlotte
Wm. 1782 w.
Chesterfield
Wm. 177– w.
Abraham 1788 i.
Henrico
Danl. 1783 w.
Isle of Wight
Samuel 1746 w.
Lunenburg
Jno. 1763 w.
Northampton
Jno. 1733 i.
Spotsylvania
Alex 1784 w.
Surry
Richd. 1679 i.
Thos. 1711 w.
Thos. 1751 w.
ADKINS
Sussex
Thos. 1764 w.
Henry 1755 i.
Jno. 1762 i.
Thos. 1770 i.
Jno. 1781 w.
Jno. 1782 w.
Jno. 1783 i.
Thos. 1796 w.

Lucy 1797 w.
Thos. 1798 i.
ADKINSON
Amherst
Hezekiah 1777 i.
Essex
James 1748 i.
Isle of Wight
Owen 1790 i.
ADKISSON
Stafford
Phill. 1730 i.
ADLEY
King George
Saml. 1776 a.
ADONGHETEE
Frederick
William 1760 w.
ADSOTH
Essex
Jno. 1719 w.
AGAR
Northumberland
Jane 1721 a.
AGER
Amherst
Cosby 1775 w.
AGNESS
Princess Anne
Thos. 1782 i.
AGNEW
Northumberland
Margt. 1746 i.
AIKEN
Amelia
Jas. 1753 i.
Chesterfield
Wm. Sr. 1757 w.
Chesterfield
Wm. Jr. 1767 w.
Cumberland
James 1795 i.
AILSTOLK
Louisa
Michael 1795 w.
AILWORTH
Accomack
Jas. 1778 w.
Jas. 1780 w.
AIMES
Accomack
Thos. 1775 w.
Jos. 1785 i.
Wm. 1785 w.
Caleb 1788 i.
Wm. 1792 i.
AINSWORTH
Fairfax
Geo. 1797 a.
AIRS
Northumberland
Thos. 1724 i.

Wm. 1749 i.
Thos. 1785 w.
Saml. 1788 i.
Jas. 1798 i.
AITCHISON
Princess Anne
Wm. 1777 w.
AKER
Augusta
Simon 1749 w.
Westmoreland
Benj. 1738 i.
AKERT
Harrison
Frederick 1793 w.
AKIN
Chesterfield
Wm. 17— i.
Eliz. 1771 w.
Wm. 1794 w.
Franklin
James 1789 a.
Henrico
Jas. Sr. 1713 w.
Sarah 1714 w.
Prince Edward
Chas. 1794 i.
AKINS
Bedford
Walter 1768 i.
Botetourt
Redman 1781 w.
AKUS
Essex
Wm. 1702 w.
ALBERTICK
Shenandoah
Charles 1795 i.
ALBERTIE
Henrico
Francis 1785 w.
ALBERTSON
Princess Anne
Warsell 1711 i.
ALBIN
Prince William
Thomas 1737 i.
ALBRIGHTON
York
Richd. 1683 w.
Richd. 1717 w.
ALBRITTON
Princess Anne
Thos. 1730 w.
York
Francis 1667 w.
Jno. 1688 w.
ALDAY
Westmoreland
Henry 1670 w.

ALDERSON
Botetourt
James 1775 i.
John 1780 w.
Cumberland
Richd. 1789 w.
Essex
James 1732 i.
Ann 1733 i.
Lancaster
Richd. 1698-9 w.
Princess Anne
Worssell 1754 w.
Richmond
Jeliff (Teliff) Jr.
1718 w.
Jno. 1757 i.
Richd. 1757 w.
Jas. 1785 w.
Jas. 1787 i.
Wm. 1790 w.
Mary 1796 w.
Jeremiah 1799 i.
Surry
Wm. 1683-4 w.
Westmoreland
Geo. 1714 w.
ALDESON
Westmoreland
Jane 1729 i.
ALDRED
Frederick
Chris. 1765 i.
ALDRIDGE
Frederick
Robert 1792 i.
Norfolk
Francis 1678 w.
ALESHITE
Shenandoah
Conrod 1776 a.
ALEWORTH
Accomack
Wm. 1686 w.
ALEXANDER
Accomack
Jas. 1708 w.
Ann 1711 w.
Thos. 1783 w.
Albemarle
Jno. 1755 i.
Hugh 1797 w.
Augusta
Wm. 1750 i.
Jas. 1778 w.
Gabriel 1779 w.
Robt. 1783 w.
Andrew 1789 w.
Francis 1792 w.
Jno. 1796 i.
Botetourt
James 1775 w.

Essex
John 1704 w.
Fairfax
Garrard 1761 w.
George 1784 w.
Philip 1790 w.
Mary 1793 w.
Robert 1793 w.
Frederick
William 1772 i.
Morgan 1783 i.
William 1797 w.
Hampshire
James 1773 w.
King George
Lucy 1781 w.
Philip T. 1783 w.
Susanna 1788 w.
Lancaster
Anguish 1743 w.
Mecklenburg
Robt. 1784 i.
Robt. 1786 w.
Norfolk
Jno. 1713 w.
Wm. 1764 i.
Northumberland
David 1743-4 i.
Robt. 1746 i.
Jno. 1749 i.
Ann 1757 i.
John 1757 w.
John 1767 w.
John 1769 i.
Gwell 1770 i.
James 1778 w.
Rappahannock
Jno. 1686 i.
Rockbridge
Archibald 1780 w.
Archibald 1796 i.
William 1797 w.
William 1799 i.
Stafford
Robt. 1704 w.
Philip 1705 i.
Robt. 1736 i.
Anne 1739 i.
Philip 1753 w.
Surry
James 1797 i.
ALFORD
Frederick
John 1748 w.
Northampton
Thos. 1755 w.
ALGAR
Richmond
Saml. 1770 i.
ALGAIR
Richmond
Saml. 1750 w.

ALGER
Richmond
Mary 1762 w.
ALGIER
Richmond
Saml. 1765 w.
ALGOOD
Amelia
Edwd. 1787 i.
ALKINS
Prince Edward
Robert 1777 w.
ALLAN
Culpeper
James 1758 w.
William 1799 w.
Orange
William 1743 a.
Stafford
Geo. 1755 w.
ALLDAY
Charlotte
Thos. 1782 i.
ALLDIN
Middlesex
Jno. 1727 w.
Jno. 1747 w.
Jno. 1765 a.
ALLEGREE
Fluvanna
Judith 1782 w.
Henrico
——— 1783 w.
ALLEN
Accomack
Stephen 1750 w.
Jas. 1761 i.
Jno. 1767 w.
Edward 1768 w.
Moses 1791 w.
Zadock 1797 w.
Jos. 1798 w.
Albemarle
Wm. 1752 w.
Jno. 1754 w.
Wm. 1760 w.
Mary 1789 w.
Amherst
Jesse 1780 w.
Saml. 1799 w.
Augusta
Benj. 1747 i.
Mary 1751 i.
Reuben 1751 i.
Hugh 1779 i.
David 1779 w.
Robt. Jr. 1789 w.
Robt. 1791 w.
Jas. Sr. 1791 w.
Bedford
Robert 1773 w.
Reynolds 1778 i.

Reynolds 1779 w.
Charles 1780 i.
Berkeley
Frederick 1788 w.
Botetourt
Malcolm 1792 w.
Charles City
Saml. 1771 i.
Charlotte
Jos. 1771 w.
Eliz. 1786 w.
Culpeper
Benjamin 1777 i.
William 1780 w.
Cumberland
Abraham 1751 w.
Isaac 1769 w.
Sarah 1774 w.
Mary 1778 w.
Moses 1782 i.
Essex
Erasmus 1720 w.
Wm. Jr. 1739 w.
William 1739 w.
Erasmus 1739 i.
Thomas 1742 i.
Erasmus 1743 i.
Thomas 1743 i.
John 1750 i.
Dinah 1751 w.
John 1762 i.
Elizabeth 1774 w.
Samuel 1779 w.
Henry 1783 w.
Andrew 1785 i.
Fauquier
John 1761 w.
Allen 1762 i.
Henry 1775 i.
John 1775 i.
Ursla 1793 w.
Fincastle
Thomas 1773 a.
Frederick
Patrick 1753 i.
Robert 1769 w.
Francis 1773 w.
Robert 1791 w.
John 1794 w.
Greensville
Arthur 1792 i.
Halifax
Chas. 1792 w.
Henrico
Isham 1783 w.
Littleberry 1785 w.
Timothy 1785 w.
Julius 1786 w.
David 1788 i.
Agnes 1789 w.
Robt. 1789 i.
Jno. 1797 w.

Richd. Royal 1798 w.
Isle of Wight
John 1677 w.
George 1679 i.
George 1694 i.
Henry 1695 i.
Thomas 1711 w.
Martha 1719 w.
Thomas 1741 w.
Joseph 1751 i.
Joseph 1766 w.
Randall 1786 w.
King George
Jno. 1752 i.
Mathew 1753 i.
Jno. 1754 i.
Mathew 1761 i.
Archibald 1762 w.
Loudoun
Wm. 1777 w.
Wm. 1799 w.
Lunenburg
Joel 1756 w.
Chas. Sr. 1759 w.
Mecklenburg
Wm. Sr. 1789 w.
Middlesex
Richard 1715 w.
Arthur 1779 w.
Northampton
Jno. 1670 w.
Northumberland
Jas. 1711 i.
Jno. 1726-7 i.
Orange
Reuben 1741 a.
Prince Edward
Danl. 1793 i.
James Sr. 1793 w.
Princess Anne
Wm. 1758 i.
Thos. 1788 w.
Prince William
George 1736 i.
Rockbridge
Hugh 1796 w.
Shenandoah
Reuben Sr. 1779 w.
Jackson 1786 w.
Reuben 1796 i.
Spotsylvania
Thos. 1743 w.
Jno. 1750 w.
Eliz. 1754 w.
Nathl. 1754 a.
Jos. 1783 w.
Stafford
Jno. 1709 i.
Wm. 1744 w.
Surry
Jno. 1700 w.
Arthur 1710 w.

James 1711 w.
Joseph 1717 i.
Arthur 1728 i.
Thos. 1733 w.
Jno. 1742 w.
James 1744 w.
Wm. 1793 w.
Westmoreland
Wm. 1718 w.
York
Thos. 1668 w.
Wm. 1679 i.
Jane 1720 w.
Susanna 1720 w.
Geo. 1736 i.
Hudson 1784 w.
ALLENTHORPE
Stafford
Jno. 1747 w.
ALLERTON
Westmoreland
Isaac 1702 w.
Willoughby 1724 w.
Isaac 1739 w.
Gawen 1754 i.
Willoughby 1759 w.
ALLFORD
Bedford
Silvator 1777 w.
Middlesex
Richd. 1714 i.
ALLGOOD
Mecklenburg
Moses 1796 i.
Jno. 1748 i.
Northumberland
Jno. 1748 i.
ALLIGOOD
Northampton
Thos. 1686 w.
Richd. 1716 i.
ALLIGRE
Albemarle
Giles 1776 w.
ALLIN
Accomack
Edmond 1711 i.
Frederick
Patrick 1751 a.
King George
Jonas 1723 i.
Middlesex
Richd. 1733 w.
John 1744 w.
Eliz. 1766 a.
Northumberland
Teag 1724 i.
Surry
Eliz. 1735 w.
York
Wm. 1713 w.
Ann 1750 w.

ALLINNE
Isle of Wight
Henry 1694 i.
ALLISON
Augusta
Robt. 1769 w.
Berkeley
Matthew 1772 w.
Montgomery
John 1792 w.
Richmond
Henry 1768 i.
Bethsheba 1794 w.
Westmoreland
Thos. 1701 i.
Thos. 1704 i.
Thos. 1757 i.
ALLISTON
Norfolk
Richd. 1723 nw.
ALLMAN
Isle of Wight
William 1771 w.
ALLMAND
Isle of Wight
Talton 1769 w.
Norfolk
Edmond 1795 w.
ALLOWAY
Richmond
Gabriel 1745 w.
Alexander 1755 w.
Gabriel 1760 w.
ALLSTIN
Surry
Thos. 1762 w.
Mary 1776 w.
ALLVERSON
Richmond
Teleaf 1718 i.
ALLWORTHY
Westmoreland
Robt. 1718 w.
ALMAND
Isle of Wight
James 1757 w.
Augustus 1793 nw.
Isaac 1793 w.
ALMON
Northumberland
Jno. 1795 w.
ALMOND
Isle of Wight
Edward 1777 i.
Northumberland
Jno. 1794 i.
Spotsylvania
Catherine 1765 w.
ALSOBROOK
Surry
Saml. 1697 i.

Sussex
Saml. 1759 i.
Jno. 1784 w.
Rachel 1788 w.
ALSOP
Spotsylvania
Wm. 1778 w.
ALSTEN
York
Jno. 1698 i.
ALSUP
Richmond
Geo. 1719 i.
ALTMAN
Isle of Wight
John 1694 i.
Thomas 1712 w.
ALTON
Fairfax
John 1787 w.
ALTRITH
Frederick
Christopher 1765 w.
ALVERSON
Northumberland
Jno. 1743-4 w.
ALWORTH
Accomack
Jonathan 1754 w.
AMBARGER
Orange
Conrad 1742 a.
AMBLER
York
Richd. 1766 w.
AMBROSE
Richmond
Jos. 1752 w.
AMERSON
Middlesex
Jas. 1768 i.
AMES
Accomack
Jos. 1709 i.
Thos. 1754 w.
Jos. Sr. 1770 w.
Thos. Sr. 1779 i.
Jno. 1792 w.
Churchel 1796 w.
Nathl. 1796 w.
Eliz. 1797 i.
Northampton
Jno. 1796 w.
AMISS
Frederick
Gabriel 1770 w.
Surry
Silvester 1764 w.
AMMINGHAM
Prince Edward
Alex. 1778 w.

AMMON
King George
Thos. 1742 i.
Shenandoah
Ernest 1786 w.
AMMONET
Charlotte
Israel 1790 i.
Chesterfield
Andrew 1761 w.
AMMONS
King George
Jos. 1733 i.
AMONE
Augusta
Arnest 1777 i.
AMONETT
Chesterfield
Jno. 17— w.
Cumberland
Andrew 1776 w.
Jacob 1771 w.
AMOS
Isle of Wight
William 1721 w.
Louisa
Nicholas 1796 w.
Lunenburg
James 1786 w.
AMOSS
Cumberland
Francis 1770 i.
Ann 1799 i.
Goochland
Valentine 1732 i.
AMRY
Surry
Thos. 1676 i.
ANCHOROM
King George
Joel 1793 w.
ANCRAM
Loudoun
James 1796 i.
ANCRUM
Stafford
Jno. 1735 i.
ANDERS
Accomack
Jno. 1716 i.
Frederick
Earnest 1790 i.
ANDERSON
Accomack
Wm. 1698 w.
Mary 1703 i.
Roger 1738 i.
Ralph 1750 i.
Jno. 1753 i.
Albemarle
Thos. 1758 w.
David 1793 w.

Amelia
Henry 1753 w.
Jno. 1766 w.
Wm. 1769 i.
Jas. 1773 w.
Jas. 1781 i.
Jas. 1782 w.
Francis Sr. 1787 w.
Francis 1795 w.
Augusta
Isaac 1749 w.
Alex. 1763 i.
Margt. 1763 w.
Thos. 1776 i.
Jas. 1779 w.
Jno. 1787 w.
Geo. Sr. 1789 w.
Wm. 1794 w.
Bedford
George 1778 w.
Richard 1783 i.
Eliz. 1799 w.
Charlotte
Jno. 1773 w.
Chesterfield
Eliz. 1759 w.
Claiborne 1773 w.
Jno. 1780 w.
Doctor 1785 w.
Cumberland
Lawrence 1781 w.
Jas. 1782 w.
Chas. 1783 w.
Wm. 1795 i.
Essex
Jos. 1729 i.
Jos. 1735 w.
Hudson 1764 w.
Fairfax
William 1788 i.
Frederick
Thomas 1747 w.
Thomas 1748 w.
Calvert 1749 i.
Thomas 1751 i.
Bartholomew 1754 w.
Colbert 1764 w.
Halifax
Jno. 1796 w.
Hampshire
William 1794 w.
Henrico
Jno. 1733 w.
Henry 1734 w.
Jno. 1735 i.
King George
Jno. 1721 i.
Mark 1726 i.
Walter 1733 i.
Cyprian 1744 a.
Lancaster
Thos. 1740 w.

Robert 1747 i.
Webster 1760 i.
Loudoun
John 1784 i.
Louisa
Elkanah 1767 i.
David 1781 w.
Pouncey 1791 w.
Robert 1782 a.
David 1785 a.
Robt. 1785 a.
David 1787 a.
Eliz. 1789 a.
Richd. 1793 i.
Eliz. 1794 w.
David 1795 a.
Pouncey 1975 i.
Micajah 1797 w.
Madison
George 1798 w.
Mecklenburg
Thos. 1780 w.
Thos. 1793 w.
Middlesex
Henry 1718 i.
Ann 1724 w.
Norfolk
James 1769 i.
John 1769 i.
Northampton
Barrett 1648 w.
Northumberland
Wm. 1668 w.
Jno. 1741 i.
Robt. 1742 w.
Andrew 1762 i.
John 1782 w.
Jno. 1792 i.
Jno. 1795 i.
Orange
Geo. 1744 a.
Augustine 1798 w.
Pittsylvania
Richd. 1796 i.
Prince Edward
Janestith 1768 i.
Wm. 1799 w.
Prince George
Chas. 1718 w.
Matthew 1718 w.
Jno. 1725 w.
Peter 1726 w.
Rockbridge
James 1798 w.
Richmond
Agnes 1770 i.
Shenandoah
John 1798 i.
Surry
Jno. 1722 w.
James 1752 w.
Geo. 1765 i.

Rebecca 1770 w.
Sussex
Robt. 1773 i.
James 1778 w.
Jno. 1778 i.
David 1782 i.
Washington
Jacob 1785 w.
Westmoreland
Abraham 1719 i.
Walton 1765 i.
York
Sarah 1683 a.
Alex. 1687 w.
Andrew 1752 w.
ANDERTON
Brunswick
Isaac 1787 w.
Eliz. 1792 i.
Lancaster
Jno. 1718 i.
Prince William
Richard 1739 i.
Sussex
Geo. 1775 w.
Geo. 1789 i.
ANDREW
Augusta
Thos. 1777 w.
Northampton
Wm. 1657 i.
Spotsylvania
Jno. 1764 a.
ANDREWS
Accomack
Nathaniel 1721 w.
Nathl. 1725 i.
Andrew 1747 i.
Robt. 1750 i.
Wm. 1763 w.
Mary 1764 w.
Jacob 1770 w.
Wm. 1778 w.
Margt. 1784 w.
Ishmael 1794 w.
Augusta
Robt. 1767 i.
Berkeley
David 1781 i.
Brunswick
Joseph 1774 w.
William 1799 i.
Chesterfield
Benj. 17— i.
Thos. 1754 w.
Jane 1756 w.
Jas. 1757 i.
Lewis 1785 w.
Isham Sr. 1792 w.
Wm. 1799 w.
Cumberland
Mark 1775 w.

Kitty 1784 i.
Wiatt 1789 w.
Essex
Jno. 1754 w.
Thomas 1779 w.
Halifax
Wm. 1777 w.
Henrico
Thos. 1731 w.
Isle of Wight
John 1728 i.
Drury 1797 w.
Loudoun
John 1770 w.
Lunenburg
Robt. 1762 i.
Abraham 1799 w.
Mecklenburg
Wm. 1772 i.
Norfolk
Wm. 1676 w.
Jno. 1700 w.
Northampton
Wm. 1655 w.
Robt. 1657 w.
Wm. 1673 w.
Jno. 1688 w.
Andrew 1700 i.
Robt. 1718 w.
Andrew 1728 w.
Nathl. 1739 w.
Jno. 1741 i.
Pearl 1757 i.
Wm. 1762 w.
Jno. 1766 w.
Southy 1778 i.
Andrew 1787 w.
Northumberland
Thos. 1794 i.
Pittsylvania
Jno. 1784 i.
Rappahannock
James 1685 i.
Rockbridge
Moses 1784 w.
Southampton
Robt. 1767 i.
Wm. 1772 w.
Ann 1794 i.
Faithy 1795 w.
Jno. 1796 w.
Spotsylvania
Charles 1756 a.
Stafford
Geo. 1703 i.
Surry
David Jr. 1716 i.
Richd. 1750 i.
Benj. 1736 w.
Bartholomew 1752 i.
Eliz. 1761 i.
Jno. 1787 w.

David 1789 w.
Blackburn 1793 w.
Wm. 1795 w.
Mary 1796 w.
Sussex
Jno. 1764 w.
Wm. 1769 w.
Fredk. 1780 w.
Stephen 1787 w.
Richd. 1795 w.
Robt. 1798 i.
York
Henry 1705-6 i.
John 1719 w.
ANDRICK
Shenandoah
Frederick 1772 w.
ANDROS
Surry
Thos. 1695 w.
ANDRUS
Goochland
Jno. 1740 a.
Surry
Bartholomew 1726 w.
Robt. 1728 w.
Thos. 1737 w.
Eliz. 1741 w.
ANGEL
Berkeley
Michael 1794 w.
Lancaster
Samuel 1772 w.
Northumberland
Robert 1757 w.
Wm. 1770 w.
ANGELL
Lancaster
Wm. 1659 w.
Uriah 1716 w.
Robt. 1726 w.
John 1744-5 w.
John 1766 i.
Northumberland
Amos. 1789 w.
ANGELLA
Cumberland
Wm. Sr. 1769 w.
ANGIER
Westmoreland
Jno. 1666 w.
ANGLEA
Cumberland
Wm. Sr. 1796 w.
ANGLIN
Pittsylvania
Jno. 1796 i.
ANGUISH
Norfolk
Jno. 1734 w.

ANGUS
Princess Anne
Patrick 1700 i.
Patrick 1701 i.
James 1717 i.
Hannah 1722 i.
Surry
Jno. 1774 i.
ANNANDALE
King George
Wm. 1755 w.
Wm. 1757 i.
ANNATOIR
Norfolk
Joseph 1799 i.
ANNIS
Westmoreland
Jno. 1671 i.
ANSELL
Norfolk
Caleb 1798 i.
ANSLEY
Loudoun
Wm 1798 w.
ANSTICE
Northampton
Thos. 1648 i.
ANTHONY
Accomack
Geo. 1719 w.
Bedford
John 1760 w.
Essex
Jno. 1725 w.
Henry
Joseph 1785 w.
Louisa
Marcy 1796 w.
Surry
Wm. 1794 i.
York
Wm. 1730 i.
ANTLE
Frederick
Peter 1771 w.
ANTON
Essex
James 1789 i.
Westmoreland
Alex. 1782 w.
APLETON
Fairfax
John 1750 i.
APPERSON
Halifax
Jno. 1768 w.
Jno. 1773 i.
Spotsylvania
Jno. 1786 w.
Mary 1788 a.

APPINGER
Augusta
Peter 1761 i.
APPLEBEE
Northumberland
Norman 1789 w.
Richmond
Richd. 1745 i.
APPLEBERRY
Albemarle
Wm. 1776 i.
APPLEBY
Northumberland
Jno. 1723 i.
Jno. 1750 i.
Norman 1788 i.
Richmond
Elizabeth 1761 w.
Eliz. 1799 w.
APPLETON
Lancaster
Abraham 1659 w.
Westmoreland
Jno. 1676 i.
APPLEWHAITE
Isle of Wight
Henry 1704 w.
Thom. 1732 w.
John 1735 w.
Thom. 1737 i.
Martha 1739 w.
Henry 1740 i.
Henry 1741 w.
Ann 1747 w.
Ann 1758 w.
Arthur 1766 w.
John 1758 w.
Henry 1770 w.
Thomas 1771 w.
Jane 1780 w.
Henry 1784 w.
Henry 1772 i.
Eliz. 1794 w.
Josiah 1794 w.
Arthur 1799 w.
APPLEWHITE
Southampton
Henry 1783 w.
Thos. 1787 w.
Ann 1795 w.
Jno. 1796 i.
APPLING
Spotsylvania
Thos. 1743 w.
Richd. 1751 w.
Jno. C. Jr. 1763 i.
Jno. 1773 w.
APSHONE
Goochland
Wm. 1743 i.

ARBUCKLE
Accomack
Wm. 1751 w.
Katherine 1758 i.
Jas. 1785 w.
Greenbrier
Mathew 1781 i.
ARBUTHNOT
Fairfax
Thomas 1742 w.
Henrico
Dorotha 1782 i.
ARCHDEACON
Norfolk
James 1782 i.
Prince Edward
Jas. 1759 w.
Edw. 1794 i.
ARCHER
Augusta
Jas. Jr. 1778 w.
Jno. 1780 w.
Rebeckah 1789 w.
Chesterfield
Geo. 17— i.
Wm. 17— i.
Sarah 17— i.
Wm. 1750 w.
Jno. 1773 w.
Sarah 1774 w.
Jno. 1784 i.
Field 1784 w.
Jno. 1784 i.
Eliz. 1785 w.
Edw. 1789 w.
Mary 1790 w.
Jno. 1794 w.
Jno. 1796 i.
Frederick
Jeremiah 1765 i.
Henrico
Geo. 1675-6 o. p.
Geo. 1731 w.
Madison
James 1797 w.
Norfolk
Edward 1771 w.
Shenandoah
Henry 1787 w.
York
Jno. 1695 i.
Jas. 1697 i.
Eliz. 1726 w.
Abraham 1752 w.
Thos. 1783 w.
ARDIES
Accomack
Edwd. 1735 i.
ARDIN
Pittsylvania
Abraham 1778 i.

ARDIS
Accomack
Robt. 1767 w.
Jas. 1767 i.
Wm. Chance 1782 i.
Edwd. 1788 w.
ARELL
Fairfax
David 1792 w.
Richd. 1796 a.
Saml. 1795 w.
ARESS
Berkeley
Thom. 1779 i.
AREW
Accomack
Jno. 1689 w.
ARISS
Westmoreland
Saml. 1726 i.
Jno. 1730 w.
Spencer 1761 w.
ARKILL
Essex
Henry 1698 i.
ARLEDG
Northumberland
Sarah 1727 i.
ARLEDGE
Northumberland
Wm. 1724 w.
ARLINGTON
Accomack
Jno. 1793 w.
Henrico
Wm. 1702 a.
ARMER
Isle of Wight
William 1692 w.
ARMENTROUT
Augusta
Eliz. 1775 w.
ARMES
Goochland
Jno. 1743 i.
Lancaster
Danl. 1701 w.
Walter 1717 w.
ARMESTEAD
Culpeper
Bowles 1785 w.
ARMISTEAD
Essex
Jno. 1704 i.
Louisa
Robt. 1791 w.
Norfolk
Robert 1794 w.
Richmond
Francis 1719 w.
York
Ellyson 1757 w.

Jane 1767 w.
ARMITRADER
Accomack
Henry 1734 w.
Arthur 1743 i.
Henry 1750 i.
Abigail 1753 i.
Richd. 1755 w.
Henry 1761 i.
Richd. 1762 nw.
Littleton 1764 w.
Israel 1769 i.
Littleton 1771 w.
Arthur 1791 w.
Arthur 1796 i.
ARMITRADING
Northampton
Henry 1663 w.
ARMITRADINGE
Northampton
Alice 1664 w.
ARMS
Fairfax
Aaron 1794 a.
Lancaster
John 1795 w.
ARMSLEY
Westmoreland
Jno. 1659 w.
ARMSTEAD
Cumberland
Jno. 1769 w.
Jno. 1795 i.
ARMSTRONG
Accomack
Henry 1677 i.
Augusta
Robt. 1754 w.
Jas. 1759 nw.
Jas. 1763 w.
Robt. 1763 w.
Thos. 1776 w.
Saml. 1788 w.
Robt. 1793 w.
Robt. 1794 w.
Eliz. 1795 w.
Wm. 1796 w.
Saml. 1799 a.
Bath
John 1799 i.
Berkeley
Alexander 1784 nw.
Botetourt
Elenor 1791 w.
Essex
John 1741 i.
John 1748 w.
Richd. 1750 w.
John 1751 i.
Ambrose 1768 w.
Halifax
Jno. 1779 w.

Jno. 1782 i.
King George
Jos. 1748 i.
Jno. 1751 i.
Thos. 1759 w.
Jos. 1763 i.
Louisa
Lancelot 1745 w.
Thos. 1781 i.
John 1784 w.
Lancelot 1794 w.
Northumberland
Adam 1741 i.
Prince Edward
Thos. 1791 w.
Richmond
Jno. 1718 w.
Stafford
Jas. 1783 i.
Sussex
Joseph 1762 i.
Washington
Henry 1798 w.
ARNELL
Accomack
Lawrence 1757 i.
ARNET
Loudoun
Alex. 1770 w.
ARNETT
Louisa
James 1781 w.
ARNOLD
Accomack
Wm. 1728 i.
Wm. 1737 i.
Albemarle
Saml. 1765 w.
Bedford
Wm. 1777 i.
Cumberland
Wm. 1774 w.
Fauquier
John 1780 w.
Humphrey 1790 i.
Hampshire
Richard 1758 w.
King George
Thos. 1726 i.
Jas. 1728 i.
Grace 1733 i.
Thos. 1743 i.
Isaac 1758 w.
Jno. 1768 a.
Jas. 1770 w.
Mary 1775 w.
Lancaster
Jno. 1683 w.
Loudoun
Justice 1794 i.
Louisa
Jonathan 1751 w.

Mecklenburg
James 1777 i.
Jno. 1784 w.
Spotsylvania
Isaac 1770 w.
Wm. 1775 w.
Edmund 1778 w.
Anthony 1786 w.
Westmoreland
Weedon 1754 w.
York
Wm. 1683 w.
ARNOLL
Mecklenburg
Jos. 1776 w.
James 1781 w.
ARNOTT
Norfolk
James 1771 w.
ARNST
Orange
Paul 1792 w.
ARRINGTON
Accomack
Jno. 1762 w.
Albemarle
Wm. 1749 w.
Goochland
Saml. 1731 i.
Henrico
———— 1700 a.
Isle of Wight
William 1725 w.
Southampton
Jno. 1761 w.
Jno. Jr. 1761 w.
Jesse 1792 i.
Westmoreland
Jno. 1712 w.
Thos. 1715 w.
Mildred 1727 i.
ARROWSMITH
Westmoreland
Richd. 1695 i.
Richd. 1752 w.
ARTHUR
Bedford
John 1793 w.
Campbell
Wm. 1783 w.
ARTIS
Middlesex
John 1779 w.
ARTISS
Southampton
Abraham 1772 i.
ARTRIP
Shenandoah
William 1776 a.
ARTRUP
Spotsylvania
Colbert 1752 a.

ARTS
Frederick
George 1762 i.
George 1767 w.
ARTZ
Shenandoah
Jacob 1789 i.
ARVIN
Lunenburg
Mordica 1779 w.
Jno. 1782 w.
ASBEE
Stafford
Robt. Sr. 1764 w.
ASBOROUGH
Spotsylvania
Jno. 1763 a.
ASBURY
Richmond
Thos. 1734 w.
Thos. 1767 i.
Ann 1797 i.
Stafford
Geo. 1759 i.
Westmoreland
Henry 1707 w.
Henry 1740 w.
Henry 1752 i.
Anne 1755 w.
Henry 1755 i.
ASCEW
Lunenburg
Jno. 1780 w.
ASCOUGH
Richmond
Thos. 1701 w.
ASGRIFIN
Richmond
Wm. 1746 i.
ASH
Accomack
Bridget 1732 i.
Fauquier
Francis 1774 w.
Northampton
Jos. 1758 i.
Mary 1761 i.
ASHALL
Norfolk
Geo. 1672 w.
ASHBE
Halifax
Joseph 1779 w.
ASHBEY
Princess Anne
Wm. 1777 i.
ASHBROOK
Chesterfield
Peter 1756 w.
Peter Jr. 1759 i.
Peter 1759 i.
Martha 1792 i.

Wm. 1796 w.
Henrico
Peter 1714 i.
Jennet 1718 w.
ASHBROOKE
Frederick
Aaron 1751 w.
ASHBURN
Northumberland
Thos. 1724 i.
Peter 1750 w.
Thos. 1750 w.
John 1772 w.
Geo. 1797 i.
ASHBY
Accomack
Rachel 1751 i.
Wm. 1770 i.
Jno. 1792 w.
Geo. 1795 w.
Thos. 1795 i.
David 1796 w.
Ezekiel 1797 w.
Nancy 1797 w.
Wm. 1797 w.
Rachel 1798 i.
Fauquier
Nimrod 1774 i.
Robert 1792 w.
Frederick
Thom. 1753 i.
Wm. 1773 i.
Princess Anne
Wm. 1697 a.
Wm. 1702 i.
Jno. 1721 i.
Wm. 1776 w.
York
Matthew 1771 w.
ASHER
Culpeper
John 1798 w.
ASHFORD
Fairfax
Eliz. 1774 i.
Michael 1794 w.
Lancaster
Jno. 1713 nw.
Prince William
Ann 1734 w.
Michael 1734 w.
ASHLEN
Fluvanna
Jno. 1795 w.
ASHLEY
Middlesex
May 1770 w.
Norfolk
Jno. 1751 w.
Edmd. 1753 w.
William 1753 w.
Jno. 1760 i.

Wm. 1760 i.
James 1763 w.
Nancy 1798 w.
Princess Anne
Edwd. 1720 i.
Wm. 1731 w.
ASHLIN
Fluvanna
Chris. 1796 i.
ASHLOCK
Halifax
Wm. 1768 i.
ASHLY
Accomack
Chas. 1735 w.
Ezekiel 1764 w.
ASHMAN
Princess Anne
Jno. 1743 i.
Westmoreland
Richd. 1726 i.
ASHMOND
Spotsylvania
Thos. 1791 a.
ASHMORE
Prince William
John 1737 i.
John 1784 w.
ASHTON
King George
Mary 1779 a.
Chas. 1783 w.
Jno. 1788 w.
Norfolk
John 1799 i.
Rappahannock
Jno. 1682 w.
Westmoreland
Jno. 1677 i.
Chas. 1724 w.
Henry 1731 w.
—— 1740 w.
Burdett 1746 i.
Mary 1756 i.
Henry 1758 i.
Burdett 1760 w.
ASHURST
Amelia
Henry 1790 w.
Chesterfield
Jacob 1778 i.
Francis 1784 w.
Halifax
Jos. 1763 i.
Henrico
Robt. 1745 i.
Westmoreland
Jno. 1732 i.
ASHWITH
Pittsylvania
Jno. 1780 i.

ASHWORTII
Charlotte
Isaac 1771 w.
Lunenburg
Jonathan 1759 w.
ASKEW
Goochland
Jno. 1758 w.
Mary 1769 w.
Isle of Wight
John 1683 i.
Nicholas 1728 i.
ASKIN
Fairfax
Jno. 1796 w.
Jno. 1797 i.
ASKLY
Princess Anne
Edmd. 1724 a.
ASQUE
Isle of Wight
John 1713 w.
ASSELIN
Amelia
David 1792 w.
ASTIN
Richmond
Anne 1713 w.
Westmoreland
Robt. 1663 w.
ASTON
Goochland
Chas. 1792 i.
ASTROP
Augusta
Robt. 1790 w.
ATCHISON
Lancaster
William 1768 i.
Northampton
Saml. 1782 w.
ATKERSON
Goochland
Mary 1791 i.
Mecklenburg
Lucy 1782 i.
Sussex
Joseph 1797 i.
ATKINS
Charlotte
Wm. 1782 i.
Chesterfield
Jno. 1786 w.
Jno. 1787 i.
Essex
James 1744 w.
Henrico
Jno. 1713 i.
Isle of Wight
John 1799 w.
Lancaster
Mark 1721 i.

Pittsylvania
Wm. 1784 w.
Prince Edward
Robt. 1778 i.
Prince George
Richd. 1718 w.
Prince William
Thom. 1780 i.
Randolph
John 1798 i.
Southampton
Mial 1782 i.
Surry
Anthony 1781 i.
Sussex
Wilmoth 1771 i.
ATKINSON
Accomack
Jas. 1699 i.
Chesterfield
Jas. 1782 w.
Cumberland
Saml. 1794 w.
Essex
Charles 1703 i.
Chas. 1761 w.
Nicholas 1773 w.
James 1782 w.
Goochland
Sarah 1730 i.
Eliz. 1738 i.
Robt. 1742 w.
Jos. 1773 i.
Isle of Wight
Thomas 1688 w.
Susanna 1698 i.
James 1723 w.
James 1739 w.
Thomas 1739 i.
Thomas 1744 i.
Mary 1760 w.
Christopher 1763 w.
Joseph 1765 w.
Joseph 1776 w.
Isle of Wight
Benjamin 1795 w.
Greensville
James 1794 i.
Thomas 1796 w.
Aaron 1797 w.
Mecklenburg
Jno. 1779 w.
Ohio
Mathias 1778 a.
Southampton
Thos. 1771 w.
Eliz. 1774 i.
Timothy 1777 w.
Thos. 1782 i.
Mial 1781 w.
Hardy 1784 i.
Saml. 1785 w.

Hardy 1787 w.
Ann 1795 w.
Wm. 1796 i.
Spotsylvania
Geo. 1790 w.
Surry
Jno. 1737 w.
Robt. 1749 w.
Anthony 1756 i.
Jno. 1796 w.
Saml. 1797 w.
Sussex
Henry 1755 w.
Thos. Jr. 1767 w.
Thos. 1774 w.
Thos. 1777 i.
Joseph 1795 w.
Benj. 1797 w.
York
Alex. 1721 i.
ATKISON
Sussex
Jno. 1794 w.
Surry
Thos. 1726 w.
ATKISSON
Goochland
Wm. 1778 w.
Surry
Wm. 1735 i.
James 1777 i.
ATQUIRE
Chesterfield
Jacob 1776 i.
ATTKINS
Westmoreland
Robt. 1731 i.
ATTWELL
Prince William
William 1797 w.
ATTWOOD
Essex
Francis 1749 i.
Princess Anne
Edwd. 1709 w.
Thos. 1720 w.
Wm. 1720 w.
Westmoreland
Jno. 1750 i.
ATWELL
Prince William
Thos. 1789 w.
Westmoreland
Thos. 1703 w.
Jno. 1713 w.
Eliz. 1718 i.
Francis 1725 w.
Youell 1731 i.
Jno. 1770 w.
Thos. 1776 i.
Richd. 1785 w.
Jno. 1788 i.

Jno. 1791 w.
Youell 1791 w.
ATWOOD
King George
Jno. 1789 a.
Middlesex
Jno. 1677 a.
Nicholas 1717 i.
Prince Edward
James 1771 w.
James Sr. 1773 i.
Princess Anne
Jno. 1723 w.
Edwd. 1772 w.
Anthony 1793 w.
York
Richd. 1669 w.
Westmoreland
Gilbert 1715 i.
AUBLIN
Northumberland
Henry 1726 i.
Peter 1726-7 i.
AUBREY
Prince William
Francis 1741 w.
AUBRY
Charlotte
Saml. 1768 i.
Henrico
Andrew 1715 w.
AUCHIN
Prince Edward
Chris. 1761 w.
AUDLEY
Henrico
Jno. 1710 i.
AUGHNEY
Hampshire
Darbey 1795 w.
Anna 1796 w.
AULT
Ohio
Mathias 1791 w.
AUSTEN
Northumberland
John 1751 i.
AUSTIN
Chesterfield
Reubin 1796 w.
Charles City
Wm. 1794 w.
Cumberland
James 1792 w.
Henrico
Jas. 1736 i.
Mary 1787 w.
Lancaster
Thos. 1731 i.
Lunenburg
Richd. 1759 w.
Jno. 1760 w.

Pittsylvania
Hannah 1784 i.
Wm. 1786 i.
Princess Anne
Cornelius 1770 w.
Danl. 1775 w.
Richmond
Henry 1706 w.
Southampton
Wm. 1778 w.
York
Jno. 1799 w.
AUTER
Berkeley
James 1797 i.
AUTON
Loudoun
Wm. 1773 i.
AVARY
Surry
Jno. 1752 w.
Sussex
Wm. 1783 w.
York
Geo. 1665 w.
AVENT
Sussex
Jno. 1755 w.
Thos. 1757 w.
Wm. 1771 i.
Thos. 1795 w.
AVERETH
Lunenburg
Thos. 1757 w.
AVERIES
Surry
Thos. 1751 i.
AVERIS
Brunswick
Wm. 1767 i.
AVERY
Brunswick
Jno. 1781 w.
Edwd. 1797 i.
Southampton
Robt. 1776 w.
Fortune 1780 w.
Joell 1782 i.
Surry
Richd. 1685 w.
Sussex
Jno. 1769 i.
Richd. 1776 w.
York
Mary 1713 w.
AVES
Norfolk
William 1779 w.
AVIS
Norfolk
William 1752 w.
John 1792 i.

Princess Anne
Jno. 1749 w.
AVOIES
Brunswick
Wm. 1770 i.
AVORISS
Surry
Jno. 1762 w.
AVORIT
Lunenburg
Thos. 1759 w.
AVORY
Lunenburg
Thos. 1757 i.
Amelia
Iyes 1760 w.
Wm. 1795 i.
AWBARY
Fairfax
Geo. 1754 w.
AWBORNE
York
Richd. 1681-2 i.
AWBREY
Essex
Henry 1694 w.
Richd. 1697 w.
Fairfax
Jno. 1744 w.
Loudoun
Thos. 1787 w.
Westmoreland
Jno. 1726 w.
Chandler 1756 w.
AWBURY
Fairfax
Richd. 1744 w.
AX
Berkeley
William 1782 i.
AXFORD
Orange
Jno. 1744 a.
Higgins 1744 i.
AXSTEAD
Princess Anne
Jno. 1724 i.
Wm. 1784 i.
Wm. 1789 i.
AXSTELL
Norfolk
Jno. 1686 w.
AXWELL
Norfolk
Thos. 1678-9 w.
AYERS
Accomack
Richd. 1796 i.
AYLETT
Westmoreland
Wm. 1744 w.

AYLWARD
York
Wm. 1706 i.
AYMES
Accomack
Jas. 1737 w.
AYRES
Accomack
Widow 1696 i.
Richd. Hill 1718 w.
Edmd. 1719 w.
Francis 1721 w.
Richd. 1721 w.
Francis 1723 i.
Richd. Hill 1724 i.
Jacob 1782 w.
Jacob 1788 i.
Richd. 1798 w.
Amherst
Saml. 1784 w.
Bedford
James 1797 w.
Essex
William 1705-6 i.
Thos. 1721 w.
Thos. 1726 i.
Thos. 1734 i.
Thos. 1756 w.
William 1792 w.
Isle of Wight
Francis 1676 w.
Richmond
Robt. 1719 l.
Pittsylvania
Nathaniel 1778 w.
AYRTON
Essex
Abraham 1711 i.
AYSCOUGH
Henrico
Henry 1703-4 i.

B
BABB
Isle of Wight
Mary 1757 w.
Frederick
Philip 1762 i.
Thomas 1779 w.
Isle of Wight
Robert 1782 i.
Robert 1793 i.
York
Wm. 1717 w.
Mary 1719 w.
BABBICOM
Henrico
Jas. 1692 w.
BABER
Albemarle
Robert 1749 w.
John 1758 i.

Edward 1798 w.
Bedford
George 1771 i.
Campbell
Robert 1786 w.
Fluvanna
Thos. Sr. 1778 w.
King George
Benj. 1799 w.
Wythe
Jas. 1798 w.
BACCUS
Westmoreland
Thos. 1757 i.
BACH
Madison
John 1794 a.
BACHELDER
Richmond
Mary 1746 w.
BACHELLER
Norfolk
Jas. 1734-5 w.
BACHELOR
Norfolk
Richard 1682 w.
John 1782 w.
BACHLER
Frederick
John 1778 w.
BACKER
Accomack
John 1713 w.
BACKHOUSE
Rockbridge
Joseph 1778 w.
BACKHURST
Charles City
James 1774 i.
York
James 1727 w.
BACON
Henrico
Langston 1755 w.
Lunenburg
John 1759 w.
Lyddal 1775 w.
Norfolk
Richard Sr. 1720 w.
Richard 1778 w.
Richard 1797 i.
Northumberland
Wm. 1659 i.
Westmoreland
Thos. 1657 i.
York
Nath'l 1691-2 w.
BADCOCK
Berkeley
Wm. 1787 i.

BADEN
Middlesex
Henry 1752 i.
BADGER
Accomack
Jacob 1754 i.
Reignold 1748 w.
John Sr. 1769 w.
Abbegal 1773 w.
Nathl. 1795 w.
Northumberland
Leeanna 1778 w.
Northampton
Ezekiel 1777 i.
BADGET
Chesterfield
Thos. (179-) i.
BADGETT
Surry
Thos. 1777 w.
Eliz. 1781 w.
Jno. 1794 i.
BADUM
Northampton
Jno. 1661 i.
Bargara 1662 w.
BAGAM
Middlesex
Jno. 1701 i.
BAGBEY
Powhatan
Henry 1790 w.
BAGBY
Louisa
Jno. 1789 w.
BAGE
Surry
Thos. 1700 w.
Thos. 1740 i.
Thos. 1795 w.
BAGET
Cumberland
Sarah 1775 w.
BAGG
Accomack
Sam'l. 1775 i.
BAGGALY
Accomack
Gervas 1705 i.
BAGGE
Accomack
Wm. 1772 w.
Sam'l. 1774 w.
Anne 1798 w.
Wm. 1799 i.
Essex
Mary 1726 w.
Edmond 1734 w.
Robt. 1755 w.
John 1726 w.
Westmoreland
Mary 1713 w.

BAGGETT
Fairfax
Ignatious 1783 i.
BAGGOTT
Spotsylvania
Jno. 1777 w.
BAGGS
Rockbridge
Alexander 1786 w.
BAGLEY
Amelia
Geo. 1769 w.
James 1787 i.
Norfolk
Wm. 1776 w.
Northampton
Thos. 1672 w.
Surry
Peter Sr. 1684/5 i.
Peter 1735 w.
Jno. 1736 w.
Eliz. 1756 w.
Sussex
Peter 1758 w.
BAGNAL
Isle of Wight
James 1702 w.
Nathan 1736 w.
Ann 1754 w.
Richard 1773 w.
Nathan 1784 w.
Wm. 1784 w.
BAGNALL
Isle of Wight
Roger (1647) w.
Robert 1719 w.
Nathan 1736 w.
BAGNEL
Isle of Wight
Richard 1779 i.
BAGWELL
Accomack
Jno. 1686 w.
Thos. 1689 w.
Edwd. 1708 w.
Thos. 1712 w.
Thos. 1714 i.
Jno. 1729 i.
Henry Jr. 1734 w.
Henry Sr. 1735 w.
Thos. 1740 i.
Eliz. 1749 w.
Jno. Sr. 1749 w.
Jno. 1751 i.
Wm. 1753 i.
Heli 1761 w.
Isiah 1764 w.
Thos. 1764 w.
Thos. 1766 i.
Thos. 1771 w.
Isaiah 1771 i.
Spencer 1779 w.

Chas. 1793 w.
Amherst
Jno. G. 1799 i.
Brunswick
Richard 1790 w.
Northampton
Alex. 1722 w.
Rappahannock
Roger 1679 w.
Westmoreland
Amos 1737 i
BAGWILL
Accomack
Jno. 1796 w.
Sophia 1797 w.
Jno. 1798 i.
BAIDEN
Middlesex
Thos. 1730 i.
BAILES
Northumberland
Jno. 1660 w.
BAILEY
Accomack
Jno. 1768 i.
Albemarle
Wm. 1762 w.
Robertson 1783 w.
Callem 1787 w.
Jno. 1792 w.
Jno. 1794 w.
Amelia
Benj. Jr. 1788 i.
Brunswick
Walter 1760 w.
Berkeley
Tarpley 1798 i.
Campbell
Jno. 1783 i.
Chesterfield
Jas. 1762 w.
Culpeper
Robert 1780 i.
Cumberland
Noah 1762 w.
Essex
David 1785 w.
Fauquier
Carr 1771 w.
James 1772 i.
James 1777 i.
Jno. 1779 w.
Fluvanna
Thos. 1789 w.
Goochland
Thos. 1775 w.
Greensville
Wm. 1796 i.
Henrico
Jos. 1783 w.
King George
Stephen 1794 w.

Lancaster
Jas. 1674 w.
Geo. 1677 w.
Wm. 1704 w.
Wm. 1734 w.
Jno. 1739 i.
James 1749 w.
Jas. 1759 i.
John 1762 w.
Eunice 1772 w.
John 1784 w.
Lunenburg
Henry 1761 w.
Norfolk
Walter 1722 w.
Jas. 1724 i.
Wm. 1777 i.
Wm. 1783 w.
Isaac 1785 w.
Margaret 1785 w.
Dinah 1797 w.
Northampton
Margaret 1736 w.
Northumberland
Jacob 1720 i.
Stephen 1771 i.
Wm. 1771 i.
Wm. 1772 i.
Richmond
Jno. 1736 i.
Jno. 1751 w.
Wm. 1759 i.
Jno. 1780 w.
Katey 1780 w.
Rockbridge
Chas. 1779 a.
Southampton
Wm. 1773 w.
Sarah 1774 w.
Robt. 1775 w.
Barnaby 1783 w.
Benj. 1785 w.
Mary 1788 i.
Hartwell 1798 i.
Surry
Robt. 1712 w.
Anselm Sr. 1759 w.
Edwd. 1762 w.
Edwd. Jr. 1763 i.
Anselm 1772 w.
Thos. 1771 i.
Benj. 1779 w.
Benj. 1785 w.
Jno. 1786 w.
Saml. 1796 w.
Sussex
Abidon 1796 w.
Michael 1798 w.
Westmoreland
Basil 1695 w.
Stephen 1697 w.
Jno. 1736 w.

Wm. 1748/9 w.
Eliz. 1759 i.
Jas. 1775 i.
Jno. 1776 i.
Wm. 1782 w.
Danl. 1786 w.
Jeremiah Garland
1791 w.
BAILIFF
Berkeley
Daniel 1777 i.
BAILIS
Northumberland
Jno. 1786 w.
Stafford
Jno. 1747 i.
BAILLEUL
Albemarle
Peter 1770 w.
BAILY
Accomack
Jno. 1717 w.
Richd. 1737 i.
Wm. 1774 w.
Chas. 1782 w.
Norfolk
——— (1723?) w.
Samuel 17(83?) i.
BAINE
Henrico
Robt. 1785 w.
Sussex
Jno. 1780 i.
BAINES
Norfolk
Jno. Jr. 1783 w.
Sussex
James 1788 w.
BAINTON
York
Saml. 1690 w.
BAIR
Shenandoah
Henry 1794 a.
BAIRD
Sussex
Jno. 1778 w.
Reubin 1787 w.
Wm. 1792 w.
BAISSE
Goochland
Edwd. 1730 i.
BAISEY
Northumberland
Josias 1756 i.
BAITES
Prince George
Isace 1714 i.
BAITS
Fairfax
Jno. 1779 i.

BAKER

Accomack
Edwd. 1664 w.
Jno. 1730 i.
Mary 1763 i.
Jno. 1764 i.
Wm. 1774 i.
Jno. 1775 w.
Wm. 1782 w.
David 1790 i.
Jno. Sheperd 1796 w.
Salathiel 1796 w.

Albemarle
Francis 1760 w.

Berkeley
John 1798 w.
Walter 1786 w.
John 1799 w.

Botetourt
Martin 1782 i.

Brunswick
Wm. 1742 i.

Charlotte
Theodorick 1797 w.

Chesterfield
Thos. 1774 w.
Sarah 1778 w.
Jerman 1792 w.
Jno. Sr. 1798 w.

Culpeper
Mary 1754 i.

Cumberland
Henry W. 1795 i.

Essex
Joseph 1720 w.
Henry Sr. 1743 w.
Amy 1745 w.
John 1789 w.
John 1794 i.

Fauquier
John 1793 w.

Frederick
Charles Jr. 1760 i.
John 1763 w.
John Nicholas 1764 i.
Joshua 1765 w.
Samuel 1796 w.

Hardy
Wm. 1793 w.

Henrico
Jas. 1706 i.
Geo. 1752 w.
Danl. 1754 w.

Isle of Wight
Francis 1669 w.
Henry 1712 w.
Mary 1734 w.
Benj. 1756 w.
Lawrence 1760 w.
Richard 1772 w.
Richard 1775 i.
Lawrence 1794 i.

Lancaster
Thos. 1698 i.

Loudoun
Jno. 1767 i.
Nathan 1775 w.
Wm. 1782 w.
Philip 1786 w.

Louisa
Jno. 1791 i.
Thos. 1775 i.

Lunenburg
Saml. 1752 i.

Middlesex
Wm. 1782 w.

Montgomery
Joseph 1786 i.
Joseph (1787) i.

Mecklenburg
Jane 1794 w.
Zachariah 1773 w.

Northampton
Danl. 1667 w.
Hugh 1664 w.
Wm. 1700 w.
Jno. 1719 w.
Timothy B. 1773 w.
Elijah 1799 w.

Prince Edward
Martha 1759 w.
Robt. 1759 w.
Mary 1760 w.
Dugless 1765 w.
Robt. Sr. 1773 w.
Douglass 1778 w.
Joshua 1777 w.
Robt. 1780 i.
Saml. 1782 w.
Saml. 1971 w.
Christian 1795 w.
Douglass 1797 w.

Princess Anne
Edw. 1701 w.
Lewis 1761 w.

Prince William
George 1798 i.

Richmond
Saml. 1718 i.
Bartholomew 1723 w.
Wm. 1735 i.
Wm. 1782 w.
Saml. 1798 w.

Shenandoah
Joseph 1781 a.
Philip 1781 i.

Surry
Lawrence 1681 w.
Henry 1700 w.
Jno. 1779 i.

Washington
Isaac 1796 w.

Westmoreland
Saml. 1698 i.

Susannah 1721 w.
Thos. 1723 w.
Jno. 1749 w.
Wm. 1751 i.
Jno. 1758 i.
Jno. 1762 w.
Jno. 1764 w.
Butler 1764 w.
Wm. 1769 i.

York
Jno. 1659 i.
Saml. 1673 w.
Wm. 1686 w.
Mary 1719 nw.
Richd. 1736 w.
Wm. 1777 w.
Jno. (F(rederick)
   1780 w.
Wm. 1793 i.

BALANCE

Norfolk
Ephraim 1778 i.

BALBRIDGE

Westmoreland
Wm. 1659 w.
James 1659 w.
Dorothy 1662 w.
James 1664 w.

BALD

Northampton
Thos. 1721/2 w.

BALDERSON

Richmond
Ebenezer 1775 i.

BALDOCK

Amherst
Richd. 1778 i.

BALDRIDGE

Westmoreland
Jas. 1655 i.
Thos. 1655 i.

BALDRY

York
Robt. 1675 w.

BALDWIN

Accomack
Jno. 1757 i.

Amelia
Francis 1747 a.
Wm. 1760 w.
Jno. 1770 w.

Berkeley
Wm. 1785 w.

Botetourt
Samuel 1793 w.

Campbell
Zabulon 1795 i.

Isle of Wight
Wm. 1696 i.
Benj. 1708 w.
Wm. 1736 i.

Essex
Nicholas 1744 i.
Isle of Wight
Wm. 1796 i.
Prince Edward
John 1799 w.
BALE
York
Jas. 1748 w.
BALEE
Surry
Robt. 1719 i.
BALENDINE
Fairfax
John 1782 w.
BALEY
Accomack
Henry 1741 i.
Jno. 1759 w.
Robt. 1760 i.
Wm. 1775 i.
Cumberland
Christopher 1762 w.
Goochland
Henry 1735 w.
Halifax
Henry 1756 i.
Isle of Wight
John 1712 w.
Lancaster
Jno. 1694 w.
Westmoreland
Stephen 1746 i.
Wm. 1749 i.
Stephen Sr. 1753 w.
Jas. 1756 i.
Stephen 1759 i.
BALL
Accomack
Alphonso 1661 i.
Amherst
Valentine 1769 w.
Chesterfield
Jas. 1782 i.
Culpeper
Samuel 1751 w.
Essex
Wm. 1696 i.
John 1707-8 w.
John 1752 i.
John Sr. 1779 w.
Ansten 1782 w.
Abner 1798 w.
Fairfax
John 1766 w.
Moses 1792 w.
Fauquier
John 1773 i.
James 1794 w.
Frederick
Wm. 1796 w.

King George
Jeduthan 1750 i.
Lancaster
Wm. 1680 w.
Wm. 1694 w.
Hannah 1695 w.
Thos. 1702 i.
Margaret 1709 w.
Joseph 1711 w.
Richd. 1726 w.
David 1732 w.
Sarah 1742 w.
Wm. Jr. 1742 i.
Wm. 1744 w.
James Jr. 1747 i.
Mary Ann 1749/50 w.
James 1754 w.
Benjamin 1765 w.
Jesse 1778 w.
Margaret 1783 w.
Wm. 1785 w.
Lettice 1788 w.
James 1789 w.
James 1794 i.
James 1795 w.
Loudoun
John 1768 i.
John 1777 i.
Norfolk
Saml. 1690 w.
Benj. 1756 w.
Wm. 1758 i.
Northumberland
Jas. 1721 w.
Wm. 1745 i.
Geo. 1746 w.
John 1751 w.
Grace 1752 w.
Spencer 1767 w.
Jesse 1769 w.
Geo. 1770 w.
Joseph 1779 w.
David 1780 w.
Joseph 1781 i.
Richard 1784 w.
Ann 1784 i.
Jas. 1786 w.
Spencer Mottrom
1787 w.
Geo. 1791 w.
Betty 1794 w.
Ann 1795 w.
Geo. 1799 w.
Princess Anne
Geo. 1760 w.
Prince William
Edward 1742 i.
Richmond
Geo. 1754 i.
Williamson 1794 w.
Stafford
Benj. 1786 w.

Westmoreland
Wm. 1670 w.
Robt. 1723 w.
Gerard 1737 w.
Geo. 1743 w.
Emanuel 1749/50 w.
BALLANCE
Norfolk
Richard 1736/7 w.
Moses 1758 w.
Richard 1782 i.
Richard 1792 w.
BALLANDINE
Lancaster
Wm. 1736 w.
BALLANDS
Norfolk
Wm. 1700 w.
BALLANTINE
Greenbrier
William 1792 i.
Henrico
Hugh 1735 i.
BALLARD
Albemarle
Jno. 1780 w.
Thos. 1782 w.
Bedford
William 1794 w.
Charles City
Wm. T. 1799 w.
Henrico
Jno. 1691 w.
Isle of Wight
Peter 1748 i.
Mecklenburg
Jno. 1787 w.
Isle of Wight
Sally 1798 w.
Norfolk
John 1678/9 nw.
Elizabeth 1787 w.
Princess Anne
Robt. 1772 i.
Spotsylvania
Bland 1792 w.
York
Thos. 1711 w.
Wm. 1719 ab.
Matthew 1718 w.
Robt. 1735 i.
Matthew 1741 i.
Jno. 1745 w.
Jno. 1751 i.
BALLENCE
Norfolk
Ephraim 1777 w.
BALLENDINE
Prince William
Frances 1793 w.
Frances 1798 i.
Thomas W. 1797 nw.

BALLENGER
Culpeper
  Edward 1780 w.
Fairfax
  Daniel 1778 i.
  William 1778 w.
Goochland
  Jos. 1744 w.
BALLENTINE
Norfolk
  Geo. Sr. 1733 w.
  John 1734 w.
  Richard 1734 i.
  William 1747 w.
  David 1753 w.
  John 1763 i.
  Wm. 1763 i.
  Samuel 1784 w.
  David 1786 w.
  Richard 1790 w.
  Paul 1791 i.
  Joshua 1797 i.
Westmoreland
  Jno. 1792 i.
BALLINGTINE
Norfolk
  Alex. 1715 w.
BALLINTINE
Norfolk
  Geo. 1702 w.
BALLETT
Frederick
  James 1799 i.
BALLEW
Henrico
  Dorothy 1701 i.
BALLINGER
Frederick
  Josiah 1748 w.
BALLOW
Albemarle
  Leonard 1749 i.
  Thos. 1752 w.
  Bernett 1753 w.
  Susanna 1756 w.
Bedford
  Leonard 1783 i.
Cumberland
  Charles 1767 w.
  Temperance 1768 w.
  Wm. 1795 i.
Henrico
  Wm. 1700 w.
  Chas. 1727 w.
Powhatan
  Thos. 1794 w.
BALMER
Surry
  Francis 1730 i.
BALONS
Lunenburg
  Wm. 1748 i.

BALSON
Northampton
  Francis 1725 w.
BALSOM
York
  Eliz. 1776 i.
BALSOR
Fairfax
  Gasper 1782 w.
BALTEZER
Westmoreland
  Peter Jas. 1729 i.
BALTHORP
Westmoreland
  Jno. 1762 w.
BALTHROP
King George
  Francis 1754 i.
BALY
Norfolk
  Betty 1742 w.
Northampton
  Richd. 1661 w.
  Margt. 1736 i.
Surry
  Danl. 1679 i.
  Thos. 1713 i.
BAMPTON
Isle of Wight
  William 1697 i.
BANCKS
Northumberland
  Eliz. 1720 w.
  Robt. 1727 i.
BANDY
Accomack
  Mary 1776 i.
Botetourt
  Richard 1795 w.
BANE
Frederick
  William 1765 i.
Montgomery
  James 1790 w.
BANETT
Norfolk
  Smith 1784 i.
BANISTEN
Princess Anne
  James 1754 i.
BANISTER
Augusta
  Mark 1777 i.
Westmoreland
  Geo. 1762 w.
BANISTOR
Bedford
  William 1767 w.
BANK
Northampton
  Harrison 1717/18 w.

BANKHEAD
Westmoreland
  Jas. 1786 w.
BANKS
Accomack
  Christopher 175– i.
Albemarle
  Wm. 1763 i.
Amherst
  Gerard 1776 w.
Bedford
  Thomas 1755 w.
Brunswick
  James 1798 i.
Chesterfield
  Thos. 1799 w.
Essex
  James 1785 w.
  Richard 1793 w.
  Robert 1799 i.
Halifax
  Thos. 1775 w.
  Thos. 1777 i.
Norfolk
  Jno. 1675 w.
  Thomas 1752 i.
Northampton
  Thos. 1718 w.
  Thos. 1727 i.
Orange
  Gerard 1768 w.
Princess Anne
  Wm. 1695 i.
  Thos. 1698 i.
  Jno. 1699 i.
  Harrison 1774 w.
  Thos. 1784 w.
  Rebecca 1790 w.
Sussex
  James 1758 w.
  Burrell 1769 i.
BANNAN
Essex
  Nicholas 1779 i.
BANNER
Berkeley
  John 1783 w.
BANNERMAN
Middlesex
  Mark 1727 w.
BANSDELL
Orange
  Jesse 1792 i.
BANTON
Lancaster
  Thos. 1698 i.
  Edwd. 1701 i.
  Rebeccka 1754 i.
  Rebekah 1757 w.
Powhatan
  Wm. Sr. 1779 w.

Spotsylvania
Jno. 1735 w.
BANUM
Northampton
Wm. 1735 i.
Wm. 1738 i.
BAPTIST
York
Morgan 1706 i.
Jno. 1729 i.
Edwd. 1747 w.
Eliz. 1747 w.
Jno. 1761 w.
Jno. 1781 i.
Margt. 1782 w.
Edwd. 1797 w.
BARBAR
York
Wm. 1669 w.
Mary 1676 w.
Jane 1686/7 w.
Jane 1700 a.
Thos. 1709 w.
Thos. 1711 w.
Thos. 1718 w.
William 1719 a.
Thos. 1727 w.
Wm. 1733 w.
Jas. 1742/3 i.
Eliz. 1750 i.
Jno. 1750 i.
BARBARY
Northampton
Wilson 1786 nw.
BARBAY
Stafford
Andrew 1702 i.
BARBE
Stafford
Thos. 1752 w.
BARBEE
Essex
Jno. 1750 w.
John 1730 w.
Ann 1766 w.
William 1757 i.
Fauquier
Andrew 1795 w.
Middlesex
Wm. 1720 w.
Powhatan
Thos. 1788 w.
BARBER
Accomack
Thos. 1745 i.
Augusta
Geo. 1750 i.
Norfolk
Matthew 1792 w.
Frederick
James 1777 w.

Henrico
Wm. 1753 i.
Northumberland
Jno. 1672 w.
Princess Anne
Jacob 1757 w.
Prudence 1758 w.
Rappahannock
Richd. 1678 w.
Richmond
Wm. 1721 w.
Chas. 1726 w.
Saml. 1735 w.
Thos. 1747 i.
Thos. 1752 i.
Thos. 1754 w.
Saml. 1761 w.
Ann 1763 i.
BARBEY
Fauquier
Thomas 1777 i.
BARBOUR
Culpeper
James 1775 w.
Sarah 1788 w.
Orange
Richard 1794 w.
Philip 1797 i.
BARCLAY
Essex
Patrick 1749 w.
BARDEN
Loudoun
Thomas 1798 i.
Middlesex
Edw. 1759 a.
BARDON
Loudoun
Thomas 1775 i.
Middlesex
Jno. 1786 i.
BARECRAFT
Northampton
Thos. 1778 w.
Thos. 1725 w.
Lucretia 1745 i.
BARECROFT
Northumberland
Geo. 1780 i.
Wm. 1784 w.
BAREFOOT
Essex
Adam 1710 w.
Surry
Noah 1711 i.
BARGER
Augusta
Casper 1760 i.
Berkeley
Peter 1790 w.

BARHAM
Southampton
Robt. 1760 w.
Benj. 1779 w.
Thos. 1786 i.
Chas. 1791 w.
Jas. 1791 w.
Robt. 1797 w.
Surry
Thos. 1767 i.
Robt. 1770 w.
Jno. 1771 w.
Wm. 1772 i.
Wm. 1774 i.
Jesse 1780 i.
Jno. 1787 w.
Sussex
Thos. 1784 w.
York
Benj. 1764 i.
BARHAW
Fauquier
Peter 1780 w.
BARINGTON
Norfolk
Benj. 1714 i.
Samuel Jr. 1785 i.
BARKALOO
Hampshire
James 1796 w.
BARKER
Accomack
Wm. 1783 i.
Brunswick
Lucy 1798 i.
Chesterfield
Jno. 1792 w.
Culpeper
James 1779 w.
Fairfax
John 1792 a.
Moses 1792 w.
Fauquier
John 1784 i.
William 1788 w.
John 1795 i.
Goochland
Thos. 1782 i.
King George
Edmund 1756 w.
Jos. 1771 w.
Lancaster
Thos. 1703 w.
Thos. 1710 w.
Wm. 1710/11 i.
Pittsylvania
Wm. 1778 w.
Geo. 1796 i.
Princess Anne
Maison 1782 i.
Prince William
Joshua 1791 i.

Maright 1792 w.
Richmond
Jos. 1713 w.
Larnce 1716 i.
Wm. 1757 i.
Jas. 1760 w.
Southampton
Wm. 1781 w.
Surry
Jno. 1714 w.
Grace 1725 w.
Jno. 1740 w.
Jno. 1742 w.
Geo. 1744 i.
Jethro 1747 w.
Grace 1750 w.
Richd. 1753 i.
Jethro 1754 w.
Jno. 1758 w.
Josiah 1761 w.
Arthur 1771 w.
Jethro 1772 i.
Jno. 1777 w.
Thos. 1782 w.
Faithy 1787 w.
Saml. 1789 w.
Richd. 1799 w.
Sussex
Henry 1758 i.
Jno. 1764 w.
Joseph 1771 i.
James 1772 i.
Joseph 1772 i.
Jehu 1773 i.
Mary 1779 w.
Drewry 1782 w.
Jehu 1782 w.
Nathl. 1785 w.
Westmoreland
Youell 1740 i.
York
Chas. 1710 w.
BARKLEY
Loudoun
Barbara 1785 w.
BARKSDALE
Albemarle
Wm. 1796 w.
Charlotte
Wm. 1771 i.
Collier 1774 w.
Halifax
Nathl. 1790 w.
Henry
Henry 1788 w.
Spotsylvania
Danl. 1789 w.
Washington
John 1779 i.
BARLEY
Albemarle
Samuel 1797 w.

Norfolk
Robt. 1682 w.
BARLOW
Albemarle
Thos. 1778 w.
Culpeper
Adam 1786 i.
Isle of Wight
Thomas 1679 w.
George (1719) w.
Sarah 1729 w.
Thomas 1749 w.
John 1754 w.
Benjamin 1759 w.
Martha 1760 w.
Jesse 1780 i.
William 1781 w.
John 1782 w.
Benjamin 1793 i.
Francis 1796 i.
Thomas 1796 w.
Nathaniel 1797 i.
Thomas 1798 i.
William 1798 w.
Norfolk
Henry 1760 w.
Northampton
Henry 1762 i.
Surry
Jno. 1728 w.
Sussex
Wm. 1766 w.
Chas. 1775 i.
Northampton
Ralph 1652 w.
BARNACLE
Henrico
Henry 1677 nw.
BARNARD
York
Saml. 1720 w.
BARNATT
Isle of Wight
Robert 1670 w.
BARNELL
Isle of Wight
John 1685 w.
BARNER
Powhatan
Jno. 1788 i.
Surry
Francis 1729 w.
BARNES
Accomack
Wm. 1705 i.
Jno. 1714 w.
Jno. 1799 w.
Charles City
Marmaduke 1773 i.
Charlotte
Henry 1787 i.
Jas. 1796 i.

Cumberland
James 1751 w.
Essex
John 1755 i.
Fairfax
Abraham 1785 w.
Sarah 1786 w.
Sarah 1796 i.
Isle of Wight
Thomas 1683 w.
James (1720?) w.
Jacob 1721 i.
John 1737 w.
Jacob 1738 i.
Middlesex
Henry 1718 i.
Northumberland
Thos. 1712/13 w.
William 1770 w.
Norfolk
Thomas 1718 i.
Powhatan
Jno. 1787 w.
Prince Edward
Wm. 1760 w.
Princess Anne
Jno. 1758 w.
Saml. 1770 i.
Princess Anne
Joshua 1798 w.
Richmond
Abraham 1743 i.
Richd. 1761 w.
Wm. 1769 i.
Geo. 1775 nw.
Newman Brocken-
brough 1779 w.
Southampton
Joshua 1762 w.
Edwd. 1762 w.
Thos. 1765 i.
Thos. 1770 w.
Benj. 1779 w.
Burwell 1782 i.
Peninah 1792 i.
Jacob 1796 w.
Spotsylvania
Thos. 1753 w.
Surry
Jno. 1758 w.
Henry 1760 w.
Sussex
James 1792 w.
Westmoreland
Thos. 1728 w.
York
Matthew 1734 w.
Mary 1755 i.
BARNET
Botetourt
Joseph 1771 i.

Westmoreland
Jno. 1754 w.
BARNETT
Fluvanna
John 1786 w.
Goochland
Jno. Jr. 1756 w.
Isle of Wight
Robert 1670 i.
Montgomery
James 1791 w.
Orange
Jno. 1750 w.
James 1797 i.
Shenandoah
Michael 1788 w.
Spotsylvania
Thos. 1734 a.
Westmoreland
Eliz. 1760 i.
Richd. 1776 i.
BARNEY
Norfolk
John 1741/2 w.
Ann. 1743/4 w.
BARNEW
Amherst
Robt. 1786 w.
BARNHESLE
Culpeper
Leonard 1799 i.
BARNISER
Berkeley
Catherine 1781 w.
BARNS
Accomack
Jno. 1738 w.
Jno. 1753 i.
Arthur 1757 w.
Wm. 1773 w.
Wm. 1776 i.
Jno. Sacker 1777 w.
Augusta
Peter 1778 i.
Berkeley
James 1783 i.
Stephen 1784 w.
Culpeper
John 1799 w.
Greenbrier
Ozias 1782 i.
Northumberland
Edwd. 1749 w.
Henry 1790 w.
Neddey 1791 w.
Mary 1794 i.
Princess Anne
Anthony 1730 w.
Anthony Sr. 1734 i.
Jno. 1758 i.
Saml. 1758 i.
Absolom 1794 w.

Spotsylvania
Isaiah 1759 a.
BARNUM
Northampton
Eliz. 1771 w.
BARNWELL
Isle of Wight
Robert 1669 i.
BARR
Northumberland
John 1776 w.
BARRACLE
Culpeper
John 1779 i.
BARRADELL
York
Henry 1729 w.
BARRAT
Northumberland
Geo. 1748 i.
Richmond
Eliz. 1720 i.
BARRATT
Frederick
John 1770 i.
Northumberland
Nathl. 1751 i.
Rappahannock
Maggue 1684 w.
York
Thos. 1693 w.
BARRET
Albemarle
James 1789 w.
Goochland
James 1740 w.
Louisa
Mary 1746 w.
Mary 1785 i.
Richmond
Jno. 1717 i.
Southampton
Jacob 1768 i.
BARRETT
Amherst
Thos. 1794 a.
Augusta
Dominick 1793 i.
Frederick
Arthur 1745 w.
John 1763 w.
Benjamin 1778 w.
Mary 1781 w.
James 1782 w.
William 1791 w.
Louisa
Chas. 1771 a.
Norfolk
John 1785 w.
Northumberland
Wm. 1763 i.
Wm. 1774 w.

John 1775 i.
Wm. 1792 i.
Orange
James 1797 w.
Southampton
Edmond 1754 w.
Wm. 1782 w.
Wm. 1788 w.
Wm. Jr. 1788 i.
Westmoreland
Thos. 1673 i.
BARRICK
Essex
David 1725 i.
Ann 1732 w.
Middlesex
David 1769 w.
Jno. Jr. 1787 w.
Richmond
Geo. 1782 w.
Elizabeth 1794 w.
Surry
Geo. 1767 w.
BARRIER
Augusta
Casper 1760 a.
Jacob 1794 i.
BARRINGER
Lunenburg
Michael 1774 w.
BARRINGTON
Norfolk
William 1744/5 w.
Lemuel 1784 w.
Samuel Sr. 1784 w.
Lemuel 1799 w.
Shenandoah
Ann 1796 w.
BARRNES
Norfolk
Peter 1652 w.
BARRON
Greensville
Richard 1786 i.
York
Jas. 1662 w.
BARROT
Northumberland
Wm. 1743 w.
Pittsylvania
Jno. 1791 w.
Princess Anne
Thos. 1740 i.
BARROW
Frederick
Thomas 1777 w.
Rappahannock
Jno. 1685 w.
Richmond
Edwd. 1721 w.
Edwd. 1733 w.

Southampton
John 1777 w.
Surry
Thos. 1685 i.
Edmund 1721 i.
BARRY
Fairfax
Edward 1748 w.
John 1776 i.
Louisa
Geo. 1754 w.
Lunenburg
Jno. 1752 i.
Wm. T. 1798 i.
Mecklenburg
Hugh 1782 w.
Norfolk
Garrett 1685 i.
Spotsylvania
Thos. 1749 a.
BARSLEY
Princess Anne
Thos. 1694 w.
Wm. 1694 i.
BARTEE
Norfolk
Robert 1711 w.
Samuel 1765 w.
William 1772 w.
John 1782 w.
Robert 1782 w.
Robert 1783 w.
William 1784 i.
Isaac 1794 w.
Andree 1795 w.
Thomas 1796 w.
Samuel 1797 w.
BARTHOLOMEW
Brunswick
Jno. 1735 i.
Princess Anne
Richd. 1696 i.
Rockbridge
John 1786 i.
BARTLE
Fluvanna
Thos. 1798 w.
BARTLET
Princess Anne
Darby 1722 i.
BARTLETT
Berkeley
William 1777 w.
William 1792 i.
Isle of Wight
Robert 1679 nw.
King George
Thos. 1748 i.
Eliz. 1765 i.
Pittsylvania
Joshua 1772 i.

Richmond
Jas. 1747 w.
Thos. 1783 w.
Spotsylvania
Wm. 1775 w.
Surry
Walter 1699 w.
Westmoreland
Jno. 1773 i.
York
Michael 1670 w.
BARTLEY
Westmoreland
Chas. 1727 i.
Lunenburg
James 1762 w.
BARTON
Brunswick
Jno. 1738 i.
Essex
William 1783 i.
Frederick
Underhill 1797 w.
Norfolk
Walter 1691/2 w.
Northumberland
Robt. 1711 i.
Prince George
Susanna 1715 w.
Prince William
Valentine 1739 i.
Surry
Jno. 1679 i.
Westmoreland
Jno. 1698 w.
BARWEN
King George
Jno. 1770 a.
BARZEY
Middlesex
Wilkinson 1792 w.
BASBEECH
Chesterfield
Jno. 1777 w.
BASDEN
Isle of Wight
Joseph 1742 i.
BASHAW
Fluvanna
Spencer 1797 i.
Westmoreland
Peter 1745 w.
Warner 1796 w.
BASKERVILLE
Cumberland
Norvell 1750 w.
Jno. 1788 w.
Saml. 1795 i.
Mecklenburg
Geo. 1777 w.
Jno. 1797 i.

Powhatan
Jno. 1793 w.
BASKERVYLE
York
Jno. 1680 i.
Mary 1693 w.
Hugh 1747 w.
BASKET
Essex
Thomas 1724 i.
Middlesex
Henry 1720 w.
BASKETT
Cumberland
Wm. 1773 i.
BASKINS
Augusta
Robt. 1750 a.
BASLOR
Isle of Wight
Francis 1763 i.
BASNET
Fairfax
Thomas 1755 w.
BASNETT
Stafford
Abram 1749 i.
Princess Anne
Jno. 1697 w.
BASS
Amelia
Wm. 1793 w.
Edwd. 1795 w.
Brunswick
James 1771 w.
Thos. 1786 w.
Wm. 1785 w.
Chesterfield
Wm. 1746/7 w.
Wm. 1769 w.
Thos. 1769 w.
Cicily 1769 w.
Christopher 1772 w.
Christopher 1775 i.
Jos. 1777 w.
Jeremiah 1780 w.
Henry 179– w.
Jos. 1794 w.
Greensville
Burwell 1787 w.
Samuel 1796 w.
Henrico
Wm. 1695 w.
Norfolk
William 1742 w.
William Sr. 1756 i.
Southampton
Charles 1780 w.
Joshua 1779 w.
BASSAM
Cumberland
William 1768 w.

BASSET
Accomack
Jno. 1710 i.
Goochland
Nathl. 1732 w.
BASSETT
Norfolk
Wm. 1687 w.
BASTIANSON
Northampton
Peter 1668 i.
BASTINENSON
Northampton
Peter 1667 w.
Francis 1725 w.
BASY
Northumberland
Edmd. 1723/4 w.
BASYE
Culpeper
Edmond 1796 i.
Joseph 1799 w.
Northumberland
Isaac 1739 w.
Edmd. 1746 w.
Elesha 1768 w.
Jesse 1768 i.
John 1769 w.
John 1782 i.
BATCHELOR
Norfolk
John 1782 i.
BATCHELDER
Middlesex
Jno. 1720 w.
Sarah 1720 w.
Wm. 1727 w.
Saml. 1742 w.
Jas. 1750 a.
Saml. 1757 w.
Henry 1760 i.
Eliz. 1785 i.
Jos. 1785 w.
Jno. 1791 i.
Norfolk
James 1754 i.
BATCHELLOR
Westmoreland
Thos. 1719 w.
BATCHELOR
Frederick
John 1788 i.
Middlesex
Jno. 1769 i.
BATE
Lancaster
Jonathan 1680 w.
BATEMAN
Isle of Wight
Richard 1733 a.

BATEN
Isle of Wight
Richard 1732 w.
William 1731/2 w.
Middlesex
Wm. 1784 i.
BATES
Albemarle
Isaac 1752 w.
Amelia
Thos. 1775 w.
Abner 1789 w.
Bedford
John 1777 w.
Essex
Jno. Jr. 1733 w.
Jno. 1746 w.
Fairfax
Edward 1762 w.
Halifax
Jno. 1766 i.
Jno. 1777 w.
James 1788 i.
Madison
William 1794 w.
York
Jno. 1667 w.
Geo. 1677 w.
Jno. 1720 w.
Jno. 1721 a.
Jas. 1723 w.
Jno. 1723 w.
Jno. Jr. 1724 i.
Sarah 1768 w.
Jas. 1769 i.
Fleming 1784 w.
BATH
Isle of Wight
Kath. 1687 nw.
BATHIN
Fairfax
David 1746 i.
BATHURST
Essex
Lawrence 1705-6 w.
BATES
Brunswick
Robt. 1766 w.
BATMAN
Stafford
Jno. 1750 i.
BATSON
Northampton
Jno. 1704 w.
Jacob 1720 w.
Francis 1725 i.
Thos. 1725 w.
Ralph 1726 w.
Eliz. 1733 i.
Jonathan 1738 i.
Jos. 1738 w.
Jno. 1740 w.

Jonas 1748 w.
Jacob 1752 i.
Nehemiah 1752 w.
Anne 1755 w.
Jno. 1758 i.
Ralph 1764 w.
BATT
Berkeley
Thomas 1797 i.
Essex
Anthony 1704 i.
BATTAILE
Essex
John 1706-7 w.
Spotsylvania
Catherine 1757 a.
BATTALEY
Spotsylvania
Moses 1758 w.
Jno. 1770 w.
Eliz. 1771 w.
Eliz. 1788 w.
BATTALY
Fauquier
Ann 1783 w.
BATTE
Chesterfield
Chamberlaine 1757 i.
Wm. 1766 w.
Henry 1770 w.
Richd. 1781 w.
Greensville
William 1789 w.
Lewis 1790 w.
Henrico
Thos. Jr. 1691 i.
Prince George
Henry 1727 w.
BATTEN
Isle of Wight
Danl. 1703 w.
Danl. 1741 i.
Jno. 1762 w.
Saml. 1786 i.
Princess Anne
Wm. 1790 w.
Geo. Sr. 1799 w.
Richmond
Jno. 1712 w.
York
Ashaell 1666 w.
Jno. 1697 i.
BATTEMAN
Westmoreland
Wm. 1716 w.
BATTHROP
Westmoreland
Jno. 1762 i.
BATTIN
Isle of Wight
Danl. 1784 w.

Princess Anne
Jno. 1752 w.
BATTELL
Surry
Jno. Sr. 1728 w.
BATTLE
Southampton
Wm. 1767 w.
Surry
Mathew 1681 a.
Sussex
Hamlin 1774 w.
Chas. 1776 w.
Mary 1786 w.
BATTS
Brunswick
Geo. 1745 i.
Northampton
Wm. 1632 nw.
Westmoreland
Wm. 1675 w.
Surry
Wm. 1742 w.
Jno. 1785 w.
Mary 1797 i.
BATTSON
Loudoun
James 1778 w.
Northampton
Wm. 1720 w.
BAUFIELD
Accomack
Jno. 1764 w.
Wm. 1788 w.
BAUGH
Brunswick
Joseph 1798 w.
Chesterfield
Jas. 17— i.
Thos. 1751 w.
Wm. 1753 w.
Jno. 1762 i.
Jno. 1772 w.
Peter 1773 w.
Richd. 1777 w.
Jas. 1778 w.
Jno. 1784 w.
Francis 1784 w.
Richd. 1785 i.
Peter Sr. 1788 w.
Robt. 1791 w.
Alex. 1793 w.
Frances 1793 w.
Francis 1795 i.
Henrico
Wm. 1687 w.
Jno. 1726 w.
Lunenburg
Jno. 1770 i.
Powhatan
Joseph 1777 w.
Rachel 1786 i.

Rachel 1787 w.
Creacher 1791 i.
Abraham 1797 w.
Prince Edward
Jno. 1795 i.
BAUGHAN
Amherst
Mitchell 1766 i.
Bedford
Samuel 1776 i.
Campbell
Ariss 1786 w
Essex
James 1749 i.
Cary 1785 a.
James 1791 w.
Augusta
Henry 1758 i.
Shenandoah
Henry 1785 w.
BAULDWIN
Isle of Wight
William 1691 i.
Prince Edward
Wm. 1799 w.
BAULKE
York
Wm. 1644 i.
BAUSTICK
Halifax
Jno. 1796 w.
BAUTH
York
Robt. 1692 i.
BAXTER
Augusta
Andrew 1753 w.
Goochland
Robt. 1745 i.
Northumberland
John 1770 i.
Ohio
John 1783 w.
Southampton
David 1752 i.
Rappahannock
Nathl. 1677 w.
Stafford
Thos. 1700 i.
Wm. 1749 w.
Westmoreland
Mary 1716 w.
Edwd. 1761 w.
Ambrose 1724 i.
York
Jno. 1645 w.
Danl. 1775 i.
BAXTOR
King George
Jno. 1754 w.

BAYAN
Frederick
Joseph 1747 a.
BAYARD
Westmoreland
Jno. 1728 i.
BAYES
Goochland
Peter 1729 w.
Pittsylvania
Jno. 1794 i.
BAYLE
York
Jno. 1740 i.
BAYLES
Northumberland
Thos. 1758 w.
BAYLEY
Accomack
Bagwell 1752 i.
Edmd. 1757 w.
Henry 1777 i.
Thos. Jr. 1781 w.
Robt. 1782 w.
Shadrach 1783 i.
Culpeper
John 1751 i.
Fairfax
Robert 1782 i.
Henrico
Thos. Sr. 1711 i.
Abraham 1713 i.
King George
Jos. 1741 i.
Loudoun
Joseph 1789 w.
Norfolk
Ann 1758 w.
Powhatan
Wm. 1779 w.
Richmond
Wm. 1728 w.
Westmoreland
Jos. 1717 w.
Ann 1732 w.
BAYLIE
Northumberland
Daniel 1754 i.
BAYLIS
Fairfax
Thomas 1780 w.
Richmond
Thos. 1699 w.
Sarah 1703 w.
Stafford
Hannah 1751 nw.
Richmond
Robt. 1725 nw.
Stafford
Jno. 1747 w.
Sussex
Humphrey 1774 w.

BAYLS
Rockbridge
Charles 1783 w.
BAYLY
Accomack
Richd. 1708 w.
Chas. 1716 w.
Edwd. 1717 w.
Edmd. 1718 w.
Edmd. 1725 w.
Richd. 1728 w.
Edmd. 1751 w.
Edwd. 1752 i.
Eliz. 1757 i.
Jno. 1768 w.
Richd. 1769 w.
Robt. 1771 i.
Chas. 1772 w.
Patience 1772 i.
Richd. 1772 i.
Chas. 1783 i.
Jno. 1793 w.
Richd. 1793 w.
Eliz. 1799 w.
Fairfax
William 1782 w.
William 1786 i.
Richmond
Saml. 1710 w.
Robt. 1725 i.
Saml. 1727 w.
Saml. 1763 w.
Surry
Edwd. 1736 w.
BAYN
Westmoreland
William 1778 w.
BAYNE
Norfolk
Alexander 1759 w.
Martin 1767 i.
Elizabeth 1783 w.
Pittsylvania
Richd. 1798 i.
Westmoreland
Mathew Sr. 1771 w.
Jno. 1783 i.
Mathew 1797 w.
Ellinor 1798 i.
BAYNES
Middlesex
Thos. 1709 w.
Norfolk
John 1790 w.
Westmoreland
Jno. 1783 w.
BAYNHAM
Halifax
Gregory 1794 i.
Louisa
Joseph 1786 i.

BAYNTON
Northampton
Benj. 1707 i.
Robt. 1730 w.
BAYS
Richmond
Jonathan 1763 w.
BAYSHAW
Norfolk
Thomas 1791 w.
BAYSIE
Northumberland
Elisamond 1756 w.
Wm. 1762 w.
BAYTON
Isle of Wight
Richard 1737 i.
BEACH
Accomack
Benj. 1727 i.
Jos. 1772 w.
Fairfax
James 1743 a.
Thomas 1790 w.
Fauquier
Peter 1779 w.
Isle of Wight
William 1737 w.
Lancaster
Geo. 1656 i.
BEACHAM
Northumberland
Rebeckah 1772 w.
John 1784 w.
Thos. 1790 i.
Danl. 1798 w.
Jno. W. 1798 i.
BEACHING
Lancaster
John 1696 nw.
BEACHUM
Northumberland
Danl. 1742 w.
BEADLES
Orange
Robt. 1783 w.
Delilah 1796 i.
BEADS
Princess Anne
Robt. 1771 i.
BEAKER
Prince Edward
Caleb 1754 w.
BEAL
Cumberland
John 1757 i.
Isle of Wight
Benj. 1714 i.
Benj. 1744 w.
Benj. 1786 w.
Jacob 1795 w.

Southampton
Jno. 1772 i.
Jno. 1778 i.
Priscilla 1783 i.
Sarah 1784 i.
Benj. 1787 w.
Ephraim 1795 i.
Richd. 1797 w.
BEALE
Frederick
Jeremiah 1772 w.
Isle of Wight
William 1765 w.
Lancaster
John Eustace 1790 i.
Orange
Tavener 1756 w.
Richd. 1771 w.
Eliz. 1773 w.
Richmond
Elizabeth 1729 w.
Thos. Sr. 1729 w.
Thos. 1732 w.
Chas. 1764 w.
Chas. 1766 i.
Jno. 1767 w.
Wm. 1778 w.
Thos. 1799 w.
Shenandoah
Charles 1777 a.
Southampton
Hardy 1779 w.
Wm. 1779 w.
Benj. 1796 w.
Joshua 1796 i.
Westmoreland
Thos. 1749 i.
Thos. 1787 w.
York
Alice 1702 w.
BEALEY
Norfolk
William 1776 w.
BEALL
Fairfax
Sophia 1782 w.
Hampshire
Benjamin 1765 w.
George 1797 w.
Southampton
John 1778 w.
BEALY
Augusta
Drury 1754 i.
BEAMAN
Middlesex
Eliz. 1770 w.
Northampton
Richd. 1642 i.
Northumberland
Mary 1785 i.

BEAMON
Middlesex
Jno. 1786 i.
BEAN
Augusta
Isaac 1747 i.
Hardy
Robt. 1791 w.
Montgomery
James Sr. 1790 i.
Northumberland
John 1755 w.
Peter 1787 w.
Prince William
William 1735 i.
BEAR
Fauquier
Andrew 1762 i.
Frederick
Justice 1796 i.
King George
Saml. 1749 i.
Shenandoah
Henry 1796 i.
BEARBLOCK
Rappahannock
Wm. 1682 a.
BEARCROFT
Northumberland
Jno. 1744 w.
Peter 1746 w.
Thos. 1748 i.
Peter 1752 i.
Winefred 1758 w.
Jno. 1785 w.
Richd. R. 1795 i.
BEARD
Augusta
Thos. 1769 w.
Thos. 1780 i.
Bedford
Adam 1778 w.
Elesabeth 1778 w.
John 1780 w.
John 1787 w.
Adam 1788 w.
Adam 1797 i.
Fauquier
George 1764 i.
Fincastle
William 1775 a.
Frederick
Andrew 1765 w.
Montgomery
William 1777 i.
Surry
Thos. 1749 w.
Westmoreland
Thos. 1698 w.
Anth. 1707 w.
Thos. 1716 w.
Geo. 1720 i.

Geo. 1724 i.
Jno. 1740 w.
Geo. 1768 w.
BEAREMORE
Northumberland
Jno. 1676/7 w.
BEARIFORD
Amherst
Jno. 1763 w.
BEARRY
Princess Anne
Geo. 1753 w.
BEARY
Chesterfield
Joannah 1751 w.
BEASELEY
Chesterfield
Stephen 1766 w.
BEASLEY
Amelia
Richd. 1771 w.
Charlotte
Wm. 1789 i.
Chesterfield
Stephen 1752 w.
Robt. 1762 w.
Tabitha 1771 w.
Thos. 1775 i.
Benj. 1781 w.
Wm. 1789 w.
Stephen 1791 w.
Wm. 1792 i.
Leroy 1793 i.
Orange
Bennet 1758 w.
Prince Edward
Peter 1797 w.
BEATH
Stafford
Peter 1702 w.
BEATIE
Washington
Francis 1791 w.
BEATON
Frederick
Hector 1790 i.
Isle of Wight
Edward 1771 i.
BEATTY
Berkeley
William 1799 i.
BEATY
Loudoun
James 1796 i.
Washington
John 1790 w.
BEAUCHAMP
Accomack
Jno. 1791 w.
BEAUFORD
Amelia
Josiah 1786 i.

Richmond
Robt. 1745 w.
BEAUGH
Chesterfield
Robt. 1792 i.
BEAUMONT
Middlesex
Wm. 1700 i.
BEAVAN
Accomack
Wm. 1746 i.
BEAVANS
Accomack
Thos. 1766 w.
Joshua 1786 i.
Wm. 1791 w.
Nathl. 1792 w.
Saml. 1797 i.
BEAVENS
Accomack
Wm. 1769 i.
Jno. 1777 w.
Tabitha 1757 w.
Wm. 1761 w.
Wm. 1765 i.
Mary 1784 w.
Mary 1798 w.
Nathl. 1799 i.
BEAVER
Loudoun
Thomas 1770 w.
Wm. 1782 i.
BEAVERSHAM
King George
Jno. 1752 w.
BEAZLEY
Essex
Wm. 1744 w.
Jno. 1759 w.
Benjamin 1758 i.
John 1777 w.
Orange
Jno. 1782 w.
BEAZLY
Chesterfield
Wm. 1764 w.
BEBBE
Northampton
Edmd. 1696/7 i.
BEBEE
Northampton
Edmd. 1660 w.
BECHINO
Isle of Wight
Edward 1679 w.
BECK
Augusta
Stephen 1788 w.
Brunswick
Andrew 1761 w.
Henrico
Jas. 1701 a.

Lancaster
Ellinor 1733 i.
Loudoun
Edward 1774 i.
Louisa
Wm. 1770 a.
Norfolk
Benj. 1718/9 nw.
Jeremiah 1719 i.
Powhatan
Robt. 1779 i.
Princess Anne
Ann 1701 w.
Edwd. 1701 i.
BECKETT
Culpeper
John 1760 i.
Frederick
John 1768 w.
Robert 1769 i.
Sarah 1780 w.
Prince William
Robert 1737 i.
BECKFORD
Norfolk
Robt. 1698 w.
BECKHAM
Essex
Ann 1760 w.
Frederick
George 1755 w.
Orange
Simon 1746 i.
Richmond
Thos. 1732 w.
Ann 1736 w.
Geo. Tomlin 1752 i.
BECKINGHAM
Lancaster
Robt. 1675 w.
BECKINS
Isle of Wight
George 1687 w.
BECKLEY
Northumberland
Francis 1757 i.
BECKLY
Amherst
Jno. 1792 w.
BECKNER
Botetourt
Jacob 1797 i.
BECKWITH
Richmond
Marmaduke 1790 i.
BEDDLE
Northampton
Danl. 1640 i.
BEDDINFIELD
Mecklenburg
Thos. 1786 i.

BEDDINGFIELD
Sussex
Nathl. 1767 i.
BEDEL
Amelia
Abraham 1795 w.
BEDFORD
Charlotte
Stephen 1773 w.
Thos. 1785 w.
Cumberland
Benj. 1772 w.
Stephen 1758 w.
BEDGOOD
Surry
Saml. 1793 i.
BEDINGER
Berkeley
Magdalene 1797 w.
Frederick
Henry 1772 w.
BEDINGFIELD
Surry
Henry 1747 w.
Henry 1781 w.
Henry 1786 i.
BEDMON
Richmond
Saml. 1749 w.
BEE
York
Barthlin 1687/8 i.
Ann 1696 w.
Robt. 1711 w.
Ralph 1715 nw.
Rebecca Jr. 1720 w.
Rebecca 1724 w.
Isaac 1740 w.
BEECH
Accomack
Saml. 1703 w.
Benj. 1727 w.
Saml. 1740 i.
Saml. 1767 w.
Wm. 1769 w.
Tabitha 1781 w.
Jno. 1792 w.
Ezekiel 1799 w.
Fauquier
Alex. 1762 w.
Halifax
Wm. 1789 w.
Thos. 1799 w.
Rockbridge
Waldron 1784 i.
BEED
Frederick
Ann 1782 i.
BEEKLE
Northumberland
Francis 1757 w.

BEEKLEY
Northumberland
Ralph 1750 i.
BEEKLY
Northumberland
John 1750 i.
BEEL
Isle of Wight
Benjamin 1713 w.
William 1772 w.
Southampton
Thos. 1763 w.
Jno. 1769 w.
Sarah 1782 w.
Jos. 1789 i.
BEELE
Southampton
John 1763 i.
BEELER
Fairfax
Christopher 1779 w.
Frederick
Frederick 1764 w.
BEEN
Isle of Wight
James 1733 i.
BEERE
Northampton
Henry 1765 i.
BEES
Frederick
Morris 1769 i.
BEESON
Frederick
Edward 1746 i.
Richard 1749 i.
BEESWELL
Orange
Jno. 1738 a.
BEETLEY
Northumberland
Jos. 1792 w.
BEEZLEY
Essex
John 1778 i.
Wm. 1719 w.
BEGG
Amelia
Jno. 1764 i.
BEGGERLEY
Middlesex
Chas. 1711 i.
BEGGS
Rockbridge
Sarah 1794 i.
BEIER
Shenandoah
Jacob 1788 w.
BELAND
Northumberland
Mary 1792 i.

BELCHER
Amelia
Isaac 1778 i.
Edwd. 1781 w.
Wm. 1796 w.
Chesterfield
Richd. 17— i.
Jno. 1776 w.
Thos. 1786 w.
Thos. 1799 w.
Henrico
Thos. 1718 i.
Richmond
Bartholomew 1770 w.
BELFIELD
Culpeper
Joseph 1770 w.
Joseph 1774 i.
Richmond
Jos. 1737 w.
Mary 1750 nw.
Westmoreland
Jos. 1754 i.
BELL
Accomack
Tabitha 1713 w.
Thos. 1715 w.
Robt. 1724 w.
Robt. 1727 i.
Edwd. 1743 w.
Wm. 1744 w.
Nathl. 1745 w.
Jeodah 1750 w.
Elias 1752 i.
Jos. 1759 w.
Jno. 1760 w.
Mary 1760 w.
Jos. 1761 w.
Chas. 1762 i.
Mary Scarburgh
  1765 w.
Wm. 1765 i.
Thos. 1768 w.
Robt. 1771 w.
Rachel 1772 w.
Eliz. 1774 w.
Robt. 1777 i.
Scarburgh 1777 w.
Geo. 1779 w.
Robt. 1779 w.
Wm. 1779 w.
Robt. Jr. 1780 i.
Wm. 1785 i.
Jacob 1788 w.
Oliver 1791 w.
Geo. 1792 w.
Jno. Selby 1795 w.
Thos. 1795 w.
Aner 1798 w.
Savage 1798 w.
Nathl. Sr. 1799 w.
Wm. 1799 w.

Amelia
Thos. 1741 i.
Amherst
David 1791 a.
Henry 1797 w.
Geo. 1785 a.
Bath
William 1798 i.
Culpeper
John Miller 1791 w.
Essex
Thos. 1748 w.
Fauquier
Francis 1795 w.
Frederick
John 1779 w.
John 1792 w.
Goochland
David 1744 w.
Halifax
James 1786 i.
Isle of Wight
Richard 1700 i.
George Sr. 1702 w.
John 1722 w.
Benjamin 1755 i.
Patience 1772 w.
William 1781 w.
James 1783 i.
Augusta
Jas. 1751 w.
Robt. 1757 w.
Wm. 1757 w.
Jos. 1758 a.
Jno. 1759 a.
Jos (malloto) 1760 i.
Jno. 1773 i.
David 1780 w.
Jno. 1783 w.
Saml. 1788 w.
Jas. Sr. 1792 w.
Jas. 1795 w.
Jno. 1797 w.
King George
Jno. 1743 i.
Lancaster
Henry 1695 w.
Phyllis 1733 i.
Jno. 1743 w.
Elizabeth 1750 w.
William 1750 i.
Charles 1781 w.
Thomas 1790 w.
Louisa
Geo. 1787 w.
Samuel 1792 w.
Mecklenburg
Wm. 1778 w.
Norfolk
Alex. 1688/9 w.
Thomas 1788 w.
Alex. 1789 w.

Northampton
Thos. Sr. 1678 w.
Thos. 1697 i.
Robt. 1709 w.
Geo. 1723 w.
Hannah 1736 w.
David 1751 i.
Ezekiel 1751 w.
Geo. Sr. 1772 w.
Thos. 1772 w.
Robt. 1791 w.
Robt. 1797 i.
Northumberland
Mary 1742 i.
Wm. 1744 w.
Wm. 1752 i.
John 1769 w.
Wm. 1773 w.
Orange
Roger 1774 w.
Wm. 1780 w.
Wm. 1786 i.
Orange
John 1790 i.
William 1790 i.
Thomas 1796 w.
Thomas 1798 w.
Prince Edward
John 1788 w.
Prince George
Jno. 1723 w.
Princess Anne
Robt. 1719 i.
Rockbridge
John 1792 i.
John 1795 i.
James 1797 w.
Stafford
Jas. 1785 i.
Jas. 1786 i.
Surry
Jno. 1713 i.
Wm. 1725 i.
Joseph 1733 w.
Richard 1734 w.
Jno. 1746 w.
Jno. 1750 i.
Benj. 1751 w.
Ann 1777 w.
Micajah 1779 w.
Sylvya 1784 w.
Stephen 1789 w.
Robt. 1796 w.
Sussex
Balaam 1755 w.
Hannah 1768 w.
James 1778 w.
James 1796 i.
Washington
Samuel 1780 w.
Westmoreland
Mary 1660 w.

Jno. 1670 w.
Richd. 1722 i.
Thos. 1749 w.
York
Wm. 1674 w.
Jno. 1681 i.
Wm. 1711 w.
Thos. 1723 i.
Nathl. 1732 i.
BELLEMY
Sussex
Eliz. 1762 w.
BELLEN
Princess Anne
Adam 1700 w.
BELLENGER
Fairfax
Judith 1746 w.
BELLEMAN
Goochland
Jno. 1729 w.
BELLEW
Greenbrier
Lenord 1785 w.
Westmoreland
Richd. 1724 i.
BELLFIELD
Richmond
Thos. Wright 1743 w.
Jno. 1793 i.
BELLONY
Princess Anne
Adam 1700 i.
BELOAT
Northampton
Jno. 1722 w.
Hezekiah 1795 w.
BELOTE
Accomack
Noah 1764 i.
Hancock 1765 w.
Caleb 1774 w.
Hancock 1798 i.
Northampton
William 1709 w.
Jonah 1729 i.
Eliz. 1735 i.
Edwd. 1736 i.
Rebekkah 1738 i.
Jno. 1743 w.
Geo. 1752 w.
Jonah 1763 i.
Jno. 1764 .i
Laban 1764 w.
Edwd. 1766 i.
Wm. 1789 w.
Wm. 1793 i.
BELSCHES
Louisa
Patrick 1764 w.
Judy 1768 w.

BELSHER
Amelia
Joel 1778 w.
Jos. 1782 w.
Henrico
Edmd. 1685 i.
Jno. 1706 i.
BELVAIRD
Lancaster
Robert 1784 w.
BEN
Chesterfield
Danl. 1781 i.
Isle of Wight
Tristram 1772 w.
BENBRIGG
Isle of Wight
Geo. 1720 w.
BENDALL
Amelia
Margt. 1745 a.
Sussex
Isaac 1792 i.
BENDER
Augusta
Jno. 1773 w.
Pittsylvania
Jno. 1774 w.
BENDRY
Essex
Wm. 1701 w.
BENFIELD
Stafford
Jno. 1708 i.
BENFORD
Charles City
Jno. 1795 w.
BENGER
Richmond
Jno. 1725 w.
Spotsylvania
Elliott 1751 a.
Dorothea 1759 a.
Jno. 1766 w.
Betty 1772 a.
BENGEY
Richmond
Richd. 1717 w.
BENHAM
Loudoun
Jno. 1782 w.
BENISON
Lancaster
Abia 1677 i.
Thos. 1684 i.
Abia 1685 w.
BENJAFIELD
York
Jos. 1710 i.
BENN
Isle of Wight
Christopher 1659 w.

Margaret 1674 i.
James 1697 w.
Arthur 1728 w.
James 1733 w.
Geo. 1759 i.
Jno. 1759 w.
Arthur 1762 w.
James 1763 w.
Tristram 1772 i.
Elizabeth 1782 w.
Pampy 1796 w.
BENNATT
Cumberland
Rice 1770 w.
BENNEHAM
Richmond
Alex. 1719 i.
Alex. 1770 i.
Dudley 1750 w.
BENNET
Amelia
Benj. 1767 w.
Stephen 1780 w.
Franklin
Wm. 1792 i.
Isle of Wight
Richard 1710 w.
Lancaster
Jno. 1749/50 i.
Northumberland
Jno. 1667 i.
Southampton
Jno. 1766 w.
Surry
Jno. 1751 w.
Wm. 1761 i.
York
Thos. 1750i.
BENNETT
Bedford
Peter 1778 w.
Berkeley
Geo. 1785 i.
Brunswick
Benj. 1783 w.
Culpeper
Thos. 1793 w.
Cumberland
Rice 1773 i.
Essex
Wm. 1711 w.
Fairfax
Eliz. 1787 w.
Jos. 1793 w.
Halifax
Robt. 1782 i.
Isle of Wight
Ambrose 1680 w.
Richard 1720 w.
Jno. 1770 w.
Lancaster
Robt. 1697/8 w.

Jno. 1710 i.
Catherine 1723 w.
Saml. 1685 w.
Northumberland
Jno. 1660 w.
Pittsylvania
Jno. 1792 i.
Prince William
—— 1784 w.
Richmond
Wm. 1719 i.
Southampton
Jno. 1791 w.
Wm. 1792 i.
Surry
Jonas 1696 w.
James 1752 w.
Saml. 1773 w.
Nathaniel 1778 w.
Westmoreland
Wm. 1697 w.
Wm. 1703 w.
Cossom 1718 w.
Jno. 1730 w.
Easter 1731 i.
Wm. 1758 w.
Thos. 1763 i.
Thos. Sr. 1763 w.
Cossom 1766 w.
Cossom 1770 i.
Danl. 1785 w.
Thos. 1789 w.
York
Thos. 1795 w.
BENNEY
Princess Anne
Richd. 1709 w.
BENNIHAM
Richmond
Dominick 1716 w.
BENNIT
Brunswick
James Sr. 1752 w.
Fairfax
Thos. 1742 i.
Robt. 1782 w.
Isle of Wight
Jno. 1771 i.
Wm. 1778 w.
Surry
Richd. 1719 i.
BENNITT
Brunswick
Jno. 1798 w.
Essex
William 1711 i.
Thos. 1749 w.
Isle of Wight
James 1785 w.
Surry
Richd. 1735 i.

York
Mary (als Collier)
1700 i.
Jas. 1720 w.
BENSKIN
Henrico
Jerrimiah 1703 w.
BENSON
Accomack
Saml. 1745 w.
Saml. 1758 i.
Rebecca 1759 i.
Micajah 1768 i.
Jonas Sr. 1776 w.
Jonas 1779 i.
Massey 1780 w.
Moses 1794 i.
Jonah 1796 w.
Sturgis 1796 i.
Jas. 1797 w.
Jonah 1798 i.
Bath
Matthias 1795 w.
Henrico
Wm. 1735 i.
Isle of Wight
Wm. 1739 w.
King George
Thos. 1734 i.
Robt. 1756 w.
Wm. 1773 a.
Norfolk
Robt. 1799 w.
Northampton
Jno. 1737 w.
Jno 1757 i.
Princess Anne
Thos. 1703 w.
Richd. 1718 w.
Wm. 1753 w.
Stafford
Hugh 1699 w.
BENSTON
Accomack
Wm. 1704 w.
Francis 1709 w.
Wm. 1718 w.
Francis 1723 w.
Wm. 1729 w.
Ambrose 1733 w.
Jas. 1734 w.
Ambros 1737 i.
Jas. 1739 i.
Alex. 1742 w.
Jonathan 1747 w.
Jos. 1751 w.
Jno. 1754 w.
Edwd. 1756 w.
Hannah 1759 i.
Edy (Edith) 1762 w.
Ezekiel 1762 w.
Nathl. 1775 w.

Massey 1785 i.
Saml. 1785 w.
Jas. 1786 i.
Moses 1791 w.
Jno. 1796 w.
BENT
Accomack
Kanutus 1702 w.
BENTHALL
Norfolk
Harrison 1798 i.
Northampton
Jos. 1711 w.
Jos. 1712 w.
Mary 1713-14 w.
Danl. 1719 w.
Wm. 1716 i.
Wm. 1732 i.
Danl. 1752 w.
Anne 1753 w.
Matthew 1755 w.
Wm. 1773 w.
Wm. 1784 w.
Azel 1785 i
Eliz. 1789 w.
Azel 1790 w.
Joab 1794 w.
Robt. 1795 w.
BENTHELL
Northampton
Thos. 1734 w.
BENTLEY
Amelia
Jno. 1770 w.
Nancy 1786 w.
Saml. 1795 w.
Henrico
Thos. 1785 w.
Lunenburg
Danl. 1791 i.
Middlesex
Math. 1686 w.
Richmond
Danl. 1721 w.
Surry
Jno. 1710 i.
Thos. 1723 w.
BENTLY
Northumberland
Jno. 1719 i.
Wm. 1742 i.
BERBRIDGE
Shenandoah
Robt. 1782 a.
BERFORD
Norfolk
St. Lawrence 1750 w.
BERGER
Shenandoah
Andrew 1778 a.

BERGERON
Northampton
Jas. 1728 w.
BERKELEY
Middlesex
Edmund 1718 w.
Lewis 1745 i.
Edmund 1767 w.
Westmoreland
Wm. 1772 w.
BERKLEY
Fairfax
Burgess 1755 i.
Wm. 1762 w.
King George
Jno. 1751 i.
Loudoun
Benj. 1768 i.
Saml. 1770 i.
Elizabeth 1772 w.
Barba 1786 i.
Reuben 1787 w.
Westmoreland
Henry 1727 i.
Jno. 1792 w.
Jno. 1794 i.
BERKLY
Loudoun
Wm. 1783 i.
BERNARD
Cumberland
Eliz. 1750 i.
Essex
Noel 1749 w.
Goochland
David 1735 w.
Henrico
David 1715 i.
King George
Wm. 1783 w.
Richard 1785 w.
Westmoreland
Robt. 1724 w.
BERNER
Goochland
David 1738 i.
BERRICK
Essex
Ann 1722 w.
Richmond
Geo. 1770 w.
Geo. 1773 i.
BERRIDGE
Rappahannock
Jno. 1676 w.
BERRIMAN
Surry
Wm. 1768 i.
Gilson 1782 w.
BERRY
Accomack
Jas. 1782 w.

Keziah 1787 i.
Augusta
Jas. 1750 i.
Jno. 1771 w.
Chas. 1789 w.
Chas 1799 i.
Brunswick
Geo. 1782 w.
Chesterfield
David 1791 w.
Culpeper
John 1779 w.
Elijah 1781 w.
Essex
Geo. Pley 1720 w.
Fauquier
Winnefred 1795 i.
Frederick
Patrick 1750 w.
Jno. 1773 w.
King George
Wm. 1721 i.
Jos. 1749 i.
Henry 1750 i.
Withers 1755 i.
Grace 1757 w.
Enock 1763 w.
Wm. 1763 i.
Reuben 1774 a.
Jas. 1783 w.
Thos 1798 i.
Lancaster
Jno. 1691 w.
Lunenburg
Jno. 1755 i.
Madison
Jno. 1798 i.
Middlesex
Jno. 1726 w.
Mary 1727 w.
Thos. 1761 a.
Jno. 1767 w.
Jno. Jr. 1772 i.
Norfolk
Geo. 1767 w.
Northampton
Wm. 1651 i.
Cornelius 1717 w.
Jno. 1738 w.
Northumberland
Thos. 1700 w.
Wm. 1722-3 i.
Thos. 1743 w.
Geo. 1756 i.
Wm. 1761 w.
Winifred 1775 w.
Jno. 1784 i.
Princess Anne
Robt. 1730 i.
Thos. 1735 w.
Hillery 1771 i.
Mary 1772 w.

Richd. 1773 w.
Jno. 1774 w.
Matthew 1779 i.
Wm. 1779 w.
Geo. 1782 w.
Jno. 1782 i.
Jesse 1790 i.
Willoughby 1798 w.
Rappahannock
Henry 1677 w.
Rockbridge
Wm. Sr. 1793 w.
Stafford
Jas. 1739 i.
Richd. 1754 i.
Wm. 1764 i.
Surry
Nathaniel 1709 i.
Washington
James 1779 i.
Wm. 1781 w.
Jno. 1786 w.
Thos. 1799 w.
York
Wm. 1717 nw.
BERRYMAN
Fairfax
Benj. 1748 w.
Fauquier
Robt. 1795 i.
King George
Rose 1791 w.
Lancaster
Jno. 1787 w.
Northampton
Wm. 1648 i.
Stafford
Gilson 1750 w.
Surry
Jno. 1711 w.
Augustine 1736 w.
Ann 1748 w.
Westmoreland
Benj. 1729 w.
Eliz. 1763 w.
James 1773 w.
Wm. 1784 w.
BERTRAND
Lancaster
Jno. 1701 w.
Wm. 1761 w.
BERY
Albemarle
Badley 1795 i.
BESHOP
Southampton
Jos. 1797 w.
BESINGER
Wythe
Paul 1799 i.

BESKIARS
Berkeley
Zephaniah 1798 w.
BESON
Frederick
Richard 1748 w.
BESOUTH
York
Jas. 1681 w.
BESS
Augusta
Abraham 1765 w.
BEST
Bedford
Thos 1780 i.
Jno. 1790 i.
Isle of Wight
Martha 1695 w.
Peter 1698 w.
Henry 1706-7 i.
Mary 1724-5 w.
Wm. 1740 i.
Thos 1757 i.
Peter 1759 i.
Martha 1766 i.
Loudoun
Jno. 1770 w.
Norfolk
Henry 1791 w.
Jno. 1792 i.
Malachi 1792 i.
Henry 1793 i.
Josiah 1798 i.
Thos. 1648 w.
BESWICK
Northumberland
Robt. 1745 w.
BETHEL
Henrico
Thos. 1783 w.
BETHELL
Frederick
Wm. 1756 i.
Henrico
Thos. 1792 i.
Stafford
Edwd. 1758 w.
BETHEN
Fairfax
David 1746 a.
BETHILL
Henrico
Thos. 1755 w.
BETHSHARES
Brunswick
Thos 1799 i.
BETTELL
Isle of Wight
Robt. 1679 w.
BETTESWORTH
King George
Chas. 1784 w.

BETTS
Isle of Wight
Thos 1773 i.
Lunenburg
Elisha 1784 w.
Wm. 1795 i.
Middlesex
Thompson 1748 w.
Northampton
Wm. 1714 w.
Isaac 1723 w.
Northumberland
Chas. Sr. 1711 w.
Wm. 1752 w.
Wm. 1756 w.
Ann 1749 w.
Chas. 1760 w.
Jonathan 1761 i.
Chas. 1762 w.
Maryanne 1765 w.
Jno. 1766 w.
Royston 1783 w.
Danl. 1787 i.
Wm. 1794 i.
BETTY
Brunswick
Jno. 1751 w.
Thos. 1798 w.
Henry
Abel 1783 i.
Stafford
Wm. 1700 i.
BEUFORD
Pittsylvania
Ambrose 1782 i.
BEVAN
Isle of Wight
Mary 1719-20 i.
Thos. 1735 w.
Peter 1736 i.
Norfolk
Geo. 1752 w.
Geo. 1773 i.
BEVEN
Isle of Wight
Thos. 1714 w.
BEVER
Madison
Christian 1797 i.
BEVERLEY
King George
Robert G. 1797 w.
Middlesex
Robt. 1687 w.
Spotsylvania
Harry 1730-1 w.
Robt 1733 w.
Harry Stanard
1794 w.
BEVERLY
Norfolk
Wm. 1761 i.

Surry
Mary 1793 w.
BEVERS
Chesterfield
Jas. 1770 w.
BEVILL
Amelia
Thos. 1761 i.
Danl. 1767 w.
Wm. 1771 w.
Thos. 1778 w.
Essex 1778 w.
Archer 1785 w.
James 1785 w.
Geo. 1798 i.
Chesterfield
Jno. 1767 w.
Francis 1794 w.
Henrico
Essex 1682 w.
Essex 1729 w.
Robt. 1733 w.
Eliz. 1732 w.
Jno. 1735 w.
Mecklenburg
Edwd. Sr. 1793 w.
BEVIN
Frederick
Samuel 1779 w.
Henrico
Wm. 1685 w.
BEVINS
York
Thos. 1681 w.
BEVIS
Fairfax
Zachariah 1750 a.
BIBB
Amherst
Jno. 1781 w.
Thos 1781 w.
Charlotte
Jno. 1791 w.
Goochland
Jno. 1769 w.
Louisa
——— 1750 w.
Thos. 1761 w.
Benj. 1768 w.
Ann 1790 w.
Mary 1791 w.
Benj. 1793 i.
BIBBE
Northampton
Edmd. 1696 w.
Jon. 1720 w.
BIBBERY
Princess Anne
Jno. 1707 w.
BICKARDICK
Norfolk
Richd. 1769 w.

BICKERDICK
Norfolk
Mary 1793 w.
Northumberland
Major 1782 i.
BICKERS
Orange
Robt. Jr. 1762 i.
BICKLE
Augusta
Adam 1799 i.
BICKLEY
Louisa
Jos. 1750 w.
Chas. 1757 or 8 w.
Wm. 1772 i.
Jas. 1776 w.
Mary Ann 1793 w.
Westmoreland
Peter 1787 w.
BIDDLE
Accomack
Thos. 1732 i.
Princess Anne
Jno. 1768 w.
Wm. 1769 w.
Joshua 1797 w.
BIDDLECOMB
Northumberland
Sarah 1747 i.
Richmond
Jas. 1716 i.
BIDGOOD
Isle of Wight
Jno. Jr. 1726 w.
Wm. 1748 w.
Wm. 1764 i.
Surry
Saml. 1791 w.
BIEDLER
Berkeley
Jacob 1787 i.
BIGARBY
Accomack
Francis 1785 w.
BIGBIE
Prince William
Geo. 1784 i.
Elijah 1798 i.
BIGERBY
Accomack
Wm. 1767 w.
BIGG
Norfolk
Jabez 1692-3 w.
Jno. 1696-7 w.
BIGGARS
Prince Edward
Jno. 1783 i.
BIGGER
Louisa
Wm. 1785 w.

Prince Edward
Jno. 1782 w.
BIGGERBEE
Accomack
Wm. 1727 i.
BIGGINS
Sussex
Wm. 1767 i.
BIGGS
Northampton
Jas. 1778 w.
Jno. 1779 i.
Jas. 1781 i.
Anne Sr. 1784 w.
Tabitha 1795 w.
Ohio
Benj. 1782 a.
Princess Anne
Jno. 1704 i.
York
Wm. 1734 i.
BIGHAM
Augusta
Jno. 1774 i.
BIGNAL
Westmoreland
Thos. 1726 i.
BIGUIN
Albemarle
Abraham 1749 i.
BILBO
Lunenburg
Jno. Peter 1751 w.
Mecklenburg
Jas. 1799 w.
BILBRO
Prince George
Thos. 1718 w.
Surry
Jno. 1773 w.
Burwell 1790 w.
Sussex
James 1780 w.
BILES
Frederick
James 1765 i.
BILDERBACK
Ohio
Chas. 1790 w.
BILLING
Halifax
Jaspar 1763 i.
BILLINGS
Halifax
Jaspar 1768 i.
Northumberland
Solomon 1784 i.
Pittsylvania
Jno. 1784 i
Westmoreland
Katherine 1726 i.

BILLINGSBY
Fauquier
Clement 1796 i.
Clement 1799 i.
BILLINGTON
Essex
Jno. 1700 i.
Mary 1727 w.
Rappahannock
Luke 1672 w.
Barbary 1674 w.
Luke 1687 w.
BILLINS
Westmoreland
Jno. 1773 i.
BILLIPS
Berkeley
John 1781 w.
BILLUPS
Lunenburg
Chris. 1794 w.
Mecklenburg
Robt. 1798 w.
BINCKS
Westmoreland
Jno. 1730 w.
BINFORD
Henrico
Thos. 1752 w.
Jas. 1782 w.
Eliz. 1789 w.
Wm. 1791 i.
BINGAMAN
Augusta
Jno. 1756 i.
BINGERMAN
Berkeley
Henry 1779 w.
BINGHAM
Culpeper
Stephen 1794 w.
BINGLEY
Cumberland
Jos. 1761 w.
Powhatan
Matthew 1785 w.
BINKS
Westmoreland
Thos. 1740 w.
BINNS
Charles City
Mary 1791 w.
Surry
Thos. 1699 i.
Thos. 1723 w.
Chas. 1749 w.
Chas. 1755 i.
Thos. 1765 w.
Eliz. 1784 i.
BINYEAR
Mecklenburg
Jno. 1777 i.

BIRCH
Goochland
Saml. 1739 w.
Stafford
Jno. 1746 i.
BIRCHETT
Brunswick
Edwd. 1790 w.
Southampton
Jas. 1782 i.
BIRD
Accomack
Edwd. 1697 w.
Jno. 1727 w.
Major 1751 i.
Danl. 1752 i.
Danl. 1758 n.w.
Nathl. 1780 w.
Jacob 1783 w.
Solomon 1784 w.
Jacob 1785 i.
Solomon 1788 i.
Jacob 1794 w.
Augusta
Andrew 1751 i.
Jno. 1756 i.
Essex
Randall 1703 i.
Franklin
Alex. 1798 i.
Frederick
Lewis 1770 w.
Isle of Wight
Robt. 1658 w.
Prince William
Wm. 1784 i.
Richmond
Philemon 1752 w.
Joaner 1765 i.
Shenandoah
Mounce 1793 a.
Patrick
Abraham 1794 i.
York
Jno. 1647 i.
BIRDSONG
Sussex
Jas. 1756 i.
Jno. 1785 w.
BIRDWELL
Bedford
Geo. 1781 w.
BIRK
Montgomery
Jos. 1786 a.
BIRKADIKE
York
Arthur 1720 a.b.
BIRKET
Richmond
Jno. 1719 w.

BIRWELL
Essex
Eliz. 1777 w.
BISCOE
King George
Jno. 1760 i.
Lancaster
Robt. 1748 i.
Jno. 1773 w.
Jno. 1792 i.
Geo. 1795 i.
Powhatan
Robt. 1779 i.
Mary 1795 i.
BISHAW
Fluvanna
Spencer 1782 i.
BISHOP
Accomack
Jacob 1757 w.
Jno. 1785 w.
Brunswick
Jos. 1764 i.
Mason 1783 w.
Wm. 1773 w.
Norfolk
Jesse 1765 i.
Northampton
Jacob 1675 w.
Dorothy 1728 i.
Jacob 1729 w.
Margt. 1730 i.
Muns 1744 i.
Wm. 1766 w.
Wm. 1767 w.
Princess Anne
Jno. 1763 w.
Jno. 1767 i.
Jacob 1783 w.
Jno. 1783 i.
Jno. 1784 w.
Prince George
Jno. Sr. 1716 w.
Sarah 1722 w.
Wm. 1718 w.
Rappahannock
Robt. 1677 w.
Southampton
Jos. 1797 i.
Surry
Jno. 1676 a.
Jno. 1758 w.
Mason 1781 w.
Jas. 1786 w.
Jno. 1798 w.
Sussex
Nathan 1792 w.
BISICK
Northumberland
Jno. 1706 w.

BITTLE
Brunswick
Jno. 1758 w.
Isle of Wight
Robt. 1681 i.
Southampton
Jno. 1760 w.
Wm. 1764 w.
Drewry 1782 i.
Robt. 1795 w.
BIVANS
Lancaster
Thos. 1786 i.
BIZWELL
Essex
Sarah 1716 w.
Rosamond 1732 w.
Robt. 1761 i.
Erasmus 1732 w.
Jeremiah 1732 i.
Wm. 1740 i.
BIZWICK
Accomack
Jas. 1731 i.
BLACK
Fairfax
Thos. 1791 a.
Accomack
Wm. 1737 w.
Albermarle
Saml. 1770 w.
Catherine 1798 i.
Augusta
Jno. 1758 w.
Anthony 1762 i.
Alex. 1765 i.
David 1769 w.
Saml. 1783 w.
Cutlip 1790 w.
Jno. 1795 w.
Chesterfield
Jno. 1769 i.
Wm. 1782 w.
Wm. 1784 w.
Frederick
Jno. 1747 w.
Margaret 1773 i.
Halifax
Wm. 1789 i.
Robt. 1793 i.
King George
Michael 1792 nw
Lancaster
Jos. 1677 i.
Jas. 1717 i.
Prince Edward
Robt. 1794 i.
Rockbridge
Thos. 1796 i.
BLAKAMORE
Lancaster
Edward 1778 i.

BLACKBORN
Cumberland
John 1757 w.
BLACKBOURNE
Mecklenburg
Thos. 1784 w.
BLACKBURN
Frederick
Archibald 1749 i.
Jno. 1755 w.
Samuel 1776 w.
Middlesex
Wm. 1749 i.
Wm. 1779 w.
Wm. 1788 i.
Norfolk
Jno. 1745-6 i.
Orange
Arthur 1742 a.
Surry
Wm. 1710-11 w.
Wm. 1732 w.
Jos. 1733 i.
Washington
Geo. 1778 w.
Wm. 1781 i.
Arthur 1782 w.
BLACKBURNE
Essex
Christopher 1694 w.
Surry
Wm. 1756 w.
BLACKE
Accomack
Wm. 1703 i.
BLACKERBY
Lancaster
Eliz. 1781 i.
Northumberland
Wm. 1780 w.
Jos. 1783 w.
Frances 1788 w.
Richmond
Jas. 1744 w.
Jas. 1758 i.
BLACKFORD
Berkeley
Benj. 1784 i.
Ebenezar 1796 w.
Middlesex
Wm. 1680 a.
BLACKGROVE
Surry
Saml. 1728 w.
BLACKLEY
Middlesex
Robt. 1726 w.
Jane 1788 i.
Frances 1790 w.
Northumberland
Thos. 1775 w.

BLACKLOCK
Accomack
Thos. 1677 w.
BLACKMAN
Henrico
Wm. 1698 w.
Prince George
Thos. 1715 w.
Westmoreland
Edwd. 1729 i.
BLACKMORE
Berkeley
Jas. 1790 i.
Laurence O. 1795 i.
Frederick
Geo. 1757 i.
Lancaster
Edwd. 1738 w.
Edwd. 1777 w.
Middlesex
Jas. 1675 w.
Washington
Jno. 1782 i.
Westmoreland
Geo. 1746 w.
BLACKSTON
Accomack
Jno. 1754 w.
Lunenburg
Jno.1770 w.
BLACKSTONE
Accomack
Leah 1789 w.
Essex
Argol 1722 w.
Argol 1732 i.
Franky 1750 i.
York
Argoll 1688 w.
Alice 1690-1 i.
BLACKWELL
Albemarle
Wm. 1775 w.
Culpeper
Jas. 1783 i.
Jno. 1770 w.
Jos. 1780 w.
Fauquier
Wm. 1774 w.
Wm. 1786 i.
Jos. 1787 w.
Wm. 1793 i.
Goochland
Jno. 1780 w.
Lunenburg
Robt. 1789 w.
Northumberland
Samuel 1762 w.
Eliz. 1764 i.
Saml. 1768 w.
Jno. 1769 w.
Jos. 1771 i.

Wm. 1780 i.
Saml. 1786 w.
Saml. 1789 i.
Geo. 1792 w.
Sarah 1792 w.
BLACKWOOD
Augusta
Wm. 1779 w.
Saml. 1799 w.
BLADES
Accomack
Jesse 1787 w.
Chesterfield
Geo. 1779 i.
BLAGG
Henry
Jno. 1781 w.
Westmoreland
Abraham 1697 w.
Abraham 1716 w.
Margt. 1726 w.
BLAGRAVE
Lunenburg
Henry 1782 w.
BLAHO
Accomack
Dennis 1760 w.
BLAICK
King George
Henry 1751 i.
BLAIR
Accomack
Thos. 1740 w.
Thos. 1743 i.
Thos. 1750 i.
Amherst
Rachel 1770 i.
Wm. 1777 a.
Augusta
Jno. 1758 a.
Jos. 1777 i.
Jno. 1789 w.
Alex. 1791 w.
Eliz. 1793 w.
King George
Sarah 1778 a.
Northampton
Henry 1721 w.
Barbara 1725 w.
Henry 1734 i.
Henry 1736 i.
Clark 1737 i.
Henry 1747 w.
Jno. 1777 w.
Jno. 1779-i.
Orange
James 1796 w.
Princess Anne
James 1750 i.
Anne 1753 w.
Westmoreland
Jas. 1773 i.

York
Jno. 1771 w.
BLAISE
Middlesex
James 1700 w.
Eliz. 1708 w.
BLAKE
Accomack
Thos. 1690 i.
Wm. 1692 w.
Joan 1696 w.
Jos. 1703 w.
Elias 1709 w.
Jno. 1726 w.
Dianer 1728 w.
Jos. 1733 i.
Wm. 1757 i.
Jno. 1761 i.
Elias 1766 w.
Jno. 1774 w.
Chas. 1779 i.
Jos. 1782 w.
Amelia
Fredk. 1750 a.
Cumberland
Martin 1791 i.
Isle of Wight
Jno. 1697 i.
Thos. 1709 w.
Wm. 1746 w.
Middlesex
Jno. 1744 w.
Jno. Sr. 1753 w.
Eliz. 1755 w.
Geo. 1760 i.
Jno. 1763 a.
Jno. 1768 i.
Wm. 1774 w.
Jacob 1781 w.
Jno. Sr. 1784 w.
Jacob 1792 i.
Thos. Sr. 1793 w.
Geo. Sr. 1793 w.
Norfolk
Robt. 1672 w.
Princess Anne
Arthur 1726 w.
Norfolk
Richard 1779 w.
Joshua 1796 w.
Rappahannock
Elias 1674 w.
Richmond
Augustine 1716 i.
Southampton
Benj. 1798 w.
Thos. 1789 w.
Spotsylvania
Jno. 1744 w.
BLAKELEY
Pittsylvania
Jas. 1799 w.

Amelia
Wm. 1786 w.
BLAKEMORE
Lancaster
Edwd. 1782 i.
BLAKEY
Culpeper
Jno. 1782 w.
Middlesex
Mary 1740 w.
Robt. 1749 a.
Spotsylvania
Geo. 1783 a.
York
Wm.1736 w.
BLAMIRE
Princess Anne
Anthy. 1766 w.
BLANCHE
Henrico
Danl. 1702 w.
Lancaster
Thos. 1698 w.
Norfolk
Thos. 1674 w.
Eliz. 1681 w.
Wm. 1718 w.
York
Richd. 1719 i.
BLANCHETT
Amelia
Isaac 1773 w.
BLANCHEFLOWER
Westmoreland
Benj. 1701 w.
Temperance 1712 w.
BLANCHEVILLE
Henrico
Chas. 1694 i.
BLANCKENSHIP
Henrico
Jas. 1749 w.
BLAND
Amelia
Jno. 1777 i.
Peter Randolph
1779 w.
Theodorick 1784 w.
Eliz. 1784 w.
Fauquier
Benj. 1771 i.
Mary 1782 w.
Thos. 1788 w.
Loudoun
Robt. 1760 i.
Mecklenburg
Merit 1773 w.
Norfolk
Thos. 1797 w.
Prince George
Richard 1720 w.

Stafford
Jas. 1708 w.
BLANEY
Isle of Wight
David 1799 w.
BLANK
Frederick
Christian 1772 w.
BLANKENBEECKLER
Orange
Jno. Nich. 1743 w.
BLANKENBEEKER
Culpeper
Matthias 1763 w.
BLANKINBECKER
Culpeper
Balthasar 1774 w.
Christopher 1781 w.
BLANKENBICER
Madison
Zachariah 1794 w.
BLANKINSHIP
Amherst
Noel 1774 w.
Bedford
Wm. 1799 i.
Chesterfield
Fred. 17— i.
Jas. 1749 i.
Jno. 1751 w.
Ralph 1754 w.
Ralph 1758 w.
Francis 1759 w.
Ephraim Jr. 1785 i.
Joel 1789 i.
Joel 1789 w.
Ephraim 1791 i.
Geo. 1792 i.
Henrico
Ralph 1714 i.
Wm. 1745 w.
Lunenburg
Asa 1794 i.
BLANKS
Brunswick
Ingram 1762 w.
James 1769 i.
Ingram 1771 w.
Charles City
James 1793 w.
Charlotte
Wm. 1767 i.
Greensville
Richard 1785 w.
Lunenburg
Thos 1752 w.
Jos. 1752 i.
Pittsylvania
Henry 1794 w.
Sussex
David 1772 i.

BLANSHARD
Amelia
Jno. 1758 w.
BLANTON
Essex
Thos. 1697 w.
Spotsylvania
Richd. 1734 w.
BLARE
Northampton
Wm. 1665 w.
BLASE
Middlesex
Wm. 1674 w.
BLATT
Essex
Thos. 1720 w.
Thos. 1743 w.
Fairfax
Jno. 1783 nw.
BLAWS
Henrico
Robt. 1729 i.
Norfolk
Robert 1760 i.
Princess Anne
Robt. 1780 w.
BLAXTON
Accomack
Jno. 1753 w.
Essex
Argyle 1748 i.
York
Dianah 1721 i.
BLAYDES
Spotsylvania
Wm. 1785 w.
Jno. 1793 w.
BLAYTON
Brunswick
Eliz. 1767 w.
BLEAR
Augusta
Jas. 1789 w.
Frederick
Jno. 1773 i.
BLEARE
Accomack
Jno. 1718 w.
BLEDGINDIN
Norfolk
Wm. 1746 w.
BLEDSOE
Culpeper
Wm. 1770 w.
Northumberland
Geo. 1705 w.
Eliz. 1708 w.
Orange
Howard 1777 i.
Spotsylvania
Moses 1764 a.

BLENCOW
Essex
Jno. 1754 i.
BLESSING
Shenandoah
Jacob Sr. 1790 w.
BLEWS
Norfolk
Samuel 1779 w.
BLICK
Brunswick
Benj. 1799 w.
Thos. 1773 w.
BLINCO
Northumberland
Jno. 1757 i.
BLINCOE
Northumberland
James 1759 w.
Jno. 1782 w.
BLISFED
Rappahannock
Thos. 1677 w.
BLIZARD
Sussex
Chas. 1773 i.
BLOODWORTH
Orange
Jos. 1743 w.
BLOSS
Fairfax
Adam 1792 w.
BLOW
Isle of Wight
Richard 1746 i.
Southampton
Saml. 1766 w.
Richd. 1786 w.
Henry 1796 w.
Surry
Geo. 1717 i.
Saml. 1796 w.
Sussex
Richd 1762 w.
Michael 1799 w.
BLOWS
Augusta
Conrod 1775 i.
BLOXAM
Accomack
Ezekiel 1771 w.
Nicho. 1772 i.
Sarah 1772 w.
BLOXHAM
Fairfax
James 1793 i.
BLOXOM
Accomack
Jno. 1714 w.
Mary 1716 w.
Wm. 1748 w.
Richd. 1751 i.
Jno. 1770 w.

Nicho. 1770 w.
Abel 1776 i.
Jno. 1776 i.
Levy 1779 i.
Lucy 1780 i.
Woodman 1781 w.
Moses 1782 w
Littleton 1783 i.
Thos. 1784 w.
Woodman 1788 w.
Wm. 1789 w.
Woodman 1792 w.
Wm. Sr. 1793 w.
Joshua 1795 w.
Louisa
Richd. 1787 a.
Northampton
Savage 1737 w.
Wm. 1796 w.
York
Richd. 1720 a.b.
BLOXSOM
Accomack
Richd. 1793 w.
BLOXSUM
Accomack
Nicholas 1704 i.
BLOXUM
Accomack
Argill 1798 w.
BLOZE
Augusta
Conrad 1774 w.
BLUE
Berkeley
Jno. 1798 i.
Hampshire
Jno. 1770 w.
Jno. Sr. 1791 w.
BLUFORD
Richmond
Geo. 1723 i.
BLUNDALL
Northumberland
Jno. 1758 w.
Elijah 17— i.
Wm. 1771 i.
Wm. 1796 i.
Westmoreland
Thos. 1732 w.
Wm. 1736 w.
Absolem 1774 w.
Susannah 1777 w.
Gardiner 1764 i.
Wm. 1789 i.
BLUNDER
Orange
Robt. 1752 i.
BLUNDLE
Northampton
Wm. 1721 w.

BLUNDON
Northumberland
Judal 1791 w.
Wm. 1793 w.
Seth 1798 w.
BLUNHERD
Lancaster
Will 1658 n.w.
BLUNT
Culpeper
Chas. 1773 w
Isle of Wight
Wm. 1687 i.
Richd. 1688 i.
Wm. Sr. 1780 i.
Eliz. 1782 w.
Southampton
Priscilla 1752 w.
Benj. 1753 i.
Henry 1758 w.
Thos. 1778 w.
Priscilla 1782 w.
Thos. 1786 i.
Wm. Sr. 1787 w.
Eliz. 1795 w.
Geo. 1795 w.
Surry
Thos. 1709 w.
Thos. 1719 w.
Wm. 1737 i.
Richd. 1747 w.
Sussex
Richd. 1774 w.
Jane 1779 w.
Jno. 1785 w.
Wm. 1794 w.
Frances 1795 w.
BLY
Shenandoah
Jacob 1795 i.
BLYE
Shenandoah
Philip 1786 w.
BOADE
Essex
Samuel 1744 i.
BOAKE
Surry
Alex. 1774 i.
BOAMAN
Lancaster
Wm. 1750 i.
BOARDMAN
Surry
James 1761 i.
BOAT
Lancaster
Jno. E. 1778 i.
BOATMAN
Lancaster
Henry 1722 w.
Jno. 1738 i.

Henry 1743 w.
Edwd. 1746 i.
Mary 1746 i.
Robt. 1749-50 w.
Richd. 1764 w.
Apphia 1789 w.
Pittsylvania
Robt. 1789 i.
BOATRIGHT
Cumberland
Daniel 1797 w.
BOAZ
Pittsylvania
Thos. 1795 i.
BOAZE
Northumberland
Jno. Jr. 1713-14 i.
BOBB
Frederick
Stephen 1760 w.
BOBBELL
Bedford
Lucy 1788 w.
BOBBIT
Sussex
Thos. 1759 i.
BOBBITT
Halifax
Jas. 1761 w.
BOBIT
Halifax
Jas. 1763 i.
BOBO
Prince William
Gabriel 1790 w.
Richd. 1792 w.
BOCHEN
Shenandoah
Saml. 1797 w.
BOCOCK
Albemarle
Saml. 1783 i.
BODDIE
Isle of Wight
Jno. 1720 w.
BODDINGHAM
Frederick
Jas. 1748 a.
BODDINGTON
King George
Jas. 1735 i.
BODEKER
Bedford
Wm. 1770 w.
BODIE
Isle of Wight
Wm. 1717 w.
BODINE
Loudoun
Cornelius 1781 w.
Jacob 1783 i.

BODINGTON
Westmoreland
Jno. 1766 i.
BODKIN
Shenandoah
Ann 1796 i.
BODMAN
Princess Anne
Thos. 1713 i.
BODNAM
Princess Anne
Wm. 1746 w.
BODOIN
Richmond
Jno. 1786 w.
Jno. Jr. 1791 i.
BODY
Isle of Wight
Mary 1732 w.
BOEHM
Shenandoah
Jacob 1798 w.
BOGAR
Loudoun
Frederick 1796 i.
BOGARD
Augusta
Johannes 1748 i.
BOGART
Hampshire
Gysbert 1778 w.
BOGEST
Augusta
Antoine 1763 w.
BOGG
Northampton
Wm. 1799 i.
BOGGAS
Northumberland
Robt. 1662 w.
BOGGES
Northumberland
Mary 1742-3 w.
Bennet 1745 w.
BOGGESS
Fairfax
Robt. 1773 i.
Henry 1785 i.
Robert 1786 w.
Fauquier
Thos. 1772 w.
Loudoun
Henry 1785 i.
Henry 1788 i.
Norfolk
Jno. 1768 i.
Northumberland
Henry 1727 8-i.
BOGGS
Accomack
William 1718 i.
Mackemie 1768 w.

Wm. 1769 i.
Mekemie 1773 w.
Jos. 1795 w.
Berkley
Wm. 1791 w.
Northampton
Wm. 1797 w.
Ohio
Andrew 1798 w.
BOGIE
Essex
Jno. 1786 i.
BOGLE
Rockbridge
Jas. 1787 i.
BOHAM
Frederick
Samuel 1782 i.
BOHANAN
Essex
John 1773 i.
BOHANNAN
Augusta
Jean 1747 w.
Essex
Wm. 1742 w.
Culpeper
Elliott 1781 w.
Madison
Ambrose 1798 a.
BOHANON
Orange
Duncan 1754 w.
BOISE
Sussex
Jacob 1783 i.
BOLD
Northampton
Henry 1728 i.
BOLDING
Amelia
Susanah 1771 w.
BOLES
Cumberland
Benj. 1788 i.
BOLEY
Berkeley
Benj. 1786 i.
Simon 1786 w.
Northumberland
Simon 1723-4 w.
BOLING
Amherst
Edwd. 1769 w.
Fairfax
Robt. 1746 w.
Jos. 1756 i.
BOLITHOE
Princess Anne
Jno. 1728 i.
Jno. 1729 w.

BOLLENTINE
Norfolk
Jno. 1761 w.
BOLLIN
Orange
Ann 1790 w.
Rappahannock
Jno. 1675 w.
BOLLING
Chesterfield
Jno. 1749 w.
Henrico
Jno. 1729 w.
Cumberland
Wm. 1757 i.
Goochland
Jas. 1731 i.
Pittsylvania
Jas. 1772 w.
Prince George
Edwd. 1715 i.
Drury 1726 i.
Prince William
Geo. 1736 i.
Surry
Stith 1727 w.
BOLLY
Lancaster
Geo. 1677 i.
BOLSER
Fairfax
Gasper 1782 i.
BOLT
Fauquier
Thos. 1774 i.
Princess Anne
Thos. 1784 i.
York
Roger 1709 i.
Frances 1739 w.
BOLTON
Chesterfield
Bolling 1795w.
Jno. 1795 w.
Benj. 1797 i.
Isle of Wight
Jno. 1729 i.
Mecklenburg
Jno. 1796 w.
Norfolk
Jno. 1650 w.
BOMAN
Chesterfield
Jno. 1766 w.
Essex
Edwd. 1766 w.
Halifax
Jno. 1799 i.
BOMAR
Essex
Edwd. 1766 w.

Halifax
Wm. 1794 w.
BOMER
Essex
Alex. 1786 w.
BONAM
Westmoreland
Saml. 1703 w.
Katherine 1715 i.
Thos. 1717 w.
Saml. 1726 w.
BONCE
Princess Anne
Thos. 1704 rp.
BOND
Culpeper
Jno. 1760 w.
Cumberland
Wm. 1759 w.
Page 1763 w.
Nancy 1782 w.
Essex
Wm. 1776 w.
Fairfax
Thos. 1794 w.
Isle of Wight
Jno. 1669 w.
Dorothy 1684 w.
Jno. 1688 w.
Frederick
Samuel 1791 w.
Lancaster
Jno. 1699 i.
Wm. 1762 i.
Jno. 1764 i.
Alice 1796 w.
Louisa
Thos. 1798 w.
Middlesex
Robert 1752 a.
Norfolk
Wm. 1713 w.
Princess Anne
Francis 1699 w.
Spotsylvania
Robt. 1725 w.
York
Jno. 1742-3 i.
Wm. 1743 w.
Jno. 1750 i.
BONDREY
Essex
Wm. 1702 i.
BONDS
Sussex
Robt. 1793 w.
York
Nich. 1670 i.
BONDURANT
Goochland
Jno. Peter 1734 w.

BONES
Amherst
Wm. 1794 a.
BONEVAL
Richmond
Jno. 1740 w.
BONEWELL
Accomack
Jas. 1702 i.
Jas. 1721 w.
Joakim Michael
1783 w.
Jacob 1791 w.
Jane 1799 w.
BONGE
Charles City
James 1791 w.
BONFIELD
Princess Anne
Jas. 1767 i.
BONFILL
Norfolk
Benj. 1769 w.
BONIFIELD
Culpeper
Gregory 1794 w.
BONIWELL
Accomack
Jacob 1793 i.
BONNER
Halifax
Thos. 1792 w.
Middlesex
Peter 1760 i.
Orange
Jno. 1745 i.
Sussex
Mary 1770 w.
BONNERWELL
Accomack
Thos. 1758 w.
BONNETS
Harrison
Samuel 1789 i.
BONNEWELL
Accomack
Thos. 1743 w.
Richd. 1746 w.
Jas. 1767 w.
BONNEY
Princess Anne
Edwd. 1720 i.
Jno. 1724 w.
Wm. 1732 w.
Wm. 1745 w.
Wm. 1762 i.
Wm. 1763 i.
Jno. 1766 w.
Jno. 1770 w.
Moses 1774 i.
Jonathan 1779 w.
Nathan 1780 w.

Jonathan 1789 w.
Jno. Sr. 1794 w.
BONSEL
Spotsylvania
Moses 1799 w.
BONNY
Princess Anne
Jno. 1758 w.
BONTRUE
Spotsylvania
Nich. C. 1740 a.
BONUM
Northumberland
Thos. 1741 i.
Thos. 1753 w.
Westmoreland
Margt. 1695 i.
Philpot 1726 w.
Danl. 1732 w.
Saml. 1748 w.
BONWELL
Accomack
Jeames 1667 i.
Thos. 1719 i.
Geo. 1721 w.
Jno. 1728 i.
Jno. 1775 w.
Jno. Jr. 1778 i.
Northampton
Sarah 1659 w.
BOOCOCK
Westmoreland
Jno. 1674 w.
Thos. 1675 i.
BOOKER
Amelia
Edwd. 1750 w.
Judith 1750 w.
Wm. 1755 w.
Edmd. Sr. 1758 w.
Edwd. 1760 w.
Richd. 1760 w.
Edwd. 1761 w.
Richd. 1760 w.
Anne 1783 i.
Saml. 1788 w.
Geo. 1791 w.
Edmd. 1793 w.
Edwd. 1794 i.
Edmd. 1795 w.
Jno. 1795 w.
Richd. 1797 w.
Peter 1798 i.
Edwd. 1799 w.
Efford 1799 i.
Chesterfield
Richd. 1793 w.
Essex
Ann 1775 w.
Jas. 1794 w.
Halifax
Edwd. 1767 w.

Parham 1786 w.
Jno. 1793 w.
Lunenburg
Richd. 1794 w.
Norfolk
Wm. 1785 w.
Prince Edward
Wm. 1783 w.
York
Martha 1742-3 w.
Richd. 1743 w.
BOOKEY
Surry
Edwd. 1712 w.
BOOL
Northampton
Richd. 1762 i.
Jno. 1747 i.
Jno. 1796 w.
BOOLE
Northampton
Richd. 1728 i.
BOOLOCK
Northumberland
Edwd. 1752 i.
BOOLTEN
Chesterfield
Bolen 1798 i.
BOON
Isle of Wight
Jas. 1770 i.
Ratcliff 1773 i.
Randliff 1799 w.
King George
Jno. 1776 w.
Wm. 1795 w.
BOOT
Accomack
Nicholas 1668 w.
BOOTEN
Culpeper
Wm. 1787 w.
BOOTH
Accomack
Jno. 1706 w.
Geo. 1755 w.
Geo. 1762 w.
Jamamiah 1781 w.
Albemarle
Geo. 1797 w.
Amelia
Geo. 1767 w.
Thos. Sr. 1769 w.
Wm. 1783 w.
Jno. 1793 w.
Wm. Sr. 1795 i.
Phoebe 1795 i.
Philip 1796 w.
Brunswick
Reubin 1775 w.
Essex
Humphrey 1702 i.

Frederick
Wm. 1790 w.
King George
Jno. 1751 i.
Loudoun
Robert 1760 w.
Lunenburg
Nathl. 1785 w.
Northumberalnd
Richd. 1739 w.
Wm. 1744 w.
Jas. 1750 w.
Richd. 1755 i.
Martha 1757 w.
Adam 1758 i.
Anne 1779 i.
Wm. 1795 i.
Jno. 1799 w.
Princess Anne
Jno. 1752 i.
Geo. 1790 w.
Jno. 1796 w.
Randolph
Daniel 1797 i.
Richmond
Jno. 1726 i.
Southampton
Robt. 1760 w.
Arthur 1770 w.
Faitha 1771 w.
Shelly 1771 w.
Robt. 1777 w.
Moses 1794 w.
Surry
Thos. 1751 w.
Sussex
Geo. 1763 w.
Michael 1792 i.
Geo. 1793 i.
Westmoreland
Geo. 1698 i.
Wm. 1702 w.
Eliz. 1708 w.
York
Whitten 1692 w.
Wm. 1692-3 i.
Margt. 1696 n.w.
Michael 1710 w.
Thos. 1725 i.
Thos. 1728 i.
Boaz 1789 w.
Geo. 1791 w.
Jno. 1799 w.

BOOTIN
Accomack
Wm. 1751 w.

BOOTON
Accomack
Jno. 1768 w.
Culpeper
Ambrose 1775 i.

BOOZE
Northumberland
Wm. 1745 i.
BORCUS
Lancaster
Wm. 1656 i.
BORDAS
Norfolk
Wm. 1667 w.
BORDEN
Augusta
Benj. 1753 w.
Frederick
Benj. 1743 w.
Shenandoah
Frederick 1799 i.
BORELAND
Augusta
Jno. 1765 i.
BOREMAN
Prince George
Jas. 1714 i.
Matilda 1718 i.
Spotsylvania
Chas. 1749 w.
BORER
Hampshire
Jacob 1778 w.
Northampton
Geo. 1692 w.
BORGER
Shenandoah
Michael 1794 w.
BORHAM
York
Wm. 1763 i.
BORKERT
Berkeley
Martin 1789 w.
BORNAR
Halifax
Jno. Sr. 1799 w.
BORNDRAGAR
Botetourt
Andrew 1798 w.
BORRO
Princess Anne
Wm. 1701 i.
BORROUGHS
Princess Anne
Chris. 1797 w.
BORROW
Sussex
Tabitha 1760 i.
BORTON
Chesterfield
Jno. 1754 w.
BORNUM
Halifax
Jno. 1785 w.
Jno. 1797 i.

BOSANG
Augusta
David 1777 w.
Jno. 1799 i.
BOSELEY
Middlesex
Jacob 1699 i.
Eliz. 1700 w.
BOSEWELL
Accomack
Jas. 1783 i.
BOSOMWORTH
York
Geo. 1774 i.
BOSOSWELL
Louisa
Wm. 1750 w.
BOSS
Middlesex
Thos. 1755 w.
Jos. 1782 i.
Mary 1795 w.
BOSTEYOUN
Frederick
John 1798 i.
BOSTICK
Goochland
Jno. 1761 w.
Greenbrier
Moses 1799 i.
Halifax
Chas. 1782 w.
Moses 1786 w.
Jno. 1796 i.
BOSTON
Orange
Jno. 1774 w.
BOSWELL
Accomack
Jas. 1779 w.
Berkeley
Walter 1778 w.
Brunswick
Wm. 1783 i.
Thos. 1791 w.
Fauquier
Wm. 1773 i.
Louisa
Jno. 1788 w.
Ann 1790 w.
Jno. 1790 i.
Lunenburg
Eliz. 1798 w.
Mecklenburg
Ransom 1792 w.
Jos. 1794 w.
Northumberland
Jno. 1772 w.
Spotsylvania
Jno. 1741 w.
BOSWORTH

Westmoreland
Edwd. 1740 i.
BOTT
Chesterfield
Thos. 1776 w.
Jno. 1797 i.
Mecklenburg
Ann 1779 w.
BOTTOM
Amelia
Thos. 176J w.
Thos. 1781-w.
Wm. 1795 w.
Culpeper
Jos. 1753 i.
Henrico
Jno. 1711 w.
Jno. 1737 w.
Jno. 1781 w.
Thos. 1789 w.
Wm. 1789 w.
Wm. 1790 i.
BOTTOMLY
Henrico
Thos. 1689 i.
BOTTS
Culpeper
Wm. 1792 i.
Loudoun
Aaron 1778 i.
Joshua 1797 w.
Orange
Jno. 1747 i.
Prince William
Joshua 1781 w.
Stafford
Thos. 1742 w.
Sabina 1785 i.
BOUDLER
Frederick
Jas. 1746 i.
BOUGARD
Augusta
Johannes 1747 w.
BOUGHAN
Culpeper
Mordecai 1792 w.
Essex
Jno. 1697 w.
Jas. 1712 nw.
Jas. 1718 w.
Jno. 1720 w.
Jas. Sr. 1722 w.
Henry 1736 w.
Jno. 1748 w.
Augustine 1751 w.
Jno. 1776 w.
BOUGHMAN
Shenandoah
Henery Sr. 1779 w.
Andrew 1785 a.

BOUGHTON
Essex
Joshua Sr. 1731 w.
Joshua 1772 w.
John 1772 w.
Henry 1787 w.
BOUGHTRIGHT
Cumberland
David 1774 i.
BOULDIN
Charlotte
Thos., the Elder,
1783 w.
BOULDING
Prince Edward
Thos. 1769 i.
BOULDWIN
Prince Edward
Thos. 1767 w.
BOULGER
Isle of Wight
Thos. 1706 w.
BOULIN
Essex
Simon 1711 i.
BOULING
Norfolk
Richd. 1669 w.
BOULT
Princess Anne
Thos. 1784 w.
Jno. 1799 w.
BOULTON
Franklin
Robert 1787 a.
Isle of Wight
Jno. 1727 w.
Middlesex
Daniel 1679 a.
Norfolk
Wm. 1722 w.
Aaron 1752 w.
Wm. 1796 i.
Jno. 1797 w.
Northumberland
Francis 1652 w.
BOULWARE
Amherst
Jesse 1777 w.
Essex
Jno. 1714 w.
Jas. 1718 w.
Benj. 1727 w.
Jno. 1743 w.
Nicho. 1751 i.
Jas. 1752 w.
Mark 1754 w.
Jno. 1761 w.
Eliz. 1777 w.
Margt. 1780 w.
Thos. 1785 w.
Younger 1791 w.

BOUNCHER
Hanover
Wm. 1733 i.
Jno. 1733-4 w.
BOUND
Essex
Jno. 1726 i.
BOURCHER
Northumberland
Jno. 1713 a.
BOURHEY
Isle of Wight
Daniell 1668 w.
BOURING
Norfolk
Jno. 1677 w.
BOURLAND
Augusta
Jas. 1762 a.
Jno. 1791 i.
BOURN
Amelia
David 1741 a.
Culpeper
Jno. 1774 i.
Geo. 1778 w.
Andrew 1790 w.
Louisa
Wm. 1782 w.
Orange
Robt. 1757 i.
Spotsylvania
Robt. 1727 w.
BOURNE
Essex
Jno. 1721 w.
Peter 1720 w.
Wm. 1739 w.
Jno. 1747 w.
BOUSH
Norfolk
Saml. 1738-9 w.
Saml. 1743 i.
Saml. 1759 w.
Maximillion 1761 w.
Saml. 1765 i.
Arthur 1779 w.
Goodrich 1782 w.
Arthur 1784 i.
Saml. 1784 w.
Goodrich 1784 i.
Horatio 1793 i.
Princess Anne
Maximillian, the
Elder, 1728 w.
Sarah 1733 w.
Maximillian, the
Elder, 1736 w.
Saml. 1770 w.
Zachariah 1778 i.
Saml. 1779 i.
Maximilion 1782 w.

Jas. 1799 w.
BOUSHELL
Norfolk
John 1785 i.
Wm. Jr. 1790 w.
Wm. 1795 w.
BOUTWELL
Princess Anne
Adam 1694 i.
Adam 1698 i.
BOW
Louisa
Jacob 1782 w.
Northampton
Moses 1713-14 i.
BOWCOCK
Westmoreland
Jas. 1742 w.
Anthony 1777 w.
Thos. 1785 w.
York
Henry 1742 i.
Henry 1778 w.
BOWCOCKE
York
Henry 1729-30 w.
BOWDEN
Isle of Wight
Jno. 1790 i.
Middlesex
Geo. 1717 i.
Northampton
Jno. 1717 w.
Jno. 1775 w.
Southampton
Robt. 1787 w.
BOWDIN
Isle of Wight
John 1788 w.
BOWDOIN
Northampton
Peter 1745 w.
Jno. 1776 i.
Grace 1799 i.
BOWE
Northampton
Moses 1713-14 w.
BOWEN
Accomack
Jno. 1678 w.
Augusta
Jno. 1761 w.
Moses 1761 i.
Jno. 1767 w.
Frederick
Jacob 1799 w.
Henry 1784 w.
Greenbrier
Anthony 1787 w.
King George
Stephen 1749 i.
Susannah 1761 i.

Stephen 1770 a.
Wm. 1771 w.
Jno. 1795 i.
Mecklenburg
Hicks 1787 w.
Jesse 1797 w.
Northumberland
Jno. 1747 i.
Rappahannock
Jno. 1686 w.
Richmond
Saml. 1708 i.
Jno. 1722 i.
Southampton
Jno. 1762 w.
Stafford
Mathew 1785 i.
Washington
Lilly 1780 w.
York
Wm. 1783 i.
BOWER
Botetourt
Martin 1796 i.
Frederick
Jacob 1799 i.
BOWERS
Berkeley
Henry 1788 i.
Brunswick
Jno. 1746 i.
Essex
Thos. 1747 i.
Norfolk
Jno. 1705-6 w.
Jas. 1717 a.
Bartleme 1779 i.
Robt. 1782 w.
Robt. 1793 i.
Princess Anne
Philip 1784 i.
Southampton
Wm. 1777 w.
BOWES
Northumberland
Jno. 1704 w.
BOWIN
Albemarle
Ephraim 1792 w.
Essex
Mary 1719 i.
Isle of Wight
Richd. 1728 w.
Northumberland
Edwd. 1746 i.
Southampton
Jno. 1759 w.
Jno. 1762 i.
BOWIS
York
Robt. 1736 w.

BOWKER
Bedford
Achilles 1779 i.
Cumberland
Achilles 1761 w.
Northampton
Abraham 1728 w.
Spotsylvania
Parmenas 1748 a.
BOWLER
Goochland
Wm. 1761 w.
Northumberland
Maurice 1726-7 w.
Rappahannock
Thos. 1679 w.
York
Jno. 1696 i.
BOWLERDE
York
Jno. 1698 a.
BOWLES
Accomack
Thos. 1674 w.
Amherst
David 1777 a.
Chesterfield
Joshua 1766 w.
Jas. 1783 w.
Joshua 17— i.
Cumberland
Jno. 1793 w.
Goochland
Gideon 1799 w.
Henrico
Thos. 1784 w.
Montgomery
Wm. 1798 w.
Northampton
Zachariah 1720 w.
Richmond
Chas. 1750 i.
Phillis 1758 w.
BOWLIN
Spotsylvania
Jesse 1792 w.
BOWLING
Fairfax
Jno. 1779 i.
Gerrard 1780 w.
Simon 1786 w.
King George
Jno. 1731 i.
Orange
Wm. 1772 i.
Stafford
Simon 1736 i.
Westmoreland
Wm. 1762 i.
BOWLS
Accomack
Thos. 1709 w.

Goochland
Zachariah 1761 i.
Norfolk
Thos. 1719 w.
BOWLY
Northumberland
Sarah 1738 w.
Wm. 1745 w.
BOWMAKER
Fairfax
Jas. 1771 w.
BOWMAN
Accomack
Edmond 1691 w.
David 1786 w.
Catherine 1791 i.
Amelia
Robt. 1745 w.
Wm. 1797 i.
Augusta
Peter 1763 a.
Geo. 1766 a.
Chesterfield
Henry 17— nw.
Abraham 1782 w.
Jno. Jr. 1783 w.
Jno. 1796 w.
Cumberland
David 1791 i.
Frederick
Andrew 1749 i.
Andrew 1764 i.
Christian 1764 w.
George 1769 w.
Christian 1771 i.
Geo. 1771 i.
Jos. 1780 w.
Geo. 1789 i.
Halifax
Nathl. 1790 w.
Wm. 1790 w.
Henrico
Jno. 1725 w.
Edwd. 1727 i.
Lancaster
Wm. 1750 w.
Middlesex
Peter 1759 a.
Montgomery
Samuel 1793 i.
Peter 1796 w.
Shenandoah
Jacob 1774 a.
Jacob 1778 a.
Christian 1783 a.
Jno. 1783 a.
Geo. Adam 1797 w.
Stafford
Saml. 1742 w.
Surry
Thos. 1699 i.
Jeane 1706 w.

BOWMAR
Halifax
Wm. 1791 i.
Wm. 1795 i.
BOWRY
Charles City
Mary 1773 w.
BOWS
Norfolk
Henry 1711 nw.
BOWSER
Princess Anne
Jno. 1778 i.
BOWYER
Augusta
Anthony 1763 i.
Jno. 1768 i.
Bedford
Fredk. 1777 w.
Botetourt
Thos. 1785 w.
Montgomery
Henry 1782 i.
BOXLEY
Louisa
Jos. 1788 w.
BOYCE
Halifax
James 1761 w.
Hampshire
Richd. 1791 w.
Rappahannock
Geo. 1686 i.
BOYCSS
Rappahannock
Geo. 1685 w.
BOYD
Albemarle
Saml. 1770 w.
Augusta
Andrew 1750 w.
Robt. 1752 a.
Alex. 1766 i.
Jno. 1793 w.
Bedford
Wm. 1761 w.
Wm. 1769 i.
Wm. 1794 w.
Berkeley
Wm. 1777 w.
Wm. 1783 i.
Thos. 1791 i.
Franklin
William 1798 w.
Frederick
Samuel 1790 i.
Halifax
Jno. 1757 w.
Patrick 1762 w.
Jas. 1771 i.
Andrew 1780 i.
Geo. Jr. 1781 w.

Geo. 1783 i.
Patrick 1784 i.
Wm. 1785 w.
Jno. 1788 w.
Wm. 1788 i.
Wm. 1789 i.
Isle of Wight
Thos. 1710 w.
Lancaster
Jno. 1781 w.
Loudoun
Wm. 1776 i.
Wm. 1781 w.
Jno. 1786 i.
Northumberland
Robt. 1711 i.
Jno. 1741 w.
Robt. 1747 i.
Robt. 1750 i.
Alex. 1755 w.
Frances 1764 w.
David 1781 w.
Margt. 1782 w.
Richmond
David 1728 i.
Surry
Jas. 1753 w.
BOYER
Northampton
Jno. 1713 w.
Northumberland
Henry 1762 i.
BOYES
Essex
Wm. 1783 w.
BOYESS
Rappahannock
Geo. 1686 w.
BOYKIN
Isle of Wight
Edward 1728 w.
Jno. 1729 i.
Edwd. 1730 i.
Wm. 1732 w.
Edwd. 1737 i.
Southampton
Simon 1788 w.
Wm. 1789 w.
Jno. 1795 w.
BOYLE
Frederick
Jas. 1758 w.
King George
Thos. 1729 i.
Margt. 1732 i.
BOYLES
Accomack
Jas. 1749 i.
Berkeley
Henry 1795 i.
Frederick
Jas. 1765 i.

BOYS
Lancaster
　Robt. 1692 i.
Westmoreland
　Thos. 1657 w.
BOZIER
Frederick
　Jno. 1765 i.
BOZMON
Fairfax
　Mary 1754 w.
　Thos. 1754 w.
BOZWORTH
Frederick
　Jno. 1760 w.
　Jno. 1764 i.
BRABIN
Prince William
　Eliz. 1737 i.
BRABNER
King George
　Geo. 1775 a.
BRABSON
Berkeley
　Jno. 1782 w.
BRACEGIRDLE
York
　Jno. 1672 nw.
Norfolk
　Fred. 1773 w.
BRACEY
Isle of Wight
　Francis 1721 i.
　Hugh 1762 w.
　Eliz. 1770 w.
Norfolk
　Wm. 1746 i.
BRACK
Norfolk
　Benj. 1719 i.
BRACKENRIDGE
Lunenburg
　Jean 1746 w.
BRACKET
Norfolk
　Wm. 1795 w.
BRACKETT
Amelia
　Thos. 1772 w.
　Benj. 1792 w.
Henrico
　Jno. 1785 w.
BRACPEIL
Augusta
　Isaac 1767 w.
BRACY
Isle of Wight
　Michael 1754 w.
BRACYES
Southampton
　Francis 1782 i.

BRADBERRY
Henry
　Richd. 1798 i.
Essex
　Jas. 1748 i.
BRADBOURN
Orange
　Wm. 1757 w.
Louisa
　Sarah 1782 i.
BRADBURN
Orange
　Sarah 1771 w.
BRADCHEN
Cumberland
　Chas. 1761 w.
BRADDY
Isle of Wight
　Patrick 1697 nw.
　Elias 1737 w.
　Wm. 1739 i.
　Ellias 1741 w.
　Olive 1753 i.
　Mason 1785 w.
Southampton
　Margaret 1750 w.
Surry
　Edwd. 1721 i.
BRADEN
Loudoun
　Robt. 1795 w.
BRADFIELD
Northumberland
　Jno. 1751 i.
BRADFORD
Accomack
　Nathaniel 1690 i.
　Wm. 1735 w.
　Nathl. 1744 i.
　Noah 1749 i.
　Eliz. 1763 w.
　Chas. 1764 i.
　Fisher 1764 w.
　Wm. 1765 w.
　Abel 1771 i.
　Jno. 1771 w.
　Levin 1772 w.
　Mary 1772 w.
　Jno. 1773 i.
　Laben 1774 w.
　Ezekiel 1778 w.
　Jacob 1784 w.
　Jno. 1784 i.
　Neomy 1784 w.
　Nathl. 1785 w.
　Wm. 1785 w.
　Zephaniah 1794 i.
　Brown 1795 w.
　Jas. 1795 w.
　Robt. 1795 w.
　Sarah 1795 w.

　Thos. B. 1795 w.
　Jno. 1796 w.
　Absolem 1797 w.
　Benston 1797 i.
　Kendall 1797 w.
　Custis 1798 w.
Augusta
　Anne 1794 w.
Brunswick
　Jno. 1735 w.
Fauquier
　Wm. 1760 w.
　Mary 1783 w.
Northampton
　Leahannah 1795 w.
Shenandoah
　David 1785 a.
BRADGG
Isle of Wight
　Mary 1736 w.
BRADHURST
Accomack
　Jno. 1723 w.
BRADLEY
Amelia
　Ann 1790 w.
Augusta
　Jemima 1784 w.
Charles City
　Benj. 1768 i.
　Jno. 1770 w.
　Walter 1791 i.
　Jos. 1795 w.
　Walter 1797 i.
Culpeper
　Laurence 1788 w.
　Wm. 1794 w.
Cumberland
　Jno. 1782 w.
Fairfax
　Wm. 1777 i.
Fauquier
　Hugh 1795 w.
Goochland
　Wm. 1738 i.
Lancaster
　Jno. 1710 w.
Norfolk
　Geo. 1695 w.
　Wm. 1785 w.
Northumberland
　Henry 1658 w.
　Wm. 1670 i.
　The Widow 1670 i.
　Robt. 1727 w.
　Eliz. 1729 i.
Orange
　Robt. 1786 w.
　Richd. 1785 w.
Richmond
　Thos. 1705 w.

Eliz. 1723 w.
Patrick 1727 i.
Sussex
Wm. 1765 w.
Henry 1773 w.
Wm. 1797 i.
BRADNNOR
Richmond
Thos. 1742 i.
BRADSHAW
Accomack
Morgan 1731 i.
Augusta
Thos. 1779 w.
Cumberland
Chas. 1762 i.
Goochland
Larner 1750 w.
Benj. 1761 w.
Ann 1777 w.
Jno. 1777 i.
Jno. 1794 i .
Isle of Wight
Wm. 1698 i.
Jno. 1706 w.
Nich. 1727 w.
Wm. 1739 w.
Jno. 1745 w.
Richd. 1785 w.
Lancaster
Edwd. 1655 w.
Middlesex
Feliz 1727 w.
Judith 1727 w.
Prince Edward
Jno. 1788 w.
Jno. 1796 i.
Princess Anne
Edwd. 1733 i.
Northumberland
Jno. 1656 w.
Robt. 1660 w.
Southampton
Jos. 1762 w.
Jos. 1778 w.
Arthur 1782 i.
Eliz. 1785 i.
Martha 1791 w.
Benj. 1792 w.
Thos. 1798 w.
York
Jas. 1726 i.
BRADWATTER
Accomack
Wm. 1726 w.
BRADY
Halifax
Owen 1771 w.
Lancaster
Eliz. 1727 i.
Eliz. 1778 w.

Surry
Jno. 1676 w.
BRAFORD
Augusta
Saml. 1789 w .
BRAG
Isle of Wight
Jas. 1670 w.
BRAGG
Amelia
Hugh 1736 w.
Chesterfield
Wm. 1792 w.
Culpeper
William 1777 i.
Isle of Wight
Jas. 1728 w.
Mary 1736 w.
Richmond
Mary 1731 i.
Jos. Sr. 1747 w.
Eliz. 1758 i.
Chas. 1759 i.
Wm. 1774 i.
Moore 1792 w.
Jas. 1794 i.
Westmoreland
Jos. 1793 i.
BRAGGER
Norfolk
Edwd. 1678 i.
BRAHAN
Fauquier
Jno. 1775 w.
BRAINE
Henrico
Edwd. 1709 w.
BRAISEY
Isle of Wight
Eliz. 1770 i.
BRAITHWAITE
Princess Anne
Jas. 1780 w.
BRAITHWAIT
York
Jno. 1720 i.
BRAKE
Frederick
Jacob 1762 i.
BRAKES
Norfolk
Henry 1640 i.
BRALLY
Wythe
Jno. 1798 w.
BRAMBLE
Norfolk
Willis 1778 w.
BRAME
Essex
Cath. 1761 w.

Halifax
Saml. D. 1799 i.
Mecklenburg
Richd. 1789 w.
Thos. 1789 i.
Reubin 1792 i.
Jno. 1793 w.
Richins 1793 i.
Eliz. 1795 w.
BRAMHAM
Richmond
Richd. 1728 w.
Richd. 1739 w.
Jno. 1755 w.
BRAMLETT
Bedford
Jas. 1758 w.
Wm. 1779 w.
BRAMMELL
Amelia
Wm. 1786 i.
BRANAN
Lancaster
Jno. 1750 w .
Richmond
Barbara 1794 w.
BRANCH
Bedford
——— 1787 i.
Chesterfield
Jas. 1726 w.
Wm. 1741 w.
Mary 1750 w.
Jno. 1751 i.
Benj. 1760 w.
Betty 1765 w.
Thos. 1765 w.
Matthew 1768 w.
Thos. 1769 w.
Johan 1769 w.
Matthew 1772 w.
Christopher 1772 w.
Thos. 1778 w.
Martha 1773 w.
Olive 1779 w.
Edwd. 1781 w.
Benj. 1782 w.
Matthew 1786 w.
Saml. 1789 w.
Saml. Jr. 1790 i.
Saml. 1790 i.
Wm. 1796 w.
Danl. 179- w.
Garner 17— i.
Henrico
Chris. 1681-2 w.
Thos. 1688 w.
Eliz. 1697 w.
Saml. 1700 w.
Benj. 1706 i.
Edwd. 1726-7 i

Matthew, Sr. 1726 w.
Christopher 1727 w.
Thos. Sr. 1728 w.
Jas. 1737 w.
Henry 1748 i.
Isle of Wight
Geo. 1688 i.
Francis 1720 w.
Lancaster
Arthur 1673-4 i.
Powhatan
Danl. 1782 w.
Southampton
Eliz. 1750 w.
Wm. 1769 w.
Geo. 1770 w.
Martha 1772 w.
Howell 1781 w.
Ogborne 1785 w.
BRAND
Augusta
Jas. Sr. 1795 w.
Westmoreland
Nicholas 1784 w.
BRANDAKIN
Essex
Tarent 1747 i.
BRANDER
Bedford
Jno. 1778 w.
BRANDON
Halifax
David 1778 w.
Wm. 1778 w.
Francis 1789 w.
Irvine 1791 w.
Wm. 1792 i.
Jno. N. 1795 i.
David 1797 w.
David 1798 i.
BRANHAM
Louisa
Benj. 1795 w.
Northumberland
Jas. 1753 nw.
Orange
Jno. Sr. 1761 w.
Jno. 1787 i.
Spotsylvania
Danl. 1794 w.
Stafford
Jno. 1749 i.
Westmoreland
Michael 1762 w.
BRANIKIN
King George
Wm. 1797 w.
BRANKER
Norfolk
Nathl. 1685-6 w.

BRANN
Northumberland
Nicholas 1799 i.
Richmond
Jos. 1778 w.
Westmoreland
Jno. 1792 i.
BRANNAN
Richmond
Caran 1750 w.
Jas. 1752 nw.
Jos. 1752 w.
Jas. 1791 w.
BRANNER
Shenandoah
Casber 1792 i.
BRANSCOM
Brunswick
Richd. 1775 w.
BRANSDON
Northumberland
Jno. 1752 i.
BRANSFORD
Chesterfield
Jno. 1767 w.
Powhatan
Jas. 1782 w.
BRANSON
Frederick
Thos. 1744 w.
Jno. 1770 w.
Hampshire
Jos. 1780 w.
Hardy
Amos 1793 i.
BRANSTON
Northampton
Francis 1709 w.
BRANTLEY
Isle of Wight
Edwd. 1721 i.
Edwd. 1737 w.
Jno. 1725 i.
James 1741 i.
Jas. 1756 i.
Benj. 1759 i.
Benj. 1778 i.
Francis 1779 w.
Surry
Hester 1727 w.
BRANTLY
Isle of Wight
Edwd. 1688-9 w.
Edwd. 1721 w.
Jno. 1730-31 w.
Edwd. 1737 w.
Edwd. 1754 i.
Clay 1755 w.
Jno. 1761 i.
Southampton
Jas. 1794 i.

Etheldred 1798 i.
BRANWELL
Isle of Wight
Robt. 1668 w.
BRAROWILL
Isle of Wight
Robt. 1668 i.
BRASHEAR
Berkeley
Sephaniah 1798
Henry
Philip 1798 w.
BRASIE
Isle of Wight
Wm. 1701 w.
BRASSE
Isle of Wight
Wm. 1732 w.
BRASSEE
Isle of Wight
Wm. 1732 w.
BRASSEY
Isle of Wight
Eliz. 1752 w.
BRASSIE
Isle of Wight
Wm. 1752 w.
BRASWELL
Isle of Wight
Richd. 1724-5 w.
Richd. 1745 w.
Susanna 1713 w.
Susannah 1732 w.
Sarah 1735 w.
BRATTEN
Accomack
Wm. 1776 w.
Wm. 1781 w.
BRATTON
Augusta
Robt. 1785 w.
Shenandoah
Jno. 1784 a.
BRAUGHTON
Norfolk
Jas. 1751 i.
Northumberland
Job 1767 w.
BRAWFORD
Augusta
Ann 1795 i.
BRAWNER
Fairfax
Mary 1765 w.
BRAY
Essex
Chas. 1772 w.
Jno. 1783 i.
Winter 1790 i.

Fauquier
Jno. 1798 i.
Lancaster
Richd. 1690 nw.
Middlesex
Jno. 1772 i.
Norfolk
Robt. 1681 w.
Princess Anne
Robt. 1719 w.
Plomer 1722 i.
Edwd. 1727 w .
Olive 1728 w.
BRAZER
Essex
John 1712 w.
Northampton
Richd. 1761 i.
Comfort 1781 w.
BRAZIEE
Prince William
Eliz. 1797 w.
BRAZIER
Essex
Richd. 1717 w.
BREAD
Isle of Wight
Richd. 1691 w.
BREAM
Frederick
Henry 1793 i.
Middlesex
Jno. 1774 i.
Jno. 1760 w.
BRECHIN
Louisa
Sarah 1753 w.
Westmoreland
Jas. 1723 i.
BRECKENRIDGE
Botetourt
Robt. 1773 w.
Orange
Alex. 1744 nw.
Wythe
Geo. 1790w.
BRECKNELL
Essex
Richd. 1719 i.
BREDEN
Augusta
Jno. Thos. 1772 w.
Spotsylvania
Richd. 1791 a.
BREECHIN
Westmoreland
Jas. 1722 w.
BREEDING
Culpeper
Richd. 1773 i.

Shenandoah
Briant 1783 i.
BREEDLOVE
Charlotte
Robt. 1792 w.
Jno. 1799 w.
Essex
Chas. 1758 i.
Lucrecy 1772 i.
Alaman 1775 w.
Nathan 1786 w.
BREHON
Frederick
Abraham 1771 w.
BRELAIN
Frederick
Wm. 1776 i.
BRENAN
Westmoreland
Owen 1740 w.
BRENAUGH
Fairfax
Geo. 1750 a.
BRENT
Charlotte
Jno. 1781 w.
Lancaster
Hugh 1716 i.
Wm. 1740 w.
Geo. 1748 w.
Hugh 1750 w.
Jas. 1750 w.
Hugh 1750-1 w.
Catherine 1761 w.
Stockley 1765 w.
Eliz. 1770 w.
Richd. 1771 i.
Chas. 1772 w.
Stockley 1772 i.
Geo. 1778 w.
Hugh 1778 w.
Thos. 1782 w.
Margt. 1784 w.
Jas. 1792 w.
Ann 1795 w.
Newton 1795 w.
Vincent 1799 w.
Loudoun
Geo. 1785 w.
Northumberland
Wm. 1738 i.
Elizab. 1770 w.
Richmond
Morris 1782 w.
Stafford
Geo. 1700 w.
Wm. 1742 i.
Benj. 1747 i.
Chas. 1756 w.
Hannah 1762 w.
Wm. 1786 i.

Westmoreland
Mary 1658 w.
Edmund 1659 w.
BRENTY
Shenandoah
Philip 1795 w.
BRERETON
Northumberland
Thos. 1699 w.
Thos. the younger
1725 i.
Richmond
Henry 1713 i.
Willoughby 1728 i.
BRESSE
Isle of Wight
Jno. 1675 i.
BRESEY
Isle of Wight
Hugh 1727 w.
BRESSIE
Halifax
Jno. 1762 w.
Lunenburg
Francis 1762 w.
Mecklenburg
Eliz. 1782 w. '
Norfolk
Samuel 1779 w.
Henry 1782 w.
BRETT
Augusta
Jno. 1773 w.
Brunswick
Jas. 1778 w.
Isle of Wight
Wm. 1744 w.
Norfolk
Elinor 1757 i.
Westmoreland
Henry 1674 i.
BREURTON
Stafford
Wm. 1750 w.
BREW
Norfolk
Joyce 1796 i.
BREWER
Amelia
Edmund 1747 i.
Ann 1771 w.
Brunswick
Peter 1741 i.
Geo. 1744 w.
Geo. 1760 w.
Geo. Jr. 1762 i.
Jas. 1785 w.
Greensville
Nicholas 1788 i.
Isle of Wight
Jno. 1669 nw.

Thos. 1729 w.
Wm. Sr. 1749 w.
Michael 1778w.
Lancaster
Paul 1655 i.
Loudoun
Henry 1793 w.
Northumberland
Thos. 1699-1700 w.
Northampton
Jno. 1708 w.
Princess Anne
Jas. 1792 w.
Mary 1764 w.
Prince William
Thos. 1778 i.
Southampton
Jno. 1780 w.
Surry
Nicholas 1730 i.
Westmoreland
Wm. 1769 i.
Jas. 1781 i.
York
Mary 1720 ab.
Francis 1770 i.
BREWSTER
Fairfax
Thos. 1756 i.
Henrico
Sackvile 1745 w.
Surry
Eliz. 1675 i.
BREWTON
Stafford
Jno. 1707 w.
Wm. 1739 w.
BRIAN
Lancaster
Robt. 1680 i.
BRIAND
Isle of Wight
Jas. 1763 w.
BRIANT
Norfolk
Jno. 1711 i.
BRIAR
Northampton
Wm. —— w.
BRICE
Accomack
Wm. 1782 i.
Essex
Henry 1724 w.
Susanna 1724 w.
BRICKELL
Loudoun
Wright 1775 w.
BRICKEN
Powhatan
Geo. 1795 w.

BRICKEY
Bedford
Jarret 1790 w.
Richmond
Jno. 1733 i.
Westmoreland
Peter 1796 i.
BRICKHOUSE
Northampton
Geo. 1688 w.
Jedediah 1736 w.
Major 1750 w.
Wm. 1760 w.
Geo. Sr. 1796 w.
Robt. 1798 i.
Princess Anne
Hezekiah 1792 w.
BRICKLY
Richmond
Jno. 1762 w.
BRIDE
Ohio
P. M. 1778 i.
BRIDELL
Isle of Wight
Francis 1712 w.
BRIDGE
Middlesex
Francis 1675 w.
Francis 1678 a.
Norfolk
Thos. 1686-7 w.
Hester 1693-4 w.
York
Geo. 1677 w.
BRIDGEFORTH
Essex
Thos. 1764 w.
Lunenburg
Thos. 1794 i.
Thos. 1795 i.
BRIDGER
Isle of Wight
Jos. 1686 w.
Jos. 1713 w.
Saml. 1713 w.
Eliz. 1717 w.
Eliz. 1727 w.
Jos. Jno. 1728 w.
Wm. 1730 w.
Wm. 1732 w.
Jos. 1751 w.
Jos. 1758 i.
Jos. 1771 i.
Robt. 1764 w.
Jno. 1779 i.
Jas. 1782 w.
Jno. 1785 w.
Wm. 1785 w.
Jos. 1786 w.
Saml. 1786 w.

Martha 1789 w.
Jas. Allen 1793 w.
Wm. 1793 w.
Jos. 1795 w.
Princess Anne
Lawrence 1722 i.
BRIDGES
Frederick
Jos. 1797 i.
King George
Wm. 1724 i.
Prince George
Timothy 1723 i.
Prince William
Wm. 1744 w.
Spotsylvania
Wm. 1794 w.
Westmoreland
Wm. 1723 i.
Jno. 1746 i.
York
Edwd. 1686-7 w.
Thos. 1705 w.
BRIER
Princess Anne
Jno. 1738 i.
BRIDGEMAN
Northumberland
Arthur 1711 i.
Jno. 1720 i.
BRIDGEWATER
Cumberland
Saml. 1772 w.
Henrico
Jas. 1784 w.
Wm. 1793 w.
BRIDGFORD
Lancaster
Thos. 1744 i.
Thos. 1784 i.
Ann 1785 i.
BRIDGFORTH
Amelia
Jno. 1760 w.
BRIDGMAN
Northumberland
Jos. 1748 i.
Wm. 1756 w.
Grace 1758 w.
Thos. 1758 w.
Jos. 1774 i.
Surry
Edwd. 1679 i.
BRIDGWATER
Henrico
Wm. 1794 i.
BRIES
Lancaster
Thos. 1657 w.

BRIGGS
Brunswick
Howell 1774 w.
Henry 1782 w.
Goochland
Geo. 1734 w.
Isle of Wight
Richd. 1679 w.
Margt. 1682 w.
Jas. 1727 i.
Mary 1728 w.
Henry 1735 i.
Edmund 1755 i.
Jas. 1757 w.
Chas. 1758 w.
Ann 1762 w.
King George
Jno. 1768 a.
Mary 1773 w.
Lancaster
Ralph 1689 i.
Northampton
Robt. 1728 w.
Ohio
Jno. 1783 i.
Southampton
Henry 1781 w.
Saml. 1799 w.
Surry
Henry 1686 w.
Geo. 1698-9 w.
Chas. 1730 w.
Saml. 1737 w.
Henry 1738 i.
Henry 1739 w.
Wm. 1748 w.
Benj. 1751 w.
Lucy 1751 i.
Mary 1756 a.
Sussex
Wm. 1763 i.
Howell 1775 w.
Thos. 1776 i.
Lucy 1779 w.
Geo. 1785 w.
Nathl. 1788 w.
Lucy 1790 i.
BRIGHOUSE
Northampton
Geo. 1713 w.
BRIGHT
Bedford
Edwd. 1784 w.
Fairfax
Wendall 1785 w.
Norfolk
Jas. 1790 w.
BRIGHTING
York
Saml. 1672 w.

BRIGHTMAN
Lancaster
Wm. 1703 w.
BRIKEY
Westmoreland
Jno. 1718 i.
BRINAGUM
Essex
Edwd. 1710 i.
BRIMINGTON
Surry
Bryan 1714 i.
BRIMMER
Accomack
Robt. 1710 w.
BRINDLE
Princess Anne
Lawrence 1739 w.
BRINK
Hampshire
Hybert 1778 w.
BRINKER
Frederick
Henry 1772 w.
Geo. 1785 w.
BRINON
Westmoreland
Owen 1749 i.
BRINNON
Westmoreland
Jno. 1778 i.
Jno. 1778 w.
Geo. 1799 w.
BRINSON
Norfolk
Thos. 1676 w.
Mathew 1681 w.
Princess Anne
Matthew 1700 i.
Jno. Jr. 1721 i.
Jno. 1738 w.
Thos. 1741 i.
Wm. 1771 w.
Richd. 1772 w.
Mary 1774 w.
Kesiah 1798 w.
BRINTLE
Amelia
Wm. 1764 w.
BRIOUNT
Southampton
Jno. 1785 w.
BRISCO
Norfolk
Jno. 1740 w.
Westmoreland
Jas. 1727 w.
BRISCOE
Berkeley
Jas. 1779 w.
Jno. 1789 w.

King George
Jno. 1755 i.
Middlesex
Wm. 1700 w.
Pittsylvania
Sarah 1781 w.
Westmoreland
Jas. 1729 i.
Margt. 1729 w.
Danl. 1790 w.
BRISENDINE
Essex
Richd. 1744 w.
BRISTER
Southampton
Saml. 1795 w.
Ishamuel 1798 w.
BRISTOE
Lancaster
Wm. 1789 i.
BRISTOW
Middlesex
Jno. 1716 w.
Nicholas 1740 i.
Wm. 1742 w.
Mary 1744 w.
Chas. 1750 w.
Jno. 1756 i.
Jas. 1765 a.
Edwd. 1775 w.
Wm. 1781 w.
Edwd. 1783 i.
Benj. 1788 w .
Benj. 1792 i.
Richd. 1793 i.
Benj. 1795 i.
Prince William
Benj. 1794 w
BRITAIN
Frederick
Jos. 1796 i.
Henrico
Jas. 1798 w.
Southampton
Elisha 1780 i.
BRITEMAN
Lancaster
Wm. 1704 i.
BRITON
Norfolk
Bennit 1773 i.
BRITT
Accomack
Billings 1759 i.
Albemarle
Obediah 1797 w.
Brunswick
Henry 1765 w.
Edith 1780 w.
Essex
Jno. 1758 i.

Goochland
Wm. 1787 w.
Jno. 1797 i.
Greensville
Jesse 1796 i.
Norfolk
Eleanor 1746 w.
Southampton
Jno. 1779 w.
Benj. 1785 w.
Edwd. 1790 w.
Jno. 1792 w.
BRITTAIN
Isle of Wight
Jno. 1769 i.
Southampton
Jno. 1760 i.
BRITTINGHAM
Accomack
Wm. Sr. 1709 w.
Saml. 1727 w.
Jno. Sr. 1728 w.
Nathl. 1735w.
Nathl. 1741 w.
Christian 1743 w.
Jno. 1743 i.
Jedidiah 1768 i.
Jno. 1795 w.
BRITTLE
Sussex
Wm. 1766 w.
Wm. 1793 w.
Mary 1797 w.
BRITTON
Chesterfield
Wm. 1770 w.
Jno. 1775 w.
Wm. 1793 w.
Halifax
Wm. 1798 w.
Norfolk
Bennet 1773 w.
BRITTOON
Princess Anne
Jno. 1707 w.
BRIZENDINE
Charlotte
Isaac 1799 i.
Jno. 1798 i.
Essex
Frances 1776 w.
Jno. 1780 w.
Eliz. 1794 w.
Francis 1797 i.
Wm. 1729 i.
BROABACK
Shenandoah
Adam 1779 w.
BROADBACK
Augusta
Adam 1784 w.

BROADBECK
Shenandoah
Adam 1779 i.
BROADDUS
Madison
Richard 1794 w.
BROADHURST
Fauquier
Wm. 1793 i.
Norfolk
Mary 1772 w.
Princess Anne
Jno. 1701 w.
BROADIE
Chesterfield
Archibald 1774 w.
BROADLY
Essex
Abra. 1698 i.
BROADNAX
Brunswick
Wm. 1771 w.
Ann 1789 w.
Sussex
Wm. 1782 i.
York
Jno. 1657 w.
BROADRIB
Sussex
Thos. 1762 i.
BROADRIBB
Surry
Benj. 1751 w.
York
Wm. 1731 i.
BROADRICK
Stafford
Christopher 1745 i.
BROADWATER
Accomack
Elias 1750 w.
Elias 1752 i.
Caleb 1756 w.
Jacob 1771 i.
Wm. 1774 w.
Wm. 1783 w.
Caleb 1784 w.
Jesse 1785 w.
Wm. 1787 w.
Wm. 1791 w.
Caleb 1792 w.
Wm. Sr. 1792 i.
Jacob 1796 w.
Jas. 1797 w.
Loudoun
Guy 1773 i.
Prince William
Chas. 1734 i.
BROADWAY
Henrico
Robt. 1704 i.

BROCK
Albemarle
Geo. 1751 w.
Augusta
Rudal 1748 w.
Henry
Jno. 1784 w.
Isle of Wight
Susanna 1727 w.
Wm. 1740 i.
Robt. 1748 i.
Richd. 1749 w.
Benjamin 1758 w.
Susannah 1759 w.
King George
Thos. 1722 i.
Margt. 1744 eb.
Mary 1750 i.
Princess Anne
Jeffery 1697 w.
Wm. 1712 i.
Thos. 1716 w.
Thos. 1727 w.
Jno. 1734 i.
Jas. 1740 i.
Wm. 1765 i.
Frances 1766 i.
Thos. 1782 w.
Wm. Jr. 1795 w.
Southampton
Thos. 1798 w.
Spotsylvania
Jos. 1743 w.
Henry 1763 w.
Wm. 1768 w.
Jno. 1792 a.
BROCKE
Norfolk
Wm. Sr. 1687 w.
Princess Anne
Francis 1712 i.
BROCKENBROUGH
Richmond
Austin 1717 w.
Wm. 1733 w.
Newman 1742 w.
Katherine 1745 nw.
Wm. 1778 w.
Moore 1793 i.
Thos. 1795 w.
BROCKES
Henrico
Thos. 1694 w.
BROCKMAN
Amherst
Jno. 1795 a.
Orange
Jno. 1756 w.
Saml. 1766 w.
Samuel 1792 i.
James 1795 i.

BRODIE
Norfolk
Martha 1765 w.
Lodowick 1794 i.
York
Jas. 1782 w.
BRODY
Northumberland
Jno. 1746 i.
BROCKWELL
Brunswick
Jno. 1739 w.
Prince Edward
Wm. 1799 i.
BRODHURST
Westmoreland
Walter 1658 w.
BRODNAX
York
Jno. 1719 w.
BROIL
Culpeper
Jacob 1763 w.
BROK
Norfolk
Jno. 1685 i.
BROMFIELD
Isle of Wight
Jno. 1681 i.
York
Thos. 1665 w.
BRONAUGH
Fairfax
Agness 1747 i.
Eliz. 1763 i.
Jeremiah 1744 a.
Jno. 1745 a.
Jeremiah 1750 i.
Geo. 1750 i.
Simpha Rosa Ann
Field 1762 w.
Wm. 1775 i.
Henry 1793 a.
Fauquier
Jno. 1778 i.
King George
David 1774 w.
Louisa
Wm. 1792 a.
Prince William
Saml. 1741 w.
Richmond
Wm. 1718 w.
BROOCH
Princess Anne
Wm. 1701 w.
BROOCK
Essex
Isaac 1761 i.

BROOCKE
Essex
Wm. 1744 i.
Peter 1759 i.
Robert. 1777 w.
Thos. 1776 w.
Wm. 1779 w.
Richd. 1729 i.
Richd. 1784 w.
Thos. Henry 1796 w.
BROOK
Chesterfield
Jno. 1771 i.
Wm. 1797 i.
Essex
Robt. 1758 i.
Princess Anne
Job 1720 w.
Southampton
Thos. 1798 i.
BROOKE
Chesterfield
Rebecca 1750 w.
Essex
Peter 1710 w.
Wm. 1735 i.
Robt. 1744 w.
Wm. Sr. 1761 w.
Humphrey 1763 w.
Sarah 1764 w.
Wm. 1764 w.
Saml. 1765 w.
Sarah 1768 w.
Robin 1779 w.
Leonard 1780 i.
Richd. 1785 i.
Jno. 1788 w.
Robt. 1790 w.
Christopher 1792 w.
Jno. 1796 i.
Fairfax
Walter 1798 i.
Fauquier
Thos. 1795 w.
Loudoun
Hannah 1776 w.
Northampton
Francis 1709 w.
Princess Anne
Ezra 1741 w.
Spotsylvania
Richd. 1792 a.
York
Jno. 1712 w.
Eliz. 1716 nw.
Jno. 1729 w.
BROOKES
Campbell
Jno. 1794 i.
Charlotte
Geo. 1791 i.

Lancaster
Frances 1744 i.
Middlesex
Wm. 1720 i.
Northampton
Wm. 1695 w.
York
Wm. 1747 w.
BROOKESHAW
Essex
Margt. 1786 i.
BROOKING
Madison
Chas. 1795 w.
BROOKS
Albemarle
Peter 1759 w.
Amelia
Thos. 1767 i.
Thos. 1770 i.
Augusta
Jno. 1763 i.
Jno. 1794 w.
Berkeley
Saml. 1790 w.
Wm. 1799 w.
Brunswick
Jno. 1751 w.
Peter 1779 w.
Campbell
Jno. 1788 w.
Jno. 1795 i.
Chesterfield
Christopher 1788 i.
Thos. 179- i.
Wm. 1796 w.
Essex
Wm. 1742 i.
Wm. 1734 w.
Robt. 1758 w.
Jno. 1772 i.
Jno. 1777 i.
Eliz. 1796 i.
Fairfax
Josiah 1752 i.
Fauquier
Wm. 1767 w.
Frederick
Matthew 1755 i.
Eliz. 1760 w.
Goochland
Thos. 1772 i.
Thos. 1777 i.
Halifax
Thos. 1775 w.
Robt. 1779 i.
Hanover
Richd. 1734 w.
Lancaster
Saml. 1773 i.
Jemima 1774 w.

Loudoun
Wm. 1799 i.
Louisa
Richd. 1799 i.
Middlesex
Jonathan 1744 w.
Philip 1745 w.
Caleb 1745 i.
Henry 1750 a.
Wm. 1761 i.
Jno. 1774 i.
Rachel 1777 w.
Wm. 1783 i.
Norfolk
Robt. 1719 i.
Northampton
Joan 1709 i.
Princess Anne
Patrick 1753 i.
Prince Edward
Isaac 1789 w.
Prince George
Geo. 1726 i.
Rappahannock
Thos. 1681 w.
Richmond
Jos. 1748 i.
Southampton
Wm. 1788 w.
Jno. 1798 w.
Surry
Wm. 1729 i.
Washington
Castleton 1778 i.
Westmoreland
Henry 1662 w.
York
David 1782 w.
BROOSHAW
Prince William
Wm. 1736 i.
BROOKSHIRE
Fairfax
Sarah 1752 i.
BROOME
Richmond
Thos. 1713 w.
BROOMFIELD
Northampton
Wm. 1744 i.
BROSTER
York
Jno. 1706 i.
Agatha 1736 nw.
BROTHERS
Albemarle
Francis 1752 i.
BROTHERTON
Accomack
Edwd. 1721 w.
Edwd. 1727 w.

BROUGIITON
Isle of Wight
Adam 1773 i.
Northumberland
Thos. 1661 i.
Mary 1662 w.
Loudoun
Wm. 1783 i.
Princess Anne
Thos. 1719 i.
Wm. 1782 w.
Chas. 1791 w.
BROW
Southampton
Jno. 1768 i.
BROUN
Henrico
Robt. 1785 w.
BROWN
Accomack
Jas. 1727 i.
Jas. 1728 i.
Albemarle
Andrew 1753 i.
Benj. 1762 w.
Amelia
Thos. 1784 i.
Amherst
Jno. 1786 a.
Jacob 1789 w.
Augusta
Saml. 1750 w.
Henry 1758 i.
Wm. 1762 i.
Geo. 1769 i.
Jno. 1770 w.
Thos. 1777 i.
Thos. 1786 i.
Jas. 1796 i.
Bath
Henry 1796 i.
Bedford
Jno. 1778 w.
Lynah 1781 i.
Jas. 1790 w.
Jos. 1795 w.
Danl. Sr. 1797 w.
Henry 1799 w.
Berkeley
Archibald 1775 i.
Jas. 1776 w.
Jno. 1797 w.
Brunswick
Burwell 1750 w.
Wm. 1763 i.
Richd. 1773 w.
Urvin 1776 w.
Mary 1778 w.
Frances 1781 w.
Beverly 1791 w.

Campbell
Wm. W. 1782 w.
Charles City
Abraham 1790 w.
Sarah 1791 w.
Charlotte
Wm. 1796 i.
Chesterfield
Francis 1755 w.
Wm. 1784 w.
Culpeper
Jas. 1751 i.
Wm. 1754 i.
Thos. 1758 w.
Danl. 1772 i.
Danl. 1777 i.
Jno. 1780 w.
Jas. 1784 w.
Thos. 1786 w.
Jno. C. 1793 w .
Jno. 1795 w.
Cumberland
Richd. 1762 i.
Jas. 1776 w.
Saml. 1780 w.
Essex
Wm. 1705-6 w.
Danl. 1708 i.
Francis 1709 w.
Richd. 1721 i.
Chas. 1727 w.
Jos. 1727 w.
Henry 1734 w.
Burkenham 1735 w.
Chas. 1748 w.
Francis 1760 w.
Catherine 1761 w.
Keziah 1765 w.
Richd. 1787 w.
Bennett 1790 i.
Fairfax
Jno. 1744 a.
Jas. 1745 a.
Richd. 1745 w.
Jno. 1748 a.
Jas. 1753 i.
Jas. 1754 i.
Graie 1783 w.
Windsor 1785 i.
David 1795 i.
Fauquier
Jno. 1761 w.
Dixon 1781 i.
Mary 1784 w.
Molly 1796 w.
Jonathan 1799 w.
Franklin
Richd. 1791 w.
Lucy 1797 w.
Frederick
Thos. 1750 w.

Jas. 1767 w.
Wm. 1776 i.
Jno. 1786 i.
Burwell 1791 i.
Richd. 1795 i.
Jas. 1796 i.
Greenbrier
Samuel 1793 w.
Hampshire
Daniel 1780 w.
Halifax
Martin 1766 i.
Jno. 1773 w.
Geo. 1776 i.
Jas. 1793 w.
Dorothy 1796 w.
Henrico
Jno. 1684 i.
Jeremiah 1690 w.
Saml. 1697 i.
Peter 1703 w.
Saml. 1782 i.
Jos. 1786 w.
Nicholas 1790 w.
Jas. Pride 1799 w.
Isle of Wight
Jno. 1662 i.
Edwd. 1669 w.
Jno. 1715 i.
Edwd. 1725 i.
Edwd. 1730 i.
Jos. 1734 i.
Saml. 1736 i.
Saml. 1741 i.
Chas. 1750 i.
Jno. 1754 w.
Jno. 1763 i.
Robt. 1764 w.
Adam 1783 w.
Jas. 1791 w.
Jas. 1793 i.
King George
Wm. 1722 i.
Jno. 1737 i.
Jas. 1742 i.
Maxfield 1745 i.
Newman 1751 i.
Robt. 1751 i.
Lancaster
Richd. 1717 i.
Jno. 1724 w.
Benj. 1728 w.
Jos. 1750 i.
Wm. 1797 w.
Loudoun
Jas. 1772 i.
Thos. 1793 w.
Thos. 1794 w.
Wm. 1785 w.
Wm. 1794 w.
Benj. 1796 w.

Isaac 1796 w.
Wm. 1797 i.
Lunenburg
Wm. 1751 w.
Jno. 1754 w.
Richd. 1757 i.
Israel 1760 w.
Valentine 1776 i.
Jacob 1778 w.
Geo. 1791 i.
Middlesex
Saml. 1707 w.
Robt. 1741 w.
Mecklenburg
Thos. 1794 w.
Henry 1797 w.
Jno. 1796 i.
Thos. 1796 i.
Montgomery
Abraham 1786 w.
Abraham 1789 w.
Norfolk
Wm. 1711 w.
Edwd. 1711 w.
Wm. 1750 i.
Margt. 1757 i.
Wm. 1757 i.
Patrick 1761 w.
Jno. 1762 w.
Sarah 1762 w.
Jno. 1768 w.
Jonas 1774 w.
Thos. 1781 w.
Henry 1782 w.
Wm. 1783 i.
Jno. 1792 w.
Ivey 1793 w.
Rubin 1793 i.
Abel 1794 w.
Wm. 1794 n.w.
Northampton
Thos. 1705 w.
Wm. 1716 w.
Northumberland
Wm. 1721 i.
Thos. 1738 w.
Jno. 1751 w.
Mauly 1751 w.
Jno. 1755 i.
Jas. 1764 i.
Jos. 1772 i.
Philip C. 1772 i.
Vincent 1787 w.
Jos. 1794 i.
Orange
Danl. 1747 w.
Pittsylvania
Richd. 1784 w.
Princess Anne
Jno. 1697 a.
Wm. 1699 a.

Susannah 1713 i.
Jas. 1723 i.
Alice 1723 i.
Wm. 1729 i.
Edwd. 1753 i.
Thos. 1770 i.
Hezekiah 1772 i.
Richd. 1774 i.
Ruth 1778 w.
Willis 1782 w.
Jno. 1784 w.
Jno. 1786 i.
Moses 1791 w.
Jas. 1785 w.
Thos. 1786 w.
Jno. 1789 w.
Jno. Sr. 1790 i.
Smith 1798 w.
Prince Edward
Alex. 1775 w.
Prince William
Wm. 1744 a.
Jas. 1780 i.
Jas. 1782 w.
Eliz. 1784 w.
Alex. 1794 i.
Richmond
Manly 1750 w.
Richd. 1750 i.
Jno. 1751 w.
Chas. 1757 i.
Jno. 1783 w.
Thos. 1774 w.
Christopher 1777 w.
Chas. 1778 w.
Jno. 1778 w.
Geo. 1780 w.
Jno. 1785 i.
Vincent 1783 i.
Thos. Sr. 1789 w.
Ellen 1793 w.
Hannah 1795 w.
Rockbridge
John 1788 i.
Shenandoah
Geo. Fred. 1798 i.
Southampton
Thos. 1765 w.
Jno. 1767 w.
Jno. 1781 w.
Olive 1795 w.
Stafford
Jno. 1760 w.
Joshua 1786 i.
Surry
Jno. 1714 i.
Mary 1737 w.
Thos. 1737 w.
Wm. 1747 w.
Saml. 1758 i.
Hannah 1771 i.

Edwd. 1796 w.
Sussex
Wm. 1776 w.
Wm. 1777 i.
Abraham 1785 w.
Washington
Nathaniel 1778 i.
Westmoreland
Philip 1670 w.
Wm. 1672 i.
Original 1698 w.
Thos. 1707 w.
Jos. 1711 i.
Jno. 1712 i.
Wm. 1714 i.
Thos. 1720 i.
Wm. Jr. 1723 i.
David 1721 i.
Jno. 1723 i.
Geo. 1724 w.
Wm. (Mulatto) 1726 i.
Jno. 1725 w.
David 1730 w.
Jno. 1741 i.
Wm. 1741 i.
Nathl. 1744 i.
Jno. 1751 i.
Richd. 1751 i.
Ann 1752 i.
Original 1757 w.
Wm. 1759 w.
Eliz. 1771 w.
Jno. 1771 w.
Jno. 1775 i.
Chas. 1775 i.
Wm. 1776 w.
Wm. 1778 i.
York
Wm. 1718 i.
Geo. 1721 i.
Chas. 1738 w.
Thos. 1741 w.
Stephen 1752 w.
Richd. 1795 w.
BROWNE
Cumberland
Thos. 1762 i.
Essex
Bennett 1789 w.
Eliz. 1701 w.
Isle of Wight
Wm. 1708 i.
Jno. 1721 w.
Saml. 1740 w.
Lancaster
Nathl. 1693 w.
Norfolk
Thos. 1666 w.
Thos. 1670 w.
Jno. 1670-1 w.

Henry 1670-1 w.
Christopher 1677 w.
Norfolk
Anne 1680 i.
Ann 1681 i.
James 1681 i.
Margaret 1757 w.
Henry 1798 w.
Northampton
Jno. 1655 w.
Hugh 1685-6 i.
Susanna 1719 w.
Northumberland
Robt. 1669 i.
Manley 1711 w.
Princess Anne
Jno. 1702 w.
Rappahannock
Wm. 1677 w.
Richmond
Philip 1713 i.
Wm. 1724 w.
Southampton
Thos. 1765 i.
Tabitha 1768 i.
Jesse 1770 w.
Jesse 1781 w.
Benj. 1789 i.
Jean 1790 w.
Surry
Edwd. 1679 i.
Wm. Sr. 1705 w.
Edwd. 1732 w.
Henry 1734 w.
Thos. 1737 i.
Wm. Jr. 1744 w.
Saml. 1749 i.
Andrew 1752 i.
Henry 1762 w.
Wm. 1786 w.
Wm. (2) 1786 w.
Wm. 1799 w.
Westmoreland
Mary 1730 i.
Original 1760 i.
York
Geo. 1713 w.
BROWNING
Culpeper
Francis 1761 w.
Frances 1792 w.
Mary 1789 i.
Fauquier
Nicholas 1774 i.
Caleb 1791 i.
Westmoreland
Thos. 1726 w.
BROWNLIE
Princess Anne
Jno. 1785 w.
BROWNTIE

Princess Anne
Jno. 1785 i.
BROWNLEY
Fairfax
Thos. 1778 i.
BROYL
Spotsylvania
John 1733-4 w.
BROYLE
Culpeper
Jno. 1785 i.
BROZIER
Lancaster
Jos. 1727 i.
BRUCE
Albemarle
Jno. 1752 i.
Amelia
Jno. 1779 w.
Augusta
Alex. 1767 a.
Brunswick
James 1767 w.
Jno. 1783 w.
Culpeper
Wm. 1792 i.
Frederick
Jno. 1748 w.
Isle of Wight
Robt. 1678 i.
King George
Wm. 1749 i.
Chas. 1754 w.
Wm. 1765 i.
Jno. 1768 a.
Elijah 1778 a.
Elijah 1787 a.
Norfolk
Abraham 1711 a.
Jno. 1720 w.
Mary 1734 w.
Thos. 1743 i.
Jno. 1746 w.
Jonas 1757 w.
Thos. 1760 w.
Alex. 1764 w.
Lemuel 1764 w.
Jos. 1768 i.
Abraham 1772 w.
Jas. 1772 w.
Ann 1785 w.
Jno. 1785 w.
Wm. Moore 1794 w.
Ohio
Saml. 1793 w.
Orange
Chas. 1792 i.
Richmond
Geo. 1715 w.
Henry 1722 i.
Henry 1727 w.

Jno. 1731 i.
Jno. 1740 i.
Andrew 1745 i.
Wm. 1752 i.
Benj. 1753 i.
Jos. 1761 i.
Thos. 1764 w.
Wm. 1788 w.
Wm. 1796 i.
Spotsylvania
Margt. 1765 w.
Stafford
Geo. 1785 i.
Surry
Jno. 1752 w.
Westmoreland
Geo. 1742 w.
BRUGE
Amelia
Thos. 1768 i.
BRUGHS
Botetourt
Harmon 1795 i.
BRUIN
Stafford
Wm. 1752 i.
BRUKS
Norfolk
Jno. 1687 w.
BRUMALL
Henrico
Jno. 1748 w.
BRUMFIELD
Charlotte
Wm. 1799 w.
Goochland
Moses 1760 w.
BRUMIGAN
Frederick
Jas. 1748 a.
BRUMLEY
Fairfax
Margaret 1750 i.
Lancaster
Saml. 1748 w.
Wm. 1792 w.
Sarah 1795 w.
Spotsylvania
Wm. 1753 w.
BRUMLOE
Richmond
Edwd. 1717 i.
BRUMIT
Fairfax
Jno. 1746 a.
BRUMMAL
Chesterfield
Jno. Sr. 1796 w.
BRUMMALL
Chesterfield
Wm. 1795 w.

BRUMMIT
Fairfax
Jno. 1747 i.
BRUMWELL
Middlesex
Peter 1721 w.
BRUNTEY
Frederick
Michael 1749 a.
BRUSH
Augusta
Richd. 1764 i.
Lancaster
Abeel 1731 i.
York
Jno. 1726 w.
BRUSTER
Fairfax
Wm. 1752 i.
BRUSTON
Fairfax
Thos. 1756 w.
BRUTNALL
Essex
Richd. 1717 i.
BRUTON
Surry
Jas. 1735 w.
Sarah 1745 w.
BRYAN
Augusta
David 1767 w.
Bedford
Wm. 1764 w.
Campbell
Jno. 1799 w.
Essex
Thos. 1732 w.
Frederick
Jos. 1747 i.
Isle of Wight
Saml. 1778 w.
King George
Richd. 1748 i.
Seth 1765 i.
Jno. 1789 w.
Middlesex
Jno. 1702 i.
Norfolk
Roger Sr. 1708 w.
Susan 1721 w.
Northampton
Henry 1788 i.
Martha 1790 w.
Prince Edward
Thos. 1764 w.
Princess Anne
Jno. 1720 i.
Richmond
Ellenor 1719 w.
Thos. Sr. 1719 w.

Edwd. 1736 w.
Jno. 1743 i.
Ann 1756 i.
Southampton
Robt. 1750 w.
Surry
Fred. 1748 w.
Martha 1759 i.
Benj. 1767 i.
Fred. 1778 w.
Sussex
Thos. 1781 w.
Westmoreland
Robt. 1737 i.
Martin 1752 i.
York
Jno. 1747 w.
Wm. 1750 i.
Mann 1757 i.
Martha 1767 w.
Fred. 1771 w.
Fred. 1789 w.
BRYAND
Culpeper
Thos. 1781 w.
BRYANT
Accomack
Wm. 1723 i.
Albemarle
Jno. 1757 w.
Jno. 1765 w.
Amherst
Anderson 1799 i.
Brunswick
Richd. 1739 i.
Culpeper
Mark 1781 w.
Essex
Susanna 1726 w.
Fairfax
Philip 1751 i.
Fluvanna
Jno. 1780 w.
Goochland
Thos. 1777 w.
Isle of Wight
Jas. 1763 i.
Middlesex
Jno. 1758 a.
Jno. 1772 i.
Norfolk
Jno. 1711 a.
Northampton
Jno. 1728 i.
Orange
Jeremiah 1741 a.
Powhatan
Jas. 1783 w.
Chas. 1786 w.
Prince William
Wm. 1792 i.

Richmond
Thos. 1720 i.
Thos. 1727 w.
Wm. 1733 i.
Jas. 1734 w.
Thos. 1741 w.
Peter 1746 w.
Eliz. 1743 w.
Chas. 1754 w.
Almorian 1762 w.
Fauntleroy 1764 w.
Jos. 1764 i.
Jesse 1778 w.
Moses 1779 w.
Saml. 1783 w.
Moses 1785 i.
Alex. 1785 w.
Southampton
Robt. 1751 i.
Lewis 1762 w.
Lewis Jr. 1762 i.
Mary 1762 w.
Lewis 1785 w.
Jno. 1786 i.
Wm. 1798 w.
Stafford
Richd. 1704 w.
Nathl. 1733 i.
Westmoreland
Wm. 1716 w.
Timothy 1716 i.
BRYARLY
Frederick
Thos. 1792 w.
BRYCE
Fairfax
Jno. 1787 i.
BRYDON
Chesterfield
Jas. 1772 i.
BRYERS
Chesterfield
Sarah 1750 w.
Thos. 1795 w.
BRYMER
Accomack
Saml. 1733 i.
Jno. 1751 i.
BRYSON
Orange
Jno. 1770 w.
BUAKE
Frederick
Jno. Jr. 1762 w.
BUBBER
Hampshire
Samberd 1774 w.
BUCE
York
Jno. 1705 i.

BUCHANAN
Augusta
Jean 1747 i.
Jas. 1759 i.
Wm. 1762 w.
Jas. 1765 w.
Jno. 1769 i.
Jno. 1770 i.
Jas. 1781 w.
Jno. 1790 w.
Wm. 1791 i.
Chesterfield
Neill 1797 i.
Cumberland
Duncan 1773 i.
Middlesex
Henry 1740 w.
Princess Anne
Elinor 1751 w.
Prince William
Jos. 1738 w.
Rockbridge
Jas. 1798 i.
Stafford
Jas. 1786 i.
Washington
Robt. 1779 i.
Andrew 1794 w.
BUCHER
Hardy
Philip 1796 i.
BUCK
Charles City
Benj. 1789 w.
Halifax
Richd. 1789 i.
Middlesex
Thos. 1792 i.
Princess Anne
Anne 1701 i.
Jno. 1700 a.
Geo. 1722 i.
York
Matthew 1724 i.
Benj. 1727 nw.
Thos. Jr. 1728 w.
Thos. 1729 w.
Jos. 1732 w.
Stephen 1767 i.
Mary 1787 w.
BUCKE
York
Thos. 1648 i.
Thos. 1659 w.
BUCKAN
Lancaster
Catherine 1794 i.
BUCKANAN
Fairfax
Eliz. 1782 w.

Fauquier
Michael 1799 w.
Frederick
Jno. 1789 i.
Washington
Saml. 1783 w.
Wythe
Alexander 1798 w.
BUCKEY
Ohio
Jno. 1779 i.
BUCKLES
Berkeley
Mary 1777 w.
Robt. 1790 w.
Jas. 1797 w.
Lancaster
Jno. 1734 w.
Ann 1775 w.
BUCKLEY
Fairfax
Jas. 1793 i.
Frederick
Joshua 1750 i.
Lancaster
Frances 1703 nw.
Thos. 1703-4 w.
Jno. 1733 i.
Loudoun
Wm. 1789 w.
Northampton
Nicholas 1762 i.
Northumberland
Jos. 1785 w.
Pittsylvania
Jas. 1788 w.
Westmoreland
Abraham 1701 w.
Abraham (2) 1701 w.
Jno. 1732 w.
Richmond
Edwd. 1722 i.
BUCKMASTER
Henrico
Robt. 1734 i.
Norfolk
Thos. 1666 i.
Norfolk
Eliz. 1667 w.
BUCKNALL
Amherst
Wm. 1780 w.
BUCKNER
Albemarle
Jean 1789 w.
Essex
Jno. 1695 i.
Fairfax
Peyton 1752 i.
Halifax
Anthony 1780 w.

Louisa
Philip 1762 w.
Prince George
Larrance 1720 i.
Spotsylvania
Mary 1787 w.
Mordacai 1788 w.
Stafford
Philip 1700 w.
Jno. 1748 w.
Jno. 1752 w.
Susannah 1755 i.
Sussex
Edwd. 1767 w.
Westmoreland
Richd. 1794 w.
York
Wm. 1716 w.
BUCKSOME
Rappahannock
Ananias 1679 w.
BUDD
Accomack
Thos. 1721 w.
Thos. 1725 i.
Zorobabel 1767 w.
Northumberland
Richd. 1659 w.
York
Jno. 1750 i.
BUEL
Southampton
Wm. 1767 i.
BUFORD
Amelia
Josiah 1786 a.
Bedford
Thos. 1774 w.
Wm. 1797 i.
Culpeper
Jno. 1787 w.
Lunenburg
Peter 1778 i.
Thos. 1793 w.
Middlesex
Henry 1720 w.
Thos. 1761 w.
Pittsylvania
Ambrose 1781 w.
BUFFIN
York
Chesley 1772 w.
BUFFINGTON
Hampshire
Wm. 1784 w.
BUFFKIN
Southampton
Jno. 1778 i.
BUGERSBEE
Accomack
Wm. 1725 w.

BUGG.
Chesterfield
Benj. 1760 w.
Cumberland
Jno. 1750 w.
Fluvanna
Wm. 1798 w.
Lunenburg
Saml. Sr. 1759 w.
Sherwood 1762 i.
Mecklenburg
Jacob 1773 w.
Anselm 1772 i.
Saml. 1777 w.
Jacob 1788 w.
Jesse 1792 w.
Martha 1796 w.
Sherwood 1798 i.
BULGER
Essex
Wm. 1732 i.
Isle of Wight
Sarah 1720 w.
Richmond
Jane 1789 w.
Westmoreland
Edmund 1736 w.
Jno. 1771 w.
BULL
Accomack
Tobias 1687 w.
Tobias 1760 w.
Tobias 1761 w.
Jno. 1789 i.
Jno. 1797 w.
Richd. 1797 w.
Danl. 1782 w.
Benj. 1771 w.
Culpeper
Wm. 1784 i.
Northampton
Nicholas 1788 w.
BULLARD
Spotsylvania
Ambrose 1756 w.
BULLING
Stafford
Jno. 1734 i.
BULLINGTON
Henrico
Margery 1691 w.
Nicholas 1691 w.
Jos. 1718 i.
Jno. 1726 w.
Jno. 1747 i.
Wm. 1783 w.
Josiah 1785 w.
BULLITT
Prince William
Cuthbert 1791 w.
Cuthbert 1797 i.

Helen 1797 w.
Fauquier
Benj. 1766 w.
Thos. 1778 w.
Jos. 1792 w.
BULLARD
Isle of Wight
Thos. 1713 w.
Jos. 1769 i.
Thos. 1772 i.
Joel 1788 i.
Jos. 1780 w.
Willis 1782 w.
Wm. 1787 w.
BULLOCK
Campbell
Jas. 1785 i.
Isle of Wight
Thos. 1711 w.
Jos. 1751 w.
Jno. 1762 i.
Jos. 1762 i.
Louisa
Jno. 1785 w.
Northampton
Isaac 1709 i.
Thos. 1736 i.
Sarah 1742 i.
Thos. 1784 w.
Solomon Jr. 1785 w.
Princess Anne
Geo. 1727 w.
Prince William
Richd. 1739 w.
Spotsylvania
Jno. 1791 a.
Jno. 1795 w.
Surry
Richd. 1703 w.
Sussex
Robt. 1755 w.
Jeremiah 1758 w.
Amey 1765 w.
York
Jas. 1681 i.
BULLS
Southampton
Wm. 1767 w.
Isle of Wight
Martha 1736 i.
BULLY
Norfolk
Jno. 1790 i.
BULMAN
Princess Anne
Jno. 1776 i.
BUMBARY
Essex
Robt. 1699 i.

BUMGARDNER
Culpeper
Adam 1770 i.
Joel 1773 w.
Orange
Fredk. 1745 w.
Frederick
Jno. 1767 i.
Augusta
Jno. 1751 w.
BUMGARNER
Shenandoah
Jno. 1790 i.
BUMLEY
Lancaster
Saml. 1782 i.
BUMPASS
Charlotte
Diggs 1780 i.
BUNBURY
King George
Thos. 1779 w.
Thos. 1783 w.
Jno. 1791 w.
BUNCH
Accomack
Ann 1771 w.
Louisa
David 1776 w.
Jno. 1777 w.
Saml. 1783 w.
Saml. 1794 i.
BUNDICK
Accomack
Richd. 1764 w.
Justice 1769 w.
Jno. Abbott 1784 w.
Abbot 1784 w.
Abbot 1788 i.
Richd. 1790 w.
Wm. 1795 w.
Agnes 1798 i.
Northampton
Richd. Jr. 1692 w.
BUNDOCK
Accomack
Richd. 1731 w.
BUNDRICK
Accomack
Geo. Jr. 1751 w.
BUNKER
Frederick
Geo. 1785 i.
BUNKLEY
Charlotte
Joshua 1780 w.
Isle of Wight
Robt. 1727 i.
Jno. 1729 w.
Jno. 1735 i.
Geo. 1742 nw.

Joshua 1798 w.
BUNLING
Culpeper
Jas. 1795 i.
BUNN
Lancaster
Jno. 1676 w.
BUNNER
Wythe
Adam 1796 i.
BUNNILL
Surry
Hezekiah 1709 w.
BUNTIN
Norfolk
Richd. 1755 w.
Jas. 1761 w.
Benj. 1785 w.
BUNTINE
Accomack
Rebecca 1740 nw.
BUNTING
Accomack
Jonathan 1764 w.
Jno. Smith 1765 i.
Smith 1770 w.
Elisha 1776 w.
Wm. B. 1777 w.
Elisha 1778 i.
Smith 1786 i.
Solomon 1787 w.
Jonathan 1791 w.
Kendall 1796 w.
Northampton
Holloway 1776 w.
Tamer 1780 i.
Norfolk
Richd. 1713 w.
Wm. 1718-19 w.
Wm. 1778 w.
Richd. 1788 w.
Benj. 1796 i.
Keziah 1796 w.
BUNYAN
Richmond
Milly 1796 w.
BURBERY
Northumberland
Malachi 1751 w.
BURBERRY
Northumberland
Malachi 1720 w.
BURBRIDGE
Spotsylvania
Mary 1727-8 w.
Thos. 1728 a.
Wm. 1744 a.
Benj. 1770 a.
Jno. 1782 a.
Wm. 1782 a.
Thos. 1791 w.

BURBURY
Northumberland
Jas. 1726-7 w.
BURCH
Albemarle
Thos. 1776 w.
Botetourt
Harmon 1794 w.
Brunswick
Jno. 1756 i.
Richd. 1772 w.
Essex
Wm. 1717 i.
Wm. 1718 i.
Norfolk
Jos. 1669 i.
Northumberland
Jno. 1723-4 i.
Jno. 1743 i.
Westmoreland
Jno. 1729 i.
Jno. 1737 i.
BURCHAM
Frederick
Jno. 1760 i.
BURCHER
York
Bartho. 1736 i.
Jno. 1756 nw.
Jas. 1759 i.
Jas. 1771 i.
Jno. 1782 w.
Lucy 1786 i.
BURCHETT
Lunenburg
Benj. 1788 w.
BURDET
Franklin
Humphrey 1794 w.
BURDETT
Accomack
Wm. 1780 w.
Northampton
Francis 1640 w.
Wm. 1643 w.
York
Jno. 1746 w.
BURDGES
Norfolk
Amy 1762 w.
BURDITT
Richmond
Henry 1725 w.
BURDYNE
Culpeper
Richd. 1761 w.
Jno. 1786 w.
BURFOOT
Princess Anne
Ambros 1733 w.
Ambrose 1755 w.

York
Thos. 1758 w.
Thos. 1751 i.
Lawson 1765 w.
Eliz. 1780 w.
Amherst
Danl. 1787 w.
BURG
Amelia
Wm. 1770 w.
BURGAIN
Greenbrier
Thos. 1787 i.
BURGAME
Goochland
Jno. 1730 w.
BURGANNY
Henrico
Jno. 1713 i.
BURGE
Amelia
Richd. 1761 i.
Charlotte
Drury 1794 i.
Drury 1796 w.
Stafford
Edwd. 1759 w.
BURGER
Albemarle
Manus 1780 w.
Henrico
Govert 1736 i.
BURGES
Lancaster
Chas. 1732 w.
Norfolk
Emanuel 1745 i.
Amanuel 1772 i.
Richmond
Wm. 1712 nw.
Southampton
Henry Jno. 1797 w.
Westmoreland
Wm. 1792 i.
BURGESS
Augusta
Robt. 1793 i.
Bedford
Wm. 1778 w.
Brunswick
Jas. 1793 i.
Fauquier
Garner 1790 w.
Norfolk
Mary 1753 w.
Robt. 1761 w.
Amy 1774 i.
Nathaniel 1782 w.
Thos. 1787 i.
Esiah 1796 i.
George Wright 1797 i.

Orange
Moses 1797 w.
Pittsylvania
Thos. 1792 i.
Wm. 1798 w.
Princess Anne
Henry 1756 w.
Richmond
Danl. 1759 i.
Stafford
Edwd. 1759 i.
Robt. 1762 i.
Surry
Robt. 1683 w.
Jno. 1796 w.
BURGHILL
Berkeley
Wm. 1798 i.
BURGIN
Lancaster
Laughly 1750 w.
BURGIS
Norfolk
Emanuel 1750 i.
Princess Anne
Henry 1792 w.
BURGISS
Norfolk
Geo. 1724 i.
Princess Anne
Wm. 1798 w.
Ann 1766 w.
BURGOMY
Goochland
Peter 1735 w.
BURGURT
Shenandoah
Michael 1796 i.
BURGYS
Fauquier
Francis 1770 w.
BURK
Augusta
Wm. 1754 w.
Wm. 1782 i.
Wm. 1786 w.
Berkeley
Luke 1796 i.
Culpeper
Jno. 1759 i.
Richd. 1760 i.
Thos. 1767 w.
Essex
Thos. 1765 w.
Hardy
Jno. 1795 i.
Isle of Wight
Thos. 1766 i.
Mary 1778 i.
Thos. 1779 w.

Middlesex
Thos. 1715 i.
Montgomery
Jos. 1786 i.
Thos. 1798 w.
BURKE
Essex
Jno. 1790 w.
BURKER
Isle of Wight
Danl. 1667 i.
BURKHAM
Frederick
Jno. 1783 i.
BURKHEAD
Shenandoah
Simon 1799 w.
York
Wm. 1697-8 a.
Saml. 1720 i.
BURKS
Albemarle
Chas. 1752 i.
Saml. Jr. 1753 w.
Saml. 1756 w.
Amherst
Saml. 1784 a.
Bedford
Jno. Partree 1775 i.
Isle of Wight
Ann 1772 i.
Prince Edward
Geo. 1793 w.
BURLEY
Accomack
Peter 1741 w.
Peter 1752 i.
Princess Anne
Robt. 1752 w.
Robt. 1755 i.
York
Geo. 1694 i.
BURN
Fairfax
James 1750 a.
Danl. 1751 w.
Frederick
Jas. 1762 i.
Northumberland
Eliz. 1722 w.
Thos. 1740 w.
Richmond
Jno. 1714 i.
Thos. 1732 i.
Southampton
David 1779 w.
Patience 1779 w.
Surry
Christopher 1777 w.
Thos. 1778 i.

Westmoreland
Jas. 1726 w.
BURNE
Isle of Wight
Owen 1705 nw.
Essex
Jas. 1748 i.
Northumberland
Jno. 1718 w.
BURNELL
Southampton
Charity 1773 w.
BURNER
Berkeley
Gasper 1779 i.
Shenandoah
Jacob 1782 w.
Jacob 1790 w.
BURNES
Berkeley
Benj. 1795 i.
Shenandoah
Cornelius 1787 a.
BURNET
Essex
Wm. 1717 i.
Jos. 1772 i.
Isle of Wight
Ann 1729 i.
Northumberland
Thos. 1742 i.
BURNETT
Essex
Lucretia 1709 w.
Jno. 1717 w.
Thos. 1749 w.
Jno. 1773 w.
Leonard 1777 w.
Isle of Wight
Robt. 1679 w.
King George
Chas. 1785 a.
Pittsylvania
Jas. 1798 i.
Benj. 1799 w.
Surry
Thos. 1702 i.
Mecklenburg
Jno. 1775 w.
Wm. 1781 w.
BURNHAM
Fairfax
Ramond 1778 i.
Lancaster
Rowland 1656 w.
York
Thos. 1718 w.
Lockey (Miles).
1761 w.

BURNITT
Brunswick
Richd. 1770 w.
BURNLEY
Halifax
Joel 1781 i.
Orange
Garland 1793 w.
BURNN
Ohio
Jonathan 1778 a.
BURNETT
Isle of Wight
Ann 1729 w.
BURNS
Augusta
Peter 1776 w.
Robt. 1782 w.
Dennis 1791 nw.
Henry
Chas. Sr. 1789 w.
Lancaster
Jas. 1721 nw.
Princess Anne
Wm. 1696 i.
Jno. 1792 i.
BURNSIDE
Augusta
Jno. 1794 w.
Martha 1794 w.
Jno. 1795 w.
Jno. 1795 nw.
Martha 1795 nw.
BURR
Berkeley
Peter 1795 w.
Northampton
Richd. 1715 w.
BURRADELL
York
Henry 1747 i. -
BURRAS
Orange
Jno. 1783 w.
Stafford
Mary 1747 w.
BURREL
Richmond
Richd. 1782 w.
Northampton
Robt. 1665 i.
BURRESS
Amherst
Jno. B. 1783 w.
BURRIDGE
Middlesex
Jno. 1734 w.
Westmoreland
Walter 1725 i.

BURRISS
Richmond
Benj. 1781 w.
BURRO
Princess Anne
Ben. 1705 w.
BURRODALE
York
Henry 1743 i.
BURROSS
Richmond
Wm. 1733 i.
Michell 1734 i.
BURROUGHS
Henrico
Bartho. 1695 i.
Wm. 1717 w.
Princess Anne
Wm. 1700 w.
Mary 1714 i.
Jno. 1719 i.
Christopher 1738 w.
Patience 1750 w.
Robt. 1755 i.
Anthony 1758 w.
Prince William
Jno. 1783 i.
Jno. 1787 w.
York
Eliz. 1758 i.
BURROW
Charlotte
Peter 1787 i.
Sussex
Thos. 1760 i.
Wm. 1770 w.
BURROWE
Norfolk
Christopher 1653 i.
BURROWGH
Princess Anne
Benj. 1719 w.
Benj. 1734 i.
Martin 1744 w.
BURROWS
Frederick
Jno. 1748 i.
Henrico
Bartho. 1690 i.
Richmond
Matthew 1733 i.
Sarah 1761 i.
Prince William
Jno. 1786 w.
BURRUS
Amherst
Chas. 1799 w.
Orange
Thos. 1789 w.

BURRUSS
Orange
Edmund 1780 w.
Richmond
Jno. 1752 i.
BURSON
Loudoun
Benj. 1769 w.
Geo. 1786 w.
Benj. 1791 w.
BURSTON
Fairfax
Wm. 1746 a.
BURT
Greensville
Wm. 1783 w.
Isle of Wight
Jno. 1752 i.
Mecklenburg
Mathew 1778 i.
Northampton
˙ Jno. 1691 w.
Surry
Philip 1772 i.
Wm. 1777 i.
Westmoreland
Jno. 1674 w. ˎ
York
Richd. 1719 ab.
Moody 1735 i.
Richd. 1745 w.
Moody 1747 i.
Josias 1758 i.
Philip 1798 w.
BURTON
Accomack
Wm. 1695 w.
Saml. 1728 w.
Wm. 1730 w.
Thos. 1735 w.
Amey 1746 w.
Saml. 1751 i.
Amy 1760 w.
Caleb 1762 i.
Jos. 1762 i.
Mary 1767 w.
Rebecca 1768 i.
Abner 1777 w.
Garrison 1788 i.
Albemarle
Jno. 1776 w.
Wm. 1778 w.
Amelia
Abraham 1736 w.
Anne 1745 w.
Abraham 1758 w.
Jno. Jr. 1762 w.
Jno. 1776 w.
Sarah 1781 w.
Amherst
Jas. A. 1783 a.

Brunswick
Abraham 1750 w.
Campbell
Jesse 1795 w.
Charles City
Wm. 1796 w.
Eliz. 1798 w.
Charlotte
Jas. 1783 w.
Chesterfield
Eliz. 1757 w.
Benj. 1770 i.
Thos. 1771 w.
Hardin 1788 w.
Wm. 1791 w.
Thos. 1792 w.
Wm. 1792 i.
Wm. 179- w.
Jno. 1797 i.
Jno. 1799 w.
Cumberland
Wm. 1749 w.
Wm. Allen 1767 w.
Seth 1774 i.
Jno. 1780 i.
Goochland
Robt. 1748 w.
Noel 1770 i.
Henrico
Jno. 1679 w.
Jno. Jr. 1682 i.
Thos. 1685 i.
Jno. 1689 w.
Jno. 1747 w.
Wm. 1751 w.
Jno. 1784 w.
Martin 1792 w.
Sarah 1795 w.
King George
Wm. 1778 a.
Wm. 1781 a.
Loudoun
Wm. 1799 i.
Mecklenburg
Nowel 1766 w.
Hutchings 1767 i.
Hutchins 1778 w.
Youngnightengale
1781 i.
Jno. 1789 w.
Micajah 1796 i.
Peter Jr. 1796 w.
Robt. 1798 w.
Middlesex
Jno. 1677 a.
Jas. 1757 w.
Northampton
Jno. 1746 w.
Wm. 1770 w.
Jno. 1786 w.

Pittsylvania
Jos. 1784 w.
Prince Edward
Saml. 1799 w.
Surry
Anthony 1733 i.
York
Lewis 1701 i.
Lewis 1718 i.
BURTT
York
Josiah 1768 w.
BURWELL
Lancaster
Nathaniel 1790 i.
Mecklenburg
Thacker 1780 w.
Lewis 1784 w.
Northampton
Wm. 1643 w.
York
Lewis 1710 w.
Jas. 1718 w.
Lucy 1719 a.
Nathl. Bacon 1749 i.
Bacon 1751 i.
Jas. 1776 i.
Anne 1779 w.
BUSBY
Prince George
Thos. 1723 w.
BUSH
Augusta
Michael 1775 a.
Bedford
Jno. 1774 w.
Culpeper
Edwd. 1775 w.
Essex
Richd. 1700 w.
Bilby 1748 i.
Jno. 1765 i.
Jno. 1767 w.
Ruebn 1779 i.
Goochland
Francis 1793 i.
Francis 1795 i.
Lancaster
Abraham 1687 w.
Ann 1690 w.
Isaac 1726 i.
Hannah 1737 i.
Jno. 1761 i.
Jas. 1766 w.
Margt. 1782 i.
Lunenburg
Wm. 1798 w.
Norfolk
Saml. 17— w.

Northumberland
Reuben 1778 i.
Westmoreland
Edwd. 1741 w.
Washington
Josiah 1781 i.
Stafford
Geo. 1758 i.
Princess Anne
Saml. 1772 w.
Orange
Jno. 1745 w.
Philip 1772 w.
BUSHELL
Norfolk
Wm. 1795 w.
BUSHROD
Frederick
Mildred 1785 w.
Westmoreland
Jno. 1720 w.
Jno. 1760 w.
York
Thos. 1677 w.
BUSKEY
Princess Anne
Moses 1712 i.
Jno. 1753 i.
Jno. 1758 w.
Sarah 1774 w.
Willoughby 1778 i.
Rebeckah 1784 w.
Jonathan 1792 w.
BUSKIN
Norfolk
Saml. 1785 w.
BUSSE
York
Jno. 1704 i.
BUSSELL
King George
Wm. 1795 w.
Northumberland
Jno. 1750 i.
Mathew 1760 i.
Jack 1795 i.
Norfolk
Josiah 1753 i.
BUSTARD
Wythe
Wm. 1795 w.
BUSTIAN
Norfolk
Christopher 1672 i.
Jno. 1688 w.
Margt. 1688 w.
Wm. 1752 w.
BUSTIN
Norfolk
Benj. 1773 w.
Christopher 1784 w.

Princess Anne
Thos. 1787 w.
BUSSY
Stafford
Henry Sr. 1764 w.
BUTCHER
Augusta
Valentine (Melchoir)
1774 i.
Essex
Jno. 1710 w.
Fairfax
Helenor 1753 i.
Jno. 1797 a.
Loudoun
Saml. 1798 w.
Middlesex
Jno. 1698 w.
Northumberland
Catherine 1723 w.
Wm. 1768 w.
Washington
Joshua 1782 i.
BUTLER
Amelia
Jno. 1759 w.
Archer 1792 i.
Bedford
Phillip 1776 i.
Wm. 1794 w.
Berkeley
Pearce 1786 i.
Saml. 1798 w.
Charles City
Saml. 1774 i.
Chesterfield
Saml. 1756 w.
Culpeper
Jno. 1757 w.
Walter 1772 w.
Walter 1774 i.
Cumberland
Jno. 1754 w.
Aaron 1776 w.
Essex
Jno. 1703 i.
Wm. 1716 i.
Jno. 1717 w.
Thos. 1771 w.
Jno. 1791 i.
Frederick
Cornelius 1752 i.
Thos. 1764 i.
Goochland
Saml. 1732 i.
Edmund 1747 w.
Greensville
Jos. 1785 i.
Halifax
Saml. 1790 i.

Henry
Henry 1791 i.
Isle of Wight
Jno. 1728 i.
Ann 1733 i.
Christopher 1748 i.
Jno. 1758 i.
Jacob 1780 i.
Jas. Sr. 1780 w.
Jno. 1784 w.
Jno. 1785 w.
Peter 1786 i
Chas. 1797 i.
King George
Joshua 1725 i.
Richd. 1735 i.
Mary 1745 a.
Wm. 1748 i.
Jas. 1754 nw.
Jas. 1755 i.
Griffin 1784 w.
Lancaster
Peter 1716 nw.
Loudoun
Lewin Smith 1795 i.
Norfolk
Chas. 1770 w.
Northampton
Robt. 1677 i.
Northumberland
Jno. 1754 i.
Jas. 1760 w.
Jno. 1783 i.
Jno. 1792 i.
Prince William
Laurence 1787 i.
Jos. 1793 w.
Prince George
Jno. 1719 w.
Rappahannock
Eliz. 1673 w.
Jno. 1677 w.
Amory 1678 w.
Jno. 1686 i.
Spotsylvania
Jno. 1760 a.
Jas. 1774 a.
Stafford
Thos. 1705 i.
Jas. 1732 w.
Thos. 1743 w.
Christopher 1767 i.
Surry
Wm. 1677 a.
Wm. 1679 a.
Sussex
Thos. 1784 w.
Westmoreland
Tobias 1698 w.
Caleb 1709 w.
Jno. 1712 w.

Thos. 1714 w.
Jas. 1714 i.
Jno. 1714 i.
Caleb 1715 i.
Jas. 1720 i.
Christopher 1729 w.
Jno. 1733 i.
Lawrence 1733 w.
Wm. 1734 w.
Catherine 1743 w.
Jas. 1743 i.
Caleb 1750 i.
Eliz. 1750 w.
Grace 1750 i.
Jno. 1750 i.
Wm. 1750 nw.
Jas. 1752 w.
Thos. 1756 w.
Thos. 1757 w.
Lawrence 1766 i.
Ann 1768 w.
Jno. 1768 i.
Mary 1773 i.
Wm. 1774 w.
Wm. 1781 w.
Lawrence 1777 w.
Wm. 1784 w.
Sarah 1785 w.
Jane 1792 w.
Nathl. 1792 w.
Ann 1796 i.
Christopher 1798 w.
York
Geo. 1724 i.
Harry 1737 i.
BUTRIDGE
Charlotte
Henry 1790 i.
BUTT
Berkeley
Jos. 1793 w.
Richd. 1799 w.
Norfolk
Robt. 1676 w.
Thos. 1710 a.
Henry Sr. 1711 w.
Robt. 1721 w.
Robt. 1722 w.
Stanhope 1722 w.
Henry Sr. 1731 w.
Jno. 1731 w.
Robt. Sr. 1731 w.
Arthur 1744-5 nw.
Thos. 1745 w.
Richd. 1746 w.
Nathl. 1750 w.
Benj. 1753 w.
Lemuel 1753 w.
Wm. 1755 i.
Radford 1756 i.
Radford 1759 i.

Wm. 1760 w.
Catherine 1762 i.
Henry 1762 w.
Jas. 1762 w.
Jeremiah 1763 i.
Thos. 1764 w.
Robt. 1765 w.
Solomon Sr. 1767 w.
Thos. 1769 w.
Anthony 1770 i.
Henry 1770 i.
Caleb 1771 w.
Mary 1772 w.
Edwd. 1773 w.
Wm. 1776 w.
Caleb 1777 w.
Saml. 1777 w.
Thos. 1777 w.
Anthony 1778 w.
Ede. 1778 w.
Josiah Sr. 1781 w.
Rasha 1782 i.
Edwd. 1783 i.
Jno. 1783 i.
Solomon 1783 i.
Read 1787 w.
Nathl. 1788 w.
Amy 1791 i.
Caleb 1791 i.
Peter 1791 w.
Saml 1791 i.
Malaba 1792 w.
Hillary 1793 w.
Mary 1794 w.
Rachel 1795 w.
Eliz. 1796 w.
Jno. 1796 i.
Trinigin 1796 i.
Rebeccah 1798 i.
Pittsylvania
Zachariah 1799 i.
Princess Anne
Carthright 1797 w.
Rockbridge
Wm. 1778 a.
BUTTERWORTH
Bedford
Isaac 1767 i.
York
Jno. 1744 w.
BUTTLER
Accomack
Judah 1780 w.
Richmond
Jas. 1716 w.
BUTTON
Culpeper
Jno. 1785 i.
Fauquier
Harmon 1790 w.

Frederick
Jos. 1798 i.
BUTTS
Culpeper
Wm. 1784 w.
Greensville
Jno. 1795 w.
Southampton
Peter 1780 w.
Benj. 1795 w.
Jas. 1796 i.
Eliz. 1798 w.
York
Anthony 1688 i.
Anthony 1718 w.
BUYER
Accomack
Jonathan 1741 i.
BUXTON
Lancaster
Ann 1738 i.
Jno. 1738 i.
BUZZARD
Augusta
Peter 1777 i.
BYARD
Westmoreland
Jas. 1720 w.
BYARS
Louisa
Jno. 1782 w.
BYBE
Goochland
Thos. 1729 w.
BYERLEY
Middlesex
Abraham 1707 i.
BYERLY
Berkeley
Michael 1788 w.
BYERS
Lancaster
Alex 1745 i.
BYLAND
Loudoun
David 1776 w.
BYLES
Accomack
Danl. 1696 w.
BYNAM
Surry
Jno. 1715 i.
BYNUM
Brunswick
Drury 1761 i.
Southampton
Wm. 1764 i.
Eliz. 1773 w.
Michael 1773 w.
Wm. 1774 w.

BYRAM
Northumberland
Abraham 1668 w.
Stafford
Wm. 1785 i.
BYRD
Accomack
Ebun. 1768 w.
Henrico
Eliz. 1678-9 w.
Thos. 1710 i.
Richmond
Jno. 1761 w.
Southampton
Jno. 1781 w.
Jas. 1798 i.
BYRN
Frederick
Jno. 1780 w.
BYRNE
Spotsylvania
Edmund 1744 w.
BYROM
Essex
Henry 1718 i.
Peter 1719 w.
Jas. 1749 w.
Fautle (roy) 1788 w.
BYRUM
Essex
Jno. 1778 w.
BYTON
Surry
Richd. 1708 i.
BYWATERS
Culpeper
Thos. 1785 i.

C

CABINESS
Amelia
Geo. 1744 w.
Matthew Jr. 1788 w.
CABANISS
Prince George
Henry 1720 w.
CABINETT
Westmoreland
Wm. 1703 nw.
CABLE
Northampton
Edwd. 1678 i.
Thos. 1743 w.
S (orrowful) Margt.
1750 w.
CABORN
Prince William
Robt. 1737 i.

CACKLEY
Frederick
Jacob 1790 i.
CADDEN
Augusta
Thos. 1760 i.
CADDON
Augusta
Thos. 1759 a.
CAFFREY
Campbell
Jno. 1790 w.
CAGE
Charlotte
Benj. 1792 i.
CAGEY
Shenandoah
Rudolph 1795 a.
CAHERNE
Northampton
Bryan 1669 w.
CAHILL
Henrico
Barney 1783 w.
CAHILLE
Princess Anne
Bryan 1700 w.
CAHOE
Prince William
Jno. 1797 w.
Westmoreland
Alex. 1714 i.
CAIGOW
York
Alex 1734 i.
CAILE
Augusta
David 1794 w.
CAIN
Accomack
Jno. 1763 w.
Martha 1769 w.
Augusta
Jno. 1759 a.
Greensville
Geo. 1793 i.
Geo. Sr. 1793 w.
Norfolk
Richd. 1720 i.
Shenandoah
Richd. 1796 i.
Sussex
Jas. 1770 w.
Jas. 1783 w.
Isham 1785 w.
Peter 1792 i.
CAINE
Accomack
Wm. 1774 w.

CAINS
Accomack
Jno. 1765 i.
CAIRON
Henrico
Jno. 1715 w.
CALBERT
Augusta
Wm. 1763 i.
CALCOTE
Isle of Wight
Thos. 1753 w.
Jos. 1754 i.
CALDBREATH
Augusta
Thos. 1788 i.
CALDER
Surry
Wm. 1789 i.
CALDWELL
Amelia
Geo. 1743 w.
Augusta
Robt. 1783 w.
David 1794 w.
Jno. 1795 w.
Eliz. 1797 w.
Jno. 1797 w.
Berkeley
Andrew 1790 w.
Charlotte
David 1769 w.
Frederick
Wm. 1746 i.
Robt. 1755 i.
Andrew 1758 i.
Halifax
Jno. 1796 i.
King George
David 1729 i.
Loudoun
Jos. 1793 w.
Lunenburg
Thos. 1747 i.
Jno. 1751 w.
Wm. 1751 w.
Henry 1752 w.
Jas. 1757 w.
Wm. 1761 w.
Prince Edward
Thos. 1772 w.
Thos. Sr. 1774 w.
CALE
King George
Alice 1732 i.
Lancaster
Nathl. 1690 w.
CALELOUGH
Isle of Wight
Thos. 1737 i.

CALFEE
Shenandoah
Jno. 1786 w.
CALHOON
Prince Edward
Adam 1796 i.
CALHOUN
Wythe
Wm. 1791 w.
Andrew 1794 w.
Eliz. 1797 i.
CALL
Isle of Wight
Chas. 1774 i.
King George
Isaac 1750 i.
Mecklenburg
Bowling 1778 w.
CALLAHAM
Surry
Morris 1721 w.
Lancaster
Darby 1687 w.
CALLAHAN
Lancaster
Jno. 1741 i.
CALLAND
Cumberland
Jos. 1791 i.
CALLAWAY
Bedford
Geo. 1773 w.
Jas. 1773 i.
Zachariah 1781 i.
Isle of Wight
Richd. 1688 i.
Benj. 1712 i.
Princess Anne
Wm. 1782 i.
CALLECOTE
Isle of Wight
Harwood 1797 i.
CALLEGAM
Halifax
Jas. 1791 w.
CALLEHAN
Lancaster
Mary 1761 i.
CALICOT
Prince Edward
Jas. 1778 w.
CALLIHAM
Lunenburg
Lightfoot 1778 i.
David 1799 w.
CALLIS
Louisa
Martha 1791 a.
Lunenburg
Jas. 1798 w.

Norfolk
Geo. 1797 w.
Richmond
Ambrose 1773 i.
Westmoreland
Ambros 1737 i.
Wm. 1750 w.
Jno. 1755 i.
Wm. 1758 w.
Francis 1770 w.
CALLISON
Augusta
Jas. 1789 w.
CALLISS
Richmond
Robt. 1785 w.
CALLOWAY
Amherst
Jas. 1787 w.
Princess Anne
Alese 1780 i.
CALLOWHILL
York
Francis 1714 w.
Nathl. 1716 w.
Jas. 1718 w.
Ann 1722 w.
CALLY
Augusta
Jno. 1761 i.
CALMES
Frederick
Marquis 1757 i.
Wm. 1773 w.
Marques 1794 w.
CALTHORP
York
Chris. 1662 i.
Chas. 1718 w.
Elystrange 1727 i.
Anne 1734 i.
CALTHORPE
Southampton
Chas. 1763 w.
Chas. 1771 i.
Elener 1775 w.
Jno. 1791 w.
Jas. 1793 w.
Jas. B. 1795 i.
York
Jas. 1690 w.
Chris. 1694 w.
Jas. 1711 i.
Elimelech 1734 i.
Jas. 1744 w.
CALVERT
Culpeper
Geo. 1782 i.
Jno. 1790 w.
Frederick
Josiah 1748 a.

Robt. 1757 i.
Richd. 1770 w.
Middlesex
Philip 1712 w.
Norfolk
Jonathan 1744 i.
Cornelius 1747 w.
Mary 1762 w.
Sanders 1763 w.
Maxemelian 1782 w.
Saml. 1782 i.
Saml. 1783 w.
Orange
Jno. 1739 w.
Prince William
Reuben 1778 i.
Jno. 1788 i.
Southampton
Christopher 1790 i.
York
Wm. 1666 w.
Robt. 1693 w.
CALWELL
Isle of Wight
Jno. 1720 w.
CAMARON
Norfolk
Osborne 1671 w.
CAMBELL
Lancaster
Ezekeil 1757 w.
Loudoun
Jas. 1796 w.
CAMBRIDGE
Middlesex
Edmd. 1720 w.
CAMELL
York
Chas. 1674-5 w.
CAMERELL
Norfolk
Wm. 1679 w.
CAMERER
Culpeper
Blace 1793 w.
Amherst
Duncan 1794 a.
Henrico
Wm. 1797 i.
CAMM
York
Jno. 1779 i.
Eliz. 1780 i.
Jno. 1780 i.
CAMMACK
Richmond
Margaret 1715 w.
Jno. 1717 i.
Spotsylvania
Francis 1778 w.
Wm. 1783 w.

CAMMEL
Lancaster
Jas. 1767 i.
Westmoreland
Patrick 1703 i.
CAMMELL
Lancaster
Jas. 1747 i.
Jas. 1763 w.
Jas. 1766 i.
Northampton
Jas. 1688 w.
Chas. 1790 w.
CAMMERON
Henry
Jacob 1780 i.
CAMMILL
Spotsylvania
Alex 1727 w.
CAMMUSKA
Westmoreland
Sarah 1739 i.
CAMP
Brunswick
Thos. 1780 w.
Culpeper
Ambrose 1769 w.
Halifax
Jno. Jr. 1779 w.
Sabra 1797 w.
Mecklenburg
Jno. 1784 w.
York
Jno. 1774 w.
CAMPBELL
Amherst
Henry 1772 w.
Neill 1776 w.
Geo. 1776 w.
Wm. 1786 a.
Neill 1788 a.
Geo. 1791 w.
Geo. 1794 a.
Augusta
Gilbert 1750 w.
Jas. 1754 w.
Alex. 1758 w.
Wm. 1759 w.
Malcolm 1763 w.
Chas. 1767 w.
Robt. 1768 i.
Hugh 1775 a.
Robt. 1777 w.
Chas. 1778 w.
Robt. 1782 w.
Robt. 1793 w.
Bedford
Wm. 1781 w.
Moses 1792 w.
Berkeley
Dugall 1772 w.

Francis 1773 w.
Jno. 1791 w.
Robt. 1797 w.
Botetourt
Archibald 1775 i.
Archibald 1777 w.
Jas. 1777 i.
Brunswick
Walter 1751 w.
Campbell
Jas. 1789 w.
Culpeper
Duncan 1761 i.
Jno. 1780 w.
Essex
Jas. 1750 i.
Jas. 1774 w.
Hugh 1791 w.
Thacker 1792 i.
Frederick
Jno. 1749 i.
Isle of Wight
Robt. 1762 i.
Eliz. 1773 w.
King George
Jno. 1749 i.
Lancaster
Alex. 1742 i.
Wm. 1743 w.
Jno. 1776 w.
Winifred 1781 w.
Loudoun
Robt. 1779 i.
Matthew 1782 w.
Lunenburg
Matthew 1763 w.
Madison
Elias 1794 w.
Jno. 1794 w.
Mecklenburg
Archibald 1797 i.
Middlesex
Jas. 1751 a.
Northampton
Simon 1740 w.
Joanna 1746 i.
Nicholas 1755 i.
Thos. 1727 i.
Thos. 1744 i.
Northumberland
Sarah 1753 w.
Wm. 1772 i.
Orange
Jno. 1741 a.
Jno. 1746 i.
Wm. 1744 w.
Archd. 1786 i.
Princess Anne
Chas. 1776 w.
Duncan 1782 w.

Prince William
Geo. 1784 i.
Isaac 1784 i.
Rockbridge
Dougal 1795 w.
Patrick 1778 w.
Shenandoah
Richd. 1782 w.
Alex. 1786 w.
Spotsylvania
Colling 1727 a.
Mary 1798 w.
Surry
Colin 1780 w.
Washington
Margt. 1778 w.
Jno. 1781 i.
Wm. 1782 w.
David 1791 w.
Jas. 1793 w.
Jacob 1795 w.
Westmoreland
Jas. 1702 w.
Archibald 1775 i.
Archibald 1781 i.
Archibald 1798 w.
Wythe
Jas. 1799 w.
York
Wm. 1709 w.
CAMPER
Botetourt
Peter 1789 i.
CAMPERLANE
Shenandoah
Saml. 1773 a.
CAMPERLIN
Frederick
Peter 1750 a.
CAMPIN
Lancaster
Wm. 1770 w.
CAMPLESHON
Accomack
Chas. 1708 w.
Chas. 1726 i.
CAMPLIN
Prince William
Jno. 1737 i.
CANADA
Bedford
Wm. 1791 w.
Westmoreland
Jno. 1702 i.
CANADAY
Essex
Jas. 1775 w.
Princess Anne
Wm. 1764 w.
Middlesex
Edwd. 1702 i.

CANDLER
Bedford
Danl. 1766 w.
CANDON
Frederick
Abraham 1746 a.
CANE
Accomack
Wm. 1774 i.
Albemarle
Nicho. 1787 w.
Middlesex
Ann 1756 w.
Northampton
Sebastian 1670 w.
Richmond
Jno. 1727 i.
CANFIELD
Westmoreland
Richd. 1723 i.
CANN
Norfolk
Jno. 1767 w.
Jas. 1796 w.
CANNADAY
King George
Jno. 1773 w.
Orange
Jno. 1744 i.
Westmoreland
Jas. 1783 w.
CANNADEY
Isle of Wight
Saml. Sr. 1711 w.
CANNAN
Isle of Wight
Robt. 1736 i.
Richmond
Thos. 1749 w.
CANNIFAX
Cumberland
Jno. 1752 w.
CANNON
Albemarle
Wm. 1749 i.
Brunswick
Jno. 1796 w.
Culpeper
Wm. 1782 i.
Goochland
Jeremiah 1767 w.
Henrico
Jno. 1696 w.
Jno. 1734 w.
Norfolk
Eliz. 1684 w.
Thos. 1684 w.
Thos. 1784 i.
Princess Anne
Edwd. 1701 w .
Thos. 1719 i.

Jno. 1733 w.
Edwd. 1734 w.
Eliz. 1735 w.
Edwd. 1782 w.
Free Lovey 1791 w.
Thos. 1795 w.
Eliz. 1796 w.
Prince William
Mary 1778 i.
Surry
Jno. 1741 w.
Jno. 1758 i.
York
Jno. 1795 w.
CANT
Albemarle
Jas. 1759 w.
CANTERBUAROY
Richmond
Jno. 1717 i.
CANTERBURY
Fairfax
Ruth 1750 a.
Saml. 1764 w.
CANTERDINE
Norfolk
Ann 1764 i.
CANTON
Loudoun
Mark. 1785 w.
CANTRELL
Bedford
Sarah 1784 w.
CANTRIL
Frederick
Zebulon 1752 i.
CAPE
Amelia
Ann 1752 a.
CAPEL
Northampton
Jno. 1745 i.
CAPELL
Northampton
Nathl. 1716 w.
Thos. 1718-19 w.
Sussex
Thos. 1769 w.
CAPLE
Northampton
Hannah 1730 w.
Jno. 1745 w.
Edwd. 1749 w.
Wm. 1791 w.
CAPLENGER
Augusta
Jacob 1773 i.
CAPLINER
Augusta
Geo. 1773 w.

CAPLINGER
Augusta
Saml. 1770 i.
CAPS
Princess Anne
Edwd. 1764 i.
CAPPS
Princess Anne
Wm. 1697 w.
Frances 1703 i.
Francis 1703 a.
Richd. 1720 w.
Wm. 1728 w.
Wm. 1744 w.
Geo. 1753 w.
Jno. 1753 w.
Edwd. 1764 w.
Horatio 1765 w.
Henry 1771 w.
Eliz. 1782 i.
Edwd. 1782 w.
Jno. 1784 w.
Jno. 1786 i.
Benj. 1795 w.
Wm. 1796 w.
Tully 1797 w.
Wm. 1798 w.
Hillary 1798 w.
CAR
Goochland
Joel 1730 i.
Prince Edward
Hugh 1785 w.
CARBY
Berkeley
Jno. 1791 w.
CARBERY
Norfolk
Phillip 1782 w.
CARDEN
Goochland
Robt. 1785 w.
Rappahannock
Robt. 1685 w.
CARDER
Culpeper
Jno. 1785 i.
CARDILL
Rockbridge
Miles 1794 w.
CARDIN
Essex
Jno. 1739 i.
CARDWELL
Charlotte
Richd. 1780 w.
Cumberland
Thos. 1751 i.
Frederick
Andrew 1757 w.

Middlesex
Wm. 1745 i.
Prince Edward
Jno. 1795 w.
Westmoreland
Richd. 1716 w.
Richd. 1726 i.
CARE
Accomack
Ezekiel 1762 i.
CAREY
Westmoreland
Edwd. 1663 w.
Hardy
Peter 1787 w.
Isle of Wight
Nicholas 1713 w.
Jno. 1763 i.
Patience 1779 w.
Middlesex
Thos. 1720 w.
Princess Anne
Francis 1763 i.
Isaac 1789 w.
Prince Edward
Wm. 1784 w.
CARFORD
Fairfax
Jno. 1752 w.
CARFREE
Chesterfield
Jas. 1792 w.
CARGILL
Charlotte
Danl. 1778 w.
Lunenburg
Hannah 1758 w.
Surry
Jno. 1732 w.
Jno. 1744 i.
(Jno.?) 1748 i.
Eliz. 1753 w.
Sussex
Jno. 1777 w.
Ann 1781 w.
CARLER
Lancaster
Jno. 1689 i.
CARLETON
Mecklenburg
Thos. 1787 w.
CARLILE
Augusta
Jas. 1753 i.
Jno. 1796 w.
Saml. 1799 i.
Greenbrier
David 1786 i.
Surry
Robt. 1711 i.

CARLTON
Essex
Sebell 1769 w.
Middlesex
Isaac 1793 i.
Norfolk
Geo. 1775 w.
CARLYLE
Cumberland
Jno. 1762 w.
Fairfax
Jno. 1780 w.
CARMICHAEL
Princess Anne
Jno. 1789 i.
CARNABY
Norfolk
Edwd. 1745 i.
Richmond
Anthony 1699 w.
Westmoreland
Geo. 1733 i.
CARNAGEE
Shenandoah
Jas. 1780 w.
CARNAGGIE
Culpeper
David 1799 w.
CARNAL
Essex
Jno. 1790 w.
CARNALL
Essex
Patrick 1728 w.
CARNARADS
Norfolk
Lucus 1674 w.
CARNE
Lancaster
Wm. 1656 w.
Shenandoah
Henry 1781 a.
CARNEGIE
Northumberland
Jno. 1712 i.
CARNEY
Berkeley
Jno. 1775 w.
Fairfax
Thos. 1744 a.
Norfolk
Wm. 1683 w.
Richd. Sr. 1710-11 w.
Jno. 1717 w.
Jas. 1719 w.
Thos. 1756 w.
Philip 1758 w.
Barnaby 1760 w.
Jno. 1765 w.
Barnaby 1773 w.
Jas. 1775 i.

Wm. 1778 w.
Richd. 1779 w.
Saml. 1780 i.
Ann 1790 w.
Barnaby 1796 i.
CARNOCK
Norfolk
Joshua 1758 i.
CARNS
Bedford
Geo. 1769 i.
CARNY
Richmond
Patrick 1717 w.
CARPENTER
Botetourt
Nathaniel 1779 i.
Thos. 1779 i.
Jos. 1792 w.
Culpeper
Jno. 1782 w.
Fairfax
Richd. 1750 w.
Harrison
Nicholas 1791 w.
King George
Jos. 1765 i.
Lancaster
Thos. 1695 i.
Nathaniel 1726 w.
Thos. 1728 w.
Nathaniel 1757 w.
Jno. 1767 w.
Frances 1769 i.
Madison
Andrew 1795 w.
Northampton
Chas. 1709 w.
Stephen 1748 w.
Jno. 1761 w.
Chas. Sr. 1766 w.
Chas. Sr. 1786 w.
Richd. 1790 w.
Richd. 1798 i.
Northumberland
Sarah 1784 w.
Orange
Wm. 1746 w.
Richmond
Mary 1721 w.
Jno. 1789 w.
Spotsylvania
Jonathan 1763 a.
Jonathan 1798 a.
Surry
Mary 1699 i.
Westmoreland
Ann 1729 w.
Wm. 1773 w.

CARPINDER
Surry
Wm. 1695 w.
CARPINTER
Orange
Wm. 1747 w.
CARR
Albemarle
Gideon 1794 w.
Goochland
Dabney 1773 w.
Henrico
Roger 1717 i.
Isle of Wight
Jno. 1734 w.
Robt. 1735 w.
Hardy 1763 i.
Spencer 1778 w.
Abraham 1786 w.
Jno. 1794 w.
Louisa
Saml. 1777 w.
Jno. 1778 w.
Barbara 1795 w.
Loudoun
Jno. 1795 w.
Jno. Sr. 1796 i.
Thos. 1796 w.
Norfolk
Edwd. 1753 w.
Ralph 1771 i.
Prince William
William 1791 w.
Spotsylvania
Wm. 1760 w.
Southampton
Robt. 1763 w.
Jesse 1799 i.
Jno. 1786 w.
Surry
Jno. 1677 w.
Thos. 1694 i.
Jno. 1737 w.
Washington
Wm. 1779i.
Westmoreland
Wm. 1703 w.
Sarah 1727 w.
Jos. 1741 w.
Jas. 1743 i.
Wythe
Jno. 1799 i.
CARRALL
Princess Anne
Jas. 1784 i.
CARRAWAY
Norfolk
Jno. 1669 i.
Ann 1692 w.
Princess Anne
Jno. Jr. 1719 w.

Jas. 1761 w.
Wm. 1761 i.
Jas. 1795 w.
CARREL
Brunswick
Danl. 1773 w.
Isle of Wight
Thos. 1773 i.
Princess Anne
Jas. 1784 w.
Sussex
Nathan 1795 i.
CARRELL
Brunswick
Thos. 1757 w.
Fauquier
Sanford 1777 w.
Goochland
Roger 1796 w.
Wm. 1797 w.
Henrico
Roger 1727 w.
Isle of Wight
Jno. 1714 w.
Thos. 1717 w.
Mary 1719 i.
Jos. 1734 w.
Saml. 1740 w.
Jas. 1748 i.
Mary 1749 w.
Richd. 1775 w.
Wm. 1790 i.
Loudoun
Demse 1776 w.
Princess Anne
Nathan 1773 w.
Surry
Benj. 1749 w.
Joyce 1753 i.
Jas. 1773 w.
Priscilla 1795 w.
Sussex
Wm. 1791 w.
York
Danl. 1671 w.
CARRICO
Stafford
Thos. 1748 i.
CARRIL
Princess Anne
Wm. 1770 w.
CARRIER
Shenandoah
Jno. 1773 a.
Westmoreland
Jno. 1697 w.
CARRIGAN
Botetourt
Patrick 1795 w.

CARRILL
Isle of Wight
Thos. 1772 w.
Princess Anne
Wm. 1772 w.
Surry
Wm. 1708 i.
Westmoreland
Jno. 1716 i.
CARRINGTON
Cumberland
Geo. 1785 w.
Halifax
Thos. 1789 i.
CARROL
Fairfax
Nicholas 1745 a.
Frederick
Wm. 1759 w.
Goochland
Wm. 1734 w.
CARROLL
Albemarle
Stew(ard) 1771 i.
Susanna 1789 w.
Essex
Wm. 1750 w.
Edwd. (Edmd.)
1754 w.
Fairfax
Danl. 1787 i.
Frederick
Jos. 1762 w.
Isle of Wight
Thos. 1774 i.
Wm. 1785 w.
Lancaster
Jno. 1695 w.
Southampton
Thos. 1774 w.
Surry
Jno. 1706 i.
Benj. 1767 i.
Westmoreland
Danl. 1714 i.
CARROTHERS
Accomack
Tabitha 1758 w.
CARROWAY
Princess Anne
Edwd. 1723 w.
Jno. 1728 w.
CARRUTHERS
Accomack
Robt. 1754 w.
Fairfax
Jas. 1748 a.
Norfolk
Jos. A. 1795 w.
Rockbridge
Saml. 1779 w.

CARSON
Accomack
Alex. 1748 i.
Augusta
Henry 1751 i.
Isaac 1783 w.
Thos. 1786 w.
Agness 1788 w.
Bedford
Jno. 1762 w.
Fairfax
Thos. 1773 w.
Halifax
Thos. 1788 i.
Andrew 1793 w.
Norfolk
Obediah 1796 i.
Shenandoah
Simon 1795 a.
CARSS
Accomack
Jno. 1794 i.
CARSTAPHEN
Southampton
Jno. 1799 w.
CARSWELL
Washington
Henry 1777 i.
CART
Accomack
Monser (Monsieur)
1755 w.
CARTER
Accomack
Henry 1708 w.
Amherst
Chas. 1766 w.
Job. 1779 w.
Elisha 1788 w.
Peter 1790 w.
Solomon 1784 w.
Brunswick
Thos. 1751 i.
Geo. 1771 w.
Charles City
Eliz. 1792 w.
Charlotte
Jno. 1777 w.
Chesterfield
Armstead 1795 w.
Culpeper
Chas. 1782 i.
Jno. 1783 i.
Lunsford 1795 i.
Cumberland
Jno. 1773 i.
Mary 1784 w.
Essex
Richd. 1699 i.
Richd. 1700 i.
Saml. 1720 w.
Wm. 1748 w.

Henry 1781 w.
Fauquier
Peter 1790 i.
Frederick
Jas. 1758 w.
Jos. 1767 i.
Wm. 1779 i.
Benj. 1796 w.
Jas. 1798 w.
Goochland
Thos. 1735 w.
Thos. 1738 w.
Edwd. 1749 w.
Thos. 1763 w.
Chas. 1777 w.
Robt. 1794 i.
Halifax
Jno. 1781 w.
Richd. 1787 i.
Richd. 1796 i.
Henrico
Giles 1701-2 w.
Theodorick 1737 w.
Eliz. 1751 w.
Jno. 1786 w.
Eliz. 1795 w.
Sherwood 1797 w.
Benj. 1798 w.
Henry
Baynes 1788 i.
Isle of Wight
Thos. 1673 i.
Thos. 1710 w.
Geo. 1736 i.
Thos. 1736 w.
Geo. 1740 i.
Katherine 1747 w.
Mary 1783 w.
Mary 1788 i.
King George
Wm. 1744 i.
Giles 1745 i.
Chas. 1764 w.
Jno. 1776 w.
Lancaster
Jno. (1669) 1722 w.
Jno. 1689 w.
Jno. Jr. 1690 w.
Thos. Sr. 1700 w.
Peter 1721 w.
Thos. 1733 w.
Thos. 1735 w.
Wm. 1735 w.
Moses 1740 w.
Wm. 1740 i.
Edwd. 1743 i.
Henry 1743 w.
Catherine 1749 w.
Aaron 1756 i.
Wm. 1757 i.
Danl. 1759 i.
Josiah 1763 i.

Jos. 1765 w.
Jos. 1771 w.
Dale 1776 w.
Thos. 1776 w.
Thos. 1781 w.
Martha 1782 i.
Jno. 1783 i.
Edwd. 1784 w
Harry 1784 w.
Catherine 1788 w.
Geo. 1789 i.
Wm. 1790 i.
Geo. 1791 w.
Mary 1792 w.
Danl. 1794 w.
Loudoun
Jno. 1789 i.
Nicholas 1793 i.
Mecklenburg
Robt. 1787 i.
Thos. 1796 w.
Middlesex
Wm. 1711 w.
Margt. 1756 a.
Jno. 1742 w.
Norfolk
Jas. Sr. 1764 w.
Mary 1764 w.
Robt. 1775 w.
Northampton
Edwd. 1727 i.
Hannah 1741 i.
Southy 1753 i.
Sarah 1766 i.
Jos. 1777 i.
Northumberland
Jno. 1772 i.
Chas. 1782 i.
Powhatan
Danl. 1798 i.
Prince Edward
Theodorick 1778 w.
Waddell 1782 w.
Prince George
Jos. 1721 w.
Jno. 1725 i.
Prince William
Giles 1785 w.
Wm. 1794 w.
Richmond
Wm. 1720 i.
Wm. 1752 i.
Wm. 1774 w.
Landon 1779 w.
Robt. Wormeley
1797 w.
Spotsylvania
Jos. 1751 w.
Danl. 1766 a.
Henry 1775 w.
Jno. 1783 w.
Eliz. 1791 w.

74   VIRGINIA WILLS AND ADMINISTRATIONS

Edwd. 1792 w.
Stafford
Jas. 1743 w.
Solomon 1760 i.
Wm. 1762 w.
Surry
Thos. 1739 i.
Sussex
Richd. 1763 w.
Richd. 1771 i.
Eliz. 1773 w.
Jno. 1794 i.
Ursley 1796 w.
Washington
Chas. 1778 i.
Susannah 1781 w.
Westmoreland
Frances 1706 w.
Dorcas 1719 i.
Jas. 1745 i.
Edwd. 1761 i.
Robt. 1779 w.
Jane 1781 w.
Jane 1781 i.
Jno. 1783 i.
Mary 1786 i.
Ann 1789 w.
Lucy 1792 i.
York
Jno. 1741-2 i.
Thomasine 1743 w.
Surry
Robt. 1744 i.
CARTMELL
Frederick
Martin 1749 w.
Dorothy 1751 i.
Nathan 1758 w.
Nathan 1795 w.
CARTMILL
Botetourt
Henry 1787 w.
CARTON
Cumberland
Robt. 1759 w.
CARTOIS
Lunenburg
Thos. Sr. 1763 i.
Thos. Jr. 1763 i.
CARTRIGHT
Princess Anne
Jno. 1704 i.
CARTWIGHT
Surry
Robt. 1676 w.
CARTWRIGHT
Princess Anne
Robt. 1719 w.
Wm. 1725 i.
Jno. 1727 i.
Ann 1730 w.
Wm. 1731 i.

Jno. 1733 i.
Wm. 1753 w.
Mary 1762 w.
Spotsylvania
Thos. 1750 a.
Surry
Robt. 1699 w.
CARTY
Augusta
Jas. 1767 i.
Northumberland
Jno. 1745 i.
Princess Anne
Ann 1712 i.
Jut (Justinian?)
    1704 a.
Jno. 1705 i.
CARUTHERS
Accomack
Robt. 1785 i.
Robt. 1773 w.
Tabithia 1769 i.
Augusta
Rebecca 1779 w.
Rockbridge
Robt. 1781 w.
CARVER
Frederick
Henry 1780 w.
King George
Mary 1789 a.
Chas. 1799 w.
CARVEY
Northampton
Richd. 1734 w.
CARVIN
Augusta
Wm. 1762 a.
CARY
Accomack
Jno. 1695 w.
Solomon 1750 w.
Jas. 1751 w.
Jesse 1772 i.
Amelia
Mary 1767 w.
Chesterfield
Henry 1748 w.
Eliz. 1750 w.
Thos. 1754 w.
Dorothy 1761 w.
Hannah 1781 w.
Robt. 1782 i.
Thos. 1784 w.
Archibald 1787 w.
Nathl. 1789 w.
Sarah 1795 w.
Essex
Hugh 1753 w.
Halifax
Jas. 1785 w.

Henrico
Henry Jr. 1733 w.
Isle of Wight
Nicholas 1713 i.
Wm. 1756 i.
Jas. 1789 w.
Middlesex
Wm. 1703 i.
Princess Anne
Wm. 1694 w.
Wm. 1695 a.
Isaac 1790 i.
Wm. 1791 w.
Southampton
Miles 1766 w.
Miles 1778 i.
Ann 1787 i.
Surry
Jos. 1777 i.
York
Danl. 1750 w.
Judith 1758 i.
Jno. 1763 w.
Ann 1768 w.
CARYE
Accomack
Timothy 1719 w.
CASADY
Halifax
Wm. 1794 w.
CASEWELL
Norfolk
Matthew 1703-4 w.
Jabes 1718 i.
CASEY
Fairfax
Jno. 1794 w.
Frederick
Wm. 1752 i.
Isle of Wight
Richd. 1748 w.
Thos. 1758 w.
Nicholas 1763 w.
Richd. 1763 i.
Constant 1770 w.
King George
Jno. 1769 w.
CASH
Amherst
Howard 1772 w.
Joel 1773 a.
Benj. 1776 w.
Robt. 1781 w.
Ruth 1785 a.
Stephen 1798 w.
King George
Jas. 1782 w.
Sarah 1795 w.
Stafford
Peter 1760 w.
Westmoreland
Wm. 1708 w.

CASHATT
Fairfax
Jno. 1749 i.
CASHION
Chesterfield
Jas. 1791 w.
Jas. 1795 i.
CASHON
Chesterfield
Jas. 1759 w.
CASHOON
Chesterfield
Sarah 1761 w.
CASHEY
Ohio
Jos. 1795 w.
CASS
Princess Anne
Thos. 1782 i.
CASSLY
Surry
Mickell 1739 w.
CASSLEY
Surry
Michael 1781 w.
CASON
Halifax
Larkin 1775 w.
Princess Anne
Jas. 1722 w.
Thos. 1737 w.
Jas. 1761 w.
Wm. 1766 w.
Jas. Sr. 1785 w.
Jno. Jr. 1792 w.
Jno. Sr. 1792 w.
Jas. 1795 w.
Kader 1796 w.
Prince Edward
Edwd. 1784 w.
Seth 1799 w.
CASSEDY
Augusta
Neal 1767 i.
CASSEY
Northumberland
Thos. 1793 w.
CASSIDAY
Montgomery
Andrew 1797 i.
CASSON
King George
Francis 1770 a.
Norfolk
Thos. 1651 i.
CASTEEN
Norfolk
Mary 1791 w.
Princess Anne
Jno. 1769 i.
CASTELLO
Fairfax

Bridget 1769 i.
CASTLE
Northampton
Robt. 1672 w.
CASTLIN
Henrico
Jno. 1795 i.
CASTON
Essex
Class 1720 i.
Class 1740 w.
Jno. 1748 i.
CASWELL
Essex
Patrick 1728 w.
CASY
York
Jno. 1703-4 i.
CATCHMAY
Northumberland
Henry 1657 i.
CATEN
Princess Anne
Wm. 1709-10 w.
CATHCART
York
———— 1705 i.
CATHERILL
Princess Anne
Wm. 1715 i.
CATHON
Chesterfield
Wm. 17— i.
Southampton
Jno. 1771 i.
CATHRITE
Norfolk
Chas. 1696 w.
CATLETT
Culpeper
Lawrence 1782 w.
Alice 1796 i.
Thos. 1797 i.
Essex
Wm. 1699 w.
Jno. 1724 w.
Lawrence 1724 w.
Wm. 1742 w.
Fauquier
Jno. 1778 w.
Frederick
Peter 1767 w.
Peter 1779 i.
Peter 1791 w.
Jas. 1797 w.
King George
Alice 1767 a.
Orange
Jno. 1745 w.
CATLIN
Henrico
Wm. 1704 w.

CATO
Brunswick
Burwell 1769 w.
Greensville
Danl. Jr. 1794 i.
Jno. 1795 w.
Danl. 1797 w.
Jno. 1797 w.
Norfolk
Mary 1752 w.
CATON
Norfolk
Jno. 1735 i.
Sussex
Eliz. 1776 w.
Henry 1790 w.
CATTON
York
Benj. 1768 w.
CATUR
Brunswick
Geo. 1734 w.
CAUDLE
Brunswick
Stephen 1759 i.
Richd. 1771 w.
Jno. 1782 i.
Mary 1782 w.
CAUFILL
Surry
Wm. 1782 w.
CAUGHLAND
Essex
Mary 1765 i.
CAUGLE
Berkeley
Jno. 1782 i.
CAUL
Augusta
Timothy 1791 w.
Northampton
Danl. 1748 i.
Danl. 1750 w.
Jos. 1750 w.
COUN
Norfolk
Sarah 1778 i.
CAUSEBY
York
Jno. 1714 i.
CAUSEN
Middlesex
Alice 1728 w.
Thos. 1728 i.
CAUSEY
Northumberland
Judith 1792 i.
CAWBY
Augusta
Margt. 1793 i.

CAWLEY
Augusta
Jno. 1775 w.
CAUSON
Norfolk
Margaret 1784 w.
CAUTHORN
Essex
Thos. 1741 i.
Wm. 1759 i.
Henry 1783 w.
Vincent 1792 w.
Thos. 1793 w.
Rice 1798 w.
CAUTHORNE
Essex
Thos. 1734 w.
Richd. 1748 w.
Rappahannock
Richd. 1687 w.
CAVE
Culpeper
Robt. 1755 i.
David 1792 w.
Fauquier
Thos. 1797 w.
Orange
Eliz. 1735 a.
David 1756 w.
Benj. 1762 w.
David 1764 i.
Stafford
Wm. 1742 w.
CAVEN
Norfolk
Patrick 1723 i.
CAVENAUGH
Essex
Thos. 1766 i.
Orange
Philemon 1744 w.
CAVENDAR
Princess Anne
Jno. 1789 i.
Thos. 1789 w.
Charlotte
Hugh 1789 w.
CAVENDER
Westmoreland
Henry 1772 w.
Thos. 1796 w.
CAVENER
Fairfax
Jno. 1755 w.
CAVENISH
Mecklenburg
Wm. 1772 i.
CAVERNER
Richmond
Danl. 1719 i.
Thos. 1719 i.

CAVERNOR
Richmond
Frances 1722 i.
CAVIN
Loudoun
Jno. 1793 w.
Jos. 1798 i.
CAWFIELD
Westmoreland
Richd. 1721 i.
CAWSON
Norfolk
Christopher 1757 w.
Princess Anne
Jonas 1760 w.
CAWTHORN
Fluvanna
Thos. 1794 w.
Goochland
Robt. 1755 i.
Gideon 1799 w.
Prince Edward
Jno. 1792 w.
CAYCE
Chesterfield
Chas. 1766 w.
Chas. 1777 i.
York
Jno. 1758 i.
CAYNEHOOE
York
Wm. 1644 i.
CEATON
Princess Anne
Solomon 1753 w.
CECILL
Montgomery
Saml. 1786 i.
CELEY
Brunswick
Martha 1789 w.
CEMP
Henrico
Robt. 1794 w.
CHACE
Accomack
Wm. 1689 i.
CHADDOK
Lancaster
Richd. 1682 i.
CHADWELL
King George
Bryan 1745 i.
Stafford
Jno. 1732 w.
CHAENEY
Essex
Philip 1785 i.
CHAFFIN
Charlotte
Jno. 1779 i.
Jno. 1789 i.

Cumberland
Jno. 1767 w.
Chris. 1769 i.
CHALKLEY
Chesterfield
Benj. 1798 w.
CHALMERS
Isle of Wight
David 1785 w.
Stafford
Jno. 1735 w.
CHAMBERLAIN
Berkeley
Jonas 1798 i.
Brunswick
Saml. 1752 w.
Essex
Leonard 1709 w.
Jno. 1725 w.
Jno. 1787 w.
Jas. 1795 a.
Norfolk
Geo. 1762 w.
Eliza. 1773 i.
CHAMBERLAYNE
Fauquier
Jas. 1775 i.
CHAMBERLIN
Norfolk
Jno. 1714 w.
CHAMBERLDIN
Montgomery
Jas. 1786 i.
CHAMBERS
Accomack
Caleb 1798 i.
Amelia
Richd. 1752 w.
Hugh 1770 w.
Mary 1776 w.
Saml. 1788 i.
Cumberland
Geo. 1782 w.
Frederick
Edmund 1746 i.
Jno. 1748 a.
Halifax
Jno. 1785 w.
Henrico
Wm. 1703 i.
Wm. 1748 w.
Lancaster
Robt. 1654 w.
Louisa
Wm. 1770 a.
Stephen 1778 a.
Lunenburg
Thos. Sr. 1798 w.
Norfolk
Richd. 1687 w.
Prince Edward
Josiah 1785 w.

Surry
Wm. 1677 w.
Wm. 1718 w.
Jno. 1727 i.
Jonathan 1735 i.
Olive 1720 i.
Ohio
David 1787 w.
Stafford
Danl. 1758 w.
Westmoreland
Thos. 1743 w.
Wm. 1748-9-w.
CHAMBLE
Orange
Thos. 1744 w.
CHAMBLES
Brunswick
Henry 1784 w.
CHAMBLESS
Lunenburg
Nathl. 1761 w.
Jno. 1780 w.
CHAMBLETT
Lancaster
Randolph 1659 w.
CHAMBLIN
Loudoun
Wm. 1791 w.
CHAMBLISS
Greensville
Henry 1795 w.
CHAMBON
Henrico
Gideon 1715 w.
Pennina 1726 w.
CHAMBOON
Goochland
Gideon 1739 i.
CHAMBRISS
Amelia
Mary 1777 i.
CHAMPBELL
Brunswick
Robt. 1763 w.
CHAMPE
Culpeper
William 1784 w.
King George
Jno. 1763 w.
Jno. 1765 i.
Jane 1767 w.
Jno. 1775 w.
Loudoun
Jno. 1763 w.
Stafford
Wm. 1748 i.
CHAMPION
Berkeley
Jos. 1778 w.
Northumberland
Moses 1758 i.

Joshua 1767 i.
Jas. 1789 i.
Surry
Benj. 1735 w.
Eliz. 1736 i.
Chas. 1755 i.
Jno. 1757 w.
CHAMPNEY
Fairfax
Wm. 1751 w.
CHANCE
Accomack
Wm. 1726 i.
Jno. 1744 i.
Wm. 1751 w.
Wm. 1754 i.
Elijah 1775 w.
CHANCELLOR
Westmoreland
Thos. 1761 w.
Catherine 1767 i.
CHANDLER
Accomack
Jno. 1728 w.
Solomon 1756 w.
Anne 1762 w.
Hathan Fettipace
1763 w.
Jno. 1781 w.
Thos. 1784 w.
Caleb 1786 w.
Caleb 1788 i.
Jno. 1788 i.
Patience 1789 w.
Patience 1792 i.
Thos. 1793 i.
Caleb 1794 i.
Levy 1795 w.
Mitchel 1796 w.
Mitchell 1799 i.
Cumberland
Joell 1755 w.
Goochland
Jno. 1747 i.
Halifax
Wm. 1779 w.
Wm. 1789 w.
Robt. 1792 w.
Lunenburg
Jos. 1764 w.
Mecklenburg
David 1793 w.
Norfolk
Thos. 1784 w.
Northampton
Littleton 1776 w.
Littleton 1785 i.
Orange
Jos. 1791 w.
Wythe
David 1794 i.

Westmoreland
Eliz. 1726 w.
Wm. 1730 i.
Jos. 1760 w.
Eliz. 1781 i.
York
Robt. 1669 w.
CHANEY
Middlesex
Penelope 1720 w.
CHANIL
Essex
Jno. 1702 i.
CHANLER
Fluvanna
Richd. 1782 w.
CHANLOR
Westmoreland
Thos. 1726 w.
Wm. 1729 w.
CHANNEL
Randolph
Jeremiah 1798 w.
CHANNELL
Isle of Wight
Jas. 1766 w.
Jeremiah 1785 w.
Southampton
Jas. 1785 i.
CHANNIS
Prince George
Henry 1719 w.
CHAPEL
Princess Anne
Jno. 1774 w.
Sussex
Thos. 1770 i.
CHAPELL
Halifax
Wm. 1799 w.
CHAPIN
Fairfax
Benj. 1781 w.
CHAPLEN
Norfolk
Benj. 1756 i.
CHAPLEER
Frederick
Wm. 1752 w.
CHAPLIN
Lancaster
Jas. 1682-3 nw.
York
Henry 1788 w.
CHAPLINE
Frederick
Wm. 1760 w.
CHAPLY
Northampton
Jacob 1737 i.

CHAPMAN
Accomack
Wm. 1720 w.
Silas 1749 nw.
Henry 1755 i.
Amelia
Saml. 1773 w.
David 1773 w.
Brunswick
Jno. 1743 w.
Jno. 1763 w.
Wm. 1770 w.
Culpeper
Thos. 1782 i.
Fairfax
Nathaniel 1762 i.
Constant 1791 w.
Constant 1798 w.
Frederick
Jas. 1785 a.
Thos. 1797 i.
Hampshire
Wm. 1796 w.
Isle of Wight
Chas. 1710 w.
Jos. 1729 w.
Chas. 1749 w.
Wm. 1773 i.
Chas. 1777 w.
Chas. 1789 i.
Jno. 1737 w.
Jno. 1761 i.
Jordan 1769 w.
Jos. 1792 w.
Jno. 1796 i.
Rhoda 1797 i.
King George
Wm. W. 1786 w.
Lancaster
Wm. 1703-4 i.
Wm. 1709 w.
Lunenburg
Moses 1764 i.
Middlesex
Eliz. 1778 w.
Montgomery
Jno. 1794 i.
Northampton
Phillip 1644 w.
Philip 1650 i.
Pearce 1733 i.
Pierce 1738 i.
Northumberland
Winter 1652 i.
Orange
Isaac 1747 i.
Princess Anne
Nicklas 1726 i.
Jas. 1729 i.
Henry 1734 i.
Jas. 1760 i.
Jno. 1773 w.

Prince William
Jos. 1736 w.
Jno. 1783 i.
Thos. 1785 w.
Jno. 1791 w.
Thos. 1791 i.
Spotsylvania
Geo. 1747 w.
Jno. 1776 w.
Stafford
Jno. 1735 i.
Taylor 1749 w.
Surry
Benj. 1720 i.
Mary 1736 w.
Westmoreland
Jno. 1738 w.
York
Walter 1751 w.
Hudson 1763 w.
Ann 1770 w.
Allen 1794 w.
Jno. 1799 w.
CHAPPEL
Chesterfield
Abraham 1781 w.
Princess Anne
Jonas 1704 i.
Chas. 1783 i.
Chas. 1784 i.
Geo. 1788 i.
Sussex
Ransom 1782 i.
CHAPPELL
Amelia
Jno. 1766 i.
Jas. 1770 w.
Jno. 1774 w.
Prudence 1778 i.
Miles 1784 w.
Lunenburg
Thos. 1790 w.
Robt. 1794 w.
Prince George
Robt. 1724 w.
Richmond
Henry 1701 w.
Surry
Saml. 1749 w.
Sussex
Eliz. 1761 w.
Jas. 1769 w.
Jas. 1778 w.
CHAPPIN
Fairfax
Benj. 1782 i.
CHAPPLE
Princess Anne
Jno. 1774 i.
CHARERON
Albemarle
Anthony 1755 w.

CHARITY
Surry
Shorod 1782 w.
CHARKE
Louisa
Rosamond 1786 i.
CHARLES
Accomack
Jno. 1708 w.
Brunswick
Eliz. 1781 w.
Lewis 1784 w.
Margt. 1785 w.
Charles City
Lydia 1795 w.
Philip 1792 w.
Willis Sr. 1792 w.
Henrico
Thos. 1694 i.
Lancaster
Thos. 1743 w.
Southampton
Rebecca 1760 w.
Mathew 1795 w.
Jethro 1797 i.
Eleanor 1798 w.
Sussex
Thos. 1787 w.
Westmoreland
Thos. 1713 i.
CHARLESWORTH
Amelia
Robt. 1745 a.
CHARLETON
Surry
——— 1676 i.
CHARLTON
Cumberland
Abraham 1790 w.
Fairfax
Andrew 1757 i.
Montgomery
Jno. 1790 w.
Northampton
Stephen 1654 w.
York
Geo. 1749 i.
Lydia 1760 w.
Richd. 1779 w.
Francis 1798 i.
CHARMOIE
Norfolk
Saml. 1652 w.
CHASE
Accomack
Wm. 1737 i.
CHASEE
Louisa
Jas. 1793 a.
CHASTAIN
Cumberland
Jno. 1762 w.

Goochland
Martha 1740 w.
Henrico
Magdalen 1731 w.
CHASTAINE
Goochland
Peter 1728 w.
Stephen 1739 w.
CHATEAU
York
Louis 1786 i.
CHATTIN
Lancaster
Thos. 1736 w.
Thos. 1748 i.
Margt. 1758 w.
CHATTING
Lancaster
Thos. 1699 i.
CHAVERS
Louisa
Jas. 1791 i.
CHAVIS
Henry
Manoah 1789 w.
CHAVONS
Mecklenburg
Henry 1798 w.
CHATWIN
Lancaster
Eliz. 1722 w.
CHATTWIN
Lancaster
Thos. 1698-9 w.
CHEADLE
Goochland
Frances 1740 i.
Middlesex
Thos. 1724 w.
CHEANEY
Essex
Wm. 1744 i.
Philip 1785 w.
CHEAP
Middlesex
Patk. 1744 w.
CHEATHAM
Chesterfield
Christopher 17 (50?) i.
Wm. 1751 w.
Thos. 1756 w.
Thos. 1762 i.
Benj. 1765 w.
Christopher 1770 w.
Thos. 1770 w.
Obedience 1771 w.
Thos. 1771 i.
Francis 1773 i.
Jas. 1774 i.
Jas. 17— i.
Obediah 1778 i.
Stephen 1783 w.

Benj. 1785 i.
Francis 1785 w.
Henry 1793 w.
Josiah 1793 w.
Thos. 1794 w.
Isham 1795 i.
Wm. Sr. 1795 w.
Jas. 1797 w.
Eliz. 1798 w.
Leonard 1798 w.
Henrico
Thos. 1726 w.
Mecklenburg
Leonard 1778 w.
Prince Edward
Jonathan 1761 i.
Surry
Marmaduke 1766 w.
Jos. 1782 i.
Jno. 1789 w.
CHEATOM
Lancaster
Jno. 1755 i.
CHEATWOOD
Chesterfield
Mathias Jr. 1773 i.
Cumberland
Marthias 1755 w.
Matthew 1755 i.
Powhatan
Wm. 1787 w.
CHECKS
Pittsylvania
Wm. 1790 i.
CHEESMAN
Stafford
Thos. 1750 i.
CHEESEMAN
York
Edmd. 1735 w.
CHEETON
Westmoreland
Eliz. 1797 i.
CHEILES
Spotsylvania
Henry 1763 w.
CHEIVRALL
Stafford
Thos. 1736 i.
CHELTON
Halifax
Chas. 1795 w.
Lancaster
Henry 1730 w.
Thos. 1738 i.
Nicholas 1738 w.
Prince William
Jno. 1744 i.
CHENALT
Bedford
Stephen 1770 i.

CHENAULT
Essex
Howlett 1738 i.
Jno. 1740 w.
CHENEY
Essex
Jno. 1749 i.
Middlesex
Thos. 1745 i.
Dorothy 1757 w.
CHENEWOTH
Botetourt
Thos. 1780 w.
CHENOWETH
Berkeley
Absolem 1773 w.
Jos. 1785 w.
Wm. 1785 w.
Frederick
Jno. 1771 w.
Wm. 1772 w.
CHERMESON
York
Jos. 1712 w.
CHERRIEHOLME
Isle of Wight
Marmaduke 1691 w.
CHERRY
Augusta
Edwd. 1751 i.
Frederick
Thos. 1760 w.
Wm. 1765 w.
Norfolk
Saml. 1734 w.
Wm. 1737 w.
Thos. 1748 w.
Jno. 1750 i.
Jno. 1751 i.
Jeremiah 1756 i.
Hillary 1761 w.
Spring 1761 w.
Bathiah 1769 i.
Joseph 1792 w.
Caleb 1794 w.
Mary 1798 i.
CHESEY
Norfolk
Thos. 1654 w.
CHESHIRE
Cumberland
Tennison 1794 w.
Fairfax
Jno. 1748 a.
Jno. 1759 i.
Jno. 1760 i.
Norfolk
Richd. 1724 w.
Princess Anne
Richd. 1725 w.
Susannah 1749 w.

CHESLEY
York
Philip 1674 w.
CHESLOAM
Charlotte
Wm. 1792 w.
CHESNUT
Frederick
Alex. 1749 a.
CHESSELL
Middlesex
Wm. 1733 i.
CHESSER
Prince William
Jno. 1780 w.
CHESSETT
Surry
Thos. 1700-1 i.
CHESSUTT
Surry
Jas. 1710 w.
CHESTER
Frederick
Thos. 1754 w.
CHESTNUT
Augusta
Wm. 1789 i.
CHESTNUTT
Isle of Wight
Alex. 1690 i.
CHETTWOOD
Franklin
Jno. 1798 w.
CHETWINE
Isle of Wight
Edwd. 1649 w.
CHETWOOD
Lancaster
Thos. 1678 i.
Thos. 1742 i.
CHEW
Fairfax
Mercy 1776 w.
Roger 1792 a.
Orange
Thos. 1782 w.
Spotsylvania
Larkin 1729 w.
Hannah 1743 a.
Jno. 1756 w.
Larkin 1770 w.
Robt. 1778 w.
Robt. Beverley
1792 w.
Jno. 1789 w.
York
Jno. 1652 w.
CHEWNING
Lancaster
Geo. 1717 w.

Louisa
Geo. 1785 w.
CHEYNEY
Essex
Wm. 1727 i.
Erasmus 1740 i.
Jno. 1740 i.
Wm. 1744 w.
Dinah 1752 w.
Jno. 1761 w.
Jno. 1773 i.
CHICHESTER
Fairfax
Richd. 1796 w.
Lancaster
Jno. 1728 i.
Ann 1729 w.
Richd. 1734 w.
Richd. 1744 w.
Jno. 1754 w.
Norfolk
Wm. 1698 w.
CHICK
Loudoun
Wm. 1797 i.
Northampton
Thos. Jr. 1708 w.
Pittsylvania
Wm. 1790 w.
Prince William
Jno. 1789 w.
CHIDDICK
Campbell
Wm. 1786 i.
CHILCOTT
Norfolk
Nicholas 1747-8 i.
CHILD
Culpeper
Wm. 1770 w.
CHILDERS
Albemarle
Abraham 1764 w.
Henrico
Abraham 1698 w.
Philemon Sr. 1717 w.
Henry 1727 w.
Wm. 1727 i.
Robt. 1731 i.
Thos. 1735 w.
Fredk. 1785 w.
Robt. 1797 i.
Lunenburg
Henry 1761 w.
Norfolk
Thos. 1763 i.
CHILDRES
Charlotte
Benj. 1779 i.
Prince Edward
Robt. 1789 w.

CHILDRESS
Amherst
Benj. 1775 w.
Lucy 1792 w.
Halifax
Abraham 1791 i.
Henrico
Benj. 1783 w.
Fredk. 1786 w.
Jacob 1797 w.
Pittsylvania
Thos. 1775 i.
CHILDREY
Amelia
Jno. 1741 a.
Charlotte
Jeremiah 1791 w.
Benedict 1795 i.
Henrico
Thos. 1783 w.
Thos. 1787 w.
Prince Edward
Robt. 1791 i.
CHILDS
Southampton
Jos. 1775 i.
Spotsylvania
Richd. 1751 w.
CHILE
Richmond
Danl. 1724 i.
CHILES
Albemarle
Micajah 1799 w.
Amelia
Henry 1747 w.
Walter 1761 i.
Bedford
Henry 1758 w.
Culpeper
Susannah 1784 w.
Halifax
Paul 1761 w.
Louisa
Jno. 1774 w.
Lunenburg
Henry 1756 w.
Orange
Malachi 1770 w.
Anna 1773 w.
CHILTON
Fauquier
Wm. 1776 i.
Jno. 1777 w.
Chas. 1793 i.
Lancaster
Thos. 1699 i.
Geo. 1709 w.
Stephen 1718 w.
Geo. 1728 w.
Benoni 1732 w.
Chas. 1739 w.

Wm. 1741 w.
Wm. 1749 w.
Wm. 1752 i.
Ezikiel 1754 w.
Wm. 1755 w.
Geo. 1759 w.
Stephen 1761 w.
Judith 1766 w.
Edwin 1771 w.
Thos. 1777 i.
Chas. 1777 i.
Ann 1778 i.
Moses 1778 w.
Stephen 1778 i.
Jno. 1784 i.
William 1787 i.
Wm. 1791 w.
Loudoun
Geo. 1771 w.
Martha 1772 w.
Wm. 1781 i.
Steerman 1785 w.
Jno. 1792 i.
Middlesex
Thos. 1711 i.
Peter 1718 w.
Mary 1744 i.
Northumberland
Andrew 1761 w.
Stephen 1766 w.
Wm. 1771 i.
Mary 1773 w.
Prince William
Jno. 1744 a.
Westmoreland
Jno. Sr. 1708 w.
Chas. 1717 i.
Jno. 1726 w.
Mary 1737 w.
Thos. 1765 w.
Thos. 1766 i.
Thos. 1781 i.
Thos. 1783 i.
CHIMINO
Goochland
Jno. 1736 i.
CHINAWETH
Frederick
Jno. 1746 i.
CHINGE
Surry
Walter 1720 i.
CHINN
Fauquier
Chas. 1788 w.
Lancaster
Jno. Sr. 1692 w.
Rawleigh 1741 w.
Easter 1751 w.
Rawleigh 1756 i.
Thos. 1768 w.

Jos. 1774 w.
Ann 1784 i.
Rawleigh 1784 i.
Robt. 1784 w.
Jno. 1791 w.
Rawleigh 1799 w.
Loudoun
Christopher 1770 w.
Elijah 1771 w.
Richmond
Chitto 1747 i.
Stafford
Rawleigh 1760 w.
CHINWORTH
Frederick
Wm. 1773 i.
CHIPPEN
Middlesex
Philip 1734 a.
CHISELDINE
King George
Henry 1757 w.
CHISM
Halifax
Jas. 1786 i.
CHISMAN
Washington
Isaac 1777 i.
York
Edmund 1673 w.
Thos. 1715 w.
Eliz. 1717 a.
Jno. 1728 w.
Jno. 1735 w.
Geo. 1741-2 w.
Jno. 1755 i .
Eloner 1767 w.
Thos. 1770 w.
Thos. 1782 i.
Edmd. 1784 w.
Jno. Sr. 1785 i.
Geo. 1786 i.
CHISRELDINE
King George
Jas. Kerby 1757 eb.
CHISSAM
Orange
Rebecca 1746 i.
CHISSUM
Orange
Jno. 1742 a.
CHISUM
Amelia
Jno. 1793 w.
CHISWELL
Fauquier
Geo. 1788 i.
Lunenburg
Uriah 1754 i.

CHITTAM
Augusta
Peter 1753 w.
Philip 1754 i.
CHITTY
Southampton
Edwd. 1758 i.
CHITWOOD
Lancaster
Wm. 1788 w.
CHIVERAL
King George
Clement 1783 w.
CHIVERS
Frederick
Jas. 1752 i.
CHOCALAT
Northumberland
Richd. 1728 i.
CHOICE
Henry
Lully 1785 w.
CHORTON
Richmond
Thos. 1719 i.
CHOWNING
Lancaster
Thos. 1688 w.
Chattin 1771 i.
Chattin 1773 w.
Geo. 1773 i.
Middlesex
Robt. 1698 i.
Ann 1699 w.
Thos. 1721 w.
Geo. 1744 i.
Geo. 1761 a.
Jane 1780 w.
Jno. 1780 i.
Thos. 1782 w.
Wm. 1786 w.
Eliz. (1) 1789 w.
Eliz. (2) 1789 w.
Wm. 1790 i.
CHRISLER
Madison
Abraham 1795 a.
CHRISMAN
Augusta
Jno. 1773 w.
Frederick
Jos. 1762 a.
Henry 1781 i.
Montgomery
Abraham 1798 w.
CHRISTALL
Northumberland
Henry 1743 w.
CHRISTEE
Northumberland
Jno. 1756 i.

CHRISTIAN
Albemarle
Robt. 1749 w.
Jas. 1759 w.
Chas. 1767 i.
Amherst
Jas. 1772 w.
Drury 1783 a.
Geo. 1785 a.
Jas. 1772 w.
Robt. 1785 w.
Saml. 1797 w.
Augusta
Wm. 1770 a.
Wm. 1779 w.
Jno. 1783 w.
Jno. 1791 w.
Robt. 1794 w.
Botetourt
Eliz. 1789 w.
Charles City
Richd. 1769 i.
Wm. 1771 i.
Gideon 1797 w.
Chesterfield
Turner Hunt 1781 w.
Frederick
Francis 1788 w.
Francis Humphrey
1790 i.
Goochland
Thos. 1737 w.
Thos. 1743 w.
Chas. 1784 w.
Greenbrier
Ellison 1795 i.
Lancaster
Olier 1702 w.
Christopher 1793 i.
Montgomery
Israel 1784 w.
Nathaniel 1779 a.
Norfolk
Matthias 1794 w.
Northampton
Michael 1735 w.
Wm. 1773 w.
Geo. 1783 w.
Michael 1783 w.
Eliz. 1787 w.
Michael 1795 w.
Prince Edward
Ann 1793 w.
Washington
Sampson 1785 i.
CHRISTIE
Brunswick
Robt. 1750 w.
Hardy
Jas. 1795 w.
Norfolk
Adam 1748 i.

Westmoreland
Geo. 1767 i.
CHRISTLE
Greenbrier
Wm. 1796 w.
CHRISTMAN
Frederick
Jacob 1778 w.
Mary 1785 w.
CHRISTMAS
Louisa
Jno. 1771 w.
York
Doctoris 1655 w.
CHRISTLER
Culpeper
Thebolt 1776 w.
CHRISTOPHER
Charlotte
Wm. 1772 w.
Lancaster
Jno. 1795 i.
Lunenburg
Nichol 1754 w.
Jacobus 1774 w.
Mecklenburg
David 1784 w.
Northumberland
Robt. 1725-6 w.
Henry 1726-7 w.
Wm. 1726-7 w.
Geo. 1748 i.
John 1753 w.
Henry 1794 w.
CHRITCHER
Fairfax
Jadwin 1750 i.
CHROUCH
Goochland
Jno. 1780 i.
CHRYSTALL
Accomack
Wm. 1751 w.
CHUBB
Westmoreland
Henry 1701 i.
Jno. Everly 1778 i.
CHUM
Accomack
Geo. 1776 w.
CHUMLEY
Amelia
Jno. 1782 w.
CHUMNEY
Amelia
Jno. 1784 i.
CHURCH
Amelia
Richd. 1779 w.
Norfolk
Richd. 1705-6 w.
Eliz. 1710 a.

Richd. 1743 w.
Jos. 1767 w.
Northampton
Thos. Jr. 1677 w.
Thos. 1717 w.
CHURCHELL
Northumberland
Saml. 1702 w.
CHURCHILL
Fauquier
Henry 1762 i.
Jno. 1796 i.
Middlesex
Wm. 1710 w.
Wm. 1714 i.
Eliz. 1716 w.
Jos. 1724 i.
Armistead 1763 w.
Hannah 1774 w.
Hannah 1776 w.
Willoughby 1780 i.
CHURNELL
Westmoreland
Jos. 1698 w.
CILLINGWORTH
Stafford
Mary 1734 w.
CIRCUS
Shenandoah
Jno. 1787 w.
CLACK
Albemarle
Moses 1792 w.
Brunswick
Sterling 1751 w.
Jas. 1757 w.
Mary 1763 w.
Lancaster
Nicho. 1709 w.
Mecklenburg
Jno. 1799 w.
Jno. Sr. 1799 i.
Surry
Ann 1754 i.
CLAGGETT
Loudoun
Chas. 1791 w.
CLAIBORNE
Chesterfield
Mary 1796 w.
Lunenburg
Richd. 1776 w.
Norfolk
Thos. 1778 w.
Sussex
Wm. Presley 1786 w.
Augustine 1787 w.
Mary 1799 w.
Stafford
Thos. 1735 w.
CLAMMONS
Brunswick

Jno. 1742 i.
CLANTON
Brunswick
Edwd. 1741 i.
Sarah 1748 w.
Edwd. 1763 w.
Surry
Wm. 1726 w.
Mary 1751 w.
Richd. 1751 i.
Sussex
Nathl. 1759 w.
Jno. 1781 w.
Drury 1782 w.
Jno. 1790 w.
Jno. 1792 i.
Jno. 1794 i.
CLAPHAM
Fairfax
Josias 1749 w.
Lancaster
Wm. Jr. 1660 w.
Wm. 1675 i.
CLARE
Frederick
Edwd. 1795 w.
Middlesex
Jno. 1777 i.
CLAREY
Sussex
Thos. 1779 i.
CLARK
Accomack
Jos. 1705 w.
Jas. 1726 w.
Major 1740 i.
Blake 1741 i.
Thos. 1760 w.
Geo. 1762 i.
Eliz. 1768 w.
Albemarle
Micajah Jr. 1774 i.
Benj. 1776 i.
Amelia
Henrietta-Maria
  1746 a.
Jas. 1746 a.
Henrietta 1750 a.
Henry 1776 w.
Thos. 1777 w.
Amherst
Benj. 1776 w.
Benj. Jr. 1781 w.
Nathl. 1796 i.
Augusta
Wm. 1753 w.
Robt. 1760 i.
Wm. 1766 i.
Jas. 1778 w.
Eliz. 1781 w.

Bath
Jas. 1791 w.
Berkeley
Eliz. 1772 w.
Walter 1792 i.
Botetourt
Jno. 1798 i.
Brunswick
Henry 1736 w.
Saml. 1736 w.
Nathl. 1761 i.
Simon 1772 i.
Geo. 1775 w.
Joshua 1775 w.
Robt. 1779 i.
Henry 1782 w.
Charlotte
Jno. 1791 w.
Chesterfield
Ellison 1766 w.
Allison 1769 w.
Culpeper
William 1787 w.
Jas. 1789 w.
Oliver 1791 w.
Essex
Edwd. 1736 w.
Wm. 1749 i.
Edwd. 1749 i.
Chas. 1761 i.
Jno. 1772 w.
Susannah 1782 w.
Robt. 1790 w.
Fairfax
Jno. 1775 w.
Aaron 1776 i.
Jno. 1786 w.
Rose 1786 w.
Jno. 1797 a.
Fauquier
Benj. 1797 w.
Frederick
Jas. 1749 i.
Hezekiah 1766 i.
Goochland
Jos. 1743 i.
Edwd. 1778 w.
Greenbrier
Alex. 1794 w.
Greensville
Joshua 1782 w.
Henry 1784 w.
Joshua 1789 i.
Joshua 1790 w.
Peter 1799 w.
Halifax
David 1797 w.
Henrico
Edwd. 1736 i.
Thos. 1736 i.
Peter 1785 w.

Wm. 1799 w.
Henry
David 1790 w.
Isle of Wight
Humphrey 1656 w.
Jas. 1672 i.
Thos. 1675 i.
Wm. 1708 i.
Jno. 1723 i.
Wm. 1742 w.
Jno. 1759 w.
Jos. 1759 w.
Jno. 1775 w.
Benj. 1776 w.
King George
Wm. Jr. 1770 a.
Lancaster
Arthur 1718 w.
Wm. 1764 i.
Louisa
Christopher 1754 w.
Francis 1770 w.
Benj. 1771 a.
Jos. 1774 w.
Mecklenburg
Jesse 1770 w.
Archibald 1792 i.
Jno. 1795 i.
Middlesex
Edwd. 1748 w.
Jno. 1784 i.
Norfolk
Lewis Lathur 1792 w.
Northampton
Robt. 1703 i.
Mary 1709 w.
Northumberland
Robt. 1744 i.
Orange
Jas. 1791 w.
Pittsylvania
Mary 1771 w.
Wm. 1795 w.
Prince Edward
Thos. 1790 w.
Richd. 1797 w.
Princess Anne
Wm. 1727 i.
Rappahannock
Richd. 1678 w.
Henry 1679 w.
Richmond
Maurice 1710 w.
Thos. 1718 w.
Wm. 1726 w.
Alex. 1744 i.
Jno. 1755 w.
Jas. 1767 i.
Geo. 1774 w.
Robt. 1774 nw.
Robt. 1785 i.

Jno. 1793 i.
Thos. 1796 w.
Rodham 1797 i.
Southampton
Thos. 1752 w.
Peter 1761 w.
Jno. 1783 w.
Stafford
Jno. 1733 i.
Geo. 1736 i.
Surry
Edwd. 1713 i.
Jno. 1717 w.
Robt. Sr. 1723 w.
Benj. 1744 i.
Jas. Sampson 1754 w.
Benj. 1756 i.
Jas. 1757 w.
Thos. 1757 w.
Wm. 1757 w.
Jno. 1758 i.
Benj. 1766 w.
Jno. 1767 i.
Joyce 1775 w.
Sussex
Jno. 1778 w.
Westmoreland
Wm. 1698 i.
Wm. 1702 i.
Jas. 1782 i.
Margt. 1791 w.
York
Jno. 1689 w.
Wm. 1700 a.
Jno. 1710 w.
Jno. 1713 i.
Francis 1718 i.
Jno. 1719 i.
Robt. 1734 w.
CLARKE
Amelia
Jas. 1746 a.
Richd. 1752 w.
Lucy 1754 w.
Henrietta 1755 w.
Thos. 1778 i.
Alex. 1786 i.
Brunswick
Saml. 1753 w.
Nathl. 1759 w.
Robt. 1774 w.
Geo. 1776 i.
Elisha 1791 w.
Charles City
Nathl. 1792 i.
Wm. 1792 w.
Sarah 1797 w.
Chesterfield
Jno. 1763 w.
Cumberland
Richd. Jr. 1775 i.

Wm. 1799 i.
Essex
Jos. 1698 i.
Jno. 1699 w.
Jas. 1777 i.
Margt. 1798 w.
Fluvanna
Jesse 1778 w.
Thos. 1780 i.
Goochland
Wm. 1779 w.
Jeffery 1786 i.
Halifax
Chas. 1792 w.
Thos. 1796 i.
Henrico
Wm. 1713 w.
Robt. 1754 i.
Wm. 1756 i.
King George
Jno. 1761 w.
Isle of Wight
Margt. 1686 w.
Jno. 1722 w.
Lancaster
Wm. 1688 i.
Louisa
Rosamond 1785 w.
Isaac 1787 w.
Mecklenburg
Jas. 1785 w.
Norfolk
Michaell 1665 w.
Northampton
Geo. 1651 i.
Richd. 1665 w.
Robt. 1698 w.
Geo. 1735 w.
Thos. 1749 w.
Jane 1761 w.
Robt. 1783 w.
Robt. 1785 i.
Jno. 1786 w.
Edwin 1792 i.
Chas. 1797 i.
Powhatan
Chas. 1785 w.
Prince Edward
Jno. Jr. 1792 w.
Thos. 1792 i.
Richd. 1798 i.
Princess Anne
Francis 1772 i.
Rappahannock
Joane 1683 w.
Richmond
Henry 1700 w.
Robt. 1705 w.
Wm. 1726 i.
Jas. 1768 i.
Mary 1775 nw.

Robt. 1784 w.
Southampton
Wm. 1797 w.
Surry
Henry 1678 w.
Henry 1721 w.
Sampson 1778 w.
Washington
Wm. 1796 w.
Westmoreland
Wm. 1697 w.
York
Jno. 1658 w.
Wm. White 1659 i.
Nicholas 1660 w.
Thos. 1666 w.
Robt. 1668 i.
Jno. 1681 w.
Nicholas 1687 w.
Jno. 1694 w.
Nicholas 1694 w.
Stephen 1699 i.
Michael 1715 i.
CLARKSON
Albemarle
Jno. 1795 i.
Charlotte
Jos. 1790 i.
Goochland
Jno. 1759 w.
Jno. 1789 i.
CLARY
Brunswick
Harwood 1790 w.
Surry
Thos. 1707 w.
Wm. 1725 w.
Benj. 1735 i.
Chas. 1762 w.
Jordan 1771 w.
Barnes 1772 i.
Sussex
Thos. 1763 w.
Thos. 1769 w.
Bird 1770 w.
Jas. 1773 w.
CLATON
York
Thos. 1702 i.
CLAUD
Prince George
Phill 1720 i.
Southampton
Philip 1773 w.
Joshua 1775 w.
Joshua 1777 w.
Jno. 1794 w.
Edwin 1797 w.
CLAUGHTON
Lunenburg
Jno. 1791 i.

Northumberland
Jas. 1652 i.
Pemberton 1711 i.
Jno. 1726 w.
Jno. 1751 w.
Jno. 1760 w.
Pemberton 1773 w.
Richd. 1773 w.
Richd. Sr. 1773 w.
Jas. 1778 i.
Griffithello 1782 i.
Thos. 1783 w.
Jno. 1796 w.
Jas. 1797 w.
Jno. 1798 i.
CLAUSE
Princess Anne
Sarah 1719 w.
CLAWR
Culpeper
Michael 1763 w.
CLAWSON
Berkeley
Richd. 1776 w.
CLAXON
York
Jno. 1659 w.
CLAY
Amelia
Jas. 1756 i.
Jno. Sr. 1782 w.
Chas. 1792 i.
Chesterfield
Henry Sr. 17— i.
Henry 1749 w.
Chas. 1754 w.
Jno. 1761 w.
Chas. 1765 i.
Cumberland
Henry 1764 w.
Henry 1768 a.
Halifax
Caleb 1786 i.
James 1791 w.
Henrico
Chas. 1686 i.
Isle of Wight
Jno. 1675 w.
Wm. 1675 w.
Wm. 1683-4 i.
Jno. 1685 i.
Montgomery
David 1792 i.
Northampton
Thos. 1691 i.
Thos. 1697 i.
Severn 1706 w.
Jno. 1732 i.
Jno. 1737 w.
Powhatan
Chas. 1789 w.

Pittsylvania
Henry 1777 w.
Prince George
Thos. 1726 w.
Princess Anne
Ann 1782 i.
Peter 1782 w.
Westmoreland
Francis 1667 w.
CLAYBORN
Amelia
Jas. 1755 w.
CLAYBROOK
Amelia
Mary 1798 w.
Peter 1798 w.
Amherst
Milly 1792 w.
Henry
Jos. 1791 w.
CLAYCOMT
Berkeley
Conrad 1784 i.
CLAYE
Surry
Thos. 1679 w.
CLAYLAND
Lancaster
Allen 1688 i.
CLAYPOLE
Augusta
Wm. 1759 i.
Loudoun
Jos. 1784 w.
CLAYPOOL
Greenbrier
Jas. 1785 w.
Jos. 1790 i.
CLAYPOOLE
Hardy
Jas. 1789 w.
CLAYTON
Brunswick
Geo. 1776 w.
Chesterfield
Frances 1771 w.
Culpeper
Philip 1786 w.
Frederick
Saml. 1784 i.
Essex
Saml. 1735 w.
Hanover
Arthur 1733 a.
Isle of Wight
Jno. 1759 w.
Wm. 1778 w.
Lancaster
Jno. 1787 w.
Wm. W. 1794 i.

Louisa
Jno. 1767 w.
Northumberland
Jno. 1726 w.
Richmond
Alex. 1718 i.
Spotsylvania
Jacob 1771 w.
CLAYTOR
Fauquier
Jno. 1773 i.
King George
Eliz. 1767 w.
Wm. 1773 a.
Richmond
Thos. 1735 i.
Mary 1797 i.
Westmoreland
Thos. 1718 w.
Katherine 1720 w.
Alvin 1755 i.
Thos. 1756 w.
Jno. 1773 i.
Wm. 1783 w.
CLEAR
Botetourt
Geo. 1790 i.
CLEARE
Middlesex
Jno. 1777 i.
CLEATON
Chesterfield
Jno. 1785 w.
Lancaster
Judith 1710 i.
Mecklenburg
Poythress 1784 i.
Wm. 1796 w.
CLEAVELAND
Albemarle
Alex. 1776 w.
Jno. 1786 w.
Loudoun
Wm. 1788 w.
Orange
Jno. 1778 w.
CLEAVELEY
Henrico
Francis 1695 a.
CLEAVER
Middlesex
Wm. 1768 i.
CLEAVES
Richmond
Patience 1714 w.
CLEEVE
Northampton
Jno. 1677 w.
CLEEVES
Norfolk
Jas. 1764 w.

CLEFT
Northampton
Jno. 1736 w.
CLEGG
Northampton
Jno. 1704 w.
Henry 1711 i.
Ezekiel 1732 i.
Henry 1737 w.
Ann 1743 w.
Henry 1748 i.
Peter Sr. 1749 w.
Abigail 1750 w.
Holloway 1752 w.
Hilary 1755 w.
Peter 1761 w.
Isaac 1784 w.
Esther 1787 w.
Hillery 1792 w.
Isaac 1795 w.
Peter 1796 w.
CLEM
Shenandoah
Davis 1789 a.
Jno. David 1789 i.
CLEMENS
Accomack
Ann 1751 w.
Lancaster
Wm. 1688 i.
Norfolk
Wm. 1688 w.
Northampton
Peter 1728 i.
Surry
Saml. 1728 w.
CLEMENT
Amelia
Wm. Sr. 1760 w.
Wm. 1761 i.
Wm. 1766 w.
Charlotte
Francis 1767 w.
Pittsylvania
Benj. 1780 w.
Susannah 1788 i.
Webster 1790 i.
Stafford
Edwd. 1733 w.
CLEMENTS
Amelia
Wm. 1741 a.
Jno. Jr. 1783 i.
Jno. 1791 w.
Jno. 1793 i.
Ama 1797 w.
Augusta
Jacob 1759 w.
Jacob 1793 i.
Brunswick
Robt. 1784 i.

Reuben 1790 i.
Charlotte
Benj. 1783 w.
Essex
Jno. 1767 w.
Pitman 1778 w.
Henry H. 1794 w.
Ewen 1797 i.
Goochland
Stephen 1746 w.
Thos. 1776 i.
Isle of Wight
Francis 1717 w.
Jno. 1744 i.
Montgomery
Jos. 1787 a.
Pittsylvania
Jas. 1780 i.
Jas. 1792 i.
Southampton
Benj. 1778 w.
Benj. 1780 w.
Benj. Jr. 1782 w.
Thos. 1789 i.
Spotsylvania
Jno. 1781 w.
Stafford
Edwd. 1702 i.
Surry
Jno. 1710 w.
Bartholomew 1713 w.
Francis 1721 w.
Wm. 1753 i.
Sussex
Thos. Sr. 1785 w.
Westmoreland
Jno. 1701 i.
David 1713 w.
CLEMET
Frederick
Alex. 1753 w.
CLEMMONS
Accomack
Stephen 1786 w.
CLEMON
Augusta
Catherine 1793 w.
CLEMONDS
Mecklenburg
Edmund 1785 w.
CLEMONS
Accomack
Ann 1752 i.
Amelia
Wm. 1774 w.
Augusta
Christian 1783 w.
Christian 1790 i.
Brunswick
Jno. 1741 w.

Charlotte
Francis 1773 i.
Surry
Jno. 1721 i.
CLENDENNING
Augusta
Archd. 1749 w.
Archd. 1764 i.
CLEPHORN
Lancaster
Chas. 1748 w.
CLERK
Lancaster
Wm. 1750 w.
CLERKE
Henrico
Richd. 1675-6 op.
Jno. 1678 w.
Allenson 1710 w.
CLESKIN
Frederick
Jno. 1764 i.
CLEVELAND
Loudoun
Jas. 1791 w.
Frances 1794 w.
Jas. 1799 i.
Southampton
Wm. 1782 w.
Surry
Jas. 1766 w.
Peggy 1784 i.
CLEVINGER
Shenandoah
Jos. 1783 w.
CLEWES
Loudoun
Jos. 1792 w.
CLEWSIS
Loudoun
Thos. 1784 nw.
CLIBORN
Chesterfield
Jno. 1764 w.
Jonas 1795 i.
CLICE
Loudoun
Jno. 1789 i.
CLICK
Northampton
Jno. 1712 i.
CLIFF
Westmoreland
Jas. 1796 i.
CLIFFORD
York
Jno. 1694 w.
CLIFT
Culpeper
Wm. 1750 i.

Wm. 1783 w.
King George
Jno. 1799 w.
Pittsylvania
Thos. 1798 i.
Stafford
Jno. 1758 i.
CLIFTON
Fairfax
Wm. 1772 i.
Eliz. 1773 w.
Thos. 1794 a.
King George
Wm. 1781 w.
Prince George
Thos. 1724 i.
Southampton
Benj. 1772 w.
Thos. 1779 i.
Thos. 1781 w.
Cordey 1798 i.
Stafford
Burdit 1762 w.
Sussex
Wm. 1756 w.
York
Mary 1724 i.
Benj. 1728 w.
CLINCH
Brunswick
Christopher 1768 i.
Culpeper
Jacob 1777 w.
Surry
Christopher 1679 w.
Christopher 1737 w.
Hannah 1739 w.
Jas. 1747 i.
Jos. Jno. 1756 i.
Philip 1768 i.
Wm. 1786 w.
CLINKER
Middlesex
Thos. 1728 i.
CLINTON
Essex
Eliz. 1726 w.
Thos. 1734 i.
CLITHRELL
York
Jno. 1748 i.
CLONINGER
Augusta
Valentine 1784 w.
CLOPTON
Cumberland
Reubin 1796 i.
Robt. 1783 w.
Goochland
Benj. 1791 i.
Benj. C. 1797 w.

York
Mary 1678 w.
CLORE
Albemarle
Jacob 1759 w.
Culpeper
Geo. 1751 w.
Peter 1762 w.
Eliz. 1766 i.
Jno. 1785 w.
Jno. 1787 i.
CLOTTIER
Isle of Wight
Jno. 1727 i.
CLOTWORTHY
Henrico
Walter 1701 i.
CLOUD
Frederick
Mordecai 1789 w.
Shenandoah
Henry 1788 w.
CLOUDAS
Charlotte
George 1783 i.
Essex
Jno. 1791 w.
Abner 1794 i.
Goochland
Geo. 1789 w.
Middlesex
Wm. 1780 w.
CLOUGH
Powhatan
Molly 1779 w.
CLOUSER
Frederick
Henry 1772 a.
CLOVELL
Accomack
Peter 1692 w.
CLOWDAS
Essex
Jno. 1775 w.
Middlesex
Wm. 1770 i.
CLOWES
Princess Anne
Wm. 1700 i.
CLOWSER
Frederick
Henry 1764 i.
CLOYD
Augusta
Jno. 1761 i.
Jno. 1767 a.
Rockbridge
David 1789 w.
David 1792 w.
Eliz. 1797 w.
Andrew 1798 i.

CLUTTEN
Lancaster
Jesse 1792 i.
CLUTTON
Lancaster
Jno. 1784 w.
CLYBORN
Henrico
Jno. 1685 i.
Jno. 1689 i.
Frances 1712 i.
CLYBORNE
Chesterfield
Jonas 1798 i.
COALE
Lancaster
Jno. 1700 i.
COANE
Northumberland
Jno. 1761 w.
Martha 1768 w.
COARTNEY
Westmoreland
Jno. 1749 i.
COAT
Norfolk
Agnis 1783 i.
COATES
Essex
Saml. 1780 w.
Mary 1785 w.
Henrico
Jno. 1692 i.
Richmond
Saml. 1718 i.
Surry
Jno. 1744 w.
COATS
Halifax
Judith 1760 i.
Saml. 1797 i.
Lancaster
Thos. 1749 i.
Jno. 1765 i.
Geo. 1769 w.
Norfolk
Jno. 1714 w.
Princess Anne
Willis 1779 w.
Jesse 1788 i.
COBB
Accomack
Ingold 1708 w.
Amelia
Theodosha 1782 w.
Chesterfield
Jno. 17— i.
Matthew 1766 w.
Isle of Wight
Nicholas 1686 nw.
Pharoah 1701 i.

Edward 1730-31 w.
Edward 1742 w.
Norfolk
Paul 1724 i.
Northampton
Jno. 1688 w.
Jno. 1766 w.
Wm. 1796 i.
Prince Edward
Sarah 1787 w.
Southampton
Nicholas 1756 w.
Wm. 1757 w.
Michael 1763 w.
Jos. 1778 i.
Wm. 1778 i.
Hardy 1782 i.
Saml. 1789 w.
Jno. 1792 w.
Henry 1795 w.
Michael 1795 w.
COBBS
Albemarle
Thos. 1761 w.
Amelia
Saml. 1757 w.
Edith 1761 w.
Bedford
Edmund 1799 i.
Reuben 1799 i.
Campbell
Jno. 1795 i.
Chesterfield
Jno. 1777 i.
Ambrose 1783 w.
Halifax
Robt. 1769 w.
Isle of Wight
Jos. 1653 w.
Louisa
Saml. 1758 w.
York
Robt. 1682-3 i.
Ambrose 1684-5 i.
Edmund 1693 w.
Thos. 1702 w.
Wm. 1705 i.
Ambrose 1718 w.
Robt. 1725 w.
Robt. 1727 w.
Thos. 1750 w.
Edmd. 1759 i.
Thos. 1774 w.
Thos. 1777 w.
Mary 1778 w.
Eliz. 1785 w.
COBNALL
Essex
Simon 1705-6 i.

COBORNE
York
Henry 1685 i.
COBURN
Augusta
Jas. 1749 i.
COCHRAN
Amherst
Wm. 1786 a.
Augusta
Jno. 1765 i.
Jno. 1783 i.
Frederick
Wm. 1795 w.
Ohio
Wm. 1783 i.
COCHREN
Westmoreland
Christian 1708 w.
COCK
Culpeper
Chas. G. 1798 i.
York
———— 1764 i.
COCKARELL
Northumberland
Jno. 1781 i.
COCKARILL
Northumberland
Eliz. 1719 w.
Richd. 1762 w.
Paley 1797 w.
COCKBURN
Middlesex
Adam 1729 i.
COCKE
Albemarle
Jno. 1759 w.
Amelia
Abraham 1760 w.
Stephen 1795 w.
Brunswick
Brazure 1770 w.
Thos. 1773 w.
Charles City
Littleberry 1773 w.
Rebecca H. 1793 w.
Jane 1794 w.
Fairfax
Wm. 1758 i.
Goochland
Francis 1799 w.
Thos. 1799 i.
Henrico
Wm. 1693 w.
Thos. 1696 w.
Jno. 1700 i.
Richd. 1706 w.
Thos. 1707 w.
Thos. 1711 w.
Henry 1714 w.

Wm. 1717 w.
Wm. 1736 i.
Thos. 1737 a.
Jas. Powell 1747 w.
Pleasants 1749 i.
Jas. Powell 1751 w.
Eliz. 1752 w.
Jas. 1783 w.
Loudoun
Wm. 1794 w.
Lunenburg
Jas. 1753 w.
Jas. 1761 w.
Abraham 1782 w.
Middlesex
Nicho. 1687 w.
Maurice 1696 w.
Jane 1694 w.
Norfolk
Argent 1737 w.
Powhatan
Chastaine 1796 w.
Princess Anne
Peter 1697 i.
Thos. 1697 w.
Christopher 1716 w.
Southampton
Hartwell 1793 w.
Surry
Wm. 1720 w.
Wm. 1732 i.
Walter Flood 1738 w.
Nicholas 1748 w.
Thos. 1750 w.
Hannah 1752 w.
Lemuel 1756 w.
Benj. 1763 w.
Wm. 1763 w.
Wm. 1765 i.
Jane 1766 w.
Hartwell 1772 w.
Richd. 1772 w.
Henry 1777 w.
Allen 1781 w.
Sarah 1781 w.
Jno. 1782 i.
Thos. 1783 w.
Jesse 1786 w.
Jno. Hartwell 1791 w.
Wm. 1792 i.
Benj. 1794 w.
Saml. 1795 w.
Henry 1796 i.
Robt. 1797 i.
Jno. 1798 w.
Benj. Allen 1799 w.
Sussex
Jno. 1786 w.
COCKEN
Princess Anne
Richd. 1716 i.

COCKER
Isle of Wight
Arthur 1750 i.
Surry
Wm. 1677 w.
COCKERANE
Culpeper
Patrick 1790 w.
COCKERHAM
Lunenburg
Henry 1757 w.
Letty 1790 w.
Mecklenburg
Philip 1776 w.
Surry
Wm. 1706 w.
Thos. 1717 w.
COCKERILL
Fairfax
Sampson 1791 w.
Loudoun
Thos. 1778 w.
Northumberland
Wm. 1784 w.
Eliz. 1797 w.
COCKET
York
Jas. 1744 i.
COCKETT
York
Ephraim 1747 i.
COCKINS
Isle of Wight
Wm. 1678 i.
COCKLEY
King George
Geo. 1785 a.
COCKRALL
Northumberland
Thos. 1760 w.
COCKRAN
Botetourt
Peter 1771 i.
COCKRELL
Fauquier
Jos. 1772 i.
Anderson 1792 w.
Frederick
Thos. 1755 i.
Lancaster
Presley 1783 i.
COCKRIL
Northumberland
Jno. 1747 i.
COCKRILL
Fairfax
Jos. 1795 w.
Loudoun
Christopher 1796 i.
Northumberland
Thos. 1770 w.
Jno. 1780 w.

COCKRILLE
Northumberland
Jno. 1704 w.
COCKROFT
Princess Anne
Jno. 1728 w.
Thos. 1736 i.
COCKRUFFT
Princess Anne
Thos. 1707 w.
COCKRUFT
Norfolk
Wm. 1686-7 w.
COCKRUM
Henry
Nathan 1778 i.
COCKS
Frederick
Wm. 1769 w.
Surry
Jno. 1782 w.
Wm. 1798 w.
Charity 1799 w.
Sussex
Jno. 1774 w.
Jas. 1785 w.
COCKSEY
Isle of Wight
Wm. 1747 w.
COCKSHUD
Northumberland
Edwd. 1660 w.
COE
Accomack
Timothy 1688 w.
Sarah Sr. 1718 i.
Benj. 1721 i.
Fairfax
Wm. 1793 w.
COELL
Northampton
Benj. 1703 i.
COFER
Culpeper
Thos. 1791 w.
Fairfax
Francis 1744 a.
Prince William
Mary 1741 w.
COFEY
Essex
Edward 1716 i.
COFFEE
Prince Edward
Peter 1771 w.
COFFELTS
Frederick
Peter 1767 i.
COFFER
Fairfax
Thos. Withers 1782 w.

Isle of Wight
Wm. 1769 w.
COFFETS
Shenandoah
Geo. 1787 a.
COFFETT
Shenandoah
Elias 1778 w.
COFFEY
Albemarle
Jno. 1775 w.
Essex
Edwd. 1716 w.
Spotsylvania
Timothy 1738 w.
COFFIN
King George
Sudrath 1740 a.
COFFMAN
Augusta
Jno. Nicholas 1770 i.
Henry 1770 i.
Berkeley
Jno. 1781 i.
Jacob 1787 w.
Shenandoah
Jacob 1774 a.
Jno. 1782 i.
Michael 1789 w.
COFFY
Lancaster
Hugh 1717 i.
COGBILL
Chesterfield
Thos. 1782 w.
Edwd. 1785 w.
Geo. 1786 w.
Chas. 1789 w.
Ann 1791 w.
Ann 1793 i.
Jas. 1797 w.
Jesse 1798 w.
Henrico
Geo. 1698 i.
COGER
Franklin
Jacob 1798 i.
COGGAN
Isle of Wight
Wm. 1728 i.
Robt. 1738 w.
Jno. 1782 w.
Southampton
Jno. 1767 i.
COGGEN
Surry
Wm. 1716 i.
COGGIN
Essex
Ann 1710 i.
Thos. 1707-8 w.

Isle of Wight
Robt. 1785 w.
Catherine 1799 w.
Northumberland
Thos. 1655 i.
Surry
Wm. 1677 w.
Thos. 1737 i.
COGHILL
Essex
Jas. 1748 i.
Fredk. 1758 w.
Fredk. 1768 i.
Thos. 1786 w.
Thos. 1790 i.
Rappahannock
Jas. 1685 w.
COHAGAN
Fairfax
Michael 1793 a.
COHEN
Fairfax
Jacob 1798 w.
COHENOUR
Shenandoah
Henry 1789 i.
COHOREN
Westmoreland
Wm. 1707 i.
COIL
Washington
Jas. 1780 w.
COINER
Augusta
Michael 1794 i.
Michael 1797 w.
COKE
Accomack
Richd. 1764 w.
York
Jno. 1767 w.
COKEE
Norfolk
Eliz. 1677-8 w.
COKELEY
King George
Jas. 1789 a.
COKER
Greensville
Jas. 1793 w.
Southampton
Jno. 1789 i.
Henry 1790 w.
Henry 1796 i.
Nathl. 1792 i.
Surry
Jno. 1720 w.
Margt. 1721 w.
COKERAN
Fincastle
Wm. 1773 i.

COLBERT
York
Richd. 1795 i.
COLBIRD
Accomack
Isaac 1788 i.
COLBOURNE
Accomack
Robt. 1698 w.
COLBREATH
Lunenburg
Jno. 1759 w.
COLBURN
Accomack
Robt. 1701 i.
COLBURT
Northumberland
Reuben 1720 w.
COLCLOUGH
Northumberland
Geo. 1662 i.
Stafford
Hannah 1700 w.
Alex. 1739 nw.
Rachel 1748 w.
COLE
Accomack
Robt. 1722 i.
Robt. 1732 i.
Peter 1791 w.
Amelia
Jas. 1745 a.
Berkeley
Jacob 1788 w.
Charles City
Anthony 1797 i.
Charlotte
Jas. Jr. 1782 w.
Chesterfield
Anthony 17— i.
Robt. 1755 w.
Hamblin Sr. 1778 w.
Hamblin 1780 i.
Robt. 1781 w.
Robt. Sr. 1782 i.
Robt. Sr. 1794 i.
Culpeper
Jno. 1757 w.
Susannah 1761 w.
Essex
Wm. 1710 i.
Wm. 1735 w.
Thos. 1750 i.
Asael 1754 i.
Eliz. 1757 i.
Geo. 1770 i.
Isaiah 1772 w.
Robt. 1773 i.
Wm. 1784 w.
Goochland
Mary 1770 w.

Henrico
Jno. 1691 i.
Robt. 1718 w.
Jos. 1728 i.
Henry
Walter King 1795 i.
Isle of Wight
Wm. 1670 i.
Jno. 1777 i.
Lancaster
Francis 1658 w.
Louisa
Richd. 1781 w.
Wm. 1795 a.
Middlesex
James 1727 i.
Norfolk
Jno. 1723 i.
Northumberland
Robt. 1728-9 w.
Edmond 1751 i.
Jno. 1777 i.
Wm. 1784 w.
Prince William
Danl. 1797 w.
Jno. 1797 i.
Rappahannock
Robt. 1682 w.
Richmond
Saml. 1710 w.
Jno. 1790 w.
Washington
Wm. 1776 w.
Hugh 1780 w.
Jos. 1785 w.
Isaac 1792 w.
Westmoreland
Richd. 1664 w.
Robt. 1707 w.
Jno. 1712 i.
Morrice 1762 i.
Wythe
Jean 1794 i.
COLEBRAITH
Mecklenburg
Edwd. 1770 w.
COLEBURN
Accomack
Robt. 1752 w.
Wm. 1752 w.
Eliz. 1768 w.
Jno. 1776 w.
Jno. 1784 i.
Robt. 1785 w.
Wm. 1790 w.
Thos. 1791 i.
Cathren 1795 w.
Jas. 1797 i.
COLELOUGH
Fairfax
Benj. 1782 w.

Loudoun
Robt. 1762 i.
COLEMAN
Albemarle
Jas. 1796 w.
Amelia
Wm. 1745 w.
Godfrey 1752 w.
Wm. Sr. 1768 w.
Jos. 1771 w.
Danl. Jr. 1789 w.
Peter 1794 w.
Abraham 1795 i.
Isaac 1798 i.
Amherst
Jno. 1778 w.
Jno. Danl. 1784 w.
Danl. 1785 w.
Geo. 1787 w.
Millie 1799 w.
Culpeper
Robt. 1793 w.
Cumberland
Danl. 1763 w.
Patience 1771 w.
Danl. 1772 w.
Essex
Robt. 1713 w.
Spilsbee 1727 i.
Geo. 1733 w.
Geo. 1753 w.
Thos. 1760 w.
Robt. Spilsbe 1761 w.
Jno. 1794 w.
Whitehead 1799 w.
Goochland
Saml. 1748 w.
Isle of Wight
Robt. 1715 w.
Lancaster
Richd. 1743 i.
Richd. 1745 i.
Loudoun
Richd. 1764 w.
Jno. 1775 i.
Mecklenburg
Jas. 1797 i.
Cluverius 1799 w.
Northumberland
Jno. 1744 w.
Mary 1764 i.
Chas. 1778 i.
Orange
Jas. 1764 w.
Robt. 1795 w.
Jas. 1797 i.
Pittsylvania
Stephen 1798 w.
Richmond
Richd. 1710 w.
Jas. 1712 i.

Spotsylvania
Spilbe 1757 w.
Jno. 1763 w.
Richd. 1783 a.
Clayton 1788 w.
Richd. 1788 w.
Richd. Jr. 1793 a.
Edwd. 1795 w.
Westmoreland
Wm. 1665 w.
Jas. 1723 w.
Jane 1723 i.
Jno. 1726 i.
Jas. 1736 w.
COLES
Amelia
James 1745 i.
Halifax
Walter 1782 w.
Mary 1793 w.
Walter 1793 w.
Mildred 1799 w.
Wm. 1799 w.
Henrico
Jos. 1734 i.
Jno. 1747 w.
Isle of Wight
Sarah 1721 i.
Northumberland
Mary Ann 1749 i.
Jno. 1757 w.
Edwd. 1764 w.
Jno. 1773 w.
Jno. 1799 w.
COLESON
Brunswick
Jesse 1737 w.
Jos. 1737 i.
COLESTON
Isle of Wight
Saml. 1779 w.
COLESTRAM
Westmoreland
Jas. 1670 w.
COLEY
Goochland
Francis 1777 i.
COLFER
Princess Anne
Jas. 1792 w.
COLGAN
Middlesex
Jno. 1753 a.
COLHOON
Prince Edward
Adam 1796 w.
COLIER
Isle of Wight
Robt. 1670 i.

COLLARD
Fairfax
Saml. 1786 i.
COLLEE
Accomack
Sylvanus 1720 w.
COLLENS
Norfolk
Giles 1674 w.
Washington
Wm. 1796 i.
COLLEROW
Essex
Jno. 1701 i.
COLLET
Berkeley
Moses 1782 w.
Frederick
Abraham 1754 i.
COLLETT
York
Jno. 1750 w.
Susan 1752 w.
COLLEY
Augusta
Jno. 1760 w.
Jno. 1767 nw.
Goochland
Francis 1776 w.
Mecklenburg
Edwd. 1798 w.
Norfolk
Edwd. 1751 w.
Jno. 1753 w.
Jno. 1758 w.
Jno. 1763 w.
Sander 1768 w.
Edwd. 1784 i.
Wm. 1785 i.
Edwd. 1794 w.
COLLIAR
Southampton
Geo. 1764 w.
COLLICK
Norfolk
Alex. 1753 w.
COLLICOTT
Amelia
Wm. 1765 w.
COLLIER
Augusta
Jno. 1765 i.
Brunswick
Wm. 1759 w.
Thos. 1760 w.
Jno. 1769 i.
Amos. 1771 i.
Isaac 1771 w.
Chas. 1775 w.
Lewis 1790 i.
Wm. 1798 i.

Charlotte
Thos. 1787 w.
Benj. 1791 w.
Jno. 1793 w.
Greensville
Moses 1784 i.
Mary 1786 w.
Moses 1791 i.
Thos. 1795 i.
Mecklenburg
Nathl. 1774 i.
Howell 1785 w.
Fredk. 1798 w.
Northampton
Peter 1703 i.
Peter 1705 i.
Prince Edward
Chas. 1795 i.
Richmond
Mary 1766 w.
Stafford
Jno. 1704 i.
Surry
Jno. 1677 i.
Jno. 1716 i.
Jno. 1727 w.
Thos. 1727 w.
Jno. 1732 w.
Benj. 1736 i.
Jno. 1754 w.
Benj. 1767 i.
Jno. 1768 i.
Ann 1770 w.
Thos. 1771 w.
Henry 1777 w.
Thos. 1777 i.
Lucy 1778 i.
Charity P. 1785 w.
Benj. 1786 i.
Lucy 1791 w.
Jno. 1795 i.
Jas. 1796 i.
Wm. 1797 w.
Stephen 1798 i.
Polly W. 1788 i.
Samson 1788 w.
Saml. 1788 i.
York
Thos. 1704 w.
Chas. 1721 w.
COLLIFER
King George
Shadrach 1741 i.
COLLIN
Lancaster
Jas. 1705 i.
COLLINGS
Accomack
Thos. 1765 w.
Isle of Wight
Wm. 1768 w.

Norfolk
Jno. 1710 a.
Eliz. 1712 w.
Princess Anne
Giles 1708 w.
Gilles 1714 i.
COLLINGSWORTH
Westmoreland
Thos. 1691 w.
Thos. 1735 w.
Thos. 1751 w.
Jno. 1772 w.
Jno. Sr. 1781 w.
Willoughby 1782 w.
Sarah 1790 w.
COLLINS
Accomack
Jno. 1711 w.
Jno. (elder) 1740 i.
Jno. 1743 w.
Joshua 1768 w.
Mary 1769 w.
Elijah 1770 w.
Jas. 1783 w.
Thos. 1788 w.
Martha 1789 i.
Jos. 1795 i.
Augusta
Jno. 1775 a.
Charlotte
Richd. 1784 i.
Culpeper
———— 1755 i.
Jas. 1781 w.
Essex
Wm. 1765 i.
Frederick
Wm. 1786 i.
Goochland
Matthew 1760 w.
Isle of Wight
Wm. 1687 i.
Jno. 1695-6 i.
Alice 1699 i.
Lancaster
Catherine 1762 i.
Middlesex
Anthony 1742 i.
Jas. 1782 w.
Wm. 1782 w.
Norfolk
Andrew 1743 i.
Timothy 1775 w.
Geo. 1792 w.
Northampton
Thos. 1687 w.
Jno. 1735 i.
Northumberland
Jas. 1724-5 i.
Timothy 1747 i.

Orange
Jno. 1770 w.
Pittsylvania
Wm. 1781 w.
Princess Anne
Johanna 1710 w.
Henry 1714 i.
Giles 1728 w.
Henry 1740 w.
Ann 1745 w.
Geo. 1766 w.
Jno. 1778 w.
Nathl. 1782 w.
Henry 1791 w.
Rappahannock
Jno. 1686 i.
Richmond
Wm. 1717 i.
Chris. 1781 w.
Chris. 1786 i.
Spotsylvania
Thos. 1748 w.
Thos. 1752 w.
Jos. 1757 w.
Thos. 1777 a.
Surry
Jno. 1694 i.
Jno. 1750 i.
Robt. 1795 w.
Wm. 1796 i.
Westmoreland
Jno. 1731 i.
Thos. 1795 i.
York
Henry 1692-3 w.
Ann 1693 nw.
Matthew 1697 i.
COLLINSWORTH
Richmond
Edmd. 1752 w.
Westmoreland
Thos. 1775 i.
Jno. 1795 i.
COLLOCK
Norfolk
Alex. 1753 w.
COLLOM
King George
Jno. 1776 a.
COLLONS
Princess Anne
Jno. 1790 w.
COLLONY
Accomack
Owen 1693 w.
Owen 1716 w.
COLLWELL
Norfolk
Jas. 1735 w.

COLLYER
York
Isaac 1688 w.
COLONY
Accomack
Bryan 1744 i.
Benj. 1776 w.
Jno. 1788 i.
COLQUET
Cumberland
Jno. 1769 w.
COLQUHOON
Spotsylvania
Jas. 1783 a.
COLQUHOUN
Goochland
Chas. 1778 i.
COLQUIT
Essex
Jas. 1774 w.
Halifax
Anthony 1774 w.
Francis 1799 i.
COLSON
Spotsylvania
Chas. 1770 w.
Sussex
Wm. 1779 w.
Sarah 1785 w.
COLSTON
Frederick
Thos. 1789 w.
Northumberland
Travers 1751 w.
Richmond
Wm. 1701 w.
Wm. 1721 w.
Chas. 1724 i.
Rebecca 1726 w.
Wm. 1781 w.
COLTIER
Surry
Jno. 1679 a.
COLTON
Northumberland
Jno. 1740 i.
COLVARD
Albemarle
Benj. 1786 w.
Benj. 1794 i.
COLVILL
Fairfax
Jno. 1756 w.
Thos. 1767 w.
Frances 1773 w.
COLVILLE
Frederick
Jos. 1758 w.
Jas. 1777 w.

COLVIN
King George
Jno. 1757 i.
Norfolk
Jno. 1773 i.
Westmoreland
Chas. 1725 i.
COLWELL
Surry
Wm. 1772 w.
COLWILL
Washington
Andrew 1797 i.
COLYER
Augusta
Jno. 1765 w.
COMAN
York
Wm. 1712 i.
COMB
Frederick
Henry 1767 w.
COMBES
Middlesex
Jno. 1675 a.
Richmond
Jno. 1716 w.
COMBS
Amelia
———— 1762 i.
Fauquier
Jno. Jr. 1781 nw.
Halifax
Geo. 1799 i.
Isle of Wight
Henry 1678 w.
King George
Archdell 1735 i.
Loudoun
Andrew 1774 w.
Elisha 1780 i.
Richmond
Wm. 1719 i.
Stafford
Jno. 1785 w.
Shenandoah
Robt. 1781 i.
Robt. 1782 a.
COMER
Charles City
Chas. 1799 w.
Charlotte
Eliz. 1790 w.
Lunenburg
Jno. 1764 i.
COMERS
Halifax
Saml. 1788 w.
Lunenburg
Jno. 1796 i.

COMES
Westmoreland
Philip 1731 i.
COMINGS
Middlesex
Geo. 1698 i.
COMINS
York
Nich. 1656 w.
COMINGER
Cumberland
Cor'n'l 1757 w.
COMMINGS
Princess Anne
Benj. 1744 w.
COMMINS
Northumberland
Henry 1772 i.
COMMUSKY
Westmoreland
Edwd. 1732 i.
COMOSKEY
Westmoreland
Cornelius 1720 i.
COMPTON
Amelia
Jno. Sr. 1772 i.
Jno. 1783 w.
Botetourt
Jno. 1778 i.
Jno. 1780 i.
Culpeper
Zackariah 1790 i.
Essex
Richd. 1748 w.
Wm. 1751 w.
Fairfax
Jno. 1797 a.
Middlesex
Jas. 1744 i.
Pittsylvania
Wm. 1774 i.
York
Jno. 1675-6 w.
CONAH
Northampton
Terrence 1724 w.
CONALLY
Berkeley
Jenkins 1786 i.
Norfolk
Matthew 1760 w.
CONAWAY
Norfolk
Jas. 1777 w.
CONDALL
Norfolk
Frances 1765 w.
CONDON
Middlesex
David 1743 i.

Norfolk
Patrick 1717 w.
Princess Anne
Jas. 1746 i.
CONDUIT
Essex
Nathl. 1730 w.
Susannah 1736 w.
Nathl. 1757 w.
Jno. 1774 w.
CONE
Lancaster
Jno. 1701-2 w.
CONELLY
Lancaster
Patrick 1738 i.
Westmoreland
Timothy 1751 i.
CONER
Westmoreland
Sarah 1741 i.
CONEY
Westmoreland
Thos. 1742 i.
CONIER
Westmoreland
Tarence 1738 w.
CONLEY
Richmond
Wm. 1746 i.
CONLY
Goochland
Bryant 1784 i.
CONN
Berkeley
Saml. 1799 i.
Loudoun
Hugh 1772 w.
CONNALEY
Essex
Thos. 1713 i.
CONNAR
Accomack
Patrick 1721 w.
CONNARD
Hampshire
Jas. 1796 w.
CONNELL
Fairfax
Simon 1744 w.
Henrico
Susannah 1796 i.
Mecklenburg
Robt. 1779 w.
Northumberland
Jno. 1753 i.
Prince George
Timothy 1727 i.
Richmond
Michael 1718 w.

CONNELLY
Augusta
Jas. 1752 i.
Bedford
Jas. 1780 w.
Brunswick
Wm. 1783 i.
Essex
Edmd. 1738 i.
Frederick
Thos. 1759 i.
Wm. 1760 i.
Lancaster
Geo. 1785 w.
Montgomery
Thos. 1793 i.
Richmond
Jno. 1754 i.
CONNELY
Augusta
Thos. 1794 w.
Frederick
Derbe 1749 i.
Darby 1751 i.
CONNER
Campbell
Allen 1799 w.
Culpeper
Philemon 1774 w.
Essex
Martin 1748 i.
Greenbrier
Jno. 1791 w.
Loudoun
Saml. 1768 i.
Edwd. 1770 i.
Chas. 1778 i.
Chas. 1778 i.
Norfolk
Lewis 1697-8 w.
Anthony 1742-3 i.
Jno. 1750 w.
Lewis 1753 w.
Craford 1757 w.
Chas. 1777 w.
Princess Anne
Monica 1757 w.
Spotsylvania
Chas. 1768 a.
Westmoreland
Jno. 1746 i.
CONNERS
Accomack
Jas. 1721 w.
CONNERY
Shenandoah
Jno. 1782 i.
CONNESY
Shenandoah
Jno. 1781 a.

CONNIL
Fairfax
Jas. 1777 w.
CONNLY
Augusta
Darby 1779 i.
CONNOLLY
Lancaster
Geo. 1772 w.
Richmond
Wm. 1778 i.
CONNOLY
Frederick
Con. 1743 a.
CONNOR
Culpeper
Margerit 1751 w.
Lancaster
Jas. 1730 i.
Norfolk
Keader 1721 w.
Lewis 1723 w.
York
Gearold 1696 i.
CONNOWAY
Accomack
Thos. 1695 nw.
Pittsylvania
Jas. 1798 w.
CONNS
Pittsylvania
Jos. 1796 i.
CONNYERS
Stafford
Henry 1733 w.
CONQUEST
Accomack
Nathl. 1760 i.
Wm. 1792 w.
Ann 1795 w.
Wm. Sr. 1799 w.
CONRAD
Augusta
Jno. 1759 i.
Stephen 1767 i.
Jacob 1776 w.
Frederick
Fredk. 1794 w.
Jno. 1796 i.
Loudoun
Jonathan 1796 w.
CONREE
Lancaster
Dennis 1731 i.
CONROD
Augusta
Hance 1758 a.
Botetourt
Mathias 1793 i.
Greenbrier
Geo. 1784 i.

CONRY
Lancaster
Dennis 1735 w.
CONSALVO
Princess Anne
Wm. 1758 i.
Henry 1764 i.
CONSAUL
Princess Anne
Wm. 1753 i.
Jno. 1774 i.
CONSOLVO
Norfolk
Chas. 1768 w.
CONSTANTINE
Rappahannock
Wm. 1687 w.
Essex
Wm. 1697 w.
CONWAY
Fauquier
Thos. 1784 w.
Lancaster
Eleanor 1718 w.
Peter 1753 w.
Geo. 1754 w.
Geo. 1758 i.
Edwin 1764 w.
Betty 1768 i.
Walter 1790 i.
Norfolk
Jas. 1779 i.
Northumberland
Dennis 1709 w.
Dennis 1721 w.
Jno. 1727 w.
Anne 1728 i.
Dennis 1739 i.
Geo. 1748 w.
Jno. 1755 w.
Jas. 1768 i.
Saml. 1778 i.
Dennis 1780 w.
Dennis Jr. 1780 w.
Frances Sinah 1782 w
Thos. 1782 w.
Thos. 1784 w.
Edwin 1786 w.
Edwin 1786 i.
Pittsylvania
Jas. 1777 i.
Richmond
Cloe 1774 w.
Stafford
Sarah 1756 w
CONWELL
Ohio
Yates 1784 w.
CONYER
Chesterfield
Margt. 1761 i.

CONYERRS
Stafford
Henry 1756 i.
CONYERS
Lancaster
Dennys 1656 w.
COOCK
Norfolk
Richd. 1686-7 w.
COODRAK
Northumberland
Joanna 1774 i.
COOK
Accomack
Thos. 1760 i.
Wm. 1761 w.
Rachel 1765 w.
Augusta
Patrick 1748 w.
Henry 1756 i.
Bedford
Andrew 1778 w.
Brunswick
Henry 1774 w.
Wm. 1791 i.
Charlotte
Jno. 1777 i.
Cumberland
Jno. 1775 w.
Jas. 1782 i.
Essex
Richd. 1711 i.
Jno. 1727 w.
Jno. 1733 w.
Susannah 1731 i.
Mary 1733 w.
Wm. 1733 w.
Thos. 1733 i.
Fairfax
Edwd. 1750 i.
Fauquier
Jno. 1760 w.
Greenbrier
Vallentine 1797 w.
Halifax
Jno. 1799 i.
Henrico
Mary 1737 a.
Henry
Wm. 1777 w.
Jas. 1779 i.
Benj. 1783 i.
Benj. 1791 i.
Isle of Wight
Thos. Sr. 1736 w.
Thos. 1736 w.
Reuben 1751 w.
Joel 1761 w.
Jno. 1777 w.
Nathan 1786 w.

Lunenburg
Abraham 1748 w.
Norfolk
Robt. 1747 i.
Northumberland
Jno. 1653 i.
Orange
Thos. 1793 w.
Pittsylvania
Elijah 1798 i.
Prince Edward
Sarah 1784 w.
Princess Anne
Richd. 1738 w.
Richmond
Saml. 1729 w.
Ann 1734 i.
Saml. 1737 w.
Anthony 1769 i.
Wm. 1782 i.
Shenandoah
Peter 1772 a.
Jno. 1787 i.
Spotsylvania
Robt. 1757 a.
Surry
Avis 1711 w.
Jno. 1711 w.
Wm. 1740 w.
Sussex
Reuben 1760 w.
Jos. 1764 i.
Wm. 1764 w.
Reuben 1768 w.
Wm. 1774 i.
Ann 1781 w.
Westmoreland
Jno. 1750 i.
York
———— 1764 i.
Jas. 1767 w.
Frances 1768 i.
Mary 1774 i.
Francis 1779 i.
COOKE
Amelia
Jno. 1765 i.
Berkeley
Giles 1799 w.
Brunswick
Jno. 1743 w.
Robt. 1748 w.
Chesterfield
Jacob 1752 w.
Wm. 1754 w.
Essex
Mary 1733 i.
Fairfax
Edwd. 1749 i.
Fauquier
Littleton 1782 w.

Goochland
Jno. 1737 i.
Greenbrier
Thos. 1787 i.
Henrico
Mary 1734 i.
Isle of Wight
Henry 1698 w.
Wm. Sr. 1698 w.
Jno. 1703-4 w.
Isach 1728 w.
Lancaster
Wm. 1681 i.
Jno. 1726 i.
Norfolk
Jno. 1652 nw.
Northumberland
Wm. 1759 w.
Stafford
Jno. 1732 w.
Travers 1759 w.
Elizabeth 1784 w.
Surry
Jas. 1701-2 w.
Jno. 1715 i.
Sussex
Eliz. 1765 i.
Wm. 1778 w.
Jas. 1782 i.
York
Jno. 1695 nw.
Jno. 1726 w.
Bennett 1793 w.
COOKEN
Essex
Thos. 1708 i.
COOKER
Berkeley
Henry 1786 i.
Henry 1789 w.
Brunswick
Jno. 1759 w.
COOKMAN
Northumberland
Rice 1794 w.
COOKS
Isle of Wight
Isaac 1728 i.
Jno. 1777 i.
COOKSEY
Prince William
Vincent 1783 i.
COOKSON
Henrico
Wm. 1677 w.
COOL
Hampshire
Philip 1795 w.
COOLEY
York
Mary 1778 i.

COOMS
Fairfax
Catherine 1754 w.
COON
Berkeley
Adam 1790 i.
Adam 1797 i.
COONES
Culpeper
Jos. 1795 i.
COONTZ
Berkeley
Henry 1787 w.
COOPE
Lancaster
Thos. 1713 i.
COOPER
Bedford
Wm. 1777 i.
Berkeley
Adam 1778 i.
Hazalet 1794 w.
Isaac 1798 i.
Botetourt
Jas. 1784 w.
Culpeper
John 1780 i.
Judith 1784 i.
Essex
Thos. 1694 w.
Thos. 1709-10 w.
Wm. 1730 w.
Richd. 1736 w.
Thos. 1754 i.
Eliz. 1774 w.
Jas. 1791 w.
Fairfax
Joel 1786 w.
Frederick
Jacob 1758 w.
Leonard 1766 w.
Thos. 1785 w.
Halifax
Jno. 1763 i.
Hampshire
Thos. 1799 w.
Isle of Wight
Justinian 1650 w.
Robert 1714 i.
Lancaster
Thos. 1658 i.
Loudoun
Appollos 1778 i.
Fredk. 1783 w.
Lunenburg
Jno. 1768 w.
Francis 1777 w.
Mecklenburg
Jas. 1774 w.
Norfolk
Wm. Sr. 1693 w.

Jno. 1718 w.
Jos. 1752 w.
Solomon 1761 i.
Hilary 1766 i.
Isaac 1768 w.
Jas. 1787 i.
Northumberland
Sampson 1659 w.
Geo. 1711 w.
Orange
Barbara 1735 a.
Jas. 1799 w.
Prince George
Jno. 1717 i.
Princess Anne
Edwd. 1697 w.
Chas. 1700 w.
Edwd. 1702 i.
Thos. 1726 w.
Harry 1767 i.
Henry 1780 w.
Rappahannock
Thos. 1675 w.
Rockbridge
Jas. 1781 w.
Wm. 1782 w.
Southampton
Wm. 1762 w.
Jno. 1774 i.
Jno. 1784 i.
Jesse 1794 i.
Jesse 1797 i.
Spotsylvania
Jno. 1728 a.
Surry
Jno. 1677 i.
Jas. 1734 w.
Wm. 1759 w.
Jno. 1768 w.
Geo. 1782 w.
Jno. 1795 w.
Jno. 1797 i.
Sussex
Jas. 1782 w.
Thos. 1786 w.
Richd. 1791 w.
Washington
Abraham 1779 i.
Westmoreland
Eliz. 1729 w.
Jno. 1735 w.
Hannah 1739 w.
Hugh 1746 i.
York
Jas. 1680 w.
Saml. 1720 w.
COOR
Northampton
Posthumos 1772 i.

COOTS
Goochland
Isaac 1762 i.
Lancaster
Wm. 1726 i.
COPE
Accomack
Thos. 1726 i.
Thos. 1747 i.
King George
Henry 1765 w.
Washington
Jno. 1786 w.
Westmoreland
Wm. 1744 i.
COPEDGE
Northumberland
Benj. 1724 i.
Rebeckah 1768 w.
COPELAND
Essex
Wm. 1701 w.
Nicklis 1720 w.
Rebecca 1735 w.
Isle of Wight
Jos. 1726 w.
Thos. 1728 j.
Jno. 1737 i.
Thos. 1742 w.
Sarah 1795 w.
COPES
Accomack
Mathias 1718 w.
Thos. 1721 w.
Mary 1726 w.
Giles 1730 i.
Thos. 1742 w.
Peter Parker 1760 w.
Robt. 1766 w.
Giles 1767 w.
Parker 1770 w.
Thos. 1785 w.
Giles 1790 w.
Southy 1790 w.
Hancock 1795 w.
Northampton
Giles 1696 w.
COPHER
Isle of Wight
Wm. 1769 i.
Thos. 1784 w.
Jesse 1789 w.
Jas. 1796 w.
Benj. 1797 w.
Mary 1798 w.
Christian 1799 w.
COPLANDE
Augusta
Benj. 1754 i.

COPNALL
Essex
Simon 1705 w.
COPPAGE
Northumberland
Wm. 1700 w.
COPPEDGE
Northumberland
Jno. 1727 i.
Jno. 1745 w.
Jno. 1746 i.
Chas. 1750 w.
Lazarus 1762 i.
Wm. 1766 w.
Jesse 1770 w.
Chas. 1786 w.
COPPER
Fairfax
Cyrus 1790 i.
COPPIDGE
Northumberland
Jas. 1741 w.
COPPLEY
Richmond
Richd. 1717 w.
CORAM
Fauquier
Champ 1788 i.
CORBELL
Northumberland
Jno. 1711 i.
Jno. 1751 i.
Spencer 1771 w.
Jane 1772 w.
Jno. 1779 i.
Wm. 1780 i.
Jno. 1787 w.
Jno. 1789 w.
Princess Anne
Wm. 1733 w.
Richd. 1720 w.
CORBETT
Isle of Wight
Saml. 1790 i.
Princess Anne
Caleb 1791 w.
Richd. 1795 w.
CORBILL
Isle of Wight
Benj. 1769 i.
CORBIN
Accomack
Robt. 1743 w.
David 1745 w.
Ralph 1746 nw.
Robt. 1767 i.
Geo. 1771 w.
Coventon 1778 w.
Geo. 1784 i.
Geo. Bonnewell
1787 w.

Geo. B. 1792 i.
Geo. 1793 w.
Ralph Jr. 1799 w.
Culpeper
Jno. 1786 w.
Jeremiah 1790 i.
Wm. 1797 w.
Essex
Jno. 1758 i.
Thos. 1799 w.
King George
Wm. 1733 i.
Jno. 1758 w.
Middlesex
Gawin 1790 i.
Northampton
Geo. 1713 w.
Pittsylvania
Thos. 1793 w.
Wm. 1796 i.
Richmond
Hannah 1782 w.
Westmoreland
Gawin 1760 w.
Lettice 1768 i.
CORBITT
Isle of Wight
Saml. 1789 w.
CORBPELL
Northumberland
Gilbert 1799 w.
CORD
Accomack
Arthur 1751 i.
Frederick
Isaac 1753 a.
CORDELL
Loudoun
Jacob 1799 i.
CORDER
Fauquier
Jno. 1760 i.
CORDING
Norfolk
Thos. 1699 w.
CORDON
Norfolk
Patrick 1717 w.
CORDY
Frederick
Thos. 1764 w.
CORE
Accomack
Edmd. 1779 w.
Levi 1784 w.
Edmd. 1789 i.
Zorobabel 1799 w.
Northampton
Jno. 1712 w.
Rebecca 1728 w.
Jno. 1750 w.

Edmd. Sr. 1772 w.
Posthumos 1772 w.
Eleazer 1786 w.
Eliazer 1790 i.
Zorobabel 1798 w.
COREN
Surry
Jos. 1702 w.
CORGIN
Accomack
Neil 1793 i.
CORIDON
York
Wm. 1753 w.
Mary 1754 w.
CORKER
York
Capt. 1677-8 i.
CORKERHIM
Halifax
Danl. 1767 w.
CORLEE
York
Edwd. 1731 w.
CORLEW
York
Edwd. 1749 i.
Christopher 1772 w.
Anne 1782 w.
CORLEY
Culpeper
Richd. 1790 w.
Cumberland
Jas. 1794 w.
Goochland
Nathl. Sr. 1796 w.
Halifax
Bartlett 1789 w.
Orange
Jno. 1743 a.
York
Edwd. 1735 w.
CORMICK
Northampton
Mull 1734 i.
CORMITHE
Pittsylvania
Robt. 1777 i.
CORN
Albemarle
Jno. Adam 1758 i.
Stafford
Wm. 1699 i.
CORNELIOUS
Middlesex
Jno. 1789 w.
Lancaster
Wm. 1778 i.
CORNELIUS
Amelia
Rowland 1765 i.

Lancaster
Robt. 1680 i.
Wm. 1720 w.
Rowland 1727 i.
Jno. 1740 i.
Wm. 1749-50 i.
Jno. 1775 i.
Lunenburg
Jos. 1750 i.
Northampton
Jno. 1655 w.
CORNELL
Mecklenburg
Robt. 1779 i.
Surry
Saml. 1679 i.
CORNELUSON
Loudoun
Garrett 1779 w.
CORNER
Halifax
Thos. 1794 w.
Thos. Sr. 1794 i.
York
Thos. 1702 a.
CORNETT
Sussex
Geo. 1767 i.
Martha 1772 i.
CORNETTE
Montgomery
Jas. 1797 i.
CORNEWELL
Norfolk
Joshua 1686-7 w.
CORNICK
Accomack
Jno. 1772 w.
Jno. 1774 i.
Princess Anne
Wm. 1700 w.
Martin 1701 i.
Jno. 1727 w.
Joel 1727 w.
Wm. 1753 w.
Elias 1770 w.
Henry 1771 w.
Anne 1772 w.
Lemuel 1774 w.
Frances 1776 w.
Joel 1777 i.
Horatio 1789 w.
Nathan 1790 i.
Jno. 1795 w.
CORNICKE
Princess Anne
Alice 1709 w.
CORNISH
Fairfax
Chas. 1775 w.
Eliz. 1776 w.

Northampton
Wm. 1654 w.
Wm. 1727 w.
Richd. 1750 w.
Wm. 1785 w.
Thos. 1740 w.
Princess Anne
Elisha 1774 i.
Michael 1776 i.
Elias 1782 i.
Jno. 1784 w.
Thos. 1784 w.
Nancy 1787 i.
Amy 1788 w.
CORNOCK
Norfolk
Margt. 1764 w.
CORNWALL
Prince William
Chas. 1782 i.
Noah 1791 i.
CORNWELL
Fauquier
Peter 1776 w.
Prince William
Chas. 1781 w.
Chas. 1797 w.
Surry
Saml. 1718 w.
Isaac 1727 w.
Saml. 1727 w.
Wm. 1759 i.
Jacob 1772 w.
Sussex
Saml 1762 w.
CORPERA
Princess Anne
Jno. 1701 a.
CORPEREW
Norfolk
Jno. 1700 w.
CORPREW
Princess Anne
Thos. 1722 w.
Norfolk
Jno. 1746-7 i.
Jno. 1769 i.
Thos. 1796 w.
CORRELL
Princess Anne
Wm. 1758 w.
CORRIE
Essex
Jno. 1748 i.
Jno. 1787 w.
Richmond
Hannah 1791 w.
CORROWAY
Princess Anne
Richd. 1710 w.

CORSEY
Isle of Wight
Frances 1679 w.
Richd. 1679 w.
CORSY
Isle of Wight
Jno. 1700 i.
CORY
Louisa
Edwd. 1782 w.
COSBY
Chesterfield
Jno. 1781 w.
Jno. 1791 i.
Louisa
Jno. 1761 w.
David 1770 w.
Ann 1785 w.
Jno. Sr. 1785 a.
Mary 1785 w.
Jno. 1789 a.
Jane 1790 w.
Powhatan
Wm. 1796 w.
York
Jno. 1695 i.
Sarah 1740 w.
Saml. 1743 w.
Jas. 1747 w.
Jno. 1750 i.
Mark 1752 w.
Stripling 1771 i.
Jas. 1784 i.
Stripling 1785 i
Jno. 1788 w.
Ann 1794 w.
COSEBY
York
Jas. 1718 w.
COSENS
Lancaster
Jno. 1697 nw.
COSH
Rappahannock
Robt. 1687 i.
COSIER
Northampton
Will 1665 i.
COSLEY
Halifax
Bartlett 1789 i.
COSTEN
Norfolk
Walter 1694 w.
COSTIN
Northampton
Jno. 1684 nw.
Stephen 1686 w.
Francis 1721 w.
Jacob 1743 w.
Francis 1750 w.

Wm. 1787 i.
Matthew 1799 i.
COSTON
Essex
Jasper 1724 i.
COTMAN
Halifax
Benedictus 1770 w.
COTNER
Augusta
Peter 1753 w.
COTRILL
Northumberland
Danl. 1752 i.
COTTEL
Princess Anne
Sarah 1782 i.
COTTEN
Lancaster
Thos. 1710 w.
Richd. 1718 w.
Princess Anne
Jas. 1772 w.
Surry
Thos. 1718 a.
Mary 1728 w.
COTTERELL
Westmoreland
Wm. 1736 i.
COTTINGHAM
Accomack
Thos. 1775 w.
COTTLE
Greenbrier
Uriah 1779 w.
Norfolk
Thos. 1712 w.
Thos. 1750 i.
Josiah 1751 i.
Eliz. 1758 w.
Princess Anne
Wm. 1761 w.
COTTON
Culpeper
Jas. 1786 w.
Loudoun
Wm. 1788 w.
Northampton
Wm. 1646 w.
Prince George
Richd. 1718 i.
Princess Anne
Jas. 1734 i.
Sussex
Thos. 1779 w.
Richd. 1790 w.
Nathl. 1794 w.
Harris 1797 i.
COTTRELL
Amherst
Thos. 1762 w.

Henrico
Richd. 1792 w.
Northumberland
Jno. 1726-7 w.
Andrew 1727 w.
Jno. Jr. 1729-30 i.
Eliz. 1765 i.
Thos. 1771 i.
Jno. 1792 w.
COUCH
Pittsylvania
Jno. 1772 w.
York
Lawrence 1701 w.
COUCHMAN
Berkeley
Benedick 1797 i.
Hardy
Adam 1786 w.
COUE
Goochland
Jno. 1730 i.
COUGHLAND
Essex
Francis 1720 i.
Mary 1764 w.
COUGILL
Loudoun
Jas. 1799 i.
COULBURN
Accomack
Temperance 1767 w.
COULSON
Grayson
Isaac 1795 i.
COULTER
Augusta
Jno. 1788 w.
Rockbridge
Jas. 1784 w.
COULTESS
Norfolk
Jno. 1770 w.
COULTHARD
York
Jno. 1756 w.
COUNCIL
Isle of Wight
Hodges 1699 w.
Susanna 1756 i.
Susannah 1757 w.
Peter 1761 i.
Jas. 1763 i.
Jno. 1795 w.
Joshua 1798 i.
Saml. 1796 w.
Southampton
Hodges 1762 i.
Jas. 1790 w.
Jno. 1793 w.

100   VIRGINIA WILLS AND ADMINISTRATIONS

COUNCILL
Isle of Wight
Hodges 1726 w.
Jas. 1728-9 i.
Hardy 1750 w.
Joshua 1793 w.
COUPELAND
Middlesex
Wm. 1678 a.
COUPLAND
Isle of Wight
Jos. 1776 w.
COUR
Albemarle
Claude de la 1789 w.
COURER
Mecklenburg
Saml. 1796 i.
COURTENAY
King George
Jno. 1756 w.
COURTNALL
Westmoreland
Jas. 1727 i.
COURTNEY
Accomack
Chas. 1764 w.
Fauquier
Francis 1789 i.
King George
Jno. 1756 i.
Jno. 1775 w.
Mecklenburg
Clack 1771 i.
Sampson 1795 i.
Northumberland
Jno. 1761 i.
Jas. 1770 i.
Westmoreland
Wm. 1734 i.
Mary 1756 w.
Saml. 1761 w.
Leonard Sr. 1780 w.
Jas. 1777 i.
COURTS
Culpeper
Wm. 1781 w.
COUS
Richmond
Jno. 1724 w.
COUSENS
Chesterfield
Chas. 1752 w.
Lunenburg
Peter 1775 i.
COUSER
York
Thos. 1734 w.
COUSIN
Cumberland
Eliz. 1758 i.

COUSINS
Amelia
Chas. 1759 w.
Robt. 1769 w.
Robt. 1782 i.
Jno. 1795 w.
Jno. Jr. 1795 i.
Chesterfield
Chas. 1754 i.
Geo. 1779 w.
Ann 1786 w.
Jno. 1799 i.
COUTANCEAU
Northumberland
Jacob 1664 w.
Peter 1709 w.
Jno. 1718 w.
COUTHORN
Essex
Thos. 1734 i.
COUTSMAN
Loudoun
Jacob 1780 w.
COUTTEN
King George
Wm. 1754 a.
COUTTS
Augusta
Jno. 1778 i.
Henrico
Patrick 1784 w.
Patrick 1787 w.
COVENTON
Northampton
Richardus 1774 i.
COVERLY
Accomack
Nathl. 1789 w.
Norfolk
Lemuel 1774 w.
COVINGTON
Chesterfield
Jno. 1790 w.
Wm. 1799 w.
Culpeper
Robt. 1766 w.
Thos. 1767 w.
Wm. 1784 w.
Essex
Wm. 1697 w.
Thos. 1700 i.
Mary 1701 w.
Wm. 1721 w.
Richd. 1726 w.
Thos. 1734 w.
Richd. 1759 w.
Wm. 1762 w.
Richd. 1764 i.
Luke 1783 w.
Wm. 1792 i.

Halifax
Jno. 1778 i.
Thos. 1782 w.
Lunenburg
Edmd. 1785 w.
Northumberland
Eliz. 1786 w.
Nehemiah 1799 w.
COWAN
Berkeley
Thos. 1780 i.
Hampshire
Robt. 1795 w.
Ohio
Wm. 1792 w.
Washington
Andrew 1798 i.
COWARD
Accomack
Wm. 1777 w.
Wm. 1778 i.
Wm. 1779 i.
Northampton
Saml. 1716 w.
Saml. 1755 w.
Orange
Jas. 1756 i.
Westmoreland
Wm. 1793 w.
COWDEN
Augusta
Wm. 1748 w.
COWDREY
Accomack
Savage 1783 w.
COWDRY
Northampton
Benj. 1684 w.
Thos. 1698 w.
Josias 1726 w.
Wm. 1734 i.
Thos. 1743 i.
Thos. 1778 w.
COWELL
Princess Anne
Luke 1774 w.
COWEN
Washington
Saml. 1779 i.
COWENOVER
Berkeley
Jno. 1778 w.
COWGILL
Loudoun
Ralph Sr. 1795 w.
Jas. 1799 w.
COWLES
Charles City
Thos. 1770 w.

COWLEY
Henrico
Abraham 1752 w.
Westmoreland
Jno. 1731 i.
COWLING
Isle of Wight
Thos. 1790 w.
COWN
Berkeley
Jas. 1798 w.
COWNTS
Stafford
Jos. 1730 w.
COWPER
Norfolk
Thos. 1645 i.
Ann 1795 w.
Jno. 1799 w.
COWPLAND
Chesterfield
Jas. 17— i.
COX
Accomack
Jos. 1780 w.
Albemarle
Jno. 1762 w.
Amelia
Henry Jr. 1781 w.
Judith Hughes
1791 w.
Amherst
Edwd. 1780 i.
Archelaus 1789 w.
Botetourt
Edwd. 1782 i.
Chesterfield
Henry 17— i.
Henry 1779 w.
Wm. 1780 i.
Milner 1782 w.
Judith 1785 w.
Judith 1789 i.
Milner 1792 i.
Higgason 1793 w.
Jno. 1795 w.
Hickson 1796 i.
Eliz. 1799 w.
Culpeper
Wm. 1781 i.
Cumberland
Stephen 1749 w.
Fredk. 1755 w.
Stephen 1758 w.
Nicholas 1759 w.
Judith 1774 w.
Essex
Jno. 1695 w.
Jno. 1750 i.
Ann 1751 w.
Wm. 1754 w.

Lucretia 1775 i.
Henry 1793 w.
Ann 1796 i.
Fairfax
Presley 1783 i.
Eliz. 1792 w.
Goochland
Geo. 1728 w.
Bartho. 1731 w.
Martha 1734 w.
Matthew 1736 i.
Sarah 1747 w.
Jno. 1785 w.
Jno. 1791 i.
Henrico
Jno. 1692 w.
Jno. 1710 w.
Wm. 1712 w.
Jas. 1713 w.
Martha 1734 w.
Richd. Sr. 1734 w.
Wm. 1734 i.
Mary 1735 w.
Richd. 1735 i.
Henry 1745 i.
Geo. 1785 w.
Mary 1788 w.
Edward 1798 w.
Henry
Wm. 1792 i.
Jno. 1794 w.
Isle of Wight
Francis 1734 i.
Lancaster
Jno. 1655 w.
Jno. 1693 i.
Jno. Sr. 1736 w.
Thos. 1753 w.
Mary 1763 i.
Presly 1798 w.
Lunenburg
Jno. (elder) 1764 w
Jno. 1791 i.
Mecklenburg
Jno. 1794 w.
Jno. (2) 1794 w.
Northampton
Richd. 1702 i.
Richd. 1739 w.
Moses 1765 i.
Jas. 1778 i.
Northumberland
Geo. 1762 i.
Wm. 1781 w.
Peter 1792 w.
Geo. 1799 w.
Ohio
Gabriel 1778 w.
Orange
Jas. 1738 w.
Wm. 1752 w.

Wm. 1783 w.
Powhatan
Richd. 1790 i.
Edwd. 1791 w.
Henry 1791 w.
Wm. 1791 i.
Jno. 1793 w.
Geo. 1795 w.
Wm. 1796 w.
Princess Anne
Wm. 1748 i.
Eliz. 1768 w.
Jno. 1771 w.
Edwd. 1772 w.
Wm. 1777 w.
Geo. 1789 i.
Benj. 1796 w.
Wm. 1798 i.
Rappahannock
Henry 1675 w.
Westmoreland
Vincent 1698 w.
Vincent 1713 w.
Charnock 1744 w.
Peter 1748 w.
Charnock 1749 i.
Charnock 1751 w.
Wm. 1758 i.
Peter Presley 1762 w.
Presley 1766 w.
Presley 1776.
Fleet 1791 w.
Fleet 1799 w.
York
Thos. 1693 w.
Chas. 1716 i.
Geo. 1724 ab.
Jno. 1773 i.
Cox 1776 w.
COXE
Richmond
Lem. 1710 w.
COYLE
Fairfax
Michael 1774 w.
Frederick
Jas. 1769 w.
Spotsylvania
Benj. 1783 w.
COYNE
Orange
Edwd. 1748 w.
Eliz. 1751 w.
COZHER
Northampton
Bartho. 1733 i.
COZIER
Northampton
Bartho. 1677 w.
Eliz. 1683 i.

COZLER
Northampton
Bartho. 1733 w.
CRABB
Essex
Hugh 1697 w.
Westmoreland
Osman 1719 w.
Danl. 1738 w.
Osman 1765 i.
Jno. 1779 w.
Jane 1781 w.
Vincent 1783 w.
Wm. Middleton
1784 i.
Benedict 1791 i.
Jno. 1799 w.
CRABBIN
Norfolk
Alex. 1759 i.
CRABEL
Shenandoah
Jno. 1789 w.
CRABTREE
Washington
Wm. 1777 i.
CRADDOCK
Amelia
Henry 1783 w.
Richd. 1785 w.
Wm. Cross 1795 w.
Jane 1796 w.
Wm. 1797 i.
Pittsylvania
Jno. 1793 w.
Goochland
Thos. 1752 i.
CRADOCK
Westmoreland
Richd. 1713 i.
CRAFE
Loudoun
Philip 1784 w.
CRAFFORD
Prince Edward
Thos. 1783 i.
Southampton
Henry 1771 w.
Jno. 1782 i.
Stafford
Robt. 1704 i.
Surry
Robt. 1735 w.
Carter 1743 w.
Jno. 1758 w.
Carter 1782 w.
CRAFORD
Norfolk
Wm. 1762 w.
Stafford
Jno. 1733 w.

CRAFT
Princess Anne
Joshua 1767 w.
CRAFTON
Lunenburg
Jas. 1779 w.
CRAFTS
Brunswick
Thos. 1755 w.
Isle of Wight
Thos. 1727 w.
Thos. 1794 w.
CRAGG
Lancaster
Duncan 1706 i.
Sussex
Wm. 1760 w.
CRAGUE
Fairfax
Paul 1749 i.
CRAIG
Augusta
Jno. 1756 i.
Wm. 1759 w.
Jno. 1774 a.
Robt. 1788 w.
Jas. Sr. 1791 w.
Fairfax
David 1760 i.
Frederick
Robt. 1769 w.
Thos. 1779 w.
Greenbrier
Wm. 1799 i.
Lunenburg
Jas. 1795 w.
Mary 1798 i.
Norfolk
Jas. 1671 nw.
Wythe
Robert 1794 w.
York
Wm. 1720 w.
Alex. 1776 w.
Jas. 1794 w.
Jas. 1797 i.
CRAIGE
Augusta
Jno. 1785 i.
CRAIGHEAD
Franklin
Peter 1786 w.
CRAIKE
Norfolk
Robt. 1756 i.
CRAILMANE
King George
Jane 1765 i.
CRAIN
Northumberland
Jas. 1770 w.
Stephen 1771 i.

CRAINE
Lancaster
Jas. 1789 i.
Middlesex
Jno. 1790 i.
Wm. 1795 i.
CRALLE
Northumberland
Thos. 1726-7 w.
Jno. Sr. 1728 w.
Jno. 1758 w.
Kenner 1785 w.
Kenner 1792 i.
CRAMER
Frederick
Josiah 1754 i.
CRANDALL
York
Jas. 1765 w.
CRANE
Berkeley
Jas. 1795 w.
Pittsylvania
Jas. 1794 i.
Spotsylvania
Jno. 1774 w.
Wm. 1778 w.
CRANK
King George
Wm. 1787 a.
Louisa
Henry 1796 w.
Geo. 1798 w.
Middlesex
Matt. 1718 w.
Thos. 1721 w.
CRANKSHAW
Norfolk
Thos. 1701 w.
CRANSTON
York
Benj. 1753 i.
CRAPELL
Northumberland
Dorothy 1724 i.
CRARY
Wythe
Jno. 1795 i.
CRASHLEY
Princess Anne
Peter 1717 w.
CRASK
Lancaster
Wm. 1710 i.
Rappahannock
Edmd. 1682 w.
Eliz. 1683 w.
Richmond
Jno. 1708 i.
Wm. 1744 w.
Wm. 1765 w.
Jno. 1785 w.

Sarah 1792 w.
Jas. 1794 w.
CRASWELL
Essex
Jas. 1720 i.
CRATCH
Norfolk
Thos. 1788 w.
CRATCHETT
Norfolk
Wm. 1719-20 w.
CRATCHIT
Norfolk
Jno. 1718 w.
CRAVEN
Augusta
Robt. 1762 w.
Frederick
Thos. 1748 i.
Loudoun
Thos. 1795 i.
Northumberland
Chas. 1741 w.
Fincastle
Jos. 1775 a.
CRAW
Montgomery
Jno. 1798 i.
CRAWFORD
Amherst
David 1761 w.
David 1766 w.
Benj. 1789 w.
Augusta
Jas. 1751 i.
Alex. 1765 i.
Geo. 1780 w.
Patrick 1787 w.
Geo. 1790 w.
Eliz. 1791 w.
Jno. 1791 w.
Wm. 1792 w.
Jas. 1793 w.
Saml. 1795 w.
Jas. 1798 w.
Bedford
Jno. 1778 i.
Botetourt
Andrew 1791 w.
Jno. 1796 w.
Culpeper
Wm. 1779 w.
Frederick
Jas. 1778 i.
Goochland
Jas. 1766 w.
Halifax
Wm. 1763 a.
Henrico
Jno. 1796 i.

Madison
Wm. 1793 w.
Oliver 1799 a.
Montgomery
Jno. 1779 i.
Thos. 1797 i.
Norfolk
Wm. 1700 w.
Orange
Barnet 1746 i.
Rockbridge
Wm. 1783 w.
Spotsylvania
Wm. 1734 w.
Jno. 1798 w.
Jno. 1765 a.
Surry
Robt. 1714 w.
Westmoreland
Robt. 1751 w.
CRAWLEY
Amelia
Wm. 1738 w.
Sarah 1761 w.
Wm. Sr. 1780 w.
Wm. 1784 w.
David 1787 w.
Jno. 1790 w.
Benj. 1794 w.
Augusta
Margt. 1776 i.
Halifax
Jeffry 1762 w.
Lancaster
Hugh 1729 i.
Lunenburg
Basil 1786 w.
Prince George
David 172— w.
York
Robt. 1697-8 i.
Nathl. 1717 w.
Ellinder 1739 w.
Robt. 1740 i.
Jno. 1748 w.
Robt. 1759 w.
Nathl. 1764 w.
Nathl. 1769 w.
CRAYER
Surry
Nicholas 1787 i.
CREABER (?)
Augusta
Wm. 1797 w.
CREACKON
Norfolk
Edmind 1680 w.
CREAGH
Sussex
Jno. 1784 w.

CREAGLER
Spotsylvania
Jacob 1734 a.
CREAKMUR
Norfolk
Edwd. 1739 w.
CREAL
Culpeper
Jno. 1793 i.
Northumberland
Chas. 1727 i.
Eliz. 1727 w.
CREAMER
Essex
Wm. 1701 i.
Loudoun
Jacob 1782 i.
CREASE
York
Thos 1757 w.
CREASEY
Bedford
Jno. 1793 i.
Fluvanna
Judy 1787 w.
Wm. 1799 i.
CREASY
Cumberland
Jno. 1750 w.
CREATCH
Norfolk
Mary 1713 w.
CREATCHER
Norfolk
Thos. 1718 i.
CRECKMUR
Norfolk
Jno. 1711 w.
CREDELL
Bedford
Humphrey 1780 w.
CREDLE
Campbell
Mildred 1794 w.
Mecklenburg
Briant 1777 w.
CREECH
Norfolk
Thos. 1777 w.
Henry 1779 i.
Thos. 1787 i.
CREED
Norfolk
Thos. 1785 i.
Princess Anne
Thos. 1734 w.
Dennis 1735 w.
Thos. 1736 i.
Jane 1740 w.
Martha 1746 w.
Wm. 1772 w.

Anne 1774 w.
Jno. 1782 i.
Westmoreland
Jas. 1733 w.
Jno. 1746 w.
Eliz. 1737 i.
CREEDLE
Cumberland
Wm. 1791 i.
Ann 1798 w.
Norfolk
Wm. 1747 w.
Mary 1755 w.
Mary 1771 i.
Princess Anne
Catran 1728 w.
CREEDLEY,
Princess Anne
Wm. 1720 i.
CREEKMOR
Norfolk
Jno. 1711 w.
CREEKMORE
Norfolk
Jno. 1711 a.
Edwd. 1742 i.
Willis 1742 w.
Wm. 1756 w.
David 1791 i.
CREEKMUR
Norfolk
Edmd. 1737 w.
Willis 1742 w.
Solomon 1749 w.
Jobb 1752 i.
Jos. 1761 w.
Joshua 1762 w.
John 1765 i.
Joab 1766 nw.
Mary 1766 w.
Solomon 1769 w.
Edmond 1772 w.
Foreman 1772 w.
Mary 1772 w.
Thos. 1772 i.
Abel 1779 w.
Frances 1783 w.
Edmd. 1785 w.
Jos. 1785 w.
Edmd. 1786 i.
Willoughby 1796 i.
Edwd. 1797 w.
Thos. 1798 w.
Wright 1799 w.
CREEKMURD
Norfolk
Edwd. 1747 i.
CREEL
Pittsylvania
Jno. 1788 i.

Bedford
Ann 1775 i.
Lancaster
Jos. 1750 w.
CREELE
Northumberland
Jno. 1720 w.
CREEVER
Augusta
Wm. 1798 i.
CREESE
Halifax
Wm. 1773 w.
CREIGHTON
Augusta
Jno. 1767 i.
Berkeley
Robt. 1797 w.
Rappahannock
Henry 1677 w.
CREMER
Norfolk
Jas. 1797 w.
CREMOR
Essex
Wm. 1697 i.
Norfolk
Geo. 1679 w.
CRENSHAW
Amelia
Elkanah 1772 w.
Wm. 1787 w.
Charlotte
Chas. 1794 i.
Halifax
Cornelius 1792 i.
Lunenburg
Jos. 1758 w.
Thos. 1786 w.
Cornelius 1786 w.
Nathl. 1794 i.
Danl. 1795 w.
Ananias 1799 w.
Pittsylvania
Wm. 1789 i.
Prince Edward
Jno. 1777 w.
Southampton
Thos. 1780 w.
Anne 1783 w.
Jno. 1787 w.
CREPSAP (Cressap?)
Hampshire
Michael 1775 w.
CRESSY
Henrico
Jno. 1692 w.
CRESWELL
Isle of Wight
Clement 1683 w.

CRETCHIT
Norfolk
Jno. 1718 w.
CREW
Charles City
Ellyson 1773 i.
Benj. 1792 w.
Benj. Sr. 1793 i.
Benj. 1799 w.
CREWDSON
Fluvanna
Jas. 1798 w.
Richmond
Wm. Sr. 1775 w.
CREWES
Surry
Thos. 1697-8 w.
CREWS
Amherst
Gideon 1797 i.
Charlotte
Jno. 1792 w.
Goochland
Jos. 1740 i.
Henrico
Jas. 1680 w.
Louisa
Wm. W. 1771 w.
Lunenburg
Richd. 1792 w.
Northampton
Jno. 1711 i.
Surry
Thos. 1728 w.
Wm. 1751 i.
Wm. 1772 w.
CRIBBIN
Richmond
Thos. 1727 i.
CRIBLE
Culpeper
Geo. Fredk. 1765 i.
CRIDDLE
Cumberland
Allen 1777 w.
CRIDER
Halifax
Jno. 1777 i.
CRIGHTON
York
Anne 1667 w.
Thos. 1667 i.
CRIGLER
Culpeper
Nicholas 1789 i.
Nicholas 1791 i.
CRIKHER
Fairfax
Jadwin 1750 w.

CRIMON
Fauquier
Jno. 1772 i.
CRIPPEN
Accomack
Thos. 1727 w.
Thos. 1734 w.
Geo. 1738 i.
Paul 1753 w.
Wm. 1753 i.
Robt. 1758 i.
Thos. 1759 i.
Patience 1772 w.
Wm. 1778 w.
Ann 1783 w.
Thos. 1783 w.
Thos. Sr. 1788 i.
Jno. Jr. 1791 w.
CRIPPS
Isle of Wight
Joyce 1679 w.
Geo. 1687 w.
CRIPS
Surry
Wm. 1749 w.
York
Thos. 1734 i.
Thos. 1736 w.
Thos. 1745 i.
Martha 1758 nw.
CRISMAN
Prince Edward
Danl. 1786 w.
CRISP
Chesterfield
Jno. 1778 w.
Jno. 1782 i.
Middlesex
Sarah 1786 w.
CRITCHER
Norfolk
Thos. 1717 w.
Westmoreland
Jno. 1749 w.
Richd. 1758 i.
Jno. 1768 w.
CRITCHET
Norfolk
Katherine 1715 a.
CRITTENDEN
Essex
Henry 1717 i.
Thos. 1732 i.
Thos. 1734 i.
Henrico
Wm. 1793 w.
CRITTENTTON
Essex
Richd. 1761 i.

CROCKER
Isle of Wight
Wm. 1729 w.
Wm. 1737 w.
Katherine 1750 i.
Edwd. 1752 w.
Jos. 1761 w.
Jos. 1772 i.
Wm. 1772 w.
Wm. 1776 w.
Molly 1793 w.
Wm. 1793 i.
Sarah 1788 w.
Anthony 1796 w.
Southampton
Robt. 1750 w.
Benj. 1761 i.
Elisha 1761 w.
Moses 1761 w.
Sarah 1781 w.
Hartwell 1782 i.
CROCKET
Rockbridge
Alex. 1784 w.
Washington
David 1778 i.
CROCKETT
Augusta
Robt. 1746-7 w.
Saml. 1750 w.
Jos. 1767 w.
Fincastle
Saml. 1773 i.
Prince Edward
Jno. 1777 i.
Wythe
Jno. 1798 w.
CROFT
Brunswick
Thos. 1797 i.
York
Jno. 1709 i.
CROIGDALLIE
Princess Anne
Hugh 1774 w.
CROKER
Isle of Wight
Anthony 1693 w.
Southampton
Nathl. 1781 i.
CROMER
Chesterfield
Jas. 1759 w.
CROMERTY
Lancaster
Robt. 1682 w.
CROMHER
Essex
Thos. 1722 i.

CROMPTON
Princess Anne
Wm. 1760 i.
CROMWELL
Frederick
Oliver 1762 i.
CRONE
Culpeper
Margt. 1764 w.
CRONY
Northampton
Jas. 1751 w.
CROOK
Frederick
Timothy 1769 i.
Prince William
Zephaniah 1779 w.
CROOKE
Northampton
Saml. 1738 i.
York
Paul 1674 i.
CROOM
Goochland
Danl 1735 w.
Isle of Wight
Edwd. 1750 i.
CROPPER
Accomack
Sebastian 1721 w.
Edmd. Bowman 1733 w.
Sebastian 1776 w.
Sebastian 1778 w.
Thos. Sr. 1781 w.
Bowman 1782 w.
Jno. Jr. 1783 i.
Sebastian 1784 i.
Boniman (?) 1785 i.
Sebastian 1796 w.
CROSBIE
Chesterfield
Jas. 1752 w.
CROSBY
Fauquier
Geo. 1799 i.
Isle of Wight
Jno. 1678 i.
Stafford
Geo. 1731 w.
Geo. 1737-8 w.
Geo. 1745 w.
CROSDOL
Henrico
Roger 1711 i.
CROSFIELD
Northumberland
Jno. 1751 w.
CROSHAW
York
Margaret 1665 w.

Jos. 1667 w.
Richd. 1669 w.
Richd. 1677-8 i.
CROSLEY
Hampshire
Abel 1794 w.
Northampton
Gardner 1761 i.
CROSS
Albemarle
Thos. 1788 w.
Amelia
Wm. 1782 i.
Botetourt
Wm. 1798 w.
Essex
Jos. 1750 w.
Wm. 1752 w.
Loudoun
Jos. 1780 i.
Lunenburg
Jno. 1791 w.
Richd. 1699 i.
Sussex
Wm. 1780 w.
Washington
Benj. 1778 i.
York
Nathl. 1718 i.
——— 1722 ab.
Ann 1732 w.
Edwd. 1760 w.
Frances 1764 w.
CROSSFIELD
Northumberland
Winnifred 1790 nw.
CROSSWELL
Essex
Jas. 1720 w.
CRORSTED
Lancaster
Jno. 1718 i.
CROSTHWAIT
Culpeper
Wm. 1771 w.
Orange
Wm. 1743 a.
Timothy 1756 w.
CROSTHWAITE
Albemarle
Wm. 1787 w.
CROSTICK
Henrico
Edwd. 1710 i.
CROSTON
Accomack
Francis 1733 w.
CROSWHITE
Fairfax
Anthony 1771 w.

CROSWELL
Richmond
Gilbert 1728 w.
CROUCH
Harrison
Jonathan 1786 i.
Goochland
Richd. 1766 i.
Jno. 1780 w.
Jno. 1799 i.
King George
Jos. 1742 i.
Montgomery
David 1799 i.
CROUCHER
Amelia
Dorothy 1754 w.
Richmond
Richd. 1740 w.
Wm. 1752 i.
Robt. 1705 nw.
CROUDAS
Essex
Wm. 1709 w.
CROUTCHMAN
Westmoreland
Jno. 1716 w.
CROW
Berkeley
Jno. 1775 w.
Essex
Thos. 1708 w.
Jno. 1718 w.
Eliz. 1720 w.
Jno. 1720 i.
Wm. 1752 w.
Goochland
Jno. 1773 w.
Madison
Jas. 1797 w.
CROWDAS
Goochland
Geo. 1789 i.
CROWDER
Amelia
Dorothy 1774 w.
Jos. 1778 w.
Mary 1786 w.
Mecklenburg
Isaac 1770 w.
Jno. 1777 i.
Brunswick
Mark 1781 w.
CROWEN
Greenbrier
Jno. 1792 i.
CROWLEY
Pittsylvania
Saml. 1777 i.

CROWSON
Accomack
Wm. 1757 i.
Wm. 1796 w.
CROWTHER
Lancaster
Araricum 1771 i.
Northumberland
Thos. 1758 w.
Robt. 1771 i.
Jas. 1771 i.
CROXTON
Essex
Jas. 1747 i.
Jno. 1757 w.
Saml. 1767 i.
Jno. 1775 w.
Thos. 1778 i.
Orange
Richd. 1785 w.
CROZIER
Northampton
Eliz. 1678 w.
CRUFF
Essex
Jno. 1721 w.
Sarah 1732 w.
CRUM
Shenandoah
Ann 1775 w.
CRUMBACKER
Loudoun
Jno. 1796 w.
CRUME
Shenandoah
Isaac 1791 a.
CRUMLEY
Frederick
Jas. 1764 w.
Berkeley
Adam 1781 i.
CRUMLY
Berkeley
Wm. 1793 w.
CRUMP
Accomack
Geo. 1667 w.
Bedford
Richd. 1791 i.
Cumberland
Stephen 1769 w.
Fauquier
Geo. 1789 i.
Jno. 1789 w.
Lancaster
Adam 1753 w.
Powhatan
Goodrich 1796 i.
CRUMPLER
Isle of Wight
Edmd. 1792 w.

Southampton
Wm. 1751 w.
Wm. 1771 w.
CRUMPTON
Bedford
Henry 1782 i.
Charlotte
Mary 1793 w.
CRUSS
Richmond
Patrick 1719 i.
CRUSIER
Culpeper
Wm. 1798 w.
CRUTCHER
Culpeper
Hugh 1779 w.
Essex
Henry 1780 w.
Leonard 1798 i.
CRUTCHFIELD
Spotsylvania
Stapleton 1789 w.
York
Mary 1761 w.
CRUTE
Amelia
Richd. 1767 w.
Northumberland
Richd. 1746 w.
Rebeccah 1756 w.
CRYDER
Frederick
Martin 1749 w.
CRYER
Shenandoah
Wm. 1783 a.
Surry
Geo. 1754 w.
Geo. 1762 w.
Ann 1776 w.
CRYMES
Lunenburg
Wm. 1778 w.
Thos. 1789 w.
CUBBAGE
Culpeper
Jno. 1797 w.
Frederick
Geo. 1778 w.
CUBBIDGE
Norfolk
Jno. 1654 w.
CUBBIN
Richmond
Chas. 1714 i.
CUBITS
Lancaster
Robt. 1674 i.
CUDY
Accomack
Jas. 1701 w.

CUGLEY
Northampton
Danl. 1641 i.
CUKES
Berkeley
Henry 1777 w.
CULBERT
Augusta
Wm. 1763 a.
CULBERTSON
Augusta
Jas. 1788 w.
CULBREATH
Mecklenburg
Wm. Jr. 1782 i.
Wm. 1787 w.
CULL
Rockbridge
Jas. 1790 i.
CULLAM
Sussex
Thos. 1797 w.
CULLEN
Isle of Wight
Thos. 1689 i.
CULLERS
Shenandoah
Jno. 1796 w.
CULLEY
York
Jane 1721 w.
CULLILAND
Augusta
Jno. 1761 i.
CULLINE
King George
Mary 1726 i.
CULLINS
Prince William
Jno. 1778 i.
CULLOM
Pittsylvania
Robt. 1787 w.
CULLUM
Westmoreland
Mark 1727 i.
CULLY
Isle of Wight
Jno. 1690 i.
CULPEPER
Norfolk
Henry 1699 w.
Robt. 1742-3 w.
Sarah 1747-8 i.
Mary 1752 i.
Robt. 1774 w.
Danl. 1775 w.
Thos. 1786 w.
Thos. 1792 w.
Benj. 1794 i.
Jos. 1799 i.

CULTON
Augusta
Jos. 1773 w.
Rockbridge
Robt. 1781 w.
CUMBER
Henrico
Jno. 1679 w.
CUMBERFOOT
Princess Anne
Jas. 1734 w.
Jno. 1784 i.
CUMBERLAND
Augusta
Jno. 1749 w.
CUMBO
Halifax
Jno. 1797 i.
CUMMING
Norfolk
Jas. 1720 i.
CUMMINGS
Accomack
Thos. 1754 i.
Augusta
Jos. 1757 i.
Fauquier
Malacki 1769 i.
Simon 1771 w.
Loudoun
Malachi 1788 i.
Middlesex
Angelo 1726 i.
Princess Anne
Benj. 1697 w.
Martin 1749 w.
Caleb 1798 w.
Richmond
Saml. 1742 w.
CUMMINS
Brunswick
David 1749 w.
Richmond
Mary 1758 w.
CUMPTON
Amelia
Jno. 1771 w.
Fairfax
Jno. 1746 i.
CUNARD
Loudoun
Wm. 1774 i.
CUNDIFF
Bedford
Richd. 1774 i.
Jonathan 1775 i.
Lancaster
Jno. 1775 w.
Richd. 1781 w.
Northumberland
Richd. 1723-4 w.
Richd. 1726 w.

Milley 1782 i.
Benj. 1785 w.
Sally 1796 i.
Prince William
Isaac 1744 a.
CUNINGHAM
Augusta
Jonathan 1769 w.
Berkeley
Jas. 1773 w.
Fairfax
Wm. 1797 a.
Norfolk
Jno. 1670 w.
Northumberland
Thos. 1727 w.
CUNNARD
Loudoun
Ann 1780 i.
Wm. 1783 i.
CUNNINGHAM
Augusta
Saml. 1747 i.
Isaac 1760 a.
Jacob 1760 i.
Jno. 1774 i.
David 1778 w.
Alex. 1782 i.
Thos. 1782 w.
Thos. 1785 i.
Berkeley
Jas. 1773 i.
Geo. 1778 i.
Robt. 1785 w.
Wm. 1786 w.
Botetourt
Hugh 1772 w.
Charlotte
Jas. 1780 w.
Robt. 1785 i.
Chesterfield
Wm. 17— i.
Wm. 1771 w.
Frederick
Jas. 1752 i.
Thos. 1761 w.
Robt. 1769 w.
Henry
Jno. 1788 i.
Lunenburg
Thos. 1752 w.
Andrew 1761 w.
Jas. 1762 w.
Jno. 1764 i.
Pittsylvania
Jos. 1780 i.
Thos. 1797 w.
Prince Edward
Alex. 1779 i.
Shenandoah
Robt. 1781 i.
Jno. 1782 i.

Walter 1782 a.
Thos. 1789 i.
Spotsylvania
Jno. 1752 a.
Jas. 1782 a.
Ann 1789 w.
Jas. 1789 a.
York
David 1719 w.
CUNSTABLE
Richmond
Margt. 1706 w.
CUPER
Norfolk
Edmd. 1746 w.
CUPINGHEIFFER
Westmoreland
Jno. 1771 w.
CUPPINET
Northampton
Jno. 1709 w.
CURATON
Prince George
Jas. 1716 w.
CURD
Goochland
Jno. 1752 i.
Richd. 1778 w.
Jas. 1792 i.
Sarah 1795 w.
CURETON
Essex
Jno. 1758 w.
Sussex
Archd. 1784 w.
CURL
Southampton
Thos. 1779 w.
CURLETT
Frederick
Jos. 1795 w.
CURLING
Norfolk
Jos. Sr. 1719 nw.
Anthony 1753 w.
Anthony 1789 w.
Henry 1798 w.
Jas. 1798 i.
CURLIS
Middlesex
Thos. 1748 i.
CUROTT
Chesterfield
Lewis 1791 i.
CURRAN
Loudoun
Jno. 1785 i.
CURRELL
Lancaster
Jacob 1721 w.
Abraham 1757 w.
Isaac 1762 w.

Harry 1785 w.
Geo. 1788 w.
Robt. 1797 w.
CURRER
Isle of Wight
Sarah 1699 w.
CURREY
Fairfax
Barneyby 1757 i.
CURRIE
Lancaster
David 1791 w.
York
Jas. 1738 i.
CURRY
Botetourt
Wm. 1781 i.
Frederick
Thos. 1771 i.
Stafford
Jno. 1761 i.
Westmoreland
Thaddy 1751 i.
CURSON
York
Thos. 1704 w.
CURTICE
Lancaster
Thos. 1790 i.
Northumberland
Ann 1758 w.
Geo. 1777 i.
Hillary 1792 w.
CURTIS
Brunswick
Michael 1761 i.
Chislen 1796 w.
Charlotte
Christopher 1778 w.
Culpeper
Thos. 1770 w.
Essex
Chas. 1760 w.
Lancaster
Richd. 1688 w.
Richd. 1744 w.
Middlesex
Jas. 1720 w.
Jas. Jr. 1720 w.
Chichester 1724 w.
Jas. Jr. 1728 i.
Jno. 1741 i.
Thos. 1747 a.
Christopher 1764 w.
Jno. 1791 w.
Chichester 1792 i.
Northumberland
Geo. 1728-9 w.
Pitts 1729 i.
Eliz. 1739 i.
Jno. 1749 i.
Benj. 1761 w.

Jno. 1767 w.
Wm. 1785 w.
Orange
Mary 1741 w.
Prince William
Chris. 1778 i.
Rappahannock
Jno. 1677 w.
Jno. 1678 w.
Spotsylvania
Rice, Sr. 1753 w.
Eliz. 1755 a.
Rice 1774 w.
Sussex
Jno. 1779 w.
Westmoreland
Thos. 1737 w.
Jno. 1752 i.
York
Adam 1713 w.
Robt. 1716 w.
Thos. 1723 w.
Thos. 1727 i.
Edmd. 1728 w.
Thos. Jr. 1731 i.
Edmd. 1791 w.
Robt. 1799 i.
CUSHYON
Richmond
Jas. 1720 w.
CUSTARD
Augusta
Arnold 1759 a.
Conrad 1771 a.
CUSTIS
Accomack
Edmd. 1700 w.
Rachell 1700 w.
Edmd. 1703 i.
Rachel 1721 i.
Thos. 1721 w.
Thos. 1723 i.
Wm. 1726 w.
Bridget, Jr. 1727 w.
Hancock 1729 w.
Henry 1732 w.
Jno. 1732 w.
Edwd. 1739 w.
Patience 1744 w.
Jos. 1747 i.
Thos. 1751 w.
Housy 1752 i.
Jno. 1763 w.
Jno. 1764 w.
Thos. 1764 w.
Wm. 1765 w.
Wm. 1766 w.
Edmd. 1774 w.
Bagwell 1777 w.
Leven 1777 w.
Leven 1779 i.
Jno. 1780 i.

Henry 1793 w.
Eliz. 1794 w.
Levin 1795 i.
Henry Sr. 1797 w.
Only 1797 w.
Robinson 1798 w.
Jno. 1799 w.
Fairfax
Jno. Parke 1782 i.
Northampton
Jno. 1687 w.
Jno. 1695 w.
Jno. 1713-14 w.
Jno. 1713-14 w.
Sarah 1720 w.
Theophilus 1733 i.
Jno. 1746 w.
Edmd. 1748 w.
Robinson 1750 i.
Edmd. 1752 i.
York
Frances 1715 ab.
CUTCHIN
Isle of Wight
Joshua 1759 i.
Jos. 1775 w.
Jos. 1779 w.
Jeremiah 1783 i.
Priscilla 1788 w.
Jos. 1789 i.
Matthew 1792 w.
Mary 1793 w.
Polly 1799 w.
CUTCHINS
Isle of Wight
Eliz. 1764 i.
Saml. 1770 w.
CUTERELL
Norfolk
Josiah 1784 i.
CUTHERELL
Norfolk
Gowin 1711 w.
CUTLAR
Accomack
Thos. 1778 w.
Wm. 1783 w.
Geo. 1784 w.
Saml. 1784 w.
Ebenezer 1789 i.
CUTLER
Accomack
Richd. 1733 w.
Geo. 1739 w.
Thos. 1743 w.
Richd. 1744 w.
Jno. 1745 i.
Jno. 1749 i.
Arcadia 1750 w.
Snead 1751 i.
Danl. 1760 w.
Jno. 1786 w.

Richd. 1794 w.
Northampton
Jazbis 1686 a.
CUTTER
Accomack
Wm. 1768 w.
CUTTILO
Lunenburg
Mathew 1755 w.
Edwd. 1783 w.
Abraham 1790 w.
CUTTING
Accomack
Wm. 1704 w.
CWVRY (Curry?)
Washington
Jas. 1782 i.
CYPHER
Frederick
David 1748 i.
CYPRESS
Surry
Wm. 1796 w.

D

DABBINS
Northampton
Jno. 1759 i.
DABNEY
Bedford
Cornelius 1792 w.
Henry
Wm. 1779 i.
DACON
Prince William
Thos. 1744 i.
DADE
King George
Cadwallader 1777 w.
Horatio 1782 w.
Baldwin 1783 w.
Virlindia 1798 w.
Fairfax
Townshend 1781 w.
Catherine 1792 a.
Northampton
Jos. 1736 w.
Orange
Francis 1791 w.
Prince William
Mary 1799 w.
Stafford
Langhorne 1753 w.
Henry 1754 i.
Cadwallader 1761 w.
Townsend 1761 w.
Westmoreland
Francis 1663 w.
DADUM
Northumberland
Barbary 1663 i.

DADGER
Northumberland
Jas. 1719 i.
DAFFNELL
Norfolk
Wm. 1686 w.
DAGEY
Shenandoah
Jacob 1782 a.
DAGG
Prince William
Jas. 1740 i.
Thos. 1778 w.
DAILEY
Brunswick
Wm. Sr. 1778 w.
Essex
Ann 1764 i.
Hampshire
Saml. 1791 w.
DAILY
Essex
Danl. 1759 i.
DAINGERFIELD
Essex
Jno. 1706 i.
Jno. 1720 w.
Wm. 1735 w.
Wm. 1767 w.
Apphia 1799 w.
DAINS
Norfolk
Wm. 1717 w.
DALBEY
Northampton
Wm. 1663 w.
Jno. 1689 w.
DALBY
Northampton
Edwd. 1677 i.
Ann 1710 w.
Stephen 1772 w.
Jos. 1778 i.
Jean 1785 w.
Thos. 1787 w.
Branson 1788 w.
Spencer 1788 i.
Thos. Sr. 1797 w.
DALE
Bedford
Frances 1777 w.
Lancaster
Edwd. 1695 w.
Norfolk
William 1715 w.
Henry 1717 i.
Richd. 1752 w.
Winfield 1767 w.
Wm. 1768 w.
Danl. 1769 w.
Peter 1771 w.
Wm. 1772 i.

Northampton
Eliz. 1641 w.
Northumberland
Litty 1794 w.
Princess Anne
Paul 1742 w.
Wm. 1750 w.
Prince William
Robert 1779 w.
Richmond
Abraham 1740 i.
Rubin 1768 i.
Thos. 1773 i.
Jos. 1791 w.
Alex. 1791 i.
York
Nicholas 1647 w.
DALES
Surry
Catharine 1750 w.
DALEY
Essex
Danl. 1755 w.
Orange
Timothy 1743 a.
DALHOUSE
Augusta
Chas. 1760 w.
DALLEOOR
Princess Anne
Joseph 1712 i.
DALLGAINER
Princess Anne
Geo. 1709 i.
DALLIS
Loudoun
Dennis 1767 i.
DALLISTER
Prince William
Richard 1737 a.
DALRYMPLE
Berkeley
John 1777 w.
DALTON
Bedford
Timothy 1782 i.
Fairfax
John 1777 w.
John 1789 i.
Robert 1792 a.
Pittsylvania
Robt. 1779 w.
Richmond
Mary 1734 w.
DAMERON
Albemarle
Richd. 1749 w.
Lazarus 1749 w.
Jno. 1757 i.
Lancaster
John 1782 w.
Rachel 1796 w.

Northumberland
Laurence 1660 w.
Bartholomew 1708 w.
Geo. 1721 i.
Josias 1727 i.
Eliz. 1728-9 i.
Jno. 1743 w.
Thos. 1750-1 w.
Thos. 1757 i.
Joseph 1759 w.
Onesiphrous 1762 w.
Chris. 1746 w.
Thos. 1766 w.
Bledso 1770 w.
Wm. 1773 w.
Hannah 1779 i.
Onesiphrous 1782 w.
Geo. 1784 i.
Wm. 1785 w.
Jessee 1790 w.
Mary 1799 w.
Eliz. 1797 w.
DANALIN
Essex
Edward 1703 i.
DANCE
Chesterfield
Jno. 1780 w.
Thos. 1783 w.
Henry 1784 w.
Wm. 1785 w.
Susanna 1788 w.
Fairfax
Jno. 1798 w.
DANCIE
Spotsylvania
Thos. 1768 w.
Ann 1782 w.
DANCY
Charles City
Benj. 1771 w.
Edwd. 1771 w.
Wm. 1772 w.
Jno. 1790 i.
Edwd. 1796 w.
Sussex
Wm. 1761 w.
DANDGE
Princess Anne
Tully 1796 w.
DANDRIDGE
Berkeley
Alex. S. 1785 w.
DANELL
Northumberland
Walter 1652 i.
DANELLY
Middlesex
Arthur 1723 w.
DANES
Norfolk
William 1717 a.

DANGE
Princess Anne
James 1719 w.
Jno. 1734 w.
DANGERFIELD
Spotsylvania
Wm. 1781 w.
Wm. 1783 w.
DANIEL
Accomack
Wm. 1692 w.
Henry 1745 i.
Wm. Sr. 1750 w.
Albemarle
James 1761 w.
Berkeley
Elizabeth 1796 w.
Brunswick
Wm. 1786 w.
Wm. 1792 i.
Joseph 1794 w.
Charlotte
Benj. 1778 i.
Culpeper
Robert 1760 i.
Cumberland
Abraham 1798 i.
Williams 1771 w.
Wm. 1775 i.
Essex
Robt. 1727 w.
James 1742 w.
Thomas 1738 i.
Oliver 1785 w.
Fairfax
Jno. O. 1799 w.
Goochland
James 1736 i.
Obadiah 1778 w.
Ezekiel 1790 w.
Halifax
James 1781 w.
Richd. 1784 w.
Isle of Wight
Thomas 1709 i.
John 1728 w.
Thomas 1742 i.
William 1750 w.
Louisa
John 1786 w.
Mecklenburg
Wm. 1782 w.
Middlesex
Wm. 1698 w.
Richd. 1715 i.
Robert 1720 w.
Wm. 1723 w.
Robt. 1742 w.
Garrett 1745 i.
Wm. 1746 w.
Josiah 1747 i.
Jas. 1748 w.

Margt. 1750 w.
Geo. 1758 w.
Henry 1767 w.
Robt. 1771 w.
Richd. 1771 i.
Jno. 1772 w.
Benj. 1774 w.
Henry 1775 w.
Wm. 1779 i.
Jas. 1779 w.
Benj. 1779 i.
Robt. 1781 w.
Beverley 1782 w.
Robt. 1782 w.
Robt. 1784 w.
Wm. 1784 i.
Geo. 1794 w.
Lunsford 1794 i.
Jno. 1795 i.
Orange
Reuben 1779 w.
Reuben 1790 w.
James 1792 w.
Powhatan
Wm. 1793 w.
Wm. Jr. 1798 i.
Richmond
Abraham 1761 i.
Spotsylvania
Chris. 1793 a.
Edmond 1799 w.
Westmoreland
Richd. 1726 i.
Jno. 1753 i.
York
Thos. 1673 i.
Jno. 1724 w.
DANIELEY
Westmoreland
Ursula 1745-6 w.
DANIELL
Accomack
Wm. 1696 i.
Essex
Richd. 1727 w.
Isle of Wight
John 1679 w.
Northampton
Jno. 1688 w.
Prince George
John 1716 i.
Surry
Thos. 1720 w.
DANIELS
Culpeper
Robert 1761 i.
DANILL
Orange
Robert 1799 i.
DANKS
Northumberland
George 1768 i.

DANLEY
Princess Anne
Jno. 1719 w.
Dennis 1728 w.
Jno. 1736 w.
Margt. 1702 w.
Thos. 1733 w.
DANN
Campbell
Jno. 1787 w.
DANNIELL
York
Jno. 1689 w.
DANZEE
Lunenburg
John Sr. 1783.
DARBY
Accomack
Churchill 1708 i.
Danl. 1708 w.
Dormand 1708 w.
Wm. 1711 i.
Danl. 1729 w.
Ann 1757 w.
Wm. 1757 w.
Churchill 1758 w.
Elijah 1759 w.
Jno. 1769 w.
Littleton 1769 w.
Churchel 1773 w.
Frances 1773 w.
Owen 1790 w.
Tamer 1792 w.
Tamer 1796 i.
Fairfax
Elizabeth 1799 w.
Northampton
Jno. 1750 w.
Jno. (2?) 1750 w.
Benj. 1760 w.
Rachel 1777 w.
York
Jno. 1719 i.
DARDEN
Isle of Wight
Jacob 1719 w.
Jacob 1741 w.
Jacob 1750 i.
Benjamin 1770 i.
Hardy 1792 w.
Henry 1794 i.
John 1789 w.
Mecklenburg
David 1785 i.
Southampton
Elisha 1789 w.
Holland 1792 w.
James 1795 w.
DARE
Lancaster
Wm. 1721 w.
Thos. 1729 i.

112   VIRGINIA WILLS AND ADMINISTRATIONS

DARICH
Botetourt
John 1790 w.
DARLEY
Accomack
Benj. 1793 i.
Isle of Wight
Mary 1786 i.
DARLING
Hardy
Wm. 1787 i.
DARLINGE
Northampton
———— 1677 w.
DARLINGTON
Frederick
Meredith 1783 i.
DARNABY
Spotsylvania
Edwd. 1749 a.
Wm. 1767 a.
Wm. 1785 w.
Wm. 1786 w.
DARNALL
Fauquier
Morgan 1766 nw.
William 1771 w.
David 1786 w.
Jeremiah 1795 w.
King George
Morgan 1726 i.
Morgan 1727 i.
Waugh 1727 i.
DARNEL
Washington
David 1785 w.
DARNELL
Westmoreland
Richd. 1705 i.
DAROCK
Prince William
John 1799 i.
DARR
Augusta
Geo. 1769 w.
Loudoun
Conrad 1782 i.
DARRALL
Fairfax
Mary 1795 w.
DARRELL
Fairfax
George 1771 w.
George 1776 i.
Augustus 1777 w.
Sampson 1777 w.
DARRNELL
Fairfax
Wm. 1798 w.

DARSH
Northampton
Richd. 1728 i.
DART
Rappahannock
Thos. 1677 w.
DARTING
Shenandoah
Adam 1776 w.
Philip G. 1776 w.
DARVY
Richmond
Peter 1718 i.
DARWIN
Louisa
Wm. 1786 w.
DASHPER
Louisa
Jno. 1770 w.
DAUGHERTY
Albemarle
Michael 1766 w.
Bedford
Hugh 1788 w.
Montgomery
Michael 1787 w.
DAUGHITY
Northumberland
James 1771 w.
DAUGHTRY
Isle of Wight
Joseph 1740 w.
John 1749 w.
Wm. 1752 w.
John 1755 i.
Eliz. 1758 w.
John 1758 i.
William 1781 w.
William 1783 i.
John 1784 w.
Joshua 1791 w.
Southampton
Robt. 1762 i.
Jas. 1766 i.
Eliz. 1788 w.
DAULTON
Bedford
Timothy 1775 w.
DAVENPORT
Albemarle
Richd. 1793 w.
Amelia
Geo. 1773 w.
Berkeley
Marmaduke 1778 i.
Abraham 1789 w.
Charlotte
Jack Smith 1781 w.
Cumberland
Stephen 1763 i.
Thos. Sr. 1773 w.

Thos. 1774 w.
Thos. 1780 w.
Wm. 1792 w.
Hanover
Martin 1735 w.
Halifax
James 1780 w.
King George
Geo. 1757 i.
Lancaster
Jno. 1683 w.
Wm. 1716 w.
Wm. 1719 i.
Geo. 1760 w.
Northumberland
Benj. 1786 w.
Jemima 1792 i.
Wm. 1792 i.
Jno. 1797 w.
Richmond
Geo. 1734 w.
Wm. 1772 w.
Fortunatus 1779 w.
Fortunatus 1786 i.
Spotsylvania
Wm. 1798 w.
Westmoreland
Randle 1703 i.
Jas. 1777 w.
Danl. 1771 i.
York
Jos. 1761 w.
Wm. 1770 i.
Matthew 1778 i.
Jos. 1788 w.
DAVES
Chesterfield
Thos. 1795 w.
DAVERS
Montgomery
Richard 1778 a.
DAVEY
Frederick
John 1748 a.
DAVICE
Surry
Nicholas 1730 w.
DAVID
Cumberland
Ann 1750 w.
Essex
Nicholas 1731 i.
Goochland
Peter 1730 w.
Henry
Peter 1785 w.
Loudoun
Jenkin 1775 w.
Lunenburg
Adlar 1749 w.

Northampton
Jacob 1768 w.
Shenandoah
Henry 1794 a.
Henry 1797 w.
DAVIDSON
Augusta
Jno. 1786 i.
Jno. 1798 w.
Brunswick
Wm. 1752 i.
Charles City
Philemon 1773 i.
Mary 1793 w.
Culpeper
William 1751 i.
Montgomery
Walter 1786 i.
Rockbridge
William 1793 w.
Spotsylvania
Alex. 1748 a.
Surry
Wm. 1727 w.
Mary 1737 w.
Wythe
John 1795 w.
York
Robt. 1738 w.
DAVIES
Bedford
Zachariah 1791 w.
Rockbridge
Hugh Sr. 1786 w.
Hugh Jr. 1786 w.
Thomas 1794 w.
Westmoreland
Wm. 1723 i.
Gerrard 1742 i.
DAVIS
Accomack
Jas. 1711 nw.
Wm. 1712 i.
Jas. 1713 i.
Jas. 1728 i.
Saml. 1735 i.
Jas. 1738 i.
Thos. 1740 i.
Jno. 1751 i.
Thos. 1752 i.
Wm. 1752 i.
Saml. 1761 i.
Major 1786 w.
Agnes 1792 w.
Wm. 1795 i.
Albemarle
Isham 1776 w.
Amherst
Nathaniel 1778 w.
Robt. 1782 a.
Philip 1786 w.
John 1779 w.

Israel 1796 w.
Augusta
Danl. 1751 i.
Benj. 1759 a.
Thos. 1765 i.
Jas. 1767 i.
Wm. 1773 i.
Jno. 1776 w.
Bedford
Benjamin 1764 i.
Samuel 1798 w.
Berkeley
William 1772 w.
Jacob 1780 w.
Daniel 1782 i.
John 1796 w.
Joseph 1799 w.
Brunswick
Jno. 1751 w.
Wm. 1772 w.
Wm. 1773 w.
Thos. 1779 w.
Wm. 1779 i.
Thos. 1786 i.
Charles City
Wm. 1772 w.
Charlotte
Wm. 1770 w.
Jos. 1793 w.
Jno. 1799 w.
Chesterfield
Caleb 1777 w.
Benj. 1792 i.
Hezekiah 1799 i.
Culpeper
David 1782 w.
Isaac 1783 i.
Cumberland
Carter 1767 i.
Wm. 1768 w.
Jas. 1769 w.
Peter 1776 w.
Matthew 1777 w.
Essex
Susanna 1700 w.
Thos. 1718 w.
Nick 1734 i.
Ann 1738 w.
Jno. 1748 w.
Thos. 1749 w.
Ann 1750 w.
Thos. 1751 i.
Thos. 1755 w.
Saml. 1757 w.
Thos. 1758 i.
Francis 1761 w.
Francis 1767 i.
Jno. 1770 w.
Edwd. 1771 w.
Thos. 1772 i.
Frances 1773 w.
Saml. 1773 i.

Jas. Jr. 1774 i.
Wm. 1783 w.
Wm. 1786 i.
Hannah 1793 w.
Ann 1797 i.
Thos. 1799 w.
Fairfax
Thomas 1757 w.
Benjamin 1762 i.
Edward 1770 i.
Isaac 1794 i.
Fauquier
Thomas 1768 i.
Charles 1798 w.
Franklin
William 1790 w.
Frederick
John 1749 i.
James 1758 i.
John 1772 i.
John 1774 i.
David 1790 w.
Goochland
Wm. 1730 i.
Sarah 1781 w.
Robin 1782 w.
Greensville
Jesse 1782 i.
Harrison
Jacob 1793 w.
Thomas 1794 w.
Hardy
Thos. 1793 i.
Henrico
Jno. 1684 i.
Nathl 1682 i.
Jno. 1689 i.
Thos. 1691 i.
Jno. 1701 i.
Jno. 1702 i.
Isle of Wight
Nicholas 1680 i.
Thomas 1696 i.
Hugh 1697 w.
Thomas 1693 w.
John 1714 w.
John 1720 i.
Mary 1720 w.
Thomas 1722 i.
James 1734 i.
Thomas 1734 w.
John 1736 i.
Robert 1736 w.
Samuel 1739 w.
Elizabeth 1744 i.
William 1748 i.
Samuel 1749 i.
John 1750 w.
Samuel 1751 w.
John 1753 i.
Edward 1759 w.
William 1759 w.

John 1762 w.
Arthur 1777 w.
William 1779 w.
William 1796 w.
Lancaster
Thos. 1697 w.
Caudry 1701 i.
Henry 1726 w.
Jno. 1729 w.
Richd. 1737 w.
Richd. 1749 i.
Ambrose 1750 i.
Elizab. 1750 i.
Moses 1750 w.
Susannah 1751 i.
Joseph 1758 w.
Thos. 1761 i.
Henry 1762 i.
John 1764 w.
John 1768 w.
William 1772 i.
Moses 1778 i.
William 1778 i.
Elennor 1789 w.
Leanner 1790 i.
Hannah 1799 w.
William 1799 w.
Loudoun
Thomas Jr. 1758 nw.
Sarah 1759 w.
Thomas 1759 i.
Nathan 1770 w.
John 1771 i.
John 1792 w.
Catherine 1799 i.
Louisa
Jno. 1773 w.
Lunenburg
Jno. 1757 i.
Jno. 1773 i.
Jas. 1777 w.
Jos. 1778 w.
Thos. 1779 w.
Jonathan 1790 w.
Ashley 1792 i.
Mecklenburg
Hardaway 1795 w.
Jno. 1798 w.
Middlesex
David 1712 w.
Mary 1714 w.
Benj. 1715 i.
Jno. 1716 i.
Thos. 1718 i.
Jno. 1732 w.
Jno. 1750 w.
Andrew 1759 w.
Andrew 1764 i.
Benj. 1764 i.
Geo. 1773 w.
Mary 1792 i.
Andrew 1793 w.

Williamson 1793 i.
Montgomery
Thomas 1789 w.
John 1799 w.
Norfolk
Robt. 1662 w.
Eliz. 1669 w.
Edwd. 1705 w.
Edwd. 1743 w.
Richard 1747 w.
John 1748 w.
Richard 1752 i.
Mary Bathiah 1753 i.
Richard 1773 w.
Samuel 1780 i.
Samuel 1782 w.
Stephen 1796 w.
Northampton
Thos. 1672 i.
Jas. 1682 w.
Pierce 1696 w.
Isaac 1708 w.
Jno. 1709 i.
Richd. 1724 w.
Hancock 1730 i.
Jno. 1756 i.
Reuben 1764 i.
Digby, Sr. 1766 w.
Wm. 1784 i.
Levin 1790 i.
Northumberland
Thos. 1749 w.
Robert 1751 w.
Wm. 1757 w.
John 1761 i.
Samuel 1763 w.
Barbee 1774 w.
Joseph 1778 w.
Judith 1795 i.
Jno. 1797 i.
Thos. 1799 w.
Orange
Berreman 1764 w.
Thomas 1797 w.
Pittsylvania
Saml. 1773 w.
Holder 1785 w.
Richd. 1785 i.
Wm. 1791 w.
Geo. 1796 i.
Jno. 1796 i.
Jno. 1798 i.
Princess Anne
Edwd. 1719 w.
Edwd. 1723 i.
Edmond 1740 i.
Edwd. 1766 w.
Saml. Sr. 1783 w.
Stephen 1785 i.
Horatia 1797 w.
Prince Edward
Stephen 1778 i.

Stephen 1781 w.
Peter 1785 w.
Littelberry 1799 w.
Prince George
Robt. 1713 i.
Jno. 1714 i.
Chris. 1722 w.
Prince William
John 1738 a.
Richard 1739 i.
William 1798 w.
Rappahannock
Edwd. 1682 i.
Richd. 1685 i.
Richmond
Joshua 1710 w.
Richd. 1719 i.
Jno. 1723 w.
Matthew 1724 w.
Jno. 1727 i.
Jno. 1732 i.
Robt. 1735 w.
Robt. 1784 w.
Jno. 1751 i.
Geo. 1781 w.
Jos. 1782 i.
Sally 1783 w.
Geo. 1784 i.
Rockbridge
Evan 1782 w.
Shenandoah
John 1778 i.
John 1783 i.
Southampton
Jno. 1756 w.
Thos. 1756 i.
Gideon 1759 i.
Jno. 1761 w.
Martha 1761 w.
Nathl. 1762 w.
Saml. 1768 i.
Lewis 1771 w.
Thos. 1771 i.
Lewis 1772 w.
Thos. Jr. 1776 w.
Thos. 1778 w.
David 1782 i.
Thos. 1791 w.
Henry 1798 w.
Spotsylvania
Jno. 1734 w.
Jno. 1759 w.
James 1765 w.
Benj. 1791 w.
James 1799 w.
Stafford
Joshua 1737 i.
Surry
Edwd. 1679 w.
Mary 1679 a.
Saml. 1680 a.
Mary 1684 a.

Nicholas 1717 w.
Arthur 1719 w.
Thos. 1720 w.
Edwd. 1735 w.
James Sr. 1746 w.
Richd. 1748 i.
Thos. 1748 w.
Jno. 1749 i.
Peter 1758 i.
Thos. 1766 w.
Henry 1767 w.
Henry 1772 w.
James 1782 w.
James 1784 w.
Thos. 1784 w.
Jno. 1793 w.
Sussex
Thos. 1772 w.
Jean 1779 w.
Wm. 1793 w.
Mary Dixon 1795 w.
Westmoreland
Wm. 1675 w.
Jno. 1698 w.
Eliz. 1723 w.
Peter 1730 i.
Wm. 1735 i.
Eliz. 1742 i.
Elias 1749 w.
Saml. 1750 w.
Wilson 1750 i.
Wm. 1751 i.
Hugh 1758 w.
Wm. 1759 i.
Joshua 1762 i.
Jno. 1762 w.
Eliz. 1762 w.
Anne 1763 w.
Frances 1763 w.
Anne 1764 w.
Gerard 1786 i.
Thos. 1789 i.
Elias 1790 i .
Elias 1794 w.
Wm. 1796 w.
Wythe
Abraham 1794 i.
John Sr. 1797 i.
York
Jno. 1646 i.
Wm. 1658 w.
Wm. 1688 i.
Elias 1689 w.
Edwd. 1700 i.
Owen 1705 i.
Wm. 1709 w.
Wm. 1717 i.
Wm. 1718 w.
Jno. 1719 w.
Thos. 1720 i.
Wm. 1720 i.
Jno. 1728 w.

Ann 1729 i.
Lewis 1732 w.
Wm. 1732 w.
Jno. 1734 w.
Lewis 1761 i.
Eliz. 1766 w.
Jas. 1780 w.
Jas. 1782 i.
Jno. 1783 w.
DAVISE
Culpeper
———— 1763 i.
DAVISON
Campbell
David M. 1793 w.
Edwd. 1794 w.
Halifax
Jno. 1770 w.
Northumberland
James 1760 w.
Prince Edward
John 1754 w.
Joshua 1771 i.
Richd. 1775 i.
Shenandoah
Ananias 1782 a.
DAVISS
Halifax
Jonathan 1796 w.
DAVISSON
Harrison
Hizekiah 1794 w.
DAVYE
Lancaster
Richd. 1678 nw.
DAWKINS
Northumberland
Geo. 1727 w.
Geo. 1728-9 w.
Peter 1743 i.
Penly 1783 w.
DAWLEY
Princess Anne
Margaret 1701 w.
Hillory 1766 i.
Anne 1778 i.
Dennis 1779 w.
Henry 1779 w.
Wm. 1780 i.
Princess Anne
Wm. 1783 i.
John 1785 i.
Jonathan 1786 w.
Sarah 1789 w.
DAWLEYES
Princess Anne
Lawrence 1698 i.
DAWS
Lunenburg
Joel 1778 w.
Joel 1788 w.

DAWSON
Accomack
Margt. 1784 w.
Amelia
Jno. 1740 i.
Amherst
Thos. 1770 w.
Jno. 1788 a.
Berkeley
Fredk. 1798 i.
Charlotte
Wm. 1777 w.
Frederick
David 1747 i.
Greensville
John 1783 w.
Isle of Wight
Martin 1746 w.
Middlesex
Wm. 1759 w.
Northumberland
Jno. 1711 i.
Henry 1795 w.
David 1798 i.
Ohio
Nicholas 1790 w.
Orange
Robert 1774 w.
Southampton
John 1756 w.
Henry 1773 w.
Surry
Geo. 1780 w.
Wm. 1782 w.
DAVISON
Augusta
Jno. 1749 a.
Danl. 1750 a.
Robt. 1751 w.
Jno. 1762 nw.
Jas. 1776 w.
DAWTIN
Richmond
Anthony 1771 w.
DAY
Cumberland
James 1777 i.
Frederick
Thomas 1779 i.
Halifax
Thos. 1795 i.
Isle of Wight
James 1700 w.
James 1702 i.
Thomas 1723 w.
James 1725 w.
Ann 1726 w.
James 1739 w.
James 1744 i.
Daniel 1750 w.
Thomas 1752 w.

Thomas 1772 **w.**
Thomas 1774 i.
John 1776 w.
Lancaster
  Robinson 1752 i.
Loudoun
  George 1773 i.
  Jeremiah 1795 i.
Norfolk
  Ann 1785 w.
Orange
  Henry 1795 i.
Princess Anne
  Jno. 1725 i.
Prince Edward
  Richd. 1774 i.
Southampton
  Thos. 1771 w.
  Edmd. 1783 w.
  Patty 1784 i.
Spotsylvania
  Lucy 1766 a.
Stafford
  Roger 1731 i.
Westmoreland
  Robt. 1672 w.
York
  Edwd. 1687 w.
DAYLE
Richmond
  Jno. 1716 i.
DAYLES
Stafford
  Benj. 1735 i.
DAYLEY
Essex
  Timothy 1717 i.
DAYLY
Culpeper
  Nicholas 1799 w.
DAYTON
Northampton
  Jonathan 1740 w.
DEACON
Accomack
  Thos. 1687 i.
Lancaster
  Wm. 1792 w.
Westmoreland
  Jno. 1718 i.
York
  Thos. 1648 i.
DEADMAN
York
  Chris. 1679 i.
DEAKERS
Prince William
  Thomas 1744 w.
DEAKINS
Prince William
  John 1796 i.

DEAL
Norfolk
  John 1723 i.
  Elizabeth 1755 i.
DEALE
Norfolk
  Henry 1734 w.
DEALL
Norfolk
  Henry 1716 w.
  Franince 1720 i.
DEAMORE
Princess Anne
  Robt. 1765 i.
DEAN
Augusta
  Wm. 1773 w.
Essex
  Thos. 1758 w.
Halifax
  Edwd. 1761 w.
  Jno. 1777 i.
Henrico
  Richd. 1748 i.
  Sarah 1751 i.
Middlesex
  Wm. 1786 w.
Montgomery
  Adam 1787 w.
Richmond
  Jno. 1742 w.
Stafford
  Jno. 1705 w.
Surry
  Saml. 1742 i.
DEANE
King George
  Chas. 1747 i.
  Wm. 1747 i.
  Jno. 1750 i.
  Geo. 1751 i.
  Wm. 1751 i.
  Jno. 1753 i.
  Wm. 1774 w.
  Wm. 1776 a.
Richmond
  Jno. 1712 w.
Westmoreland
  Chas. 1784 w.
DEANES
Norfolk
  Wm. 1687 w.
DEANS
Chesterfield
  Jas. 1762 w.
Norfolk
  David 1758 i.
  Reubin 1775 i.
  Solomon 1779 w.
  Thomas 1785 i.
  John 1792 i.
  Susanna 1795 w.

William 1799 w.
DEAR
Louisa
  Edmund 1795 i.
Orange
  Jno. 1781 w.
Pittsylvania
  Gilbert 1794 i.
DEARDEN
Brunswick
  Geo. 1749 i.
DEARDOR
Botetourt
  Henry 1792 i.
DEARING
Bedford
  Richd. 1792 i.
DEARLOVE
Henrico
  Richd. 1703-4 w.
DEARMORE
Princess Anne
  Richd. 1722 w.
DEATH
Frederick
  William 1783 w.
Isle of Wight
  Richd. 1647 w.
York
  Peter 1646 w.
DEATHERAGE
Culpeper
  Robt. 1777 w.
  Geo. 1792 i.
DEATLY
Richmond
  Chris. 1795 w.
DEATTERLEY
Westmoreland
  Matthew 1785 w.
DEATON
Amelia
  Levi 1799 w.
Middlesex
  Jno. 1757 a.
DEBELL
Fairfax
  John 1755 i.
Prince William
  William 1738 w.
  William 1739 i.
Richmond
  Wm. 1726 i.
DEBERRY
Isle of Wight
  Peter 1712 w.
DEBERS
Rappahannock
  ——— 1685 i.
DEBORIS
Surry
  Jno. 1772 i.

DEBUTTS
Westmoreland
Eliz. 1754 i.
Lawrence 1754 i.
DECEN
Prince William
Richard 1737 a.
DECK
Augusta
Robt. 1774 w.
DECKER
Mecklenburg
Henry 1768 i.
DEDERICK
Frederick
David 1768 w.
DEDFORD
Isle of Wight
John 1788 w.
DEDMAN
Mecklenburg
Saml. 1790 w.
Spotsylvania
Philip 1777 a.
York
Philip 1721 w.
Philip 1770 w.
Margt. 1773 w.
DEEKE
Richmond
Jos. 1718 w.
DEELY
Henrico
Edwd. 1688 w.
DEER
Culpeper
John 1781 w.
King George
Wm. 1785 w.
Madison
Andrew 1798 w.
DEERING
Campbell
Edwd. 1791 w.
Isle of Wight
James 1785 w.
Orange
Robt. 1758 w.
DEES
Isle of Wight
Manll. 1723 i.
DEFOE
Albemarle
James 1781 w.
DEFORD
Norfolk
John 1794 w.
DEFORDS
Isle of Wight
John 1788 i.

DEFORREST
York
Cornelius 1782 w.
DEGGE
Isle of Wight
Anthony 1786 w.
Middlesex
Jno. 1727 i.
Lancaster
Isaac 1793 w.
John 1795 i.
Richmond
Wm. 1762 w.
Surry
Jno. 1779 w.
Westmoreland
Wm. 1768 i.
Jno. 1779 w.
DEGGES
Westmoreland
James 1778 w.
DeGRAFFENREIDT
Lunenburg
Tscharner 1794 w.
Tscharner 1799 i.
DeGUISCARD
Norfolk
Raymond 1786 i.
DEHAVAN
Loudoun
Abraham 1771 w.
DEHINUS
Northampton
Anthony 1664 w.
DeJARNETT
Prince Edward
Danl. 1754 w.
Mary 1765 w.
Elias 1769 w.
Martha 1782 w.
Danl. 1788 i.
Jno. Thos. 1789 w.
Jno. 1790 w.
DeJOUX
Henrico
[Benj.] 1703 i.
DELABRIERE
Northumberland
Andrew 1670 w.
DELACOURT
Northampton
Peter 1701 i.
DELAFIELD
Mecklenburg
Nicholas 1795 w.
DELAHAY
York
Matthew 1696 w.
DE LA LUE
Henrico
Solomon 1702-3 w.

DELANEY
Culpeper
Nelley 1798 i.
Frederick
Michael 1754 i.
DELANY
Fairfax
Martin 1751 i.
Frederick
Michael 1751 a.
Lancaster
Wm. 1738 i.
DELAP
Stafford
Andrew 1708 i.
DELLIHAY
Brunswick
Arthur 1773 w.
DELAP
Orange
Alexr. 1744 i.
DELASTATIUS
Accomack
Peter 1743 i.
Sebastian 1743 w.
Sebastian 1745 w.
Mary 1752 w.
Mary 1755 i.
Sebastian 1760 w.
Mary 1790 w.
Sebastian 1797 w.
Eliza 1798 w.
DELAYAY
Frederick
James 1753 a.
DELESTATIUS
Accomack
Sebastian 1708 w.
DELEMARE
Princess Anne
Thos. 1726 i.
DELGARN
Prince William
John 1783 w.
DELICOAT
Northampton
Jno. 1729 i.
DELINGER
Frederick
George 1770 i.
DELK
Isle of Wight
John 1753 w.
Roger 1761 i.
Solomon 1772 i.
Surry
Roger 1773 w.
Wm. 1780 i.
Southampton
Joseph 1761 w.

DELKS
Isle of Wight
Shelton 1769 i.
DELLICOAT
Northampton
Peter 1735 i.
DELLICOURT
Northampton
Wm. 1716 i.
DELLINGER
Frederick
George 1769 w.
Shenandoah
Frederick 1783 i.
John 1799 i.
DELLISON
Middlesex
Jno. 1698 w.
DELLOACH
Isle of Wight
Mary 1756 i.
DELOACH
Brunswick
Wm. 1747 w.
Eleanor 1750 w.
Greensville
William 1784 w.
Isle of Wight
Michael 1727 w.
Thomas 1749 i.
Thomas 1750 i.
Southampton
Wm. 1778 w.
Benj. 1785 w.
Richd. 1798 i.
Sarah 1798 w.
Solomon 1797 w.
DELOATCH
Greensville
William 1786 i.
DELOCH
Isle of Wight
Thomas 1748 w.
DELONEY
Mecklenburg
Henry 1785 w.
York
Thos. 1734 i.
DELOZER
Chesterfield
Thos. 1788 w.
Thos. M. 1795 i.
DELOZIER
Westmoreland
Thos. 1765 w.
DELPEACH
King George
Jas. 1752 i.
DELPH
Culpeper
Conrod 1791 w.
Henry 1791 i.

Madison
Michael 1794 w.
DELRIA
Westmoreland
Lewis 1698 i.
DEMAVORELL
Westmoreland
Saml. 1723 w.
DEMAX
York
Robt. 1687 w.
DEMENT
Goochland
Timothy 1747 i.
DEMENET
Westmoreland
Luke 1702 i.
DEMERRETT
Richmond
Luke 1751 w.
DEMIRE
Princess Anne
Wm. 1772 w.
DEMMER
Culpeper
Philip 1797 i.
DEMMERY
Southampton
Fredk. 1781 w.
DEMOSS
Berkeley
Charles 1786 w.
Rebecca 1791 w.
Charles 1796 i.
Frederick
Lewis 1749 a.
Lewis 1744 i.
Lewis 1753 a.
DEMOVEL
Westmoreland
Hannah 1744 w.
Saml. 1736 i.
Saml. 1738 i.
DEMPSEY
Spotsylvania
Jno. 1791 a.
DEMPSTER
Rappahannock
James 1677 w.
DENBY
Norfolk
Edwd. Sr. 1718 w.
William 1753 w.
Mathias 1765 w.
Joseph 1779 i.
Nathaniel 1780 w.
Arthur 1784 w.
Charles 1785 w.
Charles 1787 i.
Princess Anne
Edwd. 1760 i.
Edwd. 1761 w.

Anne 1767 i.
DENDY
Halifax
Wm. 1758 i.
DENHAM
Essex
Alex. 1697 w.
Frederick
Joseph 1762 i.
DENHOLM
Essex
Alex. 1787 w.
DENING
Essex
Adam 1711 i.
DENISTON
Botetourt
John 1776 i.
Frederick
Matthew 1746 a.
DENNETT
Essex
Thomas 1783 w.
Francis 1792 i.
York
Thos. 1673 w.
DENNEY
Frederick
David 1774 w.
DENNING
Southampton
Jno. 1798 i.
DENNIS
Amelia
Richd. 1775 w.
Henry 1780 w.
Richd. 1782 w.
Dearest 1782 w.
Jno. 1782 w.
Botetourt
Joseph 1794 w.
Halifax
Jno. 1779 w.
Henrico
Henry 1726 w.
Richd. 1726 i.
Nathl. 1796 w.
Northampton
Jno. 1729 i.
Northumberland
Jno. [Sr.?] 1652 i.
Jno. [Jr.?] 1652 i.
Princess Anne
Thos. 1719 w.
Jno. 1769 i.
DENNISS
Halifax
Jno. 1784 i.
DENNISTON
Augusta
Danl. 1749 w.

DENNY
Bedford
John 1755 w.
Frederick
David 1777 i.
Lancaster
Wm. 1734 i.
Edmd. 1735 i.
Northumberland
Edmund 1711 i.
Saml.. 1750-1 w.
Jane 1757 i.
John 1767 w.
Wm. 1785 w.
Saml. 1786 i.
Princess Anne
Wm. 1770 w.
Wm. 1773 i.
Jno. 1777 w.
Washington
Patrick 1797 w.
DENNYS
Halifax
Edwd. 1773 i.
DENSON
Isle of Wight
William 1677 w.
William 1694-5 i.
William 1695 i.
Francis 1709 w.
James 1721 w.
William 1750 w.
John 1754 w.
Southampton
Jno. 1761 w.
Jos. 1767 i.
Francis 1771 w.
Tuke 1798 w.
DENT
Fairfax
Thomas 1751 w.
George 1757 i.
Northampton
Thos. 1716 w.
Jos. 1718-9 w.
Spotsylvania
Jno. 1756 a.
DENTEN
Hampshire
Robert 1778 w.
DENTON
Brunswick
Isaac 1735 i.
Jno. 1735 w.
Edmond 1744 w.
Edwd. 1752 w.
Wm. 1753 w.
Sarah 1754 w.
Eliz. 1766 w.
Jno. 1772 w.
Thos. 1774 i.

Frederick
John 1765 i.
Greensville
Susanna 1785 w.
Hardy
Jane 1787 w.
Middlesex
Christopher 1743 a.
Shenandoah
Abraham 1774 w.
Mary 1779 i.
John 1787 w.
Surry
Pollerd 1732 w.
Sussex
Joseph 1772 w.
Rebecca 1780 i.
DEPEW
Botetourt
Samuel 1792 i.
Samuel 1795 i.
DEPP
Cumberland
Peter 1774 w.
DEPREEST
Augusta
Chas. 1799 nw.
DEPRIEST
Campbell
Jno. 1799 w.
Goochland
Wm. 1749 i.
Henrico
Wm. 1788 w.
DERBY
Accomack
Benj. 1777 i.
Benj. 1792 w.
Charlotte
James 1767 i.
DERHAM
Essex
William 1700 i.
DERICK
Frederick
David 1768 i.
DERING
Isle of Wight
Nicholas 1741 w.
DERK
Shenandoah
Simon 1787 w.
DERMOT
King George
Owen 1723 i.
DERMOTT
King George
Margt. 1724 i.
Northumberland
Chas. 1703 w.
Hugh 1712-3 i.

DERRICK
Botetourt
John 1791 i.
Northumberland
Thos. 1771 i.
Shenandoah
Simon 1787 i.
Stafford
Thos. 1708 i.
Edwd. 1740 i.
Mattox 1746 w.
Benj. 1762 w.
DERST
Franklin
Samuel 1791 w.
DERTING
Shenandoah
Adam 1783 i.
Philip G. 1783 i.
DESASEY
Goochland
James 1737 i.
DESERNY
Princess Anne
Jno. 1704 w.
DESHERN
Princess Anne
Joseph 1704 w.
DESHEY
Isle of Wight
John 1748 w.
Mary 1748 w.
Melchizedec 1748 i.
John 1749 i.
DESHMAN
Westmoreland
Jno. 1739 w.
DESMORE,
Princess Anne
Jno. 1720 i.
James 1722 a.
DETORIS
Surry
Amara 1677 op.
DETTETT (?)
Northampton
Francis 1650 i.
DEUCHER
Richmond
Jno. 1752 w.
DEVAUGHN
Fairfax
Thomas 1793 a.
DEVENISH
Accomack
Jno. 1678 w.
DEVIN
Fairfax
James 1750 w.

DEVERALL
Richmond
Benj. 1716 w.
DEVERDALL
Middlesex
Jno. 1699 w.
DEVERDELL
Middlesex
Joane 1704 w.
DEVOLL
Westmoreland
Philip 1722 i.
DEW
Isle of Wight
John 1678 w.
Prince George
Jno. 1716 i.
Richmond
Thos. 1708 w.
Andrew 1714 w.
Ann 1717 i.
Jane 1717 w.
Andrew 1726 w.
Ishmeal 1728 w.
Thos. 1733 w.
Wm. 1769 w.
Eliz. 1778 i.
Shenandoah
George 1793 w.
DEWEES
Montgomery
Paul 1797 w.
Patrick
Cornelius 1794 w.
DEWELL
Prince George
Jno. 1714 i.
Surry
Jno. 1749 i.
James 1750 w.
Wm. 1773 w.
DEWEY
Northampton
Geo. 1696 i.
Geo. 1714 w.
Jacob 1734 w.
Geo. 1735 i.
Thos. 1759 w.
Matilda 1768 i.
DEWICK
York
Michael 1717 i.
DEWMAN
Northampton
Jacob 1734 w.
Nathl. 1737 w.
DeYOUNG
Rappahannock
John 1672 w.

DEZER
Lunenburg
Leonard 1785 w.
DEZINAT
Halifax
Elias 1784 w.
DIAL
Halifax
James 1799 w.
DIAMONDS
York
———— 1751 i.
DICE
Augusta
Geo. 1772 i.
DICK
Augusta
Henry 1774 w.
King George
Wm. 1766 w.
Westmoreland
Robt. 1773 i.
DICKASON
Louisa
Henry 1798 i.
DICKEN
Culpeper
Chris. 1778 w.
DICKENS
Goochland
Thos. 1741 w.
Powhatan
Ann 1793 w.
Sussex
Thos. 1759 i.
DICKENSON
Bath
John 1799 w.
Isle of Wight
Chris. 1734 i.
Louisa
Wm. 1764 w.
Chas. 1777 i.
Prince Edward
Wm. Jennings 1781 w.
Richmond
Thos. 1715 i.
Spotsylvania
Nathl. 1776 w.
Nathl. 1790 a.
Washington
Humphrey 1779 i.
York
Jno. 1683 i.
Charles 1687 w.
Edmd. B. 1778 w.
Mary 1799 w.
DICKER
Frederick
Henry 1799 i.

DICKERSON
Accomack
Edwd. 1754 w.
Sarah 1756 i.
Sarah 1758 i.
David 1773 w.
Geo. 1788 i.
Jesse 1790 i.
Brunswick
Metcalfe 1758 w.
Charlotte
Tarpley 1781 i.
Metcalfe 1787 i.
Jane 1791 w.
Chesterfield
Jos. 1772 w.
Essex
John 1725 i.
Peter 1748 w.
John 1778 w.
Thos. Cooper 1796 i.
Halifax
Jno. 1786 w.
Isle of Wight
Christopher 1731 i.
Stephen 1731 i.
Louisa
Wm. 1767 i.
Nathaniel 1783 a.
Griffith 1785 w.
Northampton
Peter 1784 i.
Prince Edward
Nelson 1797 i.
Shenandoah
Catherine 1788 i.
York
Richd. 1681 i.
DICKESON
Accomack
Abraham 1752 w.
Edwd. 1755 i.
Essex
Thomas Cuper 1728 i.
Surry
Edward 1677 w.
York
Arthur 1766 i.
Leonard 1687 w.
DICKIE
Halifax
Jno. 1785 i.
DICKINS
Surry
Thos. 1727 w.
DICKINSON
Augusta
Adam 1761 i.
Essex
Jno. 1725 w.
Thos. Cooper 1730 i.

Franklin
John 1792 i.
Isle of Wight
Jacob 1750 w.
Chris. 1781 w.
Chastity 1797 w.
Louisa
Nathaniel 1753 w.
Chas. 1776 w.
Wm. 1776 i.
Rachel 1797 w.
Norfolk
Thomas 1785 w.
Stafford
Edwd. 1786 w.
Westmoreland
Thos. 1737 w.
York
Arthur 1670 w.
Jno. 1676 w.
Arthur 1702 i.
DICKSON
Essex
Luke 1748 i.
Isle of Wight
Thomas 1764 i.
Louisa
Henry 1768 a.
Norfolk
John 1719 w.
James 1771 w.
Prince Anne
Marjery 1705 w.
Robt. 1777 w.
Robt. 1779 i.
Amy 1780 i.
Robt. 1782 i.
Rockbridge
James 1797 w.
Westmoreland
Eliz. 1740 w.
DICSON
Surry
Jno. 1659 w.
DIDLAKE
Middlesex
Jno. 1767 a.
DIE
Accomack
Jno. 1666 i.
DIER
Amelia
Peter 1776 w.
Chesterfield
Jno. 1779 w.
Princess Anne
Jno. 1787 w.
DIGBY
Norfolk
Robt. 1666 w.

Surry
Charles 1711 i.
DIGGE
Louisa
Jno. 1776 a.
Westmoreland
Eliz. 1755 i.
DIGGES
York
Wm. 1698 w.
Dudley 1710 w.
Anne 1776 w.
Wm. 1780 nw.
DIGGS
Westmoreland
Jas. 1735 i.
York
Eliz. 1692 i.
DIGMAN
Richmond
Jas. 1797 i.
DIGNUM
King George
Chris. 1754 i.
DIKE
Essex
Bowler 1748 i.
Jno. 1758 w.
Rappahannock
Jno. 1678 w.
DILLARD
Amherst
Joseph 1790 w.
James 1794 a.
Culpeper
William 1782 i.
Middlesex
Ed. 1757 w.
Jno. 1775 i.
Pittsylvania
Thos. 1774 w.
Spotsylvania
Thos. 1774 w.
Sussex
Nancy E. 1799 i.
DILLEHAY
Sussex
Jno. 1779 w.
DILLEN
Goochland
Wm. 1744 w.
Henry
Henry Sr. 1798 w.
DILLIARD
Culpeper
George 1790 w.
DILLING
Augusta
Jno. 1769 w.
DILLINGER

Frederick
John 1765 i.
Shenandoah
Christian 1780 w.
DILLION
Henry
William 1792 i.
DILLON
Frederick
Thomas 1762 w.
Goochland
Thos. 1744 i.
Lancaster
Michael 1752 i.
DILLYON
Northampton
Jno. 1737 w.
DIMMILLO
Essex
Joseph 1748-9 i.
DIMOCKS
Westmoreland
Mary 1756 i.
DINGLE
King George
Lucy 1761 w.
DINKINGS
Surry
Thos. 1727 i.
DINKINS
Surry
Thos. 1718 w.
Alex. 1751 i.
DINNE
Northumberland
Richd. 1743-4 w.
DINNEY
Northumberland
Wm. 1793 w.
DINNING
Princess Anne
Andrew 1706 a.
DINNIS
Brunswick
Jno. 1761 i.
Goochland
Jno. 1788 i.
DINWIDDIE
Amherst
Robt. 1794 a.
Saml. 1795 a.
Bath
Robert 1796 w.
Cumberland
Robt. 1772 w.
King George
Jno. 1726 i.
Jno. 1727 i.
DISHMAN
Essex
Peter 1764 i.

David 1794 w.
King George
Saml. 1796 w.
Westmoreland
Saml. 1727 w.
Cornelia 1730 i.
Ann 1791 w.
Jno. 1791 w.
DISK
Berkeley
Hannah 1774 i.
DISKIN
Essex
Daniel 1698 i.
DISKINS
Prince William
John 1787 i.
Richmond
Agatha 1765 i.
DISKS
Essex
John 1698 i.
DISMANG
Lunenburg
Wm. 1791 w.
DISMONG
Brunswick
Archer 1792 i.
DISON
Chesterfield
Benj. 17— w.
Benj. 1750 w.
Francis 1781 w.
Henrico
Nicholas Jr. 1701 w.
Nicholas 1715 w.
Norfolk
Pavey 1762 w.
Bailey 1774 i.
Princess Anne
Philip 1759 i.
Phillip 1769 i.
DISPONET
Frederick
Jacob 1758 i.
DITCH
Shenandoah
George 1790 i.
DIVERAZ
Henrico
Paul 1712 w.
DIVINIA
Frederick
Corneluis 1760 i.
DIVINNEY
Frederick
Hugh 1757 i.
DIX
Accomack
Isaac 1687 w.
Isaac 1708 w.

Jno. 1719 w.
Wm. 1733 i.
Isaac 1740 w.
Isaac 1751 w.
Richd. 1760 w.
Jno. 1762 w.
Sabra 1764 w.
Isaac 1765 i.
Solomon 1780 w.
Geo. 1785 w.
Wm. 1789 w.
Geo. 1790 i.
Amaziah 1793 w.
Geo. 1794 i.
Levi 1794 w.
Amaziah 1795 i.
Jno. 1795 w.
Bersheba 1799 w.
Campbell
Wm. 1779 i.
Essex
Wm. 1746 w.
Thomas 1750 i.
Mary 1772 i.
John 1785 i.
Thomas 1789 w.
Thomas 1796 i.
Pittsylvania
Jno. 1784 w.
Jas. 1790 w.
DIXCON
Princess Anne
Wm. 1703 w.
DIXON
Bedford
Thomas 1770 w.
Berkeley
Thomas 1778 i.
Campbell
Jas. 1786 w.
Halifax
Thos. 1764 w.
Ann 1773 i.
Mary 1774 w.
Stephen 1792 i.
Isle of Wight
Thomas 1670 i.
Thomas 1748 w.
William 1767 i.
Thomas 1794 w.
Norfolk
James 1719 i.
Sarah 1799 w.
Northampton
Chris. 1665 w.
Jonah 1670 i.
Michael 1733 i.
Michael 1737 w.
Chris. 1751 w.
Jno. 1764 w.
Tilney 1764 w.

Michael 1767 i.
Benj. 1772 w.
Wm. 1772 w.
Tilney 1774 w.
Ann 1778 w.
Jno. 1778 w.
Anne 1783 i.
Michael 1786 i.
Chris. 1789 w.
Ralph 1789 i.
Jno. 1792 w.
Wm. Jr. 1795 w.
Jno. 1798 w.
Prince Edward
John 1792 w.
Spotsylvania
Roger 1772 w.
Westmoreland
Thos. 1705 nw.
York
Richd. 1706 w.
Jas. 1752 w.
Rockbridge
Thomas 1796 w.
DIXSON
Essex
Thomas 1711 i.
DOACK
Montgomery
David 1787 w.
DOAK
Augusta
Saml. 1772 w.
Fincastle
Robert 1775 a.
Wythe
Nathl. 1794 i.
DOBBIE
Halifax
Wm. 1774 w.
DOBBINS
Brunswick
Jno. 1785 w.
Essex
Peter 1717 w.
Wm. 1736 w.
John 1783 w.
Lunenburg
Wm. 1751 w.
Richmond
Edmd. 1721 i.
DOBBS
Isle of Wight
Josiah 1778 i.
Lancaster
Joseph 1791 i.
York
Robt. 1697 i.
DOBBYNS
Lunenburg
Wm. 1761 i.

Richmond
Griffin 1750 i.
DOBE
Surry
Jno. 1722 w.
DOBIE
Cumberland
John 1753 w.
Sussex
Robt. 1760 w.
Robt. 1780 i.
Nathl.1793 w.
DOBIKIN
Augusta
Jno. 1746 w.
DOBINS
Brunswick
Bowler 1774 i.
DOBSON
Amelia
Thos. 1776 w.
Essex
Wm. 1768 w.
Wm. 1777 i.
DOBY
Brunswick
Wm. 1772 w.
Surry
Jno. 1737 w.
DOBYN
Brunswick
Jno. 1773 w.
DOBYNS
Essex
Danl. Sr. 1712 w.
Richd. 1726 i.
Wm. 1730 w.
Isaac 1737 w.
Danl. 1741 w.
Danl. 1748 w.
Danl. 1754 w.
Drury 1768 w.
Richmond
Chas. 1761 i.
Chas. 1781 w.
Saml. 1782 w.
Danl. 1784 w.
Thos. 1788 w.
Edwd. 1789 w.
Wm. F. 1791 w.
Ailcy 1796 w.
DODD
Chesterfield
Jno. 1767 w.
Ann 1783 i.
Fauquier
Nathl. 1784 w.
Frederick
Edwd. 1780 i.
Henrico
Wm. 1688 i.

King George
Jno. 1750 i.
Benj. 1773 a.
Jno. 1776 w.
Jos. 1777 a.
Northampton
Jos. 1737 i.
Jos. 1739 i.
Westmoreland
Jno. 1745 w.
Quisenbury 1781 i.
Benj. 1785 i.
DODDRIDGE
Berkeley
Joseph 1799 nw.
DODGGIN
King George
Wm. 1739 i.
DODGIN
King George
Jno. 1747 a.
Wm. 1754 a.
DODGSON
Isle of Wight
Chris. 1758 i.
DODLEY
Northumberland
Winefort 1780 w.
DODSON
Amelia
Stephen 1755 w.
Chesterfield
Joel 1783 i.
Wm. 1784 w.
Thos. 1793 w.
Fauquier
Abraham 1768 w.
Greeham 1777 w.
Greenham 1784 i.
Halifax
Joseph 1773 w.
Henrico
Wm. 1747 w.
Middlesex
Jno. Hackney 1726 w.
Northumberland
Gervas 1661 w.
Pittsylvania
Isaac Jr. 1769 i.
Fortunatus 1777 w.
Thos. 1784 i.
Thos. 1796 w.
Lazarus 1799 w.
Prince William
David 1740 w.
Richmond
Chas. 1705 w.
Chas. 1716 w.
Anne 1718 w.
Fortunatus 1738 i.
Thos. 1740 w.

Wm. 1753 w.
Chas. 1775 w.
Jno. 1799 w.
Shenandoah
John 1784 w.
Westmoreland
Thos. 1670 w.
DOE
Accomack
Saml. 1702 i.
Saml. 1775 w.
Eleanor 1788 w.
DOEBER
Norfolk
Fredk. A. 1777 i.
DOEPA
Northampton
Jno. 1709 i.
DOGAN
Isle of Wight
Bryan 1727 i.
DOGED
Northumberland
Wm. 1751 w.
DOGGET
Lancaster
Ann 1761 w.
Reubin 1772 w.
William 1772 w.
Reuben 1789 w.
DOGGETT
Northumberland
Jno. 1739-40 i.
Culpeper
George 1759 w.
George 1763 i.
Richard 1781 i.
Bushrod 1791 w.
Fauquier
Benj. 1779 i.
Lancaster
Benj. 1682 w.
Wm. 1716 w.
Richd. 1721 w.
Benj. 1723 w.
Mary 1737 w.
James 1758 w.
Benj. 1760 i.
Emberson 1765 i.
William 1773 i.
John 1780 i.
Elmor 1781 w.
Coleman 1782 w.
George 1785 w.
Mary Ann 1786 w.
Thomas 1786 i.
Mary 1794 w.
William G. 1794 i.
William 1795 w.
Northumberland
Benj. 1765 i.

DOGGIN
King George
Wm. 1754 w.
DOGGINS
Essex
Samuel 1797 i.
DOGON
Fairfax
John 1771 w.
DOHERTY
Northumberland
Neale 1724 w.
DOHONEY
Orange
Thomas 1798 w.
DOLBY
Accomack
Jno. 1671 w.
Northampton
Peter 1709 i.
Thos. 1717 w.
David 1733 i.
Benj. 1736 w.
Benj. 1742 i.
Wm. 1742 w.
Jno. Sr. 1745 w.
Jno. Jr. 1745 i.
Thos. 1745 w.
Waterfield 1751 i.
Esau 1752 w.
Jos. 1752 w.
Leah 1752 i.
Pettit 1752 i.
Upshur 1759 w.
Branson 1760 w.
Isaac 1760 w.
Jos. 1762 i.
Waterfield 1768 i.
Wm. 1768 i.
Jno. 1778 w.
Jos. 1778 w.
Benj. 1796 i.
DOLE
Surry
Peter 1676 i.
DOLES
Isle of Wight
Thomas 1688 i.
Southampton
Joseph 1786 w.
DOLL
Hardy
Jacob 1798 w.
DOLLAR
Princess Anne
Hannah 1719 a.
James 1731 i.
Margt. 1731 w.
DOLLARD
Henrico
Jno. 1792 i.

DOLLEY
Norfolk
Denis 1687 w.
DOLLIN
Northumberland
John 1761 i.
DOLLINGER
Albemarle
Wm. 1783 i.
DOLLINGS
Northumberland
Hannah 1765 w.
DOLLINS
Albemarle
Richd. 1774 w.
Jno. 1787 w.
Northumberland
Jno. 1725 i.
John 1770 w.
Sally 1775 i.
Orange
Presley 1779 i.
DOLMAN
Westmoreland
Wm. 1784 w.
DOLTON
Accomack
Sarah 1737 i.
Albemarle
Timothy 1767 w.
Spotsylvania
Geo. 1777 a.
DOMINE
Berkeley
John 1793 i.
DONAHOE
King George
Edwd. 1748 i.
DONAHOW
Norfolk
Mary 1761 w.
DONALD
Chesterfield
Wm. 1774 i.
Robt. 1791 w.
Henrico
Geo. 1795 w.
DONALDSON
Brunswick
Jno. 1749 i.
Benj. Chapman
1775 w.
Fairfax
William 1768 i.
James 1770 w.
James 1792 i.
Fauquier
Stephen 1778 i.
Lancaster
Andrew 1735 nw.

Loudoun
Bayly 1780 i.
Daniel 1782 w.
Westmoreland
Wm. 1733 i.
DONALEY
Augusta
Jno. 1765 a.
DONE
Princess Anne
Isaac 1782 i.
DONELLY
Augusta
Jno. 1770 i.
Chas. 1783 w.
Andrew 1786 i.
DONILLY
Augusta
Jno. 1767 i.
DONIPHAN
King George
Robt. 1744 i.
Anderson 1761 w.
Wm. 1798 i.
Richmond
Alex. 1716 w.
DONNALLY
Augusta
Francis 1761 w.
DONNE
King George
Saml. 1764 w.
Mary 1770 w.
DONNEL
Prince Edward
James 1763 w.
DONNOHOE
Accomack
Timothy 1750 i.
DONOHOE
Accomack
Mary 1752 w.
Essex
Patrick 1748 w.
Frances 1771 w.
Loudoun
Cornelius 1792 i.
DONOWAY
Northumberland
Jno. 1742-3 i.
Jno. 1744 w.
Richmond
Saml. 1797 i.
DONSTON
Orange
Jno. 1752 w.
DONUS
Accomack
Arthur 1721 w.

DOODGER
Chesterfield
Martin 1799 i.
DOOGAN
Hardy
Alex. 1790 w.
James 1792 w.
DOOLING
Westmoreland
Philip 1728 i.
Philip 1733-4 i.
DOOLY
Bedford
Thomas 1778 w.
DOONE
Montgomery
John 1791 w.
DOORES
Essex
Chas. 1716 w.
DOPSON
Hampshire
William 1798 w.
DORAN
Frederick
Daniel 1751 a.
Greenbrier
Jacob 1793 w.
Washington
James 1799 w.
DORANT
Frederick
Daniel 1748 a.
Daniel 1750 i.
DORCH
Surry
Walter 1684 i.
DOREING
Princess Anne
Jno. 1719 i.
DOREY
Princess Anne
Jno. 1735 a.
DORHAM
Orange
Thos. 1743 a.
DORMAN
Isle of Wight
Simpkin 1767 i.
Northampton
Wm. 1797 i.
DORON
Northumberland
Hugh 1782 w.
DOROTHY
Fairfax
Constantine 1778 i.
DORRELL
Fairfax
Cordelia 1782 w.

DORSET
Middlesex
Robt. 1747 i.
DORSEY
Frederick
Joshua 1778 i.
DORSON
Frederick
David 1746 a.
DORSTER
Frederick
Thomas 1749 i.
DORTCH
Mecklenburg
Noah 1781 w.
David 1782 w.
DORTON
Washington
William 1782 w.
DORY
Princess Anne
Jno. 1752 w.
DOSCHER
Augusta
Christian 1759 w.
DOSS
Cumberland
John 1780 w.
Henrico
Azariah 1754 i.
Pittsylvania
Jas. 1796 w.
DOSH
Shenandoah
Chris. Sr. 1778 w.
DOSTER
Frederick
Thomas 1748 w.
DOSWELL
York
Jno. Jr. 1718 w.
Eliz. 1727 w.
Jno. 1727 i.
Edwd. 1739 w.
DOUDGE
Princess Anne
Richd. 1786 i.
Goab 1799 w.
DOUGAL
Norfolk
Forrest 1797 i.
DOUGE
Princess Anne
Wm. 1752 i.
DOUGHARTY
Fincastle
William 1773 i.
Frederick
William 1761 a.
Norfolk
Owen 172— i.

DOUGHERTY
Augusta
Chas. 1763 a.
Michael 1763 i.
Frederick
Patrick 1750 i.
Barney 1786 i.
Daniel 1794 w.
Montgomery
Michael 1782 i.
Rockbridge
Anthony 1792 w.
Wythe
Anthony 1793 i.
DOUGHLY
Norfolk
Jacob 1794 w.
DOUGHTY
Frederick
Daniel 1795 i.
Lancaster
Enoch 1677 w.
Rappahannock
Enoch 1677 w.
DOUGLAS
Accomack
Geo. 1758 w.
Walton 1760 w.
Walter 1763 i.
Jas. 1796 i.
Bedford
David 1791 i.
Cumberland
Robt. 1785 w.
Fairfax
Jacob 1750 w.
James 1794 a.
James Jr. 1795 i.
Fincastle
John 1775 a.
Henrico
Chas. 1709 i.
Loudoun
Wm. 1783 w.
Louisa
Wm. 1798 w.
Northumberland
Gyles 1655 w.
Northampton
Edwd. 1657 w.
Jno. 1720 w.
Joan 1721-2 w.
Orange
John 1794 w.
DOUGLASS
Accomack
Geo. 1761 i.
Albemarle
Geo. 1785 w.
Augusta
Jno. 1777 i.

Brunswick
Robt. 1742 i.
Jno. 1751 i.
Campbell
Robt. 1794 w.
Fincastle
John 1775 w.
Halifax
Thos. 1789 w.
Wm. 1791 w.
Wm. 1797 a.
Louisa
Robt. 1781 i.
Loudoun
William 1783 w.
Northumberland
Edwd. 1793 i.
DOUNEY
Berkeley
Richd. 1787 i.
DOW
Frederick
John 1763 i.
DOWDALL
Spotsylvania
Patrick 1743 a.
DOWDELL
Fairfax
Thomas 1771 w.
DOWDEN
Richmond
Anthony 1727 i.
DOWDY
Goochland
Jno. 1786 i.
DOWEL
Louisa
Jno. 1761 w.
DOWELL
Albemarle
John 1797 i.
Bedford
George 1772 i.
Northampton
Morgan 1700 w.
Prince William
John 1781 w.
John 1796 w.
DOWELS
Isle of Wight
John 1731 w.
DOWER
Essex
Charles 1716 i.
DOWLEN
Northumberland
Mathew 1778 w.
DOWLES
Isle of Wight
John 1721 w.
Thoms 1721-2 i.

John 1731 w.
DOWLEY
Princess Anne
Wm. 1766 i.
DOWLIN
Loudoun
Daniel 1796 i.
DOWLING
Westmoreland
Jas. 1725 w.
York
[Jas. or] Jno.
1719-20 w.
Sarah 1720 w.
DOWMAN
Northampton
Jno. 1715 i.
Danl. 1718 w.
Prince William
Travers 1783 i.
DOWNES
Hanover
Jno. 1773 a.
Northampton
Robt. 1668 w.
DOWNEY
Augusta
Saml. 1773 w.
Shenandoah
John 1780 i.
William 1780 w.
DOWNING
Accomack
Jno. 1718 w.
Robt. 1745 i.
Hannah Scarburgh
1760 i.
John Robins 1779 w.
Bedford
John 1777 w.
Middlesex
Wm. Sr. 1698 w.
Northampton
Arthur Sr. 1760 w.
Edwin 1762 w.
Arthur 1768 i.
Jno. Sr. 1778 w.
Zorobabel 1781 w.
Arthur Sr. 1789 w.
Northumberland
Saml. 1719 i.
Thos. 1721 w.
Chas. 1740 i.
Wm. 1741 w.
Samuell 1751 i.
Samuel 1757 w.
Samuel 1769 i.
Wm. 1783 i.
Hannah 1788 w.
Sarah 1792 w.
Jno. 1793 i.

Wm. 1796 i.
Thos. 1799 w.
Westmoreland
Ralph 1716 w.
DOWNMAN
Lancaster
Wm. 1654 i.
Rawleigh 1718-19 w.
Rawleigh 1781 w.
Joseph Ball 1799 w.
Prince William
Jabez 1782 i.
Richmond
Wm. 1712 w.
Robt. 1716 w.
Million 1727 i.
Wm. 1727 w.
Travers 1723 w.
Wm. 1741 w.
Margaret 1758 w.
Jas. 1762 w.
Wm. 1765 i.
Robt. 1769 w.
Robt. Porteus 1774 w.
Lucy 1778 w.
Geo. 1781 w.
Geo. 1785 i.
Wm. 1791 w.
Wm. 1792 i.
Frances P. 1793 w.
DOWNS
Chesterfield
Wm. 1783 i.
Norfolk
Wm. 1784 i.
Northampton
Danl. 1773 w.
Thos. 1798 i.
DOWNTON
Westmoreland
Nicholas 1730 i.
DOWSING
Brunswick
Wm. 1766 w.
Lunenburg
Everard 1782 w.
York
Robt. 1736 w.
DOWTIE
Northampton
Rowland 1743 w.
DOWTIN
Essex
Anthony 1697 w.
DOWTY
Northampton
Jeptha 1757 w.
Josiah 1771 i.
Peter Sr. 1772 w.
Peter 1784 w.
Jno. 1799 i.

DOWY
Northumberland
Wm. 1711 i.
DOXEY
Northumberland
Jno. 1789 w.
DOYAL
Westmoreland
Patrick 1725 i.
DOYE
Southampton
Danl. 1767 i.
DOYEL
Southampton
Danl. 1768 a.
Edmund 1769 i.
Kinchen 1787 i.
DOYELL
Southampton
Wm. 1783 i.
DOYL
York
Richd. 1729 i.
DOYLE
Essex
Philip 1772 i.
Isle of Wight
Daniel 1720 w.
Prince William
Edward 1741 w.
Richmond
Jno. 1718 w.
Southampton
Edmund 1762 i.
Edward 1762 w.
Westmoreland
Chris. 1662 w.
DOYLY
York
Cope 1702 i.
DOZER
Richmond
Jno. 1748 i.
Westmoreland
Thos. 1779 w.
DOZIER
Lancaster
John 1758 i.
Richmond
Leonard 1733 i.
Eliza 1748 w.
Westmoreland
Richd. 1751 w.
Thos. 1781 i.
Wm. 1782 w.
Jas. 1799 i.
Richd. 1791 w.
DOZWELL
York
Rebecker 1725 w.

DRAGE
Frederick
Benjamin 1798 w.
DRAGOO
Benjamin 1799 i.
DRAKE
Amelia
Thos. 1797 w.
Augusta
Abraham 1746 i.
Abraham 1747 i.
Franklin
William 1792 w.
Goochland
Jonathan 1793 i.
King George
Clapham 1747 a.
Henry 1760 w.
Henry 1762 i.
Sarah 1765 w.
Wm. 1771 a.
Ann 1772 a.
Francis 1777 a.
Thos. 1777 w.
Jno. 1785 a.
Montgomery
Michael 1798 w.
Powhatan
James 1797 w.
James, Jr. 1799 i.
Richmond
Ann 1744 w.
Southampton
Jno. 1753 w.
Thos. 1758 w.
Richd. 1759 w.
Timothy 1762 i.
Jesse 1773 w.
Jno. 1770 w.
Ann 1775 w.
Thos. 1783 w.
Cordal 1796 w.
Barnaby, Sr. 1797 w.
Westmoreland
Richd. 1780 w.
Wm. 1780 w.
Sarah 1784 w.
Thos. 1785 i.
Wm. 1785 i.
Sarah 1787 i.
Benj. 1788 w.
Jno. 1798 w.
DRAKEFOOT
Prince William
Richd. 1741 w.
DRAPER
Amelia
Thos. 1779 w.
James 1780 w.
Solomon 1783 w.
Wm. 1786 i.

James 1793 i.
Augusta
Geo. 1750 i.
Lancaster
Jno. 1676 i.
Thos. 1688 w.
Josias 1713 w.
Mecklenburg
Joshua 1792 w.
Richmond
Thos. 1735 i.
Wm. 1766 i.
Jno. 1779 w.
Southampton
Thos. 1792 w.
Westmoreland
Jno. 1656 w.
DRAPIER
Princess Anne
Richd. 1694 w.
DRAYTON
Middlesex
Merlina 1760 i.
Prince George
Sarah 1718 i.
Roger 1718 i.
DRENN
Rappahannock
Edwd. 1678 w.
DREVER
Isle of Wight
Charles 1795 a.
DREW
Berkeley
William 1785 w.
William 1796 i.
Brunswick
Jno. 1760 i.
Frederick
Dolphin 1786 w.
Northampton
Edwd. 1650 w.
Southampton
Edwd. 1745 w.
Newitt 1775 w.
Jesse 1782 w.
Jeremiah 1785 w.
Surry
Richd. 1679 w.
Jno. 1702 w.
Sarah 1711 i.
Thos. Sr. 1734 w.
Thos. 1739 i.
David 1754 w.
Thos. 1742 w.
Thos. 1745 i.
Jno. 1764 w.
David 1776 w.
Wm. 1778 w.
Martha 1792 w.

DREWITT
Rappahannock
Jno. 1674 w.
York
Jonathan 1726 nw.
DREWRY
Norfolk
Thomas 1772 w.
Southampton
Thos. 1777 w.
Wm. 1781 w.
Saml. 1790 w.
Humphrey 1797 w.
Wm. 1797 w.
York
Edwd. 1687 i.
Jno. 1714 i.
Jno. 1727 i.
Robt. 1744 i.
Peter 1767 i.
Saml. Jr. 1767 w.
Saml. 1768 w.
Robt. 1782 w.
Henry 1783 w.
Mary 1792 w.
Wm. 1799 i.
DRIEU
Northampton
Chas. 1738 i.
DRIGGLEHOUSE
Northampton
Azarium 1738 w.
DRIGHOUSE
Northampton
Jno. (negro) 1729 i.
Thos. 1757 w.
DRILL
Essex
Ann 1736 w.
DRINEN
Greenbrier
Lawrence 1784 i.
DRING
York
Thos. 1755 i.
DRINKARD
Charles City
Mary 1771 w.
DRINKWATER
Amelia
Josiah 1781 w.
Campbell
Jno. 1784 w.
DRISCOLL
Essex
Timothy 1716 w.
Timothy 1721 i.
DRISKALL
Westmoreland
Darby 1720 w.

DRIVER
Albemarle
Jno. 1761 i.
Isle of Wight
Giles 1677 w.
Charles 1700 i.
Giles 1715 i.
Charles 1721 i.
Mary 1721 w.
John 1722 i.
Gyles 1725-26 w.
Gyles 1725 i.
Joseph 1725 i.
Robert 1736 i.
Edward 1739 w.
Giles 1744 w.
Robert 1748 w.
Edward 1752 i.
Giles 1753 i.
Oliver 1753 i.
Giles 1765 i.
Thomas 1771 w.
Charles 1772 i.
Charles 1785 w.
Powhatan
Jiles 1779 i.
York
Thos. 1752 i.
Jno. 1788 w.
DRIVOR
Isle of Wight
Thomas 1728 i.
DROUGHT
Princess Anne
Richd. 1749 w.
DROUT
Princess Anne
Caleb 1728 i.
DROUTT
Princess Anne
Robt. 1719 w.
DRUDGE
Princess Anne
Ann 1777 w.
DRUGGETT
Berkeley
Isaac 1782 i.
DRUMHELLER
Albemarle
Leonard 1797 w.
DRUMMOND
Accomack
Stephen 1710 w.
Richd. 1720 w.
Anne 1735 w.
Richd. 1735 w.
Jno. 1751 w.
Jno. Jr. 1751 i.
Richd. 1752 i.
Spencer 1759 w.
Richd. 1765 w.

Geo. 1766 w.
Wm. 1772 w.
Anne 1774 w.
Wm. 1775 w.
Wm. 1776 w.
Wm. 1779 i.
Ann 1780 i.
Wm. 1781 i.
Jno. 1784 w.
Wm. 1790 i.
Robt. 1792 w.
Drake 1794 w.
Richd. 1794 w.
David 1795 w.
Henry 1795 w.
Richd. Sr. 1795 w.
Spencer 1795 w.
Comfort 1796 w.
David 1797 i.
Dublin 1797 w.
Wm. 1797 w.
Essex
Paulin 1773 i.
Fauquier
James 1766 i.
York
Wm. 1773 w.
DRUMOND
Accomack
Jno. 1713 w.
Jas. 1723 i.
Hill 1728 w.
Richd. 1731 w.
DRUMWRIGHT
Goochland
Wm. 1752 w.
Geo. 1763 w.
Lunenburg
James 1757 i.
DRURY
Henrico
Wm. 1703 i.
Norfolk
Jno. Sr. 1750 w.
John 1752 w.
Southampton
Thos. 1777 i.
York
Wm. 1726 w.
DRYDEN
Augusta
David 1772 w.
Botetourt
Thomas 1777 w.
Washington
Nathl. 1781 i.
DRYSDALE
Northampton
Thos. 1797 w.

DRYER
Isle of Wight
Charles 1700 i.
DUBERLY
Accomack
Jno. 1734 i.
DUCH
Isle of Wight
John 1736 w.
DUCHE
Isle of Wight
William 1728 w.
John 1736 w.
William 1763 w.
Timothy 1773 w.
Jacob 1794 i.
Joseph 1797 w.
DUCKEBERRY
Essex
Mary 1715 i.
DUCKER
Fairfax
John 1747 w.
John 1747-8 a.
DUCKBERRY
Augusta
Abraham 1760 a.
DUCKSBERRY
Essex
Geo. 1715 w.
DUCKWORTH
Essex
Thomas 1737 i.
Frederick
John 1757 i.
John 1761 i.
William 1762 i.
Westmoreland
Wm. 1665 w.
DUDDEN
Rockbridge
Valentine 1797 i.
DUDDING
Essex
Andrew 1713 w.
Richard 1748 w.
DUDGEN
Charlotte
Richd. 1771 w.
DUDGEON
Charlotte
Wm. 1786 w.
Margaret 1791 w.
Halifax
Jno. 1776 w.
Jno. 1785 a.
Richd. 1778 i.
Lunenburg
Jno. 1763 i.

DUDLEY
Amelia
Marlon 1764 w.
Thos. 1774 i.
Edwd. 1781 w.
Amherst
Ann 1794 w.
Campbell
Wm. 1799 i.
Charles City
Jno. 1793 i.
Chesterfield
Thos. 1768 w.
Cumberland
Richd. 1750 i.
Essex
Richd. 1717 w.
Louisa
Roxanna 1793 a.
Middlesex
Wm. 1677 a.
Robert 1701 w.
James Sr. 1707 i.
James 1710 w.
James 1711 w.
Robert 1710 w.
James 1744 i.
Robert 1745 w.
Robt. 1747 i.
Jean 1748 w.
Thos. 1749 a.
Wm. 1760 w.
Peyton 1762 w.
Ambrose 1774 i.
Joyce 1776 w.
Lewis 1781 w.
Stanton 1782 i.
Chas. 1794 i.
Norfolk
Aurthur 1720 i.
William 1787 w.
Princess Anne
Thos. 1722 w.
Wm. 1724 i.
Richd. 1748 w.
Robt. 1746 w.
Jno. 1753 w.
Mary 1754 i.
Eliz. 1761 w.
Geo. 1780 w.
James 1780 w.
Henry 1782 w.
Robt. Sr. 1791 w.
Prince William
John 1788 w.
Richmond
Peter 1734 i.
Wm. 1752 w.
Thos. 1761 i.
Wm. 1761 i.
Mary 1764 i.

Alex. 1775 i.
Spotsylvania
Robt. 1766 w.
Robert 1777 a.
Westmoreland
Richd. 1702 w.
Mary 1722 nw.
York
Wm. 1771 w.
Prince William
John 1793 i.
DUE
York
Thos. 1691 a.
DUELING
Northampton
Jno. 1721 w.
DUERSON
Spotsylvania
Thos. 1769 w.
DUETT
Orange
Charles 1741 a.
DUFF
Fincastle
William 1775 a.
King George
Wm. Jr. 1743 i.
Wm. 1745 i.
Eliz. 1749 eb.
Sussex
Mary 1785 i.
Washington
John 1794 i.
Samuel 1796 w.
DUFFEE
Cumberland
Isaac 1774 w.
DUFFIELD
Harrison
Isaac 1798 i.
DUFFS
Cumberland
Isaac 1774 i.
DUFFY
Amelia
Jno. 1742 i.
DUGARD
Fauquier
John 1778 i.
DUGGAR
Brunswick
Mary 1783 w.
DUGLAS
Frederick
William 1784 i.
Harrison
Levi 1787 i.
Northumberland
Robt. 1655 i.

Orange
Roger 1744 w.
Geo. 1757 i.
DUGLASS
Halifax
Jno. 1780 w.
Lunenburg
Alex. 1749 i.
Norfolk
Danl. 1687 w.
Northumberland
John 1778 w.
DUKAR
Westmoreland
Jos. 1750 i.
DUKE
Berkeley
John Sr. 1789 w.
Margaret 1791 w.
John 1792 w.
William 1795 i.
Charles City
Henry 1795 w.
Goochland
Edmond 1787 w.
Henrico
Jas. 1791 w.
Louisa
Cosby 1778 w.
Clevears 1785 w.
Prince George
Henry 1719 i.
York
Jno. 1679 i.
DUKES
Isle of Wight
John 1720 w.
Lancaster
Jos. 1705 i.
DUKS
Essex
Jno. 1710 w.
DUKSBERRY
Essex
Geo. 1715 i.
DULANEY
Norfolk
Wm. 1757 i.
DULANY
Accomack
Wm. 1751 i.
Culpeper
William 1777 i.
Fairfax
Martin 1750 a.
Stafford
Edwd. 1739 i.
Edwd. 1743 i.
DULIN
Fairfax
William 1757 w.

Elizabeth 1762 i.
Edward 1782 w.
John 1791 w.
DULING
Essex
Ann 1744 w.
Fairfax
Elizabeth 1761 i.
DULY
Loudoun
Charity 1795 i.
DUMAS
Goochland
Jeremiah 1734 i.
DUN
Albemarle
John 1792 w.
Brunswick
Jno. 1753 i.
Essex
Jonathan 1770 i.
Isle of Wight
John 1694 i.
Lancaster
Alex. 1701 i.
Richmond
Robt. 1727 i.
Surry
Joel 1759 i.
Wythe
Thomas 1790 i.
DUNAVON
Henrico
Cornelius 1701 i.
DUNAWAY
Henrico
Esther 1792 w.
Lancaster
Saml. 1748 i.
Wm. 1758 i.
Saml. 1789 w.
William 1798 w.
Northumberland
Joseph 1759 i.
Richmond
Malachy 1737 i.
Westmoreland
Abraham 1727 i.
DUNBAR
Greenbrier
John 1794 w.
Mathew 1797 i.
King George
Peter 1729 i.
Westmoreland
Abigail 1762 i.
Wm. 1762 w.
Wm. 1769 i.
Jas. 1789 i.

DUNBARR
Augusta
Jno. 1774 a.
Thos. 1775 i.
Jonathan 1783 i.
York
Rich. 1700 w.
DUNCAN
Accomack
Eli. 1790 i.
Mechak 1793 w.
Albemarle
Martin 1751 i.
Amelia
Josiah 1782 i.
Amherst
David 1777 i.
Augusta
Andrew 1762 w.
Botetourt
Robert 1787 w.
Berkeley
Matthew 1789 w.
Matthew 1793 i.
Culpeper
William 1781 w.
Charles 1789 i.
Robert 1793 w.
Fairfax
Blanch Flower 1754 i.
George 1784 w.
Fauquier
John 1793 w.
Joseph 1793 w.
John Sr. 1796 a.
Lyddia 1797 w.
Fluvanna
George 1783 w.
Frederick
Patrick 1762 i.
Matthew 1766 i.
Mecklenburg
Geo. 1788 w.
Wm. 1796 w.
Northampton
Eliz. 1745 i.
Alex. 1787 w.
Prince William
John 1739 i.
Thomas 1740 a.
Richmond
Charity 1795 w.
Surry
David 1745 w.
Sussex
Nathl 1774 w.
Washington
John 1781 i.
Rawley 1786 i.
York
Wm. 1755 i.

DUNCANSON
King George
Jno. 1722 i.
Spotsylvania
Robt. 1764 a.
DUNCOM
Stafford
Benj. 1753 w.
DUNCOMBE
Lancaster
Thos. 1659 w.
DUNCUM
Stafford
Thos. 1742 w.
DUNDAS
Norfolk
Wm. 1693-4 w.
DUNE
Richmond
Patrick 1719 w.
DUNFORD
Cumberland
Philip 1764 i.
Philip 1764 i.
Southampton
John 1759 i.
Thos. 1772 w.
York
Wills 1742 i.
Anne 1780 w.
John 1782 i.
DUNGAN
Essex
Henry 1747 i.
DUNGEE
Cumberland
William 1773 i.
DUNING
Princess Anne
Andrew 1706 a.
DUNINGTON
Prince William
Wm. 1799 w.
DUNKAN
Westmoreland
Chas. 1712 i.
DUNKIN
Richmond
Henry 1772 w.
Westmoreland
Jno. 1726 w.
Jas. 1727 i.
Chas. 1742 i.
Peter 1748-9 w.
Geo. 1758 w.
Geo. 1767 i.
DUNKINS
Mecklenburg
Geo. 1788 i.

DUNKLEY
Halifax
Jno. 1774 i.
Martha 1797 w.
Princess Anne
Moses 1697 a.
Southampton
Jno. 1748 w.
Catherine 1758 w.
DUNLAP
Augusta
Jas. 1760 i.
Jas. 1763 i.
Northumberland
Jas. 1722-3 i.
Rockbridge
Robert 1782 w.
DUNLAVEY
Middlesex
Jno. 1762 a.
DUNLEAVY
Middlesex
James 1765 w.
DUNLOP
Prince William
William 1740 i.
Surry
Archibald 1793 w.
DUNMAN
Brunswick
Joseph 1741 w.
Lunenburg
Joseph 1799 w.
DUNMILLO
Essex
Jos. 1748-9 i.
DUNMORE
Norfolk
John 17— i.
DUNN
Brunswick
Daniel 1770 w.
David 1770 i.
David 1782 i.
David 1786 w.
Molly 1787 w.
Essex
Wm. 1732 w.
Wm. 1767 w.
Thomas 1771 w.
Benjamin 1779 w.
James 1782 w .
Philip 1785 w.
William 1785 w.
William 1788 i.
William 1789 i.
John Sr. 1790 w.
William 1791 i.
Catherine 1798 w.
William 1799 w.

Lancaster
Arthur 1656 w.
Norfolk
Jno. 1701 w.
John 1716 i.
John 1777 w.
Richmond
Robert 1726 w.
Southampton
Wm. 1762 i.
Spotsylvania
James 1739 a.
Wm. 1781 a.
Sussex
Thos. 1772 w.
Thos. 1773 w.
Lewis 1782 w.
Lewis 1783 i.
Allen 1784 i.
Lewis 1785 i.
Drury 1789 i.
Wm. 1792 i.
Thos. 1795 w.
Wm. 1797 w.
Westmoreland
Newman 1762 nw.
York
Chas. 1679 w.
Abrum 1733 i.
DUNNAGON
Essex
Timothy 1757 i.
DUNNEGAN
Northampton
David 1752 i.
DUNNIN
Isle of Wight
John 1677 w.
DUNNING
Isle of Wight
John 1677 i.
DUNNIVANT
Amelia
Thos. 1759 i.
Philip 1776 w.
Thos. 1778 w.
Wm. 1780 w.
Norvel 1782 w.
Daniel 1789 w.
Jno. 1791 w.
Danl. 1792 i.
Danl. 1797 i.
DUNNOCK
Norfolk
John 1749 i.
John 1752 i.
Alice 1772 i.
DUNSTER
Isle of Wight
Robert 1656 w.

DUNSTON
Isle of Wight
Thomas 1787 w.
York
Thos. 1679 w.
DUNTON
Accomack
Waterfield 1731 i.
Jacob 1763 w.
Rachel 1772 i.
Isaac 1774 w.
Wm. 1778 i.
Wm. 1783 nw.
Philender 1784 w.
Wm. 1787 i.
Jos. 1790 i.
Geo. 1793 w.
Northampton
Wm. 1709 w.
Jno. 1720 w.
Thos. 1720 w.
Thos. (2) 1720 w.
Eliz. 1727 w.
Benj. 1728 i.
Stephen 1728 i.
Wm. 1734 w.
Wm. 1735 i.
Benj. 1743 w.
Eliz. 1748 w.
Mary 1748 w.
Michael 1754 w.
Richards 1754 w.
Southy 1759 w.
Abigail 1760 w.
Elias 1760 w.
Elias 1763 i.
Stephen 1772 i.
Stephen 1773 i.
Wm. Sr. 1773 w.
Esther 1775 w.
Elias Jr. 1777 w.
Sophia 1778 w.
Elias Sr. 1780 w.
Jacob 1786 i.
Isabella 1787 w.
Levin 1793 i.
Polly 1793 i.
Eliz. 1797 w.
Benjamin 1798 w.
Betty 1799 i.
Westmoreland
Thos. 1769 i.
DUNWAY
Lancaster
Derby 1729 w.
DUNWODY
Augusta
Jno. 1775 i.
DUNWOODY
Amherst
James 1783.

DUPARKS
Northampton
Richd. 1691 w.
Thos. 1756 w.
Thos. 1702 w.
Jno. 1745 w.
DUPRA
Henrico
Jean 1734 w.
DUPREE
Charlotte
Thos. 1782 i.
Greensville
John 1788 w.
Lewis 1788 w.
Sarah 1793 i.
Robert 1796 i.
Lewis D. 1795 i.
DUPRIE
Chesterfield
Jane 17— i.
Lunenburg
Thos. 1786 w.
DUPRIEST
Amherst
Wm. 1784 a.
DUPUY
Amelia
Peter, Sr. 1777 w.
Judith 1783 w.
Cumberland
Jno. Jas. 1775 w.
Goochland
Bartho. 1743 w.
DURAND
Henrico
Jane 1709 i.
DURBIN
Halifax
Jno. 1759 w.
DURDY
Princess Anne
Wm. 1758 w.
Hugh 1760 i.
DUREING
Westmoreland
Thos. 1727 i.
DURESSE
Richmond
Theodore 1711 w.
DURFEY
York
Francis 1679 w.
DURHAM
Amelia
Jno. 1761 i.
Brunswick
Geo. 1767 w.
Chesterfield
Jos. 17— i.

Richmond
Thos. 1715 w.
Thos. 1735 w.
Jos. 1742 i.
Thos. 1774 i.
Spotsylvania
Robt. 1734 w.
Stafford
Saml. 1735 i.
DURLEY
Isle of Wight
Mary 1786 w.
DURRETT
Albemarle
Richd. 1784 w.
Pittsylvania
Wm. 1792 w.
Spotsylvania
Robt. 1765 w.
Richd. 1768 w.
Jno. 1775 w.
Eliz. 1783 w.
DURRUM
Cumberland
James 1789 w.
DURST
Shenandoah
Isaac 1777 w.
DUSKY
Montgomery
Peter 17— i.
DUST
Shenandoah
Abraham 1772 i.
Mary 1777 nw.
DUTCHEE
Surry
Melchiz. 1708 i.
DUTHAIS
Isle of Wight
Charles 1672 w.
DUTOIT
Henrico
Peter 1726 w.
DUTOY
Cumberland
Isaac 1752 w.
DUTTON
Frederick
William 1764 i.
DUVAL
Henrico
Saml. 1784 w.
Prince William
Cinnett 1796 i.
DUVALL
Franklin
Benjamin 1792 w.
DUZEN
Richmond
Thos. 1704 w.

DYAL
Prince William
Edward 1741 a.
DYAS
Accomack
Wm. 1739 w.
DYCHES
Northumberland
Richd. 1788 w.
DYE
Lancaster
John 1792 w.
Prince William
Vincent 1796 w.
Catherine 1798 i.
Dusosway 1798 i.
John, Jr. 1798 w.
Sarah 1798 i.
Richmond
Martin 1746 i.
Avery 1757 w.
DYEL
Loudoun
Wm. 1766 w.
DYER
Accomack
Jno. 1721 w.
Amelia
Thos. 1767 w.
Augusta
Peter 1749 i.
Wm. 1758 i.
Roger 1759 w.
Chesterfield ·
Jno. Sr. 1784 i.
Abraham 1795 w.
Essex
Jas. 1698 w.
Andrew 1709 w.
Wm. 1714 i.
Jeffery 1716 i.
Sarah 1756 i.
Frederick
Elisha 1762 a.
Halifax
Jno. 1774 w.
Lunenburg
Robt. 176[2?] w.
Robt. Henry 1766 w.
Norfolk
Thomas 1671 i.
Wm. 1674 w.
Princess Anne
John 1749 w.
Wm. 1749 w.
John, Sr. 1793 w.
York
Wm. 1697-8 i.
Mary 1702 w.
Henry 1710 i.
Henry 1713 i.

Edwd. 1719 w.
Saml. 1757 w.
DYES
Norfolk
Robert 1757 w.
DYHER
Louisa
Wm. 1760 w.
DYKE
Culpeper
George 1798 i.
Essex
John 1729 i.
Susannah 1756 w.
John 1758 i.
Mary 1789 w.
DYKES
Louisa
John 1786 w.
DRYMER
Lancaster
Wm. 1728 i.
Wm. 1771 i.
DYMON
Lancaster
Jas. 1679 nw.
DYMOR
Lancaster
Nicho. 1697 w.
DYNHAM
Northampton
Wm. 1650 i.
DYSON
Amelia
Benj. 1782 w.
Chesterfield
Jno. 1797 i.
Henrico
Leonard 1733 w.
Princess Anne
Philip 1745 i.
Mary 1753 w.
Mary 1766 i.

E

EACHES
Richmond
Ellinor 1710 i.
EADE
Berkeley
Robert 1788 i.
EADENS
Norfolk
Phillip 1721 i.
EADINGS
Princess Anne
Thos. 1731 i.
EAGAN
Shenandoah
Barnaby 1780 a.

Rachel 1780 w.
Richard 1792 a.
Barnaby 1779 i.
EAGER
Botetourt
Martha 1789 w.
EAGLE
Shenandoah
Timothy 1795 a.
EAKERT
Augusta
Casper 1779 w.
EAKIN
Rockbridge
James 1785 w.
EALES
Westmoreland
John A. 1721 i.
Jno. 1760 i.
EALIF
Northumberland
Thos. 1774 i.
EALLES
Rappahannock
Wm. 1677 w.
EANES
Chesterfield
Edwd. 1757 w.
EARL
Prince William
John 1790 i.
Pittsylvania
Thos. 1788 i.
Westmoreland
Saml. 1746 w.
EARLE
Frederick
Enos 1752 w.
Samuel, Jr. 1752 a.
Enoch 1753 i.
Samuel 1755 i.
Samuel 1771 w.
Northumberland
Jno. 1660 w.
Westmoreland
Saml. 1697 i.
EARLIS
Middlesex
Eliz. 1779 w.
EARLEY
Culpeper
Joseph 1783 w.
EARLY
Bedford
Jeremiah 1779 w.
Culpeper
Jeremiah 1787 w.
Franklin
Jubal 1798 i.
Henry
Joseph 1780 w.

Orange
Jno. 1774 w.
EARNEST
Isle of Wight
William 1677 i.
EARNSHAW
Fairfax
John 1790 a.
EARP
Fairfax
William 1748 a.
Joshua 1751 i.
Joseph 1771 i.
EARPE
Fairfax
John 1744 a.
EARSOM
Hampshire
John 1790 w.
Simon 1796 w.
EARTH
Richmond
Thos. 1721 w.
EASELEY
Cumberland
Stephen 1759 i.
EASHWOOD
Norfolk
Thomas 1720 i.
EASLEY
Amelia
Robt. 1736 a.
Goochland
Jno. 1746 w.
Halifax
Jno. 1782 i.
McDaniel 1786 i.
Danl. 1786 w.
Wm. 1796 i.
Henrico
Warham 1747 w.
Henry
Worham 1790 w.
Lunenburg
Thos. [1760?] i.
Pittsylvania
Wm. 1795 w.
EASON
Botetourt
Frances 1786 w.
EAST
Accomack
Southy 1795 w.
Charlotte
Wm. 1767 w.
Halifax
Jno. 1758 w.
Henrico
Thos. 1726-7 w.
Edwd. 1735 w.
Edwd. 1754 w.

Henry
William 1781 w.
Louisa
Joseph 1772 w.
Thos. 1782 eb.
Pittsylvania
Thos. 1797 i.
Richmond
Henry 1714 i.
EASTER
Norfolk
Thomas 1782 w.
Princess Anne
Wm. 1732 w.
Thos. 1756 w.
Jno. 1778 w.
Prince William
Giles 1741 nw.
EASTHAM
Lunenburg
James 1792 i.
EASTHER
Norfolk
James 1772 w.
EASTIN
Orange
Philip 1768 w.
EASTIS
Halifax
Wm. 1780 w.
EASTLAND
Mecklenburg
Thos. 1779 w.
EASTMEADE
Northampton
Thos. 1683 w.
EASTMOND
Northampton
Thos. 1685 i.
EASTON
Northumberland
Jno. 1783 i.
EASTWOOD
Norfolk
Richd. 1691-2 w.
Francis 1776 w.
Richard 1778 w.
EATEN
Essex
John 1749 i.
EATMAN
York
Chas. 1718 ab.
EATON
Accomack
Jno. 1690 i.
Lancaster
Geo. 1653 i.
Northumberland
Richd. 1677-8 w.

Princess Anne
Michael 1726 i.
Richard 1730 i.
Eliz. 1735 w.
Michael 1785 w.
James 1792 w.
Westmoreland
Peter 1719.
York
Wm. 1714 w.
Jno. 1717 w.
Saml. 1719 w.
Wm. 1719 w.
Jno. 1738 w.
Pinkethman 1761 w.
EATTLE
Westmoreland
Benj. 1715 i.
EAVANS
Goochland
Jno. 1754 w.
Accomack
Jno. 1725 w.
EAVES
Brunswick
Graves 1746 w.
Thos. 1785 w.
Stafford
Thos. 1752 w.
EBERLY
Shenandoah
Jeremias 1799 w.
EBLEN
Loudoun
Jane 1793 w.
EBLIN
Loudoun
Peter 1791 nw.
John 1797 w.
EBORNE
Accomack
Wm. 1677 i.
ECHOLS
Halifax
Isaac 1761 i.
Wm. 1771 w.
Joseph 1790 i.
Jeremiah 1792 w.
Wm. 1794 w.
Lunenburg
Abraham 1749 w.
Pittsylvania
Obadiah 1799 w.
ECKART
Loudoun
Adam 1792 i.
ECKHOLS
Bedford
John 1795 w.

ECKLES
Sussex
  Edwd. 1758 w.
  Jno. 1788 w.
EDDINGS
Lunenburg
  Isaac 1781 w.
  Wm. 1781 w.
EDDINS
Lunenburg
  Wm. 1754 w.
EDDY
Shenandoah
  Richard 1774 i.
EDELEN
King George
  Benj. 1791 w.
EDENS
Norfolk
  Phillip 1721 i.
EDERINGTON
Westmoreland
  Chris. 1741 i.
  Chris. 1745 i.
EDGAR
Culpeper
  William 1769 w.
  Susannah 1777 w.
King George
  Adam 1726 i.
Lancaster
  Alex. 1730 i.
Princess Anne
  James 1772 i.
  Absolem 1784 w.
EDGE
Essex
  Mary 1721 i.
King George
  Thos. 1733 i.
Prince William
  John 1738 w.
Spotsylvania
  Peirce 1740 a.
EDGERTON
Norfolk
  Chas. 1669 w.
EDINFIELD
Charlotte
  Thos. 1781 w.
EDINGS
Norfolk
  Doletre [1736?] w.
  Richard 1760 i.
  Richard 1761 i.
EDINGTON
Northumberland
  David 1771 i.
EDLOE
Charles City
  Jno. 1766 i.

EDMISTON
Augusta
  Robt. 1750 w.
  Mathew 1796 w.
Washington
  William 1789 w.
  Thomas 1792 w.
EDMONDE
King George
  Cornelius 1722 i.
EDMONDS
Accomack
  Jno. 1785 w.
  Geo. 1799 w.
Amherst
  Jno. 1782 w.
  Jno. [2?] 1782 w.
Fauquier
  Elias 1784 w.
  John 1799 i.
King George
  Anne 1745 i.
Lancaster
  Elias 1654 i.
  Thos. 1677 nw.
  Wm. 1741 w.
  Robert 1751 w.
  Robert 1762 i.
Northampton
  Owen 1697 w.
  David 1735 w.
  Elijah 1751 w.
Northumberland
  Elias 1743-4 i.
  Wm. 1758 w.
Princess Anne
  Jno. 1721 i.
  Wm. 1755 w.
  Abel 1792 w.
  John 1797 w.
Richmond
  Jeremiah 1749 w.
Spotsylvania
  Chas. 1725 a.
Surry
  Jno. 1752 w.
York
  Jane 1718 w.
  Hugh 1736 w.
EDMONDSON
Amelia
  Upton 1771 w.
  Upton 1772 w.
Augusta
  David 1751 i.
Charles City
  Eliz. 1791 w.
  Margt. 1794 w.
Essex
  Thos. 1715 w.
  Wm. 1717 i.

  Benj. 1727 w.
  Robt. 1731 w.
  Jno. 1733 w.
  Jas. 1734 i.
  Saml. 1734 i.
  Jas. 1735 i.
  Sarah 1735 w.
  Jas. 1741 w.
  Saml. 1748 i.
  Mary 1748 i.
  Robt. 1751 i.
  Thos. 1751 i.
  Judith 1753 w.
  Thos. 1759 w.
  Jno. 1774 i.
  Wm. 1774 w.
  Benj. 1775 w.
  Robt. 1777 w.
  Benj. 1779 w.
  Jas. 1779 w.
  Leah 1780 w.
  Jas. 1787 i.
  Jno. 1790 i.
  Jas. 1792 w.
Frederick
  Thomas 1784 w.
Lunenburg
  Thos. 1760 w.
Rockbridge
  William 1782 w.
Washington
  Robert 1780 w.
  Andrew 1781 i.
EDMONSON
Franklin
  Richard 1788 w.
EDMUNDS
Accomack
  Jonathan 1754 w.
  Jonathan 1764 i.
  Thos. 1777 w.
Brunswick
  Henry 1781 i.
  Nicholas 1789 w.
  Jno. Flood 1797 w.
Isle of Wight
  William 1771 w.
  James 1795 w.
Lancaster
  Wm. 1700 w.
  Elias 1745 w.
  Elias 1772 i.
Norfolk
  John 1717 w.
Northampton
  Robt. 1635 w.
  David, Jr. 1736 i.
  Thos. 1756 w.
  Tamar 1760 i.
  Sarah 1763 w.
  David 1786 w.

Abigail 1794 w.
Southampton
Jeremiah 1762 w.
Howell 1770 w.
Ann 1772 w.
Mary 1777 w.
David 1780 w.
Ann 1797 w.
Surry
Howell 1729 w.
Thos. 1737 i.
Wm. 1740 w.
Mary 1753 w.
Sussex
Jno. 1768 i.
Jno. 1770 w.
Gray 1773 i.
Thos. 1793 i.
Thos. 1794 i.
York
Thos. 1718 i.
EDMUNDSON
Lunenburg
Thos. 1760 i.
Benj. 1795 w.
Wm. 1799 i.
Rockbridge
James 1783 w.
Washington
William 1781 i.
William 1789 i.
EDMUNS
Princess Anne
Jno. 1721 w.
EDRINGTON
Fauquier
John 1771 i.
King George
Mary 1756 w.
Danl. 1793 w.
EDWARD
Isle of Wight
Hugh 1733 i.
Norfolk
John 1774 w.
Southampton
Michael 1771 i.
EDWARDS
Accomack
Evans 1733 w.
Edwd. 1751 w.
Francis 1754 i.
Jno. 1782 w.
Jno. 1784 i.
Edw. 1789 w.
Jno. 1793 i.
David 1797 i.
Sacker 1798 w.
Albemarle
David 1782 i.
Saml. 1791 i.

Amelia
Benj. 1772 i.
Amherst
Jno. 1763 i.
Augusta
Hugh 1753 i.
Berkeley
Jonathan 1773 i.
Joseph, Sr. 1797 w.
Brunswick
Benj. 1768 w.
Chas. 1770 i.
Nathl. [Sr.] 1771 w.
Nathl, Jr. 1771 w.
Chas. 1773 w.
Benj. 1773 i.
Chas. 1777 w.
Wm. 1778 w.
Benj. 1779 w.
Wm. 1781 w.
Wm. 1782 w.
Mary 1783 w.
Jno. Sr. 1798 w.
Charles City
Jno. 1770 w.
Wm. 1791 w.
Chesterfield
Thos. 1772 w.
Mark 1780 i.
Peter 1785 i.
Ann 1790 w.
Culpeper
John 1750 i.
Barbary 1786 w.
John 1783 w.
Cumberland
Wm. 1763 i.
Andrew 1774 w.
Essex
Thomas 1716 w.
Katherine 1722 i.
Richd. 1722 w.
Frederick
John 1749 i.
Goochland
Thos. 1768 w.
Halifax
James Cocke 1777 w.
Wm. 1780 w.
Wm. 1782 i.
Chas. 1790 w.
Chas. 1791 i.
Hampshire
Joseph 1782 w.
Henry
James 1792 w.
Henrico
Jno. 1781 w.
Isle of Wight
Robert 1681 i.
Peter 1682 w.

Robert 1685 i.
Thomas 1693 i.
Charles 1713 w.
James 1723 w.
James 1743 i.
John 1748 w.
John 1750 i.
Robert 1762 w.
Robert 1771 i.
Thomas 1772 w.
Thomas 1772 i.
William 1773 w.
Hezekiah 1774 w.
Joshua 1774 w.
Hezekiah 1776 i.
Benjamin 1780 i.
James 1782 w.
Jacob 1795 w.
Jamson 1797 w.
Richard 1798 i.
Britain 1799 i.
Robert 1799 w.
Solomon 1799 w.
King George
Jno. 1743 i.
Geo. 1780 w.
Lancaster
Frances 1731 i.
Wm. 1737 w.
Lucy 1745 i.
Franky 1750 w.
Thomas 1760 w.
Robert 1761 w.
John 1762 w.
Sarah 1771 w.
Thomas 1778 i.
George 1783 w.
Loudoun
Benj. 1764 i.
Louisa
John 1791 i.
John 1792 w.
Lunenburg
Thos. 1751 w.
Thos. 1795 w.
Middlesex
James 1740 w.
Thos. 1785 w.
Norfolk
Thos. 1648 i.
Peter 1719 i.
Thomas 1785 w.
Thomas 1793 i.
Thomas, Sr. 1794 w.
Northumberland
Thos. 1669 i.
Nicholas 1712 i.
Jno. 1741 i.
Ralph 1745 i.
Isaac 1753 w.
John 1759 i.

Enoch 1761 i.
Henry 1764 w.
Isaac 1767 w.
Thomas 1770 w.
Robart 1775 w.
Jonathan 1776 w.
Richd. 1776 w.
Robert 1778 i.
Elisha 1793 i.
Mary 1794 i.
Robt. 1796 w.
Eliz. 1797 w.
Thos. 1798 w.
Pittsylvania
Thos. 1791 w.
Powhatan
Wm. 1779 w.
Princess Anne
Wm. 1694 w.
Eliz. 1698 w.
Henry 1779 i.
Prince Edward
Simon 1758 w.
Richmond
Geo. 1783 w.
Shenandoah
John 1789 a.
Southampton
Wm. 1751 w.
Arthur 1754 i.
Benj. 1762 w.
Eliz. 1762 w.
Jno. 1762 i.
Jno. 1769 i.
Micajah 1770 i.
Micajah 1781 w.
Thos. 1781 w.
Wm. 1781 w.
Eliz. 1782 w.
Jno. 1789 w.
Jack 1794 w.
Wm. 1795 w.
Benj. 1797 w.
Spotsylvania
Uriah 1781 w.
James 1788 w.
Stafford
Philip 1701 i.
Jno. 1747 i.
Meredith 1750 i.
Ignatius 1750 w.
Mary 1763 i.
Surry
Thos. 1702 w.
Jno. 1713 w.
Wm. 1721 w.
Benj. 1722 w.
Eliz. 1744 w.
Wm. 1744 w.
Benj. 1750 i.
Thos. 1752 i.

Joseph 1756 w.
Jno. 1757 w.
Mary 1760 i.
Newitt 1762 w.
Thos. 1762 w.
Mary 1771 w.
Wm. 1771 w.
Eliz. 1772 i.
Benj. 1773 i.
Martha 1773 w.
Jno. 1777 i.
Thos. 1785 w.
Etheldred 1786 w.
Martha 1786 i.
Mary 1790 w.
Wm. 1797 w.
Richd. 1799 w.
Washington
David 1778 w.
Westmoreland
Merida 1712 w.
Wm. 1755 w.
Thos. 1774 w.
Riley 1745 nw.
Wm. 1773 i.
York
Mathew 1680 w.
EDZARD
Culpeper
William 1798 i.
King George
Esdras Theador
1763 i.
Theador 1763 w.
Jas. 1764 i.
Frances 1772 w.
EELBECK
Surry
Henry 1752 i.
EFFORD
Northumberland
Zachariah 1746 i.
Zachariah 1794 i.
Wm. 1799 i.
Richmond
Jno. 1754 w.
Francis 1757 w.
Sarah 1761 i.
Jno. 1788 i.
Zachariah 1793 w.
Zachariah 1794 i.
EGAR
Bedford
George 1765 w.
EGGINTON
York
Jas. 1740 w.
EGGLESTON
Amelia
Wm. 1780 w.
Jos. 1793 w.

Richd. 1796 w.
Wm. 1799 i.
Powhatan
Richd. Sr. 1781 w.
Jno. 1784 i.
EGMON
Charles City
Lawrence 1790 i.
EHART
Culpeper
Michael 1789 w.
John 1793 i.
Orange
Adam 1798 w.
EIDSON
Richmond
Edwd. 1732 w.
Jos. 1758 i.
Jno. 1774 w.
Susanna 1778 i.
Edwd. 1796 i.
EINGLE
Frederick
Meleger 1760 i.
EIRES
Northampton
Thos. 1657 w.
ELAM
Amelia
Martin 1738 a.
Chesterfield
Richd. 17— w.
Gilbert 1750 w.
Robt. 1750 w.
Gilbert, Jr. 1755 w.
Gilbert 1771 w.
Martha 1776 w.
Robt. Sr. 1776 w.
Richd. 1777 i.
Martin 1778 i.
Robt. 1779 i.
Wm. Sr. 1784 w.
Gilbert 1785 i.
Robt. 1785 w.
Wm. 1785 i.
Wm. 1790 i.
Robert Sr. 1791 w.
Danl. 1792 w.
Richd. 1792 i.
Jas. 1796 w.
Henrico
Wm. 1689 w.
Martin 1691 w.
Gilbert, Sr. 1694 w.
Gilbert 1697 w.
Thos. 1697 i.
Martin 1705 w.
Mecklenburg
Joel 1798 w.
Powhatan
Lodowick 1778 w.

Mary 1781 i.
ELBZEY
Fairfax
Francis 1751 w.
Mary 1791 w.
ELCIE
Stafford
Wm. 1706 i.
ELOCKE
York
Jas. 1675 w.
Hannah 1677 w.
ELDER
Henrico
Thos. 1794 w.
Rappahannock
Peter 1674 w.
Richmond
Wm. 1755 w.
Washington
Matthew 1783 w.
Mary 1792 i.
ELDRIDGE
Isle of Wight
Samuel 1667 a.
Samuel 1709 w.
Surry
Thos. 1741 w.
Sussex
Thos. 1755 i.
Judith 1760 w.
Wm. 1772 w.
ELDRIDGE
Norfolk
Griffin 17— i.
ELEMES
Isle of Wight
Thomas 1695-6 i.
ELEY
Isle of Wight
Robert, Sr. 1739 w.
Robert 1739 w.
Ely 1741 i.
Robert 1750 w.
William 1751 i.
William 1767 w.
Michail 1770 i.
John, Jr. 1772 w.
John 1776 w.
Elizabeth 1779 i.
Gale 1793 w.
Benjamin 1795 a.
Robert 1795 w.
Milley 1796 w.
Holland 1798 i.
William 1799 i.
ELGIN
Loudoun
Francis 1782 w.

ELGY
Rockbridge
John 1782 i.
ELIOT
Northampton
Jno. 1753 i.
ELIS
Norfolk
Thomas 1782 i.
ELISTONE
Stafford
Robt. 1785 i.
ELK
Princess Anne
Thos. 1753 w.
ELKES
Princess Anne
Jno. 1774 w.
ELKIN
King George
Jno. 1751 i.
Richd. 1751 i.
Richmond
Jas. 1717 i.
ELKINE
King George
Jas. 1722 i.
ELKINS
King George
Nathl. 1733 i.
Nathl. 1798 w.
Montgomery
Archibald 1791 w.
ELKS
Norfolk
James 1757 i.
Princess Anne
Thos. 1754 i.
Thos. 1782 w.
Rebecca 1788 w.
ELLBANK
Prince Edward
Eliz. 1777 a.
ELLEGOOD
Norfolk
John 1740 w.
John 1760 w.
Jacob 1768 w.
Northampton
Thos. Ward 1725 w.
Thos. 1727 w.
Peter 1746 w.
Jno. 1747 w.
Margt. 1750 w.
Thos. Ward 1754 i.
Jno. 1763 w.
Princess Anne
Wm. 1726 w.
Mathew 1743 w.
Margt. 1746 i.
Jacob 1753 w.

ELLEGOODE
Princess Anne
Peter N. 1778 i.
ELLESS
Surry
Jeremyer 1738 i.
ELLESTON
Northumberland
Eliz. 1742 w.
ELLETT
Essex
Jno. 1700 w.
Alice 1720 w.
Lancaster
Thomas 1784 i.
Norfolk
Abraham 1677 w.
Stafford
Chas. 1734 w.
ELLEY
Orange
James 1767 i.
ELLICE
Goochland
Wm. 1772 w.
ELLIDGE
Lunenburg
Francis 1751 w.
ELLIGOOD
Northampton
Jno. 1709 w.
Richd. 1716 w.
Thos. 1728 i.
Sophia 1736 i.
Jonathan 1792 w.
ELLINGTON
Amelia
David 1773 w.
Jno. 1783 w.
Lunenburg
Martha 1782 i.
ELLINGSWORTH
King George
Isaiah 1735 i.
ELLIOT
Accomack
Thos. Sr. 1796 i.
Amherst
Jno. 1764 w.
Augusta
Archd. 1779 i.
Lantz 1779 i.
Charlotte
Ann 1782 i.
Essex
Samuel 1717 w.
King George
Mary 1756 a.
Middlesex
Richd. 1768 i.

Northampton
Isaac 1750 i.
Pittsylvania
Philip 1777 w.
Thos. 1799 w.
Rockbridge
James 1799 w.
ELLIOTT
Accomack
Robt. 1744 w.
Wm. 1789 w.
Thos. 1790 w.
Ann 1795 w.
Jno. 1797 w.
Jno. 1799 i.
Augusta
Wm. 1771 w.
Charlotte
Richd. 1796 w.
Wm. 1791 i.
Chesterfield
Jno. 1750 i.
Essex
Caleb 1789 i.
Caleb 1796 w.
Fauquier
Reubin 1780 w.
John 1790 i.
Halifax
Geo. 1766 i.
Mary 1772 i.
Jno. 1773 w.
Middlesex
Eliz. 1718 w.
Eliz. 1779 w.
Norfolk
Mary 1799 w.
Northampton
Thos. 1718 w.
Jno. E. 1753 nw.
Thos. 1770 w.
Wm. 1776 w.
Jno. 1777 w.
Jas. 1784 w.
Prince Edward
Andrew 1795 w.
Robert 1786 w.
Rockbridge
William 1795 w.
Wesmtorcland
Jno. 1708 w.
Wm. 1726 w.
Jno. 1747 i.
Augustine 1750 w.
Sabella 1751 w.
Jno. 1756 w.
York
Jno. 1782 w.
Geo. 1788 w.

ELLIS
Albemarle
Charles 1760 w.
Amelia
Jno. 1762 w.
Berkeley
William 1772 w.
William 1777 i.
John 1782 w.
Enos 1783 w.
Mordeica 1785 i.
Chesterfield
Wm. 17— w.
Cumberland
William 1771 w.
Fauquier
John 1779 w.
Frederick
John 1762 w.
John 1764 i.
Henrico
Jno. Sr. 1728 w.
Jno. 1782 w.
Geo. 1783 w.
Henry 1783 w.
Jesse 1783 i.
Thos. 1783 w.
Wm. 1788 w.
Jno. 1790 i.
Thos. 1790 w.
Jos. 1793 w.
R. Jno. 1795 i.
Thos. 1796 w.
Geo. 1798 i.
Jno. 1798 i.
Jno. 1799 w.
Josiah 1799 w.
Loudoun
Robert 1766 w.
Ellis 1797 w.
Lunenburg
Jeremiah 1757 w.
Mecklenburg
James 1779 i.
Wm. 1797 w.
Middlesex
Hezekiah 1727 w.
Norfolk
Wm. 1669 i.
Sarah 1742-3 i.
Joseph 1761 i.
Ann 1762 w.
Ann 1764 i.
Kezia 1764 i.
William 1774 w.
John 1775 w.
John 1779 i.
James 1795 i.
Samuel 1797 w.
Sarah 1798 w.

Northampton
Jno. 1658 w.
Edwd. 1689 w.
Princess Anne
Peter 1751 i.
Richmond
Peter 1711 w.
Southampton
Jeremiah 1787 w.
Henry 1797 w.
Hezekiah 1792 i.
Spotsylvania
Robert 1745 w.
Wm. 1766 w.
Hezekiah 1772 w.
Stafford
Chas. 1707 i.
Surry
James 1714 w.
Jno. 1739 w.
Edwd. 1754 w.
Caleb 1762 w.
Isaac 1787 w.
Jonathan 1788 w.
Wm. 1795 i.
Sussex
Benj. 1759 w.
Richd. 1782 i.
Wm. 1795 w.
Caleb 1799 w.
Westmoreland
Wm. 1772 i.
York
Jno. 1789 w.
Danl. 1791 w.
Ann 1794 w.
ELLISON
Greenbrier
James 1791 w.
Southampton
Gerard 1796 w.
ELLISS
Chesterfield
Thos. 1757 w.
ELLISTONE
Northumberland
Jarvise 1740 w.
ELLIT
Accomack
Thos. 1777 w.
Essex
Jno. 1727 w.
ELLITT
Norfolk
Jno. [1699?] w.
Rappahannock
Richd. 1685 i.
ELLKINS
King George
Jno. 1730 i.

ELLWENE
Rappahannock
Thos. 1677 w.
ELLINS
Isle of Wight
Thomas 1680 w.
ELLYS
Chesterfield
Thos. 1776 w.
ELLYSON
Chesterfield
Gearrard 1771 w.
Enos 1788 i.
Cumberland
Gerrard 1791 w.
ELLZEY
Fairfax
Lewis 1786 w.
Lewis 1794 a.
Frederick
Thomas 1761 i.
Loudoun
William 1796 w.
Southampton
John 1775 i.
Stafford
Thos. 1699 i.
ELMES
Isle of Wight
Thomas 1695-6 i.
Surry
Mathew 1694 i.
ELMORE
Amelia
Thos. 1749 w.
Henrico
Rebecca 1746 w.
Thos. 1783 w.
Jane 1788 w.
Thos. 1789 i.
Thos. 1791 i.
Northumberland
Josiah 1762 i.
Richmond
Peter 1726 w.
Jno. 1757 w.
Wm. 1787 i.
Mary 1793 w.
ELMS
Westmoreland
Edwd. 1761 i.
ELSLEY
York
Andrew 1717 w.
ELRINGTON
York
Richd. 1646 w.
ELSON
Cumberland
Thos. 1763 i.

ELSWICK
Augusta
Jno. 1750 i.
Hampshire
John 1759 w.
ELSWOOD
Botetourt
Valentine 1797 i.
ELTON
Fairfax
John 1784 w.
Surry
Robt. 1695 a.
ELYSON
Prince Edward
Robt. 1791 i.
ELZEY
Brunswick
Jno. 1759 w.
Fairfax
Thomas 1743 a.
Southampton
John 1773 w.
EMACK
Botetourt
Matthew 1779 w.
EMANUELL
Lancaster
Francis 1690 w.
EMBERSON
Lancaster
Jno. 1721 w.
EMBERY
Prince George
Wm. 1714 i.
EMBRE
Lancaster
Wm. 1685 i.
EMBREE
Bedford
Moses 1796 w.
EMBREY
Orange
Wm. 1759 w.
Stafford
Jno. 1748 i.
EMBRY
Brunswick
Henry 1756 i.
Henry 1763 w.
Martha 1772 i.
Fauquier
Ann 1790 nw.
Robert 1790 w.
Lunenburg
Wm. 1760 w.
Orange
John 1791 i.
Stafford
Wm. 1742 i.
Jno. 1747 i.

EMERSON
Albemarle
Thos. 1790 w.
Essex
James 1777 w.
Surry
Jno. 1677 w.
EMERY
Charles City
Jno. 1770 i.
Surry
Thos. 1734 w.
Thos. Sr. 1777 w.
Wm. 1783 i.
EMMERSON
Accomack
Arthur 1765 i.
Wm. 1780 w.
Wm. 1790 i.
Princess Anne
James 1777 i.
Stafford
Thos. 1753 i.
EMMONS
Fauquier
William 1796 w.
EMPERER
Princess Anne
Tully 1722 w.
EMPEROR
Norfolk
Francis 1661 i.
William 1684 i.
EMPEROUR
Norfolk
Mary 1676 w.
Francis Tully 1711 w.
EMSON
Isle of Wight
Thomas 1678 i.
ENDERS
Frederick
Catherine 1793 i.
Gasper 1793 i.
ENGLAND
Franklin
Joseph 1791 w.
Frederick
Titus 1791 w.
Goochland
Wm. 1768 w.
Isle of Wight
Francis 1677 w.
King George
Jno. 1735 i.
ENGLE
Frederick
Mecker 1760 w.
ENGLEBURD
Botetourt
George 1778 i.

ENGLISH
Accomack
Andrew 1752 i.
Bedford
Stephen 1783 w.
Fairfax
Edmond 1745 w.
Isle of Wight
John 1678 w.
Wm. 1723 i.
Thomas 1769 i.
Sarah 1778 w.
Jacob 1779 w.
Lancaster
Alex. 1697 w.
Princess Anne
Thos. 1705 w.
Prince George
Thany 1722 w.
Rappahannock
Jno. 1678 w.
Richmond
Jas. 1773 i.
Westmoreland
Winifred [1696] i.
Walter 1701 i.
ENOCK
Amherst
David 1799 w.
ENNEVER
Culpeper
John 1792 i.
ENNIS
Albemarle
Jno. 1762 w.
Isle of Wight
Walter 1724 i.
ENNO
Stafford
Geo. 1700 w.
ENROUGHTY
Halifax
Edwd. 1776 w.
Henrico
Jno. 1712 i.
ENSWORTH
York
Jno. 1674 w.
ENTIWISLE
Norfolk
Hugh 1714 a.
ENTLER
Berkeley
Adam 1777 w.
Adam 1786 i.
ENTTER
Berkeley
Philip Adam 1799 w.
EPES
Amelia
Francis 1789 w.

Halifax
Joshua 1778 w.
Henrico
Francis 1679 i.
Eliz. 1678 w.
Isham 1717 w.
Wm. 1726-7 i.
Prince George
Jno. 1718 w.
Mary 1723 i.
Wm. Sr. 1727 w.
EPPERSON
Albemarle
David 1799 w.
Charlotte
Francis 1786 i.
Cumberland
Richd. 1758 w.
Richd. 1774 w.
Mecklenburg
Thos. 1785 i.
EPPES
Charles City
Mary 1772 w.
Peter 1773 w.
Chesterfield
Richd. 1762 w.
Henrico
Francis 1734 w.
Francis 1737 w.
Sarah 1748 w.
Lunenburg
Jno. 1790 w.
Southampton
Geo. 1767 a.
Surry
Danl. Jr. 1733 i.
Danl. 1753 w.
Sussex
James 1791 w.
Halifax
Jno. 1793 i.
EPPS
Brunswick
Francis 1778 i.
Sussex
Edwd. 1780 w.
ERNEST
Hampshire
Michael 1785 w.
ERSKEIN
Richmond
Wm. 1750 i.
ERSKINE
Amelia
Alexr. 1771 i.
Halifax
Robt. 1784 i.
Thos. 1779 w.

ERWIN
Augusta
Jno. 1762 w.
Mathew 1762 w.
Andrew 1765 w.
Edwd. 1771 w.
Francis 1791 w.
Jno. Jr. 1797 i.
Bedford
Abraham 1777 i.
Princess Anne
Wm. 1697 w.
Rappahannock
Thos. 1676 w.
Jno. 1685 i.
Richmond
Geo. 1713 nw.
Rockbridge
Robert 1789 w.
Edwin 1796 w.
Westmoreland
Jno. 1716 w.
ESDALE
Northampton
Nathl. 1728 i.
ESDALL
Northampton
Edmd. 1709 i.
Geo. 1709 i.
ESELEY
Henrico
Robt. 1711 w.
ESHAM
Northampton
Danl. 1693 w.
ESHOM
Northampton
Danl. 1718-19 w.
ESHON
Northampton
Jno. 1716 w.
Danl. 1743 w.
ESKRIDE
Sussex
Thos. 1777 i.
ESKRIDGE
Northumberland
Saml. 1771 w.
Wm. 1782 w.
Prince William
Geo. 1736 i.
Geo. 1737 i.
Richmond
Robt. 1765 i.
Sussex
Eliz. 1781 w.
Westmoreland
Geo. Jr. 1733 i.
Geo. 1735 w.
Eliz. 1744 w.
Wm. 1744 i.

Saml. 1747 i.
Geo. 1749 i.
Thos. 1749 i.
Susannah 1774 i.
Jane 1782 i.
Jane 1791 i.
ESPEY
Prince William
Thos. 1795 w.
ESTAGE
Halifax
Ambrose 1794 i.
ESTEN
Norfolk
Jno. 1788 w.
ESTES
Halifax
Wm. 1782 i.
Ambrose 1794 w.
Culpeper
Eliz. 1778 i.
Franklin
Wm. 1791 a.
Henry
Elisha 1782 w.
Lunenburg
Robt. 1775 w.
Geo. 1785 i.
Robt. 1791 w.
Bartlett 1796 i.
Spotsylvania
Abram 1782 w.
ESTILL
Augusta
Jno. 1781 w.
Washington
Benj. 1782 w.
ESTILE
Greenbrier
Walliss 1792 w.
ESTIN
Bedford
Nicholas 1771 i.
ESTIS
Franklin
Mary Ann 1790 w.
Elisha Sr. 1791 w.
Louisa
Jno. 1771 i.
Orange
Saml. 1791 w.
ESTREE
Middlesex
Richd. 1727 i.
ETHELL
Loudoun
Jno. 1766 w.
Westmoreland
Jno. 1698 w.

ETHEREDGE
Norfolk
Moses 1718-19 w.
Edwd. 1724 i.
Thos. 1724 i.
Robt. 1734-5 w.
Adam 1735 w.
Aaron 1740 w.
Jno. 1742 i.
Thos. 1752 w.
Jas. 1757 w.
Amos. 1761 w.
Bethiah 1761 w.
Margt. 1761 w.
Saml. 1762 i.
Henry 1766 i.
Eliz. 1770 i.
Luke 1772 i.
Edwd. 1791 i.
Princess Anne
Eve 1753 w.
David 1764 w.
Andrew 1786 w.
ETHERIDGE
Norfolk
Jno. Sr. 1692 w.
Jno. 1698 w.
Edwd. 1713 w.
Chas. 1715 i.
Wm. Sr. 1716 w.
Chas. 1717 a.
Thos. 1719 w.
Edwd. 1746 w.
Jeremiah 1753 w.
Thos. 1753 w.
Eliza 1768 w.
Luke 1772 w.
Attery 1782 i.
Enoch 1789 w.
Amos. 1793 w.
Enoch 1795 i.
Wm. 1795 w.
Saml. 1797 i.
Princess Anne
David 1767 i.
Anthy. 1770 i.
Anthy. 1771 i.
David 1773 i.
Mary 1776 i.
ETHERINGTON
Culpeper
Wm. 1799 i.
Fauquier
Jno. 1770 i.
Eliz. 1778 w.
Princess Anne
Thos. 1722 w.
Jno. 1724 i.
Rappahannock
Margt. 1685 w.

ETHRIDGE
Norfolk
Thos. 1671 w.
EUBANK
Albemarle
Jno. 1789 w.
Henrico
Jas. 1799 w.
Lunenburg
Jno. 1791 w.
EUSTACE
Northumberland
Jno. 1702 w.
Wm. 1739-40 w.
Hancock 1775 w.
Hancock 1781 i.
Jno. 1786 w.
Jno. 1789 i.
Jno. 1790 i.
EVANS
Accomack
Jno. 1670 w.
Jno. 1721 w.
Thos. 1751 w.
Isaiah 1754 w.
Ceasar 1760 w.
Jno. 1761 w.
Zerrobabel 1766 w.
Mark 1767 w.
Levin 1769 w.
Jesse 1776 w.
Justinian 1779 w.
Mark 1780 w.
Levin 1789 i.
Isaiah 1790 w.
Jno. 1790 w.
Isaiah 1792 i.
Jesse 1798 w.
Arcadia 1799 i.
Nathl. 1799 i.
Amelia
Wm. 1780 w.
Amherst
Thos. 1769 w.
Augusta
Mark 1749 i.
Danl. 1756 w.
Botetourt
Thos. 1785 i.
Peter 1797 w.
Isaac 1793 w.
Brunswick
Francis 1737 w.
Jno. 1755 w.
Eliz. 1759 w.
Chas. 1761 w.
Chesterfield
Isham 1786 i.
Ann 1789 i.
Mavell 1789 w.
Jas. 1794 i.

Cumberland
Wm. 1767 i.
Essex
Jno. 1692 w.
Rees 1713 i.
Rees 1723 i.
Jno. 1726 i.
Edwd. 1726 w.
Jno. 1733 i.
Wm. 1736 i.
Jno. 1748 i.
Thos. 1748 w.
Jno. 1748-9 i.
Jno. Jr. 1761 w.
Jno. 1762 w.
Greenslee 1766 w.
Micajah 1766 i.
Chas. 1770 w.
Mary 1783 w.
Fairfax
Jno. 1747 w.
Thos. 1752 i.
Jno. 1795 a.
Goochland
Jno. 1755 w.
Tabitha 1768 w.
Jno. 1781 w.
Jos. 1782 w.
Halifax
Evan 1773 i.
Geo. 1789 i.
Henrico
Griffin 1681 w.
Thos. 1781 w.
Thos. Jr. 1782 i.
Isle of Wight
Wm. 1689 w.
Wm. 1720 i.
Wm. 1723 i.
David 1736 i.
Loudoun
Jno. 1767 w.
Jno. 1770 w.
Eliz. 1772 w.
Joshua 1773 w.
Eliz. 1774 i.
Zachariah 1779 w.
Joshua 1779 i.
David 1783 i.
Mary 1788 w.
Zachariah 1795 i.
Lunenburg
Morris 1756 i.
Mecklenburg
Thos. 1788 w.
Middlesex
Jno. Sr. 1779 w.
Norfolk
Jno. 1682 i.
Benj. 1793 w.

Northampton
Wm. 1646 i.
Thos. 1689 w.
Jno. 1709 i.
Thos. 1709 w.
Eliz. 1713 w.
Jno. 1752 i.
Arthur 1754 w.
Jno. 1761 w.
Wm. 1771 i.
Esther 1778 w.
Thos. 1779 w.
Princess Anne
Jno. 1700 w.
Peter 1795 w.
Rappahannock
Jno. 1684 w.
Richmond
Jno. 1701 w.
Peter 1706 w.
———— 1736 i.
Mary 1762 i.
Rockbridge
Isaac 1786 w.
Shenandoah
Jos. 1797 i.
Elijah 1799 w.
Southampton
Eliz. 1751 w.
Benj. 1762 i.
Benj. 1776 i.
Hannah 1791 w.
Surry
Robt. 1679 w.
Robt. 1681 i.
Anthony 1710 w.
Abraham 1712 w.
Wm. 1721 i.
Jno. 1727 w.
Benj. 1728 w.
Wm. 1752 w.
Wm. 1760 w.
Anthony 1769 i.
Rebecca 1795 w.
Sussex
Sarah 1757 w.
Westmoreland
Peter 1696 w.
York
Wm. 1657 w.
Edwd. 1693 i.
Wm. 1718 ab.
Morris 1739 w.
Essex
Thos. 1727 i.
Andrew 1750 w.
EVE
Orange
Jos. 1770 w.

EVENCE
Rappahannock
Anne 1677 w.
EVENS
Essex
Thos. 1748 w.
Sussex
Sarah 1784 i.
York
Jno. 1700 w.
EVERAGE
Princess Anne
Lydia 1789 w.
EVEREST
Rappahannock
Jno. 1679 w.
EVERETT
Isle of Wight
Simon 1727 i.
Simon 1746 w.
Lancaster
Thos. 1727 w.
Northumberland
Nancy 1793 i.
Richmond
Wm. 1759 w.
EVERGONE
Accomack
Thos. 1710 i.
EVERHARD
Loudoun
Jacob 1771 w.
EVERIST
Rappahannock
Jno. 1679 w.
EVERIT
Northumberland
Geo. 1720 i.
EVERITT
Isle of Wight
Thos. 1723 w.
Saml. 1730-31 i.
Jos. 1757 w.
Wm. 1769 i.
Jos. 1782 i.
Saml. 1785 w.
Saml. 1787 i.
Lemuel 1798 i.
Sarah 1798 w.
Lancaster
Rawleigh 1757 w.
Jno. 1758 w.
Northumberland
Thos. 1769 w.
Lancaster
Thos. 1773 i.
Princess Anne
Jno. 1701 i.
Southampton
Simon 1752 w.
Jos. 1773 w.

Thos. 1781 w.
Jno. 1789 i.
York
Robt. 1681-2 w.
EVERMAN
Augusta
Jno. 1781 i.
EVERRIT
Isle of Wight
Simon 1726 w.
EVERS
Northumberland
Thos. 1720 nw.
EVERSON
Pittsylvania
Matthias 1774 w.
EVERT
Orange
Geo. 1744 a.
EVERY
Essex
Jarrat 1698 i.
EVES
Northumberland
Geo. 1729 i.
EVET
Essex
Thos. 1729 i.
EVINGTON
Chesterfield
Mardun V. 1778 w.
EVINS
Accomack
Jno. 1696 i.
Sarah 1712 w.
Brunswick
Matthew 1795 w.
Richmond
Peter 1719 i.
Sussex
Isara 1783 w.
EWEL
Accomack
Jas. 1704 w.
EWELL
Accomack
Mark 1727 w.
Geo. 1728 w.
Mark 1730 i.
Solomon 1734 w.
Jedidiah 1752 i.
Mark 1760 w.
Neomy 1766 w.
Jas. 1780 i.
Seth 1788 i.
Wm. 1791 w.
Geo. H. 1794 w.
Edwd. 1795 i.
Edwd. 1797 i.
Seth 1798 i.

Lancaster
Chas. 1722 w.
S[olomon?] 1768 i.
Jas. 1797 w.
Princess Anne
Thos. 1696 i.
Thos. 1721 w.
Thos. 1733 i.
Jas. 1735 i.
Jas. 1763 i.
Lemuel 1764 i.
Tamer 1764 w.
Tamer 1776 w.
Solomon 1788 i.
Thos. 1796 w.
Thos. 1799 i.
Prince William
Thos. Winder 1784 w.
Bertrand 1794 w.
EWEN
Northampton
Wm. 1678 i.
EWER
Albemarle
Wm. 1766 i.
Richmond
Thos. 1750 w.
EWING
Augusta
Jas. 1796 w.
Bedford
Chas. 1770 w.
Robt. 1787 w.
Berkeley
Thos. 1793 w.
Frederick
Wm. 1782 w.
Montgomery
Saml. 1786 w.
Jno. 1788 w.
Prince Edward
Saml. 1758 w.
Rockbridge
Henry 1798 i.
Wythe
Jas. 1791 w.
Wm. 1793 w.
EWINGS
Prince Edward
Wm. 1782 i.
EXUM
Isle of Wight
Wm. 1700-1 w.
Jeremiah 1720 w.
Wm. 1720 w.
Ann 1727 w.
Robt. 1739 i.
Robt. 1740 i.
Mary 1752 w.
Eliz. 1762 i.
Moses 1776 a.

Southampton
Francis 1753 w.
Wm. 1756 w.
Wm. 1763 i.
Patience 1775 i.
Benj. 1785 w.
EYLE
Essex
Jno. 1699 i.
EYLER
Frederick
Adolph 1769 w.
Godfrey 1771 w.
EYRE
Accomack
Benj. 1687 w.
Regnald 1709 w.
Lancaster
Martha 1725 w.
Northampton
Danl. 1691 w.
Thos. 1715 w.
Jno. 1719 w.
Ann 1721-2 w.
Severn 1728 w.
Neech 1737 w.
Littleton 1768 w.
Severn 1770 w.
Severn 1787 w.
Littleten 1789 w.
EZEL
Surry
Geo. 1730 w.
Brunswick
Wm. Jr. 1766 w.
EZELL
Surry
Timothy 1696 i.
Michael 1717 w.
Sussex
Timothy 1760 w.
Timothy 1768 w.
Isham 1775 w.
Eliz. 1782 w.
Thos. Sr. 1782 w.
Wm. 1786 w.
Drury 1787 w.
Thos. 1796 i.

F

FADRE
Accomack
Hillyard 1751 i.
FAGAN
Culpeper
Jas. 1794 i.
FAGEN
Northumberland
Arthur 1762 i.

FAGG
Amelia
  Thos. 1785 w.
FAIL
Henrico
  Jno. 1712 w.
FAIN
Amelia
  Wm. 1750 w.
Cumberland
  Richd. 1753 w.
FAIR
Bedford
  Jas. 1775 i.
  Jas. 1776 i.
  Jas. 1791 i.
FAIRES
Washington
  Robt. 1788 w.
FAIRFAX
Fairfax
  Wm. 1757 w.
Frederick
  Thos., Lord, 1782 w.
Northampton
  Jas. 1739 w.
Prince William
  Wm. 1793 w.
FAIRFIELD
Spotsylvania
  Wm. 1758 a.
FAIRMAN
Lancaster
  Jno. 1726 w.
FAIRWEATHER
Northumberland
  Patrick 1745 w.
  Catheron 1747 w.
FALCONER
York
  Jas. 1728 w.
FALKE
Norfolk
  Jno. 1691 w.
FALKNON
Prince William
  Thos. 1778 a.
FALLIN
Fairfax
  Agatha 1792 w.
Northumberland
  Chas. 1701 w.
  Dennis 1726-7 w.
  Wm. 1726-7 w.
  Ann 1743-4 i.
  Chas. 1752 w.
  Tignor 1768 i.
  Dennis 1772 i.
  Chas. 1773 w.
  Wm. 1783 w.
  Elisha 1787 i.

FALLIS
Frederick
  Thos. 1756 i.
FAMBOROUGH
Halifax
  Thos. 1791 w.
FANER
Essex
  Jno. 1723 w.
FANGHOUSEW
Frederick
  Jno. 1765 i.
FANING
Sussex
  Bryan 1767 w.
FANN
Surry
  Jacob 1781 w.
FANNEN
Amelia
  Bryan 1765 w.
FANNING
Greensville
  Wm. 1782 w.
FANSHAW
Norfolk
  Thos. 1669 w.
FARBUSH
Amherst
  Angus 1783 a.
FARDY
Norfolk
  Martin 1767 i.
FARECLOTH
Isle of Wight
  Wm. 1728 w.
FARES
Cumberland
  Richd. 1776 i.
FARGASON
Mecklenburg
  Sarah 1782 w.
Northumberland
  Geo. 1751 w.
FARGESON
Culpeper
  Benj. 1760 i.
  Benj. 1761 i.
  Francis 1768 w.
  Saml. 1772 w.
Essex
  Jos. 1717 w.
FARGESSON
Goochland
  Jas. 1741 w.
FARGUESON
Goochland
  Ann 1748 i.
Middlesex
  Allen 1718 i.

FARGUSON
Albemarle
  Danl. 1780 i.
Amelia
  Robt. 1768 w.
  Robt. Jr. 1768 w.
  Jas. Jr. 1771 i.
  Robt. 1778 i.
Bedford
  Jno. 1786 w.
Chesterfield
  Danl. 17— i.
  Moses 1750 w.
  Martha 1774 w.
  Martha 1778 i.
  Jas. 1784 w.
Cumberland
  Wm. 1793 i.
Essex
  Jno. 1717 w.
  Ann 1735 w.
  Danl. 1748 w.
  Jno. 1770 w.
Fairfax
  Jno. 1761 w.
Halifax
  Hugh 1787 i.
Henrico
  Jno. 1734 w.
King George
  Josiah 1750 i.
Lunenburg
  Joel 1788 w.
Westmoreland
  Jno. 1782 i.
FARGUSSON
Chesterfield
  Jno. 1752 w.
Essex
  Titus 1778 w.
FARIES
Augusta
  Jno. 1795 i.
FARIS
Augusta
  Jno. 1788 w.
Henrico
  Jno. 1746 w.
Henry
  Thos. 1797 i.
Washington
  Wm. 1777 i.
FARISH
Spotsylvania
  Robt. 1769 w.
  Judith 1793 w.
FARISS
Henrico
  Robt. 1783 w.

FARLAR
Chesterfield
    Jas. 17— i.
FARLEY
Amelia
    Peter 1757 w.
    Geo. 1771 w.
    Jno. 1766 w.
    Jos. 1782 w.
    Wm. Sr. 1782 w.
    Drucilla 1785 w.
Chesterfield
    Jno. 1754 w.
    Jos. 1761 w.
    Eliz. 1761 i.
    Forrest 1767 i.
    Jno. 1775 w.
    Jas. 1779 w.
Halifax
    Hervey 1768 w.
    Josiah 1774 w.
Hampshire
    Thos. 1782 w.
Lunenburg
    Henry 1784 w.
Montgomery
    Thos. 1796 w.
Powhatan
    Matthew 1789 i.
    Matthew 1792 w.
FARLOW
Stafford
    Ann 1707 w.
    Ambrose 1707 w.
FARMER
Chesterfield
    Peter 17— i.
    Wm. 1750 i.
    Seth 1756 w.
    Thos. 177— w.
    Mark 1771 w.
    Jos. 1778 w.
    Elam Jr. 1780 w.
    Wm. 1782 i.
    Elam 1784 i.
    Obedience 1785 w.
    Phebe 1785 w.
    Dorothy 1786 w.
    Mary 1787 w.
    Wm. 1790 i.
    Jno. 1793 w.
    Henry 1795 i.
    Jno. 1796 i.
Cumberland
    Henry 1781 w.
    Forrest 1794 i.
Essex
    Thos. 1715 i.
    Ralph 1750 w.
Halifax
    Fredk. 1782 i.

Lunenburg
    Benj. 1757 w.
    Geo. 1761 i.
    Lodowick 1780 w.
    Henry 1782 i.
    Sarah 1789 w.
Montgomery
    Jeremiah 1792 i.
Surry
    Thos. 1723 i.
FARMINGTON
Brunswick
    Jno. 1751 w.
FARNED
Northumberland
    Jas. 1758 w.
FARNEFOLD
Northumberland
    Jno. 1702 w.
FARNID
Northumberland
    Jas. 1748 w.
FARNSWORTH
Loudoun
    Adonijah 1791 i.
FARP
Westmoreland
    Henry 1717 i.
FARQUERHASON
Powhatan
    Chas. 1797 w.
FARR
Loudoun
    Jas. 1766 i.
FARRALL
Northampton
    Donnough 1667 w.
FARRANT
Northampton
    Phillip 1654 w.
    Phillip (2) 1654 w.
FARRAR
Albemarle
    Jno. 1769 w.
    Jno. 1792 i.
Amherst
    Perrin 1792 a.
Charlotte
    Chas. 1784 w.
Goochland
    Thos. 1742 w.
    Wm. 1744 w.
    Jos. 1749 w.
    Mary 1757 w.
    Thos. 1761 w.
    Jno. 1782 w.
Henrico
    Wm. 1677-8 w.
    Jno. 1684 w.
    Wm. 1715 i.

Louisa
    Perrin 1785 w.
Mecklenburg
    Geo. 1772 w.
Pittsylvania
    Shadrach 1782 w.
FARRELL
Brunswick
    Hubbard 1749 i.
Essex
    Chas. 1727 i.
Middlesex
    Edwd. 1727 i.
Prince George
    Brian 1716 w.
    Wm. 1718 w.
Surry
    Thos. 1713 w.
FARRER
Norfolk
    Geo. 1784 w.
FARRINGTON
Sussex
    Robt. 1768 a.
FARRIS
Cumberland
    Jos. 1795 i.
FARRISS
Bedford
    Jno. 1789 i.
Henrico
    Wm. 1784 w.
    Wm. 1785 i.
    Wm. 1799 w.
FARROW
Albemarle
    Amy 1798 w.
Loudoun
    Jos. 1784 w.
Prince William
    Jno. 1735 i.
    Abram 1743 w.
    Geo. 1779 i.
    Abraham 1786 a.
    Jno. 1793 w.
Stafford
    Abraham 1731 w.
FARSEY
Goochland
    Francis 1731 i.
FARTHING
Prince William
    Wm. Maria 1736 a.
York
    Edwd. 1720 i.
FARVIN
Henrico
    Richd. 1689 i.
FASON
York
    Henrich 1693 w.

FATHERBE
Surry
  Anne 1735 w.
FATHERLY
Isle of Wight
  ———— 1797 w.
Northampton
  Jno. 1773 w.
FATHERY
Northampton
  Jno. 1721 w.
  Ann 1737 w.
  Jno. 1746 w.
  Jno. 1765 w.
FAUBER
Augusta
  Valentine 1795 w.
FAUCETT
Frederick
  Jno. 1786 w.
  Richd. 1789 w.
FAUDRY
Lancaster
  Vachal 1790 i.
FAUGHT
Augusta
  Johan Paul 1761 w.
FAULCON
Surry
  Abraham 1727 w.
  Isaac 1727 w.
  Jacob 1727 w.
  Nich. Sr. 1783 w.
  Nich. Jr. 1793 w.
  Martha 1798 w.
FAULCONER
Essex
  Nich. 1743 w.
  Nich. 1789 w.
FAULK
Frederick
  Geo. 1787 w.
FAULKENER
Essex
  Edwd. 1722 i.
  Wm. 1725 i.
  Edwd. 1730 i.
  Wm. 1743 i.
  David 1751 i.
FAULKNER
Halifax
  Benj. 1784 w.
Lancaster
  Mary 1775 i.
Middlesex
  Jno. 1775 i.
  Thos. 1791 w.
Orange
  Peter 1738 a.
  Wm. 1778 w.

Prince William
  Thos. 1798 a.
Richmond
  Richd. 1709 w.
FAUNTLEROY
Essex
  Jno. 1766 w.
  Jno. [1766] w.
Northumberland
  Griffin 1750 w.
  Griffin 1756 w.
  Anne 1761 w.
  Judith 1774 w.
Rappahannock
  Moore [1664?] i.
  Wm. 1686 i.
Richmond
  Moore 1739 w.
  Margt. 1742 i.
  Wm. 1757 w.
  Moore Jr. 1758 w.
  Geo. Hale 1770 w.
  Wm. Jr. 1789 i.
  Moore 1791 w.
  Moore 1793 w.
  Wm. 1793 w.
  Griffin 1794 w.
  Wm. 1797 w.
  Jno. 1798 w.
FAQUIER
York
  Francis 1768 w.
FAVER
Culpeper
  Jno. Sr. 1783 w.
  Jno. 1790 w.
Essex
  Jno. 1723 w.
  Theophilus 1783 w.
  Thos. 1786 w.
Culpeper
  Wm. 1778 i.
FAVOR
Essex
  Theophilus 1760 w.
FAVOUR
Culpeper
  Jno. 1790 i.
FAWCETT
Essex
  Rice 1796 i.
Frederick
  Richd. 1792 i.
FAWCIT
Frederick
  Thos. 1747 i.
FAWN
Surry
  Wm. 1758 i.
FAWSETT

Accomack
  Jno. 1673 w.
FAYSON
York
  Henry 1698 w.
FAZAKERLEY
Princess Anne
  Thos. 1759 i.
FEAGAN
Fauquier
  Edwd. 1798 i.
FEAGEN
Prince William
  Edwd. 1744 i.
FEAGIN
Fauquier
  Edwd. 1780 w.
Westmoreland
  Wm. 177— w.
FEAGINS
Lancaster
  Danl. 1730 w.
Richmond
  Wm. 1778 i.
Westmoreland
  Geo. 1755 i.
FEAR
York
  Thos. 1707 w.
FEARISTON
Brunswick
  Chas. 1790 w.
FEARN
Isle of Wight
  Geo. 1781 w.
Middlesex
  Jno. 1700 i.
  Jno. Sr. 1743 w.
  Meacham 1774 w.
FEASTON
Amelia
  Wm. 1753 w.
FEATHERSTON
Amelia
  Wm. 1769 w.
  Lewis 1781 w.
  Wm. 1788 i.
Brunswick
  Mary 1786 i.
Chesterfield
  Eliz. 1759 w.
  Henry 1760 w.
  Chas. 1778 w.
  Edwd. 1792 w.
  Edwd. 1796 i.
FEBB
Lancaster
  Frances 1780 w.
FEDDEMAN
Accomack
  Mechack 1793 w.

FEDDERMAN
Accomack
Jos. 1772 w.
FEDDIMAN
Accomack
Jos. 1752 w.
FEEBARRY
Accomack
Jas. 1795 i.
FEELY
Frederick
Timothy 1782 w.
FEEN
Richmond
Jno. 1719 i.
FEEURSTER
Bath
Thos. 1798 i.
FEEZELL
Bedford
Philip 1789 w.
FEGIN
Northumberland
Tarrance 1766 w.
FEGINS
Mecklenburg
Geo. 1787 i.
FEIGHN
Mecklenburg
——— 1772 i.
FEILD
Westmoreland
Abram. 1674 w.
FEILDING
King George
Willoughby 1736 i.
FEIRST
Loudoun
Peter 1775 w.
FELGATE
York
Robt. 1655 w.
Wm. 1660 w.
FELLER
Shenandoah
Woolrick 1778 a.
FELLERDE
Shenandoah
Christian 1782 a.
FELLOWES
York
Wm. 1683 a.
FELPS
Surry
Humphrey 1714 w.
FELTS
Surry
Humphrey 1716 i.
Francis 1753 i.
Sussex
Richd. 1761 w.

Thos. 1769 w.
Nathl. 1771 w.
Thos. 1772 w.
Burwell 1778 i.
Nathl. 1785 w.
Wm. 1794 w.
FELTSMIRE
Shenandoah
Jno. 1797 w.
FELWOOD
Norfolk
Roger 1681 nw.
FENCAINT
Westmoreland
Jos. 1702 i.
FENFORD
Norfolk
Thos. 1679 w.
FENDLA
Lancaster
Jno. 1734 w.
Jno. 1762 i.
Geo. 1771 i.
FENDLEY
Richmond
Jas. 1757 i.
FENEMAN
Northampton
Jno. 1678 w.
FENICK
Norfolk
Mary 1679 w.
FENIEL
Richmond
Elias 1739 w.
FENLEY
Fairfax
Walter 1788 i.
Chas. B. 1789 w.
FENN
Accomack
Philip 1743 w.
Isle of Wight
Timothy 1688 i.
Robt. 1693 w.
Richmond
Henry 1733 i.
Westmoreland
Thos. 1716 w.
FENNE
York
Saml. 1660 w.
FENNELL
Brunswick
Jno. 1773 w.
Culpeper
Jonathan 1783 i.
Jno. 1785 i.
Elijah 1786 w.

FENNIL
Brunswick
Jno. Jr. 1775 i.
FENTON
Frederick
Robt. 1783 i.
Richmond
Wm. 1712 i.
FENTRESS
Norfolk
Geo. 1785 w.
Jas. 1788 w.
Ann 1790 w.
Geo. 1791 i.
Sophia 1792 i.
Wm. 1792 w.
Sarah 1794 w.
Geo. 1799 i.
Princess Anne
Michaell 1714 w.
Moses 1762 i.
Jno. 1770 w.
Jno. 1785 w.
Jno. 1788 w.
FENTRIS
Princess Anne
Jno. 1733 w.
Aaron 1738 w.
FENTRISS
Norfolk
Jno. 1775 w.
Princess Anne
Jas. 1744 w.
Wm. 1752 w.
Michael 1754 w.
Wm. 1771 i.
Wm. 1776 w.
Wm. 1778 i.
Aaron 1782 w.
FENWICK
Albemarle
Jno. 1790 w.
Norfolk
Mary 1679 nw.
FEEGAR
Loudoun
Jno. 1769 i.
FEGERSON
Southampton
Jno. 1778 w.
FEREBEE
Norfolk
Jas. 1753 w.
Jno. 1763 w.
Jno. 1782 i.
Chas. 1799 w.
FERGESON
Cumberland
Saml. 1795 w.

FERGESSON
York
Robt. 1682 w.
FERGUSON
Berkeley
David 1796 i.
Culpeper
Jno. 1794 w.
Fairfax
Joshua 1770 w.
Frederick
Hugh 1745 a.
Thos. 1747 a.
Hugh 1750 i.
Hugh 1782 i.
Halifax
Hugh 1789 a.
Lancaster
Robt. 1794 i.
Francis 1782 w.
Montgomery
Andrew 1792 w.
Pittsylvania
Robt. 1798 w.
Southampton
Jno. 1782 i.
Robt. 1791 i.
Westmoreland
Jno. 1746 i.
Jno. 1751 i.
York
Wm. 1737 w.
Patrick 1738 i.
Francis 1740 w.
FERGUSSON
Amelia
Jas. 1769 w.
Jno. 1778 w.
Chesterfield
Bartlet 1784 w.
FERIS
Cumberland
Jacob 1776 i.
FERMAN
Lancaster
Nicho. 1656 i.
FERN
Isle of Wight
Timothy 1651 w.
FERNANDIS
Prince William
Eleanor 1794 w.
FERNLEY
Frederick
Wm. 1748 i.
FERO
Henrico
Jno. 1686 i.
FERRABY
Surry
Benj. 1726 w.

FERRELL
Bedford
Wm. 1780 w.
Isle of Wight
Silvester 1736 w.
FERRER
Cumberland
Rachel 1766 i.
FERRES
Goochland
Wm. 1745 w.
FERRILL
Richmond
Jas. 1723 i.
FERRINGTON
Sussex
Robt. 1758 w.
FERRIS
Henrico
Richd. 1750 w.
FERRO
Albemarle
Thos. 1778 w.
FETHERINGIL
Shenandoah
Jos. 1786 i.
FETHERLING
Frederick
Jacob 1795 i.
FETHERSTONE
Henrico
Chas. 1682 i.
FETTWOLL
Norfolk
Roger 1681 i.
FEVERAREE
Isle of Wight
Jno. 1669 w.
FEWELL
King George
Henry 1725 i.
Spotsylvania
Jas. 1762 a.
FEWQUA
Charles City
Giles 1771 w.
FEY
Shenandoah
Jacob 1794 i.
FICKLIN
King George
Thos. 1778 w.
FIDDERMAN
Accomack
Jos. 1780 i.
Mechack 1796 i.
FIDELY
Frederick
Michael 1770 w.

FIEDIMASED
Shenandoah
Jacob 1790 a.
FIELD
Augusta
Henry 1767 i.
Bedford
Jno. 1778 w.
Brunswick
Theophilus 1796 i.
Culpeper
Keene 1754 i.
Abraham 1775 w.
Jno. 1775 w.
Henry 1778 w.
Henry Jr. 1787 w.
Geo. 1788 w.
Geo. 1790 i.
Elianer 1796 w.
Essex
Thos. 1725 i.
Fauquier
Danl. 1783 w.
Henrico
Jno. 1688 i.
Thos. 1688 i.
Jno. 1702 i.
Loudoun
Thos. Jr. 1775 w.
Thos. 1780 w.
Louisa
Jno. 1789 w.
Loudoun
Jamima 1794 w.
Mecklenburg
Jno. Shaw 1795 w.
Northampton
Henry Sr. 1664 w.
Prince Edward
Bartho. 1773 i.
FIELDER
Prince Edward
Thos. 1782 w.
FIELD
Sussex
Robt. 1754 i.
Richd. 1756 a.
Westmoreland
Danl. 1720 w.
Danl. 1733 w.
FIELDAN
Westmoreland
Edwd. 1791 w.
FIELDING
Fauquier
Edwin 1783 w.
Greensville
Jas. 1783 i.
Louisa
Jos. 1795 i.

Northumberland
Richd. 1667 w.
Edwd. 1694 i.
Ambrose 1750 w.
Ambrose 1764 w.
FIELDS
Augusta
Henry 1766 a.
Berkeley
Wm. 1774 nw.
Campbell
Andrew 1797 i.
Isle of Wight
Jno. [1718] i.
Surry
Jno. 1735 w.
FIERER
Prince William
Chas. 1749 w.
Chas. 1795 i.
FIERST
Loudoun
Jno. 1774 w.
FIFE
Norfolk
Nathaniel 1765 w.
FIGURES
Southampton
Jos. 1780 w.
Surry
Bartho. 1699-1700 i.
Thos. 1710-11 w.
FILBY
Accomack
Wm. 1758 i.
FILKIN
Northampton
Robt. 1678 w.
FILKINS
Prince William
Henry 1743 i.
FILLGATE
Norfolk
Phillip 1647 i.
FILLIPS
Accomack
Matthias 1778 w.
FILLPOT
York
Eliz. 1706 nw.
FILLSON
Augusta
Robt. 1767 i.
FINCH
Brunswick
Jas. 1778 w.
Wm. 1796 w.
Wm. 1799 i.
Charles City
Agnes 1772 w.
Wm. 1773 i.

Edwd. 1790 i.
Henry 1796 w.
Charlotte
Jno. 1798 i.
Fincasile
Nathl. 1773 a.
Halifax
Henry 1774 i.
Henrico
Geo. 1735 i.
Lancaster
Geo. 1749 i.
Mecklenburg
Edwd. 1790 w.
Norfolk
Francis 1672 w.
Northumberland
Sampson 1749 i.
Sussex
Jas. 1787 i.
Westmoreland
Jno. Jr. 1731 i.
Jno. 1735 w.
Jno. 1765 w.
FINCKLEY
Princess Anne
Thos. 1695 a.
Thos. 1722 i.
FINDER
Culpeper
Michael 1760 i.
Amherst
Andrew 1787 a.
FINE
Loudoun
Peter 1799 w.
FINELSON
Orange
Jno. 1748 w.
FINGLETON
Stafford
Danl. 1758 w.
FINK
Randolph
Henry 1790 i.
FINKLEY
Princess Anne
Jno. 1769 w.
FINKS
Culpeper
Mark 1764 w.
FINLAY
Fairfax
David 1794 i.
Henrico
Jas. 1789 i.
FINLEY
Albemarle
Mary 1751 w.
Augusta
Robt. 1763 a.

Robt. 1765 i.
Wm. 1789 w.
Jno. 1791 w.
Bedford
Jas. 1785 i.
Northampton
Wm. 1653 i.
Ohio
David 1785 i.
FINNACEY
Stafford
Richd. 1734 i.
FINNIE
Fauquier
Jno. 1760 w.
FINNEY
Accomack
Wm. 1738 w.
Wm. 1742 i.
Comfort 1743 w.
Wm. 1766 w.
Wm. 1767 i.
Abel 1768 w.
Abel 1771 i.
Wm. 1771 i.
Jno. 1790 i.
Wm. 1792 w.
Wm. 1796 i.
Amelia
Wm. 1759 w.
Wm. 1787 i.
Mary 1794 w.
Jno. 1798 w.
Culpeper
Jas. 1764 w.
Essex
Jno. 1710 w.
Fauquier
Jno. 1766 i.
Henrico
Wm. 1727 w.
King George
Morgan 1762 a.
Orange
Jas. 1743 i.
FINNY
Accomack
Andrew 1742 w.
Joannah 1768 w.
Halifax
Thos. 1783 w.
FINTON
Henrico
Thos. 1784 w.
FIPS
Charlotte
Jno. 1769 i.
Jno. 1777 i.
FIRESTONE
Loudoun
Jos. 1793 i.

FIRKETT
Northampton
Francis 1720 w.
FIRKLITTLE
Northampton
Hamon 1718 w.
FIRTH
Brunswick
Sarah 1798 w.
Thos. 1794 w.
Lunenburg
Danl. 1754 i.
FISH
Accomack
Jno. 1766 w.
FISHBACK
Culpeper
Fred. 1782 w.
Harmon 1783 w.
Fauquier
Jno. 1789 i.
Josiah 1799 i.
Prince William
Jno. 1734 w.
FISHER
Accomack
Phylop 1709 w.
Jno. 1713 w.
Jno. 1744 i.
Eliz. 1759 i.
Jno. 1770 i.
Shadrach 1777 w.
Jno. 1778 w.
Phillip 1794 w.
Amherst
Patrick 1795 a.
Berkeley
Jacob 1787 w.
Brunswick
Jas. 1784 w.
Culpeper
Lewis 1773 w.
Essex
Benj. 1716 w.
Benj. 1744 w.
Benj. 1799 w.
Frederick
Barak 1784 w.
Barrock 1784 i.
Barak 1787 i.
Greensville
Daniel 1795 w.
Halifax
Wm. 1795 w.
Isle of Wight
Thos. 1790 w.
Norfolk
Eldred 1772 w.
Northampton
Jno. 1639 w.
Rebecca 1658 w.

Phillip (elder)
1702 w.
Thos. 1709 i.
Jno. 1720 w.
Jno. 1724 w.
Thos. 1727 w.
Jno. Geo. 1735 i.
Maddox 1749 w.
Thos. Sr. 1772 w.
Thos .Jr. 1778 w.
Thos. 1781 i.
Polly 1785 w.
Polly 1790 i.
Jas. 1797 i.
Northumberland
Phillip 1774 w.
Phillip 1782 i.
Princess Anne
Jonathan 1796 w.
Prince Edward
Mary 1778 w.
Richmond
Martin Sr. 1701 w.
Southampton
Mary 1795 i.
Surry
Thos. 1777 w.
Westmoreland
Thos. 1729 i.
Jno. 1743 i.
Thos. 1782 i.
Thos. 1783 i.
Jos. 1786 w.
Thos. 1786 i.
FISHPOOL
King George
Geo. 1739 i.
FISHPOOLE
King George
Mary 1748 i.
FITCHET
Northampton
Jno. 1761 w.
Jno. 1762 i.
Sarah 1762 i.
Elishe 1765 i.
FITCHETT
Accomack
Weatherington 1728 w.
Withertun 1766 w.
Salathiel 1774 w.
Jno. 1782 w.
Comfort 1784 w.
Jacob 1784 w.
Jno. 1786 i.
Northampton
Joshua 1709 w.
Esther 1716 w.
Licia [Elisha?]
1725 w.
Elisha 1727 i.

Thos. 1728 w.
Nehemiah 1764 w
Anna 1766 i.
Joshua 1766 w.
Thos. 1787 w.
Surry
Jno. 1720 i.
FITCHIT
Surry
Wm. 1740 i.
FITER
Prince William
Jno. Miliord 1735 v.
FITSGARRALL
Norfolk
Katheren 1678-9 w.
Morris 1678-9 w.
Princess Anne
Henry 1721 w.
FITZER
Shenandoah
Geo. 1794 a.
FITZGARRELL
Accomack
Jno. 1687 w.
Rachel 1771 w.
Augusta
Wm. 1764 i.
FITZGERALD
Accomack
Peter 1744 i.
Jno. 1755 w.
Shadrach 1757 i.
Stephen 1760 i.
Jno. 1781 w.
Amelia
Wm. 1771 w.
Culpeper
Jno. 1798 w.
Fairfax
Jno. 1799 w.
Hampshire
Edwd. 1793 w.
Princess Anne
Henry 1710 i.
Morris 1715 i.
Jas. 1775 i.
FITZGERRALD
Accomack
Mary 1746 i.
Jas. 1771 w.
Northampton
Morris 1686 i.
Westmoreland
Morrice 1716 i
Essex
Honn. 1718 i.
FITZGERROLD
Accomack
Jas. 1774 i.

FITZGIBBONS
Norfolk
Austin 1786 w.
FITZHERBERT
Henrico
Thos. 1692 w.
Richmond
Wm. 1716 i.
FITZHUGH
Accomack
Wm. 1777 w.
King George
Henry 1778 w.
Henry 1783 w.
Wm. 1785 a.
Wm. 1791 w.
Humphrey Frances-
toye 1794 w.
Hannah 1799 w.
Richmond
Thos. 1719 w.
Stafford
Wm. 1701 w.
Jno. 1732 w.
Henry 1742 i.
Henry 1748 i.
Henry 1759 w.
Westmoreland
Danl. 1786 w.
FITZIMMONS
Essex
Mary 1756 w.
FITZJEFFREYS
Essex
Jno. 1720 i.
FITZMORRIS
Northumberland
Jas. 1758 i.
FITZPATRICK
Albemarle
Wm. 1764 w.
Sarah 1772 i.
Alex. 1783 i.
Thos. 1787 w.
Fluvanna
Jos. 1781 w.
Washington
Jno. 1778 i.
FITZSIMMONS
Frederick
Jno. 1748 i.
Powhatan
Patrick 1785 i.
FIVEASH
Isle of Wight
Peter 1702 i.
Thos. 1725-6 w.
Alice 1741 i.
Peter 1741 i.
Peter 1765 i.

FIZZLE
Isle of Wight
Joshua 1795 w.
FLABORN
Princess Anne
Jno. 1720 w.
FLACK
Accomack
Robt. 1720 i.
Charles City
Andrew 1769.
FLAGG
Berkeley
Thos. 1772 w.
FLAKE
Isle of Wight
Jno. 1799 a.
Surry
Robt. 1724 w.
Wm. 1728 i.
FLAMMON
Cumberland
Samson 1782 w.
FLANAGAN
Louisa
Jas. 1752 w.
Princess Anne
Patrick 1779 w.
FLANIGAN
Northumberland
Andrew 1727 w.
FLANIKIN
Princess Anne
Moses 1792 w.
FLARHATY
Accomack
Jno. 1794 i.
FLASHER
Augusta
Jno. 1779 w.
FLATT
Northampton
Jno. 1729 i.
Jane 1738 w.
FLATTERY
Prince William
Jno. 1782 i.
FLEARS
Princess Anne
Moor 1733 i.
FLECKNER
Berkeley
Peter 1789 i.
FLEECE
Berkeley
Jacob 1798 i.
FLEEMAN
Louisa
Thos. 1774 i.
FLEET
Lancaster
Henry 1733 w.

Wm. 1734 i.
Henry 1736 i.
Henry 1787 w.
Jno. 1793 w.
Mary 1799 w.
FLEETE
York
Jno. 1667 i.
FLEETWOOD
Norfolk
Francis [1691] nw.
FLEMING
Amelia
Robt. 1775 i.
Augusta
Wm. 1791 i.
Botetourt
Wm. 1795 w.
Campbell
Danl. 1789 i.
Chesterfield
Chas. 1793 w.
Cumberland
Jno. 1756 w.
Jno. 1767 w.
Fairfax
Thos. 1786 w.
Goochland
Tarlton 1750 w.
Tarlton 1778 w.
Thos. 1777 w.
Isle of Wight
Nathl. 1792 i.
Lancaster
Walter 1656 w.
Jas. 1717 i.
Chas. 1773 i.
Louisa
Danl. 1754 w.
Robt. 1764 w.
Jno. 1793 w.
Richmond
Alex. 1711 w.
Westmoreland
Jno. 1744 w.
Alex. 1751 i.
Wm. 1767 w.
FLEMISTER
Essex
Jas. 1760 i.
FLEMMING
Berkeley
Henry 1796 i.
Surry
Lawrence 1710 w.
Adam 1777 w.
FLEMYING
Isle of Wight
Wm. 1784 i.
Nathl. 1790 w.

FLESHER
Augusta
Jno. 1780 i.
FLESHMAN
Culpeper
Jno. 1787 i.
Greenbrier
Robt. 1798 i.
FLETCHER
Accomack
Wm. 1710 w.
Matthew 1719 w.
Wm. 1729 w.
Thos. 1735 w.
Matthew 1751 w.
Brandon 1762 w.
Reed 1772 i.
Tabitha 1775 w.
Nathan 1797 i.
Henry 1799 w.
Berkeley
Jno. 1772 w.
Brunswick
Jas. 1733 w.
Jas. 1736 i.
Jno. 1778 w.
Charlotte
Mary 1790 w.
Jas. 1791 i.
Culpeper
Francis 1781 w.
Essex
Wm. 1728 w.
Wm. 1776 i.
Fauquier
Thos. 1793 w.
Isle of Wight
Chas. 1784 w.
Norfolk
Roger 1649 i.
Roger 1655 i.
Northampton
Robt. 1694 w.
Stephen 1713 i.
Robt. 1728 w.
Wm. 1746 w.
Northumberland
Wm. 1746 i.
Wm. 1758 w.
Rockbridge
Job. 1798 i.
Robt. 1796 i.
Southampton
Benj. 1797 i.
Stafford
Geo. 1749 w.
Jas. 1785 i.
Westmoreland
Robt. 1713 i.
York
Jno. 1657 w.

FLEWELLING
Westmoreland
Jno. 1698 w.
FLIN
Amelia
Jno. 1781 w.
Lunenburg
Lawflin 1759 w.
FLINER
Greenbrier
Jas. 1787 i.
FLING
Henrico
Jno. 1706 a.
Stafford
Morris 1748 i.
Northumberland
Hannah 1758 nw.
Westmoreland
Wm. 1754 w.
FLINT
Albemarle
Rich. 1778 i.
Isle of Wight
Thos. 1798 i.
Lancaster
Richd. 1720 w.
David 1743 w.
Alex 1744 i.
Thos. 1764 w.
Northampton
Jno. 1706 w.
Northumberland
Jno. 1754 w.
Jno. 1786 w.
Sarah 1793 w.
Westmoreland
Martha 1705 i.
FLIPPEN
Cumberland
Thos. 1755 w.
Eliz. 1758 w.
Ralph 1767 w.
Wm. 1770 i.
Martha 1793 w.
Jno. 1794 w.
Jno. 1799 i.
FELTS
Sussex
Wm. 1794 w.
FLIPPING
Cumberland
Ralph 1771 i.
FLITTER
Stafford
Jno. 1736 i.
FLOOD
Augusta
Jno. 1753 a.
Charlotte
Fredk. 1789 w.

Henry
Seth 1780 i.
Northampton
Francis 1654 i.
Northumberland
Wm. 1777 w.
Richmond
Nich. 1777 i.
Nich. 1778 w.
Eliz. 1792 w.
Surry
Jno. 1679 i.
Jno. 1711 w.
Thos. 1718 i.
Walter, Jr. 1721 i.
Walter 1722 w.
Ann 1723 w.
Ann 1730 i.
Mary 1732 or 3 w.
Jno. 1739 w.
Harry 1740 w.
Westmoreland
Wm. 1775 w.
FLOR
Frederick
Adolph 1770 i.
FLORANCE
Prince William
Geo. 1792 w.
FLORIDAY
York
Morgan 1667 w.
FLOURNOY
Chesterfield
Francis, Jr. 1769 w.
Francis 1770 w.
Francis, Jr. 1773 i.
Jno. 1795 i.
Powhatan
Saml. 1780 w.
Eliz. 1791 w.
Thos. 1794 w.
Prince Edward
David 1757 w.
FLOW
Isle of Wight
Morris 1741 i.
FLOWER
Lancaster
Geo. 1682 w.
Geo. 1721 w.
Lee 1721 i.
Geo. 1749-50 w.
Geo. 1762 w.
Northumberland
Eliz. 1775 w.
Westmoreland
Jos. 1736 i.
FLOWERE
Spotsylvania
Wm. 1741 a.
Danl. 1742 a.

FLOWERS
Augusta
Saml. 1765 a.
Essex
Isaac 1723 i.
Isle of Wight
Henry 1728 i.
Lancaster
Geo. 1682-3 i.
Jno. 1698 w.
Jno. 1717 i.
Geo. 1777 i.
Surry
David 1748 i.
York
Jno. 1655 w.
Ralph 1704 i.
FLOWRANE
Lancaster
Thos. 1740 i.
FLOYD
Accomack
Berry 1797 w.
Augusta
Wm. 1771 a.
Chas. 1784 i.
Brunswick
Josiah 1790 w.
Zachariah 1795 w.
Chas. 1797 w.
Charles City
Chas. 1769 w.
Chas. 1772 i.
Culpeper
Jno. 1770 w.
Robt. 1787 w.
Fairfax
Ebenezer 1743 i.
Jno. 1743 a.
Henrico
Morris 1728 w.
Stephen 1745 i.
Joyce 1746 i.
Isle of Wight
Francis 1741 i.
Thos. 1761 i.
Francis 1765 i.
Lancaster
Edwd. 1690 w.
Lunenburg
Ann 1782 i.
Jno. 1783 i.
Mecklenburg
Richd. 1767 i.
Chas. 1788 i.
Northampton
Jno. 1687 w.
Hugh 1713 i.
Chas. 1718-19 w.
Hugh 1736 i.
Jno. 1738 i.
Jno. 1744 i.

Berry 1750 w.
Matthew 1752 w.
Matthew Sr. 1752 w.
Saml. 1753 i.
Matthew 1754 w.
Jas. 1760 w.
Berry 1771 w.
Benj. 1772 i.
Jno. 1777 i.
Chas. 1780 w.
Chas. 1785 w.
Wm. 1785 w.
Chas. 1790 i.
Berry 1795 w.
Northumberland
Nathl. 1740 i.
Princess Anne
Peter 1733 w.
Jno. B. 1799 w.
Rappahannock
Saml. 1684 w.
Stafford
Jasper 1743 w.
Surry
Joanna Joice 1743 w.
FLOYNE
Lancaster
Teage 1659 i.
York
Jno. 1647 i.
FLUD
Accomack
Keziah 1778 w.
FLUELLING
York
Robt. 1691-2 w.
FLUKER
Northumberland
David 1762 w.
FLY
Isle of Wight
Wm. 1679 i.
Jeremiah 1736 w.
FLYN
Halifax
Jno. 1780 w.
FLYNN
Mecklenburg
Wm. 1799 i.
FLYNT
Lancaster
Thos. 1783 w.
Northumberland
Richd. 1664 w.
Thos. 1719 i.
Jas. 1723 w.
Richd. 1748 w.
Thos. 1773 i.
Richmond
Richd. 1752 w.

FOALKE
Augusta
Lodwick 1760 i.
FOELKNER
Shenandoah
Adam 1793 a.
FOESE
Chesterfield
Jno. B. 17—i.
Jane 1793 w.
Frances 1796 w.
FOGELSONG
Frederick
Geo. 1773 w.
Christian 1777 w.
FOGG
Accomack
Ann 1713 w.
Wm. Watts 1748 w.
Jno. 1765 w.
Essex
Jas. 1742 i.
Jas. 1744 i.
Nathaniel 1753 w.
Wm. 1764 i.
Thos. 1784 w.
Jos. 1786 w.
Northumberland
Israel 1760 i.
FOGGS
Essex
Thos. 1795 i.
FOIL
Augusta
Robt. 1754 i.
FOISON
Henrico
Jno. 1693 i.
FOLAND
Berkeley
Geo. 1790 i.
FOLCHES
Henrico
Jno. 1732 w.
FOLCONER
Northampton
Patrick 1718 w.
FOLEY
Fauquier
Jas. 1797 w.
Frederick
Richd. 1782 w.
King George
Abraham 1779 a.
Patrick
Bartlett 1793 i.
Bartho. 1795 a.
Prince William
Jacob 1778 i.
Mary 1781 w.
Stafford
Jno. 1762 w.

FOLIO
Accomack
Jno. 1797 w.
FOLIOTT
York
Edwd. 1690 w.
FOLIS
Accomack
Jno. 1799 i.
FOLKES
Chesterfield
Jno. Sr. 17— w.
Jno. 1777 i.
Edwd. Sr. 1783 w.
Edwd. Jr. 1785 w.
Edwd. 1790 i.
Joel 1794 w.
FOLKS
Cumberland
Jno. 1785 i.
FOLLES
Frederick
Thos. 1756 w.
FOLLIN
Essex
Capewell 1756 i.
Fairfax
Wm. 1799 i.
FOLLIS
Halifax
Wm. 1767 w.
FOLTY
Shenandoah
Jno. Martin 1782 i.
FONES
Isle of Wight
Matthew 1704 w.
Robt. 1758 w.
Eliz. 1763 w.
Jno. 1766 i.
Shelly 1785 i.
Jno. 1788 i.
FONGAIL
Henrico
Peter 1712 i.
FONTAINE
Campbell
Edmd. 1792 nw.
Lancaster
Dorothy 1762 i.
Louisa
Sarah 1784 i.
Northumberland
Jas. 1746 i.
York
Francis 1749 w.
Susanna 1756 w.
Susanna 1761 i.
FOOKES
Accomack
Thos. 1722 w.

FOOKS
Accomack
Danl. 1740 w.
FOOLES
Essex
Nicholas 1704 i.
FOOSHEE
Culpeper
Wm. 1786 w.
FOOT
Northumberland
Henry 1778 w.
FOOTE
Fauquier
Geo. 1759 w.
Gilson 1770 i.
Wm. 1773 i.
Geo. 1775 w.
Geo. 1778 i.
Richd. 1780 w.
Lancaster
Wm. [1652?] a.
Prince William
Richd. 1779 w.
Richd. 1780 i.
York
Thos. 1668 w.
FOOTMAN
Westmoreland
Jno. 1739 w.
Eliz. 1744 w.
FORBES
Chesterfield
Geo. 1754 w.
Essex
Alice 1698 w.
Frederick
Robt. 1751 i.
Isle of Wight
Alex. 1726 i.
Jas. 1740 i.
Northampton
Jno. 1737 w.
Prince William
David 1789 w.
David 1793 i.
FORBUSH
Albemarle
Wm. 1772 w.
Amherst
Wm. 1781 w.
Surry
Theophilus 1694 i.
FORD
Amelia
Hezekiah 1752 w.
Fredk. 1777 w.
Jno. 1778 i.
Fredk. 1786 w.
Chris. 1788 w.
Wm. 1798 i.

Charlotte
Culverine 1797 i.
Culpeper
Jno. 1791 w.
Cumberland
Jno. 1753 w.
Essex
Danl. 1776 w.
Danl. 1791 a.
Fairfax
Thos. 1776 w.
Fluvanna
Jno. 1783 w.
Tandy 1797 i.
Goochland
Peter 1745 w.
Wm. 1751 w.
Thos. 1779 i.
Jno. 1782 i.
Wm. 1788 i.
Henrico
David 1785 w.
Saml. Sr. 1785 w.
Jno. 1796 i.
Lucy 1796 i.
Tarlton 1796 i.
Nelson 1798 i.
King George
Wm. 1782 w.
Wm. 1799 i.
Richmond
Jno. 1699 w.
Jno. 1714 i.
Jno. 1764 w.
Jane 1783 i.
Wm. 1783 i.
Southampton
Ann 1779 i.
Surry
Jos. 1703 w.
Westmoreland
Garrard 1747 w.
York
Richd. 1658 i.
FORDMAN
Norfolk
Alex. 1713 i.
FORE
Charlotte
Jno. 1795 w.
Chesterfield
Mary 1771 w.
Frederick
Adam 1771 i.
Henrico
Jno. 1748 w.
FOREAKERS
Essex
Jno. 1779 w.

FOREMAN
Norfolk
  Alex. 1688 nw.
  Alex. 1713 w.
  Alex. 1771 w.
  Jeremiah 1774 w.
  Jas. 1785 w.
  Wm. 1796 w.
Northumberland
  Benj. 1713 i.
FORESYTH
York
  Jas. 1696 w.
FORGASON
Hardy
  Robt. 1791 w.
York
  Jno. 1707-8 w.
FORGERSON
Essex
  Jno. 1770 i.
FORGESON
Franklin
  Jno. 1790 w.
Loudoun
  Francis 1782 i.
FORESTER
Botetourt
  Wm. 1799 i.
Norfolk
  Alace 1774 w.
Northampton
  Geo. W. D. 1785 w.
FORINHAUGH
Norfolk
  Jno. 1749 w.
FORISTER
Goochland
  Jno. 1757 i.
Richmond
  Jas. 1764 w.
FORLINES
Cumberland
  Darby 1777 w.
FORMAN
Frederick
  Benj. 1751 a.
Norfolk
  Alex. 1713 w.
  Jas. 1790 i.
  Abi 1798 w.
Surry
  Wm. 1702 w.
FORMISH
Orange
  Jno. 1777 i.
FORREST
Amelia
  Abraham Sr. 1759 w.
Henrico
  Alice 1715 w.
  Jno. 1715 w.

Lunenburg
  Jno. 1779 i.
Princess Anne
  Jno. 1770 i.
  Jno. 1795 w.
Richmond
  Wm. 1723 i.
FORRESTER
Frederick
  Eliz. 1785 w.
Richmond
  Wm. 1769 w.
  Robt. 1783 w.
FORRIST
Northumberland
  Benj. 1746 w.
FORSE
Northampton
  Jas. 1735 w.
FORSEE
Cumberland
  Jno. 1766 w.
  Stephen 1772 w.
Powhatan
  Stephen 1799 w.
FORSET
Frederick
  Jacob 1751 a.
FORSIE
Chesterfield
  Jno. Brush 1782 w.
Fluvanna
  Jno. 1785 w.
FORSIGH
Westmoreland
  Jno. 1722 w.
FORSITH
Northampton
  Jno. 1665 w.
FORSTER
Accomack
  Jno. 1785 w.
FORSYTHE
Prince Edward
  Jas. 1786 w.
FORT
Brunswick
  Henry 1782 w.
Isle of Wight
  Elias 1678 i.
Southampton
  Jno. 1753 w.
  Arthur 1765 w.
  Rebecca 1767 w.
  Elias 1775 i.
  Joshua 1781 w.
  Jno. 1791 i.
  Jno. 1796 w.
  Olive 1795 i.
Surry
  Elias 1724 i.
  Jno. 1725 w.

  Elias 1739 w.
Sussex
  Holiday 1773 w.
FORTHERINGALE
Frederick
  Geo. 1767 i.
FORTUNE
Albemarle
  Jno. 1790 w.
Amherst
  Benj. 1784 a.
Pittsylvania
  Jos. 1784 w.
Princess Anne
  Jas. 1785 i.
FOSCRAFT
Surry
  Thos. 1679 i.
FOSCROFT
Northampton
  Bridget 1704 w.
FOSCUE
Accomack
  Simon Sr. 1689 i.
  Simon 1717 w.
  Ann 1720 w.
FOSH
Bedford
  Andrew 1791 i.
FOSHEA
Richmond
  Jno. 1733 w.
FOSHEE
Culpeper
  Jno. 1779 w.
FOSQUE
Accomack
  Jno. 1746 w.
  Luke 1770 w.
  Nathl. 1777 w.
Northampton
  Geo. 1754 w.
FOSSAKER
Richmond
  Eliz. 1712 i.
FOSSET
Northumberland
  Wm. 1762 w.
FOSSETT
Frederick
  Thos. 1747 a.
Northumberland
  Richd. 1750 i.
FOSTER
Accomack
  Jno. 1719 w.
  Wm. 1773 w.
  Anne 1774 w.
  Joshua 1779 i.
  Jos. 1789 i.
  Joshua 1795 i.
  Leah 1797 w.

Albemarle
Jno. 1764 w.
Henry 1795 w.
Jas. 1795 w.
Amelia
Jas. 1750 a.
Jas. 1753 i.
Wm. 1767 w.
Wm. 1771 i.
Geo. 1772 w.
Thos. Sr. 1786 w.
Travis 1786 i.
Geo. 1790 w.
Berkeley
Jacob 1790 i.
Thos. 1796 i.
Charlotte
Jas. 1771 w.
Geo. 1775 i.
Geo. 1789 w.
Josiah 1797 i.
Thos. 1799 w.
Cumberland
Jas. 1782 i.
Essex
Jno. 1710 w.
Robt. 1715 w.
Robt. 1720 w.
Jno. 1734 w.
Jno. 1737 i.
Jos. 1743 i.
Goochland
Jos. 1786 a.
Isle of Wight
Jno. 1736 w.
Louisa
Robt. 1773 i.
Richd. 1783 a.
Lunenburg
Geo. 1762 w.
Middlesex
Jno. 1714 i.
Jno. 1715 i.
Norfolk
Richd. [1650?] w.
Henry 1708 a.
Isaac 1743-4 i.
Wm. 1791 w.
Northampton
Vrinson 1676 w.
Robt. 1691 w.
Edwd. 1698 w.
Wm. 1699 i.
Jno. 1714 w.
Eliz. 1714-15 w.
Wm. 1725 i.
Wm. 1736 w.
Edwd. 1745 i.
Orange
Thos. 1791 w.
Prince Edward
Wm. 1794 i.

Robt. 1796 w.
Prince William
Neal 1735 i.
Geo. 1778 i.
Wm. 1779 w.
Robt. 1783 i.
Southampton
Elias 1760 i.
Christopher 1767 w.
Newit 1767 w.
Alis 1773 w.
Jno. 1783 w.
Wm. 1791 w.
Spotsylvania
Edmund 1748 a.
Jno. 1773 a.
Anthony 1763 w.
Thos. 1764 w.
Surry
Geo. 1697 w.
Ann 1710-11 w.
Chris. 1711 w.
Wm. 1721 w.
Richd. 1795 w.
Westmoreland
Thos. 1671 w.
Robt. 1702 w.
FOTHERGILL
Lancaster
Wm. 1717 i.
FOUCH
Loudoun
Hugh 1780 w.
Isaac Sr. 1794 w.
FOUCHE
Loudoun
Hugh 1783 i.
FOUGHT
Greenbrier
Gasper 1797 i.
FOULER
Essex
Wm. 1733 i.
Norfolk
Frances 1679 w.
Geo. 1679 i.
FOULES
Halifax
Jas. 1792 w.
FOULKS
Northumberland
Richd. 1728 w.
FOUNKHOUSER
Shenandoah
Abraham 1797 i.
FOUNTAIN
Norfolk
Roger 1666 i.
Princess Anne
Roger 1765 w.
Jno. 1790 i.

FOUNTAINE
Princess Anne
Robt. 1714 w.
FOURLONG
King George
Wm. 1766 w.
FOUSHEE
Halifax
Jno. 1769 w.
Jno. 1774 i.
Lancaster
Jas. 1729 w.
Ruth 1731 w.
Northumberland
Jas. 1766 i.
Mary 1789 w.
FOUTT
Loudoun
Geo. 1784 w.
FOWCKS
Accomack
Amy 1678 w.
FOWKE
Accomack
Thos. 1674 w.
Fauquier
Eliz. 1781 w.
Gerard 1781 a.
King George
Gerrard 1781 a.
Loudoun
Robt. D. 1798 i.
Spotsylvania
Jno. 1783 w.
Stafford
Wm. Chandler 1743 i.
Chandler 1745 w.
Westmoreland
Thos. 1663 w.
FOWLE
Isle of Wight
Richd. 1692 w.
FOWLER
Amelia
Thos. 1795 i.
Amherst
Joshua 1773 i.
Brunswick
Danl. 1789 w.
Andrew 1795 w.
Chesterfield
Jno. 17— w.
Jno. 1783 i.
Josiah 1794 w.
Josiah 1795 i.
Jabalon 1797 i.
Gardener Sr. 1798 w.
Essex
Wm. 1734 i.
Fincastle
Wm. 1775 a.

Fluvanna
Robt. 1797 i.
Halifax
Jas. 1785 i.
Henrico
Saml. 1689 w.
Thos. 1745 i.
Godfrey 1747 w.
Isle of Wight
Wm. 1749 w.
Eliz. 1791 w.
Thos. 1793 w.
Eliz. 1794 i.
Jos. 1799 i.
Loudoun
Wm. 1771 i.
Mecklenburg
Andrew 1795 i.
Middlesex
Peter 1678 a.
Montgomery
Jno. 1778 a.
Norfolk
Robt. 1652 w.
Sidney 1689 w.
Powhatan
Jos. 1778 i.
Princess Anne
Geo. 1700 w.
Frances 1716 w.
Richmond
Richd. 1724 w.
Jno. 1750 w.
Alice 1767 w.
Southampton
Jas. 1777 w.
Wm. 1778 w.
Washington
Jas. 1779 i.
Saml. 1779 i.
FOWLES
Accomack
Danl. 1763 i.
FOWLS
Richmond
Geo. 1796 i.
FOX
Accomack
Golden 1751 w.
Thos. 1774 i.
Mary 1794 w.
Berkeley
Benj. 1785 i.
Culpeper
Jno. Peater 1788 w.
Frederick
Adam 1760 w.
Greensville
Jno. 1795 w.
Wm. 1798 w.

Lancaster
David 1702 w.
Saml. 1712 i.
Wm. 1718 w.
David 1722 w.
Ann 1723 w.
Saml. 1723 i.
Wm. 1729 i.
Loudoun
Wm. Sr. 1775 w.
Wm. 1794 i.
Louisa
Susanna 1790 w.
Mecklenburg
Richd. 1771 w.
Wm. 1783 w.
Mary 1795 w.
Middlesex
Jno. 1769 w.
Tabitha 1789 w.
Northampton
Jacob 1759 w.
Thos. 1759 i.
Robinson 1760 w.
Jno. 1719 ab.
Spotsylvania
Jno. 1749 w.
Jas. 1753 a.
Thos. 1792 w.
Wm. 1795 a.
Surry
Geo. 1712 i.
FOXCROFT
Northampton
Isaac 1702 w.
FOXHALL
Westmoreland
Jno. 1698 w.
FOXY
Brunswick
Wm. 1764 i.
FRACK
Rappahannock
Wm. 1635 w.
FRAISER
Isle of Wight
Fred. 1774 w.
Norfolk
Richd. 1773 i.
FRAME
Augusta
Jas. 1754 i.
Thos. 1796 w.
FRAMMEL
Halifax
Jno. 1787 i.
FRAMMELL
Loudoun
Sampson 1796 i.

FRANCE
Henry
Jno. 1778 w.
Norfolk
Jos. 1766 i.
Northumberland
Jno. 1761 i.
Thos. 1768 w.
FRANCES
Lunenburg
Jno. 1753 i.
Montgomery
Francis 1781 i.
FRANCESCO
Halifax
Peter 1762 i.
FRANCIS
Augusta
Jno. 1786 w.
Brunswick
Wm. 1766.
Campbell
Jno. 1792 i.
Charlotte
Jas. 1776 w.
Obedience 1793 w.
Chesterfield
Robt. 1776 w.
Halifax
Micajah 1775 i.
Henrico
Wm. 1789 w.
Isle of Wight
Jno. 1677 nw.
Northumberland
Robt. 1671 w.
Southampton
Wm. 1760 i.
Thos. 1766 w.
Thos. 1781 w.
Westmoreland
Martin 1745 i.
York
Richd. 1695 i.
FRANCISCO
Botetourt
Lodowick 1799 w.
FRANK
Augusta
Nicholas 1758 a.
Berkeley
Bernard 1782 w.
Essex
Thos. 1715 w.
King George
Jas. 1789 w.
Westmoreland
Sara 1725 w.
Robt. 1726 w.
Robt. 1776 w.
Henry 1796 i.

FRANKLIN
Albemarle
Benj. 1751 w.
Amherst
Henry 1782 eb.
Henry 1792 w.
Bedford
Lewis 1770 i.
Edmund 1772 i.
Maryann 1794 w.
Campbell
Owen 1792 i.
Chesterfield
Thos. 1775 w.
Jas. 1776 w.
Thos. 1777 w.
Archd. 1778 w.
Agnes 1795 w.
Halifax
David 1794 i.
Henrico
Jas. 1747 w.
Jno. 1791 w.
King George
Jno. 1724 i.
Jno. 1776 a.
Mecklenburg
Owen 1795 i.
Thos. 1799 i.
Powhatan
Jno. 1778 w.
Princess Anne
Thos. 1723 w.
Sarah 1727 i.
Danl. 1734 w.
Simon 1734 i.
Thos. 1750 w.
Wm. 1753 i.
Danl. Sr. 1789 w.
Thos. 1791 w.
Danl. 1793 w.
Prince William
Jane 1791 i.
Richmond
Thos. 1721 i.
Thos. 1746 i.
Thos. 1794 w.
Westmoreland
Edwd. 1696 i.
FRANKLING
Cumberland
Jos. 1766 i.
Goochland
Thos. 1737 w.
Henrico
Thos. 1789 w.
Zachariah 1795 w.
Mecklenburg
Owen 1791 w.
Stafford
Casper 1751 i.

FRANKLYN
Isle of Wight
Poter 1704-5 w.
King George
Geo. 1758 i.
Eliz. 1764 i.
Orange
Edwd. 1767 i.
FRARY
Richmond
Jas. 1774 i.
Richd. 1789 w.
FRASER
Chesterfield
Geo. 1762 i.
Northampton
Jno. 1759 i.
FRAUNCIS
York
Jno. 1730 w.
FRAY
Culpeper
Jno. 1791 w.
FRAYSER
Henrico
Wm. 1733 w.
Wm. 1799 w.
York
Thos. 1740 i.
FRAZER
Augusta
Jno. 1791 w.
Spotsylvania
Geo. 1765 w.
Andrew 1770 a.
Jas. 1778 a.
Jno. 1796 a.
Eliz. 1796 w.
Jas. 1799 w.
FRAZIER
Augusta
Wm. 1764 i.
Fauquier
Danl. 1765 w.
Henrico
Wm. 1695 i .
Middlesex
Alex. 1769 w.
Orange
Alex. 1771 w.
Spotsylvania
Wm. 1734 a.
FRAZOR
Northumberland
Thos. 1740 i.
FREDERICK
Berkeley
Henry 1775 i.
FREDRICKSON
Norfolk
Christian 1666 w.

FREEDLEY
Augusta
Lewis 1748 a.
Ludwick 1749 i.
FREEDLY
Norfolk
Michael 1782 w.
FREEID
Westmoreland
Winifred 1739 w.
FREEL
Augusta
Catrine 1780 i.
FREELAND
Albemarle
Jas. 1754 w.
Makel 1760 w.
Amherst ·
Jas. 1774 w.
FREEMAN
Accomack
Moses 1779 w.
Fauquier
Jas. 1792 w.
Henrico
Geo. 1735 w.
Gideon 1746 i.
Middlesex
Henry 1721 w.
Lunenburg
Arthur 1753 w.
Norfolk
Thos. 1762 w.
Saml. 1784 i.
Princess Anne
Sarah 1714 i.
Richmond
Wm. 1761 i.
Shenandoah
Henry 1797 i.
Southampton
Jas. 1782 i.
Surry
Jno. 1725 w.
Sussex
Henry 1755 w.
Agness 1759 i.
Joel 1759 i.
Nathan 1760 w.
Josiah 1774 w.
Henry 1776 w.
Henry 1778 w.
Phebe 1778 w.
Jno. 1788 w.
York
Henry 1680 w.
Robt. 1698 w.
Henry 1720 w.
Henry 1752 w.
Eliz. 1763 i.

FREEMOND
Louisa
Alex. 1767 w.
FREEZ
Augusta
Michael 1758 i.
FREEZELL
York
Hugh 1666 w.
FRENCH
Amelia
Mary 1789 i.
Mary 1791 i.
Berkeley
Jacob Sr. 1788 i.
Fairfax
Danl. 1749 w.
Danl. 1772 w.
Essex
Robt. 1743 w.
Frederick
Jno. 1750 a.
Hampshire
Jas. 1773 w.
Henrico
Seath 1704 w.
King George
Margt. 1749 i.
Hugh 1770 a.
Powhatan
Thos. 1785 i.
Princess Anne
Thos. 1735 i.
Prince William
Danl. 1736 i.
Jas. 1743 w.
Richmond
Hugh 1701 w.
Stafford
Hugh 1737 w.
Hugh Jr. 1740 w.
Angle 1744 i.
Mason 1752 nw.
Danl. 1756 w.
Surry
Saml. 1730 i.
Westmoreland
Mason 1746 i.
Danl. 1756 i.
Catherine 1759 i.
FRENDS
Essex
Robt. 1743 i.
FRESHOUR
Berkeley
Wendel 1794 i.
FRESHWATER
Northampton
Geo. Sr. 1688 w.
Jno. 1709 i.
Geo. 1717-18 w.
Jerom 1720 w.

Wm. 1724 w.
Eliz. E. 1733 w.
Thos. 1738 i.
Geo. 1739 w.
Matthew 1745 i.
Jno. 1753 i.
Mark 1762 w.
Benj. 1765 w.
Elishe 1770 w.
Jno. 1774 w.
Jno. 1775 i.
Jos. 1786 w.
Richmond
Thos. 1726 w.
Jno. 1754 i.
Thos. 1756 w.
Eliz. 1772 w.
Westmoreland
Geo. 1781 i.
Geo. 1780 w.
FRESSELL
Northampton
Geo. 1720 w.
FRETWELL
Cumberland
Wm. 1788 w.
FREW
Augusta
Jas. 1769 i.
FREY
Northumberland
Wm. 1723 w.
FREYER
Westmoreland
Jno. 1727 w.
FRICKLEY
Princess Anne
Thos. 1694 i.
FRIDLEY
Augusta
Loudawick 1772 i.
FRIEEL
Augusta
Danl. 1798 w.
FRIEND
Chesterfield
Thos. 1758 w.
Edwd. 1761 i.
Thos. 1761 i.
Thos. 1765[8?] w.
Thos. 1769 i.
Frances 1772 w.
Nathl. 1795 w.
Thos. 1797 w.
Chas. 1798 w.
Frederick
Israel 1750 i.
Israel 1751 i.
Israel 1753 w.
Henrico
Anne 1736 i.

FRIER
Berkeley
Alex. Sr. 1792 w.
Loudoun
Jas. 1771 w.
FRIETLY
Frederick
Andrew 1778 w.
FRIMYEAR
Louisa
Wm. 1773 w.
FRISEL
Princess Anne
Danl. 1733 i.
Danl. 1734 w.
FRISSELL
Isle of Wight
Jno. 1720 w.
Lancaster
Wm. 1676 w.
Norfolk
Jno. 1689 w.
Princess Anne
Margt. 1694 w.
FRISTOE
Stafford
Robt. 1764 w.
FRITH
Chesterfield
Martha 1786 i.
Rappahannock
Nathl. 1677 w.
York
Jos. 1712 i.
FRITTS
Norfolk
Christian 1775 w.
FRITZ
Berkeley
Michael 1787 w.
FRIZEL
Fairfax
Wm. 1769 w.
FRIZELL
Isle of Wight
Jno. 1693 w.
Ralph 1742 i.
Lancaster
Francisco 1732 w.
Northampton
Jno. 1666 w.
Geo. 1720 w.
Thos. 1721-2 w.
Danl. 1732 w.
FRIZER
Westmoreland
Wm. 1677 w.
FRIZZEL
Isle of Wight
Wm. 1706-7 w.
Ralph 1734 w.

FRIZZELL
Isle of Wight
Jno. 1752 w.
Jno. 1754 i.
Jas. 1759 i.
Ralph 1785 w.
Princess Anne
Jno. 1710 i.
Apphia 1775 w.
FRIZZLE
Princess Anne
Arthur 1795 w.
FRODSHAM
Westmoreland
Jno. 1677 i.
FROGG
Augusta
Arthur 1770 a.
Jno. 1774 a.
FROGGE
Bath
Jno. 1795 w.
FROGGOT
Henrico
Geo. 1710 w.
FROGMORTON
Henrico
————— 1756 i.
FROSHOUR
Berkeley
Wendle 1793 w.
FROST
Frederick
Wm. 1776 w.
Henrico
Mary 1746 w.
Norfolk
Jno. 1693-4 w.
Northampton
Thos. 1716 w.
Thos. 1744 i.
Robt. 1751 w.
Princess Anne
Thos. 1764 w.
FROTT
Prince William
Jno. 1736 i.
FROUD
Westmoreland
Jno. 1721 w.
FRUIT
Augusta
Martha 1759 w.
FRUNCK
York
Danl. 1677-8 w.
FRY
Albemarle
Joshua 1754 w.
Mary 1773 w.
Berkeley
Abraham 1797 i.

Essex
Richd. 1757 i.
Isle of Wight
Robt. 1783 w.
Mary 1794 w.
Loudoun
Henry 1778 i.
Montgomery
Geo. 1793 w.
FRYAR
Fairfax
Wm. 1777 i.
FRYATT
Berkeley
Bartho. 1793 w.
FRYE
Essex
Richd. 1695 i.
Loudoun
Andrew 1779 i.
Shenandoah
Jos. 1781 w.
FRYER
Augusta
Robt. 1752 a.
Berkeley
Alex. Jr. 1792 w.
Frederick
Wm. 1792 w.
Geo. 1795 w.
Loudoun
Jas. 1772 i.
Westmoreland
Wm. 1760 i.
FUDGES
Isle of Wight
Jno. 1776 i.
FUEL
King George
Benj. 1757 i.
FUGATE
King George
Josias 1757 w.
Washington
Francis 1781 i.
FUGE
Frederick
Benj. 1753 w.
FUGLAR
Charles City
Jno. 1770 w.
Sarah 1771 w.
Henry 1772 i.
Surry
Richd. 1762 i.
FULBY
Berkeley
Boltzer 1798 i.
FULCHER
Norfolk
Jno. 1712 w.

Orange
Jno. 1746 i.
FULFORD
Norfolk
Jno. 1756 i.
Levy 1786 w.
FULGAM
Isle of Wight
Nicholas 1724-5 w.
Jno. 1725 w.
FULGHAM
Isle of Wight
Anthony 1678 w.
Michael 1690 w.
Jno. 1711 w.
Michael 1727 w.
Anthony 1723 i.
Anthony 1730 w.
Edmond 1732 i.
Michael 1732 i.
Nicholas 1736 w.
Chas. 1748 i.
Jesse 1753 i.
Mary 1760 w.
Chas. 1765 w.
Ann 1773 w.
Edmund 1777 i.
Anthony 1780 w.
Jno. 1782 w.
Anthony 1785 i.
Edmund 1785 w.
Jos. 1785 w.
Hezekiah 1786 w.
Jas. 1791 w.
Michael 1797 w.
Edmund 1799 i.
Southampton
Mary 1796 w.
FULK
Augusta
Ludwick 1758 a.
FULKERSON
Loudoun
Benj. 1797 i.
Patrick
Frederick 1795 w.
FULLAR
Accomack
Asa 1795 i.
FULLGAM
Isle of Wight
Michell 1728 w.
FULLGHAM
Isle of Wight
Jno. 1729 i.
Nicholas 1766 w.
Anthony 1763 w.
FULLER
Fairfax
Robt. 1795 a.
Isle of Wight
Ezekiell 1723 w.

Loudoun
Andrew 1783 i.
Spotsylvania
Thos. 1754 w.
Stafford
Wm. 1744 i.
Rappahannock
Thos. 1686 w.
York
Edwd. 1709 w.
Antho. 1710 w.
Wm. 1720 w.
Geo. 1744 w.
Wm. 1758 i.
Eliz. 1793 w.
FULLERTON
Essex
Jas. 1714 w.
Jas. 1729 w.
Frederick
Henry 1781 w.
Humphrey 1782 i.
Humphrey 1796 i.
Rappahannock
Jas. 1678 w.
Joane 1678 w.
FULLING
Accomack
Hugh 1702 i.
FULSTON
Essex
Geo. 1702 i.
FULTIN
Frederick
Mary 1772 i.
FULTON
Augusta
Jas. 1753 w.
Jas. 1755 i.
Thos. 1756 i.
Jas. 1782 i.
Jno. 1790 w.
David 1797 w.
Berkeley
David 1796 i.
Frederick
Mary 1770 w.
Loudoun
Robt. 1798 w.
Pittsylvania
Jas. 1788 w.
Spotsylvania
Jas. 1780 a.
FULTZ
Augusta
Geo. 1772 w.
Shenandoah
Martin 1782 w.
FULWELL
Northampton
Jno. L. 1795 w.

FULWILDER
Augusta
Jacob 1782 i.
Jacob 1794 a.
FUNK
Campbell
Peter 1796 w.
Frederick
Jacob 1746 w.
Shenandoah
Mathias 1777 a.
Adam 1778 w.
Jno. 1784 a.
Henry 1790 w.
Henry Sr. 1797 i.
FUNKHOUSER
Frederick
John 1765 w.
Shenandoah
Christian 1793 i.
Abraham 1796 w.
Isaac 1797 w.
FUQUA
Bedford
Ralph 1770 w.
Jno. 1796 w.
Charlotte
Wm. 1775 i.
Jno. 1778 i.
Eliz. 1780 w.
Mary 1780 i.
Stephen 1782 i.
Jos. 1787 i.
Saml. 1790 w.
Cumberland
Jos. 1799 i.
Lunenburg
Wm. 1761 w.
FUQURAN
Chesterfield
Peter 1798 w.
FUREMAN
Essex
Mary 1786 w.
FURGERSON
Richmond
Robt. 1793 w.
FURGESON
Westmoreland
Margt. 1785 w.
FURKETTLE
Northampton
Jno. 1737 w.
FURLONG
Accomack
Edmd. 1667 i.
Cumberland
Jno. 1783 i.
Robt. 1793 i.
King George
Peter 1721 i.
Wm. 1766 eb.

Norfolk
Richd. 1713 w.
Richd. 1715 i.
Anne 1717 i.
FURMAN
Frederick
Tredwell 1789 i.
FURNACE
Accomack
Saml. 1771 a.
FURNALL
Middlesex
Geo. 1786 w.
FURNAM
Frederick
Augus 1792 a.
FURNISH
Orange
Jno. 1780 w.
FURR
Fauquier
Thos. 1783 w.
Prince William
Thos. 1735 w.
FUSH
Shenandoah
Catherine 1791 w.
FUSSELL
Henrico
Solomon 1782 i.

G

GABERT
Rockbridge
Matthias 1798 w.
GABBERD
Culpeper
Anne Mary 1762 w.
GABBERT
Frederick
Michael 1749 i.
GABRIEL
Middlesex
Richd. 1710 i.
GADDESS
Stafford
Alex. 1786 w.
GADDEY
Chesterfield
Wm. 1751 w.
GADDIS
Hampshire
Wm. 1773 w.
GADDY
Bedford
Geo. 1785 w.
GAHAGAN
King George
Mary 1755 i.
GAINES

Albemarle
Bernard 1749 i.
Culpeper
Richd. 1756 i.
Francis 1776 w.
Humphry 1779 w.
Wm. 1783 w.
Donatha 1786 w.
Jas. 1786 w.
Wm. 1796 w.
Essex
Jno. 1722 w.
Danl. 1757 w.
Jno. 1797 w.
Norfolk
Wm. 1757 i.
Northumberland
Danl. 1757 w.
Rappahannock
Danl. 1684 w.
Richmond
Geo. 1726 w.
Bernard 1749 w.
Shenàndoah
William 1798 i.

GAINOR
Isle of Wight
Saml. 1697 i.

GAINS
Culpeper
Wm. 1779 i.
Northumberland
Joshua 1791 w.
Spotsylvania
Robt. 1763 a.

GAITKILL
King George
Jno. 1764 i.

GALBREATH
Lancaster
Robt. 1749-50 w.

GALE
Accomack
Levin 1744 w.
Matthias 1756 i.
Matthias 1760 i.
Henrico
Jno. 1733 w.
Isle of Wight
Thos. 1732 w.
Thos. 1760 w.
Ann 1773 i.
Thos. Whitney 1791 w.
Spotsylvania
Matthew 1779 w.

GALESPIE
Prince Edward
Frances 1792 i.

GALESPY
Augusta
Jno. 1776 i.

GALEWOOD
Shenandoah
Philip 1797 w.

GALLAGHER
Augusta
Chas. 1750 w.

GALLAWAY
Bedford
Isham 1795 i.

GALLER
Surry
Henry 1731 i.

GALLESPIE
Harrison
Silas 1795 w.

GALLEY
Augusta
Christian 1760 a.
Princess Anne
Jno. 1742 w.

GALLIMORE
Charlotte
Wm. 1798 w.

GALLISPIE
Frederick
Patrick 1747 w.

GALLIVAN
Mecklenburg
Jno. 1792 i.

GALLOP
King George
Henry 1727 i.
Richmond
Robt. 1720 nw.

GALLOWAY
Augusta
Jno. 1787 i.
Botetourt
Robt. 1779 w.
Lancaster
Wm. 1789 w.
Northumberland
James 1754 i.
Stafford
Christian 1784 i.

GALLY
Augusta
Christian 1761 i.

GALT
Henrico
Gabriel 1789 i.
Northampton
Wm. 1764 i.
Dickey 1770 w.

GAMBELL
Augusta
Jos. 1780 i.

GAMBLE
Amherst
Jas. 1769 a.
Augusta
Jas. 1781 w.

York
Richd. 1756 i.

GAMES
Orange
Wm. 1780 i.

GAMEWELL
Princess Anne
Lawrence 1774 w.
Jno. 1780 w.

GAMON
Norfolk
Jno. 1693-4 w.

GAMMON
Norfolk
Robt. 1719 w.
Josiah 1798 w.
Westmoreland
Jno. 1722 i.

GANATT
Culpeper
Jno. 1786 a.

GANNOCKE
Essex
Wm. 1710 w.

GANNON
Botetourt
Jno. 1799 w.

GANNYMAN
York
Jno. 1680 i.

GANT
Shenandoah
Wm. 1787 a.

GAR
Culpeper
Larance 1754 w.

GARBER
Shenandoah
Jno. 1787 w.

GARDEN
Prince Edward
Jas. 1773 w.

GARDENHIRE
Fairfax
Jacob 1766 i.

GARDINER
Augusta
Jno. 1796 w.
Stafford
Jacob 1708 i.
Surry
Zephenia 1702 i.
York
Martin 1693 i.

GARDNER
Augusta
Thos. 1760 w.
Thos. 1764 i.
Essex
Henry 1778 i.
Frederick
Jno. 1768 i.

Luke 1790 i.
Isle of Wight
Jno. 1683-4 i.
Jas. 1698-9 i.
Wm. 1745 i.
Louisa
Jno. 1791 w.
Mary 1796 i.
Middlesex
Diana 1709 w.
Thos. 1709 w.
Thos. 1714 i.
Ringing 1715 i.
Wm. 1751 w.
Wm. 1781 w.
Norfolk
Chris. 1755 w.
Chas. Roff 1764 i.
Jno. 1785 w.
Northampton
Susanna 1792 w.
Orange
Jas. 1739 a.
Princess Anne
Richd. 1752 i.
Southampton
Jas. 1755 i.
Jno. 1782 w.
Joshua 1793 w.
Jas. 1793 w.
Jno. 1796 i.
Ann 1799 w.
Surry
Jas. Bruce 1746 i.
Geo. 1792 w.
Westmoreland
Wm. 1733 i.
Jno. 1791 w.
York
Jno. 1697 i.

GARELL
Isle of Wight
Jone 1720 w.
GAREY
Prince George
Wm. 1716 w.
GARLAND
Albemarle
Jas. 1781 w.
Nathl. 1793 i.
Amherst
Wm. 1777 a.
Hanover
Jno. 1734 w.
Isle of Wight
Peter 1700 w.
Jno. 1727 w.
Jno. 1730 i.
Jno. 1733 i.
Saml. 1755 i.

Lancaster
Jos. 1713 nw.
Louisa
Nathaniel 1783 w.
Lunenburg
David 1782 w.
Edwd. 1791 w.
Saml. 1798 i.
Richmond
Wm. 1747 w.
Wm. 1766 w.
Wm. 1770 i.
Mary 1774 w.
Wm. 1789 w.
Wm. 1797 i.
Geo. 1798 w.
Sussex
Martha 1770 i.
Westmoreland
Nathaniel 1703 w.
Wm. 1713 i.
Jeremiah 1743 i.
York
Jno. Pack 1770 w.
GARLEY
Halifax
Wm. 1793 i.
GARLINGTON
Halifax
Jos. 1787 w.
Northumberland
Chris. 1709 w.
Saml. 1740 i.
Chris. 1753 i.
Wm. 1757 w.
Maurice 1763 i.
Eliz. 1771 i.
Jno. 1775 w.
Jno. 1784 i.
GARMAN
Botetourt
Jno. 1799 i.
GARNER
Fauquier
Jno. 1764 i.
Danl. 1783 i.
Benj. 1790 w.
Vincent 1796 w.
Smith 1797 i.
Chas. 1798 i.
Henry
Thos. 1780 i.
Isle of Wight
Jas. 1748 w.
Jno. 1762 w.
Jno. 1785 w.
Lancaster
Hannah 1779 i.
Wm. 1791 w.
Loudoun
Saml. 1793 i.

Montgomery
Henry 1786 a.
Northumberland
Vincent 1710 w.
Parish 1718 w.
Jas. 1726-7 w.
Jas. 1751 i.
Jno. 1751 i.
Wm. 1751 i.
Vincent 1756 w.
Parrish 1761 w.
Mary 1767 w.
Edwd. 1769 w.
Parish 1769 w.
Geo. 1773 i.
Vincent 1773 w.
Wm. 1776 w.
Edwd. 1785 w.
Winifred 1785 w.
Jesse 1794 w.
Wm. P. 1799 i.
Richmond
Nathl. 1796 i.
Southampton
Jas. 1754 w.
Westmoreland
Jno. 1703 w.
Jno. 1713 w.
Susannah 1718 i.
Benj. 1718 w.
Abraham 1733 i.
Thos. 1743 i.
Henry 1745 w.
Archibald 1749 w.
Henry 1751 w.
Thos. 1757 i.
Abraham 1761 w.
Bradley 1770 w.
Valentine 1770 i.
Jos. 1771 w.
Jas. 1775 i.
Jos. 1777 i.
Benj. 1782 i.
Eliz. 1795 w.
Vincent 1796 w.
GARNES
Isle of Wight
Eliz. 1772 i.
GARNET
Bath
Absolom 1795 i.
GARNETT
Essex
Jno. 1714 i.
Thos. 1743 w.
Jno. 1747 w.
Thos. 1761 i.
Wm. 1761 i.
Jas. 1765 w.
Francis 1766 w.
Jno. Jr. 1772 w.

Jas. 1780 i.
Austin, Sr. 1786 w.
Ann 1789 w.
Margt. 1791 w.
GARNOR
Princess Anne
Richd. 1753 i.
GARNTSON
Ohio
Jas. 1784 a.
GARR
Madison
Adam 1795 i.
GARRARD
Culpeper
Wm. 1791 i.
Lunenburg
Jos. 1753 w.
Stafford
Wm. 1787 w.
Westmoreland
Thos. 1673 w.
Wm. 1747 w.
Aaron 1748 i.
GARRET
Accomack
Henry 1797 i.
Fairfax
Edwd. 1752 i.
Wm. 1778 w.
Fluvanna
Henry 1788 i.
Northampton
Isaac 1775 w.
Isaac 1777 i.
GARRETSON
Accomack
Richd. 1717 w.
GARRETT
Accomack
Henry 1795 w.
Brunswick
Jno. 1744 i.
Campbell
Robt. Sr. 1784 w.
Charlotte
Thos. 1798 i.
Cumberland
Jno. 1796 i.
Fairfax
Edwd. 1754 i.
Nicho. 1795 w.
Henrico
Wm. 1692 i.
Lancaster
Anthony 1678 i.
Louisa
Jno. 1771 i.
Wm. 1780 w.
Wm. 1785 i.
Henry 1791 i.

York
Jno. 1702 i.
GARRIOTT
Culpeper
Jno. 1781 i.
GARRIS
Northampton
Edwd. 1714 i.
Richd. 1721 w.
Thos. 1752 w.
Amos. 1761 w.
Thos. 1767 w.
Richd. 1770 i.
Thos. 1781 i.
Southampton
Amos 1771 w.
GARRISON
Accomack
Jonathan 1760 w.
Wm. Sr. 1776 w.
Wm. 1777 i.
Wm. 1788 w.
Jonathan 1789 w.
Geo. 1789 w.
Geo. 1790 w.
Jonathan 1794 i.
Jno. Jr. 1795 w.
Jno. 1798 i.
Geo. 1799 i.
Frederick
Fredk. 1763 i.
Loudoun
Nehemiah 1770 i.
Northampton
Cantwell 1749 i.
Spotsylvania
Thos. 1727 a.
GARRITSON
Accomack
Wm. 1708 w.
Richd. 1764 w.
GARRO
York
Wm. 1707-8 w.
GARROCK
Essex
Geo. 1752 w.
GARROT
Chesterfield
Isaac 1775 w.
Henrico
Mark 1790 i.
GARROTT
Amelia
Jno. 1744 w.
Surry
Wm. 1727 w.
GARROW
York
Jno. 1741 i.

GARTH
Louisa
Jno. 1786 w.
Wm. 1786 w.
GARTHRIGHT
Henrico
Saml. 1714 w.
GARTON
Augusta
Eliz. 1775 i.
Isle of Wight
Wm. 1799 i.
Orange
Uriah 1796 i.
Lancaster
Wm. 1709-10 w.
Anthony 1764 w.
Benj. 1793 w.
Anthony 1795 w.
Benj. 1796 w.
Richmond
Jno. 1721 i.
Spotsylvania
Uriah 1755 w.
GARTWRITE
Henrico
Michael 1691 i.
GASCOIGN
Northampton
Robt. 1712 i.
GASCOIGNE
Northampton
Henry 1699 w.
Robt. 1709 w.
Henry 1773 w.
GASCOINE
Northampton
Robt. 1675 w.
Henry 1691 w.
GASCOYN
Northampton
Wm. 1717-18 w.
GASCOYNE
Accomack
Thos. 1738 i.
Thos. 1760 i.
Eliz. 1760 i.
Wm. 1767 w.
Wm. 1771 i.
Henry 1784 w.
Northampton
Harman 1771 i.
Wm. 1772 w.
Henry 1775 w.
Northumberland
Thos. 1665 w.
GASGOINE
Accomack
Wm. Bradford
1747 w.

GASKING
Norfolk
Lemuel 1762 w.
Princess Anne
Job 1753 w.
Job. 1760 i.
Henry 1764 w.
Chas. 1772 w.
Sarah 1772 w.
Chas. 1773 i.
Henry 1782 i.
Job. 1782 w.
Robt. 1798 w.
GASKINGS
Northumberland
Jno. 1771 w.
GASKINS
Brunswick
Jno. 1785 w.
Lancaster
Phillips 1755 w.
Thos. 1793 i.
Northumberland
Isaac 1712 w.
Thos. Sr. 1726 w.
Thos. 1727 i.
Francis 1739 w.
Saml. 1743-4 w.
Jno. 1746 w.
Edwin 1748 w.
Jno. 1750 i.
Jesse 1757 w.
Josias 1757 w.
Jno. 1759 i.
Jno. 1763 w.
Jno. 1767 i.
Chas. 1773 i.
Wm. 1776 i.
Jno. 1782 i.
Thos. 1785 w.
Isaac 1791 w.
Prince William
Thos. 1740 i.
GATER
Northumberland
Matthew 1725-6 w.
Jno. 1753 i.
Mary 1754 i.
GATES
Amelia
Wm. 1736 i.
Wm. 1755 w.
Chesterfield
Jas. 17—i.
Wm. 1750-1 w.
Rebekah 1757 w.
Wm. 1760 w.
Edwd. 1761 w.
Jas. 1767 w.
Jos. 1797 w.

Fairfax
Saml. 1794 a.
Henrico
Jas. 1691 nw.
GATEWOOD
Amherst
Wm. 1789 w.
Essex
Jno. 1706-7 w.
Richd. 1730 w.
Jos. 1733 w.
Richd. 1734 i.
Ann 1740 i.
Richd. 1740 i.
Wm. 1743 w.
Patience 1745 w.
Richd. 1746 i.
Thos. 1748 w.
Jno. 1750 w.
Richd. 1751 w.
Philip 1757 w.
Wm. 1757 i.
Wm. 1758 i.
Richd. 1760 w.
Jno. 1763 w.
Isaac 1765 w.
Catherine 1769 i.
Hannah 1771 w.
Wm. 1783 w.
Jos. 1790 w.
Caleb 1795 i.
Richd. 1798 i.
Mary 1799 w.
Shenandoah
Philip 1793 w.
Spotsylvania
Henry 1777 w.
Ann 1792 w.
Henry 1799 a.
GATHAGIN
Westmoreland
Jas. 1752 w.
GATHINGS
Richmond
Cobham 1779 i.
GATHORN
Augusta
Eliz. 1775 a.
GATHRIGHT
Henrico
Ephraim 1750 w.
Ann 1781 i.
Wm. 1781 w.
Saml. 1783 w.
Wm. 1783 w.
Benj. 1785 w.
Jno. 1785 i.
Wm. Sr. 1785 w.
Wm. Sr. 1786 w.
Ephraim 1790 i.
Saml. 1791 w.

Benj. 1795 i.
Wm. 1795 w.
Ann 1797 w.
Ann 1799 i.
Jno. 1799 w.
GATLEY
Northumberland
Elinor 1760 w.
GATLIFF
Montgomery
Squiar 1777 w.
GATLIVE
Augusta
Jas. 1763 i.
GAUDWIN
Cumberland
Isaac 1751 w.
GAULDING
Campbell
Saml. 1785 w.
GAULT
Loudoun
Wm. 1799 i.
GAUNT
Berkeley
Edwd. Jno. 1791 w.
GAVIN
Goochland
Antho. 1750 w.
GAWAGAN
Northampton
Jas. 1688 a.
GAWDY
Berkeley
Jas. 1782 i.
GAY
Albemarle
Saml. Sr. 1796 w.
Augusta
Wm. 1755 w.
Jno. 1759 i.
Jno. 1760 w.
Robt. 1762 i.
Wm. 1767 i.
Jas. 1776 w.
Jno. 1777 w.
Chesterfield
Wm. 1749 w.
Wm. 1764 w.
Danl. 1794 i.
Danl. 1796 w.
Isle of Wight
Henry 1737 w.
Thos. 1750 w.
Thos. 1754 w.
Wm. 1783 w.
Joshua 1784 w.
Rockbridge
Henry 1779 w.
Jane 1780 w.
Marthew 1785 w.

Robt. 1791 w.
Southampton
Edmund 1776 w.
GAYDEN
Richmond
Geo. 1764 w.
GAYEDON
Richmond
Geo. 1717 i.
GAYERS
Middlesex
Wm. 1733 w.
GAYLE
Chesterfield
Josiah 1796 i.
GAYTON
Henrico
Thos. 1697 a.
GEARING
Westmoreland
Thos. 1739 i.
GEDDES
York
Andrew 1698 i.
GEDDY
York
Jas. 1744 w.
GEE
Brunswick
Robt. 1783 w.
Wm. 1798 w.
Halifax
Henry 1782 i.
Henrico
Eliz. 1732 w.
Gilbert 1734 w.
Norfolk
Thos. 1673 w.
Surry
Chas. 1709 i.
Sussex
Jas. 1760 w.
Jas. 1762 i.
Chas. 1768 w.
GEER
Brunswick
Wm. 1770 w.
GEFFERY
Richmond
Edwd. 1714 w.
Thos. 1740 w.
GEHENOUR
Shenandoah
Henry 1788 a.
GELDING
Northampton
Eliz. 1698 w.
Chas. 1709 w.
Chas. 1727 i.
Chas. 1799 w.

GELDINGE
Northampton
Wm. Sr. 1688 w.
GELLEFAR
Shenandoah
Christian 1784 i.
GELLESPIE
Prince Edward
Francis 1791 w.
GELLOCK
Shenandoah
Jno. 1783 w.
GEMMILL
Isle of Wight
Jno. 1745 i.
York
Jas. 1798 i.
GENELL
Culpeper
Jas. 1786 i.
GENEN
Berkeley
Saml. 1799 nw.
GENKINS
Halifax
Jno. 1799 w.
GENN
Northumberland
Jas. 1719 i.
GENNINGS
King George
Jo. 1735 i.
GENT
Isle of Wight
Jno. 1728 i.
GENTRY
Albemarle
Nicho. 1779 w.
Botetourt
Jno. 1779 w.
Cumberland
Simon 1790 w.
Louisa
Nathan 1784 a.
GEORG
Hampshire
Matthew 1782 w.
GEORGE
Albemarle
Jno. 1764 i.
Culpeper
Elmore 1749 w.
Wm. 1783 w.
Fauquier
Nich. 1779 w.
Aron 1791 i.
Parnack 1797 i.
Goochland
Leonard 1774 i.
Isle of Wight
Jno. 1678 w.

Jno. 1710-11 i.
Lancaster
Jno. 1693 w.
Nicho. 1700 w.
Wm. 1710 i.
Wm. 1717 i.
Nich. 1733 w.
Thos. 1748 i.
Elmour 1749 w.
Wm. 1749 w.
Benj. 1750-1 w.
Jos. 1751 i.
Jno. 1758 i.
Benj. 1760 w.
Eliz. 1760 w.
Wm. Sr. 1760 w.
Wm. 1762 i.
Moses 1772 w.
Wm. 1775 i.
Henry 1782 i.
Lazarus 1783 w.
Thos. 1784 w.
Nicholas 1785 w.
Baily 1796 i.
Jeduthun 1788 w.
Martin 1787 i.
Jesse 1792 i.
Anthony 1793 i.
Benj. 1793 i.
Catherine 1794 w.
Danl. 1795 i.
Judith 1795 w.
Nich. Lawson 1796 w.
Loudoun
Travers 1762 i.
Thos. 1798 w.
Middlesex
David 1726 w.
Robt. 1733 w.
Henry 1751 i.
Northumberland
Nehemiah 1794 w.
Nathl. 1795 i.
Orange
Saml. 1746 w.
Isaac 1781 w.
Jos. 1792 i.
Pittsylvania
Jas. 1799 w.
Rappahannock
Thos. 1683 w.
Richmond
Leroy 1700 w.
David 1775 i.
Southampton
Wm. 1782 w.
Stafford
Nich. 1737-8 w.
Spotsylvania
Jane 1775 w.

Surry
Wm. 1715 i.
Tenham 1776 w.
Westmoreland
Jno. 1717 i.
GEORGEHAM
Westmoreland
Jno. 1699 w.
GERRARD
Berkeley
Wm. 1782 i.
Jno. 1787 w.
King George
Mary 1777 w.
Westmoreland
Jno. 1711 w.
Susanna 1711 i.
Nathl. 1769 i.
York
Ralph 1637 i.
GERVIS
Northumberland
Jas. 1750-1 i.
GESNER
Shenandoah
Jno. 1784 a.
GEST
Middlesex
Geo. 1709 w.
Geo. 1750 w.
GETTY
Botetourt
Dennis 1779 i.
GEVIN
Charlotte
Geo. 1786 w.
GOFELLER
Shenendoah
Ulry 1778 w.
GHANT
Botetourt
Jas. 1778 i.
GHOLSON
Halifax
Anthony 1779 w.
Orange
Jno. 1790 w.
Spotsylvania
Jane 1797 a.
GHOST
Augusta
Geo. 1768 i.
GHOVAERE
Henrico
Pierre Jaques 1791 w.
GIBB
Isle of Wight
Ralph 1758 i.
Montgomery
Jas. 1785 w.

Richmond
Richd. 1723 i.
GIBBINS
Accomack
Henry 1708 w.
Isle of Wight
Jno. 1721 w.
York
Jno. 1727 w.
GIBBON
Northampton
David 1712 i.
GIBBONS
Northumberland
Morris 1746 w.
Jno. 1784 w.
Prince Edward
Jno. 1788 w.
Prince William
Jno. 1744 i.
Surry
Jno. Jr. 1770 i.
Sussex
Jno. 1770 w.
Rebecca 1780 w.
York
Thos. 1696 w.
Anne 1768 w.
Thos. 1772 w.
Jno. 1773 w.
Jno. Jr. 1783 w.
Jno. 1793 i.
Mary 1793 w.
GIBBS
Amelia
Jno. 1761 i.
Brunswick
Jno. 1778 w.
Chesterfield
Jno. 1773 w.
Mary 1776 w.
Culpeper
Zackarias 1773 w.
Frederick
Wm. 1784 i.
Halifax
Cornelius 1773 i.
Nathl. 1773 w.
Isle of Wight
Edwd. 1669 i.
Ralph 1746 i.
Ralph 1757 w.
Jno. 1762 i.
Jno. 1770 i.
Martha 1776 w.
Gabriell 1785 w.
Sarah 1785 w.
Ralph 1786 w.
Martha 1789 w.
Lancaster
Jas. 1771 i.

Middlesex
Jno. 1726 w.
Spotsylvania
Thos. 1763 a.
York
Wm. 1708 i.
Jno. 1733 i.
Stafford 1762 w.
Thos. 1782 w.
Thos. 1784 i.
GIBBURD
York
Wm. 1678 i.
GIBLER
Shenandoah
Jno. 1791 i.
GIBNEY
Fairfax
Hugh 1785 i.
GIBRANT
Northampton
Bartho. 1665 i.
GIBS
Prince William
Jas. 1740 i.
GIBSON
Accomack
Jas. 1752 i.
Amherst
Isaac 1789 a.
Augusta
Danl. 1751 w.
Robt. 1760 w.
Robt. 1783 i.
Alex 1795 w.
Bedford
Jas. 1765 w.
Wm. 1792 w.
Chesterfield
Thos. 1761 w.
Miles 1788 w.
Hannah 1791 w.
Hannah 1795 i.
Culpeper
Abraham 1780 i.
Fairfax
Sibella 1784 w.
Essex
Frances 1716 i.
Jno. 1716 i.
Fauquier
Jonathan 1791 w.
Jonathan 1797 i.
Frederick
Wm. 1799 w.
Hanover
Thos. 1734 w.
Henry
Thos. 1780 w.
Isle of Wight
Jno. 1775 i.

King George
Jonathan 1729 i.
Eliz. 1732 i.
Sarah 1736 i.
Loudoun
Ealse 1790 w.
Lancaster
Jno. 1698 w.
Edwd. 1717 i.
Rebecca 1717 w.
Ruth 1739 w.
Robt. 1740 w.
Wm. 1752 w.
Jos. 1797 i.
Middlesex
Thos. 1721 w.
Susannah 1786 w.
Norfolk
Jno. 1759 w.
Orange
Jonathan 1745 i.
Princess Anne
Chas. 1714 w.
Edwd. 1783 w.
Prince William
Jacob 1735 w.
Rappahannock
Wm. 1677 w.
Jno. 1684 i.
Magdalen 1636 w.
Richmond
Jno. 1763 w.
Rawleigh 1774 w.
Priscilla 1785 w.
Spotsylvania
Jos. 1746 a.
York
Jas. 1694 w.
Use 1709 ab.
GIDDENS
Accomack
Jno. 1775 w.
Ruben 1775 w.
Thos. 1788 w.
Fairfax
Thos. 1748 a.
Northampton
Wm. 1740 w.
Eliz. 1745 i.
Thos. 1750 i.
Wm. 1754 i.
Thos. 1764 w.
Jno. 1798 w.
GIFFIGON
Northampton
Thos. 1770 i.
GIFFITH
Fauquier
Evan 1796 w.
GILASPY
Augusta

Jas. 1769 w.
GILBART
Lancaster
Ezekiel 1744 w.
Ezekiel 1752 w.
GILBERT
Amherst
Henry 1778 w.
Jno. W. 1782 i.
Bedford
Saml. 1776 w.
Berkeley
Nathan. 1786 w.
Henrico
Robt. 1788 i.
Lancaster
Maurice 1758 w.
Northampton
Richd. 1665 w.
Northumberland
Wm. 1721 w.
Richmond
Jas. 1704 w.
Spotsylvania
Jno. 1751 w.
Surry
Eliz. 1673 w.
Roger 1725 w.
Wm. 1740 w.
Westmoreland
Michael 1717 w.
Wm. 1720 i.
Michael 1765 w.
Jane 1778 w.
Wm. 1788 w.
Martha 1789 w.
York
Henry 1711 w.
Geo. 1724 i.
Patience 1741-2 i.
GILBY
Essex
Jno. 1726 w.
GILCHRIST
Accomack
Andrew 1760 w.
Andrew 1765 i.
Geo. 1789 w.
Geo. 1791 i.
Essex
Jno. 1763 i.
Norfolk
Jno. 1773 w.
Robt. 1775 w.
Surry
Jas. 1792 w.
Norfolk
Jno. 1686-7 w.
GILDEA
Princess Anne
Thos. 1797 w.

GILDEN
Princess Anne
Alderton 1763 i.
GILES
Amelia
Arther 1752 w.
Wm. 1794 w.
Augusta
Valentine 1767 i.
Chesterfield
Nicho. 1794 w.
Henrico
Wm. 1692 w.
Nicho. 1781 w.
Nicho. 1790 i.
Arthur 1793 w.
Isle of Wight
Jno. 1715 w.
Thos. 1715 w.
Jno. 1717 i.
Jas. 1723 i.
Eleanor 1734 w.
Hugh 1751 i.
Thos. 1793 w.
Norfolk
Jas. 1745-6 w.
Northampton
Ann 1736 i.
Pittsylvania
Jno. 1799 w.
Prince Edward
Patrick 1780 i.
GILHAM
Norfolk
Jno. 1651 w.
GILKERSON
Frederick
Jno. 1795 i.
GILKESON
Augusta
Archd. 1782 w.
Robt. 1775 w.
Frederick
Wm. 1789 w.
GILKEY
Frederick
David 1756 i.
GILL
Chesterfield
Peter 17— i.
Stephen 1753 w.
Webster 1753 w.
Peter 1755 w.
Jno. 1764 w.
Jacob 1766 w.
Danl 1777 w.
Jos. 1778 w.
Danl. Sr. 1782 w.
Thos. 1787 w.
Robt. 1788 w.
Thos. 1788 i.

Jas. 1789 w.
Jas. 1794 w.
Jno. 1798 w.
Goochland
Jno. 1747 i.
Halifax
Peter 1784 i.
Henrico
Jos. 1732 w.
King George
Richd. 1736 i.
Lancaster
Michael 1726 i.
Michael 1728 i.
Mecklenburg
Wm. 1781 w.
Middlesex
Alex. 1766 a.
Alex. 1771 a.
Northampton
Jno. 1697 i.
Northumberland
Thos. Sr. 1708 w.
Thos. 1739 w.
Wm. 1747 w.
Ellis 1760 w.
Thos. 1766 i.
Ellis 1769 i.
Wm. 1780 i.
Ellis 1781 w.
York
Stephen 1653 w.
Wm. 1680 w.
Ellinor 1681 i.
Wm. 1681 i.
Henry 1721 w.
GILLAM
Halifax
Richd. 1794 w.
GILLASPAY
Frederick
Patrick 1747-8 i.
GILLASPPEY
Augusta
Jacob 1772 i.
GILLELAND
Amherst
Elanor 1774 a.
GILLENWATERS
Amherst
Thos. 1779 w.
GILLESPEY
Washington
Robt. 1778 w.
GILLESPIE
Prince Edward
Robt. 1758 w.
Patrick 1780 w.
GILLESPY
Augusta
Jno. 1775 a.

Jas. 1790 w.
Thos. 1790 w.
Botetourt
Hugh 1777 i.
GILLET
Accomack
Ayers 1779 w.
Lancaster
Jno. 1654 i.
GILLETT
Accomack
Jno. 1792 w.
Jos. 1796 w.
Jno. 1797 i.
Jos. 1799 i.
York
Jno. 1791 w.
GILLEY
Henry
Francis 1791 w.
GILLIAM
Albemarle
Eliz. 1773 w.
Jno. 1792 w.
Bedford
Richd. 1799 w.
Brunswick
Amy 1763 w.
Jno. 1770 i.
Charles City
Jeffry 1769 w.
Ann 1795 w.
Charlotte
Jas. 1794 w.
Martha 1799 i.
Culpeper
Richd. 1759 i.
Cumberland
Jno. 1768 i.
Jas. 1774 w.
Essex
Wm. 1743 w.
Goochland
Jno. 1794 w.
Taylor 1795 i.
Halifax
Richd. 1795 i.
Orange
Richd. 1757 i.
Southampton
Walter 1758 w.
Walter 1762 i.
Jno. 1765 w.
Jesse 1782 w.
Jos. 1782 w.
Robt. 1793 w.
Thos. 1793 w.
Arthur 1798 i.
Surry
Hinshea 1734 w.
Hincha 1737 i.

Saml. 1767 w.
Sussex
Fortain 1754 w.
Wm. [Sr.?] 1765 w.
Wm. 1765 w.
Chas. 1767 i.
Drury 1768 i.
Hinchea 1769 w.
Martha 1769 i.
Amy 1772 w.
Jno. 1777 w.
Mary 1777 w.
Hinchey 1794 w.
Wm. 1795 w.
Eliz. 1796 w.
Temperance 1797 w.
GILLIGAN
Norfolk
———— 1703-4 w.
GILLINGTON
Halifax
Jno. 1763 i.
Nich. 1773 w.
GILLINS
Accomack
Wm. 1761 w.
Southy 1774 w.
GILLINTINE
Amelia
Nicho. 1771 w.
GILLIS
Powhatan
Jno. 1783 i.
GILLISON
Culpeper
Jas. 1760 w.
Fauquier
Jno. 1792 a.
GILLISPY
Botetourt
Robt. 1798 w.
GILLOCK
Orange
Lawrence 1786 w.
GILLS
Chesterfield
Jacob 17— i.
Cumberland
Jno. 1752 w.
Northampton
Jonathan 1664 w.
GILLUM
Surry
Jno. 1738 w.
GILMAN
Hardy
Robt. 1799 i.
Rockbridge
Robt. 1779 a.
Sussex
Warrick 1778 w.

GILMER
Albemarle
Geo. 1795 w.
Hampshire
Jno. 1773 w.
Rockbridge
Jno. 1781 w.
York
Geo. 1757 w.
GILMORE
Augusta
Jno. 1759 a.
Jno. 1763 a.
Thos. 1763 i.
Jas. 1785 w.
Rockbridge
Robt. 1779 i.
Jas. 1783 w.
GILMOUR
Lancaster
Robt. 1782 w.
GILPIN
Middlesex
Henry 1728 w.
GILSHON
Prince William
Jas. 1744 w.
GILSON
Stafford
Thos. 1706 i.
Westmoreland
Behetherland 1720 w.
GIMBLIN
Shenandoah
Fred. 1777 a.
GIMBO
Spotsylvania
Thos. 1762 a.
GIMMETT
Franklin
Jno. 1794 i.
GINGAR
Berkeley
Gasper 1795 i.
GINKINS
Goochland
Richd. 1746 w.
Halifax
Jno. 1799 i.
Northampton
Edwd. 1646 w.
GINNEY
Orange
Jas. 1743 eb.
GIPSON
Chesterfield
Thos. 1762 i.
Thos. 1775 i.
Louisa
Gilbert 1764 a.

GIRTON
Princess Anne
Nathl. 1715 i.
GISBON
Princess Anne
Jno. 1773 w.
GISBORN
Princess Anne
Jas. 1750 w.
Eliz. 1753 w.
Edwd. 1783 w.
GISBORNE
Princess Anne
Jno. 1714 w.
Wm. 1733 w.
Jno. 1739 w.
GISBURN
Princess Anne
Wm. 1746 w.
Eliz. 1748 i.
Jas. 1794 w.
GISH
Botetourt
Christian 1796 w.
GIST
Loudoun
Jno. 1778 w.
GISTERT
Shenandoah
Chris. 1778 w.
GITTINGS
Northampton
Thos. 1710 w.
GIVEN
Pittsylvania
Geo. Homes 1796 i.
GIVENS
Augusta
Jno. Sr. 1789 w.
Bath
Wm. 1793 w.
Orange
Saml. 1741 w.
GIZBURN
Princess Anne
Edwd. 1743 w.
GLADEN
Fairfax
Frances 1758 w.
GLADDEN
Accomack
Howell 1786 w.
GLADHILL
Isle of Wight
Reubin 1715 w.
GLADIN
Accomack
Jno. 1721 w.
Fairfax
Jno. 1749 w.
Anne 1753 i.

GLADDING
Accomack
Jos. 1745 i.
Jno. 1750 i.
GLADMAN
Richmond
Edwd. 1728 i.
GLAN
Isle of Wight
Robt. 1667 w.
GLANISTER
York
Sarah 1675 w.
GLANVILLE
Northampton
Edmd. 1785 w.
Edmd. 1795 i.
GLASCO
Westmoreland
Jno. 1726 w.
GLASCOCK
Fauquier
Jno. 1765 w.
Jno. 1784 w.
Jno. 1793 w.
Norfolk
———— 1647 i.
Northumberland
Wm. 1776 w.
Richmond
Anne 1713 w.
Geo. 1714 w.
Geo. Sr. 1752 w.
Gregory 1752 i.
Jno. 1756 w.
Eliz. 1762 i.
Thos. 1777 w.
Wm. 1785 w.
Jno. 1796 w.
GLASCOE
Westmoreland
Jno. 1726 i.
GLASS
Albemarle
Wm. 1759 i.
Augusta
Jno. 1755 w.
Fluvanna
Wm. 1779 i.
Frederick
David 1775 w.
Jos. 1795 w.
Robt. 1797 w.
Hanover
Thos. Jr. 1734 i.
Lunenburg
Joshua 1751 a.
Ohio
Saml. 1796 w.
York
Jno. 1763 i.

GLASSCOCK
Richmond
  Thos. 1740 w.
  Million 1750 w.
  Jesse 1757 i.
  Judith 1770 w.
GLASSWELL
Northampton
  Jno. 1688 w.
GLAVE
Lancaster
  Jos. 1700 w.
GLAYNE
Norfolk
  Geo. 1653 i.
GLEADOWE
Henrico
  Saml. 1754 i.
GLEDHILL
Isle of Wight
  Mary 1712 w.
  Reubin 1716 i.
GLEGG
Prince William
  Wm. 1735 w.
GLENDENING
King George
  Jas. 1767 eb.
Richmond
  Jno. 1712 i.
GLENDENNING
King George
  Ann 1740 i.
  Jas. 1767 w.
GLENN
Berkeley
  Jas. 1774 w.
  Martha 1775 w.
  Jno. 1785 w.
  Jno. 1787 i.
  Jane 1793 w.
Cumberland
  Nehemiah 1777 i.
Henrico
  Matthew 1792 w.
  Oraner 1795 w.
  Jno. 1799 w.
Frederick
  Jas. 1755 w.
  Wm. 1769 w.
Lunenburg
  Tyree 1763 w.
Washington
  Jas. 1791 w.
GLEW
Richmond
  Jno. 1721 w.
GLIDWELL
Halifax
  Nash 1795 w.
  Nash 1799 i.

GLOVER
Cumberland
  Phinehas 1785 w.
  Mary 1786 w.
  Saml. 1791 i.
Frederick
  Wm. 1789 w.
Henrico
  Wm. 1691 i.
Isle of Wight
  Geo. 1728 i.
  Sarah 1734 i.
  Wm. 1758 w.
Orange
  Edwd. 1741 i.
Southampton
  Geo. 1775 w.
Surry
  Richd. 1715 w.
  Jno. 1754 i.
  Mary 1776 w.
GLYNN
Louisa
  Jeremiah 1775 w.
GOAD
Bedford
  Jno. 1771 w.
Pittsylvania
  Abraham 1799 w.
Richmond
  Abraham 1734 w.
  Mary 1736 i.
  Peter 1794 w.
GOAR
Shenandoah
  Henry 1791 w.
GOARD
Fairfax
  Mary 1777 w.
GOARE
Charlotte
  Wm. 1778 i.
Essex
  Henry 1702 i.
  Jno. 1727 w.
Middlesex
  Jos. 1727 w.
Shenandoah
  Jos. 1776 i.
GOARS
Halifax
  Henry 1791 i.
GOBBLE
Washington
  Fred. 1795 i.
GODARD
Essex
  Chas. 1736 w.
GODBEHEES
Isle of Wight
  Jno. 1669 i.

GODBY
Norfolk
  Thos. 1636-7 w.
GODBYE
Norfolk
  Thos. 1653 w.
GODDARD
Princess Anne
  Jno. 1695 i.
Westmoreland
  Edmond 1674 i.
GODDART
Berkeley
  Jno. 1777 i.
GODDIN
Middlesex
  Thos. 1714 w.
York
  Jno. 1687 w.
  Isaac 1688 i.
GODDING
York
  Jno. 1731 i.
  Lucy 1731 i.
GODFRA
Princess Anne
  Caleb 1792 w.
GODFREY
Essex
  Peter 1747 w.
Fairfax
  Wm. 1753 w.
Norfolk
  Jno. 1710 w.
  Warren Sr. 1712 w.
  Danl. 1716 w.
  Matthew 1717 w.
  Mary 1719 w.
  Peter 1723 w.
  Arthur 1740 w.
  Jonathan 1744-5 w.
  Betty 1749 w.
  Jno. 1753 w.
  Matthew 1755 w.
  Danl. 1758 w.
  Thos. 1759 w.
  Jno. 1760 i.
  Danl. 1761 i.
  Eliz. 1761 w.
  Nathl. 1762 w.
  Dinah 1765 w.
  Keziah 1777 w.
  Jno. 1778 w.
  Arthur 1783 i.
  Lamuel 1783 i.
  Jas. 1784 w.
  Danl. 1791 w.
  Jesse 1792 w.
  Danl. 1798 i.
Princess Anne
  Jno. 1707 w.

Wm. 1768 w.
Arthur 1771 w.
Thos. 1773 i.
Matthew 1784 w.
Jas. 1786 i.
Caleb 1792 i.
Rappahannock
Jno. 1677 nw.
Jno. 1678 w.
GODIN
Isle of Wight
Eliz. 1727 i.
Norfolk
Robt. 1709 w.
GODMAN
York
Simon 1705 w.
GODREY (?)
Norfolk
Jno. 1669 i.
GODSELL
Lancaster
Jno. 1675 w.
GODSEN
Isle of Wight
Thos. 1795 w.
GODSEY
Chesterfield
Thos. 1748 w.
GODSON
Rappahannock
Frances 1686 w.
GODWIN
Isle of Wight
Wm. 1720 w.
Eliz. 1727 w.
Jas. 1754 i.
Jno. 1761 w.
Jos. 1761 w.
Edmund 1762 w.
Sarah 1762 i.
Reade 1767 w.
Eliz. 1769 i.
Jonathan 1769 i.
Jas. 1778 w.
Wm. 1778 w.
Geo. 1781 w.
Jeremiah 1782 w.
Margt. 1788 w.
Edmund 1789 i.
Jonathan 1789 i.
Jno. 1790 w.
Saml. Sr. 1791 w.
Saml. 1794 i.
Jonathan 1796 i.
Jos. 1799 w.
Northampton
Devorax 1676 w.
Francis 1718-19 w.
Devorax 1726 w.
Jos. 1736 w.

Jos. 1739 i.
Wm. 1749 i.
Kendall 1788 i.
Devorax 1792 w.
Devorax 1797 i.
Westmoreland
Saml. 1735 i.
GODWYN
York
Jacob 1718 w.
GOFF
Amherst
Jno. 1763 w.
Bedford
Leonard 1773 i.
King George
Thos. 1734 i.
Randolph
Salathiel 1791 w.
Westmoreland
Wm. O'Brien 1766 w.
GOFFIGAN
Northampton
Peter Sr. 1773 i.
GOFFIGON
Norfolk
Ralph 1798 w.
Northampton
Thos. 1752 w.
Jas. 1762 w.
Jno. Sr. 1769 w.
Southy 1788 w.
GOFFOGAN
Northampton
Thos. 1720 w.
GOFFORD
Botetourt
Jno. 1799 i.
GOGGINS
Bedford
Stephen 1790 i.
GOIL
Augusta
Felty 1766 w.
GOING
Patrick
Nathan 1793 a.
GOLD
Berkeley
Thos. 1795 w.
Isle of Wight
Mary 1739 i.
Mecklenburg
Danl. 1793 w.
GOLDBURNE
Isle of Wight
Martin 1682 i.
GOLDEN
Henry
Jacob 1779 w.

Powhatan
Wm. 1798 i.
GOLDIE
Chesterfield
Robt. 1757 w.
GOLDING
Campbell
Saml. 1785 i.
Culpeper
Wm. 1771 w.
Essex
Wm. 1747 w.
Jas. 1749 i.
Ann 1777 i.
King George
Richd. 1751 i.
Northampton
Wm. 1718 w.
Westmoreland
Hamlett 1721 i.
GOLDMAN
Augusta
Jno. 1751 w.
Jacob 1752 i.
Bedford
Edwd. 1787 i.
GOLDSBY
Norfolk
Wm. 1781 w.
Richmond
Edwd. 1758 w.
Jno. 1786 i.
GOLDSMITH
Norfolk
Wm. 1692 w.
GOLEY
Amherst
Thos. 1767 w.
Loudoun
Thos. 1798 i.
GOLLADAY
Shenandoah
Jacob 1795 i.
GOLLAY
Shenandoah
Jacob 1795 w.
GOLLOGHER
Lancaster
Jno. 1750-1 w.
GOLORTHUM
Westmoreland
Martin 1733 w.
GOLSBE
Albemarle
Thos. 1753 i.
GOMAR
York
Jno. 1728 w.
GOMER
Greenbrier
Wm. 1792 i.

GONGEY
Essex
Richd. 1715 i.
GOOCH
Louisa
Wm. 1780 w.
Rowland 1794 w.
Norfolk
Jno. 1640-1 w.
GOOD
Fluvana
Jno. 1781 w.
Frederick
Matthias 1763 w.
Hampshire
Jacob 1780 w.
Middlesex
Jno. 1782 i.
Surry
Robt. 1746 i.
Westmoreland
Francis 1701 w.
GOODAKER
Norfolk
Wm. 1684 w.
Thos. 1687-8 w.
Princess Anne
Jos. 1712 w.
Wm. 1714 i.
Thos. 1725 i.
GOODAKERS
Princess Anne
Thos. 1721 w.
Thos. 1729 i.
GOODALL
Louisa
Jas. 1750 w.
Orange
Chas. 1775 w.
Jno. 1792 w.
GOODCHILD
Norfolk
Wm. 1793 w.
GOODDOY
Accomack
Wm. 1767 i.
GOODE
Amelia
Mackerness 1786 w.
Bedford
Jno. 1775 w.
Charlotte
Saml. 1793 i.
Sarah 1796 i.
Chesterfield
Jos. 1761 w.
Robt. 1763 i.
Robt. 1765 w.
Sarah 1774 w.
Jno. 1788 w.
Francis 1794 w.

Cumberland
Bennett 1771 w.
Essex
Richd. 1719 w.
Richd. 1725 w.
Jno. 1743 i.
Edwd. 1744 w.
Wm. 1785 i.
Jno. 1798 w.
Timothy 1798 w.
Henrico
Jno. 1709 w.
Robt. 1718 w.
Thos. 1718 w.
Saml. 1735 w.
Edwd. 1785 w.
Thos. 1788 w.
Henry
Jno. 1779 w.
Mecklenburg
Bennett 1785 i.
Powhatan
Thos. 1778 i.
Martha 1796 w.
Prince Edward
Saml. 1797 w.
GOODIN
Loudoun
Jno. 1770 w.
Surry
Thos. 1731 i.
GOODING
Chesterfield
Collins 1786 w.
Fairfax
Jacob 1792 a.
Norfolk
Wm. 1770 w.
Wythe
Abram 1794 w.
GOODLOE
Middlesex
Geo. 1710 w.
Spotsylvania
Henry 1749 w.
Eliz. 1751 w.
Robt. 1790 w.
Geo. 1787 a.
GOODMAN
Accomack
Jno. 1683 i.
Hanover
Benj. 1735 w.
Isle of Wight
Wm. 1715 i.
Rebecca 1726 w.
Rebecca 1732 i.
Wm. 1735 i.
Prince William
Jno. 1787 w.
Jno. 1798 i.

Surry
Thos. 1746 i.
Thos. 1748 i.
Eliz. 1748 i.
GOODPASTURE
Augusta
Jacob 1767 i.
GOODRICH
Brunswick
Briggs 1788 w.
Mary 1798 w.
Chesterfield
Geo. 1755 w.
Greensville
Edwd. 1791 w.
Isle of Wight
Jno. 1696 w.
Jno. 1698 w.
Geo. 1721 w.
Benj. 1747 i.
Jno. 1749 w.
Saml. 1753 i.
Edwd. 1759 w.
Geo. 1772 w.
Sarah 1783 w.
Eliz. 1785 i.
Eliz. 1795 w.
Wm. 1795 w.
Middlesex
Jno. 1709 a.
Henry 1711 i.
Norfolk
Edwd. 1779 w.
Rappahannock
Thos. 1679 w.
Prince George
Edwd. 1720 w.
Margt. 1723 i.
Chas. 1726 w.
Rappahannock
Thos. 1679 w.
GOODRIDGE
Lancaster
Wm. 1758 w.
Geo. 1771 w.
Richmond
Wm. 1713 w.
GOODRUM
Amherst
Thos. 1778 w.
Brunswick
Jas. 1772 i.
GOODS
Fairfax
Geo. 1794 a.
Geo. 1797 i.
GOODSON
Isle of Wight
Edwd. 1722 w.
Thos. 1729 i.
Thos. 1796 w.

York
Mary 1782 w.
Wm. 1782 w.
McWm. 1785 i.
GOODWIN
Fairfax
Mathew 1757 i.
Halifax
Peter 1799 w.
Isle of Wight
Saml. 1742 i.
Joshua 1743 i.
Jas. 1750 w.
Sarah 1750 w.
Lemuel 1751 i.
Louisa
Robt. 1789 w.
Middlesex
Jno. 1708 i.
Prince William
Geo. 1736 i.
Stafford
Jas. 1740 i.
York
Jno. 1701 i.
Eliz. 1718 w.
Martin 1718 w.
Peter 1731 w.
Peter 1747 w.
Rebecca 1748 w.
Sheldon 1751 w.
Jas. 1757 w.
Jno. 1759 w.
Peter 1763 w.
Jno. 1767 w.
Eliz. 1782 w.
Jno. 1785 i.
Brunswick
Thos. 1734 i.
GOODWYN
Isle of Wight
Jno. 1675 i.
Surry
Thos. 1731 i.
York
Blanch 1701 w.
Jas. 1719 w.
GOODY
Brunswick
Danl. 1761 a.
GOODYKUNST
Frederick
Geo. 1785 i.
GOOFF
Halifax
Chas. 1759 i.
GOOLD
Isle of Wight
Mary 1739 w.
Westmoreland
Wm. 1727 i.

GOOLSBY
Albemarle
Thos. 1774 w.
GOOSCOTT
Norflk
Jno. 1691 w.
GOOSE
Frederick
Geo. 1798 w.
Rappahannock
Thos. 1682 w.
Wythe
Stephen 1798 i.
GOOSLEY
York
Ephraim 1752 i.
GOOSELEY
York
Barbary 1764 i.
Cary 1774 i.
Martha 1780 w.
GOOTEE
Accomack
Mary 1768 i.
Jos. 1768 i.
Lisney 1795 w.
GORD
Surry
Henry 1677 w.
GORDAN
Amelia
Chas. 1796 i.
GORDEN
Shenandoah
Alex. 1791 a.
Surry
Jno. 1714 i.
GORDIN
Essex
Jno. 1721 i.
Prince Edward
Jno. 1753 w.
Surry
Jno. 1713 i.
GORDING
Accomack
Jno. 1678 w.
Essex
Wm. 1723 w.
Henrico
Wm. 1750 w.
GORDON
Brunswick
Chas. 1769 w.
Jno. 1769 w.
Chas. 1774 i.
Eliz. 1783 w.
Chesterfield
Robt. 1768 i.
Solomon 1785 w.

Culpeper
Jno. 1786 w.
Essex
Elianor 1721 i.
Wm. 1723 w.
Jane 1758 w.
Jno. 1764 w.
Wm. 1767 w.
Wm. 1770 w.
Jno. 1777 i.
Thos. 1777 i.
Thos. 1778 i.
Fairfax
David 1774 i.
Frederick
Gilbert 1767 w.
Goochland
Ann 1799 w.
Isle of Wight
Geo. 1789 w.
King George
Jno. 1779 w.
Lancaster
Jas. 1768 w.
Jas. 1794 w.
Loudoun
Robt. 1780 i.
Lunenburg
Gilbert 1762 i.
Roderick 1788 i.
Mecklenburg
Alex. 1796 i.
Middlesex
Wm. 1720 w.
Northumberland
Robt. 1740 i.
Spotsylvania
Jno. 1749 w.
Jno. 1766 a.
Westmoreland
Alex. 1698 w.
Geo. 1786 w.
York
Wm. 1730 w.
GORE
Accomack
Maximilian 1696 w.
Danl. 1720 w.
Wm. 1753 i.
Danl. 1770 w.
Danl. 1787 i.
Thos. 1797 w.
Culpeper
Jno. 1769 w.
Loudoun
Thos. 1790 w.
Middlesex
Jose 1750 i.
Norfolk
Chas. 1764 i.

Orange
Jno. 1777 w.
GOREING
Norfolk
Danl. 1714-15 w.
GORHAM
Loudoun
Jno. 1771 i.
Sanford 1773 w.
GORING
Surry
Jno. 1679 i.
Richd. 1679 w.
GORNOR
Princess Anne
Richd. 1751 w.
GORNTO
Princess Anne
Peter 1722 w.
Wm. 1734 i.
Jno. 1754 w.
Wm. Jr. 1789 w.
Jno. 1790 w.
Henry 1794 w.
GORR
Loudoun
Joshua 1785 w.
GORY
Goochland
Claudius 1737 i.
Henrico
Jno. Sr. 1709 w.
GOSLING
Prince Edward
Jno. 1799 w.
Prince William
Jno. 1740 w.
Simon 1744 w.
York
Jno. 1658 w.
GOSNEY
Culpeper
Wm. 1767 w.
GOSS
Essex
Jno. 1698 i.
Jno. 1705 w.
GOSSAGE
Surry
Richd. 1655 w.
GOSSAM
Fairfax
Wm. 1775 w.
GOSSEL
Franklin
Danl. 1796 i.
GOSSETT
Frederick
Abner 1799 i.

GOSWELL
Essex
Henry 1714 w.
GOUCH
Northumberland
Jno. 1720 w.
Geffry 1727 i.
Jno. 1746 w.
GOUGE
Orange
Jno. 1748 i.
GOUGH
Norfolk
Jas. 1770 i.
Northumberland
Benj. 1786 i.
Stephen 1795 i.
Stafford
Wm. 1762 i.
Westmoreland
Robt. 1726 i.
Augustine 1750 i.
GOULDING
Botetourt
Thos. 1779 w.
Essex
Simon 1789 w.
Simon 1795 w.
Prince Edward
Jno. 1774 i.
GOULDINGE
Norfolk
Jno. 1655 w.
GOULDMAN
Bedford
Edwd. 1774 w.
Essex
Thos. 1698 w.
Edwd. 1709 w.
Francis 1716 w.
Mary 1717 w.
Thos. 1729 w.
Francis 1763 w.
Thos. 1797 w.
Francis 1798 w.
GOURD
Surry
Richd. 1711 i.
GOUSH
Northumberland
Saml. 1761 i.
GOUT
Isle of Wight
Jno. 1728 w.
GOUTEE
Accomack
Jno. 1749 i.
GOUTY
Accomack
Jos. 1728 w.

GOVET
Lancaster
Clement 1740 i.
GOW
Norfolk
Alex. 1790 w.
GOWEN
Fairfax
Danl. 1796 i.
GOWER
Bedford
Standly 1782 w.
Brunswick
Wm. 1778 w.
Henrico
Abell 1688 w.
Richd. 1704 i.
Jane 1710 w.
Rappahannock
Jas. 1676 w.
Richmond
Stanley 1718 w.
Francis 1726 w.
Jno. 1726 w.
Winnefred 1727 w.
Stanley 1736 w.
Jno. 1762 i.
Stanley 1774 i.
Westmoreland
Pierce 1714 i.
⌐WERS
Accomack
Wm. 1668 w.
GOWTEE
Accomack
Mary 1764 w.
GRACE
Fairfax
Patrick 1786 w.
Isle of Wight
Wm. 1792 w.
Westmoreland
Jas. 1745 w.
Wm. 1769 w.
Frances 1747 w.
Jno. 1771 i.
GRADWELL
Norfolk
Edwd. 1651 w.
GRADY
Albemarle
Joshua 1796 w.
Amherst
Edwd. 1770 a.
Fairfax
Francis 1750 i.
Norfolk
Owne 1684 i.
Richmond
Eliz. 1702 w.
Wm. 1737 i.

Stafford
Patrick 1755 w.
Mary 1759 i.
GRAFFORD
Stafford
Mary 1756 w.
Westmoreland
Peter 1763 i.
GRAFTON
Northampton
Saml. 1752 w.
Hannah 1753 w.
GRAHAM
Accomack
Geo. 1764 i.
Augusta
Chris. 1746-7 a.
Chris. 1748 a.
Wm. 1749 i.
Florence 1762 i.
Robt. 1763 w.
Robt. 1765 i.
Robt. 1767 i.
David 1771 i.
Jno. 1771 w.
Robt. 1774 w.
Lanty 1780 w.
Berkeley
Jas. 1777 w.
Botetourt
Wm. 1786 w.
Brunswick
Thos. 1781 w.
Essex
Walter 1726 w.
Fairfax
Edwd. 1750 w.
Robt. 1752 i.
Halifax
David 1756 w.
Lancaster
Jno. 1717 i.
Lunenburg
Francis 1760 w.
Norfolk
Jno. 1714 w.
Jno. 1799 i.
Northumberland
Jno. 1706 w.
Jno. 1712 i.
Mary Eliz. 1791 w.
Wm. Jr. 1794 i.
Prince Edward
Mary 1757 i.
Prince William
Reginald 1784 i.
Jno. 1786 w.
Jno. 1787 w.
Richd. 1796 w.
Rockbridge
Wm. 1790 i.

Martha 1796 w.
Westmoreland
Wm. 1716 w.
Jane 1717 i.
Wm. 1725 i.
GRAINGER
Princess Anne
Thos. 1757 i.
GRAMMER
Loudoun
Andrew 1790 i.
GRANBERRY
Norfolk
Jas. 1761 w.
GRANBY
Norfolk
Chas. 1687 w.
GRANGER
Amelia
Jos. 1740 w.
Chesterfield
Jos. 1749 w.
Benj. 1783 w.
Ann 1784 w.
Allen 1794 i.
Jos. 1796 w.
Lunenburg
Jno. 1794 w.
Jno. 1796 i.
Norfolk
Jonathan 1678 i.
Caleb 1795 i.
Northampton
Thos. 1661 w.
Jno. 1724 w.
Margt. 1736 i.
GRANT
Berkeley
Danl. 1782 i.
Robt. 1799 i.
Charles City
Malcolm 1792 i.
Gregory 1782 w.
Fauquier
Jno. 1767 w.
Halifax
David 1781 w.
King George
Wm. 1733 i.
Wm. 1736 i.
Jno. 1762 w.
Andrew 1781 w.
Mary 1784 w.
Alex. 1795 i.
Norfolk
Edwd. 1719 i.
Wm. 1736 w.
Jno. Sr. 1775 w.
Northampton
Jno. 1713 i.

Pittsylvania
Jno. 1797 w.
Princess Anne
Thos. 1749 w.
Prince William
Jno. 1799 w.
Stafford
Partick 1733 i.
Ann 1736 w.
Westmoreland
Alice 1734 i.
York
Jno. 1761 i.
GRANTHAM
Fairfax
Jno. 1754 a.
Surry
Edwd. 1704 w.
Jno. 1739 w.
Thos. 1791 w.
Lewis 1796 w.
GRANTLIN
Isle of Wight
Darby 1670 w.
GRANTUM
Fairfax
Jno. 1754 i.
GRAPES
Frederick
Abraham 1797 i.
Jacob 1797 i.
GRASS
Augusta
Jacob 1785 i.
Jacob 1789 w.
GRASTY
Orange
Geo. 1787 w.
Spotsylvania
Sharshall 1745 w.
GRATTAN
Augusta
Jno. 1792 w.
GRAUNT
Essex
Duncan 1747 i.
GRAVAT
Stafford
Jno. 1741 i.
GRAVATT
King George
Jno. 1798 i.
Spotsylvania
Geo. 1798 w.
Stafford
Jno. 1757 i.
GRAVE
Isle of Wight
Jno. 1691 w.

GRAVENS
Prince Edward
Jno. 1771 i.
GRAVES
Amelia
Philander 1776 w.
Bedford
Isham 1775 i.
Chesterfield
Wm. 1755 w.
Wm. 1776 w.
Wm. 1780 w.
King 1791 w.
Armistead 1793 w.
Sarah 1797 w.
Jno. 1798 w.
Culpeper
Jas. 1781 w.
Thos. 1792 w.
Thos. 1795 i.
Essex
Jno. 1720 w.
Jno. 1725 w.
Thos. 1742 i.
Francis 1748 w.
Goochland
Ralph 1762 w.
Judith 1773 w.
Henry
Wm. 1791 w.
King George
Benj. 1747 a.
Blackley 1775 a.
Louisa
Jno. 1799 w.
Mecklenburg
Elijah 1799 w.
Middlesex
Alex. 1740 w.
Northampton
Roger 1720 w.
Geo. 1771 i.
Wm. Sr. 1771 i.
Wm. Sr. 1790 w.
Wm. 1792 i.
Orange
Richd. 1797 w.
Spotsylvania
Jno. 1747 w.
Thos. 1768 w.
Ann 1782 a.
Jos. 1786 w.
Jno. 1799 w.
Sussex
Solomon 1785 w.
Washington
Edmd. 1785 i.
York
Ralph 1667 w.
Ralph 1674 i.
Ralph 1694 i.

Ralph 1749 w.
Henry 1758 w.
Eliz. 1761 w.
Wm. 1782 w.
Chas. Henry 1796 w.
GRAY
Accomack
Jas. 1719 w.
Thos. 1728 i.
Thos. 1734 i.
Jas. 1738 nw.
Benj. 1760 w.
Soloman 1788 w.
Amelia
Jos. 1745 w.
Jos. 1783 i.
Augusta
Jno. 1751 w.
Bedford
Jno. 1786 w.
Berkeley
Hugh 1787 w.
David 1798 i.
Brunswick
Archibald 1762 w.
Charlotte
Wm. 1785 i.
Culpeper
Wm. 1753 a.
Jno. 1788 w.
Jno. 1790 i.
Essex
Jno. 1695 nw.
Warwick 1699 w.
Abner 1717 w.
Sarah 1733 i.
Wm. 1742 w.
Jas. 1768 i.
Wm. 1786 w.
Fairfax
Jno. 1784 i.
Frederick
Francis 1750 i.
Benj. 1786 w.
Halifax
Alex. 1796 i.
Isle of Wight
Richd. 1723 i.
Richd. 1726 i.
Richd. 1727 w.
Jno. 1728 w.
Richd. 1730 w.
Jno. 1738 w.
Jno. 1741 i.
Aaron 1741 i.
Eliz. 1753 i.
Jno. 1765 i.
Aron 1768 i.
Wm. 1769 i.
Matthew 1775 w.
Mourning 1775 w.

Matthew 1777 i.
Wm. 1782 w.
Nathl. 1799 w.
Louisa
Alex. 1763 w.
Middlesex
Wm. 1730 w.
Norfolk
Wm. 1771 w.
Jno. 1785 i.
Northampton
Jno. 1665 i.
Amy 1679 i.
Dingby 1742 w.
Dingly 1750 i.
Mary 1750 w.
Orange
Wm. 1737 a.
Princess Anne
Benj. Dingly 1791 w.
Prince William
Francis 1791 w.
Rappahannock
Wm. 1673 w.
Richmond
Thos. 1727 i.
Saml. 1756 i.
Susan 1761 w.
Rockbridge
Robt. 1799 i.
Southampton
Jos. 1758 i.
Thos. 1763 i.
Benj. 1766 w.
Wm. Watson 1768 i.
Jos. 1771 w.
Ann 1789 w.
Jno. 1789 i.
Edwin 1790 w.
Spotsylvania
Geo. 1766 w.
Stafford
Jno. 1766 w.
Surry
Thos. 1676 w.
Francis 1679 a.
Jno. 1683 w.
Jno. 1708 w.
Wm. 1714 w.
Wm. 1719 w.
Patrick 1726 i.
Wm. 1736 w.
Mary 1757 w.
Gilbert 1764 w.
Benj. 1766 i.
Margt. 1767 w.
Lucy 1773 w.
Henry 1774 w.
Richd. 1779 w.
Jas. 1788 w.

Washington
Benj. 1778 w.
Jno. 1795 w.
Westmoreland
Jno. 1714 i.
Nathl. 1743 w.
Francis 1775 i.
York
Thos. 1693 w.
GRAYE
Isle of Wight
Richd. 1722 w.
GRAYHAM
Essex
Walter 1726 w.
GRAYSON
Fairfax
Benj. 1768 i.
Frederick
Wm. 1790 w.
Wm. 1793 i.
Orange
Jno. 1755 i.
Prince William
Spence 1799 i.
Spotsylvania
Jno. 1735-6 a.
Ambrose 1743 w.
Ambrose 1756 w.
GREAR
Norfolk
Jos. 1771 w.
GREATHOUSE
Harrison
Wm. 1791 w.
Wm. 1797 i.
GREAVEN
Prince Edward
Jno. 1772 w.
GREBELL
Henrico
Saml. 1695 w.
GREDEY
Fairfax
Francis 1750 a.
GREECION
King George
Jas. 1740 i.
GREEG
Augusta
Thos. 1773 w.
GREEN
Accomack
Jno. 1735 i.
Amelia
Wm. 1747 w.
Eliz. 1760 w.
Henry 1776 w.
Fanny 1782 i.
Abraham 1783 w.
Thos. 1792 w.

Wm. 1792 w.
Thos. 1795 w.
Augusta
Hugh 1789 w.
Bedford
Jno. 1775 w.
Berkeley
Wm. Sr. 1780 w.
Botetourt
Geo. 1784 a.
Brunswick
Peter 1781 i.
Fred. 1787 w.
Jno. 1798 w.
Charles City
Martha 1768 i.
Charlotte
Jno. 1791 w.
Culpeper
Jas. 1766 i.
Moses 1770 w.
Wm. 1770 w.
Moses 1779 i.
Henry 1785 w.
Robt. 1789 w.
Wm. 1791 w.
Eleanor 1793 w.
Jno. 1793 w.
Jno. Wms. 1794 i.
Essex
Thos. 1703 i.
Wm. 1703 w.
Geo. 1706 i.
Saml. 1709-10 w.
Thos. 1733 w.
Sarah 1759 w.
Geo. 1764 w.
Fairfax
Chas. 1765 w.
Thos. 1797 i.
Fauquier
Duff 1766 i.
Franklin
Benj. 1786 a.
Benj. 1788 w.
Frederick
Moses 1799 i.
Hardy
Lewis 1787 i.
Mary 1787 i.
Halifax
Peter 1792 a.
Henrico
Paul 1728 i.
Robt. 1735 w.
Isle of Wight
Thos. 1686 w.
Geo. 1706-7 w.
Jno. 1718 i.
Jno. 1720 w.
Thos. 1726 i.

Wm. 1729 w.
Mary 1737 w.
Geo. 1762 i.
Jno. 1762 i.
King George
Jno. 1734 i.
Thos. 1759 w.
Geo. 1768 w.
Richd. 1778 w.
Louisa
Forest 1770 i.
Forrest 1772 w.
Jos. 1772 i.
Loudoun
Richd. 1779 i.
Jas. 1796 w.
Lunenburg
Henry 1749 w.
Henry 1761 w.
Jno. 1768 w.
Mecklenburg
Thos. 1778 i.
Norfolk
Jean 1694-5 w.
Thos. 1785 w.
Northampton
Jno. Sr. 1706 w.
Alice 1731 w.
Geo. 1750 i.
Jos. 1751 i.
Jos. Jr. 1752 i.
Geo. 1755 i.
Wm. 1771 w.
Rose 1782 w.
Jno. 1785 w.
Jno. 1788 i.
Orange
Robt. 1748 w.
Princess Anne
Walter 1701 a.
Edwd. 1774 w.
Boing 1779 w.
Prince William
Geo. 1783 i.
Thos. 1786 i.
Geo. 1789 w.
Richmond
Geo. 1719 w.
Stafford
Jane 1700 i.
Surry
Jno. 1702-3 w.
Edwd. 1706 w.
Richd. 1711 i.
Nathl. 1728 w.
Burrell 1733 i.
Peter 1745 w.
Nathl Sr. 1750 w.
Robt. 1750 w.
Wm. Sr. 1750 w.
Nathl. 1758 i.

Wm. 1782 w.
Sussex
Ann 1786 w.
Burril 1788 w.
Ann 1790 i.
Jas. 1792 i.
Washington
Jas. 1779 i.
Lewis 1785 w.
Westmoreland
Erasmus 1705 i.
Jas. 1726 i.
Wm. 1750 i.
Jas. 1778 i.
Jno. 1782 i.
Wm. 1785 w.
Jno. 1793 i.
Jno. 1795 w.
York
Jno. 1723 w.
Anne 1735 w.
Bailey 1755 w.
Sarah 1759 i.
GREENALDS
Accomack
Henry 1760 i.
GREENAWAY
Fairfax
Jos. 1795 i.
Richmond
Wm. 1748 i.
GREENBY
Henrico
David 1783 w.
GREENE
Brunswick
Peter 1795 w.
Lancaster
Jno. 1654 w.
Norfolk
Jno. 1674 w.
Wm. 1674 w.
Edwd. 1680 w.
GREENFIELD
Frederick
Jno. 1768 w.
GREENHAM
Richmond
Jeremiah 1753 w.
GREENHILL
Amelia
David 1772 w.
Eliz. 1774 w.
Charlotte
Paschall 1794 w.
Essex
Wm. 1726 w.
Jas. 1741 i.
Wm. 1741 i.
Jas. 1746 i.
Jos. 1758 w.

Ambrose 1795 w.
GREENHOW
Henrico
Jno. 1796 i.
GREENING
Westmoreland
Jno. 1731 i.
GREENINGE
Northampton
Wm. 1655 w.
GREENLEE
Augusta
Jas. 1763 i.
GREENLEESE
Stafford
Wm. 1763 i.
GREENLESS
Culpeper
Wm. 1779 w.
GREENSTEAD
Essex
Saml. 1789 w.
Northumberland
Wm. 1764 w.
GREENSTEED
Essex
Thos. 1784 w.
GREENSTREET
King George
Thos. 1742 i.
Berryman 1771 a.
GREENWAY
Fairfax
Jos. 1793 a.
GREENWOOD
Charlotte
Jno. 1779 i.
Essex
Rhodes 1775 w.
Wm. 1791 w.
Isle of Wight
Thos. 1658 w.
Mecklenburg
Robt. 1778 w.
Jas. 1781 w.
Middlesex
Thos. 1730 w.
Richd. 1748 i.
Jas. 1749 w.
Saml. 1750 a.
Northumberland
Wm. 1772 i.
Westmoreland
Danl. 1746-7 w.
GREER
Augusta
Jno. 1750 w.
Bedford
Jos. 1781 w.
Berkeley
Chas. 1787 i.

Mecklenburg
Jos. 1781 w.
Washington
Wm. 1782 w.
Wm. Sr. 1785 i.
GREGG
Albemarle
Wm. 1789 w.
Campbell
Tho's. 1799 i.
Loudoun
Jno. 1787 w.
Thos. 1792 w.
Isaac 1795 w.
Stephen 1796 w.
Prince William
Jno. 1743 w.
Stafford
Lucy 1730 w.
Jas. 1734 i.
Jno. 1736 i.
Jno. 1756 i.
Mathew 1757 w.
GREGORY
Amherst
Jno. 1798 i.
Augusta
Naphtalum 1762 i.
Jas. 1771 a.
Jas. 1774 w.
Charles City
Thos. 1773 w.
Jno. 1792 i.
Jas. 1794 i.
Stith 1795 i.
Eliz. 1797 i.
Essex
Richd. 1701 w.
Richd. 1725 w.
Isle of Wight
Robt. 1750 i.
Lancaster
Jos. 1727 i.
Abraham 1750 i.
Mecklenburg
Wm. 1785 w.
Prince William
Benj. 1798 w.
Rappahannock
Jno. 1678 w.
Surry
Jno. 1678 w.
Westmoreland
Jas. Sr. 1792 w.
Jas. 1793 i.
York
Anthony 1719 i.
GREGSON
Essex
Thos. 1705-6 w.

GREINER
Augusta
David 1789 i.
GRENALDS
Accomack
Southy 1781 i.
GRENAN
Prince William
Owin 1744 i.
GRESHAM
Brunswick
Jno. 1779 w.
Cumberland
Benj. 1771 i.
Essex
Chas. 1727 w.
Chas. 1731 i.
Robt. 1748 w.
Goochland
Eliz. 1762 w.
Jas. 1770 w.
Middlesex
Jno. 1752 a.
Anne 1761 a.
Louisa
Thos. 1760 w.
Northumberland
Jno. 1656 i.
Orange
Thos. 1740 a.
Pittsylvania
Thos. 1797 w.
Powhatan
Lieut. 1777 w.
Wm. 1778 i.
GRESHION
Isle of Wight
Jas. 1728 w.
GRESHON
Prince Williom
Jas. 1744 i.
GRESSITT
Lancaster
Thos. 1760 i.
GRESSWELL
Southampton
Wm. 1771 w.
GRESSWIT
Southampton
Wm. 1782 w.
GRESSWITT
Southampton
Thos. 1771 i.
GREY
Essex
Warwick 1699 i.
Surry
Thos. 1678 i.
Westmoreland
Francis 1667 w.

GRICE
Northampton
Peter 1709 w.
Stott 1736 i.
Wm. 1770 i.
Surry
Robt. 1720 w.
Westmoreland
Jno. 1726 i.
GRIDER
Frederick
Martin 1776 i.
GRIFEN
Norfolk
Jno. 1705-6 w.
GRIFFEN
Accomack
Emanuel 1747 i.
Essex
Jno. 1696 i.
Isle of Wight
Thos. 1670 w.
Norfolk
Thos. 1722 i.
Geo. 1747 w.
Constant 1753 w.
Princess Anne
Chas. 1715 w.
Wm. 1715 w.
Jno. 1730 w.
Jas. 1743 w.
Henry 1744 w.
GRIFFETH
Bedford
Geo. 1777 w.
Frederick
Saml. 1787 i.
Fairfax
David 1790 a.
Isle of Wight
Owen 1698 w.
Northampton
Jas. 1708 w.
Benj. 1719 w.
Jas. 1719 w.
Thos. Jr. 1745 i.
Sarah 1748 w.
Jno. 1749 i.
Benj. 1750 i.
Geo. 1750 w.
Thos. 1750 w.
Jos. Sr. 1751 w.
Anne 1752 i.
Luke 1752 w.
Nathan 1752 i.
Jno. 1765 w.
Wm. 1772 w.
Danl. 1793 w.
Richmond
Samon 1718 i.

GRIFFEY
Shenandoah
Martin 1792 a.
GRIFFIE
Augusta
Mathusalem 1750 w.
GRIFFIN
Accomack
Eliz. 1734 w.
Oliver 1752 i.
Amelia
Jos. 1747 a.
Amherst
Reuben 1776 w.
Culpeper
Thos. 1782 w.
Essex
Jno. 1697 w.
Saml. 1698 w
Thos. 1720 w.
Peirce 1738 i.
Jas. 1739 w.
Wm. 1741 w.
Mary 1742 w.
Jno. 1746 i.
Mary 1748 w.
Fairfax
Ezekiel 1754 i.
Halifax
Richd. 1767 i.
Ralph 1771 w.
Henrico
Wm. 1746 w.
GRIFFIN
Isle of Wight
Katherine 1763 w.
King George
Thos. 1780 w.
Lancaster
Thos. B. 1778 w.
Lunenburg
Wm. 1751 w.
Mecklenburg
Francis 1765 i.
Middlesex
Corbin 1701 w.
Norfolk
Jno. 1787 w.
Northumberland
Saml. 1703 w.
Thos. 1775 w.
Orange
Jno. 1743 w.
Princess Anne
Wm. 1695 w.
Geo. 1728 i.
Jno. 1741 w.
Jno. 1753 w.
Jno. 1759 w.
Jas. 1767 w.
Abigail 1774 w.

Nicholas 1776 i.
Wm. 1777 w.
Prince Edward
Jas. 1777 w.
Anthony 1779 w.
Prince William
Walter 1739 a.
Jno. 1783 i.
Rappahannock
Wm. 1681 w.
Wm. 1684 w.
Richmond
Winifred 1711 w.
Wm. 1725 w.
Thos. 1733 w.
Leroy 1750 w.
Eliz. 1761 w.
————— 1761 i.
Mary Ann 1770 w.
Leroy 1775 w.
Judith 1794 i.
Southampton
Matthew 1751 w.
Mary 1754 w.
Benj. 1781 w.
Stafford
Danl. 1751 i.
Surry
Jas. 1709 i.
Jas. 1711 w.
Jno. 1761 i.
Sussex
Richd. 1792 w.
Westmoreland
Oliver 1677 w.
York
Hannah 1712 i.
GRIFFING
Essex
Jno. 1697 w.
Jas. 1758 i.
GRIFFIS
Accomack
Danl. 1721 w.
Brunswick
Thos. 1776 i.
King George
Ann 1740 i.
Surry
Thos. 1726 w.
Thos. 1764 w.
Sussex
Edwd. 1761 w.
Edwd. 1762 w.
GRIFFITH
Accomack
Jas. 1748 i.
Augusta
Benj. 1764 a.
Morris 1764 a.

Frederick
Wm. 1750 a.
Henrico
Chas. 1733 w.
Loudoun
Wm. 1777 i.
Northampton
Jerom 1720 w.
Luke 1720 w.
Jno. 1745 i.
Thos. 1776 i.
Abraham 1780 w.
Jacob 1789 i.
Abraham 1795 i.
Pittsylvania
Wm. 1780 w.
Princess Anne
Benj. 1786 w.
Prince George
Richd. 1719 i.
Wm. 1727 w.
Eliz. 1728 w.
Thos. 1728 w.
GRIFIN
Henrico
Wm. 1677 w.
Essex
Peirce 1735 i.
Isle of Wight
Andrew 1726 w.
Princess Anne
Sarah 1716 i.
Wm. 1716 i.
GRIFING
Isle of Wight
Robt. 1727 i.
GRIFITS
Greenbrier
Thos. 1789 i.
GRIGE
Henrico
Robt. 1703 w.
GRIGG
Amelia
Jas. 1764 w.
Jno. 1764 i.
Josiah 1785 w.
Charlotte
Jas. 1773 w.
Greensville
Lewis 1787 w.
Abner 1796 w.
Loudoun
Geo. 1794 w.
Levi 1794 i.
Prince George
Wm. Jr. 1726 w.
GRIGGORY
Westmoreland
Isaac 1750 i.

GRIGGS
Essex
Jno. 1759 w.
Jno. 1761 i.
Lancaster
Robt. 1683 w.
Michael 1692 w
Thos. 1726 w.
Lee 1773 i.
Wm. 1782 w.
Norfolk
Wm. 1783 i.
Princess Anne
Jacob 1783 i.
Richmond
Robt. 1729 i.
Westmoreland
Wm. 1781 w.
GRIGORY
Rappahannock
Jno. 1678 w.
Richmond
Robt. 1717 i.
GRIGSBY
Fauquier
Jno. 1772 i.
Saml. 1781 w.
Wm. 1782 i.
Jno. 1789 w.
King George
Aaron 1764 w.
Verlinda 1764 i.
Reuben 1769 w.
Mott 1795 i.
Loudoun
Jas. 1797 w.
Rockbridge
Jno. 1794 w.
Stafford
Jno. 1730 w.
Chas. 1740 w.
Thos. 1745 w.
Jno. 1750 i.
Jas. 1752 w.
Jane 1756 w.
Jas. 1758 i.
GRILL
Essex
Jonathan 1699 w.
GRILLS
Henrico
Richd. 1732 w.
GRIM
Frederick
Chas. 1778 w.
GRIMES
Fairfax
Wm. 1757 i.
Wm. 1758 i.
Loudoun
Nicholas 1766 w.

Edwd. 1781 i.
Norfolk
Robt. 1693-4 w.
Jno. 1712 i.
Jas. 1750 w.
Charity 1753 i.
Wm. 1757 w.
Thos. 1769 w.
Jas. 1777 w.
Jas. 1779 i.
Jno. 1779 i.
Edwd. 1786 w.
Wm. 1786 w.
Wm. 1787 i.
Jas. 1788 i.
Jno. 1788 w.
Jas. 1789 i.
Chas. 1790 w.
Jas. 1792 i.
Jesse 1795 w.
Ann 1796 w.
Shenandoah
Benj. 1798 w.
York
Wm. 1656 w.
Richd. 1716 i.
GRIMMER
Isle of Wight
Robt. 1747 i.
GRIMSLEY·
King George
Jno. 1726 i.
GRIMSTEAD
Princess Anne
Danl. 1793 w.
Jno. 1798 w.
GRIMWOOD
Fairfax
Wm. 1746 a.
GRINALD
Accomack
Richd. 1724 w.
Southy 1798 w.
GRINALDS
Accomack
Richd. 1774 w.
GRINNALDS
Accomack
Thos. 1795 w.
GRINNINS
Albemarle
Robt. 1791 i.
GRINSTEAD
Henrico
Danl. 1788 i.
Jno. 1792 w.
Northumberland
Jno. 1796 i.
Princess Anne
Danl. 1784 w.
Jos. 1784 w.

GRIMSTED
Essex
Richd. 1698 i.
GRINSTED
Northumberland
Jno. 1726 i.
Adam 1726-7 w.
GRINTO
Princess Anne
Wm. 1706 i.
GRISITT
Northumberland
Thos. 1767 w.
GRISKELL
Northampton
Lawrence 1746 i.
GRISSWOOD
Isle of Wight
Jno. 1688 i.
GRISTOCK
Norfolk
Henry 1745-6 w.
Mary 1750 w.
Mary 1765 i.
GRISWITT
Surry
Marmaduke 1742 w.
GRIZARD
Southampton
Ambrose 1775 w.
Wm. 1779 w.
Sussex
Ambrose 1781 w.
GRIZER
Frederick
Wilhelm 1759 w.
GRIZZARD
Southampton
Wm. 1792 a.
GRIZZEL
Chesterfield
Geo. 1761 i.
GROMARRIN
Henrico
Gillee 1716 w.
GRONTO
Princess Anne
Wm. 1789 i.
GROOM
Middlesex
Jno. 1795 i.
GROOME
York
Rebecca 1745 w.
GROSS
Botetourt
Martin 1794 i.
Isle of Wight
Thos. 1675 w.
Thos. 1719 w.
Thos. 1742 w.

Francis 1751 w.
Jonathan 1762 i.
Francis 1772 w.
Thos. 1792 i.
Washington
Wm. 1794 w.
GROTEN
Accomack
Shadrach 1773 w.
Wm. 1774 w.
Mary 1776 w.
Wm. 1776 i.
Jno. 1777 w.
Major 1777 w.
Wm. 1777 w.
Jno. 1779 i.
Custis 1786 w.
Hnry. 1789 w.
Jonathan 1795 w.
GROTIN
Accomack
Wm. 1779 i.
GROTON
Accomack
Jonathan 1761 w.
Wm. 1771 w.
Solomon 1777 w.
GROVE
Frederick
Matthias 1782 w.
Jacob 1794 w.
GROVES
Bedford
Jno. 1793 i.
Fairfax
Jno. 1796 a.
Isle of Wight
Wm. 1677 i.
King George
Wm. 1751 i.
Lancaster
Jno. 1749 w.
Northampton
Rodger 1720 w.
Jno. 1750 w.
Eliz. 1792 w.
Geo. 1712-13 w.
Shenandoah
Christian 1786 w.
Surry
Jno. 1740 i.
Jno. 1749 i.
GRUBB
Fauquier
Wm. 1774 i.
Frederick
Jas. 1747 i.
Thos. 1752 i.
Jas. 1751 a.
Christian 1769 w.

Loudoun
Richd. 1783 i.
Prince William
Richd. 1787 i.
York
Edwd. 1685 i.
GRUBBS
Goochland
Andrew 1780 i.
GRUBS
Louisa
Jno. 1790 i.
GRUMMET
Franklin
Jno. 1795 i.
GRYMES
Augusta
Wm. 1748 a.
David 1768 a.
Lancaster
Edwd. 1653 w.
Margt. 1659 w.
Loudoun
Nicholas 1798 w.
Lunenburg
Francis 1761 i.
Middlesex
Jno. 1709 w.
Alice 1710 w.
Jno. 1748 w.
Philip 1762 w.
Chas. 1791 w.
Norfolk
Wm. 1785 i.
Orange
Mary 1790 w.
Ludwell 1795 i.
Richmond
Chas. 1743 i.
York
Wm. 1668 w.
GUALTNEY
Surry
Wm. 1732 w.
GUARRANT
Goochland
Peter 1744 i.
GUBB
Rappahannock
Nathl. 1687 w.
GUDREDG
Orange
Jno. 1782 w.
GUERANT
Goochland
Danl. 1731 i.
GUERRANT
Cumberland
Peter 1750 w.

GUESS
Prince William
Jos. 1740 i.
GUGGEY
Essex
Richd. 1715 w.
GUILLIAM
Charlotte
Wm. 1772 i.
GUIN
Pittsylvania
Geo. 1796 w.
GUISBORN
Princess Anne
Jno. 1740 i.
GUISCARD
Norfolk
Raymond de 1786 w.
GULEFORD
Berkeley
Jno. 1782 w.
GULLAN
Fincastle
Hugh 1775 i.
GULLAT
Fairfax
Jno. 1784 w.
Peter 1785 i.
GULLEDGE
Isle of Wight
Edwd. 1733 i.
GULLEY
Surry
Robt. 1696-7 w.
GULLINGTON
Halifax
Wm. 1786 i.
GULLOCK
Rappahannock
Robt. 1684 w.
Westmoreland
Thos. 1698 i.
GULLY
Culpeper
Wm. 1782 i.
Surry
Luceey 1700-1 w.
GULTRES
Brunswick
Danl. 1761 w.
GUN
Goochland
Jno. 1735 w.
GUMMERSON
Fairfax
Eliz. 1749 a.
GUNBEE
Northampton
Mathew 1646 w.

GUNN
Amelia
Thos. 1777 w.
Brunswick
Wm. 1795 i.
Wm. 1797 w.
GUNNE
Essex
Jno. 1698 w.
GUNNEL
Fairfax
Wm. 1760 w.
GUNNELL
Fairfax
Henry Jr. 1787 w.
Henry 1792 w.
Wm. 1794 w.
Wm. 1796 a.
GUNNERSON
Fairfax
Wm. 1742 a.
GUNSTOCKER
Rappahannock
Edwd. 1686 w.
GUNSTONE
Fairfax
Jno. 1757 i.
GUNTER
Accomack
Edwd. 1720 w.
Meshack 1772 w.
Abednego 1781 i.
Adrah 1783 w.
Adra 1789 i.
Zachary 1792 i.
Easter 1793 i.
Edwd. 1793 w.
Albemarle
Reuben 1796 i.
Halifax
Jno. 1791 i.
Lancaster
Chas. 1750 w.
Middlesex
Chas. 1752 a.
Northampton
Edwd. 1665 w.
GUNTHER
York
Jno. C. 1796 w.
GUNTOR
Accomack
Jos. 1758 w.
GUPTON
Fairfax
Wm. 1757 i.
Richmond
Stephen 1717 w.
Eliz. 1718 i.
Wm. 1722 i.
Stephen 1749 w.

Caty Ann 1785 w.
Wm. 1785 i.
GURLEY
Southampton
Nicholas 1762 w.
Benj. 1762 i.
Geo. 1771 w.
GURNEY
Botetourt
Henry 1792 w.
GURNTO
Princess Anne
Jno. 1694 w.
GUST
Botetourt
Jno. 1791 i.
GUTE
Loudoun
Hanson L. 1792 i.
GUTHERY
Franklin
Henry 1787 i.
Jas. 1788 a.
GUTHREY
Middlesex
Jno. 1747 a.
GUTHRIE
Isle of Wight
Danl. 1759 i.
Middlesex
Benj. 1780 w.
Wm. 1782 w.
Rockbridge
Robt. 1789 w.
GUTRE
Isle of Wight
Danl. 1757 w.
GUTRIDGE
Isle of Wight
Geo. 1722 i.
GUTRY
Middlesex
Mary 1744 i.
GUTTEREIDGE
Accomack
Severn 1777 w.
GUTTERIDGE
Isle of Wight
Jno. 1731 i.
GUTTERY
Halifax
Thos. 1787 w.
GUTTRY
Cumberland
Sarah 1771 w.
GUY
Accomack
Nicho. 1741 w.
Ann 1762 w.
Wm. 1778 w.
Wm. 1786 i.

Robt. 1796 w.
Jno. 1798 i.
Wm. 1798 i.
Augusta
Eliz. 1785 w.
Loudoun
Saml. 1793 i.
Norfolk
Jno. 1734 w.
Jno. 1737 w.
Benj. 1763 w.
Benj. 1769 i.
Jas. 1770 i.
Northampton
Major 1745 w.
Jno. 1771 w.
Wm. 1775 i.
Henry Sr. 1777 w.
Henry 1782 i.
Jno. 1795 w.
Nancy W. 1795 w.
GUYGER
Shenandoah
Jacob 1777 w.
GUYMER
Stafford
Edmd. 1741 i.
GYBSON
York
Thos. 1652 w.
GYLES
Spotsylvania
Wm. 1767 a.
GWALTNEY
Isle of Wight
Benj. 1762 i.
Benj. 1779 w.
Jas. 1780 w.
Jas. 1782 i.
Surry
Thos. 1728 i.
Jos. 1750 w.
Martha 1751 w.
Jno. 1752 w.
Wm. 1752 w.
Thos. 1798 w.
GWIN
Fairfax
Hooper 1759 i.
Isle of Wight
Boaze 1697-8 i.
Lunenburg
David 1752 w.
Jno. 1754 a.
Norfolk
Edwd. 1715 i.
Edwd. 1717 a.
Alex. 1721 i.
Princess Anne
Jno. 1728 w.
Jos. 1740 a.

Jno. 1753 i.
GWINN
Fairfax
Benj. 1796 w.
Norfolk
——— 1700 w.
Jno. 1792 i.
GWYN
Norfolk
Walter 1788 w.
Richmond
Katherine 1728 w.
David 1704 w.
GWYNN
Augusta
Wm. 1772 i.
GYE
Norfolk
Patrick 1688 w.

H

HABERT
Shenandoah
Nicho. 1787 i.
HABORN
Westmoreland
Geo. 1754 w.
HABRON
Richmond
Geo. 1719 i.
Westmoreland
Jas. 1782 i.
HACESTY
Albemarle
Jno. 1757 i.
HACK
Accomack
Geo. 1665 w.
Geo. Nicho. 1705 w.
Geo. 1712 w.
Peter 1717 w.
Geo. 1719 i.
Northampton
Geo. 1650 i.
Northumberland
Nicholas 1720 i.
Spencer 1727 w.
Jno. 1747 w.
Tunstall 1757 w.
HACKER
Frederick
Andrew 1770 i.
York
Henry 1742 w.
HACKET
Northampton
Moses 1744 i.
Orange
Chesley 1763 i.

Princess Anne
Mary Ann 1785 i.
HACKETT
Albemarle
Martin 1790 w.
Lancaster
Thos. 1656 i.
HACKLEY
Culpeper
Jno. 1769 a.
Judith 1772 w.
Essex
Jno. 1698 w.
Robt. 1738 w.
King George
Jas. 1748 i.
Eliz. 1756 w.
Jno. 1760 w.
Prince Edward
Saml. 1776 w.
HACKMAN
Cumberland
Thos. 1754 w.
Shenandoah
Christian 1789 i.
HACKNEY
Fluvanna
Jno. 1797 w.
Frederick
Charity 1762 w.
Middlesex
Wm. Sr. 1701 w.
Wm. 1753 w.
Eliz. 1761 a.
Wm. 1776 w.
Northumberland
Richd. 1729 w.
Prince William
Jno. 1744 i.
HADDAWAY
Middlesex
Wm. 1675 a.
HADDEN
Randolph
David 1791 w.
Washington
Thos. 1779 w.
HADDERSICK
Accomack
Job 1743 w.
HADDON
Middlesex
Thos. 1777 w.
Mary 1782 w.
York
Francis 1674 i.
Hudson 1745 w.
HADDUX
Fauquier
Ezekiel 1796 i.

HADEN
Goochland
Zachariah 1792 w.
HADLEY
Isle of Wight
Ambrose 1779 w.
Middlesex
Jno. 1710 w.
York
Dionisia 1714 i.
HADLY
Isle of Wight
Ambrose 1713 w.
HADRICK
Augusta
Adam 1775 w.
HADWELL
Northumberland
Jno. 1727 w.
Richd. 1750 i.
Jane 1761 w.
HAFF
Hampshire
Cornelius 1795 w.
HAGAN
Frederick
Patrick 1751 i.
HAGER
Prince William
Henry 1737 w.
HAGGIN
Frederick
Jas. 1783 i.
HAGGOMAN
Northampton
Jno. 1688 w.
Isaac 1728 w.
Jno. Sr. 1764 w.
Jno. 1764 w.
Sarah 1764 w.
Silvanus 1764 w.
Wm. 1764 w.
Margt. 1768 w.
HAGOMOND
Northampton
Jno. 1672 w.
HAGUE
Loudoun
Jno. 1767 w.
Francis 1780 w.
Northumberland
Jos. 1760 w.
Jos. 1787 w.
Princess Anne
Francis 1785 w.
HAIES
Lunenburg
Mark 1753 w.
HAIL
Albemarle
Jos. 1785 i.

Bedford
Richd. 1784 w.
Isle of Wight
Jno. 1714 nw.
Edwd. 1757 w.
Eliz. 1757 w.
Sussex
Benj. 1794 w.
HAILE
Bedford
Francis 1780 w.
Jane 1782 i.
Essex
Jonathan 1737 w.
Jno. 1744 w.
Jno. 1761 w.
Mary 1753 w.
Edward 1756 w.
Richd. Thos. 1795 w.
Isle of Wight
Jno. 1794 w.
Hannah 1799 w.
Pittsylvania
Jno. 1774 i.
Sussex
Benj. 1799 w.
HAILES
King George
Benj. 1783 w.
Westmoreland
Jno. 1753 i.
HAILESS
Montgomery
Edwd. 1797 i.
Emanuel 1797 w.
HAILEY
Fauquier
Jno. 1787 w.
Honor 1790 w.
Halifax
Humphrey 1788 w.
Lunenburg
Henry 1764 i.
Westmoreland
Richd. 1774 w.
Richd. 1776 i.
HAINES
Culpeper
Isaac 1799 i.
Essex
Wm. 1744 i.
Fauquier
Simeon 1796 i.
Frederick
Robt. 1796 w.
Lancaster
Sarah 1753 i.
HAINEY
Charlotte
Jno. 1794 w.

HAINS
Berkeley
Henry 1777 w.
Frederick
Joshua 1757 i.
Joshua 1760 i.
Loudoun
Thos. 1799 w.
HAIR
Berkeley
Saml. 1782 w.
Norfolk
Jos. 1789 w.
HAIRSTON
Campbell
Andrew 1782 w.
Saml. 1782 w.
Bedford
Hugh 1778 i.
Peter 1780 w.
Franklin
Robt. 1791 w.
HAISLES
Accomack
Moses 1761 i.
HAISTY
Southampton
Moses 1793 i.
HAITE
Surry
Thos. 1674 a.
HAITHCOCK
Brunswick
Jos. 1784 w.
HALBART
Essex
Wm. 1733 i.
HALBERT
Essex
Wm. 1723 w.
Wm. 1761 w.
Fairfax
Jno. 1780 i.
Loudoun
Michael 1796 w.
Westmoreland
Michael 1716 i.
HALBROOK
Westmoreland
Jos. 1752 i.
HALCOMB
Middlesex
Simon 1745 a.
HALCOME
Westmoreland
Geo. 1749 w.
HALDIMAN
Augusta
Jacob 1790 w.
HALE
Goochland
Wm. 1797 w.

Isle of Wight
Pool 1728 i.
Wm. 1762 i.
Northumberland
Jno. 1784 i.
Pittsylvania
Jno. 1786 i.
Southampton
Jos. 1777 i.
Surry
Edwd. 1676 w.
Westmoreland
Geo. 1786 i.
York
Chas. 1677 w.
HALES
Cumberland
Saml. 1797 i.
Henrico
Jno. 1752 i.
Jno. 1786 w.
Eliz. 1790 w.
Northumberland
Thos. 1658 w.
Westmoreland
Jno. 1728 w.
HALEY
Accomack
Benj. 1787 w.
Berkeley
Reuben 1790 w.
Brunswick
Jas. 1739 i.
Charlotte
Jno. 1781 w.
Jno. 1786 i.
Greensville
Jas. 1795 w.
Louisa
Jno. Sr. 1778 w.
Middlesex
Wm. 1760 a.
Orange
Edwd. 1753 w.
Westmoreland
Edwd. 1702 w.
HALFORD
Surry
Stephen 1752 i.
HALKUM
Henry
Grimes 1781 i.
HALL
Accomack
Thos. 1714 i.
Jno. 1725 w.
Thos. 1756 w.
Michael 1763 i.
Thos. 1775 w.
Asah 1778 i.
Danl. 1785 w.
Thos. 1788 w.

Danl. 1789 i.
Albemarle
Richd. 1760 w.
Amelia
Jno. 1779 w.
Wm. 1783 i.
Wm. 1778 w.
Ann 1788 w.
Boler 1787 w.
Augusta
Jas. 1765 i.
Edwd. 1796 w.
Bedford
Wm. 1759 i.
Jno. 1794 w.
Jno. 1799 i.
Berkeley
Geo. 1786 w.
Jno. 1787 i.
Jos. 1797 w.
Botetourt
Wm. 1773 w.
Brunswick
Hugh 1771 w.
Jas. 1783 i.
Chesterfield
Martha 1784 w.
Essex
Chas. 1708-9 i.
Mary 1788 i.
Fairfax
Wm. 1750 i.
Elisha 1751 w.
Jno. 1757 i.
Futerall 1766 i.
Michael 1788 w.
Eliz. 1795 a.
Kereni 1795 a.
Fauquier
Richd. 1774 w.
Richd. Lingen 1777 i.
Richd. 1777 i.
Frederick
Wm. 1764 w.
Wm. 1766 i.
Jas. 1798 w.
Halifax
Frances 1780 w.
Edwd. 1795 i.
Henry
Sarah 1791 w.
Isle of Wight
Jno. 1716 i.
Pool 1721 w.
Pool 1732 i.
Mary 1799 i.
King George
Jno. 1726 i.
Mary 1754 i.
Lancaster
Mary 1718 i.

Louisa
Jno. 1774 a.
Jno. 1780 w.
Loudoun
Jane 1785 w.
Jonathan 1790 i.
Richd. 1794 i.
Lunenburg
Wm. 1753 w.
Mecklenburg
Miles 1785 i.
Norfolk
Richd. 1648 w.
Edwd. 1675 w.
Durham 1750 w.
Thos. 1772 i.
Thos. 1782 w.
Edmd. 1787 w.
Thos. 1788 i.
Geo. Thos. 1789 w.
Jas. W. 1799 w.
Northampton
Nicholas 1646 w.
Emanuel 1696 w.
Jno. 1697 nw.
Jno. 1714 i.
Moses 1744 i.
Jno. 1750 w.
Jno. Sr. 1771 w.
Jno. Sr. 1777 i.
Northumberland
Thos. 1705 w.
Stephen 1726-7 w.
Thos. Jr. 1738 i.
Thos. Jr. 1742 i.
Thos. 1742 w.
Jno. 1758 w.
Rodham 1759 i.
James 1771 i.
Jno. 1778 i.
Jno. 1782 i.
Hutton 1783 i.
Stephen 1783 i.
Jno. 1791 i.
Stephen 1791 w.
Stephen 1794 i.
Pittsylvania
Jno. 1778 w.
Jno. 1788 w.
Powhatan
Saml. 1780 i.
Prince Edward
Wm. 1796 i.
Princess Anne
Thos. 1707 i.
Richmond
Eliz. 1719 nw.
Eliz. 1730 i.
Robt. 1766 w.
Wm. 1786 i.

Rockbridge
Andrew Sr. 1799 w.
Shenandoah
Jno. 1783 w.
Southampton
Geo. 1781 w.
Stafford
Jno. 1764 i.
Surry
Isaac 1730 w.
Washington
Isaac 1791 i.
Westmoreland
Thos. 1728 i.
Ann 1751 w.
Jeremiah 1770 i.
Leasure 1772 w.
York
Alex. 1655 w.
Frances 1658 i.
Wm. 1748 w.
HALLADAY
Isle of Wight
Saml. 1716 i.
HALLAM
Middlesex
Jno. 1677 a.
HALLAMAN
Isle of Wight
Thos. 1778 w.
Southampton
Wm. 1796 w.
HALLCOME
Southampton
Richd. 1795 i.
HALLE
Northampton
Emanuel 1666 w.
HALLET
Albemarle
Henry 1787 w.
HALLETT
Northampton
Wm. 1724 w.
Lettice 1754 w.
HALLEY
Bedford
Henry 1799 w.
Fairfax
Saml. 1779 w.
Jas. Sr. 1792 w.
HALLIDAY
Isle of Wight
Thos. 1773 i.
Norfolk
Jonas 1718 w.
HALLIMAN
Isle of Wight
Chris. 1691 w.
John 1751 i.

Southampton
Josiah Jno. 1765 w.
HALLING
Fairfax
Benj. 1745 a.
Jno. 1746 w.
Rubin 1746 i.
Wm. 1750 w.
HALLINGE
Fairfax
Reubin 1745 w.
HALLOMON
Northampton
Jno. 1650 w.
HALLOWELL
Isle of Wight
Sarah 1748 i.
Norfolk
Thos. 1693 w.
Jno. 1716 w.
Jno. 1752 w.
Princess Anne
Saml. 1751 i.
HALLS
Westmoreland
Jno. 1727 w.
Thos. 1727 i.
HALPENNY
Frederick
Robt. 1773 i.
HALSBUT
Northampton
Michael 1731 i.
HALSEY
Essex
Robt. 1703 i.
HALSTEAD
Norfolk
Jno. 1719 nw.
Henry 1724 i.
Jno. 1725 i.
Princess Anne
Jas. 1784 w.
HAM
Amelia
Geo. 1782 w.
Thos. 1782 w.
Thos. 1784 i.
Geo. 1794 w.
Spotsylvania
Saml. 1738 w.
Westmoreland
Manuel 1703 i.
York
Jos. 1638 w.
Jerome 1717 i.
HAMBLEN
Prince Edward
Danl. Sr. 1784 w.

HAMBLET
Pittsylvania
Morris 1780 w.
HAMBLETON
Amherst
Luke 1787 a.
Augusta
Jas. 1755 a.
Brunswick
Jos. 1785 w.
Cumberland
Martha 1763 w.
Wm. 1778 w.
Essex
Jno. 1783 i.
Fauquier
Wm. 1789 i.
Henrico
Jas. 1735 i.
King George
Wm. 1735 i.
Lancaster
Jno. 1699 w.
Louisa
David 1791 i.
Orange
Mathew 1783 w.
Powhatan
Mary 1795 i.
Prince Edward
Ester 1781 w.
Alex. 1790 w.
Westmoreland
Jas. 1727 w.
Grace 1727 w.
HAMBLIN
Chesterfield
Chas. 1797 w.
Lunenburg
Chas. Jr. 1786 w.
Prince Edward
Jno. 1786 i.
Obedience 1795 w.
Obedience 1797 w.
HAMBLING
Prince Edward
Jno. 1785 w.
HAMBRICK
Fauquier
Jas. 1778 i.
HAMBY
Northampton
Chas. 1720 w.
Wm. 1720 w.
HAMELTON
Essex
Wm. 1701 i.
Jno. 1784 i.
HAMERIN
Northampton
Wm. 1701 w.

HAMERTON
Middlesex
Edmd. 1716 w.
HAMES
Richmond
Chas. 1751 i.
Wm. 1754 w.
HAMILTON
Amelia
Andrew 1747 a.
Albemarle
Henry 1750 i.
Augusta
Jas. 1755 i.
Saml. 1783 i.
Andrew 1790 w.
Archd. 1794 w.
Wm. 1795 w.
Bedford
Thos. 1772 w.
Brunswick
Nancy 1787 w.
Botetourt
Godfrey 1795 w.
Fairfax
Jos. 1792 a.
Fauquier
Wm. 1788 w.
Henry 1790 i.
Darkis 1794 w.
Frederick
Jas. 1776 w.
Greenbrier
Andrew 1796 w.
Lancaster
Saml. 1774 w.
Ann 1777 w.
Louisa
David 1772 i.
Loudoun
Jas. 1775 w.
Robt. 1777 w.
Eliz. 1781 w.
Henry 1790 i.
Norfolk
Jno. 1755 i.
Northampton
Robt. 1703 w.
Andrew 1780 w.
Prince Edward
Jno. 1787 w.
Princess Anne
Wm. 1695 w.
Richd. 1697 w.
Gavin 1782 w.
Richmond
Gilbert 1768 w.
Ann 1784 w.
Rockbridge
Robt. 1783 w.

Stafford
Jno. 1759 i.
Sussex
Geo. 1764 i.
Westmoreland
Jno. 1755 i.
York
Jno. 1743 i.
Thos. 1783 i.
HAMLET
Amherst
Archer 1795 w.
Halifax
Wm. Sr. 1797 w.
HAMLIN
Amelia
Jno. 1783 w.
Chesterfield
Jno. 17— i.
Prince George
Richd. 1718 i.
Eliz. 1720 w.
Jno. 1725 w.
Surry
Chas. 1721 i.
Thos. 1750 i.
Sussex
Stephen 1775 w.
Stephen 1799 i.
HAMMACK
Richmond
Wm. 1730 w.
HAMMET
Culpeper
Wm. 1777 i.
HAMMETT
Westmoreland
Danl. 1750 i.
HAMMIL
Shenandoah
Peter 1790 a.
HAMMITT
Middlesex
Wm. 1740 w.
Ohio
Benj. 1791 w.
HAMMOCK
Albemarle
Jno. 1771 i.
Frederick
Rudolph 1787 w.
Rudolph 1798 i.
Lunenburg
Wm. 1785 w.
Wm. 1797 i.
Richmond
Wm. 1701 w.
Robt. 1786 w.
Westmoreland
Wm. 1724 i.

HAMMON
Cumberland
Jno. Sr. 1759 w.
Northampton
Philip 1726 w.
HAMMOND
Brunswick
Wm. 1754 w.
Botetourt
Peter 1797 i.
Frederick
Thos. 1747 a.
Lancaster
Thos. 1745 i.
Jas. 1741 i.
Norfolk
Wm. 1798 w.
Northumberland
Wm. 1727 i.
Jno. 1759 w.
Gedion 1764 i.
Pittsylvania
Edwin 1794 i.
Richmond
Martin 1734 i.
Geo. 1746 i.
Eliz. 1749 i.
Job 1758 w.
Wm. 1758 i.
Wm. 1764 i.
Jno. 1771 w.
Winifred 1777 w.
Thos. 1778 w.
Thos. 1783 i.
Thos. 1785 w.
Lancaster
Chas. 1767 w.
HAMMONS
Amelia
Jno. 1745 w.
HAMMONTREE
Cumberland
Harris 1786 a.
HAMNER
Albemarle
Robt. 1750 w.
Wm. 1780 w.
Nicho. 1794 i.
Mecklenburg
Jas. 1793 w.
York
Nicho. 1705 i.
HAMOCK
Richmond
Jno. 1707 w.
HAMON
Lancaster
Chas. 1735 w.
Richmond
Job 1718 w.

HAMOND
Northumberland
Peter Sr. 1711 w.
Richmond
William 1718 i.
Martin 1729 w.
Thomas 1734 i.
HAMONTREE
Northumberland
David 1770 i.
HAMPLTON
Northampton
Allin 1784 i.
HAMPTON
Bedford
Jno. 1778 i.
Brunswick
Henry 1794 w.
Fairfax
Jno. 1748 w.
Margt. 1773 i.
Jno. 1795 i.
Jno. 1797 a.
Fauquier
Richd. 1766 w.
Frederick
Jno. 1751 w.
Geo. 1779 w.
Thos. 1788 w.
Henry 1794 w.
Halifax
Elkanah 1778 w.
Henry
Lilyan 1779 w.
Jno. 1799 i.
Isle of Wight
Thos. 1703 w.
Thos. 1730 i.
Jno. 1735 w.
Benj. 1794 w.
Northumberland
Jno. 1652 i.
Pittsylvania
Thos. 1797 w.
Prince William
Henry 1779 i.
Jos. 1740 i.
Stafford
Thos. 1737 i.
Jno. 1747 i.
Wm. 1749 w.
HAMTON
Goochland
Henry 1735 i.
HANBACK
Culpeper
Jacob 1785 w.
HANBURY
Norfolk
Jno. 1719 i.
Jno. 1744-5 w.

Thos. 1785 w.
HANBY
Northampton
Richd. 1683 w.
Danl. 1709 w.
Jos. 1710 i.
Nathan 1766 i.
Richd. 1771 w.
Richd. 1781 i.
Jno. 1782 w.
HANCE
Orange
Adam 1747 w.
HANCHELWOOD
Goochland
Jno. 1754 i.
HANCHER
Frederick
Jno. 1794 i.
HANCKS
Richmond
Wm. 1732 w.
HANCOCK
Accomack
Wm. 1775 w.
Bedford
Geo. 1783 w.
Simon 1791 w.
Wm. 1791 i.
Brunswick
Robt. 1765 a.
Benj. 1789 w.
Henry 1795 w.
Chesterfield
Small. 1760 w.
Jno. 1768 w.
Geo. Sr. 1795 w.
Geo. 1797 i.
Cumberland
Jno. 1763 w.
Jno. 1769 a.
Frederick
Jno. 1749 i.
Henrico
Robt. 1708-9 w.
Johan 1726 w.
Princess Anne
Geo. 1720 w.
Geo. 1729 i.
Geo. 1735 w.
Wm. 1736 w.
Simon 1739 w.
Joshua 1742 i.
Wm. 1759 w.
Wm. 1782 w.
Wm. 1784 i.
Ann 1785 w.
Ann R. 1797 w.
Prince William
Scarlet 1740 w.

Southampton
Wm. 1768 w.
Saml. 1799 i.
Surry
Jno. 1732 w.
Jane 1734 w.
Susanna 1750 w.
Sussex
Clement 1759 w.
Anthony 1762 i.
Jno. 1762 w.
Sarah 1765 w.
Wm. 1765 w.
Benj. 1777 w.
Wm. 1778 w.
Mary 1784 w.
Rebecca 1786 w.
Westmoreland
Richd. 1708 i.
York
Thos. 1738 i.
HANCOCKE
Norfolk
Simon 1654 i.
Princess Anne
Ashall 1714 w.
HAND
Fauquier
Wm. 1763 i.
HANDCOCK
Henrico
Jno. 1702 i.
Princess Anne
Simon 1701 w.
Southampton
Henry 1782 i.
Surry
Jos. 1750 i.
HANDCOCKE
Norfolk
Wm. 1687 w.
HANDLEY
Greenbrier
Archibald 1796 w.
Madison
Thos. 1799 a.
Stafford
Bryant 1733 w.
HANDERLIN
Essex
Jno. 1714 w.
HANDLY
Botetourt
Alex. 1781 w.
Alex. 1782 i.
Augusta
Geo. 1756 a.
Frederick
Geo. 1782 w.
York
Robt. 1685 i.

Eliz. 1701 i.
HANES
Culpeper
Ezekiel 1781 w.
Carlele 1784 i.
HANEY
Northumberland
Isaac 1765 w.
HANGAR
Augusta
Fredk. 1799 w.
HANKINS
Charlotte
Jno. 1797 a.
Pittsylvania
Danl. 1797 i.
York
Sarah 1750 i.
HANKLE
York
Thos. 1743 i.
HANKLEY
York
Thos. 1760 i.
HANKS
Amelia
Thos. 1777 w.
Middlesex
Geo. 1792 i.
Richmond
Katherine 1779 i.
Turner 1785 i.
HANLAND
Norfolk
Agness 1717 w.
Hugh 1718 w.
HANLEY
Westmoreland
Edwd. 1702 i.
HANNA
Greenbrier
Wm. 1789 i.
Rockbridge
Jno. 1781 a.
HANNAH
Amelia
Jno. 1798 w.
Botetourt
Geo. 1799 i.
Charlotte
Geo. Sr. 1783 w.
Andrew 1793 w.
Fairfax
Nicho. 1794 a.
HANNEGAN
Shenandoah
Michael 1798 w.
HANNEY
Princess Anne
Robt. 1700 w.
Josiah 1706-7 w.

HANNON
Frederick
Thos. 1758 i.
HANOR
Spotsylvania
Harmon 1794 w.
HANSBARGER
Augusta
Stephen 1776 w.
HANSBOROUGH
Amherst
Wm. 1778 w.
Stafford
Peter 1784 i.
Jas. 1784 w.
HANSEL
Augusta
Geo. 1795 i.
HANSFORD
Culpeper
Wm. 1754 w.
Sarah 1755 i.
Sallis 1765 w.
Isle of Wight
Lewis 1786 w.
King George
Stephen 1758 i.
Stephen 1772 w.
Orange
Chas. 1762 w.
York
Jno. 1661 w.
Jno. 1668 i.
Eliz. 1678 w.
Mrs. 1678-9 nw.
Thos. 1679 i.
Chas. 1702 w.
Wm. 1709 w.
Thos. 1720 w.
Wm. 1733 i.
Wm. 1736 w.
Jno. 1750 w.
Lucy 1751 w.
Wm. 1753 w.
Lucy 1760 w.
Chas. Sr. 1761 w.
Chas. 1778 w.
Thos. 1786 i.
HANSILL
Berkeley
Michael 1781 w.
HANSLEY
Norfolk
Edwd. 1750 w.
HANSON
Accomack
Jno. 1681 i.
Isle of Wight
Chas. 1794 i.
Loudoun
Gustavus 1794 w.

Middlesex
Jno. 1711 w.
York
Mary 1710 i.
HANTHORN
Berkeley
Jas. 1776 w.
HANVELL
Brunswick
Darkis 1796 w.
HAPGOOD
Norfolk
Wm. 1783 i.
HAPPER
Norfolk
Wm. 1757 w.
Sarah 1764 w.
Saml. 1775 w.
Saml. 1783 i.
Saml. 1785 w.
Wm. 1788 w.
Wm. 1792 i.
Wm. 1797 i.
HARA
Norfolk
Timothy 1675 w.
HARBERT
Henrico
Matthew 1786 w.
Lancaster
Edwd. 1692 w.
Princess Anne
Peter 1766 w.
Thos. 1735 i.
HARBISON
Botetourt
Wm. 1775 w.
Culpeper
Mathew 1774 i.
HARBOUR
Henry
Abner 1778 w.
Patrick
Thos. 1796 w.
Pittsylvania
Elijah 1770 i.
HARBUT
Princess Anne
Wm. 1798 w.
HARCUM
Northumberland
Wm. 1712 i.
Hannah 1718 i.
Jno. 1728-9 w.
Thos. 1759 w.
Wm. 1762 w.
Cuthbert 1792 w.
Jos. 1792 w.
Wm. 1796 w.

HARDAWAY
Amelia
Stith 1767 w.
Purify 1778 w.
HARDEE
Essex
Andrew 1710 i.
Andrew 1715 i.
Middlesex
Jos. 1729 w.
HARDEN
Chesterfield
Wm. 1786 w.
Fairfax
Wm. 1781 w.
Loudoun
Eliz. 1759 w.
Chas. 1796 i.
Norfolk
Wm. 1752 i.
Northumberland
Thos. 1726 i.
Prince William
Mark 1735 w.
Sussex
Frances 1784 i.
HARDESTY
Rappahannock
Jno. 1673 w.
HARDEY
Pittsylvania
Wm. 1793 i.
HARDGRAVES
Augusta
Jas. 1773 w.
HARDICH
Westmoreland
Margt. 1672 i.
HARDIE
Isle of Wight
Thos. 1717 w.
Middlesex
Jno. 1787 w.
Northumberland
Parrot 1763 w.
Stafford
Alex. 1754 i.
Sussex
Jno. 1773 w.
HARDIGE
Richmond
Jno. 1777 w.
HARDIN
Brunswick
Saml. 1732 w.
Charles City
Robt. 1770 i.
Culpeper
Geo. 1780 i.
Frederick
Ann 1762 i.

Halifax
Geo. 1768 i.
Henrico
Thos. 1731 w.
Lancaster
Thos. 1698 i.
Middlesex
Geo. 1745 w.
Eliz. 1759 w.
Thos. 1759 w.
Surry
Benj. 1734 w.
Westmoreland
Jno. 1734 i.
HARDING
Accomack
Jonathan 1780 w.
Amherst
Groves 1781 w.
Essex
Richd. 1710 i.
Wm. 1723 w.
Goochland
Wm. 1768 w.
Wm. 1778 i.
Sarah 1797 w.
Henrico
Wm. 1746 w.
Isle of Wight
Sarah 1750 w.
Lunenburg
Thos. 1781 w.
Thos. 1782 w.
Norfolk
Thos. 1669 i.
Northumberland
Francis 1719 i
Thos. 1722 w.
Thos. 1751 i.
Thos. 1762 i.
Wm. 1762 w.
Sarah 1763 w.
Wm. 1765 i.
Mark 1775 w.
Wm. 1786 w.
Wm. 1799 i.
Stafford
Henry 1737-8 i.
Shenandoah
Wilmoth 1795 w.
HARDIWAY
Brunswick
Jno. 1780 w.
Marcum 1782 w.
Jno. 1790 i.
HARDWICH
Richmond
Geo. 1755 w.
Westmoreland
Geo. 1732 w.
Eliz. 1734 w.

Jas. 1737 w.
Jas. 1749 w.
HARDWICK
Albemarle
Thos. 1760 i.
Bedford
Robt. 1784 w.
Lunenburg
Jno. 1791 i.
Westmoreland
Jos. 1698 w.
Geo. 1704 w.
Geo. 1713 i.
Richd. 1718 i.
Wm. 1718 w.
Jos. 1727 w.
HARDY
Accomack
Peter 1778 w.
Amelia
Jno. 1767 i.
Isle of Wight
Geo. 1655 w.
Jno. 1677 w.
Geo. 1696 w.
Thos. 1717 i.
Richd. 1756 w.
Richd. 1789 w.
Thos. 1791w.
Lunenburg
Wm. 1791 w.
Jno. 1798 i.
Middlesex
Jno. 1786 w.
Northampton
Saml. 1729 i.
Pittsylvania
Thos. 1779 w.
Geo. 1795 w.
Richmond
Jno. 1701 w.
Westmoreland
Geo. 1717 i.
HARDYMAN
Charles City
Littleberry 1771 w.
John 1772 i.
Littleberry 1790 w.
Prince George
John 1716 i.
Littleberry 1726 w.
HARE
Chesterfield
Parker 1788 w.
Norfolk
Thos. 1761 w.
Josiah 1789 i.
Thos. 1790 i.
Rappahannock
Jas. 1659 i.

Surry
Wm. 1695 a.
HAREBOTTLE
Isle of Wight
Thos. 1705 w.
Rebecca 1706 w.
HARFORD
Northumberland
Jno. 1756 i.
Princess Anne
Wm. 1692 w.
Richmond
Henry 1737 w.
Henry 1776 w.
Thos. 1777 w.
HARGIS
Frederick
Francis 1752 i.
Westmoreland
Jno. 1730 w.
HARGRAVE
Surry
Richd. 1704 w.
Lemuel 1742 w.
Saml. 1755 w.
Wm. 1762 w.
Augustine 1763 w.
Mary 1769 w.
Hardah 1770 w.
Jos. 1776 w.
Richd. 1782 w.
Benj. 1784 i.
Robt. 1784 w.
Hartwell 1796 w.
Sussex
Thos. 1782 w.
Martha 1789 w.
York
Peter 1685 i.
HARGRESS
Accomack
Geo. 1750 i.
HARGROVE
Norfolk
Richd. 1686-7 w.
Benj. 1710-11 w.
Princess Anne
Jno. 1789 w.
Southampton
Michael 1777 i.
Surry
Bray 1728 i.
Benj. 1781 w.
Sussex
Josiah 1782 w.
HARISS
Sussex
Wm. 1782 w.
HARISTON
Accomack
Jno. 1733 i.

HARISTORY
Accomack
Jno. 1734 i.
HARKNEY
Prince William
Jno. 1744 a.
HARL
Loudoun
Eliz. 1796 w.
HARLAN
Berkeley
Stephen 1796 w.
Frederick
Aaron 1760 w.
Ann 1762 w.
HARLAND
Princess Anne
Hansard 1730 i.
HARLE
Fairfax
Jno. 1749 w.
Wm. 1750 w.
Jno. 1754 i.
Sarah 1784 i.
HARLES
Augusta
Philip 1772 w.
HARLEY
Frederick
Sigismund 1771 w.
HARLOE
Northampton
Jno. 1651 w.
HARLON
Berkeley
Elijah 1790 i.
HARLOW
Albemarle
Wm. 1772 w.
Fluvanna
Wm. 1784 i.
Goochland
Thos. 1751 w.
HARMAN
Accomack
Littleton 1778 i.
Rachel 1786 w.
Henry 1789 w.
Bayly 1792 w.
Henry 1797 i.
Augusta
Caleb 1763 a.
Jacob Sr. 1764 w.
Cumberland
Henry 1785 w.
Northampton
Teague 1684 w.
Wm. 1725 i.
Tabitha 1775 w.
Stafford
Chris. 1706 w.

York
Wm. 1670 w.
HARMANSON
Accomack
Argoll 1734 w.
Northampton
Thos. Sr. 1702 w.
Benj. 1703 i.
Henry 1709 w.
Thos. Sr. 1709 w.
Wm. 1709 i.
Henry 1710 i.
Jno. 1719 w.
Kendall 1720 w.
Thos. 1725 w.
Jno. 1731 w.
Wm. 1733 w.
Geo. 1735 w.
Gertrude 1738 w.
Susannah 1738 w.
Anne 1761 i.
Patrick 1775 w.
Jno. Jr. 1783 w.
Jno. Sr. 1787 w.
Jno. 1791 w.
Esther 1795 w.
HARMANTROUT
Augusta
Jno. 1757 a.
HARMAR
Northampton
Thos. 1671 i.
HARMENSON
Accomack
Barbara 1735 w.
HARMER
Albemarle
Geo. 1786 w.
HARMON
Accomack
Cornelias 1707 w.
Simon 1770 w.
Wm. 1773 w.
Littleton 1777 w.
Jno. 1779 w.
Botetourt
Jno. 1778 i.
Jno. 1779 i.
Jacob 1792 w.
Brunswick
Geo. 1797 w.
Essex
Jno. 1750 i.
Hardy
David 1791 w.
HARMOND
Princess Anne
Jno. 1739 w.
HARMONSON
Northampton
Kendall 1755 w.

Matthew 1755 w.
Eliz. 1757 w.
Geo. 1762 w.
HARMONTROUT
Botetourt
Geo. 1798 w.
HARMOR
Northampton
Thos. 1671 w.
HARNAGE
Northampton
Stephen 1722 w.
Jacob 1746 w.
HARNEDGE
Northampton
Stephen 1719 w.
HARNESS
Westmoreland
Wm. 1734 w.
HARNISON
Prince George
Thos. 1720 w.
HARPER
Amelia
Edwd. 1760 w.
Augusta
Michael 1767 i.
Berkeley
Robt. 1782 w.
Jno. 1793 w.
Brunswick
Newman 1744 w.
Nathl. 1794 w.
Thos. 1795 i.
Essex
Solomon 1699 w.
Thos. 1709 w.
Wm. 1714 i.
Fairfax
Jno. Withers 1751 i.
Robt. 1782 w.
Robt. 1789 a.
Nancy 1791 a.
King George
Thos. 1737 i.
Daniel 1744 i.
Lancaster
Robt. 1750 w.
Mecklenburg
Jno. 1794 w.
Norfolk
David 1772 w.
Jas. 1799 w.
Northampton
Francis 1673 w.
Thos. 1688-9 i.
Northumberland
Jasua 1783 w.
Orange
Saml. 1769 i.
Saml. 1777 w.

Prince Edward
Edmd. 1779 w.
Mary 1782 i.
Hannah 1791 w.
Jas. 1791 i.
Princess Anne
Richd. 1694 w.
David 1735 w.
Jno. 1749 i.
Jno. 1756 i.
Margt. 1761 i.
Wm. 1761 w.
Margt. 1762 i.
Jas. 1772 i.
Rappahannock
Thos. 1634 w.
Richmond
Wm. 1761 w.
Stafford
Thos. 1758 w.
Sussex
Wm. 1757 w.
Wyatt 1759 w.
Benj. 1760 i.
Edwd. 1765 w.
Westmoreland
Danl. 1671 w.
Wm. 1709 w.
Jno. 1799 w.
HARPIN
Westmoreland
Henry 1671 w.
HARPINE
Shenandoah
Thos. 1780 a.
HARR
Shenandoah
Simon 1799 i.
HARRA
Charlotte
Michael 1786 w.
Isabella 1789 w.
HARRAD
Northampton
Nicholas 1663 i.
HARRALSON
Hanover
Peter 1733 w.
Paul 1734 w.
HARRELL
Lancaster
Gilbert 1753 w.
HARRENSPARGER
Culpeper
Jno. 1760 w.
HARRILL
Fauquier
Jas. 1763 i.
HARRILSON
Halifax
Jno. 1765 w.

HARRINGTON
Northampton
Edwd. 1653 w.
HARRIOT
Richmond
Jas. 1754 nw.
HARRIS
Accomack
Thos. 1753 i.
Jno. 1785 nw.
Albemarle
Robt. 1765 w.
Mourning 1776 w.
Wm. 1788 w.
Jas. 1792 w.
Chris. 1795 i.
Jno. 1796 w.
Jas. 1797 w.
Jas. 1799 i.
Amelia
Benj. 1798 w.
Amherst
Lee 1792 w.
Berkeley
Jos. 1797 i.
Brunswick
Francis 1746 w.
Bowler 1782 i.
Matthew 1790 w.
Campbell
Wm. 1783 w.
Arthur Sr. 1799 w.
Charles City
Jas. 1791 w.
Charlotte
Jno. 1795 i.
Culpeper
David 1758 w.
Cumberland
Jno. 1751 w.
Sarah 1753 w.
Benj. 1759 w.
Benj. 1761 w.
Jas. 1767 w.
Peter 1771 w.
Richd. 1774 w.
Mary 1783 w.
Jas. 1794 w.
Fairfax
Jno. 1748 a.
Anthony 1778 i.
Benj. 1793 w.
Benj. 1798 a.
Fauquier
Geo. 1798 i.
Frederick
Jno. 1764 i.
Goochland
Henry 1776 w.
Henry 1778 w.

Greensville
Jas. 1784 w.
Jas. 1792 i.
Nathan 1793 w.
Henrico
Thos. 1679 w.
Peter 1689 w.
Wm. 1690 i.
Peter 1703-4 w.
Thos. Sr. 1730 w.
Mary 1745 w.
Jas. 1794 w.
Jas. 1798 i.
Henry
Moses 1779 i.
Isle of Wight
Thos. 1672 w.
Martha 1676 i.
Edwd. 1677 i.
Thos. 1688 w.
Jno. 1713 w.
Thos. 1713 i.
Geo. 1720 w.
Thos. 1729 w.
Thos. 1730-31 i.
Thos. 1732 i.
Edwd. 1734 w.
Edwd. 1740 w.
Robt. 1740 w.
Wm. 1740 i.
Thos. 1755 i.
Jno. 1785 i.
Ann 1795 i.
Jno. 1795 w.
Jno. 1798 i.
Matthew 1798 w.
Lancaster
Jno. 1685 w.
Catherine 1687 nw.
Geo. [?] 1693 w.
Jerry [?] 1694 i.
Edwd. 1726 i.
Jeriah 1777 i.
Jno. 1786 w.
Jas. 1787 i.
Jno. 1787 w.
Loudoun
Saml. 1764 w.
Wm. 1767 i.
Jno. 1778 i.
Saml. 1783 w.
Saml. 1786 i.
Louisa
Benj. 1765 w.
Benj. 1775 i.
Benj. 1784 a.
Edwd. 1799 i.
Mecklenburg
Wm. 1779 w.
Wm. 1796 i.

Montgomery
Nicholas 1784 i.
Norfolk
Jno. 1737 w.
Jno. 1739 w.
Thos. 1782 i.
Thos. 1799 w.
Northumberland
Jno. 1719 w.
Orange
Esther 1759 w.
Thos. 1782 w.
Thos. 1783 w.
Pittsylvania
Saml. 1799 w.
Powhatan
Priscilla 1778 i.
Edith 1779 w.
Ann 1787 w.
Jos. 1792 w.
Wm. 1794 w.
Prince Edward
Giles 1775 i.
Micajah 1779 w.
Matthew 1783 w.
Thos. 1784 w.
Princess Anne
Wm. 1696 a.
Robt. 1761 w.
Richmond
Hugh 1713 w.
Philip 1735 w.
Jno. 1762 w.
Wm. 1785 i.
Southampton
Martin 1750 w.
Jacob 1763 w.
Jno. 1764 w.
Simon 1769 w.
Joshua 1770 i.
Jno. 1773 w.
Simon 1773 w.
Benj. 1774 w.
Jno. 1781 w.
Nathan 1785 w.
Carter 1786 w.
Jas. 1789 w.
Henry 1791 w.
Hardy 1791 i.
West 1794 w.
Landon 1795 i.
Nathan 1792 i.
Jno. D. 1796 w.
Edmd. 1797 w.
Wm. 1797 i.
Surry
Richd. 1679 w.
Jno. 1698-9 i.
Eliz. 1711 w.
Jos. 1719 i.
Jno. 1720 w.

Margt. 1721 w.
Wm. 1721 w.
Michael 1743 w.
Edwd. 1765 w.
Jno. 1771 w.
Hopkin 1775 w.
Benj. 1777 i.
Wm. 1797 w.
Pleasant 1799 w.
Sussex
Wm. 1782 w.
Howell 1797 w.
Westmoreland
Jno. 1675 w.
Thos. 1695 i.
Arthur 1698 w.
Jas. 1698 w.
Wm. 1727 i.
Arthur 1730 i.
Jno. 1735 i.
York
Robt. 1716 w.
Jno. 1727 w.
Matthew 1727 i.
Thos. 1728 i.
Thos. 1729 i.
Robt. 1738 i.
Wm. 1739 w.
Mary 1741-2 i.
Jno. 1748 w.
Richd. 1756 w.
Wm. 1761 w.
Jno. 1783 w.
HARRISON
Accomack
Flowerdue 1720 nw.
Jno. 1747 i.
Jos. 1751 w.
Alex. 1760 w.
Stephen 1760 w.
Fliphen 1761 i.
Eliz. 1762 w.
Alex. 1765 i.
Jas. 1779 i.
Littleton 1786 i.
Caleb 1797 w.
Albemarle
Chas. 1762 w.
Amherst
Battaile 1775 w.
Wm. 1782 a.
Francis 1789 a.
Jno. 1795 i.
Augusta
Jos. 1748 i.
Gideon 1761 i.
Robt. 1761 w.
Jno. Jr. 1763 w.
Danl. 1770 a.
Danl. 1771 w.
Jno. 1771 w.

Jno. 1794 i.
Berkeley
Saml. 1789 w.
Botetourt
Jno. 1785 nw.
Jno. Sr. 1786 i.
Brunswick
Jas. 1762 w.
Jos. 1763 w.
Thos. 1770 w.
Gabriel 1779 w.
Arthur 1783 w.
Henry 1786 w.
Wm. 1786 w.
Joney 1787 w.
Benj. 1790 w.
Wm. 1791 w.
Henry 1793 i.
Benj. 1794 w.
Jas. 1796 w.
Nathl. 1796 w.
Wm. 1798 i.
Benj. 1799 w.
Nathl. 1799 i.
Charles City
Benj. 1791 w.
Benj. 1797 i.
Benj. Jr. 1799 w.
Chesterfield
Sarah 1781 w.
Culpeper
Jno. 1763 a.
Cumberland
Wm. 1753 w.
Wm. 1755 w.
Benj. 1761 w.
Carter Henry 1793 w.
Essex
Jas. 1712 i.
Andrew 1718 w.
Ann 1761 i.
Elias 1797 w.
Fairfax
Geo. 1748 w.
Jeremiah 1750 i.
Henry 1749 a.
Geo. 1752 i.
Thos. 1757 i.
Fauquier
Thos. 1774 w.
Wm. 1775 i.
Benj. 1798 w.
Frederick
Geo. 1772 w.
Thos. 1791 i.
Greensville
Mary 1785 w.
Nathl. 1785 w.
Miles 1792 i.
Halifax
Jno. 1761 w.

Peterson 1782 i.
Henrico
Edwd. 1746 i.
Isle of Wight
Wm. 1720 i.
Jno. 1725 i.
Wm. 1744 i.
Wm. 1762 w.
Wm. 1770 w.
Henry 1772 w.
Henry Jr. 1773 i.
Eliz. 1774 w.
Eliz. 1775 i.
Jno. 1791 w.
Eliz. 1798 w.
Richd. 1798 i.
Jno. 1799 i.
King George
Geo. 1749 i.
Wm. 1774 a.
Robt. 1776 a.
Obadiah G. 1795 i.
Lancaster
Danl. 1677 i.
Jos. 1700 w.
Louisa
Jos. 1788 w.
Lunenburg
Collier 1789 i.
Middlesex
Jos. 1701 i.
Montgomery
Richd. 1783 w.
Amos. 1794 w.
Northampton
Robt. 1683 w.
Silbe 1721 w.
Salathiel 1778 w.
Northumberland
Geo. 1744 w.
Anne 1754 w.
Geo. 1777 w.
Ann Nut 1778 w.
Winnifred 1784 w.
Jas. 1789 w.
Jno. R. 1795 w.
Ohio
Jno. 1783 a.
Wm. 1785 a.
Orange
Andrew 1754 i.
Pittsylvania
Benj. 1779 w.
Wm. 1796 i.
Henry 1797 i.
Prince Edward
Wm. 1765 w.
Prince George
Hannah 1714 i.
Princess Anne
Henry 1706 w.

Jno. 1748 i.
Jno. 1750 i.
Jas. 1764 w.
Henry Sr. 1788 w.
Henry 1791 i.
Prince William
Cuthbert 1780 w.
Ann 1783 w.
Burr 1791 w.
Richmond
Robt. 1720 w.
Jas. 1726 i.
Ann 1748 w.
Jas. 1757 nw.
Matthew 1767 w.
Geo. 1784 w.
Stafford
Wm. 1734 i.
Wm. 1746 i.
Southampton
Henry 1755 i.
Saml. 1776 w.
Wm. 1777 w.
Amy 1786 w.
Surry
Benj. 1712 w.
Nathl. 1727 w.
Mary 1732 w.
Solomon 1739 w.
Henry 1753 i.
Benj. 1759 w.
Mary 1769 w.
Margaret 1798 w.
Sussex
Henry 1773 i.
Jno. 1776 w.
Henry 1798 i.
Westmorcland
Geo. 1713 w.
Wm. 1726 i.
Thos. 1727 i.
Geo. 1734 w.
Willoughby 1750 w.
Wm. 1750 i.
Robt. 1761 i.
Saml. 1764 w.
Jno. 1772 w.
Danl. 1782 w.
Saml. 1784 w.
Magdalene 1786 w.
Jno. 1789 i.
Wm. 1791 i.
Hannah 1793 w.
York
Robt. 1668 i.
Jno. 1690 i.
Robt. 1710 w.
Richd. 1722 w.
Richd. 1753 i.
Jno. 1775 w.

HARRISS
Princess Anne
Eliz. 1786 w.
Southampton
Mary 1782 w.
HARRISTOY
Accomack
Jno. 1737 i.
HARROD
Sussex
Michael 1797 i.
HARROLD
Washington
Jas. 1796 i.
HARROOD
Essex
Peter 1709 w.
HARROT
Frederick
Hugh 1744 i.
HARROW
Essex
Hugh 1720 i.
Shenandoah
David 1787 w.
HARROWER
Lancaster
Alex. 1740 i.
HARROX
Norfolk
Jno. 1719 i.
HARRUP
Brunswick
Wm. 1779 i.
Jonathan 1791 i.
Sussex
Jonathan 1797 w.
HARSBERGER
Shenandoah
Barbara 1797 w.
HARSON
Fairfax
Jeryah 1751 w.
HART
Albemarle
Jno. 1796 w.
Augusta
Wm. 1760 i.
Berkeley
Thos. Jr. 1795 w.
Andrew 1796 a.
Thos. 1797 i.
Campbell
Wm. 1786 w.
Martha 1790 w.
Charlotte
Jno. 1793 w.
Thos. 1795 i.
Frederick
Danl. 1748 w.

Halifax
Francis 1787 w.
Lancaster
Jno. 1711 w.
Jno. 1717 i.
Northampton
Stephen 1779 i.
Orange
Jno. 1743 a.
Richmond
Leonard 1754 i.
Jno. 1785 w.
Rockbridge
Valentine 1792 w.
Stafford
Edwd. 1703 i.
Southampton
Eliz. 1770 w.
Henry 1770 w.
Robt. 1770 w.
Drury 1791 w.
Jno. 1792 w.
Henry 1793 w.
Saml. 1793 w.
Jesse 1796 w.
Robt. 1797 w.
Jno. 1797 i.
Surry
Robt. 1720 w.
Henry 1739 w.
Wm. 1744 w.
Edwd. 1782 w.
Wm. 1798 w.
HARTELY
Northumberland
Jno. 1787 i.
HARTFORD
Henrico
Jno. 1705 w.
Northumberland
Eliz. 1764 w.
HARTGROVE
Princess Anne
Margt. 1797 w.
HARTGROVES
Northumberland
Jno. 1740-1 w.
HARTHORN
Sussex
Joshua 1768 w.
HARTLAND
Lancaster
Wm. 1697 w.
HARTLEY
Fairfax
Jas. 1799 i.
Princess Anne
Sarah 1785 w.
Richmond
Jas. 1718 i.
Jas. 1719 i.

Sussex
Clements 1786 w.
Westmoreland
Jno. 1695 i.
Jonas 1720 i.
Jno. 1728 w.
HARTLY
Northumberland
Jno. 1728-9 i.
HARTMAN
Loudoun
Matthias 1783 w.
HARTREE
Northampton
Elias 1664 w.
Jane 1665 w.
HARTWELL
Surry
Jno. 1714 w.
HARTWILL
York
Jno. 1648 i.
HARVEY
Brunswick
Thos. 1781 w.
Ann 1782 w.
Charlotte
Thos. 1782 w.
Cumberland
Thos. 1782 w.
Isle of Wight
Jno. 1779 w.
Lancaster
Onesephorus 1732 w.
Northumberland
Jas. 1726-7 i.
Jno. 1744 w.
Wm. 1745 w.
Geo. 1764 w.
Jno. 1780 w.
Onesiphorus 1798 w.
Princess Anne
Thos. 1719 w.
Thos. 1726 i.
Alex. 1737 w.
Sarah 1746 w.
Francis 1761 i.
Chas. 1793 w.
Richmond
Chas. 1720 w.
Stafford
Jno. 1700 w.
Westmoreland
Jno. 1737 i.
Jas. 1766 i.
Mungo 1794 w.
HARVEYS
Lancaster
Richd. 1675 i.
HARVIE

Albemarle
Jno. 1768 w.
HARWAR
Essex
Thos. 1698 w.
Saml. 1710 i.
Thos. 1713 w.
HARWARD
Lancaster
Geo. 1703 w.
Ann 1742 i.
Mary 1737 w.
HARWAY
Essex
Henry 1723 w.
HARWELL
Brunswick
Thos. 1760 w.
Saml. 1767 w.
Jas. 1771 w.
Absolom 1775 w.
Prince George
Thos. 1719 i.
Sussex
Mark 1785 w.
Peter 1796 i.
HARWICK
Northumberland
Jos. 1776 i.
HARWIN
Henrico
Jno. 1689 i.
HARWOOD
Charles City
Wm. B. 1790 w.
Charlotte
Francis 1767 w.
Essex
Peter 1709 i.
Henrico
Saml. 1782 w.
Jno. 1784 w.
Wm. 1790 w.
Jno. Jr. 1792 i.
Thos. 1796 i.
Elisha 1799 w.
Lunenburg
Geo. 1751 w.
Northampton
Nicho. 1639 w.
Stafford
Wm. 1707 w.
Surry
Jno. 1753 i.
Sussex
Phillip 1778 w.
Danl. 1797 w.
Saml. 1799 w.
York
Thos. 1657 w.
Thos. 1700 w.

Thos. 1738 i.
Humphrey 1789 w.
Wm. 1799 w.
HARWY
Surry
Wm. 1704 w.
HARY
Isle of Wight
Thos. 1719 a.
HASE
Essex
Jno. 1765 w.
HASELDINE
Frederick
Humphrey 1749 i.
HASELRIGG
Westmoreland
Jas. 1713 i.
HASELTON
York
Sarah 1704 ab.
HASH
Montgomery
Jno. 1784 w.
HASKEW
Amelia
Jos. 1777 i.
Orange
Jno. 1798 i.
HASKINS
Brunswick
Aaron 1781 w.
Chris. 1795 w.
Jno. 1798 i.
Charlotte
Wm. 1799 i.
Chesterfield
Creed 1781 w.
Creed 1790 w.
Henrico
Edwd. 1727 w.
Wm. 1745 w.
Aaron 1746 w.
Powhatan
Edwd. 1789 w.
Prince Edward
Thos. 1798 w.
Edwd. 1799 i.
Princess Anne
Richd. 1716 w.
Job 1760 w.
Prince William
Jno. 1786 w.
HASLEWOOD
Essex
Geo. 1699 i.
Middlesex
Mary 1711 w.
Thos. 1729 i.

HASLIP
Fluvanna
Wm. 1782 w.
HASNETT
Norfolk
Jno. 1654 i.
HASTED
Norfolk
Henry 1730 w.
HASTELL
Norfolk
Edwd. 1678 i.
HASTENS
Amelia
Jno. 1763 w.
Wm. 1786 w.
Sutton 1795 w.
HASTINGS
Accomack
Jno. 1739 i.
Richd. 1775 w.
Scarborough 1796 nw.
Amelia
Sarah 1799 w.
Chesterfield
Geo. 1776 w.
Frederick
Job 1771 w.
HASTINS
Accomack
Wm. 1737 i.
HASTY
Southampton
Jas. 1768 w.
Moses 1798 i.
HATCH
Norfolk
Anthony 1688-9 w.
Prince George
Jno. 1722 w.
York
Wm. 1751 i.
HATCHELL
Mecklenburg
Wm. 1770 w.
HATCHER
Bedford
Edwd. 1782 w.
Reuben 1790 w.
Chesterfield
Obedience 17— w.
Henry 1761 w.
Saml. 1762 w.
Wm. 1766 w.
Nathl. 1787 w.
Wm. 1788 w.
Wm. 1789 i.
Saml. 1794 w.
Saml. Jr. 1795 i.
Saml. 1797 w.

Cumberland
Fredk. 1782 w.
Goochland
Prissila 1734 w.
Josiah 1762 w.
Thos. 1797 w.
Sarah 1798 w.
Henrico
Henry 1677 a.
Wm. 1680 w.
Wm. Jr. 1694 w.
Edwd. 1711 i.
Wm. 1715 i.
Benj. Sr. 1728 w.
Wm. 1736 w.
Henry 1746 i.
Jas. 1757 i.
Loudoun
Wm. 1781 w.
Lunenburg
Benj. 1751 w.
Powhatan
Eliz. 1789 w.
Chas. 1795 w.
HATCHETT
Amelia
Wm. 1784 w.
Charlotte
Thos. 1773 i.
Chesterfield
Jno. 1747 w.
Lunenburg
Edwd. 1789 w.
HATFIELD
Accomack
Elial 1764 i.
Southampton
Wm. 1755 w.
Josiah 1779 w.
HATHABY
Norfolk
Wm. 1673 i.
HATHAWAY
Essex
Thos. 1716 i.
Fauquier
Jno. 1786 w.
Jas. 1799 i.
Lancaster
Wm. 1772 w.
HATHEWAY
Lancaster
Francis 1719 i.
HATLY
Surry
Shard 1720 w.
HATON
Frederick
Robt. 1768 i.
Jno. 1771 w.

HATRICK
Augusta
Adam 1775 i.
HATSEL
Mecklenburg
Wm. 1772 i.
Stephen 1781 w.
HATT
Prince George
Wm. 1720 w.
HATTERSLEY
Norfolk
Margt. 1675 i.
Princess Anne
Thos. 1706 i.
HATTERSLOY
Fairfax
Wm. 1795 a.
HATTERSLY
Princess Anne
Dinah 1727 w.
HATTON
Frederick
Bartholomew 1765 i.
Isle of Wight
Thos. 1761 i.
Norfolk
Jno. 1650 w.
Robt. 1681 w.
Francis 1688 w.
Jno. 1702 w.
Robt. 1720 w.
Francis 1746 w.
Robt. 1758 i.
Lewis 1785 w.
Robt. 1785 w.
HAUL
Northumberland
Jno. 1781 w.
HAVATT
Norfolk
Mary 1671 w.
HAVEN
Montgomery
Jno. 1782 w.
Westmoreland
Stephen 1716 w.
HAVERNON
Lancaster
Simon 1721 i.
HAVENOR
Augusta
Nicho. 1769 w.
HAW
Augusta
Henry 1755 a.
HAWES
Essex
Jno. 1781 w.
Saml. 1786 w.
Isaac 1789 w.

Richmond
Henry 1717 w.
HAWKER
Pittsylvania
Basil 1798 w.
Princess Anne
Saml. 1726 i.
HAWKING
Frederick
Jos. 1771 i.
HAWKINS
Amelia
Benj. 1745 a.
Campbell
Wm. 1793 w.
Berkeley
Wm. 1798 i.
Botetourt
Benj. 1780 w.
Charlotte
Jno. 1795 i.
Culpeper
Benj. 1793 w.
Essex
Jno. 1726 w.
Thos. 1739 w.
Young 1758 w.
Wm. 1769 w.
Jno. 1771 i.
Levin 1777 w.
Wm. 1781 w.
Birkenhead 1782 w.
Thos. 1786 w.
Fairfax
Jno. 1754 i.
Mary 1777 w.
Frederick
Thos. 1748 i.
Jos. 1770 w.
Wm. 1782 w.
Henrico
Jane 1790 w.
Isle of Wight
Thos. 1694 i.
Wms. 1739 i.
Mary 1749 i.
Jno. Sr. 1761 w.
Saml. 1779 i.
Jno. 1784 nw.
Benj. 1785 w.
Wm. 1788 w.
Saml. 1797 i.
Lancaster
Jno. 1686 w.
Loudoun
Jno. 1795 i.
Lunenburg
Thos. 1759 w.
Norfolk
Jas. 1680-1 i.

Northampton
Ann 1648 w.
Jno. 1721 w.
Gideon 1729 w.
Gittings 1729 i.
Jno. Sr. 1734 i.
Frances 1757 w.
Northumberland
Jno. 1652 w.
Jno. 1742 i.
Orange
Wm. 1776 w.
Moses 1778 w.
Jas. 1786 w.
Prince Edward
Benj. 1777 w.
Jos. 1782 w.
Rappahannock
Thos. 1677 w.
Spotsylvania
Nich. 1754 w.
Jos. 1769 w.
Philemon 1779 w.
Jno. 1764 a.
Stafford
Thos. 1700 i.
Thos. 1736 i.
Thos. 1747 i.
Washington
Jno. 1794 w.
Westmoreland
Jno. 1702 i.
York
Wm. 1655 w.
Jno. 1718 w.
Matthew 1735 i.
Thos. 1744 w.
HAWKS
Amelia
Joshua 1775 w.
Geo. 1781 i.
Lunenburg
Abraham 1767 w.
HAWLEY
Accomack
Abel 1796 w.
Fairfax
Saml. 1780 i.
Frederick
Jacob 1758 i.
HAWLING
Loudoun
Jno. 1787 w.
HAWOOD
Northampton
Jas. 1703 w.
HAWS
Essex
Jno. 1783 i.

HAWTHORN
Surry
Robt. 1729 i.
Sussex
Frances 1792 w.
HAWTHORNE
Fairfax
Hannah 1787 w.
Surry
Jno. 1720 w.
Jno. 1724 i.
Jno. 1743 i.
Sussex
Peter 1754 w.
Rachel 1759 w.
Jno. 1791 i.
York
Jarrett 1671 w.
HAY
Amherst
Gilbert 1777 w.
Augusta
David 1776 w.
Charlotte
Jno. 1799 w.
Henrico
Jno. 1782 w.
Peter 1782 w.
Middlesex
Jno. 1709 i.
Jno. 1713 w.
Northampton
Thos. 1744 i.
Northumberland
Henry 1661 i.
Prince Edward
Danl. 1785 w.
Surry
Gilbert 1758 w.
Sussex
Richd. 1796 w.
Westmoreland
Wm. 1726 i.
York
Wm. 1668 w.
Robt. 1717 i.
Hannah 1726 i.
Jno. 1738 i.
Jno. 1745 i.
Mary 1748 i.
Robt. 1748 w.
Robt. 1754 i.
Jno. 1755 w.
Jas. 1759 w.
Peter 1767 w.
Anthony 1770 w.
Grissel 1778 i.
Jno. 1778 w.
Robt. 1778 w.
Jno. 1788 w.

HAYCOCK
Northampton
Jno. 1738 i.
HAYDEN
Northumberland
Saml. 1770 i.
Stafford
Wm. 1748 i.
HAYDON
Lancaster
Wm. 1754 i.
John 1773 w.
Mary 1787 i.
John 1788 i.
Northumberland
Thos. 1720 i.
Ezekiel 1788 w.
Thos. 1789 w.
Spotsylvania
Thos. 1782 w.
Jarvis 1791 w.
HAYES
Accomack
Alice 1721 nw.
Amelia
Mary 1789 w.
Augusta
Geo. 1747 a.
Brunswick
Chas. 1757 w.
Essex
Edward 1761 w.
John 1766 i.
Frederick
Sarah 1747 w.
Isle of Wight
Peter 1720 w.
Mecklenburg
John 1781 w.
Winkfield 1793 i.
Norfolk
Anne 1650 w.
Owen 1673 w.
Thos. 1685 w.
John 1743-4 w.
Northampton
Jno. 1638 i.
Robt. 1686 w.
Northumberland
Sarah 1752 i.
Peter 1756 w.
Thos. 1764 w.
Thos. 1789 w.
Thos. 1792 i.
Princess Anne
Adam 1701 w.
Westmoreland
Henry 1745 w.
HAYGOOD
Brunswick
Jno. 1777 w.

HAYLEY
Charlotte
Thos. 1795 i.
Greensville
James 1796 i.
HAYLES
Chesterfield
Jno. 1759 i.
HAYLY
Norfolk
Wm. 1694 w.
York
Jno. 1703 w.
HAYMAN
York
Ann 1724 w.
HAYMES
Amelia
Wm. Sr. 1769 w.
HAYNES
Botetourt
John 1797 w.
Nicho. 1797 w.
Bedford
William 1781 w.
Charlotte
Thos. 1777 i.
Culpeper
Jasper 1782 w.
Halifax
Joseph N. 1789 i.
Henry
Henry 1784 w.
Isle of Wight
William 1766 w.
Lancaster
Thos. 1679 w.
Jos. 1713 w.
James, Jr. 1748 w.
James 1750 w.
James 1753 i.
Lunenburg
Wm. 1747 i.
Princess Anne
James 1730 w.
Erasmus 1753 w.
James 1753 w.
Joel 1760 w.
Thos. 1762 i.
Jno. 1768 w.
Eliz. 1769 i.
Wm. 1769 w.
Joshua 1770 i.
Jno. 1778 i.
Erasmus 1783 w.
Thos. 1783 w.
Thos. 1785 i.
Henry 1786 w.
William 1795 w.
Elizabeth 1796 w.
Abner 1789 i.

HAYNIE
Culpeper
Anthony 1760 w.
Anthony 1799 i.
Charles 1799 i.
Northumberland
Anthony 1711 w.
Jno. 1713 i.
Jno. 1723 i.
Richd. 1724-5 w.
Maxamilian 1729 w.
Bridgar 1740 w.
Thos. 1741 w.
Ormsby 1743-4 i.
Sarah 1749 w.
Richd. 1750 w.
Richd. 1753 w.
Elinor 1754 w.
Stephen 1759 w.
Abraham 1760 w.
Wm. 1762 w.
Anne 1763 i.
Elias 1766 i.
Isaac 1770 i.
Henry 1773 w.
Thos. 1773 i.
Jacob 1778 w.
Peter 1778 i.
Charles 1781 i.
Ann 1784 w.
Henry 1785 w.
Saml. 1785 i.
Wm. 1785 w.
Jno. 1786 w.
Ann 1787 w.
Thos. 1787 i.
Chas. 1788 i.
Bridgar 1791 w.
Hezekiah 1792 w.
Danl. 1794 w.
Jno. (1) 1795 w.
Jno. (2) 1795 w.
Wm. 1796 w.
Jeduthun 1797 w.
Bridgar 1799 i.
HAYS
Augusta
Geo. 1747 i.
Jno. 1750 w.
Jno. 1751 a.
Richd. 1778 i.
Jno. 1778 i.
Moses 1796 w.
Berkeley
Jno. 1787 w.
Charlotte
Richd. 1788 w.
Frederick
Sarah 1750 i.
Sarah 1752 i.

Henrico
Wm. 1735 i.
Isle of Wight
Peter 1678 w.
Robt. 1771 i.
Arthur 1776 w.
Mecklenburg
Jno. 1796 i.
Eliz. 1796 i.
Montgomery
Simon 1778 a.
Northampton
Jno. 1761 i.
Wm. 1763 w.
Northumberland
Geo. 1783 i.
Rockbridge
Andrew 1782 i.
Geo. 1782 i.
Alex. 1786 w.
Andrew 1787 i.
Stafford
Jno. 1748 w.
Sussex
Jno. 1768 a.
Richd. 1788 w.
Nathl. 1739 ab.
HAYSE
Isle of Wight
Robt. 1771 w.
HAYSLOP
Accomack
Wm. 1778 w.
HAYTOR
Washington
Wm. 1797 w.
HAYWARD
Frederick
Jno. 1745 a.
Josiah 1746 i.
York
Henry 1711 w.
Wm. 1712 i.
HAYWOOD
Norfolk
Philemon 1740 w.
Princess Anne
Anthony 1714 i.
HAYWORTH
Frederick
Absolom 1752 w.
Jas. 1767 i.
HAZARD
Lancaster
Jos. 1743 i.
Richmond
Henry 1785 w.
HAZE
Northampton
Richd. 1768 w.

HAZELBRIGG
Westmoreland
Wm. 1796 i.
HAZELGROVE
Spotsylvania
Jno. 1780 w.
HAZELL
Richmond
Edmd. 1737 w.
Westmoreland
Jno. 1747 i.
HAZELRIG
Frederick
Richd. 1757 w.
HAZELRIGG
Westmoreland
Saml. 1773 i
HAZELTON
York
Constance 1704 i.
HAZELWOOD
Charlotte
Wm. 1796 i.
Southampton
Richd. 1760 i.
HAZLEDINE
Frederick
Humphrey 1749 a.
HAZLERIGG
Westmoreland
Wm. 1796 w.
HAZLOP
Accomack
Geo. 1708 w.
HAZZARD
Lancaster
Jno. 1750-1 w.
HEABRON
Westmoreland
Jas. 1781 w.
HEAD
Culpeper
Benj. 1790 w.
Hampshire
Mary Maidelan
1776 w.
Middlesex
Mary 1699 w.
Orange
Jas. 1798 i.
Richmond
Wm. 1710 i.
Wm. 1711 i.
Spotsylvania
Jas. 1748 a.
Henry 1772 w.
Washington
Anthony 1786 i.
HEADEN
Loudoun
Geo. 1796 i.

HEADLEY
Fauquier
Jas. 1793 w.
Northumberland
Luke 1795 i.
Richmond
Henry 1760 i.
Robt. 1775 w.
Andrew 1780 w.
Westmoreland
Ann 1713 w.
Jno. 1717 w.
Wm. 1746 i.
HEADLY
Richmond
Wm. 1745 w.
Westmoreland
Robt. 1741 w.
HEAGLE
Harrison
Michael 1784 i.
HEALD
Greensville
Jno. Pim. 1793 nw.
Essex
Jno. 1706 w.
HEALE
Lancaster
Geo. 1697 w.
Geo. 1697-8 w.
Geo. 1702 i.
Ellen 1710 w.
Geo. 1710 i.
Wm. 1732 w.
Geo. 1737 w.
Jno. 1737 w.
Jos. 1741 w.
Northumberland
Matthew 1726-7 i.
HEALEY
Fairfax
Mary 1790 w.
HEALING
Northampton
Wm. 1635 w.
HEARD
Albemarle
Henry 1778 w.
Bedford
Wm. 1781 w.
Lancaster
Walter 1677 w.
Henry 1680 i.
Wm. 1710 w.
Wm. 1710 nw.
Henry 1726 i.
Walter 1727 i.
Walter 1742 i.
Wm. 1744 w.
Henry 1750 w.
Jane 1750-1 w.

Pittsylvania
Stephen 1774 w.
HEARDING
Shenandoah
Henry 1779 w.
HEARN
Middlesex
Richd. 1752 a.
Westmoreland
Philip 1698 w.
HEART
Amelia
Luke 1760 i.
Northumberland
Jno. 1747 w.
HEARTFORD
Richmond
Hendre 1737 i.
HEASTAND
Shenandoah
Jacob 1795 a.
HEASTING
Shenandoah
Henry 1783 w.
HEASTINGS
Harrison
Jos. 1796 w.
HEATH
Accomack
Wm. 1732 w.
Jos. 1763 w.
Jos. 1765 w.
Jos. 1767 i.
Jos. 1769 i.
Teackle 1793 w.
Jane 1794 w.
Teackle 1797 i.
Margt. 1798 w.
Bedford
Wm. 1775 w.
Frederick
Wm. 1750 i.
Northampton
Widow 1640 i.
Jas. 1750 w.
Robt. 1750 w.
Anne 1772 w.
Benj. 1776 w.
Jas. 1778 i.
Wm. Sr. 1779 w.
Wm. 1780 w.
Luke 1781 i.
Josiah 1792 i.
Northumberland
Wm. 1719 i.
Thos. 1726 w.
Thos. 1727 i.
Jno. 1783 w.
Jno. 1787 i.
Princess Anne
Jas. 1703 w.

Thos. 1722 i.
Ann 1723 w.
Jas. 1727 i.
Jas. 1728 w.
Benony 1746 w.
Wm. 1784 i.
Spotsylvania
Henry 1770 a.
Surry
Wm. 1681 w.
Adam Sr. 1719 w.
Eliz. 1731 w.
Abraham Jr. 1734 i.
Wm. 1746 w.
Eliz. 1750 w.
Jno. 1772 w.
Sussex
Adam 1763 i.
Nathan 1793 w.
Westmoreland
Saml. 1730 i.
HEATHCOCKE
Greensville
Mary 1788 w.
HEATON
Fairfax
Jno. 1783 i.
Fauquier
Jno. 1783 i.
Wm. 1793 i.
Loudoun
Moses 1777 i.
HEAVIN
Botetourt
Jno. 1784 w.
Montgomery
Howard 1787 w.
HEAWORTH
Frederick
Jas. 1759 i.
HEBDEN
Norfolk
Seth 1789 i.
Jno. 1720 i.
HEBDON
Norfolk
Mary 1730-1 nw.
HECKS
Southampton
Wm. 1798 i.
HEDDY
Northampton
Thos. 1678 w.
HEDGECOCK
Middlesex
Thos. 1704 w.
HEDGEPETH
Isle of Wight
Sarah 1780 w.
Mary 1782 i.

HEDGES
Berkeley
Joshua 1790 w.
Mary 1797 w.
Prince William
Robt. 1795 i.
HEDGMAN
Stafford
Geo. 1760 i.
Peter 1765 w.
Wm. 1765 w.
HEDGPETH
Isle of Wight
Benj. 1781 w.
HEDLE
Richmond
Henry 1723 w.
HEDSPETH
Goochland
Geo. 1744 i.
HEETH
Sussex
Wm. Jr. 1771 w.
Jno. 1773 w.
Wm. 1777 w.
Seth 1781 w.
HEFFORD
Richmond
Zach. 1703 w.
HEIDIN
Isle of Wight
Ephraim 1723 i.
HEIFLER
Ohio
Jos. 1783 a.
HEISSER
Shenandoah
Jacob 1790 i.
HELDRETH
Wythe
Jos. 1792 w.
HELLAND
Richmond
Geo. 1717 w.
HELLWIG
Southampton
Jno. 1792 w.
HELM
Bedford
Thos. 1781 i.
Frederick
Meredith 1752 i.
Meredith Jr. 1752 a.
Leonard 1745 w.
Geo. 1769 w.
Thos. 1778 w.
Loudoun
Meredith 1789 i.
Prince William
Lynaugh 1797 i.

HELMS
Northumberland
Wm. 1719 w.
HELVAK
Shenandoah
Conrod 1783 a.
HELVESTINE
Frederick
Peter 1779 w.
HELVEY
Shenandoah
Chas. 1794 i.
Wythe
Susannah 1794 w.
HELVY
Southampton
Jno. 1793 i.
Wythe
Henry 1792 w.
HEMING
Essex
Wm. 1754 i.
HEMMINGS
Westmoreland
Jos. 1718 w.
HENCOCK
Brunswick
Robt. 1760 w.
HENDERSON
Accomack
Saml. 1798 w.
Lemuel 1797 w.
Albemarle
Jno. 1753 i.
Jno. Sr. 1787 w.
Jno. 1791 i.
Bennett 1794 i.
Jno. 1794 w.
Amherst
Wm. 1783 w.
Augusta
Jos. 1762 a.
Jno. 1766 w.
Wm. 1770 w.
Danl. 1772 i.
Archd. 1781 w.
Saml. 1782 w.
Jas. 1784 w.
Jno. 1785 w.
Jos. 1791 w.
Archd. 1799 i.
Botetourt
Jno. 1791 i.
Culpeper
Wm. 1760 w.
Jno. 1763 i.
Ann 1767 i.
Goochland
Richd. 1748 w.
Richd. 1792 i.
Jno. 1793 w.

Greenbrier
Jno. 1787 w.
Jas. 1793 w.
Jas. 1797 i.
Louisa
Thos. 1768 w.
Lunenburg
Jos. 1763 w.
Montgomery
Jno. 1788 i.
Norfolk
Jas. 1768 w.
Jas. 1793 i.
Northampton
Jno. 1721-2 w.
Gilburd 1734 w.
Jacob 1754 w.
Jno. 1756 w.
Robt. 1798 i.
Orange
Jno. 1783 w.
Sarah 1796 w.
Prince William
Jas. 1737 w.
Richmond
Jno. 1730 w.
Spotsylvania
Henry 1727 a.
Washington
Jno. 1781 i.
HENDREN
Pittsylvania
Thos. 1785 w.
Richmond
Esial Wm. 1771 i.
HENDRICK
Amelia
Wm. 1739 a.
Hans 1773 w.
Benj. 1777 w.
Bernard 1781 w.
Berkeley
Jas. Sr. 1795 w.
Charlotte
Gustavous 1786 w.
Cumberland
Adolphus 1763 w.
Zachariah 1782 w.
Obadiah 1787 w.
Obadiah 1798 w.
Frederick
Jno. 1765 i.
Halifax
Jas. 1769 w.
Moses 1796 w.
Louisa
Wm. 1791 w.
Mecklenburg
Wm. 1799 i.
Pittsylvania
Nathl. 1797 w.

HENDRICKS
Berkeley
Jno. 1796 w.
Jno. 1799 i.
Halifax
Jas. 1780 a.
HENDRON
Richmond
Wm. 1768 w.
HENDY
Frederick
Deborah 1799 w.
HENETTER
Norfolk
Paul 1774 w.
HENING
Culpeper
Saml. 1778 i.
Saml. 1784 i.
David 1798 i.
Lancaster
Geo. Jr. 1772 w.
Robt. 1772 i.
HENLEY
Essex
Wm. 1717 w.
Henrico
Wm. 1799 w.
Louisa
Leonard 1793 w.
Princess Anne
Thos. 1733 i.
Jno. 1734 w.
Chas. 1742 i.
Chas. 1747 w.
Cornelius 1753 w.
Chas. 1778 i.
Jno. 1778 w.
Thos. 1785 w.
Jno. Sr. 1791 w.
Rappahannock
Eliz. 1684 w.
Robt. 1685 i.
HENLY
Princess Anne
Jeremiah 1748 i.
Thos. 1764 w.
Surry
Jno. 1702 i.
HENMAN
Accomack
Bayly 1766 w.
Westmoreland
Benj. 1703 i.
HENMONS
Westmoreland
Jno. 1713 i.
HENNARY
Frederick
Geo. 1783 i.

HENNEGAR
Washington
Conrod 1786 i.
HENNESY
Middlesex
Jno. 1745 a.
HENNIBOURN
Northumberland
Robt. 1651 i.
HENNING
Culpeper
Saml. 1779 w.
Saml. 1781 w.
Frederick
Robt. 1777 w.
HENNINGAN
Shenandoah
Michael 1798 i.
HENNINGER
Fairfax
Fred. 1783 i.
HENNY
Botetourt
Wm. 1774 w.
HENRY
Accomack
Wm. Blair 1781 w.
Jas. 1787 w.
Wm. Blair 1787 i.
Alebmarle
Thos. 1786 w.
Amherst
Sarah 1784 w.
Charlotte
Robt. 1767 w.
Patrick 1799 w.
Essex
Danl. 1708 i.
Dorothy 1709 w.
Richd. 1716 i.
Wm. 1721 i.
Fluvanna
Wm. 1785 i.
Henry
Jno. 1796 i.
Loudoun
Jos. 1799 i.
Washington
Saml. 1786 w.
Westmoreland
Rowland 1732 w.
HENSER
Shenandoah
Henry 1790 i.
HENSHAW
Essex
Saml. 1719 i.
Saml. 1758 w.
Thos. 1758 w.
Saml. 1788 w.
Jno. 1790 w.

Fairfax
Jno. 1750 i.
HENSLEE
Orange
Saml. 1735 w.
HENSLEY
Albemarle
Benj. 1788 w.
Bedford
Saml. 1791 i.
Brunswick
Jos. 1744 i.
Martha 1752 i.
Jos. 1757 w.
Culpeper
Wm. 1777 i.
Norfolk
Edward 1750 i.
Orange
Francis 1757 i.
Spotsylvania
Saml. 1765 w.
HENSON
Albemarle
Jno. 1786 w.
Bedford
Henson 1799 i.
Loudoun
Jno. 1762 i.
Louisa
Benj. 1770 w.
Richd. 1775 w.
Stafford
Edmond 1743 i.
HENTHORN
Ohio
Susanah 1799 w.
HENTY
Princess Anne
Jno. 1779 i.
HEPBURN
Mecklenburg
Wm. 1794 w.
HERBERT
Accomack
Jno. 1761 i.
Chesterfield
Jno. 1760 w.
Whiddon 1778 w.
Fincastle
Wm. 1776 w.
Henrico
Richd. 1731 w.
Montgomery
Wm. 1778 i.
Norfolk
Jno. 1675 w.
Jno. 1679 w.
Richd. 1693-4 nw.
Princess Anne
Jno. 1728 w.

Norfolk
Thos. 1749 w.
Margt. 1749-50 w.
Markcom 1761 w.
Nathaniel 1766 w.
Christopher 1774 w.
Thos. 1774 w.
Josiah 1775 w.
Henry Sr. 1778 w.
Jonas 1782 w.
Jno. 1784 i.
Wm. 1784 w.
Argyle 1785 w.
Thos. 1790 w.
Sophia 1795 i.
Caleb 1796 w.
Eliz. 1797 w.
Rappahannock
Thos. 1685 w.
HERD
Fairfax
Jno. 1795 a.
HERDON
Surry
Mary 1679 w.
HERIFORD
Fairfax
Jas. 1744 w.
HERISON
Princess Anne
Jno. 1697 a.
HERLEY
Westmoreland
Eliz. 1747-8 w.
HERMON
Augusta
Jno. 1761 i.
HERMONS
Fauquier
Jno. 1775 w.
HERN
Sussex
Jas. 1774 i.
Gilliam 1789 w.
HERNDON
Augusta
Jos. 1763 i.
Campbell
David 1795 w.
Charlotte
Jno. 1786 w.
Essex
Jas. 1767 w.
Goochland
Benj. 1778 w.
Valentine 1799 w.
King George
Jno. 1769 w.
Madison
Geo. 1798 a.

Orange
Zachariah 1796 w.
Prince William
Wm. 1796 w.
Spotsylvania
Edwd. 1759 w.
Stephen 1765 w.
Jno. 1783 w.
Mary 1797 a.
Edwd. 1799 w.
HERNE
Lancaster
Benj. 1709 w.
Geo. 1720 i.
HERON
Sussex
Jas. 1773 w.
HERRALD
Washington
Jas. 1796 w.
HERRING
Halifax
Jno. 1768 w.
Isle of Wight
Danl. 1785 w.
Mills 1791 w.
Lunenburg
Arthur 1796 w.
Pittsylvania
Wm. 1799 w.
HERRINGE
Isle of Wight
Jno. 1672 w.
HERRITAGE
Northampton
Wm. 1737 w.
Freshwater 1788 w.
HERSBERGER
Shenandoah
Henry 1788 w.
HERSHFIELD
Berkeley
Fred. 1778 w.
HERST
Goochland
Wm. 1765 w.
HERTFORD
Richmond
Thos. 1742 w.
HERWOOD
Lunenburg
Geo. 1762 a.
HERYFORD
Fairfax
Jno. 1744 w.
Jean 1754 w.
HERRYFORD
Loudoun
Geo. 1777 i.

HESLETT
Norfolk
Wm. 1697 w.
HESS
Fairfax
Jacob 1788 w.
HESSE
Berkeley
Chas. 1782 i.
HESSER
Loudoun
Conrod 1789 i.
HESTER
Louisa
Chas. 1797 w.
Robt. 1770 w.
Mecklenburg
Abram 1785 i.
Abraham 1779 w.
Robt. 1799 i.
Northumberland
Wm. 1760 w.
Jos. 1762 w.
Jos. 1771 i.
Isaac 1772 w.
Ezekiel 1778 i.
HESTIN
Augusta
David 1778 i.
HETHERSOLL
York
Jno. 1679 w.
HEUTE
Berkeley
Geo. 1786 i.
HEWART
Northampton
Thos. 1733 i.
HEWES
Northumberland
Mary 1720 w.
Westmoreland
Thos. 1698 i.
HEWETSON
Loudoun
Benj. 1786 nw.
HEWETT
Norfolk
Jno. 1677 i.
Princess Anne
Francis 1701 w.
Surry
Jno. 1744 i.
HEWGATE
Westmoreland
Wm. 1727 i.
HEWIT
Stafford
Robt. 1743 w.

HEWITT
King George
Jas. 1763 w.
Stafford
Richd. 1784 w.
Sussex
Wm. 1765 i.
Jas. 1779 i.
Eliz. 1797 w.
York
Wm. 1732 w.
Francis 1741 i.
HEWLET
Norfolk
Jno. 1758 w.
HEWLETT
Chesterfield
Jno. 1795 i.
Norfolk
Jno. 1743-4 i.
HEWLITT
Henry
Thos. 1787 w.
Norfolk
Francis 1775 w.
HEWS
Norfolk
Edwd. 1709 w.
Prince William
Wm. 1740 i.
HEWSON
Lancaster
Wm. 1688 i.
HEYDON
Lancaster
Wm. 1765 w.
HEYNES
York
Wm. 1646 w.
HERWARD
Stafford
Jno. 1701 w.
York
Francis 1659 w.
Jno. 1660 w.
Henry 1720 w.
HIATT
Berkeley
Geo. 1787 w.
Frederick
Jno. 1764 w.
Jno. 1765 i.
Jno. 1767 i.
Orange
Jno. 1782 i.
HIBBLE
Middlesex
Jno. 1793 i.
HIBBS
Loudoun
Jos. 1795 i.

HICKERSON
Louisa
  Jno. 1775 a.
Stafford
  Thos. 1742 i.
HICKEY
Amherst
  Catherine 1778 i.
Hardy
  Jno. 1796 i.
Henry
  Jno. 1784 w.
Middlesex
  Jno. 1711 i.
HICKINGE
Isle of Wight
  Wm. 1684 w.
HICKLIN
Augusta
  Thos. Sr. 1771 w.
HICKMAN
Accomack
  Wm. 1683 w.
  Henry 1742 w.
  Roger 1751 w.
  Wm. 1761 w.
  Wm. 1767 i.
  Christian 1768 nw.
  Jesse 1778 w.
  Wm. 1779 i.
  Jesse 1782 i.
  Richd. 1784 w.
  Custis 1786 w.
  Richd. 1787 i.
  Custis 1789 i.
  Richd. 1791 i.
  Richd. 1793 w.
  Anne 1796 w.
  Richd. 1796 i.
  Ann 1797 i.
  Hampton 1799 i.
Albemarle
  Thos. 1765 i.
  Edwd. 1769 w.
Berkeley
  Ezekiel 1793 w.
Franklin
  Jacob 1789 w.
Frederick
  Isaac 1791 w.
Hampshire
  Eliz. 1792 w.
Loudoun
  Conrad 1799 i.
Northumberland
  Nathl. 1656 w.
  Thos. 1748 i.
Rockbridge
  Jno. 1784 w.
Southampton
  Wm. 1761 w.

York
  Richd. 1731 w.
HICKS
Augusta
  Chris. 1762 i.
Brunswick
  Danl. 1735 w.
  Robt. 1736 w.
  Robt. 1739 w.
  Eliz. 1740 w.
  Frances 1744 w.
  Jas. 1761 w.
  Sarah 1770 w.
  Robt. 1782 w.
  Jas. 1793 w.
Cumberland
  Jno. 1776 w.
Goochland
  Jno. 1772 w.
Greensville
  Robt. 1798 w.
Halifax
  Jos. 1797 i.
Henry
  Jas. 1780 i.
Louisa
  Peawd 1793 i.
Norfolk
  Stephen 1648 i.
  Benj. 1789 w.
Surry
  Jno. 1729 w.
  Jno. 1732 w.
Sussex
  Wm. 1786 i.
  Jos. 1787 w.
HIDE
Middlesex
  Jonathan 1718 w.
Surry
  Richd. 1710 w.
  Richd. 1719 w.
HIDER
Hardy
  Adam 1789 w.
HIDES
Lunenburg
  Thos. 1762 i.
York
  Lawrence 1679 i.
HIET
Frederick
  Wm. 1767 w.
HIFER
Shenandoah
  Philip 1785 i.
HIGBY
Northampton
  Thos. 1655 w.

HIGDON
Westmoreland
  Jno. 1718 w.
  Jno. 1720 w.
  Danl. 1739 w.
  Jno. 1771 w.
HIGGERSON
Stafford
  Jno. 1742 w.
HIGGIN
Hampshire
  Judiah 1796 w.
HIGGINBOTHAM
Amherst
  Moses 1778 w.
  Moses 1790 w.
  Aaron 1794 a.
HIGGINS
Frederick
  Jas. 1783 w.
Isle of Wight
  Roger 1672 w.
Northumberland
  Geo. 1651 w.
  Hannah 1765 w.
Westmoreland
  Jno. 1712 i.
HIGGINSON
Northampton
  Saml. 1703 w.
HIGGS
Prince William
  Thurman 1782 w.
  Truman 1783 i.
HIGH
Charlotte
  David 1795 w.
HIGHLANDER
Prince William
  Jas. 1796 i.
HIGHTOWER
Amelia
  Jno. Sr. 1764 w.
  Joshua 1772 w.
Brunswick
  Charnel 1762 i.
  Jno. 1781 i.
  Jno. 1782 i.
Lunenburg
  Jno. 1796 w.
Pittsylvania
  Thos. 1796 w.
Richmond
  Joshua 1726 w.
HILDRUP
Spotsylvania
  Saml. 1760 a.
HILL
Accomack
  Henry 1688 w.
  Richd. 1694 w.

Nicholas 1697 i.
Tabitha 1717 w.
Abraham 1767 i.
Eliz. 1780 w.
Amelia
Chas. 1740 w.
Wm. 1748 i.
Jas. 1765 w.
Jas. 1767 i.
Geo. 1774 i.
Geo. 1771 w.
Jno. Sr. 1779 w.
Jno. 1782 i.
Amherst
Thos. 1789 a.
Augusta
Wm. 1749 w.
Johnston 1761 i.
Brunswick
Robt. 1740 w.
Jno. 1780 w.
Wm. 1799 w.
Charles City
Francis 1768 i.
Turner 1772 i.
Chesterfield
Jas. 17— i.
Jas. 1750 w.
Godfrey 1760 w.
Edwd. 1780 w.
Jno. Sr. 1788 w.
Jno. 1789 w.
Jno. Jr. 1789 i.
Jno. 1792 i.
Jno. Sr. 1797 i.
Wm. 1798 i.
Culpeper
Jno. 1767 w.
Betty 1772 w.
Thos. 1778 i.
Cumberland
Thos. 1770 w.
Jos. 1772 w.
Thos. 1779 w.
Thos. Suggett 1781 w.
Wm. 1782 i.
Wm. Castilo 1788 w.
Essex
Henry 1727 w.
Leonard 1728 w.
Leonard 1732 i.
Leonard 1733 w.
Leonard 1735 i.
Leonard 1756 w.
Leonard 1759 i.
Jno. Jr. 1761 i.
Richd. 1764 w.
Wm. 1767 w.
Leonard 1776 w.
Jno. 1777 w.
Richd. 1784 w.

Leonard 1785 i.
Frederick
Richd. 1748 i.
Goochland
Luke 1743 i.
Henry
Robt. 1778 w.
Halifax
Jas. 1758 i.
Chas. 1758 i.
Ephraim 1781 i.
Jas. 1782 i.
Eliz. 1799 w.
Henrico
Nathl. 1687 w.
Jas. 1708 w.
Jos. 1718 i.
Paul 1732 w.
Isle of Wight
Nicholas 1675 w.
Nicholas 1678 i.
Nicholas 1679 i.
Silvestra 1706-7 w.
Thos. 1720 w.
Jos. 1776 w.
Frances 1791 w.
King George
Jno. 1734 i.
Thos. 1765 a.
Lancaster
Robt. 1698 i.
Job 1703-4 w.
Thos. 1728 i.
Jas. 1748 i.
Henry 1749 w.
Robt. 1762 w.
Wm. 1762 i.
Eliz. 1765 i.
Jas. 1773 i.
Nicholas 1777 i.
Jno. 1789 i.
Geo. 1792 w.
Eliz. 1796 w.
Lunenburg
Richd. 1758 i.
Mecklenburg
Wm. 1777 w.
Wm. 1787 w.
Eliz. 1794 i.
Middlesex
Jno. 1714 i.
Richd. 1732 w.
Dorothy 1745 i.
Wm. 1746 a.
Wm. 1759 a.
Needles 1776 i.
Letitia 1776 i.
Montgomery
Abigail 1787 i.
Norfolk
Richd. 1686 w.

Northampton
Henry 1649 w.
Northumberland
Saml. 1662 w.
Enoch 1719 i.
Jas. 1727 w.
Hannah 1740 w.
Jno. 1741 i.
Britain 1745 w.
Wm. 1745 w.
Ezekiel 1746 w.
Chostelo 1750 w.
Jas. 1750 i.
Luke 1750 i.
Sarah 1752 w.
Costelo 1758 i.
Jno. 1758 i.
Jno. 1759 w.
Jno. 1762 i.
Chas. 1769 w.
Spencer 1771 w.
Jos. 1784 i.
Pittsylvania
Jonathan 1795 i.
Prince Edward
Wm. 1774 w.
Davis 1782 w.
Prince George
Jno. Sr. 1718 w.
Princess Anne
Jno. 1703 a.
Luke 1716 i.
Thos. 1751 i.
Jno. 1754 i.
Chas. 1766 w.
Mary 1771 i.
Jas. 1777 i.
Morris 1782 w.
Wm. 1785 w.
Richmond
Richd. 1720 w.
Eliz. 1726 i.
Jno. 1728 w.
Geo. 1737 i.
Wm. Jr. 1741 w.
Wm. 1747 i.
Hull Chizell 1750 i.
Jesse 1760 w.
Ann 1780 i.
Rockbridge
Thos. 1781 w.
Southampton
Reubin 1792 i.
Spotsylvania
Thos. 1741 a.
Alex. 1744 a.
Geo. 1776 a.
Stafford
Jno. 1742 i.
Surry
Wm. 1675 w.

Herman 1679 i.
Benj. 1719 i.
Richd. 1722 i.
Thos. 1737 i.
Matthew 1752 i.
Moses 1782 w.
Sussex
Michael 1755 i.
Matthew 1760 i.
Jno. 1765 w.
Lucy 1765 i.
Michael 1766 i.
Amy 1768 w.
Michael 1768 i.
Benj. 1772 i.
Wm. 1773 i.
Richd. 1775 w.
Michael 1778 w.
Mildred 1798 w.
Washington
Thos. 1782 i.
Westmoreland
Richd. 1675 w.
York
Thos. 1711 w.
Saml. 1712 w.
Saml. 1718 i.
Saml. 1738 i.
Saml. 1770 w.
Hansford 1780 w.
HILLARD
Isle of Wight
Thos. 1730 i.
Lancaster
Jas. 1749 i.
HILLER
Westmoreland
Jno. 1657 w.
HILLERD
Richmond
Philip 1754 i.
HILLIARD
Brunswick
Alex. 1759 i.
Charles City
Richd. 1774 w.
Essex
Thos. 1718 w.
Frederick
Thos. 1766 w.
Washington
Wm. 1787 w.
York
Jno. 1706 ab.
Agnes 1746 w.
HILLMAN
Amelia
Nicho. 1761 w.
Lancaster
Eliz. 1744-5 w.

HILLSMAN
Amelia
Wm. 1771 i.
HILLYARD
Princess Anne
Wm. 1695 w.
HILLYEAR
Richmond
Jas. 1789 i.
HILSMAN
Amelia
Matthew 1780 w.
York
Jno. Jr. 1703-4 i.
Jno. 1704 w.
Wm. 1726 w.
HILTON
Bedford
Jas. 1786 w.
Greensville
Wm. 1784 i.
King George
Jonathan 1796 w.
Westmoreland
Wm. 1727 i.
Jno. 1765 w.
Wm. 1778 w.
Wm. 1784 i.
HILYARD
Frederick
Jno. 1761 w.
Isle of Wight
Thos. 1730 w.
HINCHER
Fairfax
Jno. 1751 a.
Spotsylvania
Mary 1790 w.
HIND
Augusta
Jno. 1783 i.
Spotsylvania
Jno. 1768 a.
Wm. 1770 a.
HINDE
Essex
Thos. 1700 i.
Jno. 1701 i.
York
Thos. 1718 i.
HINDERMAS (?)
Westmoreland
Thos. 1677 i.
HINDMAN
Accomack
Ann 1767 i.
Augusta
Jno. 1749 i.
Jno. 1750 a.

HINDMER
Westmoreland
Jno. 1713 w.
HINDS
Essex
Thos. 1709 i.
Jno. 1736 i.
Fairfax
Mathew 1750 i.
Richmond
Richd. 1720 w.
Jas. 1755 w.
Chas. 1760 w.
Josiah 1775 w.
HINE
Essex
Thos. 1699 w.
Jno. 1700 w.
Thos. 1709 w.
HINEAGE
Lancaster
Thos. 1728 i.
HINES
Charlotte
Caleb 1796 w.
Frederick
Michael 1759 i.
Goochland
Richd. D. 1790 i.
Richmond
Mary 1725 i.
Thos. 1725 i.
Southampton
David 1789 w.
Jno. 1772 w.
Joshua 1779 i.
Howell 1789 w.
Richd. 1789 i.
Sussex
Wm. Sr. 1760 w.
Thos. 1773 w.
Jos. 1782 w.
Joshua 1783 i.
Wm. 1784 w.
Wm. Jr. 1789 i.
Westmoreland
Zachariah 1697 w.
Wythe
Wm. 1796 i.
HINGART
Botetourt
Wm. 1775 i.
HINKENBARGER (?)
Hardy
Geo. 1798 i.
HINKLE
Frederick
Geo. 1788 w.
HINKLEY
Richmond
Edmd. 1727 i.

HINMAN
Accomack
Richd. 1721 w.
Eliz. 1722 w.
Benj. 1733 i.
Bayly 1744 i.
Argall 1745 w.
Jno. 1775 w.
Richd. 1775 w.
Bayley 1776 i.
Richd. 1777 i.
Jno. 1778 i.
Richd. 1779 i.
Thos. 1783 w.
Jadock 1784 w.
Geo. 1786 i.
Thany 1787 i.
Bayly 1788 w.
Jno. 1788 i.
Thos. 1793 i.
Moses 1797 w.
Northampton
Richd. 1663 i.
HINMON
Northampton
Jno. 1660 w.
HINSLEY
Northampton
Wm. 1654 w.
HINSON
Amelia
Chris. 1744 a.
Richmond
Geo. 1726 w.
Stafford
Chas. 1749 w.
Eliz. 1761 w.
Lazarus 1765 i.
Westmoreland
Jas. 1735 i.
HINTON
Amelia
Chris. 1747 w.
Richd. 1760 w.
Lancaster
Timothy 1731 w.
Saml. 1771 w.
Fleet 1778 i.
Richd. 1779 i.
Richd. 1780 i.
Fleet 1789 i.
Wm. 1791 w.
Judith 1795 i.
Mecklenburg
Wood 1794 i.
Catherine 1799 i.
Shenandoah
Thos. 1796 w.
HIPENSTALL
King George
Wm. 1762 a.

HIPKINGS
Essex
Thos. 1731 w.
Thos. 1764 i.
Middlesex
Thos. 1710 w.
Richmond
Jno. 1717 w.
HIPKINS
Essex
Jno. 1759 w.
Saml. 1764 w.
Fairfax
Lewis 1794 w.
Richmond
Saml. 1799 w.
Westmoreland
Richd. 1786 w.
Richd. 1792 i.
HIRE
Hardy
Leonard 1786 w.
Anna Maria 1793 w.
Lewis 1794 i.
HIRONS
Greenbrier
Saml. 1789 w.
HISER
Shenandoah
Henry 1787 w.
Jacob 1794 w.
HISEY
Shenandoah
Christian 1777 a.
HITCHCOCK
Albemarle
Wm. 1781 w.
Norfolk
Hester 1696-7 nw.
HITCHCOCKE
Charlotte
Russell 1795 w.
HITCHENS
Accomack
Edwd. 1756 i.
HITCHER
Essex
Wm. 1774 w.
HITCHIN
Accomack
Jarret 1708 w.
HITE
Berkeley
Jacob 1777 i.
Jno. Jr. 1777 w.
Jacob 1779 w.
Thos. 1779 w.
Jno. Jr. 1783 i.
Thos. 1783 i.
Frederick
Jost. 1761 w.

Jos. 1772 i.
Isaac 1795 w.
Sussex
Wm. 1782 i.
Ann 1787 w.
Huldy 1789 w.
Thos. 1789 w.
HITT
Fauquier
Peter 1772 w.
Jno. 1783 i.
HIX
Brunswick
Frances 1744 i.
Chas. 1745 i.
Francis 1745 i.
Chesterfield
Wm. 1796 w.
Goochland
Danl. 1735 w.
Nathl. 1735 w.
Jno. 1748 w.
Jno. 1773 i.
David 1784 i.
Lunenburg
Jos. 1785 w.
Jos. 1785 i.
Jno. 1796 w.
Mecklenburg
Amos 1786 w.
Pittsylvania
Jas. 1776 w.
Powhatan
Edwd. 1792 i.
Archibald 1796 w.
Prince Edward
Danl. 1797 i.
Sussex
Wm. 1763 w.
Wm. 1782 w.
Jas. 1788 w.
York
Thos. 1711 i.
HIXON
Loudoun
Wm. 1798 i.
HOAKINS
Richmond
Jno. 1715 w.
HOBBS
Brunswick
Jas. 1785 w.
Greensville
Jno. 1795 i.
Isle of Wight
Francis 1688 w.
Norfolk
Jno. 1745 i.
Wm. 1758 i.
Eliz. 1762 i.

Prince George
Richd. 1718 i.
Robt. 1718 w.
Rappahannock
Richd. 1683 i.
Sussex
Thos. 1761 i.
Jesse 1786 i.
Jos. 1793 w.
Westmoreland
Jas. 1750 i.
HOBBY
Henrico
Jno. 1692 i.
HOBDAY
Norfolk
Francis 1793 i.
Orange
Jno. 1795 w.
York
Wm. 1740 w.
Wm. 1746 i.
Thos. 1752 i.
Richd. 1763 w.
HOBDY
Orange
Edwd. 1785 i.
HOBGOOD
Norfolk
Thos. Sr. 1739 w.
Henry 1763 i.
Wm. 1785 w.
Wm. 1790 i.
HOBSON
Cumberland
Wm. 1764 w.
Jno. 1771 w.
Jno. 1777 i.
Adcock 1779 w.
Essex
Richd. 1720 w.
Frederick
Geo. 1748 w.
Henrico
Wm. 1733 w.
Matthew 1783 w.
Benj. 1790 w.
Benj. 1795 i.
Lunenburg
Nicho. 1758 w.
Matthew 1782 w.
Norfolk
Peter 1697 w.
Northumberland
Thos. 1721 ab.
Thos. 1726-7 w.
Wm. 1739 w.
Clark 1743 w.
Jno. 1762 w.
Judith 1766 w.

Orange
Jno. 1742 a.
Westmoreland
Jno. 1716 i.
HOCKEL
Stafford
Jno. 1755 i.
HOCKINGS
Orange
Wm. 1738 a.
HOCKMAN
Augusta
Johannes 1748 w.
Frederick
Jacob 1765 w.
Shenandoah
Jos. 1786 a.
Benj. 1788 w.
Christian 1788 a.
Christian 1799 w.
HODDGES
Henry
Esham 1782 w.
HODDLE
Frederick
Jno. 1761 i.
HODG
Isle of Wight
Roger 1720 i.
Surry
Jno. 1679 w.
HODGE
Augusta
Jno. 1751 i.
Eliz. 1752 w.
Saml. 1775 w.
Jno. 1797 w.
King George
Thos. 1778 w.
Thos. 1783 w.
Thos. 1786 a.
Norfolk
Edward 1649 w.
Robt. 1681 w.
Stafford
Archibal 1750 i.
Westmoreland
Eleanor 1753 i.
HODGEPETH
Isle of Wight
Henry 1780 i.
HODGES
Cumberland
Thos. 1750 w.
Johnson 1771 i.
Goochland
Benj. 1768 i.
Welcome Wm.
1772 w.
Isle of Wight
Robt. 1687 i.

Elias 1727 i.
Elias 1742 nw.
Benj. 1753 w.
Jno. Sr. 1770 w.
Norfolk
Jno. 1714 w.
Richd. 1751 w.
Richd. 1753 i.
Wm. 1759 w.
Jos. Jr. 1761 w.
Sarah 1761 w.
Wm. 1762 w.
Wm. 1764 w.
Jos. 1766 w.
Richd. 1766 w.
Wm. 1767 w.
Robt. 1771 w.
Benj. 1775 w.
Hillory 1775 w.
Ferebee 1779 w.
Ferebee 1784 i.
Chas. 1786 w.
Saml. 1786 w.
Joel 1787 w.
Lemuel 1791 i.
Jno. 1793 w.
Robt. 1794 i.
Sarah 1794 w.
Jas. 1796 w.
Wm. 1796 w.
Mason 1797 w.
Ruth 1797 w.
Mary 1798 i.
Wm. 1799 i.
Pittsylvania
Edmd. 1782 w.
York
Augustine 1660 nw.
HODGGES
Essex
Jno. 1794 w.
HODGFORM
Frederick
Deborah 1791 i.
HODGHES
Isle of Wight
Elias 1727 w.
HODGIS
Norfolk
Jno. 1714 w.
Roger 1716 w.
Jno. 1771 i.
Wm. 1790 w.
HODGKIN
Rappahannock
Wm. 1673 w.
HODGKINS
Accomack
Anthony 1665 w.

HODGKINSON
Lancaster
Chris. 1717 i.
Richmond
Wm. 1748 w.
HODGKSON
Richmond
Mary 1765 w.
HODGSON
Frederick
Robt. 1780 w.
Norfolk
Francis 1784 w.
Princess Anne
Jno. 1777 w.
Westmoreland
Wm. 1766 w.
HODNETT
Pittsylvania
Dyres 1779 w.
HODSDEN
Isle of Wight
William 1758 w.
Wm. 1767 i.
Wm. 1797 w.
HODSKINS
Richmond
Wm. 1719 w.
HODSON
Accomack
Jno. 1694 w.
Essex
Jno. 1717 w.
HOFFLER
Norfolk
Wm. 1798 w.
HOG
Augusta
Thos. 1775 a.
Frederick
Lewis 1747 i.
Edwd. 1786 i.
HOGAN
Lancaster
Geo. 1762 i.
Fauquier
Margt. 1767 w.
Jno. 1771 i.
Louisa
Jno. 1774 a.
Zachariah 1787 w.
Zachariah 1791 a.
Wm. 1794 a.
Northumberland
Thos. 1795 i.
Prince William
Thos. 1779 w.
Richmond
Thos. 1786 w.

HOGE
Frederick
Wm. 1750-1 i.
Edward 1783 i.
Jos. 1795 w.
Jas. 1796 i.
Loudoun
Wm. Sr. 1789 w.
HOGG
Chesterfield
Richd. 1786 i.
Frederick
Margt. 1753 i.
Northampton
Thos. Sr. 1684 w.
Thos. 1697 i.
Spotsylvania
Eleanor 1757 a.
Westmoreland
Wm. 1698 nw.
Roger 1707 i.
York
Richd. 1795 w.
HOGGARD
Isle of Wight
Patrick 1730 i.
Louisa
Jas. 1770 i.
Norfolk
Saml. 1770 i.
HOGGATT
Albemarle
Anthony 1753 w.
HOGGHER
Accomack
Kendall 1743 w.
HOGGSHEAR
Accomack
Thos. 1738 w.
HOGINS
Brunswick
Wm. 1735 i.
HOGLAND
Berkeley
Everhart 1781 i.
Frederick
Jas. 1760 i.
Ohio
Derreck 1790 w.
HOGMAN
Frederick
Jacob 1773 i.
HOGOOD
Surry
Geo. 1727 w.
HOGSHEAD
Augusta
Jno. 1756 w.
Thos. 1779 i.
Jno. 1781 i.
Jas. Sr. 1782 w.

Robt. 1786 i.
Jno. 1799 w.
HOGUE
Hardy
David 1786 w.
HOGWOOD
Prince George
Joan 1720 i.
Surry
Francis 1677 w.
Richd. 1678 a.
HOHL
Augusta
Peter 1776 w.
HOHMAN
Shenandoah
Danl. 1784 a.
HOLBROOK
King George
Jno. 1733 i.
Northampton
Jno. 1747 w.
HOLDBROOK
Stafford
Wm. 1755 i.
HOLBROOKE
Northampton
Edwd. 1756 w.
Saml. 1765 w.
Anne 1774 w.
HOLDCROFT
York
Saml. 1755 w.
HOLDEN
Accomack
Geo. 1774 w.
Ann 1788 w.
King George
Jno. 1765 i.
Northampton
Chas. 1690 w.
Southampton
Benj. 1785 w.
York
Thos. 1672 a.
HOLDER
Essex
Jno. 1750 w.
Margt. 1756 w.
HOLDERMAN
Shenandoah
Christian 1775 i.
HOLDMAN
Frederick
Danl. 1771 i.
HOLDSWORTH
Charles City
Chas. 1769 i.
King George
Jno. 1728 i.
Chas. 1749 i.

VIRGINIA WILLS AND ADMINISTRATIONS   **213**

Surry
Chas. Sr. 1764 w.
Rebekah 1779 i.
Rebecca 1789 w.
Sussex
Chas. 1799 w.
HOLDWAY
Culpeper
Timothy 1791 w.
HOLE
Isle of Wight
Jno. 1638 i.
HOLEMAN
Albemarle
Tandy 1760 w.
Shenandoah
Danl. 1784 i.
Jacob 1784 w.
Rachel 1785 a.
HOLLADAY
Isle of Wight
Anthony 1719 w.
Saml. 1762 i.
Saml. Jr. 1797 i.
Norfolk
Jonas 1719 i.
Orange
Jos. 1771 i.
HOLLAND
Amelia
Michael 1763 i.
Jos. 1779 w.
Cumberland
Jno. 1763 w.
Wm. 1769 w.
Chas. 1768 i.
Jas. 1783 w.
Goochland
Judith 1751 w.
Michael 1746 w.
Jno. 1773 w.
Jno. 1795 i.
Isle of Wight
Samuell 1777 i.
Wm. 1786 w.
Job. 1790 w.
Robt. 1799 w.
Norfolk
Marmeduck 1676 i.
Northampton
Nathl. 1743 i.
Wm. 1769 w.
Rachel 1774 i.
Jno. 1777 i.
Ann 1784 i.
Northumberland
Danl. 1672 w.
Prince Edward
Richd. 1784 w.
Westmoreland
Youell 1737 i.

Simon 1750 w.
Youell 1772 w.
York
Lewis 1731 w.
HOLLEMAN
Isle of Wight
Eliz. 1739 i.
Jno. 1751 w.
Surry
Wm. 1728 w.
Jno. 1736 w.
Mary 1736 w.
HOLLEWELL
Norfolk
Thos. 1687 w.
HOLLIDAY
Isle of Wight
Anthony 1702 w.
Jones 1758 i.
Anthony 1783 i.
Jno. 1786 w.
Orange
Wm. 1742 a.
Prince William
Jno. 1783 i.
Jno. 1796 i.
Stafford
Jno. 1744 i.
HOLLIGAN
Bedford
Patrick 1773 i.
HOLLIMAN
Isle of Wight
Eliz. 1742 i.
Susannah 1755 w.
Thos. 1778 i.
Southampton
Jas. 1758 i.
Thos. 1762 w.
Micajah 1794 w.
Surry
Jos. 1725 i.
Arthur 1778 w.
Jos. 1786 w.
HOLLINGHEAD
Fairfax
Jno. 1771 i.
HOLLINGSWORTH
Frederick
Abraham 1748 w.
Ann 1749 w.
Zebulon 1760 i.
Loudoun
Isaac 1759 w.
Jas. 1762 i.
Orange
Jos. 1738 a.
HOLLIS
Fairfax
Jno. 1768 i.

HOLLISTER
Rappahannock
Wm. 1680 w.
HOLLIWOOD
Isle of Wight
Christopher 1758 i.
HOLLODAY
Spotsylvania
Jno. 1742 w.
Wm. 1746 w.
Jno. Jr. 1781 w.
Jno. 1781 w.
Benj. 1785 w.
Jos. 1795 w.
HOLLOGAIN
Bedford
Jno. 1772 w.
HOLLOMAN
Southampton
Wm. 1798 i.
Surry
Wm. 1706 i.
Richd. 1711 w.
HOLLOWAY
Accomack
Hezekiah 1785 w.
Brunswick
Edwd. 1778 i.
Edith 1781 w.
Wm. 1784 w.
Dan 1788 i.
Lewis 1798 a.
Culpeper
Jno. 1799 w.
Cumberland
Jno. 1755 w.
Jno. 1758 w.
Jno. 1758 w.
Hannah 1777 w.
Essex
Jas. 1698 i.
Jas. 1734 i.
Lancaster
Jno. 1721 a.
Saml. 1721 w.
Lunenburg
Geo. 1759 w.
Mecklenburg
Jas. 1778 w.
Archerbel 1782 w.
Norfolk
Jno. 1719 i.
Northampton
Jno. 1643 w.
Orange
Jas. 1744 a.
Prince Edward
Elias 1796 i.
Jas. 1788 i.
Surry
Davis 1789 w.

York
Jno. 1704 w.
David 1733 i.
Jas. Jr. 1767 i.
Jas. 1788 w.
Thos. 1791 w.
Thos. 1793 i.
HOLLOWELL
Isle of Wight
Sarah 1748 w.
Wm. 1782 w.
Norfolk
Jos. 1705 w.
Jno. 1716 w.
Sarah 1717 w.
Thos. 1743-4 i.
Jno. 1752 w.
Jno. 1785 w.
Jno. 1791 i.
HOLLSTEAD
Norfolk
Henry 1685 w.
HOLLYMAN
Isle of Wight
Chris. 1731 w.
Thos. 1734 w.
Eliz. 1736 w.
Eliz. 1739 w.
HOLMAN
Cumberland
Jas. 1761 w.
Goochland
Henry 1740 w.
Wm. 1796 w.
Wm. 1799 i.
HOLMES
Frederick
Jos. 1796 i.
Halifax
Wm. Wilson 1775 i.
Henrico
Thos. 1714 w.
Isle of Wight
Christopher 1688 i.
Lunenburg
Jos. 1762 w.
Mecklenburg
Saml. 1766 w.
Isaac 1772 w.
Lucy 1796 i.
Norfolk
Henry 1678 i.
Gabriel 1717 i.
Lemuel 1772 w.
Northampton
Edwd. 1783 i.
Ohio
Obediah 1794 w.
Saml. 1799 w.
Princess Anne
Jno. 1719 i.

Lemuel 1719 w.
Wm. 1723 w.
Geo. 1725 i.
Henry 1733 w.
Edwd. 1734 i.
Henry 1753 w.
Robt. 1753 i.
Saml. 1753 w.
Robt. 1754 i.
Henry 1756 i.
Jno. Edwd. 1757 i.
Jno. 1765 w.
Jno. 1767 i.
Wm. 1774 w.
Jas. 1776 w.
Henry 1780 w.
Wm. 1780 i.
Henry 1782 i.
Prince William
Jno. 1739 w.
York
Thos. 1783 w.
Lucy 1786 i.
HOLMS
Loudoun
Wm. 1775 w.
HOLSEY
Lancaster
W—— 1688 nw.
HOLSTEAD
Norfolk
Henry 1736 w.
Eliz. 1747 i.
Simon 1770 w.
Drew 1771 w.
Simon 1775 i.
Jno. 1784 w.
Jos. 1784 i.
Thos. 1784 i.
Saml. 1785 w.
Henry 1795 w.
Matthew 1795 i.
Saml. 1797 i.
Jesse 1798 w.
HOLSTED
Norfolk
Jas. 1782 i.
HOLSWORTH
Surry
Walter 1681 a.
HOLT
Amelia
Richd. Sr. 1776 w.
Thos. 1787 w.
Bedford
Jno. 1779 i.
Jno. White Jr.
1790 w.
Charles City
Jos. 1772 w.

Charlotte
Wm. 1790 w.
Chesterfield
David 1786 w.
Cumberland
Jno. 1767 w.
Essex
Richd. 1693 w.
Robt. 1698 i.
Wm. 1734 w.
Frederick
Geo. 1797 w.
Halifax
Peter 1792 w.
Nancy 1798 w.
Henry
Richd. 1787 i.
Norfolk
Jas. 1779 w.
Northampton
Geo. 1755 i.
Geo. 1758 w.
Martin 1776 i.
Prince Edward
Plunkett 1789 w.
Princess Anne
David 1734 w.
Southampton
Jos. 1762 i.
Jesse 1766 i.
Chas. 1781 i.
Thos. 1788 w.
Surry
Randall 1679 w.
Eliz. 1709 w.
Jno. 1723 w.
Wm. 1726 w.
Thos. 1730 w.
Eliz. 1737 w.
Wm. 1753 w.
Jno. 1764 w.
Francis 1767 i.
Francis 1769 w.
Benj. 1770 w.
Randolph 1770 w.
Chas. 1773 w.
Thos. 1775 i.
Wm. 1778 i.
Jas. 1782 w.
Jno. 1783 w.
Jas. 1790 i.
Archer 1797 w.
Jos. 1799 w.
HOLTON
Fauquier
Alex. 1782 w.
HOLYHONE
Stafford
Jno. 1707 i.

HOLTZCLAW
Fauquier
Jacob 1760 w.
Jos. 1786 i.
HOLTZCLOUGH
Prince William
Henry 1778 w.
HOLTZENHILLER
Frederick
Geo. 1794 w.
HOLTZENPILLER
Frederick
Stephen 1776 w.
Jno. 1780 w.
HOLVAH
Shenandoah
Conrad 1784 w.
HOLYCROSS
Prince George
Jos. 1716 i.
HOMERSLY
Cumberland
Jane 1761 w.
HOMES
Accomack
Isaac 1742 i.
Henrico
Richd. 1712 w.
Prince William
Edwd. 1799 w.
Spotsylvania
Robt. 1733 w.
HOMMAN
Shenandoah
Michael 1791 i.
HOMMIL
Shenandoah
Peter 1791 i.
HOMMON
Shenandoah
Paul 1789 a.
HONAKER
Shenandoah
Jno. 1787 i.
HONEKAR
Wythe
Jacob 1796 w.
HOOD
Amelia
Thos. 1761 w.
Wm. 1774 w.
Tucker 1785 i.
Jno. 1798 w.
Frederick
Jno. 1744 i.
Luke 1771 w.
Lunenburg
Parker 1795 w.
Stafford
Jno. 1766 w.

Sussex
Jno. 1773 w.
Nathl. 1780 w.
Chris. 1797 w.
HOOE
King George
Housen 1773 w.
Seymour 1783 w.
Gerard 1786 w.
Prince William
Howson 1796 w.
Stafford
Rice 1748 i.
Rice 1758 w.
Francis 1759 i.
Harris 1786 w.
HOOF
Accomack
Caty 1792 w.
HOOFMAN
Culpeper
Jno. 1772 w.
HOOK
Accomack
Jos. 1738 i.
Augusta
Robt. Jr. 1773 i.
Ohio
Jno. 1781 a.
Richmond
Jeremiah 1712 i.
York
Nathl. 1722 w.
HOOKE
Berkeley
Mary 1778 w.
Isle of Wight
Jas. 1777 i.
HOOKER
King George
Stephen 1784 a.
York
Jas. 1772 w.
HOOKEY
Norfolk
Wm. 1691-2 w.
HOOMES
Culpeper
Chris. 1785 w.
Loudoun
Jno. 1777 w.
Spotsylvania
Benj. 1785 a.
HOOP
Culpeper
Chilip 1761 w.
Shenandoah
Gasper 1781 i.
Peter 1773 w.

HOOPER
Amelia
Zachariah 1775 i.
Bedford
Wm. 1760 i.
Cumberland
Jos. 1751 w.
Prince George
Thos. 1726 a.
Middlesex
Francis 1713 w.
Stafford
Thos. 1731 i.
HOOTEN
Accomack
David 1746 i.
HOOVER
Berkeley
Martin 1791 i.
Shenandoah
Wm. 1779 w.
HOPE
Accomack
Wm. 1719 i.
Geo. 1722 i.
Thos. 1734 w.
Geo. 1779 w.
Leah 1783 i.
Kendall 1785 i.
Leah 1785 i.
Thos. 1788 i.
Essex
Thomas 1698 i.
Arthur 1768 i.
Frederick
Jno. 1774 w.
Northampton
Wm. 1754 w.
HOPEGOOD
Rappahannock
Peter 1677 w.
Peter 1679 w.
HOPEWELL
Loudoun
Saml. 1795 i.
HOPEWILL
Loudoun
Jno. 1766 w.
HOPHOCK
Loudoun
Cornelious 1779 w.
HOPKINS
Albemarle
Arthur 1767 w.
Brunswick
Jno. 1748 i.
Henrico
Jas. 1707 i.
Lancaster
Robt. 1718 i.

Loudoun
Jos. 1768 i.
Louisa
Jos. 1782 w.
Peter 1790 w.
Mecklenburg
Jos. 1778 i.
Pittsylvania
Arthur 1776 w.
Princess Anne
Jno. 1694 i.
Jno. 1695 a.
Jno. 1736 w.
Jno. 1771 w.
Jonathan 1782 w.
Jno. 1791 i.
Jno. Sr. 1791 w.
Joshua 1795 w.
Rappahannock
Thos. 1659 i.
Robt. 1677 w.
Northumberland
Wm. 1677 w.
Thos. 1669 i.
Richmond
Geo. 1720 w.
Frances 1747 w.
Westmoreland
Rice 1736 i.
York
———— 1645 i.
Jos. 1764 w.
HOPMAN
Accomack
Jas. 1799 i.
HOPPAUGH
Loundoun
Elce 1797 i.
HOPPER
Culpeper
Wm. 1776 i.
Goochland
Jno. 1791 w.
Mildred 1796 i.
HOPSON
Henrico
Benj. 1736 w.
HOPWOOD
Westmoreland
Richd. 1725 w.
Northumberland
Mary 1758 w.
HORBIN
Princess Anne
Eliz. 1696 w.
HORD
Culpeper
Jno. 1783 w.
Essex
Jno. 1749 w.

Henry
Mordecai 1789 w.
King George
Jno. 1755 i.
Thos. 1766 w.
Mecklenburg
Thos. 1796 w.
Spotsylvania
Wm. 1736 a.
HORE
Stafford
Elias 1730 w.
Westmoreland
Jno. 1712 w.
Robt. 1712 i.
Jas. 1763 w.
Wm. 1753 w.
HORN
Lancaster
Henry M. 1784 i.
Sussex
Jas. 1793 w.
Jno. 1793 i.
HORNBUCKELL
Stafford
Richd. 1748 i.
Richd. 1747 i.
Westmoreland
Henry 1707 w.
HORNBY
Richmond
Danl. 1705 w.
Danl. 1750 w.
HORNE
Lancaster
Rowland 1727 w.
Henry 1749 w.
HORNER
Chesterfield
Benj. 17— i.
Benj. 1766 w.
Savinah 1773 w.
Henrico
Havaliah 1677 op.
Benj. 1734 w.
Norfolk
Geo. 1650 w.
Powhatan
Eliz. 1796 w.
HORNSBY
Accomack
Esther 1750 w.
Jno. 1750 i.
Jno. 1767 w.
Jas. 1769 w.
Mary 1772 w.
Jno. 1773 w.
Rachel 1774 w.
Argall 1775 w.
Jas. 1777 w.
Jno. 1777 i.

Levi 1778 w.
Argol 1789 w.
Elisha 1791 w.
Jno. 1791 w.
Bagwill 1795 w.
Jno. 1795 i.
Zorobabel 1796 w.
Northumberland
Jno. 1754 i.
York
Thos. 1772 w.
HORSELEY
Frederick
Richd. 1784 w.
Hanover
Robt. 1734 w.
HORSENAIL
Spotsylvania
Jas. 1730-1 w.
HORSELLE (?)
Accomack
Jno. 1761 i.
HORSLEY
Albemarle
Wm. 1760 w.
Amherst
Robt. 1786 w.
Wm. 1791 w.
Goochland
Robt. 1734 i.
Northumberland
Ralph 1656 i.
HORSY
Frederick
Morgan 1754 w.
HORSINGTON
York
Jno. 1672 w.
HORTON
Lancaster
Tobias 1669 w.
Ralph 1671 w.
Tobias 1688 i.
Robt. 1706 w.
Tobias 1745 i.
Tobias 1748 w.
Geo. 1753 w.
Geo. 1772 i.
Ellenor 1778 w.
Middlesex
Jno. 1728 i.
Prince William
Snowden 1798 i.
Spotsylvania
Benj. 1728 a.
Stafford
Hugh 1766 i.
Surry
Danl. 1718 i.
Thos. 1723 w.

Westmoreland
  Hugh 1724 i.
HOSFIELD
  Isle of Wight
  Stephen 1689.
HOSKINS
  Amelia
  Jno. 1768 i.
  Essex
  Jno. 1749 i.
  Halifax
  Saml. 1781 w.
  Wm. 1781 w.
  Princess Anne
  Jno. 1697 w.
  Surry
  Ann 1679 w.
  Nicholas 1631 i.
  Edwd. 1727 i.
HOTTEL
  Frederick
  Jno. 1760 w.
HOTZENPELER
  Frederick
  Jno. 1780 i.
  Geo. 1795 i.
HOTZLEGGER
  Shenandoah
  Alex. 1778.
HOUBURT
  Shenandoah
  Nicholas 1787 w.
HOUCHIN
  Goochland
  Chas. 1782 w.
HOUCHINS
  Goochland
  Edwd. 1765 w.
HOUET
  Hanover
  Robt. 1734 a.
HOUGH
  Accomack
  Jos. 1788 i.
  Fairfax
  Laurence Sr. 1779 w.
  Isle of Wight
  Jas. 1760 i.
  Loudoun
  Jos. 1777 w.
  Jno. Jr. 1793 i.
  Philip 1796 i.
  Montgomery
  Jno. 1795 i.
HOUGHMAN
  Frederick
  Jacob 1760 i.
  Loudoun
  Jno. 1793 i.

HOUGHTON
  Northampton
  Jacob 1778 w.
HOUISON
  Culpeper
  Thos. 1769 w.
HOULSWORTH
  Surry
  Ann 1673 w.
HOULT
  Northumberland
  Jos. 1712 i.
  Jno. 1755 w.
HOUSE
  Brunswick
  Jas. 1735 w.
  Thos. 1735 w.
  Laurence 1752 i.
  Lawrence 1753 i.
  Laurence 1754 i.
  Saml. 1773 w.
  Henry 1790 w.
  Hardy
  Jacob 1795 w.
  Isle of Wight
  Jas. 1677 i.
  Geo. 1721 w.
  Jas. 1728 w.
  Jas. 1749 i.
  Jas. 1752 i.
  Jno. 1753 i.
  Jas. 1759 i.
  Martha 1763 i.
  Saml. 1771 w.
  Middlesex
  Nicholas 1717 i.
  Surry
  Saml. 1723 i.
HOUSEMAN
  Berkeley
  David 1794 w.
HOUSMAN
  Brunswick
  Jno. 1768 i.
HOUSER
  Shenandoah
  Henry 1795 w.
HOUSTON
  Culpeper
  Wm. 1783 i.
  Rockbridge
  Mary 1793 w.
  Spotsylvania
  Eliz. 1754 a.
  Hugh 1774 a.
  Wm. 1771 w.
HOUTE
  Berkeley
  Geo. 1786 w.

HOUTZ
  Shenandoah
  Windel 1798 w.
HOVER
  Berkeley
  Martin 1794 i.
HOW
  Essex
  Alex. 1722 w.
  Frederick
  Thos. 1750 a.
  Isle of Wight
  Benj. 1755 i.
  Norfolk
  Thos. 1679 w.
  Richmond
  Jno. 1750 i.
  Geo. 1799 i.
HOWARD
  Accomack
  Nathl. 1751 w.
  Solomon 1755 nw.
  Danl. 1771 i.
  Ambrose 1772 w.
  Nathl. 1788 w.
  Amelia
  Alex. 1752 a.
  Bedford
  Wm. 1782 i.
  Wm. 1791 i.
  Berkeley
  Robt. 1779 i.
  Botetourt
  Edwd. 1785 w.
  Brunswick
  Jno. 1768 w.
  Wm. 1794 w.
  Tabitha 1798 w.
  Frederick
  Jno. 1746 i.
  Jno. 1779 i.
  Goochland
  Allen 1761 w.
  Eliz. 1775 w.
  Jas. 1778 w.
  Henrico
  Jno. 1684 i.
  Isle of Wight
  Jane 1777 w.
  King George
  Chas. 1725 i.
  Lancaster
  Martha 1717 w.
  Lunenburg
  Francis 1749 w.
  Wm. 1752 i.
  Francis 1753 w.
  Middlesex
  Geo. 1720 w.
  Youstice 1744 w.

Norfolk
Roger 1666 i.
Jno. 1795 w.
Jno. 1799 i.
Northumberland
Wm. 1716 nw.
Wm. 1725 i.
Pittsylvania
Wm. 1783 i.
Powhatan
Allen 1798 i.
Jno. 1798 w.
Prince George
Jas. 1720 i.
Prince William
Robt. 1737 a.
Richmond
Jas. 1750 w.
Stafford
Wm. 1761 i.
Surry
Henry 1789 w.
Betty 1795 w.
Westmoreland
Jno. 1716 i.
Susanna 1717 i.
Sarah 1729 i.
Philip 1750 i.
York
Ann 1747 i.
Francis 1748 i.
Henry 1753 i.
Jno. 1770 w.
Eliz. 1773 i.
Henry 1782 w.
Anne 1785 i.
HOWE
Montgomery
Jos. 1790 w.
Richmond
Mary 1762 w.
Geo. 1794 w.
Surry
Robt. 1699 i.
HOWEL
Accomack
Jno. 1762 i.
Isle of Wight
Jno. 1732 w.
Northumberland
Jno. 1727 i.
HOWELL
Albemarle
Simon 1783 i.
Amelia
Jno. 1751 a.
Jno. 1781 w.
Stephen 1772 w.
Jno. 1785 i.
Brunswick
Thos. 1779 i.

Frances 1786 i.
Frederick
Wm. 1747 w.
Wm. 1749 w.
Henrico
Thos. 1698 w.
Isle of Wight
Jno. 1680 i.
Hopkins 1687 w.
Mathey 1720 w.
Jno. 1728 i.
Jas. 1754 i.
Wm. 1755 w.
King George
Jno. 1754 w.
Lancaster
Thos. 1723 w.
Sarah 1731 w.
Jno. 1732 i.
Loudoun
Hugh 1777 w.
Timothy 1794 w.
Timothy 1797 i.
Montgomery
Benj. 1799 w.
Norfolk
Cobb (Cob) 1656 w.
Northampton
Jno. 1787 w.
Northumberland
Geo. 1728-9 w.
Prince George
Chas. 1728 i.
Rappahannock
Geo. 1681 w.
Richmond
Downing 1750 w.
Southampton
Wm. 1763 w.
Hartwell 1778 i.
Goodrich 1797 i.
Surry
Edmund 1679 w.
Jno. 1717 w.
Wm. 1720 w.
Wm. 1732 w.
Nathl. 1742 w.
Edmond 1747 i.
Sussex
Wm. 1762 i.
Westmoreland
Paul 1703 i.
Jno. 1738 w.
HOWELLS
Isle of Wight
Mathew 1721 i.
HOWELS
Isle of Wight
Thos. 1778 i.

HOWERTON
Brunswick
Jas. 1784 w.
Thos. 1795 i.
Essex
Thos. 1757 w.
Obediah 1762 w.
Jno. 1781 w.
Wm. 1781 w.
Heritage 1793 i.
Wm. 1798 i.
Spotsylvania
Jno. 1792 w.
HOWETT
Northumberland
Jno. 1658 i.
Thos. 1658 w.
HOWGATE
Westmoreland
Jas. 1726 w.
HOWILL
Isle of Wight
Jno. 1728 w.
HOWKINS (?)
Northampton
———— 1646 i.
HOWLE
Goochland
Wm. 1730 a.
HOWLET
Chesterfield
Jos. 1782 i.
HOWLETT
Chesterfield
Crowley 1750 w.
Thos. 1757 w.
Jno. 1761 i.
Judith 1769 w.
Betty 1784 i.
Thos. 1791 w.
Thos. 1795 i.
Thos. 1798 i.
Henrico
Thos. 1685 i.
Susanna 1725 w.
HOWLS
Henrico
Jas. 1727 i.
HOWS
Prince William
Wm. 1740 a.
HOWSON
Northampton
Robt. 1720 w.
Northumberland
Leonard 1704-5 w.
Richd. 1743-4 w.
Hannah 1744 w.
Judith 1772 w.

HOXFORD
Richmond
Jno. 1718 w.
HOY
Shenandoah
Jno. 1777 w.
Jno. 1784 a.
HOYLAND
Pittsylvania
Geo. 1783 i.
HOYLE
Berkeley
Jacob 1781 w.
Essex
Saml. 1707-8 i.
Saml. 1708 i.
King George
Saml. 1734 i.
Edwd. 1750 i.
Saml. 1775 a.
Saml. 1788 a.
HUBANK
York
Geo. 1686 w.
HUBARD
Amelia
Jno. 1745 w.
York
Ralph 1713 i.
Matthew 1745 w.
Jane 1748 i.
Matthew 1755 i.
Eliz. 1764 w.
Matthew 1772 i.
HUBBARD
Amelia
Eliz. 1783 w.
Halifax
Benj. 1771 w.
Joel 1781 w.
Jos. 1799 w.
Lancaster
Thos. 1717 w.
Thos. 1745 w.
Jno. 1761 w.
Jos. 1766 w.
Joshua 1783 i.
Wm. 1783 w.
Wm. 1792 i.
Chas. 1795 w.
Jos. 1795 i.
Wm. 1797 w.
Lunenburg
Matthew 1783 i.
Pittsylvania
Edmd. 1780 w.
Jno. 1793 w.
Spotsylvania
Thos. 1747 w.
Jno. 1761 a.

Sussex
Matthew 1779 w.
Jas. 1789 i.
York
Jas. 1719 w.
Thos. 1721 i.
Jno. 1732 i.
Wm. 1783 i.
Cuthbert 1790 w.
Wm. 1790 i.
Zachariah 1791 w.
HUBBERD
York
Jno. 1668 i.
HUBBERT
York
Jas. 1694 i.
Jas. 1695 i.
HUBERD
York
Matthew 1667 w.
Matthew 1670 i.
HUBELL
Washington
Justis 1796 i.
HUCKBERRY
Fairfax
Robt. 1750 a.
HUCKEY
Surry
Thos. 1740 i.
HUCKIBY
Brunswick
Thos. 1736 w.
HUCHINGS
Norfolk
Zach. 1783 w.
HUCKSTEP
Albemarle
Josiah 1774 w.
HUCKLESCOTT
Essex
Thos. 1701 w.
HUDDINGTON
Northampton
Wm. 1654 i.
HUDDLE
Botetourt
Geo. 1794 w.
Shenandoah
Jno. 1772 w.
Geo. 1787 w.
David 1788 w
HUDDLESEY
Henrico
Thos. 1726 i.
HUDDLESTON
Bedford
Abraham 1785 w.
Princess Anne
Thos. 1749 i.

HUDLESTONE
Northampton
Saml. 1727 i.
Princess Anne
Jno. 1763 i.
Thos. 1748 w.
Thos. 1778 w.
HUDGGEN
Princess Anne
Moses (1) 1782 w.
Moses (2) 1782 w.
HUDGEN
Princess Anne
Geo. 1788 w.
Jas. 1790 w.
HUDGENS
Cumberland
Wm. 1781 w.
HUDNALL
Northumberland
Jno. 1659 i.
Parton 1703-4 w.
Jos. 1709 w.
Partin 1721 i.
Jos. 1742 w.
Richd. 1752 w.
Jno. 1754 w.
Richd. 1760 w.
Rebecca 1763 w.
Judith 1775 w.
Ellis 1776 i.
Jno. 1789 w.
Wm. 1794 i.
Wm. 1797 w.
Prince William
Thos. 1740 w.
HUDSON
Accomack
Wm. 1709 w.
Wm. 1786 i.
Albemarle
Jno. 1769 w.
Jno. 1771 w.
Amelia
Jas. 1749 w.
Pheby 1762 w.
Henry 1766 i.
Nicho. 1769 w.
Jno. 1777 w.
Hall 1778 w.
Jno. 1780 i.
Robt. 1780 w.
Jno. 1782 i.
Burton 1785 w.
Peter 1786 w.
Saml. 1787 i.
Jno. 1787 w.
Chris. 1789 w.
Eliz. 1795 w.
Edwd. 1797 w.

Amherst
Martha 1784 w.
Robt. 1791 w.
Joshua 1793 a.
Charlotte
Jas. 1765 w.
Chesterfield
Robt. 1757 w.
Martha 1759 w.
Jno. 1786 w.
Sarah 1799 w.
Essex
Thos. 1706 i.
Wm. 1729 w.
Jno. 1735 i.
Jno. 1739 i.
Henry 1745 w.
Thos. 1786 w.
Fairfax
Jno. 1750 a.
Hanover
Jno. 1733-4 eb.
Henrico
Wm. 1701-2 i.
King George
Wm. 1729 i.
Rush 1735 i.
Wm. 1735 i.
Lucy 1756 w.
Jas. 1765 i.
Jno. 1765 i.
Ann 1778 a.
Joshua 1797 w.
Wm. 1797 w.
Louisa
David 1788 w.
Lunenburg
Jno. 1755 i.
Richd. 1777 w.
Jno. 1790 w.
Ward 1793 w.
Mecklenburg
Chas. 1766 w.
Chris. 1779 w.
Robt. 1796 w.
Norfolk
Ann 1782 w.
Jno. 1790 w.
Northampton
Jno. 1679 i.
Jesse 1784 w.
Northumberland
Robt. 1757 w.
Rodham 1760 i.
Thos. 1778 i.
Jno. C. 1795 w.
Prince Edward
Thos. Sr. 1796 w.
Rappahannock
Thos. 1679 w.

Shenandoah
Jno. 1793 a.
Surry
Danl. 1761 w.
Westmoreland
Joshua 1704 w.
Jno. 1703 w.
Field 1737 nw.
Joshua 1727 i.
Joyce 1729 i.
Wm. 1750 i.
Leroy 1779 i.
York
Eliz. 1660 i.
HUEBANKS
Accomack
Mary 1732 i.
HUES
Middlesex
Jno. 1678 a.
Norfolk
Edwd. 1712 i.
HUEY
Lunenburg
Humphrey 1760 w.
HUFF
Brunswick
Danl. 1777 w.
Danl. 1795 w.
Wm. Sr. 1781 w.
HUFFINGTON
Northampton
Jas. 1772 w.
HUFFINTON
Northampton
Jas. 1772 i.
HUFFMAN
Culpeper
Henry 1766 w.
Henry 1783 w.
Loudoun
Jno. 1792 w.
Madison
Adam 1796 w.
Moses 1796 a.
Orange
Jno. 1741 a.
Pittsylvania
Henry 1795 i.
Shenandoah
Philip 1784 i.
HUFMAN
Culpeper
Jno. 1772 i.
HUGART
Greenbrier
Jas. 1791 w.
HUGBIN
Northampton
Jno. 1688 w.

HUGES
Accomack
Jno. 1712 w.
HUGGART
Augusta
Jas. 1767 w.
HUGGINS
Brunswick
Wm. 1743 w.
Isle of Wight
Wm. 1712 i.
Princess Anne
Philip 1727 i.
Margt. 1737 i.
Robt. 1754 w.
Mary 1759 i.
Robt. 1773 w.
Natt 1774 w.
David 1785 i.
Marcom 1791 w.
HUGH
Westmoreland
Hugh 1773 i.
HUGHES
Accomack
Wm. 1721 w.
Albemarle
Thos. 1779 w.
Stephen 1793 w.
Augusta
Jas. 1767 i.
Bedford
Jno. 1790 i.
Berkeley
Isaac 1776 i.
Brunswick
Jno. 1784 w.
Charles City
Jno. 1769 i.
Cumberland
Ashford 1750 nw.
Stephen 1753 w.
Robt. 1755 w.
Jos. 1756 w.
Isaac 1758 w.
Robt. 1760 w.
Abraham 1761 w.
Wm. 1764 i.
Wm. 1768 nw.
Orlando 1768 w.
Martha 1769 w.
Jno. 1774 w.
Leander (1) 1775 w.
Leander (2) 1775 w.
Essex
Jno. 1694 w.
Francis 1749 i.
Franklin
Pratt 1794 w.
Frederick
Ralph 1767 w.

Goochland
Sarah 1730 w.
Hardy
Susan 1791 w.
Henrico
Jas. 1795 i.
Henry
Blackmore 1786 w.
Isle of Wight
Ephila 1782 w.
King George
Wm. 1786 a.
Louisa
David 1791 i.
Norfolk
Edwd. 1776 w.
Northumberland
Jno. 1792 i.
Orange
Thos. Sr. 1764 w.
Powhatan
Robt. 1784 w.
Martha 1785 w.
David 1796 i.
Prince Edward
Leander 1772 w.
Richmond
Edwd. 1752 i.
Spotsylvania
Thos. 1798 a.
Washington
Saml. 1783 i.
York
Wm. 1661 i.
HUGHLETT
Norfolk
Jno. 1743 w.
Northumberland
Jno. 1711 w.
Mary 1711 i.
Jno. 1719 w.
Ephraim 1727 i.
Thos. 1729 w.
Yarrott 1750 w.
Nicholas 1765 i.
Judith 1775 w.
Wm. 1794 w.
Saml. 1795 w.
Jno. 1795 w.
Winter 1795 w.
Jno. 1796 w.
Lucy 1796 i.
Jno. 1798 i.
Richmond
Jno. 1742 w.
HUGHLEY
Norfolk
Thos. 1687 w.
HUGHS
Accomack
Jos. 1733 i.

Amelia
Thos. 1753 a.
Anderson 1782 i.
Jno. 1792 w.
Mary Ann 1794 w.
Essex
Simon 1754 i.
King George
Thos. 1759 i.
Lunenburg
Anthy. 1763 w.
Princess Anne
Thos. 1779 w.
Richmond
Jno. 1715 i.
HUGING
Princess Anne
Geo. 1790 i.
HUGINS
Norfolk
Nicho. 1691-2 w.
HUGLEY
Loudoun
Abraham 1792 w.
HUGULEY
Loudoun
Chas. 1797 w.
HUIT
Accomack
Robt. 1677 w.
HULETT
Fauquier
Leroy 1782 i.
Northumberland
Thos. 1770 w.
York
Lawrence 1658 w.
HULIN
Sussex
Celea 1763 i.
Celia 1764 i.
HULING
Brunswick
Edwd. 1772 w.
HULINGS
Sussex
Israel 1761 i.
HULL
Berkeley
Henry 1794 i.
Northumberland
Jno. 1668 w.
Richd. 1719 i.
Richd. 1777 w.
Eliz. 1794 w.
Rappahannock
Jno. 1677 w.
Jos. 1750 i.
Westmoreland
Mr. 1669 i.
Anne 1671 w.

Edwd. 1704 i.
Wm. 1729 i.
Geo. 1793 i.
HULM
Amelia
Wm. 1761 i.
HULME
Amelia
Wm. 1760 w.
Sussex
Anne 1759 w.
HULSE
Berkeley
Josiah 1778 i.
Frederick
Richd. 1770 w.
Richd. 1783 i.
HULSTON
York
Nicho. 1719-20 w.
HUM
Berkeley
Jacob 1786 w.
HUMBLE
Augusta
Martin 1777 i.
Frederick
Michale 1781 w.
HUMBOUGH
Shenandoah
Henry 1790 a.
HUME
Culpeper
Geo. 1760 i.
Fauquier
Wm. 1796 i.
Frederick
Geo. 1744 a.
HUMPHREY
Culpeper
Jno. 1767 w.
Essex
Jno. 1706-7 w.
Fairfax
Saml. 1789 w.
Frederick
Ralph 1751 i.
Loudoun
Thos. 1796 w.
Isaac 1797 i.
Stafford
Elias 1703 i.
Westmoreland
Wm. 1718 i.
HUMPRES
Middlesex
Wm. 1785 w.
HUMPHREYS
Essex
Jos. 1706-7 i.

Frederick
Jno. 1783 **w.**
Greenbrier
Jas. 1795 **i.**
Henrico
Wm. 1687 **w.**
Lancaster
Jos. 1748 **i.**
Surry
Robt. 1714 **i.**
York
Jno. 1657 **i.**
HUMPHRIES
Brunswick
Jno. 1738 **w.**
Botetourt
Jno. 1796 **i.**
Loudoun
Wm. 1789 **i.**
Middlesex
Jno. 1761 **w.**
Northumberland
Wm. 1728 **i.**
Geo. 1784 **i.**
Jos. 1787 **w.**
Elias 1792 **w.**
Stafford
Walter 1739 **i.**
HUMPHRIS
Middlesex
Jno. Jr. 1795 **i.**
Northumberland
Jos. 1769 **w.**
Jno. 1782 **w.**
HUMPHRISS
Northumberland
Geo. 1756 **i.**
HUMPHREYS
Lancaster
Geo. 1746 **i.**
HUMPLETT
Norfolk
Thos. 1749-50 **w.**
HUMPRIES
Middlesex
Jno. 1768 **i.**
Ann 1768 **i.**
HUMSTON
Stafford
Thos. 1731 **i.**
HUNDLEY
Amelia
Chas. 1778 **w.**
Anthony 1784 **w.**
Josiah 1790 **i.**
Charlotte
Ambrose 1778 **i.**
Chesterfield
Margt. 1791 **i.**
Essex
Ambrose 1772 **i.**

Jno. 1798 **i.**
Middlesex
Eliz. 1746 **w.**
Pittsylvania
Geo. 1781 **i.**
Mary 1798 **i.**
HUNGARFORD
King George
Thos. 1772 **w.**
HUNGATE
Augusta
Chas. 1749 **i.**
HUNLEY
Essex
Thos. 1775 **w.**
Robt. 1778 **w.**
Jno. 1796 **w.**
York
Humphrey 1752 **w.**
HUNNICUT
Surry
Augustine 1683 **w.**
Jno. 1699 **i.**
Augustine 1710 **w.**
Margt. 1718 **w.**
Wm. 1718 **i.**
Augustine 1743 **w.**
Jno. 1762 **w.**
Robt. 1778 **w.**
Augustine 1792 **w.**
Sussex
Glaister 1781 **w.**
HUNNIFORD
Surry
Wm. 1710 **w.**
Hugh 1746 **w.**
Jane 1757 **w.**
HUNT
Bedford
Jno. 1778 **i.**
Charlotte
Chas. 1788 **w.**
Jas. 1795 **w.**
Jas. 1797 **w.**
Wm. P. 1797 **w.**
Essex
Wm. 1720 **i.**
Jno. 1748 **i.**
Jno. 1761 **w.**
Frederick
Henry 1764 **w.**
Halifax
Jos. 1756 **i.**
Jos. 1777 **i.**
Elijah 1795 **w.**
Nathl. 1795 **i.**
Nathl. 1797 **i.**
Isle of Wight
Lawrence 1720 **i.**
Prudence 1778 **i.**
Dempsey 1786 **w.**

Lancaster
Mary 1785 **i.**
Loudoun
Jas. 1768 **i.**
Wm. 1798 **i.**
Lunenburg
Jos. 1761 **i.**
Middlesex
Matth. 1723 **w.**
Northuhmberland
Geo. 1745 **w.**
Northampton
Thos. 1655 **w.**
Joane 1656 **w.**
Thos. 1701 **w.**
Ann 1709 **w.**
Thos. 1719 **w.**
Jno. 1720 **w.**
Azariah 1736 **w.**
Hillary 1741 **w.**
Gawton 1754 **w.**
Mary 1757 **w.**
Thos. 1758 **w.**
Anne 1761 **w.**
Obadiah 1772 **w.**
Azariah 1775 **w.**
Azariah 1779 **i.**
Thos. 1795 **w.**
Orange
Henry 1743 **a.**
Southampton
Miles 1795 **i.**
Stafford
Francis 1703 **i.**
Surry
Thos. 1711 **i.**
Wm. 1711 **w.**
Thos. 1726 **w.**
Wm. 1727 **i.**
Sussex
Jno. 1759 **w.**
Jno. 1773 **i.**
Thos. 1759 **w.**
Wm. Jr. 1772 **w.**
Wm. 1774 **w.**
Sarah 1779 **i.**
Goodwyn 1792 **w.**
York
Ralph 1676 **i.**
Jno. 1679 **w.**
Richd. 1679 **w.**
Jno. 1706 **w.**
Jno. 1719 **i.**
Jno. 1729 **i.**
Chas. 1795 **w.**
HUNTER
Augusta
Saml. 1765 **i.**
Jno. 1774 **w.**
Bedford
Alex. 1768 **w.**

Berkeley
Hugh 1778 i.
Campbell
Jno. 1796 w.
Essex
Ann 1717 w.
Jno. 1721 w.
Wm. 1785 i.
Sarah 1792 i.
Fairfax
Jno. 1764 w.
Geo. 1776 w.
Wm. 1792 w.
Goochland
Wm. 1767 i.
Isle of Wight
Jas. 1688 w.
Wm. 1720 w.
Jas. 1739 w.
Seth 1759 w.
Joshua 1772 w.
Eliz. 1779 w.
Louisa
Andrew 1764 w.
Norfolk
Jno. 1774 i.
Northumberland
Jno. 1726 i.
Robt. 1740 i.
Allen 1749 i.
Princess Anne
Wm. 1718 w.
Jno. 1753 w.
Jacomine 1756 i.
Thos. 1761 w.
Wm. 1764 w.
Jno. 1769 i.
Jas. 1772 i.
Jas. 1774 w.
Wm. 1777 w.
Jas. 1779 i.
Thos. 1779 w.
Wm. 1779 i.
Jacob 1780 w.
Thos. 1789 w.
Dinah 1782 w.
Spotslyvania
Wm. 1754 w.
Stafford
Jno. 1749 i.
Jas. 1785 w.
Surry
David 1783 i.
Wm. 1784 i.
Westmoreland
Jas. 1778 w.
York
Saml. 1727 i.
Mary 1733 i.
Wm. 1761 w.

HUNTLY
Westmoreland
Wm. 1740 i.
HUNTON
Albemarle
Jno. 1786 w.
Lancaster
Thos. 1746 w.
Thos. 1794 w.
Middlesex
Thos. Jr. 1793 i.
Pittsylvania
Jas. 1791 i.
Richmond
Alex. 1789 w.
Thos. 1795 i.
HUNTSMAN
Albemarle
Benj. 1791 w.
Augusta
Lawrence 1764 i.
Westmoreland
Danl. 1716 i.
HUNTZBUGER
Shenandoah
Jacob 1795 i.
HUPPOK
Loudoun
Elsey 1797 w.
HURD
York
Morris 1683-4 i.
HURDLE
Surry
Wm. 1727 w.
Eliz. 1747 w.
HURDY
Stafford
Robt. 1749 w.
HURLE
Norfolk
Jos. 1677 w.
HURLEY
Westmoreland
Jno. 1766 w.
HURNDON
Lunenburg
Humphrey 1799 i.
HURST
Brunswick
Thos. 1752 i.
Sarah 1762 i.
Penny 1776 w.
Eliz. 1779 w.
Fairfax
Jas. 1766 i.
Jno. 1790 w.
Jno. 1798 i.
Fauquier
Rosannah 1793 w.

Isle of Wight
Jno. 1727 w.
Lancaster
Toby 1656 i.
Northumberland
Thos. 1721 w.
Jno. 1745 i.
Thos. 1758 w.
Thos. 1765 w.
Kemp 1782 w.
Isaac 1786 w.
Isaac 1787 w.
Jos. 1790 w.
Kemp 1794 w.
Henry 1798 w.
Shenandoah
Wm. 1781 w.
Stafford
Geo. 1748 i.
Jno. 1748 w.
Jane 1757 w.
Southampton
Wm. 1797 w.
HURT
Amelia
Moses Sr. 1783 w.
Wm. 1795 w.
Culpeper
Jas. 1781 w.
Jas. 1789 w.
Halifax
Moza 1793 w.
Phebee 1795 i.
Norfolk
Jno. 1781 w.
Pittsylvania
Moses 1799 w.
Prince Edward
Benj. 1797 i.
HURTLEY
Accomack
Wm. 1728 i.
HUSK
Northumberland
Jno. 1711 i.
HUSKEGSON
Prince Edward
Lucritia 1795 w.
HUSKEY
Brunswick
Wm. 1799 w.
HUSKINSON
Charlotte
Jno. 1775 w.
HUSON
Henrico
Robt. 1678 i.
Sussex
Richd. 1761 w.
Jno. 1797 i.

HUST
Northumberland
Jno. 1745-6 w.
Jno. 1748 w.
HUSTARD
Montgomery
Wm. 1778 i.
HUSTON
Augusta
Jno. 1754 w.
Robt. 1761 w.
Archd. 1774 w.
Archd. 1782 i.
HUTCHASON
Goochland
Matthew 1750 w.
HUTCHERSON
Amelia
Wm. 1796 w.
Spotsylvania
Jno. 1774 w.
Wm. 1775 w.
HUTCHESON
Amelia
Chas. 1769 w.
Amherst
Jno. 1799 i.
Augusta
Jno. 1758 a.
Thos. 1772 w.
Campbell
Wm. 1793 w.
Mecklenburg
Jno. 1782 w.
Prince Edward
Wm. 1765 i.
Spotsylvania
Wm. 1763 w.
Stafford
Geo. 1735 i.
Westmoreland
Wm. 1768 w.
HUTCHING
Lancaster
Jno. 1768 i.
HUTCHINGS
Essex
Richd. 1712 i.
Richd. 1720 w.
Henrico
Jos. 1783 w.
Jno. 1785 w.
Lancaster
Jno. 1727 w.
Jno. 1758 i.
Wm. 1760 i.
Wm. 1770 i.
Richd. 1777 i.
Jno. 1785 w.
Richd. 1788 i.
Montgomery
Jno. 1787 a.

Norfolk
Jno. 1768 w.
Jno. 1786 w.
Pittsylvania
Jno. 1776 w.
Princess Anne
Danl. 1718 i.
Danl. 1720 i.
Nicholas 1730 w.
Nathl. 1731 i.
Sarah 1731 w.
Southampton
Danl. 1782 w.
Surry
Jno. 1719 i.
Westmoreland
Jno. 1792 w.
HUTCHINS
Isle of Wight
Francis 1774 w.
Lancaster
Frances 1733 w.
HUTCHINSON
Accomack
Robt. 1712 w.
Jas. 1713 w.
Stephen 1721 w.
Jas. 1767 w.
Benj. 1780 w.
Jno. 1787 w.
Botetourt
Wm. 1778 w.
Northampton
Jno. 1689 w.
Princess Anne
Robt. 1728 i.
Prince William
Jno. 1780 w.
Richmond
Thos. 1750 i.
HUTCHISON
Accomack
Jno. 1735 w.
Augusta
Janet 1747 nw.
Frances 1747 nw.
Sarah 1785 i.
Greenbrier
Jno. 1796 i.
Loudoun
Wm. 1788 i.
Benj. 1796 i.
Prince William
Wm. 1795 w.
Westmoreland
Wm. 1769 i.
HUTSELL
Wythe
Geo. 1793 w.
HUTSON
Accomack
Jno. 1724 i.

Wm. 1785 w.
Amherst
Martha 1787 w.
Northumberland
Rodham 1792 w.
Rappahannock
Edwd. 1672 w.
HUTT
Berkeley
Simeon 1798 w.
Westmoreland
Danl. 1674 w.
Gerrard 1740 w.
Thos. 1758 i.
Gerrard 1770 w.
Jno. 1772 w.
Gerrard 1773 i.
Jno. 1774 i.
Jno. 1777 i.
Jno. 1783 w.
Wm. 1799 w.
HUTTLE
Shenandoah
David 1788 i.
HUTTON
Accomack
Jno. 1709 w.
Loudoun
Jno. 1772 w.
Saml. 1787 i.
Middlesex
Jno. 1751 a.
Prince William
Benj. 1737 a.
HUTTOR
Hampshire
Michael 1796 w.
HUTTSON
Essex
Wm. 1729 i.
HUX
Surry
Wm. 1677 w.
HUXFORD
Lancaster
Henry 1688 w.
Northampton
Henry 1687 w.
HYDE
Mecklenburg
Jas. 1782 w.
Jno. 1792 w.
Jno. Sr. 1792 w.
Thos. 1792 i.
Surry
Benj. 1754 i.
York
Robt. 1718 i.
Saml. 1739 w.
Sarah 1740 i.
Anne 1743 w.
Jno. 1774 w.

Jno. 1778 i.
Eliz. 1788 w.
HYDEN
Isle of Wight
Ephram 1727-8 w.
HYDES
Isle of Wight
Ann 1700 i.
HYLTON
Chesterfield
Jno. 1773 w.
R—— 1790 w.
HYMAN
Essex
Peter 1698 i.
HYNDS
Augusta
Edwd. 1778 w.
Brunswick
Robt. 1767 w.
York
Thos. 1717-18 ab.
HYNES
Charles City
Edwd. 1796 i.
HYRON
Northampton
Mary 1736 w.
HYSLEP
Accomack
Hannah 1784 w.
HYSLOP
Accomack
Geo. 1797 w.
Smith 1797 w.
Northampton
Walter 1792 w.

I

I'ANSON
Surry
Jno. 1758 w.
Thos. 1792 i.
ICE & SNOW
Albemarle
———— 1780 i.
ICORN
Northampton
Henry 1728 i.
IDLE
Princess Anne
Edwd. 1742 w.
ILER
Frederick
Godfrey 1771 w.
ILES
York
Thos. 1677 w.
ILIFFE
Princess Anne

Thos. 1708 w.
INBRUNT
Frederick
Hildebrand 1765 w.
INCE
Norfolk
Jno. Jr. 1767 w.
Princess Anne
Edmd. 1769 i.
Jno. 1771 i.
Jno. 1773 i.
York
Jno. 1709 i.
INCH
Northampton
Eliz. 1711 w.
INEBENS
Frederick
Hillibrand 1770 i.
INGERSON
Accomack
Tabitha 1753 w.
INGHAM
Norfolk
Jno. 1761 w.
INGLASS
Lunenburg
Alex. 1749 i.
INGLE
Frederick
Melechia 1764 a.
INGLEBIRD
Botetourt
Geo. 1778 a.
INGLETHORP
Westmoreland
Thos. 1751 w.
INGLIS
Augusta
Jno. 1761 a.
Montgomery
Wm. 1782 w.
INGLISH
Augusta
Patrick 1761 w.
Isle of Wight
William 1742 i.
Jno. 1750 w.
Jno. 1751 i.
Thos. 1768 w.
Mary 1777 w.
Jos. 1782 i.
York
Wm. 1767 w.
INGLISHBY
Richmond
Mary 1765 w.
INGO
Richmond
Jas. 1724 w.
INGOE

Richmond
Jno. Sr. 1701 w.
INGRAHAM
Isle of Wight
Jeremiah 1737 w.
Southampton
Wm. 1758 w.
INGRAM
Brunswick
Jno. 1760 w.
Jno. 1763 w.
Jas. 1770 w.
Jno. 1777 i.
Moses 1784 w.
Jno. Sr. 1791 w.
Jos. Sr. 1793 w.
Benj. 1795 w.
Essex
Thos. 1714 w.
Tobias 1751 i.
Wm. 1792 i.
Isle of Wight
Roger 1669 i.
Roger 1732 i.
Roger 1734 w.
Roger 1743 w.
Jennings 1763 w.
Sarah 1774 w.
Lunenburg
Saml. 1765 i.
Robt. 1782 i.
Richd. 1788 i.
Jno. 1795 i.
Norfolk
Content 1777 w.
Northumberland
Jno. 1654 w.
Thos. 1707 w.
Jno. 1722 w.
Saml. 1743-4 w.
Geo. 1749 i.
Chas. 1760 w.
Geo. 1796 w.
Surry
Jno. 1772 i.
INGREM
Botetourt
Alex. 1783 w.
INGRUM
Isle of Wight
Jno. 1721 w.
Roger 1728 i.
Prince George
Richd. 1727 i.
INKSON
Norfolk
Richd. 1753 w.
INMAN
Surry
Robt. 1701-2 w.
John 1771 w.
Isham 1785 w.

Westmoreland
Abraham 1662 w.
INNES
Franklin
Hugh 1797 w.
INNIS
Northampton
Sarah 1687 w.
Richmond
Jas. 1710 w.
York
——— 1721 i.
INSCOE
Essex
Abner 1761 i.
INSKEEP
Culpeper
Wm. 1796 i.
INSLE
Loudoun
Henry 1761 w.
INUIN (?)
Albemarle
Jno. 1777 w.
IRBY
Amelia
Jno. 1763 w.
Chas. 1763 i.
Wm. 1765 w.
Susanna 1767 w.
Wm. 1767 i.
Chas. 1775 w.
Brunswick
Jno. 1747 w.
Wm. 1753 i.
Charles City
Eliz. 1768 i.
Hardyman 1798 w.
Chesterfield
Jno. 1761 i.
Halifax
Wm. 1775 i.
Anthony Jr. 1780 i.
Anthony 1796 w.
Henrico
Joshua 1746 w.
Northampton
Walter 1652 w.
Pittsylvania
Jas. 1779 i.
Peter 1795 w.
Francis 1795 i.
Sussex
Jno. 1761 w.
Jno. 1770 i.
Mary 1774 w.
Mary 1777 i.
York
Richd. 1718 w.

IRELAND
Harrison
Jonathan 1798 i.
Henrico
Wm. 1729 i.
Lancaster
Wm. 1655 i.
Westmoreland
Thos. 1746-7 i.
IREMONGER
Accomack
Thos. 1724 i.
IRESON
Frederick
Jas. 1767 w.
IRISH
Lancaster
Jno. 1659 i.
Richmond
Barnard 1716 i.
IRONMONGER
Accomack
Edwd. 1761 w.
Jno. 1779 i.
Major 1782 w.
Edwd. 1788 nw.
Surry
Mary 1695 a.
Thos. 1711 i.
Westmoreland
Corderoy 1675 i.
IRONS
Northumberland
Jno. 1767 w.
IRVIN
Albemarle
Jno. 1783 i.
Brunswick
Eliz. 1736 w.
Campbell
Jno. 1791 i.
Montgomery
Jno. 1779 i.
Norfolk
Robt. 1786 w.
IRVINE
Bedford
Wm. 1767 w.
Chris. 1769 w.
Campbell
Wm. 1796 w.
Halifax
Jas. 1774 w.
Alex. 1784 w.
Saml. 1789 i.
IRVING
Albemarle
Chas. 1795 i.
Campbell
Jno. 1791 w.

Essex
Wm. 1718 i.
IRWIN
Frederick
Wm. 1791 i.
Princess Anne
Wm. 1697 i.
Wm. 1698 a.
York
Thos. Wm. 1742-3 i.
Thos. Wm. 1748 i.
Eliz. 1767 w.
ISAAC
Frederick
Saml. 1749 w.
Saml. 1760 w.
Saml. 1767 i.
Northampton
Jno. 1709 i.
Jno. 1716 w.
ISACK
Richmond
Thos. 1714 i.
ISBELL
Charlotte
Jas. 1777 w.
Halifax
Geo. 1794 w.
ISDALL
Northampton
Mark 1749 i.
ISDELL
Northampton
Geo. 1687 w.
Jno. 1736 w.
Princess Anne
Jas. 1731 i.
ISH
Culpeper
Christian 1791 i.
ISHALL
Norfolk
Jno. 1796 i.
ISHAM
Henrico
Henry 1678-9 w.
Katherine 1686 w.
ISLES
Westmoreland
Jacob 1726 i.
York
Thos. 1678 i.
ISON
Amherst
Jas. 1765 i.
ISTED
York
Richd. 1711 nw.
IVES
Norfolk
Timothy 1743 w.

Geo. 1752 i.
Thos. 1757 w.
Robt. 1764 w.
Sarah 1764 w.
Jno. 1798 w.
Josiah 1778 i.
Timothy 1784 w.
Ann 1785 w.
Joshua 1796 w.
York
Alice 1722 w.
[Eliz.?] 1722 ab.
IVEY
Brunswick
Benj. 1795 w.
Norfolk
Geo. 1711 i.
Geo. 1715 i.
Wm. 1764 i.
Lamuel 1782 i.
Southampton
Jno. 1787 i.
Jno. 1791 i.
Henry 1791 w.
Sussex
Hugh 1793 w.
Adam 1795 w.
IVIE
Prince George
Eliz. 1719 w.
Surry
Jno. 1753 w.
Sussex
Henry 1771 i.
IVY
Brunswick
Hardey 1783 w.
Norfolk
Thos. Vis. 1684 w.
Geo. 1688-9 w.
Jno. 1693 w.
Jas. 1752 w.
Jno. 1752 w.
Wm. Sr. 1769 w.
Alice 1773 i.
Eliz. 1777 w.
Jno. 1779 i.
Wm. 1779 i.
Saml. 1796 i.
Princess Anne
Lemuel 1703 w.
Thos. 1713 i.
Anthony 1725 w.
Jno. 1739 a.
Lemuel 1734 w.
Thos. 1743 i.
Southampton
Jos. 1764 i.
Henry 1774 w.
Jno. 1781 w.
Jno. 1789 w.

IZARD
Isle of Wight
Richd. 1669 w.
Rebeccah 1675 w.

J

JACK
Berkeley
Jeremiah 1785 w.
Jas. 1796 w.
Loudoun
Patrick 1784 w.
JACKMAN
Fauquier
Thos. 1782 w.
Rappahannock
Anthony 1681 a.
JACKSON
Accomack
Jonah 1678 w.
Eliz. 1731 w.
Henry 1732 i.
Jno. 1737 w.
Jno. 1742 i.
Wm. 1765 i.
Archd. 1777 i.
Amelia
Thos. 1765 w.
Francis 1776 w.
Wm. 1778 w.
Danl. 1781 w.
Matthew 1783 w.
Jno. Sr. 1788 w.
Francis 1792 w.
Joel 1795 w.
Augusta
Wm. 1751 a.
Wm. 1753 i.
Jas. 1767 a.
Thos. 1773 i.
Berkeley
Jno. Sr. 1787 w.
Brunswick
Jno. 1740 i.
Ralph 1744 w.
Ambrose 1745 w.
Jno. 1746 w.
Thos. 1751 w.
Danl. 1760 w.
Peter 1765 w.
Rebecca 1765 w.
Henry 1795 w.
Mark 1797 w.
Chesterfield
Jos. 1772 w.
Ralph 1776 i.
Richd. 1781 w.
Richd. 1782 i.
Isaiah 1794 w.
Lucy 1795 w.

Josiah 1796 i.
Peter 1798 w.
Charles City
Jno. 1791 w.
Turner 1770 w.
Charlotte
Wm. 1769 i.
Ezekiel 1771 i.
Robt. 1791 w.
Lewis 1795 i.
Essex
Patrick 1698 i.
Isaac 1701 i.
Fairfax
Jno. 1785 w.
David 1790 i.
Frederick
Hugh 1767 w.
Jos. 1791 w.
Josiah 1794 w.
Greensville
Jno. 1782 w.
Henrico
Ralph 1709 w.
Jno. 1713 i.
Jennet 1746 i.
Richd. 1703 w.
Richd. 1741 w.
Mary 1761 w.
Jno. Sr. 1762 w.
Lancaster
Andrew 1710 w.
Loudoun
Lovill 1767 w.
Wm. 1795 w.
Louisa
Wm. 1783 w.
Thos. 1796 w.
Lunenburg
Edwd. 1772 i.
Josiah 1787 w.
Philip W. 1797 i.
Benj. 1792 w.
Mecklenburg
Flemmon 1797 i.
Middlesex
Jno. 1705 w.
Mary 1766 w.
Jno. 1785 w.
Gawen 1793 w.
Wm. Sr. 1793 w.
Norfolk
Jas. 1667 i.
Jas. 1702 w.
Simon 1724 i.
Richd. 1753 w.
Joel 1777 w.
Joel 1784 w.
Northampton
Jno. 1647 i.
Jno. 1735 w.

Nehemiah 1747 **i.**
Jonah 1751 **w.**
Orange
Thos. 1764 **w.**
Prince Edward
Rowland 1781 **w.**
Mark 1791 **i.**
Thos. 1792 **w.**
Matthew 1795 **w.**
Agnes 1798 **w.**
Nancy 1798 **w.**
Prince George
Thos. 1713 **i.**
Susannah 1715 **w.**
Wm. 1720 **w.**
Wm. 1727 **w.**
Princess Anne
Thos. 1694 **i.**
Sarah 1705 **w.**
Jno. 1733 **w.**
Jas. 1774 **w.**
Jonathan 1778 **w.**
Eliz. 1789 **w.**
Prince William
Lodowick 1742 **i.**
Francis 1782 **w.**
Saml. 1786 **w.**
Rappahannock
Geo. 1677 **w.**
Richmond
Danl. 1706 **w.**
Saml. 1747 **i.**
Jno. 1750 **w.**
Thos. 1751 **i.**
David 1755 **w.**
Danl. 1764 **i.**
Jos. 1767 **w.**
Nathl. 1769 **w.**
Mary 1783 **w.**
Vincent 1792 **w.**
Wm. 1794 **w.**
Vincent 1796 **i.**
Spotsylvania
Robt. 1764 **w.**
Wm. 1791 **a.**
Stafford
Wm. 1749 **i.**
Southampton
Wm. 1767 **w.**
Sarah 1778 **w.**
Kindred 1787 **w.**
Surry
Wm. 1710 **w.**
Sussex
Jno. 1770 **w.**
Westmoreland
Chris. 1748 **i.**
Chris. D. 1749 **w.**
Jos. 1755 **w.**
Richd. 1764 **i.**
Magdalene 1767 **w.**

Danl. 1770 **w.**
Wm. 1773 **i.**
Saml. 1783 **w.**
Wm. Sr. 1780 **w.**
Richd. 1789 **i.**
York
Jno. 1640 **w.**
Robt. 1646 **i.**
Wm. 1675 **i.**
Henry 1683 **i.**
Wm. 1721 **w.**
Philemon 1723 **ab.**
Robt. 1728 **i.**
Ambrose 1755 **w.**
Fips 1770 **w.**
Robt. 1781 **w.**
Geo. 1794 **w.**
Ambrose 1796 **w.**
JACOAKS
Frederick
David 1746 **w.**
JACOB
Middlesex
Nicholas 1770 **i.**
Norfolk
Wm. 1666 **i.**
Jno. 1681 **w.**
Northampton
Richd. 1662 **w.**
Thos. 1676 **w.**
Esau 1703 **w.**
Thos. 1708 **w.**
Philip 1713 **w.**
Risdon 1718 **w.**
Richd. 1719 **w.**
Wm. 1720 **w.**
Resdon 1725 **i.**
Philip 1728 **i.**
Jno. 1729 **w.**
Danl. 1733 **i.**
Isaac 1734 **i.**
Clark 1735 **w.**
Isaac 1735 **w.**
Lazarus 1736 **i.**
Jno. 1751 **i.**
Philip 1751 **w.**
Philip Jr. 1752 **i.**
Anne 1753 **i.**
Josiah 1754 **w.**
Richd. 1761 **w.**
Abraham 1763 **i.**
Isaac 1764 **i.**
Jno. 1773 **w.**
Esau 1775 **w.**
Sarah 1785 **w.**
Hancock Sr. 1787 **w.**
Wm. 1792 **w.**
Thos. Sr. 1795 **w.**
Wm. 1795 **i.**
Easer 1797 **w.**
Hancock 1797 **w.**

Richd. 1798 **w.**
Hancock 1799 **i.**
Princess Anne
Wm. 1753 **i.**
JACOBIE
Culpeper
Jno. Danl. 1767 **w.**
JACOBUS
Middlesex
Jos. 1721.
JACOBS
Accomack
Thos. Sr. 1796 **w.**
Frederick
Geo. 1750 **w.**
Isle of Wight
Jno. 1681-2 **i.**
Loudoun
Catherine 1796 **i.**
Middlesex
Eliz. 1793 **i.**
JACOBSON
Northampton
Laurence 1666 **i.**
JADWIN
Westmoreland
Robt. 1674 **i.**
Jeremiah 1697 **w.**
JAMBORN
Goochland
Giddion 1737 **w.**
JAMERSON
Norfolk
Standley 1795 **w.**
JAMES
Accomack
Jonathan 1723 **w.**
Joshua 1750 **w.**
David 1764 **w.**
Wm. 1765 **w.**
Amey 1767 **w.**
Wm. Sacker 1775 **w.**
Robt. 1787 **w.**
Wm. Sacker 1794 **i.**
Wm. 1796 **w.**
Robt. 1799 **i.**
Amelia
Wm. 1771 **w.**
Thos. 1779 **i.**
Thos. 1780 **w.**
Wm. 1786 **i.**
Augusta
Wm. 1749 **w.**
Thos. 1764 **i.**
Brunswick
Cary 1798 **i.**
Charlotte
Hugh 1775 **i.**
Chesterfield
Phebe 17— **i.**
Moses 1758 **i.**

Culpeper
Henry 1778 w.
Jos. 1783 w.
Cumberland
Francis 1760 w.
Mary 1760 w.
Esesx
Jno. 1722 i.
Wm. 1726 i.
Jno. 1734 i.
Wm. 1745 i.
Fauquier
Thos. 1776 w.
Jno. 1778 w.
Frederick
Jenkin 1763 w.
Goochland
Francis Jr. 1746 w.
Isle of Wight
Abell 1791 w.
Wm. 1794 w.
Abel 1797 w.
King George
Sarah 1750 a.
Jno. 1769 w.
Lancaster
Eliz. 1697 w.
Walter 1723 w.
Mathias 1740 w.
Ann 1748 i.
Mathias 1748 i.
Thos. 1765 w.
Thos. 1773 i.
Benj. 1774 i.
Joan 1775 i.
Thos. 1775 i.
Bartlet 1778 i.
Sarah 1779 i.
Walter 1779 w.
Isaac 1784 i.
Jno. 1789 w.
Loudoun
Elias 1789 w.
Lunenburg
Jno. 1760 i.
Norfolk
Jno. 1791 w.
Northampton
Jno. 1696 w.
David 1703 w.
Joan 1712-13 w.
Robt. 1713-14 w.
Wm. 1719 w.
Francis 1724 w.
Thos. 1726 i.
Anne 1733 i.
Robt. 1735 i.
Philip 1738 i.
Robt. 1759 i.
Jno. 1768 w.
Mary 1773 w.

Jno. 1780 w.
Northumberland
Margt. 1723-4 w.
Partin 1741 i.
Joshua 1745 w.
Thos. 1753 w.
Jno. 1755 i.
Wm. 1758 w.
Moses 1760 w.
Wm. 1770 i.
Moses 1773 i.
Orange
Saml. 1754 w.
Princess Anne
Jno. 1710 w.
Jno. 1720 i.
Edwd. 1727 w.
Edwd. 1733 i.
Jno. 1733 w.
Mary 1733 w.
Jno. 1734 i.
Wm. 1734 i.
Susannah 1735 i.
Jno. 1740 w.
Henry 1741 w.
Jno. 1759 i.
Chas. 1769 w.
Jonathan 1772 w.
Anthy 1775 i.
Edwd. 1784 w.
Eliz. 1785 w.
Wm. Sr. 1788 w.
Eliz. 1790 w.
Ann 1791 i.
Ursly 1792 i.
Rappahannock
Edwd. 1675 w.
Richmond
Thos. 1727 w.
Spotsylvania
Jno. 1725-6 w.
Jno. 1726 a.
Geo. 1753 a.
Jas. 1754 a.
Surry
Nathl. 1775 w.
Edwin 1782 i.
Sussex
Abner 1774 w.
Emanuel 1785 w.
Westmoreland
Geo. 1656 nw.
Francis 1737 w.
Francis 1774 i.
York
Nathl. 1696 i.
Jno. 1737 i.
Eliz. 1742 w.
Ann 1748 w.
Elisha 1786 w.

JAMESON
Accomack
Walter 1773 w.
Walton 1782 i.
Albemarle
Saml. 1788 w.
Amherst
Thos. 1763 i.
Augusta
Jno. 1776 w.
Charlotte
Wm. 1785 w.
Essex
David 1711 w.
Jas. 1736 w.
Norfolk
Jno. 1761 w.
Henry 1765 w.
Jas. 1783 w.
Orange
Thos. 1772 i.
Princess Anne
Alex. 1697 i.
Alex. 1699 a.
Jno. 1745 i.
Prince William
David 1794 w.
York
Mary 1771 w.
Thos. 1783 i.
JAMESTOWN
Henrico
Jno. 1726 w.
JAMISON
Augusta
Wm. 1753 w.
Norfolk
Henry 1789 i.
Rockbridge
Jno. 1790 w.
Wm. 1797 w.
Washington
Edwd. 1787 w.
JANE
Prince George
Phillip 1719 i.
JANNET
Augusta
Jno. 1746 a.
JANNEWAY
Stafford
Wm. 1707 w.
JANNEY
Fairfax
Amos 1747 a.
Loudoun
Mary 1760 w.
Mary 1767 w.
Abel 1774 w.
Saml. 1785 w.
Jacob 1787 w.

Wm. 1791 w.
Jos. 1793 w.
Saml. 1793 i.
Eliz. 1798 nw.
JAQUES
Northumberland
Wm. H. 1794 i.
JARRAD
Surry
Nicho. 1733 i.
JARRARD
Surry
Nicho. 1718 w.
JARRAT
Sussex
Jno. 1766 w.
JARRATT
Goochland
Jos. 1761 i.
Archelus 1794 w.
Sussex
Jesse 1781 w.
Henry 1784 w.
JARREL
Southampton
Benj. 1769 w.
JARRELL
Isle of Wight
Thos. Sr. 1741 w.
Thos. 1751 w.
Southampton
Thos. 1753 w.
Jno. 1757 i.
Wm. 1753 i.
Thos. 1771 i.
JARRET
Southampton
Jno. 1757 w.
Lunenburg
Robt. 1788 w.
Surry
Richd. 1672 w.
JARRETT
Surry
Chas. 1719 w.
Ferdinando 1720 w.
Henry 1720 w.
Geo. 1721 w.
Mary 1721 w.
Jno., the Elder, 1768 w.
JARRIL
Southampton
Thos. 1758 i.
JARROT
Lancaster
Thos. 1782 i.
JARROTT
Southampton
Fortunatus 1795 w.

Sussex
Nicho. 1785 w.
JARVIS
Accomack
Robt. 1750 w.
Amherst
Jno. 1799 w.
Norfolk
Thos. 1747 w.
Richd. 1785 w.
Northampton
Wm. 1710 i.
Prince William
Richd. 1778 i.
Westmoreland
Richd. 1706 i.
Jno. 1744 w.
Field 1766 i.
York
Eliz. 1724 i.
Geo. 1752 w.
Christmas 1768 i.
Thos. 1782 w.
Jno. 1786 i.
Thos. 1788 i.
JASPER
Frederick
Wm. 1741 i.
Wm. 1747 w.
Richmond
Danl. 1779 w.
York
Margt. 1752 i.
Lucy 1780 i.
JAUNCEY
Lancaster
Wm. 1697 w.
JAVINS
Fairfax
Jos. 1760 i.
JAYCOCK
Frederick
David 1746 a.
Jonathan 1747 i.
JAYNE
Wythe
Zopher 1791 w.
JEFFERIED
Isle of Wight
Richd. 1666 i.
JEFFERIS
Westmoreland
Ann 1742 i.
Edmd. 1743 i.
JEFFERISS
Essex
Wm. 1701 i.
JEFFERS
Northampton
Jos. 1764 i.

Jos. 1766 i.
Orange
Richd. 1753 i.
JEFFERSON
Albemarle
Peter 1757 w.
Jane, Jr. 1768 i.
Jane 1768 i.
Jane 1777 i.
Jane 1778 w.
Henrico
Thos. 1698 i.
Thos. 1731 w.
Lancaster
Jos. 1692 w.
Lunenburg
Geo. 1780 i.
Mecklenburg
Thos. 1784 i.
Norfolk
David 1795 w.
York
Thos. 1705 i.
Mary 1742 i.
JEFFERY
Northampton
Mary 1773 i.
JEFFRES
Surry
Jno. Jr. 1745 w.
JEFFREY
Accomack
Alex. 1769 w.
JEFFREYS
York
Wm. 1694 w.
JEFFRICE
Stafford
Thos. 1732 w.
Alex. 1762 w.
JEFFRIES
Greensville
Archilles 1794 w.
Henrico
Wm. 1708 w.
Mecklenburg
Jno. Jr. 1773 i.
Jno. 1773 w.
Wm. 1779 w
Jno. 1792 w.
Marcey G. 1795 w.
Northumberland
Sarah 1763 w.
Westmoreland
Edmd. 1736 w.
Geo. 1763 w.
Jeremiah 1766 w.
Robt. 1784 w.
Robt. 1787 i.
Robt. 1789 i.

JEFFRYS
Surry
  Jno. Sr. 1752 w.
JEFFYERS
Norfolk
  Eliz. 1797 w.
JEGITTS
York
  Jno. 1769 i.
JELKS
Southampton
  Wm. 1770 w.
Surry
  Richd. 1695 w.
JELLES
Essex
  Jno. 1699 w.
JENCO
Lancaster
  Peter 1692 w.
JENENS
Norfolk
  Jno. 1763 w.
JENINGS
Isle of Wight
  Jno. 1678-9 w.
Richmond
  Henry 1710 i.
JENKENS
Princess Anne
  Benj. 1759 w.
JENKENSON
Accomack
  Thos. 1734 i.
JENKINS
Accomack
  Jno. 1685 w.
  Wm. 1752 i.
  Mary Anne 1797 w.
Chesterfield
  Wm. 1760 w.
Essex
  David 1706 w.
  Isaac 1762 i.
Rappahannock
  Thos. 1677 nw.
Fairfax
  Thos. 1745 a.
  Wm. 1747 w.
  Ezekiel 1750 w.
  Jno. 1752 i.
  Saml. 1790 w.
  Simon 1792 w.
  Jas. Sr. 1794 a.
Frederick
  Aaron 1759 w.
  Jno. 1748-9 a.
Hampshire
  Jacob 1795 w.
Isle of Wight
  Benj. 1769 i.

Valentine 1782 w.
Lancaster
  Henry 1748 i.
Loudoun
  Saml. 1760 i.
  Jno. 1773 w.
  Amos 1778 i.
  Stephen 1791 i.
  Jno. 1796 w.
Northampton
  Thos. 1737 w.
Prince William
  Jno. 1741 i.
Richmond
  Wm. 1720 i.
  Eliz. 1739 w.
  Edwd. 1741 i.
  Mansfield 1755 w.
  Jno. 1784 i.
  Harmon 1785 w.
  Peggy 1796 w.
Shenandoah
  Saml. 1796 i.
Southampton
  Valentine 1766 w.
  Edmd. 1780 w.
  Jacob 1785 i.
  Spencer 1788 w.
Stafford
  David 1704 w.
Sussex
  Jno. 1756 i.
Westmoreland
  Nicho. 1673 w.
  Nicho. 1675 i.
  ————— 1707 i.
  Jno. 1717 i.
  Thos. 1723 w.
  Morgan 1731 i.
  Job. 1739 i.
  Richd. 1782 w.
York
  Edwd. 1681 w.
  Edwd. 1701 ab.
  Thos. 1701 ab.
JENKINSON
Accomack
  Thos. 1724 w.
  Thos. 1732 w.
  Jno. 1745 i.
  Custis 1756 i.
  Comfort 1757 w.
  Robt. 1777 w.
Essex
  Jno. 1712 w.
JENNE
Northampton
  Wm. 1794 w.
JENNEING
Goochland
  Kelley 1773 w.

JENNINGS
Amelia
  Jno. 1784 w.
Fairfax
  Alesander 1751 w.
  Danl. 1754 w.
Fauquier
  Augustine 1778 i.
  Berryman 1783 i.
  Geo. 1789 i.
Frederick
  Edwd. 1758 i.
Halifax
  Wm. 1763 i.
  Jno. Jr. 1777 w.
Henrico
  Thos. 1798 i.
Isle of Wight
  Jno. 1694 w.
  Jno. 1698 w.
King George
  Edwd. 1740 i.
  Mary 1748 i.
Loudoun
  Mary 1761 i.
  Daniel 1783 w.
Lunenburg
  Jas. 1799 a.
Norfolk
  Richd. 1669 i.
Orange
  Jno. 1735 w.
Prince Edward
  Robt. 1794 w.
Richmond
  Wm. Sr. 1733 w.
  Wm. 1733 w.
  Ann 1734 w.
  Thos. 1734 i.
  Jno. 1764 i.
  Jno. 1783 i.
JENT
Isle of Wight
  Jno. 1733 i.
JERDONE
Henrico
  Benj. 1783 w.
Louisa
  Francis 1771 w.
York
  Wm. 1750 i.
JERMAN
Albemarle
  Henry 1792 i.
JERMY
Norfolk
  Wm. 1666 w.
JESPER
Richmond
  Richd. 1702 w.
  Eliz. 1725 w.

Thos. 1748 w.
Simon 1752 w.
Richd. T. 1753 w.
Thos. 1760 w.
Jno. 1764 w.
Thos. 1793 w.
Thos. 1797 w.

JESSOX
Lancaster
Isaac 1696 i.

JESTER
Accomack
Frances 1708 w.
Saml. 1746 w.

JETER
Amelia
Thos. 1765 w.
Saml. 1793 w.

JETT
Culpeper
Jno. 1771 w.
Jas. 1795 w.
King George
Frances 1724 i.
Eliz. 1726 i.
Peter 1758 i.
Wm. 1762 w.
Frances 1766 w.
Birkett 1771 w.
Peter 1777 a.
Peter 1777 w.
Gladis 1778 w.
Peter 1784 w.
Loudoun
Wm. 1762 i.
Richmond
Jno. 1710 w.
Margt. 1739 w.
Peter 1739 w.
Jno. 1754 w.
Jno. 1762 i.
Ann 1781 w.
Thos. 1785 w.
Catherine 1787 w.
Francis 1788 i.
Jno. 1790 w.
Wm. 1791 w.

JEWELL
Brunswick
Saml. 1776 w.
Essex
Mary 1706 i.
Westmoreland
Wm. 1767 i.
Northampton
Jno. 1668 i.

JEWRY
Isle of Wight
Wm. 1651 w.

JEXSON
Accomack
Henry 1748 i.

JIMES
Northampton
Edwd. 1670 i.

JINKINS
Cumberland
Jos. 1797 i.
Frederick
Wm. 1784 i.
Northumberland
Jno. 1786 w.
Spotsylvania
Jno. Sr. 1797 w.

JINNINGS
Madison
Rachael 1799 w.

JLES
Isle of Wight
Frances 1691 w.

JOANES
Chesterfield
Francis 1752 w.
Henrico
Jas. 1713 i.
Stafford
Jno. 1735 w.

JOANS
Accomack
Richd. 1720 w.

JOB
Augusta
Caleb 1750 w.
Abraham 1750 w.
Frederick
Hannah 1748 w.
Shenandoah
Johna 1783 i.

JOELL
Norfolk
Richd. 1735 i.

JOHN
Berkeley
Wm. 1795 a.
Frederick
Danl. 1770 w.
Loudoun
Jas. 1767 w.
Mary 1767 w.
Thos. 1769 w.
Thos. 1771 w.
Elias 1784 i.
Princess Anne
Jacob 1711 i.

JOHNES
Isle of Wight
John 1771 i.

JOHNS
Amelia
Jno. 1774 i.

Amherst
Wm. 1777 a.
Robt. 1779 a.
Charlotte
Thos. 1769 w.
Jno. 1778 w.
Cumberland
Jos. 1776 i.
Jno. 1781 w.
Jos. 1784 w.
Thos. 1786 w.
Goochland
Judith 1735 w.
Philip 1787 w.
Wm. Combs 1788 w.
Isle of Wight
Jno. 1697 w.
Northampton
Roger 1654 i.
Pittsylvania
Thos. 1795 i.
Spotsylvania
Erasmus 1749 a.

JOHNSON
Accomack
Richd. 1673 w.
Geo., ye Older,
1692 w.
Alex. 1696 w.
Hendreck 1705 w.
Geo. 1732 w.
Jno. 1734 w.
Edmd. 1748 i.
Washbourne 1750 w.
Afradozy 1751 w.
Bayly 1761 w.
Rachel 1763 w.
Geo. 1765 w.
Saml. 1765 w.
Wm. 1765 i.
Saml. 1769 i.
Joshua 1782 w.
Jno. 1783 w.
Jno. 1784 i.
Solomon 1794 w.
Azariah 1793 w.
Isaiah 1793 i.
Albemarle
Thos. 1785 w.
Amelia
Chas. 1768 w.
Wm. 1769 w.
Jno. 1772 w.
Gerrard 1785 i.
Stephen 1796 i.
Amherst
Jonathan 1775 a.
Wm. 1776 w.
Mary 1781 a.
Benj. 1789 a.
Snelling 1790 a.

Jno. 1791 a.
Stephen 1793 a.
Augusta
Jno. 1756 a.
Wm. 1771 w.
Wm. 1786 w.
Bath
Bertollemy 1796 i.
Bedford
Benj. 1769 w.
Botetourt
Peter 1794 i.
Brunswick
Wm. 1758 w.
Nathl. 1762 w.
Barnes 1781 w.
James 1785 w.
Jno. 1785 w.
Thos. 1795 w.
Campbell
David 1799 i.
Charles City
Benj. 1770 i.
Jacob 1789 w.
Charlotte
Wm. 1767 i.
Thos. 1790 i.
Saml. 1791 i.
Chesterfield
Edwd. 1780 i.
Andrew 1792 i.
Cumberland
Danl. 1749 w.
Jno. 1755 w.
Collins 176/ i.
Jno. 1768 w.
Randolph 1769 w.
Danl. 1794 w.
Essex
Martin 1694 w.
Wm. 1702-w.
Henry 1703 w.
Christian 1712 w.
Saml. 1715 i.
Wm. 1729 w.
Jas. 1750 w.
Thos. 1750 w.
Jas. 1758 i.
Isaac 1764 i.
Ruth 1764 i.
Thos. 1769 w.
Richd. 1770 w.
Ann 1771 w.
Fairfax
Saml. 1773 w.
Fauquier
Jeffry 1783 w.
Smith 1793 i.
Jno. 1797 i.
Isaac 1798 w.

Frederick
Wm. 1746 i.
Ann 1748 i.
Robt. 1763 w.
Geo. 1796 w.
Goochland
Benj. 1744 i.
Jno. 1750 w.
Danl. 1754 w.
Jos. 1781 w.
Wm. 1782 i.
Drewry 1784 i.
Benj. 1785 w.
Jno. 1789 w.
Isham 1794 i.
Wm. 1796 w.
Jno. 1796 w.
Greensville
Jno. 1784 i.
Eliz. 1789 w.
Moses 1793 w.
Moses 1796 w.
Halifax
Jos. 1779 w.
Moses 1781 w.
Hampshire
Wm. 1794 w.
Harrison
Wm. 1795 i.
Henrico
Jno. 1691 i.
Michael 1786 w.
Benj. 1787 i.
Thos. Sr. 1799 w.
Isle of Wight
Jno. 1707 w.
Wm. Sr. 1719 w.
Jno. 1728 i.
Robt. 1733 w.
Wm. 1745 i.
Thos. 1746 w.
Jas. 1747 w.
Jas. 1749 i.
Robt. 1757 w.
Ann 1762 i.
Robt. 1766 w.
Rebecca 1769 w.
Wm. 1771 i.
Isbel 1774 w.
Abraham 1776 w.
Henry Sr. 1784 w.
Aaron 1785 i.
Robt. 1785 w.
Robt. 1788 w.
Robt. 1789 w.
Thos. 1789 i.
Nathan 1790 w.
Abraham 1792 i.
Sarah 1793 i.
Amos 1794 i.
Henry 1794 w.

Henry 1793 i.
King George
Jeffrey 1727 i.
Ann 1781 w.
Jno. 1783 a.
Gabriel 1796 w.
Lancaster
Jno. Sr. 1656 i.
Henry 1722 i.
Simon 1728 w.
Jane 1740 i.
Neil 1768 w.
Archd. 1769 w.
Loudoun
Jno. 1770 w.
Louisa
Benj. 1754 w.
Isham 1766 w.
Wm. 1778 i.
Collins 1782 i.
Jno. 1783 w.
David 1788 w.
Jas. 1788 w.
Thos. 1791 w.
Jas. 1793 a.
Thos. (Minor)
  1795 w.
Jas. 1797 i.
Thos. 1798 w.
Agnes 1798 w.
Sarah 1799 w.
Lunenburg
Jos. 1761 w.
David 1782 w.
Michael 1782 w.
Wm. 1783 i.
Jas. 1787 w.
Jas. 1788 w.
Isaac 1793 w.
Mecklenburg
Danl. 1767 w.
Jas. 1784 w.
Jno. Sr. 1793 w.
Middlesex
Jno. 1678 a.
Geo. 1744 i.
Wm. 1745 w.
Geo. 1750 a.
Wm. 1760 i.
Henry 1770 i.
Norfolk
Jas. 1672 i.
Jas. 1673 w.
Benj. 1677 w.
Jno. 1679 w.
Jas. 1680-1 i.
Wm. 1703-4 w.
Jos. 1756 w.
Ann 1759 i.
Jno. 1763 w.

Northampton
Thos. 1658 w.
Adolf 1665 w.
Cornelius 1696 i.
Thos. 1705 w.
Obedience 1708 w.
Jacob 1711 i.
Richd. 1713 i.
Jno. 1716 w.
Edmd. 1721 w.
Jno. 1721-2 w.
Thos. 1732 i.
Luke 1733 w.
Saml. 1735 w.
Thos. Griffen 1738 i.
Obedience Jr. 1738 w.
Harmon 1739 i.
Obedience 1739 w.
Jos. M. 1742 w.
Mary 1743 w.
Spencer 1745 w.
Jephthah 1746 w.
Edmd. 1747 w.
Elijah 1748 i.
Jno. 1749 i.
Obedience 1749 w.
Richd. 1751 w.
Robinson 1751 i.
Nathl. 1752 i.
Jno. 1754 w.
Kelly 1758 w.
Beautifila 1761 i.
Mary 1762 w.
Jepthah 1764 w.
Moses, Sr. 1764 w.
Thos. 1767 i.
Thos. 1768 w.
Ismay 1770 w.
Benj. 1773 w.
Powell 1773 i.
Benj. 1774 i.
Mary 1774 w.
Obediah 1774 w.
Wm. 1774 w.
Jno. Jr. 1775 w.
Jno. 1775 w.
Moses 1775 w.
Moses 1775 w.
Lucretia 1777 w.
Rachel 1779 w.
Edmd. 1780 i.
Jno. 1780 w.
Obedience Jr. 1782 w.
Wm. 1782 w.
Tabitha 1785 w.
Anna M (aria)
   1789 w.
Obedience 1789 i.
Robinson 1790 w.
Tabitha 1791 i.
Obedience 1795 w.

Moses 1798 w.
Jno. Sr. 1799 w.
Northumberland
Jno. 1720 w.
Eliz. 1772 w.
Orange
Wm. 1766 w.
Robt. 1770 i.
Wm. 1771 i.
Jno. 1779 w.
Jno. 1783 w.
Martin Jr. 1786 w.
Pittsylvania
Moses 1782 w.
Powhatan
Danl. 1779 i.
Prince Edward
Edwd. 1770 i.
Gabriel 1788 w.
Jesse 1791 i.
Prince George
Edwd. 1725 w.
Princess Anne
Jacob 1710 w.
Jacob Jr. 1710 w.
Ann 1716 w.
Margt. 1749 w.
Jas. 1779 i.
Saml. 1785 w.
Prince William
Jas. 1784 i.
Rappahannock
Peter 1683 w.
Thos. 1684 i.
Israel 1685 i.
Edwd. 1687 w.
Rockbridge
Thos. 1778 a.
Stafford
Jno. 1761 w.
Wm. 1761 i.
Southampton
Benj. 1752 w.
Jno. 1753 i.
Jno. 1754 w.
Richd. 1760 w.
Jacob 1763 w.
Stephen 1764 w.
Jesse 1765 i.
Benj. 1767 w.
Dency 1767 i.
Lazarus 1772 w.
Robt. 1772 w.
Job 1773 w.
Jno. 1775 w.
Jesse 1777 i.
Saml. 1779 w.
Elebey 1782 i.
Richd. 1782 i.
Robt. 1782 i.
Jno. 1783 w.

Charite 1785 w.
Jacob 1785 w.
Jos. 1782 i.
Simon 1785 i.
Abraham 1785 w.
Giles 1789 w.
Jno. Sr. 1795 w.
Josiah 1793 w.
Sarah 1798 w.
Stephen 1798 i.
Spotsylvania
Richd. 1726 a.
Wm. 1728 a.
Jael 1733 w.
Stafford
Richd. 1733 i.
Jas. 1734 i.
Bedford 1740 i.
Jno. 1744 i.
Surry
Martin 1703 w.
Wm. 1710 w.
Martin 1724 w.
Jno. 1743 w.
Richd. 1743 i.
Jno. 1745 i.
Arthur 1751 i.
Wm. 1752 w.
Thos. 1758 w.
Thos. 1767 w.
Henry 1772 w.
Leveter 1777 w.
Jno. 1782 w.
Sussex
Moses 1763 w.
Thos. 1763 i.
Stephen 1764 w.
Thos. 1772 i.
Petaway 1781 w.
Wm. 1782 w.
Lewis 1786 w.
Thos. 1793 w.
Waddill 1794 w.
Jane 1795 w.
Mildred 1796 w.
Washington
Jno. 1796 i.
Westmoreland
Jas. 1715 w.
Eliz. 1716 i.
Jas. 1748 i.
Saml. 1761 w.
York
Paul 1671 w.
Geo. 1679 w.
Saml. 1701 w.
Jno. 1734 w.
Eliz. 1736 w.
Jno. 1738 w.
Jas. 1759 i.
Josiah 1773 w.

JOHNSTON
Augusta
Jno. 1749 w.
Jno. 1756 i.
Wm. 1756 i.
Wm. 1762 w.
Arthur 1762 w.
Wm. 1772 i.
Eleanor 1791 i.
Botetourt
Ezekel 1781 w.
Charlotte
Wm. 1775 w.
Chesterfield
Edwd. 1780 w.
Andrew 1791 w.
Culpeper
Peter 1756 w.
Wm. Jr. 1765 w.
Wm. 1768 w.
Fairfax
Geo. 1767 w.
Mary 1769 w.
Saml. 1769 w.
Hannah 1771 w.
Mary 1775 i.
Fauquier
Jas. 1795 i.
Frederick
Isaac 1752 a.
Jno. 1760 i.
Wm. 1760 i.
Robt. 1764 i.
David 1796 i.
King George
Geo. 1778 a.
Wm. 1778 w.
Loudoun
Geo. 1777 w.
Louisa
Nicho. 1768 i.
Lunenburg
Jas. 1761 w.
Middlesex
Geo. 1704 w.
Robt. 1730 w.
Montgomery
David 1786 w.
Norfolk
Jno. 1698 w.
Northumberland
Wm. 1738 i.
Archd. 1740 i.
Ohio
Jacob 1787 w.
Orange
Robt. 1779 a.
Pittsylvania
Archd. 1788 w.
Prince Edward
Edwd. 1770 w.

Saml. 1776 i.
Peter 1786 w.
Prince William
Jacob 1795 i.
Danl. 1799 i.
Jas. 1799 i.
Rockbridge
Francis 1790 i.
Southampton
Henry 1770 i.
Job 1773 i.
Jos. 1781 w.
Stephen 1797 w.
Elijah 1797 i.
Spotsylvania
Aquilla 1786 a.
Aquilla 1788 w.
Richd. W. 1791 w.
Washington
Hugh 1795 i.
Curtis 1799 w.
Westmoreland
Thos. 1666 w.
Jas. 1698 w.
Wm. 1740 i.
Frances 1742 i.
Wm. 1748 i.
JOHNSTONE
King George
Robt. 1761 w.
Wm. 1761 w.
Westmoreland
Jacob 1765 i.
JOINER
Isle of Wight
Theophilus 1753 i.
Theophilus 1778 i.
Southampton
Israel 1777 w.
Jesse 1799 w
JOLIFF
Princess Anne
Eliz. 1772 w.
Matthew 1772 w.
JOLLEFFE
Frederick
Eliz. 1796 i.
Isle of Wight
Jas. 1727 w.
Jas. 1729-30 i.
JOLLEY
Jno. 1736 w.
JOLLIF
Norfolk
Martha 1762 w.
JOLLIFF
Isle of Wight
Thos. 1776 i.
Norfolk
Richd. 1779 w.
Jas. Jr. 1796 i.

JOLLIFFE
Frederick
Wm. 1770 w.
Jas. 1771 w.
Jno. 1777 w.
Jno. 1780 i.
Eliz. 1783 w.
Norfolk
Jas. 1791 w.
Wm. 1791 i.
Jas. 1793 i.
JOLLITT
Westmoreland
Morris 1732 i.
JOLLOFF
Norfolk
Jno. 1717 w.
Jno. 1777 w.
Jas. 1778 w.
JOLLY
Isle of Wight
Jno. 1750 i.
JONAS
Richmond
Elisha 1722 i.
JONATHAN
York
Cornelius 1670 w.
JONCEL
Westmoreland
Edwd. 1755 w.
JONES
Accomack
Henry 1664 w.
Dave 1703 i.
Richd. 1737 w.
Giles 1741 i.
Henry 1755 i.
Albemarle
Jno. 1760 i.
Jno. 1773 i.
Jno. 1793 w.
Orlando 1793 i.
Jas. Jr. 1799 w.
Thos. 1799 w.
Amelia
Jno. 1735 a.
Emmanuel 1743 w.
Jno. 1748 w.
Martha 1752 w.
Peter 1758 w.
Abraham 1759 w.
Edwd. 1759 i.
Richd. Sr. 1759 w.
Robt. 1770 w.
Richd. 1772 w.
Danl. 1772 w.
Nelson 1773 w.
Branch 1775 w.
Wm. 1776 w.
Richd. 1778 w.

Amy 1780 w.
Adam 1782 w.
Thos. Field 1788 w.
Wood 1790 w.
Philip 1790 i.
Thos. 1791 w.
Uriah 1792 i.
Susanna 1795 w.
Margt. 1796 w.
Martha 1798 i.
Peter, Sr. 1799 w.
Wood 1799 i.
Augusta
Isaac 1751 i.
Jas. 1754 i.
Thos. 1763 a.
Thos. 1765 i.
Bedford
Michael 1781 w.
Wm. 1781 w.
Jno. 1797 i.
Berkeley
Jas. 1779 i.
Eliz. 1781 w.
Robt. 1798 w.
Botetourt
Jno. 1773 w.
Jno. Gabriel 1779 w.
Jno. G. 1786 i.
Brunswick
Richd. 1747 w.
Hicks 1758 i.
Chas. 1768 w.
Isaac 1778 w.
Henry 1779 i.
Jno. Robt. 1781 w.
Wm. 1781 w.
Wm. 1789 i.
Binns 1791 w.
Thos. 1791 w.
Peter 1795 w.
Chas. B. 1797 w.
Jesse 1799 w.
Charlotte
Philip 1773 i.
David 1778 i.
Thos. 1780 w.
Thos. Jr. 1781 i.
Culpeper
David 1752 w.
Joshua 1761 i.
Wm. 1765 i.
Gabriel 1777 w.
Joshua 1777 i.
Jno. 1778 i.
Robt. 1784 w.
Wm. 1795 i.
Thos. 1798 w.
Cumberland
Jno. 1776 w.
Jno. 1778 i.

Danl. 1782 w.
Jno. 1785 i.
Judith 1788 w.
Elijah 1795 i.
Essex
Jno. 1693 w.
Wm. 1697 i.
Roger 1698 i.
Roger 1699 i.
Eliz. 1704 i.
Jno. 1706 i.
Jno. 1719 w.
Edwd. 1722 i.
Rice 1728 i.
Robt. 1730 i.
Robt. 1734 i.
Richd. 1735 w.
Thos. 1738 w.
Richd. 1743 i.
Wm. 1743 w.
Eliz. 1746 w.
Rice 1746 i.
Jonathan 1749 w.
Wm. 1749 w.
Richd. 1750 w.
Philip 1752 w.
Jas. 1754 w.
Richd. 1756 w.
Rice 1758 w.
Jno. 1759 w.
Wms. 1759 i.
Francis 1767 w.
Rice 1767 w.
Jas. 1785 w.
Wm. 1791 w.
Fairfax
David 1747 a.
Jno. 1751 i.
Robt. 1769 i.
Chas. 1797 w.
Fauquier
Chas. 1776 i.
Jno. 1783 i.
Brereton 1795 w.
Frederick
Josiah 1744 a.
Spencer 1748 w.
Gore 1752 w.
Jno. 1756 i.
Jno. 1759 i.
Thos. 1759 i.
Willabey 1765 i.
Jas. 1771 w.
Jos. 1793 w.
Jas. 1799 i.
Greensville
Eliz. 1788 w.
Leak 1796 w.
Halifax
Jno. 1773 w.
Wm. 1777 w.

Richd. 1779 w.
Wm. 1781 w.
Job 1786 w.
Wm. 1791 i.
Richd. 1792 i.
Richd. 1797 w.
Hampshire
Jno. 1794 w.
Peter 1795 w.
Henrico
Gilbert 1685 w.
Thos. 1688 w.
Repps 1639 w.
Wm. 1694 a.
Edwd. 1695 i.
Hugh 1705 w.
Rees 1732 w.
Saml. 1784 w.
Saml. 1797 w.
Henry
Saml. 1779 i.
Isaac 1782 w.
Jos. 1785 i.
Isle of Wight
Anthony 1649 w.
Wm. 1694 i.
Anne 1706-7 w.
Susannah 1713 w.
Richd. 1721 w.
Edwd. 1722 w.
Jos. 1727 w.
Jacob 1728 w.
Mathew 1728 w.
Edwd. 1730 w.
Jos. 1730 i.
Richd. 1735 i.
Jas. 1740 i.
Wm. 1744 w.
Eliz. 1749 i.
Thos. 1749 w.
Abraham 1758 w.
Britain 1759 i.
Eliz. 1759 i.
Mathew 1760 i.
Richd. [1762] w.
Thos. 1762 i.
Jno. 1767 w.
Jno. 1770 w.
Saml. Sr. 1771 w.
Jno. 1778 i.
Fred. 1781 w.
Jesse 1784 i.
Abraham 1790 w.
Mary 1791 w.
David 1795 i.
Jacob 1795 w.
Willis 1795 w.
Celia 1797 a.
King George
Lewis 1721 i.
David 1726 i.

Edwd. 1726 i.
Jno. 1726 i.
Richd. 1726 i.
Sarah 1726 i.
Richd. 1727 i.
Edwd. 1727 i.
Geo. 1729 i.
Mark 1731 i.
Henry 1735 i.
Jno. 1736 i.
Robt. 1737 i.
Jas. 1744 i.
Jno. 1752 w.
Jas. 1764 i.
Jas. Sr. 1764 w.
Lewis 1765 a.
Chas. 1771 w.
David 1772 a.
Wharton 1773 a.
Geo. 1783 w.
Calvert 1791 w.
Margt. 1794 w.
Nathl. 1794 w.
Lancaster
Jno. 1683 w.
Eliz. 1751 i.
Sarah 1784 w.
Lewis 1791 i.
Loudoun
Wm. 1771 w.
Jno. 1783 w.
Louisa
Richd. 1780 w.
Lunenburg
Thos. 1748 w.
Robt. 1749 w.
David 1757 i.
Reps 1778 w.
Robt. 1781 w.
Richd. 1782 w.
Mecklenburg
Robt. 1771 w.
Jas. 1773 i.
Thos. 1782 w.
Richd. 1783 w.
Robt. 1784 i.
Thos. 1787 i.
Jno. Sr. 1792 w.
Tignal Jr. 1794 w.
Wm. 1796 w.
Wm. 1798 i.
Robt. 1799 w.
Middlesex
Thos. 1675 a.
Francis 1703 w.
Wm. 1709 w.
Thos. 1713 i.
Wm. 1713 i.
Thos. 1713 w.
Humphrey 1726 w.
Roger 1741 i.

Lodowick 1742 i.
Mary 1743 w.
Jas. 1745 a.
Wm. 1747 w.
Wm. 1748 w.
Jno. 1749 w.
Humphrey 1750 i.
Jno. 1752 w.
Jno. 1758 i.
Churchill 1757 w.
Benj. 1760 i.
Thos. 1767 a.
Lodowick 1777 w.
Isaac 1780 w.
Lucy 1788 w.
Wm. 1791 i.
Norfolk
Rice 1666 w.
Richd. 1682-3 w.
Richd. 1691-2 w.
Richd. 1769 i.
Thos. 1794 w.
Caleb 1799 i.
Northampton
Wm. 1669 w.
Jno. 1733 w.
Jno. 1744 w.
Wm. 1759 w.
Grace 1787 i.
Northumberland
Robt. 1675 w.
Wm. 1711 i.
Sarah 1719 w.
Wm. 1725 i.
Maurice 1727 w.
Maurice Jr. 1728 i.
Wm. 1741 w.
Chas. 1742 i.
Judith 1742 i.
Wm. 1748 i.
Owen 1750-1 i.
Robt. 1750-1 w.
Chas. 1755 w.
Thos. 1757 i.
Leeanna 1760 w.
Eliz. 1762 w.
Semore 1762 i.
Chas. 1778 w.
Joshua 1784 w.
Robt. 1795 i.
Sarah 1798 w.
Orange
Jno. 1758 w.
Jos. 1783 w.
Nicho. 1783 i.
Thos. 1788 w.
Hugh 1791 w.
Pittsylvania
Thos. 1787 w.
Mosaias 1796 w.

Powhatan
Richd. 1778 i.
Chas. 1799 a.
Prince George
Jas. 1719 w.
Paul 1720 w.
Jas. 1725 w.
Mary 1725 w.
Peter 1726 w.
Robt. Jr. 1727 w.
Princess Anne
Edwd. 1698 i.
Sarah 1700 w.
Richd. 1720 w.
Evan 1722 w.
Solomon 1722 w.
Susannah 1726 w.
Richd. 1728 w.
Owen 1734 w.
Jno. 1739 w.
Edwd. 1740 w.
Elinor 1750 w.
Jas. 1750 i.
Elinor 1752 i.
Robt. 1771 w.
Moses 1773 w.
Sarah 1777 w.
Venus 1777 w.
Edwd. 1782 w.
Robt. 1782 w.
Sarah 1782 w.
Mary 1792 w.
Prince William
Cornelius 1735 i.
Saml. 1778 i.
Geo. 1785 i.
Wm. 1793 i.
Rappahannock
Rice 1677 w.
Richd. 1680 w.
Geo. 1684 i.
Robt. 1684 i.
Honoria 1685 w.
Richmond
Chris. 1705 w.
Edwd. 1715 w.
Jno. 1716 i.
Fookes 1717 w.
Samford 1717 w.
Jno. 1719 w.
Edwd. 1739 nw.
Owin 1741 i.
Jno. 1743 w.
Samford 1750 w.
Wm. 1754 nw.
Wm. 1758 w.
Edwd. 1759 w.
Edwd. 1762 i.
Isaac 1764 w.
Edwd. 1765 i.
Chas. 1769 w.

Jno. 1770 i.
Richd. 1776 w.
Jno. 1778 w.
Edwd. 1782 w.
Ambrose 1783 w.
Wm. 1784 i.
Wm. 1785 w.
David 1787 w.
Wm. B. 1792 i.
Chas. 1795 w.
Chas. 1795 w.
Jno. 1796 w.
Shenandoah
Jno. 1782 a.
Thos. 1784 a.
Wm. 1789 w.
Southampton
Arthur 1751 i.
Jno. 1751 w.
Matthew 1752 i.
Wm. 1757 w.
Thos. 1757 i.
Thos. 1769 i.
Wm. 1770 w.
Jos. 1770 i.
Jas. 1772 w.
Honer 1773 w.
Nathan 1777 w.
Robt. 1779 w.
Martha 1781 w.
Thos. 1782 w.
Richd. 1782 w.
Robt. 1783 i.
Jas. 1785 i.
Albridgton 1786 w.
Jas. 1786 w.
Jas. 1793 w.
Matthew 1793 w.
Wm. 1793 w.
Mary 1794 w.
Jas. 1797 i.
Saml. 1797 w.
Sarah 1798 w.
Lemuel 1799 i.
Spotsylvania
Jno. 1752 a.
Barbara 1765 w.
David 1768 a.
Thos. 1778 a.
Richd. 1779 a.
Jas. 1778 w.
Stafford
Evan 1708 i.
Swan 1734 w.
Wm. 1758 i.
Jno. 1762 i.
Surry
Susannah 1677 i.
Wm. 1712 w.
Jas. 1713 i.
Arthur 1716 w.

Eliz. 1724 w.
Wm. 1731 i.
Jas. 1742 w.
Jno. 1743 w.
Mary 1747 i.
Thos. 1748 i.
Howell 1751 w.
Sarah 1751 w.
Richd. 1752 i.
Thos. 1773 w.
Ann 1774 w.
Richd. 1774 w.
Hamilton 1781 w.
Jacobina 1781 w.
Ann 1789 i.
Hamilton 1789 i.
Richd. 1789 i.
Sussex
Nicholas 1758 w.
David 1761 i.
Edmunds 1764 w.
Jno. 1767 i.
Howell 1772 w.
Jas. 1772 w.
Richd. 1772 w.
Matthew 1773 i.
Robt. 1775 w.
Jos. 1777 i.
David 1780 w.
Holmes 1780 w.
Richd. 1780 i.
David 1784 w.
Eliz. 1784 w.
Rebecca 1784 w.
David 1786 w.
Nathl. 1788 w.
Jas. Boisseau 1789 w.
Jno. 1793 i.
Rebecca 1793 w.
Jas. 1795 i.
Saml. 1796 i.
Robt. 1797 w.
Jemima 1799 w.
Washington
Thos. 1777 w.
Westmoreland
Hugh 1655 w.
Humphrey 1660 w.
Nathl. 1662 w.
David 1671 i.
Thos. 1677 i.
Jno. 1695 w.
Thos. 1698 w.
Stephen 1703 w.
Hugh 1707 i.
Jno. 1713 w.
Robt. 1717 i.
Mary 1719 i.
Mary 1720 i.
David 1725 i.
Walter 1734 i.

Nathl. 1754 w.
Jno. 1759 i.
Katherine 1766 i.
York
Richd. 1660 w.
Gabriel 1670 w.
Rowland 1688 w.
Edwd. 1689 a.
Mrs. Rowland 1689 i.
Edwd. 1690 w.
Edwd. 1695 i.
Rice 1697 w.
Cornelius 1718 w.
Wm. 1718 i.
Orlando 1719 w.
Humphrey 1755 w.
Matthew 1762 w.
Jno. 1767 i.
Mary 1774 i.
JONS
Cumberland
Jos. 1775 w.
JONSON
Augusta
Arthur 1759 w.
Southampton
Stephen 1799 a.
JOPLIN
Henrico
Ralph 1726 i.
JOPLING
Amherst
Thos. 1789 w.
Josiah 1797 w.
Ralph 1791 w.
JORDAN
Accomack
Dorothy 1689 w.
Albemarle
Matthew 1769 w.
Amelia
Saml. 1761 i.
Saml. 1765 nw.
Wm. 1779 w.
Bedford
Jonas 1785 i.
Brunswick
Jane 1755 w.
Thos. 1768 i.
Thos. 1771 w.
James 1795 w.
Campbell
Chas. 1787 w.
Chesterfield
Lucy 1785 w.
Goochland
Charles 1774 w.
Chas. 1777 i.
Robert 1779 w.
James 1781 w.

Greensville
Michael 1793 i.
Thomas 1784 w.
Halifax
Edwd. 1791 w.
Henrico
Henry 1710 w.
Henry 1791 w.
Isle of Wight
Richard 1702 w.
John 1712 w.
Benjamin 1717 w.
Joshua 1718 w.
Richard 1724 w.
Margaret 1728 i.
James 1732 w.
Richard 1735 i.
James 1741 i.
Joshua 1743 i.
Mathew 1743 w.
Charles 1747 i.
Matthew 1748 w.
John 1758 w.
James 1762 i.
Richard 1763 i.
Sarah 1769 w.
Mathew 1770 w.
John 1778 w.
John 1781 w.
Richard 1782 i.
James 1783 i.
Matthew, Sr. 1785 w.
Josiah 1786 w.
William 1789 w.
John 1790 w.
Richard 1791 w.
Mourning 1792 w.
William 1794 w.
James 1796 w.
Joseph 1796 w.
Lewis 1797 w.
King George
Jno. Morton 1771 w.
Thos. 1789 w.
Loudoun
John 1764 i.
Lunenburg
Eliz. 1795 w.
Mecklenburg
Jno. 1795 w.
Middlesex
James 1711 i.
James 1715 w.
Norfolk
Jas. 1704 w.
James 1742 w.
Francis 1779 w.
John 1794 w.
Northampton
Wm. 1662 w.

Pittsylvania
Saml. 1783 w.
Powhatan
Robt. 1791 w.
Prince William
Thomas 1744 w.
Richmond
Wm. 1713 w.
Wm. 1757 i.
Shenandoah
Jeremiah 1788 a.
Southampton
John 1757 i.
Stafford
Alex. 1761 i.
Surry
Geo. 1678 w.
Thos. 1681 i.
Anne 1697 w.
James 1697 a.
Arthus 1698-9 w.
James 1699 i.
Richd. Sr. 1699 w.
River 1700-1 w.
Robt. 1710 i.
Geo. 1718 w.
Richd. 1751 w.
Wm. 1758 w.
Robt. 1762 i.
Wm. 1764 w.
Joseph 1770 w.
Perry 1798 i.
Westmoreland
Jno. 1696 w.
Dorcas 1708 w.
Robt. 1776 w.
Reuben 1777 w.
JORDEN
York
Williby 1796 w.
JORDON
Essex
William 1718 i.
Isaac 1786 w.
Isaac 1794 i.
Prince William
John 1793 i.
JOURNEW
Westmoreland
Sisley 1667 w.
JOURNEY
Essex
William 1705-6 w.
Lunenburg
Catherine 1775 w.
JOUSLIN
Princess Anne
James 1697 w.
JOYCE
Isle of Wight
Thomas 1762 i.

Norfolk
Martin 1679 w.
Jno. 1710 w.
Jno. 1752 w.
Martain 1782 w.
JOYNE
Accomack
Wm. 1775 w.
Abel 1782 w.
Northampton
Edwd. Sr. 1739 w.
Thos. 1747 w.
Chas. 1754 i.
Edmd. 1757 i.
Littleton 1762 i.
Major 1771 i.
Berry 1772 w.
Edmd. 1774 w.
Harmanson 1780 i.
Thos. 1784 w.
Wm. 1789 i.
JOYNER
Albemarle
Philip 1762 w.
Isle of Wight
Thomas 1695 nw.
William 1698 w.
Thomas 1708 w.
Bridgman 1719 i.
Abraham 1728 w.
Thomas Jr. 1728 w.
Alexander 1732 i.
Theophilus 1739 w.
Thomas 1740 w.
John 1745 w.
Lazarus 1746 w.
John 1748 w.
John 1772 w.
Southampton
Jonathan 1753 w.
Wm. 1758 w.
Bridgman 1754 w.
Henrietta 1762 w.
Jno. 1762 w.
Jos. 1762 w.
Joshua 1767 w.
Bridgman 1776 w.
Wm. 1777 w.
Israel 1778 i.
Jethro 1788 w.
Jonas 1788 i.
Wm. 1785 i.
Ann 1786 w.
Henry 1789 i.
Arthur 1793 i.
Jesse 1799 i.
Mary 1799 w.
JOYNES
Accomack
Wm. 1782 i.
Edwd. 1787 w.

Reuben 1789 w.
Margt. 1791 w.
Levin 1794 w.
Northampton
Jno. Sr. 1784 w.
Thos. 1785 w.
Jno. 1789 i.
JUD
Stafford
Michael 1731 i.
JUDD
Culpeper
William 1766 i.
Stafford
Michael 1734 w.
JUDE
Powhatan
Jno. 1781 w.
JUDKINS
Southampton
Jordan 1799 i.
Surry
Saml. 1705 i.
Charles 1710 w.
Wm. 1721 i.
Thos. 1732 w.
Sam 1740 w.
Ann 1757 w.
Jno. 1760 w.
Wm. 1760 w.
Nicholas 1765 i.
Benj. 1771 i.
Martha 1771 w.
Joseph 1779 w.
Jesse 1781 w.
Saml. 1782 w.
Jesse 1783 w.
Saml. Maggit 1784 i.
Wm. 1784 w.
Saml. 1793 w.
Jno. 1794 w.
Martha 1794 w.
Joseph 1795 w.
Jacob 1798 w.
Rebecca 1798 w.
Sussex
Robt. 1761 w.
Chas. 1774 w.
Robt. 1782 w.
Gray 1789 i.
Wm. 1790 w.
Jno. 1796 w.
Mary 1796 w.
Chas. 1798 w.
Sarah 1798 w.
Thos. 1798 w.
JUDY
Hampshire
Martin 1785 w.

JUFFERSON
Westmoreland
David 1757 i.
JUKE
Middlesex
Lewis 1747 w.
JULIAN
Norfolk
Sarah 1649 w.
Spotsylvania
Charles 1764 w.
JUMPE
Frederick
William 1747 a.
JUMP
Frederick
William 1752 i.
George 1776 i.
JUNAL
Halifax
Sylvester 1773 i.
JUNEL
Halifax
Silvester (Silvanus) 1773 w.
JUNKS
Halifax
Thos. 1779 w.
JURDEN
Essex
Wm. 1717 w.
JUSTICE
Accomack
Abbott 1724 i.
Ralph 1729 w.
Jno. 1744 i.
Mary 1744 w.
Ralph 1760 w.
Wm. 1761 w.
Wm. Jr. 1762 w.
Wm. 1764 i.
Richd. 1768 w.
Jas. 1769 w.
Thos. 1772 i.
Ralph 1783 i.
Richd. 1784 w.
Ralph 1794 w.
Richd. 1798 i.
Brunswick
James 1798 w.
Halifax
Jno. 1766 w.
Lunenburg
Justinian 1756 w.
Surry
Jno. 1775 w.
Jno. 1778 i.
Elizabeth 1799 w.
JUSTIS
Accomack
Robt. 1780 w.

JUY
Princess Anne
Lemuel 1704 w.
JYLES
Westmoreland
Wm. 1776 w.

K

KABLER
Culpeper
Conwright 1778 w.
Frederick 1780 w.
KAE
Isle of Wight
Robert, Sr. 1688 w.
Robert 1704 w.
Stephen 1727 i.
Robert Fenn. 1740 w.
KAFFER
Culpeper
Michael 1768 w.
KAGY
Shenandoah
Henry 1783 w.
KAIDYEE
York
Jno. 1742-3 w.
KAIN
Goochland
Wm. 1743 i.
Prince Edward
Alex. 1774 i.
KAINS
Culpeper
John 1767 w.
KAIRUS
King George
Robt. 1721 i.
KAMPER
Fauquier
Moses 1782 i.
Frederick 1784 i.
John Peter 1788 i.
KANADY
Orange
Jno. 1743 w.
KANE
Berkeley
Daniel 1781 i.
KANIDY
Isle of Wight
Morgan 1676 i.
KARFORD
Frederick
William 1780 i.
KARR
Campbell
Jas. 1786 w.

KASHWILER
Shenandoah
Jacob 1784 a.
KATE
Surry
Robt. 1730 i.
KATHEZINE
Norfolk
Mathew 1712 i.
KATRON
Wythe
Stophel 1795 i.
KAUFMAN
Augusta
Martin 1749 w.
Shenandoah
Michael 1789 i.
KAVANAUGH
Brunswick
Arthur 1733 w.
Culpeper
Philiman 1764 w.
KAVENAUGH
Orange
Phileman 1785 w.
KAVEY
Richmond
Carmock 1714 i.
KAY
Essex
James 1769 w.
Henrico
Jos. 1793 i.
King George
Jas. 1795 w.
KAYS
Princess Anne
Wm. Sr. 1789 w.
KAYSER
Greenbrier
Martin 1789 i.
KAYSS
Princess Anne
Wm. 1791 i.
KEA
Isle of Wight
Robert 1722 i.
Robert 1724 i.
Henry 1727 w.
Surry
Wm. 1711 w.
Charles 1768 w.
Bruton 1776 w.
Mary 1778 w.
Elizabeth 1784 w.
Burton 1785 i.
KEAIR
Shenandoah
Philip 1784 i.

KEALLY
Norfolk
Wm. 1710 a.
KEAR
Cumberland
Wm. 1793 w.
KEARBY
Halifax
Richd. 1782 w.
KEARNS
Norfolk
John 1799 w.
Ohio
James 1786 a.
KEATING
Westmoreland
Pierce 1730 w.
KEATON
Princess Anne
Thos. 1717 w.
KEATT
Brunswick
Josiah 1795 i.
KEAUGH
Washington
Robert 1781 i.
KEAVES
Lancaster
Mary 1751 i.
KEBLE
Northumberland
Cary 1728 i.
KECKLEY
Frederick
Jacob 1789 w.
KEE
Surry
Jno. 1762 i.
Doiley 1779 i.
KEEBLE
Cumberland
Humphrey 1783 w.
KEEFF
York
Jno. 1754 w.
KEEKLEY
Frederick
Benjamin 1780 i.
KEEL
Stafford
Jno. 1701 i.
KEELER
Frederick
George 1749 i.
KEELING
Chesterfield
Eliz. 1779 i.
Norfolk
Eliz. 1671 w.
Thorowgood 1679 w.
Adam 1683 w.

Princess Anne
Jno. 1701 i.
Alex. 1704 w.
Adam 1712 i.
Robt. 1715 w.
Thos. 1716 i.
Thos. 1724 i.
Wm. 1740 i.
Thorowgood 1743 i.
Edwd. 1748 w.
Wm. 1753 w.
Jno. 1755 w.
Barbary 1761 w.
Jno. 1762 i.
Thos. 1766 w.
Adam 1768 i.
Henry 1768 w.
Wm. 1763 w.
Amey 1770 i.
Adam 1771 w.
Nath'l 1779 i.
Wm. 1779 i.
Alex. 1783 w.
Jno. 1788 w.
KELLAM
Princess Anne
Henry 1789 w.
KEELING
Princess Anne
Robert 1790 w.
Wm. 1790 i.
John 1792 w.
Thos. 1799 i.
KEEN
Amelia
Alex. 1748 i.
Fairfax
James 1761 w.
Loudoun
Richard 1764 i.
John 1777 w.
Louisa
Richd. 1772 a.
Northumberland
Wm. 1725 w.
Stafford
Matthew 1731 w.
York
Jno. 1693 w.
KEENE
Lancaster
Geo. 1683 i.
Eliz. 1736 i.
Northumberland
Thos. 1652 w.
Jno. 1740 i.
Ruth 1760 w.
Newton 1771 w.
Anne 1776 w.
Sarah 1794 w.
Newton 1795 i.

York
Jno. 1693 i.
KEENOR
Greenbrier
Thomas 1793 w.
KEENY
Greenbrier
Michael 1791 i.
KEESACKER
Berkeley
John 1799 w.
KEESEE
Essex
George 1785 i.
KEESEY
King George
Geo. 1742 i.
KEESLEYS
Montgomery
George 1788 i.
KEETON
Mecklenburg
Jno. Sr. 1795 w.
Norfolk
Patrick 1752 w.
KEIGHLEY
Isle of Wight
John 1719 w.
KEIRCHEVAILL
King George
Lawrence 1722 i.
KEITH
Fauquier
Isham 1787 w.
Spotsylvania
Rosannah 1799 w.
York
Wm. 1744 w.
Ann 1746 w.
KEITON
Norfolk
Solomon 1782 i.
KELLAHAWN
Accomack
Wm. 1719 w.
KELLAM
Accomack
Richd. 1703 w.
Wm. 1714 w.
Richd. 1731 w.
Edwd. 1737 w.
Thos. 1756 w.
Peter 1763 i.
Abel (Alias Laban)
1769 w.
West 1769 w.
Wm. 1770 w.
Arthur 1771 i.
Jno. 1771 w.
West 1772 i.
Eliz. 1773 w.

Jno. 1773 w.
Wm. 1773 i.
Edwd. 1774 w.
Benston 1775 w.
Scarburgh 1776 w.
Benj. 1777 i.
Solomon 1777 w.
Levi 1779 i.
Ezar 1782 w.
Jno. 1782 w.
Argol 1784 w.
Edmd. 1784 i.
Jno. 1784 i.
Bridget 1784 i.
Richd. 1784 w.
Jno. 1785 w.
Nash 1786 w.
Richd. 1786 i.
Jos. 1789 w.
Abraham 1789 w.
Zerobabel 1791 w.
Matilda 1792 w.
Jno. 1793 i.
Shadrach 1794 w.
Nash 1795 i.
Sacker 1795 w.
Severn 1795 w.
Solomon 1795 w.
Jno. 1797 w.
Northampton
Moses 1773 w.
Abigail 1775 w.
Princess Anne
Henry 1790 i.
John 1797 w.
KELLAR
Shenandoah
Abraham 1787 w.
KELLAWAY
York
Wm. 1647 i.
KELLEBREW
Isle of Wight
William 1740 i.
KELLER
Berkeley
Andrew 1795 i.
Shenandoah
George 1783 w.
George 1788 w.
Barbara 1798 i.
KELLEY
Frederick
John 1751 i.
David 1757 i.
Lancaster
Letitia 1726 i.
Thomas 1749-50 i.
Wm. 1751 i.
John 1757 w.
Wm. 1757 i.

Hugh 1758 w.
Loudoun
Thomas 1783 i.
Mecklenburg
James 1784 i.
KELLEY
Norfolk
Wm. 1710-11 w.
Matthew 1774 w.
Princess Anne
Chas. 1761 w.
Frances 1773 w.
Wm. 1774 i.
Harry 1785 w.
Westmoreland
Wm. 1720 w.
KELLO
Southampton
Richd. 1789 w.
KELLOM
Accomack
Benj. 1799 i.
KELLSALL
Norfolk
Roger 1708-9 w.
KELLUM
Accomack
Sarah 1744 i.
Elijah 1766 nw.
Eliz. 1774 i.
Comfort 1778 w.
Benstone 1779 i.
Jonathan 1779 i.
Wm. 1783 i.
Matilda 1793 i.
Margt. 1795 w.
Northampton
John 1761 w.
Abigail 1778 i.
Jonathan 1792 w.
Northumberland
Richd. 1762 i.
Princess Anne
Nathaniel 1798 w.
KELLY
Accomack
Jno. 1724 w.
David 1755 i.
Jos. 1760 w.
Edmond 1762 w.
Jno. 1763 w.
Henry 1780 w.
Timothy 1782 w.
Henry 1784 i.
Thos. 1784 w.
Richd. 1784 w.
Wm. 1784 i.
Timothy 1785 i.
Wm. 1785 i.
Jno. 1787 w.
Jos. 1796 w.

Jos. 1797 i.
Augusta
Wm. 1767 i.
Bath
Owen 1796 i.
Berkeley
William 1777 w.
William 1785 w.
Brunswick
David 1783 w.
Jiles 1786 w.
Culpeper
William 1751 i.
Joseph 1757 i.
William 1760 w.
William 1799 i.
Essex
Arthur 1718 i.
Fauquier
Joseph 1783 w.
Frederick
David 1744 a.
Hardy
John 1798 i.
Henrico
Thady 1789 i.
Henry
Andrew 1782 i.
William 1783 i.
Lancaster
Roger 1683 w.
Jno. 1691 i.
Jno. 1704 i.
Giles 1718 a.
Wm. 1718 i.
Chas. 1723 i.
Martha 1750 i.
Wm. 1753 i.
Benj. 1773 i.
Hugh 1778 nw.
William 1785 i.
Loudoun
James 1798 i.
Middlesex
Patk. 1724 w.
Norfolk
Daniel 1765 w.
Northamhpton
Edmd. 1682 w.
Thos. 1727 i.
Chas. 1736 i.
Alex. Jr., 1784 i.
Pittsylvania
Hugh 1799 w.
Princess Anne
Matthew 1736 w.
Jno. 1778 w.
Richmond
Jno. 1715 w.
Alex. 1754 w.
Matthew 1772 w.

Stafford
Edmd. 1706 w.
Saml. 1750 i.
Edmond 1746 i.
Sussex
Jno. 1790 w.
Westmoreland
Thos. 1723 w.
KELP
Shenandoah
William 1793 w.
KELSHAW
Chesterfield
Jno. 1788 w.
Middlesex
Mary 1730 i.
KELSICK
Norfolk
Richard 1760 w.
Richard 1774 w.
Richard 1787 i.
Richmond
Mary 1794 w.
KELSIE
Frederick
John 1769 i.
KELSO
Frederick
John 1763 w.
Prince Edward
Nathan 1792 i.
KEM
Lancaster
Joseph 1791 w.
KEMBLE
Brunswick
Dianna 1792 w.
KEMP
Chesterfield
Susannah 1767 i.
Essex
Richd. 1714 w.
Frederick
James 1749 i.
Thomas 1749 a.
James 1791 i.
Middlesex
Matthew 1716 w.
Mary 1769 w.
Thomas 1773 w.
Mary 1791 w.
Thomas 1791 i.
Norfolk
Jno. 1648 i.
Geo. 1676 w.
Ann 1678-9 w.
Northampton
Alex. 1757 w.
Jno. 1773 i.
Susanna 1773 i.

Prince George
Jno. 1715 i.
Princess Anne
James 1707 w.
Jno. 1723 w.
Richmond
Martin 1719 nw.
KEMPE
Accomack
Jas. 1721 w.
Princess Anne
Geo. 1733 w.
James 1783 w.
KEMPER
Fauquier
John 1799 w.
KENDAL
Accomack
Jno. 1771 i.
KENDALL
Accomack
Jno. 1738 w.
Lemuel 1751 w.
Saml. 1752 i.
Joshua 1755 w.
Wm. 1758 w.
Jno. 1760 i.
Wm. 1760 i.
Robins 1780 w.
King George
Saml. 1790 w.
Moses 1793 w.
Northampton
Wm. 1686 w.
Jno. 1689 w.
Wm. 1696 w.
Wm. 1708 i.
Wm. Jr. 1718 w.
Wm. 1720 w.
Littleton 1730 w.
Henrietta 1737 i.
Geo. 1755 w.
Littleton 1760 i.
Jno. 1763 w.
Custis, Sr. 1781 w.
Geo. Sr. 1784 w.
Geo. Jr. 1784 w.
Peter 1787 w.
Custis Sr. 1795 i.
Wm. Sr. 1795 w.
Jno. Jr. 1794 w.
Bowdoin 1797 i.
Thos. 1799 w.
Prince William
William 1744 i.
Richmond
Thos. Jr. 1716 i.
Westmoreland
Jno. 1736 nw.
Saml. 1750 w.
Jno. 1754 w.

Jos. 1754 i.
York
Ann 1719 w.
Richd. 1719 ab.
KENDEL
King George
Woffendel 1795 w.
KENDELL
Norfolk
Jas. 1679 w.
York
Jno. 1701 w.
KENDOE (?)
Northampton
Richd. 1649 i.
KENDOL
Northampton
Peggy 1735 w.
Wm. 1736 w.
KENDRICK
Culpeper
Jacob 1794 i.
Shenandoah
Abraham 1782 w.
Christian 1788 a.
Washington
Solomon 1781? i.
Westmoreland
Marshall 1753 i.
KENEDAY
Berkeley
Thomas 1798 w.
KENEDY
Princess Anne
John 1799 w.
KENNA
Northampton
Danl. 1775 nw.
KENNADY
Lunenburg
Andrew 1748 i.
Louisa
Davenport 1782 a.
Northumberland
Nicholas 1774 i.
KENNAN
Randolph
Joseph 1793 i.
Richmond
Robt. 1767 i.
Jno. 1782 i.
KENNARD
Prince George
Geo. 1724 i.
KENNEBREW
Southampton
Wm. 1772 w.
Ann 1777 w.
Edwin 1781 w.

KENNEBROUGH
Sussex
Jno. 1794 w.
KENNEDY
Augusta
Matthew 1784 i.
Bedford
John 1781 w.
Frederick
Daniel 1758 w.
Louisa
Davenport 1787 i.
Mary 1791 a.
Northumberland
Richard 1760 i.
Geo. 1775 i.
Wm. 1776 i.
Mary 1777 i.
Eliz. 1778 w.
Ohio
Samuel 1778 a.
KENNEN
Richmond
Wm. 1767 i.
Jno. 1777 w.
KENNER
Fauquier
Howson 1778 w.
Rodham 1793 w.
Norfolk
John 1679 i.
Northumberland
Rodham 1706 w.
Richd. 1726-7 w.
Francis 1728 w.
Matthew 1743-4 w.
Rodham 1743 w.
Rodham 1757 i.
Brereton 1759 w.
Rodham 1761 w.
William 1762 w.
Winder 1762 w.
Wm. 1773 i.
Hannah 1777 i.
Winder 1785 w.
Rodham 1786 i.
Westmoreland
Richd. 1719 w.
KENNERLEY
Culpeper
Samuel 1749 w.
Elin 1756 w.
KENNEY
Augusta
Jno. 1793 i.
KENNITT
Northampton
Martin 1647 i.
KENNON
Chesterfield
Wm. 1759 w.

Richd. 1761 w.
Agnes 1762 w.
Ann 1766 w.
Robt. 1781 w.
Henrico
Richd. 1694 w.
Richd. 1736 w.
Henry Isham 1748 i.
Richmond
Wm. 1764 i.
KENNY
Botetourt
William 1784 i.
Northampton
Kenny 1775 i.
Rappahannock
Wm. 1677 w.
KENOE
Prince William
Francis 1797 w.
KENT
Albemarle
James 1759 i.
Botetourt
Jacob 1777 w.
Fairfax
Richard 1759 w.
Richard 1771 w.
Benoni 1774 w.
Fluvanna
Thos. 1786 w.
Goochland
Wm. 1746 i.
Halifax
Robt. 1783 w.
Luke 1789 w.
Lancaster
Henry 1765 i.
Edwin 1786 i.
Montgomery
Robert 1796 i.
Northumberland
Jno. 1665 w.
John 1765 w.
John 1766 w.
Wm. 1789 w.
KENTINE
Princess Anne
Jno. 1782 w.
KENTON
Loudoun
Mark 1785 i.
KENUMS
Bedford
Alex. 1779 i.
KENWARD
Frederick
Nich. 1760 i.
KENYON
King George
Jno. 1743 i.

Abraham 1750 i.
Richmond
Jno. 1706 w.
KER
Accomack
Edwd. 1790 w.
Orange
Jacob 1745 w.
James 1777 i.
Middlesex
David 1785 i.
KERBY
Albemarle
Jno. 1760 i.
King George
Jas. 1758 i.
Northampton
Mary 1771 w.
York
Martha 1782 w.
Wm. 1782 w.
Bennet 1783 w.
Wm. 1784 i.
Robt. 1785 w.
Jno. 1796 i.
KERCHEVALL
Essex
John 1784 w.
Dolly 1786 w.
Frederick
John 1788 w.
KERCKER
Orange
Andrew 1738 a.
KERFOOT
Frederick
William 1779 w.
George 1779 i.
KERLL
Isle of Wight
Eleanor 1728 w.
KERNEY
Berkeley
William 1787 w.
Elizabeth 1799 w.
Henrico
Hugh 1795 w.
Norfolk
John 1717 a.
Surry
James 1716 w.
KERNS
Bedford
John 1794 i.
KERR
Albemarle
James Jr. 1789 w.
Augusta
Jas. 1770 i.
Wm. 1785 w.

Bedford
George 1765 i.
William 1791 w.
Fauquier
John 1796 w.
King George
Peter 1736 i.
Middlesex
David 1772 w.
Norfolk
Robert 1778 w.
Robert 1786 i.
Powhatan
Jno. 1777 i.
Surry
Jno. 1771 w.
Sussex
Geo. 1784 i.
Geo. 1792 i.
Eliz. 1795 w.
Washington
John 1778 i.
KERRAN (?)
Hardy
Peter 1799 i.
KERSEY
King George
Barberry 1731 i.
Alice 1781 w.
Louisa
Geo. 1796 w.
Welthey Ann 1797 w.
Surry
Hannah 1761 i.
Wm. 1762 w.
KERTLY
Madison
William 1795 i.
KESLEY
Franklin
Jesse 1786 w.
John 1787 i.
KESTER
Augusta
Arnold 1759 i.
KESTERSON
Northumberland
Thos. 1719 w.
Wm. 1729 i.
John 1752 w.
Quilla 1762 w.
Geo. 1766 i.
Geo. 1786 w.
Wm. 1791 w.
KETCHNER
Frederick
Michael 1757 w.
KETOR
Norfolk
James 1792 w.

KEWE
Northumberland
Bervely 1769 w.
KEY
Albemarle
Martin 1791 w.
Essex
Robert 1726 w.
Henry
George 1799 w.
Lancaster
Jas. 1725 i.
Louisa
Eliz. 1761 w.
Lunenburg
Wm. 1764 i.
Norfolk
Ann 1791 w.
Northumberland
Jno. 1656 i.
Ralph 1661 i.
Princess Anne
Jno. 1750 w.
KEYES
Berkeley
Gershom 1783 a.
Humphrey 1793 w.
Ruth 1798 w.
KEYS
Berkeley
John 1777 i.
Chesterfield
Michael 1779 w.
Frederick
Gersham 1766 w.
Gresham 1770 i.
Rockbridge
Roger 1781 w.
Jno. 1799 w.
KEYTON
Spotsylvania
Jerrerd 1769 a.
KIBLENGER
Shenandoah
Daniel 1797 w.
KIBLER
Shenandoah
Christian 1787 w.
John 1790 a.
Henry 1797 i.
KICHEN
Isle of Wight
William 1735 i.
KID
Frederick
Daniel 1792 i.
Norfolk
John 1785 w.
KIDD
Albemarle
Aaron 1776 w.

Jno. 1785 w.
Amelia
Geo. 1797 w.
Amherst
Jno. N. 17[85?] i.
Augusta
Francis 1769 i.
Essex
Thomas 1748 w.
Isaac 1772 i.
Henry 1793 w.
Middlesex
Thos. 1727 w.
Jno. 1760 i.
Benj. 1762 i.
Jno. 1777 i.
Wm. 1792 i.
Norfolk
Alex. 1785 i.
KIDINGE
Norfolk
Thos. 1666 i.
KIDWELL
Fauquier
Mary 1795 w.
KIGAN
Isle of Wight
Karbry 1657 w.
KIGGIN
Surry
Terrence 1699 i.
KIGGON
York
Chas. 1658 i.
KILBEE
Middlesex
Wm. 1706 a.
KILBY
Culpeper
John 1772 w.
KILGORE
Princess Anne
Wm. 1786 w.
Wm. 1790 w.
David 1791 i.
Margt. 1795 w.
John 1797 w.
Spotsylvania
Peter 1727 a.
KILL
Richmond
Chas. 1718 i.
Westmoreland
Chas. 1749 w.
KILLBEE
Richmond
Wm. 1729 i.
KILLGORE
Lancaster
Peter 1709 w.

KILLE
Harrison
John 1796 w.
KILLEBREW
Isle of Wight
William 1740 i.
KILLINGWORTH
Surry
Wm. 1709 w.
KILLY
Brunswick
David 1790 w.
KILMAN
Accomack
Jno. 1797 w.
KILLMAN
Rappahannock
John 1677 w.
KILP
Frederick
Peter 1756 i.
KILPATRICK
Augusta
Chas. 1767 w.
Alex. 1786 i.
Greenbrier
Roger 1797 w.
Surry
James 1677 i.
Northumberland
Anna 1738 w.
KILPIN
Middlesex
Wm. 1717 i.
KIMBALL
Surry
Joseph 1713 i.
Westmoreland
Lydia 1698 w.
KIMBERLAND
Augusta
Jacob 1765 a.
KIMBLER
Loudoun
John 1793 i.
KIMBROW
Louisa
Jno. 1765 w.
Wm. 1765 w.
KIMPER
Fauquier
Harman 1774 i.
KINCADE
Augusta
Geo. 1759 i.
KINCAID
Bath
William 1794 i.
Greenbrier
Thomas 1795 w.

KINCHELOE
Fairfax
Daniel 1785 w.
Prince William
John 1799 i.
KINCHEN
Isle of Wight
William 1735 w.
Matthew 1736 w.
Matthew 1743 i.
KINDALL
Orange
John 1795 i.
KINDEL
Orange
Wm. 1777 w.
KINDER
Augusta
Jacob 1749 a.
Peter 1749 i.
Norfolk
Robert 1794 w.
Robert 1799 i.
KINDRED
Isle of Wight
Samuel 1729 w.
Southampton
Mary 1752 w.
Saml. 1785 w.
Benj. 1794 w.
Surry
Jno. 1677 i.
Jno. 1703 w.
KINDRICK
Shenandoah
Abraham 1790 a.
Christian 1790 i.
Washington
Thomas 1779 i.
KINEAD
Rockbridge
Robert 1799 i.
KING
Accomack
Robt. 1755 w.
Augusta
Robt. 1749 w.
Jos. 1769 w.
Jas. 1775 a.
Jno. 1795 w.
Brunswick
Jno. 1742 i.
Chas. 1768 i.
Henry 1791 w.
Essex
George 1698 i.
Fairfax
Samuel 1750 i.
John 1752 i.
James 1768 i.

Fluvanna
Danl. 1798 w.
Frederick
James 1788 i.
Halifax
Robt. 1757 i.
Jno. 1795 i.
Henrico
Jno. 1717 w.
Henry
William 1798 i.
Isle of Wight
Henry 1669 w.
Sarah 1700-1 i.
Robert 1725 w.
Robert 1751 i.
Henry 1772 w.
Augustine 1774 w.
Henry 1783 i.
Martha 1791 w.
Samuel 1793 w.
King George
Thos. 1737 i.
Lancaster
Henry 1675 i.
Wm. 1716 w.
John 1752 w.
William 1773 i.
Loudoun
John 1785 w.
Mary 1790 w.
John 1793 i.
Benj. Sr. 1795 w.
Louisa
Thos. 1798 i.
Middlesex
Jno. 1711 w.
Montgomery
William 1792 i.
Norfolk
Richd. 1686 w.
Jacob 1713 i.
Robert 1783 w.
John 1784 w.
Edmond 1797 w.
James 1797 w.
Miles 1799 w.
Northumberland
John 1777 w.
Patrick
Samuel 1797 a.
Pittsylvania
Jno. 1771 w.
Jas. 1777 w.
Jno. 1783 i.
Princess Anne
Landmon 1779 w.
James 1787 w.
Eliz. 1792 w.
Dinah 1796 w.
Jeremiah 1798 w.

Prince William
John 1797 w.
Rappahannock
Robt. 1683 i.
Jane 1685 w.
Richmond
Theophilus 1711 w.
Wm. 1736 w.
Eliz. 1741 w.
Henry 1750 w.
Jno. 1771 i.
Southampton
Katherine 1771 w.
Stafford
Wm. 1702 w.
Jos. 1733 i.
Surry
Thos. 1679 i.
Anne 1788 w.
Faithy 1756 i.
James 1759 i.
Jno. 1705 w.
Jno. 1737 i.
Philip 1772 i.
Randolph 1786 w.
Robt. 1752 i.
Thos. 1732 w.
Thos. 1751 i.
Thos. 1774 i.
Sussex
Jno. Jr. 1759 i.
Richd. 1759 i.
Wm. 1762 i.
Andrews 1766 i.
Jno. 1766 w.
Faithy 1793 w.
Joshua 1799 w.
Westmoreland
Adam 1674-5 w.
Arthur 1718 i.
Jno. 1726 w.
Smith 1739 i.
Arthur 1762 i.
York
Richd. 1727 w.
KINGARY
Franklin
Jacob 1791 a.
KINGCART
Richmond
Thos. 1716 i.
KINGMAN
Princess Anne
Robt. 1724 w.
KINGSTON
Albemarle
Geo. 1793 i.
Norfolk
Paul 1764 w.
Princess Anne
Thos. 1706 i.

KINGWELL
Northumberland
Thos. 1655 i.
KINIBLER (?)
Loudoun
John 1792 w.
KINISON
Bath
Nathaniel 1794 w.
KINKADE
Augusta
Geo. 1756 a.
KINKEAD
Albemarle
James 1763 w.
Joseph 1774 w.
Augusta
Burrows 1764 i.
Mathew 1776 w.
Washington
David 1779 w.
KINNEGAR
Washington
Conrod 1786 w.
KINNEON
Princess Anne
Jno. 1787 w.
KINNIAN
King George
Abraham 1752 a.
KINSEY
Princess Anne
Thos. 1787 w.
KINSLEY
Shenandoah
Anthony 1783 a.
KINZY
Halifax
Wm. 1776 i.
KIRBY
Accomack
Wm. 1772 w.
Halifax
Richd. 1784 i.
Northumberland
Simon 1667 w.
Pittsylvania
Jno. 1773 w.
Jno. 1795 w.
Southampton
Richd. 1761 w.
Moody 1761 w.
Wm. 1772 w.
Mary 1774 w.
Richd. 1781 w.
Turner 1783 i.
Jno. 1797 i.
Ann 1798 w.
York
Thos. 1668 w.
Robt. 1727 i.

Jas. 1737 i.
Thos. 1741 i.
Jno. 1774 w.
Augusta
Jas. 1783 w.
Jas. 1791 i.
KIRK
Culpeper
John 1788 w.
Fauquier
William 1780 w.
King George
Jeremiah 1792 w.
Lancaster
Jas. 1713 i.
Jas. 1717 w.
Chris. 1721 i.
Chris. 1722 w.
Wm. 1725 w.
Robt. 1727 w.
Thos. 1727 w.
Chris. 1736 w.
Hezkiah 1741 i.
James 1777 i.
Anthony 1764 w.
Sarah 1778 w.
Thomas 1778 w.
James 1779 i.
Anthony 1794 i.
Loudoun
Wm. 1774 w.
Northumberland
Jno. 1783 i.
Orange
James 1736 i.
Rappahannock
Eliz. 1682 w.
Richmond
Geo. 1750 w.
Rockbridge
Thomas 1782 i.
Stafford
Jno. 1730 w.
Jno. 1733 i.
Wm. 1753 i.
Westmoreland
Jno. 1765 w.
Wm. 1775 i.
Jno. 1796 i.
York
Julius 1763 i.
KIRKE
Northampton
Christopher 1652 w.
KIRKHAM
Augusta
Robt. 1749 w.
Robt. 1755 i.
Henry 1765 w.

KIRKLAND
Brunswick
Thos. 1764 w.
Fairfax
Richard 1743 w.
Lancaster
Richd. 1724 nw.
Prince George
Richd. 1726 i.
KIRKLEY
Northumberland
Geo. 1765 i.
KIRKPATRICK
Fairfax
Thomas 1785 w.
Northumberland
Edwd. 1710 i.
Rockbridge
Robert 1780 w.
Charles 1795 w.
Spotsylvania
Jno. 1747 a.
KIRKUM
Augusta
Michael 1746 a.
Robt. 1749 i.
KIRKUP
Lancaster
Geo. 1701 nw.
KIRKWOOD
Essex
Patrick 1769 i.
KIRLE
Isle of Wight
William 1720 w.
KIRSEY
Charlotte
Thos. 1796 w.
KIRTLEY
Augusta
Francis 1774 w.
Culpeper
Francis 1763 w.
Margt. 1781 w.
Madison
William Sr. 1795 i.
Thomas 1799 w.
Orange
Jno. 1775 i.
KIRTON
Westmoreland
Thos. 1691 i.
KIPP
Accomack
Benj. 1777 w.
KIPPAX
Richmond
Edwd. 1712 i.
Peter 1719 w.

KIPPERS
Amherst
Wm. 1769 w.
KISER
Shenandoah
Charles 1797 i.
KISLINGER
Augusta
Chris. 1774 i.
KISSINGER
Greenbrier
Mathias 1795 i.
KISTIN
Augusta
Christofull 1773 w.
KITCHEN
Accomack
Temperance 1738 w.
Botetourt
Henry 1792 i.
Mecklenburg
Jno. 1787 w.
Loudoun
Wm. 1775 i.
John 1784 i.
William 1788 w.
Prince William
George 1785 w.
Southampton
Jas. 1764 i.
Thos. 1768 i.
Benj. 1778 w.
Westmoreland
Sarah 1780 w.
Sarah 1780 i.
Lancaster
Wm. 1653 a.
Surry
Jno. 1720 w.
KITCHING
Southampton
James 1762 w.
Thos. 1767 w.
Stafford
Augustine 1734 i.
Anthony 1748 w.
Westmoreland
Wm. 1723 i.
KITE
Westmoreland
Jno. 1735 i.
KITSON
Accomack
Richd. 1740 w.
Eliz. 1784 w.
KITTSON
Accomack
Jno. 1782 w.
KITTY
Lancaster
Wm. 1678 i.

KIVIL
Louisa
  Thos. 1782 i.
KIZEE
Pittsylvania
  Arthur 1789 w.
  Richd. 1794 w.
KLECKHAM
Berkeley
  Conrad 1784 w.
KLEINHOOF
Chesterfield
  Geo. 1794 i.
KLEINHOFF
Chesterfield
  Geo. 1793 w.
KLUG
Middlesex
  Saml. 1794 w.
KLUGG
Culpeper
  Geo. Saml. 1764 i.
KNIBB
Charles City
  Jno. 1794 w.
Chesterfield
  Ann 1764 w.
Henrico
  Solomon 1679 i.
  Saml. 1691 w.
  Sarah 1696 w.
  Saml. 1716 w.
  Jno. 1726-7 w.
  Sarah 1736 i.
  Thos. 1747 w.
KNIGHT
Accomack
  Geo. 1728 i.
  Thos. 1765 w.
  Jno. 1776 w.
  Geo. 1779 i.
Bath
  James 1796 i.
Fluvanna
  Isaac 1797 w.
Frederick
  Solomon 1745 i.
  James 1787 w.
Henrico
  Anthony 1700 w.
Lunenburg
  Jno. 1772 w.
Mecklenburg
  Joseph 1789 w.
Norfolk
  Richard 1772 i.
  William 1799 i.
Northampton
  Danl. 1635 w.
  Jno. Sr. 1701 w.
  Eliz. 1702 i.

Jno. 1709 w.
Dixon 1735 i.
Dixon 1736 w.
Jno. 1736 i.
Southy 1738 i.
Thos. 1739 i.
Jno. 1750 w.
Dixon 1755 w.
Jonah 1760 i.
Wm. 1788 i.
Northumberland
  Peter 1705 w.
  Thos. 1709-10 w.
  Jos. 1724 w.
  Francis 1726-7 w.
  Jos. 1728-9 i.
  John 1777 i.
  Hannah 1786 w.
  Jno. 1794 i.
Princess Anne
  Henry 1773 w.
Stafford
  Thos. 1707 i.
  Wm. 1748 i.
  Wm. 1765 w.
  Benj. 1784 i.
Surry
  Jeremiah 1678 i.
  Nathaniel 1678 w.
Sussex
  Danl. 1755 a.
  Jno. 1762 w.
  Wm. 1763 w.
  Jno. 1764 i.
  Wm. 1782 i.
  Chas. 1786 w.
  Jno. 1791 w.
Westmoreland
  Terrell 1698 w.
  Wm. 1735 i.
KNIGHTON
King George
  Moses 1755 w.
York
  Henry 1680 w.
KNITE
Westmoreland
  Jno. 1726 i.
KNIVETON
York
  Susanna 1700 w.
KNOBLE
Westmoreland
  Robt. 1704 w.
KNOCK
Accomack
  Eliz. 1799 w.
KNOTT
Norfolk
  Wm. 1696-7 w.

Northumberland
  Wm. 1747 w.
  Richd. 1758 w.
  James 1766 w.
  Peter 1777 w.
  Ellanor 1784 w.
  Jas. 1797 i.
Surry
  Wm. 1717 w.
  Wm. 1727 w.
  Christian 1741 i.
  Mary 1742 i.
Washington
  Andrew 1797 w.
Westmoreland
  Jno. 1660 i.
KNOWLES
Norfolk
  James 1771 w.
Washington
  Edward 1795 i.
KNOX
Accomack
  Eliz. 1781 i.
Augusta
  Jas. 1772 w.
Berkeley
  William 1778 w.
Charlotte
  James 1774 i.
Fauquier
  Robert 1785 w.
Stafford
  Alex. 1785 i.
KNYVEXON
York
  Francis 1694 w.
KOGER
Franklin
  Jacob 1797 w.
Henry
  Jacob 1783 i.
Orange
  Nicho. 1743 eb.
  Michael 1743 i.
KOIN
Prince William
  Nicholas 1740 w.
KOLLER
Shenandoah
  John 1797 i.
KOON
Harrison
  Joseph 1798 w.
KOUGHNARVER
Frederick
  Jacob 1772 w.
KRUCK
Berkeley
  Jacob 1795 w.

KUE
Northampton
Jno. 1647 w.
KYLE
Albemarle
Wm. 1792 i.
Berkeley
Jos. 1783 w.
Botetourt
Archd. 1784 w.

L

LABARIER
Chesterfield
Nancy 1794 w.
LABARRIAIRE
Chesterfield
Ann 1798 i.
LABOURN
Augusta
Edwd. 1754 i.
LaCAZE
Henrico
Jacques 1708 w.
LACEY
Amherst
Wm. 1771 w.
Culpeper
John 1789 i.
Loudoun
Benj. 1783 i.
Thomas 1797 i.
Surry
Mary 1716 w.
Westmoreland
Jos. 1787 w.
LACIE
Surry
Robt. 1702 w.
LACKEY
Berkeley
James 1778 w.
LACKLAND
Charlotte
John 1780 w.
LACKY
Patrick
John 1793 i.
LACON
Prince William
Francis 1744 w.
LACY
Amelia
Jno. 1764 w.
Charles City
Thos. Batts 1774 w.
Chesterfield
Wm. 1774 w.
Nathl. 1781 w.

Cumberland
Vincent 1749 w.
Goochland
Stephen 1772 w.
Sarah 1794 i.
Greenbrier
Wm. Sr. 1795 i.
Halifax
Elisha 1782 i.
Pittsylvania
Theophilus 1778 i.
Westmoreland
Jos. 1787 w.
LADD
Goochland
Constant 1766 w.
Charles City
James 1770 w.
Amos 1790 w.
Anna 1792 w.
Wm. 1797 w.
Mecklenburg
Wm. 1780 w.
LADE
Augusta
Edwd. 1784 i.
LADNER
Lancaster
Hugh 1708 w.
LAFFLEY
Northampton
Edwd. 1733 w.
LAFFOON
Brunswick
Matthew 1789 w.
LAFFOTY
Accomack
Neal 1796 i.
LAFON
Essex
Nicholas 1750 i.
LAFORCE
Goochland
Rene 1728 w.
LAFORSE
Goochland
Sarah 1757 w.
LAFUITE
Goochland
Tobias 1728 w.
LAGHLIN
Augusta
Archd. 1782 i.
LAHORE
Stafford
Jno. 1733 i.
LAIN
Charlotte
James 1781 w.

LAINE
Amherst
Jno. 1778 a.
Wm. 1791 w.
Norfolk
Robert 1783 i.
Prince William
William 1742 i.
LAING
Stafford
Andrew 1741 i.
LAINHART
Bedford
John Chris. 1779 w.
LAIR
Augusta
Ferdinando 1767 a.
Ferdinando 1773 i.
LAIRD
Washington
James 1780 w.
LAKE
Essex
Mary 1710 w.
Fairfax
Richard 1775 w.
Norfolk
Jos. 1687 w.
LAKELAND
Essex
Richard 1699 i.
LALSEY
Essex
Robert 1702 i.
LAMAS
Richmond
Wm. 1719 i.
LAMASTER
Amherst
Richd. 1774 w.
LAMB
Charles City
Jno. 1792 i.
Orange
John 1794 i.
Princess Anne
James 1785 w.
Frances 1790 i.
Sussex
Jno. 1785 w.
Danl. 1786 w.
York
Anthony 1700 i.
Jno. 1735 i.
Danl. 1744 w.
Anthony 1758 w.
Martha 1776 w.
LAMBART
Princess Anne
Jno. 1724 w.

LAMBEE
Westmoreland
Wm. 1702 i.
LAMBERT
Accomack
Robt. 1687 i.
Bedford
Charles 1798 w.
Brunswick
Hugh 1765 w.
Thos. 1778 i.
Richd. 1794 w.
Charlotte
Hugh 1785 i.
Lunenburg
Lewis 1785 w.
Mecklenburg
James 1778 w.
Hugh 1782 w.
Norfolk
Thos. 1677 w.
Susanah 1710-11 i.
John 1746 w.
Solomon 1763 w.
Hilley 1779 i.
Willis 1783 i.
James 1786 w.
Northumberland
Henry 1670 w.
Prince William
Joseph 1738 a.
Richmond
Wm. 1716 w.
Ann 1743 w.
Jno. 1783 i.
Wm. 1783 i.
Shenandoah
Chris. 1786 w.
Westmoreland
Thos. 1747-8 w.
LAMBETH
Middlesex
Jno. 1759 w.
Norfolk
David 1763 w.
LAMKIN
Amelia
Griffin Lewis 1781 w.
Northumberland
James 1778 i.
Prince William
Chattin 1789 i.
Westmoreland
Jno. 1677 i.
Benj. 1724 i.
Geo. 1727 w.
Jno. 1737 i.
Saml. 1751 w.
Aston 1761 i.
Peter 1762 w.
Danl. 1769 i.

Ann 1771 i.
Mathew 1773 w.
Peter 1775 i.
Francis 1777 i.
Ashton 1796 i.
LAMKINE
Northumberland
John 1752 w.
LAMON
Richmond
Jas. 1716 i.
LAMOUNT
Princess Anne
James 1706 w.
James 1739 w.
Jno. 1746-7 w.
Thos. 1748 i.
Henry 1774 w.
Caleb 1783 i.
Henry 1793 w.
Cornelius 1795 w.
Norfolk
Henry 1773 i.
LAMPHIER
Fairfax
Venus 1769 w.
Venus 1770 w.
LAMPKIN
Northumberland
Jane 1765 w.
Lewis 1769 w.
Prince William
George 1789 i.
LAMPREY
Northumberland
Angel 1737 w.
LAMPTON
King George
Wm. 1723 i.
Richmond
Francis 1716 w.
Spotsylvania
Wm. 1760 a.
LANCASTER
Isle of Wight
Robert 1720 i.
Sarah 1722 w.
Henry 1785 w.
Northumberland
Nich. 1713 ab.
Jno. 1738 i.
Jos. 1744 w.
John 1751 w.
Wm. 1766 w.
Southampton
Jos. 1785 w.
Jas. 1796 w.
Rebecca 1798 i.
Surry
Robt. 1739 i.
Wm. 1740 i.

Saml. 1744 i.
Saml. 1761 w.
Silviah 1768 w.
LANCE
Augusta
Barnard 1786 w.
Barnet 1791 i.
Loudoun
Peter 1772 i.
LANCELETT
Westmoreland
Jane 1713 i.
LANCELOTT
Westmoreland
Wm. 1706 i.
Jno. 1712 w.
LANCISCO
Hardy
Henry 1799 w.
LANCKFIELD
Norfolk
John 1640 i.
LANCRUM
Lunenburg
Wm. 1778 w.
LAND
Norfolk
Renatris 1681 w.
Orange
Richard 1795 i.
Princess Anne
Francis 1695 a.
[Mary?] 1706 rp.
Edwd. 1722 w.
Edwd. 1726 i.
Robt. 1726 w.
Francis 1736 w.
Renatus 1740 a.
Francis 1742 w.
Edwd. 1778 w.
Robt. 1783 w.
Francis 1787 i.
Richd. 1788 w.
Willoughby 1788 w.
Southampton
Bird 1794 w.
Surry
Curtis 1729 w.
Robt. 1739 w.
Sussex
Jno. 1781 w.
Curtis 1783 w.
Webb 1784 w.
Robt. 1797 w.
Nathl. 1798 w.
LANDMAN
Frederick
Daniel 1761 i.
Richmond
Wm. 1727 i.
Catherine 1747 i.

Jno. 1750 w.
Jas. 1761 w.
LANDON
Middlesex
Thos. 1700 w.
LANDRAM
Essex
Mary 1754 w.
Eliz. 1755 w.
Patrick 1759 w.
King George
Thos. 1771 w.
LANDRUM
Essex
John 1707-8 i.
Thomas 1715 i.
James 1739 w.
Samuel 1750 i.
Austin 1764 i.
John 1788 i.
Prince William
William 1782 i.
LANE
Accomack
Israel 1788 w.
Bedford
Joseph 1773 i.
Brunswick
Simon 1782 w.
Essex
John 1782 w.
Greensville
Joseph 1796 i.
Isle of Wight
William 1751 i.
Loudoun
Wm. Car 1770 w.
John 1772 i.
Wm. 1777 i.
James 1778 i.
Jas. Hardage 1787 w.
James 1790 w.
James Sr. 1794 i.
John Hardage 1797 i.
James 1799 i.
Norfolk
Robert 1721 w.
Augustus 1782 w.
Robert 1783 w.
Princess Anne
Danl. 1700 w.
Solomon 1789 a.
Shenandoah
George 1779 a.
Surry
Thos. 1709 w.
Thos. 1721 i.
Thos. 1734 w.
Thos. 1771 w.
Jno. Sr. 1777 w.
Joseph 1778 w.

Etheldred 1782 w.
Mary 1796 w.
Wm. 1799 w.
Sussex
Joseph 1775 w.
Westmoreland
James 1719 i.
Jos. 1741 i.
Wm. 1760 w.
Wm. 1761 i.
Jos. 1786 i.
LANG
Lunenburg
Jno. 1788 i.
LANGDON
Frederick
Joseph 1760 w.
Joseph 1770 i.
LANGFORD
Isle of Wight
Thomas 1782 i.
Jesse 1791 i.
Westmoreland
Thos. 1669 w.
LANGHORNE
Cumberland
Jno. 1784 w.
Maurice 1791 i.
Mary 1797 i.
LANGLEY
Lunenburg
Jno. 1750 i.
Mecklenburg
Thos. 1796 w.
Norfolk
Joyce 1742 w.
Nathan 1742 w.
Sarah 1742-3 w.
Thomas Sr. 1747 w.
Jeremiah 1749 w.
Joseph 1749-50 w.
Sarah 1749 i.
Thomas 1750 w.
Nathaniel 1752 w.
Katherine 1753 i.
Kezsia 1753 w.
Lemuel 1753 i.
Mary 1761 w.
Absolom 1763 i.
Willis 1767 w.
Samuel 1772 w.
James 1778 w.
Joseph 1781 w.
Robert 1784 w.
James 1785 w.
Willis 1791 i.
Richard 1792 i.
James 1796 i.
Lemuel 1798 i.
Princess Anne
Jacob 1741 w.

James 1752 w.
Thos. 1768 w.
Bridger(t?) 1784 w.
Thos. 1784 w.
LANGLY
Norfolk
Wm. 1718 w.
Lemuel 1748 w.
LANGMARCH
Fairfax
Christian 1783 w.
LANGSDALE
Northumberland
Jno. 1727 i.
LANGSDON
Powhatan
Esther 1793 w.
LANGSTON
York
Mathew 1741 i.
LANGSTONE
York
Mathew 1746 i.
Mary 1794 w.
LANGTON
York
Chris. 1687 i.
LANHAM
Loudoun
Aaron 1795 w.
LANIER
Brunswick
Sampson 1743 w.
Thos. 1745 w.
Sampson 1758 i.
Nich. 1781 w.
Lucy 1782 w.
Jno. 1785 w.
Nicholas 1792 w.
Jno. 1794 w.
Greensville
Jacob 1788 w.
Mary 1798 w.
Thomas 1799 i.
Henry
Lemuell 1786 w.
Mecklenburg
Benj. 1796 w.
Prince George
Jno. 1719 w.
Surry
Robt. 1756 w.
Jno. 1765 w.
Jno. 1780 i.
Sussex
Benj. 1789 w.
LANKFORD
Henry
Nicholas 1779 i.
Isle of Wight
Thomas 1778 w.

Stephen 1786 w.
Isabella 1794 w.
Southampton
Thomas 1781 w.
LANQUISHEAR
Isle of Wight
Robert 1720 w.
LANSDELL
Northumberland
Benj. 1784 w.
Wm. 1791 w.
Sarah 1792 w.
LANSDON
Goochland
Wm. 1743 i.
LANSDOWN
Halifax
Geo. 1798 i.
Westmoreland
Wm. 1753 w.
LANSDOWNE
Westmoreland
Nich. 1665 w.
LANSFORD
Pittsylvania
Henry 1778 w.
LANTHROP
Prince George
Joseph 1719 i.
LANTHROPP
Prince George
Jno. 1718 w.
LANTZ
Shenandoah
George 1793 w.
LAPESLEY
Rockbridge
Joseph Jr. 1792 w.
LAPESLY
Rockbridge
Joseph 1788 w.
LAPRADE
Chesterfield
Andrew 1797 w.
Goochland
Jno. 1784 w.
LAPSLEY
Rockbridge
William 1780 a.
LARAMORE
Isle of Wight
Roger 1687 i.
LAREW
Frederick
Peter 1783 i.
Samuel 1783 i.
LARKE
Mecklenburg
Dennis 1773 w.
LARKINE
Botetourt
Henry 1773 w.

LARNER
Isle of Wight
Bartholomew 1720 w.
LARRICK
Frederick
John 1782 w.
LARY
Stafford
Thos. 1748 i.
Westmoreland
Timothy 1705 i.
LASEY
Stafford
Jno. 1740 i.
LASHLEY
Brunswick
Wm. 1761 w.
Wm. 1763 i.
Howell 1794 a.
Surry
Walter 1751 w.
Sussex
Jane 1779 i.
Patrick 1781 w.
Wm. 1788 w.
Mary 1795 w.
LASHLY
Surry
Patrick 1711 i.
Sussex
Thos. 1765 w.
Jno. 1767 w.
LASSWELL
Fairfax
John 1746 i.
LATANE
Essex
Lewis 1733 w.
Mary 1765 w.
LATCHUM
Accomack
Geo. 1777 i.
Geo. 1791 w.
LATEY
Essex
Jonathan 1698 w.
LATHAM
Culpeper
John 1767 i.
Joseph 1771 i.
William 1772 i.
Frances 1790 w.
Thomas 1796 w.
Orange
Jno. 1746 w.
Stafford
Jno. 1736 i.
Stephen 1747 i.
LATHER
Lancaster
Nich. 1684 i.

Surry
Jno. 1709 w.
Jane 1715 i.
Jno. 1720 i.
Jane 1741 w.
LATHROM
Northumberland
John 1753 i.
LATON
York
Jno. 1720 w.
LATTIMER
Westmoreland
Thos. 1746 i.
LATTIMORE
Augusta
Mathew 1783 w.
Lancaster
Clement 1756 w.
Northumberland
Richd. 1723 w.
Wm. 1758 w.
David 1769 i.
Wm. 1771 i.
LAUD
York
Jas. 1709 a.
LAUGHAM
York
Robt. 1647 i.
LAUGHLAN
Accomack
Cornelius 1734 w.
LAUGHLAND
Berkeley
Joshua 1783 i.
LAUGHLER
Lancaster
James 1751 i.
LAUGHLIN
Middlesex
Robt. 1749 i.
Thos. 1771 w.
LAUGHTON
York
Henry 1777 w.
LAUNCELOT
Westmoreland
Jno. 1671 w.
LAURANCE
Isle of Wight
John 1788 w.
Louisa
Henry 1763 w.
LAURENCE
Botetourt
Jas. Jr. 1773 w.
Isle of Wight
Hardy 1788 w.
Louisa
James 1795 w.

Norfolk
Michaell 1679 w.
Richd. 1687 w.
Northumberland
Jno. 1712-13 i.
Rockbridge
Samuel 1785 i.
LAURIE
Lancaster
Jno. 1719 w.
LAURRANCE
Norfolk
Jno. 1684 w.
LAVALLE
Goochland
Joseph 1784 i.
LAVENDER
Amherst
Wm. 1776 a.
Jno. 1776 a.
Northumberland
Jno. 1791 i.
Spotsylvania
Wm. 1795 a.
LAVERTY
Bath
Ralph 1792 w.
LAVIE
York
Jas. 1772 i.
LAVILLIAN
Cumberland
Anthony 1750 i.
LAVINDER
Amherst
Allen 1797 w.
LAVINGER
Frederick
Michael 1789 i.
LAW
Rockbridge
Michael 1784 w.
LAWBINGER
Frederick
Geo. M. 1783 w.
LAWLESS
Augusta
Henry 1757 a.
Goochland
Thos. 1765 i.
LAWLOR
Culpeper
John 1798 w.
LAWN
Shenandoah
Rudolph 1787 a.
LAWRANCE
Lancaster
Thos. 1686 w.

LAWRENCE
Augusta
Jno. 1750 w.
Henry 1759 i.
Brunswick
Thos. 1774 i.
Jno. 1781 i.
Essex
Jno. 1721 w.
Fauquier
Edward 1786 w.
Frederick
John 1779 w.
Isle of Wight
Robert 1720 w.
Robert 1721 w.
John 1739 w.
Robert 1744 w.
Margaret 1750 w.
Jeremiah 1756 w.
William 1757 w.
John 1758 i.
Sarah 1762 w.
John 1772 w.
Robert 1783 i.
Joseph 1785 i.
John 1794 i.
Martha 1795 i.
Rix 1798 w.
Lancaster
Wm. 1698 i.
Wm. 1721 i.
Loudoun
Moses 1787 i.
Norfolk
John 1671 i.
Bartho. 1799 i.
Northampton
Jno. 1721 w.
Susannah 1724 w.
Southampton
Robt. 1793 w.
Thos. 1793 w.
Westmoreland
Spencer 1749 i.
Chas. 1771 w.
LAWRY
Lancaster
Jno. 1729 i.
Mary 1771 i.
Gavin 1790 w.
LAWS
Accomack
Jonathan 1753 i.
Jno. 1776 w.
Wm. 1790 i.
Fauquier
John 1772 i.
LAWSON
Amelia
Claiborne 1782 w.

Bedford
Jonas 1771 w.
Charlotte
Geo. 1787 w.
Essex
Epaph. 1652 w.
[1742 rec.]
Fairfax
Robt. 1799 w.
Fauquier
Anna Steptoe 1774 w.
John 1798 w.
Halifax
Francis 1755 i.
David 1775 w.
Jno. 1782 w.
Thos. 1788 i.
Thos. 1789 i.
Thos. 1790 i.
Jno. 1794 i.
Francis 1796 i.
Henrico
Thos. 1692 i.
Lancaster
Epaphroditus 1652 w.
Rowland 1706 w.
Rowland 1716 w.
Catherine 1722 w.
Epaphroditus 1722 w.
Jane 1738 w.
Epaphroditus 1745 w.
Thomas 1747 w.
James 1749 i.
Nicholas 1750 w.
Henry 1752 w.
Anna 1753 i.
Ann 1761 w.
Elizabeth 1778 w.
Epaphroditus 1778 w.
Epaphroditus 1787 i.
William 1790 w.
John 1795 w.
Norfolk
Geo. 1678 w.
Thomas 1684 i.
Thomas 1790 w.
Northampton
Robt. 1643 w.
Prince Edward
Benj. 1789 w.
Princess Anne
Anthy. 1701 a.
Thos. 1703 w.
Thos. 1707 a.
Thos. 1735 w.
Thos. 1753 i.
Anthy. 1785 w.
Prince William
Wm. Marmaduke
1743 w.

Rappahannock
Richd. 1658 w.
Richmond
Jos. 1717 i.
Joshua 1717 w.
Thos. 1729 w.
Jno. 1761 w.
Richd. 1761 w.
Saml. 1761 i.
Thos. 1762 i.
Mary 1769 w.
Chris. 1772 w.
Danl. 1789 w.
Westmoreland
Wm. 1765 i.
Jno. 1785 i.
York
Benj. 1717 w.
Jas. 1718 w.
Robt. 1718 w.
LAWTON
Amelia
Jno. 1784 w.
Mary 1786 w.
LAWYER
Frederick
Michael 1792 w.
LAX
Halifax
Wm. 1783 w.
LAY
Fairfax
Sarah 1799 w.
Frederick
John 1798 w.
Loudoun
Silvanus 1773 i.
Abraham 1785 w.
Pittsylvania
Jno. 1797 i.
LAYER
Stafford
Edwd. 1740 i.
LAYLAND
Northumberland
John 1769 w.
Surry
Robt. 1769 w.
LAYLER
Accomack
Nicholas 1682 w.
Arthur 1721 w.
Northampton
Hannah 1713 w.
Luke 1716-17 w.
LAYLOR
Accomack
Jno. 1708 w.
Northampton
Nicho. 1751 w.

LAYMAN
Shenandoah
Benjamin 1788 w.
LAYN
Goochland
Jno. 1755 w.
LAYNE
Goochland
Benj. 1771 i.
David 1792 w.
Agnes 1795 i.
Norfolk
Anne 1680 i.
LAYTON
Essex
Frances 1734 i.
Middlesex
Thos. 1772 i.
York
David 1743 w.
Mary 1750 i.
LEA
Amelia
Wm. 1770 w.
Charlotte
John 1783 w.
Louisa
Francis 1766 w.
Anne 1783 w.
LEACH
Albemarle
Andrew 1788 i.
Middlesex
Wm. 1704 w.
Northumberland
John 1756 i.
John 1774 w.
Prince William
William 1788 w.
LEACHMAN
Prince William
Thomas 1799 w.
LEADBETTER
Charles City
Peter 1796 i.
LEADER
Northumberland
Saml. Sr. 1792 w.
Edwd. 1793 i.
LEAGUE
Amelia
Aaron 1796 w.
LEAK
Albemarle
Saml. 1776 w.
Goochland
Walter 1758 w.
Walter 1777 i.
Josiah Sr. 1795 w.
Norfolk
Willis 1799 w.

Pittsylvania
Joshua 1776 w.
LEAKE
Pittsylvania
Robt. 1773 i.
Essex
Wm. 1700 w.
LEAKER
Middlesex
Jas. 1793 i.
LEAL
Surry
Robt. 1708 w.
LEALAND
Northumberland
Jno. 1746 w.
LEAMON
Augusta
Jacob 1791 i.
LEAMOUNT
Princess Anne
Edwd. 1710 w.
Edwd. 1734 w.
LEAR
Culpeper
James 1771 w.
John 1782 w.
LEARNE
Surry
Richd. 1684 i.
LEASE
Loudoun
John 1794 w.
LEASON
Campbell
Saml. 1783 w.
LEASURE
Northumberland
Geo. 1709 w.
LEATH
Amelia
Arthur 1768 w.
Chesterfield
Peter 1792 w.
Surry
Peter 1738 w.
Sussex
Jno. 1765 i.
Mary 1765 w.
Chas. 1770 w.
Jno. 1795 i.
LEATHEAD
Lancaster
John 1749 w.
LEATHER
Spotsylvania
Jno. 1765 a.
LEATHERBERRY
Northampton
Perry 1771 w.

Accomack
Edmd. 1782 w.
Geo. 1793 w.
LEATHERBURY
Accomack
Chas. 1700 i.
Chas. 1721 w.
Edmd. 1722 w.
Thos. 1747 w.
Thos. 1751 i.
Perry 1776 w.
Chas. 1797 i.
Wm. 1799 w.
LEATHERER
Culpeper
Paul 1785 w.
LEATHERMAN
Accomack
Jno. 1761 i.
LEATON
Amelia
Hugh 1768 w.
Eliz. 1787 w.
LEAVELL
Fauquier
Joseph 1775 i.
Spotsylvania
James 1783 w.
LEAVERSAGE
Princess Anne
Wm. 1734 i.
LEAVIL
Spotsylvania
Edw. 1749 w.
LEAVILL
Culpeper
Edward 1783 w.
LEAZURE
Northumberland
Bartholomew 1721 w.
LeBARREAR
Chesterfield
Jno. 1773 w.
LECAT
Accomack
Jno. 1702 w.
Chas. 1770 i.
LECATT
Accomack
Philp Alex. 1700 w.
Jno. 1711 i.
Jno. 1748 w.
Jno. 1751 i.
Jos. 1752 w.
Nathl. 1767 i.
Littleton 1785 i.
LECOMPTS
Princess Anne
Anthy 1772 i.

LEDBETTER
Brunswick
Henry 1751 w.
Richd. 1751 i.
Mary 1779 w.
Isaac 1785 i.
Wm. 1787 i.
LEDFORD
Lancaster
John 1754 w.
Northumberland
Eliz. 1756 i.
James 1784 i.
LEDSEN
Frederick
Thomas 1762 a.
LEDWEDGE
Spotsylvania
Edwd. 1792 w.
Edwd. 1792 a.
LEE
Amherst
Ambrose 1764 w.
Wm. 1785 w.
Frank 1791 w.
Augusta
Jas. 1760 i.
Berkeley
Charles 1783 w.
John 1791 i.
Brunswick
Wm. 1761 w.
Cumberland
Joseph 1788 w.
Charles 1793 w.
Essex
John 1778 w.
Hancock 1792 w.
John 1797 i.
Fauquier
John 1763 i.
Mary 1768 i.
Richd. Lancelot
1790 w.
Goochland
Jno. 1757 i.
Jno. 1762 i.
Jno. 1771 w.
Jno. 1779 w.
Jno. 1793 i.
Isle of Wight
Francis 1716 w.
Peter 1738 i.
John 1748 w.
King George
Edwd. 1727 i.
Hancock 1765 i.
Jas. 1790 w.
Lancaster
Henry [1652?] a.
Thos. 1735 w.

Thos. 1759 w.
Susannah 1774 i.
Charles 1777 i.
Charles 1792 w.
Charles 1794 i.
Lunenburg
David 1748 w.
Mecklenburg
Waller 1771 w.
Middlesex
Thos. 1709 w.
Chas. 1720 w.
Thos. Sr. 1753 w.
Geo. 1757 w.
Jno. Sr. 1760 i.
Jno. 1779 i.
Chas. 1791 w.
Arthur 1792 w.
Norfolk
John 1779 w.
Northampton
Thos. 1638 w.
Chas. 1701 w.
Hancock 1709 w.
Richd. 1740 i.
Chas. 1741 i.
Chas. 1746 w.
Northumberland
Leeanna 1761 w.
Kendall 1780 w.
Eliz. 1784 w.
Chas. 1785 w.
Betty 1790 w.
Chas. 1795 w.
Orange
Chas. 1775 w.
Jno. 1789 w.
Prince George
Jno. 1726 i.
Prince William
Henry 1787 w.
Richmond
Wm. 1717 i.
Thos. 1719 i.
Wm. 1764 i.
Phil. Thos. 1790 i.
Francis Lightfoot
1797 w.
Surry
Henry 1752 w.
Sussex
Edwd. 1758 i.
Washington
John 1797 i.
Westmoreland
Jno. 1673-4 i.
Richd. 1715 w.
Henry 1747 w.
Thos. 1751 w.
Thos. 1758 i.
Geo. 1762 w.

Mary 1764 w.
Jno. 1767 w.
Philip Ludwell
  1782 i.
Richd. 1788 i.
Philip Thos. 1791 i.
Richd. Henry 1794 w.
Richd. 1795 w.
Philip 1796 i.
Cassius 1797 i.
Francis L. 1797 i.
Philip 1798 i.
York
  Henry 1657 i.
  Henry 1693 w.
  Wm. 1728 w.
  Francis 1753 w.
  Henry 1782 i.
  Francis 1799 w.
LEED
Henrico
  Jno. 1680 w.
LEEDY
Wythe
  Abram 1797 i.
LEEMAN
Essex
  Jos. 1755 w.
  Thos. 1758 w.
LEEPER
Augusta
  Jas. 1763 a.
LEES
Loudoun
  George 1779 i.
LEESE
Loudoun
  John 1797 i.
LEETH
Shenandoah
  George 1780 a.
  John 1783 a.
  Ephariam 1784 a.
  James 1785 a.
  Leah 1797 w.
LEFORCE
Botetourt
  Rene 1783 i.
LEFTWICH
Bedford
  Augustine 1795 w.
LEGG
Fauquier
  Davenpeart 1761 i.
Isle of Wight
  Ann 1720 i.
Westmoreland
  Robt. 1703 w.
Spotsylvania
  Jabez. 1786 a.

LEGGE
Isle of Wight
  John 1713 i.
LEGGETT
Princess Anne
  Jno. 1699 w.
  Anthony 1770 i.
  Elaxesander 1770 w.
LEGHT
Halifax
  Jno. 1790 w.
LEGIN
Henrico
  Saml. 1789 w.
LEGON
Chesterfield
  Jno. 1795 i.
LeGRAND
Goochland
  Jno. 1731 i.
Halifax
  Jno. 1784 i.
Henrico
  Jas. 1716 w.
LEGREW
Princess Anne
  Abraham 1742 w.
LEHEW
Frederick
  John 1778 w.
  Peter 1782 w.
LeHUGH
Northumberland
  Nicholas 1718 i.
LEIEDAMOOTH
Frederick
  George 1770 w.
LEIGH
Accomack
  Jno. 1764 i.
Amherst
  Wm. 1788 w.
Chesterfield
  Wm. 1786 w.
Henrico
  Walter 1753 i.
Mecklenburg
  Walter 1779 i.
  Edmund 1793 i.
Norfolk
  Francis 1782 w.
Prince Edward
  Zachariah 1770 w.
LEILE
Henrico
  Jas. 1698 i.
LEISTER
Augusta
  Jas. 1762 i.
  Jas. 1769 w.

LEITCH
Prince William
  Andrew 1780 i.
LEITH
Frederick
  George 1768 w.
  John 1787 i.
LEITZ
Montgomery
  William [1790?] i.
LELAND
Lancaster
  John 1789 w.
Northumberland
  John 1778.
  Peter 1795 w.
LEMANE
Northampton
  Richd. 1646 i.
LEMASTER
Berkeley
  Abraham 1778 i.
LEMAY
Louisa
  John 1785 a.
LEMBY
Frederick
  John 1784 w.
LEMELL
Lancaster
  Wm. 1683 w.
LEMEN
Berkeley
  John 1774 w.
  James 1777 w.
  John 1778 i.
LEMENS
Berkeley
  James 1780 i.
LEMLEY
Frederick
  John 1784 i.
LEMMAN
Northampton
  Jane 1649 i.
LEMMON
Essex
  John 1732 w.
Frederick
  James 1757 w.
  Nicholas 1761 w.
LEMMONT
Princess Anne
  Edwd. 1711 i.
LEMON
Lancaster
  Robt. 1675 i.
LEMOND
Princess Anne
  Hardis 1734 i.

LEMOUNT
Norfolk
Hardiss 1769 w.
LENDRUM
Prince William
William 1782 w.
LENEVE
Prince Edward
John 1784 i.
LENHAM
Westmoreland
Jno. 1699 w.
LENN
Chesterfield
Geo. 1778 w.
LENNARD
Henrico
Jno. 1782 w.
Jno. 1792 i.
LENNIS
Lancaster
Robt. 1721 w.
LENTOR
Botetourt
Mordecai 1780 i.
LENTZ
Shenandoah
George 1779 i.
George 1796 w.
LEONARD
Berkeley
Nicholas 1797 w.
Halifax
Alex. 1793 i.
Orange
Patrick 1758 i.
Walter 1766 i.
Shenandoah
Adam 1781 i.
Washington
Peter 1786 i.
LEONBERGER
Frederick
John 1757 w.
LENOIR
Brunswick
Robt. 1793 w.
LEP
Culpeper
John Christian
1788 w.
LEPER
Ohio
James 1776 w.
LEPRAID
Chesterfield
Andrew 1765 w.
LER
Northampton
Thos. 1638 w.

LESLAND
Norfolk
John 1718 i.
LESSENBERRY
Sussex
Mary 1784 w.
LESSENBURY
Sussex
Jno. 1764 w.
LESSLY
Augusta
Jas. Jr. 1775 w.
Jas. 1780 w.
Sarah 1792 w.
LESTEN
Princess Anne
Darces 1753 i.
LESTER
Amelia
Jeremiah 1736 a.
Brunswick
Andrew 1788 i.
Charlotte
John 1795 i.
Chesterfield
Josiah 1777 i.
Jacob 1793 w.
Fairfax
William 1776 w.
Henrico
Edwd. 1696 i.
Geo. 1746 i.
Robt. 1753 i.
Lunenburg
Bryant Sr. 1796 w.
Pittsylvania
Thos. 1788 i.
Princess Anne
Richd. 1694 i.
Wm. 1734 w.
Richd. 1745 w.
Thos. 1755 w.
Richd. 1763 w.
Wm. 1786 i.
Sussex
Andrew 1756 i.
York
Jno. 1767 w.
Sarah 1772 w.
Jno. 1773 i.
Whitehead 1783 w.
Jno. 1791 w.
Benj. 1795 w.
LeSUEUR
Cumberland
David 1769 w.
David 1771 w.
LETCH
Loudoun
Jesse 1775 w.
Jesse 1799 i.

LETCHER
Henry
William 1782 i.
Rockbridge
John 1794 i.
LEATHERBERRY
Accomack
Thos. 1673 w.
LETHERBERRY
Accomack
Perry 1709 w.
LETT
Brunswick
Jno. 1787 w.
LEVACON
Richmond
Richd. 1709 i.
LEVERING
Loudoun
Septimus 1782 w.
LEVERITT
Lunenburg
Thos. 1783 w.
LEVERSAGE
Norfolk
William 1769 w.
LEVI
Northampton
Dennis 1773 w.
LEVILLAIN
Goochland
Jean 1746 w.
John 1746 w.
LeVILLIAN
Cumberland
Anthony 1754 i.
Jno. 1768 w.
Peter 1768 i.
LEVINGSTON
Essex
John 1782 i.
Norfolk
Wm. 1681 w.
Princess Anne
Wm. 1694 w.
Washington
William T. 1778 w.
LEWELL
Augusta
Andrew 1779 w.
LEWELLEN
Norfolk
Richd. 1723 w.
LEWELLIN
Amelia
Thos. 1752 i.
Greensville
Thomas 1786 w.
Prince Edward
Danl. 1785 w.

York
Jno. 1733 w.
LEWELLING
Norfolk
Abell 1750 w.
Edward 1752 w.
Wm. 1752 w.
Edward 1755 i.
Thomas 1758 w.
Richard 1761 w.
Sarah 1762 i.
Alice 1765 w.
Alice 1771 i.
Richard 1771 i.
Benj. 1773 w.
John 1778 w.
Prince Edward
Jno. 1788 w.
Thos. 1788 w.
Wm. 1790 w.
Princess Anne
Richd. 1758 w.
Lemuel 1785 w.
LEWIS
Accomack
Jno. Sr. 1697 w.
Jno. 1702 i.
Saml. 1717 w.
Eliz. 1732 w.
Wm. 1740 w.
Jno. 1741 i.
Fenn 1749 w.
Saml. 1758 i.
Jno. 1762 w.
Josiah 1770 w.
Wm. 1770 w.
Danl. 1776 w.
Thos. 1779 w.
Jno. Sr. 1783 i.
Wm. 1783 i.
Jas. 1784 w.
Jno. 1787 w.
Abel 1795 w.
Albemarle
Robt. 1766 w.
Eliz. 1774 w.
Chas. 1779 w.
David 1779 w.
Wm. 1780 i.
Chas. 1782 w.
Isham 1789 w.
Augusta
Jno. 1763 w.
Chas. 1774 w.
Geo. 1796 w.
Jno. 1790 w.
Berkeley
Chris. 1779 i.
David Jr. 1793 i.
Botetourt
Andrew 1782 w.

John 1783 w.
Alex. 1799 i.
Brunswick
Zebulon 1799 w.
Chesterfield
Mary 179- w.
Culpeper
James 1765 i.
John 1791 w.
John F. 1792 i.
Essex
David 1725 i.
Edmund 1732 w.
Edward 1748 w.
Esther 1749 w.
Mary 1762 w.
Fairfax
Thomas 1749 w.
Stephen 1757 i.
Thomas Sr. 1771 w.
Wm. 1795 i.
Fauquier
Sarah 1778 w.
Goochland
Jno. 1746 i.
Chas. 1779 w.
Joseph Sr. 1783 w.
Joseph 1784 i.
Eliz. 1784 w.
Wm. 1791 w.
Jno. 1796 w.
Greenbrier
John 1787 w.
Hardy
Abner 1791 i.
Henrico
Jno. 1689 i.
Wm. 1707 w.
Robt. 1785 w.
Chas. 1793 w.
Wm. 1796 i.
Isle of Wight
Thomas 1670 i.
Arthur 1671 i.
Benedict 1675 i.
Morgan 1677 w.
William 1685 w.
John 1690 w.
John 1692 w.
Richard 1692 w.
Daniel 1698 w.
John 1700 w.
William 1700 i.
John 1712 i.
Zebulon 1738 w.
Anthony 1739 w.
King George
Geo. 1742 i.
Lancaster
Jno. 1729 w.
Wm. 1733 w.

Wm. 1743 i.
Richard 1763 w.
Margaret 1785 w.
Loudoun
Vincent 1766 i.
George 1771 i.
Nathan 1778 w.
Sarah 1789 i.
Vincent 1797 w.
James 1798 i.
Lunenburg
James 1764 w.
Madison
James 1793 i.
Mecklenburg
Edwd. 1781 w.
Mary 1783 i.
Benj. 1797 i.
Middlesex
Jas. 1720 w.
Jno. 1748 i.
Jno. 1758 w.
Eusebius 1761 w.
Eliz. 1768 w.
Northampton
Richd. 1796 w.
Richd. 1799 i.
Northumberland
Jno. 1702 w.
Jno. 1745 w.
Jno. 1746 i.
Jas. 1747 w.
Peter 1750 i.
Wm. 1756 w.
Mary 1774 i.
William 1784 i.
Hannah 1785 w.
Sarah Ann 1790 i.
Jos. 1793 i.
Jas. 1795 i.
Wm. B. 1797 i.
Orange
Thos. 1735 a.
Edward 1787 w.
Pittsylvania
Jno. 1794 w.
Prince George
Thos. 1714 i.
Thos. 1725 w.
Princess Anne
Gilbert 1696 w.
Richd. 1704 i.
Ruth 1704 a.
Thos. 1783 w.
Prince William
Zacharias 1793 w.
Richmond
Thos. 1709 w.
Ann 1720 i.
Chas. 1726 w.
Thos. 1749 i.

Geo. 1760 i.
Jas. 1772 w.
Jno. 1795 i.
Spotsylvania
Jno. 1749 a.
Jno. 1749-50 a.
Wm. 1763 w.
Zachary 1765 w.
Sarah 1771 w.
Jno. 1780 w.
Fielding 1782 w.
Robt. 1783 w.
Nicho. 1783 w.
Jno. 1784 w.
Sarah 1785 a.
Henry 1785 a.
Jas. 1790 w.
Wm. 1793 a.
Shenandoah
Thomas 1791 a.
Southampton
Joshua 1760 w.
Benj. 1790 w.
Surry
Chris. 1673 w.
Morgan 1718 i.
Richd. 1735 w.
Richd. 1743 i.
Washington
William 1784 w.
Westmoreland
Frances 1671 w.
Mathew 1672 i.
Francis 1675 i.
Nicho. 1698 w.
Theodorus 1716 nw.
Wm. 1719 i.
Surles 1736 w.
Eliz. 1751 w.
York
Roger 1657 w.
David 1670 w.
David 1704 i.
Mary 1775 i.
LEWRIGHT
Prince William
John 1792 i.
LEY
Essex
Thomas 1715 i.
Augustine 1720 w.
Thomas 1748 w.
Thomas 1784 i.
Isle of Wight
Francis 1717 i.
LEYBOURN
Frederick
Thomas 1747 w.
LEYCOURN
Frederick
Thomas 1747 i.

LIBBY
Accomack
Catrip 1752 i.
LIBY
Norfolk
James 1743 i.
LIDLER
Frederick
Benjamin 1783 a.
LIES
Loudoun
George 1778 w.
LIFELY
Albemarle
Mark 1752 w.
LIFSEY
Brunswick
Wm. 1757 w.
Jno. 1772 w.
LIGGIN
Henrico
Bathsheba 1792 w.
LIGGON
Henrico
Jno. 1785 w.
LIGHT
Halifax
Geo. 1778 a.
Lancaster
Geo. 1748 i.
Joseph 1751 w.
George 1766 i.
LIGHTBURN
King George
Stafford 1772 a.
LIGHTENHOUSE
York
Robt. 1701 i.
LIGHTFOOT
Brunswick
Jno. 1751 w.
Henry 1781 w.
Wm. 1782 i.
Mary 1785 w.
Culpeper
Goodrich 1778 w.
Frederick
John 1749 a.
Greensville
John 1795 w.
Isle of Wight
Henry 1754 i.
Bartho. 1775 w.
Henry 1795 w.
Orange
Jno. 1735 w.
Goodrich 1738 a.
Richmond
Danl. 1755 w.
Surry
Philip Jr. 1753 i.

York
Philip 1748 w.
Armistead 1772 i.
Mary 1775 w.
LIGON
Amelia
Wm. 1764 w.
Wm. 1796 w.
Chesterfield
Jos. 1751 w.
Jno. 1773 w.
Judith 1783 w.
Cumberland
James 1764 w.
Matthew 1764 w.
Thos. 1764 w.
Wm. 1767 i.
Goochland
Wm. 1765 i.
Powhatan
Joseph 1797 w.
Halifax
Joseph 1780 w.
Thos. 1795 i.
Henrico
Wm. 1689 w.
Mary 1703-4 w.
Thos. 1705 i.
Mary 1712 nw.
Powhatan
Richd. 1779 w.
Prince Edward
Henry 1762 i.
Henry 1779 i.
Sarah 1785 w.
Wm. 1788 w.
Wm. 1791 w.
LIKENS
Hardy
Richd. 1787 i.
LIKINS
Botetourt
Andrew 1780 w.
LILBER
Orange
Jno. 1741 a.
LILBURN
Berkeley
Francis 1778 i.
John 1778 i.
Frederick
Ann 1749 i.
Isle of Wight
Sarah 1728 i.
Norfolk
Olive 1764 w.
Princess Anne
Alex. 1710 w.
Jno. 1719 w.
Nathl. 1745 w.
Wm. 1727 i.

Wm. 1730 i.
York
Eliz. 1773 w.
Reuben 1783 i.
LILE
Isle of Wight
Thomas 1761 i.
Surry
Jno. 1711 i.
LILLARD
Madison
Wm. 1793 w.
Prince William
Martha 1734 w.
LILLASTON
Accomack
Thos. 1786 w.
LILLESTON
Accomack
Elijah 1791 w.
Eliz. 1794 w.
LILLICROP
Surry
Thos. 1675 a.
LILLISTON
Accomack
Jacob 1760 nw.
Jno. 1760 i.
LILLY
Albemarle
Jno. 1759 w.
LIMBREY
Prince George
John 1714 i.
Rebecca 1720 w.
LINNSCOTT
Isle of Wight
Giles 1689 nw.
LINARD
Shenandoah
Adam 1779 a.
LINAUGH
Stafford
Morrice 1755 w.
LINCH
Cumberland
John 1766 i.
Essex
Eliz. 1696 w.
Norfolk
John 1682 i.
LINCOLN
Rappahannock
Jno. 1687 w.
LIND
Fluvanna
Arthur 1784 w.
LINDAMUDE
Frederick
George 1772 i.

LINDER
Frederick
Simon 1751 a.
George 1766 w.
LINDLEY
Northumberland
Henry 1726 i.
LINDOL
Orange
Benj. 1747 w.
LINDSAY
Botetourt
Samuel 1784 w.
Charlotte
Francis 1799 i.
Essex
Caleb 1790 w.
Fairfax
William 1794 i.
Frederick
Thomas 1769 w.
James 1795 w.
Henrico
Jas. 1798 w.
Northumberland
Opie 1726 i.
Richmond
Jno. 1771 i.
York
Curtis 1778 nw.
LINDSEY
Botetourt
Robert 1776 i.
Brunswick
Wm. 1768 w.
Wm. 1789 w.
Essex
Caleb 1718 i.
Joshua 1718 w.
Fairfax
Robert 1784 w.
Frederick
James 1764 i.
Henry
Jacob 1779 i.
York
Wm. 1721 ab.
LINES
Culpeper
Robert 1749 w.
Fairfax
Timothy 1768 i.
LINGLE
Augusta
Philip 1777 w.
LINGO
Accomack
Wm. 1750 w.
Littleton 1771 w.
Caleb 1789 w.
Jno. 1792 i.

Caleb 1794 i.
LINGOE
Accomack
Jno. 1788 w.
LINK
Halifax
Jno. Adam 1789 w.
Shenandoah
Catherine 1799 w.
LINKHORN
Northumberland
Wm. 1770 w.
Richmond
Jno. 1719 i.
LINN
Albemarle
Josiah 1760 i.
Bedford
Adam 1772 w.
Ohio
Moses 1793 w.
LINSEY
Accomack
Eliz. 1734 w.
Jno. 1745 w.
Isle of Wight
Ann 1679 w.
John 1727 w.
LINTEN
Prince William
William 1736 i.
LINTHICUM
Pittsylvania
Thos. 1796 w.
LINTON
Accomack
Sarah 1746 i.
Rachel 1762 w.
Fairfax
Moses 1753 i.
William 1770 i.
King George
Wm. 1736 i.
Loudoun
Edmund 1759 i.
Mecklenburg
Jno. 1770 w.
Norfolk
Moses 1677 w.
Moses 1693 w.
Stafford
Jno. 1753 i.
Westmoreland
Wm. 1734 w.
Mary 1744 i.
LINUS
Norfolk
Martha 1766 w.
LIP
Culpeper
Henry 1792 w.

Madison
Daniel 1798 w.
LIPFORD
Cumberland
Edwd. 1776 w.
LIPLONG
Henrico
Jos. 1795 i.
LIPSCOMB
Amelia
Andrew 1779 i.
Benj. 1778 w.
Louisa
Thos. 1770 w.
LIPTROT
Henrico
Edmund 1735 w.
LISBORN
Norfolk
Catharine 1777 w.
LISH
Hanover
Thos. 1734 a.
LISLE
Albemarle
Jno. 1775 w.
LISNEY
Accomack
Ralph 1727 w.
LIST
Northampton
Jno. 1665 w.
LISTER
Amelia
Jeremiah 1799 i.
Lancaster
Wm. 1709 w.
York
Sarah 1783 w.
LITCHFIELD
Accomack
Wm. 1718 w.
Jacob 1744 w.
Francis 1752 w.
Wm. 1765 w.
Francis 1778 w.
Ezekiel 1779 i.
Lunenburg
Joseph 1760 i.
Northampton
Wm. 1785 i.
LITREL
Northumberland
Richd. 1786 w.
LITTEL
Rockbridge
Joseph 1787 w.
LITTEN
Washington
Burten 1779 i.

LITTER
Frederick
Mary 1779 i.
LITTIMORE
Northumberland
David 1770 i.
LITTLE
Botetourt
John 1793 w.
Frederick
Thomas 1748 w.
Samuel 1779 i.
Greensville
Robert 1789 w.
Isle of Wight
Robert 1736 w.
John 1742 w.
Barnaby 1771 w.
John 1792 w.
Kiziah 1792 i.
Northampton
Jonathan 1740 i.
Northumberland
Wm. 1661 i.
Shenandoah
John 1772 a.
Southampton
John 1764 w.
Wm. 1777 a.
Surry
Jno. 1704 w.
Wm. 1740 w.
Francis 1750 w.
Francis 1772 w.
Jno. 1784 w.
Jno. 1794 w.
Jno. 1798 i.
Westmoreland
Archibald 1695 i.
LITTLEBOY
Surry
Robt. 1730 w.
Eliz. 1732 w.
LITTLEHOUSE
Accomack
Wm. 1701 w.
Wm. 1719 w.
LITTLEJOHN
Northampton
Simeon 1764 w.
Prince Edward
Jos. 1761 w.
Stafford
Oliver 1703 w.
LITTLER
Frederick
George 1748 w.
John 1749 i.
Mary 1771 a.
Samuel 1778 w.

LITTLETON
Accomack
Southy 1679 w.
Bowman 1696 w.
Southy 1705 i.
Jno. 1721 w.
Sarah 1761 i.
Comfort 1785 w.
Wm. 1795 i.
Mark 1797 w.
Fairfax
John 1746 w.
Northampton
Ann 1656 w.
Edwd. 1663 w.
Southy 1679 w.
Nathl. 1702 w.
Southy 1712-13 w.
Nathl. 1716 i.
LITTRELL
Northumberland
John 1761 i.
Anne 1795 w.
Richmond
Jas. 1762 i.
LIVELY
Amherst
Joseph 1793 a.
Essex
Marthew 1757 i.
LIVESAY
Prince George
Jno. 1720 w.
LIVINGSTON
Essex
John 1752 i.
Margaret 1760 i.
John 1781 w.
Muscoe 1798 i.
Norfolk
John 1742 i.
Sarah 1763 nw.
John 1777 w.
Saml. 1797 i.
Spotsylvania
Wm. 1729 a.
Susanna 1745 w.
LIZENBY
Lancaster
Thomas 1745 i.
Wm. 1750 i.
Thomas 1766 i.
LLOYD
Fairfax
Peter 1762 w.
Norfolk
Cornelius 1655 i.
LOAFMAN
Henrico
Wm. 1747 i.

Mecklenburg
Wm. 1798 i.
LOAGNE
Botetourt
William 1793 i.
LOAN
Berkeley
John 1789 i.
LOCK
King George
Henry 1738 i.
Norfolk
George 1641 i.
LOCKE
Amelia
Richd. 1782 w.
Berkeley
Richard 1775 i.
Washington
Samuel 1786 i.
LOCKET
Henrico
Margt. 1708 w.
LOCKETT
Amelia
James 1759 w.
Benj. 1785 w.
Jno. 1790 i.
Bedford
Richard 1795 i.
Chesterfield
Benj. 17— i.
Jane Jr. 17— i.
Wm. 17— i.
Eleanor 1749 w.
Wm. 1756 w.
Jane 1759 w.
Chas. 1791 i.
Wm. 1794 w.
Cumberland
Joel 1769 w.
Thos. 1770 w.
Goochland
Thos. 1745 w.
Henrico
Thos. 1686 w.
Jas. 1708 w.
Mecklenburg
Abner 1790 w.
Powhatan
Judith 1782 i.
Benejah 1793 i.
Prince Edward
Stephen 1792 w.
LOCKEY
York
Edwd. 1667 w.
Eliz. 1675 w.
LOCKHART
Amherst
Butler 1791 a.

Augusta
Chas. 1767 i.
Jacob 1783 w.
Greenbrier
Jacob 1786 w.
Isle of Wight
John 1683 w.
Norfolk
John 1746 w.
James 1770 w.
Joseph 1772 i.
John 1797 i.
Samuel 1798 i.
Richmond
Eliz. 1710 w.
Rockbridge
Thomas 1783 w.
Henry
Thomas 1791 w.
Montgomery
William 1790 a.
LOCKLEY
Henrico
Jno. 1786 w.
LOCKMILLER
Frederick
Valentine 1785 w.
Shenandoah
George 1788 w.
LOCKBRIDGE
Augusta
Andrew 1791 w.
Wm. 1795 w.
LOCKRIDGE
Bath
William 1798 w.
LOCKYER
Westmoreland
Chas. 1720 i.
LODGE
Henrico
Jas. 1710 i.
LOE
Isle of Wight
Thomas 1683 w.
Lancaster
Thos. 1713 w.
Thos. 1750-1 w.
Norfolk
Henry 1717 w.
Northumberland
Chas. 1786 w.
LOES
Rappahannock
Richd. 1675 w.
LOFFLY
Northampton
Edwd. 1734 i.
LOFTIN
Frederick
Thomas 1751 w.

Elinor 1752 i.
Ezekiel 1752 i.
Thomas 1752 i.
Greensville
John 1793 i.
Surry
Corneluis 1736 w.
Sussex
Wm. 1777 w.
Corneluis 1785 w.
LOFTLAND
Princess Anne
Barnabas 1780 w.
LOGAN
Berkeley
James 1782 w.
Frederick
Hugh 1763 i.
Halifax
Richd. 1779 w.
Henrico
Jno. 1785 i.
Isle of Wight
Elizabeth 1721 i.
Lunenburg
David 1763 w.
Pittsylvania
Jas. 1771 i.
Powhatan
Chas. 1799 a.
Rockbridge
William 1791 w.
William 1795 w.
Washington
Robert 1791 w.
LOGGAN
Augusta
Jno. 1778 w.
Botetourt
John 1773 i.
LOGGINS
Charlotte
James 1798 w.
LOGIN
Cumberland
Geo. 1760 w.
LOGWOOD
Chesterfield
Edmd. 1775 w.
Archibald 1784 w.
Archibald 1798 i.
Powhatan
Edmd. 1799 w.
LOHMAN
York
Jacob 1718 w.
LOHORE
Spotsylvania
Benj. 1778 a.

LOMAN
Wythe
George 1795 w.
LOMAX
Essex
Lunsford Jr. 1771 w.
Fairfax
John 1787 w.
LONAS
Shenandoah
George 1793 w.
LONG
Accomack
Saml. 1793 w.
Amelia
James 1745 w.
Augusta
Jos. 1757 w.
Wm. 1760 w.
Wm. 1781 w.
Culpeper
Benjamin 1774 i.
Bromfill 1778 w.
Reuben 1792 w.
Frederick
Henry 1753 i.
Paul 1760 i.
Paul 1766 i.
Isle of Wight
John 1678 w.
Daniel 1698 w.
Edward 1719 w.
Robert 1719 i.
John 1724 w.
John 1728 i.
Danl. 1729 i.
Edward 1744 i.
King George
Henry 1733 i.
Loudoun
Thos. 1765 w.
Lunenburg
Jno. 1788 i.
Middlesex
Eliz. 1744 i.
Norfolk
Daniel 1747 w.
Northumberland
Josias 1719 i.
Jno. 1727 w.
Orange
Brumfield 1779 w.
Richmond
Philip 1729 i.
Shenandoah
Nicholas 1772 i.
Southampton
Arthur 1767 w.
Spotsylvania
Saml. 1740 w.
Jno. 1752 w.

Richd. 1762 w.
Geo. 1762 w.
Eliz. 1764 w.
Geo. 1764 a.
Surry
Mary 1679 w.
Arthur 1700 i.
Edwd. 1749 w.
Wm. 1753 w.
David 1754 w.
Hartwell 1783 w.
Lewis 1784 w.
Sussex
Geo. Sr. 1788 w.
Wythe
Benjamin 1797 w.
York
Roger 1670 i.
LONGBOTTOM
Surry
Wm. 1733 w.
LONGEST
Essex
Robt. 1766 w.
Timothy 1781 w.
LONGLEY
Lunenburg
Mary 1762 w.
LONGMAN
York
Richd. 1666 a.
LONGMIRE
King George
Wm. 1749 i.
LONGMORE
Prince George
Francis 1720 i.
LONGO
Accomack
Jas. 1730 w.
LONGWORTH
Lancaster
Robt. 1691 i.
Richmond
Wm. 1756 i.
Southampton
Joseph 1778 i.
Westmoreland
Jno. 1722 i.
Wm. 1724 i.
Jno. 1727 w.
Burges 1751 w.
LOOKUP
York
Jno. 1775 w.
LOOKADO
Cumberland
Peter Anty. 1768 w.
LOONEY
Augusta
Robt. Jr. 1756 i.

Danl. 1761 i.
Botetourt
Absolom 1796 w.
LONDON
Amherst
Moses 1777 a.
Charlotte
John 1777 w.
LORD
Northumberland
Robt. 1661 w.
LORIMOR
Augusta
Thos. 1768 w.
LORRIMER
Augusta
Jno. 1765 a.
Thos. 1773 i.
Middlesex
Geo. 1784 i.
LORTON
Augusta
Israel 1752 i.
LORWELL
Northampton
Jno. 1749 i.
LOTZ
Shenandoah
Jonas 1786 w.
LOUCHRIDGE
Augusta
Jno. 1799 w.
LOUD
Shenandoah
Nicholas 1772 a.
LOUDERBACK
Shenandoah
David 1793 w.
LOUDIN
Frederick
Thomas 1760 i.
LOUDON
Middlesex
David 1786 i.
LOUDOUN
Westmoreland
Wm. 1655 w.
LOUGH
Essex
Thomas 1712 i.
LOUGHEE
Middlesex
Jno. 1707 w.
LOUGHLAN
Northampton
Dorman 1688 i.
Dorman 1748 i.
LOUGHMILLER
Shenandoah
George 1789 i.

LOUMER
Augusta
Jno. 1764 a.
LOUND
Henrico
Henry 1708 w.
LOURY
Amelia
Thos. 1767 w.
Essex
Wm. 1750 w.
Jno. 1758 w.
LOUTHER
Hardy
Geo. 1787 i.
LOVE
Botetourt
Phillip 1790 i.
Brunswick
Allen 1788 w.
Hugh 1780 w.
Charlotte
John 1795 w.
Fairfax
Thomas 1793 w.
Lunenburg
Wm. 1793 w.
Montgomery
Samuel 1781 w.
Northumberland
Alex. 1727 w.
Prince William
Saml. 1787 w.
Chas. 1792 i.
Rappahannock
James 1681 w.
Rockbridge
James 1792 w.
Southampton
Elias 1760 w.
York
Silas 1713 w.
Elias 1720 w.
Justinian 1747 w.
LOVATT
Lancaster
Geo. 1718 i.
LOVEDAY
Norfolk
Robt. 1678-9 w.
LOVEGROVE
Norfolk
Wm. 1794 i.
LOVELACE
Halifax
Thos. 1792 w.
Richmond
Chas. 1756 w.
Bridget 1764 i.
Chas. 1764 i.

LOVELL
Goochland
Geo. 1778 w.
Westmoreland
Jno. 1720 i.
Robt. 1725 w.
Danl. 1734 w.
LOVERN
Amelia
Richd. 1767 w.
Wm. 1798 w.
LOVET
Princess Anne
Wm. 1720 i.
Thos. 1722 w.
Jno. 1738 w.
Adam 1739 a.
LOVETT
Loudoun
Daniel 1785 w.
Norfolk
Lancaster 1673 w.
Princess Anne
Lancaster 1703 w.
Mary 1707 w.
Adam 1722 w.
Jno. 1740 i.
Lancaster 1743 w.
Wm. 1748 i.
Lancaster 1752 w.
Wm. 1752 i.
Adam 1759 w.
Jno. 1764 w.
James 1778 w.
Amy 1782 i.
John 1784 i.
James 1789 w.
Thomas 1790 w.
LOVINE
Essex
Peter 1705 i.
LOVING
Amherst
Jno. 1786 a.
Wm. 1791w.
Bedford
William 1767 w.
LOVINGSTON
Princess Anne
Wm. 1695 a.
LOVITT
Princess Anne
Wm. 1708 w.
John 1789 i.
Susannah 1795 w.
Andrew 1797 w.
John 1797 i.
LOW
Bedford
Samuel 1767 i.

Cumberland
Thos. 1750 i.
Norfolk
Henry 1717 i.
Sarah 1743-4 w.
Northumberland
Abraham 1743 i.
Rockbridge
Michael 1792 a.
LOWARD
Norfolk
John 1794 w.
LOWD
King George
Peter 1734 i.
LOWDEN
Berkeley
William 1795 w.
LOWE
Fairfax
John 1771 i.
Norfolk
Sarah 1759 i.
Prince William
John 1791 w.
Southampton
Levi 1795 w.
Lighborn 1797 w.
Westmoreland
Jas. 1747 i.
Jno. 1761 w.
Richd. 1783 w.
LOWELL
Amelia
Jno. 1744 w.
LOWEN
Culpeper
John 1779 i.
Benjamin 1791 w.
LOWER
Berkeley
Philip 1783 i.
Philip 1779 w.
LOWERY
Norfolk
Wm. 1686-7 w.
Rockbridge
William 1780 a.
LOWERRY
Isle of Wight
Arthur 1772 i.
LOWES
Essex
Jeremiah 1702 i.
LOWICK
Rappahannock
Walter 1685 i.
LOWIN
Culpeper
Margarett 1792 w.

LOWING
Accomack
Wm. 1683 w.
LOWNEY
Augusta
Jno. 1762 i.
LOWRAINE
Augusta
David 1763 a.
LOWREY
Washington
John 1794 i.
LOWRY
Augusta
Jno. 1762 w.
Jno. 1770 w.
Jno. 1794 i.
Essex
William 1751 i.
Wm. 1762 w.
Goochland
Matthew 1794 w.
Isle of Wight
Matthew 1728 i.
Matthew 1729 w.
Joanna 1738 w.
King George
Robt. 1766 eb.
Lancaster
Jas. 1713 w.
Elias. 1743 w.
Obediah 1751 i.
Stokeley 1795 i.
Louisa
Wm. 1781 w.
Lunenburg
Thos. 1779 i.
Wm. 1786 w.
Norfolk
Jas. 1718-19 w.
Jacob 1776 w.
Northampton
Jno. 1737 w.
Northumberland
Robt. 1743 i.
Wm. 1762 i.
Elias 1766 i.
Rockbridge
Robert 1780 i.
Robert 1799 w.
Stafford
Wm. 1745 i.
LOWTHER
Northumberland
Thomas 1760 w.
Surry
Hew 1676 a.
LOYD
Essex
George 1713 w.
George 1748 i.

Frederick
David 1760 i.
James 1765 i.
James 1768 i.
James 1798 i.
Isle of Wight
Thomas 1741 w.
Mecklenburg
Jno. 1798 w.
Prince George
Thos. 1717 w.
Richmond
Joane 1703 w.
An 1718 i.
LOYDE
Essex
George 1713 i.
Stephen 1715 i.
Ruth 1775 i.
John 1787 w.
LOYER
Frederick
Michael 1792 i.
LUCAR
Northampton
Thos. 1726 i.
LUCAS
Accomack
Wm. 1729 w.
Thos. 1741 w.
Wm. 1751 w.
Robinson 1752 i.
Solomon 1752 w.
Geo. 1755 i.
Thos. 1768 i.
Jabez 1774 w.
Elijah 1790 i.
Wm. R. 1792 w.
Amherst
Thos. 1790 a.
Augusta
Richd. 1750 a.
Berkeley
Edward 1777 w.
Brunswick
Wm. 1740 w.
Wm. 1743 w.
Jno. 1744 i.
David 1760 w.
Mary 1760 i.
Wm. 1765 i.
Jno. 1766 i.
Saml. 1777 i.
Campbell
Wm. 1796 i.
Culpeper
William 1796 i.
Fairfax
Jacob 1748 i.
Thos. 1795 w.

Frederick
Rebecca 1748 w.
Greensville
Charles 1783 w.
Tabitha 1784 w.
John 1790 w.
John 1792 i.
Henrico
Edwd. 1691 i.
Loudoun
Alex 1777 w.
Samuel 1781 i.
Lunenburg
Jno. 1783 w.
Mecklenburg
Wm. 1778 w.
Northumberland
Thos. 1724 i.
Saml. 1740-1 w.
Samuel 1777 w.
Prince William
Francis 1738 a.
Orange
Jno. 1751 w.
Wm. 1758 w.
Prince William
Anthony 1797 w.
Rappahannock
Thos. 1674 w.
Richmond
Frances 1723 i.
Stephen 1737 i.
Stafford
Jos. 1703 i.
Surry
Wm. 1717 w.
Grace 1719 w.
Chas. 1758 w.
Mary 1764 w.
Saml. 1770 w.
Stephen 1773 w.
Jno. 1785 w.
Saml. 1797 i.
Chris. 1798 i.
Spotsylvania
Anthony 1751 w.
Peter 1782 w.
Westmoreland
Jacob 1703 i.
Chas. 1724 i.
LUCEY
York
Jno. 1688-9 w.
LUCK
Halifax
Joseph 1772 i.
Isle of Wight
John 1711 i.
John 1721 i.
Louisa
Tarlton B. 1795 i.

Pittsylvania
Francis 1781 w.
Spotsylvania
Saml. 1787 w.
Richd. 1799 a.
York
Jos. 1719 w.
LUCKETT
Loudoun
Thos. Hussey 1787 w.
Prince William
John Boon 1794 w.
LUCKHAM
Lancaster
Isaac 1720 i.
Wm. 1750-1 w.
LUCKS
Isle of Wight
John 1749 i.
LUCKUS
Prince William
Francis 1739 i.
LUCOR
Northampton
Chas. 1720 w.
LUCOS
Charlotte
John 1783 w.
LUCUS
Isle of Wight
Mary 1734 w.
LUCY
Brunswick
Robt. Sr. 1792 w.
Surry
Francis 1677 a.
LUDGALL
Norfolk
Nathl. 1719 w.
John [1741?] w.
LUDLOWE
York
Thos. 1660 i.
LUGG
Isle of Wight
Peter 1736 i.
LUGGE
Isle of Wight
Peter 1689 nw.
LUKE
Augusta
Richd. 1753 i.
Isle of Wight
Paul 1666 w.
King George
Jno. 1777 w.
Norfolk
Isaac 1784 w.
Northampton
Jno. 1709 w.
Jno. 1712 i.

Danl. 1735 w.
Jno. 1761 w.
Danl. 1763 w.
Jno. 1765 w.
Princess Anne
Betty 1782 w.
Westmorelad
Edwd. 1697 i.
Nicho. 1714 a.
LUKELASCO
Surry
Jno. 1721 i.
LUKER
Accomack
Jno. 1766 w.
Luke 1774 w.
Northampton
Thos. 1725 w.
Danl. 1744 i.
Jno. 1744 i.
Jno. 1750 w.
Mary 1750 w.
Speakman 1750 w.
Thos. 1771 w.
LUM
Frederick
Jonas 1744 i.
LUMBLEY
Southampton
Thomas 1762 w.
LUMKIN
Campbell
Moses 1782 i.
Essex
Mary 1780 w.
LUMSDALE
Montgomery
James 1781 w.
LUMSDEN
Franklin
John 1788 w.
LUNCEFORD
Fauquier
George 1782 i.
Northumberland
Martha 1749 i.
Joseph 1782 w.
LUND
Westmoreland
Thos. 1660 w.
LUNDAY
Brunswick
James 1746 w.
Greensville
Isham 1784 i.
Lunenburg
Richd. 1764 w.
LUNDERMAN
Charlotte
Wm. 1777 w.

LUNDIE
Brunswick
Thos. 1798 w.
LUNDY
Isle of Wight
James 1723 w.
Greensville
Mary 1785 w.
James 1798 w.
Southampton
Edwd. 1773 w.
Byrd 1778 w.
Drury 1778 i.
Edwd. 1778 w.
Jas. 1781 w.
Robt. 1783 w.
Jno. 1789 w.
Edith 1797 w.
Jno. 1799 w.
LUNE
Northampton
A[ster?] 1709 w.
LUNEY
Augusta
Thos. 1760 a.
Peter 1761 i.
Botetourt
Robert 1770 w.
LUNN
Rappahannock
Wm. 1679 w.
LUNSFORD
Amelia
Jesse 1775 w.
Jno. 1782 w.
Fauquier
Amos. 1784 i.
King George
Jas. 1724 i.
Rowley 1764 a.
Jno. 1776 w.
Lancaster
Rodham 1791 w.
Northumberland
Saml. 1739 w.
Charles 1740 i.
Alex. 1750 i.
John 1754 i.
Swanson 1758 w.
Richd. 1768 i.
Moses 1790 w.
Jno. 1794 w.
Lewis 1794 i.
Jno. 1797 i.
Eliz. 1799 w.
Surry
Swan 1791 w.
LUPO
Isle of Wight
Philip 1670 w.
Philip 1778 w.

James 1790 w.
LUPPO
Isle of Wight
James 1713 w.
LUPTON
Frederick
Joseph 1758 w.
William 1783 w.
Joseph 1791 w.
LURE
Westmoreland
Dennis 1713 i.
LURTEY
King George
Jno. 1795 w.
LURTON
Accomack
Henry 1714 w.
Wm. 1730 i.
Jno. 1748 w.
Thos. 1750 w.
Lazarus 1764 w.
Jacob 1770 w.
Rachel 1771 w.
Jacob 1786 w.
Littleton 1787 w.
Jacob 1792 i.
LUSH
Norfolk
Andrew 1777 w.
Sarah 1780 i.
LUSK
Augusta
Nathan 1748 w.
Wm. 1771 w.
Jas. 1774 w.
Rockbridge
Robert 1778 w.
LUTER
Southampton
Thos. 1779 i.
LUTESINGER
Loudoun
Philip 1775 w.
LUTRELL
Richmond
Jas. 1785 i.
LUTTRELL
Fauquier
Richard 1766 w.
Michael 1778 w.
John 1790 i.
Prince William
Simon 1779 w.
Richmond
Jas. 1781 w.
Wm. 1795 i.
Westmoreland
Simon 1723 w.

LUTWISGE
York
Mathew 1727 w.
LUTZ
Fairfax
Michael 1796 a.
LUX
Isle of Wight
Wilt. 1696 i.
LYAL
Essex
John 1770 w.
LYALL
Cumberland
Barsheba 1781 w.
Westmoreland
Wm. 1768 i.
LYBURN
Princess Anne
Jno. 1701 i.
LYCON
Frederick
Peter 1754 w.
LYDDERDALE
Lunenburg
Wm. 1759 w.
LYELL
Essex
Gerrard 1753 w.
Lancaster
Jno. 1726 i.
Richmond
Jno. 1742 i.
Jno. 1788 w.
LYGON
Henrico
Thos. 1675-6 op.
LYLE
Augusta
Jno. 1758 w.
Mathew 1774 w.
Jas. Jr. 1793 w.
Berkeley
Robert 1788 i.
Hugh 1790 w.
John 1798 w.
Fairfax
Robert Sr. 1788 w.
Loudoun
Elenor 1771 i.
Rockbridge
Daniel 1784 w.
James 1791 w.
James 1795 i.
Surry
Wm. 1713 w.
LYMAN
York
Jno. 1668 w.

LYNAUGH
Prince William
Helm 1789 w.
LYNCH
Albemarle
Chas. 1753 w.
Augusta
Patrick 1752 i.
Campbell
Chris. 1782 i.
Chas. 1798 i.
Essex
Eliz. 1696 i.
King George
Patrick 1793 w.
Orange
Jno. 1761 a.
Richmond
Mathew 1712 i.
Westmoreland
Francis 1712 i.
LYNDSAY
Northumberland
David 1667 w.
Spotsylvania
James 1766 a.
LYNE
Frederick
John 1771 a.
Lancaster
Thos. 1717 w.
Richmond
Thos. 1765 w.
Mary 1785 w.
Thos. 1785 i.
Robt. 1786 w.
LYNES
Lunenburg
Jarrott 1779 i.
LYNN
Albemarle
[Josiah?] 1758 i.
Augusta
Margt. 1768 a.
Fairfax
Adam 1786 w.
Fauquier
John 1794 w.
Prince William
William 1795 w.
Spotsylvania
Wm. 1758 w.
LYNNY (?)
Northampton
Anthony 1642 i.
LYNSEY
York
Adam 1636 w.
LYNTON
Stafford
Anthony 1738 w.

LYON
Albemarle
Peter Sr. 1764 w.
Amherst
Jno. 1763 w.
Franklin
Elisha 1787 w.
Patrick
Humberston 1794 i.
Princess Anne
Mary 1775 i.
John 1795 w.
Washington
Humbertson 1784 w.
LYSLE
Washington
John 1782 i.
LYTH
Botetourt
John 1781 w.

Mc and M

McADAM
Northumberland
Jno. 1784 w.
Jos. 1789 w.
Martha 1794 w.
Geo. Thos. 1794 w.
McADAMS
Fincastle
Samuel 1775 w.
McALESTER
Culpeper
Finley 1771 w.
McALLESTER
Madison
Eliz. 1798 a.
James 1799 a.
McALLISTER
Louisa
James 1785 i.
John 1787 a.
McALPIN
Essex
Andrew 1722 w.
McANNALLEY
Albemarle
Robt. 1758 i.
McASLEN
Mecklenburg
Duncan 1794 i.
McAUSLAND
Spotsylvania
Humphrey 1792 w.
McAVEY
Bath
John 1799 i.
McBAY
Amelia
———— 1753 a.

McBOYD
Westmoreland
Patrick 1718 w.
McBRIDE
Augusta
Benj. 1749 a.
Wm. 1754 w.
Wm. 1758 w.
Louisa
Edward 1799 i.
Norfolk
Sarah 1799 i.
McBRIGHT
Accomack
Hugh 1750 i.
McBROWN
Charles City
Allen 1796 w.
McCABE
Amherst
Hugh 1778 a.
Loudoun
Henry 1781 i.
Henry 1798 i.
Princess Anne
Laughlin 1779 w.
Daniel 1791 i.
McCADDIN
Frederick
Patrick 1743 a.
McCADE
Amelia
Jno. 1751 i.
McCAINE
Richmond
Wm. 1731 i.
McCALIN
Princess Anne
Wm. 1795 w.
McCALL
Halifax
James 1779 i.
Lancaster
George 1750-1 i.
Princess Anne
John 1786 i.
McCALLESTER
Orange
Alexr. 1789 i.
McCALLEY
Spotsylvania
Jno. 1783 w.
McCALLUM
Chesterfield
Danl. 1795 w.
McCALPEN
Rockbridge
Robert 1791 w.
McCALPIN
Rockbridge
Robert 1790 w.

McCAMPBELL
Rockbridge
David 1778 a.
Andrew 1785 w.
John 1787 i.
Andrew 1799 w.
McCAN
Albemarle
James 1757 i.
Augusta
Neil 1774 a.
McCANAHAN
Northumberland
Peter 1793 w.
McCANN
Frederick
Daniel 1799 w.
McCARMICK
Frederick
John 1769 i.
McCARROLL
Lancaster
Wm. 1744 i.
McCARTER
Northumberland
Danl. 1725-6 i.
McCARTHY
Halifax
Joseph 1798 i.
Northumberland
Mildred Smith 1795 i.
McCARTNEY
Berkeley
Benjamin 1776 i.
Sarah 1781 w.
Prince Edward
James 1775 w.
McCARTY
Culpeper
John 1796 w.
Fairfax
Dennis 1743 w.
Dennis 1749 a.
Denis 1757 w.
Daniel 1792 w.
Halifax
Jarred 1793 w.
Joseph 1797 w.
Lancaster
Thaddeus 1788 i.
Frederick 1792 i.
Frances 1794 w.
Princess Anne
Darby 1724 i.
Richmond
Danl. 1724 i.
Thaddeus 1732 w.
Billingon 1745 w.
Billington 1753 i.
Billington 1771 w.
Chas. 1785 w.

Chas. T. 1799 w.
Shenandoah
Dennis 1786 a.
James 1789 w.
Stafford
Wm. 1743 i.
Cornelius 1755 w.
Westmoreland
Danl. 1724 w.
Ann 1732 w.
Danl. 1746 i.
Danl. 1795 w.
York
Florence 1727 i.
Dionysius 1748 i.
Eliz. 1751 i.
Eliz. 1757 i.
Jno. 1757 i.
McCASTLE
Princess Anne
Saml. 1766 w.
McCAULEY
Westmoreland
Andrew 1748 nw.
MCAVE
Richmond
Jno. 1778 i.
McCAVE
Westmoreland
Jno. 1744 w.
McCAWN
Botetourt
Patrick 1773 i.
McCAY
Greenbrier
James 1780 w.
McCHESTNUT
Frederick
Alex. 1750 i.
McCINNEY
Augusta
Jno. 1762 w.
McCLAID
Amelia
Jno. 1750 a.
McCLALIN
Princess Anne
Thos. 1774 i.
Eliz. 1779 w.
McCLANAHAN
Northumberland
Jas. 1799 i.
Princess Anne
Nathl. 1713 i.
Mary 1788 i.
Westmoreland
Wm. 1771 w.
Peter 1775 w.
Wm. 1788 i.

McCLANEN
Princess Anne
Richd. Sr. 1790 w.
McCLANHAN
Princess Anne
Jno. 1734 i.
McCLANNAHAN
Lunenburg
Jno. 1759 w.
Jas. 1761 w.
McCLARREN
Isle of Wight
James 1755 w.
McCLARY
Lunenburg
Wm. 1749 i.
McCLAUGHLIN
Lunenburg
Geo. 1792 w.
McCLEAR
Frederick
William 1754 i.
McCLEARY
Augusta
Alex. 1751 w.
McCLEERY
Augusta
Jno. 1776 w.
McCLELHILL
Augusta
Jos. 1759 a.
McCLENACHAN
Augusta
Jno. 1774 w.
Wm. 1776 i.
Robt. 1791 w.
Elijah 1796 w.
Botetourt
Robert 1774 i.
McCLENAHAN
Augusta
Wm. 1774 i.
Princess Anne
Nathl. 1711 w.
Wm. 1731 i.
David 1735 w.
Eliz. 1748 w.
Nathl. 1767 w.
David 1773 w.
Wm. 1791 w.
McCLELLAND
Stafford
Chas. 1741 i.
McCLELON
Loudoun
William 1775 w.
McCLENCY
Richmond
Ed. 1719 i.

McCLENNY
Isle of Wight
Michael 1795 w.
McCLINTOCK
Augusta
Jno. 1780 i.
Wm. 1785 w.
McCLOLON
Augusta
Jos. 1762 i.
McCLOUD
Norfolk
Hezekiah 1763 i.
Daniel 1764 w.
James 1786 i.
McCLUNG
Botetourt
John 1779 w.
Greenbrier
James 1790 w.
Rockbridge
Henry 1784 w.
William 1784 w.
James 1785 w.
John 1791 i.
William 1794 w.
James 1798 w.
McCLURE
Amherst
James 1785 a.
Augusta
Patrick 1752 a.
Halberd 1754 w.
Jas. 1761 w.
Nathl. 1761 w.
Mary 1767 w.
Nathl. 1767 a.
Halbert 1771 w.
Andrew 1789 w.
Botetourt
John 1778 w.
Malcom 1791 w.
Ohio
David 1786 a.
Rockbridge
Moses 1778 i.
William 1785 w.
Alexander 1790 w.
Isabella 1798 i.
Samuel 1779 w.
Washington
Nathaniel 1792 i.
McCLYMONS
Berkeley
William 1777 w.
McCOCKLE
Montgomery
James 1794 w.
McCOLM
Rockbridge
Patrick 1784 w.

McCOLLEY
Northumberland
Chas. 1762 i.
McCOLLOCK
Albemarle
Jno. 1789 w.
Jno. 1795 w.
Ohio
John 1778 i.
McCOLLOUR
Bath
John 1797 w.
McCOMB
Accomack
Jno. 1738 w.
Augusta
Andrew 1788 w.
McCONAHUE
Loudoun
James 1779 w.
McCONALL
Loudoun
Thomas 1786 i.
McCONNEL
Frederick
Abraham 1771 i.
McCONNELL
Augusta
Alex. 1792 i.
Ohio
James 1797 w.
Rockbridge
Patrick 1785 i.
McCONNICO
Lunenburg
Wm. 1758 i.
McCONWAY
Pittsylvania
Robt. 1776 w.
McCOOL
Halifax
Andrew 1785 w.
McCOOLE
Frederick
James 1751 w.
McCORD
Albemarle
James 1761 i.
Jno. Sr. 1764 w.
Jno. 1784 w.
Wm. 1790 w.
Augusta
Martha 1749 a.
Sarah 1753 nw.
Jos. 1763 w.
Frederick
Arthur 1788 w.
McCORKLE
Augusta
Saml. 1788 w.

Rockbridge
John 1781 w.
McCORMACK
Bedford
William 1775 w.
Washington
James 1791 i.
James 1789 w.
McCORMECK
Northumberland
Francis 1720 ab.
McCORMICK
Fauquier
James 1760 i.
Frederick
John 1765 w.
King George
Neal 1744 i.
Louisa
Wm. 1753 w.
Prince William
Frances 1794 w.
McCOSKEY
Augusta
David 1788 w.
McCOWN
Augusta
Francis 1761 w.
Moses 1765 a.
Wm. 1766 i.
Francis 1773 w.
Frederick
Isaac 1770 i.
Rockbridge
John 1783 w.
McCOY
Campbell
Jno. 1783 i.
Greenbrier
John 1779 w.
William 1795 i.
Isle of Wight
Jesse 1783 w.
Loudoun
Wm. 1765 i.
Montgomery
Richard 1793 w.
Norfolk
John 1734-5 w.
Jno. 1739 w.
Richard 1750 w.
Kedar 1760 w.
John 1771 i.
Richard 1777 w.
Hugh 1784 w.
Richard 1787 i.
Josiah 1791 w.
Joshua 1792 w.
Shenandoah
James Jr. 1788 a.

Stafford
Alex. 1735 i.
McCRACKEN
Frederick
James 1756 i.
McCRADY
Westmoreland
Thos. 1749 i.
McCRAW
Powhatan
Francis 1778 w.
Jno. 1782 i.
McCRAY
Rockbridge
Joseph 1785 i.
McCREA
Norfolk
Andrew 1774 i.
McCREADY
Northampton
Ezekiel 1787 w.
McCREEMON
Campbell
Geo. 1790 i.
McCREERY
Augusta
Jno. 1768 w.
McCRONEY
Lancaster
Patrick 1725 i.
McCROSKEY
Augusta
Jno. 1758 w.
McCROY
Prince Edward
James 1770 w.
McCUE
Augusta
Patr. 1752 i.
McCULLACK
Rockbridge
Thomas 1782 w.
McCULLOCK
Albemarle
Alexr. 1783 w.
Louisa
Eliz. 1782 w.
Ohio
John Sr. 1783 a.
Westmoreland
Roderick 1746 w.
Jno. 1767 i.
McCULLOUGH
Harrison
James 1798 w.
Washington
Thomas 1780 w.
McCUNE
Augusta
Jas. 1795 w.

McCURDY
Charles City
Jno. 1769 i.
Culpeper
Joseph 1786 i.
McCURRY
Fluvanna
Richard 1785 i.
McCUTCHEN
Augusta
Jas. 1759 w.
Jennate 1789 w.
Lunenburg
Jno. 1778 w.
Rockbridge
William 1789 w.
McDANIEL
Albemarle
Thos. 1755 w.
Arthur 1757 w.
Augusta
Bryan Sr. 1758 i.
Essex
William 1746 i.
Halifax
Michael 1764 i.
Johnson 1777 i.
Wm. 1778 w.
King George
Geo. 1730 i.
Lancaster
Edmd. 1727 i.
Roger 1774 w.
Lunenburg
Terrens 1762 w.
Northumberland
Jno. 1742 i.
Andrew 1775 w.
Orange
Randolph 1744 a.
Pittsylvania
Anne 1795 w.
Princess Anne
Jno. 1777 w.
Richmond
Jno. 1749 i.
Spotsylvania
Henry 1782 a.
McDANIELL
Richmond
Wm. 1714 i.
McDANNOLD
Culpeper
Alex. 1783 w.
McDAVID
Frederick
Neill 1778 i.
Lunenburg
James 1749 w.

McDEARMANDRO
Prince Edward
Michael 1765 w.
McDONALD
Augusta
Bryan 1757 w.
Randall 1757 a.
Edwd. 1760 i.
Francis 1762 i.
Saml. 1773 i.
Berkeley
Andrew 1799 w.
Botetourt
Bryan 1777 w.
James 1778 nw.
Fairfax
Alexander 1793 w.
Frederick
Augus 1779 w.
John 1787 w.
Mary 1789 w.
King George
Danl. 1762 w.
Elender 1780 w.
Washington
Alexander 1793 w.
Charles 1794 w.
McDONOUGH
Augusta
Jno. 1783 w.
McDOWAL
Amherst
Andrew 1796 w.
Orange
Jno. 1742 a.
McDOWEL
Prince William
Thomas 1742 w.
McDOWELL
Augusta
Jno. 1747 a.
Jas. 1771 a.
Hugh 1794 w.
Greenbrier
William 1796 w.
McELDOE
Northumberland
Wm. 1721 i.
McELHENNY
Montgomery
James 1775 i.
McENTIRE
Ohio
William 1782 w.
McENTOSH
Stafford
Jas. 1751 i.
McEWEN
Fairfax
Patrick 1793 a.

McFARLANE
King George
Ralph 1754 i.
Westmoreland
Thos. 1755 w.
McFARLAND
Ohio
James 1796 w.
John 1797 w.
Rockbridge
Robert 1798 w.
McFARLIN
Halifax
Jno. 1779 i.
McFARREN
Botetourt
John 1776 w.
McFAREN
Bath
Samuel 1796 i.
McFEELY
Prince Edward
Manassa 1792 i.
McFEETERS
Augusta
Alex. 1761 w.
McFELEY
Prince Edward
Manis 1791 i.
McFERRIN
Augusta
Jas. 1761 i.
Jno. Jr. 1761 i.
McGAHEY
Loudoun
Manasah 1789 i.
McGARY
York
Martin 1719 i.
McGEACH
Loudoun
Thos. 1769 w.
McGEATH
Loudoun
Thomas 1769 i.
James 1791 i.
William 1798 i.
McGEE
Augusta
Jas. 1759 i.
Chas. 1769 i.
Frederick
James 1746 i.
Hardy
Ramsey 1791 w.
Richmond
Geo. Taylor 1757 i.
Spotsylvania
Thos. 1784 w.

McGEHEE
Cumberland
Wm. 1771 w.
Edward 1771 w.
Jacob 1794 w.
Louisa
Saml. 1794 i.
Prince Edward
Abner 1799 i.
McGEORGE
Bedford
John 1795 i.
McGILL
Stafford
Sarah 1753 w.
Westmoreland ·
Henry 1758 i.
Henry 1765 i.
McGINNESS
Halifax
Wm. 1761 i.
McGINNIS
Bedford
William 1774 i.
Shenandoah
Chris. 1780 a.
Richmond
Richard 1769 nw.
Janett 1786 i.
Richd. S. 1794 i.
McGLISTER
Wythe
Cornelius 1795 i.
McGLOUGHLER
Bath
Hugh 1799 i.
McGOO
Northumberland
Jas. 1744 i.
McGOON
Northumberland
Thos. 1753 i.
McGOURIN
Lancaster
Margaret 1743 i.
McGOVERN
Shenandoah
James 1784 a.
McGRANGHALON
King George
Wm. 1769 w.
McGRAVEY
Princess Anne
Mary 1738 w.
McGRAVY
Princess Anne
Owin 1718 w.
McGRAW
Botetourt
Brin 1771 i.

Essex
Thomas 1723 i.
Lancaster
Daniel 1749-50 i.
McGREGOR
Halifax
James 1792 i.
McGREW
Loudoun
Charles 1765 w.
McGRIGGOR
Holifax
David 1773 i.
McGRILL
Norfolk
Patrick 1788 w.
McGUIRE
Henry
Zacheriah 1788 i.
Westmoreland
Jno. 1782 w.
Travis 1782 i.
Jno. 1784 i.
McGWYER
Richmond
Mary 1721 i.
McHENRY
Frederick
Barnaby 1749 w.
McILHANEY
Loudoun
John 1773 w.
McILHANY
Rockbridge
Robert 1799 w.
McILHENY
Bedford
Thomas 1777 w.
McINNISH
Surry
Donald 1752 i.
McINTIRE
Augusta
Jno. 1761 i.
Harrison
John 1791 i.
Loudoun
Alex. 1789 w.
McINTOSH
Essex
Lauchlin 1764 i.
Fairfax
John 1769 w.
Prince William
Alex. 1797 i.
McINTURF
Shenandoah
Eliz. 1788 a.
McINTYRE
Norfolk
Dugald 1753 w.

McIVER
Fairfax
Colin 1788 w.
McLWANE
Franklin
Thomas 1798 i.
McKAN
Middlesex
Jas. 1785 i.
Mary 1794 w.
McKAY
Augusta
Robt. 1752 w.
Shenandoah
Isaac 1780 i.
Moses 1780 a.
James 1789 i.
George 1798 w.
James 1797 w.
Spotsylvania
James 1776 a.
McKEAN
Norfolk
William 1785 w.
McKEE
Frederick
[James 1746] i.
Rockbridge
James 1778 w.
John 1780 w.
John 1792 w.
Washington
Alexander 1778 i.
McKENDRE
York
Jas. 1769 i.
McKENDREE
Halifax
Mary 1784 i.
McKENNE
Westmoreland
Wm. 1732 w.
Wm. 1755 w.
McKENNEY
Augusta
Jno. Sr. 1789 w.
Wm. Sr. 1796 w.
Fauquier
John 1795 w.
Westmoreland
Danl. 1744 i.
Gerard 1761 i.
Gerard 1784 w.
Jno. Sr. 1784 w.
Vincent 1780 w.
McKENNY
Berkeley
Edward 1795 w.
Brunswick
Thos. 1783 i.
Thos. 1784 i.

Culpeper
John 1773 w.
Frederick
Peter 1748 i.
Tully 1757 i.
Isle of Wight
Gilbert 1746 i.
Mecklenburg
James 1794 w.
Richmond
Wm. 1747 i.
Jno. 1748 w.
McKENSEY
Fairfax
James 1761 i.
McKENY
Orange
Jno. 1751 w.
Westmoreland
Jno. 1726 i.
McKENZEY
Prince William
Daniel 1743 i.
McKENZIE
Norfolk
John 1759 w.
Spotsylvania
Alex. 1757 a.
Surry
Kenneth 1767 i.
York
Kenneth 1755 w.
Joanna 1767 w.
McKEY
Frederick
James 1750 i.
King George
Robt. 1722 i.
Frederick
Margt. 1760 w.
McKIE
Lunenburg
Michael 1797 w.
Stafford
Saml. 1758 i.
McKILDOE
Westmoreland
Eliz. 1797 i.
McKILLICAT
Albemarle
Alex. 1762 w.
McKINNE
Isle of Wight
Thomas 1772 i.
McKINZIE
Albemarle
Alexander 1798 i.
McKITTRICK
Augusta
Robt. Sr. 1795 w.

Spotsylvania
James 1754 a.
McKNIGHT
Brunswick
Wm. 1759 w.
Loudoun
Wm. 1794 i.
McKOOT
Frederick
James 1751 i.
McLACHLAN
Goochland
Jno. 1758 w.
Norfolk
John 1774 w.
McLAIN
Frederick
William 1754 w.
King George
Hugh 1754 w.
McLARD
Prince Edward
Danl. 1774 w.
McLAUGHLIN
Accomack
Wm. 1773 w.
Mecklenburg
Nathl. 1790 w.
Richmond
Manus 1710 w.
McLAURINE
Cumberland
Catherine 1776 w.
Robt. 1771 w.
McLEAN
Fairfax
Samuel 1793 w.
McLELAND
Chesterfield
Malcolm 1781 i.
McLEOD
Essex
Tortile 1752 i.
McLEMORE
Southampton
John 1783 w.
McLENCH
Richmond
Edmd. 1718 w.
McMACKAN
Frederick
William 1751 i.
McMACHAN
Ohio
William 1794 w.
McMAHAN
Richmond
Arthur 1734 i.
McMAHON
Augusta
Saml. 1755 i.

Jno. 1784 w.
Fairfax
Michael 1786 w.
Frederick
William 1749 w.
McMATH
Accomack
Jane 1751 i.
Botetourt
William 1782 w.
Rockbridge
James 1794 w.
McMECHEN
Ohio
William 1795 w.
McMENAS
Northampton
Jno. 1764 i.
McMERRIN
Norfolk
Lydia 1734 w.
McMICHAEL
Sussex
Wm. 1765 i.
McMIKIN
Norfolk
Hugh 1774 w.
McMILLAN
Henrico
Jas. 1731 i.
McMOON
Northumberland
Patrick 1727 i.
McMORRAN
Norfolk
James 1718-19 i.
McMULLEN
Botetourt
Edward 1783 w.
Randolph
Andrew 1787 w.
McMUN
Westmoreland
Neil 1755 i.
McMURDY
Pittsylvania
———— 1794 w.
McMURRAY
Botetourt
William 1798 i.
McMURRIN
Culpeper
David 1750 w.
McMURTREE
Bedford
James 1772 w.
James 1777 i.
McNAB
Northampton
Dunkin 1677 i.

McNABB
Rockbridge
Samuel 1790 i.
McNAIR
Augusta
Danl. 1791 i.
McNALL
Northumberland
Joshin 1755 i.
McNANCE
Frederick
Bryan 1743 w.
McNAUGHTON
Rockbridge
John 1798 w.
McNEAL
Botetourt
Hugh 1795 w.
Orange
Patrick 1786 w.
Washington
Archibald 1779 i.
McNEIL
Southampton
James 1795 w.
Westmoreland
Jas. 1797 i.
McNEILL
Augusta
Jno. 1765 w.
Botetourt
John 1773 w.
James 1778 w.
Chesterfield
Isabella 1758 w.
McNEILY
Albemarle
Robt. 1757 w.
McNEKAL
Middlesex
Jno. 1785 w.
McNERRIN
Norfolk
Lidia 1734 w.
McNEW
Washington
William 1792 i.
McNIEL
Mecklenburg
Jno. 1786 w.
McNUCKLES
Westmoreland
Jno. 1783 i.
McNUTT
Augusta
Jas. 1749 i.
McPHEETERS
Augusta
Wm. Sr. 1773 w.
Alex. 1798 w.

McQUEEN
Culpeper
Alexander 1781 w.
McQUHAE
Northumberland
Anthony 1774 i.
McQUIE
Mecklenburg
Jno. 1790 w.
McPHEETERS
Rockbridge
James 1785 i.
McPHERSON
Amherst
Alex. 1765 w.
Berkeley
Daniel 1789 w.
Frederick
Robert 1749 a.
Jacob 1750 i.
Loudoun
Stephen 1799 w.
Norfolk
Andrew 1775 w.
Daniel 1784 w.
William 1795 w.
Saml. 1798 i.
Danl. 1799 w.
McREYNOLDS
Washington
Roland 1796 i.
McROBERTS
Botetourt
Samuel 1784 i.
McSHERRY
Berkeley
Barney 1799 i.
McSPARRAN
Botetourt
Archibald 1777 w.
McSWAINE
Orange
Neal 1738 a.
McTIRE
Lancaster
Robert 1775 w.
Middlesex
Hugh 1764 a.
McTYRE
Essex
Ann 1795 w.
Josiah 1795 w.
Lancaster
Mary 1789 i.
Eliz. 1792 i.
Eliz. 1795 w.
McWILLIAMS
Albemarle
Andrew 1772 w.
Spotsylvania
Wm. Jr. 1758 a.

Benj. 1774 a.
McWHERTER
Amherst
James 1763 a.
MABRY
Brunswick
Hinchia Jr. 1755 w.
Hinchy 1762 i.
Greensville
Joel 1784 w.
Nathaniel 1795 w.
Mecklenburg
Anne 1772 w.
Surry
Chas. 1749 w.
Wm. 1750 w.
Sussex
Chas. 1769 i.
MACANTURF
Shenandoah
John 1779 w.
MACARTER
Henrico
Danl. 1733 w.
MACARTY
Accomack
Danl. 1680 w.
Princess Anne
Denis 1702 i.
MACASKOE
Henrico
Jno. 1709 i.
MACBOYD
Westmoreland
Jeoffrey 1719 i.
MACCAIL
Westmoreland
Alex. 1719 i.
MACCENEY
Richmond
Carnock 1718 i.
MACCHARTY
Stafford
Wm. 1732 w.
MACCLALLEN
Norfolk
John 1678 i.
MACCOMB
Accomack
Jno. 1684 w.
MACCOME
Accomack
Jas. 1719 i.
MACCOY
Norfolk
Richd. 1750 w.
Richard 1779 i.
MACCROW
Cumberland
Wm. 1752 w.

MACDONALD
Princess Anne
Michael 1696 w.
MACGAE
Lancaster
Jno. 1713 w.
MACHAM
Surry
James 1709 i.
Lancaster
Mathew 1734 w.
MACHEN
Middlesex
Thos. 1730 w.
MACINTURF
Shenandoah
John 1780 a.
MACK
Augusta
Rude 1750 i.
MACKAFARSON
Norfolk
Danl. 1696-7 w.
MACKALESTER
Louisa
Wm. 1765 w.
MACKANDREE
York
Sarah 1771 w.
MACKARY
Mecklenburg
Alex. 1774 w.
Eliz. 1794 w.
MACKEY
Norfolk
Wm. 1791 nw.
MACKAY
Westmoreland
Jno. 1785 w.
Barbary 1787 w.
MACKCLANHAN
Princess Anne
Jno. Sr. 1728 w.
MACKCONE
Isle of Wight
William 1712 w.
MACKDANIEL
Mecklenburg
James 1781 w.
MACKDOWELL
Isle of Wight
James 1686 w.
MACKEE
Accomack
Wm. 1763 w.
MACKEEL
Norfolk
Darman 1684-5 w.
Princess Anne
Naomy 1734 w.

MACKENDREE
Halifax
James 1764 w.
MACKENEY
Prince George
Morgan 1727 i.
MACKENNY
Essex
Jno. 1733 w.
MACKENTOSH
York
Enoch 1687 w.
Eliz. 1695 w.
Saml. 1696 w.
MACKENY
York
Jno. 1736 w.
MACKENZE
Northampton
Danl. 1714-15 w.
MACKENZIE
Orange
Markham 1741 w.
MACKERTY
York
Florence 1718 w.
MACKEY
Campbell
Walter 1786 i.
Isle of Wight
Caleb 1751 i.
Mecklenburg
Michael Sr. 1765 i.
Norfolk
Adam 1715 i.
Josias 1717 a.
Patrick 1780 w.
Princess Anne
Jonathan 1795 w.
Southampton
Danl. 1762 w.
Jno. 1762 i.
Joseph 1780 w.
MACKGEHEE
Prince Edward
Jacob 1784 w.
MACKGREGORY
Northampton
Wm. 1738 i.
MACKHONE
Isle of Wight
William 1712 i.
MACKIE
Chesterfield
David 1771 i.
Fauquier
Thomas 1788 w.
Norfolk
Josias 1716 w.
Robert 1770 w.

Princess Anne
Josiah 1718 i.
Jno. 1726 i.
Wm. 1795 w.
MACKINDO
York
Jas. 1731 i.
MACKINIAL
Isle of Wight
Thomas 1728 i.
MACKINNIE
Brunswick
Morgan 1753 i.
MACKINNY
Brunswick
Jno. 1795 w.
MACKIR
Shenandoah
Alexander 1790 w.
Angus 1791 a.
MACKLAINE
Brunswick
Jno. 1741 i.
MACKLAY
Frederick
William 1791 i.
MACKMAILL
Isle of Wight
John 1730 w.
MACKMEHAN
Prince George
Hue 1717 w.
MACKMELION
Richmond
Jno. 1705 w.
MACKMEMAS
Northampton
Jas. 1751 i.
MACKMENAS
Northampton
Jas. 1754 i.
MACKMIALL
Isle of Wight
John 1734 w.
MACKMIEL
Isle of Wight
John 1730 w.
MACKMILLION
Northampton
Thos. 1716 i.
MACKMILLON
Northampton
Thos. 1716 w.
MACKNEALS
Norfolk
Dunkin 1756 i.
MACKNYELL
Henrico
Hugh 1678-9 w.
MACKPHERSAN
Stafford

Anne 1741 w.
MACKPHERSO[N?]
Norfolk
Wm. 1777 w.
MACKTYER
Middlesex
James 1717 i.
MACKVAY
Amelia
Anne 1754 i.
MACKWILLIAM
Accomack
Finla 1687 w.
MACKY
Augusta
Jno. 1774 w.
MACLAND
Isle of Wight
John 1705 w.
MACLEMORE
Sussex
Jno. 1767 w.
Burrell 1798 w.
MACLIN
Brunswick
Wm. 1743 i.
Mary 1746 w.
Wm. Sr. 1751 w.
James 1769 w.
Jno. 1774 w.
Jno. 1779 w.
Thos. 1798 w.
Greensville
James 1794 w.
Irvin 1797 i.
Mecklenburg
Thos. 1773 w.
Surry
Wm. 1762 w.
MacMELON
Northampton
Neale 1677 w.
MacMORAN
Norfolk
James 1714 a.
MacMORRIN
Norfolk
Jas. 1714 w.
MACOANE
Isle of Wight
Neall 1680 w.
MACODINE
Isle of Wight
Phillip 1693 i.
MACOMICK
Fauquier
Stephen 1786 w.
MACON
Cumberland
Henry 1783 w.
Frances 1785 w.

Wm. 1796 w.
Powhatan
Jno. 1793 w.
MACOY
Norfolk
Michaell 1682 w.
Dennis Sr. 1705-6 w.
MacPHERSON
Chesterfield
Danl. 1772 i.
MacQUINAY
Isle of Wight
Michael 1686 w.
MACREDIE
Spotsylvania
Thos. 1753 a.
MACRORY
Middlesex
Rowland 1676 a.
MACTYER
Middlesex
Hugh 1731 i.
MACY
Isle of Wight
Thomas 1739 w.
Thomas 1750 i.
Southampton
Jane 1760 i.
MADDEN
Fairfax
Hannah 1799 w.
Prince William
George 1782 i.
Scarlett 1796 w.
Samuel 1797 i.
MADDERA
Surry
Zachariah 17— w.
Sarah 1767 w.
Wm. 1773 w.
Zacheriah 1774 i.
Christopher 1782 w.
Elizabeth 1783 w.
Jno. 1787 i.
MADDERY
Isle of Wight
Joseph 1781 w.
MADDESFORD
Lancaster
Thos. 1675 i.
MADDIN
Frederick
John 1760 i.
Isle of Wight
Henry 1687 i.
MADDING
Pittsylvania
Jno. 1780 w.
MADDISON
Rappahannock
Thos. 1674 w.

Westmoreland
Jno. 1659 w.
MADDOCKS
Lunenburg
Lazarus 1795 w.
MADDOX
Amherst
Eliz. 1772 w.
Culpeper
John 1785 w.
Mary 1787 w.
Cumberland
Wm. 1795 i.
Goochland
Michael 1748 i.
Jno. 1749 w.
Benj. 1790 i.
Jno. 1790 w.
Henrico
Wm. 1785 w.
Norfolk
Elizabeth 1769 i.
Prince William
William 1799 i.
MADDUX
Fauquier
Thomas 1783 w.
Northampton
Sarah 1697 w.
Thos. 1713 i.
Thos. 1717 i.
MADDY
Fairfax
William 1756 i.
MADEIRAS
Middlesex
Bowler 1782 w.
MADERO
King George
Jno. 1725 i.
MADISON
Augusta
Humphrey 1759 i.
Richd. 1785 nw.
Botetourt
John 1784 w.
Thomas 1798 w.
Isle of Wight
Richard 1677 w.
Orange
Ambrose 1794 i.
Spotsylvania
Ambrose 1732-3 w.
MADKINS
Mecklenburg
Thos. Durham
1794 w.
MADOCK
Henrico
Wm. 1682-3 i.

MADOX
Chesterfield
Jno. 17— i.
MAFFITT
Amherst
Thos. 1778 w.
Rappahannock
Jno. 1684 w.
MAGANN
Amherst
Merrit 1777 a.
MAGANS
Fauquier
James 1765 i.
MAGARETY
Surry
Patrick 1721 i.
MAGDUELL
Northumberland
Alex. 1655 w.
MAGEE
Prince George
Danl. 1725 i.
Surry
Robt. 1730 i.
Sussex
Robt. 1786 w.
Drury 1796 w.
MAGERT
Shenandoah
David 1775 w.
MAGERTY
Surry
Patrick 1725 i.
MAGET
Southampton
Micajah 1770 i.
Nicholas 1797 w.
Surry
Nicholas 1745 w.
Nicholas Jr. 1752 w.
MAGGEE
King George
Patrick 1725 i.
MAGGIRT
Shenandoah
Rudolph 1799 i.
MAGGET
Augusta
David 1775 i.
Frederick
Christian 1763 i.
Surry
Ann 1754 w.
MAGGOT
Sussex
Saml. 1787 w.
MAGILL
Augusta
Wm. 1749 w.

MAGKEE
Halifax
Wm. 1759 w.
MAGNUS
Henrico
Thos. 1692 i.
MAGOON
Lunenburg
Joseph 1779 w.
MAGOONE
Northumberland
John 1772 i.
MAGRAH
Essex
Thos. 1722 w.
MAGRATH
Accomack
Edwd. 1760 nw.
MAGRIGG
Halifax
David 1773 i.
MAGRUDER
Culpeper
Thomas 1788 w.
Fairfax
Thomas 1785 i.
MAGUYER
Richmond
David 1711 i.
MAGWIAR
Essex
Susanna 1698 w.
MAHAN
Northumberland
Meredith 1726-7 w.
MAHANE
Northumberland
Saml. 1740 w.
Saml. 1751 w.
Deborah 1758 i.
John 1771 i.
MAHANES
Norfolk
John 1794 w.
MAHANNES
Northampton
Margt. 1725 i.
MAHLIN
Frederick
Lydia 1769 w.
MAHON
Accomack
Jno. 1769 w.
MAHONE
Princess Anne
Jno. 1703 i.
Surry
Wm. 1795 w.
MAHORN
Accomack
Jno. 1770 i.

MAHORNER
Fauquier
Henry 1762 i.
MAHUGH
Loudoun
James 1796 i.
MAHUNNY
Albemarle
James 1753 w.
MAIHONE
Lunenburg
Abraham 1749 i.
MAIL
Albemarle
Wm. 1762 w.
MAIN
Surry
Jno. 1724 i.
MAINE
Prince George
Edwd. 1716 i.
MAJOR
Accomack
Jno. 1664 w.
Wm. 1683 w.
Peter 1711 w.
Wm. 1730 w.
Rowles 1751 w.
Jno. 1763 i.
Caleb 1774 i.
Amelia
Saml. 1770 i.
Brunswick
Edwd. 1778 i.
Charles City
Jno. 1768 w.
James 1793 i.
Bernard 1796 i.
Culpeper
Constance 1765 w.
Samuel 1799 i.
William 1799 i.
Cumberland
Wm. 1778 w.
Greensville
Harwood 1784 w.
Loudoun
Richd. 1797 w.
Madison
Samuel 1799 w.
Middlesex
Richd. 1751 w.
Northampton
Jno. 1648 w.
Jno. 1734 w.
Winefred 1745 w.
Wm. Sr. 1765 w.
Wm. 1782 w.
Jno. 1798 w.
Orange
George 1798 w.

York
Wm. 1678 i.
Saml. 1785 w.
MAKEMIE
Accomack
Eliz. 1709 i.
MAKEPEACE
Princess Anne
Ebenezer 1783 i.
MAKER
Isle of Wight
Susanna 1727 w.
MAKEY
Augusta
Jno. 1774 i.
MALAFUA
Henrico
Jno. 1703 i.
MALBON
Norfolk
Reedolphus 1746-7 w.
MALBONE
Norfolk
[Peter?] 1680 i.
Margt. 1740 w.
Mary 1743 i.
Princess Anne
Rodolphus 1728 w.
Jno. 1736 w.
Chas. 1741 w.
Margt. 1742 i.
Peter 1752 w.
Wm. 1752 w.
Reodolphus 1766 w.
Philip 1782 w.
Godfrey 1794 w.
MALCKOM
Augusta
Jno. 1761 w.
MALCOLM
Albemarle
Archibald 1762 i.
Isle of Wight
John 1795 w.
MALE
Chesterfield
Joel 1796 w.
MALEY
Northumberland
Jas. 1789 w.
Patrick 1713 w.
MALECOTE
Isle of Wight
George 1795 i.
MALIN
Frederick
David 1761 w.
MALLET
Henrico
Etinne 1712 w.

MALLEY
Rappahannock
Danl. 1686 w.
MALLICOAT
York
Wm. 1718 i.
MALLONE
Surry
Nathaniel 1732 w.
MALLORY
Culpeper
William 1779 w.
Orange
Roger 1743 w.
Henry H. 1755 i.
Jno. 1774 w.
Wm. 1784 w.
Prince George
Francis 1719 w.
MALLOW
Augusta
Michael 1773 i.
MALONE
Halifax
Danl. 1795 w.
Greensville
Nathaniel 1781 w.
Mecklenburg
Drury 1782 w.
James 1784 w.
Jones 1788 i.
Isham 1793 i.
Surry
Wm. 1745 w.
Sussex
Nathl. 1761 w.
Danl. 1781 w.
Jno. 1794 w.
Eliz. 1798 i.
Michael 1798 w.
MALOONE
Sussex
Wm. 1774 w.
MALOWE
York
Jno. 1720 i.
MALTIMOR
Northumberland
Elizab. 1751 i.
MAMAKEN
Norfolk
Wm. 1687 w.
MAMPHUS
Henrico
Thos. 1749 w.
MAN
Albemarle
Thos. 1759 w.
MAN
Augusta
Moses 1756 a.

Culpeper
Michael 1797 w.
Essex
John 1709-10 i.
Goochland
Mary 1795 i.
Henrico
Robt. 1713 w.
Robt. 1747 w.
Isle of Wight
Thomas 1690 i.
Middlesex
Jno. 1686 w.
Northumberland
Saml. 1665 w.
York
Jos. 1704 i.
MANAGHAM
Orange
Danl. 1745 w.
MANEAR
Richmond
Jno. 1717 w.
MANFEELD
Norfolk
Edmand 1793 w.
MANGAM
Isle of Wight
Henry 1795 w.
Sussex
James 1784 w.
MANGAR
Henrico
Russell 1789 w.
MANGUM
Isle of Wight
John 1737 i.
Joseph 1762 w.
Joseph 1777 i.
Brittain 1782 w.
Richard 1795 i.
Surry
Jno. 1744 i.
Nicholas 1757 i.
Martha 1761 w.
MANING
Fairfax
John 1752 i.
Isle of Wight
Eleanor 1705 i.
Norfolk
John Sr. 1716 w.
Jos. 1742 w.
John (1) 1758 w.
John (2) 1758 w.
Solomon 1760 w.
MANIRE
Amelia
Wm. 1770 i.

MANKIN
Fairfax
Josias 1766 i.
Prince William
Mark Matthew 1797 i.
MANLEY
Fairfax
John 1750 i.
John 1751 w.
Harrison 1774 w.
Prince William
John 1734 i.
Westmoreland
Wm. 1716 w.
Wm. 1727 i.
MANLOWE
Northampton
Derman 1658 w.
MANN
Amelia
Francis 1753 w.
Abel 1761 i.
Joel 1770 w.
Robt. 1782 w.
Eliz. 1796 w.
Bath
Thomas 1796 i.
Botetourt
John 1783 i.
William 1778 w.
Campbell
Barberry 1786 w.
Charlotte
Francis 1768 w.
Chesterfield
Thos. 1770 w.
Danl. 1782 w.
Francis 1782 w.
Obedience 1788 w.
Thos. 1789 w.
Martha 1796 w.
Olive 1797 i.
Jos. 1799 w.
Essex
Joseph 1783 w.
Robert 1797 w.
Halifax
Robt. 1780 w.
Stafford
Jas. 1705 w.
MANNAN
King George
Robt. 1759 w.
Clara 1782 a.
MANNEN
Brunswick
Wm. 1746 w.
King George
Moses 1749 i.

MANNER
Westmoreland
Jno. 1708 i.
MANNERING
Richmond
Stephen 1699 w.
MANNIN
Charles City
Chas. 1798 i.
Norfolk
Elisha 1779 i.
MANNING
Brunswick
Joel 1793 i.
Fairfax
John 1751 w.
Isle of Wight
James 1689 i.
Norfolk
John 1719 i.
Nicholas 1719 i.
Joseph 1742 w.
William 1764 w.
Elisha 1778 w.
John 1782 w.
Elizabeth 1784 w.
MANNING
Norfolk
William 1786 i.
Wm. 1787 i.
David 1788 w.
Sarah 1793 w.
Orange
Andrew 1783 w.
Patrick
William 1794 a.
Southampton
Saml. 1750 w.
York
Jno. 1744 w.
Mary 1757 i.
MANRY
Sussex
Henry 1772 w.
Agnes 1797 w.
MANS (?)
Norfolk
Joseph Sr. 1716 w.
MANSFIELD
Middlesex
Wm. 1769 w.
Norfolk
Alphed 1799 w.
MANSELL
Rappahannock
David 1672 w.
MANSON
Bedford
Nathaniel 1785 i.
York
Peter 1721 w.

Peter 1726 i.
Robt. 1796 w.
MANUEL
Fauquier
Francis 1793 w.
MANY
Northampton
Wm. 1648 i.
MANYARD
Isle of Wight
Hezekiah 1768 i.
MAPLE
Westmoreland
Robt. 1662 w.
MAPLES
Bedford
Richard 1774 w.
Lancaster
Geo. 1685 w.
MAPP
Accomack
Laban 1787 w.
Laban 1797 i.
Housen 1799 w.
Northampton
Bartho. 1698 i.
Jno. Sr. 1725 w.
Esther 1732 w.
Jno. 1737 w.
Saml. 1744 w.
Howsen 1757 w.
Jno. Sr. 1760 w.
Robins 1760 w.
Jno. 1784 i.
Wm. 1788 i.
Saml. 1795 w.
Betty 1799 w.
Susanna 1799 i.
MARA
Greenbrier
Francis 1791 w.
MARABLE
Charlotte
Chris. 1795 w.
Mecklenburg
Matthew 1786 w.
Geo. 1796 w.
MARBERGER
Frederick
John 1799 w.
MARCH
Lancaster
Francis 1653 w.
Richmond
Wm. 1713 i.
York
Jno. 1687 w.
MARCHANT
Accomack
Benj. 1743 w.
Cathren 1779 w.

Princess Anne
Caleb 1769 i.
Richmond
Easter 1729 i.
MARCHBANKS
Amelia
Geo. 1740 w.
MARCY
Accomack
Jno. 1765 i.
Loudoun
Charles 1759 w.
Westmoreland
Edwd. 1724 w.
MARDER
Westmoreland
Wm. 1750 i.
MARDERS
King George
Mose 1783 a.
Jas. 1787 w.
MARGARETTS
York
Jno. 1661 w.
MARGETTS
Northampton
Jno. 1688 w.
MARGRAVE
Rockbridge
Thomas 1797 i.
MARE
Richmond
Ralph 1709 i.
MARIN
Henrico
Gilley 1747 w.
York
Anthony D. 1797 w.
MARINER
King George
Geo. 1748 a.
Northampton
Jno. 1720 w.
MARK
Augusta
Jacob 1777 w.
MARKENDREE
Spotsylvania
Mary 1742 a.
MARKENNY
Essex
John 1734 i.
MARKER
Frederick
Jacob 1790 w.
MARKES
Norfolk
Peter 1656 w.
MARKHAM
Amelia
Thos. 1750 a.

Chesterfield
Jno. 1770 w.
Isle of Wight
Bryan 1708 i.
Prince William
William 1734 i.
Richmond
Margret 1720 i.
Stafford
Jas. 1741 i.
Westmoreland
Lewis 1713 w.
MARKS
Brunswick
Edwd. 1787 w.
Culpeper
John 1759 w.
Lancaster
Patrick 1727 i.
Loudoun
John Sr. 1778 w.
Isaak 1785 w.
William 1795 i.
Middlesex
Wm. 1760 w.
Norfolk
Stephen 1670 w.
Prince George
Israel 1718 i.
Matthew 1719 w.
Richmond
Wm. 1735 w.
Jno. Sr. 1791 w.
Jno. 1793 i.
Southampton
Thos. 1772 w.
Surry
Henry 1799 w.
MARLEY
Norfolk
John 1717 i.
John 1766 i.
Maximillion 1794 w.
MARLOE
Westmoreland
Jno. 1718 w.
MARLOW
Surry
James 1755 i.
MARMADUKE
Westmoreland
Miles 1695 w.
Chris. 1761 w.
Danl. 1782 i.
Lamkin 1783 i.
Mary 1792 i.
Wm. 1792 i.
Vincent 1794 i.
Danl. 1796 i.

MARNER
Accomack
Sarah 1795 w.
Norfolk
Jemima 1785 i.
MARQUES
Frederick
Thomas 1762 i.
MARQUESS
Culpeper
William 1790 a.
King George
Wm. 1754 i.
MARQUIS
Frederick
John 1794 w.
MARR
Fauquier
Mary 1778 i.
Henry
John 1794 i.
Northampton
Jno. 1733 i.
Pittsylvania
Gideon 1777 w.
Christopher 1780 w.
Prince William
John 1744 w.
Shenandoah
John 1775 a.
MARRABLE
Charles City
Benj. 1773 i.
Geo. 1796 i.
Ann 1796 i.
Sussex
Henry Hartwell
1775 w.
MARREAN
Westmoreland
Danl. 1715 w.
MARRICK
Pittsylvania
Jno. 1791 w.
MARRINER
Accomack
Geo. 1795 w.
Isle of Wight
John 1737 i.
Northampton
Giles 1736 i.
MARRINOR
Essex
Susanna 1799 w.
MARRIOT
Northampton
Robt. 1665 w.
MARRIOTT
Brunswick
Thos. 1789 w.

Northampton
Jno. 1682-3 w.
Surry
Wm. 1673 a.
Matthias 1707 w.
Wm. Jr. 1755 w.
Wm. 1767 w.
Wm. 1770 i.
Matthias 1774 w.
MARRON
Goochland
Danl. 1749 i.
MARROT
York
Jean 1717 w.
MARSDEN
Orange
James 1777 w.
MARSDON
Accomack
Robt. 1687 w.
MARSEYE
Accomack
Thos. 1767 i.
MARSH
Culpeper
John 1776 w.
Essex
Benj. 1699 i.
James 1717 w.
Henrico
Nicholas 1688 op.
Northumberland
Arthur 1726 i.
Wm. 1755 i.
Peter 1772 i.
Sarah 1781 w.
Chas. 1783 w.
Richd. 1790 i.
Jas. 1793 w.
Richd. 1793 w.
Jas. 1798 i.
Princess Anne
Geo. 1720 w.
York
Jno. 1659 i.
MARSHAL
Accomack
Chas. 1781 i.
Westmoreland
Jno. 1751 i.
MARSHALL
Accomack
Chas. 1745 i.
Mary 1757 w.
Wm. 1761 w.
Peter 1766 w.
Solomon 1766 w.
Jno. 1767 i.
Danl. 1775 w.
Skinner 1775 w.

Chas. 1779 w.
Danl. 1784 w.
Peter 1784 w.
Thos. 1785 w.
Wm. 1787 w.
Kinner 1790 i.
Patience 1791 w.
Danl. 1792 i.
Peter 1793 i.
Wm. 1794 w.
Sophia 1795 w.
Stephen 1797 w.
Patience 1799 i.
Albemarle
Richard 1799 w.
Amelia
Robt. 1767 w.
Wm. 1772 w.
Judith 1790 w.
Jno. 1785 w.
Brunswick
Jno. 1733 w.
Matthew 1742 w.
Geo. 1751 i.
Campbell
Wm. Sr. 1784 w.
Charlotte
John 1771 w.
Jno. 1773 w.
Chesterfield
Alex. 1771 w.
Culpeper
William 1772 w.
Elizabeth 1779 w.
James 1783 w.
Margaret 1784 i.
Thomas 1794 w.
Zanner 1797 w.
Cumberland
William 1769 w.
Isle of Wight
John 1688 w.
Robert 1698 w.
Humphrey 1711 w.
Joseph 1728 i.
Mary 1739 w.
Humphrey 1741 i.
Humphrey 1744 w.
Robert 1757 w.
James 1761 w.
John 1766 w.
John 1782 i.
John 1784 w.
Dempsey 1794 i.
King George
Wm. 1749 i.
Hudson 1757 i.
Edwd. 1763 w.
Wm. 1772 w.
Benj. 1778 a.
Geo. 1785 w.

Geo. 1789 w.
Rush 1789 a.
Jno. 1794 w.
Lancaster
Wm. 1676 i.
Thos. 1690 w.
Sackfeld 1710 w.
Jas. 1718 i.
Jno. 1727 i.
Thos. 1728 i.
Louisa
John 1790 i.
Mecklenburg
Jno. 1785 w.
Middlesex
Jno. 1740 i.
Mary 1742 i.
Northampton
Thos. Jr. 1687 w.
Thos. 1704 w.
Geo. 1713-14 w.
Wm. 1716 i.
Jno. 1720 w.
Mary 1724 w.
Jno. 1750 w.
Jacob 1752 w.
Thos. 1753 w.
Thos. 1761 w.
Patience 1768 w.
Northumberland
Richd. 1750-1 i.
Orange
Mungo 1758 i.
Powhatan
Francis 1781 w.
Josiah 1790 w.
Princess Anne
Saml. 1693 a.
Jno. 1746 w.
Richmond
Abraham 1709 w.
Stafford
Thos. 1730 i.
Anne 1740 w.
Surry
Robt. 1727 i.
Westmoreland
Thos. 1704 w.
Jno. 1752 w.
Jas. 1751 i.
MARSHMAN
Northampton
Henry 1686 w.
MARSON
Westmoreland
Thos. 1713 i.
MARSSEY
Accomack
Stephen 1778 w.

MARSTERS
Essex
James 1761 w.
MARSTON
Middlesex
Jno. 1729 w.
Thos. 1749 a.
Wm. 1767 i.
Surry
Jno. 1798 w.
MASSEY
Middlesex
Ralph 1716 i.
MARTAIN
Cumberland
Henry 1752 w.
Valentine 1760 w.
Brunswick
Wm. 1762 w.
Prince Edward
Saml. 1777 w.
MARTANE
Orange
Ann 1789 w.
MARTEN
Chesterfield
Eliz. 1774 w.
Henrico
Ann 1737 w.
King George
Frances 1770 eb.
MARTIAL
Accomack
Jno. 1752 i.
Loudoun
Joseph 1771 w.
MARTIALL
Accomack
Jno. 1733 w.
MARTIAN
York
Nicholas 1657 w.
MARTIN
Accomack
Edwd. 1738 i.
Peter 1761 w.
Henry 1769 i.
Edwd. 1779 i.
Albemarle
Henry 1757 w.
Joseph 1762 w.
Geo. 1777 w.
Wm. 1777 w.
Thos. 1792 w.
Mary 1798 w.
Amherst
David 1766 w.
Stephen 1768 w.
James 1771 w.
Henry 1797 w.

Augusta
Jos. 1746 i.
Andrew 1749 i.
Jacob 1765 a.
Hugh 1766 i.
Patrick 1770 w.
Bedford
John 1774 i.
Robert 1781 w.
Berkeley
Bandyah 1786 i.
Brunswick
Ann 1761 i.
Campbell
Robt. 1785 w.
Jas. 1796 i.
Charles City
Jno. Soane 1771 i.
Charlotte
Abraham 1773 w.
Chesterfield
Jas. 1750 i.
Jas. 1751 w.
Chris. 1766 i.
Jas. 1766 w.
Jno. 1778 w.
Wm. 1793 w.
Jno. 1799 w.
Culpeper
John 1793 w.
Cumberland
Henry 1752 i.
Jno. 1777 w.
Orson 1786 w.
Essex
John 1716 i.
John 1741 w.
Hannah 1778 w.
Fairfax
John 1757 w.
Nicholas 1759 i.
George 1774 i.
Fauquier
Tilmon 1779 w.
Charles 1786 w.
Joseph, Sr. 1793 w.
Fluvanna
James 1783 w.
Frederick
George 1753 i.
Thomas 1797 w.
Goochland
Gilbert 1738 i.
Jno. 1739 w.
Matthew 1768 i.
Jno. 1788 w.
Saml. 1790 w.
Wm. 1792 w.
Halifax
Isaac 1774 w.
James 1779 i.

Jno. 1788 i.
Benj. 1796 w.
Joel 1799 i.
Henrico
Andrew 1701 i.
Thos. 1707 i.
Philip 1717 w.
Richd. 1726 i.
Jno. 1736 w.
Grissel 1799 w.
Jas. 1799 w.
Henry
William 1783 i.
Isle of Wight
George 1721 i.
King George
Francis 1770 w.
Lancaster
Jno. 1684 i.
Thos. 1688 i.
Thos. 1692 i.
Thos. 1710 i.
Thos. 1713 w.
Thos. 1727 w.
Wm. 1739 w.
Nicholas 1761 w.
William 1786 i.
William 1794 i.
Loudoun
Ralph 1772 w.
James 1777 w.
Norfolk
John 1666 i.
Jonathan 1690 w.
Thomas 1738 w.
Thomas 1740 w.
Jonathan 1764 w.
Northampton
Nancy 1795 w.
Orange
Henry 1757 w.
Benj. 1766 i.
Robt. 1783 w.
Pittsylvania
Jno. 1780 i.
Thos. 1799 w.
Powhatan
Isaac 1778 w.
Prince Edward
Saml. 1778 i.
Farish 1783 i.
Jos., Sr. 1786 w.
Jno. 1788 w.
Prince George
Jno. 1719 i.
Princess Anne
Wm. 1715 w.
Jno. 1718 i.
Henry 1722 i.
Jonathan 1747 w.
Presson 1776 w.

Joshua 1797 w.
Prince William
  Elizabeth 1791 i.
  Catherine 1795 i.
Rappahannock
  Solomon 1671 w.
Rockbridge
  David 1778 i.
  David 1789 w.
Southampton
  James 1791 w.
Spotsylvania
  Jno. 1748 w.
  Henry 1749 w.
  Jno. 1794 a.
Stafford
  Richd. 1707 w.
  Jno. 1743 i.
  Leonard 1750 i.
Surry
  Wm. 1737 i.
Sussex
  Eliz. 1756 w.
Westmoreland
  Thos. 1670 w.
  Jane 1677 w.
  Jno. 1720 w.
  Mathew 1725 w.
  Jacob 1728 w.
  Sarah 1734 i.
  Jno. 1783 w.
York
  Jno. 1684-5 w.
  Robt. 1697 w.
  Geo. 1702 w.
  Arbraham 1711 w.
  Martha 1756 w.
  [Alexander] 1767 w.
  Jas. 1767 w.
MARTNDALE
Princess Anne
  Robt. 1753 w.
MARTING
Accomack
  Andrew 1758 w.
MARTINO
Accomack
  Julian 1696 w.
MARTON
Goochland
  Peter 1743 w.
MARTY
Shenandoah
  Lawrence 1794 a.
MARTYN
Northampton
  Jno. 1670 i.
MARVILL
Accomack
  Jno. 1707 i.

MAVINS
Shenandoah
  John 1795 i.
MARVIS
Shenandoah
  George 1794 a.
MARYE
Spotsylvania
  James Sr. 1768 w.
  James 1780 w.
  Sarah 1788 a.
MASCALL
Lancaster
  Robt. 1653 w.
MASEY
Accomack
  Wm. 1747 i.
Essex
  Ralph 1719 i.
MASH
Richmond
  Alex. 1715 w.
MASIE
Northumberland
  Charles 1777 i.
MASKILL
Halifax
  James 1787 w.
MASMAN
Northampton
  Luke 1691 w.
MASON
Accomack
  Robt. 1677 w.
  Wm. 1710 i.
  Sarah 1710 i.
  Ede 1748 w.
  Wm. 1759 w.
  Eleanor 1762 i.
  Bennett 1766 w.
  Edmd. 1770 i.
Augusta
  Jno. 1761 w.
Bedford
  Gilbert 1781 i.
Botetourt
  Martin 1794 i.
Brunswick
  Chris. 1778 w.
  Nathl. 1794 w.
  Joseph 1795 w.
  Sarah 1796 w.
Campbell
  Jno. 1796 w.
  Jno. Sr. 1796 w.
Culpeper
  James 1779 i.
Cumberland
  Wm. 1795 i.
Fairfax
  French 1748 w.

Charles 1756 w.
Ann 1761 w.
French 1768 i.
Philip 1779 w.
Geo. 1792 w.
Geo. 1796 w.
Geo. 1799 i.
Fauquier
  Peter 1798 i.
Greensville
  James 1784 w.
  John 1793 w.
Isle of Wight
  William 1676 i.
Lancaster
  Jno. 1737 w.
  Thomas 1755 i.
  Wm. 1765 w.
  Thomas 1769 w.
  Joseph 1777 w.
  John 1778 i.
  John 1782 w.
  Sarah 1784 w.
  William 1785 i.
  John 1799 w.
Loudoun
  Benj. 1795 w.
Lunenburg
  Nathl. 1785 w.
  William 1791 w.
Mecklenburg
  Thos. 1768 w.
  Ann 1778 w.
  Thos. 1781 w.
Norfolk
  Trustram 1678 w.
  Lemuell 1702 w.
  Ann 1705-6 w.
  George 1710 w.
  Lemuell 1711 a.
  Saml. 1711 i.
  Thomas 1711 w.
  Lemuel 1714 a.
  Mary 1714 w.
  John 1791 i.
Northumberland
  Catherine 1725-6 i.
  Edwd. 1746 i.
  John 1758 i.
  Peter 1759 i.
  Jas. 1783 w.
Orange
  Chas. 1788 w.
Prince Edward
  Jos. 1788 i.
  Jos. 1791 i.
  Wm. 1799 w.
Princess Anne
  Robt. 1753 w.
  James 1768 w.
  James 1782 w.

Nathl. 1789 w.
Obediah 1791 w.
Prince William
George 1735 i.
Richmond
Thos. 1710 i.
Jno. 1716 w.
Southampton
Isaac 1760 w.
Stafford
Geo. 1730 i.
Wm. 1733 w.
Wm. 1746 i.
Ann 1762 w.
Thomson 1785 w.
Surry
Francis 1696-7 w.
James 1702 w.
Eliz. 1713 w.
Joseph 1750 i.
Jno. 1752 i.
Sussex
Jno., Sr. 1755 i.
Isaac 1758 w.
Seth 1759 i.
Jno. 1761 i.
Isaac, Jr. 1763 i.
Wm. 1781 w.
Jno. 1785 w.
Joseph 1792 w.
Wm. 1793 w.
Jno. 1796 w.
Westmoreland
Wm. 1719 w.
Jas. 1725 w.
MASSEE
Albemarle
Thomas 1799 i.
MASSENBURG
Sussex
Nicho. 1772 w.
MASSEY
Accomack
Jno. 1764 i.
Jno. 1767 w.
Jean 1770 w.
Jno. 1774 i.
Nanny 1795 w.
Brunswick
Richd. 1740 w.
Anne 1770 w.
Essex
John 1757 w.
Greensville
Richd. 1794 w.
King George
Benj. 1765 i.
Thos. 1778 w.
Chas. 1785 a.
Sigismund 1792 w.
Robt. 1793 w.

Thos. 1795 i.
Robt. 1796 w.
Loudoun
Lewis 1769 i.
Stafford
Dade [Sr.] 1734 w.
Dade, Jr. 1734 w.
Lee 1745 i.
Sigismund 1746 i.
Robt. 1754 i.
Westmoreland
Lovell 1765 w.
Jas. 1778 w.
Lovell 1778 w.
Jno. 1794 w.
Jno. 1797 i.
MASSIE
Accomack
Alex. 1696 w.
Albemarle
Edmund 1782 w.
Brunswick
Joseph 1761 w.
Culpeper
Edward 1754 i.
Goochland
David 1755 w.
Thos. 1755 w.
Wm. 1797 i.
Henrico
Gideon 1797 i.
MASSINGALE
Sussex
Thos. 1794 w.
MASSOT
Henrico
Peter 1711 w.
MASSY
Greensville
John 1791 w.
MASTEN
Prince Edward
James 1767 w.
MASTERS
Essex
James 1761 i.
Henry
John 1799 i.
Northampton
Jno. 1728 i.
Stafford
Thos. 1737 w.
MASTERSON
Fairfax
Edward 1754 w.
MATH
Northumberland
Jno. 1724 i.
MATHANY
Westmoreland
Jno. 1797 i.

MATHEAS
Norfolk
Mathew 1731 w.
MATHENY
Stafford
Wm. 1705 w.
MATHERS
Richmond
Thos. 1736 i.
MATHES
Shenandoah
Alexander 1788 w.
Benjamin 1797 w.
MATHESON
Augusta
Alex. 1756 w.
MATHEW
Stafford
Wm. 1786 w.
Isle of Wight
Richard 1720 w.
Westmoreland
Danl. 1783 i.
MATHEWS
Accomack
Wm. 1731 w.
Jno., Sr. 1781 w.
Jno. 1782 i.
Ephraim 1784 i.
Staten 1793 i.
Augusta
Jno. 1757 w.
Jno. 1764 w.
Joshua 1765 i.
David 1790 w.
Berkeley
William 1778 i.
Botetourt
William 1772 w.
Campbell
Gregory 1791 w.
Essex
Richard 1705-6 i.
Goochland
Jno. 1740 w.
Henrico
Rosamund 1703 i.
Edwd. 1707 w.
Sarah 1710 w.
Edwd. 1727 i.
Ann 1791 w.
Anthony 1791 i.
Isle of Wight
Anthony 1681 w.
Ralph 1687 nw.
John 1739 i.
Richard 1755 w.
Richard 1789 w.
Lancaster
Samuel 1746 w.
Wm. 1755 w.

Norfolk
Jas. 1679 w.
John 1768 w.
Northampton
Henry 1685 w.
Eliz. 1696 w.
Custis 1784 w.
Martha 1788 w.
Levin 1795 w.
Princess Anne
Owen 1710 i.
Richmond
Jas. 1710 w.
Andrew 1717 i.
Saml. 1718 w.
Robt. 1734 i.
Stafford
Wm. 1758 w.
York
Francis 1674 i.
MATHEWSON
Augusta
Mathew 1787 i.
MATHIAS
Norfolk
Matthew 1669 w.
Mathew 1731-2 w.
Jno. 1751 i.
Elenor 1760 w.
Jonathan 1782 w.
MATHIS
Brunswick
Drury 1795 w.
Essex
William 1738 i.
Isle of Wight
Richard 1755 i.
Pittsylvania
Nehemiah 1790 w.
Princess Anne
Owen 1710 w.
Richmond
Robert 1734 w.
MATLOCK
Bedford
William 1769 i.
MATSON
Lancaster
Alex. 1751 i.
MATTERS
Shenandoah
Barnett 1783 a.
MATTHEIS
Cumberland
Edwd. 1775 w.
MATTHEW
Isle of Wight
Samuel 1782 w.
Lancaster
Wm. 1727 i.

MATTHEWS
Accomack
Jos. 1764 w.
Wm. 1770 w.
Thos. 1771 w.
Geo. 1772 w.
Wm. 1772 i.
Southy 1776 w.
Ephraim 1783 w.
Ezekiel 1797 w.
Jos. 1799 i.
Thos. Stockley 1799 i.
Amherst
Thos. 1783 w.
Berkeley
John 1778 w.
Brunswick
Chas. 1781 i.
Luke 1788 w.
Culpeper
John 1783 w.
Cumberland
Jno. 1795 i.
Essex
Benj. 1722 w.
Philip S. 1795 i.
Fauquier
Edward 1798 i.
John 1798 w.
Frederick
Joseph 1759 w.
William 1760 i.
Goochland
Edwd. 1785 w.
Jno. 1797 i.
Greenbrier
Barnaby 1789 i.
Archer 1790 i.
Henrico
Thos. 1737 w.
Wm. 1749 i.
Thos. 1753 w.
Anthony 1781 w.
Thos. 1783 w.
Chas. 1784 w.
Isle of Wight
Richard 1706-7 i.
Alexander 1720 w.
Zeakell 1740 w.
Joseph 1762 i.
William 1783 i.
King George
Jno. 1729 i.
Middlesex
Jno. 1747 a.
Northampton
Walter 1683 w.
Jno. 1767 w.
Jno. C. 1777 w.
Northumberland
Thos. 1712 w.

Powhatan
Gregory 1785 i.
Prince Edward
Saml. 1770 w.
Wm. 1799 w.
Spotsylvania
Benj. 1755 w.
Wm. 1758 w.
Richmond
Giles 1710 w.
Southampton
Hugh 1747 w.
Hugh 1752 i.
Edwd. 1761 i.
Jno. 1762 w.
York
Jno. 1702 i.
Patrick 1762 w.
Anne 1772 w.
Patrick 1772 i.
MATTHEWSON
Surry
Jno. 1765 i.
MATTHIAS
Loudoun
Simon 1770 i.
Griffith 1790 i.
Norfolk
Joshua 1785 w.
Robinson 1791 i.
Matt. 1792 i.
Peter 1795 w.
Princess Anne
Henry 1769 w.
Sarah 1774 w.
Jno. 1782 w.
Reuben 1785 w.
Jno. Sr. 1787 w.
Hillary 1799 w.
MATTHIS
Amelia
Eliz. 1769 w.
Brunswick
Chas. 1782 w.
Fauquier
Robert 1767 w.
Lunenburg
Matthew 1784 i.
Princess Anne
Geo. 1793 w.
MATTICOAT
York
Francis 1774 i.
MATTISON
Northampton
Jno. 1683 w.
MATTLAND
Isle of Wight
Daniel 1680 w.

MATTOCK
Amherst
Jno. 1767 a.
Culpeper
Timothy 1794 w.
Louisa
John 1785 w.
MATTOCKS
Northampton
Alex. 1660 w.
MATTOX
Brunswick
Ralph 1798 i.
Frederick
Henry 1749 i.
Tobias 1749 a.
Prince William
Jean 1794 w.
William 1797 i.
MATTUX
Princess Anne
Margt. 1720 i.
MAUCK
Frederick
Frederick 1779 w.
MAUGHON
Lancaster
Susanna 1778 w.
MAUK
Frederick
Peter 1771 w.
Frederick 1786 i.
Shenandoah
Henry 1788 a.
MAULBONE
Princess Anne
James 1794 w.
MAULDEN
Stafford
Jacob 1704 w.
MAULEY
Westmoreland
Wm. 1716 i.
MAULPIS
Stafford
Alex. 1743 w.
MAUND
Norfolk
William Jr. 1734 w.
William 1741 w.
Lott 1764 w.
Marcum 1794 i.
MAUNDER
Westmoreland
Wilkes 1666 w.
MAUNE
Norfolk
Jno. 1644 w.
MANPIN
Albemarle
Danl. Sr. 1788 w.

Gabriel 1794 i.
MAURER
Shenandoah
George 1776 w.
MAURY
Albemarle
James 1769 w.
Orange
Walker 1795 i.
Lunenburg
Matthew Fontaine
1783 w.
Abraham 1784 w.
MAUX
Northampton
Jno. 1719 w.
MAUZEY
Fauquier
Mary 1769 w.
MAUZY
Fauquier
John 1764 w.
Stafford
Peter 1751 w.
MAXEY
Cumberland
Mary 1771 w.
Wm. 1768 w.
Franklin
Walter 1791 w.
Josiah 1793 w.
Goochland
Edwd. 1740 w.
Susanah 1743 w.
Halifax
Radford 1780 a.
Jno. 1790 w.
Henrico
Edwd. 1727 i.
Powhatan
Nathl. 1779 w.
Edwd. 1782 w.
MAXFIELD
Henrico
Jno. 1717 i.
Northampton
Susanna 1710 w.
Stephen 1711 i.
Spotsylvania
Jno. 1774 a.
MAXON
Harrison
Ephraim 1795 w.
MAXWELL
Albemarle
Edwd. 1752 i.
Frederick
Solomon 1771 i.
Montgomery
John 1779 a.

Rockbridge
John 1786 i.
Alex. 1794 i.
Shenandoah
John 1777 i.
Washington
David 1795 w.
MAY
Amelia
Jno. 1767 w.
James 1773 w.
James [1783?] i.
Berkeley
Daniel 1777 w.
Charlotte
Henry 1773 w.
Danl. 1778 w.
David 1789 w.
Chesterfield
Jno. 1790 w.
Fluvanna
John 1782 i.
Frederick
William 1751 i.
Goochland
Wm. 1744 i.
Jno. 1772 w.
Isle of Wight
George 1691 nw.
Lunenburg
Wm. 1751 w.
Northumberland
Jno. 1796 w.
Spotsylvania
Thos. 1771 a.
York
Jno. 1751 i.
MAYBURY
Surry
Francis 1712 w.
Eliz. 1715 w.
Francis 1728 w.
Eleanor 1735 i.
MAYE
Princess Anne
Lucy 1772 i.
John 1791 w.
John 1795 w.
MAYES
Amelia
Wm. 1752 w.
Wm. 1753 w.
Wm. [1774?] i.
Richd. 1787 i.
Phoebe 1796 i.
Danl. 1796 w.
Wm. 1797 i.
Greensville
Matthew 1796 w.
Halifax
Wm. 1794 i.

Lancaster
Henry 1775 w.
Lunenburg
Richd. 1797 i.
Northumberland
Henry 1702 w.
Henry 1711 w.
John 1750 i.
Henry 1750 w.
John 1781 w.
MAYFIELD
Culpeper
William 1761 i.
Essex
Robert 1714 w.
MAYHEW
York
Jno. 1732 i.
MAYHUE
Loudoun
James 1794 w.
MAYLE
Norfolk
Charles 1780 i.
Charlotte 1797 w.
MAYNARD
Amelia
Wm. 1765 w.
Charles City
Nathl. 1769 i.
Wm. 1799 i.
Mecklenburg
Nicho. 1785 w.
Wm. 1792 w.
Eliz. 1796 w.
Ann 1797 w.
Prince George
Henry 1727 i.
MAYNOR
Patrick
Richard Tucker
1798 w.
MAYO
Albemarle
James 1777 w.
Chesterfield
Jno. 1785 w.
Cumberland
Danl. 1761 w.
Ann 1769 w.
Mary 1773 i.
Goochland
Wm. 1744 w.
Isle of Wight
Wm. 1715 w.
Middlesex
Valentine 1717 i.
Jno. 1724 w.
Norfolk
Trastrom 1684 i.

Powhatan
Mary 1799 a.
Surry
James 1722 i.
MAYS
Amherst
Joseph 1797 w.
Augusta
Jas. 1756 a.
Bedford
James 1795 w.
Halifax
Mattox 1773 w.
Wm. 1794 w.
Northumberland
John 1784 i.
Pittsylvania
Wm. 1783 i.
MAYSEY
Fairfax
John 1760 w.
MAYTON
Amelia
Jno. 1761 w.
MAYZE
Henry
Henry 1787 w.
MAZARETT
Westmoreland
Jno. 1794 w.
MAZE
Botetourt
William 1783 w.
MCEELLALLEN
Norfolk
Jno. 1679 w.
M'CLAIN
Amherst
Richd. 1777 a.
M'CLANAHAM
Westmoreland
Magdalin 1797 i.
M'CLANAHAN
Westmoreland
Peter 1776 i.
MCLEROY
Spotsylvania
Bryant 1733 a.
MCLOUD
Princess Anne
Jno. 1724 w.
MEACHAM
Middlesex
Joseph 1710 i.
Jno. 1712 w.
Henry 1719 w.
Jno. 1727 i.
Jno. 1764 i.
Wm. 1764 w.
Westmoreland
William 1727 w.

MEACHUM
Sussex
Henry 1758 i.
Joshua 1775 w.
Banks 1798 w.
MEACOME
Isle of Wight
Thomas 1723 i.
MEACUM
Isle of Wight
Lewis 1738 i.
MEAD
Bedford
John 1754 i.
Lancaster
Thos. 1655 w.
Loudoun
Wm. 1784 w.
Ellen 1787 w.
Richmond
Jno. 1713 w.
Spotsylvania
Thos. 1770 a.
York
Jno. 1783 i.
MEADE
Brunswick
Andrew 1795 w.
MEADER
Essex
Thomas 1717 w.
John Jr. 1720 w.
John 1721 w.
John 1723 i.
Thomas 1758 w.
William 1759 i.
Reubin 1778 w.
Richard 1780 i.
MEADES
Essex
Thos. 1717 w.
MEADOR
Amelia
Joel 1774 w.
Benj. 1797 w.
Bedford
Hambus 1795 w.
Cumberland
Jonas Sr. 1768 w.
Frances 1774 w.
Jonas 1775 i.
Essex
Richard 1716 w.
Frances 1770 w.
Meador 1770 nw.
John 1774 i.
John 1786 i.
MEAKINS
York
Richd. 1679 i.

MEAKS
Augusta
Jno. 1761 a.
MEALER
Lunenburg
Nicho. 1763 w.
Mecklenburg
Philip 1789 w.
MEALEY
Frederick
Andrew 1760 i.
Northumberland
Patrick 1727 i.
James 1769 i.
Patrick 1775 i.
Anne 1781 w.
Richmond
Humphrey 1700 w.
MEALY
Amelia
Jno. 1762 i.
Stafford
Danl. 1742 w.
MEAN
Augusta
Robt. 1755 w.
MEANLEY
Henrico
Jno. 1794 w.
Jno. 1795 i.
Lunenburg
Saml. 1783 w.
MEANLY
Amelia
Gideon 1775 i.
Goochland
Isaac 1776 w.
MEAR
Rockbridge
John 1787 w.
MEARIS
Princess Anne
Jno. 1693 i.
MEARS
Accomack
Richd. 1759 i.
Elisha Sr. 1772 w.
Elisha 1773 i.
Litt. 1778 i.
Jno. 1785 w.
Nathan 1785 w.
Sabra 1785 w.
Jno. 1788 w.
Southy 1791 w.
Levi 1793 i.
Richd. 1793 i.
Tabitha 1793 i.
Spencer 1794 w.
Geo. 1795 w.
Southy 1795 i.
Jonathan 1796 w.

Meshack 1796 i.
Elisha 1798 w.
Jonathan 1798 i.
Robt. 1798 i.
Fairfax
John 1755 i.
Norfolk
Eliz. 1795 nw.
MEAZLE
Surry
Luke 1694 i.
MECAN
Bath
Samuel 1795 i.
MECHUM
Goochland
Thos. 1754 w.
MECLOUD
Norfolk
John 1783 w.
James 1785 w.
John 1788 i.
MECOM
Southampton
Matthias 1774 w.
MECOY
Norfolk
Denniss 1724 i.
John 1739 w.
Samuel 1765 w.
Princess Anne
Anguish 1760 w.
MEDARIS
Middlesex
Chas. 1774 w.
MEDCALFE
Henrico
Jno. 1701-2 w.
Northampton
Henry 1651 i.
Northumberland
Wm. 1655 w.
MEDES
Surry
Wm. 1696 i.
MEDFORD
Richmond
Henry 1741 i.
MEDLEY
Berkeley
William 1794 w.
Culpeper
Robert 1759 w.
John 1763 w.
Essex
James Sr. 1772 w.
James Jr. 1774 w.
John 1777 w.
Halifax
Joseph 1796 i.

Lunenburg
Isaac 1762 w.
MEADORS
Essex
Reuben 1778 i.
MEECK
Augusta
Agnes 1795 i.
MEECOM
Isle of Wight
John 1720 i.
MEED
Surry
Jno. 1766 w.
MEEDS
Surry
Honour 1711 i.
MEEK
Augusta
Jno. 1761 i.
Thos. 1788 w.
Richmond
Richd. 1729 w.
MEEKS
Richmond
Ann 1761 w.
MEENS
Norfolk
Jos. Sr. 1716 w.
MEERS
Accomack
Bartholomew 1682 w.
Mary 1705 w.
Wm. 1744 w.
Jno. 1747 w.
Wm. 1755 w.
Wm. 1759 i.
Jno. 1762 i.
Bartholomew 1766 w.
Robt. 1768 w.
Richd. 1772 w.
Tabitha 1773 w.
Thos. 1775 w.
Littleton 1776 w.
Bartholomew 1778 w.
Rachel 1779 w.
Norfolk
Elijah 1790 w.
Northampton
Littleton 1728 i.
MEES
Stafford
Jno. 1733 i.
Mary 1747 w.
MEGEE
Sussex
Ralph 1770 w.
MEGEHEE
Goochland
Abraham 1743 i.

MEGGS
Essex
John 1737 w.
Humphrey 1748 w.
MEGLACH
Loudoun
Joseph 1761 w.
MEGOON
Northumberland
Thos. 1753 w.
MEHAN
Essex
Augustine 1705-6 i.
MEHOLLOMS
Northampton
Jno. 1785 w.
MEKEMIE
Accomack
Francis 1708 w.
MELBY
Accomack
Patience 1798 w.
MELDRUM
Westmoreland
Michael 1742 w.
MELEAR
Essex
William 1759 w.
MELHOLLOUR
Northampton
Jno. 1774 i.
MELHOLLOWS
Northampton
Stringer 1785 i.
Jno. 1787 i.
MELICHOP
Accomack
Jno. 1740 i.
Naomi 1745 w.
MELICK
Berkeley
Philip 1797 w.
MELLATT
Essex
John 1720 i.
MELLICHOP
Accomack
Richd. 1704 i.
Jno. 1727 i.
MELLING
Frederick
David 1766 i.
MELLINGE
Northampton
Wm. 1670 w.
Anne 1676 w.
Wm. 1684 w.
Wm. 1688 or 9 i.
MELLIS
Prince George
Jno. 1713 i.

MELMOND
Accomack
Ephraim 1798 w.
MELONEY
Amelia
Jos. 1782 i.
MELSON
Accomack
Jno. 1737 w.
Mary 1743 w.
Jno. 1759 i.
Solomon 1774 w.
Wm. 1782 w.
Wm., Jr., 1782 i.
Solomon 1783 i.
Geo. 1784 i.
Isaac 1791 i.
Levin 1795 w.
Smith 1796 w.
MELTON
Albemarle
Silas 1783 w.
Brunswick
Jno. 1773 w.
Fluvanna
John 1795 w.
Frederick
John 1751 w.
Louisa
James 1798 w.
Norfolk
Thomas 1644 i.
Prince William
Richard 1735 i.
York
Anthony 1675 i.
MELVIN
Accomack
Smith 1787 w.
Westmoreland
Wm. 1729 w.
MENDENHALL
Berkeley
John 1773 w.
Fairfax
Wm. 1796 w.
MENEFEE
Culpeper
John 1765 w.
John 1782 w.
Jonas 1784 i.
MENG
Culpeper
Mallery 1796 i.
MENNIS
York
Francis 1760 w.
Elias 1773 w.
MENTIRE
Augusta
Jno. 1759 a.

MENZIES
Northumberland
Adam 1767 w.
Geo. 1784 i.
MERCER
Berkeley
Edwd. 1783 w.
Brunswick
James 1791 i.
Essex
Isaac 1716 i.
Frederick
John 1749 w.
Edward 1763 w.
Isle of Wight
James 1734 w.
Lancaster
Isaac 1780 w.
Norfolk
Christopher 1711 a.
Thomas 1718 w.
John 1751 w.
John, Jr. 1771 w.
Turner 1793 w.
Southampton
Jno. 1775 w.
Robt. 1775 w.
Jno. 1789 i.
Spotsylvania
Hugh 1777 w.
James 1795 w.
MERCHANT
Berkeley
William 1772 w.
Frederick
Richard 1752 w.
Louisa
Thos. 1784 a.
Princess Anne
Chris. 1699 w.
Willoughby 1727 w.
MERCY
Accomack
Jno. 1734 w.
Mary 1743 w.
Wm. 1744 w.
Thos. 1760 w.
Culpeper
Edward 1754 w.
MEREDITH
Amherst
Rice 1779 a.
Rice 1787 w.
Cumberland
Jas. 1751 w.
Elisha 1799 i.
Lancaster
John 1795 w.
Prince George
Samson 1720 w.

MERENNER
Princess Anne
Jno. 1764 i.
MEREWETHER
Louisa
Thos. 1757 w.
MERIDETH
Lancaster
John 1758 i.
John 1784 w.
Brunswick
David 1782 w.
MERILL
Accomack
Wm. 1798 i.
MERION
Goochland
Richd. 1777 w.
MERIWETHER
Albemarle
Nicholas 1773 w.
Essex
Thomas 1708-9 w.
Francis 1713 i.
Thos. 1731 w.
Goochland
Nicho. 1744 w.
Nicho. 1758 w.
Henrico
Jno. 1791 w.
Louisa
Elizabeth 1762 w.
Geo. 1782 w.
Geo. 1792 i.
Surry
Francis 1676 a.
MERRELL
Accomack
Wm. 1783 w.
MERRET
Accomack
Wm. 1784 i.
MERRICK
Westmoreland
Edwd. 1718 i.
MERRIDETH
Lancaster
John 1785 i.
MERRIL
Accomack
Rebecca 1795 i.
MERRILL
Accomack
Thos. 1727 i.
Esau 1750 i.
Wm. 1750 w.
MERRIMAN
Lancaster
Jno. 1674 i.
Richd. 1696 w.
Thos. 1718 w.

Wm. 1740 w.
MERRIOT
Berkeley
George 1776 w.
Surry
Wm. 1761 i.
MERRIOTE
Berkeley
Barbara 1779 w.
MERRIOTT
Surry
Benj. 1762 i.
MERRIT
Brunswick
Mary 1789 i.
Wm. 1790 i.
Middlesex
Matth. 1679 a.
MERRITT
Brunswick
Wm. 1788 w.
Essex
Olenor 1700 w.
James 1736 i.
Lancaster
Thos. 1717 w.
Powhatan
Tapley 1783 w.
Richmond
Jas. 1728 w.
MERRIWEATHER
Surry
Wm. 1695 a.
MERRY
Charles City
David 1793 w.
Isle of Wight
Francis 1770 w.
Norfolk
Prettymon 1743-4 w.
Orange
Thos. 1756 w.
York
Jane 1700 i.
MERRYMAN
Cumberland
John 1769 w.
John 1785 w.
Lancaster
Wm. 1697 i.
Jno. 1727 i.
John 1775 w.
John 1789 i.
MERYL
Accomack
Wm. 1795 w.
MESMORE
Frederick
Peter 1760 w.

METCALF
Accomack
Thos. 1771 w.
Eliz. 1774 w.
Tabitha 1790 w.
Mark 1796 w.
Brunswick
Thos. 1761 i.
Fauquier
Chris. 1777 i.
Greensville
Andrew 1794 w.
Middlesex
Samuel 1782 w.
Northumberland
Wm. 1727 i.
Wm. 1769 i.
Richmond
Jno. 1728 w.
Gilbert 1737 w.
Susanna 1747 w.
Sussex
Warner 1760 i.
METCALFE
Accomack
Isaac 1688 w.
Jno. 1744 i.
Jno. 1751 w.
Campbell
Jno. S. 1797 w.
Northumberland
Henry 1767 i.
METEER
Augusta
Jas. 1793 w.
METHENY
Stafford
Jas. 1739 i.
MEYER
Loudoun
George 1793 i.
Shenandoah
Henry 1797 w.
MEYERS
York
Henry 1666 i.
MEYRICK
Loudoun
Griffith 1771 w.
M'HANE
Northumberland
Thos. 1746 w.
MIARS
Fairfax
Jacob 1763 i.
Norfolk
Richard 1744-5 w.
Eliza. 1758 w.
Joshua 1785 w.

MICANE
Surry
  Michaell 1672 i.
MICHAEL
Accomack
  Jno. 1684 w.
  Jno. 1691 i.
  Susannah 1772 w.
  Jno. 1785 i.
Augusta
  Jno. 1783 i.
  Fredk. 1798 w.
Isle of Wight
  John 1793 w.
Northampton
  Jockim 1707 i.
  Yardly 1716 w.
  Joachim 1752 w.
  Thos. 1759 w.
  Rose 1761 w.
  Tilney 1764 i.
  Wm. W. 1772 w.
  Wm. Wainhouse
    1780 i.
  Joachim 1783 i.
  Sarah Tabitha 1794i.
MICHAELL
Accomack
  Simon 1728 w.
Northampton
  Ann 1675 w.
  Jno. Jr. 1678 w.
  Adam 1689 w.
MICHASON
Norfolk
  Constance 1734 w.
Princess Anne
  Jno. 1729 i.
MICHAUX
Cumberland
  Jacob 1774 w.
  Jacob 1784 i.
Goochland
  Jacob 1744 w.
  Susanne 1744 w.
Halifax
  Abraham 1778 i.
Henrico
  Abraham 1717 w.
Lunenburg
  Abraham 1748 w.
Powhatan
  Paul 1779 w.
MICHEL
Goochland
  Wm. 1796 w.
MICHELL
Charles City
  Archelaus 1795 a.
Goochland
  Reuben 1783 w.

MICHIE
Albemarle
  Jno. 1777 w.
  James 1782 w.
Louisa
  James 1778 w.
  Robt. 1793 w.
MICKEL
Berkeley
  Michael 1793 w.
MICKELBURROUGH
Middlesex
  Tobias 1702 w.
  Edmund 1718 i.
MICKEY
Louisa
  Mary 1767 i.
MICKLEBURROUGH
Middlesex
  Jno. 1717 i.
MICKELBOROUGH
Middlesex
  Jas. 1779 i.
  Henry 1783 w.
  Jno. 1787 i.
MICONICO
Lancaster
  Enis 1687 w.
MICOU
King George
  Jas. 1745 i.
Essex
  Paul 1736 w.
  Margt. 1740 w.
  Paul 1742 w.
  Henry 1742 i.
  Jno. 1754 w.
  Jno. 1757 i.
  Paul, Sr. 1799 w.
MIDDLETON
Accomack
  Thos. 1708 w.
  Geo., Sr. 1719 w.
  Geo. 1746 w.
  Wm. 1759 i.
  Geo. 1773 w.
Berkeley
  Adam 1792 i.
Charlotte
  John 1766 w.
Chesterfield
  Jane 1788 w.
Essex
  Alex. 1772 i.
  Martha 1786 i.
Frederick
  William 1753 i.
King George
  Thos. 1767 w.
Loudoun
  Jane 1767 i.

Middlesex
  Alex. 1730 i.
Prince George
  Jno., Jr. 1720 w.
  Jno. 1722 w.
Surry
  Geo. 1708 i.
Westmoreland
  Robt. 1697 w.
  Jno. 1706 w.
  Jno. 1726 i.
  Eliz. 1733 w.
  Thos. 1737 i.
  Robt. 1754 w.
  Benj. 1756 w.
  Wm. 1757 i.
  Jno. 1760 i.
  Mary 1763 w.
  Jeremiah 1769 w.
  Sarah Ellen 1770 w.
  Benedict 1771 w.
  Robt. 1772 w.
  Alice 1772 w.
  Jno. 1776 i.
  Robt. 1776 i.
  Benedict 1785 w.
  Jno. 1789 w.
  Wm. 1790 w.
  Geo. 1793 w.
  Jno. 1797 i.
MIDLETON
Isle of Wight
  Robert 1675 i.
MIERS
Brooke
  Christopher 1797 w.
Frederick
  Stephen 1798 i.
MIFFLIN
Accomack
  Edwd. 1743 w.
  Mary 1775 w.
  Mary 1782 i.
  Danl. 1796 w.
MIFFORD
Botetourt
  Jacob 1798 w.
MIFLIN
Westmoreland
  Jas. 1769 i.
MIGGETT
York
  Henry 1647 i.
MIHILL
York
  Edwd. 1660 w.
MILACHOP
Accomack
  Nicholas 1742 w.

MILAM
Bedford
Thomas 1775 w.
John 1780 i.
MILBURN
Accomack
Joshua 1759 i.
Frederick
John 1761 w.
Robert 1764 i.
Elizabeth 1773 w.
MILBOURNE
Essex
John 1704-5 i.
MILBY
Accomack
Wm. 1709 i.
Jno., Jr. 1721 w.
Jno. 1723 i.
Peter 1726 w.
Jno., Sr. 1728 w.
Garrison 1737 w.
Salathiel 1749 i.
Peter 1760 w.
Jno. 1777 w.
Northampton
Jno. 1770 w.
Gilbert 1774 w.
Adial 1775 w.
Leah 1775 w.
Eliz. 1777 i.
Surry
Wm. 1796 i.
MILES
Accomack
Stephen 1713 i.
Roger 1744 w.
Robt. 1756 w.
Wm. 1767 i.
Parker 1798 w.
Augusta
Jno. 1751 i.
Chesterfield
Jas. 1777 w.
Culpeper
Charles 1777 i.
Essex
Thomas 1731 i.
Halifax
Jeremiah 1782 i.
Isle of Wight
Daniel 1688 w.
William 1698 w.
King George
Burdett 1790 w.
Lancaster
David 1674 w.
Lunenburg
Jno. 1753 i.
Prince George
Jno. 1716 i.

Surry
Jno. 1697 i.
York
Adam 1668 w.
Chas. 1788 w.
Chas. 1790 i.
Mildred 1795 w.
MILFIELD
Essex
George 1711 i.
MILL
Augusta
Robt. 1785 w.
Frederick
Lewis 1776 i.
MILLAKIN
York
Robt. 1695 i.
MILLAM
Bedford
Benjamin 1781 w.
MILLAN
Berkeley
John 1787 w.
John 1798 i.
MILLAR
Shenandoah
William, Sr. 1778 w.
Southampton
Wm. 1780 i.
MILLARD
Fauquier
William 1782 w.
Northampton
Jno. 1752 i.
Northumberland
Jos. 1739-40 w.
MILLENER
Accomack
Eliz. 1781 w.
Robt. 1781 w.
Wm. 1783 w.
Wm. 1788 i.
MILLER
Albemarle
Wm. 1752 w.
Amherst
Alex. 1781 w.
Augusta
Christian 1749-50 i.
Wm. 1755 i.
Marks 1757 i.
Henry 1759 i.
Jno. 1766 a.
David 1767 a.
Jno. 1767 i.
Jacob 1768 i.
David 1769 i.
Francis 1776 i.
Jno. 1788 i.
Danl. 1791 w.

Bedford
Joseph 1764 i.
Jacob 1785 i.
John 1785 w.
Simon 1785 w.
Berkeley
David 1782 w.
Robert 1788 i.
John 1791 w.
Hugh Sr. 1794 w.
Zacariah 1796 w.
James 1796 w.
Philip 1798 w.
Culpeper
Henry 1783 w.
Essex
Jno. 1743 w.
Benj. 1744 i.
Thos. 1751 w.
Wm. 1751 i.
Jno. 1761 w.
Simon 1765 i.
Jane 1785 i.
Apphia 1792 i.
Simon 1792 w.
Fauquier
Simon 1770 w.
Frederick
John 1746 a.
Thomas 1749 a.
Elizabeth 1750 a.
John 1756 i.
William 1758 w.
John 1765 i.
Jacob 1766 w.
Valentine 1782 w.
Michael 1793 w.
Nicholas 1794 i.
Goochland
Thos. 1742 i.
Henry 1752 w.
Wm. 1777 w.
Mary 1796 w.
Halifax
Jno. Fredk. 1787 w.
Hardy
Jacob 1787 w.
Henrico
Wm. 1793 i.
Isle of Wight
Nicholas 1706-7 i.
John 1728 i.
Edward Sr. 1733 w.
John 1740 i.
William 1746 w.
John 1749 i.
Nicholas 1749 i.
Alice 1750 w.
George 1751 w.
Thomas 1760 i.
Nicholas 1762 w.

John 1767 i.
Benjamin 1775 w.
Robert 1778 i.
Lucy 1782 w.
King George
Wm. 1726 i.
Wm. 1733 i.
Lancaster
Jno. 1717 i.
Peter 1717 w.
Wm. 1719 w.
Randolph 1721 w.
Jno. 1726 w.
Margaret 1732 w.
Jno. 1738 i.
Stephen 1744 w.
George 1761 i.
Peter 1772 i.
Martha 1776 w.
Martha 1784 i.
Loudoun
John 1769 w.
Christian 1798 i.
Middlesex
Patk. 1728 i.
Jno. 1742 w.
Christopher 1748 a.
Jno. the younger
   1748 i.
Christopher 1760 w.
Christopher 1782 w.
Corneluis 1784 i.
Christopher 1794 i.
Norfolk
Jos. 1693 w.
Thos. 1717 i.
William 1719 w.
Edward 1734-5 i.
Moses 1740 w.
William 1740 w.
Mary 1743-4 w.
Elizabeth 1751 w.
Solomon 1757 w.
Peleg 1759 w.
Henry 1760 w.
Matthias 1767 w.
Moses 1773 w.
Mason 1775 w.
Charles 1782 i.
William 1782 w.
Willoughby 1782 i.
Shaduk 1784 i.
Nathaniel 1785 w.
Pelege 1785 w.
Bateman 1786 w.
William 1792 w.
Peledge 1794 i.
Matthew 1795 w.
Bateman 1796 i.
Patrick 1796 w.
Simon 1796 w.

Benj. Sr. 1798 w.
Bartlett 1799 i.
Matthias 1799 i.
Northampton
Jno. 1678 w.
Francis 1783 w.
Northumberland
Thos. 1719 i.
Jane 1741 i.
Elizab. 1758 w.
Ohio
Joseph 1778 a.
Orange
Isaac 1758 i.
Powhatan
Thos. 1786 i.
Prince William
Richard 1739 i.
Rappahannock
Symon 1684 w.
Richmond
Simon 1720 w.
Jno. 1744 w.
Joan 1745 nw.
Rockbridge
Henry 1797 w.
Shenandoah
Abraham 1773 nw.
Jacob 1777 w.
Jacob 1781 w.
Barbara 1785 a.
Henry 1789 w.
Henry 1791 w.
William 1791 a.
Catherine 1792 w.
Philip 1797 i.
Spotsylvania
Wm. 1767 w.
Westmoreland
Jno. 1698 w.
York
Jas. 1656 w.
Jno. 1675 w.
Jas. 1678 w.
Edwd. 1726 w.
MILLERD
Northumberland
Thos. 1713 i.
MILLERSON
Princess Anne
Whiddon 1778 i.
MILLESON
Princess Anne
Jno. 1763 w.
MILLICON
Northampton
Susanna 1732 i.
MILLICOTE
Surry
Thos. 1790 w.

MILLINER
Accomack
Henry 1771 i.
Amey 1779 w.
MILLINGTON
York
Saml. 1711 i.
MILLION
Northampton
Wm. 1737 i.
Esther 1751 i.
MILLISON
Norfolk
James 1759 w.
MILMAN
Accomack
Nicho. 1753 w.
Thos. 1762 i.
MILLNER
Prince Edward
Jno. 1795 w.
Richmond
Luke 1746 w.
Luke 1754 w.
MILLON
Northampton
Alice 1663 w.
MILLS
Accomack
Thos. 1709 w.
Edwd. 1711 i.
Moses 1761 i.
Albemarle
David 1764 w.
Amelia
James 1782 i.
Amherst
Wm. 1755 w.
Augusta
Jno. 1750 a.
Gilbert 1757 w.
Botetourt
John 1782 i.
Hugh 1785 w.
Charlotte
Wm. 1769 w.
Wm. Terrel 1770 i.
Essex
Robert 1710 w.
Robert 1757 i.
John 1719 w.
Jno. 1720 w.
Vincent 1750 i.
Fairfax
Alexander 1767 w.
John 1785 i.
Jno. 1798 w.
Middlesex
Jas. 1782 w.
Norfolk
Wm. 1667 w.

Northampton
Rowland 1646 w.
Wm. 1750 w.
Wm. 1755 i.
Thos. 1760 w.
Southy 1768 i.
Edmd. 1780 i.
Prince Edward
John B. 1777 i.
Princess Anne
Abraham 1735 w.
Anne 1797 w.
Rappahannock
Peter 1677 a.
Jno. 1683 w.
Richmond
Jno. 1710 w.
Thos. 1727 i.
Surry
Alexander 1755 i.
Westmoreland
Richd. 1750 i.
Wm. 1758 w.
York
Jas. 1762 w.
MILLSAP
Augusta
Thos. 1760 w.
MILNER
Accomack
Henry 1771 w.
Greensville
Thomas 1799 i.
Henrico
Jno. 1684 a.
Isle of Wight
Betty 1763 w.
Richmond
Benj. 1733 i.
Jno. 1744 i.
York
Eliz. 1743 i.
MILSON
Accomack
Jos. 1754 w.
King George
Jno. 1777 a.
MILTON
Albemarle
Wm. 1772 w.
Prince William
William, Jr. 1779 i.
Southampton
Elisha 1797 w.
MIMS
Charlotte
Thos. 1793 w.
Goochland
Shadrack 1777 w.
David 1781 w.
David 1786 w.

MINARD
Isle of Wight
George 1746 i.
Jesse 1790 i.
MINCHIN
Princess Anne
Geo. 1694 w.
MINENTREE
Surry
David 1758 w.
MINGE
Charles City
Geo. 1772 i.
Jno. 1772 w.
MINGHAM
York
Thos. Townshend
1770 w.
MINIARD
Isle of Wight
Ann 1754 i.
Barnaby 1758 i.
MINNES
York
Chas. 1696 i.
MINNGE
Chesterfield
Jno. 1777 w.
MINNION
Accomack
Owing 1720 w.
MINNIS
King George
Robt. 1791 w.
York
Chas. 1778 w.
Holman 1784 w.
Callowhill 1785 i.
MINOKIN
York
Jno. 1682-3 w.
MINOR
Albemarle
James 1791 i.
James 1796 w.
Culpeper
Joseph 1779 w.
Armistead 1790 w.
Joseph 1791 i.
Fairfax
John 1753 w.
Nicholas 1764 w.
John 1780 w.
Daniel 1787 i.
Frederick
Stephen 1750 i.
Loudoun
John 1782 nw.
Nicholas 1782 w.
Spence 1794 i.

Louisa
Garrit 1799 w.
Lunenburg
Joseph 1785 w.
Middlesex
Doodes 1695 w.
Minor 1716 i.
Garrett 1720 w.
Orange
Dabney 1798 w.
Stafford
Jno. 1751 w.
Spotsylvania
Jno. 1755 w.
Wm. 1759 w.
Sarah 1772 w.
Thos. 1776 w.
Westmoreland
Jno. 1698 w.
Wm. 1726 w.
Nicho. 1744 w.
Jno. 1748 w.
Wm. Stewart 1751 w
Nicho. 1751 i.
Wm. 1755 i.
Blagdon 1762 i.
MINORAN
Norfolk
James 1714 w.
MINSER
Fairfax
William 1752 i.
Frederick
Jacob 1799 i.
MINSON
Lancaster
Minor 1660 i.
York
Thos. 1796 i.
MINTER
Cumberland
Jno. 1785 w.
James 1796 w.
Essex
Jno. 1743 w.
Joseph 1783 w.
Ann 1785 i.
Josiah 1792 w.
Fauquier
Jacob 1773 w.
Joseph 1774 i.
John 1778 w.
Powhatan
Richd. 1785 w.
MINTON
Cumberland
Thos. 1778 w.
King George
Jos. 1739 i.

MINTOR
King George
Thos. 1744 i.
MINTY
Richmond
Edwd. 1745 w.
Margaret 1755 w.
MINTZ
Isle of Wight
Sarah 1772 i.
John 1795 i.
Sarah 1795 w.
MINYARD
Isle of Wight
William 1734 i.
MINYARDS
Isle of Wight
Ezekiach 1768 i.
MINZIES
Northumberland
Phebe 1780 i.
MIRTLE
Spotsylvania
Peter 1734 a.
MISKELL
Richmond
Jno. 1744 i.
Geo. 1772 w.
Newman 1789 w.
Wm. 1790 i.
MISKILL
Henry 1761 w.
David 1764 i.
MITCHAM
Spotsylvania
Lucy 1798 w.
MITCHEL
Culpeper
Jacob 1778 i.
John 1798 i.
Bedford
Robert 1799 w.
Essex
John 1717 w.
Peter 1743 w.
Isaac 1752 i.
Fauquier
Jno. 1784 i.
MITCHELL
Accomack
Wm. 1685 w.
Amelia
Walter 1755 i.
James 1770 i.
Anderson 1772 w.
James 1772 w.
Thos. 1779 w.
Thos. 1782 w.
Thos. 1783 w.
Thos. 1784 w.
Evan 1796 i.

Amherst
Thos. 1767 w.
Archelaus 1799 i.
Augusta
Martha 1759 w.
Jno. 1771 w.
Jno. 1783 w.
Wm. 1796 i.
Bedford
Daniel 1775 w.
Botetourt
David 1788 i.
Brunswick
Peter 1739 i.
Jno. 1745 w.
Thos. 1747 w.
Thos. 1758 w.
Wm. 1763 w.
Thos. 1774 w.
James 1791 w.
Jno. 1799 w.
Charlotte
John 1783 w.
Culpeper
Jacob 1777 w.
Corneluis 1779 w.
William 1785 i.
Thomas 1786 w.
Essex
John 1702 i.
William 1720 i.
Elizabeth 1757 i.
William 1771 w.
Isaac 1792 w.
Fairfax
Elias 1746 i.
Frederick
William 1755 i.
Cary 1798 i.
Goochland
Thos. 1776 w.
Greensville
Nathan 1789 i.
Robert 1798 i.
Henry
Robert 1786 w.
Isle of Wight
Henry 1759 w.
James 1799 w.
Lancaster
Robt. 1702-3 w.
Jno. 1710 i.
Geo. 1717 w.
Jas. 1718 i.
Wm. 1729 w.
Wm. 1738 w.
Robt. 1748 w.
John 1759 w.
Susanna 1762 i.
John 1765 i.
Richard 1781 w.

Lunenburg
Jno. 1755 w.
Thos. 1779 i.
Mecklenburg
Jacob 1779 i.
Middlesex
Jno. 1778 w.
Jno. 1791 i.
Northumberland
Wm. 1767 w.
Richmond
Archibald 1744 w.
Mary 1750 w.
Mary 1750 nw.
Jno. 1753 i.
Robt. 1758 w.
Jas. 1776 w.
Wm. 1778 w.
Ann 1793 w.
Rockbridge
John 1790 w.
Spotsylvania
David 1730 a.
Jno. 1777 w.
Surry
Robt. 1726 i.
Henry 1751 w.
Abraham 1782 w.
Sussex
Henry 1754 w.
Thos. 1762 w.
Jno. 1770 w.
Henry 1771 i.
Wm. 1778 w.
Jno. 1782 w.
Milley 1788 w.
Jno. 1795 w.
Jacob 1797 w.
Westmoreland
David 1776 w.
York
Abraham 1697 i.
Jas. 1772 w.
Jannett 1782 w.
Wm. 1786 w.
MIZE
Lunenburg
James 1761 w.
James 1770 w.
Stephen 1792 w.
MIZELL
Surry
Luke 1695 a.
M'KENNY
Westmoreland
Jno. 1784 i.
MOBBERLY
Prince George
Edwd. 1727 w.

MOBLEY
Albemarle
James 1760 w.
Loudoun
Saml. 1769 nw.
Washington
James 1783 w.
MOFFETT
Augusta
Jno. 1749 a.
Jas. 1764 w.
Fincastle
William 1775 a.
MOFFITT
Frederick
John 1799i.
MOGGOT
Frederick
Christian 1762 w.
MOHON
Lancaster
Patrick 1721 i.
MOHONE
Accomack
Jno. 1789 i.
MOHOONE
Norfolk
Anne 1710 a.
MOHUN
Norfolk
Joel 1783 w.
MOHUNDS
Norfolk
James 1711 i.
MOILEY
Shenandoah
Daniel 1791 i.
Tobias 1791 a.
MOIR
Norfolk
James 1750 i.
MOLBURN
Princess Anne
Jonathan 1787 i.
MOLDE
Lancaster
Lawrence 1699 i.
MOLER
Berkeley
Adam, Sr. 1783 w.
Frederick
John A. 1766 w.
John Adam 1767 i.
MOLINEX
Middlesex
Jno. 1728 w.
MOLLOY
Prince Edward
Thos. 1795 w.

MOLONY
Richmond
Jno. 1728 i.
MOLSON
Norfolk
George 1752 i.
MOLTIMORE
Northumberland
Wm. 1792 w.
MONCURE
Stafford
Jno. 1764 w.
Jno. 1784 w.
MONDAY
Albemarle
Saml. 1795 w.
Cumberland
Thos. 1777 w.
King George
Mary 1772 a.
MONDY
Essex
Thomas 1718 i.
MONEY
Accomack
Nicho. 1764 i.
Fairfax
Nicho., Sr. 1799 w.
Prince William
Isaac 1797 i.
Richmond
Winifred 1727 nw.
MONFKS (?)
Northampton
Wm. 1655 i.
MONGER
Accomack
Catherine 1794 w.
Isle of Wight
John 1671 i.
MONGONG
Northampton
Philip 1727 w.
MONK
Northampton
Geo. 1744 w.
Wm. 1750 w.
Stafford
Jas. 1700 i.
Thos. 1762 w.
MONKHOUSE
Loudoun
Jonathan 1778 i.
Jonathan 1779 i.
Mary 1792 i.
MONKS
Berkeley
Owen R. 1792 i.
MONOHAM
Lancaster
John 1764 i.

MONOHAN
Augusta
Danl. 1748 i.
MONRO
Isle of Wight
Andrew 1719 i.
Sarah 1725 w.
John 1760 w.
MONROE
Fairfax
Thomas 1779 i.
Catherine 1780 i.
John 1785 w.
Fauquier
Daniel 1789 i.
King George
Thos. 1746 i.
Orange
Wm. 1769 i.
Northumberland
Catherine 1772 w.
Westmoreland
Andrew 1714 w.
Spence 1726 w.
Andrew 1736 i.
Wm. 1737 w.
Sarah 1739 w.
Spence 1748 i.
Wm. 1761 i.
Jno. 1767 i.
Andrew 1770 w.
Geo., Jr. 1771 w.
Andrew 1773 i.
Thos. 1772 w.
Spence 1774 w.
Geo. 1776 w.
Spence [1776?] w.
Wm. 1777 i.
Jemima 1786 i.
MONROW
Essex
C——— 1702 i.
Loudoun
Geo. 1769 w.
MONTAGUE
Cumberland
Thos. 1778 i.
Essex
Wm. 1710 i.
Wm. Sr. 1733 w.
Abraham 1740 w.
Charlotte 1747 w.
Abram. 1778 i.
William 1778 w.
Samuel 1785 i.
Peter 1789 i.
Thomas 1789 i.
Richard 1791 w.
Lancaster
Peter 1659 w.
William 1784 w.

Middlesex
Peter 1703 i.
Wm. 1714 w.
Wm. 1754 w.
Thos. 1756 w.
Jno. 1760 i.
Wm. 1761 a.
Wm. 1764 w.
Jno. 1774 i.
Lewis 1778 w.
Betty 1779 w.
Jas. 1781 w.
Thos. 1789 w.
Thos. 1794 i.
Richmond
Edwd. 1709 i.
Spotsylvania
Clement 1791 w.
MONTEITH
King George
Thos. 1747 i.
MONTGOMERY
Westmoreland
Geo. 1791 nw.
MONTIER
Norfolk
James 1756 w.
MONTGOMARY
Princess Anne
Geo. 1727 w.
MONTGOMERY
Accomack
Jno. 1776 nw.
Jno. 1787 i.
Amherst
Michael 1764 w.
James 1778 a.
Isle of Wight
Robert 1761 i.
Loudoun
Isaac 1786 i.
Princess Anne
Eliz. 1753 i.
Jno. 1753 w.
Jno. 1774 w.
James 1779 w.
Prince William
William 1799 i.
Rockbridge
Humphrey 1799 i.
Sussex
Jno. 1790 i.
Washington
Michael 1779 i.
Michael 1788 i.
MOODY
Augusta
Robt. 1787 nw.
Bedford
William 1795 w.

Charles City
Jno. 1772 i.
Saml. 1772 w.
Cumberland
Thos. 1797 w.
Essex
Wm. 1726 w.
Jno. 1738 w.
George 1783 w.
Fairfax
Benjamin 1784 w.
Jno. 1796 i.
Saml. 1796 a.
Frederick
James 1747 i.
Halifax
Edwd. 1781 i.
Isle of Wight
Isaac 1785 w.
Philip 1788 w.
Mecklenburg
Henry 1793 i.
Henry 1797 w.
Pittssylvania
Wm. 1795 w.
Southampton
Philip 1783 w.
Surry
Blanks 1752 i.
Mary 1760 i.
Saml. 1776 w.
York
Josias 1677 w.
Josiah 1687 i.
Philip 1719 w.
[Eliz.?] 1721 ab.
Giles 1729 nw.
Mary 1738 i.
Philip 1739 i.
Ishmael 1748 w.
Mary 1767 i.
Josiah 1770 w.
Mary 1775 w.
Matthew 1775 w.
Ishmael 1777 w.
Jno. 1778 w.
Wm. 1785 w.
Matthew 1793 w.
Jno. 1794 w.
Wm. 1794 w.
Jno. 1798 i.
MOOLER
Berkeley
Adam 1784 i.
MOON
Bedford
Jesse 1780 w.
Jacob Jr. 1781 w.
Brunswick
Thos. 1742 i.

Fairfax
Patrick 1793 a.
Frederick
Simon 1749 i.
Isle of Wight
John 1655 w.
Lunenburg
Gideon 1790 w.
Northumberland
Thos. 1711 w.
Jas. 1741 w.
Westmoreland
Jno. 1717 w.
Jno. 1727 i
MOONE
King George
Saml. 1748 i.
Lancaster
Abraham 1655 i.
MOONEY
Accomack
Nicho. 1761 w.
MOOR
Albemarle
Obadiah 1768 w.
Amelia
Jno. 1751 w.
Chesterfield
Thos. 1772 w.
Goochland
Jno. 1785 w.
Henrico
Richd. 1784 w.
Isle of Wight
Thomas 1744 i.
Lucy 1760 i.
Tristram 1739 nw.
Lancaster
Jno. 1713 w.
Louisa
Ann 1792 w.
Norfolk
Thomas 1783 i.
William 1785 w.
Northampton
Mathew 1734 w.
Thos. 1737 w.
Isaac 1745 i.
Levi 1748 i.
Thos. 1753 i.
Isaac 1756 w.
David 1723 i.
Prince George
Thos. 1719 i.
Spotsylvania
Robt. 1751 w.
Westmoreland
Wm. 1737 w.
Thos. 1750 i.

MOORAN
Albemarle
Jno. 1776 w.
MOORE
Accomack
Richd. 1713 i.
Edwd. 1717 w.
Epharm 1723 w.
Robt. 1774 w.
Jos. 1785 w.
Wm. 1785 i.
Jos. 1790 i.
Amelia
Jas. 1771 w.
Wm. 1778 w.
Jno. 1782 i.
Mary 1782 i.
Jno. 1787 w.
Amherst
Wm. 1766 w.
Benj. 1792 w.
Augusta
David 1748 w.
Andrew 1749 w.
Saml. 1754 i.
Jno. 1757 a.
Moses 1758 a.
Saml. 1758 a.
Wm. 1797 w.
Bath
William 1792 a.
Berkeley
Joseph 1781 w.
John 1784 w.
Cato 1797 w.
Botetourt
James 1780 w.
Brunswick
Jno. 1753 w.
Arthur 1754 i.
James 1761 i.
Tobias 1762 i.
Mary 1784 w.
Drury 1790 w.
Macarina 1799 w.
Campbell
Wm. 1790 w.
Charlotte
John 1792 w.
Richd. 1795 w.
Saml. 1797 w.
Chesterfield
Mark 1763 w.
Eleck 1771 w.
Thos. 1777 w.
Thos., Sr. 1779 w.
Wm. 1781 w.
Geo. Hunt 1783 w.
Jno. 1783 w.
Richd. 1790 i.
Eleazer 1792 w.

Fleming 1792 i.
Culpeper
David 1755 i.
Essex
Henry 1708 i.
Francis 1718 i.
Thomas 1745 i.
Augustine 1777 w.
Fairfax
William 1769 w.
William 1770 i.
Henry 1773 w.
Fluvanna
John 1785 w.
John 1795 w.
Frederick
Simon 1748 w.
James 1760 i.
Riley 1760 w.
Lewis 1769 i.
Peter 1786 w.
Isle of Wight
John 1688 w.
John 1692 i.
Thomas 1696 w.
John 1704 w.
George 1714 w.
Halifax
Hugh 1760 w.
Wm. 1787 w.
Francis 1797 i.
Geo. 1798 w.
Henrico
Anne 1728 i.
King George
Jno. 1759 w.
Rebecca 1760 w.
Lancaster
Francis 1702 i.
Joseph 1773 i.
Loudoun
Ann 1782 w.
Wm. 1790 i.
Louisa
Jno. 1777 w.
Peter 1784 a.
Lunenburg
Drury 1781 w.
Eddings 1781 i.
David 1785 i.
John 1789 i.
Thos. 1791 i.
Mecklenburg
Thos. 1795 w.
Norfolk
John 1681 nw.
Wm. 1683 w.
Morggon 1689 w.
William 1764 w.
Thomas 1782 w.
Samuel 1785 w.

Mathias 1790 i.
John 1795 w.
James 1797 w.
Thomas 1799 w.
Northampton
Augustine 1655 i.
Thos. 1676 w.
Gilbert 1708 w.
Robt. 1710 i.
Mathew 1717-18 w.
Isaac 1744 w.
Matthew 1770 w.
Isaac 1783 w.
Isaac 1790 i.
Wm. 1795 i.
Jno. 1796 w.
Orange
Bernard 1775 w.
Francis 1784 i.
Powhatan
Robt. 1797 i.
Prince George
Richd. 1727 w.
Princess Anne
William 1705 w.
Jean 1708 i.
James 1711 w.
Matthias 1719 w.
Cason 1720 w.
Cason 1726 w.
Thos. 1736 w.
Henry Sr. 1745 w.
Mary 1745 i.
Woodhouse 1747 w.
Jno. 1750 i.
James 1753 w.
Mary 1761 i.
James 1766 i.
Francis 1768 w.
Jno. 1769 i.
Jonathan 1769 i.
Jonathan 1771 i.
Hilliary 1772 w.
Thos. 1772 w.
Henry 1778 w.
Elilm[?] 1780 i.
Willoughby 1780 i.
Frances 1783 i.
Jacob 1785 w.
Cason Sr. 1791 w.
Samuel 1792 w.
Diannar 1794 w.
Tully 1797 w.
Richmond
Garland 1765 w.
Robt. 1779 w.
Jno. 1785 i.
Rockbridge
William 1778 a.
John 1782 i.
David 1783 w.

Robert 1784 i.
Andrew 1791 w.
William 1791 w.
Samuel 1793 i.
Alexander 1799 a.
William 1799 w.
Shenandoah
Thomas 1790 w.
Reuben 1791 i.
Southampton
Thos. 1772 w.
Jas. 1778 w.
Wm. 1784 w.
Sarah 1785 w.
Spotsylvania
Saml. 1726 w.
Jno. 1790 a.
Stafford
Jas. 1702 i.
Richd. 1737-8 i.
Surry
Richd. 1721 i.
Jno. 1734 i.
Wm. 1744 w.
James 1756 w.
Jno. 1799 i.
Sussex
Elizabeth 1761 w.
Epes 1765 i.
Thos. Sr. 1765 w.
Thos. 1767 i.
Wm. 1768 i.
Ann 1776 w.
Martha 1776 w.
Sarah 1771 w.
Wm. 1781 w.
Thos. 1782 w.
Thos. 1792 i.
Westmoreland
Thos. 1713 w.
Jas. 1713 i.
Thos. 1742 w.
Thos. 1750 w.
Saml. 1760 i.
Robt. 1762 w.
Jane 1775 w.
Robt. 1776 i.
Elijah 1779 i.
Wm. 1796 w.
York
Jas. 1671 w.
Jeffrey 1672 w.
Alex. 1675 i.
Mary 1680 i.
Amy 1700 w.
Jno. 1700 i.
Richd. 1729 w.
Starkey 1733 w.
Jane 1734 w.
Jno. Grigs 1738 i.
Jno. 1740 w.

Starkey 1745 i.
Judith 1751 w.
Danl. 1767 w.
Filmer 1776 i.
Jno. 1776 i.
Mary 1782 w.
Augustine 1788 w.
Mary 1788 w.
Merritt 1793 w.
Lucy 1797 w.
Wm. 1797 w.
MOOREFIELD
Amelia
Jos. 1737 i.
MOOREMAN
Bedford
Pleasant 1774 i.
MOORING
Surry
Chris. Sr. 1753 w.
MOORMAN
Albemarle
Thos. 1787 w.
Bedford
Silas 1777 w.
Campbell
Achilles 1783 w.
Zachariah 1789 w.
Andrew 1791 w.
Chas. 1798 w.
Louisa
Chas. 1757 w.
Eliz. 1765 w.
Chas. 1778 w.
James 1782 w.
Chas. 1783 i.
MORCE
York
Jno. 1702 w.
MORDECAI
Westmoreland
Hallbrook 1787 i.
MORE
Lancaster
Wm. 1728 w.
Middlesex
Edwd. 1716 i.
Montgomery
James 1786 i.
Norfolk
Cason 1686-7 w.
William 1784 i.
Matthias 1790 w.
Northumberland
Robert 1757 i.
Prince Edward
Geo. 1777 w.
Royall 1782 w.
Jos. 1791 w.
Geo. 1798 w.

Princess Anne
Wm. 1714 i.
Cason 1798 w.
Spotsylvania
Jno. 1777 a.
Westmoreland
Robt. 1727 i.
Jno. 1735 w.
York
Gyles 1657 i.
MORECOCK
Charles City
Isaac 1797 i.
MOREFIELD
Halifax
Edwd. 1785 i.
Lunenburg
Jno. 1751 w.
MOREHEAD
Fauquier
John 1768 w.
Charles 1783 w.
Samuel 1797 w.
Middlesex
Geo. 1747 a.
Northumberland
Alex. 1743-4 w.
Alex. 1754 i.
MORING
Surry
Wm. 1774 w.
MORELAND
Isle of Wight
Katherine 1736 i.
Thomas 1738 i.
Surry
Edwd. 1713 w.
Bartlett 1725 w.
Frances 1782 i.
Francis 1784 i.
York
Jno. 1706 w.
Jno. 1717 i.
Matthew 1736 w.
Mary 1774 w.
Young 1774 w.
Nathl. 1790 i.
MORELL
Albemarle
Wm. 1753 i.
MOREMEN
Bedford
Thomas 1766 w.
MOREN
Loudoun
Joseph 1770 w.
MOREY
Norfolk
Jno. 1753 w.

MORGAIN
Goochland
Robt. 1746 w.
Mecklenburg
Reuben 1781 w.
Saml. 1781 i.
Northumberland
David 1771 i.
MORGAN
Accomack
Wm. 1701 i.
Jno. 1751 w.
Jacob 1752 i.
Jas. 1761 w.
Arnold 1772 w.
Mary 1775 w.
Wm. 1781 w.
Wm. 1784 i.
Amelia
Saml., Sr. 1770 w.
Thos. 1770 i.
Jacob 1772 i.
Jno. 1780 w.
Jno., Sr. 1796 w.
Bedford
William 1770 i.
Berkeley
Jacob 1780 w.
Isaac 1784 w.
William 1788 w.
William 1795 w.
Morgan 1797 w.
Charles City
Robt. 1773 w.
Culpeper
Charles 1782 w.
Cumberland
Anthony 1763 i.
Essex
Jno. 1733 w.
Fairfax
Enoch 1787 i.
Fauquier
Charles 1766 w.
James 1768 a.
Randle 1773 w.
Joseph 1785 i.
Simon 1793 w.
Frederick
Evan 1747 i.
John 1747 i.
Sarah 1747 i.
Joseph 1749 i.
Isaac 1750 i.
Richard 1763 w.
Richard 1784 i.
Henry
John 1791 w.
Isle of Wight
Walter 1745 i.

Lancaster
Jno. 1682 w.
Middlesex
David 1719 w.
Wm. 1764 w.
Wm. 1767 i.
Josiah 1784 i.
Jno. 1785 w.
Norfolk
Thos. 1675 w.
Thos. 1755 i.
Northampton
Francis 1654 w.
Michaell 1709 w.
Mary 1712 i.
David 1748 i.
Pittsylvania
Geo. 1781 w.
Haynes 1795 w.
Rappahannock
Evan 1684 w.
Richmond
Wm. 1749 i.
Anthony 1750 i.
Andrew 1795 i.
Shenandoah
Maurice 1779 i.
Southampton
Wm. 1762 w.
Jno. 1773 i.
Jno. 1780 w.
Jno. 1781 w.
Wm. 1783 i.
Foster 1787 w.
Sussex
Jno. 1781 w.
Westmoreland
Jno. 1666 w.
Mary 1734 i.
Jno. 1778 w.
Benj. 1787 i.
York
Francis 1656 i.
Ellinor 1700 i.
MORGERT
Loudoun
Philip 1779 i.
MORGIN
Bedford
Thomas 1774 w.
Essex
John, Sr. 1734 w.
Richmond
Wm. 1726 w.
Westmoreland
Jno. 1778 w.
Danl. 1789 w.
MORIN
Norfolk
Wm. 1745 nw.

MORING
Surry
Wm. 1783 i.
Benj. 1787 i.
Henry 1787 i.
Henry 1799 w.
Jno. 1799 w.
MORISON
Halifax
Theodore 1774 i.
MORLAND
Isle of Wight
Edward 1729 i.
John 1743 i.
York
Jno. 1720 i.
Matthew 1755 w.
Jno. 1780 i.
MORLEY
Frederick
Charles 1748 a.
MORNIE
Northampton
Jno. 1720 w.
Wm. 1728 i.
MOROE
Westmoreland
Geo. 1773 i.
MOROR
Fauquier
Alexander 1786 i.
MORPHY
Orange
Miles 1741 a.
MORRAH
Rappahannock
Jno. 1683 w.
MORRAIN
Accomack
Jno. 1720 i.
MORRELL
Surry
Thos. 1719 w.
MORRES
King George
Jno. 1721 i.
MORRICE
York
Jno. 1720 ab.
MORRIL
Accomack
Esau 1751 i.
Wm. 1751 i.
MORRIS
Accomack
Dennis 1693 i.
Jno. 1696 w.
Eliz. 1703 w.
Dennis 1716 w.
Ester 1722 i.
Anne 1724 w.

Gilbert 1744 i.
Albemarle
Hugh 1774 w.
Jno. 1774 w.
Jno. 1784 i.
Amelia
Isaac Sr. 1750 w.
Isaac 1772 i.
Bedford
Daniel 1767 w.
Tabithy 1778 w.
Daniel 1794 i.
Brunswick
Wm. 1746 i.
Aebedona 1758 i.
Richd. 1774 i.
Wm. 1778 i.
James 1779 w.
Henry 1783 w.
James 1787 i.
Thos. 1793 a.
Charlotte
Joshua 1791 w.
Culpeper
William 1771 w.
Mary 1795 w.
Essex
John 1720 i.
Benj. 1721 i.
Frederick
Samuel 1749 w.
Elizabeth 1760 w.
James 1761 i.
Edward 1786 i.
Greensville
Thomas 1783 w.
Thomas 1784 w.
Henrico
Ann 1686 i.
Ann 1701-2 i.
Henry
Joseph 1796 w.
Isle of Wight
William 1672 w.
Richard 1677 i.
John 1711 w.
John 1772 w.
Lancaster
Wm. 1728 w.
John 1745 w.
Louisa
Silvanus 1746 w.
Geo. 1786 w.
Loudoun
John 1787 w.
Middlesex
Thos. 1710 i.
Norfolk
Thomas 1685 w.
John 1722 w.
Thomas 1761 w.

Northampton
Jacob 1751 i.
Orange
Thos. 1789 w.
Northumberland
Nicholas 1664 w.
Wm. 1759 i.
Pittsylvania
Benj. 1794 w.
Prince Edward
Isaac 1784 w.
Jas. 1798 i.
Princess Anne
Josiah 1701 i.
Thos. 1701 w.
Josiah 1703 a.
Jno. 1733 i.
Jno. 1741 w.
Wm. 1753 w.
Hillory 1763 w.
Thos. 1773 i.
Willis 1776 w.
Wm. Sr. 1790 w.
Jonathan 1791 w.
Josiah 1792 w.
Wm. 1792 i.
Dinah 1793 w.
Cader 1795 w.
John 1797 w.
Prince William
Ann 1743 w.
Richmond
Edwd. 1752 w.
Jno. Sr. 1799 i.
Southampton
Nicholas 1799 w.
Spotsylvania
Thos. 1742 w.
Jacob 1751 a.
Moses 1787 a.
Westmoreland
Jno. 1713 w.
Abraham 1725 w.
Elias 1726 w.
Jno. 1730 i.
Chas. 1797 w.
York
Geo. 1672 i.
Owen 1697 w.
Ann 1704 w.
Jno. 1734 i.
Jno. 1739 w.
Benj. 1741 i.
Eliz. 1743 w.
Jno. 1746 w.
Eliz. 1748 w.
Bethiah 1765 w.
Jno. 1765 w.
Jno. 1767 i.

MORRISBY
York
Mary 1690 i.
MORRISET
Chesterfield
Eliz. 1746 w.
Henrico
Peter 1734 i.
Princess Anne
Peter 1748 i.
MORRISETT
Chesterfield
Jno. 1782 w.
David 1793 w.
Goochland
Wm. 1797 w.
MORRISON
Accomack
Jno. 1799 w.
Albemarle
Wm. 1761 w.
Amherst
James 1763 w.
Jno. 1785 w.
Wm. 1785 w.
Jas. 1790 w.
Jno. 1795 w.
Berkeley
William 1781 i.
Elizabeth 1792 i.
Brunswick
Mercer 1796 i.
Culpeper
Hugh 1750 i.
Frederick
Andrew 1762 i.
Greenbrier
John 1798 i.
Isle of Wight
William 1761 i.
King George
Jno. 1747 i.
Jno. 1752 i.
Wm. 1759 nw.
Wm. 1760 i.
Mecklenburg
Alex. 1778 w.
Norfolk
Henry 1746 w.
Northumberland
Richd. 1799 w.
Orange
Fendley 1768 w.
Wm. 1783 w.
Thomas 1790 i.
Thomas 1793 i.
Spotsylvania
David 1748 a.
MORRISS
Berkeley
Elizabeth 1792 w.

Brunswick
Thos. 1789 w.
Loudoun
Jacob 1775.i.
Louisa
Geo. Stuart 1780 i.
Norfolk
James 1799 w.
Princess Anne
Cornelius 1789 w.
Westmoreland
Richd. 1717 i.
Francis 1718 i.
Saml. 1719 i.
Chas. 1797 i.
MORRISSETT
Princess Anne
John 1796 w.
MORRO
Brooke
William 1799 w.
MORROUGH
Accomack
Eliz. 1726 i.
Danl. 1728 i.
MORROW
Berkeley
Charles 1792 w.
Charles 1797 i.
Greenbrier
James 1798 w.
Norfolk
David Jr. 1692 w.
Jno. 1744-5 w.
MORRYES
Albemarle
Lawrence 1754 i.
MORS
Westmoreland
Obediah 1784 i.
MORSE
Essex
William 1753 i.
Isle of Wight
Richard 1722 i.
Princess Anne
Francis 1716 w.
Baron 1735 w.
Thos. 1766 w.
Thos. 1771 i.
Jno. 1772 w.
Thos. 1772 w.
Lazarus 1788 w.
Wm. 1788 w.
Frances 1790 w.
Francis 1791 i.
Barbra 1795 w.
Richmond
Thos. 1794 i.
Westmoreland
Obediah 1777 i.

MORSELEY
York
Mary 1690 i.
MORSHAM
Cumberland
John 1755 w.
MORSSUM
Cumberland
John 1755 i.
MORTAN
Frederick
Bernard 1770 a.
MORTIMER
Loudoun
Wm. 1779 nw.
Northampton
Geo. 1679 w.
MORTIMORE
Loudoun
Arthur 1765 i.
MORTON
Charlotte
Saml. 1765 w.
Jos. 1782 w.
Chas. 1783 i.
Josiah 1785 w.
Essex
Jno. 1748 w.
Fairfax
Andrew 1778 i.
Jane 1798 i.
Halifax
Joseph 1753 w.
Henrico
Thos. 1731 w.
Jno. 1752 w.
King George
Geo. 1765 w.
Jno. 1795 i.
Norfolk
Anne 1682 w.
Orange
Geo. 1744 a.
Wm. 1748 w.
Jeremiah 1757 i.
Prince Edward
Jno. 1796 w.
Richmond
Jno. 1722 w.
Westmoreland
Wm. 1794 i.
Richd. 1732 w.
Wm. 1793 w.
Mercy 1734 i.
Richmond
Jas. 1760 w.
Thos. 1777 w.
Jno. 1728 i.
Jas. 1799 i.

MORYSON
Westmoreland
Henry 1733 i.
MOSBY
Cumberland
Stephen 1763 w.
Edwd. 1769 i.
Benj. 1771 w.
Micajah 1772 w.
Jos. 1775 i.
Goochland
Richd. 1746 w.
Henrico
Benj. 1783 i.
Robt. 1788 i.
Powhatan
Jacob 1781 w.
Hezekiah 1787 w.
Geo. 1798 i.
Robt. 1798 w.
Prince George
Jos. 1727 w.
MOSCROP
Isle of Wight
Thomas 1723 w.
Susanna 1745 w.
MOSEBY
Powhatan
Susanna 1782 w.
MOSELEY
Brunswick
Wm. 1776 w.
Ann 1777 i.
Benj. 1785 w.
Chesterfield
Jos. 17— w.
Wm. 17— i.
Matthew 1768 w.
Wm. 1772 i.
Wm. 1778 w.
Thos. 1780 w.
Matthew 1789 w.
Cumberland
Benj. 1757 i.
Wm. 1763 w.
Arthur 1770 w.
Essex
Wm. 1700 w.
Robt. 1707 i.
Wm. 1707 i.
Benj. 1709 w.
Eliz. 1709-10 w.
Jno. 1717 i.
Edwd. 1727 w.
Jno. 1736 w.
Benj. 1737 i.
Eliz. 1739 w.
Henrico
Arthur 1730 w.
Robt. 1734 w.
Arthur 1736 w.

Middlesex
Marvel 1721 w.
Norfolk
Susanna 1655 i.
Wm. 1655 w.
Wm. 1671 i.
Arthur 1702 w.
William 1753 w.
Arthur 1757 w.
Chris. 1758 w.
Arthur 1761 i.
Bassett 1782 w.
William 1782 w.
Eliz. 1794 w.
Eliz. 1795 w.
Edward 1793 w.
Powhatan
Richd. 1782 w.
Benj. 1791 w.
Mary 1791 w.
Thos. 1795 w.
Arthur 1797 w.
Geo. 1798 w.
Princess Anne
Wm. 1699 w.
Wm. 1705 i.
Richd. 1712 i.
Wm. 1713 i.
Benj. 1717 w.
Geo. 1718 i.
Edwd. 1719 w.
Margt. 1723 w.
Tully 1724 i.
Jno. 1725 w.
Hillary 1730 w.
Geo. 1731 i.
Anthony 1735 w.
Edwd. 1735 w.
Isabella 1740 w.
Jno. 1740 w.
Francis 1756 w.
Frances 1759 i.
Hewlett 1762 i.
Francis 1763 i.
Anthy. 1771 w.
Jno. 1771 w.
Jno. 1773 i.
Tully 1773 w.
Wm. 1773 w.
Robt. 1774 w.
Tully 1775 i.
Abia 1777 w.
Edward Hack 1782 w.
Edwd. 1783 w.
Edwd. Hack 1783 w.
Wm. 1783 w.
Edwd. 1785 w.
Charles 1789 i.
Wm. 1790 i.
Hillary 1794 w.
Hillary 1797 w.

MOSELY
Northumberland
Jno. 1669 w.
Prince William
Robert 1787 w.
Brunswick
Geo. 1758 i.
MOSER
Augusta
Geo. 1758 a.
Peter 1758 i.
Eliz. 1765 i.
MOSES
Accomack
Austin 1752 nw.
MOSEY
Norfolk
John 1753 w.
MOSIER
Norfolk
Thos. 1679 w.
MOSLEY
Norfolk
Joseph 1712 w.
Wm. 1788 i.
Northumberland
Henry 1656 w.
Goochland
Marvil 1753 w.
Jno. 1754 i.
MOSS
Brunswick
Stephen 1758 i.
Cumberland
Wm. 1754 w.
Dorraty 1764 w.
Alex. 1772 w.
Essex
Jno. 1697 w.
Robt. 1714 w.
Wm. 1753 w.
Fairfax
Sarah 1778 w.
Thomas 1778 w.
Goochland
Rebecca 1771 w.
Hugh 1780 w.
Jno. 1785 w.
Halifax
David 1780 i.
Isle of Wight
Thomas 1669 w.
King George
Jno. 1785 w.
Thos. 1785 a.
Jno. 1796 i.
Loudoun
John 1768 w.
Louisa
Jno. 1758 w.
Jno. 1796 w.

Wm. 1797 i.
Lunenburg
Wm. 1753 w.
Jno. 1774 i.
Powhatan
James 1785 w.
Mary 1790 w.
Rappahannock
Thos. 1678 w.
Wm., Sr. 1685 w.
Southampton
Henry 1782 i.
Stafford
Jno. 1736 i.
Wm., Sr. 1746 w.
Surry
Jno. 1734 w.
Wm. 1746 i.
Sussex
Wm. 1758 i.
Benj. 1761 i.
Jno. 1761 w.
James 1772 i.
Mary 1775 w.
Jno. 1776 w.
Seth 1777 w.
Eliz. 1782 w.
Henry 1782 w.
Sampson 1782 i.
Joanna 1784 w.
Wm. 1786 w.
Edmund 1789 w.
Ephraim 1792 w.
Washington
Matthew 1780 i.
Westmoreland
Roger 1707 i.
Richd. 1728 w.
York
Edwd. 1716 w.
Jno. 1716 w.
Wm. 1718 w.
Jno. 1727 i.
Benj. 1735 w.
Eliz. 1736 w.
Benj. 1737 w.
Benj., Jr. 1737 i.
Edwd. 1738 i.
Francis 1741 i.
Robt. 1752 i.
Edwd. 1754 i.
Edwd. 1758 i.
Eliz. 1760 w.
Chas. 1761 nw.
Jas. 1762 w.
Benj. 1768 w.
Amey 1772 w.
Jno. 1772 i.
Wm. 1772 i.
Jno. 1782 i.
Edwd. 1785 w.

Edwd. 1786 w.
Benj. 1791 w.
Jno. 1796 w.
Mary 1799 w.
MOSSELEY
Princess Anne
Benj. 1753 i.
MOSSEY
Prince Edward
Shearwood 1782 i.
MOSSOM
Albemarle
Eliz. 1758 i.
MOTHERSHEAD
King George
Geo. 1747 i.
Elinor 1757 i.
Orange
Nathaniel 1781 w.
Richmond
Alvin 1735 w.
Stafford
Jonathan 1703 i.
Westmoreland
Brooks 1718 i.
Jno. 1731 w.
Jno. 1741 w.
Chris. 1745 w.
Wm. 1746 w.
Jno. 1750 w.
Chas. 1756 w.
MOTLEY
Amelia
Jos. 1763 w.
Sarah 1784 w.
Jos. 1793 i.
Paschal 1799 i.
Essex
Jno. 1736 w.
Essex
Wm. 1739 w.
Essex
Eliz. 1742 w.
John 1742 i.
Pittsylvania
Abraham 17— i.
Rappahannock
Jno. 1684 i.
MOTLIN
Rappahannock
Jno. 1684 w.
MOTT
Lancaster
Jno. 1698 w.
Jno., Sr. 1732 w.
John 1754 w.
Joseph 1775 i.
Thomas 1796 w.
Northumberland
Randolph 1743 i.
Mosley 1757 w.

Wm. 1765 i.
Isaac 1770 nw.
Wm. 1786 i.
Betty 1789 w.
Randolph 1789 w.
Eliz. 1793 i.
Moseley 1793 w.
Rappahannock
Geo. 1674 w.
Jno. 1677 w.
MOTTLEY
Pittsylvania
Abraham 1781 i.
MOTTROM
Northumberland
Jno. 1657 i.
MOUAT
Norfolk
Walter 1741 w.
MOUGHON
Lancaster
Patrick 1763 w.
James 1775 w.
MOUHON
Lancaster
Absolum 1759 i.
MOULD
Lancaster
Margaret 1722 w.
MOULIN
York
Gawin 1659 i.
MOULSON
Amelia
Wm. 1775 w.
Mary 1794 w.
Wm. 1797 i.
MOULSON
Middlesex
Richd. 1730 w.
MOULTON
Westmoreland
Thos. 1673 w.
MOUNGER
Southampton
Robt. 1752 w.
MOUNT
Frederick
Richard 1752 w.
MOUNTAGUE
Essex
Thomas 1721 w.
John 1733 i.
Orange
Peter 1746 w.
MOUNTCASTLE
Charles City
Joab 1773 w.
MOUNTFIELD
Frederick
Robert 1751 i.

MOUNTFORT
Southampton
Thos. 1787 w.
York
Thos. 1708 ab.
Jos. 1738 w.
Rose 1751 w.
Thos. 1757 w.
Thos. 1761 i.
MOUNTGOMERY
Augusta
Jas. 1757 a.
Botetourt
Samuel 1777 i.
Prince William
Thomas 1792 w.
MOUNTJOY
Fauquier
Edward 1778 i.
Richmond
Alvin 1700 w.
Alvin 1761 i.
Eleanor 1777 w.
MOUNTNEY
Lancaster
Hannah 1659 i.
MOUNTONY
Augusta
Saml. 1758 w.
MOURER
Shenandoah
[Widow] 1785 i.
Michael 1786 a.
MOURIN
Shenandoah
Mary 1785 w.
MOURNING
Norfolk
Michael 1799 i.
MOUSE
Augusta
Danl. 1751 a.
Geo. 1758 i.
Geo. 1760 a.
MOVIGNAUD
Princess Anne
Sarah 1720 a.
MOXEY
Prince Edward
Selvannis 1770 w.
MOXLEY
Fairfax
Ann 1750 a.
Thomas 1750 w.
Richard 1758 i.
William 1752 w.
Daniel 1761 w.
Thomas 1787 w.
King George
Alvin 1781 a.
Ann Dent 1795 i.

Loudoun
Joseph 1792 w.
Spotsylvania
Wm. 1789 a.
Westmoreland
Jos. 1735 w.
Wm. 1744 w.
Alex. 1762 w.
Edwd. 1768 i.
Jno. 1771 w.
Danl. 1774 w.
Richd. 1777 w.
Richd. 1784 i.
Jno. 1787 i.
Augustine 1797 w.
Richd. 1797 i.
MOXSON
Isle of Wight
Robert 1735 i.
MOXUM
Spotsylvania
Matthews 1727 a.
MOY
Augusta
Caleb 1767 a.
Princess Anne
Jno. 1723 w.
Richd. 1733 w.
MOYE
Norfolk
John 1644 i.
Northampton
Roger 1646 i.
MOYER
Botetourt
Henry 1793 i.
Jacob 1795 i.
MOYERS
Frederick
Stephen 1797 w.
Shenandoah
Henry 1773 a.
MOZINGO
Richmond
Edwd. 1712 w.
Edwd. 1754 w.
Edwd. 1783 w.
Edwd. 1795 w.
MUCKENTREE
York
Richd. 1740 nw.
MUCKLEROY
Westmoreland
Elix. 1718 w.
MUIR
Accomack
Adam 1772 w.
Francina 1785 w.
Fairfax
James 1780 w.

James 1783 i.
John 1791 w.
George 1794 i.
Loudoun
Robert 1778 w.
MULDROUGH
Augusta
Andrew 1759 w.
MULHEIES
Culpeper
John 1757 i.
MULL
Botetourt
James 1782 w.
Loudoun
David 1795 w.
MULLABIN
Norfolk
James 1668 w.
MULLEUS
Middlesex
Jno. 1717 w.
MULLIKEN
Norfolk
Jas. 1686-7 w.
MULLIN
Westmoreland
Peter 1787 i.
MULLINAX
Goochland
Jno. 1745 i.
MULLINER
Berkeley
Nathaniel 1797 i.
MULLINGS
Westmoreland
Geo. 1745 i.
MULLINS
Charlotte
Jas. 1771 i.
Jno. 1772 w.
Essex
Wm. 1794 i.
Goochland
Jno. 1783 w.
Henry 1798 i.
Jno. 1798 i.
Hanover
Wm. 1734 w.
Henrico
Wm. 1752 i.
Middlesex
Wm. 1711 w.
Wm. 1776 w.
Westmoreland
Rachel 1761 w.
Peter 1784 w.
Wm. 1784 i.
MULLIS
Lancaster
Stephen 1761 w.

MULLISS
Lancaster
Stephen 1713 i.
MULLS
Northampton
Jno. 1697 w.
MUMFORD
Amelia
Thos. 1787 w.
King George
Wm. 1745 i.
Wm. 1782 w.
MUNCASTER
Rappahannock
Henry 1684 i.
MUNCH
Shenandoah
Philip 1798 i.
MUNDAY
Essex
Thos. 1703 w.
Thos. 1719 i.
Jno. 1739 w.
Chas. 1747 i.
Mary 1748 w.
Wm. 1748 i.
Jos. 1750 i.
Jas. 1767 i.
Thos. 1769 i.
Jane 1784 w.
Stephen 1784 w.
Fairfax
William 1782 w.
Frederick
Thomas 1771 i.
King George
Thos. 1754 a.
MUNDELL
Isle of Wight
Frances 1750 w.
Southampton
John 1786 w.
York
Jno. 1745 w.
MUNDEN
Princess Anne
Jno. 1752 w.
Aquillo 1765 i.
Nathan 1798 w.
MUNDS
Norfolk
Sarah 1719 i.
John 1734 i.
Sussex
Jno. 1768 a.
MUNFORD
Amelia
Jas. 1754 w.
Robt. 1771 w.
Thos. Bolling 1780 w.
Robt. 1782 i.

Thos. 1785 w.
Wm. 1788 i.
Isle of Wight
Elizabeth 1792 w.
Mecklenburg
Robt. 1784 w.
Sussex
Thos. 1763 w.
MUNGAR
Accomack
Catherine 1795 i.
MUNGER
Surry
Nathaniel 1731 w.
MUNGOR
Isle of Wight
John 1670 w.
MUNK
Northampton
Geo. 1744 i.
Wm. 1750 i.
MUNKE
Northampton
Wm., Sr. 1716 i.
MUNN
Westmoreland
Thos. 1659 w.
MUNNS
Amelia
Robt. 1754 a.
MUNROE
Fairfax
John 1792 i.
MUNS
Amelia
Robt. 1754 i.
Norfolk
Joseph 1717 i.
MUNSEY
Wythe
Skidmore 1797 i.
MUNSH
Shenandoah
Philip 1796 w.
MUNTGALL
Washington
Richard 1797 i.
MURAY
Frederick
George 1796 i.
MURCHLAND
Brooke
Robert 1797 w.
MURDEN
Norfolk
Jno. 1695 w.
Edward 1735 w.
John 1750 w.
Maximillion 1756 i.
Martha 1763 w.
Jeremiah 1777 w.

John 1782 w.
Princess Anne
Robt. 1726 i.
Robt. 1776 w.
Jno. 1782 i.
James 1793 w.
Jeremiah 1798 w.
MURDIN
Princess Anne
Zachariah 1797 w.
MURDOCK
King George
Jeremiah 1752 w.
Jas. 1770 eb.
Jean (Jane) 1770 w.
Jos. 1770 w.
Mary 1784 w.
Stafford
Jno. 1759 w.
MURFEE
Norfolk
Jno. 1675 w.
Southampton
Richd. 1782 i.
Richd. 1789 w.
Simon 1796 w.
Stafford
Dennis 1705 i.
MURFEY
Shenandoah
Patrick 1787 i.
Surry
Simon 1754 w.
MURFFEY
Westmoreland
Bryant 1715 i.
Wm. 1719 i.
Eliz. 1721 i.
MURFREE
Isle of Wight
Sarah 1742 w.
Southampton
Simon 1796 i.
MURFREY
Isle of Wight
John 1721 w.
MURLEY
Frederick
Charles 1749 i.
Charles 1750 i.
MURPHEE
Southampton
James 1782 w.
MURPHERY
Isle of Wight
William, Jr. 1715 i.
MURPHEW
Northumberland
Danl. 1711 i.

MURPHY
Augusta
Danl. 1752 a.
Jno. 1764 i.
Bedford
Thomas 1778 w.
MURPHEY
Frederick
Thomas 1750 i.
Halifax
Jno. 1787 i.
Isle of Wight
John 1772 w.
John 1788 w.
Northumberland
Wm. 1750-1 i.
Thos. 1753 i.
Margaret 1771 i.
MURPHIE
Northumberland
Darbie 1748 i.
MURPHREE
Southampton
James 1783 i.
MURPHREY
Isle of Wight
William 1789 w.
MURPHRY
Isle of Wight
Michael 1747 i.
MURPHY
Amherst
Saml. 1770 a.
Berkeley
William 1782 i.
John 1799 w.
Culpeper
Silvester 1792 i.
Frederick
Henry 1753 a.
Darby 1769 w.
Henrico
Jas. 1794 i.
Isle of Wight
Sarah 1787 w.
Loudoun
Michael 1785 w.
Mecklenburg
Jno. 1771 w.
Northampton
Bridget 1734 i.
Danl. 1741 i.
Westmoreland
Maurice 1741 i.
Jno. 1742 w.
Jas. 1745-6 i.
Jno. 1750 w.
MURRAH
Isle of Wight
Ann 1700 nw.

Northumberland
Wm. 1719 w.
Richmond
Jeremiah 1765 w.
MURRAY
Accomack
Jno. 1735 w.
David 1788 i.
Botetourt
John 1775 w.
Fairfax
Joseph 1790 i.
Isle of Wight
Ann 1701 i.
Adam 1706-7 i.
Amey 1797 i.
Mecklenburg
Jno. 1782 w.
Susanna 1795 i.
Middlesex
Jno. 1768 i.
Frances 1780 w.
Rachel 1784 w.
Wm. 1787 w.
Jack 1788 w.
Robt. 1790 i.
Robt. 1795 i.
Norfolk
David 1693 w.
Prince Edward
Danl. 1793 i.
Princess Anne
Jno. 1728 i.
Jno. 1731 w.
Richd. 1777 w.
Matthews 1784 i.
Chris. 1791 w.
John 1791 w.
Prince William
John 1783 w.
Southampton
Alexander 1784 w.
Mary 1792 w.
MURRE
Isle of Wight
John 1719 w.
MURRELL
Charles City
Thomas 1790 w.
Goochland
Joseph 1741 i.
Lunenburg
Wm. 1780 w.
Jno. 1782 w.
Jas. 1782 i.
MURRER
Surry
Wm. 1716 w.
MURREY
Amelia

Sarah 1795 w.
Augusta
Adam 1785 w.
Isle of Wight
William 1728 i.
Princess Anne
Caleb 1758 w.
Stafford
Anthony 1750 w.
MURRILL
Albemarle
Geo. 1789 w.
MURROUGH
Accomack
Timothy 1728 i.
MURROW
Amherst
Richd. 1797 i.
Richmond
Andrew 1740 w.
MURRY
Amelia
Richd. 1783 i.
Augusta
Adam 1786 i.
Culpeper
James 1776 w.
Fauquier
James 1783 w.
Isle of Wight
John 1720 i.
John 1724 w.
John 1729 i.
George 1734 i.
Thomas 1740 w.
Sarah 1756 i.
William [1762?] i.
John 1763 w.
Ann 1781 w.
Thomas 1783 i.
Middlesex
Molly 1780 w.
Norfolk
John 1746 i.
Princess Anne
Abigail 1799 w.
MURRGE
Isle of Wight
Alexander 1698 i.
MUSCOE
Essex
Salvator 1741 w.
Mary 1750 i.
MUSCROP
Isle of Wight
Thomas 1723 i.
Susanna 1753 a.
MUSE
Lancaster
Thomas 1755 w.
John 1761 i.

Northumberland
Wm. 1789 i.
Richmond
Danl. 1784 w.
Westmoreland
Jno. 1723 w.
Ann 1726 w.
Thos. 1732 w.
Thos. 1734 w.
Eliz. 1735 w.
Chris. 1736 w.
Jno. 1751 w.
Thos. 1762 i.
Thos., Jr. 1763 i.
Jno. 1770 w.
Jno. 1772 w.
Nicho. 1774 w.
Danl. 1777 i.
Nicho. 1779 w.
Edwd., Sr. 1782 w.
Richd. 1780 i.
Danl. 1782 i.
Jane 1782 w.
Jas. 1784 w.
Jesse 1784 i.
Geo. 1791 w.
Eliz. 1791 w.
Mary 1792 w.
Saml. 1794 w.
MUSGROVE
Fairfax
John 1746 w.
Frederick
John 1751 i.
Loudoun
William 1779 i.
William 1783 i.
Prince William
Lydia 1784 w.
MUSHATOE
Shenandoah
Anthony 1795 i.
MUSICK
Spotsylvania
Geo. 1754 w.
MUSKETT
Essex
James 1799 i.
MUSON
Botetourt
James 1783 i.
MUSTIAN
Pittsylvania
Thos. 1791 w.
Jesse 1798 i.
MUSTIN
King George
Thos. 1743 i.
Thos. 1745 i.
Thos. 1799 w.

Westmoreland
Wm. 1749 i.
MUTTOONE
Northumberland
Jno. 1680 w.
MYARS
Hardy
Henry 1793 w.
MYBORNE
Halifax
Jno. 1761 a.
MYCKE
Brunswick
Frances 1748 w.
MYER
Loudoun
George 1793 w.
MYERS
Albemarle
Chris. 1798 w.
Frederick
Charles 1772 i.
Gasper 1793 i.
Lancaster
Thomas 1795 w.
Loudoun
Jonathan 1790 w.
Benj. 1796 i.
John 1797 i.
Chris. 1799 i.
Norfolk
David 1799 i.
Shenandoah
Henry 1798 i.
MYLES
Berkeley
George 1776 i.
MYRICK
Brunswick
Owen 1795 w.
Southampton
Jno. 1771 w.
Mary 1781 w.
Owen 1786 w.
Henry 1795 i.
Ann 1796 w.
Wm. 1796 i.
Howell 1798 w.

N

NAFIES
Loudoun
Geo. 1787 i.
NAILOR
Ohio
Samuel 1792 w.
NAINLEY
Fairfax
Joseph 1792 a.

NAISH
Mecklenburg
Wm. 1796 w.
NALLE
Culpeper
Martin 1780 w.
John 1782 w.
Richard 1786 w.
Martin 1788 w.
Essex
Martin 1723 w.
Mary 1734 w.
Mary 1742 i.
NALLEY
Prince William
Aaron 1798 i.
NANCE
Brunswick
Wm. 1771 w.
Charles City
Zachariah 1772 w.
Essex
John 1731 w.
Lunenburg
Jno. 1762 w.
Fredk., Sr. 1796 w.
Pittsylvania
Jno. 1782 i.
David 1780 i.
Martha 1797 i.
Prince George
Jno. 1716 w.
NANGLE
Rappahannock
Geo. 1677 w.
NANNEY
Brunswick
Jno. 1789 w.
NANNY
Brunswick
Thos. 1781 i.
Mecklenburg
Wm. 1798 i.
NAPIER
Albemarle
Robt. 1763 w.
Patrick 1775 w.
Goochland
Rene 1751 w.
Booth, Sr. 1780 w.
Westmoreland
Geo. 1657 i.
York
Patrick 1669 w.
NAPPER
Montgomery
Thomas Hugh 1799 i.
NASH
Amherst
Enoch 1772 w.

Culpeper
Betty 1772 i.
William 1754 i.
Fauquier
Elijah 1777 w.
Henrico
Thos. 1737 w.
Lancaster
Thos. 1676 i.
Wm. 1698 i.
Amey 1710 w.
Wm. 1719 w.
Jno. 1734 w.
Middlesex
Jno. 1717 w.
Arthur 1718 w.
Norfolk
Thomas 1672 i.
Francis 1687-8 w.
Thomas 1735 i.
Solomon [1741] w.
Nathl. [1751?] w.
William 1751 w.
Caleb 1759 i.
Sarah 1759 w.
William 1771 w.
Thomas 1783 w.
John 1790 w.
Dinah 1791 w.
Thomas, Sr. 1794 w.
Ann 1795 w.
Thomas 1797 i.
Northumberland
Wm. 1655 w.
Wm. 1657 i.
Wm. 1750 w.
Prince Edward
Mary 1775 w.
Jno. 1776 w.
Jno., Sr. 1781 i.
Richmond
Thos. 1733 w.
Wm. 1733 w.
Wm. 1738 i.
Fielding 1744 w.
Thos. 1749 w.
Geo. 1760 i.
———— 1764 i.
Nathaniel 1787 w.
Geo. 1790 w.
Pitman 1799 i.
Surry
Wm. 1696 i.
Westmoreland
Robt. 1748 i.
Eliz. 1762 w.
Jno. 1758 i.
Jeremiah 1773 w.
Jno. 1778 i.
Jno. 1786 i.

NAUTY
Westmoreland
Jas. 1757 w.
NAUGHTY
Westmoreland
Jas. 1762 w.
Jno. 1768 w.
Jno. 1772 i.
NAUL
Washington
James 1778 i.
NAYLOR
King George
Jno. 1735 i.
Orange
Ann 1744 w.
Prince George
Simon 1727 i.
Richmond
Avery 1704 w.
Westmoreland
Michael 1757 i.
NEADOM
Accomack
Eliz. 1755 w.
NEAL
Albemarle
Nicholas 1756 i.
Amelia
Thos. 1736 w.
Stephen, Sr. 1740 w.
Roger 1750 w.
Thos. 1758 i.
Joel 1775 w.
David 1775 w.
Wm. 1778 w.
Wm. 1782 w.
Roger 1785 w.
Ann 1794 w.
Augusta
Jno. 1791 i.
Brunswick
Jno. 1791 w.
Chesterfield
Thos. 1764 w.
Essex
William 1730 i.
Fairfax
Charles 1745 a.
Lydia 1746 i.
Presly 1749 w.
Chris. 1764 i.
Shapleigh 1777 w.
Frederick
Hugh 1746 a.
Lancaster
John 1769 i.
Lunenburg
Jno. 1789 w.
Jno. 1795 i.

Prince Edward
Stephen 1795 w.
Richmond
Chas. 1718 w.
Chas. 1737 i.
Spotsylvania
Jane 1772 a.
NEALE
Bedford
Charles 1780 i.
Charlotte
Thomas 1798 w.
Chesterfield
Thos. 17— i.
Culpeper
Charles 1778 w.
Essex
Wm. 1729 w.
Fairfax
Chris. 1761 i.
Fauquier
Joseph 1784 w.
Benj. 1785 w.
Lancaster
Arthur 1744 i.
Presly 1792 i.
Loudoun
Robt. 1780 w.
Thomas 1789 i.
Norfolk
Samuel 1795 w.
Northampton
Henry 1678 i.
Northumberland
Danl. 1700 w.
Ebenezer 1711 a.
Chris. 1721 i.
Danl. 1727 w.
Peter 1728 i.
Richd. 1728-9 w.
Chris. 1745-6 i.
Shapleigh 1747 i.
Mathew 1780 w.
Richard 1782 w.
Presley 1784 nw.
Jno. 1785 w.
Richd. 1785 i.
Orange
Fielding 1792 i.
Prince William
John 1739 i.
Rodham 1742 w.
Richmond
———— 1724 i.
Robt. 1766 i.
Spotsylvania
Wm. 1728-9 a.
Westmoreland
Danl. 1713 w.
Thos. 1733 i.
Presley 1749 i.

Margt. 1755 w.
Danl. 1759 w.
Spence 1768 i.
Rodham 1778 i.
Danl. 1782 w.
Rodham 1782 i.
Richd. 1788 i.
Jno. 1793 i.
NEALEY
Frederick
William 1757 i.
NEALLEY
Botetourt
John 1778 w.
NEALMS
Northumberland
Jno. 1726-7 w.
NEALS
Norfolk
Morris 1749-50 i.
NEALY
Pittsylvania
Wm. 1788 w.
NEAS
Shenandoah
Adam 1797 w.
NEASOM
Lancaster
Samuel 1766 i.
NEASOME
Lancaster
Wm. 1760 i.
Northumberland
John 1766 i.
NEASUM
Lancaster
Robt. 1697 i.
Robt. 1743 w.
Robt. 1747 i.
Anne 1748 i.
NEATHERCOTE
Richmond
Robt. 1721 i.
NEAVES
Goochland
Wm. 1763 w.
NEAVIL
Fauquier
George 1774 w.
NEAVILL
Fauquier
John 1768 w.
Isle of Wight
Eliz. 1747 w.
NEAVILLE
Frederick
Robert 1763 i.
Isle of Wight
John 1740 w.

NECELEY
Shenandoah
Henry 1783 a.
NEDDOM
Accomack
Jno. 1745 i.
NEDHAM
Norfolk
Thos. 1655 w.
NEDLE
Westmoreland
Danl. 1759 i
NEDOM
Accomack
Edwd. 1738 i.
NEECH
Northampton
Danl. 1703 w.
NEEDHAM
Accomack
Michael 1718 i.
Augusta
Ann 1777 w.
Jno. 1777 w.
Jno., Sr. 1777 i.
NEEDLER
York
Thos. 1678-9 w.
NEEDLES
Middlesex
Wm. 1701 i.
Dorothy 1711 i.
NEELEY
Botetourt
Robert 1780 w.
NEELS
Halifax
Stephen 1776 w.
NEELSON
Middlesex
Charlotte 1791 w.
NEELY
Montgomery
William 1796 w.
Rockbridge
William 1782 w.
NEFF
Shenandoah
John Henry 1784 w.
NEIBERGER
Shenandoah
Christian 1787 w.
NEIGLEY
Augusta
Sebastian 1772 a.
NEILL
Frederick
John 1751 w.
John 1755 i.
Lewis 1776 w.
William 1779 w.

Joseph 1796 w.
John 1797 w.
NEILSON
Randolph
Charles 1796 i.
NEISHAM
Lancaster
Anthony 1660 i.
NELLSON
Northampton
Jno. 1716-17 w.
NELMES
Lancaster
Wm. 1741 i.
NELMS
Isle of Wight
Ann 1774 w.
John 1785 w.
John 1786 w.
Northumberland
Richd. 1711 w.
Richd. 1737 i.
Wm. 1751 w.
Aaron 1753 w.
Wm. 1753 i.
Eliza. 1761 w.
Samuel 1761 w.
Wm. 1761 w.
Eliza. 1763 w.
William 1768 w.
Charles 1776 i.
Eliza. 1780 w.
Chas. 1795 w.
NELSON
Accomack
Jane 1709 i.
Provis 1721 w.
Jno. 1772 w.
Provost 1778 w.
Isaac 1785 w.
Augusta
Jno. 1765 i.
Thos. 1781 i.
Cumberland
Matthew 1781 w.
Mary 1789 w.
Fauquier
James 1771 i.
William 1777 i.
John, Sr. 1784 w.
John, Sr. 1791 w.
Goochland
Wright 1793 i.
Greenbrier
William 1794 i.
Halifax
Saml. 1770 i.
Jno. 1783 i.
Henry
Thomas 1782 w.

Isle of Wight
Thomas 1784 i.
William 1784 i.
King George
Jno. [1776?] w.
Louisa
John 1791 i.
Benj. 1794 w.
Northampton
Provost 1686 w.
Jno. 1716 i.
Jno. 1722 w.
Jno. 1753 i.
Southy 1731 w.
Joshua 1744 w.
Pittsylvania
Ambrose 1799 w.
Princess Anne
Elijah 1787 w.
Richmond
Wm. 1710 w.
Jas. 1721 w.
Spotsylvania
James 1764 w.
Wm. 1782 w.
Stafford
Henry Sr. 1750 w.
Henry 1757 i.
Alex. 1760 i.
Surry
Wm. 1782 w.
Westmoreland
Jno. 1780 i.
Wm. 1796 w.
Wythe
John 1791 i.
York
Wm. 1750 i.
Wm. 1772 w.
Nathl. 1786 w.
Thos. 1789 w.
Eliz. 1798 w.
NEOMIAH
Accomack
Shae 1754 i.
NEOSAY
Norfolk
John 1724 i.
NERN
Surry
Eliz. 1773 w.
NESBET
Rockbridge
William 1795 w.
NETHERLAND
Cumberland
Wade 1769 w.
Wade 1773 w.
Goochland
Sarah 1745 w.

Powhatan
Benj. 1780 w.
NETHERY
Mecklenburg
Thos. 1798 w.
NETHERTON
Westmoreland
Henry 1717 i.
NEVEL
Isle of Wight
John 1730 w.
NEVES
Goochland
Christian 1792 w.
Sussex
Susannah 1799 w.
NEVILL
Albemarle
James 1752 w.
Isle of Wight
John 1740 i.
Joseph 1782 i.
NEVILLE
Amherst
James 1780 w.
NEVINS
Chesterfield
Saml. 1781 w.
NEVISON
Brunswick
Jno. 1769 w.
NEW
Charles City
Richd. 1796 w.
Henrico
Edmund 1726 w.
Edmund 1727 w.
Wm. 1785 i.
Greensville
Edith 1795 i.
NEWBALL
Essex
Jas. 1699 w.
NEWBERRY
Accomack
Jno. 1749 i.
Montgomery
Samuel 1788 w.
Ohio
Thomas 1777 w.
NEWBILL
Essex
Geo. 1744 w.
Nathaniel 1743 w.
James 1770 w.
Thomas 1777 w.
Thos. 1779 w.
NEWBOROUGH
Frederick
John 1798 i.

NEWBOURGH
Richmond
Henry John 1714 w.
NEWBY
Chesterfield
Jno. 1786 i.
Wm. 1794 w.
Elijah 1796 w.
Jas. 1798 i.
Isle of Wight
Thomas 1798 w.
Lancaster
Henry 1741 w.
Mary 1762 w.
Henry 1764 i.
Robert 1772 nw.
James 1791 w.
Ozwald 1791 w.
John 1795 i.
Surry
Edwd. 1702 i.
NEWCOM
Albemarle
John 1797 i.
NEWCOMB
Henrico
Thos. 1688 i.
Richd. 1708 a.
NEWCOME
Henrico
Richd. 1698 i.
NEWELL
Fauquier
Benj. 1782 w.
Loudoun
Sarah 1786 w.
Montgomery
James 1786 w.
Samuel 1777 a.
Norfolk
Henry 1680 w.
Spotsylvania
Wm. 1793 w.
Stafford
Adam 1786 w.
Westmoreland
Jno. 1698 w.
York
Jonahan 1679 i.
NEWET
Surry
Wm. 1772 w.
NEWGENT
Fauquier
Thomas 1790 w.
Edward 1791 w.
King George
Edwd. 1729 i.
Frances 1759 w.
Westmoreland
Elias 1717 w.

NEWHOOK
Norfolk
Dinah 1757 w.
NEWHOUSE
Fauquier
Benj. 1794 i.
Surry
Thos. 1680 a.
NEWITT
Surry
Wm. 1713 w.
Eliz. 1719 w.
NEWKIRK
Frederick
Bennett 1765 w.
NEWLAND
Shenandoah
Daniel 1788 w.
NEWMAN
Amelia
Richd. 1782 w.
James 1784 w.
Augusta
Jonathan 1748 a.
Culpeper
James 1777 w.
Essex
Elias 1749 i.
Elias 1750 w.
Elias 1759 w.
Northumberland
Robt. 1655 w.
Prince George
Richd. 1725 w.
Isle of Wight
John 1695 w.
Ruth 1699 i.
Thomas 1740 w.
John 1783 w.
Thomas 1798 i.
Norfolk
Alice 1689 w.
Northampton
Matthew 1713-14 w.
Prince William
Thomas 1778 i.
Rappahannock
Jno. 1677 w.
NEWMAN
Richmond
Alex. 1711 nw.
Geo. 1734 w.
Jno. 1759 i.
Geo. 1784 w.
York
Wm. 1670 w.
Nathl. 1717 i.
Jas. 1724 i.
Jane 1726 nw.
Thos. 1798 i.

NEWMARCH
Westmoreland
Jonathan 1762 w.
Thos. 1785 i.
NEWPORT
Frederick
John 1750 i.
Orange
Jno. 1747 i.
NEWSOM
Lancaster
Robt. 1695 w.
Wm. 1700 w.
Robt. 1745 i.
Richmond
Benj. 1789 w.
Southampton
Robt. 1757 w.
Benj. 1762 i.
Priscilla 1763 i.
Jos. 1766 w.
David 1768 w.
Jacob 1778 w.
Patience 1798 w.
Surry
Geo. 1696 i.
Sussex
Charlotte 1789 w.
Isle of Wight
William 1736 i.
NEWSUM
Isle of Wight
Thomas 1745 w.
Southampton
Elizabeth 1755 w.
Nathan 1762 i.
Sampson 1779 w.
Surry
Jno. 1724 w.
Wm. 1751 w.
Jno. 1770 w.
Joseph 1771 i.
Wm. 1776 w.
Wm. 1779 i.
Sussex
Thos. 1785 w.
NEWTON
Accomack
Jos. 1691 w.
Jos. 1695 w.
Jos. 1699 i.
Sterling 1710 i.
Abriliho 1758 w.
Augusta
Jonathan 1749 a.
Cumberland
John 1795 i.
Essex
Henry 1713 w.
Eliz. 1718 w.
Henry 1733 w.

Mecklenburg
Henry 1783 w.
Norfolk
Lemuel 1721 i.
George 1762 w.
Wilson 1762 w.
Northampton
Robt. 1642 w.
Jonathan 1687 i.
Chris. 1721 w.
Princess Anne
James 1731 i.
Nathl. 1767 i.
Rebecca 1779 w.
Lemuel 1782 w.
Richmond
Edwd. 1710 w.
Gerard 1711 i.
Southampton
Wm. 1761 i.
Alice 1798 i.
Spotsylvania
Edmund 1797 a.
James 1799 w.
Stafford
Jno. 1700 i.
Benj. 1732 i.
Surry
Saml. 1703 w.
Washington
Shadrack 1785 i.
Westmoreland
Jno. 1697 w.
Jno. (2) 1697 w.
Rose 1712 w.
Wm. 1722 w.
Thos. 1727 w.
Jno. 1767 w.
Willoughby 1767 w.
Wm. 1782 i.
Jno. 1786 i.
NIBLET
Accomack
Richd. 1700 w.
Burnal 1728 w.
Caleb 1770 nw.
NIBLETT
Lunenburg
Francis 1777 w.
Southampton
James 1779 i.
NICADEMAS
Frederick
Fredk. 1771 a.
NICHEL
Augusta
Jno. 1774 w.
NICHOLAS
Augusta
Saml. 1772 w.
Saml. 1775 i.

Goochland
Nicholas 1733 i.
Fairfax
George 1762 w.
Norfolk
Andrew 1655 w.
Henry 1677 w.
Eliz. 1684 w.
Isaiah 1789 w.
Princess Anne
Wm. 1730 w.
Jno. 1744 w.
Jno. 1747 w.
Nathl. Sr. 1747 w.
Andrew 1754 w.
Susanna 1780 i.
Nathl. 1792 i.
Richmond
Hannabal 1718 i.
Spotsylvania
Nich. 1733 a.
NICHOLASON
Brunswick
Robt. 1773 w.
NICHOLDS
Richmond
Chas. 1739 i.
NICHOLES
Richmond
Chas. 1762 i.
Thos. 1762 i.
NICHOLLS
King George
Saml. 1729 i.
Middlesex
Jno. 1705 w.
Henry 1718 i.
Northumberland
Wm. 1652 i.
Norfolk
Jno. Sr. 1750 w.
Northampton
Wm. 1683 i.
Rappahannock
Geo. 1677 w.
Richmond
Zachariah 1713 i.
Surry
Roger 1708 i.
NICHOLS
Bedford
Nehemiah 1794 i.
Halifax
Jno. 1774 w.
Bird 1786 a.
Lancaster
John 1779 w.
Loudoun
James 1791 w.
Henry 1794 w.

Norfolk
Richd. 1677 w.
Jno. 1697 w.
Henry 1772 w.
Powhatan
Mathias 1790 w.
Princess Anne
Richd. 1761 i.
Lunenburg
Wm. 1763 w.
Shenandoah
Richard 1792 w.
NICHOLSON
Accomack
Wm. 1728 w.
Geo. 1753 i.
Wm. 1761 i.
Wm. 1765 i.
Frederick
John 1757 i.
George 1795 w.
Goochland
Joshua 1796 w.
Isle of Wight
Richard 1673 i.
Louisa
Samuel 1797 w.
Mecklenburg
Henry 1799 w.
Middlesex
Clement 1790 w.
Norfolk
Alice 1748 w.
John 1765 w.
Joshua 1768 w.
James 1778 w.
Robert 1796 w.
William 1796 w.
William 1799 w.
Princess Anne
Thos. 1739 i.
Robert 1784 i.
Chas. 1786 w.
Southampton
Joshua 1765 w.
Joshua 1781 w.
Saml. 1783 w.
Sarah 1784 w.
Mary 1795 w.
Chas. 1798 w.
Surry
Geo. 1716 w.
Robt. 1719 w.
Ann 1720 w.
Geo. 1721 w.
James 1723 w.
Parkes 1752 i.
Michael 1777 w.
Sussex
Mary 1776 w.
Jno. 1777 w.

Flood 1781 w.
Jno. 1783 i.
Wm. 1797 w.
NICKASON
Middlesex
Michaell 1678 a.
NICKEN
Lancaster
Edwd. 1735 w.
Northumberland
Thomas 1778 w.
NICKHOLS
Northumberland
Jno. 1711 a.
NICKLESS
Accomack
Hancock 1749 i.
Eleanor 1760 w.
Princess Anne
Richd. 1721 w.
NICKLIN
Frederick
John 1751 w.
Susannah 1764 i.
NICHLIS
Norfolk
Wm. 1693-4 w.
Henry 1694 w.
Princess Anne
Eliz. 1716 i.
NICKLSON
Princess Anne
Jno. 1776 w.
NICKOLS
Loudoun
John 1782 i.
Louisa
Jeremiah 1757 w.
Northumberland
Jno. 1727 w.
NICKOLLS
Norfolk
Judath 1721 w.
NICKOLSON
Princess Anne
Malacai 1754 w.
NICKSON
York
Jno. 1693 i.
Humphrey 1718 w.
NICODEMUS
Frederick
Adam 1772 i.
NICOLLS
Westmoreland
Jno. 1724 i.
NICOLS
Fauquier
John 1772 i.

NICOLSON
Surry
Wm. 1760 i.
Sussex
Jno. 1754 w.
Robt. 1762 w.
NIE
Shenandoah
Ulry 1784 w.
NIEL
Frederick
John 1798 i.
Halifax
Susanna 1788 w.
NIGHTINGALE
Essex
John 1705 w.
NIGHTENGALE
Westmoreland
Jno. 1660 i.
York
Chas. 1717 w.
NIMMO
Essex
James 1755 i.
Princess Anne
James 1753 w.
James 1759 i.
Jacob 1764 w.
Gersham 1765 i.
Wm. 1770 w.
Johnson 1784 i.
Wm., Sr. 1791 w.
Nathl. 1799 w.
Wm. 1799 w.
NIPPER
Brunswick
Jno., Sr. 1741 w.
Ann 1752 w.
James 1794 w.
Northumberland
Jno. 1719 i.
NISBETT
Prince William
James 1783 i.
NISBETT
York
Jos. 1762 w.
NISELY
Shenandoah
Anthony 1778 w.
NISEWANDER
Frederick
John 1788 w.
NISEWANGER
Frederick
Jacob 1754 i.
Abraham 1785 i.
John 1789 i.

NISWINGER
Ohio
Peter 1783 a.
NIX
Hanover
Edwd. 1734 a.
Spotsylvania
Geo. 1746 w.
NIXON
Isle of Wight
Augustine 1738 i.
Loudoun
Jonathan 1791 i.
Middlesex
Henry 1709 w.
Norfolk
Wm. 1761 i.
NIXSON
Halifax
Jonothan 1799 i.
NOBELL
Westmoreland
Robt. 1704 i.
NOBLE
Accomack
Jas. 1693 i.
Edwd. 1762 i.
Augusta
Jno. 1752 w.
Berkeley
Thomas 1794 w.
Lunenburg
Robt. 1752 w.
Robt. 1754 w.
Northampton
Jas. 1695 a.
Stafford
Joshua 1765 w.
NOCK
Accomack
Wm. 1726 w.
Wm. 1738 w.
Jno. 1740 w.
Eliz. 1742 w.
Geo. 1743 w.
Jno. 1749 w.
Jno. Jr. 1750 i.
Comfort 1757 i.
Jno. 1758 i.
Jno. 1759 i.
Benj. 1766 w.
Elijah 1790 w.
Benj. 1791 w.
Wm. 1791 w.
Thos. 1796 i.
Jno. 1797 i.
NODEN
Prince George
Chas. 1724 w.

NOEL
Essex
Bernard 1749 w.
James 1765 w.
Joseph 1771 w.
Presly 1799 i.
NOELL
Cumberland
John 1776 w.
Essex
Ralph 1695 i.
Cornelius 1697 w.
James 1733 i.
James 1741 w.
William 1762 i.
Scott 1766 i.
Cornelius 1767 i.
Larkin 1767 w.
Samuel 1768 i.
Anna 1770 i.
Cornelius 1770 i.
Daniel 1770 i.
Reuben 1778 i.
Martha 1779 w.
Sarah 1779 w.
Milley 1785 w.
Richard Sr. 1789 w.
James 1791 w.
Milly 1792 i.
NOLAND
Loudoun
Philip 1785 i.
Philip Jr. 1785 w.
Philip 1794 w.
Prince William
Philip 1735 i.
NOLLEBOY
Isle of Wight
Daniel 1704 nw.
NOLLEY
Isle of Wight
Needham 1761 i.
Greensville
Daniel 1784 w.
NOLUN
Goochland
Thos. 1730 i.
NOOE
Culpeper
John 1784 i.
NORCUTT
Norfolk
Thos. 1710-11 w.
William 1746 w.
Thomas 1753 i.
NORDEN
Prince George
Robt. 1726 i.
NORFLETT
Southampton
Cordall 1788 w.

NORGATE
Northumberland
Philip 1711 i.
NORLY
Northampton
Thos. 1703 w.
Esther 1710 w.
NORMAN
Culpeper
Courtney 1770 w.
Isaac 1777 i.
Joseph 1784 w.
Isaac 1792 i.
King George
Webster 1781 w.
Middlesex
Robt. 1709 w.
Moses 1727 i.
Thos. 1727 w.
Robt. 1747 i.
Norfolk
Jno. 1684-5 w.
Northumberland
Wm. 1738 i.
Thos. 1773 i.
Prince William
Thomas 1797 i.
Southampton
Wm. 1763 w.
Stafford
Thos. 1785 w.
NORMANT
Mecklenburg
Wm. 1786 i.
NORRIE
Westmoreland
David 1671 w.
NORRIS
Chesterfield
Wm. Sr. 1765 w.
Jno. 1783 w.
Jno. 1784 i.
Jas. 1787 w.
Fauquier
Septimus 1799 i.
Lancaster
Jno. 1720 i.
Wm. 1733 w.
Mary 1738 i.
Northumberland
James 1778 nw.
Lancaster
John 1778 w.
Joseph 1784 w.
Joseph 1788 i.
John 1789 w.
William 1792 i.
Northumberland
Joseph 1778 i.
Princess Anne
Geo. 1771 i.

Chas. 1774 i.
Mary 1795 w.
Surry
Mary 1681 i.
Saml. 1752 w.
NORRISS
Lancaster
William 1789 w.
NORTEN
Prince George
Francis 1717 i.
NORTH
Bedford
William 1782 i.
Charlotte
Thos. 1794 w.
Cumberland
Anthony 1773 i.
Essex
Anthony 1700 w.
William 1706-7 w.
Anthony 1726 w.
Fairfax
John 1757 i.
Jean 1765 i.
Henrico
Wm. Sr. 1748 i.
Wm. 1748 w.
Prince Edward
Wm. 1790 w.
Shenandoah
Edward 1782 a.
Surry
Jno. 1673 w.
NORTHAM
Accomack
Wm. 1758 nw.
Wm. 1769 i.
Jno. 1796 w.
Jno. 1798 i.
NORTHCOTT
Norfolk
Thomas 1791 w.
Thomas 1793 i.
NORTHCROSS
Brunswick
James 1773 a.
NORTHCUT
Northumberland
Richd. 1742 i.
Powhatan
Jno. 1781 w.
NORTHCUTT
Norfolk
Amos 1779 w.
NORTHEN
Richmond
Edwd. 1739 i.
Edmd. 1747 w.
Geo. 1795 i.
Margaret 1799 w.

Edmund 1783 i.
NORTHINGTON
Sussex
Starling 1773 i.
Nathan 1777 w.
Nathan 1785 i.
NORTHROP
Brunswick
James 1763 i.
NORSWORTHY
Isle of Wight
John 1670 i.
William 1707 w.
Thomas 1723 w.
Tristram 1724 w.
George 1724-5 w.
Christian 1727 w.
Charles 1735 w.
Tristram 1736 i.
George 1741 i.
George 1752 w.
Joseph 1758 w.
John 1760 w.
Joseph 1761 w.
Rachel 1761 w.
George 1774 w.
Joseph 1778 w.
Patience 1781 w.
George 1782 w.
Tristram 1784 w.
John 1793 i.
Elizabeth 1797 w.
Nathaniel 1799 i.
Southampton
Joseph 1761 i.
NORTON
Frederick
John H. 1797 w.
Lancaster
Wm. 1675 i.
Rappahannock
Patrick 1677 w.
Richmond
Nathl. 1731 i.
Southampton
Joseph, Jr. 1762 w.
NORVELL
Spotsylvania
Wm. 1728 a.
NORWOOD
Culpeper
Andrew 1784 i.
Isle of Wight
Elizabeth 1733 i.
Richard 1731 i.
James 1736 i.
William 1736 w.
William 1741 i.
Richmond
Jno. 1777 i.

Surry
Wm. 1703 w.
NOSAY
Norfolk
Thomas 1764 w.
Thomas 1766 i.
Daniel 1782 w.
Thomas 1794 i.
NOSY
Norfolk
Thomas 1791 w.
NOURSE
Berkeley
James 1785 i.
NOTINGHAM
Accomack
Sarah 1725 i.
Princess Anne
Joseph 1795 w.
NOTT
Northumberland
Geo. 1655 w.
Washington
Andrew 1798 i.
Westmoreland
Jno. 1698 i.
NOTTENHAM
Accomack
Eliz. 1796 i.
NOTTING
Northampton
Richd. 1737 i.
NOTTINGAM
Bath
William 1799 w.
NOTTINGHAM
Northampton
Richd., Sr. 1692 w.
Robt. 1698 w.
Benj. 1716 i.
Wm. 1718-19 w.
Jos. 1721 w.
Richd. 1729 w.
Clark 1736 w.
Jonathan 1736 i.
Mary 1737 i.
Robt., Jr. 1744 w.
Elishe 1745 w.
Robt., Sr. 1745 w.
Eliz. 1746 w.
Jacob 1747 w.
Michael 1753 w.
Jno. 1758 i.
Joshua 1758 w.
Richd., Sr. 1758 w.
Mary 1762 i.
Jos. 1765 w.
Isaac 1769 i.
Addison 1773 w.
Robt., Jr. 1774 w.
Jno. 1778 w.

Addison 1783 i.
Wm. 1783 w.
Joanna 1784 w.
Mary 1785 w.
Leah 1786 w.
Thos., Jr. 1788 w.
Jacob 1789 w.
Thos. 1791 i.
Thos., Sr. 1797 w.
Robt. 1798 i.
NOURSE
Westmoreland
Sarah 1774 i.
NOVELL
Halifax
James 1771 w.
NORVEL
Essex
Edward 1756 i.
Wythe
Edwd. 1794 i.
NOWELL
Lunenburg
Hugh 1760 w.
Sussex
Wm. 1764 i.
NOWLAND
Amelia
Michael 1752 i.
Henry
Richard 1782 i.
NOWLIN
Goochland
James 1749 w.
David 1777 w.
Prince George
Richd. 1715 w.
NOWLING
Pittsylvania
Saml. 1770 i.
NOX
Accomack
Elijah 1776 w.
NOYALL
Isle of Wight
William 1746 w.
Norfolk
Nicholas 1785 w.
Wm. 1791 w.
NUCKOLDS
Goochland
Wm. 1793 i.
NUCKOLS
Goochland
Wm. 1796 w.
Louisa
Chas. 1767 w.
NUGENT
Fauquier
Ann 1785 w.

King George
Peter 1750 i.
NULL
Augusta
Nicho. 1767 i.
NULTON
Frederick
Maria 1790 w.
NUNALEY
Henrico
Richd. 1727 w.
NUNALLY
Amelia
Eliz. 1785 w.
Chesterfield
Jno. P. 1789 i.
NUNN
Chesterfield
Thos. 17— i.
NUNNALLEE
Chesterfield
Walter 1784 w.
NUNNALLY
Chesterfield
Jno. 1765 w.
Walter 1773 i.
Danl., Jr. 1777 i.
Noel [1784?] w.
Henry 1787 w.
Samson 1797 i.
Powhatan
Archelaus 1795 i.
NUNNELLY
Chesterfield
David 1794 i.
NUNNERY
Campbell
Bartlett 1797 i.
NURSE
Westmoreland
Robt. 1673 i.
Jno. 1761 i.
NUTEN
Essex
Nickles 1708 w.
NUTT
Augusta
Nicholas 1758 i.
Northumberland
Philip 1661 w.
Wm. 1668 i.
Wm. 1712-13 w.
Ann 1718 i.
Richd. 1718 i.
Benj. 1728 w.
Benj. 1741 i.
Richd. 1746 w.
Wm. 1748 i.
Eliza. 1753 i.
Farnefold 1762 i.
Joseph 1766 w.

Benjamin 1767 i.
John 1768 w.
Farnifold 1772 i.
Richd. 1778 i.
Lancaster
James 1794 w.
NUTTING
York
Thos. 1717 w.
Eliz. 1735 w.

O

OAGE
Northampton
Robt. 1786 i.
OAKEHAM
Princess Anne
Ruth 1695 a.
OAKEN
Princess Anne
Wm. 1782 w.
OAKES
Orange
John 1796 w.
Pittsylvania
Chas. 1795 w.
OAKHAM
Princess Anne
Jno. 1706 i.
Jno. 1707 w.
Wm. 1753 w.
OAKLEY
Accomack
Jno. 1727 i.
Henrico
Jno. 1754 i.
OAKLY
Henrico
Mathew 1691 i.
OAKS
Cumberland
Eliz. 1784 w.
OAKUM
Princess Anne
Jonathan 1795 w.
OAKWOOD
Washington
Henry 1792 w.
OALER
Augusta
Wm. 1766 i.
OART
Washington
Francis 1794 w.
OAST
Princess Anne
Godwin 1727 i.
Norfolk
Sudden 1753 w.

OBANION
Berkeley
Briant 1784 w.
OBANON
Fauquier
John 1774 w.
Bryan 1762 w.
OBANNON
Fauquier
George 1777 w.
John 1797 w.
OBERETT
Westmoreland
Wm. 1674 w.
OBERRY
Southampton
Thos. 1768 w.
OBERT
Lancaster
Barham (Bertram)
1659 w.
OBRIAN
Greenbrier
James 1781 i.
York
Wm. 1761 w.
OBRISSELL
Middlesex
Thos. 1699 w.
O'BRYAN
Augusta
Cornelius 1751 w.
OBRYANT
Frederick
John 1755 i.
OBURN
Berkeley
James 1782 w.
O'CAIN
Stafford
Richd. 1762 i.
OCAINE
Accomack
Thos. 1706 i.
O'CAY
Northampton
Eliz. 1709 i.
OCCANY
Westmoreland
Danl. 1716 w.
OCHELTREE
Botetourt
Michael 1799 w.
O'DANNALY
Fairfax
Patrick 1748 a.
O'DAUGHITY
Northumberland
Neale 1725 i.

ODEAN
Norfolk
Wm. 1771 i.
O'DEER
Northampton
Jos. 1759 i.
Stephen 1774 w.
ODELL
Shenandoah
Jeremiah 1777 w.
Samuel 1780 w.
Elijah 1798 w.
ODEN
Loudoun
Thomas 1798 i.
Norfolk
Charles 1795 i.
ODEON
Norfolk
Wm. 1662 w.
William 1743-4 w.
ODER
Culpeper
Thomas 1796 i.
O'DONLEY
Augusta
Michael 1770 i.
O'DONNAL
Augusta
Michael 1767 a.
ODYER
Westmoreland
Gabriel 1660 i.
ODINEAL
Louisa
Timothy 1766 w.
ODUR
Northampton
Wm. 1795 w.
OFFENBACKER
Shenandoah
Jacob 1775 w.
Jacob 1783 w.
OFFILE
Westmoreland
Wm. 1712 i.
OFFLEY
Norfolk
Henry 1678 w.
OFFNER
Shenandoah
John 1798 i.
O'FRIEL
Augusta
Morris 1778 w.
OGBORN
Isle of Wight
Symond 1669 w.
OGBORNE
Brunswick
Jno. 1774 w.

OGBOURN
Surry
Jno. 1719 i.
Isle of Wight
Nicholas 1692 i.
Norfolk
Thomas 1785 i.
Thomas 1788 i.
OGBURN
Berkeley
Jonathan 1779 w.
Sussex
Edmund 1782 w.
Jno. 1790 w.
OGELBY
Goochland
Richd. 1731 i.
OGELVEY
Middlesex
Peter 1763 a.
OGG
Orange
John 1798 i.
OGILBY
Amelia
Richd. 1795 w.
OGLE
York
Cuthbert 1755 i.
OGLEBY
Amelia
Richd. 1750 w.
Richmond
Jno. 1736 i.
Edwd. 1775 nw.
OGLESBY
Bedford
Sarah Sr. 1780 w.
Campbell
Thos. 1787 w.
Richd. 1790 w.
Isle of Wight
Peggy 1763 i.
Fluvanna
Shadrack 1778 w.
Frederick
Alexander 1794 w.
OGLETHROPE
Isle of Wight
Thomas 1687-8 w.
O'GRAHAN
Accomack
Danl. 1736 w.
OGRAHON
Accomack
Danl. 1708 i.
O'GULLIAN
Franklin
Hugh 1775 a.

O'HARRA
Charlotte
Michael 1787 i.
Isabella 1792 i.
O'HARROW
Lancaster
Thomas 1764 i.
O'KEAN
Fairfax
Henry 1746 w.
OKEHAM
Norfolk
John 1670 i.
OLATHMAN
Westmoreland
Teague 1668 w.
OLD
Amelia
Jno. 1768 w.
James 1772 i.
Wm. 1798 w.
Norfolk
Willoughby 1782 w.
Princess Anne
Edwd. 1718 w.
Edwd. 1738 w.
Edwd. 1743 i.
Cockruft 1760 w.
Thos. 1782 w.
Thomas 1790 w.
Caleb 1791 w.
Mary 1793 w.
Penbrook 1793 w.
OLDACRE
Loudoun
Henry, Jr. 1787 i.
OLDAKER
Fauquier
Abram 1795 w.
OLDAM
Northumberland
Jas. 1712-13 i.
OLDENBROUCH
Shenandoah
Daniel 1786 w.
OLDERHEAD
Westmoreland
Peter 1731 i.
OLDHAM
Bath
William 1799 w.
Brunswick
Chas. 1785 w.
Fairfax
James 1752 i.
King George
Edwd. 1795 i.
Lancaster
William 1777 i.
Northumberland
John, Sr. 1753 w.

John, Jr. 1753 w.
Geo. 1758 w.
Tarpley 1763 w.
Rawleigh 1765 i.
Caleb 1782 w.
Jas. 1787 i.
Geo. 1789 i.
Wm. 1789 i.
Eliz. 1791 i.
Wm. 1791 w.
Wm. 1792 i.
Wm. 1797 i.
Richmond
Wm. 1728 w.
Peter 1734 i.
James 1740 w.
James 1754 w.
Jno. 1762 w.
OLDNER
Princess Anne
Thos. 1763 i.
Thos. 1785 i.
OLDSHOE
Botetourt
Jacob 1795 i.
OLDUM
Richmond
Peter 1735 i.
OLERHOLDER
Shenandoah
Samuel 1783 w.
OLIFF
Westmoreland
Geo., Sr. 1748 w.
Sarah 1799 w.
OLINGER
Augusta
Philip 1787 w.
OLISS
Surry
Wm. 1677 w.
OLIVANT
Norfolk
Wm. 1673 w.
OLIVE
Essex
Jane 1727 w.
Powhatan
Jno. 1788 i.
Spotsylvania
Wm. 1787 a.
Westmoreland
Jno. 1750 i.
OLIVER
Amelia
Jas. 1787 w.
Augusta
Aron 1773 w.
Jno. 1791 w.
Middlesex
Francis 1794 w.

Bath
John 1799 i.
Brunswick
Lucy 1766 w.
Jno. 1766 w.
Charlotte
Joseph 1787 w.
John 1796 w.
Frederick
James 1795 w.
Henrico
Edwd. 1695 a.
Isle of Wight
John 1655 w.
King George
Thos. 1785 w.
Lancaster
Martha 1750 i.
William 1768 w.
Ellison 1773 i.
Mecklenburg
Asa 1796 w.
Jno., Jr. 1799 i.
Norfolk
Emanuell 1679 w.
Lovey 1784 w.
Ellener 1719 w.
Northumberland
Lowry 1779 w.
Orange
Durrett 1771 i.
Pittsylvania
Drury 1781 w.
Princess Anne
Jno. 1734 w.
Eliz. 1762 w.
John 1792 i.
Prince William
Thomas 1796 w.
Sussex
Thos. 1760 w.
Wm. 1795 i.
Surry
Edwd. 1677 i.
Jno. 1725 w.
OLLARD
Lancaster
James 1773 i.
Northumberland
Judith 1784 i.
OLLIFF
Richmond
Geo. 1779 w.
OLLIVER
Lancaster
Wm. 1742 i.
Wm. 1750-1 i.
Princess Anne
Peter 1723 w.

OLSCHLAGLE
Culpeper
John E. 1793 w.

OMEHUNDRO
Fairfax
Richd. 1745 w.

O'MEHUNDRO
Loudoun
Ann 1763 w.

OMOHUNDRO
Westmoreland
Richd. 1698 w.
Thos. 1732 i.
Jno. 1765 w.
Jane 1767 i.
Wm. 1778 i.
Thos. 1788 w.
Jas. 1790 w.
Bruce 1797 w.
Thos. 1799 i.

OMSBY
Mecklenburg
Matthew 1785 w.

O'NEAL
Augusta
Jno. 1757 i.
Jas. 1778 i.
Essex
John 1741 w.
John 1769 w.
Culpeper
John 1783 w.
Fairfax
Chas. 1747 i.
Frederick
Hugh 1750 i.
Hugh 1751 i.
Middlesex
Jno. 1761 i.
Northampton
Henry 1725 w.
Richmond
Jas. 1738 i.
Spotsylvania
Mary 1784 a.
Stafford
Timothy 1744 i.
Westmoreland
Garrett 1722 w.

ONEALE
Essex
Brigett 1716 i.
Greenbrier
John 1792 w.
Loudoun
Ferdinand 1781 i.

ONEANS
Accomack
Jno. 1716 w.

ONEBY
Essex
Arthur 1737 i.

ONEIL
Prince William
Daniel 1783 w.

ONELY
Accomack
Wm. 1738 i.

ONEY
Southampton
Leonard 1779 w.
John 1784 w.

ONIONS
Accomack
Selby 1728 w.
Thos. 1738 w.
Eliz. 1744 w.
Jno. 1751 w.
Wm. Silby 1764 i.
Richd. 1771 i.

ONLEY
Accomack
Fairfax 1738 w.
Wm. Jr. 1751 i.

ONLY
Accomack
Jno. 1722 i.
Jno. 1794 w.

OPIE
Frederick
Eliz. 1794 i.
Northumberland
Jno. 1723 w.
Ann 1724-5 w.
Ann 1724-5 nw.
Lindsay 1746 w.
John 1759 i.
Thos. 1770 i.
Lindsay 1785 w.
Thos. 1798 w.

OPPLING
York
Richd. 1694 i.

OQUILLION
Frederick
Duncan 1754 w.

ORANG
Henrico
Lewis 1735 i.

ORCHARD
Surry
Jno. 1677 a.
Westmoreland
James 1703 w.
York
Robt. 1756 i.

ORGAN
Prince William
Sarah 1793 w.

ORGIN
Prince William
Matthew 1736 i.

ORLEY
Northumberland
Thos. 1662 w.

ORIAR
Prince William
Daniel 1737 w.

ORILL
Middlesex
Law. 1749 w.

ORME
Fairfax
Aaron 1795 i.

ORMESTON
York
Jno. 1769 i.

ORMSBY
Amelia
Jno. 1759 i.

ORNDORFF
Frederick
John 1798 w.

ORR
Charlotte
James 1767 w.
Shadrack 1777 w.
Culpeper
Samuel 1767 i.
Isle of Wight
William 1779 w.
Norfolk
Hugh 1797 i.
York
Hugh 1764 w.

ORRANGE
Amelia
Peter 1754 a.

ORRICK
Berkeley
Nicholas 1781 w.
Nicholas 1786 i.

ORRILL
Middlesex
Martha 1761 w.

ORTAN
York
Richd. 1757 w.

ORTH
Westmoreland
Emanuel 1746 i.

ORTS
Shenandoah
Jacob 1789 a.

OSBOND
Middlesex
Henry 1698 w.

OSBONS
Prince William
Thomas 1737 i.

OSBORN
Accomack
Jno. 1737 w.
Amelia
Jno. 1752 a.
Fairfax
Robert 1743 w.
Richard 1750 w.
Henrico
Edwd. 1707 i.
Lunenburg
Thos. 1755 i.
Westmoreland
Thos. 1718 i.
OSBORNE
Accomack
Jno. 1692 w.
Albemarle
Arthur 1752 w.
Amelia
Wm. 1787 w.
Eliz. 1794 w.
Branch 1799 w.
Chesterfield
Jno. 1760 w.
Thos. 1781 w.
Edwd. 1781 w.
Edwd. 1783 w.
Jno. 1788 i.
Francis 1791 w.
Ann 1792 w.
Frances 1793 w.
Thos. 1795 w.
Henrico
Thos. Sr. 1691 w.
Edwd. 1696 w.
Edwd. 1732 a.
Thos. 1733 w.
Prince Edward
Thos. 1787 w.
Prince George
Elias 1716 a.
OSBOURN
Loudoun
John 1787 w.
Richd. 1799 i.
OSBOURNE
Isle of Wight
Edward 1732 i.
OSBURN
Berkeley
David 1783 w.
Loudoun
Nicholas 1787 w.
OSBURNE
Accomack
Jenifer 1736 w.
OSGRIFFEN
Richmond
Jane 1765 i.

OSHEAL
Northumberland
Philip 1724 i.
Norfolk
John 1750 i.
OSLEN
Cumberland
Samuel 1769 w.
Jesse 1774 i.
Saml. 1779 i.
Martin 1780 w.
OSLIN
Henrico
Saml. 1793 w.
OSMAN
Essex
James 1708 w.
Northampton
Joan 1709 w.
OSTIN
Accomack
Rebecka 1726 i.
OSWALD
Essex
Henry 1726 w.
Mary 1728 w.
OTTERSON
Princess Anne
Joseph 1734 w.
Mary 1774 i.
Joseph 1777 i.
OTTO
Frederick
Tobias 1765 w.
OULDAKERS
Loudoun
Henry Sr. 1785 w.
OULTEN
Accomack
Jno. 1767 i.
OUTLAND
Isle of Wight
William 1792 w.
John 1796 nw.
John 1798 w.
OUTLAW
Norfolk
Edward 1714 w.
OUTTEN
Accomack
Abraham 1786 w.
Samuel 1788 i.
Purnell 1798 w.
OVEAHOLSER
Shenandoah
Samuel 1784 i.
OVERALL
Prince William
John 1742 w.

OVERBAGER
Shenandoah
Jacob 1775 a.
OVERBY
Brunswick
Jno. 1783 i.
Mecklenburg
Adam 1780 w.
Nicholas 1791 i.
OVERSTREET
Bedford
Thomas, Sr. 1792 w.
Lancaster
Richard 1775 w.
Prince Edward
Wm. 1757 i.
York
Thos. 1694 i.
Mary 1701 i.
Jeffery 1702 w.
Jno. 1710 i.
Thos. 1720 i.
OVERSY
Northumberland
Simon 1662 i.
OVERTON
Amelia
Saml. 1761 i.
Thos. P. 1796 i.
Charlotte
Wm. 1779 i.
Louisa
James 1790 w.
Richmond
Edmd. 1712 i.
OWDEN
Prince William
Francis 1779 i.
OWEN
Accomack
Jonathan 1717 w.
Timothy 1720 w.
Timothy 1731 i.
Jno. 1758 w.
Jonathan 1759 i.
Rachel 1766 w.
Saml. 1780 i.
Botetourt
Thomas 1775 i.
Brunswick
Gronow 1770 w.
Essex
Richard 1716 i.
Owen 1749 i.
Augustine 1766 w.
Goochland
Barnet 1782 w.
Halifax
Richd. 1756 w.
Jno. 1771 w.
Evan 1777 i.

Abraham 1785 i.
Joseph 1791 w.
Jno. 1796 i.
Henrico
Thos. 1689 i.
Even 1691 i.
Margery 1691 i.
Wm. 1784 w.
Thos. 1794 i.
Thos. 1795 w.
Nancy 1797 w.
King George
Richd. 1765 i.
Lancaster
Humphrey 1663 i.
Lunenburg
Walter 1765 w.
Middlesex
John (1) 1720 w.
John (2) 1720 w.
Aug. 1726 w.
Wm. 1765 a.
Wm. 1776 w.
Jacob 1790 i.
Jno. 1791 i.
Wm. 1792 i.
Montgomery
David [1799?] w.
Pittsylvania
Jno. 1786 w.
David 1797 w.
Powhatan
Geo. 1794 w.
Prince Edward
Jno. 1767 w.
Miss 1770 i.
Jesse 1794 i.
Spotsylvania
Jacob 1760 a.
Mary 1771 a.
Jacob 1787 a.
Mary 1787 a.
Surry
Bartholomew 1677 i.
Robt. 1717 w.
Sussex
Wm. 1763 w.
Robt. 1772 w.
Westmoreland
Edmund 1718 i.
OWENS
Albemarle
Wm. 1791 w.
Essex
Richard 1717 i.
Fairfax
John 1787 i.
Fauquier
Jeremiah 1773 w.
Halifax
Wm. 1753 w.

Wm. 1782 w.
King George
Richd., Sr. 1763 w.
Saml. 1767 w.
Margt. 1774 a.
Montgomery
Thomas 1791 a.
Norfolk
Wm., Sr. 1711 w.
John 1773 i.
Paul 1787 w.
William 1788 w.
James 1790 w.
Northumberland
Mary 1744 w.
Wm. 1758 i.
Princess Anne
Thos. 1717 w.
Thos. 1757 i.
Nathl. 1774 i.
Thos. 1782 w.
Prince William
Joshua 1778 i.
Richmond
Jno. 1712 i.
Sussex
Robt. 1795 i.
Westmoreland
Wm. 1751 i.
OWIN
Accomack
Peter 1761 i.
Surry
Jno. 1740 i.
Hannah 1743 i.
Sussex
David 1790 w.
Hannah 1796 w.
Jno. 1783 i.
OWING
York
Even 1687 i.
OWINGS
Norfolk
Wm. 1711 a.
John 1769 w.
OWINS
Norfolk
Thomas 1757 w.
Edward 1762 i.
John 1767 w.
OWLET
York
Valentine 1783 w.
OWLETT
York
Wm. 1769 w.
OWNES
Accomack
Saml. 1737 i.

OWSLEY
Fairfax
Thomas 1751 w.
Loudoun
Wm. 1762 i.
John 1767 i.
Stafford
Thos. 1701 i.
OXFORD
Roger 1759 w.
Thos. 1782 w.
OXLEY
Loudoun
Everet 1777 i.
Henry 1777 w.
Rachel 1779 w.
OYSTEN
Princess Anne
Danl. 1776 i.

P

PACE
Goochland
Joseph 1765 w.
Jno. 1790 w.
Middlesex
Jno. Sr. 1720 w.
Spotsylvania
Wm. 1761 a.
PACK
Surry
John 1716 w.
PACKERILL
Surry
Wm. 1701-2 w.
PACKETT
Richmond
Gabriel 1741 i.
Jeremiah 1761 i.
Richd. 1791 w.
Westmoreland
Wm. 1792 w.
PACKSTON
Rappahannock
Jno. 1674 w.
PADDERSON
Prince William
Caroline 1739 w.
PADON
Princess Anne
Wm. 1790 w.
PAERMONTO
Isle of Wight
John 1715 i.
PAGE
Essex
Jno. 1721 w.
Fairfax
William 1792 i.

Goochland
Jacob 1763 i.
Jesse 1793 i.
James 1797 i.
Robt. 1787 w.
Winifred 1790 w.
Isle of Wight
John 1701 w.
Thomas 1720 w.
William 1746 w.
Lunenburg
Jno. 1786 w.
Northampton
Jas. 1721-2 w.
Orange
Jno. 1789 w.
Prince William
John 1744 w.
Rappahannock
Thos. 1676 w.
Jonas 1686 w.
Spotsylvania
Mann 1781 w.
Ann Corbin 1785 w.
York
Stephen 1658 i.
Jno. 1691-2 w.
Francis 1692 w.
Richd. 1694 w.
Alice 1698 w.
Richd. 1721 w.
PAGET
Essex
Edmund 1722 w.
Ephraim 1723 w.
Shenandoah
Reuben 1795 i.
PAGETT
Essex
Francis 1735 i.
Abraham 1737 i.
Henry 1745 w.
John 1745 w.
Mary 1758 i.
Mary 1761 w.
Ephream 1763 i.
Loudoun
Frances 1795 w.
Norfolk
John 1645 i.
PAGIT
Loudoun
Francis 1795 w.
PAIFIELD
Surry
Nicholas 1701 w.
PAIN
Bedford
Flayl 1784 w.
Henrico
Chas. 1747 w.

Northampton
Orlando 1739 i.
Spotsylvania
Barnett Jr. 1740 a.
Jno. 1770 w.
PAINE
Essex
Thomas 1761 w.
Henrico
Thos. 1710 w.
King George
Jno. 1725 i.
Lancaster
Wm. 1700 w.
Richd. 1709 w.
Norfolk
Saml. 1715 w.
Northampton
Danl. 1709 w.
Rappahannock
Thos. 1664 a.
Richmond
Robt. 1717 w.
Westmoreland
Wm. 1697 w.
Jno. 1702 i.
Edwd. 1702 i.
Jno. 1729 i.
York
Eliz. 1702 i.
PAINTER
Augusta
Cath. 1764 i.
Adam 1773 a.
Adam 1793 i.
Frederick
Peter 1768 i.
John 1770 i.
John 1771 w.
Shenandoah
Peter 1788 a.
PAIR
Sussex
Wm. 1757 w.
PAISE
King George
Thos. 1725 i.
PALFRY
Northumberland
Mary 1742 w.
Westmoreland
Ann 1748 i.
PALLASON
Isle of Wight
Charles 1762 w.
PALLET
Princess Anne
Matthew 1703 w.
Matthew 1758 i.

PALLETT
Princess Anne
Jno. 1719 w.
Jno. 1777 w.
PALLISERES
Stafford
Stephen 1705 i.
PALLISTER
Prince William
Richard 1737 i.
PALMER
Accomack
Thos. 1687 w.
Augusta
Wm. 1797 w.
Botetourt
William 1772 i.
Berkeley
Thomas 1797 w.
Culpeper
Joseph 1798 i.
Cumberland
John 1763 w.
Wm. 1786 w.
King George
Benj. 1743 i.
Margt. 1744 i.
Loudoun
John 1774 w.
Lunenburg
Parmenas 1761 w.
Richd. 1761 i.
Northampton
Saml. 1709 w.
Jno. 1790 w.
Jas. 1791 w.
Northumberland
Jos. Sr. 1704 w.
Thos. 1709 w.
Isaac 1748 w.
Thos. 1749 i.
Wm. 1765 i.
Nargalsharezer 1770 w.
Joseph 1771 i.
Robt. 1783 w.
Hannah 1793 w.
Rodham 1794 i.
Rappahannock
Jno. 1686 w.
Richmond
Robt. 1733 w.
Jas. 1740 w.
Jos. 1750 w.
Jno. 1773 i.
Rawl. 1787 i.
Westmoreland
Sarah 1718 w.
Thos. 1764 i.
York
Eliz. 1716 w.

Jas. 1718 i.
Wm. 1758 w.
Benj. 1785 i.
PAMER
York
Edwd. 1715 w.
Ann 1716 w.
PAMPLIN
Essex
Nicholas 1750 w.
Wm. 1752 w.
Sarah 1758 w.
Nicholas 1760 w.
Middlesex
Robt. 1785 i.
PANCOAST
Fairfax
David 1786 i.
PANEWELL
Northampton
Jno. 1691 w.
PANKEY
Chesterfield
Stephen 1788 w.
Stephen 1790 w.
Cumberland
John 1750 w.
Prince Edward
Mary 1799 w.
PANKY
Lunenburg
Dorothy 1772 w.
PANNEL
Richmond
Thos. 1718 w.
PANNELL
King George
David 1774 a.
Northampton
Saml. 1666 w.
Rappahannock
Thos. 1677 w.
Richmond
Wm. 1716 w.
Spotsylvania
Saml. 1762 a.
PANNIL
Pittsylvania
Jno. 1793 w.
PANNILL
Culpeper
William 1750 w.
William 1757 i.
Orange
Jno. 1763 w.
PANNY
Westmoreland
Aliace 1753 i.
PAPPENE
Cumberland
Margaret 1758 i.

PAPTICOE
Northumberland
Wm. 1719 a.
PARADICE
Accomack
Jno. 1763 i.
PARADISE
Stafford
Eliz. 1763 i.
PARDO
Isle of Wight
Phillip 1678 i.
PARDUE
Isle of Wight
Phillip 1720 i.
PARFITT
Lancaster
Thos. 1709 w.
PARHAM
Amelia
Gower 1767 w.
James 1787 i.
Danl. 1798 w.
Brunswick
Matthew 1743 i.
Frances 1744 w.
James 1763 w.
Wm. 1763 w.
Jno. 1779 w.
Wm. 1780 w.
James 1791 w.
Ephraim 1793 w.
Surry
Edwd. 1709 w.
Ephraim 1726 w.
Wm. 1733 i.
Sussex
Wm. 1758 w.
Ephraim 1763 w.
Jno. 1764 i.
Robt. 1767 i.
Mathew 1772 w.
Thos. 1772 i.
Wm. 1775 w.
Thos. 1781 w.
Mary 1788 w.
Rebeckah 1790 w.
Jno. 1791 w.
James 1793 w.
Stith 1793 w.
Mathew 1795 w.
Nathl. 1795 w.
Anderson 1797 w.
Rebecca 1798 w.
PARIS
Prince Edward
James 1797 w.
PARISH
Brunswick
James 1758 i.

Goochland
Jno. 1752 i.
Henry 1753 w.
Louisa
Jolley 1783 w.
Mecklenburg
Saml. 1785 w.
Peter 1786 w.
Jno. 1787 w.
Spotsylvania
Joel 1791 w.
PARK
Accomack
Jno. 1727 i.
Mary 1733 w.
Berkeley
John 1784 w.
James 1791 i.
Brunswick
Joseph 1749 w.
Essex
Geo. 1697 w.
PARKE
Berkeley
Samuel Sr. 1793 w.
Prince Edward
James 1769 w.
Shenandoah
Roger 1794 a.
PARKENS
Norfolk
John 1785 i.
PARKENSON
Isle of Wight
John 1784 w.
Northampton
Jos. 1767 w.
PARKER
Accomack
Geo. 1674 w.
Jno. Sr. 1695 w.
Wm. 1697 w.
Chas. 1708 i.
Geo. Sr. 1713 w.
Geo. 1718 i.
Jno. 1720 w.
Philip 1721 w.
Wm. 1721 w.
Geo. 1724 w.
Henry 1727 w.
Dorothy 1729 w.
Geo. 1733 w.
Sacker 1738 w.
Geo. 1738 w.
Chas. 1740 i.
Philip 1741 i.
Geo. 1748 w.
Thos. 1750 w.
Jno. 1755 w.
Caleb 1756 i.
Sacker 1756 w.

Sarah Anne 1756 i.
Jno. 1757 i.
Wm. 1758 w.
Jno. 1758 w.
Hancock 1759 w.
Agnes 1760 i.
Sacker 1760 w.
Anderson 1762 i.
Jno. 1766 w.
Levin 1763 w.
Naomi 1769 i.
Levin 1771 i.
Wm. 1772 w.
Sarah 1773 w.
Levin 1774 i.
Robt., Sr. 1774 w.
Edwd. 1776 w.
Robt. 1776 i.
Robt. 1777 w.
Anderson 1778 w.
Clement 1783 w.
Philip 1783 w.
Geo. 1784 w.
Wm. 1784 w.
Geo. 1785 i.
Sarah 1785 w.
Susannah 1786 w.
Wm. 1792 i.
Thos., Jr. 1793 w.
Eliz. 1795 w.
Peggy 1795 w.
Chas. 1796 w.
Jno., Jr. 1799 i.
Bedford
Mildred 1768 i.
Brunswick
Jno. 1774 w.
Jane 1790 w.
Chesterfield
Allen 1760 i.
Cumberland
Wm. 1756 w.
David 1776 i.
Sarah 1790 w.
Essex
Thomas 1697 w.
John 1712 i.
John 1715 i.
William 1722 i.
Robert 1731 i.
Alexander 1750 w.
Thos. 1761 w.
Robt. 1764 w.
Robert 1792 w.
Fauquier
William 1775 w.
Alex. 1785 w.
Frederick
Gilbert 1750 w.
Halifax
Obadiah 1777 w.

Richd. 1782 w.
Mary 1795 i.
Richd. 1797 w.
Henrico
Richd. 1726-7 w.
Jno. 1787 i.
Isle of Wight
Thomas 1685 w.
John 1700-1 i.
Francis 1717 w.
Nathaniel 1730 w.
George 1734 w.
Thomas 1736 w.
William 1744 w.
George 1747 w.
Nathaniel 1762 i.
Wilkinson 1758 w.
Martha 1768 w.
Frederick 1777 w.
William 1782 w.
Thomas 1788 w.
William 1791 w.
Elias 1794 w.
Lancaster
Jos. 1733 i.
Lunenburg
Wm., Sr. 1766 i.
Norfolk
Thomas 1798 w.
Northampton
Geo. 1698 w.
Thos. 1720 w.
Eliz. 1724 w.
Jno. 1735 i.
Northumberland
Jonathan 1664 w.
Jas. 1713 i.
Wm. 1719 i.
Jane 1726 w.
Wm. 1742 i.
Toulson 1796 w.
Wm. 1798 w.
Prince George
David 1717 w.
Prince William
Sarah 1738 w.
Rappahannock
Robt. 1637 w.
Richmond
Jno. 1699 w.
Henry 1707 w.
Southampton
Drury 1789 w.
Spotsylvania
Wm. 1797 w.
Wm. 1798 a.
Surry
Jno. 1679 a.
Judith 1679 i.
Richd. 1750 w.
Richd., Jr. 1751 w.

Dolly 1793 w.
Sussex
Sarah 1760 w.
Wm. 1768 w.
Wm. 1779 w.
Westmoreland
Richd. 1780 i.
PARKERSON
Northampton
Hancock 1778 w.
PARKES
Accomack
Henry 1686 i.
Benj. 1780 i.
Northampton
Chas. 1694 w.
PARKHURST
Culpeper
Samuel 1797 i.
PARKIN
York
Jno. 1745 i.
PARKINS
Frederick
Isaac 1774 w.
Joseph 1784 w.
Leah 1784 i.
Elisha 1795 w.
PARKS
Accomack
Edmd. Baley 1742 w.
Wm. 1742 w.
Jno. 1743 w.
Sacker 1752 i.
Sarah 1752 i.
Mary 1753 i.
Jno. 1760 w.
Benj. 1776 w.
Mark 1776 w.
Chas. 1792 w.
Albemarle
Thos. 1761 w.
Amherst
Wm. 1769 w.
Wm. 1778 a.
Jno. 1786 a.
Brunswick
Joseph 1749 i.
Frederick
William 1743 i.
Greensville
Aaron 1782 w.
Joseph 1785 w.
Louisa
Richard 1788 w.
Mecklenburg
James 1786 i.
Powhatan
Edwd. 1796 i.
Prince Edward
Mary 1774 w.

Rockbridge
John 1793 w.
Rebecca 1796 w.
York
Wm. 1750 w.
PARLER
Lancaster
Mesheck 1750 i.
PARMER
Amherst
Pledge 1795 a.
King George
Jno. 1799 i.
PARNELL
Isle of Wight
Thomas 1688 w.
John 1716 w.
PARNAL
Isle of Wight
Joseph 1737 w.
PARNALL
Isle of Wight
Thomas 1758 i.
William 1763 w.
James 1770 w.
John 1785 w.
PARNOLD
Isle of Wight
Joshua 1772 i.
PARR
Brunswick
Richd. 1759 w.
Essex
Philip 1701 w.
Henry
Henry 1788 i.
Isle of Wight
Thomas 1766 i.
Anthony 1776 w.
Princess Anne
Peter 1797 w.
Surry
Wm. 1738 i.
PARRADICE
Accomack
Wm. 1763 i.
PARRAM
Prince George
Thos. 1717 w.
PARRAMORE
Accomack
Thos. 1774 w.
Thos. 1783 i.
Northampton
Thos. 1716 w.
Robins 1756 i.
Richd. 1761 i.
Jno. 1764 i.
Obedience 1767 w.
Eliz. 1769 w.
Bridget 1771 w.

Bridget 1778 w.
Ezra 1783 w.
Richd. 1775 w.
PARRELL
Frederick
Hugh 1748 w.
PARRETT
Northumberland
Mary 1755 w.
PARRIMORE
Northampton
Jno. 1728 i.
Jno. 1730 i.
PARRIS
Louisa
Saml. 1759 w.
PARRISH
Accomack
Agnes 1771 w.
Edwd. 1771 w.
Brunswick
Chas. 1756 i.
James 1754 w.
Jno. 1754 i.
Joseph 1782 w.
Charles City
Eliz. 1793 w.
Goochland
Humphrey 1743 w.
Humphrey 1773 w.
Nelson 1780 i.
Jno. 1786 w.
Wm. 1790 w.
James 1792 w.
Lancaster
Anne 1755 w.
Lunenburg
Chas. 1764 w.
Peter 1779 w.
Abraham 1785 i.
Chas. 1797 i.
PARRON
Essex
Thomas 1784 w.
PARROT
Northumberland
Lawrence 1746 i.
Pittsylvania
Curtis 1794 w.
PARROTT
Halifax
John 1779 w.
Jas. 1779 i.
Lancaster
Wm. 1744 w.
Northumberland
William 1778 w.
Shenandoah
George 1777 a.

PARRUS
Augusta
Wm. 1791 w.
PARRY
Essex
Samuel 1707 i.
Mary 1735 w.
Middlesex
Wm. 1772 w.
Northumberland
Elizab. 1750 w.
PARRYMORE
Northampton
Jno. 1728 w.
PARSE
Northumberland
Jno. 1667 w.
PARSINGER
Botetourt
Jacob 1795 i.
PARSON
Isle of Wight
John 1719 w.
Northumberland
James 1754 i.
Orange
Richd. 1738 a.
York
Jno. 1753 w.
PARSONS
Culpeper
Jesse 1793 i.
Fairfax
James 1785 w.
Hardy
Jonathan 1796 i.
Henrico
Woodson 1797 w.
King George
Jno. 1743 i.
Middlesex
Jno. 1706 w.
Norfolk
William 1744 i.
Willis 1772 w.
Willoughby 1795 i.
Abijah 1798 w.
Willis 1799 w.
Northampton
Eustice 1692 i.
Wm. 1751 i.
Mariot 1773 i.
Sarah 1783 w.
Thos. 1796 w.
Pittsylvania
Richd. 1785 w.
Princess Anne
Wm. 1763 w.
Wm. 1773 w.
Francis 1778 w.
John 1794 w.

John 1796 w.
Stafford
Jno. 1732 w.
Surry
Jacob 1783 i.
Sussex
Robt. 1777 w.
York
Jno. 1699 w.
Jno. 1718 i.
Jas. 1728 w.
Jas. 1735 w.
Armiger 1736 i.
Jas. 1797 w.
Westmoreland
Jno. 1716 i.
Dorothy 1717 w.
PARTESON
Prince George
Joseph 1713 w.
PARTIN
Chesterfield
Jno. 17—i.
Surry
Eliz. 1733 i.
Sussex
Wm. 1787 w.
PARTLETT
Richmond
Edwd. 1714 i.
PARTLOW
Spotsylvania
Jno. 1790 w.
PARTRIDG
Accomack
Hugh 1671 nw.
PARTRIDGE
Henrico
Jno. 1677 a.
Isle of Wight
James 1695 nw.
Northumberland
Jno. 1783 i.
Middlesex
Saml. 1675 a.
Sussex
Nicholas 1756 w.
Wells 1765 w.
Nicholas 1791 w.
Westmoreland
Richd. 1750 w.
Jane 1761 w.
Matthew 1771 w.
Matthew 1792 i.
York
Robt. 1668 i.
PARVIN
Westmoreland
Jno. 1674 w.

PASLEY
Fluvanna
Mary 1781 w.
PASSATT
Middlesex
Richd. 1712 w.
PASSMORE
Surry
Geo. 1751 w.
PASQUET
Lancaster
Chas. 1723 i.
Jerome 1728 w.
Eliz. 1729 w.
Walter 1729 w.
William 1763 w.
York
Jno. 1761 w.
PASQUETT
Lancaster
Jerosme 1705 i.
John 1750 w.
William 1776 w.
PASQUIT
Lancaster
Margret 1788 w.
PASSON
Westmoreland
Jas. 1727 i.
PASTERIDGE
Westmoreland
Thos. 1747 i.
PASTEUR
York
Jno. 1741 w.
Martha 1746 w.
PASTUER
Isle of Wight
John 1795 w.
PASTURE
Henrico
Chas. 1736 i.
PATE
Bedford
John 1767 w.
Edward 1768 w.
Botetourt
Jeremiah 1797 w.
Goochland
Thos. 1747 i.
Halifax
Jeremiah 1799 i.
Southampton
Edward 1756 w.
Surry
Jacob 1752 w.
Jacob 1786 i.
Sussex
Thos. 1774 w.
York
Thos. 1703 w.

PATEMAN(?)
Middlesex
Thos. 1715 i.
PATEN
Westmoreland
Anthony 1733 w.
PARY
Westmoreland
Wm. 1738 w.
PATERSON
Lancaster
Jno. 1728 i.
Northampton
Jas. 1735 w.
Princess Anne
Robt. 1771 w.
York
Wm. 1703 i.
PATES(?)
Halifax
Thos. 1771 i.
King George
Wm. 1765 w.
PATMAN
Henrico
Jno. 1796 i.
PATRAM
Chesterfield
Francis 1759 w.
Danl. 1795 i.
PATRICK
Accomack
Jno. 1739 i.
Albemarle
Charles 1797 w.
Augusta
Robt. 1761 w.
Northampton
Mathew 1689 w.
Wm. 1694 i.
Judith 1697 w.
York
Walter 1679 i.
Jno. 1732 i.
Thos. 1753 i.
Jno. 1754 w.
Curtis 1785 w.
Wm. 1794 i.
Lucy 1797 w.
PATTEN
Essex
Robert 1744 i.
Stafford
Wm. 1760 w.
PATTERSON
Accomack
Jno. 1709 i.
Andrew 1737 i.
Wm. 1740 w.
Anderson 1760 w.

Augusta
Jno. 1749 w.
Nathan 1752 w.
Martha 1767 i.
Jno. 1770 w.
Jane 1772 w.
Robt. 1774 w.
Thos. 1795 i.
Bedford
Irvins 1777 i.
Berkeley
William 1782 w.
Botetourt
George 1789 w.
Essex
Phillip 1773 i.
John 1778 i.
Fairfax
John 1768 w.
Fleming 1778 w.
Thomas 1792 w.
Susanna 1799 w.
Henrico
Jno. 1746 w.
King George
Anne 1769 w.
Isle of Wight
Sanford 1777 i.
Loudoun
Mary 1763 i.
Samuel 1763 i.
Lunenburg
Danl. 1751 w.
Erwin 1761 w.
Jonathan 1774 w.
Middlesex
Jno. 1760 i.
Richd. 1765 a.
Jas. 1773 i.
Jno. 1792 i.
Montgomery
William 1788 i.
Northampton
Jas. 1736 i.
Ohio
John 1791 w.
Pittsylvania
Littlebury 1798 w.
Surry
Dennis 1713 w.

PATTESON
Chesterfield
Jas. 1767 w.
PATTEY
Halifax
James 1759 w.
PATTIE
Culpeper
James 1785 w.

PATTINSON
Westmoreland
Chas. 1742 i.
PATTISHALL
King George
Wm. 1727 i.
PATTISON
King George
Jno. 1760 w.
York
Thos. 1742-3 w.
PATTON
Augusta
Jas. 1755 w.
Jacob 1755 i.
Jno. 1757 w.
Amherst
Alex. 1784 a.
Frederick
Samuel 1756 w.
Harrison
Francis 1797 w.
PATTRICK
Northampton
Richd. 1675 w.
PATY
Lancaster
Herebert 1687 w.
PAUCHEE
Henrico
Jno. 1717 i.
PAUL
Augusta
Wm. 1757 w.
Berkeley
William 1779 w.
John 1782 w.
Chesterfield
Jas. 1783 i.
Robt. 1783 i.
Frederick
Hugh 1749 w.
Robert 1770 i.
Rockbridge
John Sr. 1795 w.
Spotsylvania
Wm. 1774 w.
PAULETT
Charlotte
John 1795 w.
Louisa
Thos. 1771 w.
Wm. 1776 i.
PAUTRY
York
Henry 1648 i.
PAVELY
Charles City
Jno. 1796 w.

PAVEY
Spotsylvania
Adam 1756 a.
PAVORY
Amelia
Thos. 1768 w.
PAXTON
Augusta
Jos. 1755 w.
Saml. 1756 w.
Thos. 1762 w.
Botetourt
Joseph 1794 i.
Rockbridge
John 1787 w.
Thomas 1788 w.
James 1789 i.
John Sr. 1789 i.
William 1796 i.
PAYLOR
Richmond
Jno. 1730 i.
Westmoreland
Wm. 1776 i.
PAYN
Northumberland
Elisha 1755 w.
Lancaster
Frances 1779 i.
Princess Anne
Thos. 1783 i.
Spotsylvania
David 1758 a.
PAYNE
Accomack
Saml. 1738 w.
Saml. 1799 w.
Bedford
John 1798 w.
Essex
Thos. 1696 i.
Robt. 1701 w.
Catherine 1704 i.
John 1710 i.
Robert 1725 w.
Moneca 1726 i.
Fairfax
William 1776 w.
William 1782 w.
Josias 1783 i.
Sanford 1792 w.
Fauquier
William 1780 i.
Fluvanna
Robt. Burton 1785 w.
Goochland
Geo. 1744 w.
Robt. 1764 i.
Robt. 1770 w.
Jesse 1771 w.
Geo. 1784 w.

Jno. 1784 w.
Jesse 1789 w.
Jno. 1795 w.
Halifax
Wm. 1771 w.
King George
Geo. 1745 i.
Charles 1749 i.
Jno. 1752 i.
Maredith 1752 i.
Barbary 1757 w.
Wm. 1770 w.
Jno. 1772 w.
Lancaster
Wm. 1700 i.
Wm. 1726 w.
Judith 1748 w.
Wm. 1749 i.
George 1761 w.
Wm. 1762 i.
Richard 1768 w.
Wm. 1769 i.
Merryman 1773 w.
Daniel 1779 w.
George 1779 i.
George 1780 i.
Merryman 1780 w.
John 1788 w.
Loudoun
Benj. C. 1790 i.
Northampton
Rowland 1639 i.
Francis 1673 w.
Orlando 1738 w.
Northumberland
Wm. 1726 w.
George 1770 w.
Pittsylvania
Jno. 1773 w.
Mark 1775 w.
Jno. 1781 w.
Josias 1785 w.
Robt. 1791 w.
Prince William
Henry 1796 i.
Rappahannock
Robt. 1675 w.
Richmond
Geo. Sr. 1711 w.
Southampton
Thos. 1799 i.
Spotsylvania
Jno. 1772 a.
Westmoreland
Jno. [1668?] w.
Jno. 1697 w.
Elinor 1737 i.
Richd. 1779 i.
Richd. 1780 i.
Geo. 1790 w.

PAYRAS
York
Jno. 1752 w.
PAYNTAR
Princess Anne
John 1792 w.
PAYNTER
Sussex
Jno. 1772 i.
PAYTE
Montgomery
Anthony 1782 i.
PAYTON
Culpeper
William 1787 w.
Westmoreland
Carnaby 1773 i.
Jno. 1778 w.
Geo. C. 1791 w.
Wm. 1791 w.
Anthony 1791 i.
PEACH
King George
Thos. [1778?] w.
Surry
Matthias 1679 a.
Westmoreland
Geo. 1725 w.
Jos. 1750 i.
PEACHEY
Essex
Samuel 1784 w.
Prince William
Samuel 1779 w.
Richmond
Saml. 1712 w.
Mary 1713 w.
Saml. 1714 i.
Saml. 1750 w.
Saml. 1795 w.
PEACOCK
Frederick
William 1785 i.
Princess Anne
Andrew 1743 w.
Spotsylvania
Richd. 1760 a.
Surry
Wm. 1722 w.
PEAD
King George
Phillips 1751 i.
Jas. 1757 w.
Philip 1768 i.
Norfolk
Jno. 1678 w.
Princess Anne
Wm. 1719 w.
Norfolk
Wm. 1784 i.

PEAK
Fairfax
William, Jr. 1756 w.
Northampton
Jno. 1789 i.
PEAKE
Fairfax
William 1761 w.
Humphrey 1785 w.
William 1794 w.
Fauquier
John 1780 w.
PEALE
Princess Anne
Robt. 1705 w.
PEAR
Shenandoah
Philip 1799 i.
PEARCE
Accomack
Edwd. 1781 w.
Cumberland
Edmund 1785 i.
Jeremiah 1792 w.
Fauquier
Peter 1768 w.
Frederick
Lewis 1764 i.
Henrico
Francis 1792 w.
Francis 1794 w.
Jos. 1795 i.
Isle of Wight
Philip 1728 w.
Thomas 1742 w.
Richmond
Jno. 1721 i.
Surry
Richd. 1712 i.
Westmoreland
Jno. 1698 i.
Copland 1777 i.
PEAREY
Orange
Charles 1792 w.
PEARIS
Frederick
George 1752 w.
Sarah 1753 i.
PEARL
Accomack
Comfort 1769 w.
Richmond
Richd., Jr. 1716 i.
PEARLE
Fauquier
William 1785 w.
King George
Richd. 1725 i.

PEARMUN(?)
Goochland
Edwd. 1733 i.
PEARS
Frederick
Hugh 1749 a.
Westmoreland
Jno. 1698 w.
PEARSE
Isle of Wight
——— 1693 i.
Westmoreland
Geo. 1740 w.
PEARSON
Brunswick
Jno. 1798 w.
Fairfax
Thomas 1744 w.
Samuel 1753 i.
Simon 1798 w.
Frederick
Abel 1745 i.
Enoch 1752 i.
Lancaster
John 1782 w.
Richmond
Jno. 1767 i.
Stafford
Simon 1733 w.
Simon 1736 i.
Hannah 1748 w.
Ann 1748 w.
York
Wm. 1778 i.
PEART
Northumberland
Francis 1742-3 i.
PEASCUD
York
Robt. 1705 i.
PEASELEY
York
Michell 1647 w.
PEATEL
Essex
Thos. 1700 w.
Jno. 1700 i.
PEATON
Norfolk
Timothy 1746 w.
PEATRASS
Montgomery
Matthew 1798 i.
PEATROSS
Essex
Thomas 1716 w.
PEBWORTH
Norfolk
William 1760 w.
Wm. 1768 i.

Princess Anne
Martha 1768 i.
Wm. 1792 w.
Molton 1795 w.
PECK
Accomack
Benj. 1785 i.
King George
Wm. 1754 i.
Wm., Sr. 1754 w.
Robt. 1771 w.
Reuben 1776 w.
Reuben 1779 a.
Mary 1780 w.
Jno. 1785 w.
Princess Anne
Robt. 1776 i.
Richmond
Jno. 1719 i.
Jno. 1795 w.
PEDDICOAT
Stafford
Jno. 1736 i.
PEDDENTON
Northampton
Henry 1647 i.
PEDDON
Isle of Wight
James 1694 w.
PEDIN
Isle of Wight
James 1784 w.
James 1749 i.
Mary 1752 w.
PEDINGTON
Surry
Thos. 1702 w.
PEEBLES
Brunswick
Jno. 1772 w.
Joseph 1782 w.
Greensville
William 1784 w.
Surry
Thos. 1743 i.
Sussex
Thos. 1782 w.
PEEBODY
Fairfax
John 1784 w.
PEED
King George
Jas. 1757 i.
Philip 1779 w.
Jas., Sr. 1780 a.
Jno. 1798 i.
Norfolk
Thomas 1787 w.
Northumberland
Isaac 1783 i.

Princess Anne
Jno. 1742 w.
Wm. 1780 i.
Joel 1784 w.
PEEK
Prince Edward
John Sr. 1776 w.
PEEKENS
Montgomery
William 1786 w.
PEEL
Accomack
Robert 1769 i.
PEEPLES
Sussex
Jesse 1782 w.
PEER
Shenandoah
Jacob 1799 i.
PEEREE (?)
Orange
Wm. 1761 a.
PEERIE
Augusta
Thos. 1763 w.
PEERS
Amelia
Wm. 1773 i.
Goochland
Anderson 1793 w.
Jno. M. 1797 i.
PEERSE
Accomack
Jno. 1740 i.
PEERY
Augusta
Jno. 1762 w.
Thos. 1786 i.
PEETE
Greensville
Richard 1782 w.
PEETERS
Norfolk
Simon 1679-80 w.
PEGRAM
York
Danl. 1726 w.
Sarah 1727 w.
Jno. 1753 i.
PEIRCE
Frederick
Lewis 1762 w.
Michael 1781 w.
Isle of Wight
Philip 1728 i.
Thomas 1740 w.
King George
Jno. 1735 i.
Lancaster
Thos. 1723 i.

Middlesex
Edward 1698 a.
Southampton
Eliz. 1794 w.
York
Richd. 1687 w.
PEIRCEHOUSE
Montgomery
Thomas 1782 i.
PELLS
Rappahannock
Timothy 1677 w.
PELSERF
Accomack
Francis 1780 i.
PEMBERTON
Cumberland
Richd. 1769 w.
Frederick
Geoge 1757 w.
Joseph 1758 i.
Louisa
Abishai 1797 i.
Norfolk
Mary 1780 i.
Richmond
Wm. 1710 i.
Spotsylvania
Wm. 1786 w.
PEN
Loudoun
Saml. 1780 i.
PENCE
Augusta
Jacob 1751 i.
Valentine 1761 w.
Shenandoah
Jacob 1779 i.
PENDALL
Amelia
Margett 1746 i.
PENDERGRASS
Westmoreland
Edmd. 1727 i.
PENDLETON
Amherst
Wm. 1774 w.
Berkeley
Nathaniel 1793 w.
Culpeper
James 1763 w.
Eliz. 1769 w.
James 1793 w.
Henrico
Nathl. 1791 a.
PENENTON
Surry
Thos. 1727 w.
PENICK
Hanover
Jno. 1734 a.

Prince Edward
Jno. 1787 w.
Charles 1798 w.
PENIX
Amelia
Wm. 1750 w.
Hanover
Edwd. 1734 w.
Prince Edward
John 1788 i.
PENLEY
Richmond
Wm. 1746 i.
PENLY
Northumberland
Thos. 1742-3 i.
PENMAN
York
Thos. 1759 w.
PENN
Brunswick
Philip 1774 i.
Amherst
Moses Jr. 1774 w.
Wm. 1776 w.
Jos. 1792 a.
Gabriel 1794 w.
Geo. 1796 w.
Brunswick
Moses 1781 w.
Northampton
Crispiani 1637 w.
Rappahannock
Jno. 1677 w.
Spotsylvania
Jno. 1772 w.
Wm. 1781 w.
Mary 1786 w.
Thos. 1793 w.
PENNCELLOR
Frederick
Nicholas 1770 w.
PENNELL
Northampton
Jno. 1660 w.
Katherine 1660 w.
Westmoreland
Thos. 1698 w.
PENNER
Wythe
Peter 1798 i.
PENNEY
Isle of Wight
Ralph 1728 w.
Middlesex
Edwd. 1678 a.
Norfolk
Bryan 1743-4 w.
PENNINGTON
Brunswick
Edwd. 1752 w.

Wm. 1784 w.
Sack 1794 w.
Goochland
Paul 1730 i.
Mecklenburg
Jno. Geo. 1797 w.
Sussex
Jno. (1) 1766 w.
Jno. (2) 1766 w.
Moses 1766 i.
Joseph 1768 w.
Joshua 1768 w.
Jno. 1770 i.
Moses 1770 i.
Thos. 1772 w.
Jno. 1773 w.
David 1781 w.
David 1783 w.
Thos. 1785 i.
PENNY
Isle of Wight
Richard 1694 w.
William 1695 w.
John 1717 w.
John 1735 w.
John 1758 i.
Northumberland
Jno. 1740 i.
Stafford
Jas. 1737 w.
PENTECOST
Brunswick
Francis 1799 i.
Scarborough 1795 w.
PEPER
Frederick
Joseph 1785 i.
Westmoreland
Jno. 1698 i.
PEPPER
Surry
Stephen 1746 w.
Sussex
Richd. 1759 w.
Washington
Elisha 1781 i.
York
Jno. 1668 i.
PERAULT
Henrico
Chas. 1717 w.
PERCIFFULL
Lancaster
Eppa A. 1789 i.
PERCIFULL
Northumberland
Thos. 1718 w.
John 1751 i.
PERDUE
Chesterfield
Josiah 1794 w.

PERE
Norfolk
Henry 1673 w.
PEREGOY
Frederick
Henry 1765 w.
PERFECT
Lou
Christopher 1791 w.
PERKEY
Augusta
Henry 1762 w.
PERKINS
Albemarle
Joel 1793 w.
Essex
Henry 1736 w.
Griffing 1745 i.
Fluvanna
Richd. 1787 w.
Abram 1799 w.
Goochland
Constant, Jr. 1769 w.
Constantine 1769 i.
Philimon 1769 i.
Obedience 1771 i.
Stephen 1772 w.
Nicholas 1777 w.
Walker 1782 i.
James 1784 w.
Mary 1797 w.
Halifax
Nicholas 1762 w.
Robt. 1790 w.
Jno. 1798 w.
Henrico
Nicholas 1710 i.
Nicholas 1712 w.
Isle of Wight
Edward 1686 w.
Lancaster
Thomas 1750 w.
Louisa
Jesse 1796 w.
Norfolk
William 1722 w.
Orange
Elisha 1742 w.
Pittsylvania
Constant 1790 w.
Philemon 1795 i.
Rappahannock
Thos. 1684 w.
Stafford
Wm. 1701 i.
Mathew 1708 i.
York
Jno. 1694 w.
Susannah 1696 i.

PERKINSON
Amelia
Seth 1782 w.
Jeremiah 1789 w.
Matthew 1792 w.
Field 1799 i.
Wm. 1798 i.
Chesterfield
Francis 1768 w.
Wm. 1778 w.
Jno. 1786 w.
Henrico
Seth 1735 w.
Northampton
Edwd. 1683 i.
PEROUNEY
Fairfax
William 1756 i.
PERRIN
Charlotte
Joseph 1773 w.
Halifax
Saml. 1785 i.
Jane 1786 w.
Saml. 1795 i.
Jane 1796 i.
Henrico.
Thos. 1689 a.
Richd. 1695 w.
Richd. 1704 i.
Anne 1711 w.
PERROT
Middlesex
Mary 1767 i.
PERROTT
Middlesex
Richd., Sr. 1686 w.
Margt. 1687 w.
Henry 1706 a.
Robt. 1723 i.
Curtis 1740 w.
PERROW
Campbell
Stephen 1792 i.
PERRY
Accomack
Jno. 1708 w.
Thos. 1779 i.
Brunswick
Micajah 1760 i.
Charles City
Eliz. 1771 i.
Nicho. 1770 w.
Littleberry 1793 w.
Chesterfield
Jno. 1789 i.
Patience 1799 w.
Essex
John 1724 i.
Fluvanna
Geo. 1785 i.

Isle of Wight
Phillip 1667 w.
Orange
Benj. 1782 w.
Jno. 1797 i.
Pierce 1796 w.
Princess Anne
Joseph 1718 i.
Edwd. 1740 w.
Shenandoah
John 1795 i.
Samuel 1795 w.
Westmoreland
Jno. 1743 i.
PERRYMAN
York
Robt. 1705 i.
PERSE
Henrico
Wm. 1712 w.
PERSINGER
Augusta
Philip 1761 i.
Botetourt
Jacob 1789 i.
PERSON
Brunswick
Thos. 1771 i.
Thos. 1774 i.
Greensville
Thomas 1783 w.
Henry
Joseph 1784 i.
Isle of Wight
Samuel 1754 w.
James 1757 i.
Samuel 1762 w.
Lunenburg
Chris. 1760 w.
Southampton
Jno. 1752 w.
Thos. 1754 w.
Henry 1759 w.
Jno. 1767 w.
Wm. 1768 w.
Jno. 1773 w.
Collier 1782 w.
Philip 1782 w.
Anthony 1799 w.
Jno. 1799 w.
Surry
Jno. 1738 w.
Francis 1758 i.
York
Langhone 1678 i.
PERSONS
Northampton
Wm. 1707 i.
York
Christopher 1697-8 i.

PERVIS
Amherst
Geo. 1794 w.
PERY
Essex
Mary 1735 w.
PESCUD
York
Thos. 1783 i.
PESTELL
Surry
Jno. 1695 i.
PESTRIDGE
Stafford
Eleanor 1749 w.
PETER
Surry
Jno. 1763 w.
Robt. 1789 w.
York
Margaret 1742 i.
PETERS
Frederick
Otho 1757 i.
Fauquier
John 1781 w.
John 1795 i.
Middlesex
Wm. 1782 w.
Princess Anne
James 1709 w.
Rappahannock
Henry 1674 w.
Randolph 1684 w.
Shenandoah
Ulrick 1776 w.
Philip 1792 a.
Surry
Joannah 1721 i.
Sussex
Thos. 1760 i.
Thos. 1774 w.
Thos. 1777 w.
York
Jno. 1671 w.
Eliz. 1679 w.
Robt. 1727 i.
Edwd. 1757 i.
Jno. 1758 i.
Eliz. 1759 nw.
Francis 1778 w.
PETERSON
Brunswick
Batte 1752 i.
Jno. 1769 w.
Greensville
Batt 1795 w.
Isle of Wight
John 1731 w.
Lancaster
Edwd. 1727 a.

Rappahannock
Neale 1678 w.
Southampton
Gomer 1795 i.
Spotsylvania
Jos. 1766 w.
PETEWAY
Surry
Wm. 1710-11 i.
PETIT
Henrico
Josue 1707 w.
York
Jno. 1670 w.
PETNEY
Essex
Jno. 1743 w.
PETREE
Princess Anne
James 1753 i.
Frances 1760 i.
PETRIE
Surry
Wm. 1763 i.
PETTAWAY
Surry
Wm. 1699-1700 w.
Sussex
Sterling 1792 w.
PETTE
Essex
John 1737 w.
Norfolk
Thos. 1674 w.
PETTER
Northampton
Robt. 1714 i.
PETTERSON
Norfolk
Ann 1786 w.
PETTEWAY
Sussex
Jno. 1781 w.
PETTICREW
Campbell
Mathew 1798 w.
PETTIGREW
Accomack
Jas. 1772 w.
Leah 1773 w.
PETTIJOHN
Northampton
Jas. 1665 i.
PETTIS
Isle of Wight
Roger 1677 i.
Roger 1678 i.
PETTIT
Accomack
Jno. Jr. 1772 nw.
Jno. 1779 i.

Jno. 1785 w.
Essex
Thomas 1694 w.
Thomas 1720 w.
Northampton
Justinian 1712 i.
Jacob 1747 i.
Jno. Sr. 1750 w.
Wm. 1756 i.
Francis 1760 i.
Jacob 1760 i.
Henry 1760 i.
Jonathan 1761 i.
Thos. 1777 w.
Wm. 1784 i.
PETTITE
Northampton
Mary 1704 w.
PETTITT
Northampton
Ann 1650 w.
Francis 1688 w.
Thos. 1716 w.
Bartho. 1734 w.
Wm. 1755 w.
Amey 1764 w.
Wm. 1769 w.
Leah 1784 w.
PETTIWAY
Surry
Burwell 1784 w.
PETTOTH
Fairfax
John 1780 i.
PETTS
Richmond
Jeremiah 1755 i.
PETTUS
Charlotte
Dabney 1788 w.
Jno. 1799 w.
Halifax
Chas. 1797 w.
Eliz. 1799 w.
Louisa
Jno. 1770 w.
Thos. Waters 1791 w
Lunenburg
Thos. 1779 w.
Jno. Sr. 1781 w.
Sarah 1798 w.
Jno. 1799 i.
Mecklenburg
Thos. 1797 i.
Harriott 1799 i.
Spotsylvania
Wm. 1798 w.
PETTWAY
Brunswick
Frances 1770 w.
Jno. 1770 w.

Greensville
Edward 1795 w.
Elizabeth 1795 w.
Surry
Robt. 1728 w.
Joseph 1745 w.
Thos. 1755 w.
Joseph 1765 i.
Edwd. 1766 w.
Sarah 1772 w.
Jno. 1799 w.
Sussex
Robt. 1757 w.
Robt. 1772 w.
Edwd. 1773 w.
Wm. 1774 w.
Edwd. 1779 w.
Robt. 1784 w.
Hinchey 1791 w.
Edwd. 1795 i.
PETTY
Culpeper
Zachariah 1799 w.
Orange
Thos. 1750 w.
Geo. 1752 w.
Jno. 1770 w.
Princess Anne
Edward 1793 w.
Wm. 1796 w.
Prince William
Joseph 1784 w.
Richmond
Geo. 1726 w.
Chris. 1727 w.
Jno. 1727 i.
Chris. 1740 w.
PETTYCREW
Rockbridge
James 1799 w.
PETTYJOHN
Princess Anne
Wm. 1712 i.
PETTYPOOL
Lunenburg
Wm. Sr. 1774 w.
Prince George
Wm. 1726 w.
PEW
Henrico
Henry 1711 w.
Northumberland
Jas. 1742-3 i.
Princess Anne
Hugh 1720 i.
Stephen 1720 w.
Mary 1722 i.
PEYSONIE
Fairfax
William 1755 i.

PEYTON
Culpeper
William 1771 w.
John 1782 w.
Thomas 1782 w.
Fairfax
Valentine 1796 w.
Frederick
Henry, Jr. 1776 w.
Henry 1779 i.
Loudoun
Craven 1781 w.
Norfolk
John 1763 w.
Prince William
Henry 1781 w.
Valentine 1786 w.
Stafford
Jno. 1760 w.
Westmoreland
Henry 1659 w.
Valentine 1665 w.
Gerrard 1687-8 w.
PFIPER
Shenandoah
Henry, Sr. 1778 w.
PHARIS
Louisa
Chas. 1779 a.
PHARLOW
Surry
Joseph 1679 w.
PHEASANT
Southampton
John 1755 w.
PHELING
Norfolk
Jno. 1790 w.
PHELPS
Albemarle
Wm. 1749 w.
Thos. 1751 w.
Thos. 1772 i.
Bedford
John 1772 w.
Cumberland
John 1777 i.
Saml. 1790 w.
Goochland
Jno. 1747 w.
Halifax
Jno. 1794 w.
Jno. 1796 i.
Westmoreland
Thos. 1671 w.
York
Edwd. 1678 nw.
PHENIX
Brunswick
Abraham 1750 w.
Drury 1784 w.
Ann 1786 i.

Jno. 1791 w.
PHIERPACK
Orange
Henry Fredk. 1745 w
PHILBEE
Accomack
Geo. 1750 w.
PHILBY
Accomack
Stephen 1687 w.
Geo. 1743 i.
Geo. 1751 i.
PHILIP
Berkeley
Christian 1793 w.
PHILIPS
Accomack
Jacob 1790 w.
Mathias 1792 i.
Berkeley
Thomas 1780 i.
Fairfax
John 1755 w.
Jno. 1798 i.
King George
Thos. 1733 i.
Benj. 1768 w.
Loudoun
Thos. Sr. 1766 w.
Benj. 1781 w.
Jenkin 1785 w.
Thomas 1796 w.
Norfolk
John 1775 i.
Northumberland
Jno. 1742 i.
Stafford
David 1731 i.
Sussex
James 1782 w.
York
Eliz. 1745 w.
PHILIPSON
York
Robt. 1754 w.
PHILLIPPS
Norfolk
Daniel 1720 w.
PHILLIPS
Accomack
Wm. Sr. 1730 w.
Jno. 1760 w.
Jno. 1775 w.
Rachel 1778 nw.
Benj. 1795 w.
Jno. 1798 w.
Susanna 1799 w.
Amelia
Richd. 1793 w.
Amherst
Thos. 1778 w.
Matthew 1791 w.

Leonard 1798 i.
Wm. 1799 i.
Bedford
Stephen 1788 w.
Brunswick
Joseph 1777 w.
Charles City
Henry 1774 i.
Culpeper
Dawnil 1769 w.
Essex
Phinehas 1741 i.
Wm. 1747 i.
Jno. 1751 w.
Frederick
Solomon 1786 w.
Halifax
Jno. 1759 w.
Greensville
John 1799 w.
Isle of Wight
William 1681 i.
John Sr. 1795 w.
Lancaster
Jno. 1655 w.
Jas. 1690 w.
Ann 1768 w.
Louisa
Richd. 1776 i.
Thos. 1779 a.
Thos. 1783 i.
Richard 1791 i.
Katherine 1794 w.
John 1795 w.
Lunenburg
Jno. 1761 w.
Priscilla 1765 w.
Geo. 1786 w.
Mecklenburg
Martin 1781 w.
Martin 1794 i.
Norfolk
Lawrence 1654 i.
Daniel 1782 i.
Northumberland
Geo. 1795 i.
Jas. 1796 i.
Sarah 1797 i.
Princess Anne
Lemuel 1696 a.
Henry 1772 i.
Courtney 1773 i.
Mitchell 1782 i.
Eleanor 1789 w.
Richmond
Jno. 1701 w.
Mary 1712 w.
Jno. 1714 i.
Geo. 1716 w.
Jas. 1716 i.
Susannah 1726 w.
Tobias 1740 w.

Jno. 1744 w.
Betty 1750 i.
Wm. 1753 w.
Joshua 1758 w.
Jno. 1775 w.
Jos. 1778 w.
Southampton
Aaron 1771 w.
Joseph 1774 i.
Jno. 1779 w.
Moses 1792 w.
Surry
David 1696 i.
Jno. 1699 i.
Jno. 1714 i.
Wm. 1720 w.
Mary 1727 w.
Wm. 1734 w.
Wm. 1737 i.
Nathaniel 1738 w.
Jno. 1749 i.
Ann 1750 i.
Wm. 1750 i.
Jno. 1759 w.
Benj. 1767 i.
Wm. 1778 w.
Hannah 1783 i.
Washington
James 1781 i.
Westmoreland
Jno. 1746 i.
York
Edwd. 1709 w.
Nicholas 1715 w.
Thos. 1774 w.
Thos. 1781 w.
Aaron 1783 w.
Wm. 1785 w.
PHILPOT
Norfolk
Lettissue 1780 w.
Princess Anne
Henry 1737 i.
Chris. 1754 w.
Mary 1763 w.
Jno. 1782 i.
PHIPS
Brunswick
Wm. 1770 i.
PHIPPS
Brunswick
Wm. 1771 i.
Botetourt
Joseph 1772 w.
Frederick
Elinor 1745 i.
Lancaster
Mary 1709 w.
PHIN
Norfolk
John 1761 w.

PHINNEY
Accomack
Wm. 1766 i.
PHOBIN
Northampton
Paul 1705 w.
PHRIPP
Norfolk
John 1776 w.
Matthew 1780 w.
PHROND
Lancaster
Phillip 1745 w.
Benj. 1746 i.
PICKE
Henrico
Geo. 1752 w.
PICKINGS
Bedford
John 1772 i.
PICKENBERGER
Shenandoah
Abraham 1781 w.
PICKERELL
Westmoreland
Henry 1703 i.
PICKERIN
Northumberland
Wm. 1712 w.
PICKERING
Frederick
William 1789 w.
John 1796 w.
PICKETT
Essex
Henry 1702 w.
William 1743 w.
Fauquier
Wm. 1766 w.
William Sanford
1798 w.
Frederick
Henry 1797 i.
Stafford
Joyce 1703 i.
PICKLES
Westmoreland
Jno. 1733 i.
PICKRELL
Northumberland
David 1770 w.
Spencer 1774 w.
PICKREN
Northumberland
Geo. 1664 w.
Geo. 1751 w.
David 1771 i.
PICKRON
Northumberland
Wm. 1798 w.

PIECROFT
Westmoreland
Nath. 1695 w.
PIED (?)
Norfolk
John 1678 i.
PIERCE
Amherst
Wm. 1783 a.
Frederick
Hugh 1749 i.
Charles 1756 i.
Michael 1781 i.
Henrico
Richd. 1688 op.
Wm. 1754 w.
Jos. 1792 w.
Isle of Wight
George 1705 i.
Jeremiah 1729 i.
Thomas 1740 w.
John 1752 w .
Honour 1761 w.
Peter 1772 w.
Peter 1790 i.
William 1791 w.
John 1793 i.
William 1793 i.
Loudoun
John 1778 i.
John 1790 i.
Norfolk
Ignatious 1797 w.
Northumberland
Richd. 1740 w.
Jos. 1792 i.
Southampton
Rice B. 1796 a.
Surry
Jeremiah 1793 w.
Westmoreland
Wm. 1702 w.
Wm. 1733 w.
Wm. 1782 w.
Wm. 1784 i.
Jos. 1798 w.
York
Edith 1739 w.
Matthew 1737 w.
Matthew 1755 i.
PIERSON
Augusta
Geo. 1793 i.
PIFER
Frederick
Joseph 1769 w.
PIGEON
Orange
Wm. 1745 i.
Prince George
Richd. 1718 w.

PIGG
Chesterfield
Francis 1783 w.
Pittsylvania
Paul 1767 w.
Jno. 1785 w.
Hezekiah 1785 w.
Spotsylvania
Edwd. Jr. 1733 w.
Edw. 1741 w.
PIGGOTT
Henrico
Jno. 1702 w.
Loudoun
Samuel 1799 i.
Norfolk
Sarah 1689 w.
PIGOT
Northampton
Francis 1684 w.
Wm. 1738 i.
Ann 1739 w.
Culpeper 1752 i.
Ralph 1752 w.
Ralph 1756 w.
Jno. 1772 w.
PIGOTT
Northampton
Ralph 1705 i.
Ralf 1715 i.
Jno. 1773 i.
PIGHTHING
Princess Anne
Phillip 1701 w.
PIKE
Loudoun
Jonathan 1790 i.
Northampton
Henry 1723 w.
Stafford
Jno. 1699 i.
PILAND
Isle of Wight
James 1740 i.
James 1756 i.
William 1769 w.
Surry
Geo. 1745 w.
Richd. 1757 w.
Mary 1760 w.
Wm. 1777 w.
PILCHER
Accomack
Peggy 1797 w.
Lancaster
Wm. 1710 i.
PILE
Berkeley
Richard 1780 i.
PILES
Bath
Francis 1798 i.

Essex
Vincent Godfrey
1737 i.
John 1758 i.
Ludo 1764 i.
Cathron 1770 w.
Samuel 1779 w.
Halifax
Godfrey 1780 w.
Jno. 1781 w.
Southampton
Vincent 1782 i.
PILKERTON
Brunswick
Richd. 1787 w.
PILKINGTON
Isle of Wight
Wm. 1730-31 i.
Norfolk
John 1734 i.
PILKINTON
Brunswick
Agness 1794 w.
Richd. 1798 i.
Essex
William 1748 w.
Isle of Wight
William 1729 i.
PILLION
Westmoreland
Jno. 1792 i.
PILLISTOR
Prince William
Richd. 1744 a.
PIMMET
Fairfax
Geo. 1744 w.
PIMMIT
Fairfax
Sarey 1748 w.
Moses 1750 w.
PIMMITT
Fairfax
Edward 1751 w.
PINCHBACK
York
Thos. 1707 w.
PINCKARD
Lancaster
Jno. 1734 w.
Jno. 1738 i.
Thos. 1740 w.
Jno. 1743 w.
Mary 1749 w.
James 1751 w.
James 1754 i.
William 1762 i.
Thomas 1768 w.
James 1769 i.
Spencer 1769 i.
Thomas 1783 w.
Thomas 1784 i.

Jeduthum 1785 i.
Mary 1785 w.
James 1790 w.
Thomas 1795 w.
Northumberland
Robt. 1787 i.
Richmond
Elizabeth 1763 w.
Elizabeth 1770 i.
Westmoreland
Thos. 1776 w.
PINDER
Northampton
Jos. 1720 w.
PINES
Northumberland
Margt. 1752 w.
Spotsylvania
Lewis, Jr. 1787 w.
Lewis 1788 w.
PININGTON
Surry
Edwd. 1728 w.
PINKARD
Franklin
John 1788 i.
Henry
John 1782 w.
Lancaster
Jno. 1690 w.
Eliz. 1699 i.
PINKERTON
Norfolk
James 1784 w.
James 1791 i.
Sarah 1798 i.
Stafford
Jno. 1763 i.
PINKETHMAN
York
Timothy 1705 i.
Rebecca 1707-8 w.
Timothy 1709 i.
Wm. 1712 w.
PINKETT
York
Thos. 1715 i.
PINKSTONE
Fairfax
Greenbury 1772 i.
PINN
Halifax
David 1797 w.
PINNER
Isle of Wight
Thomas 1765 w.
Mary 1778 i.
John 1785 w.
Josiah 1794 w.
Norfolk
Wm. 1667 w.

PINNICK
Prince Edward
Edwd. 1759 w.
PINOR
Culpeper
Thomas 1777 w.
PINQUITE
Loudoun
Esther 1799 w.
PINSON
Lunenburg
Aaron, Sr. 1758 w.
PIPER
Fairfax
David 1766 i.
Harry 1780 w.
King George
Wm. 1792 w.
Ann 1798 w.
Shenandoah
Henry 1798 i.
Westmoreland
Jno. 1673 w.
Jno. 1707 i.
Jno. 1759 w.
Jonathan 1766 w.
PITCHER
Culpeper
John 1774 w.
Loudoun
Edwd. 1795 w.
PITHINGTON
Essex
Ambrose 1777 i.
PITMAN
Accomack
Jos. 1683 w.
Isle of Wight
Thomas 1730 w.
Edward 1746 i.
King George
Wm. 1731 i.
Wm. 1734 i.
Wm. 1735 i .
Isaac 1747 i.
Wm. 1775 a.
Moses [1778?] w.
Lancaster
Jno. 1702 w.
Elizabeth 1710 w.
Wm. 1719 i.
Benjamin 1762 w.
Benjamin 1785 i.
Robert 1787. i.
Thomas 1790 i.
Benjamin 1792 i.
Northumberland
Thos. 1742-3 w.
Robt. 1773 i.
Wm. 1778 i.
Southampton
John 1781 w.

PITSENBERGER
Shenandoah
Abm. 1782 i.
PITT
Accomack
Robt. 1672 i.
Robt. 1714 w.
Robt. 1756 w.
Robt. 1759 i.
Anne 1772 w.
Tabey 1774 w.
Jno. 1779 w.
Robt. 1794 w.
Isle of Wight
Robert 1674 w.
Thomas 1688 w.
Thomas 1691 i.
William 1692 i.
John 1702-3 w.
Mary 1711 i.
Robert 1712 w.
Henry 1719 w.
Thomas 1728 i.
Henry 1734 i.
John 1734 w.
Thomas 1746 i.
Henry 1748 w.
John 1748 w.
Thomas 1748 i.
Henry 1757 w.
John 1761 w.
Joseph 1764 i.
Sarah 1765 i.
Henry 1775 w.
Thomas 1775 i.
Jacob 1781 w.
Henry 1785 w.
Joseph 1789 i.
Isham 1794 w.
James 1799 w.
Northampton
Andrew 1715 w.
Surry
Charles 1750 w.
York
Sarah 1773 w.
Geo. 1776 i.
PITTMAN
Accomack
Jno. 1687 w.
Montgomery
Joshua 1796 w.
PITTS
Accomack
Jno. 1745 w.
Isaac 1747 w.
Wm. 1751 w.
Hannah 1752 w.
Wm. 1753 i.
Saml. 1767 i.
Culpeper
Joseph 1797 w.

Essex
John 1730 w.
Reuben 1782 i.
David 1783 w.
David 1793 w.
Norfolk
Thomas 1685 w.
Northampton
Thos. 1730 w.
Edmd. 1749 w.
Hillary 1755 i.
Jacob 1761 w.
Jno. 1761 w.
Major 1762 w.
Jno. 1770 w.
Jacob 1779 i.
Geo. 1788 w.
Orange
Jno. 1738 a.
Surry
Charles 1751 i.
Hannah 1779 w.
PITZER
Frederick
Wolsey 1770 w.
Loudoun
Harman 1783 i.
PIWELL
Accomack
Chas. 1708 w.
PLAILE
King George
Jno. 1734 i.
PLATT
Henrico
Gilbert 1691 w.
Mary 1700 w.
Powhatan
Henson Honor 1794 i.
Prince George
Randall 1719 w.
Spotsylvania
Barnett 1764 a.
York
Lawrence 1692-3 w.
PLAYSTEAD
Norfolk
William 1799 i.
PLEASANT
Surry
Buford 1784 w.
Sussex
Geo. 1782 w.
PLEASANTS
Chesterfield
Wm. 1785 i.
Cumberland
John 1763 w.
Goochland
Wm. 1772 i.
Thos. 1775 w.
Thos. 1776 w.

Richd. 1778 w.
Mary 1797 w.
Henrico
Jno. 1690 w.
Jno. 1698 w.
Jane 1709 w.
Jno. 1714 w.
Jos. 1725 w.
Jane 1726-7 w.
Jos. 1728 i.
Jno. 1733 w.
Thos. 1745 w.
Robt. 1751 w.
Jno. 1783 w.
Jno. (2) 1783 w.
Jonathan 1783 w.
Jacob 1784 w.
Jno. 1784 w.
Jos. 1785 w.
Jno. 1789 i.
Sarah 1790 i.
Thos. 1790 w.
Robt. 1794 i.
Thomas 1796 w.
Jos. 1798 i.
PLEDGE
Goochland
Wm. 1779 w.
Wm. 1781 w.
Francis 1785 i.
PLEDGER
Isle of Wight
Thomas 1752 w.
Martha 1782 w.
PLEY
Essex
Robt. 1697 w.
Geo. 1701 w.
Eliz. 1719 w.
PLOMTON
Princess Anne
Richd. 1722 w.
PLOTNER
Berkeley
John 1791 i.
PLOVER
Rappahannock
Junipher 1661 ? i.
PLOVIER
York
Peter 1677-8 w.
PLOWMAN
Spotsylvania
William 1733 w.
PLUMBE
Northampton
Eliz. 1670 i.
PLUMER
Norfolk
Lawrence 1654 w.

PLUMMER
Princess Anne
George 1792 w.
Richmond
Thos. 1749 w.
Betty 1751 nw.
Jno. 1771 w.
PLUNKETT
Orange
Jno. 1758 w.
PLUNKITT
Norfolk
Garrett 1744 w.
PNILLER
Shenandoah
Catherine 1792 a.
POACK
Augusta
Robt. 1774 w.
POAGE
Augusta
Jno. 1789 w.
Thos., Jr. 1794 w.
Mary 1794 w.
Wm. 1799 w.
Botetourt
George 1786 w.
Robert 1788 w.
John 1789 w.
Orange
Seth 1740 a.
POAKE
Surry
Jno. 1725 w.
POE
Essex
Samuel 1725 i.
Samuel 1726 i.
POINDEXTER
Cumberland
Benj. 1766 w.
Louisa
Jno. 1753 w.
Richd. 1776 a.
Christian 1779 w.
Wm. 1779 i.
Wm. 1793 a.
Thos. 1796 w.
Mecklenburg
Philip 1790 w.
Sarah 1790 w.
POINTER
Halifax
Saml., Sr. 1799 w.
Norfolk
Seth 1784 w.
POKE
Shenandoah
Barbara 1794 a.
POKER
Frederick
John 1750 w.

Ulrick 1751 i.
POLAND
Berkeley
Samuel 1780 w.
Loudoun
Samuel 1782 i.
POLE
Northampton
Godfrey 1729 w.
POLEY
Richmond
Jno. 1743 w.
POLK
Loudoun
Moses 1779 i.
POLLAND
Chesterfield
Thos. 1754 w.
POLLARD
Amelia
Wm. 1782 i.
Wm. 1787 i.
Jos. 1789 w.
Wm. 1792 i.
Bedford
Francis 1771 w.
Chesterfield
Walter 1768 w.
Culpeper
Richard 1770 w.
James 1779 i.
Frederick
Joseph 1773 w.
Goochland
Joseph 1792 w.
King George
Richd. 1778 nw.
Lancaster
Robt. 1709-10 w.
Richd. 1721 i.
John 1750-1 i.
Thomas 1751 w.
George 1760 w.
William 1762 w.
Margaret 1768 w.
Thomas 1770 w.
Lunenburg
Wm. 1761 w.
Orange
Wm. 1746 w.
Spotsylvania
Ann 1754 w.
Sarah 1789 a.
POLLEY
Pittsylvania
David 1785 i.
POLLICK
Northumberland
Patrick 1716-17 w.
POLLIN
York
Jno. 1720 ab.

POLLING
York
Jno. 1720 w.
POLLOCK
Berkeley
Allen 1798 w.
Goochland
Jno. 1754 w.
Shenandoah
James T. 1797 i.
POLLOTH
Fairfax
John 1777 i.
POLLSON
Botetourt
Benjamin 1770 w.
POLSON
York
Wm. 1755 i.
Rebecca 1773 w.
POLLY
Henrico
Saml. 1692 i.
POND
Shenandoah
John A. 1794 i.
Southampton
Richd. 1778 w.
Danl. 1786 w.
Richd. 1796 w.
Mary 1799 w.
Surry
Danl. 1783 w.
York
Jno. 1697-8 ab.
Jno. 1718 w.
PONDS
Southampton
Mason 1797 i.
PONSONBY
Isle of Wight
William 1761 w.
PONTIN
Stafford
Edwd. 1741 w.
POOCH
Norfolk
Henry 1675 i.
POOL
Loudoun
Benjamin 1773 w.
Thomas 1783 w.
Rebeccah 1791 w.
Lunenburg
Thos. 1758 i.
Northumberland
Peter 1785 i.
Shenandoah
Conrod 1795 i.
POOLE
Essex
John 1698 i.

Lancaster
Jos. 1677 w.
Norfolk
Richd. 1674 w.
Geo. 1761 i.
Isle of Wight
Joseph 1669 w.
Thomas 1682 w.
Richard 1689 w.
Mecklenburg
Wm. 1777 w.
Norfolk
Nicholas 1772 w.
Princess Anne
Rose 1706 rp.
Geo., Jr. 1717 i.
Geo. 1719 w.
Easter 1730 w.
Richd. 1738 w.
Wm. 1738 w.
Alex. 1768 i.
Spotsylvania
Geo. 1744 w.
Eliz. 1798 w.
York
Wm. 1767 w.
POOPE
Northampton
Jno. 1642 i.
POOR
Bedford
Micaell 1760 i.
Goochland
Thos. 1788 w.
Henry
Jeremiah 1784 i.
Montgomery
Peter 17[83?] i.
Westmoreland
Lawrence 1727 i.
Chas. 1799 w.
POORE
Goochland
Abram 1792 w.
Halifax
Moses 1791 i.
Norfolk
Jno. 1679 w.
Richmond
Jno. 1718 w.
POPE
Accomack
Thos. 1768 i.
Isle of Wight
Thomas 1691 w.
Robert 1699 w.
Ri[chard?] 1704-5 i.
Henry 1728 w.
Richard 1733 w.
William 1744 i.
Joseph 1749 w.
William 1750 i.

John 1752 w.
Robert 1761 w.
Priscilla 1769 w.
Richard 1774 w.
Edward 1782 w.
Ephraim 1793 w.
Norfolk
Wm. 1690-1 w.
Northumberland
Jno. 1723 w.
Leroy 1746 w.
Joseph 1767 w.
John Sr. 1776 w.
Nicholas 1777 w.
Wm. 1784 w.
Richd. 1793 w.
Sarah 1794 i.
Southampton
Jno. 1751 w.
Eliz. 1757 w.
Henry 1758 w.
Stephen 1760 w.
Benj. 1762 w.
Richd. 1762 i.
Wm. 1763 w.
Henry 1766 w.
Joshua 1769 w.
Nathan 1769 w.
Jno. 1772 w.
Nathan 1772 i.
Jos. 1777 i.
Wm. 1777 w.
Jno. 1779 w.
Patience 1779 w.
Henry 1783 i.
Wm. 1783 i.
Jno. 1787 i.
Wm. 1789 w.
Henry 1790 i.
Hardy 1791 w.
Henry 1791 i.
Jesse 1794 w.
Simon 1796 i.
Westmoreland
Nathl. 1660 w.
Nathl. (2) 1660 w.
Humphrey 1696 i.
Nathl. 1719 i.
Jno. 1722 i.
Lawrence 1723 w.
Humphrey 1734 w.
Jno. 1735 i.
Nathl. 1737 i .
Thos. 1741 w.
Worden 1749 w.
Jane 1752 w.
Jas. 1752 i.
Humphrey 1760 w.
Humphrey 1762 i.
Jno. 1774 i.
Jno. 1785 w.

York
Matthew 1792 w.
Betty 1796 w.
POPEJOY
Prince William
William 1799 i.
POPHAM
Culpeper
Job 1782 i.
Westmoreland
Jno. 1739 w.
POPPLEWEL
Northumberland
Arthur 1723-4 i.
PORCH
Greensville
Bridges 1791 i.
King George
Richd. 1750 i.
Mary 1753 eb.
Wm. 1762 w.
Richmond
Thos. 1716 i.
Southampton
James 1788 w.
Stafford
Robt. 1747 i.
Surry
James 1732 w.
Sussex
Henry 1765 w.
Henry 1775 w.
James Sr. 1776 w.
Peter 1779 w.
Israel 1783 w.
Henry 1794 w.
POREGOS
Frederick
Henry 1766 i.
PORT
Richmond
Robt. 1716 i.
PORTEEN
Norfolk
Danl. 1714 w.
William 1722 i.
PORTEN
Norfolk
Sarah 1678 w.
Wm. 1678 w.
Westmoreland
Danl. 1716 w.
PORTEOUS
Southampton
John 1757 i.
PORTER
Accomack
Abell 1687 i.
Botetourt
William 1790 i.

Cumberland
Thos. 1767 w.
Eliz. 1772 w.
Wm. 1775 w.
Fauquier
Thomas 1799 w.
Henrico
Jno. 1689 i.
Martha 1726 w.
Wm. 1747 i.
Wm. 1750 w.
Isle of Wight
Charles 1735 i.
Lancaster
Francis 1680 i.
Loudoun
Edward 1771 w.
Louisa
Pleasant 1790 a.
John Sr. 1791 w.
Middlesex
Wm. 1706 w.
Norfolk
Robert 1667 w.
Jno. 1675 w.
James 1633 w.
Samuel 1718 w.
John 1743 i.
Willoughby 1744 i.
John 1745 i.
William 1760 w.
Wm. 1764 i.
Orange
Benj. 1761 w.
Charles 1791 w.
Pittsylvania
Ambrose 1773 w.
Powhatan
Jno. 1784 w.
Isaac 1786 i.
Stephen 1795 w.
Isaac 1796 w.
Thos. 1797 w.
Prince Edward
John 1781 w.
Rockbridge
William 1782 w.
Southampton
James 1794 w.
Jno. 1782 i.
Thos. Jr. 1788 w.
Stafford
Thos. 1740 w.
Westmoreland
Robt. 1670 i.
Edwd. 1705 i.
Edwd. 1725 i.
Wm. 1749 i.
Wm. 1768 w.
Elender 1779 w.
Danl. 1783 w.

Demcey 1796 w.
York
Jno. 1660 i.
PORTEUS
Augusta
Jas. 1751 a.
PORTIS
Isle of Wight
John Jr. 1704 w.
John 1707 w.
Surry
Edwd. 1722 w.
PORTLOCK
Isle of Wight
Charles 1752 w.
Norfolk
John Sr. 1715 w.
John 1717 a.
John 1743-4 w.
Paul 1743-4 w.
Nathl. 1752 w.
William 1756 w.
William 1759 w.
Charles 1761 w.
Edward 1767 w .
Elizabeth 1769 w.
Simon 1773 i.
Martha 1775 w.
John 1778 w.
Matthew 1788 w.
Matthias 1790 i.
Seth 1791 i.
Matthew 1795 w.
John 1799 i.
Sussex
Charles 1797 w.
PORTWOOD
Charlotte
Thos. 1784 w.
PORY
Northumberland
Jane 1652 i.
POSEY
Halifax
Allison 1786 w.
Louisa
Belain 1750 w.
POSELETT
Norfolk
Edwd. 1669 w.
POSTON
Loudoun
Francis 1777 w.
POTERFIELD
Berkeley
Alex. 1799 w.
POTESS
Brunswick
Jno. 1760 i.

POTES
Stafford
Wm. 1734 i.
POTHOR
Isle of Wight
George 1692 i.
POTSON
Frederick
Richard 1753 i.
POTT
Northampton
Mathew 1644 w.
Francis 1658 w.
POTTER
Accomack
Nicholson 1794 w.
Augusta
Jno. 1775 i.
Henrico
Jno. 1703 i.
Louisa
Geo. 1786 w.
Northampton
Jno. 1735 i.
Surry
Roger 1695 w.
Westmoreland
Wm. 1718 w.
Jas. 1754 i.
York
Jos. 1719 w.
Jno. 1723 w.
Edwd. 1757 w.
Edwd. 1774 w.
POTTINGER
Berkeley
Robert 1778 i.
POTTS
Botetourt
Amos 1780 w.
John 1782 i.
Nathan 1779 i.
Essex
Jno. 1738 w.
Lancaster
Thomas 1795 w.
Loudoun
David 1768 w.
Jonas 1768 w.
Northumberland
Robert 1779 w.
Ezekiel 1782 i.
Robert 1782 i.
Prince George
Thos. Sr. 1716 i.
POULDEN
Northampton
Morgan 1700 w.
POULSON
Accomack
Geo. 1763 nw.

Edmd. 1771 w.
Edmd. 1773 i.
Edmd. 1779 i.
Jno. 1799 w.
POULTNEY
Fairfax
Richard 1748 i.
Loudoun
John 1759 w.
John 1792 i.
POUND
Halifax
Thos. 1769 i.
Thos. 1770 w.
Richmond
Jno. 1717 w.
Jno. 1719 i.
Thos. 1719 i.
Deborah 1726 i.
York
Stephen 1717 w.
POUNTNEY
Northumberland
Henry 1655 w.
POVALL
Cumberland
Richard 1771 w.
Henrico
Robt. 1733 w.
Robt. 1785 w.
Robin 1785 w.
POVEALL
Henrico
Robt. 1728 w.
POW
Northumberland
Jonathan 1753 i.
POWE
Spotsylvania
Marsom 1782 w.
POWEL
Accomack
Jas. 1740 i.
Nathl. 1778 w.
Peter 1793 w.
Albemarle
Jno. 1762 i.
Culpeper
Elias 1757 w.
Cumberland
Wm. 1780 i.
Essex
Place 1717 i.
King George
Elias 1736 i.
Stafford
Grace 1734 w.
POWELL
Accomack
Jno. 1730 i.
Thos. 1778 i.

Jonathan 1780 w.
Anaritta 1783 nw.
Nicho. 1785 w.
Jno. 1786 nw.
Jno. 1787 i.
Nickless 1795 w.
Peter 1796 i.
Jas. 1797 w.
Sarah 1798 w.
Amelia
Jno. 1753 w.
Jno., Sr. 1764 w.
Henry 1764 w.
Jno. 1783 i.
Mary 1795 w.
Robt., Sr. 1796 w.
Wm. 1798 w.
Amherst
Richd. 1766 w.
Thomas 1783 w.
Wm. 1797 i.
Augusta
Ambrose 1783 w.
Brunswick
Thos. 1757 w.
Wm. 1760 w.
Jno. 1791 w.
Campbell
Moses 1797 w.
Culpeper
John 1763 i.
Benjamin 1768 w.
Honorias 1773 i.
Ambrose 1788 w.
Cumberland
Wm. 1776 w.
Essex
John 1699 i.
Thos. 1701 w.
Edward 1702 i.
John 1703 i.
John 1748 i.
Jno. 1749 w.
Goochland
Saml. 1799 w.
Greensville
Seymour 1781 w.
Edward 1785 w.
Jane 1789 w.
Robert 1791 w.
Thomas 1796 w.
Halifax
Ann 1759 i.
Hesikeah 1764 i.
Edwd. 1773 w.
Joshua 1781 w.
Hezekiah 1794 i.
Henrico
Herbert 1690 i.
Jno. 1728 i.
Isle of Wight

Nathaniel 1678 i.
Thomas 1687-8 w.
James 1692 w.
William 1695 w.
John 1716 i.
Nathaniel 1729 w.
John 1731 w.
William 1734 w.
William 1747 w.
John 1748 w.
Thomas 1752 w.
William 1758 i.
John 1762 w.
George 1774 w.
Sarah 1776 w.
John 1779 i.
Benjamin 1784 w.
Joshua 1788 w.
Martha 1793 w.
John 1795 w.
Lancaster
Rawleigh 1686 w.
Loudoun
Elisha 1796 w.
Lunenburg
Richd. 1751 w.
Jno. 1784 w.
Middlesex
Wm. 1763 a.
Norfolk
Richard 1673 i.
Jno. 1688 w.
Wm. 1691 w.
Richd. 1713 w.
William 1715 w.
Grace(?) 1717 i.
Lemuel 1718 w.
Lemuel 1759 i.
John 1772 w.
John 1774 w.
Richard 1774 w.
Lemuel 1777 w.
Richard 1777 w.
Joshua 1780 w.
Francis 1784 i.
Richard 1784 i.
Joseph 1785 w.
Joshua 1790 i.
Northampton
Saml. 1666 w.
Nicho. 1670 w.
Jno. 1702 w.
Jno. 1710 w.
Saml. 1711 i.
Jno. 1718 w.
Sarah 1718 w.
Saml. 1719 w.
Nathl. 1732 w.
Nicho. 1732 w.
Yardly 1734 i.
Jno. 1740 i.

Jno. 1742 i.
Sarah 1742 w.
Jno. 1750 w.
Jos. 1753 w.
Susanna 1758 w.
Abel 1760 w.
Jas. 1760 i.
Nicholas 1761 w.
Jno. 1765 i.
Geo. 1767 w.
Nathl. 1793 w.
Seth 1794 w.
Geo. 1798 w.
Orange
Honorias 1768 i.
Simon 1771 w.
James 1776 w.
Princess Anne
Mark 1721 i.
Prince William
William 1788 w.
Richmond
Pythogaras 1703 w.
Wm. 1714 i.
Jno. 1745 i.
Southampton
Jos. 1760 w.
Jas. 1768 i.
Jas. 1795 i.
Spotsylvania
Thos. 1797 a.
Stafford
Philip 1707 i.
Chas. 1744 i.
Wm. 1746 i.
Sussex
Seymour 1794 w.
Jno. 1798 w.
Westmoreland
Michael 1670 i.
Wm. 1708 i.
Thos. 1714 i.
York
Hester 1717 w.
Thos. 1739 w.
Thos. 1749 w.
Wm. 1764 w.
Robt. 1780 nw.
Seymour 1782 w.
Thos. 1782 w.
Peter 1783 i.
Lucy 1784 w.
Benj. 1791 w.
Thos. 1796 w.
POWER
Fairfax
James 1745 w.
Loudoun
Joseph 1794 w.
Norfolk
Sampson 1711 i.

Sampson 1765 w.
Eliza. 1776 w.
Northumberland
Jno. 1742 w.
Nancy 1771 w.
Lidday 1771 w.
Joseph 1779 w.
Wm. 1784 w.
Princess Anne
Saml. 1751 w.
Lowery 1764 i.
Saml. 1774 w.
Westmoreland
Robt. 1720 w.
York
Henry 1692-3 i.
Jno. 1720 w.
Danl. 1727 w.
Jno. 1768 w.
POWERS
Brunswick
Sarah 1777 w.
Culpeper
Ann 1790 w.
Goochland
Major 1792 w.
Harrison
Major 1788 w.
Isle of Wight
Edward 1729 w.
Princess Anne
Saml. 1752 i.
Saml. 1774 w.
James 1777 w.
Rappahannock
Margt. 1684 i.
Southampton
Chas. 1782 i.
York
Henry 1692 w.
Edwd. 1719 w.
Chas. 1720 w.
Eliz. 1732 w.
POWES
Norfolk
Robt. 1651 w.
POYELLS
Isle of Wight
William 1694 i.
POYNER
Halifax
James 1782 i.
Norfolk
Jonathan 1770 w.
Robert 1770 i.
POYTHRESS
Isle of Wight
Edwd. 1781 w.
Prince George
John 1724 w.

PRAT
Goochland
Roger 1730 i.
PRATHAR
Bedford
Jonathan 1772 w.
PRATHER
Bedford
James 1759 w.
PRATT
Accomack
Baly 1757 w.
Moses 1783 w.
Culpeper
Jonathan 1781 w.
Fairfax
Shubael 1785 w.
King George
Jno. 1725 i.
Thos. 1796 i.
Thos. 1797 w.
Orange
Wm. 1748 w.
Richmond
Wm. 1795 w.
Wm. 1797 i.
Stafford
Jno. 1739 i.
Thos. 1766 w.
Birket 1761 i.
Westmoreland
Jno. 1714 w.
Jno. 1725 i.
Philemon 1773 i.
PRATTON
Northampton
Jno. 1787 w.
PREESON
Northampton
Thos. 1723 w.
Eliz. 1733 w.
Hannah 1739 w.
Thos. 1759 w.
PRENTIS
Richmond
Thos. 1716 i.
York
Wm. 1765 w.
Mary 1768 w.
Wm. 1773 w.
Jno. 1775 w.
PRESCOAT
Richmond
Henry 1775 i.
PRESCOTT
Essex
Henry 1719 i.
Fairfax
John 1776 i.
Norfolk
Moses 1724 i.
Moses [1750?] w.

Thomas 1753 w.
William 1771 w.
Prince William
Roger 1795 w.
Richmond
Jane 1714 i.
Westmoreland
Edwd. 1662 w.
PRESGRAVE
Fairfax
Jeremiah 1752 i.
PRESLEY
Northumberland
Peter 1719 i.
Peter 1750 w.
Peter 1781 i.
PRESLY
Northumberland
Wm. 1656 w.
PRESSON
Surry
Richd. 1764 i.
Jno. 1789 w.
Jno. 1790 i.
Lucy 1795 w.
Sussex
Thos. 1785 w.
York
Jas. 1753 w.
Jno. 1767 w.
Jas. 1776 w.
Saml. 1776 w.
Danl. 1783 w.
Thos. 1786 w.
Thos. 1790 i.
Robt. 1791 w.
Thos. 1792 i.
Saml. 1796 w.
PRESTAGE
Pittsylvania
Jno. 1791 w.
PRESTON
Augusta
Jno. 1747 a.
Bedford
Phillip 1775 i.
Thomas 1798 w.
Brunswick
Thos. 1798 w.
Fairfax
Robert 1757 w.
Montgomery
William 1783 w.
Northampton
Thos. 1733 i.
Washington
John 1797 w.
PRESTREDGE
Stafford
Thos. 1732 w.

PRETLOW
Isle of Wight
John 1788 w.
Southampton
Thos. 1787 w.
Surry
Joseph 1742 i.
Wm. 1767 i.
Rebecca 1772 **w.**
Saml. 1782 w.
Saml. 1790 w.
Saml. 1796 i.
Sussex
Joshua 1762 i.
PRETLOWE
Surry
Thos. 1754 w.
PRETTYMAN
Lancaster
Thos. 1659 nw.
PREWIT
Accomack
Wm. 1759 w.
Goochland
Jno. 1788 [1794] w.
Halifax
Danl. 1755 w.
PRICE
Accomack
Elias 1709 w.
Richd. 1709 i.
Berkeley
Ignatius 1795 w.
Brunswick
Jno. 1772 i.
Seaward 1782 i.
Charlotte
Wm. 1793 w.
Culpeper
Kalem 1761 w.
Cumberland
Jos. 1779 w.
Richd. 1781 w.
Ann 1782 w.
Augusta
Jno. 1797 w.
Essex
William 1718 w.
Richard 1718 i.
William 1719 w.
John 1772 w.
John 1785 i.
Fairfax
David 1785 w.
John 1786 w.
Fauquier
Bennett 1775 i.
Bennett 1779 w.
Frederick
Aaron 1759 i.
George 1797 w.

Goochland
Leonard 1772 w.
Halifax
Jno. 1772 w.
Henrico
Jno., Sr. 1711 w.
Saml. 1782 w.
Danl. 1783 w.
Jno. 1783 i.
Jno. W. 1791 w.
Barrott 1795 w.
Chas. 1797 w.
Isle of Wight
Thomas 1723 i.
Joseph 1728 w.
Richard 1747 i.
King George
Meredith 1726 i.
Richd. 1735 i.
Richd. 1757 i.
Bourn 1758 w.
Jno. 1767 w.
Thos. 1778 a.
Wm. 1782 a.
Anthony 1798 w.
Lancaster
Wm. 1688 i.
Elenor 1702 w.
Loudoun
Evan 1770 w.
Thos. 1791 w.
Louisa
Wm. 1775 w.
Wm. 1778 a.
Wm. 1779 w.
Middlesex
Robt. 1689 w.
Jno. 1726 w.
Jno. 1731 i.
Thos. 1761 a.
Robt. 1764 a.
Hannah 1773 w.
Montgomery
Henry 1797 w.
George 1799 w.
Norfolk
Henry 1746 w.
Henry 1756 i.
Northampton
Walter 1682 w.
Chas. 1691 w.
Chas. 1697 i.
Walter 1709 w.
Ellenor 1709 w.
Northumberland
Mary 1663 w.
Rebecca 1712 w.
Wm. 1720 i.
Mary 1726 i.
Richd. 1726 i.
Mary 1744 w.

Orange
Ajalon 1773 w.
Pittsylvania
Thos. 1792 w.
Prince Edward
Pugh 1775 w.
Danl. 1789 i.
Chas. 1790 w.
Josiah 1796 i.
Princess Anne
Wm. 1693 i.
Mary 1716 i.
Lewis 1779 i.
Prince William
Richard 1741 i.
Richmond
Jno. 1708 w.
Shenandoah
Edward 1787 w.
John 1784 w.
Spotsylvania
Roderick 1736 w.
Surry
Francis 1721 w.
Richd. 1735 i.
Jno. 1748 w.
Saml. 1767 w.
James 1772 w.
James 1777 i.
Elizabeth 1778 i.
Randolph 1778 w.
Sussex
Ann 1765 i.
Westmoreland
Meriday 1708 w.
Thos. 1717 w.
Jno. 1745-6 w.
Meredith 1751 w.
Evan 1755 w.
Wm. 1756 w.
Evan 1756 w.
Wm. 1794 w.
PRICHARD
Grayson
James 1796 w.
Middlesex
Joseph 1771 w.
Northumberland
Swanson 1740 i.
Westmoreland
Thos. 1771 a.
York
Robt. 1683 i.
PRICHETT
Culpeper
William 1774 w.
PRICKETT
Accomack
Richd. 1666 i.
Northumberland
Thos. 1658 w.

PRIDAM
Richmond
Chris. 1731 w.
PRIDDY
Fluvanna
Wm. 1792 w.
Halifax
Robt. 1791 i.
Geo. 1795 i.
PRIDE
Amelia
Jno., Sr. 1773 w.
Francis 1776 w.
Rowlett 1780 w.
Jno., Sr. 1794 w.
Chesterfield
Wm., Jr. 1749 w.
Wm. 1764 i.
Thos. 1779 w.
Jno. 1795 w.
Jno. 1797 i.
Halifax
Wm. 1791 w.
Sussex
Halcott 1774 w.
PRIDHAM
Northumberland
John. 1758 i.
Richmond
Chris. 1739 w.
Edmon 1774 w.
Frances 1782 w.
PRIEST
Bedford
Henry 1789 i.
Fauquier
William 1781 w.
Thomas 1795 w.
PRILLIMAN
Franklin
Jacob 1796 w.
PRIM
King George
Wm. 1794 a.
PRIME
Isle of Wight
John 1726 w.
PRIMER
Isle of Wight
Thomas 1767 i.
Thomas 1770 i.
PRINCE
Fauquier
Hubbard 1779 i.
Fincastle
William 1775 a.
King George
Jno. 1727 i.
Prince William
Hubbard 1782 a.
Sussex
Hannah 1783 w.

PRINGLE
King George
Richd. 1784 w.
Spotsylvania
Robt. 1738 a.
York
Jno. 1775 i.
PRINCE
Shenandoah
Philip 1795 i.
PRINULES
Shenandoah
Frederick 1774 i.
PRISE
Essex
John 1713 i.
Henrico
Danl. 1692 i.
PRITCHARD
Amherst
Richd. 1783 w.
Culpeper
Jane 1781 w.
Essex
Roger 1721 w.
Frederick
Rees 1758 w.
William 1770 w.
Lancaster
Frances 1680 w.
Robt. 1697 w.
Jas. 1718 i.
Robt. 1737 i.
Northumberland
Swanson 1743 i.
Charles 1780 w.
Surry
Marris 1748 w.
Rappahannock
James 1683 i.
PRITCHATT
Greensville
Elizabeth 1799 w.
PRITCHET
Accomack
Wm. 1736 w.
Joshua 1752 i.
Culpeper
William 1749 i.
Goochland
Jno. 1735 i.
PRITCHETT
Accomack
Wm. 1753 i.
Griffin 1763 w.
Albemarle
John 1798 w.
Brunswick
Wm. 1795 w.
Essex
Andrew 1726 i.

Greensville
John 1797 i.
King George
Chris. 1730 i.
Richmond
Rodham 1791 w.
Thos. 1795 i.
Stafford
Philip 1744 i.
Westmoreland
Thos. 1762 w.
Thos. 1765 i.
PRITLOW
Southampton
Mary 1793 w.
PRITT
Rappahannock
Robt. 1685 w.
PROBART
Accomack
Wm. 1754 w.
PROCTOR
Amelia
Wm. 1763 i.
Brunswick
Robt. 1758 w.
Isle of Wight
Ambrose, Jr. 1672 w.
Ambrose 1689 w.
Reuben 1729 w.
John 1710 w.
Jeremiah 1744 i.
Richmond
Isaac 1767 i.
Spotsylvania
Geo. 1738 w.
Wm. 1753 w.
Chas. 1787 w.
Wm. 1778 a.
Stafford
Thos. 1700 i.
Surry
Geo. 1679 i.
Joshua 1719 w.
Joshua 1744 i.
PROPHET
Goochland
Sylvester 1767 w.
PROSSER
Essex
John 1706-7 w.
Roger 1711 i.
Samuel 1726 w.
Northampton
Wm. 1701 i.
Rappahannock
Jno. 1677 w.
Richmond
Jno. 1786 i.
Stafford
Anthony 1734 i.

York
Jos. 1688 w.
PROU
Richmond
Cyprian 1712 w.
PROUD
Isle of Wight
Thomas 1698 w.
PROVERTS
Middlesex
Wm. 1710 i.
PROVINCE
Frederick
Thomas 1773 i.
PROVOE
York
Jno. 1788 w.
PRUCE(?)
Botetourt
Peter 1796 i.
PRUDEN
Isle of Wight
Nathaniel 1779 w.
PRUIT
Accomack
Benj. 1772 i.
PRUITT
Accomack
Catherine 1737 i.
Wm. 1741 i.
PRYER
Chesterfield
Thos. 1797 i.
PRYOR
Amelia
Jno. 1785 w.
Saml. 1790 w.
Botetourt
Luke 1785 w.
Charlotte
Robt. 1780 w.
Goochland
David 1746 i.
Jno. 1755 w.
Nicho. 1746 i.
Saml. 1773 i.
Wm. 1777 w.
Pittsylvania
Jno. 1797 i.
Princess Anne
Dickison 1778 i.
Middlesex
Wm. 1786 nw.
Wm. 1789 i.
York
Wm. 1646 w.
Croxton 1776 w.
PUCKET
Halifax
Anthony 1799 i.
Henrico
Abraham 1735 w.

Richd. 1737 a.
PUCKETT
Charlotte
Dougless 1794 i.
Chesterfield
Jno. 17— w.
Jno. 1765 w.
Jno. 1772 w.
Thos. 1781 w.
Thos. 1787 w.
Thos. 1789 i.
Nathan 1797 i.
Henrico
Jno. 1675-6 op.
Eliz. 1735 i.
Henry
Thomas 1784 i.
PUGGETT
Norfolk
Cisar 1644 i.
PUGH
Charlotte
Willoughby 1790 w.
Thos. 1793 i.
Thos. 1795 i.
Hardy
Jesse 1797 i.
Frederick
Thomas 1789 w.
Loudoun
Saml. 1782 i.
Norfolk
Edward 1773 w.
Shenandoah
Joseph 1783 i.
Joseph 1799 w.
Richmond
Henry 1766 w.
Westmoreland
David 1783 i.
PUGHE
Mecklenburg
Jno. 1770 w.
PULISTONE
Surry
Jno. 1707 w.
PULLEN
Bedford
Jeremiah 1786 i.
Moses 1790 w.
Lancaster
Wm. 1698 i.
Brian 1756 w.
Mary 1761 w.
William 1769 i.
Jonathan 1791 i.
Loudoun
Charles 1797 w.
Northumberland
Thomas 1781 w.
Richmond
Jehu 1790 w.

PULLETT
York
Jos. 1767 i.
PULLEY
Surry
Wm. Sr. 1777 w.
PULLIAM
Amelia
Wm. 1774 i.
Halifax
James 1779 w.
Hanover
Jno. 1734 w.
Louisa
Drury 1772 i.
John 1779 w.
Prince Edward
Geo. 1786 w.
Mecklenburg
Benj. 1792 w.
Spotsylvania
Thos. 1758 w.
David 1794 w.
Patterson 1758 a.
James 1764 a.
PULLIN
Northumberland
Nathan 1791 i.
Westmoreland
———— 1717 i.
PULLUM
Northumberland
Thos. 1759 i.
PULLY
Surry
Wm. 1738 w.
PUMROY
Westmoreland
Jacob 1799 i.
PUNCH
Henrico
Page 1727 w.
PUNTER
Charles City
Henry 1792 i.
PURCEL
Lancaster
Tobias 1710 w.
Westmoreland
Tobias 1743 i.
PURCELL
Halifax
James 1793 w.
Isle of Wight
Arthur 1729 w.
Lancaster
Thos. 1733 w.
Geo. 1761 i.
Geo. 1763 i.
Thomas 1764 i.
Middlesex
Patk. 1742 i.

Norfolk
David 1775 w.
Prince William
William 1784 w.
Richmond
Jno. 1752 w.
Tobias 1767 i.
PURCELLY
Westmoreland
Thos. 1753 i.
PURDIE
York
Alex. 1779 w.
PURDIEN
Bedford
Minter Pin 1798 i.
PURDY
Norfolk
Hugh 1679 i.
Princess Anne
Joanna 1705 i.
Geo. 1730 w.
Thos. 1736 w.
Wm. 1750 w.
Evan 1779 w.
PURKINS
Essex
Henry 1739 w.
Tabitha 1740 w.
Griffin 1745 i.
Henry 1780 w.
Goochland
Abram 1742 w.
Louisa
John 1799 w.
Mecklenburg
David 1785 w.
Westmoreland
Jno. 1701 i.
PURKINSON
Amelia
Caleb 1782 i.
Ralph 1788 w.
Chesterfield
Burrell 1781 w.
Jno. 1793 w.
Henrico
Jno. 1736 w.
PURKS
Essex
Joseph 1791 i.
PURLAND
Westmoreland
Matthew 1757 w.
PURLEY
Fairfax
Jane 1769 w.
PURLINE
Frederick
William 1760 i.

PURNALL
Frederick
William 1760 w.
Pittsylvania
Chesed 1772 i.
PURRINGTON
Louisa
Sarah 1794 i.
PURSEL
Richmond
Jno., Jr. 1778 i.
PURSELL
Essex
Elizabeth 1717 w.
Isle of Wight
Arthur 1745 w.
Phillip 1752 w.
Richmond
David 1719 i.
Tobias 1761 w.
Southampton
Arthur 1769 w.
Martha 1795 w.
Jno. 1799 w .
PURSLEE
Westmoreland
Patrick 1726 w.
PURSLY
Loudoun
Thomas, Sr. 1779 w.
PURTLE
Frederick
Nicholas 1796 i.
PURVINE
Princess Anne
Thos. 1694 w.
Lewis 1697 w.
Richd. 1718 i.
Jno 1719 w.
Lewis 1732 w.
Thos. 1738 i.
PURVIS
Essex
Thomas 1734 w.
Spotsylvania
Francis 1789 w.
James 1798 w.
PURYEAR
Goochland
Hezekiah 1796 w.
Henrico
Thos. 1784 w.
Mecklenburg
Jno. 1785 w.
Seymour 1788 w.
PUTLEE
Rappahannock
Nich. 1685 w.
PUTMAN
Culpeper
Zaceriah 1753 w.

Essex
Zachariah 1748 w.
PUTNEY
Greensville
Daniel 1797 w.
Surry
Richd. 1778 w.
PUY
Essex
Eliz. 1719 w.
PYCRAFT
Richmond
Winnifred 1731 i.
PYKE
Berkeley
Michael 1775 w.
William 1776 w.
PYLAND
Isle of Wight
James 1728 w.
Elizabeth 1758 i.
William 1770 i.
William 1783 w.
Surry
Geo. 1777 i.
Nicholas 1777 w.
Wm. 1779 i.
Wm. 1782 w.
Robt. 1796 w.
Fairfax
David 1789 w.
PYNE
Lancaster
Jno. 1736 w.
PYOTT
Loudoun
John 1787 w.
PYPER
Lancaster
Wm. 1675 i.
PYRTLE
Henry
John 1793 w.

Q

QUARAM
Northumberland
Thos. 1749 i.
QUARLES
Brunswick
Hubbard 1780 w.
Mary 1781 w.
Jno. 1788 w.
James 1791 w.
Campbell
Jno. 1790 w.
Wm., Jr. 1792 w.
Fauquier
Betty 1773 w.
Louisa
Wm. 1797 i.

Spotsylvania
Wm. 1796 w.
QUASK
Albemarle
Charles 1798 w.
QUASOM
Northumberland
Mary 1754 w.
QUEEN
Prince William
John 1739 i.
QUESENBURY
Westmoreland
Nicho. 1755 w.
Ann 1779 w.
Eliz. 1785 w.
Chris. 1756 i.
QUIDLEY
King George
Jas. 1731 i.
Stafford
Mary 1749 i.
QUIGLEY
Frederick
Patrick 1755 i.
QUINN
Culpeper
Darby 1756 w.
Thomas 1781 w.
John 1789 i.
Richard 1790 w.
Richard 1791 w.
Frederick
James 1749 a.
QUINTO
Accomack
Southy 1775 i.
QUINTON
Accomack
Philip 1708 w.
QUIRE
Spotsylvania
Raymon 1781 a.
QUIRK
Lancaster
Jas. 1718 i.
QUISENBERRY
King George
Humphrey 1723 i.
Jno. [1775?] w.
Orange
Aaron 1795 i .
Prince William
James 1786 w.
Westmoreland
Jno. 1717 w.
Nicho. 1750 i.
Jno. 1756 i.
Wm., Sr. 1762 w.
Wm. 1767 i.
Humphrey 1776 w.

James 1796 i.
Jas. 1794 w.
QUOANES
Westmoreland
Eliz. 1664 w.

R

RABBLING
Stafford
Jno. 1749 i.
RABISHAW
Accomack
Wm. 1671 i.
RABYSHAW
Northampton
Wm. 1728 w.
RACKCLIFF
Accomack
Chas. 1666-7 i.
RACKEE
Fairfax
William 1752 w.
RACLYFE
Isle of Wight
Richard 1686 w.
RADFORD
Cumberland
John 1772 w.
Essex
George 1746 w.
Lancaster
Roger 1658 nw.
RADLEY
Richmond
Thos. 1701 w.
RADY
Augusta
Michael 1753 i.
RAE
King George
Robt. 1753 w.
RAFFERTY
Washington
Thomas 1780 w.
RAGAN
Westmoreland
Timothy 1717 i.
RAGEN
Fairfax
William 1754 i.
RAGLAND
Goochland
Isaac 1754 i.
Greensville
Stephen 1794 i.
Halifax
Edwd. 1789 i.
Evan 1795 w.
Henrico
Jno. 1791 w.

Louisa
Jno. 1772 w.
Wm. 1782 i.
John 1785 w.
Wm. 1792 i.
Saml. 1797 w.
RAGSDAILE
Henrico
Jno. 1710 i.
RAGSDADLE
Amelia
Geo. 1787 w.
Chesterfield
Drury 1749 w.
Eliz. 1750 i.
Henrico
Godfrey 1703 w.
Godfrey 1731 w.
Peter 1747 w.
Lunenburg
Godfrey 1751 w.
Edwd. Sr. 1780 w.
Jno. 1787 w.
Joshua 1790 w.
Jno. 1793 w.
Mecklenburg
Benj. 1772 w.
Jno. 1794 w.
RAKE
Ohio
John 1781 a.
RAIBONE
Henrico
Richd. 1732 w.
RAIFIELD
Northampton
Thos. 1776 i.
RAIFORD
Isle of White
William 1773 w.
RAILEY
Amherst
Miles 1772 w.
Augusta
Michael 1753 a.
Chesterfield
Jno. 1778 w.
Frederick
Terrill 1758 i.
RAINES
Northumberland
Wm. 1792 w.
Surry
Jno. 1731 w.
Simon 1738 i.
RAINEY
Brunswick
Susanna 1796 i.
Greenbrier
Michael 1784 w.

Mecklenburg
Wm. 1798 i.
Northumberland
Peter 1720 ab.
Princess Anne
John 1753 w.
Marget 1776 w.
Thos. 1789 w.
Sussex
Wm. 1769 w.
Nathl. 1783 i.
RAINS
Lancaster
John 1784 i.
Sussex
Robt. Wynne 1773 i.
RAJOR
Pittsylvania
Paul 1792 i.
RAKESTRAW
Spotsylvania
Jno. 1761 a.
RALEY
Chesterfield
Jas. 1797 i.
Loudoun
Mathias 1792 i.
RALLINGS
King George
Margt. 1789 w.
Jos. 1795 w.
Norfolk
Edwd. 1687 w.
Westmoreland
Jno. 1740 i.
Saml. 1750 w.
Jno. 1754 i.
RALLINS
Westmoreland
James 1754 w.
Benj. 1755 w.
Richd. 1757 i.
RALLS
Stafford
Jno. Jr. 1763 w.
Edwd. Sr. 1785 w.
RALSON
Augusta
Wm. 1767 w.
RALTON
Essex
Thomas 1718 i.
RAMAGE
Middlesex
Alex. 1783 w.
RAMBO
Augusta
Barbara 1749 i.
RAMBOE
Lunenburg
Chris. 1747 w.

RAMEY
Fairfax
Benj. 1751 i.
Frederick
Wm. 1759 w.
Henry
John 1791 i.
Loudoun
Benj. 1779 i.
Shenandoah
Thos. 1787 i.
Prince William
Thos. 1787 i.
Richmond
Saml. 1752 i.
Westmoreland
Jacob Sr. 1721 w.
RAMPHORN
Isle of Wight
Elizabeth 1766 i.
RAMPHON
Isle of Wight
Rhoda 1790 w.
RAMSAY
Albemarle
Jno. 1770 w.
Essex
William 1776 i.
Betty 1788 w.
Fairfax
Anthony 1753 i.
Ann 1785 i.
Amelia 1792 a.
Lancaster
Jane 1765 w.
Norfolk
George 1759 w.
Princess Anne
Jno. 1780 w.
RAMSBOTTOM
Northampton
Jno. 1719 w.
Lettice 1720 w.
RAMSEY
Accomack
Jno. 1790 i.
Saml. 1798 i.
Augusta
Robt. 1760 i.
Jas. 1761 i.
Jno. 1783 w.
Danl. 1784 w.
Mary 1786 w.
Bedford
Bartholomew 1793 w.
Brunswick
Richd. 1785 w.
Essex
William 1744 i.
Thos. 1745 w.
Francis 1767 w.

Francis 1797 i.
Fairfax
John 1784 i.
William 1785 w.
Franklin
John 1787 a.
Henry
John 1782 w.
Lancaster
Martha 1698 i.
Thos. 1698 i.
Henry 1721 i.
John 1752 w.
Alex. 1768 w.
Mecklenburg
Gilbert 1787 w.
Northumberland
Robert 1770 i.
Pittsylvania
Thos. 1790 w.
Jas. 1792 i.
Rockbridge
William 1789 w.
Polly 1795 w.
Southampton
Jas. 1771 w.
Catherine 1795 w.
RAND
Isle of Wight
Wm. Sr. 1771 w.
York
Jno. 1702 i.
RANDALL
Augusta
Jas. 1750 i.
Brunswick
Jno. 1753 w.
Hardy
Able 1792 w.
King George
Thos. 1759 w.
Norfolk
Richard 1722 i.
Richmond
Robt. 1767 i.
Francis 1777 w.
Geo. 1783 i.
Spotsylvania
Nicho. 1748 a.
Surry
Geo. 1711 w.
Geo. 1742 i.
Sussex
Geo. 1772 i.
Westmoreland
Thos. 1795 i.
RANDE
York
Jno. 1704 a.

RANDEL
Westmoreland
Thos. 1789 i.
RANDELL
Westmoreland
Geo. 1789 w.
RANDLE
Brunswick
Wm. Sr. 1771 w.
Barnett 1781 i.
Greensville
Thos. Graves 1799 w.
RANDOL
Surry
Peter 1741 i.
RANDOLPH
Accomack
Edwd. 1703 i.
Albemarle
Henry 1778 w.
Berkeley
John 1790 w.
James 1795 i.
Chesterfield
Henry 1769 w.
Eliz. 1775 w .
Jno. 1775 w.
Eliz. 1777 i.
Goochland
Isham 1742 w.
Wm. 1742 w.
Wm. 1745 w.
Jane 1761 w.
Thos. Mann 1794 w.
Henrico
Henry 1693 i.
Wm. 1713 w.
Henry 1726-7 w.
Richd. 1749 w.
Beverly 1750 w.
Peter 1783 w.
Peyton 1784 w.
Ryland 1785 w.
Richd. 1786 w.
Norfolk
Giles 1725 i.
Giles 1750 w.
Solomon 1758 i.
Maxmillan 1785 i.
Thomas 1788 w.
Wm. 1789 w.
Rachel 1794 i.
William 1794 i.
Princess Anne
James 1757 w.
Willis 1767 i.
Mary 1785 w.
Prince William
John 1790 w.
William 1792 w.
Southampton
Temperance 1798 i.

Sussex
Mary 1754 w.
Peter 1786 w.
Frances 1791 w.
Westmoreland
Francis 1704 i.
York
Edwd. 1704 i.
Peyton 1775 w.
Betty 1782 w.
RANES
Fairfax
John 1755 w.
RANEY
Mecklenburg
Wm. 1798 w.
Princess Anne
Robt. 1726 i.
Sussex
Wm. 1770 i.
Phebe 1781 w.
Wynn 1782 w.
RANFRO
Botetourt
William 1789 w.
RANGER
Lancaster
Chas. 1677 i.
RANKIN
Augusta
Geo. 1760 w.
Thos. 1789 i.
Geo. 1792 w.
Richd. 1792 w.
Thos. 1792 i.
Berkeley
Benjamin 1787 w.
Frederick
David 1768 w.
Gray
William 1799 i.
King George
Jos. 1767 a.
RANKINS
King George
Robert 1748 i.
RANNELL
Richmond
Henry 1723 w.
RANSDELL
Fauquier
Wm. Sr. 1776 w.
Wharton 1786 w.
Wm. 1788 i.
Thomas 1794 i.
Thomas 1796 i.
Richmond
Amy 1729 w.
Westmoreland
Edwd. 1724 w.
Wharton 1758 w.
Edwd. 1773 w.

Sarah 1781 w.
RANSOM
Brunswick
Richd. 1748 w.
Surry
James 1740 w.
RANSOME
Cumberland
Ambrose 1762 w.
Middlesex
Geo. 1675 w.
RANSON
York
Robt. 1746 i.
RANSUM
Essex
Jno. 1698 w.
RANTZ
Shenandoah
Susanna 1773 w.
RANY
Princess Anne
Jno. 1784 w.
RANYE
Prince George
Wm. 1722 w.
RAPENE
Cumberland
Margaret 1756 w.
RAPFIELD
Northampton
Jno. 1780 i.
RAPHEL
Accomack
Halbert 1752 i.
RAPIER
Westmoreland
Suzanna 1674 w.
RAPPEEN
Goochland
Antho. 1737 w.
RAREDON
King George
Denie 1725 i.
RARTLEY
Bath
Lazarus 1798 w.
RASCOE
Northampton
Peter 1726 i.
Eliz. 1734 i.
Eliz. 1738 i.
Jno. 1751 i.
Jas. 1760 i.
Peter 1760 i.
Jas. 1763 i.
Joanna 1778 w.
RATCHFIELD
Accomack
Thos. 1741 nw.

RATCLIF
Chesterfield
Isham 1761 i.
RATCLIFF
Accomack
Eliz. 1686 w.
Fairfax
Barbara 1796 w.
Isle of Wight
Richard 1718 w.
John 1743 i.
Cornelius 1762 w.
Loudoun
John 1759 i.
Edward 1789 i.
York
Richd. 1716 i.
Wm. 1726 i.
Wm. 1784 w.
Jno. 1792 w.
RATCLIFFE
Essex
John 1698 i.
Fairfax
Jno. 1797 a.
RATHERFORD
Louisa
Adam 1761 w.
RATLIFT
Bedford
Thomas 1781 i.
RAUENING
Norfolk
Edward 1684 i.
RAULSTON
Greenbrier
Andrew 1782 i.
RAVEN
Norfolk
William [1745?] w.
RAVENS
Princess Anne
Mary 1707 w.
RAVEWELL
Richmond
Henry 1725 i.
RAVENHILL
Frederick
Francis 1797 i.
RAWLEIGH
York
Jno. 1740 i.
RAWLETTE
King George
Wm. 1791 w.
RAWLINGS
Bedford
Anthony 1774 i.
Benj. 1777 w.
Brunswick
Martha 1783 w.
Wm. 1787 w.

Greensville
James 1799 w.
Northumberland
Jno. 1665 w.
Prince William
Wm. 1781 i.
Southampton
Jno. 1778 i.
Edwin 1798 i.
Spotsylvania
Thos. 1749 a.
James 1757 w.
Thos. 1769 a.
James 1785 w.
Thos. 1786 w.
Surry
Jno. 1674 w.
Roger 1694 w.
Jno. 1703 w.
Sussex
Gregory 1755 w.
Hannah 1757 w.
Jno., Jr. 1764 i.
Gregory 1769 w.
Westmoreland
Anthony 1716 w.
RAWLINS
Richmond
Jno. 1739 i.
Spotsylvania
Peter 1793 w.
York
Nicholas 1691 i.
RAWLY
Goochland
Wm. 1748 i.
RAWSER
Orange
Eliz. 1742 a.
RAY
Amelia
Jno. 1766 w.
Augusta
David 1755 i.
Amherst
Jno. 1764 w.
Moses 1766 w.
Bedford
Joseph 1767 w.
William 1779 i.
Berkeley
Lucas 1794 i.
Southampton
Wm. 1775 w.
Jno. 1797 w.
Surry
Joseph 1721 w.
Wm. 1731 i.
Wm. 1736 w.
Francis 1739 w.
Sussex
Jno. 1771 i.

York
Thos. 1655 w.
RAYE
York
Geo. 1699 w.
RAYFIELD
Accomack
Peter 1787 w.
Jno. 1794 w.
Major 1798 w.
RAYFORD
Isle of Wight
Phillip 1724 w.
RAYLEY
Loudoun
John 1771 i.
Nathan 1779 i.
Princess Anne
Thos. 1722 w.
RAYMAN
Northampton
Arthur 1651 i.
RAYNE
Orange
Simon 1740 a.
RAYNER
Isle of Wight
Francis 1719 w.
Norfolk
Jno. 1691 w.
RAYNEY
Amelia
Moses 1743 a.
RAYNOLDS
Richmond
Anne 1736 w.
Geo. 1778 w.
Geo. 1781 w.
REA
Amherst
Fargus 1763 a.
Henry
James 1789 w.
Benjamin 1799 i.
Prince George
Francis 1718 w.
Stafford
Jas. 1741 i.
York
Thos. 1696 w.
REACH
Augusta
Archd. 1774 i.
READ
Accomack
Henry 1695 w.
Mary 1708 i.
Jno. 1721 i.
Jno. 1723 i.
Henry 1734 w.
Richd. 1749 i.
Richd. 1757 i.

Tabitha 1763 i.
Richd. 1771 w.
Henry 1773 i.
Jno. 1777 w.
Jno. 1781 i.
Absabath 1783 w.
Richd. 1783 i.
Ann 1784 w.
Jno. 1787 i.
Tabitha 1787 w.
Tabitha, Jr. 1788 i.
Ann 1791 i.
Caleb 1797 w.
Zorobabel 1798 w.
Albemarle
Thos. 1765 w.
Augusta
Wm. 1760 a.
Bedford
John 1773 w.
William 1798 w.
Brunswick
Wm. 1764 w.
Robt. 1774 w.
Thos. 1774 i.
James 1796 w.
Charlotte
Clement 1771 w.
Isaac 1778 w.
Clement 1782 w.
Mary, Sr. 1787 w.
Mary 1787 w.
Jonathan 1796 w.
Chesterfield
Jno. Sr. 1753-4.
Culpeper
John 1765 w.
Theophilus 1773 i.
Frederick
Daniel 1762 w.
William 1749 a.
Isle of Wight
William 1746 w.
Henrico
Elisha 1745 i.
Lancaster
Nicho. 1717 w.
Jno. 1741 i.
Loudoun
Joseph 1762 w.
Lunenburg
Clement 1765 i.
Mecklenburg
James 1799 w.
Northumberland
Andrew 1723-4 i.
Prince Edward
Robt. 1766 i.
James 1778 w.
Princess Anne
James 1723 w.

Richmond
Eli 1739 w.
Southampton
John 1790 w .
Westmoreland
Andrew 1697 w.
Andrew Jr. 1698 i.
Coleman 1748 w.
Robt. 1761 nw.
Mary 1772 w.
York
Eliz. 1686-7 w.
Benj. 1692-3 w.
Thos. 1719 w.
Mary 1722 w.
READE
Middlesex
Eliz. 1783 w.
Brunswick
Wm. 1795 w.
Lancaster
Alex. 1685 i.
Middlesex
Alex. 1760 w.
Northampton
Jno. 1696 w.
Northumberland
Archabell 1657 i.
Thos. 1657 i.
Princess Anne
Jno. 1778 w.
Chas. 1784 w.
Westmoreland
Ruth 1768 w.
York
Robt. 1712 w.
Mary 1723 i.
Saml. 1758 w.
Mary 1773 w.
Mildred 1775 w.
Wm. 1783 w.
READER
Augusta
Adam 1773 i.
Mecklenburg
Robt. 1782 w.
Shenandoah
Adam 1784 i.
York
Andrew 1677 i.
Andrew 1680 w.
READING
King George
Thos. 1766 w.
READS
Stafford
Thos. 1748 w.
READY
Shenandoah
Barnett 1787 i.

READYHOE
Surry
Richd. 1707 i.
REAGAN
Frederick
John 1767 w.
Fairfax
Michael 1773 w.
Michael 1784 w.
REAGER
Augusta
Hance 1759 i.
REAGER
Berkeley
Burket 1782 w.
Hardy
Martin 1797 i.
REAGH
Frederick
Adam 1789 w.
REAGLAND
Augusta
Nathan 1778 w.
Nathan 1785 w.
REAGLES
Frederick
Adam 1789 i.
REAHO
York
Ollester 1667 w.
REALY
Augusta
Michael 1753 i.
REAMS
Amelia
Thos. 1773 w.
Fredk. 1785 w.
REAMY
Henry
Mary 1798 w.
Loudoun
Sandford 1788 w.
REANALDS
Richmond
Jafral 1721 w.
REANE
Norfolk
Susanah 1680 nw.
REANOLD
Westmoreland
Jno. 1673 i.
REANOLDS
Richmond
Robt. 1722 i.
REAPHEW
Frederick
Peter 1763 i.
REAPMAN
Culpeper
Christian 1763 i.

REARDON
Fairfax
John 1778 i.
REASON
Lancaster
Michael 1735 i.
Northumberland
Jno. 1720 i.
Jno. 1747 w.
Thos. 1754 w.
REASOE
Wythe
Peter 1798 i.
REAVELL
Accomack
Jno. 1727 w.
REAVEN
Norfolk
Wm. 1690-1 w.
REAVES
Lancaster
Marcy 1753 i.
John 1790 i.
REBOONE
Northampton
Anthony 1665 i.
REBURN
Augusta
Jno. 1798 w.
Montgomery
Henry 1792 i.
RECLIFF
Middlesex
Chas. 1746 a.
RECTOR
Bedford
Jacob 1779 w.
Fauquier
John 1773 w.
John 1777 i.
Henry 1781 w.
Harmon 1789 w.
Spencer 1793 i.
Jacob 1795 i.
Henry 1799 w.
Prince William
John 1742 i.
REDBURN
Surry
Peter 1768 w.
REDCROSS
Lunenburg
Danl. 1777 w.
REDD
Spotsylvania
Mordicai 1783 w.
James 1784 w.
REDDERICK
Surry
James 1695 pw.

REDDICK
Brunswick
Margaret 1782 w.
REDDIN
Fauquier
Timothy 1760 i.
REDDING
Isle of Wight
Richard 1678 w.
REDFORD
Augusta
Thos. 1770 i.
Chesterfield
Jno. S. 1773 w.
Goochland
Wm. 1752 w.
Halifax
Maxey 1771 w.
Henrico
Francis 1682 w.
Jno. 1752 w.
Jno. 1754 i.
Jno. 1784 w.
Milner 1785 w.
Jas. 1799 w.
REDGAN
Frederick
John 1768 i.
REDING
Surry
Thos. 1676 a.
REDISH
Stafford
Jas. 1736 w.
Edwd. 1743 i.
REDMAN
Berkeley
Robert 1790 i.
Charlotte
Wm. 1780 i.
Fauquier
Richd. 1759 i.
Halifax
Benj. 1774 w.
King George
Ann 1758 w.
Loudoun
John 1797 w.
Richmond
Solomon 1749 w.
Jno. 1773 w.
Stewart 1786 w.
Mary 1791 i.
Westmoreland
Jno. 1673 w.
Robt. 1704 w.
Francis 1716 w.
Cornelius 1717 i.
Solomon 1719 i.
Wm. 1761 w.
Jno. 1775 i.

Solomon 1783 w.
Wm. 1799 w.
REDMON
Frederick
Thomas 1762 i.
REDMOND
Charlotte
Geo. 1790 i.
Wm. 1779 w.
Fauquier
John 1796 i.
Loudoun
Andrew 1764 w.
REDSLEEVES
Hardy
Michael 1787 i.
REED
Accomack
Southy 1779 w.
Augusta
Wm. 1761 i.
Robt. 1788 i.
Robt. 1794 w.
Botetourt
Samuel 1793 w.
Fairfax
Thomas 1794 w.
Hugh 1796 a.
Frederick
Edward 1748 i.
William 1752 i.
Mary 1755 w.
Joseph 1766 w.
Edward 1777 w.
Mary 1794 w.
Halifax
John 1799 i.
King George
Saml. 1750 i.
Jno. 1759 w.
Loudoun
Jonathan 1791 w.
Andrew 1798 i.
Norfolk
John 1798 w.
Prince Edward
John 1763 w.
Saml. 1763 w.
Richmond
Thos. 1719 w.
Wm. 1720 w.
Wm. 1756 i.
Rockbridge
Joseph 1798 w.
Southampton
Alexander 1772 i.
Westmoreland
Saml. 1698 w.
Jno. 1723 w.
Jane 1724 a.

REEDER
Halifax
Joseph 1798 w.
Loudoun
Joseph 1770 w.
Shenandoah
Benjamin 1793 i.
REEKES
Surry
Richd. 1709 w.
REEKS
Surry
Thos. 1744 w.
Sussex
Jno. 1763 i.
REES
Albemarle
David 1753 i.
Augusta
Thos. 1754 a.
Halifax
Jacob 1789 w.
Frederick
Morris 1763 w.
Henry 1771 w.
Thomas 1785 w.
Shenandoah
Joel 1787 a.
Westmoreland
Henry 1726 i.
REESE
Accomack
Edwd. 1771 w.
Tabitha 1773 w.
Augusta
Thos. 1752 w.
Southampton
Jos. 1779 w.
Edwd. 1782 i.
Jno. 1794 i.
Olive 1794 i.
Prince George
Richd. 1723 i.
REEVE
Prince William
George 1779 w.
James 1791 i.
REEVES
Essex
James 1707 i.
Elizabeth 1711 w.
Joseph 1717 w.
Samuel 1730 i.
John 1736 w.
Henry 1729 w.
Sarah 1739 w.
Henry 1745 w.
Jos. Jr. 1745 w.
Henry 1749 i.
James 1762 w.
Joseph 1783 w.

Lancaster
Jno. 1731 w.
Pheebe 1733 w.
Northumberland
Robt. 1727 w.
Thos. 1729 i.
Prince William
Geo. 1780 i.
Mary 1781 w.
John 1782 w.
Spotsylvania
Geo. 1754 w.
Thos. 1760 a.
Henry 1760 a.
REGAN
Stafford
Wm. 1745 i.
Surry
Francis 1727 w.
REGANS
Prince William
William 1742 i.
REGAR
Frederick
Daniel 1787 a.
Spotsylvania
Jno. 1763 a.
REGNEY
Pittsylvania
Jno. 1791 i.
REGS
Accomack
Jos. 1766 w.
REID
Accomack
Wonney 1763 w.
Southy 1765 i.
Albemarle
Andrew 1751 w.
Wm. 1760 i.
Thos. 1767 i.
James 1790 w.
Amherst
Andrew 1765 w.
Jno. N. 1799 w.
Fairfax
Joseph 1750 w.
Thos. 1794 i.
Greenbrier
James 1796 i.
Isle of Wight
John 1774 i.
Lancaster
Nicholas 1769 i.
Middlesex
Adam 1751 a.
James 1763 w.
Loudoun
John 1797 i.
Rockbridge
Adam 1789 w.

Spotsylvania
Wm. 1743 w.
Jno. 1747 w.
Stafford
Jno. 1762 i.
REIDFORD
Lancaster
John 1748 w.
REIDINGS
Isle of Wight
Richard 1678 i.
REILEY
Berkeley
John 1779 i.
John 1793 w.
Botctourt
Francis 1779 w.
Frederick
Terrill 1760 i.
REILLY
Stafford
Thos. 1731 i.
REINIER(?)
Northampton
Jno. 1663 w.
REIVES
Brunswick
Geo. 1773 i.
Surry
Jno. 1720 i.
RELE
Westmoreland
Jno. 1729 i.
REMEY
Loudoun
Jacob, Sr. 1787 w.
Sandford 1788 i.
REMNANT
Fairfax
John 1787 w.
REMY
Shenandoah
Thomas 1787 w.
Westmoreland
Jacob 1727 w.
Jacob 1736 i.
Wm. 1738 w.
Jno. 1740 i.
REN
Surry
Joseph 1750 i.
RENALDS
Augusta
Robt. 1750 w.
RENICK
Greenbrier
Thomas 1791 w.
RENICKS
Frederick
Thomas 1751 a.

RENIX
Augusta
 Robt. 1757 a.
RENKIN
Augusta
 Jno. 1790 w.
RENKING
Northampton
 Henry 1663 w.
RENN
Sussex
 Joseph 1788 w.
RENNARD
Henrico
 Richd. 1797 w.
RENNELLS
Isle of Wight
 Henry 1729 i.
RENNIX
Augusta
 Robt. 1763 i.
RENNOLDS
Essex
 Thomas 1712 w.
 James 1724 w.
 Jas. 1731 w.
 Martha 1753 w.
 William 1762 w.
 James 1772 w.
 Eliz. 1774 w.
 Sarah 1774 w.
 Robert 1781 w.
 John 1794 w.
 John 1795 i.
 John 1797 i.
Fauquier
 John 1769 i.
 James 1776 w.
Hanover
 Jas. 1733 i.
Orange
 Benj. 1776 i.
Surry
 Robt. 1709 i.
RENO
Prince William
 Thomas 1779 i.
RENOLDS
Norfolk
 Thomas 1672 i.
Surry
 Grace 1711 w.
RENTFRO
Bedford
 Joseph 1776 w.
RENWICKE
Isle of Wight
 Edward 1715 w.
RENY
Princess Anne
 Robt. 1712 i.

RENZES
Frederick
 Fredk. 1768 i.
REPASS
Wythe
 Jacob 1794 i.
RESPES
Northampton
 Henry 1730 w.
RESPESS
Northampton
 Jno. 1791 w.
 Susanna 1792 w.
Surry
 Thos. 1758 w.
RESTRICK
Norfolk
 William 1719 i.
RETTERFORD
Essex
 Robert 1726 i.
 John 1743 i.
 Mary 1753 w.
 John 1755 i.
REVEIRS
Lancaster
 Peter 1737 i.
REVEL
Accomack
 Jno. 1769 i.
 Edwd. 1793 i.
REVELL
Accomack
 Edwd. 1687 w.
 Francis 1697 nw.
 Edwd. 1753 w.
 Anne 1756 nw.
 Rebecca 1757 w.
Isle of Wight
 Randall 1739 w.
REVIL
Southampton
 Sampson 1781 w.
REVOL
Accomack
 Jno. 1764 i.
REW
Accomack
 Jno. 1714 w.
 Comfort 1772 w.
 Absolem 1795 w.
Isle of Wight
 John 1748 w.
REYNOLD
Isle of Wight
 Chris. [1654?] w.
 Henry 1679 w.
REYNOLDS
Albemarle
 Wm. 1790 w.

Amherst
 Absolom 1784 a.
Bedford
 Jonas 1793 w.
Botetourt
 William 1796 i.
Campbell
 Wm. M. 1798 w.
 Jno. M. 1798 i.
Culpeper
 John, Sr. 1784 w.
Cumberland
 Wm. 1755 i.
 Jno. 1760 w.
Essex
 John 1717 w.
 Cornelius 1735 w.
 Thomas 1735 i.
 James 1751 w.
 Martha 1755 i.
 Elizabeth 1761 w.
Henrico
 Thos. 1794 i.
 Wm. 1798 w.
Henry
 David 1788 i.
Isle of Wight
 John 1669 w.
 Richd. 1707 i.
 Richd. 1712 w.
 Chris. 1733 i.
 Sharpe 1754 w.
 Rebecca 1755 w.
 George 1762 i.
 Chris. 1763 w.
 Christian 1764 i.
 Pitt 1774 i.
 Richard 1774 i.
 Isham 1778 w.
 Sharp 1784 w.
King George
 Hillary 1751 i.
Orange
 Cornelius 1757 i.
Pittsylvania
 Wm. 1791 w.
Rappahannok
 Cornelius 1685 w.
Richmond
 Wm. 1700 w.
 John 1761 w.
 Wm. 1784 i.
 Betty 1796 w.
Spotsylvania
 Thos. 1796 a.
Surry
 Robt. 1702 w.
Westmoreland
 Robt. 1744 w.
York
 Thos. 1682-3 i.

Jas. 1749 i.
Thos. 1759 w.
Susanna 1768 w.
RHAPFOLD
Northampton
Jno. 1779 w.
RHINE
Augusta
Michael 1764 i.
RHOADS
Middlesex
Hezekiah 1717 w.
Surry
Benj. 1789 w.
RHODES
Middlesex
Randolph 1749 i.
Jno., Jr. 1752 w.
Loudoun
Moses 1769 w.
Mecklenburg
Wm. 1788 w.
Northampton
Jos. 1787 i.
Orange
Wm. 1744 w.
Hezekiah 1762 w.
Stafford
Jno. 1748 w.
York
Clifton 1745 w.
RHODRY
Prince William
John 1735 i.
RIANT
Northampton
Wm. 1732 i.
RIBOT
Henrico
Francois 1707 w.
RICABOKER
Shenandoah
Henry 1780 w.
RICE
Amelia
James 1784 i.
Bedford
Nathaniel 1787 i.
Brunswick
Michael 1752 i.
Charlotte
Thos. 1796 w.
Fluvanna
Tandy 1795 i.
Frederick
Simeon 1760 w.
John 1785 w.
Edward W. 1797 w.
John 1798 i.
Patrick 1799 w.
Goochland

Michael 1737 w.
Edwd. 1770 w.
Charles 1785 w.
Hanover
Wm. 1734 w.
Lancaster
Augustine 1776 w.
Louisa
Wm. 1786 a.
Middlesex
Geo. 1750 w.
Northampton
Henry 1718 w.
Northumberland
Mary 1726 w.
Richd. 1742 w.
John 1762 w.
Eliz. 1783 w.
Wm. 1786 i.
Jno. 1787 w.
Wm. 1792 w.
Orange
Henry 1747 i.
Henry, Jr. 1754 i.
Michael 1784 w.
Prince Edward
Wm. 1760 i.
Jos. 1763 i.
Jos. 1766 w.
Matthew 1775 i.
Chas. 1779 w.
Princess Anne
Abraham 1757 w.
Jno. 1761 i.
Jno. 1763 i.
Thos. 1767 i.
Jno. 1772 w.
Rappahannock
Dominick 1685 w.
Ann 1686 w.
Spotsylvania
Wm. 1734 a.
Stafford
Jno. 1750 i.
Westmoreland
Jno. 1696 w.
Jno. 1706 i.
Wm. 1733 w.
Wm. 1750 i.
Wm. 1755 i.
Zerubabel 1758 w.
Wm. 1785 i.
RICH
Fauquier
Daniel 1784 i.
Frederick
John 1750 a.
Conrod 1771 i.
Henry 1799 i.
Goochland
Timothy 1736 i.

Lancaster
Daniel 1793 i.
RICHARD
Rappahannock
Bridgett 1685 w.
RICHARDS
Accomack
Michael 1757 w.
Richd. 1758 i.
Campbell
Thos. 1788 w.
Essex
John 1773 w.
Fairfax
Benj. 1747 i.
George 1789 a.
Frederick
John 1757 w.
Henry 1793 w.
Greenbrier
Josiah 1787 w.
James 1791 w.
Isle of Wight
Anne 1684 w.
William, Sr. 1711 w.
Thomas 1726 w.
Robert 1728 w.
William 1732 nw.
Robert 1733 w.
Thomas 1740 w.
Robert 1748 i.
William 1761 i.
Martha 1768 w.
King George
Robt. 1735 i.
Margt. 1748 i.
Lunenburg
Eliz. 1785 w.
Northampton
Thos. 1701 i.
Jno. 1764 w.
Orange
William 1790 w.
Rappahannock
Bridget 1685 w.
Richmond
Wm. 1785 i.
Stafford
Jno. 1784 w.
Westmoreland
Eliz. 1786 w.
York
Thos. 1736 w.
RICHARDSON
Accomack
Jno. 1709 i.
Danl. 1774 w.
Wm. 1774 w.
Chas. 1778 w.
Danl. 1779 w.
Wm. Martial 1781 w.

Zorobabel 1783 w.
Jno. 1785 w.
Solomon 1785 w.
Wm. 1792 w.
Jacob 1794 w.
Rachel 1795 w.
Wm. 1795 w.
Augusta
Danl. 1753 w.
Bedford
Jonathan 1773 w.
Randolph 1782 w.
Berkeley
Joseph 1790 i.
Campbell
Jno. 1788 w.
Charlotte
John 1767 i.
Mary 1791 w.
Chesterfield
Jno. 1794 w.
Brunswick
Wm. 1792 i.
Cumberland
Jno. 1753 w.
Isham 1788 w.
Essex
John 1791 w.
Fairfax
John 1745 w.
Fluvanna
Robert 1783 w.
Halifax
Skip 1788 w.
Jno. 1798 w.
Jeffrey 1799 i.
Henrico
Melchizedek 1701 op.
Saml. 1747 i.
Jno. 1789 w.
Isle of Wight
William 1685 w.
John 1690 w.
William 1762 i.
King George
Mary 1727 i.
Honour 1749 a.
Clapham 1750 i.
Thos. 1755 w.
Wm. 1771 a.
Lancaster
Nathl. 1677 i.
Loudoun
James 1779 w.
Madison
Richard 1794 a.
Mecklenburg
Geo. 1798 i.
Norfolk
Thomas 1718-19 w.
———— 1722 i.

Elizabeth 1724 i.
Wm. 1771 i.
John 1777 i.
Mary 1796 w.
Northampton
Geo. 1655 i.
Northumberland
Eliz. 1724 w.
Pittsylvania
Jas. 1799 w.
Prince William
Nicklis 1740 i.
Richmond
Rodger 1716 w.
Jno. 1767 w.
Shenandoah
Isabella 1797 w.
Spotsylvania
Wm. 1762 w.
Stafford
Wm. 1701-2 w.
Surry
Wm. 1746 w.
Jno. 1747 w.
Sussex
Jno. 1773 w.
Arthur 1775 i.
Benj. 1785 w.
Amey 1798 w.
Westmoreland
Jonathan 1746 w.
RICHASON
Augusta
Ephraim 1779 w.
Princess Anne
Jno. 1714 w.
Thos. 1716 i.
RICHERSON
Louisa
Sally 1773 a.
Norfolk
Moses 1759 w.
RICHESON
Accomack
Chas. 1730 i.
Middlesex
James 1760 a.
RICHEY
Amelia
Alex. 1749 w.
Frederick
Robert 1760 w.
James 1763 i.
RICHIE
Prince Edward
Hugh 1766 w.
RICHISON
Lancaster
Wm. 1705 i.

RICHMOND
Princess Anne
Robt. 1699 a.
Jno. 1720 w.
Robt. 1735 w.
Wm. 1740 w.
Robt. 1743 i.
RICKARDS
Northampton
Michael 1688 w.
RICKABOCKER
Shenandoah
Henry 1780 i.
RICKELL
Halifax
Wm. 1765.
RICKES
Isle of Wight
Jno. 1717 w.
James 1730 w.
RICKMAN
Halifax
Thos. 1761 w.
RICKS
Isle of Wight
Jacob 1706-7 i.
Isaac 1724 w.
Robert 1743 w.
Abraham 1746 w.
Southampton
Eliz. 1754 i.
Robt. 1764 w.
Robt. 1770 i.
Richd. 1779 w.
Mary 1785 w.
Ann 1792 i.
Surry
Benj. 1754 w.
RICORD
Loudoun
Simon 1795 i.
RIDDELL
Montgomery
William 1784 i.
York
Geo. 1779 w.
RIDDICK
Brunswick
Margaret 1783 i.
Isle of Wight
George 1727 w.
RIDDLE
Brunswick
Eliz. 1797 w.
Goochland
Jno. 1771 w.
Orange
Wm. 1777 w.
Pittsylvania
Sarah 1777 w.

RIDENBAUGH
Loudoun
Fredk. 1789 i.
RIDER
Culpeper
Alexander 1786 i.
Northumberland
Henry 1726-7 w.
Jno. 1738 w.
Winifred 1741 w.
John 1750 i.
Princess Anne
Tho. 1695 i.
Shenandoah
William 1797 i.
York
Andrew 1660 i.
RIDGE
York
Robt. 1704 w.
RIDGES
Brunswick
Godfray 1744 i.
RIDGEWAY
Berkeley
John 1794 i.
RIDGWAY
Frederick
Josiah 1783 w.
Richard 1785 w.
Josiah 1796 i.
Middlesex
Jno. 1743 a.
Anthony 1748 i.
RIDING
King George
Danl. 1765 i.
Wm. 1789 w.
Geo. 1795 i.
RIDLEHURST
Charles City
Richd. 1771 w.
Jno. 1772 w.
RIDLEY
Isle of Wight
Nathaniel 1719 w.
William 1761 w.
Southampton
Nathl. 1753 w.
Nathl. 1776 w.
Jas. Day 1779 i.
Jas. 1781 w.
Matthew 1795 w.
Surry
Thos. 1719 i.
RIGDON
Fairfax
Edward 1772 w.
RIELY
Frederick
Ferrell 1757 w.

Martin 1790 w.
RIEVES
Brunswick
Harmon 1776 w.
Greensville
Benjamin 1791 w.
Sussex
Frances 1770 w.
Christopher 1773 i.
RIFE
Shenandoah
Christian 1794 i.
RIGBY
Lancaster
Peter 1660 i.
Princess Anne
Paul 1745 w.
Stafford
Alex. 1753 w.
RIGG
Frederick
Richard 1785 w.
Princess Anne
James 1795 w.
Westmoreland
Jas. 1762 i.
RIGGAN
Surry
Jno. 1767 i.
RIGGIN
Isle of Wight
Daniel 1744 w.
RIGGINS
Accomack
Jno. 1798 i.
RIGHT
Accomack
Jacob 1798 w.
Bedford
John 1767 i.
Lancaster
James 1757 w.
Southampton
Mary 1781 w.
RIGIN
Isle of Wight
Ann 1728 nw.
RIGINS
Isle of Wight
Daniell 1721 i.
RIGGS
Accomack
Abraham 1726 w.
Isaac 1742 w.
Joshua 1772 w.
Sarah 1774 w.
Isaac 1777 w.
Abraham 1785 w.
Jno. 1788 w.
Jno. 1793 i.

Northampton
Watson 1750 i.
Princess Anne
John 1796 w.
RIGLESWORTH
Norfolk
Peter 1652 w.
RIGNEY
Pittsylvania
Chas. 1791 w.
RILEE
Middlesex
Jno. 1788 w.
RILEY
Accomack
Thos. 1724 w.
Jno. 1740 i.
Thos. 1772 w.
Wm. Jr. 1778 w.
Jno. 1785 w.
Thos. 1786 w.
Raymond 1789 w.
Wm. 1791 w.
Augusta
Pharoah 1762 i.
Fauquier
John 1793 w.
Middlesex
Jno. 1745 w.
Westmoreland
Jas. 1799 i.
RILY
Accomack
Thos. Sr. 1697 w.
RIMINGTON
York
Wm. 1720 i.
RIND
York
Wm. 1773 i.
Wm. 1774 i.
RINEHART
Shenandoah
Michael 1783 a.
RING
York
Jos. 1702 w.
RINGO
Loudoun
Philip 1790 i.
RINHARD
Augusta
Michael 1751 i.
RINKER
Frederick
Henry 1796 w.
Shenandoah
Jacob 1797 w.
RION
Berkeley
John 1788 w.

RIONDON
Richmond
───── 1726 i.
RIPLEY
Essex
Richard 1711 w.
RIPP
Botetourt
Frederick 1790 i.
RIPPEY
Berkeley
Joseph 1774 w.
RIPPIN
Northampton
David 1749 i.
RIPPING
York
Edwd. 1734 w.
Mary 1744 w.
RISE
Norfolk
Judith 1704 w.
RISK
Augusta
Jas. 1774 a.
Jno. 1774 w.
RISKE
Middlesex
James 1717 i.
RITCHASON
Richmond
Thos. 1719 w.
RITCHEY
Augusta
Jas. 1782 i.
Jno. 1787 i.
Botetourt
William 1777 i.
John 1780 w.
Charlotte
Alexander 1771 i.
Rockbridge
James 1797 w.
John 1799 a.
Essex
Archibald 1784 w.
Prince Edward
Jno. 1770 i.
Jane 1785 w.
Chas. 1788 w.
Eliz. 1794 w.
Chas. 1794 i.
RITCHIE
Spotsylvania
Robt. 1790 w.
RITE
Accomack
Wm. 1733 i.
RITTENHOUSE
Louisa
Henry 1797 i.

RITTER
Franklin
Johr 793 w.
RITTERFORD (?)
Essex
Mary 1753 w.
RIVEER
Lancaster
Elizabeth 1776 i.
Richard 1778 i.
Bushrod 1782 i.
John 1787 w.
John 1790 i.
RIVERS
Brunswick
Thos. 1789 w.
Greensville
Robert 1792 w.
Isle of Wight
George 1707 w.
Prince George
Jno. 1720 w.
Surry
Wm. 1698-9 w.
Sussex
Jno. 1774 w.
RIVES
Brunswick
Geo. 1773 w.
Jno. 1776 w.
Simon 1787 i.
Mecklenburg
Wm. 1787 i.
Surry
Geo. 1746 w.
Jno. 1750 i.
Sussx
Wm. 1778 w.
Wm. 1782 i.
Geo. 1795 w.
RIXEY
Prince William
Richard 1786 i.
ROACH
Accomack
Michael 1750 w.
Amelia
Wm. 1798 w.
James 1799 w.
Charles City
Henry 1791 w.
James 1796 w.
Wm. 1798 i.
Goochland
Patrick 1789 i.
King George
Price [1778?] w.
Lancaster
Jno. 1718 i.
Wm. 1744 i.
Solomon 1744-5 i.

Loudoun
Richd. 1797 i.
Orange
James, Sr. 1777 w.
Jno. 1778 i.
Northampton
Widow 1638 i.
Westmoreland
Edwd. 1725 i.
ROADES
York
Jno. 1708 w.
ROADS
Berkeley
John 1793 w.
Henrico
Geo. 1726 i.
ROAN
Northampton
Wm. 1708 w.
ROANE
Essex
Wm. 1757 w.
Sarah 1760 w.
William 1785 w.
William 1791 i.
Middlesex
Wm. 1770 w.
Sarah 1780 w.
ROB
Lancaster
James 1747 i.
Agatha 1775 i.
Marget 1777 w.
ROBARDS
Essex
John 1727 i.
John 1728 i.
John 1734 i.
ROBBINS
Accomack
Wm. 1725 w.
ROBBINSON
Goochland
Thos. 1743 i.
ROBERDS
Essex
William 1740 i.
ROBARDS
Goochland
Jno. 1755 w.
Wm. 1783 w.
Ohio
William 1783 w.
ROBARTS
Louisa
Joseph 1747 w.
ROBASEN
Richmond
Jno. 1716 i.

ROBB
Lancaster
Thomas 1782 i.
ROBBARDS
York
Mary 1749 w.
ROBBERSON
Lancaster
Giles 1755 w.
ROBBERTS
Albemarle
Ellender 1791 w.
ROBBORDS
Surry
Jno. 1740 w.
ROBBOSSON
Surry
Chris. 1727 i.
ROBEARDS
York
Robt. 1705 i.
ROBERDEAU(?)
Frederick
Daniel 1795 w.
ROBERSON
Cumberland
Jno. 1768 w.
Isle of Wight
John 1737 w.
Lancaster
Alex. 1710 w.
Giles 1785 w.
Lunenburg
Jno. 1764 w.
Abraham 1763 i.
Northumberland
Joseph 1756 i.
Westmoreland
Thos. 1756 w.
ROBERT
Accomack
Foreman 1791 i.
Amherst
Elliott 1788 w.
Fairfax
Saml. 1796 a.
Franklin
Thomas 1798 w.
Norfolk
Willis 1763 i.
ROBERTS
Accomack
Francis 1697 w.
Arthur 1702 i.
Francis 1706 i.
Hugh 1721 w.
Arthur 1740 w.
Francis 1745 w.
Saml. 1748 i.
Thos. 1753 i.
Abel 1761 w.

Abot 1761 i.
Hugh 1770 w.
Rose 1770 w.
Hugh 1773 i.
Hugh 1778 i.
Joakim 1791 w.
/ Arthur 1797 w.
Sarah 1797 i.
Arthur 1799 i.
Amelia
Thos. 1737 w.
Jno. 1764 w.
James 1784 w.
Sarah 1797 w.
Albemarle
Morris 1760 w.
Martha 1783 w.
Bedford
Daniel 1781 w.
Thomas 1781 w.
Berkeley
Samuel 1799 w.
Charlotte
Jno. 1778 w.
Thos. 1780 i.
Jno. 1786 i.
Francis 1789 i.
Francis 1791 i.
Chesterfield
Morris 17— w.
Joshua 1757 w.
Jessee 1764 i.
Culpeper
George 1775 w.
Benjamin 1782 w.
Benjamin J. 1783 i.
Benjamin 1793 i.
Essex
Griffin 1694 w.
Edmond 1705-6 i.
William 1728 w.
Jean 1747 i.
Fairfax
John Sr. 1750 w.
Franklin
John 1775 i.
Frederick
Joseph 1759 i.
William 1768 w.
Elizabeth 1784 w.
Halifax
Jno. 1776 w.
Jno. 1781 i.
Francis 1793 w.
Jane 1795 w.
Jno. 1795 i.
Jane 1796 i.
Michael 1798 i.
Henrico
Bartholomew Jr.
1693 i.

Roger 1703 i.
Thos. 1709 i.
Jno. 1717 w.
Henry
Joseph 1778 w.
Isle of Wight
Jane 1713 w.
John Sr. 1762 w.
Thomas 1775 w.
John 1794 w.
Lancaster
Eleanor 1730 nw.
John 1793 i.
Loudoun
Richard 1762 w.
Owen 1775 w.
Owen 1780 w.
Lunenburg
Francis 1779 i.
Madison
Hugh 1794 w.
Mecklenburg
Thos. 1770 i.
Jno. 1779 w.
Alex. 1781 w.
Lark 1793 w.
Jno. 1798 w.
Middlesex
Willet 1718 i.
Norfolk
Samuel 1715 w.
Richard 1718 w.
Benj. 1719 i.
Joseph 1719 i.
Joseph 1743 w.
John 1746 i.
Henry 1750 w.
Lemuel 1766 w.
Humphrey 1791 w.
Northampton
Jno. 1662 w.
Wm. 1677 w.
Sarah 1700 w.
Obedience 1709 w.
Thos. 1713 w.
Arthur 1719 w.
Jacob 1730 w.
Eliz. 1731 w.
Elias 1735 i.
Jno. 1742 w.
Obedience Sr. 1744 w.
Isaac 1747 i.
Arthur 1748 w.
Wm. 1748 i.
Edwd. 1749 w.
Wm. 1749 i.
Jno. 1750 i.
Littleton 1750 w.
Zorobabel 1750 w.
Jacob 1752 i.
Moses 1754 w.

Obedience 1755 w.
Archibald 1764 i.
Ezekiel 1764 i.
Francis Jr. 1764 w.
Jno. 1765 w.
Francis 1769 w.
Jno. 1774 i.
Isaac 1779 w.
Edmd. 1784 w.
Mark 1787 w.
Obedience 1787 w.
Moses 1792 w.
Mark 1795 i.
Orange
Joseph 1780 w.
Pittsylvania
Geo. 1773 w.
Princess Anne
Jno. 1727 w.
Mary 1728 w.
Mark 1753 i.
Moses 1760 w.
Jno. 1773 w.
Elias 1778 w.
Rappahannock
Thos. 1683 w.
Elias 1684 i.
Spotsylvania
John 1724 w.
Surry
Nat. 1795 w.
Sussex
Willet 1767 w.
Faithy 1773 w.
Wilett 1779 w.
Benj. 1782 w.
Washington
David 1779 w.
Westmoreland
Maurice 1701 w.
York
Constant 1668 w.
Eron 1673 w.
Wm. 1702 w.
Jno. 1719 w.
Thos. 1719 w.
Jno. 1739 w.
Saml. 1746 w.
Robt. 1748 w.
Eliz. 1755 i.
Robt. 1755 i.
Gerrard 1757 i.
Thos. 1763 w.
Gerard 1767 w.
Saml. 1768 i.
Thos. 1768 i.
Sarah 1774 i.
Thos. 1785 w.
ROBERTSON
Amelia
Chris. 1749 i.

Elnore 1750 i.
Edwd. 1769 w.
Mary 1776 w.
Henry 1782 w.
Wm. 1784 w.
Matthew 1798 i.
Albemarle
James 1752 w.
Amherst
Rebecca 1784 w.
Augusta
Jas. 1754 w.
Eliz. 1759 i.
Wm. 1765 w.
Alex. 1770 i.
Jno. 1771 i.
Matthew 1786 w.
Bedford
James 1783 i.
Berkeley
James 1798 i.
Charlotte
Jesse 1797 i.
Chesterfield
Wm. 17— i.
Jas. 1757 w.
Wm. 1757 w.
Wm. 1764 w.
Jno. 1765 w.
Jno. 1766 i.
Frances 1768 w.
Jno. 1768 w.
Wm. 1774 w.
Geo. 1775 w.
Lodowick 178- w.
Jeoffery 1784 w.
Elijah 1795 w.
Geo. 1795 w.
Christopher 1796 w.
Jno. 1796 w.
Eliah 1797 i.
Wm. 1797 w.
Essex
Mary 1736 w.
Fairfax
James Sr. 1769 w.
George 1782 w.
John 1792 a.
Fauquier
Benj. 1783 i.
Halifax
Walter 1783 a.
Martha 1785 w.
Walter 1786 i.
Christopher 1791 w.
Henrico
Geo. 1745 i.
Wm. 1783 w.
Wm. 1785 w.
Geo. Sr. 1797 w.

Isle of Wight
Jonathan 1737 w.
William 1782 w.
King George
Jas. 1729 i.
Robt. 1754 a.
Robert 1759 i.
Lancaster
Andrew 1795 w.
Loudoun
Henry 1769 w.
Susannah 1791 i.
Wm. 1791 w.
Lunenburg
Jno. 1766 i.
Francis 1778 w.
Francis 1787 i.
Mecklenburg
Richd. 1775 i.
Norfolk
John 1745-6 w.
Moses 1799 i.
Northumberland
Moses 1747 w.
Thos. 1749 i.
Prince Edward
Christopher 1765 i.
Isaac 1766 w.
Princess Anne
Thos. 1788 i.
Moses 1788 i.
Surry
Nathaniel 1711 i.
Nathaniel 1735 w.
Eliz. 1751 w.
Wm. 1752 i.
Eliz. 1752 i.
Sussex
James 1793 w.
Westmoreland
Priscilla 1717 w.
Jno. 1735 i.
York
Andrew 1725 i.
Robt. 1783 w.
ROBESON
Accomack
Thos. 1783 w.
Cumberland
David 1795 i.
Henrico
Jeffery 1734 i.
Northumberland
Jno. 1797 w.
ROBINET
Botetourt
Samuel 1772 i.
ROBINS
Accomack
Edwd. 1728 w.
Edwd. 1730 i.

Jno. 1732 w.
Sarah 1744 i.
Jos. 1747 w.
Jno. 1752 w.
Spencer 1778 w.
Leonard 1780 w.
Michael 1789 w.
Norfolk
Richard 1745 i.
Northampton
Obedience 1662 w.
Saml. 1662 w.
Obedience 1683 i.
Arthur 1693 w.
Jno. Sr. 1709 w.
Scarbo 1709 i.
Littleton 1718-19 w.
Jno. Jr. 1720 w.
Jno. Jr. 1727 i.
Jno. Jr. 1734 w.
Jno. Sr. 1740 w.
Obedience 1740 w.
Jno. Sr. 1742 i.
Arthur 1747 i.
Katharince 1754 w.
Jno. Sr. 1772 w.
Teackle 1774 w.
Edward Sr. 1779 w.
Joshua 1789 w.
Arthur Sr. 1792 w.
Edwd. 1793 w.
Joshua 1793 i.
Margt. 1794 w.
Susanna 1794 w.
Orange
Wm. 1774 i.
Rappahannock
Alex. 1684 w.
Richmond
Wm. 1782 w.
Southampton
James Francis 1763 i.
Westmoreland
Simon 1703 w.
Thos. 1725 i.
Hannah 1778 w.
York
Thos. 1729 w.
Jno. 1791 w.
ROBINSON
Accomack
Lawrence 1673 w.
Tully 1724 w.
Ann 1727 i.
Jas. 1775 i.
Jas. 1783 i.
Patience 1795 w.
Albemarle
Richd. 1785 w.
Jno. 1788 w.

Amherst
Jno. 1796 w.
Augusta
Jas. 1749 i.
Jas. 1751 w.
Jas. 1753 a.
Jno. 1757 i.
Geo. 1763 w.
Wm. 1765 a.
Geo. 1766 i.
Wm. 1769 i.
Jas. 1768 w.
Isaac 1775 w.
Geo. 1776 w.
Jno. 1776 w.
Jas. 1777 w.
Bath
William 1794 w.
Bedford
James 1778 w.
Botetourt
Elizabeth 1772 i.
David 1788 w.
Brunswick
Wm. Sr. 1777 w.
Littleberry 1784 i.
Jno. 1795 w.
Culpeper
William 1771 w.
Israel 1784 w.
Cumberland
Nathan 1773 i.
Edwd. 1782 i.
Field 1785 w.
Josiah 1786 w.
Jones 1793 i.
Hezekiah 1796 w.
Essex
Henry 1721 w.
Duncan 1734 w.
Molly 1761 w.
Fairfax
Thomas 1745 a.
Thomas 1753 i.
Joseph 1786 w.
Fauquier
Joseph 1782 w.
Benj. 1785 w.
William 1791 w.
Frederick
Thomas 1745 a.
Francis 1749 a.
Richard 1749 a.
John 1754 i.
John 1757 i.
William 1798 w.
Goochland
James 1748 w.
Greenbrier
William 1797 i.

Halifax
Wm. 1774 w.
Robt. 1784 i.
Harrison
William Jr. 1799 i.
Isle of Wight
Richard 1737 w.
James 1749 i.
Jonathan 1772 w.
King George
Wm. 1743 i.
Philip 1759 i.
Gerrard 1770 a.
Maximilian 1777 w.
Wm. 1777 w.
Lancaster
Isaac 1713 w.
Wm. 1724 w.
Archibald 1729 nw.
Giles 1735 w.
Jno. 1735 i.
Jane 1737 i.
James 1764 w.
Giles 1766 w.
William 1767 w.
Aaron 1768 w.
Eleazer 1783 w.
Jesse 1789 w.
Loudoun
John 1782 w.
Louisa
James 1748 w.
James 1776 a.
Wm. 1782 i.
Lunenburg
Abraham 1762 i.
Jno. 1767 i.
Mecklenburg
Nathaniel 1792 w.
Middlesex
Christopher 1693 w.
Judith 1720 w.
Christopher 1727 i.
Wm. 1758 a.
Christopher 1768 w.
Sarah 1772 w.
Christopher 1784 w.
Chas. 1787 w.
Jno. 1787 w.
Norfolk
Nicholas 1677 w.
Robert 1773 w.
Tully 1796 w.
Northampton
Jno. 1661 w.
———— 1668 w.
Jeremiah 1670 w.
Jno. 1678 i.
Richd. 1695 w.
Benj. 1715 w.
Leonard 1735 i.

Northumberland
Jno. 1700 w.
Francis 1719 ab.
Thos. 1720 i.
Saml. 1721 w.
Anthony 1724 w.
Benj. 1725 i.
Nicholas 1727 w.
John 1751 i.
Jesse 1766 w.
Winfield 1787 w.
Ohio
Andrew 1781 a.
Edward 1783 w.
Princess Anne
Wm. 1696 w.
Wm. 1741 w.
Mary 1742 i.
Wm. 1760 w.
Anne 1768 i.
Mary 1773 i.
Tully 1773 w.
Wm. 1783 i.
Moses 1787 w.
Thos. 1787 w.
Wm. 1787 w.
Mark 1791 i.
John 1795 w.
Rappahannock
John 1679 w.
Wm. 1683 i.
Richmond
Rebecca 1718 i.
Wm. 1721 i.
Rockbridge
John 1789 w.
Shenandoah
William 1778 a.
Spotsylvania
Wm. 1734 a.
Benj. 1791 a.
Benj. 1795 a.
Henry 1770 w.
Jno. 1786 w.
Wm. 1792 w.
Benj. 1795 w.
Stafford
Henry 1753 w.
Surry
Andrew 1677 i.
Ann 1678 i.
James 1697 i.
Sussex
Geo. 1768 w.
Seymour 1780 w.
Washington
John 1792 w.
Westmoreland
Thos. 1720 w.
Jno. 1725 w.
Wm. 1731 w.

Jno. 1756 i.
Michael 1758 w.
Jane 1768 i.
Hannah 1778 w.
Harry 1778 w.
Wm. 1782 w.
Wm. 1786 i.
Jas. 1798 w.
Solomon 1799 w.
York
Jno. 1687 w.
Wm. 1691 i.
Anthony 1727 w.
Peter 1734 w.
Jno. Jr. 1737 i.
Anthony Jr. 1738 i.
Jno. 1738 i.
Wm. 1748 i.
Ann 1752 i.
Anthony 1756 w.
Anne 1758 i.
Diana 1762 w.
Anthony 1772 i.
Peter 1773 w.
Anthony 1776 w.
Ann 1781 nw.
Thos. 1788 w.
ROBISON
Northampton
Geo. 1728 w.
Westmoreland
Jno. 1730 i.
ROBOTTOM
Westmoreland
Wm. 1717 i.
ROBUCK
Northumberland
Robt. 1751 w.
Wm. 1763 w.
Wm. 1790 i.
ROCHELL
Sussex
Jno. 1759 w.
Nathl. 1792 w.
Prince George
Wm. 1714 a.
Southampton
Jno. 1794 w.
ROCHESTER
Isle of Wight
William 1749 w.
Richmond
Wm. 1767 w.
Westmoreland
Jno. 1755 i.
Wm. 1755 w.
Jno. 1796 i.
ROCK
Lancaster
Constantine 1786 i.
Francis 1794 i.

ROCKET
Henrico
Baldwin 1782 w.
ROCKETT
Henrico
Baldwin 1731 w.
RODDEN
Essex
John 1789 w.
RODDY
Shenandoah
Charles 1782 a.
RODEAVER
Culpeper
John 1791 i.
RODEHEDVEL
Culpeper
John 1790 w.
RODES
Albemarle
Jno. Sr. 1775 w.
David 1794 w.
Augusta
Mathias 1774 w.
Fluvanna
Geo. 1788 i.
Middlesex
Jno. 1759 w.
RODEWELL
Isle of Wight
John 1720 w.
RODGERS
Accomack
Peter 1722 i.
Richd. 1742 nw.
Jacob 1750 i.
Danl. 1752 w.
Jno. 1757 w.
Edwd. 1763 i.
Major 1763 w.
Norwich 1764 i.
Richd. 1764 i.
Thos. Wise 1767 w.
Major 1768 i.
Jno. 1769 i.
Isaac 1770 w.
Jas. 1770 w.
Jno. 1770 i.
Babel 1776 w.
Sarah 1776 w.
Peter 1779 w.
Levin 1787 i.
Richd. 1787 w.
Jerobabel 1789 w.
Jno. Sr. 1791 w.
Jno. Sr. 1794 w.
Jno. 1795 w.
Jas. 1795 w.
Tibney 1799 w.
Zorobabel 1799 i.

Augusta
Geo. 1767 i.
Charlotte
Thos. 1786 w.
Fairfax
William 1793 a.
Greenbrier
David 1785 i.
King George
Jno. 1795 w.
Norfolk
Wm. 1685 w.
Northampton
Littleton M. 1769 i.
Jackson 1774 i.
Lydia 1778 w.
Richmond
Nicholas 1718 w.
RODIN
Essex
Homer 1716 i.
RODWAY
Isle of Wight
John 1752 w.
RODWELL
Surry
Jno. 1703 i.
ROE
Isle of Wight
Robert 1675 w.
Norfolk
William 1722 w.
Princess Anne
Kiteley 1753 w.
Richmond
Jno. 1745 i.
Surry
Robt. 1770 w.
Sussex
Cannon 1761 i.
Westmoreland
Sutton 1716 i.
Henry 1725 w.
Bunch 1743 w.
Bunch 1756 w.
Henry 1783 w.
ROEBUCK
Culpeper
William 1782 w.
Robert 1793 w.
Northumberland
Robert 1752 i.
ROFFE
Mecklenburg
Wm. 1786 w.
ROGER
Shenandoah
Michael Sr. 1794 i.
ROGERMAN
Norfolk
Thos. 1734-5 i.

ROGERS
Accomack
Jno. 1674 w.
Peter 1719 w .
Jno. 1721 w.
Peter 1731 i.
Wm. 1731 w.
Jno. 1735 i.
Wm. 1738 i.
Richd. Sr. 1740 w.
Richd. 1740 w.
Reuben 1749 w.
Jno. 1757 i.
Richd. 1761 w.
Saban 1764 w.
Albemarle
Caroline 1752 i.
Giles 1794 w.
Amelia
Wm. 1798 i.
Augusta
Jas. 1760 i.
Bedford
William 1759 w.
Culpeper
Joseph 1762 w.
John 1763 i.
Bernard 1783 w.
Fairfax
Richard 1742 a.
Fauquier
George 1792 w.
John 1794 w.
Robert 1795 i.
Frederick
John 1763 i.
James 1797 i.
Goochland
Robt. 1740 w.
Addustin 1749 i.
Wm. 1777 i.
Greenbrier
John 1798 i.
Halifax
Abraham 1762 w.
Peter 1785 w.
Isle of Wight
Edward 1683-4 w.
Michael 1710 w.
King George
Thos. 1758 w.
Wm. 1778 a.
Benj. 1796 w.
Benj. 1797 i.
Lancaster
Noah 1717 i.
Thos. 1718 i.
Eliz. 1728 w.
Wm. 1728 w.
Mary 1731 w.
John 1752 w.

Jane 1760 w.
John 1760 w.
John 1765 w.
William 1768 w.
Richard 1769 i.
Richd. 1777 i.
John 1788 w.
Charles 1793 w.
Lunenburg
Wm. 1751 w.
Andrew 1756 w.
Mecklenburg
Richd. 1769 i.
Norfolk
Samon 1719 w.
Saml. 1751 w.
Phillis 1760 w.
Northampton
Jacob 1751 w.
Nathl. 1754 w.
Abel 1764 i.
Lazarus 1773 w.
Northumberland
Jas. 1711 i.
Jas. 1712 w.
Edward 1755 w.
Geo. 1784 i.
Orange
William 1794 w.
Pittsylvania
Thos. 1781 w.
Josiah 1793 i.
Richmond
Wm. 1718 nw.
Southampton
Collin 1798 i.
Spotsylvania
Henry 1747 a.
Wm. 1779 w.
Lucy 1787 w.
Thos. 1786 w.
Stafford
Jno. 1760 w.
Wm. 1761 i.
Surry
Richd. 1678 w.
Jno. 1697 i.
Wm. 1701 w.
Wm. 1727 w.
Benj. 1744 i.
Sussex
Wm. 1770 w.
Benj. 1778 w.
Wm. 1778 w.
Thos. 1783 i.
Washington
John 1782 i.
Westmoreland
Jos. 1746 w.
Jno. 1752 i.

York
Thos. 1709 i.
Adduston 1728 i.
Jno. Adduston 1729 i.
Wm. 1739 w.
Jas. 1745 w.
Theodosia 1752 w.
Adduston 1762 w.
Chas. 1772 i.
Clayton 1773 w.
Sarah 1778 w.
Margt. 1781 w.
Wm. Adeuston
1785 w.
ROHRER
Shenandoah
Jacob 1773 w.
Daniel 1788 i.
ROLAND
Bedford
Henry 1794 i.
Sussex
Joseph 1760 i.
Jno. 1761 i.
Burwell 1782 i.
ROLEMAN
Augusta
Jacob 1773 i.
ROLEN
Orange
Edwd. 1749 w.
ROLLER
Princess Anne
Hannah 1719 i.
ROLLIN
Rockbridge
James 1794 w.
ROLLING
Fairfax
John 1785 i.
ROLLINGS
Sussex
Geo. 1777 a.
Richd. 1795 w.
ROLLINS
King George
Jas. 1785 w.
Richmond
Eliz. 1750 i.
Westmoreland
Wm. 1718 w.
ROLLINSON
York
Eliz. 1750 w.
Jno. 1784 i.
ROLLISON
York
Jno. 1780 w.
ROLLSTONE
Pittsylvania
Robt. 1781 w.

ROLT
Rappahannock
——— 1685 i.
Jno. 1685 i.
ROMINE
Loudoun
Peter 1788 w.
John 1797 i.
Peter 1797 i.
RONALD
Henrico
Andrew 1799 w.
Powhatan
Wm. 1793 i.
RONALDSON
Isle of Wight
Patrick 1791 w.
RONEY
Richmond
James 1738 i.
RONSHELL
Norfolk
William Sr. 1795 i.
RONVIEVE
Princess Anne
Geo. 1759 i.
ROOFF
Loudoun
John 1796 i.
ROOGER
Shenandoah
James 1791 w.
ROOKARD
Prince William
William 1799 w.
Fauquier
Thomas 1799 w.
ROOKINGS
Surry
Wm. 1679 w.
Wm. 1714 w.
Wm. 1750 i.
ROOKSBY
York
Anthony 1678 w.
ROOLFE
Northumberland
Thom. 1668 i.
ROOSE
Accomack
Jno. 1742 w.
ROOTS
Lancaster
Thos. 1660 w.
ROPER
Brunswick
Jas. 1767 a.
Charles City
Jno. 1766 i.
Thos. 1769 w.

Greensville
David 1783 w.
Henrico
Jno. 1793 i.
Loudoun
Thomas 1792 i.
Powhatan
Shadrack 1784 w.
Susannah 1791 w.
RORACK
Wythe
James 1794 i.
RORER
Northampton
Jane 1739 i.
Shenandoah
Daniel 1788 a.
ROROOK
Northumberland
Richd. 1723-4 i.
ROSCOE
Northampton
Arthur 1720 w.
ROSE
Accomack
Thos. 1722 w.
Thos. 1724 i.
Richd. 1742 i.
Jacob 1747 w.
Jas. 1762 i.
Jos. 1799 w.
Albemarle
Robt. 1751 w.
Amherst
Henry 1779 w.
Hugh 1794 w.
Berkeley
Jonathan 1785 w.
Conrod 1796 w.
Brunswick
Henry 1752 i.
Henry 1753 i.
Absolom 1776 i.
Jno. 1781 w.
Alex. 1786 i.
Jno. 1792 w.
Fairfax
John 1744 a.
Frederick
George 1746 i.
Daniel 1748 i.
Isle of Wight
William 1771 w.
William 1773 i.
King George
Wm. 1752 w.
Eliz. 1785 a.
Alexander 1786 w.
Norfolk
Alexander 1686-7 w.
Robt. 1710 w.

Peter 1777 w.
Daniel 1792 w.
Peter 1793 i.
Northampton
Thos. 1786 w.
Jacob 1792 w.
Prince Edward
Hugh 1765 i.
Prince William
John 1784 w.
Southampton
Richd. 1765 w.
Surry
Richd. 1736 w.
Wm. 1766 w.
Wm. 1797 w.
Sussex
Richd. 1754 w.
Richd. 1768 w.
Richd. 1770 w.
Wm. 1792 w.
Westmoreland
Chas. 1761 w.
Francis 1793 w.
Jno. 1799 i.
ROSS
Accomack
Andrew 1724 w.
Ezekiel 1798 w.
Bedford
William 1781 w.
Berkeley
Stephen 1780 w.
Brunswick
Chas. 1744 w.
Frederick
Alex. 1748 w.
David 1748 w.
John 1748 i.
Stephen 1750 i.
James 1751 w.
George 1781 w.
James 1784 w.
Greensville
Charles 1792 i.
Henrico
Adam 1699 w.
King George
Andrew 1753 a.
Norfolk
John, Sr. 1713 w.
Alexander 1761 i.
John 1763 w.
John 1784 i.
John 1799 i.
Northampton
David 1768 w.
Jno. 1778 i.
Prince William
William 1786 w.

Stafford
Alex. 1730 i.
Wm. Sr. 1758 i.
York
Jno. 1782 w.
ROSSE
York
Robt. 1686-7 w.
ROSSER
Campbell
David 1790 w.
Jonathan 1795 a.
Brunswick
Jno. 1775 w.
Fauquier
John 1783 w.
Greensville
Eliz. 1796 w.
King George
Wm. 1747 eb.
Richd. 1754 a.
Jas. 1757 i.
Orange
Eliz. 1742 w.
ROSSON
Culpeper
Jerome 1796 w.
Lancaster
William 1763 w.
Northumberland
Wm. 1789 w.
Wm. 1794 i.
ROSSOR
Sussex
Thos. 1767 i.
ROSZELL
Loudoun
Stephen 1792 w.
ROTCHELL
Southampton
John 1754 w.
ROTHEFEFFER
Shenandoah
David 1773 w.
ROTHERY
Norfolk
Daniel 1761 w.
Henry 1769 w.
Matthew 1772 w.
ROTHGAB
Augusta
Jno. Jacob 1753 w.
ROTTENBERRY
Sussex
Susannah 1767 w.
Silvanus 1769 i.
ROTTENBURY
Surry
Jno. 1751 w.

ROTTINGBURY
Lunenburg
Henry 1753 w.
ROUGH
Chesterfield
Geo. 1756 w.
Loudoun
John 1797 w.
ROULTON
Norfolk
William 1795 w.
ROUMIERE
Princess Anne
Geo. 1759 w.
ROUNDTREE
Augusta
Noah 1770 a.
Isle of Wight
William 1796 w.
Goochland
Randal 1788 w.
ROURAIN
Lunenburg
Saml. 1770 i.
ROUSAU
Westmoreland
David 1748 i.
ROUSE
Norfolk
Robt. 1687 w.
Northampton
Mouns 1663 i.
ROUSSAU
Fauquier
William 1798 w.
ROUT
Northumberland
Richd. Sr. 1713 w.
Geo. 1727 w.
John 1772 i.
Stafford
Richd. 1733 i.
ROUTE
Northumberland
Geo. 1727 i.
ROUTH
York
Anthony 1758 i.
ROUTHLEDGE
Prince Edward
Robt. 1766 i.
ROUTON
Bedford
Richard 1792 w.
ROUTT
Fauquier
James 1795 i.
Northumberland
Richd. 1752 w.
John 1759 w.
Thomas 1779 w.

Richd. 1790 w.
Ann 1794 w.
Anthony L. 1797 w.
Stafford
Peter 1765 w.
ROUZEE
Essex
Lodowick 1726 w.
ROVARDES
Brunswick
Bartho. 1741 w.
ROW
Fluvanna
Stephen 1796 i.
Isle of Wight
John 1733 i.
Middlesex
Joseph 1749 a.
York
Wm. 1718 w.
ROWALDSON
Isle of Wight
Patrick 1792 i.
ROWBOTOM
Westmoreland
Eliz. 1739 w.
Washington
Matthew 1778 i.
ROWDEN
Lancaster
Isaac 1727 nw.
ROWE
Brunswick
Deadmond 1779 w.
Fluvanna
Wm. 1788 w.
Westmoreland
Wm. 1768 w.
Wm. 1778 i.
ROWELL
Surry
Edwd. 1729 w.
Richd. 1746 w.
Robt. 1752 i.
Richd. 1782 w.
ROWLAND
Bedford
Henry 1773 w.
Henry 1782 i.
Botetourt
William 1777 nw.
Robert 1782 w.
Cumberland
Michael 1757 w.
Ann 1789 i.
Henry
John 1780 w.
Mary 1791 w.
Northumberland
Robt. 1754 w.

Surry
Joshua 1752 w.
Westmoreland
David 1711 w.
ROWLATE
Henrico
Wm. 1736 i.
ROWLEN
Charlotte
Joseph 1794 i.
ROWLES
Accomack
Jno. 1709 w.
Major 1731 w.
Danl. 1735 w.
Danl. 1739 w.
Jno. 1749 w.
Jonathan 1749 i.
Jno. 1750 w.
Phebe 1755 w.
Major 1762 i.
Hancock N. 1763 w.
Stafford
Jas. 1762 i.
ROWLETT
Chesterfield
Jos. 17— w.
Mary 17— i.
Peter 1749 w.
Wm. 1760 i.
Jno. 1774 w.
Mary 1777 w.
Thos. 1780 w.
Wm. 1785 w.
Francis 1793 w.
Henrico
Peter 1702 w.
Wm. 1735 w.
Lunenburg
Peter 1754 w.
Prince Edward
John 1776 w.
ROWLEY
Accomack
Richd. 1744 w.
Richd. 1747 i.
Wm. 1747 w.
Jno. 1753 i.
Arthur 1776 w.
King George
Wm. Sr. 1754 w.
Wm. 1774 w.
Ann 1794 w.
Lancaster
Rowland 1679 w.
ROWLING
Fairfax
Elizabeth 1757 i.
ROWNTREE
Goochland
Wm. 1766 w.

Wm. 1776 w.
ROWS
Isle of Wight
John 1734 i.
ROWSE
Norfolk
George 1739 w.
ROWZEE
Essex
Lodowick 1699 w.
Jno. 1699 w.
Ralph 1719 w.
Edward 1720 i.
Edwd. 1726 w.
Benj. 1738 i.
Ralph 1741 i.
John 1748 i.
Martha 1748 i.
Edwd. 1761 w.
Edwd. 1764 w.
John 1778 w.
Edwd. 1790 w.
Richard 1791 w.
Ralph 1799 w.
William 1799 w.
ROWZIE
Rappahannock
Edwd. 1677 w.
ROY
Berkeley
Renold 1776 i.
Essex
Mungo 1758 w.
James 1779 w.
James 1793 w.
Ralph L. 1799 w.
Spotsylvania
James 1741 w.
Jno. Beverley 1774 a.
ROYAL
Accomack
Benj. 1792 i.
Halifax
Joseph 1760 w.
Jno. 1766 w.
Mecklenburg
Sarah 1792 w.
ROYALL
Accomack
Benj. 1753 i.
Amelia
Richd. 1774 w.
Richd. (2) 1774 w.
Eliz. 1777 w.
Jos. 1783 w.
Jno. 1791 w.
Richd. 1797 w.
Chesterfield
Littleberry 1749 w.
Jos. 1783 w.
Eliz. 1794 w.

Henrico
Henry 1747 w.
Jos. 1748 w.
Isle of Wight
James 1666 i.
Thomas 1790 i.
Lunenburg
Joseph 1755 i.
Surry
Wm. 1767 i.
ROYL
Isle of Wight
James 1666 w.
ROYLE
York
Jos. 1766 w.
ROYLEY
Essex
Brian 1698 i.
ROYSTER
Charles City
Peter 1767 w.
Geo. 1797 i.
Halifax
Peter 1795 w.
Peter 1796 i.
Henrico
Jno. 1787 i.
Jno. 1788 w.
Mecklenburg
Geo. 1797 i.
Jacob 1798 w.
ROYSTON
Spotsylvania
Jno. 1748 a.
ROZIER
Westmoreland
Jno. 1660 w.
Jno. 1702 i.
Bridget 1704 w.
Jno. 1705 w.
RUBLE
Frederick
Ulrick 1761 w.
Wooley 1761 i.
RUBSAMEN
Chesterfield
Jacob 1792 w.
RUBY
Shenandoah
Jacob 1791 w.
RUCK
Henrico
Thos. 1695 i.
King George
Jas. 1760 i.
RUCKER
Amherst
Jno. 1779 w.
Reuben 1782 a.

Culpeper
Cornelius 1761 w.
Thomas 1763 w.
Esther 1777 w.
James 1784 w.
Madison
Ephraim 1798 i.
Orange
Jno. 1742 w.
Peter 1743 w.
John 1794 w.
Peter 1794 i.
RUCKMAN
Augusta
Jno. 1753 i.
RUCKS
Chesterfield
Wm. 1777 i.
Wm. Sr. 1777 w.
RUD
Chesterfield
Jno. 1744 w.
RUDD
Chesterfield
Wm. 17— i.
Avis 1759 w.
Hannah 1771 w.
Jas. 1785 i.
Fredk. 1790 i.
Thos. 1790 i.
Jno. 1791 w.
Robt. 1791 i.
Thos. Jr. 1791 w.
Thos. Sr. 1792 w.
Thos. Sr. 1793 i.
Jos. 1797 w.
Mecklenburg
Jno. 1766 w.
Wm. 1771 i.
Joseph 1779 w.
RUDDELL
Botetourt
Cornelius 1798 w.
Shenandoah
John 1781 w.
Archible 1787 w.
RUDDER
Lunenburg
Alex. 1798 i.
RUDDERFORD
Lancaster
Ralph 1738 w.
RUDDICK
Isle of Wight
George 1727 i.
RUDDLE
Augusta
Jno. Jr. 1749 w.
Shenandoah
Elizabeth 1792 a.

RUDNY
Westmoreland
Sutton 1673-4 w.
RUDOLPH
Frederick
Adam 1789 i.
Westmoreland
Geo. 1784 i.
RUE
Culpeper
William 1780 w.
RUFF
Rockbridge
Jacob 1795 w.
RUFFIN
Mecklenburg
Jno. 1775 w.
Jno. 1777 w.
Southampton
Benj. 1784 w.
Surry
Eliz. 1714 w.
Robt. 1720 w.
Wm. 1774 w.
RUFFNER
Shenandoah
Peter 1778 w.
RUKLE
Shenandoah
Conrod 1795 w.
RULE
Accomack
Jas. 1765 i.
RULEY
Princess Anne
Dorothy 1700 w.
RUMBOW
Norfolk
Isaac 1750 i.
RUMNEY
Fairfax
William 1783 nw.
RUMSEY
Berkeley
James 1793 w.
RUNALS
Goochland
Wm. 1730 w.
RUNDELL
Norfolk
Wm. 1736 w.
RUNELS
Isle of Wight
Henry 1729 w.
RUNGOE
Loudoun
Philip 1786 i.
RUSH
Berkeley
Leonard 1788 w.

Culpeper
James 1788 w.
Frederick
William 1796 i.
Orange
Wm. 1735 a.
RUSK
Augusta
Jas. 1764 i.
Robt. 1786 w.
RUSH
Westmoreland
Wm. 1708 i.
Wm. 1712 i.
RUSSEL
Accomack
Chas. 1668 w.
Robt. 1772 i.
Berkeley
Rebeccah 1781 i.
Cumberland
Thos. 1763 i.
Richmond
Jos. (Youngest)
1748 w.
RUSSELL
Accomack
Saml. 1762 w.
Solomon 1777 w.
Geo. Sr. 1783 w.
Berkeley
Rebecca 1780 w.
Brunswick
Richd. 1761 i.
Saml. 1761 i.
Campbell
David 1784 i.
Robt. 1791 w.
Charles City
Edwd. 1791 w.
Charlotte
Wm. 1774 i.
Wm. 1788 w.
Chesterfield
Jno. 1766 w.
Cumberland
Thos. 1761 w.
Sarah 1772 i.
Culpeper
Sarah 1757 w.
William 1758 w.
Michael 1777 w.
Essex
George 1764 i.
Frederick
Robert 1760 w.
William 1777 w.
Halifax
Wm. 1777 w.
Henrico
Wm. 1798 w.

Loudoun
Anthony 1779 w.
Francis 1782 i.
Lunenburg
Jno. 1759 i.
Philemon 1778 w.
Mecklenburg
Richd. 1768 w.
Burnel 1797 w.
Norfolk
Richard 1667 w.
Thomas 1684 i.
Joseph 1746 nw.
Northampton
Jno. 1645 i.
Northumberland
Richd. 1711 i.
Thos. 1789 i.
Orange
Peter 1746 i.
Princess Anne
Jno. 1697 w.
Thos. 1698 w.
Jno. 1755 i.
Wm. 1790 w.
Anne 1795 w.
Prince William
Nathaniel 1734 a.
Rappahannock
Jno. 1675 nw.
Richmond
Geo. 1731 w.
Thos. 1748 w.
Jos. Jr. 1749 w.
Jno. 1765 w.
Joan 1771 nw.
Sarah 1775 w.
Shenandoah
John 1787 a.
Washington
William 1793 i.
Westmoreland
Andrew 1729 w.
Wm. 1770 i.
York
Jno. 1667 w.
Thos. 1783 w.
RUST
Bedford
George 1775 w.
Campbell
Jeremiah 1787 w.
Cumberland
Jeremiah 1774 w.
Essex
Benjamin 1787 w.
Fauquier
John 1778 i.
John 1798 i.
Loudoun
Daniel 1796 i.

Richmond
Saml. 1752 i.
Benj. 1754 w.
Saml. 1769 w.
Westmoreland
Wm. 1699 w.
Saml. 1718 w.
Jno. 1727 w.
Martha 1729 w.
Jeremiah 1731 w.
Jeremiah 1738 i.
Wm. 1741 i.
Saml. 1741 i.
Martha 1745 w.
Saml. 1746 i.
Henry 1750 i.
Mathew 1751 w.
Wm. 1754 w.
Winifred 1755 w.
Frances 1761 w.
Peter 1762 w.
Peter 1782 w.
Jno. 1786 w.
Geo. 1788 i.
Jno. 1788 i.
Vincent 1794 w.
Jeremiah 1799 i.
Saml. 1799 w.
RUTH
Northumberland
Richd. 1718 w.
RUTHE
Norfolk
Robert 1799 i.
RUTHERFORD
Augusta
Jas. 1767 w.
Thos. 1769 a.
Margt. 1774 w.
Berkeley
Robert 1785 i.
Thomas 1796 w.
Essex
Jno. 1742 w.
Frederick
Reuben 1764 i.
Reuben 1766 i.
King George
Eliz. 1753 i.
Lunenburg
James 1759 i.
RUTLAND
Stafford
Simon 1702 i.
RUTLEDGE
Amelia
Thos. 1741 i.
Augusta
Jas. 1750 i.
Jno. 1751 w.
Jas. 1753 a.

Edwd. 1787 w.
Thos. 1791 w.
Rosanna 1799 w.
Henrico
Jas. 1712 i.
Prince Edward
Wm. 1759 w.
RUTT
Isle of Wight
Abraham 1681 i.
RUTTER
Frederick
Mathias 1794 w.
Isle of Wight
William 1729 i.
William 1730-31 i.
Norfolk
John 1784 i.
Richmond
Ralph 1712 w.
Westmoreland
Robt. 1776 i.
York
———— 1721 ab.
RUTTERS
Isle of Wight
Walter 1698 i.
William 1728 w.
RYAL
Richmond
Jno. 1778 i.
RYALL
Isle of Wight
Thomas 1709 w.
RYAN
Amherst
Jno. 1785 a.
Augusta
Michael 1762 i.
Culpeper
John 1772 w.
Goochland
Philip 1764 i.
Halifax
Danl. 1756 w.
Northumberland
Edward 1759 i.
Ohio
Thomas 1780 a.
Shenandoah
Edward 1784 w.
Westmoreland
Patrick 1704 i.
RYDINGE
Northampton
Thos. 1682 i.
RYE
Lancaster
Henry 1659 w.

RYEVES
Surry
Timothy 1716 i.
RYLAND
Essex
Joseph 1772 w.
York
Wm. 1716 i.
Mary 1718 i.
RYLEY
Augusta
Pharoah 1761 a.
Westmoreland
Edwd. 1741 i.
Edwd. 1754 i.
RYLIE
Middlesex
Jno. 1771 i.
Betty 1772 w.
RYLY
Northumberland
Tinny 1718 i.
RYMER
Richmond
Mark Jr. 1716 w.
RYNDLE
Augusta
Patrick 1791 w.
RYNEHART
Northampton
Jno. 1672 i.
RYNER
Culpeper
Christian 1784 w.

S

SABAGR (?)
Northampton
Jno. 1681 i.
SABASTINE
King George
Chas. 1761 i.
SABATIE
Henrico
Peter 1712 i.
SABLES
York
Richd. 1679 w.
SACHEVERIL
Northumberland
Timothy 1720 w.
SACKER
Accomack
Wm. 1688 w.
Franc. 1690 i.
SACRY
King George
Thos. 1764 w.
Thos. 1765 i.
Francis 1785 a.

SADDLER
Chesterfield
Thos. 1780 w.
SADLER
Amelia
Jeremiah 1778 i.
Brunswick
Thos. 1793 w.
Edwd. 1795 i.
Thos. Sr. 1796 w.
Essex
Aaron 1744 i.
Fluvanna
Wm. 1795 i.
John 1796 i.
Goochland
Benj. 1791 w.
Henrico
Thos. 1713 i.
Middlesex
Jno. 1710 w.
Richmond
Wm. 1796 i.
SAFER
Shenandoah
William 1792 i.
SAGE
Mecklenburg
Henry 1797 w.
ST. CLARE
Prince William
Abraham 1741 i.
ST. CLAIR
Montgomery
Ann 1789 a.
ST. CROIX
Norfolk
Clement 1785 i.
ST. JOHN
Essex
Thos. 1696 w.
Thos. 1698 w.
Thomas 1718 i.
Wm. 1723 w.
Richard 1734 w.
William 1742 w.
Thomas 1780 w.
Spotsylvania
Isaac 1786 a.
SAISE
King George
Wm. 1726 i.
SALE
Amherst
Thos. 1797 w.
Essex
Edwd. 1725 w.
Wm. 1735 w.
Cornelius 1746 w.
Ann 1767 w.
Cornelius 1775 w.

James 1775 w.
Leonard 1776 w.
Cornelous 1779 i.
Thomas 1790 w.
Thomas 1796 i.
John 1797 w.
Accomack
Arthur 1766 i.
SALISBURY
Accomack
Jno. 1795 w.
Northampton
Robt. 1640 i.
SALKELD
Fairfax
Henry 1755 i.
SALLARD
Lancaster
Simon 1679 i.
Simon 1747 w.
Richmond
Simon 1748 i.
Simon 1770 w.
Blanche 1777 i.
Jno. 1782 w.
Chas. 1794 w.
SALLE
Cumberland
Pierre 1752 w.
Goochland
—— 1731 i.
SALLEE
Chesterfield
Magdalen 1756 w.
Henrico
Abraham 1730 w.
Powhatan
Frances 1777 w.
SALLING
Augusta
Jno. Peter 1755 w.
Rockbridge
George 1788 w.
SALLIS
Essex
Samuel 1704 i.
Samuel 1730 w.
SALLIX
Augusta
Wm. 1770 a.
SALLMON
Norfolk
Jno. 1679 w.
SALMON
Albermarle
Thos. 1786 i.
Bedford
John 1791 w.
Culpeper
Thomas 1751 w.

Cumberland
John 1764 w.
Isle of Wight
James 1730-31 w.
Princess Anne
Wm. 1707 w.
Wm. 1754 w.
Richard 1788 i.
SALMONDS
Goochland
Benj. 1794 w.
SALMONS
Goochland
Jas. 1799 w.
Princess Anne
Jno. 1737 w.
Anthy 1775 w.
SALSBURY
Northumberland
Thos. 1657 w.
SALT
Middlesex
Thos. 1752 w.
Northampton
Balmforth 1764 i.
SALTER
Accomack
Silvester 1727 w.
Norfolk
Christopher 1744 w.
Surry
Wm. 1779 w.
Wm. 1799 w.
Spotsylvania
Eliz. 1771 w.
SALTS
Northampton
Wm. 1785 w.
SALYER
Culpeper
Charles 1757 i.
SAMFORD
Accomack
Thos. 1794 w.
Brunswick
Wm. Sr. 1763 w.
Wm. Keen 1795 w.
Richmond
Jas. 1704 w.
Isabelle 1725 w.
Giles 1727 w.
Saml. 1736 w.
Jas. 1742 w.
Thos. 1762 w.
Thos. 1764 nw.
Jno. 1768 w.
SAMM
Spotsylvania
Jno. 1727 a.

SAMMONS
Princess Anne
Wm. 1707 rp.
Sussex
James 1765 w.
Jno. 1766 w.
James 1781 w.
SAMMS
Spotsylvania
James 1726 w.
James 1768 a.
SAMPLE
Augusta
Saml. 1776 w.
Frederick
Samuel 1788 w.
SAMPHLIN
Prince William
John 1737 a.
SAMPSON
Bedford
Benjamin 1774 i.
Culpeper
John 1778 w.
Goochland
Bridgett 1757 w.
Stephen 1768 w.
Mary 1774 w.
Chas. 1776 w.
Saml. 1782 i.
Saml. Smith 1782 w.
Charles 1783 i.
Isle of Wight
James 1689 w.
James 1728 w.
Lancaster
Thos. 1709 i.
George 1798 w.
Northampton
Francis 1742 i.
Jno. 1764 i.
Stephen 1781 w.
Northumberland
Jos. 1782 w.
Rappahannock
Jno. 1685 w.
Shenandoah
Edward 1774 a.
Westmoreland
Jno. 1654 i.
Richd. 1675 i.
SAMSON
Goochland
Francis 1744 w.
Lunenburg
Mary 1751 w.
SAMUEL
Culpeper
James 1795 i.
Essex
Anthony, Sr. 1731 w.

Henry 1748 w.
James 1759 w.
Anthony 1760 w.
Mark 1763 w.
Averelah 1795 w.
Spotsylvania
Anthony 1744 w.
SAMUELS
Loudoun
Shadrack 1784 i.
SANBOURNE
Isle of Wight
Daniel 1712 w.
SANDAGE
Albemarle
James 1763 i.
SANDE
Lancaster
Anthony 1685 i.
SANDERFORD
Middlesex
Jno. 1715 w.
Wm. 1717 i.
SANDEFUR
Cumberland
Abraham 1789 i.
Jno. 1795 w.
York
Jonathan 1757 w.
Gerard 1764 w.
SANDER
Berkeley
Rudolph 1785 i.
SANDERLAND
Mecklenburg
Mary 1798 w.
SANDERLIN
Princess Anne
Richd. 1755 i.
SANDERS
Accomack
Mary 1728 w.
Jno. 1752 i.
Jas. 1755 i.
Richd. 1759 w.
Amy 1786 i.
Albemarle
Wm. 1765 w.
Brunswick
Edwd. 1784 w.
Essex
Thomas 1708-9 i.
Thomas 1714 i.
Fauquier
Robert 1791 i.
Isle of Wight
Robert 1731 w.
Henry 1733 i.
Solomon 1758 i.
John 1772 w.

Lancaster
Duke 1713 w.
Jno. 1741 i.
William 1780 w.
William 1790 i.
Loudoun
Philip 1769 w.
James 1778 w.
John 1797 w.
Lunenburg
Francis 1760 w.
Middlesex
Jno. 1761 a.
Mary 1762 a.
Jno. 1767 i.
Jno. 1779 i.
Northampton
Eustis 1667 w.
Jas. 1715 w.
Esther 1737 w.
Esther (2) 1737 w.
Northumberland
Wm. 1704-5 i.
Pittsylvania
Jas. 1772 i.
Princess Anne
Jonna 1701 i.
Prince William
Elenor 1739 w.
John 1796 w.
Mathew 1798 w.
Richmond
Jno. 1719 i.
Geo. 1754 w.
Geo. 1795 i.
Wm. Sr. 1796 w.
Sussex
Wm. 1764 w.
Sarah 1769 w.
Westmoreland
Philip 1723 w.
Wm. 1726 w.
Jno. 1751 i.
Hugh 1781 w.
York
Jno. 1700 w.
SANDERSON
Cumberland
Wm. 1782 i.
Northampton
Jno. 1716 w.
Jane 1720 w.
SANDFORD
Accomack
Saml. 1711 w.
Jno. 1785 i.
Ann 1794 w.
Eliz. 1796 w.
Lunenburg
Jno. 1762 w.

Princess Anne
Jno. 1693 i.
SANDIDGE
Albemarle
Wm. 1777 w.
Wm. 1787 w.
Spotsylvania
Wm. 1747 w.
SANDIFORD
Northumberland
Thos. 1722 w.
SANDIFUR
Cumberland
Abraham 1784 w.
Southampton
Wm. 1755 w.
SANDIVOR
York
Jno. 1691-2 w.
SANDRES
Accomack
Jno 1795 w.
SANDREWS
Accomack
Amey 1784 w.
SANDS
Loudoun
Edmund 1775 w.
Isaac 1789 i.
Surry
Saml. 1736 i.
SANDY
Richmond
Jno. 1770 w.
Westmoreland
Vincent 1759 i.
SANDYLAND
Mecklenburg
James 1784 w.
SANDYS
Westmoreland
Thos. 1733 i.
SANFORD
Brunswick
Wm. K. 1799 w.
Fairfax
Robert 1769 w.
Richd. 1799 w.
Fauquier
Richard 1798 w.
Halifax
Robt. 1782 w.
Daniel 1795 w.
Orange
Robt. 1787 w.
Richmond
Richd. 1794 i.
Barberry 1797 w.
Westmoreland
Thos. 1726 i.
Jno. 1735 i.

Robt. 1737 w.
Robt. 1738 w.
Jno. 1741 w.
Wm. 1748-9 w.
Jos. 1751 w.
Thos. 1752 w.
Richd. 1759 w.
Robt. 1760 w.
Winifred 1766 w.
Thos. 1770 w.
Robt. 1772 i.
Jno. 1778 w.
Wm. 1784 w.
Thos. 1784 i.
Margt. 1785 w.
Augustine 1785 w.
Willoughby 1786 w.
Edwd. 1786 w.
Youell 178-w.
Thos. 1790 i.
Wm. 1790 i.
Saml. 1797 w.
Wm. 1798 i.
SANGSTER
Fairfax
Thos. 1796 a.
Thos. 1798 i.
Loudoun
John 1778 i.
SANTCLAR
Loudoun
Margt. 1764 w.
SANTON
Prince George
Wm. 1717 w.
SAPPINGTON
Accomack
Hartly 1796 w.
SARE
Rockbridge
James 1789 w.
SARGEANT
Essex
Jas. 1702 w.
SARGENT
Rappahannock
Wm. 1683 w.
Richmond
Elizabeth 1745 i.
Jno. 1745 i.
SARGIANT
Orange
Jno. 1738 a.
SASSEEN
Chesterfield
Alex. 1777 w.
Elias 1777 w.
SATCHEL
Accomack
Henry 1747 w.
Eliz. 1749 w.

Wm. 1796 i.
Northampton
Southy 1759 w.
SATCHELL
Accomack
Henry 1779 w.
Northampton
Wm. 1679 w.
Jno. 1696 w.
Jno. 1750 w.
Sarah 1784 w.
Chas. 1786 i.
Chas. 1789 w.
Chas. Sr. 1791 i.
Wm. Sr. 1794 w.
Mary 1795 w.
Mary 1797 i.
Wm. 1737 w.
SATCHWELL
Princess Anne
Matthew 1782 w.
SATERWHITE
Prince Edward
Thos. 1757 i.
SATTER
Southampton
John 1782 i.
SATTERWHITE
Essex
John 1779 w.
SAUL
Southampton
Eliz. 1754 w.
Jno. 1765 i.
SAULS
Isle of Wight
Abraham 1730 w.
SAUNDERS
Accomack
Rachel 1774 w.
Brunswick
Edwd. 1785 i.
Cumberland
John Hyde 1768 w.
Essex
Alexander 1778 w.
Fairfax
Joseph 1793 w.
Henrico
Wm. 1795 i.
Isle of Wight
Solomon 1756 i.
Henry 1761 w.
Thomas 1784 w.
Thomas 1787 i.
Henry 1793 i.
Robert 1793 w.
Elizabeth Sr. 1794 w.
John 1797 i.
Lancaster
Phillip 1697 w.

Mecklenburg
Merry Arthur 1772 i.
Edwd. 1777 i.
Middlesex
Wm. 1741 i.
Richd. 1757 i.
Thos. 1770 w.
Geo. Sr. 1787 w.
Geo. 1789 w.
Thos. Sr. 1789 w.
Norfolk
John 1751 w.
Northampton
Jas. 1675 i.
Esther 1737 w.
Richd. 1758 w.
Jas. 1778 w.
Princess Anne
Jno. 1700 a.
Jno. 1734 w.
Jonathan 1765 i.
Eliz. 1772 i.
Richmond
Geo. 1794 w.
Westmoreland
Wm. 1727 i.
SAUNDERSON
Cumberland
Lucy 1794 w.
Wm. Sr. 1781 w.
Stafford
Jno. 1761 w.
SAVAGE
Accomack
Griffeth 1685 w.
Jno. 1708 w.
Thos. 1709 nw.
Rowland 1717 w.
Robt. 1720 w.
Rowland 1729 w.
Jno. 1730 w.
Mary 1732 i.
Abel 1738 i.
Griffith 1739 w.
Richd. 1739 w.
Jno. 1751 i.
Parker 1753 i.
Robt. 1762 w.
Parker 1763 i.
Patience 1769 w.
Griffeth 1770 w.
Jonathan 1774 w.
Robt. 1777 i.
Francis 1778 w.
Griffeth 1778 i.
Esther 1779 w.
Wm. 1781 w.
Chas. 1784 w.
Jacob 1784 w.
Patience 1785 i.
Rowland 1785 w.

Wm. 1785 w.
Wm. Hope 1787 i.
Jno. 1788 i.
Sarah 1788 w.
Geo. 1791 w.
Jno. 1792 w.
Wm. Hope 1792 w.
Littleton Sr. 1793 w.
Abel 1794 w.
Abel 1795 w.
Robt. 1795 w.
Nancy 1796 w.
Robt. 1796 w.
Wm. 1797 w.
Abel 1798 i.
Peter 1798 w.
Robt. 1798 i.
Geo. 1799 i.
Wm. H. 1799 i.

Essex
Jno. 1701 w.

Northampton
Jno. 1678 w.
Benj. 1717-18 w.
Elkenton 1719 w.
Jno. 1720 w.
Thos. Sr. 1721-2 w.
Geo. 1728 w.
Thos. 1728 w.
Nathl. 1729 w.
Thos. 1730 i.
Geo. 1730 i.
Thos. 1737 w.
Jno. 1747 w.
Thos. 1747 w.
Jno. 1749 i.
Esther 1764 w.
Mary 1770 w.
Nathl. 1771 w.
Geo. 1772 i.
Jonathan 1772 w.
Nathl. 1777 i.
Wm. 1779 w.
Wm. 1781 i.
Jno. Sr. 1784 w.
Richd. 1786 i.
Jno. 1789 i.
Abel 1797 w.
Jno. 1798 w.

Prince George
Wm. 1720 w.
Jno. 1722 i.

Southampton
Moses 1759 w.

Stafford
Nathl. 1739 i.
Jno. 1745 i.

Surry
Henry 1741 a.

SAVEAL
Northumberland
Richd. 1721 a.

SAVEDGE
Surry
Wm. 1777 w.

SAVELL
Norfolk
Richd. 1686 w.
Solomon 1769 w.
James 1790 w.
Daniel 1799 w.

SAVIDGE
Surry
Robt. 1698 w.
Henry 1711 i.
Charles 1718 w.
Lovelis 1729 w.
Benj. 1768 w.
Jno. 1795 i.
Nathaniel 1796 w.

SAVIGE
Accomack
Wm. 1727 w.

SAVILL
Norfolk
James 1799 w.
Solomon 1799 w.

SAWER
Lunenburg
Eliz. 1757 i.

SAWOUR
Botetourt
Elizabeth 1790 w.

SAWYER
Augusta
Robt. 1757 i.
Jas. 1783 w.

SAWYERS
Augusta
Jas. 1790 w.
Jas. Sr. 1791 i.
Lunenburg
Wm. 1761 i.

SAX
Halifax
Wm. 1783 i.
Lancaster
Thos. 1654 w.

SAXTON
Westmoreland
Nicholas 1670 w.
Wm. 1708 i.

SAYER
Frederick
James 1761 w.
Norfolk
Francis 1707 a.
Thos. 1707 a.
Richard 1720 w.

Princess Anne
Chas. 1740 w.
Arthur 1745 w.
Margt. 1754 w.
Margt. 1759 i.
Arthur 1761 w.
Arthur 1763 i.
Eliz. 1765 w.
Arthur 1766 i.

SAYERS
Augusta
Robt. 1746 w.
Robt. 1756 nw.
Montgomery
William 1781 w.

SAYLER
Accomack
Arthur 1764 w.

SAYLOR
Mecklenburg
Alex. 1799 i.

SAYMAN
Shenandoah
Catherine 1788 a.

SAYMOUR
Chesterfield
Wm. 1760 w.

SAYRES
Essex
Robt. 1756 w.

SCABOTH
Isle of Wight
William 1736 w.

SCAILS
King George
Thos. 1742 i.

SCALES
Henry
Joseph 1796 (?) w.

SCAMMEL
Isle of Wight
John 1774 i.

SCAMMELL
Surry
Richd. 1799 w.

SCANDLIN
Accomack
Jas. 1763 i.

SCANDRETT
Essex
Isaac 1769 i.

SCANELL
Northampton
Jno. 1695 w.

SCANLIN
Fairfax
Thomas 1747 i.

SCANNEL
Northampton
Anguish 1710 w.

SCANTHING
Princess Anne
Wm. 1790 w.
SCARBOROUGH
Brunswick
Hubbert 1795 w.
Southampton
John 1782 w.
Surry
Wm. 1717 i.
SCARBRO
Prince George
Thos. 1722 w.
Surry
Wm. 1679 i.
SCARBROUGH
Accomack
Jno. 1676 w.
Brunswick
Edwd. 1782 i.
Lewis 1797 w.
Southampton
Mary 1796 i.
SCARBROW
Surry
Edwd. 1716 i.
SCARBRUGH
Accomack
Mary 1691 w.
SCARBURG
Accomack
Wm. 1757 i.
SCARBURGH
Accomack
Chas. 1702 w.
Edmd. 1711 w.
Eliz. 1719 w.
Chas. 1725 i.
Bennet 1734 w.
Henry 1735 w.
Henry 1740 i.
Bennet 1741 i.
Jno. 1743 w.
Henry 1744 w.
Wm. 1756 w.
Winifred 1756 w.
Tabitha 1757 i.
Chas. 1757 i.
Wm. 1757 i.
Winifred 1757 i.
Hannah 1759 w.
Chas. 1762 w.
Mitchel [Michael?]
1763 w.
Chas. 1764 i.
Edmd. 1764 w.
Mitchell 1764 w.
Edmd. 1765 i.
Bennett 1767 w.
Eliz. 1768 w.
Henry 1770 w.

Henry 1772 i.
Littleton 1772 w.
Americus 1774 w.
Dorothy 1775 w.
Henry 1794 w.
Chas. 1796 w.
Bennet 1799 w.
Northampton
Jno. 1794 w.
York
Edmd. 1753 w.
SCARLING
Fairfax
Thomas 1748 a.
SCARSBROOK
Isle of Wight
William 1794 w.
York
Jno. 1679 w.
SCATERDAY
Loudoun
George 1768 w.
SCATES
Richmond
Jos. 1795 w.
SCHERER
Henrico
Geo. 1783 w.
SCHOFIELD
Amherst
Wm. 1790 w.
Lancaster
Robt. 1699 w.
Thomas 1778 i.
William 1785 i.
Northumberland
Henry 1791 w.
SCHOGINS
King George
Richd. 1767 a.
SCHOLFIELD
Lancaster
Robt. 1699 w.
Robt. 1747 i.
SCHOLLER
Hanover
Wm. 1734 a.
SCHOOLAR
King George
Thos. 1755 w.
Spotsylvania
Leanna 1782 a.
SCHOOLCRAFT
Harrison
Mathias 1784 i.
SCHOOLER
King George
Thos. 1755 i.
SCHOOLEY
Loudoun
Samuel 1782 w.

Samuel 1787 w.
SCHREVER
Northumberland
Bartho. 1720 w.
Bartho. 1728 w.
Eliz. 1738 w.
SCLALLAGHAM
Richmond
Bartho. 1726 i.
SCLATER
York
Jas. 1724 w.
Jas. 1727 w.
Mary 1744 w.
Wm. Sheldon 1757 w.
Sacheveral 1773 w.
Richd. 1777 w.
Wm. S. 1785 i.
Jno. 1797 w.
Jno. 1799 i.
SCOGGAN
King George
Sarah 1775 a.
SCOGGEN
Surry
Jno. Sr. 1727 i.
SCOGGIN
Brunswick
Wm. 1757 w.
Halifax
Jno. 1782 i.
Surry
Jno. 1725 i.
Sussex
Richd. Jr. 1779 i.
SCOGGING
Brunswick
Jno. 1741 i.
SCOGGINS
Fauquier
Charles 1782 i.
SCOGIN
Halifax
Jno. 1760 i.
Richd. 1770 w.
Mary 1780 w.
SCOLL
Hardy
Benj. 1790 w.
SCOOLY
Augusta
Isaac 1754 a.
SCOPUS
Princess Anne
Thos. 1767 w.
SCOT
Accomack
Thos. 1735 i.
Walter 1799 w.
Augusta
Jno. 1751 a.

Alex. 1753 i.
Jas. 1753 w.
Jno. 1754 i.
Halifax
Robt. 1797 w.
Lancaster
Wm. 1681 nw.
SCOTT
Accomack
Radolphus 1748 i.
Walter 1751 i.
Robt. 1754 i.
Geo. 1775 w.
Jas. 1778 w.
Jno. Jr. 1785 i.
Danl. Roe 1786 w.
Albemarle
John 1798 w.
Augusta
Saml. 1749 w.
Robt. 1774 w.
Thos. 1786 i.
Wm. 1794 w.
Amelia
Jos. 1748 w.
James 1761 w.
Jno. 1772 w.
Jno. 1774 i.
Bedford
William 1794 w.
Berkeley
George 1788 w.
Botetourt
James 1783 w.
Brunswick
James 1759 i.
Campbell
Jno. 1795 w.
Charles City
Wm. 1769 w.
Charlotte
Thos. 1799 w.
Chesterfield
Reaves 1771 w.
Walter Sr. 1782 w.
Walter 1784 i.
Wm. Sr. 1794 w.
Culpeper
Anthony 1764 w.
Ambrose 1777 w.
Cumberland
Saml. 1755 i.
Danl. 1755 i.
Mary 1758 w.
Seymour 1788 i.
Hannah 1798 i.
Essex
Jno. 1697 w.
Wm. 1716 w.
Fairfax
Thomas 1769 i.

Wm. 1787 w.
James 1794 a.
Fauquier
James Jr. 1779 w.
John 1786 w.
Sarah 1799 i.
Fluvanna
Joseph 1778 w.
Goochland
Jno. Jr. 1730 w.
Edwd. 1738 w.
Halifax
James 1758 i.
Thos. 1767 w.
Wm. 1779 w.
Robt. 1785 i.
Eliz. 1787 w.
Jno. 1793 w.
Henrico
Walter 1746 w.
Isle of Wight
Robert 1711 w.
Wm. 1718 w.
Robert 1728 i.
John 1729 w.
Robert 1743 w.
Thomas 1749 w.
Thomas 1754 i.
Joannah 1756 w.
William 1757 w.
James Took 1765 i.
Eliz. 1770 i.
Thos. 1783 w.
Wm. 1789 i.
Thos. 1798 i.
King George
Jas. 1722 i.
Loudoun
Jos. 1777 w.
Saml. Sr. 1782 w.
Jacob 1787 i.
Lunenburg
Robt. Jr. 1790 w.
Robt. 1794 w.
Madison
Thos. 1797 w.
Middlesex
Bartho. 1751 w.
Thos. 1768 i.
Delphus 1784 i.
Delphias 1794 i.
Norfolk
Robt. 1698 w.
Thos. 1734 i.
Thos. Sr. 1719 w.
Jno. 1751 w.
Alexander 1763 w.
Richard 1766 w.
Thos. 1773 i.
Jno. 1775 w.
Sarah 1775 w.

Saml. 1780 i.
Northampton
Thos. 1678 w.
Jno. 1709 w.
Wm. Sr. 1712 i.
Henry 1732 w.
Thos. 1736 i.
Wm. Sr. 1741 w.
Wm. 1742 i.
Thos. 1745 w.
Tatum 1748 i.
Jos. 1749 w.
Danl. 1750 i.
Wm. 1750 w.
Mary 1752 w.
Tatum 1752 i.
Mary 1759 i.
Benj. 1760 w.
Baily 1768 w.
Caleb 1771 i.
Bailey 1772 i.
Henry 1772 w.
Henry 1774 i.
Thos. 1774 w.
Thos. 1776 i.
Wm. 1784 w.
Zorobabel 1784 w.
Laban 1788 i.
Mary 1789 w.
Zerobabel 1789 i.
Thos. Jr. 1792 i.
Thos. Sr. 1792 i.
Danl. 1797 i.
Orange
Wm. 1789 w.
Mary 1793 i.
Powhatan
Wm. 1797 w.
Prince Edward
John 1786 w.
Mildred 1793 w.
Prince George
Jno. 1724 w.
Jno. Jr. 1724 i.
Bethia 1725 i.
Princess Anne
David Sr. 1716 w.
David 1727 w.
Thos. 1729 w.
David 1742 i.
Frances 1742 i.
Jno. 1764 w.
Richd. 1766 i.
Walter 1773 w.
Bridgett 1777 w.
Geo. 1779 w.
Geo. 1780 i.
Ann 1792 w.
James 1782 w.
Robert 1783 w.
Sarah 1784 w.

Richard 1792 i.
Wm. 1795 w.
Rappahannock
Saml. 1677 w.
Richmond
Jas. 1718 w.
Thos. 1750 w.
Rockbridge
Thos. 1797 w.
Southampton
Wm. 1752 w.
Eliz. 1755 w.
Jno. 1758 i.
Jas. Jordan 1775 w.
Spotsylvania
David 1749 a.
Isaac 1757 a.
Stafford
Alex. 1738 w.
Wm. 1742 w.
Wm. 1784 w.
Surry
Jno. 1705 nw.
Sussex
Jno. 1783 w.
Washington
Archibald 1785 i.
Robert 1796 i.
Westmoreland
Jno. 1701 w.
Thos. 1782 w.
SCRAMAGE
King George
Saml. 1784 a.
SCREWS
Isle of Wight
John 1727 w.
John 1731 w.
Mary 1742 i.
SCRIVENER
Frederick
John 1748 i.
York
Thos. 1772 w.
SCROSBY
Middlesex
James 1760 w.
James 1772 w.
SCRUGGS
Amherst
Susannah 1748 w.
Bedford
Gross 1788 w.
Cumberland
Jno. Sr. 1762 w.
Jesse 1774 w.
Robt. 1780 w.
Drury 1782 w.
Wm. 1785 w.
Henry 1793 w.
Jno. 1796 i.

Goochland
Wm. 1796 i.
Powhatan
Jno. 1783 w.
SCRUGS
Cumberland
Theaah 1784 w.
Thos. 1788 w.
Goochland
Edwd. 1787 w.
SCULLY
Isle of Wight
Cornelius 1675 i.
SCULTHORPE
Orange
Anthony 1744 a.
SCURLOCK
King George
Wm. 1762 a.
Lancaster
Michael 1699 i.
Richmond
Jno. 1718 w.
Thos. 1757 w.
Danl. 1764 w.
Alexander 1773 i.
SCURR
Princess Anne
Thos. 1791 w.
SCURRY
Cumberland
John 1762 w.
SCUTT
Westmoreland
Robt. 1718 i.
Jas. 1745 nw.
SEA
Augusta
Geo. 1751 a.
Fredk. 1764 a.
Greenbrier
John 1795 i.
SEABLETON
Frederick
Robert 1755 i.
SEABORN
Frederick
James 1792 w.
Sussex
Benj. 1782 w.
Wm. 1791 w.
SEABROOK
Henrico
Nicholas Brown
1793 i.
SEABROOKE
York
Chas. 1752 w.
SEABURN
Berkeley
George 1796 w.

SEADY
Northampton
Anthony 1718 w.
SEAGAR
Richmond
Henry 1718 w.
SEAGER
Middlesex
Randolph 1700 i.
SEAGOOD
King George
Geo. 1725 i.
SEAL
King George
Sarah 1762 i.
SEALE
Frederick
Thomas 1750 a.
King George
David 1755 i.
Sarah 1797 i.
Prince William
Anthony 1781 w.
SEALEY
Princess Anne
Ann 1716 w.
SEAMAN
Berkeley
Jeremiah 1783 i.
Jonah 1783 w.
Jonathan 1785 w.
Frederick
Jonathan 1743 i.
Richmond
Jos. 1729 w.
SEAMANS
Richmond
Moses 1742 w.
SEAMON
Fauquier
Thomas 1762 i.
SEAMORE
Washington
Joseph 1799 i.
SEAMON
Richmond
Jos. 1726 i.
SEARCY
Hanover
Robt. 1733 w.
SEARES
Essex
William 1752 w.
SEARGEANT
Essex
James 1703 i.
SEARIGHT
Augusta
Geo. 1785 i.
Rockbridge
Alexander 1791 i.

SEARLE
Northampton
  Gabriel 1649 i.
Surry
  Richd. 1684 i.
SEARLES
Essex
  Edward 1725 w.
  Mary 1769 w.
SEARS
Norfolk
  John 1750 i.
Rockbridge
  James 1790 i.
Westmoreland
  Edwd. 1767 w.
SEAT
Halifax
  Robt. 1797 i.
Lunenburg
  Josiah 1761 w.
Surry
  Robt. 1708 i.
  Joseph 1737 w.
Sussex
  Robt. 1792 w.
SEATON
Brunswick
  Liswell 1769 w.
Fauquier
  William 1782 w.
Stafford
  Jas. 1744 w.
  Jno. 1751 i.
SEAWELL
King George
  Benj. 1773 w.
SEAY
Albemarle
  Abraham 1772 w.
Amelia
  James 1775 i.
  Jacob, Sr. 1790 w.
  Jno. 1795 w.
Amherst
  Reuben 1785 a.
Fluvanna
  Jno. 1797 w.
Lunenburg
  Gedion 1777 i.
SEAYRES
Essex
  John 1750 w.
  William 1753 i.
  Robert 1756 w.
  John 1779 i.
SEBASTIAN
Fairfax
  Benjamin 1770 w.
  Benjamin 1772 i.
  Elizabeth 1773 w.

  Priscilla 1773 i.
  Benjamin 1774 i.
Stafford
  Isaac 1735 i.
  Joshua 1735 i.
  Isaac 1750 i.
  Wm. 1755 i.
  Jos. 1762 w.
SEBASTINE
Lancaster
  Joseph 1771 i.
Spotsylvania
  Chas. 1781 a.
Stafford
  Nicholas 1736 i.
SEBREE
Northumberland
  Mary 1753 w.
  James 1767 w.
  Wm. 1784 w.
  Jas. 1785 w.
  Moses 1785 w.
  Wm. 1788 w.
  Moses 1789 i.
  Mary 1790 w.
SEBRELL
Southampton
  Benj. 1767 i.
Surry
  David 1742 w.
  Mary 1748 w.
  Saml. 1748 w.
  Moses 1754 i.
  Joseph 1759 w.
York
  Nicholas 1710 ab.
  Anthony 1714 w.
  Nathl. 1721 w.
SECCAFOOSE
Augusta
  Jacob 1780 i.
SEDDON
Stafford
  Katherine 1744 i.
SEDGRAVE
Northumberland
  Robt. 1652 i.
SEGRAVES
Isle of Wight
  Francis 1727 w.
  Francis 1780 w.
SEDGWICK
Frederick
  Benjamin 1783 w.
  James 1790 w.
York
  Wm. 1704 w.
SEE
Augusta
  Jno. 1756 a.

Hardy
  Geo. 1797 i.
SEEBRE
Northumberland
  Richd. 1743 i.
SEED
Montgomery
  Francis 1777 a.
SEERS
Middlesex
  Joseph 1740 w.
Powhatan
  Jeremiah 1795 w.
SEEVER
Berkeley
  Peter 1781 w.
SEEVERS
Frederick
  John 1796 w.
SEGAR
Isle of Wight
  Oliver 1782 i.
Lancaster
  Oliver 1659 w.
Middlesex
  Randle 1694 w.
  Oliver 1699 i.
  Jno. 1740 w.
  Oliver 1741 a.
  Wm. 1741 i.
  Jno. 1758 a.
  Jno. 1771 i.
  Wm. 1780 w.
  Ann 1791 w.
SEHUT
Henrico
  Tertulian 1700 i.
SEIBERT
Shenandoah
  Francis 1789 i.
SEIVER
Berkeley
  Peter 1791 a.
SEIZER
Cumberland
  Geo. 1771 i.
SELBY
Accomack
  Wm. 1793 w.
Amelia
  Jno. 1750 a.
Essex
  Thos. 1729 w.
York
  Parker 1746 w.
SELDEN
Lancaster
  Eliz. 1766 w.
  Richd. 1771 w.
  Jno. 1789 i.
  Mildred 1793 w.

Powhatan
Saml. 1799 w.
SELDON
Lancaster
James 1784 i.
SELERS
Frederick
Matthias 1764 i.
SELEVEN
Fairfax
John 1753 w.
SELF
Cumberland
Wm. 1786 w.
Loudoun
Thomas 1781 w.
Northumberland
Thos. 1758 w.
Wm. 1771 w.
James 1776 w.
James 1779 i.
Jas. 1794 i.
Saml. 1799 i.
Richmond
Jeremiah 1788 i.
Westmoreland
Robt. 1717 w.
Jno. 1733 w.
Francis 1737 i.
Stephen 1751 i.
Wm. 1762 w.
Henry 1776 i.
Stephen 1789 i.
Jno. 1791 w.
Peter 1792 i.
Moses 1794 w.
Stephen 1797 i.
Wm. 1797 i.
SELLAWAY
Isle of Wight
John 1724 w.
John 1752 w.
Richard 1764 a.
SELNEY
Accomack
Tobias 1681 w.
SELZER
Frederick
Mathias 1763 w.
SEM
Shenandoah
Peter 1782 i.
SEMMS
Northumberland
James 1780 i.
SEMPLE
Prince William
John 1790 w.
SEMPSON
Prince William
Thomas 1734 a.

SENDERS
Berkeley
————— 1788 i.
SENECA
Princess Anne
Wm. 1782 w.
Wm. (2) 1782 w.
Mary 1784 w.
Jonathan 1794 w.
Sarah 1794 w.
SENIOR
Northampton
Jno. 1728 i.
SENKLIAR
Fauquier
John 1776 i.
SENNER
Northampton
Jno. 1709 w.
Jno. 1728 w.
SENTER
Montgomery
Alexander 1786 a.
SEPHTON
Lancaster
Jno. 1702 i.
SERETON
Frederick
John 1770 i.
SERGENT
Rappahannock
Wm. 1683 w.
SERISP
Norfolk
Thomas 1712 i.
SERTIN
Culpeper
John 1760 w.
SERVERS
Botetourt
Casper 1782 w.
SESSIONS
Henrico
Thos. 1708 i.
SESSOMS
Surry
Nicholas 1716 w.
SETTLE
Culpeper
Isaac 1783 i.
Fauquier
Martin 1769 i.
Wm. 1781 w.
Gayton 1788 w.
Eliz. 1790 i.
King George
Jno. 1738 i.
Benj. 1752 a.
Francis 1752 w.
Sarah 1755 w.
Francis 1757 i.

Margt. 1780 w.
Eliz. 1795 i.
Abraham 1799 i.
Louisa
Wm. 1789 w.
Joseph 1790 i.
Richmond
Henry 1702 w.
Francis 1707 w.
Thos. 1749 w.
Henry 1772 w.
Westmoreland
Wm. 1761 w.
SEVERN
Accomack
Peter 1668 w.
SEVERNE
Northampton
Jno. 1644 i.
Jno. 1665 i.
SEVERT
Shenandoah
Francis 1783 a.
SEVILL
Norfolk
Kedar 1771 i.
SEWARD
Brunswick
Benj. 1766 w.
Isle of Wight
John 1706-7 w.
William 1721 w.
Loudoun
Nicholas 1763 w.
Middlesex
Jno. 1779 w.
Surry
Jno. 1699 i.
Jno. 1702 i.
Wm. 1703 w.
Ann 1712 w.
James 1727 w.
Jno. 1749 i.
Wm. 1761 w.
Henry 1763 w.
Wm. 1771 w.
Wm. Cofield 1782 i.
SEWELL
Berkeley
John 1794 i.
Fairfax
Wm. 1771 i.
Henrico
Wm. 1725 w.
Norfolk
Henry 1796 i.
SEX
Washington
John 1778 i.

SEXTON
Norfolk
Isaac 1796 w.
SEYBOLD
Loudoun
Jesper 1788 w.
SEYLER
Augusta
Jacob 1789 w.
SEYMOUR
Accomack
Wm. 1776 w.
Leah 1796 w.
Northampton
Digby 1751 w.
Digby 1756 i.
Rose 1761 w.
Geo. 1762 i.
SHABER
Botetourt
Peter 1798 w.
SHACKELFORD
Halifax
Wm. 1778 w.
SHACKLE
Brunswick
Richd. 1769 i.
SHACKLEFORD
Culpeper
William 1779 i.
Richmond
Richd. 1794 w.
Richd., Jr. 1795 i.
Spotsylvania
Richd. 1774 w.
SHACKLETON
Chesterfield
Jonathan 1758 i.
Henrico
Jno. 1785 i.
SHADBURN
Prince William
John 1735 i.
John 1736 i.
SHADDOCK
Essex
James 1795 w.
Northumberland
Jno. 1746 i.
SHADDON
Augusta
Mathias 1766 i.
SHADOW
Augusta
Ladowak 1774 w.
SHADRACK
Fauquier
John 1759 w.
SHADRICK
Orange
Job 1790 w.

SHAE
Accomack
Neomy 1757 i.
Danl. 1761 i.
Wm. 1785 i.
SHAFFER
Shenandoah
William 1791 a.
SHALLEY
Surry
Philip Sr. 1704 w.
SHALTER
Stafford
Henry 1700 i.
SHAMBLIN
Botetourt
Aaron 1789 w.
SHANDS
Sussex
Thos. 1755 w.
Jno. 1758 i.
Wm. 1759 w.
Jno. 1760 i.
Nazareth 1764 w.
Wm. 1776 w.
SHANER
Augusta
Paul 1773 i.
SHANK
Shenandoah
John 1774 a.
SHANKLAND
Augusta
Thos. 1774 w.
SHANKLIN
Augusta
Jno. 1768 w.
Robt. 1768 w.
Greenbrier
Robert 1791 i.
SHANKS
Mecklenburg
Jno. 1792.
SHANNAN
Amelia
Wm. 1762 w.
Amherst
Thos. 1772 w.
SHAPLEIGH
Northumberland
Thos. 1703 i.
Hannah 1728 w.
Jno. 1741 w.
SHARBRO
Middlesex
Jno. 1675 w.
SHARINTON
Surry
Wm. 1739 w.

SHARKEY
Botetourt
Patrick 1786 w.
SHARLOCK
Accomack
Jno. 1792 w.
SHARP
Albemarle
Robt. 1787 w.
Botetourt
Edward 1770 w.
Fauquier
David 1782 i.
Frederick
Thomas 1762 w.
Henrico
Isaac 1788 i.
Richd. 1791 w.
Isle of Wight
Richard 1700 w.
Lancaster
Margaret 1709-10 w.
Jno. 1710 w.
Thos. 1726 w.
Thomas 1751 w.
Mecklenburg
Mark 1779 i.
Spotsylvania
Stephen 1735 w.
Jno. 1763 a.
Surry
Wm. 1742 i.
Jno. 1759 w.
Burwell 1799 w.
Washington
Edward 1777 i.
Westmoreland
Thos. 1677 w.
Thos. 1750 i.
SHARPE
Augusta
Jno. 1749 a.
Henrico
Nicholas 1700 i.
Richd. 1726 w.
Robt. 1783 w.
Wm. 1783 w.
King George
Elias 1745 i.
Lincefield 1759 w.
Norfolk
John 1682 i.
Northampton
Wm. 1679 w.
Northumberland
Robert 1655 w.
Southampton
Richd. 1785 i.
Stafford
Jno. 1730 i.

Surry
Francis 1739 w.
SHARPLIE
Accomack
Wm. 1747 i.
SHARPLY
Accomack
Wm. 1742 w.
SHARRO
Isle of Wight
Elizabeth 1737 w.
SHARROD
Accomack
Henry 1799 i.
SHARTLE
Campbell
Jacob 1786 i.
SHARWOOD
Princess Anne
James 1775 i.
John 1796 w.
SHATTEIN
Henrico
Francis 1703 a.
SHAVER
Berkeley
Michael 1785 i.
Frederick
Peter 1781 i.
Elizabeth 1787 w.
Harrison
John 1791 i.
SHAVNE
Culpeper
Shadrack 1776 i.
SHAW
Bedford
John 1786 w.
Culpeper
William 1791 w.
Fairfax
Jane 1768 w.
William 1775 w.
Thomas 1777 w.
William 1777 i.
John 1783 i.
William 1783 i.
Frederick
James 1765 i.
Isle of Wight
Mathew 1687-8 i.
Elizabeth 1753 w.
Lancaster
Jno. 1706 w.
Loudoun
John 1768 i.
Middlesex
Thos. 1745 w.
Thos. 1751 w.
Norfolk
Wm. 1679 i.

Northumberland
Jno. 1667 i.
Thos. 1671 i.
Richmond
Jas. 1716 i.
Westmoreland
Thos. 1717 w.
Thos. 1724 i.
Jas. 1735 i.
Wm. 1736 w.
SHAWL
Frederick
Adolph 1788 a.
SHAY
Accomack
Danl. 1783 w.
Jno. 1790 w.
Jno. 1794 i.
SHAUP
Augusta
Mathias 1750 w.
SHEA
Washington
Derby 1779 i.
SHEADRICK
Westmoreland
Thos. 1716 w.
SHEAN
Shenandoah
Moses 1782 i.
SHEAPARD
Henrico
Saml. 1781 i.
SHEARE
Middlesex
Jno. 1700 w.
SHEARER
Berkeley
John 1777 i.
Campbell
Jas. 1785 i.
SHEARMAN
Lancaster
Martin 1771 w.
Thomas 1792 i.
Martin 1793 w.
Richmond
Martin 1727 w.
Rockbridge
Patrick 1778 a.
Patrick 1799 i.
Sussex
Ebenezer 1777 i.
SHEARWOOD
Accomack
Wm. 1751 i.
Jacob 1789 w.
Franklin
Robert 1794 w.
Princess Anne
Jno. 1753 w.

SHEASTER
Frederick
George 1749 w.
SHEATHS
Middlesex
Joane 1702 i.
SHEDD
Loudoun
James 1778 i.
SHEEPHARD
Isle of Wight
John 1688 w.
SHEETZ
Berkeley
Philip 1794 w.
SHEFFER
Shenandoah
Michael 1793 w.
SHEHORN
Albemarle
Jno. Darby 1750 i.
Brunswick
Stephen 1761 i.
SHEILD
Accomack
Job 1743 w.
Sacker 1762 i.
Asa 1791 i.
Norfolk
Moss 1794 w.
York
Robt. 1753 w.
Robt. 1767 i.
Robt. 1773 w.
Rebecca 1775 w.
Robt. 1782 w.
Jno. 1783 w.
SHEILDS
Accomack
Jno. 1792 i.
Isle of Wight
Charles 1772 i.
Norfolk
Matthew 1777 w.
York
Robt. 1681-2 i.
Matthew 1766 w.
SHELBURN
York
Benj. 1776 i.
SHELBY
Washington
Evan 1798 w.
SHELDON
Augusta
Jno. 1764 i.
York
Jos. 1686-7 i.
Wm. 1727 w.

SHELFORD
Middlesex
Richd. 1709 i.
SHELL
Brunswick
Jno. 1794 w.
Charles City
Jno. Sr. 1774 w.
SHELLEY
Amelia
Jno. 1750 i.
Isle of Wight
Thomas 1751 w.
Jane 1759 i.
James 1767 w.
SHELLY
Isle of Wight
John 1720 w.
Jane 1758 w.
Thomas 1782 i.
Surry
Philip 1716 w.
Wm. 1756 i.
Washington
Abraham 1793 w.
Benjamin 1794 i.
York
Jno. 1689 i.
SHELTON
Albemarle
Wm. 1789 w.
Saml. 1793 w.
Henry 1799 w.
Brunswick
Silvanus 1783 w.
Culpeper
John 1773 i.
Goochland
Wm. Parks 1778 w.
Halifax
Chas. 1796 i.
Jesiah 1797 w.
Henry
Zebulon 1777 i.
James 1785 w.
Ralph 1789 w.
Isle of Wight
John 1704 w.
Lancaster
Benj. 1750-1 i.
Benj. 1754 w.
John 1772 i.
Louisa
Joseph 1784 w.
David 1797 w.
Lunenburg
James 1798 w.
Mecklenburg
Jno. Sr. 1778 w.

Middlesex
Ralph 1733 w.
Thos. 1743 i.
Mary 1744 i.
Norfolk
Malbone 1784 i.
Pittsylvania
Abraham 1789 w.
Crispin 1794 w.
Wm. 1794 i.
Abraham 1797 i.
SHEMELL
Norfolk
George 1775 i.
SHEPARD
Essex
John 1723 w.
Elizabeth 1724 i.
Jeremiah 1744 w.
John 1749 w.
Jacob 1760 w.
Goochland
Wm. B. 1779 w.
Henrico
Jos. 1783 i.
Middlesex
Henry 1775 w.
Jeremiah 1788 i.
Princess Anne
Smith 1750 w.
Spotsylvania
Geo. 1751 w.
SHEPEARD
Northampton
Thos. 1709 w.
SHEPHARD
Accomack
Wm. 1718 w.
Jno. 1740 i.
Essex
Jeremiah 1754 i.
Jeremiah 1786 i.
Northampton
Thos. 1648 w.
Jno. 1719 w.
SHEPHEARD
Accomack
Jno. 1709 w.
Northampton
Thos. 1697 w.
Jno. 1702 w.
Wm. 1702 w.
Wm. 1714 i.
SHEPHERD
Accomack
Jno. 1741 i.
Jacob 1743 w.
Jno. 1769 w.
Jno. 1780 i.
Albemarle
Christopher 1779 i.
Christopher 1789 w.

Amelia
Geo. 1743 w.
Amherst
David 1782 w.
Berkeley
Thomas 1776 w.
Thomas 1792 w.
Eliza. 1793 w.
Chesterfield
Wm. 1782 w.
Essex
Wm. 1720 w.
Jeremiah 1747 i.
Ephraim 1782 w.
Anner 1798 i.
Ephraim 1798 i.
Fluvanna
John 1797 w.
Frederick
John 1746 w.
Sarah 1770 w.
Loudoun
John 1792 w.
Middlesex
Henry 1765 w.
Henry D. 1795 i.
Norfolk
John 1741-2 w.
Samuel 1762 w.
Northampton
Jno. 1703 i.
Ohio
David 1795 w.
Prince William
Elizabeth 1738 w.
Northumberland
Wm. 1757 w.
Princess Anne
Saml. 1718 w.
Wm. 1764 w.
Isaac 1772 w.
Smith Sr. 1799 w.
Westmoreland
Geo. 1702 nw.
SHEPPARD
Henrico
Wm. 1783 w.
Jos. 1794 w.
Jos. 1795 i.
Benj. 1796 w.
Northampton
Jos. 1732 w.
Sarah 1732 w.
Orange
Micha 1740 a.
Spotsylvania
Edwd. 1739 a.
Westmoreland
Geo. 1703 i.
SHEPPERD
Goochland
Robt. 1797 i.

Henrico
Saml. 1706 i.
Northumberland
Geo. 1795 w.
SHEPPERSON
Louisa
John 1793 w.
SHERDON
Richmond
Jno. 1709 w.
SHERER
Frederick
John 1764 w.
SHERHORN
Brunswick
Stephen 1761 i.
SHERIDON
Fairfax
John 1768 w.
SHERIFF
Frederick
John 1797 w.
SHERLEY
Culpeper
James 1791 i.
King George
Wm. 1749 i.
Northumberland
Richd. 1728 i.
Prince George
Jno. 1719 i.
Spotsylvania
Jno. 1764 a.
SHERLOCK
Rappahannock
Jno. 1676 w.
Richmond
Jas. 1709 i.
SHERMAN
Henrico
Henry 1687 w.
Jno. 1687 w.
Henry 1695 w.
Cesly 1703-4 w.
Lancaster
Thos. 1779 w.
Rappahannock
Quintellian 1675 w.
Richmond
Quintilian 1715 i.
York
Wm. 1708 i.
SHERRER
Isle of Wight
John 1706-7 w.
Sarah 1733 i.
SHERROD
Surry
Arthur 1747 i.

SHERWIN
Amelia
Saml. 1744 w.
SHERWOOD
Accomack
Francis 1666 i.
Wm. 1728 i.
Lewis 1764 i.
Essex
Jacob 1717 i.
John 1799 w.
Princess Anne
James 1701 i.
Grace 1740 w.
Michael 1750 i.
Westmoreland
[Francis?] 1657 i.
SHERY
Norfolk
James 1796 i.
SHETFORD
Berkeley
Simon 1783 w.
SHEVELY
Frederick
Daniel 1765 i.
SHEVERS
Frederick
John 1764 i.
SHEWCRAFT
Norfolk
Simon 1783 w.
Princess Anne
Wm. 1768 w.
Wm. 1793 w.
SHEWGAR
Isle of Wight
Margarett 1687 i.
SHEWMAKE
Isle of Wight
Arnell 1697 w.
SHIBLEY
Frederick
Daniel 1768 w.
SHIELD
Accomack
Delight 1743 w.
Wm. 1743 i.
Wm. Sacker 1752 i.
Ruben 1767 w.
Richd. 1785 w.
Wm. Sacker 1789 w.
Nicho. 1790 w.
Augusta
Thos. 1781 i.
Jno. 1773 w.
York
Dunn 1732 w.
Jno. 1770 w.
Robt. 1783 i.

SHIELDS
Amherst
Jane 1794 w.
Augusta
Jas. 1750 i.
Isle of Wight
Charles 1771 w.
Pittsylvania
Patrick 1770 w.
Jas. 1779 w.
Powhatan
Wm. 1796 i.
York
Jas. 1727 w.
Robt. 1728 i.
Hannah 1739 i.
Jas. 1750 w.
SHIFFLEY
Henrico
Saml. 1749 w.
SHIFLETT
Albemarle
Jno. 1794 w.
Orange
Stephen 1777 i.
SHILLIDEARY
Wythe
George 1792 w.
SHINKENS
Henrico
Geo. 1702 i.
SHINGLETON
Norfolk
John 1682 i.
SHIMM
Stafford
Geo. 1784 i.
SHIP
Culpeper
Richard 1781 w.
Essex
Josiah 1705-6 w.
Richard 1724 w.
Richard 1727 i.
William 1755 i.
SHIPHAM
Accomack
Wm. 1794 w.
SHIPLEY
Essex
Ealse 1715 w.
John 1720 i.
SHIPP
Accomack
Matthew 1688 w.
Essex
Josiah 1706 i.
Fauquier
John 1778 w.
Middlesex
Joseph 1675 a.

Norfolk
Francis 1657 i.
Mary 1657 i.
Princess Anne
Francis 1695 i.
Frances 1696 a.
Francis 1719 w.
Wm. 1735 w.
Jno. 1741 w.
Wm. 1762 w.
Wm. 1764 i.
Wm. 1786 i.
Jonathan 1789 w.
Josiah 1794 w.
Simon 1799 w.
SHIPPEE
York
Richd. 1673 w.
SHIPPEY
Essex
Mary 1721 w.
Wm. 1731 w.
Richmond
Richd. 1708 i.
SHIPPY
Essex
James 1717 i.
James 1731 w.
Henrico
Thos. 1684 i.
Thos. 1688 w.
King George
Ellen 1741 i.
SHIPWASH
Norfolk
Ambrus 1725-6 w.
John 1769 w.
Andrew 1785 i.
Ambrose 1791 w.
Willis 1795 w.
Thomas 1798 i.
Keziah 1799 w.
SHIPWELL
Norfolk
Wm. 1654 i.
SHIPWORTH
York
Alex. 1666 w.
SHIRLEY
Frederick
Walter 1755 w.
King George
Wm. 1747 eb.
Princess Anne
Jno. Sr. 1718 w.
SHIRLY
Northumberland
Jno. 1742 w.
SHEVERAL
Northumberland
Allen Long 1789 w.

SHIVERS
Isle of Wight
Jonas 1777 i.
Surry
Wm. 1681 i.
SHNIDO
Botetourt
John 1772 i.
SHOALS
Greenbrier
Martin Henry 1793 w.
SHOARES
Westmoreland
Wm. 1695 w.
SHOATS
Westmoreland
Geo. 1790 w.
SHOBE
Hardy
Martin 1792 w.
SHOCKEY
Surry
Alice 1738 w.
SHOCKLEY
Pittsylvania
Jas. 1796 w.
SHOE
Shenandoah
Jacob 1785 a.
SHOECORAFT
Princess Anne
Cary 1786 i.
SHOMAN
Shenandoah
Stephen 1774 w.
SHOOK
Hardy
Harmon 1789 w.
Jno. 1790 w.
SHOOMAN
Franklin
Jacob 1792 w.
SHORE
Fairfax
Richard 1751 w.
Richard 1759 i.
Norfolk
Robert 1762 w.
John 1777 w.
George 1798 w.
Westmoreland
Arthur 1664 w.
SHORES
Fairfax
Richard 1752 i.
SHOREY
Henrico
Wm. 1732 i.
SHOMAKER
Frederick
George 1783 i.

SHORT
Brunswick
Wm. Sr. 1769 w.
Wm. Sr. 1787 w.
Chesterfield
Saml. 1780 w.
Essex
Thomas 1740 w.
Elizabeth 1775 w.
Frederick
Adam 1762 i.
Halifax
Cornelius 1762 i.
Cornelius 1764 i.
Henry
Henry 1789 i.
King George
Anne 1788 w.
Jno. 1798 i.
Thos. 1798 w.
Loudoun
John 1791 w.
Mecklenburg
Jno. 1799 i.
Northumberland
Wm. 1743 i.
Thos. 1747 i.
Robt. 1748 w.
Thos. 1750-1 i.
Richmond
Patrick 1726 w.
Surry
Wm. 1675 w.
Wm. 1741 w.
Susannah 1743 w.
Wm. 1757 w.
Wm. 1782 i.
Stafford
Jno. 1764 w.
Westmoreland
Wm. 1711 i.
Thos. 1749 i.
Jno. 1789 i.
SHORTER
Middlesex
Jno. 1728 w.
SHORTHOSE
Essex
Henry 1736 w.
SHORTRIDGE
Fairfax
William 1783 i.
SHORTT
Chesterfield
Wm. Jr. 1763 w.
Wm. 1765 w.
Young 1795 w.
Essex
Catherine 1771 i.
Northumberland
Benedick 1784 w.

SHORTWATER
York
Benj. 1704 w.
SHORTZRAETZ
Princess Anne
John 1791 w.
SHOTWELL
Culpeper
John 1757 i.
Robert 1785 w.
Mecklenburg
Jno. 1798 w.
SHOUGH
Greenbrier
Anthony 1785 i.
SHOUND
Augusta
Leonard 1783 w.
SHOWLE
Frederick
Adam 1787 i.
SHREAVES
Accomack
Wm. 1789 w.
SHREEFES
Norfolk
Wm. 1687 w.
SHREVE
Fairfax
Daniel 1750 w.
William 1750 i.
Loudoun
Wm. 1763 w.
Benj. 1791 w.
SHREWSBURY
Bedford
Samuel 1786 i.
SHRIEVES
Accomack
Wm. 1797 w.
SHROCKES
Frederick
Nicholas 1774 i.
SHROPSHIRE
King George
Wm. 1791 w.
Westmoreland
St. Jno. 1718 i.
SHROUSBY
Surry
Francis 1678 w.
James 1679 i.
SHROWSBERY
Surry
Thos. 1695 w.
SHRYOCKS
Berkeley
Leonard 1782 i.
SHUMATE
Fauquier
John 1784 w.

Daniel 1785 i.
SHUNAMAN
Frederick
George 1755 i.
SHURLEY
Frederick
Walter 1756 i.
Middlesex
Richd. 1709 i.
Thos. 1727 w.
Northumberland
Jno. 1738 w.
Daniel 1768 i.
SHURLY
Princess Anne
Jno. 1701 a.
SHURMAN
Frederick
John 1756 i.
SHUTE
Prince William
Fanny 1784 w.
John 1792 i.
SIAS
Fauquier
John 1779 w.
SIBBALDS
Northumberland
Robert 1770 w.
SIBLEY
Fairfax
John 1750 w.
SIBSEY
Norfolk
John 1652 w.
SICKES
Norfolk
James 1742 w..
SICKLEMORE
Princess Anne
Saml. 1716 w.
SICKS
Norfolk
Jeremiah 1790 i.
SIDEY
Essex
John 1714 i.
SIDNEY
Norfolk
Jno. 1663 nw.
SIDNOR
Lancaster
Fortunatus 1683 i.
SIDWAY
Surry
Thos. 1695 w.
SIEVELY
Shenandoah
John 1782 w.
Joseph 1783 i.

SIGES(?)
Richmond
Jno. 1703 w.
SIGNER
Northumberland
Edwd. 1712-13 w.
SIKES
Halifax
Jonas 1784 w.
Isle of Wight
Thomas 1708 w.
John 1719-20 w.
Thomas 1730-31 w.
Andrew 1782 i.
Adam 1783 w.
Norfolk
Walter 1710 w.
Costin(?) 1719 i.
John 1719 w.
James 1742-3 i.
John 1758 w.
Joseph 1759 w.
William 1772 w.
Jesse 1773 w.
Jeremiah 1789 w.
Daniel 1793 i.
Josiah 1794 w.
Thomas 1795 w.
Hannah 1796 i.
Princess Anne
Solomon 1785 w.
SILBORN
Berkeley
Francis 1774 w.
SILES
Hardy
Geo. 1790 w.
SILEY
Essex
Thos. 1729 w.
SILIVANT
Accomack
Dormand 1692 w.
SILL
Accomack
Gowen 1768 w.
Jno. 1774 w.
SILLEY
Essex
Thomas 1729 i.
Elizabeth 1733 i.
SILLIVAN
Accomack
Danl. 1798 w.
SILLOWAY
Isle of Wight
Richard 1762 w.
SILLS
Greensville
David 1783 w.

SILVER
Essex
William 1709-10 w.
Augusta
Jacob 1761 i.
SILVERTHORN
Accomack
Sebastian 1754 w.
Leavin 1776 w.
Jno. 1786 w.
Jno. 1789 i.
Arthur 1796 i.
SILVERTHORNE
Accomack
Sebastian 1712 w.
SILVESTER
Norfolk
Richd. Wm. 1762 w.
Richard 1782 w.
Dorcas 1794 w.
David 1797 w.
Westmoreland
Philip 1669 w.
SIMCO
Essex
Edward 1778 i.
SIMCOE
Essex
Thomas 1760 i.
SINICOCK
Accomack
Jno. 1708 w.
SIMES
Accomack
Robt. 1667 w.
Northampton
Thos. 1695 w.
Prince William
Richard 1741 w.
SIMKINS
Accomack
Wm. 1704 i.
Northampton
Wm. Sr. 1793 w.
Isaac D. 1797 w.
Wm. 1797 w.
SIMMEON
Botetourt
Jacob 1789 i.
SIMMONDS
Fairfax
James 1749 a.
Lancaster
John 1767 i.
James 1788 i.
Richmond
Jno. 1715 w.
SIMMONS
Bedford
George 1798 i.

Brunswick
Henry 1766 w.
Peter 1768 w.
Thos. 1774 w.
Henry 1781 w.
Susanna 1793 w.
Campbell
Chas. 1794 w.
Fairfax
Thomas 1744 w.
Isle of Wight
James 1748(?) i.
James 1754 i.
Samuel 1788 w.
Lancaster
John 1750 i.
Elizabeth 1774 w.
Lunenburg
Chas. 1752 i.
Mecklenburg
Saml. 1794 w.
Eliz. 1797 i.
James 1798 i.
Norfolk
Mary 1724 i.
Jas. 1742 w.
James 1743-4 i.
John 1760 w.
Jean 1763 w.
John 1778 w.
Elizabeth 1781 i.
Northumberland
Jas. 1721 i.
Prince Edward
Wm. 1780 w.
Prince George
Jno. 1721 i.
Princess Anne
Henry 1728 w.
Thos. 1729 w.
Wm. 1740 w.
Geo. 1742 w.
Joel 1761 w.
Lemuel 1770 i.
Southward 1770 w.
Richd. 1771 w.
Jno. 1773 i.
James 1775 i.
Amy 1779 i.
Uriah 1779 w.
James 1784 w.
Mary 1784 w.
Amy 1785 w.
Southampton
Jno. (1) 1749 w.
Jno. (2) 1749 w.
Stephen 1757 i.
Jno. 1759 i.
Wm. 1764 i.
Chas. 1769 i.
Chas. 1771 w.

Benj. 1772 w.
Wm. 1778 w.
Jos. 1782 w.
Sarah 1782 i.
Jno. 1792 i.
Henry 1799 i.
Surry
Wm. 1693 w.
Eliz. 1696-7 w.
Thos. 1733 w.
Wm. 1733 w.
Jno. 1738 w.
Wm. 1778 w.
Sarah 1779 w.
Wm. 1793 i.
Sussex
Martha 1785 w.
Westmoreland
Lawrence 1698 w.
Wm. 1704 i.
York
Jane 1729 i.
SIMMS
Botetourt
Ignatius 1786 w.
Brunswick
Geo. 1763 w.
Wellington 1767 i.
Geo. 1768 i.
Jno. 1778 w.
Prince William
John 1779 i.
Jane 1782 w.
Rappahannock
Richd. 1677 w.
Spotsylvania
Wm. 1760 a.
Westmoreland
Alex. 1745 w.
SIMON
Southampton
Augustine 1760 w.
York
Richd. 1647 w.
SIMONDS
Norfolk
James 1717 a.
SIMONS
Fairfax
Ann 1768 w.
Halifax
Hanary 1767 i.
Norfolk
James 1717 i.
Thomas 1717 i.
Lemuel 1734 i.
Princess Anne
Mary 1719 i.
Wm. 1719 i.
Surry
Mary 1678 w.

SIMPKINS
Accomack
Wm. 1766 w.
Sabrah 1779 w.
Loudoun
John 1772 i.
Lunenburg
Jno. 1754 w.
SIMPSON
Accomack
Thos. 1728 i.
Jno. 1742 w.
Wm. 1751 w.
Saml. 1760 w.
Thos. 1760 w.
Mary 1761 i.
Laban 1767 w.
Southy 1779 w.
Comfort 1785 i.
Wm. 1790 w.
Selby 1799 w.
Amherst
Wm. 1787 a.
Augusta
Jas. 1762 i.
Jas. 1756 a.
Jas. 1764 a.
Campbell
Robt. 1782 w.
Chesterfield
Andrew 1766 w.
Culpeper
John 1776 w.
Jane 1785 i.
Fairfax
Richard 1762 w.
Sarah 1766 w.
Gilbert 1773 w.
Moses 1780 i.
George 1782 w.
Moses Sr. 1787 w.
Sybil 1792 a.
Moses 1792 i.
French 1795 a.
Joseph 1796 w.
Frederick
Thomas 1796 w.
King George
Saml. 1732 i.
Jno. 1744 eb.
Wm. 1749 i.
Saml. 1778 nw.
Lancaster
Jno. 1684 w.
Ann 1690 w.
Ann 1695 i.
Montgomery
John 1786 i.
Norfolk
Wm. 1674 i.
Jonathan 1768 w.

Prince William
Thomas 1741 i.
Richmond
Jos. 1762 i.
Jos. 1764 i.
Southampton
Saml. 1782 i.
Spotsylvania
Abraham 1771 a.
Francis 1795 a.
Stafford
Geo. 1750 w.
Jno. 1756 w.
Surry
James 1777 w.
Ann 1796 w.
SIMS
Albemarle
William 1797 i.
John 1798 w.
Brunswick
Adam 1771 w.
David 1773 w.
Wm. 1780 w.
Jno. 1797 i.
Charlotte
Sally 1799 w.
Culpeper
Jeremiah 1768 w.
William 1769 w.
William 1777 w.
Edward 1784 i.
Thomas, Sr. 1785 w.
Greensville
Robert Wall 1798 w.
Halifax
Keziah 1778 w.
Wm. 1778 w.
David 1784 w.
Mathew 1791 i.
Wm. 1797 i.
Louisa
Micajah 1793 i.
Northumberland
Thos. 1741 i.
Thos. 1763 i.
Orange
Richd. 1747 i.
Pittsylvania
Jas. 1773 w.
Prince William
James 1778 i.
Richmond
Wm. 1716 w.
Westmoreland
Edwd. 1763 i.
Henry 1774 i.
York
Jas. 1774 w.

SIMSON
Accomack
Thos. 1725 w.
Lancaster
Percival 1703-4 w.
Prince William
Thomas 1734 w.
Surry
Jno. 1717 i.
SINACA
Princess Anne
Nathl. 1761 w.
SINCKLER
Loudoun
Wayman 1762 w.
SINCLAIR
Loudoun
John 1798 i.
Middlesex
Wm. 1753 a.
Surry
Arthur 1792 w.
SINCLEARE
Fauquier
John 1771 w.
SINCOCK
Frederick
John 1744 a.
SINERALL
Frederick
James 1798 w.
SINGER
Northumberland
Jno. 1747 w.
SINGLETON
Amelia
Robt. 1760 i.
Bedford
Phillip 1775 i.
Brunswick
Chas. 1762 i.
Norfolk
Anthony 1771 w.
Ann 1790 w.
Orange
Daniel 1794 w.
Princess Anne
Peter 1790 w.
Richmond
Joshua 1732 w.
Ann 1734 w.
Joshua 1773 w.
Joshua 1779 i.
Robt. 1781 w.
Robt. 1789 i.
York
Anne 1765 w.
Richd. Hunt 1774 i.
SINKLER
Fairfax
Amos 1744 w.

Northumberland
Edmd. 1662 w.
Richmond
Jno. 1716 i.
SINKLIAR
Fauquier
William 1798 w.
SINTON
Accomack
Wm. 1754 i.
Prince William
Setine 1741 ab.
SIRCLE
Shenandoah
John 1790 a.
Michael 1794 a.
SIRLES
Essex
James 1798 nw.
SISER
Cumberland
David 1771 w.
SISES
King George
Ralph 1729 i.
SISSON
Brunswick
Stephen 1772 i.
Orange
Bryan 1771 w.
William 1795 i.
Richmond
Wm. 1719 i.
Geo. 1744 i.
Henry 1775 w.
Surry
Thos. 1731 w.
Westmoreland
Frances Butler
1697-8 w.
SITES
Brunswick
David 1744 i.
SITLINGTON
Augusta
Wm. 1773 i.
SITTINGTON
Bath
John 1798 w.
SITTLE
Shenandoah
William 1786 a.
SITTLER
Frederick
Benjamin 1783 i.
SIVER
Augusta
Jacob 1758 i.
SIVIL
Norfolk
Abraham 1795 w.

SIX
Shenandoah
John 1772 a.
SKAINE
Augusta
Mathew 1748 a.
SKARRATT
Amelia
Jno. 1773 w.
SKEARMAN
Shenandoah
Adam, Sr. 1797 w.
SKEATS
Spotsylvania
Jno. 1778 a.
SKEEN
Augusta
Mathew 1749 i.
Rockbridge
Robert 1795 w.
SKELDERMAN
Rappahannock
Hannan 1684 w.
SKELDING
Berkeley
John 1789 i.
SKELTON
Charles City
Bathurst 1771 w.
Isle of Wight
John 1704 i.
John 1706-7 i.
Thomas 1730-31 w.
Mecklenburg
Wm. 1769 w.
SKERME
Henrico
Edwd. 1700 w.
Mary 1710 w.
SKEVINGTON
Norfolk
Thos. 1690-1 w.
Princess Anne
Thos. 1691 w.
SKEY
Essex
John 1716 i.
SKIDMORE
Augusta
Jos. Sr. 1778 w.
Bedford
Jeremiah 1774 i.
SKILEREN
Augusta
Wm. 1746 w.
SKILLERN
Orange
Wm. 1745 w.
SKILMAN
Loudoun
John 1777 w.

SKIN
Harrison
Benjamin 1791 w.
SKINER
Westmoreland
Peter 1735 i.
SKINKER
King George
Saml. 1752 w.
Saml. 1770 w.
Peggy 1778 w.
Jno. 1798 w.
SKINNER
Berkeley
William 1793 w.
Henrico
Alex. 1789 w.
Isle of Wight
Richard 1677 w.
Loudoun
Phenelias 1795 i.
Stafford
Jno. 1750 i.
SKIPER
Norfolk
Francis 1679 i.
SKIPP
Amelia
Jno. 1775 i.
Princess Anne
Jno. 1779 w.
SKIPWITH
York
Henry 1736 w.
SKOOT
Surry
Adam 1734 i.
SKRINE
King George
Wm. 1729 i.
SKY
Essex
John 1717 i.
SLADE
Northampton
Jeremiah 1766 i.
Prince William
William 1784 w.
Southampton
Wm. 1790 w.
Surry
Thos. 1757 i.
Mary 1774 i.
Sarah 1781 w.
SLADYEN
Goochland
Arthur 1787 w.
SLATE
Brunswick
Wm. 1777 i.
Edwd. 1750 w.

Jno. 1761 i.
SLATER
Hardy
Saml. 1798 i.
Greenbrier
Joseph 1795 i.
Richmond
John 1746 i.
York
Richd. 1718 w.
SLATTER
Norfolk
Wm. 1760 i.
SLAUGHTER
Albemarle
John 1797 i.
Culpeper
Francis 1766 w.
Robert 1769 w.
Mary 1771 i.
George Clayton
1790 w.
John 1796 w.
Essex
Pheby 1710 w.
Robt. 1726 w.
Fairfax
Ann 1798 w.
Princess Anne
Hillary 1784 i.
Rappahannock
Francis[1656 or 7?]w.
Richmond
Francis 1718 w.
Shenandoah
Francis 1776 w.
SLEDD
York
Josuah 1717 w.
Dodman 1726 i.
SLEDGE
Surry
Chas. 1725 w.
Mary 1728 w.
Jno. 1750 w.
Amos 1780 w.
Amos 1791 i.
Sussex
Chas. 1771 i.
Jno. 1793 i.
SLEET
Orange
Weedon 1773 w.
SLEETH
Harrison
John 1794 i.
SLEMING
Prince William
William 1740 i.

SLINKER
Bedford
Christopher 1795 w.
SLOCUM
Berkeley
Isaac 1794 i.
SLIVEA
Shenandoah
Philip 1784 a.
SLOAN
Bath
James 1792 w.
Loudoun
John 1774 i.
SLOANE
Pittsylvania
Jno. 1769 w.
SLOCOMB
Accomack
Thos. 1784 w.
Loudoun
Robt. 1782 i.
SLOCUM
Accomack
Robt. 1727 i.
SLOCUMB
Accomack
Robt. 1741 w.
SLOWN
Culpeper
James 1760 w.
SLY
Fairfax
Richard 1745 a.
SMALECOMBE
York
Lieut 1675 i.
SMALL
Amherst
James 1771 a.
Frederick
James 1760 i.
John 1760 w.
Lancaster
Jno. 1719 i.
Middlesex
Joseph 1749 a.
Northampton
Andrew 1688 w.
Patrick
John 1791 w.
SMALLEY
Accomack
Jno. 1688 w.
Loudoun
Isaac 1781 w.
Ezekiel 1799 i.
SMALWOOD
Loudoun
Luke 1794 i.

SMALLWOOD
Norfolk
Charles 1772 i.
Charles 1783 w.
Charles 1796 i.
Spotsylvania
James 1793 w.
SMARR
Loudoun
John 1795 w.
SMART
Essex
Johannah 1728 w.
SMAW
Norfolk
Andrew 1774 w.
Northampton
Andrew 1735 w.
Henry 1777 w.
SMELLY
Isle of Wight
William 1692 w.
Lewis 1724-5 w.
SMELLEY
Isle of Wight
Robert 1734 w.
Thomas 1762 w.
John 1765 w.
Sarah 1775 w.
John 1781 w.
Robert 1785 i.
Southampton
Giles 1755 w.
SMELSER
Bedford
Paulser 1778 w.
SMELT
Essex
Jno. 1765 w.
Lunenburg
Mary 1784 w.
SMETHER
Essex
William 1763 i.
William 1766 i.
Philip 1769 i.
William 1782 w.
William 1785 i.
SMILEY
Augusta
Alex. 1749 i.
Northampton
Alex. 1784 i.
Rockbridge
Alexander 1797 i.
Shenandoah
Ann 1797 i.
SMILY
Rockbridge
Mary 1784 i.

SMITH
Accomack
Wm. 1674 w.
Edwd. 1675 w.
Jno. 1677 w.
Joshua 1683 w.
Eliz. 1688 nw.
Geo. 1703 i.
Jas. 1709 w.
Thos. 1710 i.
Simon 1721 w.
Valentine 1731 i.
Wm. 1734 i.
Jno. 1741 w.
Danl. 1746 i.
Jno. 1746 i.
Simon 1747 i.
Robt. 1756 w.
Eliz. 1760 w.
Wm. Robinson
  1760 w.
Isaac 1760 w.
Geo. 1761 nw.
Richd. 1764 w.
Henry 1765 w.
Jno. 1765 w.
Huet 1766 w.
Richd. 1767 i.
Susanna 1768 w.
Fairfax 1771 w.
Isbell 1773 w.
Jno. 1774 w.
Margaret 1774 i.
Wm. 1774 w.
Jno. 1775 i.
Jno. 1779 w.
Jno. 1782 i.
Wm. 1784 w.
Thos. 1785 i.
Darby 1789 i.
Wm. 1789 i.
Geo. 1791 w.
Eliz. 1795 w.
Bayly 1797 w.
Albemarle
Larkin 1763 w.
Chas. 1765 i.
Stephen J. K. 1775 i.
Thos. 1783 w.
Thos. 1788 w.
Thos. 1791 w.
Amelia
Wm. Thornton
  1749 a.
Thos. 1763 i.
Agnes 1774 w.
Wm. 1785 i.
Amherst
Wm. 1797 w.
Jos. 1798 w.
Augusta
Jno. 1756 w.

Wm. 1756 w.
Jno. 1757 a.
Jno. 1760 a.
Andrew 1762 w.
Jno. 1770 w.
Zachariah 1788 w.
Bedford
Bowker 1768 w.
Guy 1781 w.
Samuel 1784 i.
Berkeley
William 1786 i.
Thomas 1791 w.
John 1798 w.
Botetourt
James 1780 i.
David 1782 i.
John 1783 w.
William 1786 i.
Brunswick
Roger 1735 w.
Patrick 1739 i.
Richd. 1750 w.
Richd. 1752 i.
Ambrose 1761 w.
Wm. 1762 w.
Christopher 1767 w.
Peter 1768 w.
Roger 1768 i.
Edwd. 1772 w.
Cuthbert 1780 w.
Jesse 1782 i.
Joseph 1783 w.
Burwell 1784 i.
Edwd. 1786 w.
Henry 1791 w.
Aaron 1793 w.
James 1793 w.
Richd. 1799 w.
Charles City
Isaac 1769 w.
Charlotte
Wm. 1777 i.
Reuben 1777 i.
Conrodmercer 1778 w.
Robt. 1778 w.
Saml. C. 1794 i.
Peter 1791 i.
Chesterfield
Jno. 17— i.
Robt. 1757 w.
Alex. 1761 w.
Jno. 1770 w.
Martin 1776 w.
Obediah 1777 w.
Jno. 1795 i.
Saml. 1797 i.
Culpeper
John 1751 i.
John 1752 i.
John Michael 1761 w.
John 1776 w.

Thomas 1779 i.
Edwin 1784 i.
Joel 1790 i.
Cumberland
Jno. 1757 w.
Jas. 1759 w.
Humphrey 1766 w.
Ann 1768 w.
Jno. 1771 i.
Catherine 1790 w.
Jno. 1792 w.
Essex
Anthony 1693 i.
John 1694 w.
Richd. 1696 w.
Jno. 1703 w.
Charles 1710 i.
Henry 1716 i.
Joseph 1728 w.
Samuel 1736 w.
Thomas 1743 i.
John Sr. 1744 w.
Daniel 1745 i.
Rebecca 1745 w.
John 1746 i.
Ann 1753 w.
Nicholas 1757 w.
John 1759 w.
William 1761 w.
Benj. 1762 w.
Francis 1762 w.
Nicholas 1764 i.
Francis 1765 i.
Susanna 1767 w.
Alexander 1773 w.
John 1777 w.
Mary 1781 w.
Thomas 1784 w.
Elizabeth 1785 i.
William 1785 w.
Meriwether 1795 i.
William 1795 i.
Wm. 1797 i.
Fairfax
Jacob 1750 w.
James 1751 w.
William 1751 w.
William 1757 i.
Thomas 1764 w.
Margery 1776 w.
William 1786 w.
Saml. 1799 w.
Fauquier
Alex. 1761 i.
John 1777 w.
Joseph 1777 i.
Augustine 1780 i.
John 1783 i.
Matthew 1782 w.
Susannah 1782 i.
John 1784 i.
Joseph 1793 w.

James D. 1794 i.
William 1798 w.
Fluvanna
John 1795 i.
Franklin
Thomas 1787 w.
Gideon 1788 i.
Frederick
John 1748 a.
George 1749 w.
John 1750 i.
Susannah 1750 a.
William 1756 i.
Frederick 1761 i.
Stephen 1764 i.
Daniel 1768 w.
Charles 1776 w.
George 1778 i.
Joseph 1782 i.
Jeremiah 1787 w.
Daniel 1794 i.
Jeremiah 1794 w.
Goochland
Jno. 1754 i.
Wm. Sharp 1783 w.
Greensville
Earl 1782 w.
Thomas 1782 w.
William 1788 w.
Elizabeth 1790 w.
William 1790 i.
David 1799 w.
Halifax
Luke, Jr. 1757 w.
Luke 1758 w.
Chas. 1760 i.
Duncan 1761 i.
Jno. 1764 w.
Benj. 1770 w.
Edwin 1773 w.
Richd. 1780 w.
Geo. 1782 i.
Richd. 1783 a.
Thos. 1787 i.
Stephen 1789 i.
Wm. 1792 i.
Harrison
Thomas 1795 i.
Henrico
Philip 1732 w.
Obadiah 1746 w.
Mary 1754 w.
Jno. 1781 w.
Eliz. 1789 w.
Jno. Sr. 1790 w.
Eliz. 1791 i.
Jacob 1791 w.
Humphrey 1792 i.
Jacob 1797 i.
Isle of Wight
Virgus 1677 nw.

Robert 1678 w.
Arthur 1693 w.
Nicholas 1695 w.
Arthur 1697 w.
William 1704 w.
Jane 1710 w.
Mary 1715 w.
Stephen 1718 w.
Mary 1720 w.
Thomas 1738 i.
Nicholas 1740 i.
Thomas 1741 w.
Arthur 1742 w.
William 1747 w.
Hannah 1748 w.
Lawrence 1748 w.
Martha 1749 i.
Thomas 1752 w.
William 1753 w.
Arthur 1754 i.
Arthur 1755 i.
Jesse 1758 i.
Mary 1758 i.
Joseph 1759 i.
Elizabeth 1761 w.
Nicholas 1765 i.
John 1766 w.
Steven 1768 w.
Joseph 1778 i.
Joseph 1779 i.
Nathaniel 1780 w.
William 1780 w.
Thomas 1785 w.
Joseph 1790 i.
Thomas 1790 i.
Nicholas 1795 w.
Thomas 1799 w.
King George
Nicholas 1734 i.
Wm. 1741 i.
Jarret 1743 i.
Nicholas 1743 a.
Thos. 1760 w.
Henry 1782 w.
Wm. [1793 or 4] w.
Margt. 1793 w.
Lancaster
Saml. 1688 w.
Elizabeth 1735 w.
John 1765 w.
Burgess 1776 i.
Loudoun
John 1761 i.
William 1778 w.
Henry 1784 w.
Samuel 1786 i.
John 1789 i.
Clator [Cayton?] 1793 w.
John 1795 i.
Mary 1798 w.

Louisa
Chas. 1768 w.
James, Jr. 1777 w.
David 1778 w.
James 1778 i.
Thos. Ballard 1778 w.
James 1784 w.
B. Thos. 1791 w.
Ann 1794 i.
Elizabeth 1796 i.
Thomas 1797 w.
Lunenburg
Wm. 1751 w.
Richd. 1760 w.
Zachariah 1761 i.
Thos. 1780 w.
Joseph 1794 w.
Madison
Nicholas 1797 w.
Mecklenburg
Robt. 1777 w.
Peartree 1779 w.
Drury 1783 w.
Augustine 1790 w.
Jno. 1792 w.
Anderson 1794 i.
Benj. 1798 w.
John 1798 w.
Middlesex
Robt. 1683 w.
Jno. 1696 w.
Jos. 1699 i.
Thos 1705 w.
Thos. 1715 i.
Jno. 1722 w.
Thos. 1723 w.
Eliz. 1727 i.
Jno. 1727 w.
Wm. 1727 i.
Jas. 1728 w.
Jas. (2) 1728 w.
Edwd. 1741 i.
Cary 1743 w.
Anthony 1745 w.
Jno. 1746 w.
Jos. 1746 w.
Ann 1749 w.
Frances 1750 w.
Jno. 1751 i.
Eliz. 1758 w.
Benj. 1762 i.
Jas. 1771 w.
Eliz. 1773 w.
Augustine 1774 w.
Eliz. 1775 i.
Margt. 1782 w.
Montgomery
Samuel 1787 a.
Eloner 1795 i.
Norfolk
William 1669 i.

Robt. 1679 w.
Thomas 1685 i.
Robt. 1686-7 w.
John 1711 w.
John 1719 w.
John 1733 w.
Mary 1734-5 w.
John 1735 i.
Samuel 1739 w.
Samuel 1756 w.
Josiah 1761 w.
Peter 1761 w.
Butler 1763 w.
John 1766 w.
Charles 1773 w.
Richard, Jr. 1773 i.
William 1777 w.
Charles 1778 i.
John 1778 i.
Sarah 1780 w.
Samuel 1783 i.
George 1785 w.
Soloman 1785 w.
Henry 1787 w.
John 1787 i.
Mathias 1788 w.
Richard 1788 w.
George 1789 w.
Samuel 1789 w.
William 1789 w.
Samuel 1797 i.
James 1799 w.
John 1799 w.

Northampton
Wm. 1636 w.
Richd. 1659 w.
Argol 1661 w.
Wm. 1668 i.
Jno. 1697 w.
Peter 1705-6 i.
Wm. 1709 w.
Isaac 1712 i.
Jno. 1712 w.
Jno. 1713 i.
Geo. 1715-16 w.
Richd. 1716 w.
Jno. 1720 w.
Jos. 1720 w.
Thos. 1728 i.
Thos. 1730 w.
Levin 1736 i.
Levin 1737 i.
Jacob 1738 i.
Richd. 1738 i.
Geo. 1741 w.
Abraham 1749 w.
Isaac 1750 w.
Wm. 1750 w.
Jonathan 1751 i.
Wm. 1751 w.
Jno. 1753 i.

Obadiah 1757 w.
Jno. 1761 w.
Wm. 1761 w.
Jno. 1763 w.
Jonathan 1778 w.
Thos. 1784 w.
Wm. Jr. 1794 w.
Richd. 1797 w.
Esau 1798 i.

Northumberland
Robt. 1660 w.
Jno. 1663 w.
Richd. 1710 ab.
Richd. 1726-7 w.
Bryant 1728 i.
Thos. 1729-30 w.
Wm. 1729 w.
Saml. 1740 w.
Lazarus 1742 i.
Hannah 1743 w.
Philip 1743 w.
Hannah 1745-6 w.
Saml. 1746 i.
Jno. 1748 w.
Richd. 1748 w.
Edwin 1750 w.
Saml. 1750-1 i.
Wm. 1751 i.
Wm. 1752 w.
Wm. 1754 i.
John 1756 w.
Thos. 1758 w.
Hannah 1762 w.
Baldwin Mathews
   1763 i.
John 1763 w.
Wooldridge 1763 w.
James 1768 w.
Thomas 1771 i.
Woldridge 1771 i.
Peter 1774 i.
John 1777 w.
William 1777 w.
Thos. 1779 i.
Richard 1782 i.
Woolridge 1783 i.
Geo. 1791 i.
Thos. 1795 i.

Ohio
Geo. 1783 w.
James 1788 w.
James 1791 w.

Orange
Augustine 1736 w.
Jno. 1738 a.
Jno. (2) 1738 a.
Wm. 1739 w.
Eliz. 1739 w.
Edwd. 1756 w.
Ambrose 1770 w.
Chas. 1772 i.

Geo. 1779 i.
Stephen J. K. 1784 w.
Paris 1799 w.
Stephen 1799 w.
Pittsylvania
Jno. 1776 w.
Thos. 1781 w.
Jno. 1784 w.
Orlando 1790 w.
Powhatan
Robt. 1785 i.
Thos. 1786 w.
Magdalen 1787 w.
Wm. 1790 w.
Prince Edward
Charles 1760 i.
Jonathan 1785 w.
Geo. 1789 w.
Prince George
Thos. 1718 w.
Jno. 1726 i.
Richd. 1726 w.
Princess Anne
Robt. 1701 w.
James 1706 i.
Geo. 1708 w.
Richd. 1709 w.
Richd. 1711 i.
Geo. 1724 w.
Wm. Jr. 1725 w.
Wm. Sr. 1727 w
Eliz. 1728 w.
Wm. 1728 w.
James 1730 w.
Benoni 1745 i.
Wm. 1745 w.
Jno. 1746 w.
West 1757 w.
Danl. 1763 i.
Jno. 1782 w.
Thos. 1784 w.
Prince William
William 1736 i.
Thomas 1743 i.
Thomas 1744 i.
Caleb 1778 w.
Thomas 1778 i.
Peter 1792 w.
Rappahannock
Toby [1658?] w.
Thos. 1679 w.
Henry 1684 w.
Richmond
Eve 1705 w.
David 1711 i.
Thos. 1711 i.
Wm. 1714 i.
Thos. 1717 w.
Jno. 1718 w.
Jos. 1718 i.
Wm. 1721 i.

Wm. 1724 w.
Jno. 1726 nw.
Thos. 1726 w.
Wm. 1728 w.
Wm. 1743 w.
Thos. 1749 i.
Jane 1774 w.
Robt. 1776 w.
Robt. 1778 i.
Thos. 1782 w.
Betty 1785 i.
Wm. 1786 w.
Thos. 1791 i.
Jno. 1794 w.
Jno. 1797 i.
Jno. Jr. 1797 w.
Shenandoah
John 1778 a.
Elizabeth 1780 i.
Henry 1782 i.
Joseph 1782 w.
John 1786 a.
Henry 1790 w.
Ulrick 1791 a.
John 1793 i.
Samuel 1793 i.
Southampton
Geo. 1749 i.
Virgis 1753 w.
Jas. 1754 w.
Turner Jno. 1756 w.
Jane 1758 w.
Absolem 1768 i.
Jno. 1780 w.
Martha 1783 w.
Matthew 1785 w.
Wm. 1785 i.
Aaron 1798 w.
Spotsylvania
Wm. 1734 a.
Francis 1746 a.
Jno. 1746 a.
Oswald 1748 a.
Jno. 1753 a.
Jno. 1761 a.
Ralph 1769 a.
Chas. 1770 a.
Eliz. 1772 w.
Peyton 1782 a.
Wm. 1794 w.
Stafford
Henry 1702 i.
Jas. 1732 i.
Jno. 1754 i.
Thos. 1757 nw.
Jno. 1762 w.
Chas. 1764 i.
Surry
Jno. 1679 w.
Jno. 1711 i.
Richd. 1713 w.

Nicholas 1719 w.
Jno. 1720 w.
Thos. Sr. 1722 w.
Wm. 1751 w.
Wm. 1757 w.
Henry 1764 w.
James 1777 i.
Wm. 1777 w.
Nicholas 1785 w.
Willis 1787 w.
Lucy 1798 w.
Sussex
Thos. 1761 i.
Jno. 1764 w.
Saml. 1764 w.
James 1765 i.
Thos. 1779 i.
Jno. 1781 i.
William 1782 w.
Joseph 1790 w.
Lawrence 1794 w.
Isham 1795 w.
Arthur 1799 w.
Westmoreland
Herbert 1663 w.
Wm. 1671 w.
Jno. 1677 i.
Neomiah 1695 i.
Isaac 1698 w.
Robt. 1702 i.
Wm. 1707 w.
Chas. 1714 w.
Jas. 1714 w.
Anne 1716 w.
Anne (2) 1716 w.
Jos. 1718 w.
Caleb 1725 w.
Jno. 1725 w.
Stephen 1725 i.
Francis 1729 i.
Wm. 1734 i.
Wm. 1735 i.
Jno. 1736 w.
Thos. 1738 i.
Thos. 1740 i.
Jno. 1741 i.
Peter 1741 w.
Lazarus 1742 w.
Jos. 1750 w.
Jas. 1750 i.
Robt. 1750 w.
Stephen 1762 w.
Jas. 1770 i.
Jno. 1772 w.
Peter, Sr. 1774 w.
Peter 1774 w
Peter 1776 i.
Spence 1775 w.
Saml. 1776 w.
Jno. 1778 w.
Sarah 1779 w.

Stephen 1781 i.
Philip 1782 i.
Wm. 1782 w.
Wm. 1786 w.
Thos. 1789 w.
Jacob 1789 w.
Eliz. 1792 i.
Jacob 1792 i.
Lewis 1792 w.
Jas. 1793 w.
Washington
Tobias 1781 i.
Alexander 1785 w.
Thomas 1786 i.
York
Richd. 1645 w.
Jas. 1672 w.
Wm. 1679 i.
Sarah 1710 w.
Sarah 1712 i.
Abraham 1719 i.
Jno. 1720 w.
Lawrence 1738 w.
Edmd. 1750 w.
Mildred 1754 w.
Thos. 1763 w.
Robt. 1775 i.
Robt. 1777 w.
Lawrence 1778 w.
Lawrence 1788 w.
Jas. 1792 i.
SMITHER
Culpeper
Thomas 1749 w.
Essex
Wm. 1762 w.
John 1794 w.
John 1796 i.
Lancaster
George 1756 w.
Thomas 1782 i.
Northumberland
John 1782 w.
Geo. 1786 w.
Judith 1795 i.
Richmond
Gabriel 1785 w.
SMITHERS
Accomack
Moses 1772 i.
Norfolk
Thos. 1687 w.
SMITHSON
Lunenburg
Jno. 1761 w.
Jno. 1783 i.
Francis 1784 w.
Wm. 1797 w.
Francis 1797 i.
Sarah 1797 i.
Wm. 1799 i.

SMOOT
Fauquier
John 1796 w.
Northumberland
Thos .1757 i.
Sarah 1761 i.
Chas. 1787 i.
Jno. 1792 w.
Orange
Caleb 1797 w.
Prince William
Thomas 1783 w.
Richmond
Wm. 1716 w.
Wm. 1784 w.
Westmoreland
Wm. 1707 w.
SMOTHERS
Northampton
Jno. 1687 w.
SMOTT
Berkeley
Edward 1793 w.
SMYTH
Botetourt
Ad. 1786 w.
Cumberland
Robt. 1768 w.
Northumberland
Danl. 1740 i.
Princess Anne
Geo. 1707 rp.
Richd. 1707 rp.
Wm. 1710 w.
Tully 1723 w.
Geo. 1739 w.
Jno. 1741 w.
Richd. 1746 w.
Sarah 1748 i.
Chas. 1749 w.
Tully Robinson 1753 i.
Richmond
Wm. 700 w.
York
Jno. 1670 w.
Jno. 1687-8 w.
Jno. 1697 i.
SMYTHE
Botetourt
James 1790 w.
SNAFFER
Frederick
Mary 1762 w.
SNAIL
Princess Anne
Wm. 1710 i.
SNAILE
Norfolk
Henry 1655 w.
Princess Anne
Henry 1721 w.

Henry 1738 w.
Henry 1769 i.
Hillary 1769 i.
SNAILL
Princess Anne
Thos. 1713 i.
SNALE
Norfolk
Thomas 1760 i.
SNALLEN
Chesterfield
Alex. 17[54?] w.
SNAPP
Frederick
John 1762 w.
John 1786 w.
Shenandoah
Lawrence 1782 w.
Peter 1789 w.
Lawrence 1790 a.
Joseph 1791 w.
SNAVELEY
Frederick
Jacob 1790 i.
SNAVELY
Montgomery
John 1790 a.
SNEAD
Accomack
Robt. 1712 w.
Robt. 1721 w.
Chas. 1727 w.
Chas. 1733 i.
Anne 1746 w.
Mary 1748 i.
Katherine 1751 w.
Thos. 1755 w.
Jno. 1780 w.
Smith 1782 w.
Chas. 1784 w.
Robt. 1785 w.
Thos. 1787 w.
Chas. 1795 i.
Smith 1795 i.
Eliz. 1796 w.
Thos. 1796 i.
Northampton
Smith 1792 w.
Geo. 1794 i.
Smith 1797 i.
Wm. 1798 w.
Margt. 1799 i.
Richmond
Chas. 1724 w.
Sarah 1759 w.
SNEADE
Hanover
Alex. 1734 w.
Matthew 1734 a.

SNEED
Fluvanna
Archibald 1781 w.
Henrico
Thos. 1781 w.
Wm. 1783 w.
Pittsylvania
Zachariah 1783 i.
SNEIDER
Amherst
Jno. 1774 w.
Culpeper
John 1760 i.
Orange
Henry 1747 w.
SNELGROVE
Surry
Henry 1721 i.
SNELL
Albemarle
Philamon 1797 i.
Orange
Joseph 1760 i.
Jno. 1786 w.
Spotsylvania
Jno. 1733 a.
SNELLET
Accomack
Wm. 1696 nw.
SNELLING
Fauquier
Benj. 1774 w.
King George
Alex. 1760 w.
Lancaster
Jno. 1703 i.
Shenandoah
John 1777 a.
SNELLOCK
Isle of Wight
John 1679 w.
SNELSON
Louisa
Wm. 1780 w.
Sarah 1789 w.
SNICKERS
Frederick
Edward 1791 w.
SNICKNERS
Frederick
Henry 1749 i.
SNIDER
Berkeley
Jacob 1790 w.
Shenandoah
Jacob 1779 w.
John 1779 a.
George 1785 w.

SNIDOW
Montgomery
Phillip 1793 i.
SNIDUS
Shenandoah
Christopher 1786 i.
SNIPE
Stafford
Nathl. 1785 w.
SNIPES
Surry
Robt. 1721 i.
Ann 1774 i.
SNODGRASS
Augusta
Jno. 1758 a.
Berkeley
John 1788 w.
Botetourt
Joseph 1782 w.
Elizabeth 1783 i.
William 1791 w.
Montgomery
Elenor 1793 a.
Ohio
Mary 1796 w.
Rockbridge
Robert 1795 w.
Spotsylvania
David 1758 a.
Washington
John 1796 w.
SNOW
Albemarle
Jno. 1784 w.
Bedford
Henry 1778 i.
Thomas 1781 w.
Berkeley
Guy 1783 i.
Northumberland
Saml. 1745 w.
Surry
Josiah 1709 i.
SNOWDALL
Westmoreland
Wm. 1674 w.
SNOWDEN
Berkeley
Joseph 1799 w.
Isle of Wight
Richard 1746 i.
Westmoreland
Thos. 1724 i.
SNOXEL
Stafford
Edwd. 1736 i.
SNUTE
Loudoun
John 1782 i.

SNYDER
Berkeley
Jacob 1798 i.
Shenandoah
Martin 1777 w.
SOANE
Henrico
Jno. 1699 w.
Wm. 1714 w.
Saml. 1731 w.
SOAREY
Princess Anne
Francis 1784 i.
Peter 1785 i.
Wm. 1785 i.
Caleb 1799 i.
SOARY
Princess Anne
Wm. 1784 w.
SOBLET
Albemarle
James 1750 a.
Cumberland
Peter Lewis 1755 w.
Goochland
Jas. 1741 w.
SOCOMB
Accomack
Thos. 1785 i.
SOLESBERY
Accomack
Jno. 1732 w.
SOLLEY
Princess Anne
Thos. 1700 w.
Westmoreland
Thos. 1663 w.
SOLOMON
Albemarle
Ann 1795 i.
Surry
Lewis 1743 w.
Sussex
Lewis 1795 w.
SOLWAY
Surry
Jno. 1678 w.
SOMERBY
Spotsylvania
Phil 1773 a.
SOMERS
Northampton
Thos. 1729 i.
Thos. 1730 i.
SOMERSETT
Northampton
Thos. 1679 w.
SOMERVELL
Essex
Alexander 1724 i.
King George
Colin 1771 w.

SOMERVILLE
King George
Jas. 1752 i.
Northampton
Chas. 1694 w.
SOMERWELL
York
Mungo 1706 ab.
SOMMER
Shenandoah
Michael 1783 i.
George 1787 w.
SOMMERS
Fairfax
John 1790 i.
Michael 1782 i.
SOMMERVILLE
Westmoreland
Jno. 1717 i.
SONGSTER
Loudoun
John 1787 i.
SOPER
York
Jno. 1717 w.
SOREY
Princess Anne
Frances 1753 w.
Andrew 1783 w.
Peter 1784 w.
SORN
Augusta
Jacob 1755 a.
SORREL
Amherst
Jno. 1780 w.
Westmoreland
Jno. 1773 i.
Thos. 1797 i.
Jas. 1799 i.
SORRELL
Essex
John 1693 a.
Jno. 1700 w.
Joseph 1773 w.
Loudoun
Thos. 1774 w.
John 1783 w.
Reuben 1785 w.
Spotsylvania
Jno. 1799 a.
Westmoreland
Thos. 1726 w.
Jno. 1758 i.
Judith 1786 w.
SORRILL
Richmond
Thos. 1745 i.
SORSBY
Surry
Wm. 1758 i.

Thos. (elder) 1768 w.
Alexander 1771 w.
Thos. 1788 w.
SORY
Princess Anne
Francis 1753 i.
Andrew 1783 w.
SOSBURY
Richmond
Thos. 1733 i.
SONDERS
Berkeley
John 1793 a.
SOULIE
Goochland
Nicholas 1738 i.
SOUTH
Middlesex
Jno. 1793 w.
Westmoreland
Geo. 1720 w.
SOUTHALL
Amelia
Stephen 1748 w.
Charles City
Henry 1795 w.
James 1794 w.
Cumberland
James 1776 i.
Wm. 1789 w.
Henrico
Philip 1790 w.
Turner 1791 w.
Spotsylvania
Edwd. 1728 a.
Edward 1786 a.
Surry
Jno. 1796 i.
SOUTHARD
Fauquier
Francis 1779 w.
Loudoun
William 1794 i.
SOUTHER
Culpeper
Henry 1784 w.
SOUTHERLAND
Norfolk
[John] 1711 i.
Jno. 1720 w.
Wm. 1724 i.
Ann 1766 w.
John 1772 w.
York
Jas. 1752 i.
SOUTHERN
Essex
Wm. 1783 w.
Middlesex
Edmd. 1767 a.

Geo. 1774 i.
Princess Anne
Henry 1697 i.
Henry 1747 w.
Richmond
Wm. 1713 i.
SOUTHIN
Rappahannock
Geo. 1685 i.
SOUTHREN
Middlesex
Jno. 1728 w.
SOUTHWOOD
Frederick
Edward 1749 a.
SOUTHWORTH
Orange
Thos. 1738 w.
Wm. 1739 i.
Southampton
Thos. 1760 i.
Sussex
Jno. 1766 i.
SOWEL
Charlotte
Thos. 1795 w.
Chesterfield
Geo. 1770 i.
SOWELL
Albemarle
Thos. 1763 i.
Thos. 1766 w.
SOWERBY
Surry
Francis 1717 w.
Francis 1723 i.
Jno. 1727 w.
SOWERS
Frederick
Jacob 1785 w.
SOWERSBY
Surry
Saml. 1743 i.
SOXMAN
Shenandoah
Frederick 1796 w.
SPADDEN
Loudoun
William 1785 i.
SPADY
Northampton
Jas. 1688 i.
Wm. 1725 i.
Jas. 1771 i.
Wm. 1780 w.
Thos. Sr. 1793 w.
Eliz. 1795 w.
Jas. 1799 w.
SPAIN
Amelia
Thos. 1760 w.

Sussex
Jno. 1783 w.
SPALDING
Accomack
Geo. 1796 w.
Henrico
Jasper 1750 i.
SPAN
Northumberland
Richd. 1668 w.
Jno. 1724 i.
Saml. 1726 i.
Richd. 1728 w.
Saml. 1728 i.
Grace 1738 w.
Cuthbert 1753 w.
Richard 1764 w.
SPANGLER
Franklin
Daniel 1787 w.
George 1793 a.
George 1794 a.
Shenandoah
John 1793 a.
Wythe
Peter 1796 w.
SPANN
Northumberland
Dorothy 1711 w.
Jno. 1722 w.
Princess Anne
Wm. 1748 w.
SPANNS
Princess Anne
Wm. 1782 i.
SPARK
Prince William
John 1787 i.
Westmoreland
Wm. 1767 w.
York
Nimrod 1795 w.
SPARKES
Culpeper
Henry 1770 w.
Essex
John 1786 w.
Prince William
William 1735 w.
SPARKS
Culpeper
William 1781 w.
Thomas 1787 w.
Fairfax
Jeremiah 1750 a.
Prince William
Wm. 1788 w.
Spotsylvania
James 1758 a.

Westmoreland
Wm. 1767 w.
Alex. 1783 w.
SPARLIN
Northampton
Margt. 1697 i.
SPARROW
Accomack
Jno. 1775 w.
Mary 1776 w.
Mecklenburg
Eliz. 1781 w.
Norfolk
Richd. [1740?] w.
James 1777 w.
James 1784 i.
Peter 1784 w.
Richard 1795 w.
George 1799 w.
Princess Anne
Geo. 1771 w.
Wm. 1789 i.
Westmoreland
Robt. 1717 i.
Matthew 1726 i.
SPEAKMAN
Northampton
Wm. 1779 i.
Rachel 1792 w.
SPEAR
Augusta
Jno. 1760 w.
Goochland
Jno. 1743 w.
Henrico
Jane 1755 i.
Jno. 1787 w.
Robt. 1789 w.
Robt. 1791 i.
SPEARE
Henrico
Robt. 1735 w.
SPEARMAN
Essex
John 1772 w.
Susanna 1785 w.
SPEARS
Albemarle
James 1761 i.
James 1763 i.
Chesterfield
Wm. 1767 w.
Mary 1781 w.
Mary 1789 i.
Cumberland
Wm. Sr. 1796 w.
Goochland
Robt. 1740 i.
Powhatan
Nicholas 1799 w.

SPEARY
Frederick
Thomas 1766 i.
SPECIAL
Isle of Wight
Samuel 1733 i.
SPEED
Mecklenburg
Jno. Jr. 1774 w.
Jno. 1785 w.
Southampton
Geo. 1762 i.
Wm. 1771 i.
Mary 1778 w.
Robt. 1791 i.
Robt. 1793 w.
Chas. 1798 w.
Sussex
James 1773 i.
Westmoreland
Ralph 1716 w.
SPEEDE
Rappahannock
Jno. 1675 w.
Sussex
Thos. 1797 w.
SPEERS
Goochland
James 1732 w.
SPEIRS
Accomack
Jno. 1763 i.
SPEKE
Westmoreland
Thos. 1659 w.
SPELL
Prince George
Geo. 1716 i.
SPELLMAN
Westmoreland
Thos. 1718 i.
SPELLOWAY
Isle of Wight
Richard 1762 i.
SPELMAN
York
Thos. 1691 i.
SPELMONDS
Norfolk
William 1794 w.
SPENCE
Augusta
Wm. 1799 i.
Fairfax
John 1760 i.
Greensville
John 1791 w.
Northumberland
David 1726 w.
Jno. 1727 i.

Richmond
Alex. 1716 i.
Eliz. 1720 i.
Robt. 1763 w.
Southampton
Wm. 1758 w.
Surry
Danl. 1760 w.
Westmoreland
Alex. 1704 w.
Jno. 1736 i.
Jas. 1739 i.
Patrick 1740 w.
Thos. 1750 i.
Jeremiah 1755 w.
Patrick 1765 i.
Thos. 1765 i.
Jno. 1771 i.
Smith 1785 i.
SPENCER
Albemarle
Abraham 1761 w.
Jno. 1753 i.
Jno. 1789 w.
Abraham 1795 w.
Campbell
Chas. 1796 i.
Charlotte
Sion 1775 w.
Jas. 1781 w.
Thos. 1793 w.
Chesterfield
Richd. 1785 i.
Cumberland
James A. 1797 i.
Halifax
Thos. 1776 w.
Margaret 1786 w.
Henry
James, Jr. 1783 w.
Lancaster
Geo. 1691 w.
Louisa
Benj. 1751 w.
Montgomery
William, Sr. 1794 w.
Northumberland
Peter 1760 i.
Orange
Edwd. 1753 i.
Edwd. 1762 w.
Prince George
Richd. 1719 i.
Southampton
Edmund 1784 w.
Westmoreland
———— 1696 i.
Anne 1696 w.
Jno. 1708 w.
Francis 1720 w.
Frances 1727 i.

SPENDERGRASS
Richmond
Jas. 1718 i.
Jno. 1733 w.
SPENSOR
Surry
Jno. 1675 w.
Robt. 1679 w.
SPERRY
Botetourt
Jacob 1798 i.
Frederick
Thomas 1766 w.
Peter 1773 w.
SPHEAR
Frederick
John M. 1770 w.
SPIAS
Essex
Joh. 1703 i.
SPICER
Accomack
Jno. 1693 nw.
Brunswick
James 1768 w.
Culpeper
William 1751 i.
Moses 1798 w.
King George
Jno. 1721 i.
Jno. 1727 i.
Arthur 1749 i.
Jos. 1781 w.
Orange
Rawson 1768 w.
Prince William
Rocer 1744 i.
Richmond
Arthur 1700 w.
SPICHARDS
Botetourt
Phillip 1793 i.
SPIERS
Accomack
Wm. 1755 w.
Wm. 1757 i.
Wm. 1786 w.
Robt. 1788 i.
Newberry 1789 i.
Leah 1790 w.
Comfort 1794 w.
Jno. 1796 w.
Essex
John 1744 i.
SPILLER
Westmoreland
Dorothy 1722 w.
SPILLMAN
Westmoreland
Thos. 1740 i.
Wm. 1760 w.

Wm. 1770 i.
SPILMAN
Culpeper
Robt. 1786 i.
James 1790 w.
Jacob 1760 i.
King George
Thos. 1782 w.
Westmoreland
Wm. 1760 i.
SPILTIMBER
Surry
Jno. 1656 a.
Jno. 1677 i.
SPINDLE
Spotsylvania
John 1783 w.
SPINKS
Fairfax
John 1779 w.
Westmoreland
Enoch 1724 i.
SPINNEY
Norfolk
William 1795 w.
SPINNY
Northampton
———— 1663-4 w.
SPIERS
Accomack
Jno. 1724 i.
SPIRING
Middlesex
Jno. 1699 i.
SPITTELL
Surry
James 1725 w.
SPIVEY
Norfolk
Matthew 1719 w.
Matthew 1724 i.
Matthew 1757 i.
SPIVY
Norfolk
Matthew 1758 i.
Southampton
Jno. 1794 i.
Wm. 1794 w.
Wm. 1798 i.
SPOE
Richmond
Mary 1731 nw.
Chas. 1740 w.
SPOO
Richmond
Chas. 1731 w.
SPOONER
King George
Saml. 1761 w.

SPOTSWOOD
Middlesex
Eliz. 1791 w.
Orange
Alex. 1740 w.
Spotsylvania
Robt. 1733 w.
Jno. 1758 w.
SPOUEL
Augusta
Margt. 1781 w.
SPOYLDING
Cumberland
Francis 1772 w.
SPRABORROUGH
Brunswick
Jno. 1774 w.
SPRADLIN
Albemarle
William 1798 i.
Hanover
Jno. 1733-4 eb.
SPRADLING
Pittsylvania
Jno. 1768 w.
SPRAGGINS
Campbell
Wm. 1797 w.
Charles City
Thos. 1795 w.
SPRAGIN
Halifax
Wm. 1759 w.
SPRAGINS
Charles City
Wm. 1773 w.
Halifax
Thos. 1795 w.
SPRATLEY
Surry
Jno. 1728 w.
Jno. 1758 w.
Mary 1773 w.
Walter 1777 w.
Benj. 1792 w.
Jno. 1796 i.
SPRATLING
Northampton
Henry 1732 i.
SPRATT
Middlesex
Robt. 1792 w.
Norfolk
Henry 1686-7 w.
Princess Anne
Isabel 1700 w.
Thos. 1729 w.
Henry 1736 w.
Thos. 1746 w.
James 1799 w.

SPRATTE
Princess Anne
Henry 1749 w.
SPRATTING
Northampton
Eliz. 1734 i.
SPRIGG
Prince William
Richard 1781 i.
SPRIGGS
Northumberland
Joseph 1784 w.
SPRING
Norfolk
Robert 1678 i.
Robt. 1679 w.
Aaron 1693-4 w.
Moses 1700 w.
James 1793 w.
York
Robt. 1683 w.
SPRINGER
Frederick
Dennis 1760 w.
SPRINGSTONE
Augusta
Jacob 1780 i.
SPROUL
Berkeley
Samuel 1785 i.
SPROULL
Rockbridge
William 1798 w.
SPROUT
Augusta
Jno. 1755 w.
Bath
John 1796 w.
SPROWLE
Norfolk
John 1773 i.
SPROWEL
Wythe
William 1799 w.
SPRUKER
Shenandoah
Andrew 1795 a.
SPURLING
Westmoreland
Jeremiah 1726 w.
SPURLOCK
Albemarle
Wm. 1751 w.
Wm. 1759 i.
Goochland
Anne 1759 w.
Henrico
Wm. 1754 w.
Mecklenburg
Stephen 1774 w.

SPURR
Loudoun
James 1760 w.
SPYCER
York
Wm. 1658 w.
SQUIRES
Fauquier
John 1779 i.
Loudoun
Thos. 1780 w.
SROTLAR
Goochland
Nicholas 1739 w.
SSECH
Shenandoah
Jacob 1786 i.
STACY
Sussex
Simon 1784 w.
York
Jos. 1728 i.
Jno. 1770 w.
STAFFORD
Fairfax
William 1751 i.
Montgomery
Ralph 1794 w.
Norfolk
John 1744 i.
William 1761 w.
Joseph 1789 i.
William 1798 w.
Prince George
Cuthbert 1726 i.
Sussex
Thos. 1761 w.
STAGG
Isle of Wight
Edward 1765 i.
York
Chas. 1736 i.
STAIGE
York
Theo. 1747 i.
STAINBACK
Brunswick
Francis 1779 w.
Francis 1790 w.
Geo. 1796 w.
STAKES
Accomack
Henry 1727 w.
Wm. 1770 i.
Northampton
Simon 1728 w.
Wm. 1732 w.
Job 1755 w.
Peggy 1761 i.

STALAKER
Harrison
John 1796 i.
STALEY
Berekley
Jacob 1793 w.
STALKER
Halifax
Saml. 1759 i.
STALLARD
Essex
Saml. 1720 w.
Samuel 1725 i.
Rappahannock
Walter 1684 w.
STALLE
Augusta
Wm. 1773 i.
STALLINGS
Isle of Wight
John 1788 w.
STALMAKER
Randolph
Jacob 1792 w.
STALNAKER
Augusta
Saml. 1755 a.
STALP
Augusta
Wm. 1773 w.
STALZER
Washington
Martin 1780 i.
STAMP
York
Richd. 1748 i.
STAMPER
Middlesex
Powell 1727 i.
Jno. 1774 w.
STAMPS
Fauquier
Thomas 1763 w.
William 1772 w.
Goochland
Wm. 1746 i.
King George
Timothy 1731 i.
Lancaster
Timothy 1698 i.
Wm. 1746 i.
STANARD
Middlesex
Wm. 1733 i.
Eliz. 1747 w.
Spotsylvania
Beverly 1765 w.
STANBACK
Mecklenburg
George 1788 w.

STANDARD
Middlesex
  Geo. 1794 i.
STANDLEY
Amelia
  Wm. 1768 w.
Madison
  Thomas 1799 i.
Spotsylvania
  Moses 1761 a.
STANDLY
Northumberland
  Thomas 1790 w.
STANFELD
Halifax
  Thos. 1797 w.
STANFIELD
Richmond
  Thos. 1726 w.
STANFILD
Essex
  Robard 1696 i.
STANDORD
Lancaster
  Vincent 1658 w.
STANHOPE
York
  Jno. 1693 w.
STANLEY
Amelia
  Dacey 1757 w.
Berkeley
  Isaac 1794 w.
Frederick
  Richard 1747 i.
Henry
  William 1784 w.
Northumberland
  Jno. 1747 i.
Pittsylvania
  Jos. 1789 nw.
Surry
  Ann 1657 w.
STANLY
Henrico
  Edwd. 1726 w.
  Edwd. 1727 i.
Norfolk
  Roger 1752 i.
Northumberland
  Jno. 1660 w.
  Jno. 1726 i.
  Joseph 1751 i.
STANNOP
York
  Jno. 1694 i.
STANTON
Accomack
  Jno. 1719 i.
  Lemuel 1786 i.

Charlotte
  John 1784 w.
Culpeper
  William 1763 i.
Essex
  Jno. 1718 w.
King George
  Mary 1745 i.
  Sarah 1745 eb.
Middlesex
  Theophilus 1711 w.
Orange
  Thos. 1741 w.
Southampton
  James 1789 w.
Surry
  James 1719 w.
Washington
  Richard 1782 i.
York
  ——— 1686-7 i.
  Elisha 1693-4 i.
  Elisha 1700 ab.
STANUP
York
  Richd. 1707-8 i.
STAP
Henrico
  Joshua 1695 w.
STAPELTON
Frederick
  Robert 1755 w.
Loudoun
  Thomas 1773 i.
Middlesex
  Thos. 1706 w.
  Jno. 1710 i.
  Geo. Jr. 1720 w.
Montgomery
  Charles 1799 w.
STAPLES
Amherst
  Saml. 1776 a.
  Saml., Jr. 1777 a.
  John 1797 w.
Charlotte
  Wm. 1795 w.
Henrico
  Jno., Sr. 1788 w.
Lunenburg
  Thompson 1777 w.
STAPP
Orange
  Joshua 1783 w.
STARBUCK
King George
  Richd. 1773 a.
STARCHY
York
  Peter 1702 w.

STARK
Essex
  Thomas 1742 w.
Isle of Wight
  Thomas 1734 i.
Loudoun
  Wm. 1772 w.
Stafford
  Jas. 1754 w.
  Ann 1762 i.
Westmoreland
  Wm. 1727 i.
York
  Richd. 1704 i.
  Rebecca 1713 w.
STARKE
Henrico
  Bolling 1788 w.
  Jno. 1789 i.
STARKEY
York
  Peter 1677 w.
STARKS
Richmond
  Jas. 1726 w.
STARLING
Princess Anne
  Saml. 1729 w.
STARLINGE
Norfolk
  James 1653 i.
STARNELL
Norfolk
  Richd. 1655 w.
STARNS
Washington
  Frederick 1779 w.
  Joseph 1779 i.
STARY
Berkeley
  Daniel 1787 i.
STATHAM
Louisa
  Love 1781 w.
STATLER
Frederick
  Lewis 1744 i.
STATON
Accomack
  Jos., Sr. 1711 i.
  Jos. 1725 i.
  Warrington 1761 w.
Amherst
  Wm. 1782 a.
  Thos. 1785 a.
Bedford
  Thomas 1778 w.
Essex
  John 1735 i.
  John 1737 i.

STAYTON
Accomack
Geo. 1795 i.
STEAL
Stafford
Jos. 1739 i.
STEARS
Spotsylvania
Abel 1778 w.
Abel 1794 a.
STEDMAN
Frederick
Lucas 1749 i.
STEED
Brunswick
Francis 1734 w.
Jno. 1789 w.
Norfolk
Robert 1773 w.
Northumberland
Thos. 1670 w.
STEEL
Amherst
Augustine 1790 w.
Augusta
Andrew 1764 w.
Saml. 1790 w.
Lancaster
Saml. 1706-7 nw.
Louisa
Wm. 1783 w.
Prince Edward
Robt. 1775 i.
Northampton
Francis 1720 w.
Danl. 1726 i.
Mary 1729 i.
Northumberland
Samuel 1772 w.
Jno. 1784 w.
Jane 1787 i.
Richmond
Saml. 1736 i.
Katherine 1741 i.
STEELE
Rockbridge
William 1791 i.
STEEL
Westmoreland
Jno. 1736 w.
Jno. 1743 w.
Margt. 1750 i.
Catron 1792 w.
STEELE
Augusta
David 1747 w.
Nathl. 1796 w.
Saml. 1796 w.
Saml. 1799 w.
Middlesex
Thos. 1716 i.

Northumberland
Jno. 1669 i.
Westmoreland
Chas. 1741 w.
Richd. 1772 i.
York
Mary 1767 w.
STEEP
Frederick
Frederick 1771 w.
STEEN
Frederick
Thomas 1786 i.
James 1792 i.
STEEP
Orange
Joseph 1735 a.
STEEPS
Frederick
Frederick 1772 i.
STEER
Northampton
Timothy 1712 i.
York
Thos. 1701 i.
STEERE
Northampton
Agnes 1690 w.
STEEVENS
Northampton
Jno. 1667 i.
STEGALL
Amelia
Jno. 1769 w.
STEGAR
Cumberland
Francis 1769 w.
Powhatan
Thos. H. 1798 w.
STEGER
Amelia
Hans Hinrick
1761 w.
STEGOR
Cumberland
Janett 1785 i.
STEMBRIDGE
Lunenburg
Wm. 1787 w.
STEMSON
Stafford
Wm. 1703 w.
STEMON
Bedford
Martin 1768 w.
STEP
Culpeper
John 1752 i.
STEPHANS
Accomack
Molly 1795 w.

STEPHEL
Loudoun
Martin 1789 i.
STEPHEN
Augusta
Robt. 1794 w.
Southampton
Thos. 1773 i.
STEPHENS
Accomack
Christopher 1751 w,
Jas. 1775 i.
Jno. 1791 i.
Jno. 1796 w.
Richd. 1799 w.
Amherst
Augustine 1795 w.
Berkeley
Richard 1797 i.
Essex
John 1724 i.
Fauquier
Robert 1773 w.
Frederick
Peter 1757 w.
Alexander 1768 w.
Lawrence 1776 w.
Joseph 1796 w.
Goochland
Joshua 1735 w.
Jno. 1738 i.
Isle of Wight
William 1738 i.
Elizabeth 1789 w.
King George
Lilly John [1780?]w.
Lancaster
Wm. 1679 i.
Jos. 1742 i.
Christopher 1748 i.
Wm. 1749 i.
Daniel 1753 i.
Richard 1762 w.
Richd. 1773 w.
Wm. 1779 i.
Loudoun
Giles 1773 w.
Richard 1785 w.
Ellener 1790 nw.
James 1798 w.
Samuel 1799 i.
Lunenburg
Thos. 1758 i.
Mecklenburg
Mary 1791 w.
Thos. 1795 i.
Northampton
Walker 1750 i.
Jno. 1784 w.
Jno. 1787 i.

Northumberland
John 1791 i.
Orange
Wm. 1767 w.
Prince William
Joseph 1798 w.
Rappahannock
Jno. 1677 w.
Surry
Edwd. 1740 i.
Westmoreland
Robt. 1726 w.
York
Phillips 1658 i.
Richd. 1661 w.
STEPHENSON
Amherst
Edwd. 1766 w.
Augusta
Wm. 1759 w.
Robt. 1772 w.
Adam 1791 i.
Berkeley
Hugh 1776 w.
Richard 1776 w.
Richard 1777 w.
Richard 1795 w.
Fauquier
James 1790 i.
Frederick
Richard 1765 w.
Isle of Wight
John 1737 w.
Wm. 1737 i.
Loudoun
Wm. 1796 i.
Jane 1797 nw.
Northampton
Nathl. 1786 i.
Shenandoah
Wm. 1784 a.
Wm. 1785 w.
Southampton
Katherine 1753 w.
Peter 1761 i.
Thos. 1770 w.
Ann 1774 w.
Geo. 1774 i.
Eliz. 1775 i.
Simon 1781 i.
Thos. 1788 w.
Sally 1799 w.
STEPP
Essex
Abraham 1714 i.
STEPPING
Northumberland
Danl. [1652] w.
STEPTO
Northumberland
Jno. 1741 w.

Wm. 1750 w.
Lancaster
Thomas 1744 i.
John 1755 w.
Wm. 1782 w.
STEPTOE
Northumberland
Anner 1757 w.
Westmoreland
Jas. 1757 w.
Geo. 1784 w.
STERLING
Accomack
Richd. 1710 i.
Jno. 1771 i.
Wm. 1775 w.
Wm. 1782 i.
Richd. 1787 w.
Richd. 1789 i.
Northampton
Wm. 1698 w.
Washington
Edwd. 1792 i.
STERN
Amelia
Anne 1773 w.
Tabitha 1786 w.
Washington
Frederick 1779 i.
Leonard 1782 i.
Richmond
Francis 1713 w.
STEUART
Bath
Wm. 1797 w.
Cumberland
Alex. 1791 w.
Fairfax
James 1781 w.
Andrew 1778 w.
Louisa
Garret 1752 w.
Middlesex
Hugh 1732 w.
York
Eliz. 1737 w.
STEVENS
Accomack
Wm. 1684 w.
John 1789 w.
Bedford
Thos. Jr. 1779 i.
Charlotte
Geo. 1767 i.
Cumberland
John 1763 w.
Halifax
James 1795 w.
Isle of Wight
Jno. 1784 w.
Jno. 1785 i.

Elizabeth 1790 i.
Lancaster
Richd. 1728 w.
Hannah 1741 w.
Middlesex
Richd. 1705 a.
Jno. 1751 i.
Richd. 1759 w.
Jno. 1782 i.
Prince George
Jno. 1720 w.
Spotsylvania
Chas. 1727 w.
Jeremiah 1772 w.
Stafford
Saml. 1733 i.
Surry
Richd. 1662 w.
York
Wm. 1778 w.
Ann 1748 w.
STEVENSON
Augusta
Adam 1760 a.
Jno. 1770 a.
Thos. 1785 w.
Brunswick
Wm. 1783 i.
Cumberland
Jno. 1763 i.
Jno. 1772 w.
Fauquier
William 1790 i.
Frederick
James 1762 a.
Isle of Wight
John 1726 w.
John 1737 w.
Lunenburg
Thos. 1795 w.
Northampton
Nathl. 1782 w.
Powhatan
Saml. 1780 i.
York
Wm. 1778 w.
Wm. 1784 w.
Wm. 1786 i.
STEWARD
Accomack
Danl. 1728 i.
Danl. 1752 i.
Bedford
James 1784 w.
Chesterfield
Sarah 1783 i.
Culpeper
Joseph 1785 w.
Frederick
Alexander 1758 w.

King George
Jno. 1769 w.
Price 1794 **w.**
Lancaster
Jno. 1727 i.
Louisa
Catherine 1761 w.
Geo. 1776 w.
Norfolk
John 1710 a.
Pittsylvania
Jas. 1777 i.
Prince William
William 1742 i.
Richmond
Jno. 1740 nw.
Spotsylvania
Chas. 1750 a.
Jno. 1785 a.
Surry
Jno. 1705 w.
Hannah 1768 **w.**
Jno. 1792 w.
York
Jno. 1721 w.
STEWART
Accomack
Andrew 1745 w.
Sarah 1756 w.
Benj. 1767 i.
Jas. 1767 i.
Levin 1784 w.
Geo. 1789 i.
Augusta
Jas. 1757 a.
Jas. 1758 a.
Archibald 1761 **w.**
Jas. 1764 i.
David 1767 w.
Wm. 1768 w.
Jno. 1771 w.
Jas. 1772 a.
Jas. 1775 a.
Jno. 1778 i.
Jas. 1779 i.
Berkeley
George 1792 w.
John 1799 w.
James 1765 i.
James 1767 w.
Chas. 1777 w.
Chesterfield
Edwd. 1780 i.
Culpeper
Robert 1790 i.
Cumberland
Jno. 1774 w.
Jno. 1787 w.
Alex. 1797 i.
Essex
Patrick 1794 i.

Fauquier
James 1781 w.
Frederick
Alexander 1760 i.
Greensville
John 1783 w.
Thomas 1791 w.
Henrico
Jno. 1706 i.
Jno., Sr. 1707 i.
Jno. 1714 w.
King George
Chas. 1764 i.
Loudoun
Daniel 1799 i.
Louisa
Robt. 1791 i.
Mecklenburg
Martha 1780 w.
Norfolk
Robert 1723 w.
Robert 1747 nw.
John 1752 w.
Joseph 1753 w.
Andrew, Jr. 1785 w.
Andrew 1789 w.
Andrew 1791 i.
James 1798 i.
Northumberland
Jas. 1745 i.
Jas. 1746 i.
Prince Edward
George 1766 i.
Richmond
Wm. 1717 i.
Southampton
Benj. 1795 w.
Spotsylvania
Chas. 1784 a.
Surry
Richd. 1759 a.
Jno. 1786 w.
James 1789 i.
Elizabeth 1792 i.
Jno. 1795 i..
Wm. 1795 i.
Sussex
Mourning 1788 w.
Richd. 1798 w.
Westmoreland
Jno. 1702 i.
STHRESHLY
Essex
Thomas 1735 w.
Thomas 1737 i.
STICIKAR
Accomack
Jas. 1724 w.
STICKLEY
Frederick
John 1770 w.

Shenandoah
Benjamin 1796 **w.**
Jacob 1798 i.
STIEN
Frederick
James 1785 w.
STIFF
Middlesex
Thomas 1710 w.
Jacob 1762 w.
Jas. 1790 w.
STIFFLER
Loudoun
Martin 1789 w.
STIGLAR
King George
Benj. 1777 w.
STIGLER
Frederick
James 1796 i.
King George
Jas. 1765 w.
STILES
Chesterfield
Jno. 1778 w.
Henrico
Wm. 1745 i.
Isle of Wight
John [1652]w.
STILL
Amelia
Geo. 1779 w.
Pittsylvania
Patrick 1774 i.
STIMPSON
Pittsylvania
Jeremiah 1777 w.
STIMSON
Essex
John 1697 i.
STINESYFER
Culpeper
John 1757 w.
John 1761 i.
STINNETT
Amherst
Benj. 1764 w.
STINSON
Fauquier
James 1789 w.
STIP
Berkeley
Peter 1782 i.
STIPP
Berkeley
Martin 1795 w.
STIRLING
Princess Anne
Jno. 1720 w.

STITH
Brunswick
Drury 1740 i.
Drury 1771 w.
Elizabeth 1771 w.
Drury 1789 w.
Edmunds 1789 w.
Buckner 1791 lw.
King George
Robt. 1791 w.
Northampton
Griffin, Sr. 1784 w.
Griffen 1794 w.
Wm. 1794 w.
Surry
Eliz. 1774 w.
STIVER
Frederick
David 1746 a.
STOAKES
Essex
John 1701 i.
Rappahannock
Wm. 1674 w.
Sussex
Saml. 1773 a.
Thos. 1777 i.
York
Francis 1659 i.
STOAKLEY
Northampton
Jno. 1716 i.
STOAKES
Essex
William 1719 w.
STOATT
Northampton
David 1708 w.
STOBO
Norfolk
Jacob 1794 w.
Jacob 1797 i.
STOCK
York
Richd. 1671 i.
STOCKBRIDGE
Shenandoah
Herbert 1778 a.
STOCKDELL
Essex
Philip 1737 w.
Madison
John 1794 a.
STOCKELY
Accomack
Francis 1698 w.
STOCKLEY
Accomack
Jno. 1737 w.
Jos. 1748 w.
Rebecca 1749 w.

Jos. 1760 w.
Ezebel 1761 w.
Naomi 1762 w.
Alex. 1763 w.
Chas. 1764 w.
Jos. 1769 w.
Anne 1771 w.
Jos. 1772 i.
Nathl. 1773 w.
Northampton
Francis 1655 w.
Jno. 1736 w.
Anne 1771 w.
Thos. 1736 w.
Francis 1744 w.
Ann 1746 i.
Woodman 1748 i.
Wm. 1756 w.
Francis 1777 i.
Frances 1777 i.
STOCKLY
Accomack
Jno. 1673 w.
Wm. 1686 w.
Chas. 1719 w.
Thos. 1719 w.
Chas. 1737 i.
Hannah 1739 w.
Jno. 1739 i.
Eyre 1741 i.
Francis 1741 w.
Christopher 1744 i.
Elias 1758 i.
Thos. 1768 w.
Naomi 1769 w.
Elijah 1778 w.
Nehemiah 1778 w
Alex 1787 w.
Wm. 1790 w.
Kendall 1796 w.
Northampton
Jno. 1712-13 w.
Jno. 1736 i.
STOCKMAN
Frederick
Jacob 1765 i.
STOCKSLAGER
Shenandoah
Daniel 1790 i.
STOCKTON
Albemarle
Joseph 1762 w.
Richd. 1775 w.
Thos., Sr. 1783 w.
Bedford
Wm. 1795 w.
Frederick
Robert 1772 i.
Robert 1785 i.

STODGHIL
Orange
James 1753 i.
STODGHILL
Essex
James 1784 w.
Goochland
Jno. 1773 w.
STOE
Charlotte
Joel 1781 w.
Pittsylvania
Joel 1784 i.
STOKELEY
Northampton
Thos. 1736 i.
Jacob 1772 i.
STOKES
Amelia
Frances 1752 w.
Brunswick
Silvanus 1778 w.
Charles City
Jno. 1768 w.
Essex
Richd. 1711 w.
Richd. 1728 i.
Thomas 1760 i.
John 1762 i.
Halifax
Chas. 1780 w.
Silvanus 1783 w.
Lunenburg
Eliz. 1751 w.
Young 1770 w.
Allen 1787 w.
David 1794 w.
Sterling 1794 i.
David, Sr. 1797 i.
Mecklenburg
David 1798 i.
David, Jr. 1799 i.
Pittsylvania
Sylvanus 1798 w.
Surry
Silvanus 1748 w.
Sussex
Jno. 1764 w.
Silvanus 1766 w.
Saml. 1771 w.
Sarah 1772 i.
Cecelia 1786 w.
Cecelia 1789 w.
York
Christopher 1646 w.
STOKLY
Accomack
Christopher 1728 w.
STOLE
Norfolk
Barbara 1765 w.

STONE
Amelia
Wm. 1749 i.
Bedford
Stephen 1778 i.
Micajah 1799 w.
Brunswick
Thos. 1795 w.
Campbell
Wm. 1799 w.
Charles City
Jno. 1772 w.
Chesterfield
Danl. 1774 w.
Culpeper
Simon 1782 i.
Fairfax
John 1780 i.
Samuel 1785 w.
Eli 1792 w.
Fluvanna
Wm. 1778 w.
Frances 1791 i.
Halifax
Richd. 1761 i.
Henrico
Thos. 1781 w.
Thos. 1784 i.
Wm. 1786 w.
Wm. 1788 i.
Henry
William 1796 w.
Eusabius 1798 i.
King George
Wm. 1740 i.
Francis 1749 i.
Sarah 1752 a.
Geo. 1772 a.
Wm. 1772 w.
Mary 1776 a.
Lunenburg
Wm. 1761 i.
Wm. 1791 i.
Richd. 1797 w.
Mecklenburg
Elijah 1771 i.
Thos. 1779 i.
Jno., Sr. 1782 w.
Mary 1795 w.
Pittsylvania
Saml. 1794 i.
Prince Edward
Thos. 1760 i.
Princess Anne
Jno. 1765 w.
Eliz. 1772 w.
John 1784 i.
Lemuel 1784 w.
Prince William
Francis 1740 i.
Francis 1741 i.

Thomas 1791 w.
Richmond
Wm. 1707 w.
Francis 1716 i.
Sarah 1717 w.
Joshua 1719 i.
Wm. 1772 w.
Ann 1774 w.
Joshua 1775 w.
Joshua 1777 i.
Thos., Jr. 1785 w.
Thos. 1786 i.
Stafford
Jno. 1750 i.
Barton 1786 w.
Westmoreland
Thos. 1718 w.
Jos. 1771 w.
York
Jas. 1647 i.
Wm. 1729-30 w.
Sarah 1730 w.
STONEBANKS
Goochland
Jno. 1749 i.
STONER
Cumberland
Danl. 1762 w.
Frederick
Woolrich 1768 i.
York
Thos. 1715 i.
STONEHAM
Lancaster
Henry, Sr. 1713 w.
Henry 1738 w.
John 1782 i.
STONEHOUSE
Westmoreland
Thos. 1736 i.
Eliz. 1742 w.
STONHAM
Lancaster
Wm. 1750-1 w.
STONUM
Lancaster
Jno. 1717 w.
Henry 1770 i.
Richmond
Wm. 1719 i.
Geo. 1784 i.
Wm. 1791 w.
STOOP
Rockbridge
Robert 1797 w.
STOPPER
Westmoreland
Christopher 1691 w.
STORER
Chesterfield
Jno. 1755 w.

STORIES
Princess Anne
Eliz. 1764 i.
STORKE
King George
Francis 1799 w.
Stafford
Wm. 1733 i.
Westmoreland
Wm. 1677 w.
Jno. 1758 i.
STORRS
Henrico
Joshua 1783 w.
Joshua 1786 w.
Susanna 1789 i.
Southampton
Thos. 1771 i.
STORY
Augusta
Thos. 1777 w.
Essex
James 1698 i.
Isle of Wight
John 1681 w.
Lawrence 1710 w.
Thomas 1727 w.
Orange
Jno. 1744 a.
Princess Anne
Thos. 1763 i.
Richmond
Jas. 1716 i.
Southampton
Danl. 1753 i.
Jas. 1784 w.
STOTSLAGER
Shenandoah
Alexander 1780 i.
STOTT
Accomack
Danl. 1752 i.
Bedford
John 1778 i.
Lancaster
Thos. 1671 w.
Bryan 1704-5 w.
Jas. 1710 i.
Bryan 1729 i.
Luke 1734 w.
John 1746 i.
Thomas 1747 w.
James 1751 i.
John 1762 w.
Wm. 1763 i.
William 1781 w.
Thomas 1786 w.
Richard 1788 i.
Elizabeth 1791 w.
Northampton
Henry 1692 w.

Jonathan 1699 i.
Jonathan 1735 w.
Danl. 1736 w.
Henry 1738 i.
Nehemiah 1751 w.
Wm. 1752 w.
David 1759 w.
Wm. 1760 w.
Jno. 1764 w.
David, Jr. 1765 w.
Jonathan 1767 w.
Mary 1769 w.
Jonathan 1778 w.
Jno. 1781 w.
Jonathan 1783 w.
Elias 1784 w.
David 1795 w.
Teackle 1799 w.
Northumberland
Stephen 1757 i.
Richmond
Bryant 1768 w.
Raleigh 1772 w.
Robt. 1795 w.
York
Jno. 1748 w.
STOTTS
Orange
Jno. Michael 1741 a.
STOUT
Culpeper
Abel 1797 i.
Frederick
Daniel 1770 w.
Harrison
Bonam 1791 i.
Ezekiel 1795 w.
STOVALL
Amherst
Geo., Jr. 1779 a.
James 1787 w.
Bedford
John 1778 w.
Campbell
Geo., Jr. 1782 w.
Geo. 1786 w.
Henry
Thomas 1792 i.
Mecklenburg
Thos. 1772 w.
Powhatan
Bartho. 1777 a.
Bartho. 1796 w.
STOVEALL
Goochland
Wm. 1736 i.
STOVER
Augusta
Isaac 1764 a.
Frederick
Jacob 1779 i.

Franklin
Henry 1798 w.
Orange
Jno. Casper 1734 w.
Jacob 1741 a.
Shenandoah
Elizabeth 1791 i.
Peter 1799 w.
STOWE
Charlotte
Mathew 1782 w.
Joel 1792 i.
STOWELL
Northumberland
Ann 1723 w.
STOWERS
Henrico
Jno. 1694 w.
Richmond
Saml. 1786 w.
Westmoreland
Jno. 1751 i.
Wm. 1757 i.
Saml. 1771 w.
STRACHAN
Henrico
Peter 1793 i.
Lancaster
Jas. 1710 w.
STRAHAN
York
Adam 1667 w.
STRAITON
Lancaster
James 1749 i.
STRANGE
Campbell
Nathl. 1799 i.
Brunswick
Owen 1794 w.
Campbell
Nathl. 1799 i.
Cumberland
Joseph 1749 w.
Essex
George 1775 w.
Powhatan
Thos. 1784 i.
STRANGWIDGE
Northampton
Wm. 1656 w.
STRATFORD
Isle of Wight
William 1669 nw.
STRATON
Lancaster
Jas. 1739 w.
Norfolk
Henry 1679 w.

STRATTON
Accomack
Jno. 1697 w.
Eliz. 1707 w.
Bedford
Henry 1799 w.
Chesterfield
Thos. 17— i.
Thos. 1773 w.
Thos. 1775 w.
Henrico
Martha 1692 w.
Edwd. 1698 w.
Edwd. 1731 i.
Northampton
Thos. 1666 w.
Thos. 1701 w.
Benj. 1717 w.
Jno. 1751 w.
Thos. 1754 w.
Benj. 1760 i.
Nathl. 1770 i.
Elishe 1780 w.
Elishe 1781 i.
Benj. 1784 i.
Benj., Sr. 1784 w.
Jno., Sr. 1795 w.
Powhatan
Wm. 1780 w.
Richd. 1796 i.
Judith 1797 i.
Stafford
Benoni 1751 i.
STRAUGHAN
Northumberland
Jas. 1741 i.
Jas. 1742 i.
Winifred 1745-6 i.
David 1763 w.
Richd. 1779 w.
STRAUGHAIUN
Stafford
Hugh 1745 i.
STRECHBURY
Loudoun
Richard 1763 i.
STRETCHLEY
Lancaster
Alice 1701 w.
STRECKLEY
Frederick
John 1771 i.
STREEP
Norfolk
John 1765 w.
STREET
Amherst
Anthony 1788 w.
Essex
Henry 1784 w.
Katherine 1791 w.

Halifax
Joseph 1782 w.
Henrico
Danl. 1737 i.
Wm. 1788 w.
Isle of Wight
John 1711 w.
Maddison 1732 w.
Middlesex
Richd. 1744 w.
Richd. 1750 i.
STREETE
Richmond
Henry 1722 i.
Ann 1726 i.
Henry 1726 nw.
STREETMAN
Loudoun
Martin 1778 i.
STRESHLEY ,
Essex
Thos. 1735 w.
Lancaster
Jno. 1698 w.
STRETTON
Essex
Thomas 1705 i.
Northumberland
Thos. 1711 ab.
STRIBLING
Frederick
William 1749 i.
Taliaferro 1774 w.
William 1794 i.
King George
Jno. 1738 i.
Benj. 1752 i.
Benj. 1754 i.
Stafford
Wm. 1765 i.
STRIBLINGE
Northampton
Christopher 1669 w.
STRICKLER
Augusta
Abraham 1746 i.
Shenandoah
Jacob 1784 a.
Abraham 1786 a.
Benj. 1795 a.
Jos. 1795 w.
STRICKLIN
Isle of Wight
Samuel 1720 w.
STRICKLAND
Isle of Wight
Mathew 1730 w.
STRIDER
Berkeley
Isaac 1794 w.

STRIKLER
Hardy
Joshua 1796 w.
STIRIN
Princess Anne
Geo. 1779 w.
STRINGER
Accomack
Thos. 1747 w.
Jacob 1761 w.
Thos. 1764 w.
Elisha 1767 w.
Jno. 1769 i.
Fereby 1779 w.
Smart 1781 w.
Rachel 1786 w.
Benj. 1797 w.
Chesterfield
Jno. 1783 w.
Middlesex
Danl. Sr. 1790 w.
Northampton
Jno. 1689 w.
Jno. 1698 w.
Hillary 1721-2 w.
Jacob 1737 w.
Hillary 1744 i.
Jno. 1751 w.
Elisha 1760 w.
Jno., Jr. 1761 w.
Hillary 1774 w.
Wm. 1774 w.
Hillary, Sr. 1791 w.
Thos. 1793 w.
Jno., Sr. 1795 w.
Jno., Jr. 1796 i.
STRINGFELLOW
King George
Wm. 1746 i.
Reuben 1770 w.
STRINGFIELD
Isle of Wight
John 1790 i.
STRIP
Accomack
Wm. 1703 w.
STRIPE
Princess Anne
Wm. 1723 i.
STRIPLING
Frederick
Thos. 1755 i.
Stafford
Joel 1739 i.
STRIPES
Princess Anne
Eustice 1775 w.
Lewis 1779 w.
STRODE
Berkeley
Jeremiah 1785 w.

James 1795 w.
STRONG
Essex
John 1718 w.
Norfolk
Edwd. 1780 i.
STROOP
Berkeley
Elizabeth 1781 w.
Henry 1787 w.
Frederick
William 1767 i.
STROOPE
Frederick
Wm. 1767 i.
STROTHER
Culpeper
Francis 1752 w.
James 1761 i.
Benj. 1763 i.
Geo. 1767 w.
Francis 1777 w.
Ann 1788 w.
John 1795 w.
Fauquier
James, Sr. 1778 i.
King George
Wm. 1726 i.
Wm. 1733 i.
Robt. 1735 i.
Wm. 1738 i.
Benj. 1752 i.
Benj., Sr. 1752 w.
George 1761 w.
Richd. 1761 w.
Geo. 1763 i.
Jos. 1763 i.
Jos., Jr. 1763 w.
Jos. 1766 w.
Enoch 1772 a.
Wm. 1773 w.
Nicholas 1779 w.
Tabitha 1790 w.
Orange
Jeremiah 1741 w.
Sarah 1774 w.
Richmond
Wm., Sr. 1702 w.
Jas. 1716 w.
Stafford
Jas. 1763 w.
Anthony 1766 w.
Eliza. 1785 i.
Westmoreland
Wm. 1750 nw.
Margt. 1799 w.
STROUD
Brunswick
Thos. 1739 w.
Joshua 1741 a.

Frederick
Edward 1749 i.
Mecklenburg
Jno. 1776 w.
Norfolk
Matthew 1756 w.
Mary 1770 w.
York
Jos. 1696 i.
Jos. 1782 w.
STROUP
Frederick
Wm. 1766 w.
STROWD
Loudoun
Saml. 1765 w.
STRUPE
Ohio
Conrad 1787 pw.
STUART
Accomack
Andrew 1697 w.
Amelia
Gilbert 1758 w.
Wm. 1774 w.
Jno. 1777 w.
Mary 1781 w.
Wm. 1782 i.
Amherst
Jno. 1784 w.
Augusta
Thos. 1789 w.
Jno. 1790 w.
Jno. 1792 w.
Brunswick
Charles 1753 w.
Anne 1754 i.
Chesterfield
Edwd. 1761 w.
Sarah 1782 w.
Culpeper
Robert 1789 w.
Halifax
Chas. 1780 w.
Thos. 1784 i.
King George
Wm. 1735 i.
Wm. 1798 w.
Wm. G. 1798 i..
Lancaster
Charles 1752 i.
Middlesex
Jno. 1730 i.
Stafford
Alex. 1743 i.
David 1748 w.
Jas. 1758 i.
Sussex
Jno. 1791 i.
Washington
Thos. 1798 i.

STUBBLEFIELD
Culpeper
Edwd. 1750 w.
Thos. 1758 w..
Jas. 1777 w.
Fairfax
Thos. 1785 i.
Spotsylvania
Geo. 1752 w.
Catherine 1777 w.
STUBBS
Henrico
Thos. 1704 w.
STUBBLEFIELD
Frederick
Benj. 1795 i.
STUCKBERRY
Fairfax
Robt. 1751 i.
STUCKEY
Isle of Wight
Simon 1760 i.
Edmund 1791 i.
York
Edmd. 1765 w..
STUCKY
Richmond
Job Sims 1799 w.
STULZNAKER
Augusta
Henry 1773 i.
STUMP
Bedford
John 1787 w.
Hardy
Katherine 1794 w.
STURDIVANT
Brunswick
Sarah 1797 w.
Lunenburg
Jno. 1797 i.
Surry
Matthew 1728 i.
Sussex
Holam 1757 w.
Abner 1765 i.
Henry 1772 w.
Jno. Anderson
1777 w.
Matthew 1782 w.
Jno. 1796 i.
Allen 1799 w.
STURDY
Isle of Wight
Robt. 1702 w.
Stafford
Wm. 1700 w.
STURGEON
Southampton
Jno. 1780 w.

STURGES
Accomack
Eliz. 1685 w.
Danl. 1726 i.
STURGIS
Accomack
Jno. 1684 w.
Richd. 1696 w.
Richd. Sr. 1744 nw.
Danl. 1751 i.
Wm. 1751 i.
Wm. 1755 i.
Adah 1767 w.
Absolum 1773 w.
Susannah 1773 w.
Richd. 1795 w.
Abraham D. 1799 i.
Northampton
Jacob 1752 w.
Danl.. 1755 i.
STURMAN
Campbell
Valentine 1789 w.
Fairfax
Wm. 1746 a.
Westmoreland
Ann 1654 w.
Richd. 1669 w.
Richd. 1691 w.
Jno. 1723 w.
Wm. 1723 w.
Thos. 1737 w.
Thos. 1758 i.
Richd. 1762 i.
Foxhall 1771 i.
Elliott 1792 w.
STWORD
Accomack
Danl. 1727 w.
STYLES
York
Saml. 1728 w.
STYNSON
Frederick
Jas. 1763 i.
SUBBLETT
Charlotte
Wm. 1780 w.
SUBLET
Charlotte
Abram, Sr. 1782 w,
Wm. 1782 i.
SUBLETT
Charlotte
Abraham 1782 i.
Powhatan
Peter 1783 i.
SUCKETT
Essex
Geo. 1693 w.

SUDARTH
Amherst
Wm. 1761 w.
SUDBURY
Chesterfield
Ezekiel 1757 w.
SUDDARTH
Stafford
Henry 1732 i.
Thos. 1737 i.
Robt. 1762 w.
SUDDATH
Fairfax
Benj. 1792 w.
Benj. 1794 i.
SUDDEARTH
Fluvanna
Manuel 1795 w.
SUDDUTH
Fauquier
Wm. 1795 w.
Stafford
Jas. 1753 w.
SUEL
Prince William
Margaret 1779 w.
SUELL
Berkeley
John 1793 w.
SUETER
Southampton
Thos. 1782 i.
SUGARS
Isle of Wight
John 1727 w.
SUGERT
Shenandoah
Zackaria 1796 w.
SUGG
Norfolk
Geo. 1734 w.
SUGGET
Northampton
Jno. 1774 i.
Richmond
Edgcum 1724 i.
SUGGETT
Richmond
Jno. 1772 w.
Jno. 1773 i.
Elizabeth 1784 w.
SUGGITT
Richmond
Jno. 1704 w.
Thos. 1713 i.
Jas. 1734 i.
Thos. 1742 w.
Edgecombe 1753 w
Elizabeth 1788 i.
Jno. 1788 i.

SUGGS
Norfolk
Wm. 1708 w.
Wm. 1718 i.
Jos. 1764 w.
Moses 1791 w.
SUILEVANT
Northumberland
Danl. 1704-5 w.
Danl. 1721 w.
SUILLIVANT
Essex
Timothy 1734 w.
SUITER
Montgomery
Alexander 1787 i.
SULIVAN
Botetourt
John 1783 i.
SULLENGER
Essex
Peter 1706-7 i.
SULLEVANT
Halifax
Chas. 1777 w.
SULLINS
Halifax
Richd. 1771 i.
Josiah 1773 w.
SULLIVAN
Amelia
Ann 1742 w.
Brunswick
Michael 1737 w.
Essex
Daniel 1760 w.
Fairfax
Danl. 1797 a.
Fauquier
George 1779 i.
King George
Francis 1765 i.
Northumberland
Jos. 1742 i.
Peter 1747 w.
Cornelious 1761 w.
Charles 1767 w.
Moses 1763 i.
Dennis 1789 i.
Princess Anne
Jno., Jr. 1697 i.
Jno. 1698 w.
Jno., Sr. 1698 i.
Spotsylvania
Nich. 1752 a.
Wythe
Morris 1790 nw.
SULLIVANT
Brunswick
Michael 1772 i.

Charlotte
Wm. 1769 w.
Wm. 1782 i.
Jno. 1797 i.
Halifax
Chas. 1799 i.
King George
Darby 1729 i.
Wm. 1791 w.
Lancaster
Dennis 1747 i.
Joseph 1782 i.
Lunenburg
John 1750 w.
Princess Anne
Dinah 1749 w.
Jno. 1761 i.
Westmoreland
Darby 1699 w.
York
Timothy 1731 i.
SUMBERS
Accomack
Robt. 1759 w.
SUMMER
Shenandoah
George 1787 i.
Stafford
Jos. 1734 i.
SUMMERELL
Isle of Wight
Thomas 1737 i.
SUMMERRELL
Isle of Wight
Thomas 1739 w.
John 1746 w.
Southampton
Gwin 1763 i.
Jno. 1784 w.
Jacob 1795 w..
SUMMERS
Fairfax
John 1788 w.
Wm. 1799 w.
Frederick
Michael 1784 w.
Middlesex
Jno. 1702 w.
Northumberland
Wm. 1761 i.
Shenandoah
Michael 1782 w.
SUMMERTON
King George
Wm. 1744 i
SUMMERVILLE
Surry
James 1762 i.
Westmoreland
Jno. 1717 w.

SUMNER
Surry
Francis 1677 a.
SUMPTER
Chesterfield
Jno. 1798 i.
SUMTER
Louisa
Wm. 1752 w.
SUMERVOLT
Frederick
Andrew 1765 i.
SUNAFRANK
Loudoun
Jacob 1797 i.
SUNDERMAN
Lunenburg
Abraham 1764 w.
SUNNINGBROOK
Northumberland
Florentine 1653 i.
SURBER
Frederick
Henry 1754 i.
Shenandoah
Henry 1778 w.
Henry 1795 i..
SURBEY
Isle of Wight
John 1712 i.
SURGEON
Middlesex
Jno. 1767 i.
SURGINOR
Isle of Wight
John 1728 w.
SURLOCK
Richmond
Wm. 1740 i.
SUTE
Prince William
Edward 1739 w.
SUTER
Southampton
Jno. Sr. 1788 w.
Wm. 1795 w.
Arthur 1798 i.
SUTHERLAND
Norfolk
John 1773 i.
Spotsylvania
Jno. 1765 w..
Jno. (2?) 1765 a.
Westmoreland
Jno. 1720 nw.
SUTHERN
Richmond
Thos. 1704 w.
SUTTEN
Northumberland
Wm. 1755 i.

Elizabeth 1780 w.
Thos. 1786 w.
SUTTENFIELD
Bedford
John 1781 i.
SUTTLE
King George
Amy 1792 w.
Prince William
Strother 1792 w.
Westmoreland
Thos. 1752 i.
Benj. 1778 i.
SUTTLES
King George
Wm. 1782 a.
SUTTON
Essex
John 1716 i.
Middlesex
Rowland 1782 w.
Norfolk
Ashbury 1761 w.
Northumberland
Richd. 1712 w.
Jno. 1742 w.
John 1750-1 i.
Richd. 1754 i.
Lazarus 1771 w.
Isaac 1786 w.
Moses 1796 w.
Orange
Saml. 1784 i.
Spotsylvania
Amey 1738 w.
Westmoreland
Richd. 1747-8 w.
Jas. 1754 i.
Mary 1755 w.
Wm.. 1786 i.
Elijah 1787 i.
Josiah 1792 w.
Jesse 1794 i.
Josiah 1794 i.
Jacob 1799 i.
SWAFFER
Frederick
Mary 1763 i.
SWAIN
Northumberland
Jos. 1793 i.
SWAINE
Charles City
James 1791 i.
Lancaster
Jno. 1690 i.
SWAN
Lancaster
Alex. 1710 w.
Mary 1721 w.
Jno. 1722 i.

Surry
Matthew 1702 w.
SWANEY
Norfolk
Marg. 1790 w.
SWANN
Frederick
Philip 1789 w.
Henrico
Saml. 1799 w.
Powhatan
Thompson 1779 w.
Thos. T. 1799 i.
SWANSON
Amherst
Jno. 1799 w.
Brunswick
Edwd. 1745 i.
Jno. 1783 i.
Joyse 1798 w.
Henry
John 1787 i.
Northumberland
Ann 1745 i.
Benj. Nice 1750-1 w.
John 1752 w.
Dennis 1755 w.
John 1755 w.
Winney 1757 i.
Denis 1760 w.
Aaron 1768 i.
Stephen 1773 w.
Ann 1783 w.
Stephen 1794 w.
SWART
Loudoun
Adrian 1799 i.
John 1798 w.
SWATLEY
Augusta
Mark 1773 i.
SWEARINGEN
Berkeley
Thomas 1780 w.
Thomas 1786 w.
Van 1788 w.
Van 1792 w.
Sarah 1799 w.
Frederick
Thomas 1760 w.
Thomas 1773 i.
Ohio
Vann 1794 w.
Zachariah 1799 w.
SWEATNHAM
Lancaster
Joshua 1703-4 w.
SWEENY
Norfolk
Lazarus 1734 i.

York
Eliz. 1729 w.
SWENEY
Pittsylvania
Moses 1785 w.
SWEET
King George
Henry 1736 i.
SWELLIVANT
Rappahannock
Dennis 1675 w.
SWENEY
York
Meritt 1764 i.
Danl. 1773 i.
SWENY
Norfolk
Samuel 1753 w.
Daniel 1761 w.
Charles 1763 i.
Ann 1767 w.
Samuel 1773 i.
York
Edmd. 1728 i.
SWEPSON
Mecklenburg
Richd., Sr. 1788 w.
SWETT
Isle of Wight
Conny 1767 i.
Surry
Robt. 1696 i.
SWIFT
Berkeley
Godwin 1798 w.
Hanover
Wm. 1734 i.
Louisa
Richard 1785 i.
Northumberland
John 1776 i.
William 1778 w.
Wm. 1785 w.
SWIGAR
Berkeley
Jacob 1775 w.
SWILL
Princess Anne
Jno. 1695 w.
SWILLE
Goochland
Nicolas 1735 w.
SWILLEVANT
Northumberland
Danl. 1747 w.
Rappahannock
Cornelius 1673 w.
SWILLIVAN
King George
Jno. 1764 a.

SWILLIVANT
King George
Wm. 1754 i.
SWILLS
Norfolk
Absolom 1798 i.
SWINDLER
Loudoun
Henry 1793 i.
SWINGLE
Berkeley
Peter 1798 i.
SWINK
Loudoun
Adam 1782 w.
SWINNEY
Chesterfield
Abraham 1770 w.
SWINTON
Northampton
Jas. 1737 i.
SWITZER
Botetourt
Henry 1798 w.
SWOOB
Augusta
Widow 1760 i.
SWORD
Frederick
William 1796 w.
Washington
Henry 1779 i.
SYBLEY
Fairfax
John 1754 a.
SYDNER
Frederick
Wiiliam T. 1798 i.
SYDNOR
Halifax
Epaphroditus 1783 w.
Henrico
Fortunatus 1783 w.
Lancaster
Fortunatus 1723 w.
Ruth 1740 w.
Wm. 1751 w.
William 1794 w.
Moore 1798 w.
Northumberland
Anthony 1779 w.
Fortunatus 1781 w.
Eliz. 1785 w.
Jno. 1791 w.
Richmond
Anthony 1755 i.
Epaphroditus 1756 w.
Anthony 1759 w.
Elizabeth 1778 w.
Anthony 1789 w.
Dewanna 1789 w.

Richd. 1795 w.
Richd. 1799 i.
SYFRETT
Frederick
Laurence 1796 i.
SYKES
Isle of Wight
Thomas 1731 i.
Mary 1793 w.
Orange
Francis 1771 i.
Prince George
Bernard 1718 i
Sussex
Wm. 1776 i.
SYMMONS
Northumberland
Eliz. 1663 w.
SYMONDS
Northampton
Jno. 1636 w.
SYMONS
Henrico
Robt. 1700 w.
Northumberland
Francis 1662 w.
SYMOOR
Lunenburg
Thos. 1749 w.
SYMPSON
Botetourt
Solomon 1785 w.
SYMES
Louisa
Wm. 1769 i.
SYMS
Brunswick
Adam 1733 w.
Louisa
Robt. 1748 w.

T

TABB
Amelia
Thos. 1769 w.
Berkeley
Robert 1776 i.
Cumberland
Thomas 1782 w.
Mecklenburg
Jno. 1776 i.
Norfolk
William 1764 w.
Jno. 1784 i.
York
Wm. 1721 w.
Eliz. 1731 w.
Edwd. 1732 w.
Edwd., Jr. 1741 w.
Edmd. 1762 w.

Edwd. 1771 w.
Wm. 1785 i.
Mary 1790 w.
Bailey Seaton 1793 i.
TABER
Henrico
Wm. 1713 w.
TABERNER
Isle of Wight
Joshua 1656 w.
TABOR
Norfolk
Thos. 1700-1 w.
John 1717-19 i.
TABOROR
Isle of Wight
Thomas 1694 w.
TACKETT
Prince William
William 1783 w.
TADLOCK
Essex
Joshua 1722 i.
TAFF
Richmond
Peter 1716 i.
Eliz. 1746 w.
Saml. 1785 i.
TAGEY
Shenandoah
Jacob 1782 i.
TAILER
Northampton
Thos. 1710 i.
TAIT
Louisa
Jno. 1769 w.
Jas. 1793 i.
Lunenburg
Wm. 1751 w.
TAITE
Louisa
Jas. 1776 i.
Northumberland
Wm. 1767 w.
Wm. 1772 i.
TALBERT
Loudoun
Anne 1784 w.
Richmond
Saml. 1726 w..
TALBOT
Bedford
Matthew 1758 w.
Chas. 1779 w.
Jas. 1782 i.
Jas. 1784 i.
Jas. 1788 i.
Campbell
Chas. 1788 i.

Essex
Thos. 1698 i.
Norfolk
Sarah 1764 i.
Isaac 1774 w.
Wm. 1775 w.
Richmond
Catheron 1783 w.
Westmoreland
Jas. 1698 i.
TALBOTT
Chesterfield
Wm. 1765 w.
Haley 1797 w.
Peter 1798 w.
Frederick
Edward 1793 w.
King George
Mark 1758 w.
Loudoun
Jos. 1798 w.
Norfolk
Keader 1752 w.
Jno. 1755 w.
Shadrack 1761 i.
Thos. 1777 w.
Wm. 1777 i.
Jno. 1799 i.
Prince George
Michael 1718 w.
Wm. 1719 i.
Richmond
Wm. 1713 i.
Westmoreland
Henry 1657 nw.
TALBUT
Fauquier
Jno. 1796 w.
TALBUTT
Fairfax
Daniel 1779 i.
Saml. 1779 i.
Loudoun
Jno. 1789 i.
Norfolk
Jacob 1732 w.
Jas. 1751 i.
Rappahannock
Wm. 1678 w.
Richmond
Benj. 1726 w.
Hannah 1729 i.
TALER
Accomack
Edwd. 1727 w.
Wm., Sr. 1774 w.
Henrico
Wm. 1790 w.
TALIAFERRO
Amherst
Chas. 1791 w.

Jno. B. 1795 w.
Zachariah 1797 w.
Essex
Francis 1710 i.
Eliz. 1717 i.
Jno. 1720 w.
Chas. 1726 i.
Chas. 1728 i.
Lawrence 1726 w.
Robt. 1726 w.
Zachariah 1745 w.
King George
Richd. 1727 i.
Jno. 1756 i.
Jno. 1798 i.
Orange
Lawrence 1798 w.
Wm. 1798 w.
Richmond
Richd. 1715 i.
Sarah 1718 w.
Spotsylvania
Robt. 1728 w.
Jno. 1744 w.
Jno. 1751 w.
Francis 1758 w.
Mary 1771 w.
Jno. 1751 w.
TALLARD
Augusta
Mark 1760 i.
TALLAUGH
Isle of Wight
Jas. 1744 i.
TALLETT
Surry
Geo. 1748 i.
TALLEY
Mecklenburg
Abraham 1767 i.
Jno. 1768 i.
Abraham 1784 w.
TALLION
Pittsylvania
Redmond 1785 w.
TALLY
Amelia
Jno. 1740 w.
Thos. 1780 w.
Tucker 1782 w.
Lodwick 1782 w.
Wm. 1794 w.
Bedford
Jas. 1776 i.
Halifax
Henry 1778 w.
TALOR
Augusta
Wm. 1767 w.

TANCEL
Westmoreland
Edwd. 1755 i.
TANCOCKE
Henrico
Eliz. 1703 w.
Philip 1703 w.
TANDY
Essex
Silvanus 1699 i.
Henry 1705 i.
Henry 1741 w.
Silvanus 1761 i.
TANKARD
Northampton
Jno. 1779 w.
TANKERSLEY
Charlotte
Jno. 1785 i.
King' George
Geo. 1758 w.
Richd. 1765 i.
Mary 1782 w.
TANKRED
Accomack
Jno. 1749 w.
Eliz. 1752 i.
Jno. 1752 i.
Wm. 1760 w.
Northampton
Jno. 1689 w.
Sarah 1718-19 w.
Wm. 1752 w.
TANER
Norfolk
Josiah 1757 i.
Princess Anne
Jno. 1785 w.
Jno. 1797 w.
TANNER
Albemarle
Mary 1760 w.
Amelia
Thos. 1765 w.
Edwd. 1770 w.
Lodwick 1773 w.
Branch 1793 w.
Branch [Jr.] 1794 w.
Field 1799 i.
Bedford
Michael 1777 w.
Nathl. 1781 w.
Chesterfield
Jos. 1757 w.
Harrison
Edward [17—] i.
Henrico
Jos. 1698 i.
Isle of Wight
Thomas 1666 i.
Madison
Christopher 1797 i.

Mecklenburg
Lewis 1766 i.
Norfolk
Danl. 1653 w.
Northampton
Paul 1709 w.
Pittsylvania
Anne 1794 i.
Floyd 1799 w.
Surry
Edwd. 1685 w.
Westmoreland
Thos. 1708 w.
Martha 1733 w.
TANNY
Halifax
Wm. 1769 w.
TAPP
Culpeper
Wm. 1785 i.
Wm. 1791 w.
Vincent 1791 w.
Frederick
Vincent 1752 i.
Northumberland
Wm. 1719 i.
TAPSCOT
Lancaster
Henry 1727 i.
Northumberland
Jas. 1770 w.
Henry 1781 w.
Edney 1782 w.
Mary 1791 w.
TARBACK
Northampton
Thos. 1712-13 w.
TARBERT
Princess Anne
Isaac 1731 w.
TARGEAR
Loudoun
Mary 1797 i.
TARKLESON
Northumberland
Tarkle 1742 w.
TARLETON
Isle of Wight
Roger 1729 w.
TARNEY
Norfolk
John 1783 i.
TARP
Prince William
John 1737 a.
TARPLEY
Brunswick
James 1781 w.
Chas. 1796 i.
Hosea 1796 i.
Charlotte
James 1792 w.

Wm. 1794 w.
Frederick
John 1753 i.
Lancaster
Elizabeth 1789 w.
Richmond
Jas. 1713 w.
Jno., Jr. 1736 i.
Jno. 1739 w.
Betty 1777 w.
York
Edwd. Ripping
1763 w.
TARPP
Prince William
John 1743 i.
TARRENT
Essex
Leonard 1718 w.
Mary 1749 i.
Henry
Leonard 1779 w.
TARRILL
Essex
Henry 1718 i.
TART
Norfolk
Elnathan 1702 w.
Eliz. 1710 a.
Elnathan 1717 i.
Alice 1723 w.
Jno. 1743 i.
Jas. 1765 i.
Enos. 1766 w.
Reubin 1775 i.
Mary 1778 w.
Wm. 1778 w.
Thos. 1778 w.
Mary 1779 i.
Thos. 1782 i.
Ann 1790 i.
Jno. 1795 i.
Jas. 1799 i.
TARTT
Norfolk
Thomas 1773 w.
TARVER
Surry
Thos. 1712 w.
TASKER
Westmoreland
Jno. 1654 w.
TASSEY
Frederick
James 1747 i.
TATAM
Prince George
Mary 1716 i.
Saml. 1715 i.
Nathl. 1719 w.

TATE
Augusta
Jas. 1781 w.
Bedford
Charles 1792 nw.
Campbell
Henry 1793 w.
Essex
Arthur 1764 i.
Frederick
Magnus 1749 i.
Onor 1750 i.
Louisa
Jas. 1776 w.
Wm. 1782 i.
Wm. 1784 a.
Zedekiah 1784 w.
Abigail 1792 w.
York
Jas. 1665 w.
TATEM
Norfolk
Nathl. 1739 w.
Ann 1744 i.
Trimagen 1762 w.
Nathl. 1771 w.
Dinah 1784 w.
Nathl. 1787 w.
Jno. 1788 i.
Wm. 1792 w.
Solomon 1797 i.
Solomon 1799 w.
Princess Anne
Anne 1768 w.
TATHAM
Accomack
Edmd. 1723 w.
Thos. 1776 w.
Thos. 1780 i.
Ezekiel 1791 w.
Richd. 1791 w.
Jno. 1797 w.
Jas. 1798 i.
TATHOM
Accomack
Esther 1786 w.
TATNALL
Lancaster
Thos. 1691 i.
TATUM
Brunswick
Edwd. 1744 w.
Peter 1755 i.
Peter 1772 i.
Jos. 1782 w.
Paul 1787 w.
Henry
Jesse 1790 i.
Northampton
Jno. 1725 w.
Southampton
John 1774 i.

Joshua 1775 w.
Surry
Edwd. 1739 w.
Christopher 1751 i.
Peter 1751 w.
Sussex
Jno. 1766 w.
Christopher 1769 w.
Thos. 1782 w.
TAUTEE
York
Wm. 1677 w.
TAVENER
Richmond
Jno. 1711 w.
TAVERNER
York
Gyles 1655 w.
Wm. 1721 w.
TAVENOR
York
Giles 1720 i.
Wm. 1751 w.
TAYLER
Accomack
Wm. 1687 w.
Thos. 1703 i.
Jno. 1721 w.
Essex
Daniel 1735 i.
Orange
Wm. 1737 a.
Rappahannock
Thos. 1687 w.
Richmond
Geo. 1706 w.
Rockbridge
Jas. 1791 i.
Stafford
Chas. 1730 i.
Surry
Richd. 1715 w.
Westmoreland
Wm. 1762 i.
TAYLOE
Lancaster
Jos. 1716 i.
Barbara 1726 w.
Wm. 1770 i.
Richmond
Wm. 1710 w.
———— 1718 i.
Jno. 1747 w.
Jno. 1779 w.
TAYLOR
Accomack
Walter 1672 w.
Saml. 1696 w.
Thos. 1696 w.
Jno. 1698 w.
Wm. 1698 i.
Jas. 1703 w.

Thos. 1708 w.
Jno. 1709 w.
Thos. 1709 w.
Elias 1717 w.
Elias 1717 nw.
Thos. 1723 i.
Saml. 1727 w.
Jas. 1728 i.
Thos. 1730 i.
Joshua 1731 i.
Chas. 1735 w.
Wm. 1741 i.
Elias 1743 nw.
Mary 1743 i.
Jno., Sr. 1744 w.
Wm. 1744 i.
Jos. 1745 w.
Nehemiah 1749 i.
Jno. 1751 w.
Jos. 1751 w.
Robt. 1752 i.
Sarah 1758 i.
Geo. 1760 w.
Abraham 1765 w.
Bartholomew 1766 w
Wm. 1768 i.
Jas. 1769 w.
Levin 1772 w.
Jno. 1774 w.
Thos. Teackle
1774 w
Levin 1775 w.
Jos. 1776 w.
Teackle 1776 w.
Chas. 1779 w.
Jas. 1779 w.
Jno. 1779 w.
Levin 1779 i.
Jno. 1780 w.
Saml. 1780 w.
Chas. 1783 i.
Saml., Sr. 1783 w.
Jno. 1784 w.
Pharoah 1784 w.
Wm. 1784 i.
Bartholomew 1785 w.
Molly 1786 w.
Mary 1788 i.
Jacob 1792 w.
Wm. 1792 i.
Danl. 1794 w.
Bartholomew 1795 w.
Deadamy 1795 i.
Edwd. 1795 i.
Geo. 1795 i.
Alex. 1796 w.
Ezekiel 1796 w.
Jno. 1796 i.
Saml. 1797 w.
Jacob 1798 w.
Alex 1798 i.
Abel 1799 w.

Iffiniah 1799 w.
Danl. 1799 i.
Amherst
Virginia 1795 a.
Augusta
Jno. 1747 i.
Jno. (2) 1747 i.
Thos. 1749 i.
Wm. 1749 i.
Jno. 1772 w.
Wm. 1778 w.
Bedford
Henry 1777 w.
Isaac 1778 w.
Berkeley
Isaac 1780 i.
Saml. 1786 w.
Jno. 1793 w.
Brunswick
Edwd. 1784 w.
Jos. 1794 i.
Charlotte
John 1790 w.
Culpeper
Benj., Jr. 1767 i.
Benj. 1776 w.
Cumberland
Jno. 1758 w.
Jas. 1773 w.
Jeremiah 1782 i.
Saml. 1792 i.
Essex
Robt. 1700 w.
Wm. 1735 w.
Mary 1737 w.
Richd. 1742 w.
Wm., Jr. 1742 i.
Wm. 1763 w.
Jos. 1769 w.
Jas. 1798 w.
Fairfax
Jno. 1748 w.
Saml. 1751 i.
Thos. 1777 w.
Henry 1784 i.
Fauquier
Henry 1792 i.
Frederick
Jacob 1760 w.
Richd. 1760 i.
Saml. 1762 w.
Benj. 1798 w.
Goochland
Chas. 1742 w.
Halifax
Jas. 1769 w.
Edwd. 1791 i.
Henrico
Thos. 1725 w.
Jno. 1727 i.
Mary 1727 w.
Michael 1736 w.

Matthew 1749 i.
Wm. 1755 i.
Thos. 1798 w.
Isle of Wight
Wm. 1677 nw.
Edwd. 1735 w.
Jno. 1785 w.
Geo. 1791 w.
King George
Wm. 1743 i.
Jno. 1748 i.
Henry 1751 i.
Geo. 1767 a. .
Lancaster
Jno. 1654 i.
Richd. 1683 i.
Thos. 1703 i.
Thos. 1718 w.
Jno. 1722 w.
Jno. 1728 i.
Jos. 1737 i.
Theriat 1738 i.
Thos. 1744-5 i.
Jno. 1746 i.
Moses 1748 w.
Jno. 1749-50 w.
Thos. 1751 w.
Eliz. 1751 w.
Edwd. 1758 w.
Isaac 1764 w.
Richd. 1774 w.
Richd. 1784 i.
Jno. 1785 i.
Richd. 1789 i.
Loudoun
Henry 1771 w.
Geo. 1789 w.
Wm. 1790 w.
Evan 1793 i.
Thos. 1797 w.
Louisa
Jno. T. 1776 w.
Geo. 1795 w.
Lunenburg
Danl. 1781 w.
Madison
Charles 1798 w.
Mecklenburg
Thos. 1772 w.
Wm. 1772 w.
Goodwyn 1786 w.
Jesse 1792 w.
Middlesex
Benj. 1723 w.
Eliz. 1765 a.
Wm. 1775 i.
Ann Chowning
1795 i.
Montgomery
Isaac 1781 w.
Norfolk
Sarah 1640 i.

Mary 1666 w.
Richd. 1678 i.
Margt. 1679 w.
Richd. 1679 w.
Theodore [1703] w.
Andrew 1718 w.
Richd. 1734 i.
Thos. 1744 w.
Jno. 1744-5 w.
Archibald 1746 w.
Thos. 1746-7 w.
Peter 1753 w.
Thos. 1763 w.
Wm. 1771 w.
Jno. 1772 w.
Margt. 1775 w.
Ann 1779 w.
Jas. 1782 w.
Sarah 1783 w.
Margt. 1785 w.
Richd. 1785 w.
Eliz. 1786 w.
Jno. 1787 i.
Thos. 1789 i.
Eliz. 1791 w.
Arthur 1795 w.
Jas. 1798 w.
Northampton
Elias 1640 i.
Philip 1646 i.
Stephen 1649 i.
Philip 1656 i.
Jno. 1680 i.
Paul 1730 i.
Wm. 1734 i.
Matilda 1745 i.
Jno. 1776 i.
Jno. 1777 i.
Will 1734 w.
Jas. 1783 w.
Thos. T. 1796 w.
Northumberland
Thos. 1721 i.
Jno. 1722-3 i.
Lazarus 1726-7 w.
Jno. 1727 w.
Thos. 1741 i.
Lazarus 1743-4 w.
Ann 1746 w.
Wm. 1746 w.
Aaron 1747 i.
Jno. 1751 w..
Thos. 1754 i.
Argil 1758 w.
Thos. 1758 i.
Jno. 1768 w.
Michael 1771 i.
Judith 1776 w.
Jos. 1782 w.
Wm. 1782 w.
Jos. 1783 i.
Moses 1797 w.

Orange
Jno. 1763 w.
Jas. 1763 i.
Martha 1763 w.
Zachary 1768 i.
Richd. 1779 w.
Hancock 1774 w.
Jas. 1784 w.
Geo. 1792 w.
Erasmus 1795 w.
Frances 1799 w.
Pittsylvania
Geo. 1794 i.
Jas. 1797 i.
Powhatan
Mark 1781 i.
Martha Jane 1795 w.
Princess Anne
Joseph 1700 i.
Jacob 1703 w.
Rose 1712 i.
Thos. 1744 w.
Richd. 1745 w.
Prince William
Chas. 1740 i.
Chas. 1741 i.
Rappahannock
Richd. 1679 w.
Richmond
Thos. 1713 w.
Robt. 1719 i.
Thos. 1727 w.
Simon 1728 w.
Robt. 1730 i.
Thos. 1730 w.
Jno. 1741 i.
Eliz. 1747 w.
Geo. 1748 w.
Septimus 1748 i.
Geo. 1750 i.
Geo. 1757 w.
Eliz. 1767 i.
Rockbridge
Jno. 1778 a.
Jno. 1779 w.
Eliz. 1799 w.
Thos. 1799 w.
Shenandoah
John 1778 a.
Chas. 1785 w.
Christopher 1786 a.
Southampton
Thos. 1754 w.
Etheldred 1755 w.
Katherine 1765 w.
Patience 1766 w.
Jas. 1771 i.
Wm. 1772 w.
Chas. 1773 w.
Lucy 1776 w.
Etheldred 1777 w.
Harris 1778 w.

Henry 1781 w.
Jas. 1782 w.
Charlotte 1791 w.
Etheldred 1791 w.
Robt. 1793 w.
Temperance 1798 i
Spotsylvania
Jas. 1743 w.
Geo. 1791 a.
Stafford
Edwd. 1703 w.
Jno. 1735 i.
Jno. 1739 i.
Surry
Jas. 1655 i.
Edwd. 1708 i.
Etheldred 1716 w.
Jno. 1725 i.
Edwd. 1727 i.
Robt. 1735 i.
Wm. 1736 w.
Edwd. 1749 i.
Thos. 1758 w.
Wm. 1770 w.
Jas. 1786 w.
Westmoreland
Jos. 1722 i.
Jas. 1723 i.
Isaac 1727 i.
Thos. 1736 w.
Edwd. 1740 i.
Jas. 1751 w.
Wm. 1762 i.
Thos. 1773 w.
Mary 1781 w.
York
Henry 1674-5 w.
Jno. 1695 i.
Thos. 1708 i.
Danl. 1712 w.
Henry 1718 ab.
Sarah 1724 i.
Walter 1743 w.
Danl. 1744 i..
TAZEWELL
Brunswick
Littleton 1758 i.
Northampton
Wm., Jr. 1750 i.
Wm. 1752 w.
Sophia 1754 w.
TEACKLE
Accomack
Jno. 1722 i.
Caleb 1740 w.
Jno. 1760 w.
Thos. 1769 w.
Taylor 1769 w.
Upshur 1774 w.
Wm. 1777 w.
Upshur 1777 i.
Wm. 1779 i.

Margt. 1782 w.
Thos. 1784 w.
Arthur 1791 w.
TEACLE
Accomack
Thos. 1695 w.
TEAGUE
Northampton
Richd. 1660 w.
Simon 1718 w.
Thos. 1733 w.
Danl. 1750 w.
TEAS
Augusta
Wm. 1778 w.
TEASLY
Isle of Wight
John 1738 i.
Richard 1759 w.
John 1765 w.
TEATER
Orange
Geo. 1744 a.
TEBBS
Prince William
Daniel 1742 w.
James 1785 i.
Foushee 1790 i.
John 1799 i.
Mary 1793 w.
Richmond
Elizabeth 1798 i.
Westmoreland
Danl. 1762 w.
Danl. 1776 w.
Danl. (2) 1776 w.
Danl. 1783 i.
Danl. 1788 i.
TEBOE
Richmond
Chas. 1705 w.
TEDDER
Surry
Jno. 1721 i.
TEDFORD
Rockbridge
Alexander 1781 w.
David 1784 w.
Robert, Sr. 1791 w.
Alexander, Sr.
1793 w.
TEEHARY
Accomack
Rachel 1792 w.
TEES
Augusta
Jos. 1756 w.
TEGINS
Richmond
Jno. 1764 w.

TELNEY
Accomack
Wm. 1707 i.
TEMHAM
Louisa
Robt. 1769 w.
TENNOCK
York
Robt. 1725 w.
TEMPEST
Northumberland
Edwd. [1652] i.
TEMPLE
Northumberland
Jno. 1658 w.
Rappahannock
Jno. [1658?] w.
York
Peter 1695 i.
TEMPLEMAN
Westmoreland
Thos. 1752 w.
Dozer 1763 i.
Thos. 1794 w.
TEMPLETON
Amelia
David 1742 a.
TENANT
Princess Anne
Saml. 1771 w.
James 1779 w.
Eliz. 1783 w.
TENCH
Lunenburg
Henry 1781 w.
TENENT
Princess Anne
James 1726 w.
TENER
Middlesex
Stephen 1757 a.
TENHAM
Louisa
Elizabeth 1784 w.
York
Jno. 1735 w.
Jno. 1770 w.
Jno. 1789 i.
TENNANT
Norfolk
Timothy 1747 w.
Princess Anne
James 1741 w.
TENNELL
Prince William
Francis 1779 w.
TENNISON
Amherst
Henry 1786 w.
Jno. 1794 a.
Prince William
William 1783 i.

TENOE
Middlesex
Stephen 1760 i.
TERALL
Isle of Wight
Blackabee 1733 w.
TERIMGEMS (?)
Westmoreland
Jno. 1695 i.
TERNALL
Accomack
Roger 1695 w.
TERREL
Augusta
Edwd. G. 1797 nw.
Charles City
Richmond 1797 i.
TERRELL
Albemarle
Joell 1774 w.
Reuben 1776 w.
Reuben 1785 i.
Halifax
Wm. 1797 w.
Isle of Wight
Joane 1720 i.
Louisa
Richmond 1765 w.
Ann 1795 w.
Samuel 1798 w.
Orange
Robt. 1786 w.
TERRETT
Fairfax
William Henry
1758 w.
Richmond
Francis 1715 i.
TERREY
Louisa
James 1792 i.
TERRIER
King George
Philip 1764 i.
TERRIL
Ohio
Jurud 1799 w.
TERRILL
Louisa
Richmond 1771 w.
Thos. 1781 w.
Culpeper
Edmund 1784 w.
John 1790 i.
TERRY
Halifax
Cheslen 1761 i.
Nathl. 1780 w.
Henry
James 1788 w.
Louisa
Champness [1758]w.

James 1783 w.
Mecklenburg
Saml. 1765 w.
Northampton
Jno. 1721-2 w.
Jno. 1736 w.
Pittsylvania
Benj., Sr. 1771 w.
Champness 1784 i.
Henry 1784 w.
Jos. 1785 w.
Stephen 1797 w.
TESDALE
Amelia
Wm. 1752 w.
Louisa
John 1785 w.
TETER
Augusta
Mathias 1758 a.
TEW
Westmoreland
Jno. 1655 w.
THACKER
Albemarle
Benjamin 1799 w.
Essex
Saml. 1713 w.
Middlesex
Edwin 1704 w.
Henry 1709 w..
Eliz. 1714 w.
Henry 1714 i.
Edwin 1746 i.
Eliz. 1751 a.
Henry 1766 w.
Mary Eliz. 1776 w
THACKSTON
Prince Edwd.
James 1799 w.
THALLAWELL
Essex
James 1717 i.
THARKELSON
Lancaster
Nicholas 1749 w.
Joseph 1792 w.
THARP
Sussex
Hardy 1767 i.
THARPE
Essex
Thomas 1704 w.
Southampton
Joseph 1762 w.
Surry
Robt. 1719 i.
Joseph 1726 w.
THATCHER
Berkeley
Samuel 1776 w.

King George
Silvester 1725 i.
Wm. 1742 i.
Thos. 1751 i.
Lancaster
Wm. 1698 w.
Gabriel 1744 w.
James 1752 w.
Judith 1755 w.
Gabriel 1757 w.
Loudoun
Richard 1781 w.
Richmond
Silvester 1718 w.
THATCHWELL
Lancaster
Wm. 1659 a.
THEAD
Westmoreland
Richd. 1783 i.
THEBO
York
Jno. 1720 w.
THELABALL
Norfolk
Francis 1704-5 w.
Jas. 1711 w.
Dyer 1714 i.
Jas. 1767 w.
Lewis 1767 w.
Jas., Sr. 1773 w.
Wm. 1777 w.
Elizabeth 1783 w.
Princess Anne
Saml. 1718 i.
Francis 1727 i.
Lemuel 1727 w.
Jas. 1741 w.
Lemuel 1746 w.
THELIBAL
Norfolk
Jas 1779 i.
THELWALL
Essex
Jas. 1713 i.
THENABALL
Norfolk
Geo. 1796 w.
THERIOT
Lancaster
Domine 1675 i.
Wm. 1691 i.
THILABALL
Norfolk
Jas. 1693 w.
Princess Anne
Lemuel 1791 w.
THILMAN
Middlesex
Paul 1714 i.
Paul 1731 i.
THISTLETHWAITE

York
Christopher 1766 w.
THOM
Culpeper
Alexander 1791 i.
THOMAS
Accomack
Saml. 1737 i.
Solomon 1739 i.
Geo. 1772 w.
Geo. 1774 w.
Geo. 1779 i.
Levin 1785 w.
Bridget 1793 w.
Susanna 1797 w.
Albemarle
Edward 1759 w.
Jno. 1760 w.
Jos. 1797 i.
Amelia
Wm. 1772 i.
Amherst
Cornelius 1775 w.
Augusta
Jacob 1749 a.
Jacob 1752 i.
Morgan 1753 i.
Jno. 1756 i.
Rees 1759 w.
Berkeley
Geo. 1796 i.
Botetourt
Lodowick 1778 w.
Richd. 1782 w.
Richd. 1794 w.
Brunswick
Thos. 1760 w.
Richd. 1762 i.
Thos. 1781 i.
Chesterfield
Eliz. 1786 w.
Culpeper
Massey 1776 i.
John 1785 w.
Cumberland
David 1756 w.
Philip 1762 w.
Job 1787 w.
Essex
Edwd. 1699 w.
Jno. 1712 i.
Katherine 1712 i.
Robert 1714 i.
Jas. 1740 i.
Wm.C[atlett]1742 w.
Wm. Sr. 1745 w.
Meredith 1755 i.
Elizabeth 1757 w.
John 1765 i.
Wm., Sr. 1771 w.
Jno. 1775 i.
Wm. 1790 w.

Angelinah 1794 i.
Lewis 1795 w.
Edwd. 1799 i.
Fairfax
Mark 1746 a.
Wm. 1755 w.
David 1765 i.
Robt. 1768 w.
Thos. 1786 i.
Fauquier
William 1799 w.
Frederick
Owen 1750 i.
Lewis 1751 a.
Evan 1755 w.
Lewis 1756 i.
Ellis 1763 w.
Enos 1763 w.
Nathaniel 1763 w.
John 1786 w.
John 1794 i.
Rachel 1795 i.
Halifax
Even 1775 w.
Madling 1778 w.
Hardy
Morris 1796 w.
Henrico
Jno. 1727 i.
Christopher John 1783 w.
Isle of Wight
Philip 1702-3 w.
John 1725-6 w.
Wm. 1728 i.
Wm. 1741 w.
Richd. 1762 w.
Jacob 1766 i.
King George
Mary 1773 a.
Benj. 1781 w.
Lancaster
Tarpley 1791 i.
Loudoun
Evan 1757 w.
Joseph 1786 i.
John 1793 w.
Catherine 1794 w.
David 1796 w.
Madison
John 1793 w.
Middlesex
Chas. 1728 i.
Chas. 1741 i.
Montgomery
Benj. 1787 a.
Norfolk
Henry 1717 i.
Charles 1783 w.
Charles 1791 i.
John 1797 w.

Northampton
Simon 1682 w.
Jno. 1723 w.
Wm. 1745 i.
Geo. 1773 i.
Jno. 1786 w.
Jno. 1798 i.
Northumberland
Jno. 1719 i.
Richd. 1741 w.
Philip 1744 i.
Peter 1765 i.
Wm. 1767 w.
Jno. 1771 w.
Jno., Jr. 1772 w.
Jno. 1777 w.
Jas. 1780 nw.
Richd. 1783 w.
Peter 1790 i.
Wm. 1790 w.
Wm. 1791 i.
Robt. 1792 i.
Jno. 1796 w.
Orange
Jno. 1744 a.
Jos. 1773 w.
Robt. 1788 w.
Sarah 1795 w.
Pittsylvania
Geo. 1770 i.
Wm. 1795 i.
Nathl. 1799 w.
Princess Anne
Jno. 1708 i.
Prince William
Geo. 1781 w.
Benj. 1793 w.
Rappahannock
David 1672 w.
Job 1683 i.
Richmond
Rebecca 1700 w.
Jno. 1724 i.
Geo. 1726 w.
Humphrey 1732 w.
Evan 1743 w.
Moses 1746 i.
Wm. 1774 i.
Shenandoah
Saml. 1788 i.
Southampton
Richd. 1752 i.
Jno. 1770 w.
Henry 1772 w.
Henry 1792 i.
Wm. 1795 w.
Nathan 1796 i.
Spotsylvania
Wm. 1726 a.
Joshua 1745 a.
Owen 1760 w.
Owen 1772 w.

Stafford
Richd. 1748 nw.
Benj. 1760 w.
Surry
Wm. 1719 w.
Wm. 1723 w.
Priscilla 1733 w.
Westmoreland
Wm. 1696 i.
Jno. 1698 i.
David 1703 i.
Hugh 1718 w.
Ann 1719 i.
Henry 1730 i.
Jas. 1743 w.
Jas. the younger
1743 i.
Jno. 1771 i.
Geo. 1780 i.
Wm. 1791 i.
York
Edwd. 1693 w.
Edwd. 1714 w.
Jno. 1718 i.
Mary 1759 w.
Hillsman 1761 w.
THOMASIN
Stafford
Simon 1701 w.
Patience 1703 i.
THOMASON
Brunswick
Jas. 1787 i.
Fluvanna
Thos. 1794 i.
Louisa
Geo. 1783 w.
THOMKINS
York
Saml. 1701 i.
THOMMER
Augusta
Jacob 1752 a.
THOMPSON
Accomack
Mary 1754 i.
Wm. 1754 i.
Albemarle
Jos. 1759 i.
Jos. 1765 w.
David 1770 w.
Robt. 1778 w.
Wm. 1799 w.
Amelia
Robt. 1762 w.
Richd. 1769 w.
Isham 1777 i.
Robt. 1783 w.
Peter 1785 w
Mary 1788 w.
Amherst
Robt. 1787 w.

Augusta
Matthew 1753 w.
Thos. 1760 i.
Hugh 1762 w.
Thos. 1764 a.
Thos. 1766 w.
Adam 1769 w.
Jas. 1773 w.
Mary 1779 i.
Wm. 1781 w.
Bedford
Wm. 1763 w.
Jno. 1778 w.
Brunswick
Richd. 1778 w.
Campbell
Wm. 1783 i.
Jno. 1792 w.
Charles City
Ling 1767 i.
James 1773 w.
Mary 1794 i.
Charlotte
Sarah 1777 w.
Chesterfield
Robt. 1751 w.
Mary 1753 w.
Culpeper
Geo. 1764 w.
Jno. 1772 w.
Wm. 1783 i.
Jno. 1796 i.
Cumberland
David 1765 i.
Jno. 1786 i.
Fairfax
Jos. 1773 i.
Wm. 1785 i.
Fluvanna
Geo. 1777 w.
Frederick
Reuben 1793 w.
Neil 1753 i.
Ralph 1771 w.
Benjamin 1777 i.
Goochland
Geo. 1767 w.
Mary 1771 w.
Richd. 1778 w.
Greenbrier
Thomas 1795 i.
Halifax
Jno. 1766 i.
Wm. 1781 w.
Jno. 1795 w.
Wm. 1799 i.
Henrico
Robt. 1697 i.
Jas. 1747 w.
King George
Dekar 1769 w.
Wm. 1793 w.

Lancaster
  Thos. 1694 w.
  Thos. 1722 i.
Isle of Wight
  William 1795 i.
Loudoun
  Edward 1774 w.
  Andrew 1792 w.
  Israel 1795 w.
Louisa
  Robt. 1775 a.
  Geo. 1786 w.
  Matthew 1790 i.
Lunenburg
  James 1794 w.
Mecklenburg
  Wells 1769 w.
  Jno. 1770 i.
Middlesex
  Thos. 1706 w.
Montgomery
  William 1796 i.
Norfolk
  Benedictus 1746 w.
  Cyprian 1759 w.
  Cyprian 1769 i.
  Thomas 1771 w.
  Robert 1773 w.
  Wm. 1774 i.
  Isaac 1780 w.
Northampton
  Jno. 1702 i.
  Robt. 1744 i.
  Chas. 1752 i.
  Robt. 1761 i.
Northumberland
  Wm. 1665 w.
  Simon 1714 i.
  Richd. 1746 w.
  James 1750 i.
Orange
  Samuel 1794 i.
Pittsylvania
  Geo. 1799 w.
Powhatan
  Patience 1797 i.
Prince Edward
  Jno. 1795 w.
Prince George
  Henry 1720 w.
Rockbridge
  James 1795 w.
Surry
  Jno. 1699 w.
  Saml. 1721 a.
  Nicholas 1725 w.
  Wm. 1732 w.
  Saml. 1752 i.
  Wm. 1752 w.
  Jno. 1755 w.
  Wm. 1762 w.
  Jno. 1763 w.

  Jno. 1766 i.
  Jno. 1767 w.
  Jno. 1768 i.
  Anne 1768 i.
  Nicholas 1773 w.
  Philip 1777 w.
  Ann 1792 w.
  Philip 1799 w.
Sussex
  Nicho. 1777 a.
  John, Sr. 1779 w.
  Francis Read 1785 w.
  Arthur 1789 w.
Washington
  Robt. 1798 w.
Westmoreland
  Michael 1691 i.
  Thos. 1716 w.
  Thos. 1744 i.
  Jno. 1751 w.
  Thos. 1744 i.
  Wm. 1752 i.
  Wm. 1764 i.
  Jas. 1770 i.
  Andrew 1770 w.
  Andrew 1772 i.
Wythe
  Samuel 1791 i.
  William 1798 w.
York
  Jas. 1732 w.
  David 1749 i.
  Chas. 1770 i.
THOMSON
Accomack
  Christopher 1704 w.
  Jno. 1735 w.
  Robt. 1745 i.
  Jno. 1765 i.
Amelia
  Saml. 1779 w.
Augusta
  Moses 1778 w.
Cumberland
  John 1785 w.
Frederick
  Neal 1751 a.
Louisa
  Saml. 1753 w.
  Thos. 1774 w.
  Robt. 1776 i.
  Wm. 1778 w.
  Matthew 1785 a.
  Robt. 1789 w.
Northampton
  Richd. 1739 i.
Northumberland
  Jas. 1743 w.
  Ann 1747 w.
Prince William
  Samuel 1797 i.

Spotsylvania
  Wm. 1728 w.
Surry
  Jno. 1702 w.
Westmoreland
  Wm. 1785 w.
THORN
Augusta
  Henry 1750 w.
Essex
  John 1739 i.
Fairfax
  William 1773 w.
Loudoun
  Humphrey 1771 w.
THORNBERRY
Berkeley
  Francis 1779 i.
Essex
  Wm. 1697 w.
Fauquier
  Samuel 1797 i.
  John 1799 w.
Prince William
  Richard 1743 i.
Stafford
  Saml. 1755 w.
THORNBOROUGH
Berkeley
  Thomas 1789 w.
THORNBROUGH
Berkeley
  Benjamin 1795 i.
  Sarah 1795 w.
THORNE
Accomack
  Arthur 1706 i.
Richmond
  Jas. 1718 i.
Surry
  Martin 1695 w.
Westmoreland
  Geo., Jr. 1698 w.
  Geo., Sr. 1704 i.
THORNEBURY
Accomack
  Thos. 1703 i.
THORNHILL
Bedford
  Wm. 1793 w.
Culpeper
  Bryant 1780 w.
  Jos. 1782 w.
Fauquier
  Bryant 1785 w.
Richmond
  Bryan 1709 nw.
THORNLEY
King George
  Aaron 1728 i.
  Jno. 1779 a.
  Ann 1792 w.

THORNSMON
Accomack
Obediah 1780 i.
THORNTON
Accomack
Edwd. 1703 w.
Jas. 1741 w.
Wm. 1758 w.
Edwd. 1759 w.
Jno. 1760 i.
Wm., Jr. 1761 i.
Edwd. 1795 w.
Mary 1795 w.
Edwd. 1799 w.
Brunswick
Wm. 1790 w.
Halifax
Reuben 1792 i.
Henrico
Sterling 1787 w.
Isle of Wight
John 1688 w.
Jno. 1695 i.
Wm. 1726 i.
Thos. 1732 i.
King George
Francis 1726 i.
Rowland 1742 i.
Wm. 1743 i.
Frances 1744 eb.
Rowland 1755 i.
Francis 1767 w.
Wm. 1776 a.
Wm. [1778] w.
Francis 1780 nw.
Francis 1784 w.
Lancaster
Thos. 1741 w.
Loudoun
Jno. 1780 i.
Jno. 1783 i.
Jno. 1785 w.
Thos. 1793 i.
Northumberland
Presly 1770 w.
Orange
Jas. 1750 i.
Jno. 1780 i.
Jas. 1791 w.
Princess Anne
Wm. 1795 w.
Prince William
Charles 1778 i.
Richmond
Luke 1718 i.
Mark 1721 i.
Luke 1725 w.
Mathew 1727 w.
Thos 1729 w.
Roger 1730 i.
Robt. 1737 i.
Wm. 1741 i.

Eliza 1742 w.
Hopkins 1742 i.
Thos. 1763 i.
Crask 1771 w.
Thos. 1771 w.
Thos. 1773 i.
David 1777 w.
Jesse 1779 i.
Jno., Sr. 1791 w.
Elizabeth 1794 w.
Robt. 1795 i.
Shenandoah
Christian 1774 i.
Spotsylvania
Francis 1749 w.
Francis 1795 w.
Frances 1794 a.
Stafford
Anthony 1757 w.
York
Anna Maria 1760 w.
THOROGOOD
Isle of Wight
John 1671 i.
Norfolk
Adam 1640 i.
Adam 1685-6 w.
Princess Anne
John Harper 1796 w.
THOROWGOOD
Norfolk
Adam 1644 i.
Princess Anne
Pembrook 1695 a.
Argoll 1700 w.
Jno. 1701 w.
Robt. 1703 w.
Adam 1710 i.
Adam 1719 w.
Argoll 1719 i
Jno. 1719 w.
Francis 1723 i.
Wm. 1723 w.
Thos. 1727 w.
Francis 1741 w.
Argoll 1755 w.
Robt. 1755 i.
Jno. 1757 w.
Jno. 1759 i.
Fran. 1761 i.
Jno. 1763 w.
Adam 1769 w.
Robt. 1779 i.
Wm. 1780 w.
Sally 1783 w.
Norfolk
Francis 1785 i.
Princess Anne
Lemuel 1785 w.
Jno. 1787 w.
Jno. 1788 i.
Thos. Scarborough

1788 w.
Wm., Jr. 1788 w.
THORP
Bedford
Amos 1776 i.
Campbell
Francis 1791 i.
Essex
Wm. 1757 i.
Thos. 1763 i.
Thos. 1768 w.
Franklin
Wm. 1794 w.
Frederick
Zebulun 1780 w.
Surry
Christopher 1777 w.
Sussex
Jos. 1780 w.
THORPE
Southampton
Timothy 1751 w.
Timothy 1763 w.
Aaron 1772 i.
Jno. 1772 w.
Peterson 1779 i.
Jno. 1781 w.
Jno. 1785 i.
Jno. 1786 w.
Timothy 1789 w.
Moses 1790 w.
Joshua 1792 w.
Jeremiah 1793 w.
Martha 1794 w.
Susanna 1794 w.
Jno. 1795 w.
Joshua 1799 i.
Surry
Jno. 1721 i.
Wm. 1724 i.
Wm. 1727 w.
Wm. 1777 i.
Joseph 1792 i.
York
Richd. 1660 w.
Otho 1686-7 w.
Katherine 1695 i.
THORPP
Isle of Wight
Thomas 1711 w.
THOW
Stafford
Jas. 1758 w.
THRAILKILL
Westmoreland
Jas. 1761 i.
Jno. 1783 i.
THRASHER
Frederick
Richard 1768 w.
THREADGALL
Norfolk

Siball 1730 w.
THREADGILL
Brunswick
Jno. 1772 w.
THREEWETS
Surry
Jno. 1749 w.
THREEWITTS
Sussex
Ann 1756 w.
Jno. 1756 w.
Ann 1760 i.
Frances 1767 i.
THRELDKELD
King George
Christopher 1757 w.
THRELKEILD
Northumberland
Christopher 1711 w.
THRELDKILL
Culpeper
Henry 1776 i.
Stephen 1793 i.
King George
Jessey 1763 i.
Wm. 1766 w.
THRESH
Rappahannock
Clement [1659?] w.
THRESHLEY
Essex
William 1750 i.
THRIFT
Fairfax
Absolom 1773 i.
Charles 1790 w.
Geo. 1798 i.
Richmond
Nathaniel 1736 w.
Jos. 1764 i.
Wm. 1776 w.
Jesse 1777 w.
Jesse 1778 i.
Job 1783 w.
Jno. 1789 w.
Jno. 1790 w.
THRILKIL
Richmond
Henry 1731 w.
THRILKILL
Richmond
Geo. 1747 w.
THRILLWIND
Princess Anne
Thos. 1734 w.
THROCKMORTON
Berkeley
John 1775 w.
Job 1780 w.
Robert 1796 w.
William 1797 i.

Fauquier
Frances 1790 w.
Frederick
Albion 1796 w.
THROPP
Isle of Wight
John 1721 w.
Westmoreland
Wm. 1656 i.
THROWER
Brunswick
Hezekiah 1787 w.
Princess Anne
Jno. 1696 w.
Alice 1709 w.
Surry
John 1730 i.
Thos. 1730 w.
Edwd. 1738 w.
Tabitha 1740 i.
THUM
Fairfax
Adam 1795 a.
THUMMY
Berkeley
Jacob 1783 w.
THURMER
York
Robt. 1758 w.
THURMOND
Albemarle
Philip, Sr. 1774 w.
THUSTIN
Berkeley
John 1779 i.
William 1782 i.
THURSTON
Culpeper
William Plummer
    1789 w.
Goochland
Francis 1774 w.
Duel 1777 w.
Frances 1778 i.
Reuben 1786 i.
Eliz. 1799 w.
Middlesex
Jno. 1745 w.
Jno. 1760 i.
Jno. 1771 i.
Robt. 1784 i.
Saml. 1794 i.
Orange
Thos. 1742 a.
James 1742 i.
Ann 1790 i.
THUSON
Middlesex
Henry 1794 w.

THRUSTON
Middlesex
Carter 1791 i.
Norfolk
Malachy 1699 w.
John 1709 w.
Martha 1745-6 i.
Edward 1762 w.
THWEAT
Brunswick
Burwell 1781 w.
Judith 1773 w.
Peterson 1779 w.
THWEATT
Greensville
David 1789 w.
Lunenburg
Danl. 1775 w.
Edward 1784 w.
Southampton
Wm. 1763 w.
TIBBONS
Sussex
Jno. 1770 i.
TIBBOO
Culpeper
John 1781 i.
TIBBS
Prince William
Foushee 1784 w.
TIBNEY
Northampton
Jno. 1741 w.
TICKELL
Louisa
Joseph 1768 a.
TICKTOM
Augusta
Richd. 1750 w.
Richd. 1755 i.
TIDMARSH
Prince George
John 1718 w.
Richd. 1725 w.
TIDMASH
Isle of Wight
Giles [1729-30] w.
TIDWELL
Westmoreland
Jno. 1760 i.
Robt. 1761 w.
Hannah 1764 w.
Robt. 1764 w.
Ann 1786 w.
Ann B. 1789 i.
TIFFEY
Westmoreland
Geo. 1783 i.
TIGNAL
Accomack
Dennis 1775 w.

Philip 1797 w.
TIGNOR
Lancaster
Wm. 1657 i.
Northumberland
Wm. 1702 w.
Martha 1750-1 w.
Philip 1776 w.
Jas. 1777 i.
TILFORD
Amherst
Jas. 1787 i.
TILLAR
Powhatan
Jane 1778 i.
Southampton
John 1794 w.
TILLARY
Spotsylvania
Saml. 1728-9 w.
TILLER
Chesterfield
Thos. 1765 w.
Thos. 17—i.
Essex
Wm. 1718 w.
King George
Wm. 1750 i.
Isle of Wight
Susannah 1727 w.
Richmond
Wm. 1718 w.
Stafford
Merrimond 1755 i.
Sussex
Major 1790 w.
TILLEROY
Berkeley
Andrew 1780 w.
TILLERS
Isle of Wight
John 1720 i.
TILLERY
Northumberland
Jas. 1785 i.
Jas. 1786 i.
Richmond
Thos. 1705 w.
Job 1730 w.
Job 1733 w.
Jno. 1746 w.
Geo. 1751 w.
TILLESON
Northampton
Gideon 1652 i.
TILLETT
Loudoun
Saml., Sr. 1798 w.
Prince William
John 1734 i.
Giles 1736 i.

John 1736 i.
TILLEY
Berkeley
Geo. 1795 i.
Brunswick
Michael 1795 i.
TILLMAN
Brunswick
Geo. 1756 w.
Mecklenburg
Roger 1767 w.
Prince George
Susannah 1716 w.
TILLOTSON
Chesterfield
Jno. 1766 w.
TILLSON
Northampton
Gideon 1652 w.
TILLY
Orange
Lazarus 1744 a.
TILLYARD
York
Arthur 1712 w.
TILMAN
Brunswick
Roger 1761 i.
David 1782 w.
Jno. 1785 i.
Fluvanna
Nathl. 1781 w.
Mecklenburg.
Henry 1781 w.
Henry 1782 w.
TILNEY
Accomack
Wm. 1741 i.
Wm. 1774 w.
Northampton
———— 1701 w.
Jno. 1728 i.
Jno. 1741 i.
Jonathan 1750 i.
TILSON
Westmoreland
Roger 1702 w.
TIMBERLAKE
Charles City
Jas. 1793 i.
Louisa
Philip 1789 w.
Middlesex
Francis 1727 i.
Richard 1782 i.
Richard 1795 i.
Northumberland
Francis 1762 w.
Shenandoah
John 1782 a.

York
Jno. 1714 i.
TIMMONS
Stafford
Thos. 1734 i.
TIMSON
York
Saml. 1695 w.
Francis 1702 w.
Saml. 1704-5 i.
Jno. 1709 w.
Wm. 1719 w.
Wm. 1726 w.
Jno. 1738 w.
Saml. 1739 w.
Jno. 1742 w.
Saml. 1748 i.
Wm. 1757 w.
Jno. 1777 i.
Saml. 1782 w.
Mary 1783 i.
TINCHER
Greenbrier
Saml. 1791 w.
TINDAL
Halifax
Thos. 1790 i.
TINDALL
Albemarle
Thos. 1774 w.
Goochland
Thos. 1742 i.
Prince William
Jos. 1737 a.
York
Geo. 1702 w.
Eliz. 1705 w.
TINDSLEY
Madison
Edwd. 1799 a.
TINEY
Halifax
Susanna 1785 w.
TINGLE
Berkeley
Geo. 1777 w.
TINLEY
Accomack
Wm. 1707 i.
TINNIE
York
Jas. 1796 i.
TINNIS
Halifax
Wm. 1783 w.
TINNY
Middlesex
Wm. 1718 w.
TINNYS
Halifax
Wm. 1774 i.

TINSLEY
Amelia
Isaac 1776 w.
Amherst
Edwd. 1782 a.
Wm., Jr., 1790 a.
Charlotte
Jno. 1767 i.
Essex
Thos. 1715 w.
Thos. 1764 w.
Halifax
Jno. 1762 w.
Louisa
Wm. 1799 i.
Madison
Jno. 1798 w.
Prince Edward
Thos. 1778 i.
TIPLADY
York
Jno. 1689 w.
Ralph 1697 w.
TIPLING
Princess Anne
Jno. 1782 w.
TIPPETT
Richmond
Thos. 1710 w.
TIPSHOD
Northampton
Wm. 1682 w.
TIPTON
Montgomery
Mordacai 1795 w.
TISDALE
Louisa
Jno. 1785 i.
Mecklenburg
Edwd. 1796 i.
TISEKER
Accomack
Jno. 1738 w.
TITTIMAN
Accomack
Saml. 1701 w.
TIVENDALE
Richmond
David [1752] i.
TIZAKER
Accomack
Jos. 1765 w.
Wm. 1788 i.
TIZECKER
Accomack
Eliz. 1780 w.
TIZEKER
Accomack
Wm. 1786 w.

TIZZAKER
Accomack
Robt. 1754 w.
TOAKE
Surry
Wm. 1721 i.
TOAP
York
Nicholas 1679 i.
TOBE
Northumberland
Jane 1729 w.
TOBEN
Westmoreland
Michael 1746 w.
TOBIN
Loudoun
James 1774 w.
Northumberland
Thos. 1745 i.
TOBIT
Loudoun
John George 1770 i.
TOBY
Stafford
Jno. 1752 i.
Jno. 1757 i.
TODD
Charlotte
Thos. 1777 i.
Chesterfield
Betty 1777 w.
Essex
Thomas, [Jr.]
1714 w.
Thomas 1720 i.
William 1748 i.
Henrico
Geo. 1746 i.
Loudoun
Robert 1793 w.
Louisa
Andrew 1791 w.
John 1793 w.
Montgomery
Mary 1792 i.
Northumberland
Cornelius 1750 i.
Pittsylvania
Richd. 1795 i.
Richmond
Jeane 1724 i.
Rockbridge
James 1789 i.
Stafford
Richd. 1737 w.
Hayward 1755 w.
Sussex
Saml. 1773 w.
Washington
Patrick 1798 i.

Westmoreland
Robt. 1761 w.
TODHUNTER
Loudoun
John 1771 w.
John 1783 i.
TOELL
Norfolk
Richard 1734 w.
TOFF
Middlesex
Thomas 1787 w.
Richmond
Jno. 1780 w.
TOLBERT
Fairfax
Osborn 1788 i.
TOLEMAN
Northampton
Jos. 1739 i.
Henry 1761 w.
Wm. 1798 w.
Wm., Jr. 1799 i.
TOLER
Bedford
Joshua 1792 i.
Goochland
Jas. 1796 i.
Jno. 1780 i.
James 1781 i.
Pittsylvania
Wm. 1799 w.
TOLLE
Fauquier
Stephen 1792 nw.
TOLMAN
Northampton
Ebenezer 1758 i.
TOLSON
Northumberland
Wm. 1738 w.
Mary 1742 w.
Jno. 1745 w.
Stafford
Benj. 1764 w.
Geo. 1785 w.
TOMASON
Mecklenburg
James 1780 w.
TOMER
York
Jno. 1717 w.
Jas. 1752 i.
TOMKINS
Northampton
Anne 1798 w.
Westmoreland
Jno. 1762 i.
York
Bennet 1740 i.

TOMLIN
Fauquier
John 1796 i.
Essex
Thos. 1704 w.
William 1709 i.
Rebecca 1714 w.
Isle of Wight
Mathew 1684 w.
James 1702 w.
John 1752 w.
John, Sr. 1753 i.
Joseph 1753 i.
Matthew 1756 w.
Benjamin 1758 i.
John 1759 i.
Martha 1761 w.
James 1782 i.
Matthew 1782 w.
Nathan 1785 w.
Martha 1793 w.
Nicholas 1797 w.
Richmond
Geo. 1705 w.
Lancaster
Stephen 1704 w.
Edwd. 1722 i.
Stephen 1733 w.
Mary 1742 w.
Richmond
Robt., Sr. 1761 w.
Robt., Jr. 1794 w.
Robt. 1795 w.
Spotsylvania
Mary 1773 a.
TOMLINSON
Amelia
Henry 1749 w.
Brunswick
Wm. 1757 (8?) w.
James 1782 i.
Greensville
John 1782 w.
Lunenburg
Benj. 1789 w.
Norfolk
Samuel 1785 i.
Richmond
Edwd. 1755 w.
Northampton
Henry 1759 w.
Surry
Wm. 1732 w.
Richd., Jr. 1750 w
Thomas 1750 w.
Richd. 1751 w.
Sussex
Benj. 1759 w.
Wm. 1760 w.
Jno 1762 w
Burrell 1765 w

Jno. 1766 i.
Nathl. 1782 w.
Henry 1786 w.
Henry 1789 i.
Wm. 1792 w.
Thos. 1793 w.
Burwell 1795 w.
Benj. 1797 w.
Mary 1797 w.
Burwell 1799 w.
Mary 1799 w.
TOMPKENS
Accomack
Edmd. 1757 i.
TOMPKINS
Albemarle
Giles 1795 w.
Loudoun
James 1794 w.
Northampton
Jno. 1757 w.
Pittsylvania
Saml. 1796 w.
York
Mary 1741-2 w.
Saml. 1763 w.
Saml. 1772 i.
TOMPSON
Northampton
Jno. 1682 w.
TOMSON
Charles City
Jeffry 1769 i.
Frederick
Saml. 1744 i.
Halifax
Jno. 1782 i.
Middlesex
Wm. 1727 w.
Northampton
Robt. 1703 a.
Geo. 1729 i.
Jno. 1738 i.
Northumberland
Richd. 1725 w.
Frances Ann 1749 w.
Barbary 1753 w.
TONEY
Goochland
Chas. 1776 w.
TONY
Northampton
Kinge (negro)
1677 w.
TOOK
Isle of Wight
James 1662 w.
TOOKE
Brunswick
Jno. 1752 w.
Wm. 1753 i.

Surry
Jno. 1675 w.
Wm. 1675 w.
Jno. 1720 w.
TOOL
King George
Jno. 1752 i.
Middlesex
Garret 1785 w.
TOOLE
Northampton
Jas. 1768 i.
TOOLEY
Princess Anne
Thos. 1702 w.
Jane 1703 i.
Jas. 1729 w.
Adam 1767 i.
Jas. 1782 i.
Sarah 1792 w.
TOOMBS
Charlotte
Eliz. 1766 w.
Ambrose 1772 i.
TOOMER
York
Thos. 1727 i.
Anne 1786 nw.
Jno. 1795 w.
TOOMS
Charlotte
Wm. 1765 w.
TOON
Richmond
Thos. 1769 w.
TOONE
Rappahannock
Jas. 1677 w.
Richmond
Jas. 1718 w.
Jno. 1742 w.
Tarpley 1763 i.
TOOTEY
Amherst
Chas. 1782 i.
TOPING
Accomack
Saml. 1782 w.
TOPLADY
York
Saml. 1702 w.
Isabella 1714 w.
TOPLIS
York
Wm. 1729 i.
TOPPIN
Norfolk
Arthur 1671 w.
Wm. 1745-6 w.
Northumberland
Henry 1660 i.

TORENCE
Campbell
  Moses 1783 i.
TORIAN
Halifax
  Seare 1780 w.
  Mary 1781 i.
  Andrew 1793 w.
  Andrew 1798 i.
TOSELEY
Middlesex
  Thos. 1710 w.
TOSH
Augusta
  Tasker 1767 i.
Botetourt
  Wm. 1773 w.
  Thos. 1778 w.
  Jonathan 1782 w.
TOSHER
Augusta
  Christian 1758 a.
TOTTE
Fauquier
  Roger 1780 w.
TOTTY
Chesterfield
  Wm. 1758 w.
  Thos. 1771 w.
  Thos. 1780 i.
  Jno. 1794 w.
  Jesse [1795] i.
  Jno., Sr. 1796 w.
Henrico
  Thos. 1732 w.
TOULSON
Northumberland
  Thos. 1738 i.
  Mary 1752 w.
  Jas. 1774 i.
  Thos. 1794 w.
  Jas. 1798 i.
TOUNZEN
Northumberland
  Elizab. 1784 w.
TOURNER
Northumberland
  Jno. 1794 w.
TOWARD
Stafford
  Jno. 1732 w.
TOWERS
Surry
  Jno. 1675 w.
TOWERSAY
Lancaster
  Jno. 1718 i.
TOWLER
Frederick
  Wm. 1771 i.

TOWLES
Accomack
  Henry 1721 w.
  Job 1723 w.
  Thos. 1744 w.
  Kendal 1751 w.
  Danl. 1765 i.
Charlotte
  Japheth 1791 w.
Culpeper
  Stokley 1757 w.
  Jos. 1783 w.
Lancaster
  Henry 1734 w.
  Ann 1736 w.
  Stockly 1765 w.
  Henry 1799 w.
Middlesex
  Henry 1749 w.
Spotsylvania
  Oliver 1770 a.
TOWNES
Amelia
  Jno. 1751 a.
  Jno. 1752 i.
  Wm. 1783 w.
  Richd. 1760 i.
Charlotte
  Wm. 1777 w.
Halifax
  Stephen 1789 i.
TOWNLEY
Essex
  James 1785 w.
  Jno. 1792 w.
TOWNS
Halifax
  Stephen 1783 w.
TOWNSAND
Isle of Wight
  Henry 1728 i.
TOWNSEN
Accomack
  Jno., Sr. 1709 w.
Mecklenburg
  Wm. 1766 w.
TOWNSEND
Accomack
  Thos. Jr. 1720 w.
  Thos. 1728 w.
  Henry 1744 i.
  Thos. 1744 i.
  Jas. 1748 nw.
  Richd. 1750 w.
  Mary 1751 nw.
  Eliz. 1755 w.
  Richd. 1765 i.
  Stephen 1767 w.
  Stephen 1769 w.
  Jno. 1770 w.
  Littleton 1773 w.

  Littlton 1779 i.
  Caleb 1783 w.
  Jno. 1784 w.
  Jno. 1793 w.
  Henry 1795 i.
  Jno. 1799 i.
Augusta
  Jno. 1788 w.
Lunenburg
  Joseph 1786 i.
Middlesex
  Thos. 1710 w.
Norfolk
  Jos. 1693 w.
  Dorman 1799 i.
Northampton
  Jeremiah 1730 w.
Northumberland
  Wm. 1771 i.
  Joshua 1772 i.
  Presly 1796 i.
Prince George
  Wm. 1714 i.
York
  Henry 1674 w.
  Wm. 1687 w.
TRABUE
Chesterfield
  Jos. 1756 w.
  Jos. 17— i.
  Jacob 1767 w.
  David 17— i.
  Jacob 17— i.
  Joshua 17— i.
  Joshua 1772 w.
  Jno. Jas. 1775 w.
  Wm. 1785 w.
  Mary 1789 w.
  Jno. 1791 w.
  Mary 1795 i.
Goochland
  Antho 1743 w.
Henrico
  Anthony 1726 i.
TRACEY
Augusta
  Jno. 1759 a.
TRADAN
Frederick
  John 1749 w.
TRADER
Accomack
  Armey 1795 w.
  Henry 1797 i.
TRADWELL
Norfolk
  Edward 1651 i.
TRAFFORD
Rockbridge
  Charles, Cecil 1782 w.

TRAIN
Frederick
John 1783 i.
TRAMELL
Fairfax
John 1758 i.
TRAMMELL
Fairfax
John 1755 w.
William 1776 i.
Gerrard 1786 w.
Wm. 1799 i.
TRAMMILL
Halifax
Jno. 1793 i.
TRANET
Northumberland
Thos. 1668 w.
TRANT
Amelia
Jno. 1762 i.
Judith 1771 w.
TRASEY
Westmoreland
Eliza. 1741 i.
TRAVALLEY
Frederick
James 1757 i.
TRAVELLOR
Northampton
Geo. 1642 w.
TRAVERS
Berkeley
John 1778 w.
Northumberland
Wm. 1796 i.
Rappahannock
Wm. 1687 w.
Richmond
Rawleigh 1701 w.
Stafford
Rawleigh 1733 w.
Rawleigh 1749 w.
TRAVERSE
King George
Thos. 1736 i.
TRAVILLIAN
York
Saml. 1673 i.
TRAVIS
Fairfax
John 1749 i.
Stafford
Jno. 1735 i.
Wm. 1765 w.
Southampton
Piland 1797 w.
York
Edwd. C. 1779 w.
Jno. 1796 i.

TRAVISS
Lancaster
Jno. 1717 w.
TRAYLER
Chesterfield
Jesse 1795 w.
TRAYLOR
Chesterfield
Geo. 1771 w.
Robt. 1773 w.
Jno. 17— i.
Jno., Sr. 1774 w.
Jos. 1777 w.
Eliz. 1782 w.
Humphrey 1790 w.
Geo. 1793 w.
Geo. [1795] i.
Fredk. 1799 w.
Halifax
Edwd. 1791 w.
Lunenburg
Wm. 1762 w.
TREAGAN
Mecklenburg
Henry 1767 i.
TREEBLE
Essex
Mary 1777 w.
TRENDALL
Northampton
Paul 1679 i.
TRENN
Fairfax
Henry 1752 w.
TRENT
Albemarle
Jno. 1760 i.
Amherst
Henry 1793 w.
Chesterfield
Wm., Sr. 1768 w.
Cumberland
Alex.1751 w.
Henrico
Henry, Sr. 1701 w.
Alexander 1703 w.
Henry 1726 w.
Powhatan
Alex. 1793 w.
Richmond
Jas. 1707 w.
TREVETHAN
Princess Anne
Wm. 1702 a.
Sampson 1729 i.
Sampson 1730 w.
Ann 1736 w.
Anne 1743 w.
TREVILLIAN
Albemarle
James 1794 w.

TREWETT
Accomack
Geo., Sr. 1670 w.
TRIBBLE
Halifax
Shadrake 1759 w.
TRIBLE
Essex
Peter 1738 w.
William 1746 w.
John 1749 i.
Halifax
Peter 1793 w.
TRICE
Amelia
James 1775 i.
Goochland
Wm. 1775 i.
Louisa
Mary 1788 w.
Norfolk
John 1733-4 i.
TRIGG
Bedford
William 1773 w.
Middlesex
Danl. 1716 w.
Spotsylvania
Danl. 1769 a.
James 1786 a.
Jno. 1778 w.
Westmoreland
Wm. 1718 i.
TRIGGER
Westmoreland
Thos. 1717 i.
TRIGGS
Norfolk
Paul 16[79]? w.
TRIMBLE
Augusta
Jno. 1765 i.
Jno., Sr. 1790 w.
Botetourt
James 1776 w.
Rockbridge
James, Jr. 1779 i.
John 1783 w.
Sarah 1787 i.
William 1794 w.
Washington
Moses 1783 i.
TRINIMAN
Accomack
Benj. 1676 w.
TRIPLET
Prince William
Thos. 1737 i.
TRIPLETT
Culpeper
Thos. 1778 w.

Hannah 1781 w.
John 1790 i.
Fairfax
Francis 1758 w.
Thos. 1780 i.
Fauquier
Francis 1795 w.
King George
Jas. 1754 a.
Isabella 1760 w.
Francis 1767 w.
Prince William
James 1789 i.
Richmond
Francis 1701 w.
Westmoreland
Wm. 1794 i.
Wm. 1795 i.
Jas. 1798 w.
TRIPONNEY
Isle of Wight
John 1674 i.
TRIPPE
Princess Anne
Henry 1770 i.
TROOP
Halifax
Alexander 1771 w.
Northumberland
Wm. 1766 i.
TROP
Northumberland
Moses 1761 i.
TROTTER
Brunswick
Jas. 1783 w.
Amherst
Wm. 1784 w.
Brunswick
Jas. 1787 i.
Isham 1791 w.
Isham 1799 i.
Cumberland
Thos.1796 w.
Frederick
Mathew 1794 w.
Princess Anne
Jas. 1772 w.
Jno. Giles 1780 w.
Sarah 1782 i.
York
Thos. 1646 i.
Richd. 1699 w.
Ann 1700 w.
Wm. 1733 w.
Jno. 1745 w.
TROUGHTON
Prince George
Wm. 1721 i.

TROUP
Henry
Jacob 1782 i.
TROUT
Augusta
Nicho. 1753 i.
Loudoun
Jeremiah 1778 i.
Frederick
Jacob 1790 w.
TROUTWINE
Frederick
Geo. S. 1783 w.
TROWER
Northampton
Robt. 1756 w.
Henry 1744 w.
Wm. 1795 w.
Princess Anne
Henry 1772 w.
Henry 1776 i.
Robert 1794 w.
Thos. 1795 w.
TROHARD
Essex
Jos. 1727 w.
TROWTEN
Princess Anne
Geo. 1782 w.
TROWTON
Northampton
Andrew 1699 i.
TROY
Accomack
Bridget 1794 w.
TRUE
Spotsylvania
Jno. 1749 a.
Martin 1759 a.
Martin 1766 a.
TRUEHEART
Goochland
Mary 1779 w.
TRUEMAN
Bedford
Wm. 1797 w.
Henrico
Richd., Sr. 1754 w.
Mary 1783 w.
Richd. 1783 w.
Jno. 1784 w.
Richd. 1797 w.
TRUGEN
Fairfax
Edwd. 1795 i.
TRUHITE
Amelia
Levy 1780 w.
TRUIT
Accomack
Henry 1676 w.

Elias 1745 w.
Henry 1719 w.
TRULY
Amelia
Hector 1761 w.
TRUMAN
Henrico
Abraham 1796 w.
Campbell
Henry 1799 w.
TRUSS
Norfolk
Gideon 1778 w.
Josiah 1780 w.
TRUSSELL
Northumberland
Jno. 1660 w.
Jno. 1754 bw.
Westmoreland
Jno. 1667 w.
TRUSSILL
Northumberland
Wm. 1748 i.
TRUTON
Northampton
Andrew 1698 w.
TRYLER
Frederick
Geo. 1764 i.
TUCK
Halifax
Edwd. 1781 w.
Thos. 1788 w.
Edwd. 1790 i.
Thos. 1792 i.
Edwd. 1795 i.
TUCKER
Amelia
Robt. 1750 w.
Robt. 1765 i.
Robt. 1769 w.
Jno.1769 w.
Francis 1774 w.
Robt. 1778 i.
Mathew, Sr. 1784 w.
Wm. 1785 w.
Wm., Jr. 1786 i.
Francis 1793 w.
Campbell
Mathew 1796 w.
Essex
Jno. 1793 w.
Frederick
Saml. 1746 i.
King George
Jno.1735 i.
Henrico
Jno. 1799 w.
Lunenburg
Geo., Jr. 1781 i.
Geo. 1784 w.

Mecklenburg
Jas. 1770 w.
Nat. 1777 w.
Jas. 1778 i.
Norfolk
Thos. 1677 w.
Wm. 1710 w.
Jno. 1719 w.
Robert 1722 w.
Jno. 1743 i.
Aaron 1749 i.
Jno. 1750 i.
Geo. 1752 i.
Mary 1761 w.
Jno. 1762 w.
Robert 1767 w.
Wm. 1774 w.
Robert 1780 w.
Wm. 1785 w.
Wm. 1798 i.
Powhatan
Wm. 1791 w.
Prince Edwd.
Joseph 1798 w.
Prince George
Jno. 1716 w.
Francis 1723 w.
Rappahannock
Leornydon (?)
1658 i.
Southampton
Benj. 1779 w.
Surry
Wm. 1719 i.
Sussex
Joel 1772 i.
Joseph 1782 w.
Robt. 1779 w.
Robt. 1791 i.
Westmoreland
Jno. 1671 w.
Eliz. 1722 w.
York
Dorothy 1665 i.
Sarah 1743 i.
TUCKUR
Accomack
Mansfield 1777 i.
TUCKWILLER
Shenandoah
Thomas 1774 i.
TUDER
Sussex
Henry 1771 w.
Eliz. 1779 w.
TUDOR
Mecklenburg
Jno. 1798 i.
TUELL
York
Matthew 1774 w.

TUFLEY
Rappahannock
Wm. 1672 w.
TUGGEY
Rappahannock
Jno. 1668 a.
TUGGLE
Prince Edward
Benj. 1778 i.
Benj. 1779 w.
Goochland
Jno. 1793 i.
Middlesex
Henry 1743 w.
Jos. 1745 w.
Benj. 1749 w.
Thos. 1754 w.
Jno. 1759 w.
Anne 1760 w.
Jno. 1760 i.
Henry 1770 i.
Henry 1771 a.
Catherine 1782 w.
TUKE
Middlesex
Thos. 1729 w.
TULEY
Albemarle
Jno. 1750 w.
Arthur 1754 i.
Arthur 1755 i.
James 1781 w.
TULLAGH
Isle of Wight
James 1698 w.
TULLET
Henrico
Jno. 1726 a.
TULLIS
Berkeley
Moses 1777 w.
TULLIT
Henrico
Hanna 1737 w.
TULLOS
Fauquier
Richard 1759 w.
Northumberland
Jno. 1742 i.
TULLY
Accomack
Katherine 1702 w.
TUNBRIDGE
Westmoreland
Geo. 1698 w.
TUNDLE
Accomack
Scarburgh 1757 w.
TUNE
Richmond
Mark 1718 w.

Jas. 1742 i.
Harris 1752 w.
Wm. 1755 w.
Anthony 1776 w.
Anthony 1796 w.
Saml. 1796 w.
TUNELL
Accomack
Nathaniel 1696 w.
TUNNAL
Accomack
Robt. 1783 w.
TUNNEL
Accomack
Nathl. 1739 w.
Washburn 1772 w.
Wm. 1778 w.
Wm. 1780 i.
Scarbrough 1782 w.
Mary 1783 i.
Jos. 1789 w.
TUNNELL
Accomack
Edmd. 1750 w.
Nehemiah 1797 nw.
Southampton
Mary 1789 i.
TUNSTALL
Pittsylvania
Thos. 1788 w.
Louisa
Sarah 1792 a.
TURBERVILE
Orange
Edward 1751 i.
Sarah 1761 w.
TURBERVILL
Lancaster
Jno. 1728 i.
TURBERVILLE
Richmond
Geo. Lee 1798 w.
TURBEVILLE
Westmoreland
Geo. 1742 w.
TURBERVILLE
Westmoreland
Geo.. 1793 w.
TURBEVILLE
Westmoreland
Jno. 1799 w.
TURBYFILL
Brunswick
Jno. 1783 w.
Wm. 1786 w.
Wilson 1786 i.
TUREMAN
Culpeper
Robert 1754 w.
Ignatius 1782 w.
John 1778 i.

Spotsylvania
Ignatius 1784 w.
TURK
Augusta
Robt. 1772 w.
TURLAND
King George
Wm. 1754 i.
TURLEY
Fairfax
John 1756 w.
James 1771 i.
Paul 1772 w.
Jane 1773 i.
Paul 1777 w.
Henry
Peter 1782 w.
Loudoun
Sarah 1792 w.
TURLINGTON
Accomack
Peter 1749 w.
Thos. 1767 w.
Wm. 1781 w.
Wm. 1785 w.
Wm. 1786 i.
Peter 1784 w.
Ann Mary 1793 i.
Jas. 1793 w.
Jacob 1799 i.
TURMAN
Botetourt
Benjamin 1784 w.
TURNALL
Accomack
Thos. 1723 w.
Robt. 1763 w.
Tabitha 1783 w.
TURNBULL
King George
Jas. 1768 w.
Westmoreland
Stephen 1784 w.
Geo., Jr. 1785 nw.
TURNER
Accomack
Abraham 1768 w.
Richd. 1769 w.
Richd. 1769 i.
Albemarle
Jerisha 1772 i.
Charles 1789 w.
Amherst
Stephen, Jr. 1794 a.
Bedford
Richard 1769 w.
James 1793 i.
Berkeley
Mary 1782 w.
John 1792 i.

Brunswick
Joseph 1737 i.
Jas. 1743 w.
Jno. 1743 i.
Jas. 1746 i.
Wm. 1774 w.
Arthur 1777 w.
Jno. 1794 w.
Campbell
John 1796 nw.
Charlotte
Jno. 1792 i.
Keziah 1795 w.
Chesterfield
Wm. 1782 w.
Hannah 1795 i.
Matthew 1795 i.
Culpeper
John Baker 1781 w.
Nathan 1784 w.
Cumberland
Micajah 1762 i.
Essex
Michael 1708-9 i.
Jas. 1765 w.
Ann 1774 i.
Fairfax
Peter 1745 a.
Chas. 1780 i.
Franklin
Jas. 1789 a.
Frederick
Thos. 1744 w.
Anthony 1762 w.
Anthony 1769 i.
Anthony 1768 i.
Goochland
Jas. 1734 w.
Henry 1735 w.
Henry 1760 w.
Greensville
Jno. 1797 w.
Wm. 1797 w.
Halifax
Jas. 1756 i.
Jas. 1762 i.
Jno. 1764 w.
Jas. 1773 w.
Jno. 1781 w.
Jas. 1783 a.
Jas. 1785 w.
Tandy 1793 w.
Henrico
Patience 1733 w.
Abel 1734 w.
Henry
Izrareal 1777 w.
Shadrack 1784 w.
Isle of Wight
John 1705 w.
Joshua 1728 i.

Jas. 1736 w.
John 1737 i.
Thos. 1752 i.
Jno. 1761 w.
Martha 1761 w.
Joshua 1773 w.
Thos. 1775 w.
Mathew 1782 i.
Joshua 1784 i.
Wm. 1789 i.
King George
[Harry 1752] w.
Thos. 1758 w.
Jane 1795 i.
Loudoun
Fielding 1794 w.
Louisa
Wm. 1784 a.
Lunenburg
Robt. 1759 i.
Matthew 1783 w.
Middlesex
Danl. 1771 w.
Jas. 1785 w.
Thos. 1792 i.
Northampton
Richd. 1649 i.
Eliz. 1654 w.
Christopher 1668 w.
Edwd. 1728 w.
Judith 1732 w.
Richard 1734 w.
Jno. 1741 i.
Geo. N[icholas] 1741 w.
Sarah 1744 w.
Geo. Nicholas 1745 i.
Margt. 1745 w.
Maddox 1751 w.
Sarah 1753 w.
Edwd. 1754 w.
Geo. 1754 w.
Andrew 1760 w.
Jno. 1782 i.
Edwd. 1786 w.
Revell 1798 w.
Northumberland
Edwd. 1738 w.
Jno. 1742 w.
Geo. 1746 w.
Henry 1752 i.
Hannah 1754 i.
Jno. 1794 w.
Jno. 1796 w.
Wm. 1798 i.
Orange
Robt. 1744 w.
Prince Edward
John 1759 i.
Princess Anne
Thos. 1711 i.

Jno. 1750 w.
Thos. 1778 w.
Wm. 1782 i.
Jno. 1783 w.
Prince William
John 1744 ab.
Rappahannock
Hezekiah 1677 w.
Southampton
Simon 1762 w.
Wm. 1764 i.
Wm., Sr. 1766 w.
Simon 1767 w.
Jas. 1768 w.
Thos. 1771 w.
Sampson 1772 w.
Wm. 1773 i.
Jno. 1774 w.
Jos. 1774 w.
Simon 1775 i.
Jas. 1777 i.
Wm. 1779 w.
Benj. 1781 w.
Wm. 1782 i.
Arthur 1782 i.
Benj. 1783 w.
Littleton 1783 i.
Jacob 1784 w.
Thos. 1788 w.
Henry 1791 w.
Pass 1791 w.
Thos. 1791 i.
Henry 1792 w.
Benj. 1795 w.
Willie 1795 w.
Arthur 1797 i.
Jacob 1797 w.
Ann 1799 i.
Jno. 1799 w.
Stafford
Jos. 1747 i.
Jno. 1750 i.
Surry
James 1711 i.
Daniel 1735 w.
Jno. 1735 i.
Sussex
Edmund 1785 w.
James 1794 w.
James 1799 i.
Westmoreland
Robt. 1724 i.
Thos. 1787 w.
York
Jno. 1696 w.
Jno. 1775 w.
TURNHAM
Culpeper
John 1790 i.

TURNLEY
Spotsylvania
Francis 1769 w.
Francis 1797 w.
TURNOR
York
Abra. 1648 i.
TURPEN
Greenbrier
James 1777 w.
TURPIN
Botetourt
Solomon 1778 i.
Chesterfield
Philip 1763 i.
Eliz. 1767 w.
Henry, Sr. 1782 w.
Ann [1791] ? i.
Philip 1794 w.
Philip [1797] ? i.
Goochland
Obedience 1746 w.
Halifax
Michael 1794 w.
Henrico
Matthew 1688 w.
Michael [1701] w.
Lusby, Sr. 1791 w.
Jno. 1795 w.
Michael 1796 w.
Henry
James 1782 w.
Powhatan
Peterfield 1790 w.
Thos. 1790 w.
Thos. 1797 w.
TURTON (?)
Norfolk
Timothy 1684 i.
Princess Anne
Leonard 1734 i.
TUTE
Lunenburg
Partrick 1750 i.
TUTT
Culpeper
Richard 1771 w.
James 1773 i.
Reuben 1776 i.
Charles 1778 i.
James 1789 w.
King George
Richd. 1729 i.
Jos. 1750 i.
Jno. 1767 a.
Martha 1770 w.
Spotsylvania
Richd. 1767 w.
TUTTJE
Norfolk
Jno. 1669 w.

TWARTON
Accomack
Margt. 1711 w.
TWEDLE
Pittsylvania
Wm. 1794 w.
TWENTYMAN
Fauquier
Edward 1760 w.
TWIFORD
Accomack
Danl. 1779 w.
Jas. 1786 w.
Northampton
Wm. 1709 w
Jas. 1721 w.
Jno. 1729 i.
TWIFOOT
Accomack
Bartholomew 1759 w.
Northampton
Jno. 1725 i.
TWISDELL
Essex
John 1721 i.
TWITTY
Lunenburg
Jno. 1755 i.
TWYFORD
Surry
Jno. 1679 i.
Accomack
Hillery 1761 i.
TWYMAN
Middlesex
Geo. 1703 i.
Spotsylvania
Geo. 1734 w.
TYLER
Amherst
Danl. 1795 a.
Augusta
Wm. 1749 a.
Charlotte
Lewis 1777 w.
Essex
Richard 1734 w.
John 1757 w.
Richd. 1761 w.
Fairfax
Charles 1779 i.
Loudoun
Charles 1768 i.
Fauquier
Mary 1768 i.
King George
Jno. 1757 w.
Esther [1778?] w.
Wm. 1784 w.
Loudoun
Ann 1769 w.

Louisa
Henry 1773 a.
Mecklenburg
Wm. 1780 w.
Middlesex
Wm. 1741 a.
Northampton
Thos. 1692 w.
Jno., Sr. 1774 w.
Sarah 1788 i.
Prince William
Joseph 1786 i.
John 1792 i.
William 1794 w.
Southampton
Jeremiah 1789 w.
Sussex
Henry 1774 w.
Wm. 1792 w.
Westmoreland
Chas. 1723 i.
Jane 1723 i.
Jos. 1737 w.
Wm. 1773 i.
York
Hugh 1659 nw.
Henry 1729 w.
Jno. 1773 w.
Overton 1783 w.

TYNDLE
Accomack
Wm. 1750 nw.

TYNES
Halifax
Wm. 1795 w.
Isle of Wight
Timothy 1752 w.
Thomas 1771 w.
Robt., Jr. 1773 w.
Timothy 1773 i.
Martha 1778 w.
Henry 1781 i.
Celia 1782 w.
Robert 1794 w.
Benjamin 1799 w.

TYNGEY
Northumberland
Jno. 1667 w.

TYNON
Westmoreland
Wm. 1739 w.

TYNOR
Isle of Wight
Nicholas 1708-9 w.

TYPPETT
King George
Wm. 1729 i.

TYRE
Accomack
Thos. 1739 w.

TYREE
Charles City
Francis 1769 w.

TYRIE
York
Jas. 1786 w.

TYSON
Northampton
Nathl. 1792 w.

TYUS
Greensville
Lewis 1794 w.
Surry
Jno. 1725 w.
Thos. 1726 i.
Sussex
Thos. 1763 i.
Jno. 1763 w.
Agnes 1764 i.
Absolem 177- i.

TYUSS
Surry
Mary 1736 i.

U

UHLE
Bedford
Michael 1791 w.

ULMAN
Frederick
Mary 1768 w.

ULRICK
Frederick
Gasper 1762 i.

UMPRIESS
Princess Anne
Jno. 1792 w.

UNDERHILL
Accomack
Danl. 1788 w.
Thos. 1797 w.
Northampton
Thos. 1728 i.
Amos 1744 i.
Surry
Giles 1724 w.
Sussex
Isham 1779 w.
Henry 1781 w.
Henry 1791 w.
Howell 1795 w.
York
John 1672 w.
Jno. 1693 i.

UNDERWOOD
Augusta
Jas. 1764 i.
Brunswick
Jno. 1771 w.
Thos. 1774 w.

Culpeper
Lot 1773 w.
Wm. 1774 w.
Isle of Wight
Thos. 1702 w.
Thos. 1717 w.
Wm. 1723 i.
Thos. [1734] w.
Sampson 1799 w.
King George
Jno. 1723 i.
Wm. 1726 i.
Thos. 1752 w.
Wm. 1772 w.
Louisa
Elizabeth 1798 w.
Middlesex
Nathaniel 1716 i.
Prince William
John 1734 i.
Richmond
Wm. 1717 w.
Shenandoah
Geo. 1795 a.
Sussex
Beedles 1761 i.
Southampton
John 1787 w.
Sussex
Esther 1798 w.
Westmoreland
Mary 1707 w.

UNSEL
Ohio
Henry 1778 a.

UPCHURCH
Brunswick
Jas. 1765 w.
Jas. 1783 w.
Jas. 1784 w.
Michael 1796 i.
Surry
Michael 1681 a.

UPSHAW
Essex
Wm. 1720 w.
Jeremiah 1746-7 w.
Richard 1755 w.
Hannah 1758 i.
Forrest 1759 i.
Wm. 1760 w.
Wm. 1762 w.
Hannah 1763 w.
Sally 1771 w.

URQUHART
Loudoun
Jno. 1767 i.
Northumberland
Thos. 1711 i.
Thos. 1719 i.

USSERY
Lunenburg
Jno. 1752 i.
Jno. 1784 i.
UPSHUR
Accomack
Arthur 1708 w.
Arthur 1738 w.
Abel 1754 w.
Arthur 1784 w.
Caleb 1784 i.
Abel 1792 i.
Leah 1792 w.
Northampton
Thos. 1750 w.
Thos., Sr. 1793 w.
Thos., Sr. 1793 w.
Jno., Sr. 1799 w.
Thos. 1799 i.
UPTON
Albemarle
Mary 1775 w.
Isle of Wight
John 1652 w.
URIE
Middlesex
Jno. 1756 w.
UTLEY
Goochland
Jno. 1762 w.
UTT
Augusta
Caspar 1756 i.
UTTERBACK
Culpeper
Henry 1799 w.
UTZ
Culpeper
Geo. 1766 w.
Michael 1790 w.
UZZELL
Isle of Wight
Thos 1751 w.

V

VACHUB
Rockbridge
Mathew 1785 i.
Joseph 1787 w.
VADEN
Chesterfield
Wm. 1770 w.
Jno. 1790 w.
Danl. 1792 w.
Geo. 1798 w.
Henrico
Henry 1755 i.
VAHAN
Accomack
Edwd. 1682 w.

VAIDEN
Goochland
Jno. 1781 w.
VALENCIER
Chesterfield
Gilbert 1776 w.
VALENTINE
Isle of Wight
John [1652] w.
James 1677 w.
Surry
Peter 1792 w.
York
Bartholomew 1720 i
Jos. 1771 w.
Benj. 1782 i.
VALLENTINE
Surry
Nicholas 1737 a.
VANARSDALE
Berkeley
Cornelius 1782 i.
VANBEBBER
Botetourt
Isack 1776 i.
VANCE
Augusta
Jno. P. 1782 w.
Bedford
John 1759 a.
Berkeley
Hugh 1792 w.
Joseph 1799 w.
Frederick
James 1751 w.
Andrew 1754 w.
John 1760 w.
James 1762 w.
David 1768 w.
Elizabeth 1785 w.
William 1792 w.
Greenbrier
Jacob 1798 i.
Isle of Wight
Hugh 1756 w.
Lydia 1771 i.
Rockbridge
Patrick 1791 i.
Washington
Samuel 1778 w.
York
Patrick 1747 w.
VANDAGESTEEL
Stafford
Giles 1700 w.
VANDEGRAUGH
Accomack
Obediah 1744 i.
VANDEN
York
Richd. 1762 i.

VANDERHOOD
Henrico
Henry 1734 w.
Henry 1735 w.
VANDEWALL
Henrico
Nathl. 1783 w.
VANDIVAN
Prince George
Jno. 1726 w.
VANDIVER
Loudoun
Geo. 1764 w.
VANELSON
Accomack
Cuzaline, (the
  younger) 1742 w.
Elias 1772 w.
Selby 1784 w.
Selby 1786 i.
VANGEMUNDAY
Augusta
Philip Chas. 1765 w.
VANGOVER
Lancaster
Jno. 1726 w.
Princess Anne
Blazen 1790 w.
VANHORN
Loudoun
Bernard 1799 i.
VANLANDENHAM
Northumberland
Francis 1740 w.
VANLANDINGHAM
Northumberland
Francis 1753 i.
Geo. 1774 w.
Henry P. 1791 i.
Benj. 1795 w.
Richd. 1796 i.
VAN LEAR
Augusta
Jacob 1783 w.
VAN MATRE
Frederick
Isaac 1749 i.
VANMATRE
Botetourt
Isaac 1798 i.
VANMETER
Berkeley
Abraham 1783 w.
Henry 1793 w.
VAN METER
Frederick
John 1745 w.
VANMETER
Hardy
Garrett 1788 w.

VANMETRE
Ohio
    Joseph 1781 a.
    Abram 1782 a.
VANNER
York
    Wm. 1758 i.
VANOVER
Montgomery
    Cornelius 1797 i.
VARNER
Chesterfield
    Edwd. 1785 w.
    Edwd. 1791 i.
VARNUM
York
    Lewis 1708 i.
VASS
Essex
    Vincent 1727 w.
    John 1755 w.
    William 1788 i.
Middlesex
    Henry 1795 i.
Spotsylvania
    Vincent 1766 a.
    Jno. 1768 a.
VASSEN
Amelia
    Wm. 1754 w.
    Mary 1772 w.
VASSER
Isle of Wight
    John [1650?] w.
    Peter 1709 w.
    William 1724 w.
    Peter 1729 i.
    John 1736 w.
Southampton
    Jacob 1758 i.
    Benj. 1762 w.
    Nathan 1770 w.
    Elijah 1775 i.
    Lydia 1776 w.
    Jos. 1788 w.
VASTEEN
Augusta
    Wm. 1795 i.
VAUGAN
Mecklenburg
    Wm. 1786 w.
VAUGHAN
Amelia
    Thos. 1751 w.
    Henry 1756 w.
    Abraham 1765 i.
    David 1769 i.
    Geo. 1771 w.
    Stephen 1776 i.
    Robt. 1779 w.
    Saml. 1781 w.

Jeen 1795 i.
Amherst
    Cornelius 1779 w.
Brunswick
    Abraham 1748 w.
    Richd. 1749 w.
    Wm. 1754 i.
    Wm. 1755 i.
Charles City
    Rabley 1772 w.
    Wm. S. 1791 w.
Charlotte
    Abraham 1796 w.
    Edwd. 1796 w.
    Molly 1799 w.
Culpeper
    Jacob 1774 i.
Goochland
    Matthew 1798 i.
Greensville
    Pierce 1786 w.
    Rebecca 1791 i.
    Faitha 1797 w.
    Tabitha 1797 w.
    William 1798 w.
Halifax
    Wm. 1777 w.
Isle of Wight
    John 1741 w.
    Samuel 1763 w.
    Henry 1782 i.
Lunenburg
    James 1750 w.
Mecklenburg
    Drury 1783 i.
    Claibourne 1787 i.
    Mildredge 1791 w.
    Jeremiah 1792 w.
    James 1797 i.
Norfolk
    Wm. 1688 w.
Northampton
    Richd. 1656 w.
Pittsylvania
    Thos. 1788 w.
Powhatan
    Edmund 1796 w.
Prince George
    Saml. 1718 w.
Princess Anne
    Jno. 1694 w.
Southampton
    Wm. 1769 w.
    Wm. 1779 w.
    Henry 1784 w.
    Wm. 1794 w.
    Lydia 1796 w.
Spotsylvania
    Eliz. 1778 w.
Surry
    James 1731 w.

Sussex
    Thos. 1788 w.
    Dorothy 1796 w.
Westmoreland
    Jno. 1664 w.
    Saml. 1677 i.
    Jno. 1718 i.
    Corderoy 1735 w.
VAUGHN
Brunswick
    James 1735 w.
Henry
    Reuben 1798 i.
VAULX
Northumberland
    Robt. 1722 i.
Westmoreland
    James 1711 w.
    Robt. 1721 w.
    Robt. 1755 w.
York
    Robt. 1659 i.
    Robt. 1681-2 i.
VAUX
Westmoreland
    Robt. 1756 i.
VAWTER
Culpeper
    John 1752 w.
    Margaret 1756 w.
    Bartho. 1777 i.
Cumberland
    Saml. 1789 i.
Northampton
    Wm. 1735 i.
Essex
    Bartho. 1717 w.
    Benj. 1736 i.
    Edward 1779 w.
    Angus 1785 w.
    Richard 1799 w.
VEALE
Essex
    Wm. 1693 w.
Norfolk
    Morrice 1705-6 w.
    Lemuel 1757 i.
    Geo. 1773 w.
    George 1776 w.
    Thomas 1793 w.
    Samuel 1796 i.
Westmoreland
    Morris 1696 w.
VEATCH
King George
    Jno. 1758 w.
VEEL
Westmoreland
    Jno. 1718 w.

VEIL
Princess Anne
Martha 1791 w.
VELDEN
Lancaster
Francis 1733 i.
VELE
Frederick
Ezekel 1773 i.
VELLINES
Isle of Wight
Thaits 1798 w.
VELLINS
Isle of Wight
Samuel 1788 w.
VENABLE
Albemarle
Wm. 1772 i.
Cumberland
Jno. 1782 w.
Fluvanna
Wm. 1781 i.
Louisa
Abraham 1769 w.
Prince Edward
Abraham 1778 w.
Abrim 1780 i.
VENABLES
Hanover
Abraham 1734 a.
VENELSON
Accomack
Chas. 1748 w.
VENNAMAN
Frederick
George 1752 i.
VERDEE
Berkeley
James 1786 i.
VERE
Northampton
Wm. 1796 w.
VERNON
Fairfax
John 1793 i.
VERSER
Amelia
Jonas 1767 w.
Joel 1782 w.
VESSELLS
Accomack
Ephraim 1774 w.
Anne 1776 w.
VESSELS
Accomack
Jas. 1754 w.
Elijah 1797 i.
Elijah 1799 w.
Sophia 1799 w.

VEST
Amelia
Vollentine 1751 i.
Chesterfield
Jno. 1765 w.
Valentine 1776 w.
Jas. 1794 w.
Berkeley
Daniel 1790 i.
VESTAL
Frederick
William 1746 i.
VESTALL
Berkeley
John 1776 i.
VESTE
Norfolk
Widow 1669 i.
VETE
Frederick
Ezekiel 1773 w.
VIA
Amherst
Jno. 1781 w.
Henrico
Margt. 1795 w.
VIALE
Loudoun
William 1793 w.
VIAR
Albemarle
Wm. 1783 w.
VIATT
Norfolk
John 1782 w.
VICK
Greensville
John 1789 w.
Howell 1795 i.
Sarah 1795 w.
Isle of Wight
Robert 1735 w.
Southampton
Richd. 1758 w.
Joshua 1767 w.
Jos. 1770 w.
Wm. 1778 w.
Arthur 1780 w.
Arthur, Sr. 1782 i.
Wm. 1784 w.
Saml. 1785 w.
Matthew 1788 w.
Richd. 1789 w.
Shadrock 1789 i.
Jacob 1789 w.
Robt. 1789 w.
Matthew 1792 i.
Wm. 1794 w.
Jacob 1795 i.
Jas. 1796 w.
Simon 1799 w.

VICKARS
Isle of Wight
John 1678 w.
VICKERS
Isle of Wight
Robert 1747 w.
VICKERY
Orange
Hezekiah 1736 w.
VICTON
York
Michell 1647 i.
VICTORY
Rockbridge
John 1784 i.
VIER
Augusta
David 1766 w.
VIGNE
Goochland
Adam 1728 w.
VIGOR
Westmoreland
Jacob 1797 i.
VIGOUR
Westmoreland
Wm. 1767 w.
VILET
Fairfax
Edward 1773 w.
Ewel 1771 w.
VILEY
Fairfax
John 1786 i.
VINCE
Lancaster
Jno. 1688 w.
VINCENT
Greensville
John 1789 w.
Joseph 1798 i.
Norfolk
Wm. 1654 w.
Surry
Peter 1728 i.
Westmoreland
Henry 1666 w.
Jos. 1701 w.
Thos. 1752 i.
VINCENTO
Norfolk
Nicholas 1654 i.
VINES
Sussex
Wm. 1787 w.
Mary 1790 i.
York
Thos. 1731 i.
Thos. 1737 w.

VINEY
Washington
  Stephen 1795 w.
VINEYARD
Botetourt
  Christian 1798 w.
VINSON
Brunswick
  Thos. 1771 i.
Surry
  Jno. 1699 i.
  Katherine 1705 w.
VINTON
Spotsylvania
  Margt. 1750 a.
VINTOY (?)
Northampton
  Wm. 1652 i.
VIOLET
Fairfax
  Whaley 1794 i.
VIOLETT
Loudoun
  Edwd. 1797 i.
VIRGETT
Essex
  Job 1713 i.
VIRT
Loudoun
  Peter 1799 i.
VIVIAN
Isle of Wight
  Thomas 1670 i.
Northumberland
  Wm. 1726-7 i.
VIVION
Orange
  John 1793 a.
Middlesex
  Jno. 1705 w.
  Jno. 1722 w.
Westmoreland
  Thos. 1761 w.
VOAKS
Northumberland
  Wm. 1724-5 i.
VODEN
Chesterfield
  Danl. 1793 i.
  Gardner 1794 w.
  Jno. 1795 i.
VODIN
Henrico
  Henry 1747 w.
VOLCKNER
Shenandoah
  Adam 1787 w.
VOSS
Norfolk
  Israel 1714 w.
Northampton
  Henry 1662 i.

Anne 1690 w.

W

WACKAWAMP
Northampton
  (Indian Emperor)
  1656 w.
WADDEL
Fauquier
  Jno. 1788 w.
WADDELL
Norfolk
  Jno. 1798 w.
WADDEY
Northumberland
  Jas. 1725 w.
  Sarah 1749 w.
  John 1750-1 i.
  James 1772 w.
  Thos. 1794 w.
WADDILL
Chesterfield
  Wm. 1754 w.
WADDINGTON
Northumberland
  Jno. 1721 i.
WADDLE
Augusta
  Thos., Sr. 1784 w.
Culpeper
  Wm. 1797 i.
WADDY
Louisa
  Saml. 1764 w.
  Mary 1773 w.
  Jno. 1776 w.
  Frances 1778 w.
  Saml., Jr. 1780 w.
Northumberland
  Thos. 1739 i.
  Benj. 1741 i.
  Jno. 1748 w.
  Jno. 1750 i.
  Sarah 1750 i.
  Eliz. 1758 i.
  John 1775 w.
  Penelope 1775 w.
  Benj. 1781 w.
WADE
Albemarle
  David 1793 i.
Amherst
  Pearce 1769 w.
  Jno. 1785 w.
Bedford
  Jeremiah 1772 w.
  Jeremiah 1779 i.
Brunswick
  Wm. 1781 i.
Cumberland
  Jeremiah 1798 i.

Fairfax
  Zephaniah 1747-8 i.
Franklin
  John Attly 1798 w.
Goochland
  Richd. 1757 w.
  Grisle 1768 w.
  Wm. 1772 w.
  Richd. 1794 w.
Halifax
  Robt. 1765 w.
  Andrew 1756 w.
  Robt. 1770 N.
  Ann 1774 i.
  Robt., Jr. 1774 i.
  Edwd. 1776 w.
  Wm. 1782 w.
  Hampton 1783 i.
  Andrew 1789 i.
  Edwd. 1785 a.
  Jno. 1786 w.
Henrico
  Edwd. 1796 i.
  Jos. 1799 i.
Isle of Wight
  Chris. 1687-8 i.
  Edwd. [1720] i.
Lancaster
  Jno. 1688 w.
Loudoun
  Zephaniah 1794 i.
Mecklenburg
  Wm. 1779 w.
  David 1786 i.
Prince Edward
  Chas. 1782 w.
  Leonard 1783 i.
  Philip 1795 w.
  Lewis 1799 i.
  Philip 1799 i.
Princess Anne
  Thos. 1791 i.
Richmond
  Jno. 1734 w.
  Jno. 1750 i.
Shenandoah
  Zachary 1774 a.
Southampton
  Chris. 1782 w.
  Wilson 1798 i.
Surry
  Danl. 1695 w.
Sussex
  Thos. 1772 w.
York
  Arminger 1677 w.
  Edwd. 1677 w.
  Arminger 1708 w.
  Edwd. 1719 i.
  Jno. 1722 w.
  Thos. 1755 w.
  Jos. 1762 w.

Jno. 1744 w.
WADKINS
Louisa
Jno. 1769 w.
WADLE
Botetourt
Martin 1783 w.
WADLOW
Goochland
Thos. 1773 w.
Pittsylvania
Wm. 1795 w.
WADSON
Powhatan
Wm. 1799 w.
WAFF
Norfolk
Geo. 1763 i.
WAGAMAN
Accomack
Hendrick 1682 w.
WAGENER
Fairfax
Peter 1776 i.
Peter 1798 w.
WAGER
Greensville
Elizabeth 1784 w.
Surry
Robt. 1755 i.
WAGGAMAN
Accomack
Jonathan 1724 w.
WAGGENER
Essex
Saml. 1729 w.
Christianna 1730 i.
Herbert 1743 w.
Richard 1767 i.
Frederick
Thomas 1760 i.
WAGGERMAN
Accomack
Ephraim 1758 w.
WAGGMAN
Accomack
Ephraim 1768 i.
WAGGNER
Essex
John 1716 w.
Rachel 1718 w.
WAGGOMAN
Accomack
Jos. 1795 w.
WAGGONER
Berkeley
Chris. 1794 w.
Culpeper
Gransley 1798 i.
Essex
John 1697 w.
Benj. 1748-9 w.

WAGNER
Surry
Jno. 1798 i.
WAGONNER
Montgomery
Adam 1786 w.
WAGSTAFF
Lunenburg
Francis 1760 w.
York
Basil 1719 w.
Basil 1726 i.
Albrighton 1735 i.
Jno. 1775 w.
Jno. 1781 w.
WAIGHT
Rappahannock
John 1679 w.
WAIL
Isle of Wight
Nicholas 1776 w.
WAILE
Isle of Wight
John 1785 w.
Rachel 1787 w.
WAILLES
Isle of Wight
Nicholas 1711 i.
WAILS
Isle of Wight
Ann 1778 w.
John 1786 i.
WAINHOUSE
Accomack
Francis 1720 w.
Francis 1724 i.
Francis 1760 w.
Bridget 1761 i.
Francis 1764 w.
WAINWRIGHT
Isle of Wight
William 1737 i.
William 1750 i.
Norfolk
John 1764 i.
George 1798 i.
WAIT
Accomack
Wm. 1708 w.
Botetourt
George 1798 w.
WAITE
Fauquier
William 1787 i.
Jane 1794 w.
WAKE
Middlesex
Wm. 1715 w.
Robt., Jr. 1765 w.
Ambrose 1782 i.
Jno., Sr. 1789 i.

Norfolk
Richard 1648 i.
Northumberland
Matthew 1669 i.
WAKEFEILD
Norfolk
Thomas 1709-10 w.
Edward 1710-11 w.
John 1712 w.
WAKEFIELD
Lancaster
Jno. 1660 w.
Norfolk
John 1734-5 w.
Geo. 1753 i.
William 1765 w.
Princess Anne
Lemuel 1785 w.
Ann 1787 i.
WAKELY
Isle of Wight
Mathew 1680 i.
Lunenburg
Wm. 1753 i.
WAKEMAN
Richmond
Mary 1710 i.
WAKUP
Lunenburg
James 1750 w.
WALDEN
Campbell
Richd. 1793 i.
Halifax
Saml. 1779 w.
Middlesex
Mary 1750 i.
Pittsylvania
Richd. 1790 w.
Mourning 1794 w.
WALDER
Lancaster
Edwd. 1698-9 w.
WALDIN
Brunswick
Matthew 1762 i.
WALDON
Brunswick
Jno. E. 1761 i.
Shenandoah
William 1793 a.
WALDRON
York
Henry 1656 w.
WALDROPE
Pittsylvania
Jas. 1772 w.
WALE
Accomack
Wm. 1714 w.
Isle of Wight
Nicholas 1777 i.

Lancaster
Geo. 1674 i.
Geo. 1688 i.
Benj. 1709 w.
Geo. 1721 i.
John 1749 i.
George 1767 w.
William 1777 w.
John 1784 i.
Lawson 1785 w.
WALEING
Surry
Wm. 1775 w.
WALES
Frederick
Mary 1748 i.
Henrico
Jno. 1786 i.
Isle of Wight
John 1677 i.
WALFORD
Berkeley
Martin 1781 w.
WALK
Princess Anne
Thos. 1703 i.
WALKDEN
Northumberland
Jas. 1738-9 i.
WALKE
Amelia
Jno. 1798 i.
Norfolk
Thos. 1693-4 w.
Princess Anne
Thos. 1704 i.
Thos. 1761 w.
Thos. 1764 i.
Anthony 1782 w.
Mary 1788 w.
Mary 1795 w.
William 1795 w.
John Bassett 1796 w.
Thomas 1797 w.
Thos. 1723 w.
WALKER
Accomack
Peter 1696 w.
Henry 1704 i.
Peter 1704 i.
Nathl. 1719 w.
Mary 1723 w.
Nehemiah 1745 i.
Jno. 1746 w.
Jos. 1747 w.
Jno. 1749 i.
Eliz. 1751 i.
Jno. 1762 i.
Jos. 1767 w.
Stephen 1768 w.
Naomy 1770 i.

Danl. 1771 w.
Robt. 1772 i.
Wm. B. 1780 w.
Wm. 1794 w.
Jno., Sr. 1796 w.
Jno., Jr. 1796 w.
Levin 1798 w.
Albemarle
Thos. 1794 w.
Eliz. 1796 w.
Amelia
Jno. 1760 i.
Edmund 1768 w.
Wm. 1785 w.
Edmund 1795 w.
Amherst
Joel 1794 w.
Augusta
Alex., Jr. 1770 a.
Alex. 1775 w.
Andrew 1778 w.
Bedford
Robert 1767 w.
Saml. 1777 i.
Botetourt
Alexander 1771 nw.
Brunswick
Alex. 1755 i.
Freeman 1766 w.
Geo. 1780 w.
Danl., Jr. 1786 w.
Wm. 1789 w.
Campbell
Saml. 1788 w.
Charles City
Lockey 1774 w.
Alex. 1790 i.
Wm. 1790 i.
Freeman 1790 i.
Alex. 1791 i.
Rebecca 1794 w.
Richardson 1794 w.
Charlotte
Eliz. 1796 i.
Chesterfield
Michael 1754 w.
Francis 1767 w.
Culpeper
Edwd. 1776 w.
Jno. 1776 w.
Cumberland
Wm. 1752 w.
Judith 1768 w.
Benj. 1781 w.
Warren 1785 w.
Frederick
Jno. 1756 w.
Goochland
Jno. Jr. 1740 w.
David 1741 w.
Jno. 1767 w.

David, Jr. 1772 w.
David, Sr. 1774 w.
Mary 1777 w.
Jno. 1794 w.
Agnes 1798 w.
Philip 1798 w.
Henrico
Eliz. 1728 w.
Isle of Wight
Danl. 1678 w.
Jno. 1755 i.
King George
Robt. 1777 a.
Loudoun
Isaac 1782 w.
Lunenburg
Judith 1752 w.
Tandy 1752 i.
Mecklenburg
Edwd. Brodnax
1773 w.
Silvanus 1786 w.
Henry 1792 w.
Middlesex
Thos. 1721 w.
Richd. 1727 w.
Richd. 1728 i.
Jno. 1745 w.
Northampton
Peter 1655 i.
Nathl. 1683 w.
Wm. 1684 i.
Jno. 1709 w.
Northumberland
Edwd. 1656 w.
Mary 1711 i.
Nathl. 1728 i.
Thos. 1744 i.
Richd. 1747 i.
Jane 1750 w.
Jos. 1752 w.
Leonardo 1752 i.
Thos. 1756 i.
Manuel 1757 w.
Wm. 1761 w.
Richd. 1772 w.
Jno. 1777 w.
Jno. 1778 w.
Jos. 1784 i.
Risdon 1785 i.
Francis 1789 i.
Geo. 1791 i.
Thos. 1792 w.
Edmd. 1795 i.
Rachel 1796 w.
Richd. 1798 w.
Orange
Thos. 1770 w.
Pittsylvania
Jas. 1778 i.
David 1780 i.

Susannah 1783 i.
Catherine 1788 i.
Prince Edward
George 1773 w.
Henry 1780 i.
Wm. 1797 i.
Princess Anne
Thos. 1703 w.
Wm. 1777 i.
Wm. 1779 i.
Thos. R. 1788 w.
Prince William
Jno. 1737 w.
Rappahannock
Sarah 1679 w.
Richmond
Jno. 1706 w.
Jno. 1726 i.
Wm. 1736 i.
Thos. 1747 w.
Wm. 1751 i.
Wm. 1754 w.
Jeremiah 1755 i.
Thos. 1759 w.
Rockbridge
Alex. 1784 w.
Alex. 1785 w.
Jas. 1787 i.
Saml. 1794 i.
Jno. 1795 i.
Jno. 1797 w.
Stafford
Wm. 1749 w.
Wm. 1767 i.
Surry
Timothy 1706 w.
Washington
John 1778 w.
Saml. 1779 w.
Westmoreland
Richd. 1664 w.
Jno. 1665 w.
Richd. 1672-3 w.
Thos. 1715 i.
Thos. 1716 w.
Chas. 1716 i.
Thos. 1726 w.
Wm. 1727 i.
Wm. 1733 w.
Geo. 1744 w.
Peter 1745 w.
Edmd. 1746 i.
Benj. 1749 i.
Jno. 1761 w.
Danl. 1762 i.
Peter 1776 i.
Jno. 1777 i.
Jas. 1778 w.
Martha 1779 i.
Jas. 1783 i.
Saml. 1786 i.

WALKER
York
Eliz. 1656 w.
Ralph 1702 w.
Jos. 1723 w.
Chapman 1737 i.
Jno. 1799 i.
WALKINS
Surry
Jno., Sr. 1797 w.
WALKTON
York
Robt. 1674 i.
WALL
Augusta
Jno. 1761 a.
Jno. (2) 1761 a.
Adam 1764 w.
Brunswick
Danl. 1736 i.
Michael 1749 w.
Wm. 1751 w.
Jno. 1758 w.
Michael 1758 i.
Jno. 1761 w.
Mary 1763 w.
Geo. 1768 i.
Jas., Jr. 1777 w.
Rebecca 1777 w.
Geo. 1781 w.
Geo. 1791 i.
Essex
James 1753 i.
Dorothy 1762 w.
Greensville
James 1788 w.
Sarah 1794 w.
Willis 1799 i.
Halifax
Geo. 1761 w.
Isham 1777 w.
Burgess 1785 w.
Jno. 1787 w.
David 1789 w.
Jno.. 1795 i.
Montgomery
Adam 1799 w.
Northumberland
Jno. 1711 i.
Orange
Jacob 1736 w.
Prince George
John 1717 w.
Surry
Thos. 1663 i.
Jno. 1673 w.
Joseph 1727 w.
Jno. 1763 w.
Aron 1783 w.
Jonathan 1789 w.

WALLACE
Albemarle
Wm. 1766 w.
Andrew 1785 w.
Amelia
Jeff. 1763 i.
Augusta
Saml. 1764 i.
Saml. 1765 w.
Widow 1766 i.
Wm. 1779 i.
Jas. 1780 w.
Brunswick
Susannah 1757 w.
Greenbrier
Moses 1786 i.
King George
Michael 1767 w.
Lancaster
James 1791 w.
Lunenburg
Wm. 1783 i.
Middlesex
Wm. 1744 a.
Norfolk
Richard 1765 w.
William 1768 w.
David 1783 w.
John 1785 w.
Kedar 1789 w.
Wm., Sr. 1797 w.
Richmond
Walter 1763 w.
Rockbridge
Adam 1781 w.
Andrew 1781 w.
John 1782 w.
Peter 1786 w.
Samuel 1786 w.
William 1796 w.
WALLARD
Prince William
Burr 1737 i.
WALLENTINE
Loudoun
Joseph 1790 w.
WALLER
Essex
Charles 1725 w.
William 1746 i.
Fauquier
John 1795 i.
Lunenburg
James 1788 w.
Norfolk
Hardress 1778 w.
Ann 1784 i.
Robert 1790 i.
Mason 1794 w.
Northumberland
Ephraim 1744 i.

Jas. 1744 w.
Southampton
John 1784 i.
Spotsylvania
Jno. 1754 w.
Dorothy 1758 w.
Wm. 1760 w.
Jno. 1775 a.
Jno. 1776 w.
Agnes 1779 w.
Thos. 1787 w.
Pomfrett 1799 w.
Stafford
Wm. 1703 w.
Susannah 1749 w.
Catherine 1749 w.
Edwd. 1754 w.
Edwd. 1785 w.
Jno. 1785 w.
Surry
Thomas 1721 w.
Thos. 1750 i.
Mary 1752 i.
Edwd. 1782 w..
Benj. 1788 i.
York
Wm. 1799 i.
WALLES
Norfolk
Wm. 1753 w.
WALLICE
Amelia
Jno., Sr. 1755 w.
Mary 1773 w.
Norfolk
Thos. 1705-6 w.
Thos. 1718 i.
WALLING
Montgomery
Jas. 1786 w.
WALLIS
Accomack
Wm. 1678 i.
Jno. 1695 w.
Amelia
Matthew 1759 i.
Brunswick
Susanna 1758 w.
Fairfax
Saml., Jr. 1795 a. .
Lancaster
Francis 1734 w.
Norfolk
Jno. 1701 w.
Wm. 1711 i.
Richd. 1719 w.
Wm. 1753 w.
Ann 1762 w.
Jno. 1765 w.
Jno. 1768 w.
Solomon 1768 w.

Wm. 1768 i.
Northumberland
Hugh 1712-13 w.
Jos. 1740 i.
Prince William
Burr 1736 a.
Thos. 1743 i.
Surry
Thos., Sr. 1749 w.
Sussex
Jas. 1755 i.
WALLOP
Accomack
Jno. 1693 w.
Skinner 1718 i.
Jno. 1751 w.
Jno. 1754 i.
Wm. 1769 i.
WALLS
Berkeley
George 1786 i.
George 1788 w.
Frederick
Mary 1746 w.
WALLTON
Brunswick
Jno. 1795 w.
WALPOLE
Brunswick
Jno. 1777 w.
Thos. 1792 w.
Prince George
Richd. 1718 i.
WALSH
Norfolk
Richd. 1765 w.
Westmoreland
Richd. 1747 i.
WALSHAM
King George
Robt. 1774 w.
WALSTEN
Norfolk
Saml. 1686-7 w.
WALSTON
Isle of Wight
Mary 1725 w.
Norfolk
Thos. 1782 i.
Princess Anne
Hester 1727 w.
WALSTONE
Princess Anne
Wm. 1697 i.
Jno. 1704 a.
Joseph 1728 i.
Thos. 1731 i.
WALTER
Accomack
Richd. 1787 w.

WALSWORTH
Princess Anne
Wm. 1706 w.
WALTER
Northampton
Benj. 1703 w.
Jno., Sr. 1718-19 w.
Jno. 1743 w.
Mary 1755 w.
Jno. 1772 w.
Orange
Michael 1798 w.
WALTERS
Accomack
Richd. 1789 i.
Pittsylvania
Thos. 1796 w.
Henrico
Jno. 1735 w.
Isle of Wight
Walter 1731 w.
Walter 1732 w.
Lancaster ·
Miles 1721 w.
Montgomery
Jas. 1786 a.
Northumberland
Roger 1669 w.
Spotsylvania
Isaac 1726 w.
WALTHALL
Amelia
Henry 1756 w.
Chris. 1778 w.
Richd. 1782 i.
Wm., Sr. 1782 w.
Wm. 1792 w.
Robt. 1794 w.
Wm. 1798 w.
Chesterfield
Francis 17—i.
Thos. 17—i.
Jeremiah 1747-8 w.
Richd. 1763 w.
Henry 1764 w.
Richd. 1764 i.
Henry 1766 w.
Francis 1770 w.
Henry 1773 w.
Benj. 1774 i.
Martha 1774 w.
Henry 1775 i.
Thos. 1776 w.
Wm. 1782 i.
Wm. 1788 w.
Jeremiah 1790 w.
Wm. 1791 w.
Gerrard 1792 w.
Jas. 1792 i.
Jno. 1792 w.
Gerrard 1794 i.

Henrico
Dinah 1715 w.
Richd. 1715 w.
Wm. 1715 w.
Henry, Sr. 1733 w.
Mary 1736 w.
Richd. 1745 i.
Prince Edward
Chris. 1799 w.
WALTHAM
Accomack
Eliz. 1702 w.
Charlton 1722 i.
Jno. 1773 w.
Jno. 1775 i.
Teackle 1777 w.
Northampton
Stephen 1773 w.
Jno. 1778 w.
Stephen 1728 w.
WALTHORN
Accomack
Jno. 1698 i.
WALTMAN
Loudoun
Emanuel 1784 w.
WALTON
Brunswick
Geo. 1767 w.
Isaac Row 1770 w.
Eliz. 1775 w.
Thos. 1789 w.
Wm. 1789 w..
Cumberland
Robt. 1750 w.
Thos. 1771 w.
Josiah 1776 i.
Martha 1798 w.
Frederick
Moses 1764 w.
Moses 1782 w.
Goochland
Wm. 1747 w.
Isle of Wight
John 1705 w.
Thomas 1754 i.
Louisa
John 1794 i.
Northumberland
Robt. 1671 w.
Prince Edward
Jesse Hughes 1791 w.
Geo. 1797 w.
Washington
William 1797 i.
WALTUM
Northampton
Jno. 1650 w.
WAMSLEY
Augusta
Jno., Sr. 1782 w.

WAPPLE
Surry
Jno. 1716 i.
WARBURTON
Henrico
Wm. 1750 w.
WARCUP
Henrico
Jno. 1727 i.
WARD
Accomack
Thos. 1718 i.
Isaac 1788 w.
Albemarle
Eliz. 1793 w.
Amelia
Henry 1765 w.
Jno. 1779 w.
Henry [1780] i.
Benj. [1783?] i.
Richd. 1785 w.
Benj. 1787 w.
Amherst
Benj. 1761 a.
Bedford
John 1782 w.
Berkeley
Joseph 1787 w.
Joshua 1792 i.
Brunswick
Jno. 1761 w.
Campbell
Mark 1795 w.
Charlotte
Seth 1794 w.
Jno. 1796 w.
Seth 1797 w.
Wm. 1799 w.
Chesterfield
Leonard 1772 w.
Seth 1772 w.
Seth 1773 w.
Benj. 1783 w.
Blackman 1789 w.
Culpeper
William 1749 w.
Margaret 1777 w.
Jacob 1791 w.
Essex
John 1727 i.
Abel 1730 i.
Fairfax
William 1794 w.
Frederick
Francis 1748 i.
Sarah 1753 i.
Henrico
Richd. 1682 w.
Mary 1727 i.
Richd. 1728 i.
Benj. 1732 w.

Benj. 1734 i.
Seth 1734 w.
Jos. 1788 w.
Isle of Wight
Thomas 1693 i.
Thomas 1728 w.
John 1740 w.
Benjamin 1752 i.
Joseph 1768 w.
Joseph 1770 i.
Francis 1776 w.
Thomas 1777 i.
Wills 1782 i.
Lancaster
William 1795 i.
Louisa
Wm. 1799 w.
Lunenburg
Richd. 1762 w.
Middlesex
Wm. 1703 i.
Norfolk
Thos. 1654 w.
Edwd. 1669 w.
John 1710 a.
Thomas 1744-5 w.
William 1748 i.
Thomas 1773 w.
Thomas 1783 i.
Godfree 1785 w.
Northampton
Benoni 1694 w.
Michael 1799 w.
Prince Edward
Robt. B. 1795 w.
Prince George
Collingwood 1719 i.
Princess Anne
Jno. 1733 w.
Jno. 1735 i.
Robt. 1756 w.
James 1757 i.
Thos. 1764 w.
Arthur 1782 i.
Geo. 1782 w.
Caleb 1785 w.
Simon 1785 w.
Randolph
George 1791 w.
Richmond
Thos. 1709 i.
Spotsylvania
Jno. 1785 a.
Surry
Thos. 1676 w.
Jno. 1715 w.
Saml. 1720 w.
Robt. 1783 i.
Elizabeth 1799 w.
Westmoreland
Jno. 1718 w.

Henry 1741 w.
Wm. 1754 i.
York
Plany 1733 w.
WARDE
Orange
Jonathan 1741 a.
Princess Anne
Mary 1778 i.
WARDEN
Fairfax
Robert 1743 w.
James 1785 w.
Frederick
William 1754 i.
Norfolk
James 1739 w.
John 1741 w.
John 1747 i.
John 1773 w.
Wm. 1790 w.
WARDLAW
Augusta
Wm. 1762 w.
WARE
Amherst
Edwd. 1779 w.
Chesterfield
Caleb 1740 w.
Goochland
Peter 1741 w.
Henrico
Jacob 1709 i.
Susanna 1735 w.
Isle of Wight
Thomas 1676 w.
King George
Henry 1751 i.
Middlesex
Edwd. 1774 w.
Jas. 1778 i.
Jane 1787 w.
Northampton
Wm. 1725 i.
Westmoreland
Jno. 1704 w.
WARRENTON
Accomack
Elleck Sander 1721 i.
WARFORD
Princess Anne
Wm. 1692 i.
WARINER
Richmond
Jno. 1736 w.
WARING
Essex
Thos. 1754 w.
Thos., Sr. 1761 w.
Francis 1771 w.
Epaphroditus Lawson

1772 w.
Henry 1780 w.
Thos. Robinson
1795 w.
Robert Payne 1799 w.
Fairfax
John 1760 i.
WARINTON
Princess Anne
Geo. 1718 i.
WARMAN
Loudoun
Thos. 1789 i.
WARMOTH
Northumberland
Thos. 1782 w.
WARNALL
. *Loudoun*
Roby 1785 w.
WARNER
Accomack
Sophia 1784 w.
Augusta
Edwd. 1778 w.
Culpeper
Martin 1796 i.
Essex
Danl. 1761 w.
Frederick
Adam 1751 w.
Henrico
Jno. 1757 i.
Stafford
Jno. 1742 w.
Richmond
Wm. 1782 i.
WARNOCK
Middlesex
Jno. 1747 i.
WARREN
Accomack
Sophia 1780 w.
Augusta
Jacob 1770 w.
Amherst
James 1769 w.
Robt. 1769 a.
Brunswick
Benj. 1778 w.
Jno. 1779 w.
Benj. 1792 w.
Essex
Rachel 1706 w.
Isle of Wight
Wm. 1672 w.
Wm. 1734 i.
Thos. 1736 w.
Mecklenburg
Marriott 1799 w.
Norfolk
Eliz. 1752 w.

Jno., Sr. 1752 w.
Jas. 1758 w.
Jno. 1759 i.
Peter 1763 w.
Christian 1764 w.
Christian 1770 i.
Wm. 1790 w.
Wm. 1798 w.
Northampton
Robt. 1679 w.
Jos. 1691 w.
Henry 1693 w.
Jos 1723-4 w.
Jno. 1725 w.
Jno., Sr. 1725 w.
Argil 1728 w.
Jno. 1729 w.
Jas. 1735 w.
Henry, Sr. 1740 w.
Jos 1741 w.
Jos. 1750 i.
Mary 1752 i.
Matthew 1752 i.
Robt., Sr. 1752 w.
Devorax 1760 w.
Henry 1760 i.
Jno. 1762 w.
Solomon 1765 i.
Henry 1770 i.
Peter 1781 w.
Rose 1784 w.
Wm. 1790 i.
Hillery 1795 w.
Southampton
Jno. 1766 w.
Jos. 1778 w.
Faith 1781 w.
Benj. 1798 w.
Spotsylvania
Wm. 1727 w.
Thos. 1750 w.
Eliz. 1751 w.
Saml. 1780 w.
Surry
Jno. 1674 i.
Edwd. 1676 w.
Wm. 1702 i.
Thos. 1721 w.
Robt. 1728 i.
Eliz. 1730 w.
Jno. 1731 i.
Allen, Jr. 1733 w.
Robt. 1752 w.
Robt. 1754 i.
Thos. 1759 w.
Jno. 1767 w.
Drury 1773 w.
Allen 1780 w.
Saml. 1783 w.
Wm. 1785 i.
Lucy 1786 i.

Jno. 1791 i.
Jno. 1794 i.
Arthur 1798 w.
Jno. Darden 1798 w.
Saml. 1798 i.
York
Jno. 1711 i.
WARRENER
Northampton
Jas. 1724 w.
Rappahannock
Ralph 1669 w.
WARRICK
Northumberland
Richd. 1728-9 w.
Wm. 1750 i.
Richmond
Obadiah 1784 i.
WARRIN
Northampton
Hillary 1737 w.
Surry
Allen 1744 w.
WARRINER
Henrico
Danl. 1707 w.
Richd. 1783 i.
Thos. 1783 i.
Benj. 1793 w.
Jno. 1793 i.
Northampton
Ezekiel 1736 i.
Rappahannock
Ralph 1674 w.
WARRINGTON
Accomack
Stephen 1708 w.
Jonathan 1744 w.
Stephen 1745 w.
Walter 1749 w.
Jno. 1755 w.
Abbott 1760 w.
Edmond 1767 w.
Wm. 1768 w.
Alex. 1770 w.
Benj. 1771 w.
Tabitha 1771 w.
Geo. 1775 w.
Wm. 1777 i.
Geo. 1782 w.
Jas. 1784 w.
Southy 1785 w.
Jas. 1786 i.
Jno. 1790 w.
Josephus 1798 i.
Princess Anne
Geo. 1719 w.
WARTHEN
Randolph
Raphael 1798 w.

WARWELL
Surry
Jno. 1675 a.
Thos. 1675 i.
WARWICK
Amelia
Edwd. 1748 i.
Brunswick
Wm. 1796 w.
Henrico
Fredk. 1784 i.
Middlesex
Thos. 1678 a.
Thos. 1718 i.
Philip 1719 w.
Jno. 1744 i.
Philip 1744 w.
Jno. 1782 i.
Geo. 1785 i.
WASCOTTE
Northampton
Jno. 1733 w.
WASH
Louisa
Thos. 1780 w.
John 1785 i.
WASHBOURN
Culpeper
Thomas 1785 w.
WASHBURN
Culpeper
John 1779 w.
WASHBURNE
Accomack
Jno. 1721 w.
WASHINGTON
Albemarle
Henry 1788 w.
Berkeley
Samuel 1781 w.
Susannah 1783 w.
Thornton 1787 w.
Ferdinand 1798 i.
Charles 1799 w.
Brunswick
Thos. 1775 i.
Fairfax
Lawrence 1752 w.
Edward 1792 w.
George Augustine
1793 w.
Geo. Augustine
1796 a.
Lund 1796 w.
Lawrence 1799 w.
Isle of Wight
Sarah 1764 w.
King George
Augustine 1743 i.
Jno. 1782 w.
Thacker 1798 w.

Middlesex
Henry 1765 w.
Rappahannock
Lawrence 1677 w.
Southampton
Jno. 1754 w.
Eliz. 1758 i.
Thos. 1758 i.
Arthur 1761 w.
Geo. 1763 w.
Wm. 1763 w.
Jno. 1767 w.
Geo. 1783 w.
Arthur 1787 w.
Stafford
Jno. 1742 w.
Townsend 1744 w.
Henry 1748 w.
Jno. 1752 w.
Surry
Richd. 1725 w.
Eliz. 1735 w.
Thos. 1749 i.
Westmoreland
Jno. 1677 w.
Jno. 1697 w.
Lawrence 1698 w.
Jno. 1713 i.
Lawrence 1740 w.
Henry 1746-7 i.
Jno. 1753 i.
Augustine 1762 w.
Robt. 1765 w.
Ann 1774 i.
Lawrence 1774 w.
Augustine 1778 i.
Jas. 1782 i.
Geo. 1782 i.
Lawrence 1782 i.
Jno. 1787 w.
Jno. Augustine
1787 w.
Wm. 1788 w.
Thos. 1794 w.
Jno. 1795 w.
WASON
Washington
James 1780 w.
WASS
Brunswick
Rebecca 1778 i.
WATERFIELD
Accomack
Jacob 1773 i.
Northampton
Wm. 1720 w.
Wm. (2) 1720 w.
Southy 1742 w.
Jno. 1748 w.
Wm. 1748 i.
Jacob, Sr. 1766 w.

Jno., Jr. 1772 w.
Southy 1773 i.
Elias 1779 i.
Jno. 1779 i.
Thos. 1784 w.
Wm. 1788 w.
WATERHOUSE
Fauquier
Charles 1793 a.
Northampton
Thos. 1748 i.
WATERMAN
Princess Anne
Solomon 1745 w.
Chas. 1782 i.
WATERS
Amelia
James 1753 w.
Amherst
Jno. 1776 a.
Bedford
Joseph 1773 i.
Essex
John 1692-3 i.
John 1695 i.
Jno. 1711 w.
John 1719 i.
Hugh 1778 w.
Frederick
Thos. 1760 i.
Norfolk
Henry 1697 i.
Northampton
Wm. 1688 w.
Wm. 1721 w.
Wm. 1730 i.
Northumberland
John 1751 i.
John 1764 i.
Princess Anne
Joseph 1796 w.
Rappahannock
Roger 1685 w.
Stafford
Edwd. 1745 i.
Westmoreland
Jno. 1716 i.
Dorothy 1717 w.
York
Wm. 1767 w.
WATERSON
Northampton
Jno. 1679 w.
Frances 1703 w.
Wm. 1722 w.
Jno. 1734 i.
Richd. 1734 i.
Wm. 1741 i.
Tamar 1754 w.
WATERTOWN
Northampton
Jacob 1728 i.

WATERWORTH
Norfolk
Jos. 1769 w.
WATHEN
Surry
Jas. 1723 w.
WATKINS
Albemarle
Nathl. 1798 i.
Amelia
Stephen 1755 w.
Bedford
Thos. 1773 w.
Botetourt
Jno. 1784 w.
Charlotte
Wm. 1784 w.
Chesterfield
Stephen 1758 w.
Daniel 1778 w.
Benj. 1781 w.
Jos. 1783 w.
Essex
Wm. 1789 w.
Chesterfield
Jos. 1798 i.
Cumberland
Thos. 1760 w.
Edwd. 1765 w.
Jno. 1765 w.
Culpeper
Edwd. 1787 w.
Essex
Thos. 1707 w.
John 1748 w.
Eustis 1751 i.
Lewis 1754 i.
Frederick
Evan 1765 w.
Evan 1772 i.
Goochland
Jos. 1734 i.
Benj. 1753 w.
Thos. 1776 w.
Jane 1778 w.
Benj. 1794 w.
Thos. 1797 i.
Benj. 1799 w.
Halifax
Jno. 1763 w.
Micajah 1780 w.
Geo. 1782 w.
Eliz. 1784 i.
Wm. 1794 w.
Micajah 1797 i.
Benj. 1798 i.
Micajah 1798 i.
Wm. 1799 w.
Henrico
Henry 1714 w.
Thos. 1781 i.
Thos. 1783 w.

Thos., Jr. 1787 w.
Isle of Wight
Jno. 1694 w.
Geo. 1720 w.
Jas. 1720 i.
Wm. 1775 i.
Jesse 1778 w.
Honour 1783 w.
Wm. 1789 w.
Priscilla 1796 w.
Mary 1798 i.
Sarah 1798 w.
Louisa
Stephen 1787 i.
Jas. 1794 w.
Jos. 1795 i.
Norfolk
Jno. 1649 w.
Thos. 1669 i.
Thos. 1713 i.
Jno. 1760 w.
Pittsylvania
Jno. 1791 i.
Prince Edward
Jno. 1770 w.
Joel 1776 w.
Henry, Sr. 1799 w.
Prince William
Wm. 1780 i.
Surry
Geo. 1673 w.
Henry 1679 i.
Jno. 1708 w.
Ann 1722 i.
Jno. 1722 w.
Fortune 1753 w.
Henry 1744 i.
Jno.. 1749 w.
Jno. 1753 i.
Robt. 1766 w.
Robt. 1767 i.
Henry 1770 w.
Jno., Sr. 1777 w.
Nicholson 1793 w.
Jno., Jr. 1798 i.
Sussex
Wm. 1764 w.
Jos. 1797 w.
York
Richd. 1681-2 w.
Thos. 1687 w.
Henry 1701 i.
Wm. 1703 w.
Thos. 1717 i.
Wm. 1740 w.
WATKINSON
Accomack
Peter 1688 w.
Peter 1740 w.
Cornelius 1749 w.
Thos. 1762 i.
Susanna 1769 w.

WATLINGTON
Halifax
Francis 1788 i.
Norfolk
Rowland 1791 i.
WATSON
Accomack
Richd. 1688 w.
Robt. 1703 w.
David 1709 w.
Jno. 1709 w.
Eliz. 1720 w.
Benj. 1735 w.
Benj. 1737 w.
Sarah 1742 i.
David 1751 i.
Jno. 1751 i.
Moses 1751 w.
Robt. 1751 i.
Solomon 1755 w.
Peter 1758 w.
Moses 1760 w.
Arthur 1761 i.
Benj. 1762 w.
Sarah 1764 w.
Benj. 1765 i.
Thos. 1765 i.
Abel 1766 w.
Moses 1767 w.
Bartho. 1768 w.
Benj. 1772 w.
Mitchel 1774 w.
Zorobabel 1775 w.
Peter 1776 w.
Edmd. 1777 w.
Benj. 1778 i.
Edmd. 1778 i.
Levi 1778 w.
Peter 1782 i.
Benj. 1784 nw.
Robt. 1786 w.
America 1790 w.
Americus 1795 i.
Zorobabel 1795 w.
Patty 1795 i.
Jno. 1799 i.
Albemarle
Wm. 1783 w.
Amelia
Wm. 1752 w.
Augusta
Jos. 1747 i.
Jno. 1776 i.
Berkeley
John 1778 i.
Thomas 1778 w.
John, Sr. 1785 w.
Brunswick
Jno. 1748 i.
Jno. 1796 w.

Charlotte
Matthew 1777 i.
Matthew 1778 w.
Eliz. 1790 w.
Matthew 1794 w.
Fairfax
John 1770 i.
Frederick
William 1765 i.
Greensville
Alexander 1782 w.
Gershom 1794 w.
Daniel 1798 i.
Henrico
Jno., Sr. 1706 w.
Benj. 1714 w.
Jno. 1750 w.
Jos. 1752 w.
Henry
John 1784 w.
John 1795 i.
Isle of Wight
Robt. 1651 nw.
John 1666 i.
Sarah 1672 w.
John 1673 i.
Elizabeth 1676 w.
Richard 1687 i.
William 1688 nw.
Thomas 1742 i.
James 1774 w.
William 1787 i.
Loudoun
Robert 1768 i.
Thomas 1778 i.
Louisa
James 1776 w.
David 1777 i.
Barbary 1778 w.
Nehemiah 1789 w.
Randolph 1789 i.
Lunenburg
Jno. 1763 w.
Mecklenburg
James 1772 w.
Isaac 1783 w.
Jno. 1784 i.
Burwell 1792 i.
Henry 1795 i.
Norfolk
Thomas 1656 i.
Henry 1667 i.
Robert 1791 w.
Northampton
Jno. 1733 w.
Robt. 1761 i.
Ruhamah 1770 i.
Edmd. 1795 w.
Northumberland
Hugh 1767 w.
Margt. 1772 w.

Prince Edward
Thornton 1794 i.
Rappahannock
Jno. 1684 w.
Shenandoah
John 1798 i.
Joseph 1798 i.
Washington
Patrick 1788 w.
Westmoreland
Thos. 1721 i.
York
Ralph 1645 i.
WATSON
Norfolk
Sarah 1794 i.
WATT
Accomack
Jas. 1716 w.
Adam 1751 w.
Wm. 1765 i.
Jas. 1774 w.
Northampton
Jas. 1686 w.
WATTER
Princess Anne
Leavin 1797 w.
WATTERS
Northumberland
Thos. 1721 nw.
Princess Anne
Sarah 1796 w.
Richmond
Catherine 1718 w.
WATTERSON
Augusta
Thos. 1778 w.
Montgomery
William 1791 i.
Henry 1792 i.
William 1794 i.
WATTEY
Westmoreland
Geo. 1714 i.
WATTFORD
Norfolk
Jno. 1694 w.
WATTRON
Accomack
Robt. 1708 w.
WATTS
Accomack
Jno. 1684 w.
Jno. 1726 w.
Priscilla 1730 w.
Jno. 1735 i.
Jno. 1742 i.
Wm. 1743 w.
Wm. 1746 i.
Wm. 1748 i.
Jno. 1776 w.

Albemarle
Jno. 1776 i.
Amherst
Hannah 1790 w.
Thos. 1798 i.
Bedford
Edwd. 1795 w.
Campbell
Wm. 1798 w.
Charlotte
John 1771 w.
Culpeper
Thos. 1749 w.
Thos. 1764 w.
Joel 1781 w.
Benj. 1790 w.
Thos. 1796 w.
Thos. 1799 i.
Essex
David 1731 i.
Dorothy 1763 i.
Thos. 1767 w.
Fauquier
Thos. 1769 i.
Francis 1770 w.
Thos. 1770 i.
Francis 1788 i.
Frederick
David 1774 w.
Henrico
Thos. 1678 w.
Henry
Thos. 1783 i.
Isle of Wight
Jno. 1697-8 w.
Jno. 1720 i.
Jno. 1722 i.
Thos. 1728 nw.
Mecklenburg
Mary 1782 w.
Richd. 1789 w.
Middlesex
Jno. 1715 i.
Hugh 1720 w.
Ralph 1789 w.
Northampton
Jno., Sr. 1696 i.
Jno. 1715 w.
Thos. 1726 w.
Smith 1738 w.
Jno. W. 1752 w.
Jno. W. 1767 w.
Thos. 1769 i.
Rachel 1770 i.
Thos. 1773 w.
Northumberland
Henry 1670 w.
Robt. 1726-7 i.
Jno. 1738 w.
Richd. 1777 w.
Wm. 1796 w.

Orange
Robt. 1741 w.
Esther 1772 w.
Prince Edward
Sarah 1787 w.
Surry
Jno. 1713 i.
Westmoreland
Jas. 1699 w.
Wm. 1713 i.
Richd. 1716 w.
Richd. 1744 i.
Jno. 1754 w.
Youell 1767 i.
Jno. 1769 i.
Youell 1726 w.
York
Edmund 1676 w.
Anthony 1704 i.
WATTSON
Accomack
Peter 1704 i.
Danl. 1728 w.
WAUGH
Augusta
Isaac 1789 w.
Lancaster
Wm. 1726 i.
Elizabeth 1745 w.
Wm. 1760 i.
Jas. 1767 w.
Orange
Alexander 1793 w.
Stafford
Jno. 1706 i.
Jno. 1743 w.
Jos. 1748 w.
Million 1748 w.
Jas. 1750 w.
Mary 1758 w.
Travers 1766 i.
Gowry 1783 w.
WAUGHOP
Northumberland
John 1749 i.
Elizab. 1770 w.
WAVERBORE
Frederick
Jacob 1758 i.
WAX
Botetourt
Henry 1797 w.
WAY
Lancaster
Wm. 1747 w.
Northumberland
Richd. 1750 w.
Richd. 1779 nw.
Betsy 1791 w.
Davenport 1792 i.
Jno. 1799 i.

WAYLAND
Culpeper
Adam 1781 w.
Spotsylvania
Patrick 1763 a.
WAYLES
Charles City
Jno. 1773 w.
WAYMAN
Essex
Jno. 1798 w.
WEAKLEY
Frederick
Jno. 1780 i.
Halifax
Robt., Sr. 1798 w.
WEANHOUSE
Northampton
Francis 1717-18 w.
WEATHER
Sussex
Wm. 1764 w.
WEATHERALL
Isle of Wight
Aquilla 1745 i.
WEATHERELL
Isle of Wight
Jno. 1706 i.
WEATHERFORD
Charlotte
Major 1774 w.
Cumberland
Wm. 1772 i.
Henry
David 1799 i.
Lunenburg
Richd. 1756 w.
Susanna 1758 w.
Wm. 1799 i.
WEATHERS
Frederick
Wm. 1780 w.
Lancaster
Eliz. 1763 i.
Richmond
Saml. 1729 i.
Surry
Thos. 1744 w.
Sussex
Lyddia 1776 w.
Thos. 1788 i.
Benj. 1793 w.
Edmund 1797 i.
WEATHERSPOON
Lancaster
Jas. 1721 w.
Orange
Jno. 1778 i.
WEAVER
Augusta
Jno. Geo. 1789 w.

Berkeley
 Christopher 1788 w.
Brunswick
 Wm. 1761 i.
 Jno. 1769 w.
Campbell
 Jno. 1785 w.
Charlotte
 Eliz. 1784 i.
Cumberland
 Samuel 1769 i.
Fauquier
 Tilman 1760 w.
Halifax
 Richd. 1758 i.
Lancaster
 Isaac 1778 w.
Loudoun
 Jno. 1787 i.
Northumberland
 Isaac 1663 w.
 Richard 1759 w.
Surry
 Henry 1719 i.
 Jno. 1719 w.
Sussex
 Edwd. 1772 w.
 Edwd. 1777 w.
 Wm. 1789 w.
Westmoreland
 Adam 1771 w.
 Benj. 1783 w.
 Jno. 1784 w.
 Abraham 1785 i.
 Wm. 1785 i.
 Zachariah 1796 i.
York
 Wm. 1679 i.
WEB
Henry
 Silvanus 1777 i.
WEBB
Accomack
 Thos. 1709 i.
 Scarbrough 1718 w.
 Thos. 1757 w.
 Thos. 1763 i.
Albemarle
 Wentworth 1752 i.
Amherst
 Cuthbert 1777 w.
Brunswick
 Eliz. 1774 w.
Essex
 Richard 1710 w.
 Thos. 1710 i.
 Jno. 1713 w.
 Jas. 1716 w.
 Jas. 1722 i.
 Richd. 1722 w.
 Jas. 1723 i.

Isaac 1729 w.
Sarah 1748 w.
Edwd. 1749 w.
Jno. 1758 i.
Hannah 1761 i.
Jno. 1767 w.
Jas. 1771 w.
Jas. 1774 w.
Thos. 1784 w.
Mary 1786 w.
Richd. 1786 i.
Lillian 1792 w.
Griffin 1796 i.
Fauquier
 Jno. 1778 w.
Franklin
 Theodorick 1794 w.
Halifax
 Jno. 1794 w.
Henrico
 Thos. 1712 i.
 Giles 1713 w.
Henry
 Merry Sr. 1779 w.
Isle of Wight
 Jas. 1675 i.
 Wm., Jr. 1700 w.
 Wm. 1713 w.
 Jas. 1720 w.
 Wm. 1728 i.
 Richd. 1748 w.
 Richd. 1752 i.
 Samuel 1764 w.
 Wm. 1771 i.
 Mathias 1785 w.
 Samuel 1794 w.
 Anne 1799 w.
Lancaster
 Jas. 1693 i.
 Jno. 1738 i.
 Jno. 1761 w.
 Jas. 1765 w.
 Geo. 1775 i.
 Jas. 1778 w.
 Frances 1781 i.
Lunenburg
 Isaac 1774 w.
 Jordan 1794 i.
Norfolk
 Robert 1761 w.
 Jas. 1792 w.
Northampton
 Edwd. 1709 i.
 Wm. 1710 i.
 Jno. 1728 i.
 Chas. 1737 i.
Northumberland
 Jno. 1700 w.
 Thos. 1702 w.
 Jno. 1709 w.
 Ann 1719 w.

Jno. 1720 w.
Thos. 1721 w.
Jno. 1743-4 i.
Moses 1743 w.
Wm. 1747 w.
Mary 1750 w.
Samuel 1750 w.
Wm. 1755 i.
Elizabeth 1757 i.
Aaron 1760 i.
Wm. 1762 i.
Wm. 1763 w.
Jno. 1765 w.
Jos. 1765 w.
Betty 1769 w.
Moses 1769 i.
Giles 1771 w.
Jno. 1771 w.
Wm. 1777 w.
Thos. 1783 w.
Jno. 1784 w.
Jno. S. 1784 w.
Jno. 1785 i.
Leanna 1785 i.
Eliz. 1786 nw.
Isaac 1786 i.
Jno. Span 1788 i.
Homer 1795 w.
Cuthbert 1797 w.
Aaron 1798 w.
Orange
 Milley 1768 w.
 Wm. 1783 w.
Patrick
 Isham 1799 w.
Princess Anne
 Thos. 1697 w.
 Thos. 1698 a.
 Saml. 1704 w.
 Geo. 1782 w.
Richmond
 Jno. 1725 i.
 Giles 1732 w.
 Jas. 1750 w.
 Jno. Spann 1756 i.
 Isaac 1760 w.
 Betty 1762 w.
 Wm. 1765 w.
 Wm. 1768 i.
 Jas. 1775 w.
 Jas. 1777 i.
 Jas. 1779 i.
 Cuthbert 1782 w.
 Francis 1783 i.
 Francis 1784 nw.
Southampton
 Chas. 1758 w.
 Chas. 1771 i.
Stafford
 Benj. 1702 w.

Surry
Nicholas 1734 i.
Sussex
Robt. 1771 w.
Chas. 1782 w.
Robt. 1782 w.
Westmoreland
Wm. 1670 w.
Wm. 1698 w.
Michael 1698 w.
Moses 1741 i.
Wm. 1742 a.
York
Jno. 1703 i.
Wm. 1738 i.
WEBBER
Cumberland
John 1794 w.
Tahpenes 1794 w.
Philip 1796 w.
Goochland
Augustine 1759 i.
Wm. 1794 w.
Northumberland
Jno. 1671 w.
WEBLEY
Rappahannock
Richd. 1666 a.
WEBLIN
Lancaster
William 1790 i.
Norfolk
Jno. 1686-7 w.
Princess Anne
Jno. 1719 w.
Mary 1723 i.
Wm. 1724 i.
Wm. 1728 i.
Geo. 1744 i.
Wm. 1747 w.
Wm. 1754 i.
Geo. 1756 w.
Geo. 1760 i.
Geo. 1763 i.
Sarah 1771 i.
Willoughby 1786 i.
WEBSTER
Amelia
Peter 1774 w.
Thos. 1785 w.
Wm. 1796 w.
James 1799 i.
Chesterfield
Prudent 17— i.
Essex
John 1703 w.
Goochland
Jno. 1733 w.
Henrico
Thos. 1689 w.
Thos. 1691 i.

Thos. 1748 w.
Isle of Wight
Alex. 1690 nw.
Northampton
Jno. 1650 i.
Simpson 1656 i.
Saml. 1664 w.
Wm. 1665 w.
Sampson 1697 i.
Richmond
Henry 1721 i.
Elizabeth 1727 w.
Spotsylvania
Jno. 1744 a.
Stafford
Chas. 1762 w.
Surry
Thos. 1678 i.
Westmoreland
Alex. 1703 w.
WEEBB
Henrico
Jno. 1726 w.
WEEB
Henrico
Jno. 1736 w.
WEEDING
Halifax
James 1764 w.
WEEDON
Westmoreland
Geo. 1704 w.
Benj. 1712 i.
Jordan 1717 i.
Geo. 1723 i.
Geo. 1734 w.
Thos. 1734 i.
Jno., Sr. 1740 w.
Augustine 1763 w.
Jean 1767 w.
Jno. 1777 i.
WEEKS
Essex
Charles 1790 w.
Middlesex
Abraham 1692 w.
Albemarle
Martin 1785 i.
Amelia
Richd. 1772 i.
Richmond
Elizabeth 1755 i.
Surry
Thos. 1676 w.
Stephen 1677 w.
Westmoreland
Jos. 1716 w.
Ann 1784 w.
Benj. 1788 i.

WEIGHT
Essex
Henry 1728 i.
WEIR
Amherst
Robt. 1772 w.
Halifax
Geo. 1775 w.
Northampton
Jas. 1795 w.
Rockbridge
Hugh 1779 w.
George 1781 w.
WEIRBACK
Frederick
John 1768 a.
WEIRE
Rappahannock
Jno. 1684 i.
WELBURN
Accomack
Danl. 1766 i.
Francis 1769 w.
Danl. 1777 i.
WELBURNE
Accomack
Thos. 1702 i.
Benj. 1721 w.
Saml. 1728 w.
Danl. 1733 w.
WELCH
Accomack
Wm. 1781 w.
Wm. 1795 i.
Amherst
Jno. 1790 w.
Bedford
Nicholas 1768 w.
Jno. 1775 i.
Essex
Mary 1713 w.
Reubin 1729 i.
Michael 1785 i.
Isle of Wight
Wm. 1704 w.
Jno. 1772 w.
Mary 1786 w.
Northumberland
Silvester 1754 w.
Benj. 1785 w.
Mary 1793 w.
Benj. 1796 w.
Pittsylvania
Josiah 1790 i.
Shenandoah
Thos. 1791 a.
Stafford
Wm. 1750 i.
Westmoreland
Garratt 1716 w.
Wm. 1749 i.

Matthew 1750 i.
Matthew 1776 i.
WELDEN
Pittsylvania
Jonathan 1782 w.
WELDON
Henrico
Saml. 1748 w.
Richmond
Ann 1737 i.
Sussex
Benj. 1756 w.
WELDY
Goochland
Rebecca 1770 w.
WELILY
Accomack
Jno. 1723 i.
WELLAND
Northampton
Thos. 1742 w.
WELLCH
Richmond
Thos. 1722 w.
WELLCOM
Fairfax
Eliz. 1750 a.
WELLENS
Southampton
John 1790 w.
WELLINGHAM
Halifax
Jarrald 1792 i.
WELLINGTON
Westmoreland
Michael 1706 w.
Jno. 1737 w.
WELLONS
Southampton
Jno. 1778 w.
Henry 1784 w.
WELLS
Accomack
Richd. 1788 i.
Amelia
Baker 1774 w.
Chesterfield
Thos. 17—i.
Isham 1795 w.
Wm. 1798 w.
Henrico
Thos. 1695 w.
King George
Thos. 1728 i.
Lancaster
Jno. 1697 w.
Robt. 1709 i.
Jno. [1710] w.
Robt. [1710] w.
Wm. 1710 w.
Robt. 1736 w.

Loudoun
Thos. Wm. 1768 i.
Thos. Wm. 1774 i.
Louisa
Robt. 1751 w.
Lunenburg
Geo. 1761 w.
Mecklenburg
David 1799 w.
Northumberland
Stephen 1718 w.
Ohio
Benj. 1794 w.
Rappahannock
Barneby 1686 i.
Richmond
Stephen 1723 i.
Eliz. 1725 w.
Jno. 1730 w.
Stafford
Thos. 1704 i.
York
Geo. 1754 w.
WELSH
Berkeley
Jacob 1787 w.
Michael 1787 i.
Essex
Robt. 1746 w.
Fairfax
Jno. 1796 a.
Frederick
John 1788 a.
Jonathan 1789 w.
Middlesex
Andrew 1680 a.
Norfolk
Richd. 1765 i.
Northampton
Thos. 1726 i.
Jno. 1728 i.
Northumberland
Elinor 1725-6 i.
Pittsylvania
Joshua 1790 w.
WELSHIRE
Montgomery
Nathaniel 1776 w.
WELTON
Frederick
John 1749 i.
Richmond
Henry 1710 i.
WEM
Westmoreland
Alice 1791 i.
WEMS
Richmond
Alice 1791 i.

WENDELL
Shenandoah
Valentine 1793 w.
WENDLE
Shenandoah
Christopher 1791 w.
WENTWORTH
Isle of Wight
Mary 1768 w.
York
Edwd. 1658 w.
WERNER
Shenandoah
Philip 1799 i.
WESCOT
Northampton
Jno., Sr. 1786 w.
WESCOTT
Norfolk
Wright 1784 i.
Wm. 1793 i.
Samuel 1796 i.
George 1798 i.
Northampton
Jno. 1733 w.
WESGATE
Norfolk
Henery 1655 w.
WESIGER
Chesterfield
Danl. 1784 w.
WESSLEY
Norfolk
Thos. 1712 w.
WESSON
Brunswick
Edwd. 1788 w.
WEST
Accomack
Jno. 1703 w.
Benony 1708 w.
Jno., (elder) 1708 w.
Anthony 1717 w.
Alexander 1727 w.
Jonathan 1727 w.
Jno. 1730 w.
Edwd. 1732 i.
Wm. 1734 i.
Argol Yardley
1735 w.
Eliz. 1753 w.
Jno. 1755 w.
Chas. 1757 w.
Agnes 1760 w.
Parker 1760 w.
Scarburgh 1760 w.
Alex. 1761 w.
Chas. 1763 i.
Judith 1766 i.
Jno. 1772 w.
Jno. 1773 w.

Benj. 1775 w.
Jno. 1775 i.
Benj. 1777 i.
Anthony, Sr. 1778 w.
Isaac 1779 w.
Jonathan 1787 w.
Richd. 1788 w.
Benj. 1790 w.
Jeremiah 1793 w.
Anthony 1795 w.
Geo. 1795 w.
Benj. 1796 w.
Philip Parker 1796 w.
Eliz. 1797 w.
Edmund 1798 i.
Jno. 1799 w.
Jno., Jr. 1799 i.
Scarburgh 1799 w.
Albemarle
Thos. 1796 w.
Amelia
Francis 1738 w.
Jno. 1742 w.
Jno. 1746 w.
Jno. 1767 w.
Robt. 1789 i.
Augusta
Thos. 1774 w.
Thos. 1777 i.
Bedford
Wm. 1777 i.
Charles City
Wm. 1772 w.
Chesterfield
Wm. 1783 w.
Jno. Tommast
[1785?] i.
Saml. 1785 w.
Geo. 1789 w.
Essex
Richd. 1693 w.
Richd. 1711 i.
Eliz. 1722 w.
Fairfax
Hugh 1754 w.
Hugh 1767 w.
Thos. 1773 i.
Jno. 1777 w.
Jno., Jr. 1777 w.
Geo. 1786 w.
Sybil 1787 w.
Hugh 1791 a.
Wm. 1793 w.
Fairfax
Geo. Wm. 1796 w.
Jos. 1796 a.
Margaret 1798 w.
Fauquier
Ignatius 1793 w.
Halifax
Reuben 1798 i.

Harrison
Edmond 1784 w.
Henrico
Jno. 1687 i.
Jno. 1753 i.
Eliz. 1790 i.
Jno. 1790 i.
Drury 1791 w.
Edwd. 1794 w.
Isle of Wight
Wm. 1708-9 w.
Robt. [1713] w.
Francis [1717] w.
Richard 1747 w.
Richard 1751 i.
Ann 1752 w.
Everett 1752 i.
Robert 1752 w.
Giles 1770 w.
Richard 1781 w.
King George
Jas. 1784 w.
Lancaster
Wm. 1692 w.
Thomas 1778 w.
Loudoun
Wm., Jr. 1763 w.
William 1769 w.
Thomas 1776 w.
Charles 1787 w.
Norfolk
William 1685 i.
Northampton
Robt. 1646 i.
Anthony 1652 w.
Jno. 1719 w.
Chas. 1797 w.
Northumberland
Wm. 1720 i.
John 1750 i.
John, Jr. 1750 i.
Thos., Jr. 1750 w.
John 1759 w.
Lucy 1760 w.
John 1762 i.
Princess Anne
Wm. 1764 w.
Lemuel 1769 i.
Caleb 1772 w.
Lemuel 1772 i.
Amey 1771 w.
Willoughby 1772 w.
Thos. 1784 w.
William. Sr. 1790 w.
Caleb 1798 w.
Southampton
James 1759 i.
Joseph 1762 w.
Josiah 1762 i.
Stafford
Jno. 1744 w.

Surry
Sarah 1750 w.
Philip 1786 i.
Westmoreland
Richd. 1698 w.
York
Jno. 1721 i.
Mary 1735 w.
Mary 1743 w.
WESTBROOK
Amelia
Wm. 1770 i.
Wm. 1774 w.
Chas. 1777 w.
Phoebee 1787 w.
Henrico
Jas. 1737 i.
Isle of Wight
John 1733 w.
James 1749 w.
Southampton
Jno. 1761 w.
Saml. 1761 w.
Thos. 1767 w.
Wm. 1767 w.
Jas. 1773 w.
Thos. 1777 w.
Elias 1777 w.
Saml. 1782 w.
Jno. 1785 w.
Saml. 1785 w.
Helen 1787 w.
Miday 1787 w.
Mary 1788 w.
Joshua 1795 w.
Hellica 1798 i.
Henry 1798 w.
WESTCOAT
Norfolk
Susanna 1769 w.
WESTCOMB
Westmoreland
Jas. 1716 w.
WESTCOT
Northampton
Jno. 1728 w.
WESTCOTT
Norfolk
Wright 1760 w.
Geo. 1787 w.
Wm. 1787 w.
WESTEL
Frederick
Martin 1761 i.
WESTER
Southampton
Wm., Jr. 1795 i.
WESTERHOUSE
Northampton
Wm. 1683 w.
Adrian 1705 w.

Wm. 1720 w.
Nicholas 1728 w.
Thos. 1734 w.
Newton 1738 i.
Wm. 1760 w.
Peleg 1765 i.
Wm. 1772 w.
Ann 1797 w.
WESTERLINKE
York
Martin 1658 i.
WESTFALL
Augusta
Euric 1753 a.
Joel 1779 i.
Hardy
Jno. 1789 w.
WESTHOPE
Surry
Jno. 1656 a.
WESTMORELAND
Brunswick
Robt. 1791 i.
WESTON
Isle of Wight
Jno. 1690 w.
Stephen 1723 w.
Benj. 1738 w.
Benj. 1739 w.
Jos. 1750 w.
Mary 1762 i.
Samuel [1769?] i.
William 1777 w.
Charlotte 1794 i.
Norfolk
Samuel, Sr. 1785 w.
Benj. 1798 w.
Surry
Wm. 1727 i.
York
Robt. 1671 w.
WESTONE
Isle of Wight
Jno. 1718 i.
WESTRAY
Isle of Wight
Robt. 1737 i.
Jno. 1756 w.
Edwd. 1760 i.
Hardy 1760 w.
Jno. 1763 w.
Benj. 1781 w.
Robt. 1790 w.
Mathew 1792 i.
Edmund 1795 w.
WESTRY
Isle of Wight
Eliz. 1750 w.
WETHERALL
Culpeper
Jno. 1763 w.

WETHERBURN
York
Henry 1760 w.
WETHERS
King George
Saml. 1750 i.
WETHERSPOON
Essex
Jas. 1768 i.
WETZELL
Frederick
Chris. 1799 w.
WEVER
Culpeper
Peter 1763 w.
WEYMAN
Essex
Jno. 1796 nw.
York
Jno. 1710 w.
WEYMOUTH
Richmond
Thos. 1799 i.
WHALEY
Accomack
Solomon 1744 i.
Thos. 1750 i.
Lancaster
Oswald 1718 w.
Oswald 1726 nw.
Stephen 1726 w.
Loudoun
Jas. 1784 w.
Jas. 1796 w.
Northampton
Joshua 1797 i.
Northumberland
Thos. 1792 w.
Richmond
Jas. 1750 w.
York
Jas. 1701 w.
WHARTON
Lancaster
Francis 1700 w.
Jno. 1744 w.
Wm. 1765 i.
Ann 1766 w.
Jno. 1776 w.
Culpeper
Jno. 1755 w.
King George
Saml. 1733 i.
Jno. 1736 i.
Thos. 1752 w.
Zachariah 1766 a.
Chas. 1767 w.
Sarah 1772 w.
Mary 1778 a.
Isaac 1798 a.

Lancaster
Thos. 1742 w.
Sarah 1744 w.
Jos. 1749 w.
Middlesex
Abraham 1752 a.
Orange
Thos. 1747 i.
Jos. 1773 w.
Jno. 1788 w.
Princess Anne
Jno. 1697 w.
Richmond
Jno. 1720 i.
Spotsylvania
Saml. 1738 w.
Westmoreland
Henry 1706 i.
York
Thos. 1745 w.
WHEADON
Isle of Wight
Philip 1735 w.
Jos. 1744 w.
James 1758 i.
WHEALER
Northumberland
Moses 1795 w.
Pittsylvania
Jno. 1772 i.
WHEALEY
Lancaster
Jas. 1722 w.
WHEALOR
Northumberland
Moses 1793 i.
WHEALTON
Accomack
Wm. 1763 w.
Nehemiah 1782 i.
WHEALY
Stafford
Oswell 1701 i.
WHEARY
Albemarle
Jas. 1773 i.
WHEAT
Ohio
Conrod 1781 w.
WHEATCROFT
Northampton
Edwd. 1694 i.
WHEATELY
Northampton
David. 1667 i.
WHEATHERALL
Isle of Wight
Wm. 1719 i.
WHEATLEY
Fauquier
Jas. 1795 i.

John 1796 i.
Jos. 1796 i.
Geo. 1798 i.
Isle of Wight
Jno. 1670 w.
Norfolk
Francis Ann 1769 i.
John 1769 i.
Prince George
Thos. 1717 w.
WHEATTON
Accomack
Elisha 1799 i.
WHEDDON
Isle of Wight
Joyce 1752 w.
WHEELER
Albemarle
Robert Woodson
1799 w.
Essex
Thos. 1700 w.
Thomas 1719 i.
Fairfax
Richard 1751 w.
Rebecca 1763 w.
Isle of Wight
Jacob 1795 w.
Lancaster
Maurice 1784 i.
Maurice 1788 i.
Lunenburg
Mary 1760 i.
Northampton
Jas. 1752 w.
Thos. 1762 i.
Jas. 1789 w.
Jas. 1792 i.
Jno. 1798 w.
Stafford
Jno. 1746 w.
Westmoreland
Thos. 1716 w.
Wm. 1762 w.
York
Francis 1659 i.
Ellias 1660 w.
WHEELLER
Northampton
Jas. 1753 i.
WHEELOR
Northumberland
Jno. 1794 w.
WHEELTON
Accomack
Thos. 1770 i.
Jas. 1773 w.
WHEELWRIGHT
Accomack
Jno. Taylor 1775 i.

WHEETTON
Accomack
Jno. 1758 i.
WHELDEN
Accomack
Ebenezer 1789 i.
WHELER
Rappahannock
Humphrey 1686 i.
WHELTON
Accomack
Jno. 1717 w.
WHETZELL
Frederick
Martha 1760 w.
WHEWELL
York
Andrew 1637 w.
WHIDDON
Norfolk
Augustine 1693 w.
William, Sr. 1721 w.
Jno. 1729 w.
John 1796 w.
Northumberland
Jno. 1745 i.
WHIDICK
Norfolk
Henry 1711 a.
WHIDON
Norfolk
Eliz. 1710-11 i.
John 1710-11 i.
John 1750 w.
WHILTON
Louisa
John 1785 w.
WHISHARD
Norfolk
John 1707 a.
WHISTON
Westmoreland
Jno. 1670 w.
WHITACRE
Loudoun
Geo. 1785 w.
WHITAKER
Middlesex
Thos. 1759 a.
York
Simon 1766 w.
WHITBY
Brunswick
Jno. 1781 i.
Middlesex
Wm. 1677 w.
York
Wm. 1669 w.
Thos. 1711 w.

WHITCOMB
Stafford
Richd. 1746 i.
WHITE
Accomack
Henry 1669 w.
Jno. 1682 w.
Wm.1683 i.
Wm. 1709 i.
Chas. 1721 i.
Simcock 1721 w.
Benj. 1742 i.
Chas. 1744 i.
Henry 1760 w.
Jno. 1760 i.
Rixon 1760 i.
Jacob 1767 w.
Wm. 1767 w.
Henry, Sr. 1771 w.
Wm. 1771 i.
Jacobus 1775 i.
Hezekiah 1778 w.
Geo. 1778 w.
Robt. 1784 i.
Solomon 1785 w.
Chas. 1786 w.
Galen 1790 w.
Joachim 1790 w.
Jacob 1790 w.
Nathan 1795 i.
Levin 1797 i.
Robt. 1797 i.
Sarah 1797 w.
Wm. 1797 w.
Albemarle
Robt. 1755 w.
Jeremiah 1777 w.
Amelia
Geo. Chris. 1772 w.
Amherst
James 1783 a.
Augusta
Geo. 1757 a.
Stophel 1761 i.
David 1775 i.
Isaac 1782 w.
Berkeley
John 1795 i.
Brunswick
Geo. 1736 w.
Saml. 1771 w..
Valentine 1782 w
Wm. 1783 w.
Sarah 1789 w.
Danl. 1795 i.
Geo. 1799 w.
Charlotte
Saml. 1780 i.
Jno. 1782 w.
Jas. 1783 i.

Culpeper
John 1784 i.
Ann 1786 w.
Daniel 1790 w.
Armistead 1791 i.
Essex
Robt. 1698 w.
Fauquier
Pleasant 1769 w.
Frederick
Robert 1755 i.
Benjamin 1760 w.
William 1766 w.
Isaac 1767 i.
Thos. 1779 i.
Richard 1794 i.
Mary 1796 w.
Halifax
Catherine 1792 w.
Henrico
Chas. 1700 nw.
Danl. 1781 i.
Elisha 1781 w.
Elisha. Jr. 1782 i.
Catherine 1788 w.
Jas. 1796 w.
Thos. 1798 w.
Isle of Wight
Jno. 1719 w.
Jno. 1729 w.
Wm. 1729 w.
Henry 1733 w.
Ann 1742 w.
Jno. 1754 w.
Jno. 1776 i.
King George
Richard 1723 i.
Patrick 1725 i.
Wm. 1733 i.
Geo. 1738 i.
Daniel 1748 i.
Danl. 1750 i.
Aaron 1754 w.
Margt. 1756 w.
Danl. 1759 w.
Simon 1760 w.
Ann 1762 w.
Danl. 1770 w.
Danl. 1771 a.
Saml. 1783 w.
Mary 1795 w.
Lancaster
Wm. 1678 w.
Wm. 1686 w.
Thos. [1710] w.
Thos. [1713] i.
Abraham 1776 i.
Presley 1791 w.
Loudoun
Richard 1791 w.
Jas. 1798 i.

Louisa
Richd. 1780 a.
Richd. 1786 i.
Wm., Sr. 1787 w.
Moses 1794 a.
Lunenburg
Jno. 1796 w.
Jno. 1797 w.
Madison
Jeremiah 1796 a.
Mecklenburg
Jas. 1798 i.
Norfolk
Jno. 1640 i.
Jno. 1681 w.
Wm. 1684 w.
Patrick 1713 i.
Eliz. 1714 i.
Patrick 1761 w.
Mary 1762 w.
Archibald 1765 w.
Keder 1773 w.
Gidion 1774 w.
Wm. 1799 w.
Northampton
Nicholas 1638 w.
Nicholas 1639 w.
Lewis 1656 w.
Henry 1709 w.
Wm. 1712 i.
Jno. 1718 w.
Rebecca 1724 w.
Anne 1728 w.
Jno. 1728 w.
Caleb 1730 i.
Mary 1730 i.
Mary 1740 w.
Caleb 1744 w.
Jos. 1744 w.
Edwd. 1752 i.
Wm. 1755 w.
Jno. 1758 w.
Thos. 1759 w.   •
Thos. 1760 i.
Eddeniah 1764 w.
Obedience, Sr.
  1764 w.
Abel 1775 w.
Susannah 1786 i.
Caleb 1787 w.
Obedience 1789 w.
Caleb 1791 i.
Rachel 1794 w.
Hannah 1796 w.
Abel 1797 w.
Patience 1797 w.
Wm. 1797 i.
Northumberland
Richd. 1661 w.
Jane 1723-4 w.
Griffin 1747 i.

Robt. 1748 i.
Edwd. 1764 i.
Simon 1792 w.
Ohio
Samuel 1778 w.
Orange
Jeremiah 1796 i.
Pittsylvania
Epa 1785 i.
Princess Anne
Patrick 1691 i.
Eliz. 1693 w.
Jas. 1716 w.
Jas. 1718 i.
Jos. 1727 i.
Solomon 1734 i.
Solomon 1735 w.
Aliff 1738 i.
Isaac 1743 w.
Major 1760 i.
Jos. 1784 w.
Prince William
John 1744 a.
Rappahannock
Wm. 1660 i.
Jno. 1679 w.
Henry 1684 w.
Richmond
Richard 1703 w.
Jno. 1714 i.
Thos. 1715 w.
Thos. 1733 i.
Thos. 1786 w.
Wm. 1786 w.
Rockbridge
Jno. 1780 a.
Shenandoah
Wm. 1772 w.
Ann 1780 i.
Southampton
Arthur 1752 i.
Baker 1773 i.
Mary 1775 i.
Spotsylvania
Agnes 1757 w.
Basil 1786 w.
Roderick 1790 w.
Geo. 1797 w.
Thos. 1782 a.
Surry
Wm. 1677 w.
Jno. 1679 w.
Thos. 1694 w.
Charles 1710 w.
Mary 1721 w.
Jno. 1728 w.
Jno. 1729 w.
Walter 1745 w.
Chas. 1747 w.
Robt. 1750 i.
Thos. 1772 i.

Thos. 1773 w.
Wm. 1787 i.
Jno. 1788 w.
Wm. 1788 i.
Henry 1797 w.
Washington
Samuel 1780 i.
William 1781 w.
Moses 1797 w.
Westmoreland
Dennis 1677 w.
Philip 1698 i.
Thos. 1701 i.
Philip 1741 i.
Wm. 1750 i.
Jno. 1750-1 w.
Jno. (2) 1751 w.
Benj. 1756 i.
Danl. 1759 i.
Sarah 1762 w.
Jas. 1763 w.
Mary 1765 w.
Jas. 1768 w.
York
Martha 1660 w.
Henry 1671 w.
Henry 1687 w.
Jos. 1710 w.
Jno. 1720 ab.
Dennis 1721 i.
Henry 1736 i.
[WHITE?]
York
Wm. 1721 a.

WHITCOTTON
Stafford
Mealy 1733 i.
Geo. 1744 i.
Sarah 1762 w.
WHITECOTTON
King George
Hutband 1767 a.
Melia 1784 a.
WHITEFIELD
Sussex
Matthew 1767 w.
WHITEHARD
Princess Anne
John 1792 i.
WHITEHEAD
Amherst
Richd. 1785 a.
Jno. 1787 a.
Bedford
Joseph 1778 w.
Joseph 1783 i.
Culpeper
Anthony 1796 i.
Frederick
Edward 1782 i.

James 1779 i.
Saml. 1790 i.
Isle of Wight
Arthur [1711] w.
Arthur 1749 w.
Arthur, Jr. 1754 i.
Lazarus 1775 w.
Mecklenburg
Benj. 1781 w.
Northampton
Wm. 1752 i.
Stephen 1770 w.
Hannah 1777 w.
Northumberland
Thos. 1721 i.
Eliz. 1726-7 i.
Princess Anne
Jno. 1771 i.
Margt. 1776 i.
Wm. 1782 w.
Charles 1790 i.
John, Sr. 1797 w.
Joshua 1798 w.
Rappahannock
Saml. 1685 i.
Southampton
Arthur 1751 w.
Arthur 1760 i.
Lewis 1759 w.
Jno. 1793 i.
Mary 1795 w.
Wm. 1798 i.
Surry
Robt. 1731 i.
Sussex
Math. 1765 w.
York
Thos. 1660 w.
WHITEHERST
Norfolk
Robt. 1679 w.
WHITEHILL
Richmond
Jno. 1753 w.
WHITEHORN
Sussex
Jno., Sr. 1780 w.
Essex
Ann 1715 w.
WHITEHOUSE
Princess Anne
Thos. 1786 w.
Spotsylvania
Wm. 1747 a.
Essex
Danl. 1700 w.
WHITEHURST
Norfolk
Ellen 1654 w.
William 1757 w.
Richard 1765 w.

Princess Anne
Saml. 1711 w.
James, Sr. 1721 w.
James, Jr. 1721 w.
Jno. 1721 w.
Henry 1726 w.
Jno. 1727 w.
Wm. 1732 w.
Jno. 1733 i.
Eliz. 1734 w.
Hugh 1734 w.
Mary 1737 w.
Thos. 1740 w.
James 1741 w.
Willis 1748 w.
David 1749 i.
Mary 1749 w.
Robt. 1749 w.
Anthony 1753 i.
Batson 1753 i.
Arthur 1754 w.
Chas. 1754 w.
Lemuel 1755 i.
Nathl. 1755 w.
Jno. 1756 w.
Batson 1759 w.
Henry 1761 w.
Flowerence 1767 i.
Wm. 1767 w.
Margt. 1768 i.
Wm. 1768 i.
Jno. 1771 w.
Richd. 1771 i.
Sarah 1772 w.
Jas. 1773 w.
Thos. 1777 w.
Carraway 1778 w.
Jas. 1780 w.
Peter 1784 w.
Jas. 1785 w.
Jno. 1785 w.
Solomon 1785 w.
Wm. 1785 w.
Eliz. 1786 w.
Jas. 1786 i.
Thos. 1786 i.
Amey 1787 w.
Jonathan 1787 w.
Christopher 1788 w.
Jno. 1789 w.
Wm. 1789 i.
Hosea 1790 i.
Jonathan 1791 w.
Nathl. 1791 w.
Robert 1791 w.
Jno. 1792 w.
Richd. 1792 w.
Francis 1794 w.
Amey 1795 w.
Enoch 1795 w.
Hillary 1795 w.

Wm. 1795 w.
Lemuel 1797 w.
Reuben 1797 w.
Thos., Sr. 1797 w.
Cason 1799 w.
Jno. 1799 w.
WHITELY
Loudoun
Wm. 1790 i.
WHITEMAN
Henrico
Jno. 1690 i.
King George
Jno. 1735 i.
WHITESIDE
Rockbridge
Moses 1795 w.
WHITETENS
Princess Anne
Samuel 1795 w.
WHITFIELD
Isle of Wight
Thos. 1702 w.
Mary 1739 w.
Wm. 1750 w.
Jno. 1758 i.
Samuel 1758 w.
Harrison 1779 i.
Miles 1783 w.
Samuel 1785 w.
Abraham 1787 w.
Samuel 1788 i.
Samuel 1789 i
Milley 1795 i.
Southampton
Benj. 1796 w.
Sussex
Thos. 1794 w.
WHITFORD
Norfolk
David 1686-7 nw.
WHITHURST
Norfolk
Jno. 1691-2 w.
Richard 1791 w.
WHITING
Berkeley
Francis 1778 i.
Matthew 1792 i.
Fauquier
Jno. 1786 i.
Jno. 1786 w.
Fairfax
Anthony 1793 nw.
Frederick
Henry 1787 w.
Henry 1799 i.
Middlesex
Henry 1765 w.
Joyce 1772 w.
Prince William
Henry 1797 i.

Westmoreland
Thos. 1758 w.
WHITKER
Isle of Wight
Jno. 1689 nw.
WHITLEDGE
Prince William
Wm: 1782 w.
WHITLER
Spotsylvania
Jane 1773 a.
Jacob 1789 a.
WHITLEY
Botetourt
Paul 1772 w.
Brunswick
Thos. 1756 i.
Fairfax
Robert 1744 i.
Isle of Wight
John 1695 i.
Thos. [1716] w.
Arthur [1725] i.
Mary 1728 i.
Mary 1742 i.
Thos. 1751 i.
John 1758 i.
Jno. 1761 w.
Mary 1766 w.
Randolph 1785 w.
Geo. 1792 i.
Nathan 1798 i.
Nathaniel 1798 w.
Middlesex
Thos. 1778 w.
Rockbridge
Moses 1788 w.
WHITLIFF
Westmoreland
Isaac 1726 i.
WHITLIFFE
Westmoreland
Eliza 1727 i.
WHITLOCK
Essex
Jas. 1758 w.
Thos. 1784 i.
Goochland
Grizel 1759 w.
Jno. 1775 i.
Halifax
Thos. 1780 w.
Henrico
Mary 1786 w.
Louisa
Jas. 1749 w.
Thos. 1778 w.
Prince Edward
Josiah 1770 w.
Rappahannock
Thos. 1659 w.
Thos. 1678 w.

Wythe
Charles 1796 i.
WHITLOE
Henrico
Wm., Sr. 1726 w.
Anne 1727 w.
WHITLOW
Goochland
Wm. 1768 w.
Henry 1788 w.
Halifax
Cox 1788 w.
Thos. 1797 w.
Henrico
Wm. 1752 i.
Wm. 1788 w.
Jno. 1798 w.
Mecklenburg
Henry 1783 w.
James 1782 i.
WHITLY
Isle of Wight
John 1695 i.
WHITMAN
Orange
Wm. 1767 i.
WHITMILL
Stafford
Richd. 1753 i.
WHITMON
Berkeley
Frederick 1784 i.
WHITMOYE
Shenandoah
David 1796 i.
WHITMYER
Shenandoah
David 1794 a.
WHITNEY
Berkeley
Elizabeth 1795 i.
Isle of Wight
Joshua 1736 w.
Southampton
Joshua 1762 w.
Giles 1783 i.
WHITRICK
Frederick
Daniel 1756 w.
WHITSON
Shenandoah
Charles 1782 i.
George 1783 a.
Stafford
Saml. 1701 i.
Thos. 1732 i.
Thos. 1734 i.
Thos. (elder)
1739 w.
Surry
Jno. 1683 a.

WHITT
Halifax
Jno. 1789 w.
WHITTACRE
Lancaster
Jos. 1676 w.
WHITTALL
Louisa
Francis 1751 w.
WHITTEMORE
Brunswick
Wm. 1743 i.
Mecklenburg
Abraham 1772 w.
Lewis 1777 w.
WHITTEN
Amherst
Jeremiah 1778 a.
WHITTHERST
Norfolk
Wm. 1702 w.
WHITTMORE
Prince George
Nicholas, (elder)
1718 i.
Nicholas, Jr. 1718 i,
WHITTINGTON
Accomack
Wm. 1741 i.
Wm. 1757 i.
Eliz. 1762 w.
Southy 1790 w.
Southy 1797 w.
Brunswick
Wm. 1751 w.
Mary 1756 w.
Greensville
John 1791 w.
Northampton
Wm. 1659 w.
WHITTLE
Loudoun
Richd. 1789 i.
Louisa
Sarah 1782 a.
Richmond
Thos. 1719 w.
WHITTMIRE
Lancaster
Jos. 1677 i.
WHITTNEY
Isle of Wight
Joshua 1736 w.
WHITTY
Montgomery
William 1789 a.
WORTH

s. 1769 w.
s. 1775 i.
smus 1779 i.
raham 1798 i.

Prince Edward
Jno. 1793 i.
WHOREDOM
Northumberland
Peter 1728 i.
WHYT
Norfolk
Patrick 1713 i.
WHYTE
Lancaster
William 1793 i.
WIAT
Accomack
Jno. 1737 i.
Fauquier
William 1762 i.
WIATT
Norfolk
Shadrick 1773 w.
John 1782 i.
WICERS (?)
Northumberland
Henry 1669 w.
WICKENS
Princess Anne
Jno. 1772 w.
Jno. 1785 w.
Wm. 1787 w.
WICKER
Princess Anne
Richd. 1701 w.
Wm. 1717 w.
Wm. 1727 w.
WICKERS
Westmoreland
Thos. 1704 w.
WICKERSHAM
Frederick
Samuel 1785 w.
WICKHAM
York
Mary 1705 w.
WICKINS
Isle of Wight
Edmund 1679 i.
WICKLIFF
Prince William
Nathaniel 1790 i.
Moses 1799 i.
WICKLIFFE
Fairfax
Robert 1782 w.
Westmoreland
Robt. 1698 w.
Henry 1699 w.
WIDDON
Norfolk
William 1721 i.
WIDGEON
Northampton
Robt.,Sr. 1735 w.
Wm. 1738 i.

Jacob 1742 i.
Thos. 1748 w.
Robt. 1750 i.
Jos. 1759 i.
Edwd. 1760 w.
Jno. 1760 w.
Thos. 1774 w.
Southy 1775 w.
Jno. 1780 w.
Levin 1780 w.
Abel 1781 w.
Jno. 1782 i.
Esther 1784 w.
Jno. 1786 w.
Robt. 1799 w.
WIDGING
Stafford
Margt. 1743 i.
WIDROM
Goochland
Jno. 1761 w.
WIER
Amherst
Robt. 1794 w.
Pittsylvania
Thos. 1775 w.
WIERE
Rappahannock
Walter 1680 w.
WIESE
Accomack
Otto William 1748 w.
Sarah 1755 i.
WIGEON
Princess Anne
Isaac 1790 w.
WIGGEN
Northampton
Robt. 1677 w.
WIGGENS
Northumberland
Isaac 1771 i.
WIGGIN
Princess Anne
Wm. 1750 w.
WIGGINTON
Loudoun
James 1766 w.
Roger 1778 w.
Stafford
Wm. 1733 w.
Henry 1736 w.
Westmoreland
Roger 1712 w.
Wm. 1721 w.
Francis 1733 w.
Wm. 1733 i.
Henry 1748 w.
WIGGINS
Princess Anne
Eliz.1768 i.

Surry
Thos. 1710 w.
WIGGONS
Southampton
John 1772 w.
WIGGS
Isle of Wight
Henry [1712] w.
Katherine 1729 w.
Sarah 1732 w.
George 1747 w.
Luke 1758 i.
WIGHTWICK
York
Edwd. 1711 i.
WIGINTON
Fairfax
Roger 1752 w.
WIGLER
Frederick
Henry 1785 w.
WIGLESWORTH
Spotsylvania
Jno. 1750 a.
WIGLEY
Westmoreland
Job 1782 w.
WILBORN
Sussex
Jno. 1764 w.
WILBORNE
Halifax
Gunnery 1790 i.
Powhatan
Danl. 1799 w.
Sussex
Burril 1797 w.
WILBOURN
Cumberland
Thos. 1774 w.
WILBOURN
Halifax
Judith 1799 i.
Sussex
Jno. 1771 w.
Ann 1772 w.
Wm. 1783 w.
WILBOURNE
Sussex
Benj., Jr. 1798 w.
WILBUR
Princess Anne
Jno. 1752 i.
Eliz. 1753 i.
Wm. 1769 w.
Sarah 1771 w.
WILBURN
Frederick
Robert 1760 i.
Goochland
Richard 1759 i.

Lunenburg
Jno. 1758 w.
Sussex
Mary 1772 i.
Joel 1776 i.
WILLBURN
Frederick
Thos. 1746 i.
WILBY
Accomack
Salathiel 1735 i.
WILCOCKS
Northampton
Jno. 1662 w.
WILCOX
Frederick
Jno. 1748 i.
Lancaster
Jno. 1726 i.
Sussex
Eliz. 1772 i.
York
Wm. 1757 i.
WILCOXON
Fairfax
Lewis 1744 i.
WILCOXSON
Loudoun
Jno. 1765 w.
WILDBORE
Princess Anne
Jno. 1792 w.
WILDE
York
Robt. 1647 i.
WILDER
Culpeper
Jas. 1763 w.
Lancaster
Jas. 1788 w.
Jonathan 1788 w.
Geo. 1793 i.
Nathaniel 1794 i.
Norfolk
Edwd. 1687 w.
Michael 1717 w.
Francis 1725 i.
Jno. 1767 i.
Jacob 1769 i.
Prince William
Rhuben 1779 i.
WILDERS
Norfolk
Jacob 1772 i.
WILDES
Isle of Wight
Thos. 1675 i.
WILDEY
Lancaster
Michael 1746 w.

Northumberland
Wm.1681 w.
Jane 1701 w.
Motley 1748 w.
Elizabeth 1765 w.
Joseph 1769 w.
WILDS
Lunenburg
Luke 1749 w.
Stephen 1762 w.
WILDY
Northumberland
Wm. 1726 w.
Jos. 1748 w.
Wm. 1759 w.
Jane 1760 w.
Frederick 1768 i.
WILES
Isle of Wight
Zacharias [1718] w.
Jos. 1741 w.
Mecklenburg
Robt. 1771 w.
Norfolk
Lemuel 1750 w.
Samuel 1764 i.
Princess Anne
Thos. 1744 w.
Saml. 1755 i.
Thos. 1768 i.
Thos. 1769 w.
Thos. 1771 i.
Martha 1785 w.
WILEY
Augusta
John 1749 i.
Culpeper
Jno. 1791 w.
Essex
Jno. 1764 w.
Orange
David 1746 i.
WILFORD
Southampton
Jno. 1761 w.
WILLHOIT
Culpeper
Adam 1763 w.
Jno. 1776 i.
Lewis 1783 w.
Daniel 1790 i.
WILHOITE
Culpeper
Tobias 1762 w.
WILIE
Norfolk
Thos. 1792 w.
WILKASON
Surry
Jno. 1700 w.

Westmoreland
Jno. 1764 i.

WILKERSON
Accomack
Thos. 1775 w.
Mary 1788 w.
Amelia
Wm. 1759 i.
Eliz. 1760 i.
Mary 1774 i.
Charles City
Richd. 1796 w.
Harrison
Gabriel 1790 i.
King George
Chas [1778?] w.
Taylor 1784 w.
Thos. 1785 w.
Jas. 1788 w.
Jarriot 1789 w.
Settle 1793 w.
Molly 1796 i.
Weedon 1799 w.
Norfolk
Arnall 1654 w.
Powhatan
Jno. 1795 w.
Nicholas 1795 w.
Spotsylvania
Robt. 1779 w.
Sussex
Jno. 1758 w.
Jno. 1761 w.
Eliz. 1766 i.
Wm. 1799 w.
Westmoreland
Jno. 1764 w.

WILKEY
Fairfax
Jno. 1757 i.

WILKIN
Shenandoah
Godfrey 1785 a.

WILKINGS
Mecklenburg
Jas. 1781 w.

WILKINS
Augusta
Thos. 1751 i.
Cumberland
Jas. 1779 w.
Jno. 1791 i.
Fairfax
Jno. 1752 i.
Middlesex
Robt. 1741 i.
Norfolk
Wm. 1747 w.
Lemuel 1752 w.
Robert 1762 w.

James 1764 w.
Lemuel 1765 i.
John 1768 w.
John 1775 w.
Joshua 1777 w.
William 1777 w.
Willis 1785 w.
Sally 1788 w.
Malachi 1790 w.
James 1793 w.
John 1793 w.
John 1797 w.
Keziah 1797 w.
Smart 1799 i.
Northampton
Jno. 1650 w.
Jno. 1709 w.
Nathl. 1713 i.
Argall 1725 w.
Jno. 1726 w.
Thos. 1726 w.
Nathl. 1730 i.
Jno. 1737 w.
Argill 1742 i.
Esther 1742 i.
Jonathan 1747 i.
Nathl., Jr. 1747 i.
Nathl. 1750 w.
Wm., Sr. 1750 w.
Stockley 1752 w.
Thos. 1752 w.
Watkins 1752 w.
Thos. 1753 i.
Esther 1761 i.
Patrick 1761 w.
Henry 1770 w.
Wm., Sr. 1770 w.
Elishe 1771 w.
Jno. 1771 i.
Jas. 1774 i.
Jno. 1775 w.
Jno., Sr. 1777 i.
Sarah 1777 w.
Santica 1778 w.
Sarah 1779 i.
Joakim M. 1786 w.
Jno. 1787 w.
Argil 1788 w.
Eliz. 1797 w.
Wm., Sr. 1797 w.
Northumberland
Chas. 1742 w.
Jno. 1742 i.
Sarah 1749 i.
Charles 1750 i.
Jane 1752 i.
Thos. 1759 i.
John 1761 w.
Jane 1766 w.
Daniel 1768 i.
John 1768 i.

Dorothy 1791 i.
Wm. 1791 i.
Princess Anne
John 1785 i.
Solomon 1786 w.
Shenandoah
Godfrey 1787 i.
York
Jas. 1684 i.

WILKINSON
Accomack
Thos. 1746 i.
Jacob 1760 w.
Thos. 1777 w.
Amelia
Jane 1779 w.
John 1779 w.
Thos 1782 w.
Charles City
David 1795 w.
Richd. 1799 i.
Chesterfield
Edwd. 17— i.
Jos. 1750 w.
Anthony 1768 w.
Edwd. 1771 w.
Jos., Sr. 1773 w.
Eliz. 1778 i.
Richd. 1784 w.
Jos. 1789 i.
Wm. 1791 i.
Thos. [1796] i.
Fairfax
Thomas 1752 i.
Thomas 1790 a.
Harrison
Joseph 1789 w.
Samuel 1795 w.
Henrico
Jos. 1733 w.
Martha 1736 w.
King George
Geo. 1742 i.
Isle of Wight
Richard [1715] w.
Richard [1717] w.
Richard, Jr. 1727 i.
William 1741 w.
Richard 1742 w.
Jane 1793 w.
Lancaster
Isaac 1685 i.
Thos. 1719 i.
Mecklenburg
Wm. 1797 i.
Powhatan
Royal 1799 i.
Richmond
Chas. 1727 i.
Southampton
John 1784 w.

Surry
Jno. 1700 i.
Matthew 1752 w.
Sussex
Jno. 1758 i.
Averis 1779 i.
Westmoreland
Chas. 1733 i.
Wm. 1750 i.
Tyler 1760 w.
Taylor 1761 i.
York
Robt. 1655 w.
Thos. 1668 w.
Saml. 1739 w.
Geo. 1768 i.
WILKISON
Loudoun
Evan 1780 i.
York
Geo. 1717 w.
WILKS
Brunswick
Joseph 1784 w.
Charlotte
Minor 1794 w.
Benj. 1795 i.
Henrico
Richd. 1710 i.
Lancaster
Thos. 1686 i.
Loudoun
Francis 1784 i.
Powhatan
Thos. 1788 w.
WILKTON
Isle of Wight
John 1700 i.
WILLARD
Essex
Thomas 1718 i.
Martin 1745 w.
Sarah 1767 w.
Northampton
Thos. 1742 w.
WILLAROY
Princess Anne
James 1783 i.
WILLCOCK
Richmond
Godfrey 1766 i.
WILLCOCKS
Rappahannock
Mathew 1678 w.
WILLCOX
Charles City
Thos. 1773 i.
Wm. 1799 i.

WILLCOXTON
Ohio
Henry Hardy
1792 w.
WILLDY
Lancaster
Nathaniel 1730 w.
Northumberland
Wm. 1742 w.
WILLE
Princess Anne
Eleanor 1714 w.
WILLEROY
Princess Anne
Abraham 1759 i.
WILLESS
Goochland
David 1750 i.
WILLET
Accomack
Jno. 1763 i.
Thos. 1782 w.
Thos. 1784 i.
Botetourt
John 1773 i.
Northampton
Wm., Jr. 1725 w.
Hillary 1735 w.
Wm. 1739 w.
WILLETT
Accomack
Wm. 1719 w.
Jno. 1762 w.
Ambrose 1798 w.
Northampton
Jno. 1680 i.
Thos. 1752 w.
Douglas 1782 i.
WILLEY
Augusta
John 1748 w.
Brunswick
Jno. 1735 w.
Essex
John 1764 i.
Greenbrier
Henry 1796 w.
Princess Anne
Owen 1720 i.
WILLHEIT
Orange
Michael 1746 w.
WILLIAM
Frederick
David 1777 i.
Halifax
Saml. 1773 i.
Isle of Wight
John 1734 w.
John 1744 w.
David 1754 w.

Sussex
Chas. 1798 w.
WILLIAMES
Mecklenburg
Jones 1789 w.
WILLIAMS
Accomack
Jno. 1668 w.
Henry 1692 w.
Jones 1708 w.
Finley M. 1762 w.
Planner 1789 i.
Amelia
Jonas 1754 a.
Jonas 1756 w.
Chas. [1773?] i.
Billington 1785 w.
Philip, Sr. 1786 w.
Amherst
Francis 1789 w.
Augusta
Jno. 1763 a.
Jno. 1775 a.
Moses 1791 w.
Berkeley
Jerom 1792 i.
Brunswick
Chas. 1752 i.
Thos. 1755 w.
Jno. 1763 w.
Jane 1771 w.
Jno. 1772 w.
William 1775 w.
Danl. 1779 w.
Hugh 1781 w.
Jno. 1781 w.
Thos. 1787 w.
Jno. 1790 i.
Wm. 1792 i.
Ogburn 1793 w.
Charles City
Edwd. 1772 i.
Brazure 1793 w.
Charlotte
Wm. 1775 w.
Wm. 1777 w.
Jonathan 1797 i.
Chesterfield
Jno. 1794 w.
Jno. 1796 i.
Culpeper
John 1777 w.
William 1778 w.
Susannah 1786 w.
James 1790 w.
Cumberland
Wm. 1761 i.
Matthias 1780 i.
Thos. 1782 w.
Essex
John 1712 w.
William 1712 i.

Jno. 1713 w.
John 1714 w.
Emanuell 1737 i.
Richard 1738 i.
Thomas 1744 i.
John 1747 i.
Hugh 1749 i.
James 1758 i.
Fairfax
Howell 1743 a.
Thomas 1743 w.
William 1745 a.
Richard 1748 a.
William 1749 a.
William 1750 a.
William 1752 i.
John 1776 w.
John Locke 1776 i.
Owens 1776 w.
Geo. 1794 w.
Jonas 1795 i.
Geo. 1797 a.
Jno. 1797 a.
Sarah 1798 w.
Fauquier
George 1786 w.
Frederick
Samuel 1745 i.
Joseph 1747 i.
Paul 1747 i.
Ralph 1750 a.
Owen 1766 i.
Geo. 1781 i.
Barnett 1795 w.
Goochland
Edwd. 1731 i.
Jno. 1740 i.
Philemon 1760 i.
Zachariah 1766 i.
Zachariah 1772 i.
Wm. 1783 w.
Wm., Sr. 1783 i.
Eleazer 1789 i.
Philip 1792 i.
Frances 1797 w.
Greenbrier
Samuel 1784 w.
Greensville
Winfred 1783 w.
Benj. 1784 w.
Halifax
Abraham 1780 i.
Jno. 1797 i.
Hanover
Jno. 1735 a.
Henrico
Robt. 1699 a.
Thos. 1733 a.
Jno. 1748 w.
Jno. 1783 w.
Thos. 1783 w.

Thos. 1784 i.
Thos. 1785 i.
Jesse 1791 w.
Jno. 1792 i.
Isle of Wight
Morgan 1669 i.
Geo. 1672 w.
Rowland 1678 nw.
David 1687 w.
Jno. 1687 w.
Jno. 1690 w.
Jno., Sr. 1692 w.
Thos. 1693 w.
Jno. 1708 w.
Richard [1709] i.
Jno. 1719 i.
Thos. 1721 i.
Richard 1726 i.
Thos. [1727] w.
Epaproditus 1728 w.
Peter 1729 i.
Jno. 1734 w.
Mary 1734 w.
Garret 1735 w.
Jno. 1737 w.
Richard 1737 w.
Jno. 1741 w.
Margaret 1741 w.
Rachell 1742 w.
Geo. 1744 w.
Jno. 1745 i.
Richard 1750 i.
Wm. 1750 i.
Mathew 1751 i.
David 1754 i.
Jno. 1754 w.
Jos. 1756 w.
Jos. 1759 i.
Jos. 1773 i.
Jno. 1774 w.
Jno. 1776 w.
Jno. 1789 i.
David 1791 w.
Jno. 1794 w.
Josiah 1797 w.
King George
Nathaniel 1725 i.
David 1748 i.
Thos. 1750 i.
Lancaster
Roger 1702 w.
Thos. 1752 i.
Loudoun
Walter 1767 i.
Wm. 1786 w.
Richd. 1797 w.
Lunenburg
Jno. 1755 i.
Jno. 1767 w.
Richd. 1770 w.
Jno. 1776 w.

Thos. 1783 w.
Richd. 1784 i.
Thos. 1786 i.
Lazarus 1790 i.
Nicho. 1791 i.
Jno. 1795 w.
Jno. 1797 w.
Mecklenburg
Jno. 1794 w.
Middlesex
Geo. 1678 a.
Thos. 1701 w.
Chas. 1706 w.
Jno. 1764 w.
Benj. 1789 w.
Norfolk
Evan 1671 w.
Nicholas 1679 w.
Richd. 1694-5 w.
Jno. 1735 w.
Robt. 1751 w.
Lemuel 1752 i.
Jno. 1762 w.
Edwd.1765 w.
Willis 1765 w.
Jno. 1771 w.
Thos. 1782 w.
Wm. 1782 i.
Willis 1782 i.
Jno. 1783 i.
Jas. 1785 w.
Charles 1787 i.
Jno. 1792 w.
Wm. 1794 w.
Northampton
Henry 1661 w.
Morgan 1709 i.
Thos. 1709 i.
Wm. 1725 w.
Jacob 1734 w.
Frances 1757 w.
Jno. 1757 w.
Thos. 1758 i.
Abigail 1760 w.
Peter 1780 w.
Jas. 1789 w.
Northumberland
Thos. 1707 w.
Wm. 1723 i.
Thos. 1744 w.
Thos. 1794 i.
Jno. 1797 w.
Thos. 1799 w.
Aron 1751 w.
Wm. 1752 i.
John 1760 w.
Ephraim 1770 w.
John 1770 i.
Moses 1772 w.
Thos. 1777 i.

Orange
Francis 1766 w.
Pittsylvania
Wm. 1780 w.
Lucy 1788 w.
Thos. 1795 i.
Prince George
Wm. 1717 i.
Jno. 1726 i.
Princess Anne
Thos. 1710 i.
James 1758 i.
James 1762 i.
James 1772 i.
Hillary 1777 i.
James 1777 i.
Jno. 1782 w.
Prince William
William 1741 i.
David 1743 i.
Jonas, Jr. 1744 w.
Evan 1783 i.
Rappahannock
Walter 1672 w.
Roger 1677 w.
Richmond
Rice 1701 w.
Henry 1703 w.
Jno. 1706 w.
Luke 1706 w.
Shadrack 1709 i.
Jno. 1715 i.
Luke 1717 i.
Thos. 1718 i.
Jno. 1720 i.
David 1726 w.
Edwd. 1726 i.
Francis 1726 i.
Mary 1726 w.
Thos. 1733 w.
Jonas 1744 w.
Henry 1745 w.
Elizabeth 1750 i.
Jno. 1751 w.
Abraham [1760] i.
Henry 1760 w.
Jno., Sr., 1762 w.
Jane 1765 w.
Jno. 1767 i.
Roger 1767 w.
Saml. 1777 w.
Eliz. 1783 i.
Priscilla 1783 w.
Abraham 1785 i.
Luke 1786 w.
Sarah S. 1787 w.
Wm. 1791 w.
Betty Ann 1795 i.
Shenandoah
Benjamin 1777 a.
Benjamin 1782 i.

Southampton
Sarah 1750 w.
Matthew 1751 i.
Thos. 1759 w.
Arthur 1761 w.
Geo. 1766 i.
Thos. 1766 w.
Jonah 1771 w.
Jacob 1772 i.
Nathan Robt. 1773 w.
Sarah 1774 w.
Drury 1779 i.
Jacob 1779 i.
Michael 1781 i.
Henry 1782 i.
Wm. 1783 w.
Benj. 1787 w.
Jno. 1787 i.
Elias 1789 w.
Epaphroditus 1791 w.
Isaac 1791 i.
Nicho. 1791 w.
Richd. 1796 i.
Richd. 1797 w.
Matthew 1796 i.
Jacob 1798 w.
Geo. 1799 w.
Sion 1799 w.
Spotsylvania
James 1735 w.
James 1784 w.
Jno. 1769 a.
Saml. 1791 a.
Eliz. 1792 a.
Stafford
Antho. 1700 w.
Wm. 1703 i.
Wm. 1731 i.
Geo. 1750 w.
Thos. 1753 nw.
Jennett 1755 w.
Morgan 1784 i.
Surry
David 1676 w.
Lewis 1679 w.
Geo. 1703 i.
Roger 1709 w.
Jones 1718 w.
Chas. 1721 w.
Wm. 1741 w.
Roger 1744 w.
Roger 1745 w.
Catharine 1752 w.
Geo. 1757 i.
Wm. 1779 w.
Wm. 1784 i.
Sussex
Jas., Sr. 1770 w.
Jas. 1771 i.
Westmoreland
Morgan 1698 i.

Jno. 1702 w.
Wm. 1714 i.
Henry 1717 i.
Rice 1718 i.
Thos. 1726 i.
Morgan 1727 i.
Edwd. 1734 w.
Jno. 1737 w.
Jno. 1742 w.
Wm. 1745-6 i.
Thos. 1761 w.
York
Jno. 1697 i.
Jno. 1697-8 a.
Jno. 1711 i.
Wm. 1751 i.
Hannah 1759 i.
Simon 1769 w.
Simon 1771 i.

WILLIAMSON
Albemarle
Jas. 1750 i.
Amelia
Benj. 1761 i.
Frances 1769 w.
Augusta
David 1777 w.
Brunswick
Exum 1767 w.
Jno. 1773 w.
Jno. 1782 i.
Campbell
Robt. 1784 w.
Chesterfield
Jas. 1771 w.
Geo. 1778 w.
Culpeper
Thos. 1774 w.
Cumberland
Geo. 1756 w.
Essex
Thos. 1694 w.
Henry 1699 w.
Jno. 1701 w.
Jas. 1718 i.
Wm. 1743 w.
Jno. 1744 w.
Edwd. 1748 w.
Wm. 1748 i.
Wm. 1753 w.
Thos. 1765 w.
Thos. 1773 i.
Wm. 1775 w.
Jas. 1778 w.
Jno. 1791 w.
Fairfax
Henry 1757 w.
Jno. 1782 i.
Wm. 1787 i.
Fluvanna
Jno. 1795 w.

Goochland
  Geo. 1742 i.
Greensville
  Jno. 1796 w.
  Robt. 1799 w.
Isle of Wight
  Robt. 1670 w.
  Geo. 1722 w.
  Francis 1737 nw.
  Francis 1743 w.
  Francis, Sr. 1744 i.
  Ann 1753 w.
Henrico
  Jno. (younger)
    1763 i.
  Prudence 1795 w.
  Saml. 1799 w.
Loudoun
  Benj. 1766 i.
Louisa
  ―――― 1794 i.
Lunenburg
  Thos. 1755 w.
Mecklenburg
  Robt. 1796 w.
Middlesex
  Robt. 1726 w.
  Benj. 1726 w.
  Wm. 1764 w.
Norfolk
  Jno. 1677 w.
  Jno. 1711 i.
  Jno. 1716 i.
  Thos. 1752 w.
  Jno. 1763 w.
  Joshua 1767 w.
  Roger 1769 w.
  Robt. 1775 w.
  Jno. 1782 w.
  Jno. 1782 w.
  Jas. 1798 w.
Ohio
  Jas. 1782 a.
  Moses 1792 w.
Pittsylvania
  Thos. 1776 w.
  Thos. 1795 i.
Princess Anne
  Bartho. 1698 w.
  Jas. 1711 w.
  Jas. 1713 i.
  Richd. 1723 w.
  Chas. 1734 i.
  Chas. 1736 i.
  Jas. 1746 i.
  Bartho. 1749 w.
  Jno. 1750 w.
  Roger 1750 w.
  Dinah 1753 i.
  Jno. 1754 w.
  Jas. 1758 i.

Chas. 1764 w.
Jas. 1767 i.
Jas. 1769 i.
Lemuel 1777 w.
Reuben 1782 w.
Tully 1782 w.
Mary 1784 w.
Geo., Sr. 1791 w.
Geo. 1792 i.
Wm. 1794 w.
Willoughby 1795 w.
Joshua 1796 w.
Charles 1797 w.
Sarah 1797 w.
Rappahannock
  James 1657 i.
  James 1665 i.
Rockbridge
  Jno. 1781 a.
Shenandoah
  Joseph 1795 a.
  Joseph 1798 i.
Southampton
  Joseph 1753 w.
  Joseph 1757 i.
  Arthur 1772 w.
  Benj. 1772 w.
  Ann 1774 i.
  Francis 1782 w.
  Hannah 1782 i.
  Thos. 1787 w.
  Robt. 1788 w.
  Wm. 1788 i.
  Celah 1791 i.
  Burwell 1792 w.
Surry
  Jno. 1732 w.
  Cuthbert 1736 i.
Sussex
  Arthur 1781 w.
  Thos. 1782 w.
  Valentine 1784 w.
York
  Eliz. 1757 w.
WILLIARD
Essex
  Sarah 1768 i.
WILLICOME
Spotsylvania
  Wm. 1763 a.
WILLIE
King George
  Wm. 1721 i.
Sussex
  Wm. 1777 w.
  Eliz. 1788 w.
WILLIFORD
Isle of Wight
  John 1746 i.
Southampton
  John 1762 i.

Jno. 1783 w.
WILLIMOT
Richmond
  Jno. 1712 w.
WILLINGHAM
Halifax
  Jared 1792
Lunenburg
  Jno. 1751 w.
WILLIS
Accomack
  Danl. 1737 i.
  Danl. 1749 w.
  Henry 1750 w.
  Peter 1769 w.
  Solomon 1779 i.
Berkeley
  Robert Carter
    1783 w.
  Richard 1798 w.
Brunswick
  Jno. 1767 w.
  Mildred 1769 w.
Charles City
  Eady 1794 w.
Culpeper
  Francis 1789 i.
Fairfax
  Thomas 1747 w.
Fluvanna
  Willis 1782 w.
Goochland
  Robt. 1755 i.
  Robt. 1767 i.
  Ellender 1795 w.
Hanover
  Edwd. 1735 w.
Henrico
  Edwd. 1798 i.
Isle of Wight
  Thomas 1752 w.
  Miles 1794 i.
King George
  Jno. 1728 i.
  Jno. 1753 a.
  Eliz. 1767 w.
Lunenburg
  Jno. 1759 i.
  Edwd. 1760 w.
Mecklenburg
  Richd., Sr. 1777 w.
  Isabella 1796 i.
  Edwd. 1796 i.
Middlesex
  Danl. 1678 a.
  Jno. 1688 w.
  Richd. 1700 i.
  Thos. 1783 i.
Norfolk
  Nicholas 1682 i.
  Walter 1799 i.

Northampton
Geo. 1681 w.
Geo. 1720 w.
Geo. 1727 w.
Thos. 1771 i.
Thos. 1797 w.
Northumberland
Jas. 1655 w.
Orange
Jno. 1750 i.
Jno. 1762 w.
Princess Anne
Jno. 1771 w.
Thos. 1782 i.
Richmond
Jno., Sr. 1715 w.
Wm. 1717 i.
Spotsylvania
Mildred 1747 a.
Sussex
Jno. 1797 i.
Westmoreland
Wm. 1714 i.
Bridget 1717 i.
Wm. 1720 i.
York
Oliver 1688-9 w.
WILLISON
Surry
James 1787 w.
WILLMORE
Goochland
Cicilla 1740 w.
WILLOUGHBY
Amherst
Hugh 1768 w.
Fauquier
John 1783 i.
Norfolk
Thomas 1671 i.
Sarah 1672 i.
Sarah 1673 w.
Sarah 1682 i.
Thos. 1710-11 w.
Thos. 1712 w. .
Sarah 1739-40 w.
Thomas 1753 w.
Ann 1758 w.
Lemuel 1764 w.
John, Sr. 1776 w.
Martha 1778 w.
Thomas 1784 w.
John 1791 w.
Princess Anne
Thos. 1736 i.
Jno. 1740 w.
John 1789 i.
Rappahannock
Henry 1686 w.

WILLS
Amelia
Thos. 1761 i.
Lawrence 1784 w.
Matthew 1798 i.
Essex
John 1720 i.
Halifax
Harwood 1762 w.
Philmer 1769 i.
Isle of Wight
Joseph 1741 i.
Thomas 1751 w.
Miles 1763 i.
John 1770 w.
John 1772 w.
Micajah 1778 w.
Mary 1788 w.
John S. 1794 w.
Miles 1798 w.
Lunenburg
Richd. 1758 i.
Jno. 1760 a.
Middlesex
Jno. 1730 i.
Northampton
Thorn 1725 i.
Eliz. 1735 w.
Eliz. 1737 i.
Southampton
Francis 1749 w.
Surry
Geo. 1746 i.
Geo. 1781 w.
Jno. Geo. 1782 w.
Washington
Jacob 1795 i.
WILLSON
Accomack
Wm. 1683 i.
Amelia
Richd. 1768 w.
Jno. [1780?] i.
Danl., Jr. 1783 i.
Danll 1786 w.
Ann 1795 i.
Peter 1799 i.
Jno. 1798 i.
Augusta
Robt. 1788 w.
Botetourt
Patrick 1774 w.
Brunswick
Ralph 1751 i.
Chesterfield
Edwd. 17— i.
Geo. 1753 w.
Geo. 1760 w.
Geo. 1761 i.
Jas. 1766 w.

Goochland
Richard 1735 w.
Henrico
Jno., Sr. 1685 i.
Jno., Sr. 1716 w.
Richd. 1736 a.
Isle of Wight
Jas. 1720 w.
Jno. 1694 i.
Nicholas 1696 i.
Lancaster
William 1773 i.
Loudoun
Geo. 1777 w.
Lunenburg
Wm. 1796 w.
Norfolk
Hugh 1689 w.
Thos. 1702 w.
Northampton
Alice [16—?] w.
Austine (?) 1641 i.
Jas. 1720 w.
Northumberland
Jno. 1722 i.
Robt. 1727 w.
Richmond
Jno. 1709 w.
Jas. 1738 w.
Winnifred 1738 i.
Jas. 1743 w.
Jno. 1760 w.
Morton 1799 w.
Westmoreland
Jno. 1719 w.
Robt. 1726 w.
WILLY
Princess Anne
Owen 1698 w.
WILMORE
Cumberland
Daniel 1773 w.
WILMOT
York
Mary 1754 i.
WILMOTH
Isle of Wight
Edwd. [1647?] w.
WILMOTT
Isle of Wight
Wm. [1700] i.
WILSFORD
Westmoreland
Thos. 1667 w.
Thos. 1703 w.
WILSHER
Amherst
Jos. W. 1777 w.
WILSON
Accomack
Thos. 1707 w.

Wm. 1738 w.
Amelia
Wm. 1771 w.
Mary 1781 w.
Jno. 1795 w.
Augusta
Robt. 1745 w.
Robt. 1748 i.
Jno. 1754 w.
Jno. 1757 w.
Josiah 1758 a.
Jno. 1759 i.
Saml. 1760 w.
Saml. 1760 w.
Jas. 1768 i.
Robt. 1768 w.
Wm. 1768 i.
Jno. 1773 a.
Thos. 1773 w.
Saml. 1774 w.
Thos. 1777 i.
Robt. 1799 w.
Bath
William 1795 w.
Bedford
Matthew 1771 w.
Jno. 1780 w.
Berkeley
Jos. 1778 i.
Jno. 1783 w.
Jos. 1795 w.
Thos. 1797 nw.
Botetourt
Richd. 1779 w.
David. 1789 i.
Mathew 1795 w.
Geo. 1799 i.
Brunswick
Henry 1775 w.
Charlotte
John 1779 i.
Daniel 1798 i.
Chesterfield
Wm. 1777 w.
Jas. 1798 w.
Essex
Hugh 1776 w.
Frederick
Jno. 1762 w.
Robt. 1770 i.
Jas. 1777 w.
Robt. 1779 w.
Robt. 1784 i.
Robt. 1792 w.
Goochland
David 1752 i.
Greenbrier
Jas. 1781 w.
Jas. 1786 w.
Halifax
Peter 1764 w.

Thos. 1771 w.
Thos. 1777 w.
Stephen 1782 w.
Henrico
Jno. 1732 i.
Richd. 1732 w.
Henry
Jas. 1777 w.
Jas. 1793 w.
Isle of Wight
Jas. 1665 nw.
Jas. 1683-4 i.
Margaret 1697 i.
Margaret 1698 nw.
Jno. 1719 w.
Goodrich 1742 w.
Jno. 1745 i.
Geo. 1758 w.
Rosamond 1760 i.
Henry 1762 i.
William 1665 i.
Willis 1785 w.
Samuel 1789 w.
Solomon 1799 w.
King George
Robt. 1739 i.
Jno. 1790 w.
Loudoun
John 1788 w.
Louisa
Robt. 1785 a.
Madison
James 1798 i.
Mecklenburg
Jno. 1794 i.
Jno. 1796 w.
Middlesex
Edwd. 1774 w.
Norfolk
Thos. 1693 w.
Jno. 1695-6 w.
James 1712 w.
Thomas 1714 w.
James 1718 w.
Thomas 1725 i.
Willis 1750 w.
William 1752 w.
James, Sr. 1756 w.
Thomas 1757 w.
Thos. 1759 i.
Willis 1760 w.
James 1761 w.
Thomas 1766 w.
Dinah 1771 w.
James 1777 i.
John 1780 w.
Goodrich 1785 w.
John 1785 i.
Malachi 1787 w.
William 1787 w.
Caleb 1789 w.

James 1789 w.
Josiah 1792 i.
Caleb 1794 i.
Henry 1794 i.
Malachi 1794 w.
Grace 1795 w.
Josiah 1795 w.
Thomas, Sr. 1796 w.
Willis 1798 w.
Northampton
Richd. 1639 i.
Robt. 1650 w.
Richd. 1659 i.
Jas. 1725 w.
Thos. 1732 w
Richd. 1735 i.
Thos. 1737 w.
Hannah 1739 i.
Solomon 1750 i.
Williams 1764 w.
Jno. 1766 w.
Thos. 1770 w.
Jno. 1772 w.
Jno., Jr. 1773 i.
Thos. 1773 w.
Thos. 1777 i.
Jno. 1787 w.
Northumberland
Jane 1751 i.
Moses 1775 w.
Nathl. 1796 i.
Prince Edward
James 1786 i.
Princess Anne
Saml. 1710 i.
Baswell 1770 i.
Prince William
Henry 1778 w.
Sarah 1786 w.
Rappahannock
Hugh 1661 i.
Richmond
Elias 1699 w.
Elias 1706 w.
Jas. 1712 w.
Henry 1737 w.
Jas. 1746 w.
Martha 1754 w.
Richd. 1758 i.
Jno. 1796 i.
Rockbridge
Seth 1790 w.
Thomas 1793 i.
David 1795 i.
Seth 1795 i.
Robert 1798 i.
Southampton
Wm. 1779 w.
Spotsylvania
Hugh 1766 a.

Surry
Sampson 1750 i.
Thos. 1768 w.
Capt. ——— 1774 i.
James 1788 i.
Elizabeth 1790 w.
Westmoreland
Jno. 1671 w.
Henry 1713 w.
Thos. 1720 i.
Allen 1753 w.
York
Cornelius 1707 i.
Rosanna 1783 w.
Geo. 1793 w.
Geo. 1798 i.

WILT
Frederick
Peter 1761 i.

WILTON
Essex
Richard 1711 i.
Mecklenburg
Richd. 1780 w.
Richd. 1793 w.
Northampton
Jno. 1650 i.
Richmond
Henry 1710 i.

WILTSHIRE
Amherst
Benj. 1777 a.

WILY
Culpeper
James 1791 i.
Halifax
Wm. 1783 w.

WIMBISH
Halifax
James 1770 w.
Prince Edward
Jas. 1761 w.
Benj. 1774 w.
Benj. 1775 i.
Benj. 1776 i.
Benj. 1799 i.

WIMBROUGH
Accomack
Wm. 1731 i.
Jos. 1771 w.
Solomon 1776 i.

WIMMER
Bedford
John 1780 w.

WIMPIE
Lunenburg
Jno. 1762 w.

WINBERRY
Northampton
Jno. 1675 w.

WINBROUGH
Accomack
Jno. 1759 i.
Paul 1764 i.

WINDER
Northumberland
Wm. 1711 nw.

WINDHAM
Isle of Wight
Reuben 1745 i.
Southampton
Benj. 1782 i.

WINDLE
Shenandoah
Augustine 1792 w.
Christopher 1792 i.
Augustine 1795 i.

WINDLEKITE
Augusta
Jno. 1752 i.

WINDOM
Accomack
Geo. 1731 w.
Surry
Griffin 1721 i.

WINDOW
Accomack
Jno. 1755 i.
Eliz. 1767 w.
Jno. 1772 w.
Babel 1774 w.
Eli. 1775 i.
Jno. 1775 w.
Jno. 1779 i.
Levin 1786 w.
Violater 1793 w.
Robt. 1797 w.

WINDSOR
Fairfax
Thos. 1792 w.

WINDZOR
Westmoreland
Anthony 1698 w.

WINEFORD
Cumberland
Wilmoth 1768 i.

WINEGARDNER
Loudoun
Harbard 1779 w.

WINFELL
Norfolk
Jno. 1698 w.

WINFIELD
Brunswick
Joel 1762 i.
Sussex
Wm. 1770 w.
Peter 1788 w.
Wm. 1798 w.

WINFREE
Amelia
Jno. 1780 w.
Gideon 1782 w.
Cumberland
Jacob 1772 w.
Jno. 1793 w.
Chesterfield
Henry 1793 w.
Valentine 1795 w.
Wm. 1797 i.

WINFREY
Chesterfield
Henry 1779 w.
Cumberland
John 1795 i.
York
Mary 1793 w.

WING
King George
Jos. 1737 i.

WINGATE
Fairfax
Henry 1793 a.
Norfolk
Jno. 1773 w.
Northampton
Elishe 1797 i.

WINGET
Northampton
Geo. 1758 w.

WINGFIELD
Goochland
Robt. 1791 w.
Louisa
Robt. 1769 w.
Sussex
Jarvis 1756 i.
Amelia
Abraham 1776 w.

WINGO
Jno. 1755 w.
Thos. 1765 w.
Thos., Jr. 1768 i.
Charlotte
Wm. 1793 i.

WINGORD
Augusta
Jno. 1759 i.

WINKELLS
Surry
Wm. 1733 w.

WINKFIELD
Amherst
Mathew 1778 a.
Fauquier
Honor 1799 w.

WINLOCK
Westmoreland
Jos. 1726 i.

WINN
Amelia
 Jno. 1781 w.
Fauquier
 Minor 1778 w.
Lunenburg
 John 1768 w.
 Thos. 1781 w.
 Washington 1794 i.
 Jno. 1795 w.
 David 1799 w.
Richmond
 Jno. 1745 i.
 Mary 1745 i.
WINNEFERD
Cumberland
 David 1794 i.
WINNEFORD
Cumberland
 David 1771 w.
 David 1776 w.
 Chas. 1780 w.
WINNIFRED
Cumberland
 Geo. 1758 i.
WINSETT
Berkeley
 Richard 1791 i.
WINSLOW
Essex
 Thos. 1726 w.
 Benj. 1751 w.
Spotsylvania
 Beverly 1793 w.
WINSOR
Prince William
 Christopher 1735 w.
WINSTEAD
Northumberland
 Saml., Sr. 1726 w.
 John 1761 i.
 Eliz. 1765 i.
 Samuel 1774 w.
 Jas. 1785 i.
 Danl. 1793 w.
 Lewis 1794 i.
WINSTON
Henrico
 Peter 1784 w.
Louisa
 Saml. 1758 w.
WINT
King George
 Jas. [1777] w.
WINTER
Northumberland
 Roger 1758 w.
 Thos. 1763 w.
 Wm. 1768 i.
 Betty 1778 i.

Richmond
 Jno. 1743 i.
Westmoreland
 Jno. 1724 i.
York
 Andrew 1679 i.
WINTERBERDY
Frederick
 Jno. 1752 i.
WINTERTON
Norfolk
 Nicholas 1771 i.
WINTZEL
Loudoun
 Adam 1772 w.
WIRE
Augusta
 Francis 1779 w.
WIRICK
Wythe
 Nicolas 1792 w.
WIRRECK
Norfolk
 Henry 1711 w.
WIRT
Loudoun
 Peter 1798 w.
WISDALE
King George
 Richd. 1734 i.
WISDOM
Orange
 Jno. 1762 w.
Pittsylvania
 Francis 1794 w.
 Thos. 1798 i.
Spotsylvania
 Jno. 1769 a.
WISE
Accomack
 Jno., Sr. 1695 w.
 Jno. 1717 w.
 Matilda 1723 w.
 Jno., Sr. 1741 w.
 Geo. 1764 i.
 Thos. 1764 w.
 Wm. 1764 nw.
 Jno. 1767 w.
 Wm., Sr. 1769 w.
 Jno. 1770 w.
 Jno. 1774 w.
 Tully Robinson
  1778 w.
 Saml. 1779 w.
 Jno. 1782 i.
 Jno., Sr. 1782 w.
 Samuel 1782 i.
 Wm. 1782 w.
 Saml. 1785 i.
 Jas. 1791 w.
 Wm. 1797 i.

 Johannis 1798 w.
 Jno. 1799 i.
Brunswick
 Wm. 1752 i.
Culpeper
 John 1798 w.
Frederick
 Jacob 1768 w.
 John 1770 i.
Henrico
 Jno. 1785 i.
Norfolk
 Nicholas 1669 i.
Northampton
 Jno. 1778 i.
Northumberland
 Spencer 1765 w.
 Edwd. 1798 w.
York
 Chas. 1712 w.
 Wm. 1718 w.
 Sarah 1718 w.
 Rachel 1719 w.
 Wm. 1723 w.
 Chas. 1740 w.
 Robt. 1773 i.
WISEGARBER
Frederick
 John 1783 i.
WISEMAN
Augusta
 Peter 1798 w.
Shenandoah
 Thomas 1797 i.
WISENT
Frederick
 Joseph 1779 i.
WISH
Essex
 Margt. 1732 i.
WISHARD
Accomac
 Thos. 1755 w.
Princess Anne
 James 1717 w.
 Thos. 1728 w.
 Mary 1735 w.
 Mary 1736 w.
WISHART
Accomac
 Jas. 1750 w.
 Thos. 1757 i.
 Wm. 1765 i.
King George
 Jno. 1774 w.
Norfolk
 Jas. 1679/80 w.
 William 1750 w.
 Francis 1771 w.
Princess Anne
 Wm. 1736 w.
 Geo. 1766 w.

Thos. 1772 w.
Geo. 1777 w.
Wm. 1784 w.
Mary 1795 w.
WISHEART
Fairfax
Henry 1776 w.
WISLEY
Montgomery
Frederick 1782 i.
WISMAN
Shenandoah
Philip 1778 w.
WITAKER
Isle of Wight
John 1688 i.
WITBOURN
Greensville
William 1798 i.
WITCH
Cumberland
John 1769 i.
WITE
Berkeley
James 1799 i.
WITCHELL
Augusta
Jno. 1759 a.
WITHERALL
Culpeper
George 1781 w.
WITHERINGTON
Surry
Nicholas 1712 w.
Katherine 1713/14 w.
Westmoreland
Edwd. 1677 w.
WITHERS
Berkeley
William 1785 w.
Fauquier
James 1784 w.
James 1791 w.
Thomas 1794 w.
Frederick
Ralph 1790 w.
Rappahannock
Jno. 1687 w.
Stafford
Wm. 1703 w.
Jas. 1746 w.
WITHEY
Rappahannock
Augustine 1659 w.
WITT
Albemarle
Wm. 1755 w.
Amherst
Jno. 1781 w.
Jane 1796 a.
Littleberry 1797 i.

Bedford
Lewis 1774 i.
Halifax
Chas. 1782 w.
WITTEN
Wythe
Thomas 1795 i.
WITTON
Mecklenburg
Richd. 1781 i.
WIXON
Goochland
Danl. 1744 i.
WOCKER
Shenandoah
George Adam 1799 w.
John 1799 w.
WOFFENDALE
King George
Mary 1762 w.
WOFFENDALL
King George
Wm. 1747 i.
Mary 1762 i.
Richmond
Adam 1704 w.
WOFFENDELL
King George
Wm. 1794 a.
WODROP
Northumberland
Robt. 1768 i.
WOLDROP
Amelia
Jos. 1775 w.
WOLF
Shenandoah
Jacob 1779 a.
Augustine 1782 a.
Jacob 1799 w.
WOLFE
Frederick
Michael 1766 w.
Peter 1779 w.
WOLFINBERGER
Shenandoah
John 1789 a.
WOLGAMOTT
Berkeley
David 1799 i.
WOLLARD
Richmond
Elizabeth 1788 w.
WOLTZ
Berkeley
Peter 1785 w.
WOMACK
Bedford
Jesse 1782 w.
Campbell
Alex. 1784 w.

Charlotte
Wm. 1790 w.
Chesterfield
Mary 1750 w.
Thos. 1780 w.
Thos. 1782 w.
Joel 1783 i.
Sarah 1785 w.
Jesse 1797 i.
Cumberland
Wm. 1786 w.
Nathan 1798 w.
Goochland
Wm. 1762 w.
Henrico
Thos. 1697 w.
Richd. 1730 a.
Abraham 1733 w.
Thos. 1733 w.
Prince George
Jno. 1725 w.
Southampton
James 1787 i.
Thos. 1795 w.
WOMBELL
Isle of Wight
Thomas 1687/8 w.
Thomas 1740 w.
Thomas 1785 w.
Joseph 1797 i.
WOMBLE
Isle of Wight
John 1773 i.
Joseph 1784 w.
WOMBRELL
Isle of Wight
Joseph 1746 w.
WOMBWELL
Isle of Wight
Joseph 1793 i.
Britain 1797 i.
Mary 1798 w.
Southampton
Jesse 1774 w.
Surry
Jno. 1746 w.
WOMECK
Henrico
Richd. 1684 i.
WONYCOTT
Norfolk
Nicholas 1774 w.
Aphia 1782 w.
WOOBANK
Surry
Robt. Smith 1750 i.
WOOD
Albemarle
Henry 1774 w.
Jno. 1777 i.
Ann 1781 w.

Amelia
  Jas. 1767 i.
  Jas. 1775 i.
Amherst
  Jno. 1783 w.
Augusta
  Wm. 1782 w.
Bedford
  Thos. 1766 i.
  Thos. 1793 w.
Botetourt
  Andrew 1781 w.
Brunswick
  Richd. 1746 w.
  Thos. 1762 i.
  Wm. 1772 w.
Charlotte
  Jno. 1790 w.
Chesterfield
  Wm. 1758 w.
Culpeper
  Jas. 1773 i.
  Jno. Scott 1778 w.
  Saml. 1782 w.
  Edwd. 1785 w.
  Jos. 1791 w.
Essex
  Jno. 1698 w.
  Jno. 1700 w.
  Thos. 1709/10 i.
  Jno. 1753 w.
Fairfax
  Jno. 1785 i.
Fauquier
  Robt. 1763 i.
  Saml. 1777 i.
Frederick
  Jos. 1749 i.
  Tobias 1752 w.
  Jas. 1760 w.
  Thos. 1786 w.
Goochland
  Henry 1757 i.
  Valentine 1781 w.
Greensville
  Reuben 1784 i.
Halifax
  Jas. 1769 w.
Henrico
  Moses 1715 w.
  Jno. 1733 i.
  Jno. 1789 i.
Isle of Wight
  Thos. [1716] w.
  Eliz. 1721 w.
  Geo. 1734 i.
King George
  Henry 1722 i.
  Jno. 1757 w.
  Saml. 1775 w.
Lancaster
  Richard 1722 w.

  Jno. 1744 i.
Louisa
  Christopher 1790 w.
  Wm. 1791 w.
Lunenburg
  Stephen 1782 w.
  Jno. 1787 i.
Middlesex
  Wm. 1733 w.
  Wm. 1734 w.
  Wm. 1750 w.
  Saml. 1765 w.
Norfolk
  Dinah 1794 w.
  Joshua 1797 i.
Northumberland
  Jno. 1739 w.
  Jno. 1759 w.
Orange
  Jos. 1792 i.
  Absolom 1796 w.
Princess Anne
  Edward 1735 i.
  Mark 1735 w.
  Wm. 1769 w.
  Jas. 1770 i.
Richmond
  Thos. 1727 w.
Southampton
  Benj. 1765 i.
  Geo. 1770 w.
  Hannah 1773 i.
  Joshua 1783 w.
Spotsylvania
  Jno. 1753 a.
  Lancelot 1754 a.
Stafford
  Wm. 1706 w.
  Elijah 1734 i.
Surry
  Benj. 1797 w.
Sussex
  Chas. 1785 w.
Washington
  Archelaus 1783 i.
Westmoreland
  Edwd. 1713 i.
  Wm. 1731 i.
  Saml. 1794 w.
York
  Richard 1695 i.
  Robt. 1739 w.
WOODALL
Goochland
  Jno. 1750 w.
  Wm. 1797 w.
WOODARD
Norfolk
  Caleb Sr. 1784 w.
Princess Anne
  Joel 1773 w.
  Josiah 1786 w.

  Wm. 1791 i.
  Joel 1796 w.
Southampton
  Saml. 1752 w.
  Chas. 1781 w.
Surry
  Wm. 1727 i.
Sussex
  Susanna 1789 w.
WOODBRIDGE
Richmond
  Wm. 1726 w.
  Jno. 1770 i.
WOODBURN
Isle of Wight
  Jno. [1672] i.
WOODCOCK
Chesterfield
  Thos. 1777 i.
Henrico
  Isaac 1786 i.
Richmond
  Wm. 1735 i.
WOODDING
York
  Jno. 1698 i.
WOODEN
Norfolk
  Thos. 1712 w.
Surry
  Amey 1742 w.
WOODFIELD
York
  Thos. 1714 w.
WOODFORD
Fauquier
  Catesby 1792 w.
Westmoreland
  Henry 1786 i.
WOODHOUSE
Norfolk
  Henry 1655 w.
  Henry 1686/7 w.
  Richard 1762 w.
Princess Anne
  Jno. 1693 w.
  Wm. 1700 w.
  Henry 1703 i.
  Jno. 1715 w.
  Henry, (Elder)
    1719 w.
  Horatio 1719 w.
  Horatio 1724 w.
  Philip 1734 w.
  Eliz. 1741 w.
  Henry 1743 w.
  Philip 1752 w.
  Mary 1760 i.
  Francis 1765 w.
  James 1768 w.
  Henry 1770 i.
  Wm. 1774 w.

Jno. 1775 w.
Jonathan 1775 w.
Aliph 1782 w.
Horatio 1782 w.
Philip 1782 i.
Wm. 1783 w.
Henry 1784 w.
Henry 1785 w.
Thos. 1787 w.
Thos. 1788 i.
John 1793 w.
Jonathan 1797 w.
York
Edwd., Jr. 1735 i.
WOODIER
Westmoreland
Thos. 1719 i.
WOODIN
Norfolk
William 1770 w.
WOODING
Halifax
Robt. 1797 w.
WOODLAND
Accomack
Jos. 1698 i.
Brunswick
Jno. 1749 i.
Prince George
Jno. 1721 i.
Princess Anne
Jno. 1778 w.
Sussex
Wm. 1795 w.
WOODLEIF
Amelia
Robt. 1757 w.
Louisa
Catherine 1773 w.
Jno. 1773 i.
Catherine 1779 i.
WOODLEY
Augusta
Jno. 1749/50 w.
WOODLIEFE
Prince George
Edwd. 1718 w.
WOODLEY
Isle of Wight
Andrew 1720 w.
John [1725/6] w.
Henry 1754 w.
Thomas 1754 w.
John 1779 i.
John, Sr. 1791 w.
WOODLOCK
Westmoreland
Thos. 1703 w.
WOODMAN
Shenandoah
Philadelphia 1788 w.

Westmoreland
Cyprian 1744 i.
WOODFIN
Powhatan
Wm. 1797 i.
WOODROFF
Greensville
Joel 1793 w.
WOODROOF
Albemarle
David 1761 i.
Greensville
Richard 1789 w.
Richmond
Jas. 1733 i.
WOODRUFF
Greensville
John 1782 w.
Spotsylvania
Geo. 1771 w.
Richd. 1795 w .
WOODS
Accomack
David 1753 i.
Albemarle
Michael 1762 w.
Nathan 1783 w.
Jno. 1791 w.
Amherst
James 1781 w.
Saml. 1781 w.
Augusta
Wm. 1758 a.
Jno. 1763 i.
Wm. 1784 i.
Bedford
Thomas, Sr. 1764 i.
Botetourt
Arthur 1774 i.
Michael 1777 w.
Archibald 1784 i.
Henry
William 1790 i.
Greenbrier
William 1782 w.
King George
Jno. 1757 i.
Montgomery
Joseph 1793 w.
Orange
Jno. 1785 w.
Richmond
Richd. 1721 w.
Rockbridge
Richard 1778 w.
Southampton
Benj. 1763 i.
Washington
John 1790 w.
WOODSON
Albemarle
Tucker, Jr. 1779 w.

Jno. 1779 w.
Chesterfield
Tarlton 1761 w.
Richd. 1766 i.
Cumberland
Benj. 1754 i.
Sanburn 1756 w.
Josiah 1781 w.
Wm. 1784 w.
Drury 1788 w.
Jno. 1791 w.
Jno. 1793 w.
Jno. (D. W.) 1793 i.
Stephen 1794 w.
Fluvanna
Benj. 1778 w.
Goochland
Robt., Jr. 1729 w.
Joseph 1734 w.
Benj. 1735 w.
Josiah 1736 w.
Stephen 1736 w.
Benj. 1750 i.
Robt. 1750 w.
Jno. 1754 w.
Bouth 1757 w.
Susanna 1757 w.
Jacob 1762 i.
Lewis 1771 w.
Tarlton 1774 i.
Joseph 1784 i.
Joseph, Sr. 1784 w.
Robt. 1784 i.
Jno. 1790 w.
Matthew 1794 w.
Tucker 1795 w.
Henrico
Jno., Sr. 1684 w.
Jno., Jr. 1700 w.
Sarah 1704 w.
Mary 1710 w.
Jno. 1715 w.
Saml. Tucker 1718 w.
Jno. 1727 w.
Jacob 1728 w.
Robt., Sr. 1729 w.
Jno. 1733 a.
Jno. 1735 a.
Jos. 1752 i.
Powhatan
Chas., Jr. 1789 w.
Chas. 1790 i.
Jos. 1791 w.
Chas. 1796 i.
Prince Edward
Obadiah 1767 w.
Constant 1773 w.
Richd. 1775 w.
Obadiah 1776 w.
Chas. 1787 w.
Anthony W. 1796 i.

WOODWARD
Bedford
  Isaac 1782 i.
  Richd. 1786 w.
Culpeper
  Richd. 1793 i.
Fairfax
  Jas. 1788 w.
Goochland
  Mary 1753 w.
  Jno. 1777 i.
Isle of Wight
  Thos. 1677 w.
  Thos. 1681 i.
  Katherine 1684 w.
  Oliver 1741 w.
  Jno. 1753 i.
  Wm. 1797 w.
  Jno. Geo. 1798 w.
Lancaster
  Wm. 1704 i.
Norfolk
  Francis 1679 w.
Princess Anne
  John 1785 i.
  Josiah 1786 i.
  Henry 1794 w.
Sussex
  Jno. 1783 w.
  Jno. 1787 w.
WOODY
Amherst
  Thos. 1784 a.
Hanover
  Moor 1734 i.
  Simon 1734 w.
WOODYARD
Prince William
  Jno. 1795 w.
WOODYATES
Richmond
  Thos. 1707 w.
WOOHNAN
Shenandoah
  David 1787 w.
WOOLAM
Berkeley
  Jacob 1778 w.
WOOLARD
Loudoun
  Wm., Sr. 1787 i.
Richmond
  Jno. 1759 w.
  Sarah 1764 w.
WOOLBANKS
Goochland
  Wm. 1785 i.
WOOLDRIDG
Cumberland
  Jno. 1772 w.

WOOLDRIDGE
Accomack
  Thos. 1752 i.
Campbell
  Richard 1782 i.
Chesterfield
  John 1780 w.
  John 1783 i.
  Robert 1784 w.
Cumberland
  Thos. 1762 w.
Northumberland
  Edwd. 1727 i.
WOOLEY
Middlesex
  Geo. 1699 w.
Richmond
  John 1714 i.
WOOLF
Augusta
  Jno. 1749 i.
WOOLFENBARGO
Culpeper
  Geo. 1785 w.
WOOLFFAILLIER
Augusta
  Jno. 1748 a.
WOOLFOLK
Halifax
  Jno. 1779 w.
Louisa
  Wm. 1780 w.
Orange
  Jos. 1778 w.
Sussex
  Francis 1794 w.
WOOLLARD
Loudoun
  Mary 1788 w.
Richmond
  Richard 1743 i.
  Isaac 1749 w.
  Jos. 1760 i.
  Richd. 1774 i.
  Saml. 1787 w.
WOOLWINE
Augusta
  Wm. 1786 i.
WOORY
Isle of Wight
  Jos. 1693 i.
WOOLSEY
Brunswick
  Jno. 1782 w.
Washington
  Thos. 1794 w.
WOOTEN
Isle of Wight
  Richard 1686 w.
WOOTON
Halifax
  Wm. 1762 i.

WOOTTEN
Southampton
  Richd. 1773 i.
WOOTTON
Northampton
  Richard 1655 w.
WORAS
Princess Anne
  Chas. 1773 w.
WORD
Lancaster
  Wm. 1792 w.
Richmond
  Thos. 1717 w.
Spotsylvania
  Margaret 1798 a.
  Margaret (2) 1798 a.
WORDEN
Westmoreland
  Jno. 1716 w.
  Jno. 1727 a.
WORKMAN
Norfolk
  Thos. 1654 w.
  Jno. 1675 w.
Northampton
  Richard 1650 i.
WORLEY
Amelia
  Wm. 1773 w.
Bedford
  Francis 1780 w.
  Wm. 1787 w.
Northampton
  Jno. 1649 w.
Stafford
  Wm. 1753 i.
York
  Edwd. 1724 w.
  Edwd. 1738 i.
WORLEY
Cumberland
  John 1758 w.
WORMAN
Northumberland
  Jno. 1771 w.
WORME
Berkeley
  Michael 1792 i.
WORMELEY
Lancaster
  John 1785 w.
Middlesex
  Eliz. 1693 w.
  Christopher 1701 w.
  Ralph 1701 w.
  Ralph 1714 w.
  Eliz. 1761 w.
  Ralph 1791 w.
WORMINGTON
Norfolk
  Wm. 1763 i.

Abraham 1789 w.
Saml. 1797 i.
WORMINTUN
Norfolk
Wm. 1762 w.
WORNEM
Northumberland
Jean 1743 w.
WORNER
Wythe
Jacob 1794 i.
WORNOM
Northumberland
Thos. 1742/3 w.
Thos. 1743/4 w.
Jane 1743/4 w.
Thos. 1768 w.
Thos. 1789 w.
WORREL
Southampton
Wm. 1766 i.
Richd. 1788 w.
WORRELL
Isle of Wight
Richard [1716] w.
Wm. 1736 w.
Southampton
Wm. 1765 w.
Josiah 1798 i.
Richd. 1799 w.
WORRICK
Lancaster
Richard 1759 i.
WORRINGTON
Accomack
Jno. 1728 i.
Princess Anne
Martha 1720 i.
Clifton 1722 w.
WORSHAM
Amelia
Jno. 1757 i.
Jno. 1758 w.
Drury 1767 i.
Thos. 1776 w.
Jno. 1779 w.
Danl. 1780 w.
Wm. 1783 w.
Geo. 1784 w.
Kennon 1788 i.
Henry 1789 w.
Henry 1795 w.
Chesterfield
Jno. 1751 w.
Wm. 1752 w.
Essex 1758 w.
Jos. 1758 i.
Peter 1760 i.
Ann 1768 w.
Jno. Jr. 1768 w.
Jno. 1769 w.

Essex 1772 w.
Wm. 1772 w.
Rosamond 1774 w.
Wm. 1780 w.
Edwd. 1792 w.
Henrico
Chas. 1712 i.
Jno. 1726 i.
Danl. 1728 i.
Geo. 1728 i.
Jno. 1729 w.
Chas. 1735 w.
Geo. 1735 w.
Chas. 1736 w.
Geo. 1736 i.
Jno. 1736 i.
Jno., Jr. 1745 w.
Wm. 1748 w.
Pittsylvania
Joshua 1771 w.
Patty 1778 w.
Prince Edward
Daniel 1793 i.
WORTHAM
Brunswick
James 1770 w.
Essex
Wm. 1744 i.
Jno. 1766 w.
Middlesex
Chas. 1743 w.
Geo. 1752 w.
Jno. 1759 w.
Saml. 1784 i.
Jas. 1786 i.
WORTHINGTON
Berkeley
Robert 1779 w.
Ephraim 1787 w.
Frederick
Jacob 1750 i.
Ohio
Thos. 1778 w.
Orange
Saml. 1739 w.
Robt. 1736 w.
Saml. 1742 i.
WORTHY
Charlotte
Jno. 1770 i.
Thos. 1778 i.
WORTON
King George
Sarah 1767 a.
WOSAY
Norfolk
Danl. 1783 i.
WOSLEY
Norfolk
Thos. 1712 w.

WOSTER
Bedford
Hinmon 1797 w.
WOTHERSPOON
Goochland
Reuben 1792 w.
WOTTEN
Isle of Wight
Jno. 1767 i.
York
Thos. 1783 i.
WOTTON
Isle of Wight
Thos. 1670 w.
WRAY
Brunswick
Jno. 1774 w.
Henrico
Wm. 1794 i.
Norfolk
Jno. A. 1799 i.
York
Jas. 1750 i.
WRAYTREE
York
Jas. 1752 i.
WREN
Charlotte
Temperance 1770 i.
Fairfax
Thos. 1768 w.
Isle of Wight
Francis 1719 w.
Jno. 1736 i.
King George
Jno. 1750 i.
Jno. 1752 w.
Wm. 1766 w.
Margt. 1782 w.
Lancaster
Nicho. Sr. 1701 w.
Wm. 1710-11 w.
Wm. 1736 w.
Lunenburg
Thos. 1762 i.
Thos. 1763 w.
Surry
Jos. 1750 w.
Sussex
Nathan 1777 w.
Jos. 1789 i.
WRENCH
Isle of Wight
Jno. 1728 w.
Jno. 1784 w.
WRENN
Brunswick
Jno. 1772 w.
Greensville
Francis 1787 w.
Jas. 1798 w.

Isle of Wight
Francis 1684 i.
Thos. 1728 w.
Elizabeth 1737 i.
Olive 1744 nw.
Mary 1747 w.
Jas. 1749 i.
Jno. 1752 w.
Jno. 1757 i.
Jos. 1757 i.
Wm. 1773 w.
Frances 1775 w.
Jno. 1786 w.
Thos. 1798 w.
Loudoun
Susannah 1779 i.
Thos. 1779 i.
Surry
Jno. 1713 i.
Richd. 1717 w.
Thos. 1775 w.
Sussex
Jos. 1782 w.
Thos. 1793 w.
WRESSELL
Northampton
Chas. 1691 i.
WRIDINGS
Essex
Jno. 1734 i.
Jno. 1755 i.
WRIGHT
Accomack
Wm. 1759 i.
Henry 1785 w.
Mack Williams
1786 w.
Albemarle
Jno. 1754 i.
Amelia
Thos. [1773] w.
Jno. 1790 w.
Wm. 1791 i.
Stephen 1796 w.
Amherst
Francis 1766 i.
Augustine 1777 a.
Benj. 1799 w.
Augusta
Thos. 1751 a.
Ann 1752 i.
Thos. 1755 w.
Wm. 1755 a.
Jno. 1762 w.
Wm. 1776 w.
Wm. 1777 w.
Jos. 1782 i.
Jos. 1795 a.
Bedford
Thos. 1763 w.

Botetourt
Peter 1793 w.
Brunswick
Saml. 1775 w.
Robt. 1783 w.
Uriah 1784 i.
Jas. 1793 i.
Labon 1795 w.
Mary 1795 i.
Culpeper
Jno. 1769 w.
Richard 1783 w.
Cumberland
Jno. 1772 i.
Saml. 1773 i.
Geo. 1774 w.
Thos. 1781 i.
Geo. 1789 w.
Thos. 1790 w.
Geo. 1791 i.
Essex
Robt. 1698 w.
Geo. 1769 w.
Geo. 1770 w.
Ambrose 1771 w.
Geo. 1773 i.
Wm. 1773 i.
Elizabeth 1775 w.
Fairfax
Abraham 1773 i.
Fauquier
Jos. 1760 w.
Jno. 1792 w.
Frederick
Jas. 1760 w.
Jas. 1764 w.
Mary 1764 w.
Thos. 1766 i.
Isaac 1777 i.
Wm. 1786 i.
Goochland
Jno. 1730 w.
Maridy 1735 i.
Halifax
Francis 1787 i.
Henrico
Patrick 1787 w.
Isle of Wight
Thos. 1701 w.
Geo. 1702 w.
Jno. 1736 w.
Martha 1739 w.
Jos. 1746 i.
Jno. 1757 w.
Jno. 1758 w.
Jno. 1759 i.
Henry 1763 i.
Hannah 1778 w.
Lancaster
Frances 1691 i.
Mottram 1701 w.

Saml. 1706 i.
Arthur 1752 w.
Louisa
Richd. 1773 w.
Thos. 1792 w.
Lunenburg
Jno. 1755 i.
Mecklenburg
Reuben 1777 w.
Middlesex
Wm. 1679 a.
Norfolk
Thos. 1654 w.
——— 1718 i.
Stephen 1748 w.
Thos. 1748 w.
Jno. 1761 w.
Thos. 1762 w.
David 1773 w.
Francis 1777 i.
Stephen 1779 w.
Geo. 1795 w.
Jno. 1795 nw.
Anne 1796 w.
Northumberland
Richard 1663 w.
Richard 1720 w.
Jno. 1797 w.
Orange
Thos. 1736 w.
Pittsylvania
Jno. 1791 w.
Prince Edward
John 1779 w.
Princess Anne
Thos. 1772 w.
Joshua 1782 w.
Christopher 1785 w.
Jacob 1785 i.
Jas. 1787 w.
Jas. 1788 i.
Jeremiah 1789 w.
Reuben 1796 w.
Prince William
Francis 1742 w.
Rappahannock
Wm. [1657?] i.
Thos. 1666 w.
Thos. 1672 w.
Richmond
Jno. 1736 i.
Jno. 1737 nw.
Thos. 1751 w..
Edwd. 1791 i.
Shenandoah
Ignatius 1778 a.
Southampton
James 1778 w.
Jas. 1762 w.
Mary 1781 i.
David 1791 i.

Spotsylvania
Mary 1729 a.
Alex. 1772 a.
Jacob 1777 a.
Stafford
Richard 1701 i.
Surry
Thos 1712 w.
Timothy 1717 i.
Edwd. 1781 w.
Washington
Jacob. 1799 w.
Westmoreland
Francis 1713 i.
Jno. 1714 w.
Saml. 1725 i.
Richd. 1741 w.
Francis 1776 i.
Francis 1793 w.
York
Edwd. 1658 a.
Jno. 1695 w.
Augustin 1732 w.
Edwd. 1735 w.
Wm. 1735 w.
Wm. 1737 i.
Jno. 1752 w.
ᴸLawrence 1753 i.
Ann 1757 i.
Dudley 1761 w.
Wm. 1778 i.
Edwd. 1779 w.
Eliz. 1780 i.
Edwd. 1790 w.
Benj. 1793 w.
Jno. 1797 i.

WRITEE
Frederick
Jacob 1769 i.
WRO
Richmond
Sarah 1791 i.
WROE
King George
Sutton [1780?] w.
Richmond
Jeremiah 1775 i.
Nathaniel 1782 w.
Jno. 1783 w.
Jno. 1794 w.
Thos. 1799 i.
Westmoreland
Wm. 1730 w.
Richd. 1762 i.
Original 1774 w.
Wm. 1781 w.
Richd. 1785 i.
WYAT
Fauquier
Wm. 1761 i.

Greenbrier
Edwd. 1787 i.
Westmoreland
Wm. 1729 i.
Jas. 1734 i.
WYATT
Accomack
Thos. 1771 i.
Wm., Sr. 1774 w.
Kendall 1776 w.
Littleton 1784 i.
Wm. 1788 i.
Thos. 1791 w.
Joshua 1793 w.
Joshua 1799 i.
Charlotte
Richard 1782 w.
Chesterfield
Thos. 1759 i.
Loudoun
Thos. 1772 w.
Norfolk
Amy 1753 w.
Anne 1753 w.
Jno. 1797 i.
Prince George
Anthony 1721 a.
Edwd., Sr. 1726 w.
Nicholas 1720 w.
Richmond
——— 1737 i.
Spotsylvania
Jno. 1785 w.
WYBOURNE
Halifax
Jno. 1761 i.
WYCHE
Brunswick
Henry 1735 w.
Frances 1749 i.
Peter [1757] w.
Wm. 1758 i.
Sarah 1777 w.
Greensville
Geo. 1781 w.
Surry
Henry 1712 w.
Wm. 1720 w.
Jas. 1749 w.
Sussex
Geo. 1757 w.
Jas. 1761 i.
Benj. 1768 i.
Benj. 1772 i.
Nathl. 1777 w.
Jas. 1782 i.
WYEBOUGH
Frederick
Jacob 1751 w.

WYER
Loudoun
Wm. 1796 i.
WYN
Lancaster
Henry 1685 i.
WYNN
Surry
Thos. 1718 w.
Sussex
Jno. 1784 i.
WYNNE
Amelia
Wm. 1750 i.
Brunswick
Sloman 1780 w
Campbell
Joshua 1789 w.
Greensville
Mary 1788 w.
Pittsylvania
Wm. 1778 w.
Prince George
Joshua 1715 a.
Frances 1726 w.
Sussex
Robt. 1754 w.
Wm. 1758 i.
Sloman 1761 w.
Thos. 1773 w.
Wm. 1793 w.
Jno. 1794 i.
Jno. 1796 w.
Jno. 1797 i.
Matthew 1798 w.
Rich. 1798 w.
York
Jno. 1772 w.
Thos. 1794 w.
WYRE
Northampton
Jno. 1680 i.
WYSE
Brunswick
Wm. 1752 w.
WYTH
York
Jno. 1712 i.

Y

YAAR
Madison
Adam 1793 w.
YAGER
Culpeper
Nicholas 1781 w.
Nicholas 1793 w.
Madison
Adam 1794 w.
Michael 1794 w.

YALDEN
Isle of Wight
   Edwd. 1669 i.
YANCEY
Albemarle
   Jeremiah 1789 i.
Culpeper
   Lewis 1784 w.
   Lewis Davis 1788 w.
   Philemon 1789 i.
Louisa
   Robt. 1746 w.
   Archelaus 1764 w.
   Joel 1774 w.
   Robt. 1774 w.
   Henry 1784 w.
   Stephen 1793 a.
   John 1799 w.
Mecklenburg
   Richd. 1780 w.
   Mary 1796 w.
YANCY
Culpeper
   Charles, Jr. 1795 i.
Lunenburg
   Jno. 1761 i.
Mecklenburg
   Hezekiah 1782 w.
YANKSHAW
Fairfax
   Laurence 1752 i.
YARBOROUGH
Bedford
   Jeremiah 1759 w.
   Jeremiah 1765 i.
Brunswick
   James 1777 w.
YARBROUGH
Amelia
   Wm. 1748 w.
   Wm., Jr. 1749 i.
   Hezekiah 1754 w.
   Moses 1756 w.
   Thos. 1769 w.
   Jordan 1770 w.
Brunswick
   Abraham 1754 i.
Cumberland
   Edwd. 1757 w.
Prince Edward
   Wm. 1771 w.
YARDLEY
Northampton
   Argoll 1655 i.
   Argall 1683 w.
Norfolk
   Francis 1655 i.
YARINGTON
Essex
   John 1792 w.

YARRANTON
Middlesex
   —— 1710 i.
YARRETT
Isle of Wight
   William 1682 w.
YARRINGTON
Essex
   John 1796 i.
Middlesex
   Massey 1756 w.
   Anne 1760 a.
YARROW
Essex
   Mathew 1759 w.
YATES
Culpeper
   George 1788 w.
Loudoun
   Joseph 1761 w.
Mecklenburg
   Edwd. Randolph
     1792 w.
Middlesex
   Bartholomew 1769 i.
   Bartholomew 1771 i.
   Harry B. 1790 w.
Norfolk
   John 1648 i.
   Joane [1666?] w.
   Richd. 1679 w.
Pittsylvania
   Eliz. 1795 w.
Richmond
   Wm. 1713 i.
Westmoreland
   Benj. 1736 i.
York
   Thos. 1694 w.
YAXLEY
Henrico
   Robt. 1755 w.
Norfolk
   John 1748 w.
YEAGER
Augusta
   Andrew 1787 i.
Shenandoah
   Adam 1782 i.
YEAMAN
Fairfax
   Jno. 1798 i.
YEARGAIN
Brunswick
   Thos. 1790 w.
YEARGER
Augusta
   Andrew 1790 i.
YEARGIN
Chesterfield
   Anner 1797 w.

YEATES
Loudoun
   Samuel 1778 w.
Northumberland
   Richd. 1750 i.
Richmond
   Francis 1724 i.
York
   Thos. 1658 w.
YEATMAN
Richmond
   Jno. 1737 i.
   Jno. 1753 i.
   Thos. 1760 i.
   Ellen 1766 i.
York
   Thos. 1690 w.
   John 1739 i.
   Chas. 1740 i.
YEATS
Frederick
   Abraham 1746 i.
Essex
   Richard 1722 i.
Rappahannock
   James 1685 w.
Richmond
   Wm. 1754 i.
   Jno. 1725 i.
Westmoreland
   Travis 1771 i.
YEATTS
Pittsylvania
   Jno. 1778 w.
YELDEN
Isle of Wight
   Edward 1670 nw.
YELLOP
Westmoreland
   Thos. 1742 w.
YEO
Accomack
   Wm. 1718 w.
YERBY
Lancaster
   Thos. 1716 w.
   Ann 1720-21 w.
   Jno. 1737 nw.
   Thomas 1756 w.
   Hannah 1761 w.
   George 1765 w.
   Elizab. 1772 w.
   John 1777 w.
   Elizabeth 1779 i.
   William 1786 w.
   James 1788 i.
Northumberland
   Chas. 1794 w.
Richmond
   Jno. 1776 w.
   Geo. 1793 w.

YERLEY
Northumberland
Thos. 1792 w.
YEWELL
Princess Anne
Thos. 1696 a.
YOACON
Augusta
Valentine 1768 i.
YOAKAM
Frederick
Francis 1752 i.
YOAKUM
Augusta
Valentine 1764 a.
Hardy
Geo. 1789 w.
YOEL
Berkeley
Henry 1779 w.
YOPP
Lancaster
William 1788 i.
William 1789 i.
Samuel 1793 w.
YOSTFRUNK
Shenandoah
John 1791 i.
YOUELL
Westmoreland
Thos. 1695 w.
Hannah 1725 i.
YOULLAN
Pittsylvania
Phil. 1785 i.
YOUND
Halifax
James 1796 i.
YOUNG
Accomack
Francis 1733 w.
Jno. 1750 w.
Jno. 1769 w.
Jno. 1775 i.
Wm., Sr. 1781 w.
Ezekiel 1786 w.
Jno. 1795 w.
Ezekiel 1796 i.
Jno. 1798 i.
Amelia
Saml. 1777 w.
Martha 1781 w.
Susanna 1798 i.
Amherst
James 1772 a.
Augusta
Jno. 1747 i.
Jas. 1760 i.
Patrick 1761 w.
Jno., Jr. 1783 w.
Jno. 1783 w.
Jas. 1790 w.

Robt. 1793 w.
Bedford
James 1778 w.
Berkeley
Nicholas 1796 w.
Noah 1796 w.
Daniel 1779 i.
Brunswick
Michael, Jr. 1762 w.
Chesterfield
Nathl. 1777 i.
Culpeper
Richard 1775 w.
Essex
Wm. 1693 w.
Wm. 1697 w.
William 1718 w.
William 1720 i.
John 1749 w.
Henry 1750 w.
Williamson 1750 w.
William 1783 w.
Mary 1791 w.
Fairfax
David 1770 i.
John 1792 a.
Fauquier
William 1791 w.
James 1799 i.
Franklin
Allin Redly 1792 w.
Frederick
James 1749 w.
Goodman 1765 i.
John 1766 i.
Greensville
James 1781 i.
James 1782 w.
Ann 1792 i.
Halifax
James 1795 w.
Henrico
Judith 1783 w.
Alex. 1796 w.
Alex. 1797 i.
Isle of Wight
Alexander 1728 w.
Francis 1795 i.
Elizabeth 1799 w.
Lancaster
Christopher 1679 i.
Robt. 1705 w.
Louisa
Lenard 1785 w.
Laurence 1799 w.
Mecklenburg
Jane 1792 w.
Norfolk
Robt. 1679 i.
William 1762 i.
Lawrence 1792 i.

Northampton
Gawton 1750 i.
Henry 1751 i.
Northumberland
Mary 1738 w.
Prince Edward
Henry 1783 w.
Henry 1792 w.
Prince William
Edward 1740 i.
Edward 1743 i.
Robert 1790 i.
Shenandoah
Edwin 1793 i.
John 1794 i.
Edwin 1799 i.
John (3) 1799 i.
Spotsylvania
Lewis 1795 a.
Lawrence 1799 w.
Stafford
Wm. 1700 w.
Henry 1734 i.
Surry
Jno. 1714 w.
Sussex
Thos. 1771 w.
Katherine 1774 w.
Thos. 1776 w.
Thos. 1780 i.
Jno. 1782 w.
Drury 1785 w.
Washington
James 1777 i.
Jacob 1798 w.
York
Alex. 1701 w.
Jno. 1719 w.
Francis 1729 i.
Martha 1773 w.
YOUNGE
Accomack
Wm. 1748 w.
Lunenburg
Lemuel 1755 i.
Jno. 1758 i.
Joseph 1770 i.
YOUNGER
Essex
Alexander 1727 w.
Alexander 1733 i.
Halifax
Thos. 1791 w.
YOUNGHUSBAND
Henrico
Isaac 1795 w.
YUILLE
Henrico
John 1747 i.
Halifax
Thos. 1792 w.

YOUT
Loudoun
John 1776 i.
YOWEL
Madison
David 1793 w.
David 1794 a.
John 1795 w.
YOWELL
Culpeper
Christopher 1762 i.
Christopher 1764 i.
James 1778 i.

Z

ZACHARY
Amelia
David 1782 i.
David, Jr. 1782 i.
David 1784 w.
Brunswick
Benj. 1791 w.
Culpeper
John, Jr. 1785 w.

Prince Edward
Bartho. 1786 w.
ZACKARY
Madison
John 1797 w.
ZAMWALL
Frederick
Andrew 1765 w.
ZANTZ
Shenandoah
Frederick 1782 i.
ZEE
Augusta
Geo. 1752 i.
ZELL
Sussex
Eliz. 1762 w.
ZELLS
Surry
Lambert 1751 i.
ZERN
Shenandoah
Peter 1782 a.

ZIGLAR
Culpeper
Leonard 1758 w.
Leonard 1772 w.
ZILLS
Sussex
Lambert 1764 w.
John 1777 w.
Morris 1795 w.
ZIMMERMAN
Berkeley
Adam 1789 w.
Culpeper
Christopher 1781 w.
Orange
Christopher 1748 w.
Shenandoah
John 1799 i.
ZORN
Augusta
Jacob 1756 a.
ZUILLE
Fairfax
Robert 1778 w.

APPENDIX

APPENDIX

NORFOLK CITY HUSTINGS COURT
(1784–1800)

Abyvon, Marian 1795w; Allen, Hugh 1790w; Anderson, Robt. 1786w; Archer, Dinah 1794w; Archer, John 1794w; Armstrong, Jno. 1799i; Avery, Isaac 1799w; Bacon, Samuel 1794w; Bacon, Samuel 1795w; Ballentine, Eliza 1792w; Bathgate, William 1798w; Bayley, Wm. Armstead 1792w; Biggar, Matthew 1794w; Blaws, Thos. 1798w; Boggess, John 1790w; Booth, Thos. 1791w; Boush, Jno. 1792w; Boyer, Elias 1798w; Bradley, Jas. Whital 1786i; Brehm, Chas. 1794w; Brown, John 1785w; Brown, Bristol 1788w; Brown, Francis 1792i; Browne, Jas. 1796w; Bruce, Jno. 1799a; Brunet, Peter 1797w; Brunet, Peter 1798w; Burke, Saml. 1795w; Butler, Jno. 1792w; Calvert, Thos. 1785w; Calvert, Jonathan 1793i; Calvert, Jno. Savage 1796w; Campbell, Donald 1795w; Campbell, Duncan 1795w; Campbell, Wm. 1792i; Campbell, Alex. Jr. 1796i; Carter, Lemuel 1795i; Clark, Wm. 1796w; Cody, Simon 1796i; Cornick, Henry 1794w; Cowan, Ebenezer 1799w; Cunningham, Wm. 1797i; Denby, Jas. 1794w; Diack, Patrick 1789n.w; Donayhua (Donahoe), Edwd. 1797w; Donnell (Donald), Hugh 1790w; Driscol, Thos. 1796w; Edey, Solomon 1789w; Faulder, Thos. 1797a; Finn, Jas. 1794i; Flyn, Jas. 1785i; Frazer, Robt. 1799w; Gibbs, Polly 1798i; Godfrey, Nathaniel 1797w; Gow, Anne 1797w; Gornto, Nathaniel 1797w; Gwyn, Thos. 1788w; Hall, Armestead 1797w; Hand, Jos. 1795i; Harwood, Peggy 1796w; Hatteredge, Robt. 1792w; Hatton, Thos. 1797w; Hayes, Robt. 1796i; Hunter, Jas. 1795w; Hunter, Jno. 1795w; Hutchings, Eliz. 1792w; Inkson, Eliz. 1799w; Ivy, Mason 1794w; Jones, Saml. 1798w; Keith, Ann 1796i; Kelley, George 1796w; Kelsick, Eliz. 1789w; Lathbury, Geo. 1786w; Lee, Jno. 1797w; Leitch, Jas. 1787w; Lindsay, Wm. 1798w; McClod, Geo. 1799a; McFarlain, Alex. 1799n; McGown, Archd. 1792w; McNeal (McNeil), Jno. 1792w; McNeil, Jno. 1792w; Maclean, Jno. 1799i; Maxwell, Jas. 1795w; Maxwaull, Simon 1791i; Mayle, Lydia 1792w; Miles, Chas. 1796w; Moore, Jno. 1793w; Morris, Thos. 1789w; Nassaw (Nashaw), Richd. 1785w; Nichols, Jas. 1787w; Neilson, Jos. 1784i; Newton, Thos. 1795w; Ogbourn, Wm. 1795i; Owens, Edwd. 1795w; Parker, Patrick 1796w; Payne, Isaac 1795w; Peters, Jno. 1797i; Phil, Herman 1791i; Portlock, Saml. 1788w; Portlock, Saml. 1790w; Precious, Matthias 1791w; Price, Thos. 1786w; Price, Lydia 1788w; Pryor, Jno. 1792w; Ramsay, Jas. 1797w; Rea, Sampson 1794w; Redman, Isaac 1796w; Reid, Jas. 1795w; Reid, Jno. 1795w; Reynolds, Saml. 1798w; Robertson, Jno. 1795a; Robinson, Jno. 1796a; Rothery, Danl. 1795w; Ross, Jno. 1793i; Ross, Jno. 1795i; Russell, Jesse 1796w; Scott, Robt. 1795w; Selden, Mary Ann 1799w; Sharp, Alex 1798i; Shellsman, Jno. 1796i; Smallwood, Jno. 1799i; Smith, Jno. 1794i; Smith, Temperance 1797a; Smith, Wm. 1785w; Smith, Wm. 1790i; Stetson, Geo. 1796w; Street, Benj. 1797i; Sweeney, Anne 1790w; Talbot, Diane 1789w; Terry, Thos. 1784a; Thompson, Francis 1794i; Tucker, Gawen Corbin 1789i; Valentine, Jno. 1796a; Vaughan, Jas. 1797w; Walke, Mary 1798w; Walker, Jas. 1796i; Wallace, Wm. 1799w; Watson, Jas. 1789w; Webb, Jno. 1794i; West, Charlotte 1795w; Williams, Jacob 1784i; Williams, Mary 1789w; Williams, Fredk. 1796i; Willoughby, Geo. Abyvon 1791w; Winter, Jas. 1796a.

FREDERICKSBURG HUSTINGS COURT
(1782–1800)

Abbott, Saml. 1785w; Armistead, Henry 1787w; Atkinson, Geo. 1792w; Bingey, Jno. 1796i; Brown, Thos. 1790w; Campbell, Lachlan [1789]w; Callender, Eliezer 1793i; Dick, Chas. 1782w; Dick, Alex. 1785w; Duncanson, Jas. 1791w; Evans, Philip 1792w; Hackley, Jas. 1784w; Harvey, Wm. 1798w; Hobson, Wm. 1782w; Johnston, Robt. 1789w; Laporte, Bajean 1782w; Legg, Jno. 1793w; Madden, Jas. [1793]i; McCoull, Neil 1791w; Mitchell, Henry 1793w; Nairne, Alex. 1794w; Patterson, Leonard 1788w; Pottinger, Jas. 1793i; Robinson, Michael 1784w; Robinson, Jas. 1785w; Robinson, Jno. 1795w; Stone, Thos. 1793w; Taylor, Jno. 1799i; Walker, Thos. 1786w; Washington, Mary 1788w; Weedon, Geo. 1793w; Wilson, Jonathan 1782i; Woodfolk, Nancy 1796w; Wright, Wm. 1788w.

KANAWHA COUNTY (NOW WEST VIRGINIA)
(1789–1800)

(Entries from Deed Book "A" and Order Book 1788–1803)

Bailey, Jno. 1794w; Bryan, Jas. 1798w; Clindenen, Geo. 1797i; Erwin (Arwin), Edwd. 1798a; Graham, Wm. 1789i; Haile (Hale), Jas. 1791i; Harraman, Shedrick 1794i; Hill, Jas. 1793i; Hughes, Thos. 1793w; Maze, Jas. 1799w; McClung, Edwd. 1793a; Morris, Wm. 1794w; See, Michael 1793i; Stares, Conrod 1798a; Smith, Wm. 1796a; Tacket, Francis 1798a; Tacket, Thomas 1797a; Tyler, Isaac 1798a; Upton, Thos. 1795w; Van Bibber, Peter 1797i; Wheeler, Roland 1793i; Wheeler, Roland 1795i.

NOTTOWAY COUNTY
(1789–1800)

Anderson, Jno. 1794w; Anderson, Henry 1795w; Anderson, Reinard 1797w; Baldwin, Wm. 1793w; Baldwin, Jno. 1793w; Bagley, Jas. 1795w; Bagley, Geo. 1796w; Bennett, Wm. 1789w; Beasley, Jno. 1794w; Bentley, Saml. Sr. 1797i; Bentley, Saml. Jr. 1797i; Bell, Wm. 1799i; Bolling, Stith 1797w; Borum, Richd. 1789w; Borum, Edmd. 1791w; Bridgeforth, Jas. 1798i; Brown, Lawrence 1797w; Bruce, Alex. Sr. 1795w; Buford, Henry 1791w; Burks, Richd. Sr. 1797w; Cabiness, Matthew 1790w; Cabiness, Elijah 1795w; Cabiness, Elijah 1798i; Cabiness, Geo. 1799w; Chambers, Saml. 1793a; Chapman, Wm. 1794i; Cheatham, Joel 1797i; Clarke, Geo. 1790i; Clardy, Benj. 1792w; Clark, Jno. 1794w; Clardy, Benj. 1795i; Clardy, Henry 1799i; Cocke, Stephen 1793w; Connally, Chas. Sr. 1791w; Connally, Catherine 1791w; Craddock, Edwd. 1797w; Crenshaw, Wm. 1789w; Crenshaw, Jane 1793a; Crenshaw, Wm. 1794w; Cross, Wm. 1792w; Dupuy, Jno. Bartho. [1791]w; Dupuy, Mary 1793w; Ellett, Jno. 1796w; Epes, Mary 1795i; Epes, Thos. 1798i; Farguson, Peter 1796w; Featherstone, Chas. H. 1790w; Foard, Abraham 1797w; Forrest, Abraham 1793w; Forrest, Jno. 1795i; Foster, Richd. 1796w; Fowlkes, Jos. Sr. 1789w; Fowlkes, Gabriel 1793w; Fowlkes, Jno. 1799w; Frank, Nehemiah 1798i; French, Robt. 1789w; Gooch, Francis 1799i; Grammer, Jos. 1795w; Greenhill, Philip 1795w; Greenhill, Saml. 1799i; Hall, Ann 1791w; Hall, David 1791i; Harrison, Christopher 1796i; Hastings, Henry 1795w; Hatchett, Margaret 1792w; Heightower, Jonathan Sr. 1794w; Holland, Zachariah 1796w; Holmes, Isaac 1793i; Howson, Jno. 1799w; Hudson, Mary 1793w; Hundley, Jno. 1795w; Hundley, Josiah 1797a; Hurt, Wm. 1796w; Irby, Elizabeth 1799w; Jackson, Burwell 1792w; Jackson, Edwd. Sr. 1793w; Jackson, Abigail 1796i; Jeffress, Thos. Sr. 1794w; Jennings, Jno. 1795w; Jennings, Robt. 1798w; Johns, Nathl. 1790w; Johns, Mary 1796w; Jones, Danl. 1795w; Jones, Thos. 1796w; Jones, Batte 1797w; Jones, Robt. 1799i; Jordan, Benj. 1799i; Lamkin, Peter 1797w; Leath, Sarah 1793w; Ligon, Wm. 1791i; May, Jno. 1798w; Mayes, Danl. Sr. 1793i; Munford, Jane 1790i; Oliver, Isaac Sr. 1799w; Osborne, Wm. 1793w; Osborne, Abner 1794i; Palmer, Elijah 1795i; Parham, Jas. 1793i; Parham, Wm. 1797w; Pincham, Saml. 1797w; Ramsey, Richd. 1793w; Robertson, Robt. 1791i; Robertson, Nathl. 1794w; Robertson, Tralusia 1790w; Robinson (Robertson), Jas. 1792w; Sherwin, Saml. 1789w; Smith, Samuel 1790w; Smith,

Wm. [1791]i; Smith, Hezekiah 1795i; Smith, Wm. 1796w; Smith, Richd. 1797i; Smith, Richd. 1798w; Spragins, Melchijah 1797i; Stow, Wm. 1797w; Tanner, Joel Jr. 1793i; Thompson, Medkip 1790w; Thompson, Judah 1795w; Thompson, Judith 1797i; Walker, Thos. 1793w; Waller, Major 1794w; Watkins, Saml. 1796i; Ward, Rowland Jr. 1794i; Williams, Billington 1794w; Williams, Thos. R. 1798w; Wills, Edmd. Sr. 1797w; Winfree, Ann 1794w; Winn, Susanna 1796w; Winn, Jno. 1797i; Wood, Wm. 1798w; Worsham, Jno. 1796w; Yates, Wm. 1790i.

PENDLETON COUNTY (NOW WEST VIRGINIA) (1787–1800)

Aur, Staphel 1797a; Blizard, Jno. 1799i; Botkin (Batkin), Jno. Sr. 1790w; Boyd, Jno. 1791i; Buzard, Henry 1791i; Cayle, Geo. 1794w; Clifton, Wm. 1796w; Cowder (Cowger, Geo. 1788i; Dice, Geo. 1795i; Dice, Matthias 1799w; Douglass, Thos. 1793w; Evick, Geo. 1795a; Eye, Christopher 1797w; Fleisher, Conrad 1797w; Fusell (Fesell, Fezel), —— 1796w; Gragg, Wm. 1795i; Hanns, Richd. 1799w; Harper, Philip 1799w; Henkle, Justus 1794i; Hoover, Sebastian 1791 g.b.; Johns, Isaac 1797w; Life, Martain 1797w; Lough, Adam 1789w; Lutz, —— 1792i; Marrall, Jno. 1795w; McCoy, Jno. Sr. 1797w; Miller, Matthias 1794i; Moyer, —— [1795]i; Miller, Stephen 1799w; Props, Jno. Michael 1789w; Rexroth (Rexroad, Rexroade), Zachariah 1799w; Richards, Saml. 1798w; Roy, —— 1798w; Seybert, Henry 1795w; Smith, Fredk. 1797i; Smith, Henry 1797i; Snider, Jno. 1798i; Teter, Geo. 1798w; Waggoner, Lewis 1790w.

PRINCE GEORGE COUNTY
(From Volume of Deeds, &c., 1787–1792)

Armistead, Margaret 1792w; Avery, Edwd. Sr. 1789w; Avery, Edwd. 1790w; Black, David 1789i; Bland, Richd. 1789i; Bland, Theodorick, 1790w; Bonner, Silvia 1789w; Bonner, Wm. 1791i; Boyd, Robt. 1787a; Braceberry, Nicho. 1789a; Brockwell, —— 1786w; Brown, Wm. 1789w; Brown, Thos. 1790w; Burge, Jas. 1791w; Burrow, Jno. 1790i; Chiles, Robt. 1787i; Cotton, Wm. 1787w; Cureton, Thos. 1791i; Daniel, Lucrese (Lucretia) 1787w; Daniel, Jno. 1788a; Denhart, Rebecca 1789w; Draper, Jno. 1791i; Dunn, Nathl. 1790a; Edwards, Edwd. 1781i; Edwards, Jno. 1789a; Epes, Amy 1789i; Field, Theophilus 1788i; Field, Jas. 1789w; Fletcher, Jas. 1789a; Fletcher, Rebecca 1789a; Goodgame, David 1788w; Goodgame, David 1791w; Gordon, Jno. 1787a; Gordan, Ann Isham 1790w; Grammer, Timothy 1787w; Grammer, Grief 1787w; Grammer, Jno. 1789w; Green, Wm. 1789w; Gregory, Chas. 1787a; Haddon, Francis 1792i; Hall, Eliz. 1790i; Hamblin, Lucy 1787w; Harrison, Nathl. 1787a; Harrison, Robt. 1788w; Harrison, Benj. 1790w; Harrison, Richd. 1792w; Harrison, Nathl. 1792w; Harrison, Benj. 1792i; Heath, David 1787a; Hobbs, Mary 1790i; Hobbs, Edwd. 1792w; Holloway, Jno. 1789a; Imray, Jno. 1788w; Lacey, Wm. 1790i; Leath, Peter 1790div; Lee, Peter 1787i; Lee, Jno. 1787i; Lewis, Agnes 1789w; Littlewood, Thos. 1787i; Marten, Jas. 1790w; Mattox, Jos. 1792i; Moody, Peter 1791i; Morison, David 1788i; Morison, Ann 1789i; Morison, Jno. 1790w; Newell, Edwd. 1792w; Peterson, Thos. 1789w; Poythress, Mary 1788w; Raines, Nathl. 1789w; Raines, Phoebe 1789w; Raines, Ephraim 1792w; Rives, Wm. 1787a; Rives, Isham 1789a; Robertson, Alex. 1787a; Ruffin, Edwd. 1791w; Scott, Edwd. 1786w; Sherman, Eliz. 1787w; Simmons, Wm. 1790w; Stewart, Richd. 1791w; Sturdivant, Ann 1787i; Sturdivant, Joel 1789a; Sturdivant, Jane 1791i; Sykes, Barnard 1791n.w; Stainback, Geo. 1788i; Stannings, Judith 1787a; Tatum, Epes 1789w; Thomas, Isham 1789w; Warthen, Eliz. 1788w; Warthen, Eliz. 1791w; Wilkins, Benj. 1789i; Williams, Jos. 1789w; Williams, David 1790a; Williams, Jas. 1791i; Williams, Lessenberry 1791w; Williamson, Jno. 1791a; Womack, Jno. 1787w.

DISTRICT OF WEST AUGUSTA
(1774-5-1776)

This District divided by Virginia Assembly Oct. 1776 into the counties of Ohio, Yohogania and Monongalia. In an attempt to gather a list of the wills and inventories of people dying in this section while it was *under Virginia's jurisdiction* the court houses of Ohio County, West Virginia (at Wheeling) and Monongalia County, West Virginia (at Morgantown), and of Washington County, Pennsylvania (at Washington, Pennsylvania) were visited, this last for any items of residents in Yohogania County. The items obtained from Ohio County are given in the body of this "Index" under the individual surnames found; and there remain no records of wills and administrations prior to 1800 for Monongalia County in the court house at Morgantown. The list given below is from examination of the volume of wills at Washington, Pennsylvania 1778-1786 and a list of *"Old Virginia Wills in Washington County Pennsylvania"* appearing in Boyd Crumrine's *"Records of Deeds for the District of West Augusta, Virginia . . . Annals of Carnegie Museum (of Pittsburg) Part 2, Vol. III.* Those marked (Pa) will be found in the volume at Washington, Pennsylvania; those marked (BC) will be found in Boyd Crumrine's work referred to above. Only wills of those persons who described themselves as of Yohogania County, or West Augusta, have been listed here.

Bleakley, Jno. 1779w (BC); Chapin, Wm. 1778w (BC); Cribs, Christian 1784w (Pa); Daley, Chas. 1783w (BC); Devoor, Jas. 1779w (BC); Dickerson, Jno. 1785w (Pa); Ellis, Ellis 1776w (BC); Fowler, Jas. 1782w (Pa); Freeman, Jas. 1778w (BC); Gass, Robert 1782w (Pa); Kellar, Jacob 1787w (Pa); Kirkwood, Jos. 1777w (BC); Lamb, Jacob 1777w (BC); Lamb, Catherine 1779w (BC); Maines, Francis 1784w (Pa); McKnight, Jas. 1781w (Pa); Moor, Jno. 1784w (Pa); Owens, Jno. 1785w (Pa); Pearce, Jas. 1778w (BC); Pearce, Jno. Sr. 1778w (BC); Reed, Jonathan 1777w (BC); Richards, Stephen 1780w (Pa); Robertson, Lane 1784w (Pa); Robins, Jno. 1777w (BC); Rogers, David 1783w (Pa); Ross, Jas. 1781w (BC); Vance, Jno. 1778w (BC); Vaughan, Abraham 1778w (BC); Veneman, Nicholas 1782w (Pa).

CHESTERFIELD COUNTY
(Some items 1752-1756)

Thomas Nelson 1753i; James Hall 1754i; Wm. Geddy 1752i; John Fanning [1753?]i; Robt. Easeley, Jr. 1752i; Eliz. Martin 1753i; Francis Jones 1753i; Richd. Green 1753i; Jos. Rough 1755i; Godfrey Ragsdale 1755i; Richd. Walthall [1755?]i; Josiah Sellars 1754i; Alexander Gordon 1756i.

PETERSBURG HUSTINGS COURT
(1784-1799 inclusive)

Ager, John 1786a; Alexander, Joseph 1789w; Allen, John 1786i; Arbuckle, John 1785w; Armistead, Thomas 1792i; Bagnal (Bagnell), William 1786a; Baily (Bailey), Jesse 1790w; Bartleman, Robert 1791i; Bessor (Byser, Boisser), Peter 1786w; Blakeley (Blaikley), James 1794w; Bradley, William 1785i; Broadie, Archibald 1795w; Brown, Francis 1795i; Brown, James 1798w; Buchanan, Archibald 1786w; Buchanan, William 1790nw; Cathcart, John 1790w; Clarke, Joseph 1797nw; Cobb, John 1791i; Colvin, William, Sr.,1784w; Cooper, Joseph 1799i; Crumpler, John 1794w; Cunningham, Robert 1790i; Daves, Peter 1785i; Davis, Gressett 1791w; Dean, James Allen 1790i; Delane, Samuel 1799i; Dobbie (Dobie) Robert 1786i; Dudgeon, George 1789w; Dudgeon, Martha 1790i; Edwards, Margaret 1790w; Exell, Jesse 1796i; Falkner, Ralph 1787w; Fawcett, James

1789w; Fletcher, Thomas 1796w; Galbraith, Charles 1795w; Garratt, Nicholas Potter 1796w; Garrettson, Richard 1796i; Gerard (Gerrard), Thomas 1793i; Gibson, John 1795a; Gibson, Elizabeth 1795a; Gilbert, Stephen 1797w; Glass, Samuel 1793w; Godfry (Godfrey), Rebecca 1793i; Gordon, Alexander 1785i; Gordon, Alexander 1787i; Grammer, Robert 1788i; Grammer, Pleasant 1796w; Hamilton, Andrew 1794w; Harjesheimer, Peter 1792i; Heathcote, Michael 1793w; Heblethwaite, Robert 1798i; Holliday, Elizabeth 1795a; Holliman, Mary 1789a; Hood, Benjamin 1794w; Holt, Daniel 1795w; Hope, Thomas 1793w; Horsburgh, Alexander 1798w; Horton, William 1788i; Hunter, Thomas T. 1789i; Hunter, Hugh 1796w; Jackson, Joseph 1784w; Jasper, Jack, 1793w; Jeffers, John, 1796w; Johnston, Andrew 1785w; Kerr, Thomas 1790i; Lesslie (Lessley), George 1785w; Linch (Lich) Henry 1794w; Livingston, Thomas 1798w; Lloyd, Henry 1794nw; Long, George 1784i; Majeville, John 1797i; Manley, Devereux J. 1797w; Mathews, Thomas 1788w; May, Ephraim 1794w; Middlemast, Archibald 1799i; Miller, George 1786i; Minge, Daniel 1786a; Minitree, Archibald 1792w; Morgan, Richard 1790i; Morrison, Alexander 1797a; Morriss, William 1785w; Murray, James 1786a; McFarlan, John 1790i; McFarquhar, John 1794i; McCloud, John 1795w; McDowell, James Jr., 1790i; McNabb, Alexander 1788w; Nebeker, George 1797w; Pagan, David 1788w; Parke, Thomas 1796w; Parke, John 1798w; Reeves (Rives), Elizabeth 1797w; Renaud, John 1798i; Rinny, David 1797i; Roberts, Elenor 1798w; Russell, James R. 1796w; Shuler, Jacob 1793w; Smitton, John 1791i; Stabler, Edward 1785w; Steger, William 1791w; Stevens, John 1792a; Stewart (Stuart) Richard 1799w; Smith, John 1799i; Swail, Simon 1799w; Taylor, William 1794i; Tilley, Henry 1788i; Thomson, John 1785w; Thomson, John 1799w; Tucker, Robert 1791w; Tulloch, Hugh 1787i; Turnbull, James 1784w; Uncle (Unkle), Lewis 1792w; Watlington, John 1789i; Wiat, Stephen 1789w; Willcox, Edward 1798w; Williams, John 1799w; Young, William 1792i.